Knowledge-Based Systems

# AN INTRODUCTION TO EXPERT SYSTEMS

OTHER BOOKS AND MONOGRAPHS
BY ROBERT J. MOCKLER AND D. G. DOLOGITE

**Joint Authorship**

Using Computers (2nd edition)
Knowledge-Based Systems for Strategic Corporate Planning

**Robert J. Mockler**

Strategic Management: A Methodological Approach, 4th ed. (co-author)
Strategic Management: Case Studies
Strategic Management: An Integrated Situational Management Orientation
Computer Software to Support Strategic Management Decision Making*
Entreprenuerial New Venture Situations: The Strategic Management Processes Involved
Strategic Planning for Multinational Operations: The Decision Making Processes Involved
Developing Knowledge-Based Systems Using an Expert System Shell*
Situations Involving Major Social Factors: The Strategic Management Processes Involved
Knowledge-Based Systems for Management Decisions
Knowledge-Based Systems for Strategic Planning
Business Planning and Policy Formulation
Developing Information Systems for Management
Management Decision Making and Action in Behavioral Situations
The Business Management Process: A Situational Approach
Guidelines for More Effective Planning and Management of Franchise Systems
The Management Control Process
Business and Society
New Profit Opportunities in Business Publishing (editor and contributing author)
Putting Computers to Work More Effectively in Business Publishing (editor and contributing author)
Readings in Business Planning and Policy Formulation (editor and contributing author)
Readings in Management Control (editor and contributing author)

**D. G. Dologite**

Using Computers (3rd ed.)
Developing Expert Systems Using VP-Expert with Sample Prototype Systems*
Using Microcomputers
Using BASIC
EXSYS: An Expert System Tutorial
Using Small Business Computers

*Published by Macmillan

Knowledge-Based Systems

# AN INTRODUCTION TO EXPERT SYSTEMS

ROBERT J. MOCKLER
St. John's University

D.G. DOLOGITE
Baruch College, City University of New York

Macmillan Publishing Company
*New York*

Maxwell Macmillan Canada
*Toronto*

Maxwell Macmillan International
*New York Oxford Singapore Sydney*

Editor: Ed Moura and Vernon R. Anthony
Developmental Editor: Peggy H. Jacobs
Production Editor: Linda H. Bayma
Art Coordinator: Peter A. Robison
Text Designer: Anne Flanagan
Cover Designer: Robert Vega
Production Buyer: Pamela D. Bennett



This book was set in New Baskerville by Clarinda Company and was printed and bound by R. R. Donnelley & Sons Company. The cover was printed by Lehigh Press, Inc.



Level5 Object software for Figures 21–10, 21–11, 21–12, and 21–13 courtesy of Information Builders, Inc., New York, New York; M.1 software courtesy of Cimflex Teknowledge Corporation, Palo Alto, California; NeuroShell software for Figures 22–2, 22–3, 22–5 courtesy of Ward Systems Group Inc., Frederick, Maryland; ObjectCraft software for Figures 21–1, 21–4 (top), and 21–6 courtesy ObjectCraft, Inc., San Francisco, California; PKWare software courtesy of PKWare, Inc., Brown Deer, Wisconsin; and VP-Expert software for Figures 3–14, 4–9, 4–12, 4–13, 5–3, 5–6, 5–8, 5–17, 5–20, 5–21, 6–1, 6–2, 6–3, 6–4, 6–9, and 6–11 courtesy Wordtech Systems, Inc., Orinda, California.



Macmillan Publishing Company
866 Third Avenue
New York, New York 10022

Macmillan Publishing Company is part of the Maxwell Communication Group of Companies.

Maxwell Macmillan Canada, Inc.
1200 Eglinton Avenue East, Suite 200
Don Mills, Ontario M3C 3N1

**Library of Congress Cataloging-in-Publication Data**
Mockler, Robert J.
An introduction to expert systems : knowledge-based systems / by Robert J. Mockler and D.G. Dologite.
p. cm.
Includes index.
ISBN 0–02–381897–2
1. Expert systems (Computer science)
I: Dologite, D. G. (Dorothy G.). 1941– .
II. Title.
QA76.76.E95M63 1992
006.3′3—dc20 91–38956
CIP

Printing: 2 3 4 5 6 7 8 9 Year: 3 4 5

# THE MACMILLAN SERIES IN INFORMATION TECHNOLOGY

| | |
|---|---|
| BARKER | *Developing Business Expert Systems Using Level5,* 0-675-20951-X, 1988 |
| CHANDLER/ LIANG | *Developing Expert Systems for Business Applications,* 0-675-21102-6, 1990 |
| DOLOGITE | *Developing Knowledge-Based Systems Using VP-Expert,* 0-02-381886-7, 1992 |
| DUGGAL | *Business Programming Using dBASE IV: A Structured Approach to Systems Development,* 0-02-330588-6, 1992<br>*Business Programming Using FoxPro,* 0-02-330585-1, 1992 |
| ELIASON | *Online Business Computer Applications, Third Edition,* 0-02-332481-3, 1991 |
| ELLZEY | *Data Structures for Computer Information Systems, Second Edition,* 0-02-332610-7, 1989 |
| KHAN | *Beginning Structured COBOL,* 0-675-21174-3, 1990 |
| KROENKE | *Database Processing: Fundamentals, Design, Implementation, Fourth Edition,* 0-02-366875-X, 1992 |
| LAUDON/ LAUDON | *Management Information Systems: A Contemporary Perspective, Second Edition,* 0-02-368101-2, 1991 |
| LUCAS | *Managing the Information Services,* 0-02-372231-2, 1989 |
| MARTIN, M. | *Analysis and Design of Business Information Systems,* 0-675-20852-1, 1991 |
| MARTIN/ DEHAYES/ HOFFER/ PERKINS | *Managing Information Technology: What Managers Need to Know,* 0-02-328231-2, 1991 |
| McLEOD | *Management Information Systems, Fourth Edition,* 0-02-379431-3, 1990<br>*Introduction to Information Systems: A Problem-Solving Approach,* 0-02-379464-X, 1990 |
| MOCKLER | *Computer Software to Support Strategic Management Decision Making,* 0-02-381895-6, 1992<br>*Developing Knowledge-Based Systems Using an Expert System Shell,* 0-02-381875-1, 1992 |

| | |
|---|---|
| MOCKLER/ DOLOGITE | *Knowledge-Based Systems: An Introduction to Expert Systems,* 0-02-381897-2, 1992 |
| NEWCOMER | *Select . . . SQL: The Relational Database Language,* 0-02-386693-4, 1992 |
| OLSON/ COURTNEY | *Decision Support Models and Expert Systems,* 0-02-389340-0, 1992 |
| RAMOS/ SCHROEDER/ SIMPSON | *Data Communication and Networking with Novelle Netware,* 0-02-407791-7, 1992 |
| REGAN/ O'CONNOR | *Automating the Office: Systems and End-User Computing,* 0-02-399165-8, 1989 |
| ROCHE | *Managing Information Technology in Multinational Corporations,* 0-02-402690-5, 1992 |
| ROWE | *Business Telecommunications, Second Edition,* 0-02-404104-1, 1991 |
| TURBAN | *Decision Support and Expert Systems: Management Support Systems, Second Edition,* 0-02-421663-1, 1990<br>*Expert Systems and Applied Artificial Intelligence,* 0-02-421665-8, 1992 |
| WENIG | *Introduction to C.A.S.E. Technology Using the Visible Analyst Workbench,* 0-675-21367-3, 1991 |

*Dedicated to the late Colman M. Mockler Jr., former Chief Executive Officer of Gillette, brother and mentor of the authors, one of business's truly great leaders and an extraordinary human being*

# ACKNOWLEDGMENTS

A unique feature of this book is the inclusion of actual prototype knowledge-based systems (KBS), complete with expert system shells that enable developing and running KBS.

The disks accompanying this book contain the following shells:

- VP-Expert (runtime version and educational development version) from Wordtech Systems, Inc.
- LEVEL5 OBJECT (special version developed for this text) from Information Builders, Inc. and ObjectCraft (demonstration version) from ObjectCraft Inc.
- M.1 (educational development version) from Cimflex Teknowledge.
- NeuroShell runtime version) from Ward Systems Group, Inc.

We wish to thank our many friends at each of these companies, especially Jay Brownfield, William Draper, Paul Harmon, Rob Savette, Terry Schussler, and Steve Ward, who helped develop the versions of their systems included in this book and who gave their permission to use their software.

The disks accompanying this book also provide knowledge-based systems for performing and staffing the many tasks involved in the KBS development cycle and in the KBS development effort management job. In addition, several sample KBS used in such areas as fault diagnosis, tax fraud detection, financial planning, logistics planning, career planning, and pricing strategies are given on the accompanying disks.

The inclusion of actual systems on disks grew out of our experiences in teaching KBS development. Students clearly seem to learn effectively from studying models or samples of these systems.

We wish to thank our many colleagues in business and in teaching for their inspiration and help in developing this book, including Alan Brody, consultant; Justin Carey and Pat Lyons of St. John's University; Jim Euchner, New York Telephone Company; Robert Flast and Paul Clancy, Metropolitan Life Insurance Company; Paul Gray, Claremont School of Management; B. Loernic Helft and Bill Ferns, Baruch College, City University of New York; Medhi Khosprowpour, Pennsylvania State University; Dorothy Leonard-Barton, Harvard Business School; Jay Liebowitz, George Washington University; Donald Lotufo, Halbrecht Associates; Ed Mahler, DuPont; Laurence Mauer, St. John's University; the late Colman Mockler, CEO of Gillette; Mike Prietula, Carnegie-Mellon University; Jack Rahaim, Digital Equipment Corporation; Neantro Saavedra Rivano, University of Tsukuba, Japan; Alan Rowe, University of Southern California; Bernard Taylor, The Management College, Henley, England; and Ephraim Turban, Eastern Illinois University. We also wish to thank our students who contributed to the development of this book, including Nancy Chan, Jean Chang, James Diver, John Egan, Andrea Fiorletta, Paul Inselman, Brian Jaffe, Noreen Joyce, Irene Kaczmarzyk, Marlena Kobylinska, Ingrid Marshall, Andreas Nolas, Jill Perri, and Katherine Vasalopoulis. Special thanks to the reviewers of the final draft, whose thoughtful comments proved invaluable: Paul Alpar, Tel Aviv University, Israel; Carl Clavadetscher, California Polytechnic State University; David Doss, Illinois State University; Brian Forst, George Washington University; Shohreh Hashemi, University of Houston; Michael Pazzani, University of California, Irvine; and John Sviolka, Harvard University. Particular thanks as well to others who helped shape the initial concept of the book: Terry Byrd, Florida State University; Orakwue Arinze, Drexel University; James Courtney, Texas A&M; Allen Greenwood, Northeastern University; Gail Yaverbaum, Temple University; David Yen, Miami University of Ohio; and Bayard Wynne, University of Indiana, Bloomington.

In addition, the following people played major roles in developing systems and text descriptions of the systems included in this book: Patricia Lynch, analyzing power plant/turbine performance; Neil Radar, product pricing strategy in the computer industry; John Merseburg, initial screening for an expert-driven KBS project, feasibility studies and risk evaluation for KBS development projects, and career strategy planning; Nicholas Marino, income tax auditing; and Orlando Calderon, logistics planning.

Special thanks go to Mark Aune, Sweelim Chia, Constanza Garrido-Pullo, Dane Gobin, Nathaniel Kanner, Michael Lang, Ricky Lin, Helen Ly, Janice Smith, Peter Smith, Sharon Wajswol, and Nancy Ward for their help in preparing the draft for publication. Vern Anthony, our editor at Macmillan, is one of that rare breed of editors who retains those very high professional standards abandoned by so many publishers today—and is at the same time a valued friend who helps when needed. Our thanks to developmental editor Peggy Jacobs for her help in shaping the book at its inception and her continuing insistence on correctness of detail, Jeff Smith for his work on the software accompanying this book, Peter Robison for his work on the graphics, Linda Bayma for her work on the production of this book, and Dave Boelio, whose early interest in the project was extremely helpful. Very particular thanks goes to John Merseburg, without whose continuing help—from inception to completion—this book probably never would have been written.

# Contents

# Part Four

## MANAGING KBS DEVELOPMENT EFFORTS

# Introduction

This introductory chapter covers:

- Intended users of this book
- How to use this book
- The growing importance of knowledge-based systems (KBS) in business
- Problems inhibiting the growth of KBS
- Integrated decision making
- Nature of the KBS development cycle—a decision-making and implementation process
- Overview of the book
- Actual prototype KBS described in the text and given on the disks accompanying this book

Knowledge-based systems— generally referred to as KBS throughout this book—are computer systems designed to replicate functions performed by a human being. For example, KBS developed at E. I. duPont & Company, Inc., a U.S. based multinational company, perform such tasks as selecting the right grade and kind of rubber for customers, diagnosing equipment failures, and scheduling machines on the factory floor. Other similar systems exist which give advice in auditing, sales management, media selection, configuring computer systems, assigning rooms to guests at hotels, and many other areas of management planning and decision making.

Typically, knowledge-based systems enable users with a problem to consult a computer system as they would an expert advisor to:

- diagnose what may be causing a problem
- figure out how to solve a problem, perform a task, or make a decision

Like a human expert, such a computer system can extract additional information from a user by asking questions related to the problem during a consultation. It can also answer questions asked by a user about why certain information is needed. It can make recommendations regarding the problem or decision at the end of a consultation, and it can explain the reasoning steps gone through to reach its conclusions when asked by a user.

## INTENDED USERS OF THIS BOOK

This book is written for three types of readers:

- individuals wishing to learn how to develop KBS—including experts developing their own systems or experts working with systems developers (knowledge engineers) in developing KBS
- knowledge engineers working with experts/users
- KBS development project managers working on larger projects in more complex organizational environments

The first category includes not only computer information systems technicians but also nontechnical managers with no computer training, who wish in some way to improve their job performance using KBS or to work more effectively with knowledge engineers and experts in creating a KBS. Individuals working on their own, as well as students in a graduate or undergraduate course or in an executive seminar wishing to learn how to develop KBS, are included in this category.

The second category refers to those who wish to function as knowledge engineers and work with experts and with software engineers in developing knowledge-based systems. This includes not only programmers, software engineers, computer information systems (CIS) personnel, and computer scientists, but also those from any field wishing to explore knowledge engineering's potential usefulness to them. Knowledge engineers come from all fields—anthropology, sociology, liberal arts, CIS, computer science, or just about any field providing training and experience in the cognitive and interpersonal skills needed to do KBS development.

The third category refers to those readers who are exploring or doing KBS project management. This would include management information systems (MIS) personnel, as well as anyone else from the above categories of readers wishing to learn, or improve, their KBS development management skills.

Draft versions of this book have been used by both nontechnical managers and by CIS and other professionals to help them learn about KBS development in training seminars and in college courses at both the undergraduate and graduate level.

## HOW TO USE THIS BOOK

The first category of readers, individuals developing their own systems or taking an introductory course in KBS development, would focus on the chapters in Part One, Part Two (Chapters 3–6), Part Five, and the Appendices. These chapters provide step-by-step guidance on developing small prototype systems using expert system development shells. They are useful in courses aimed at computer information systems students, as well as in courses designed for students unfamiliar with computers.

The readers in the second category, more advanced systems developers, would focus on Parts One, Two, Three, Five, and Six, and the Appendices. These chapters provide guidance on working with experts and users in developing larger systems.

The third category, readers interested in KBS development project management, would focus on the whole book, excluding perhaps the chapters in Parts One and Two if they are already familiar with knowledge-based systems and their development.

Many readers of early drafts of this book have said they find it easier to understand the text if they can visualize what a knowledge-based system is and see it actually work. Those readers who feel the same way might find it useful to examine an actual system, such as one of those described in Chapters 15 through 20 or in the articles in the Appendices, before going on to Chapters 1 and 2. They might also want to consult one of the systems given on the disks accompanying the book.

## THE GROWING IMPORTANCE OF KNOWLEDGE-BASED SYSTEMS (KBS) IN BUSINESS

The importance of knowledge-based systems in business is increasingly being recognized, judging by the number of companies involved in developing them, the amount of money spent on them, and the number of systems already developed and in operation (for examples see: AAAI 1991; Brody 1990; Cullen 1988; Feigenbaum 1988; Humpert 1988; Mahler 1986; Mockler 1989; Schorr 1989; Schutzer 1987; World Congress 1991).

The importance of these systems is likely to increase in the future, especially systems designed to support and replicate lower- and middle-level management tasks. This is the level at which shortages of managerial personnel arising from the "baby bust" will be occurring over the next twenty years. These shortages are already showing up in the retail and service areas today. A wide range of knowledge-based systems can be useful in helping fill this management gap.

Their importance is also likely to increase as KBS become more and more integrated with conventional computer systems. KBS ultimately are just another computer information systems tool among the many available which can be used to help managers make more effective decisions.

## PROBLEMS INHIBITING THE GROWTH OF KBS

Enormous problems have been encountered in introducing KBS technology into business. In one study, half the systems failed (Cullen 1988). Rose (1988) describes another somewhat typical project, in which two years and $300,000 were spent in developing an 80-rule system that is not being used. Such stories can be discouraging to those thinking about entering this area.

In addition to technological limitations, a key problem inhibiting rapid growth of these systems is that considerable work still needs to be done in defining in precise detail how the thousands of management and operational decisions occurring daily in business are made. Solving this problem is difficult largely because a sufficient number of business managers and experts do not have the time or financial incentive to do this work. Yet, as with other types of decision support systems, input from these managers about the thinking processes (heuristics) involved in their decision making is an extremely important ingredient in creating effective KBS (Cupello 1988, DeLong and Rockart 1986, Keen 1981, Leonard-Barton 1987, and Mockler 1991, 1992).

This detailed decision-definition work needs to be done before a wide range of larger, more complex, and comprehensive KBS can be developed, as has been pointed out by AI researchers such as Daniel Dennett of Tufts University (Linden 1988, p. 63). Books such as this one, written from a nontechnical manager viewpoint, are designed to help overcome this problem.

These kinds of difficulties and failures are not unexpected, however, at this stage of a newly emerging technology, such as knowledge-based systems.

Introducing any computer technology into an organization requires integrating technological and user requirements. The job is especially difficult when introducing knowledge-based system technology because:

- The technology (hardware and software) is relatively new and still developing rapidly, so that neither the technology nor its benefits and applications are yet widely understood.
- Many advocates of the technology have promised more than the technology can deliver, given the present state of the art (Bulkeley 1990; Fox 1990), causing many to become disenchanted with the technology.
- Developing these systems requires some skills that are substantially different from those required for conventional computer system development, creating major problems for CIS personnel.

- Expert/user involvement in the development process can be much greater than that found in conventional computer system development, creating substantial management and organization problems in knowledge-based systems development efforts.
- There are few readily available, detailed accounts of, on the one hand, how these expert systems affect an existing company organization situation and the people in it, or, on the other hand, what type of organization and management style is best for developing and deriving maximum benefit from these systems.
- There is resistance to KBS because the need for such systems is not as apparent to managers as is the need for conventional computer systems, such as those found in the financial and accounting areas.

This book is an attempt to help overcome some of these problems, through describing ways to:

- encourage more expert/manager/user participation in developing these systems
- overcome management resistance to these systems
- improve development project management by defining skill requirements and developing ways to staff and train personnel to meet them
- examine the accounts of many companies that have planned and managed KBS development projects

The book provides an integrated approach to handling a wide range of KBS development situations and developer skill levels.

## INTEGRATED DECISION MAKING

Planning and carrying out KBS development efforts involves integrating technical, human, and organization factors. This process can be complicated by the fact that development situations can vary so widely.

At one extreme, a company situation may involve smaller systems and a single or small group of users/operating managers who are computer literate or have access to expert systems development shells and who perceive expert systems as being potentially useful in their jobs. At the other extreme, application development situations may involve a large, diversified group of users who are in sales or another primarily nontechnical job, who have varying degrees of computer literacy, who are not aware of the potential benefits of expert systems, who are of widely varying ages and work experience, and who work in widely dispersed geographic locations for a large diversified company.

The range of system technology and complexity can also vary, from small user-developed systems employing personal computers (PCs) and PC expert system shells, to very large systems developed by computer scientists using mainframe or dedicated computer hardware technology.

This range of possible development situations suggests that rather than just focusing on a single approach to organizing and implementing knowledge-based systems development projects, it is useful to also consider a situational decision-making orientation.

*Situational decision-making approaches to management* are fairly common and have a long history. Simply stated, they give models or approaches for either handling specific management decision-making situations or adapting general processes to specific business situations.

In the organizational behavior area, for example, over twenty years ago Fred Fiedler (1967) developed a contingency theory of leadership, in which he categorized different kinds of work-group situations and the leadership style most effective in each. A summary of the early work done in this field is given in "The Situational Theory of Management" (Mockler 1971).

A situational orientation, rather than a technique approach, is a logical one for business managers, since they very often think first in terms of specific money-making tasks, rather than in terms of techniques or general precepts (Marks 1989). The validity of this orientation is substantially documented in research literature, beginning with early intuitive and anecdotal support (Dewey 1938) and continuing later with more empirical evidence (Simon 1969; Morton 1971; and Nutt 1986).

A structured situational orientation is an especially effective disciplined approach to carrying out and managing KBS development. It is the basis of this book.

## NATURE OF THE KBS DEVELOPMENT CYCLE: A DECISION-MAKING AND IMPLEMENTATION PROCESS

The KBS development life cycle shown in Figure I–1 is based on situation requirements analysis, as can be seen from an examination of the steps involved in it:

- situation selection and definition
- situation knowledge analysis and representation
- situation knowledge transformation
- system design
- system development
- system testing and implementation
- system maintenance

The cycle is situationally based, because the system developed must replicate the specific expertise in the situation under study. This requires not only accurate analysis of the situation requirements, but constant referral to them during the system development process.

The *situational management process,* which encompasses both making decisions and carrying out those decisions, is also the approach used in KBS project

**Figure I–1.** Knowledge-Based Systems Development Life Cycle

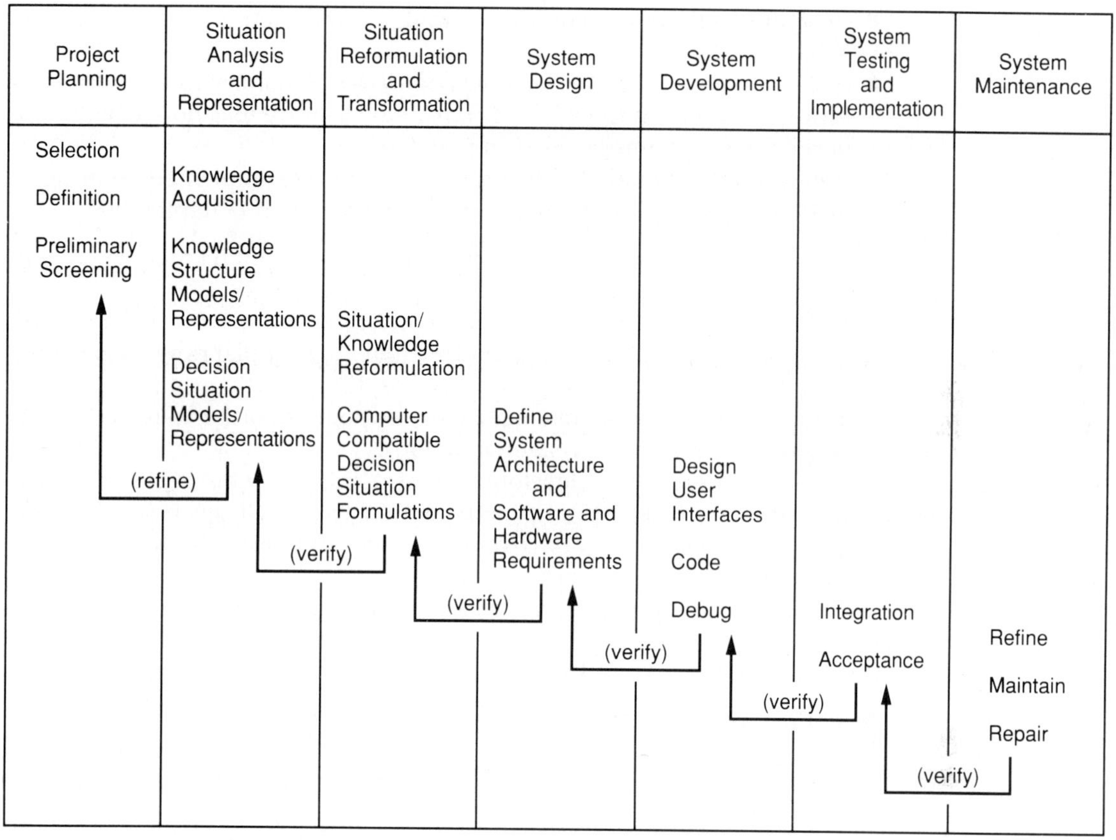


management planning and implementation. For this reason, Figure I–1 is repeated throughout the book in order to give a consistent focus to the discussions in each chapter where it is relevant.

## OVERVIEW OF THE BOOK

In Part One, Chapter 1 gives a basic introduction to knowledge-based systems. Chapter 2 covers the KBS development life cycle, from project selection and definition through structured situation analysis and system design to putting the system into the computer. Chapters 3, 4, 5 and 6 in Part Two guide readers through developing a small prototype KBS using an expert systems development shell, VP-Expert.

In Part Three, a chapter is devoted to each of the major tasks in the KBS development life cycle:

- structured situation analysis: knowledge acquisition and representation (Chapter 7)
- system design and development: knowledge transformation and system representation (Chapter 8); software and hardware selection (Chapter 9); developing user interfaces (Chapter 10)
- system implementation: interpersonal and other implementation tasks, including testing, validating, and refining a system (Chapter 11)

These chapters cover in detail the major technical tools and techniques used in KBS development.

Part Four covers the basic strategies, tasks, and tools needed for KBS development in the critical management function areas of planning, organizing, monitoring, controlling and directing, and staffing. Each of these areas is approached from a situational management viewpoint, in order to focus on how to get the job done in specific reader situations.

Part Five describes the development of a number of sample prototype knowledge-based systems. These prototype systems are all given on the disks accompanying this text. Part Six covers two areas important to KBS development: objects and neural networks.

The Appendices describe the experiences of several companies in developing larger KBS for on-the-job applications. The sample systems in Part Five and the Appendices serve several functions:

- They introduce readers to developing more advanced KBS.
- Several of the systems are designed to assist in KBS development, so the description of their development helps reinforce the material described earlier in the book.
- Many of the systems described give a feeling for the different kinds of KBS which can be developed and the way different companies went about developing them.
- These systems provide examples of how an integrated approach is applied to KBS development, for an individual working alone, a knowledge engineer, or a KBS development project manager.
- Since many of these systems are on the disks accompanying this book, they give the reader an opportunity to examine KBS, and their complete knowledge bases in detail.

## ACTUAL PROTOTYPE KBS DESCRIBED IN THE TEXT AND GIVEN ON THE DISKS ACCOMPANYING THIS BOOK

This book is the first in the area to include both a wide range of actual prototype KBS and a choice of rule-based and object-oriented expert system shells that make possible the developing and running of KBS.

The shells included are:

- VP-Expert (runtime version and educational development version)
- LEVEL5 OBJECT and ObjectCraft (educational and demo versions)
- M.1 (limited educational development version)
- NeuroShell (runtime version)

The fourteen KBS included with the book cover a wide range of knowledge areas, as seen from the table of contents and the acknowledgments at the beginning of the book. The inclusion of actual systems on disks grew out of the experiences of the authors in teaching KBS development. People seem to learn most effectively through observing models or samples of these systems.

For this reason, a library of systems and shells is made available to students at each of the authors' schools. Many of the systems from these libraries are included in this book and in other books by the authors listed below. Once such a library was provided, much less class time was needed to cover simple mechanics, substantially more interest was generated among students, and the quality of systems produced by students greatly improved. Those instructors who have had similar experiences are invited to also make use of the authors' two supplemental texts of additional systems, *Developing Knowledge-Based Systems Using an Expert System Shell* (Robert J. Mockler) and *Developing Knowledge-Based Systems Using VP-Expert* (D. G. Dologite), both published by Macmillan.

## REFERENCES

Brody, Alan. "Artificial Intelligence Comes of Age." *Ad Week's Marketing Computers,* January 1990, pp. 26–30.

Bulkeley, William M. "Bright Outlook for Artificial Intelligence Yields to Slow Growth and Big Cutbacks." *The Wall Street Journal,* July 5, 1990, pp. B1, B3.

Cullen, J., and A. Bryman. "The Knowledge Acquisition Bottleneck." *Expert Systems,* August 1988, pp. 216–25.

Cuppello, James M., and David J. Mishelevicksy. "Managing Prototype Knowledge/Expert System Projects." *Communications of the ACM,* May 1988, pp. 534–41.

DeLong, David W., and John F. Rockart. *Identifying the Attributes of Successful Executive Support System Implementation.* Center for Information Systems Research, Sloan School of Management, Cambridge, MA: MIT, November 1986.

Dewey, John. *Logic: The Structure of Inquiry.* New York: Putnam, 1938.

Dologite, D. G. *Developing Knowledge-Based Systems Using VP-Expert.* New York: Macmillan, 1992.

Feigenbaum, Edward, Pamela McCorduck, and H. Penny Nii. *The Rise of the Expert Company.* New York: Times Books, 1988.

Fiedler, Fred E. *A Theory of Leadership Effectiveness.* New York: McGraw-Hill, 1967.

Fox, Mark S. "AI and Expert System Myths, Legends, and Facts." *IEEE Expert,* February 1990, pp. 8–22.

Humpert, Benedikt, and Patrick Holley. "Expert Systems in Financial Planning." *Expert Systems,* May 1988, pp. 78–100.

Keen, Peter G. W. "Value Analysis: Justifying Decision Support Systems." *MIS Quarterly,* March 1981.

Leonard-Barton, Dorothy. "Technology Implementation as Integrative Innovation: The Case of an Expert System." *Sloan Management Review,* October-November 1987, pp. 84–109.

Linden, Eugene. "Putting Knowledge to Work." *Time,* March 28, 1988, pp. 60–63.

Mahler, Ed. "The Business Needs Approach." *Knowledge-Based Systems: A Step-by-Step Guide to Getting Started (The Second Artificial Intelligence Symposium).* Austin, Texas: Texas Instruments Company, 1986, pp. 1–18 to 1–25.

Marks, Neil B., and Richard H. McClure. "A First Step Toward Teaching *Modelling* Rather Than *Model.*" *OR/MS Today,* December 1989, pp. 28–29.

Mockler, Robert J. *Developing Knowledge-Based Systems Using an Expert System Shell.* New York: Macmillan, 1992.

Mockler, Robert J. *Knowledge-Based Systems for Management Decisions.* Englewood Cliffs, NJ: Prentice-Hall, 1989.

Mockler, Robert J. "The Situational Theory of Management." *Harvard Business Review,* May/June 1971, pp. 146–55.

Mockler, Robert J. *Strategic Management: Strategic Planning and Implementation, An Integrated Decision Making Approach,* New York: D & R Publishing Company, 1991.

Morton, Michael S. Scott. *Management Decision Systems: Computer-Based Support for Decision Making.* Cambridge, MA: Division of Research, Harvard, 1971.

Nutt, P. C. "Decision Style and Strategic Decisions of Top Executives." *Technological Forecasting of Social Change,* 30 (1), 1986, pp. 39–62.

Rose, Frederick. "An 'Electronic Clone' of a Skilled Engineer Is Very Hard to Create." *Wall Street Journal,* August 12, 1988, pp. 1, 14.

Schorr, Herbert, and Alain Rappaport. *Innovative Applications of Artificial Intelligence.* Menlo Part, CA: AAAI Press, 1989.

Schutzer, Daniel. *Artificial Intelligence.* New York: Van Nostrand Reinhold, 1987.

Simon, H. A. *The Science of the Artificial.* Cambridge, MA: MIT Press, 1969.

*World Congress on Expert Systems,* Orlando, FL: International Association of Knowledge Engineers, European Coordinating Committee for Artificial Intelligence, IEEE Technical Committee on Expert Systems Applications, December 1991.

# Part One

## KNOWLEDGE-BASED SYSTEMS DEVELOPMENT

# 1

# Knowledge-Based Systems

The objective of this chapter is to help readers understand:

- What knowledge-based systems (KBS) are
- The way knowledge is represented in a knowledge-based system
- The ways knowledge-based systems "think" or "reason": the inference engine
- Knowledge-based system programming languages and shells
- The role and importance of prototyping
- The KBS development life-cycle
- Skills useful in KBS development
- The situational decision-making orientation of the book

## WHAT KNOWLEDGE-BASED SYSTEMS (KBS) ARE

### Some Basic Definitions

As shown in Figure 1–1, knowledge-based systems are a branch of artificial intelligence (Bowerman 1988; Charniack 1985; Harmon 1990; Feigenbaum 1988; Martin 1988; Mockler 1989; Patterson 1990). Such systems can function at the assistant, colleague, or expert level.

**Figure 1–1.** Branches of Artificial Intelligence

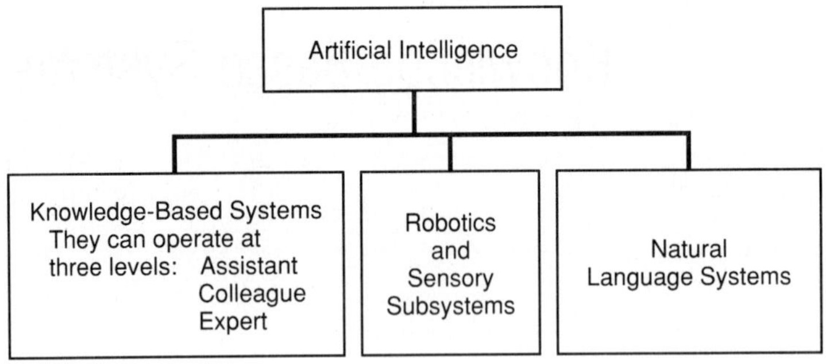


**Artificial intelligence** is the capability of a device, such as a computer, to perform functions or tasks that would be regarded as intelligent if they were observed in humans.

A **knowledge-based system** is a computer system that attempts to replicate specific human expert intelligent activities. Human experts make decisions and recommendations, such as whom to give bank loans to or what steps to take to fix a turbine malfunction, and perform tasks, such as adjusting temperature controls in a manufacturing plant. They also assist and train others to perform tasks and make decisions. Knowledge-based systems can do these intelligent activities. Typically, knowledge-based systems (KBS) enable users with a problem to consult the computer system as they would an expert human advisor.

Like a human expert, such a computer system can extract additional information from a user by asking questions related to the problem during a consultation. It can also answer questions asked by a user about why certain information is needed. It can make recommendations regarding the problem or make a decision at the end of the consultation, and can explain the reasoning steps used to reach its conclusions. In some situations, it can analyze a problem and take corrective action directly.

Figure 1–2 gives a list of commercial business applications of KBS. These systems range from ones that help in capital- or personal-investment planning to ones that troubleshoot telephone circuit breakdowns and configure computer systems for individual customers (Feigenbaum 1988; Schorr 1989).

Knowledge-based systems—computer systems in which the knowledge base and inferencing mechanism are separate—are often integrated with conventional procedural computer systems in a variety of ways. For example, financial-planning systems often contain traditional financial simulation applications, which are combined with knowledge-based systems that evaluate the more subjective decision criteria, such as planning assumptions. Knowledge-based systems are also found as so-called front-ends of database management systems (Schur 1988). As Chapnick (1988) points out, while there will always be a need for some true stand-alone knowledge-based systems, the bulk of these systems in

**Figure 1–2.** Commercial Business Applications

ACE (AT&T) provides trouble-shooting reports and analyses for telephone cable maintenance

AS/ASQ (Arthur Young) helps in auditing procedures

AUDITOR (U. of Illinois) selects auditing procedures for the verification of a firm's accounts receivable

AUTHORIZER'S ASSISTANT (American Express) helps in fighting credit card fraud

BUSINESS PLAN (Sterling Wentworth Corp.) advises self-employed professionals and business owners about all aspects of financial planning

CASH VALUE (Heuros Ltd.) provides capital projects planning

COMPASS (GTE Corp.) troubleshoots telephone circuit breakdowns

CONCEPT (Tyashare) produces models of consumer markets

DELTA (GE) helps diagnose and repair diesel electric locomotives

DRILLING ADVISOR (Teknowledge) advises drilling rig supervisors on ways to avoid problems related to drilling and sticking

EDP AUDITOR (Brigham Young and U. of Florida) assists auditors in working with advanced electronic data processing systems

EXPERTAX (Coopers & Lybrand) provides tax accounting advice

FIN PLAN (Wright Patterson Air Force Base) provides personal financial planning

FINANCIAL ADVISOR (Palladian) gives financial advice on projects, products, and mergers and acquisitions

FOLIO (Stanford) helps portfolio managers determine client investment goals and selects portfolios that best meet those needs

GENESIS (IntelliCorp) assists genetic engineers in analyzing DNA molecules

INTELLIGENT SECRETARY (Nippon T&T) manages the schedules of personnel in a company

MORTGAGE LOAN ANALYZER (Arthur Andersen) assists underwriters in making approval decisions on residential mortgage loans

PERSONAL FINANCIAL PLANNER (A.D. Little) prepares total financial plans for individuals with incomes of $25K-100K

PLANPOWER (Applied Expert Systems) gives professional financial planning advice

(R1)XCON (Digital Equipment Corp/Carnegie-Mellon) configures computer systems to meet individual customer specifications

STRATEGIC MANAGEMENT OF TECHNOLOGY (A.D. Little) assists in the planning of research and development investments for key corporate technologies

SYNTELLIGENCE has an expert system to advise insurance underwriters in evaluating commercial risk

TAXADVISOR (U. of Illinois) provides estate planning tax advice

TICOM (U. of Minnesota) models a computer company's internal control systems

TRADER'S ASSISTANT (A.D. Little) assists securities traders in assessing the state of the stock market

XSEL (Digital Equipment) acts as an expert selling assistant to assist DEC salespersons the future will probably integrate in some way with conventional systems and processes already in place and in use or under development. In this sense, it is useful to think of knowledge-based systems and related artificial intelligence areas not as a distinct market in themselves, but rather as a group of techniques that have applications in many different markets (Bulkeley 1990).

**Knowledge bases** are collections of expertise or expert knowledge. They can include anything from basic information about a field of knowledge to guidelines for reasoning about that information in order to make decisions and perform tasks. This explains why the systems discussed in this book are commonly referred to as "expert systems," a term which is an abbreviated version of the term "expert knowledge-based systems (EKBS)" (Turban 1990, p. 424).

The relation of knowledge-based systems and expert systems is easy to define. KBS are systems in which the knowledge base is in large measure distinct from the inferencing mechanism or procedure. **Expert systems** is a general term used to describe a wide range of more advanced computer systems variously described as:

- interactive decision support systems (DSS)
- executive information systems (EIS), which are more focused management information systems (MIS) that generate reports for top management
- executive support systems, which often combine DSS and MIS capabilities

Because the term *expert systems* is used sometimes to refer to both conventional and knowledge-based systems, it is avoided in this book, even though it is recognized that knowledge-based systems are in practice almost always referred to as expert systems for simplicity's sake.

Where the term *expert* is used in relation to the KBS development situations in this book, it is used in a relative sense. It refers to persons who do their jobs very well or professionally. The actual job can range from order-entry clerk, to troubleshooting repair person, to product planner, to production or operations manager, to strategy developer. The absolute importance of the decision, problem, or task is not what makes it "expert."

### Different Kinds of Knowledge-Based Systems

Knowledge-based systems are sometimes classified by the area to which they can be applied, such as medicine and chemistry. They are also classified by the generic problem areas they are concerned with, such as those given in Figure 1–3. These generic categories range from well-defined areas, such as diagnosis, monitoring, and debugging, to less well-defined areas, such as planning, design, and interpretation. Such a classification system helps potential users to determine if their own problem might be appropriate for knowledge-based systems technology. Knowledge-based systems for management decision making generally fall into the less well-defined categories listed in Figure 1–3, such as planning, designing, and interpreting.

**Figure 1–3.** Generic Categories of Expert System Applications

| Category | Problem Addressed | Types of Systems |
|---|---|---|
| Diagnosis | Infers system malfunctions from observations | Medical, electronic, financial analysis, auditing, machine repair |
| Monitoring | Compares observations in order to identify variations | Management control, nuclear power plant regulation |
| Debugging | Prescribes remedies for malfunctions | Computer software |
| Repair | Executes a plan to administer a prescribed remedy | Automobile, computer, telephone |
| Instruction | Diagnoses, debugs, and corrects student behavior | Tutorial, remedial |
| Control | Interprets, predicts, repairs, and monitors system behaviors | Air traffic control, battle management, manufacturing process control |
| Prediction | Infers likely consequences of given situations | Weather forecasting, crop estimation, financial forecasting |
| Interpretation | Infers situation descriptions from sensor data | Speech understanding, image analysis, surveillance, mapping |
| Design | Configures objects within situation constraints | Circuit layout, budgeting, automatic program generation |
| Planning | Develops guidelines for action | Strategic planning, process scheduling, military planning |
| Classification | Prescribes categories for given sets of criteria | Planning, scheduling, layout, remedial, auditing, forecasting |

Well-known early systems had such names and applications as:

| *Name (and University/Institute)* | *Application* |
|---|---|
| DENDRAL (Stanford) | Chemical analysis |
| HASP/SIAP (Stanford) | Military ship identification |
| HEARSAY-II (Carnegie-Mellon) | Speech understanding |
| INTERNIST/CADUSEUS (University of Pittsburgh) | Medical diagnosis |
| MACSYMA (MIT) | Algebraic simplification and integration |
| MYCIN (Stanford) | Medical diagnosis |
| PROSPECTOR (Stanford Research Institute) | Evaluation of mineral deposit potential |
| PUFF (Stanford) | Medical diagnosis |

Thanks largely to popular works of fiction, such as the movie *Star Wars,* the most widely recognized knowledge-based systems are those involving robotics and military weapons systems. Robotic applications of artificial intelligence techniques are fairly common today in manufacturing and the military.

### The Evolution of Knowledge-Based Systems and Their Use in Business

The concept of artificial intelligence has been around for a very long time. Meaningful development work on knowledge-based systems only began, however, in the 1960s. During the 1970s many knowledge-based systems were developed.

Early knowledge-based systems were developed mainly at major universities such as Stanford, Carnegie-Mellon, and Massachusetts Institute of Technology (MIT). These systems involved such areas as agriculture, chemistry, computer systems, electronics, engineering, geology, information management, law, manufacturing, mathematics, medicine, meteorology, military science, physics, process control, and space technology. By far the most popular areas were medicine and chemistry.

More recently, increased attention has been paid to developing knowledge-based systems for a wide range of business applications using a variety of integrated techniques from many different areas (Bulkeley 1990).

While most of the early systems were developed for research or were doctoral dissertation research projects, considerable progress has been made in the 1980s in developing commercial business applications. Examples of these are given in Figure 1–2. A more complete list of these systems is given in Feigenbaum (1988), Schorr (1989), Liebowitz (1990), and the quarterly *Sigart Newsletter,* published by the Association of Computing Machinery (ACM), 11 West 42nd Street, New York, NY 10036.

Knowledge engineering companies such as CGI (Carnegie Group), Inference Corporation, and IntelliCorp were active in the knowledge-based systems development field in the early 1990s. Developing systems for business is a significant part of their work.

Major development activity is also evident within business firms. In 1990, there were many thousands of knowledge-based systems in existence or under development. For example, Ed Mahler of DuPont noted in September 1990 at an IEEE Conference on Managing KBS that his company already had hundreds of knowledge-based systems in use or under development, even though DuPont's KBS development project was only three years old. By 1991, DuPont had over 1,000 such functioning systems. These systems cover a variety of functional and operating areas from manufacturing to marketing to decision-support applications.

The architectural and engineering firm of Skidmore, Owings & Merrill has announced that it intends to work on KBS for a variety of design functions during the 1990s, including stairwell design, planning elevators, washroom layout, and coordinated core design. It has already developed a KBS that it uses in designing beams and columns for office buildings with thousands of structural members (Leaman 1989). As another example, IBM has announced that it is developing a wide range of knowledge-based systems for internal company use and expects to become a major supplier of them commercially during the 1990s.

Westinghouse Corp took five years to develop a major AI system to detect potential steam turbine generator failures. During that period, the basis was created for developing a wide range of other knowledge-based systems in the manufacturing area. A number of systems in manufacturing are described by Barker (1989), Bonnett (1989), O'Brien (1989), and Rowan (1989).

A great deal of work is also being done in the accounting and auditing area. For example, the Internal Revenue Service (IRS) is actively developing knowledge-based systems. They have gone so far as to send a large number of employees, at full pay, to spend two years studying AI theory and applications at the graduate level (Rogers 1988).

Many major banks, insurance companies, and financial service companies, such as American Express, have extensive in-house knowledge-based systems programs ("Expert Systems—Applications in Finance" 1988; Humpert 1988). General Motors is reportedly working on a wide range of financial knowledge-based systems, including ones which integrate strategic planning applications with financial applications.

While there is evidence of considerable activity, the exact number of systems being developed and in use in business today is not known because many of the systems being developed by corporations provide a major competitive advantage in the market place. Many companies, therefore, are often unwilling to discuss their KBS in any detail. Nevertheless, overall the evidence indicates that corporations are on the threshold of a major expansion of knowledge-based systems development. Presumably, this will eventually be followed by a growth in commercially available applications.

While artificial intelligence and its KBS segment are a large and growing market, this market does not appear to be as large as originally estimated. Instead of the originally projected market of $4.5 billion in annual sales, more recent estimates of the anticipated market are closer to $600 million. In addition, that market is also expected to be highly fragmented, since the technology is integrated with many other conventional computer markets (Bulkeley 1990).

### Distinguishing Characteristics of Knowledge-Based Systems

Figure 1–4 shows the components of a knowledge-based system: a knowledge base, an inference engine and control mechanism, a user interface, and computer hardware.

The major characteristics that distinguish knowledge-based computer systems from conventional computer systems are that they:

1. Contain a knowledge base about a specific decision domain or situation, which is in large measure distinct from the mechanism used to

**Figure 1–4.** Essential Components of a Knowledge-Based System

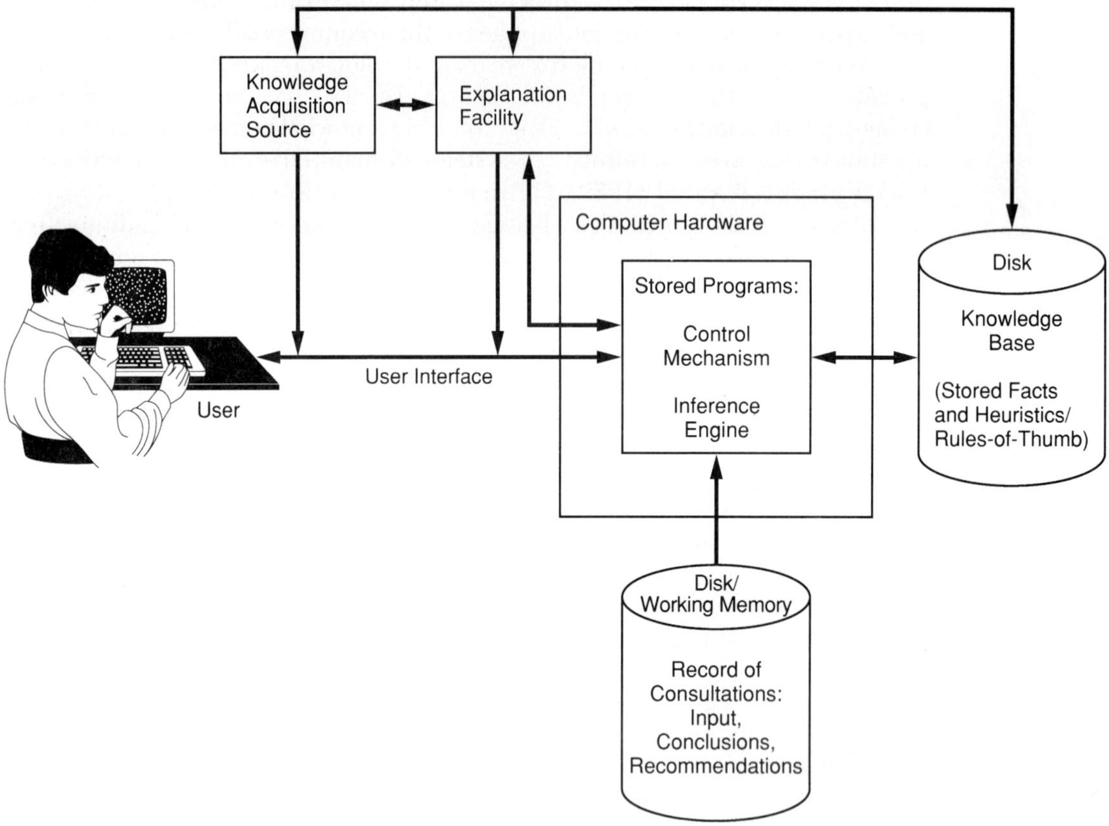


manipulate the knowledge to reach a decision (a process referred to as *inferencing*). This critical difference leads to two distinctive points:

- KBS are normally easier to modify, allowing a programmer or nontechnical user to modify segments of programs relatively easily; hence these systems are easier to maintain and update than conventional computer systems, where the expert knowledge and the procedural mechanism are not separate
- KBS allow users without much programming experience to read and even write the source code of a rule-based KBS program

2. Contain an inference engine, or inferential reasoning capability, which is in large measure distinct from the knowledge base and which in some ways mimics the way a human decision maker thinks

Other distinguishing characteristics of knowledge-based systems are that they:

3. Have a facility to explain their advice or reasoning process, so that a user can see why and how a conclusion was reached
4. Contain symbolic programming and reasoning capabilities
5. Use IF-THEN rules extensively, but not necessarily exclusively, and so are more readily understandable to nontechnical users
6. Can handle uncertain, unknown, and conflicting data
7. Very often require a high level of involvement of a human expert in their development

The following sections discuss the two major components of KBS, knowledge bases and inference engines. The discussion provides a basis for the sample system development work described in the following chapters (2, 3, 4, 5, and 6).

## REPRESENTING KNOWLEDGE IN A KBS

The following discussion briefly covers the ways knowledge is most often represented in KBS currently in use.

### IF-THEN Rules

IF-THEN rules are the most common way to represent knowledge in current knowledge-based systems. Examples of IF-THEN rules are given in Figure 1–5. Such rules contain premises or conditions in the IF clauses, and conclusions in the THEN clauses. The example in Figure 1–5 shows an IF-THEN rule used in a company's strategic planning knowledge-based system.

IF-THEN rules in knowledge-based systems differ from similar ones in conventional computer systems—they can be modified much more easily to meet changing needs. Digital Equipment Corporation, for example, first used conventional programming for a system that was designed to configure computer equipment into complete units (or systems) appropriate for specific customer needs. Digital found conventional programming rules could not meet the requirements of their production process, since their product line required frequent changes to meet individual customer needs. They switched to a knowledge-based system (called XCON) with IF-THEN rule capability, since it was easier to update.

**Figure 1–5.** Sample of IF-THEN Rules from a Knowledge Base and of the Inference Engine Search Process: Strategic Planning Prototype System

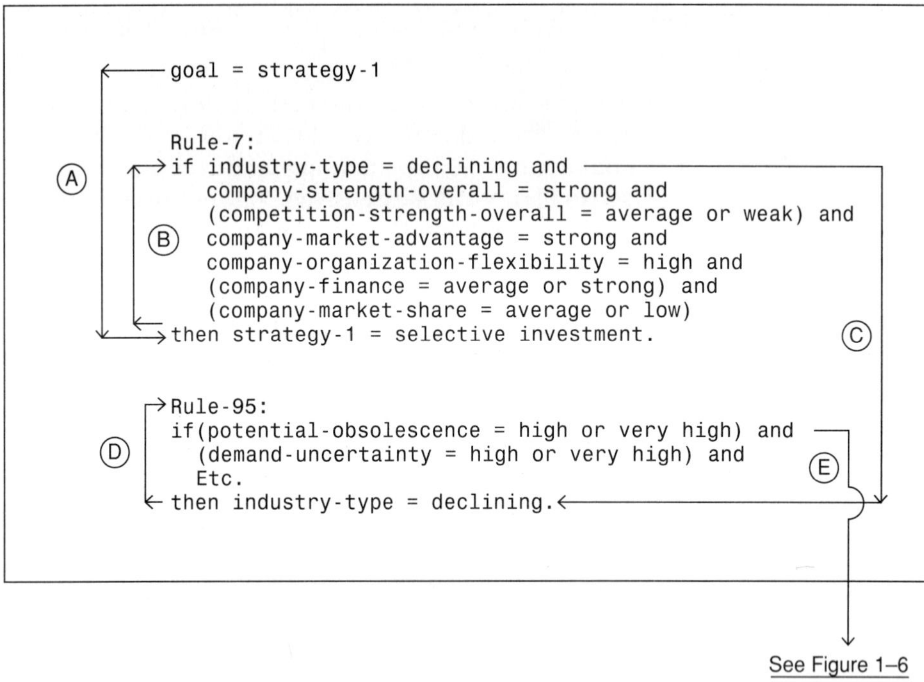


Rule-based systems, as well as other kinds of knowledge-based systems, also have the capability to ask users questions about information needed to deal with specific problems during consultations. Figure 1–6 gives an example of such questions.

### Objects or Frames

Objects or frames are a kind of template for holding related clusters of data, facts, rules, hypotheses, or any other knowledge in a single conceptual unit. They often require conceptual reorganization of situation data around key controlling concepts, as in the example of a frame given in Figure 1–7.

Frame-based, also called object-oriented, systems can deal with more complex decision situations than systems that contain only rules and questions. Since people generally think in clusters, especially in decision situations such as strategic planning, frames can sometimes come closer to mimicking the ways human beings reason and remember.

**Figure 1–6.** Sample of Knowledge Base Questions and a User Query: Strategic Planning Prototype System

```
question(potential-obsolescence) = 'How would you characterize
                                    the potential for
                                    technological obsolescence
                                    in this industry segment
                                    [very low, low, average,
                                    high, very high]?'

question(demand-uncertainty) = 'How would you assess the
                                uncertainty of future demand in
                                this industry segment [very low,
                                low, average, high, very high]?'
```

The first question above, which is stored in the system's knowledge base, causes the system to print the following on a user's computer screen:

```
      How would you characterize the potential for technological
obsolescence in this industry segment [very low, low, average,
high, very high]?

      >> (A user types an answer in here.)
```

Frames make use of slots to hold information about an item or object. This information usually covers an object's attributes and values, as well as procedures and pointers for getting data and information from other frames in the knowledge base. Frames may also contain rules and questions involving information in the frame. In addition to the items shown in Figure 1–7, they can contain and display material. They may even contain default values, which are values assumed when no other values are available.

Frames can be linked to other frames, to form a frame hierarchy. Pointers and procedures can, for example, direct the system to search other frames for related data. They can even be manipulated by the inference engine to draw new information from other frames. An example of frame hierarchies is given in Figure 1–8.

Since frame-based systems are more complex than simple rule-based systems, they are not yet as widely used in personal computer KBS applications as IF-THEN rules. Their potential in KBS development, however, is enormous, and their popularity is growing with the introduction of more frame-based development tools, such as LEVEL5 OBJECT and Nexpert Object (Aiken 1990).

**Figure 1–7.** Segment of Product/Customer Matching Frames: Marketing Planning System (Initial Prototype)

```
                              PRODUCT

Characteristics - Type:  High Quality Skis
                  Name:  Brand X
                  Specifications: Low volume, high margins;
                                  rapidly changing, high-tech;
                                  specialty/fashionable sports; short
                                  selling season; etc.

Factors affecting success: Familiarity with latest technology
                           and fashions to maintain up-to-date,
                           high quality image; ability to adapt
                           to rapid changes; not especially
                           price sensitive; ability to obtain
                           outlets and endorsements of champions/
                           winners; etc.

Opportunities:  Growing customer market, with rapidly expanding
                disposable income, etc.

Interconnecting-           Rule-6-1, etc.
  Procedures-Pointers
Rules:                     Rule-5-1, Rule-9-1, etc.
Questions:                 Question (....), etc.
```

```
                              CUSTOMER

Category:  Young Adult

Attributes:  (age) 22-29
             (income) $36,000 - 52,000
             (education) 16 years + etc.

Controlling
   concepts:  Experimental, growing, changeable, high disposable
              income, well educated, etc.

Product
 Implications: Fashionable and current; image of high quality; price is not
               barrier, image of new, up to date, technology, etc.
Interconnecting-                    Rule-6-1, etc.
 Procedures-Pointers
Rules                               Rule-5-1, Rule-9-1, etc.
Questions:                          Question (....), etc.
```

**Figure 1–8.** Frame Hierarchy Chart

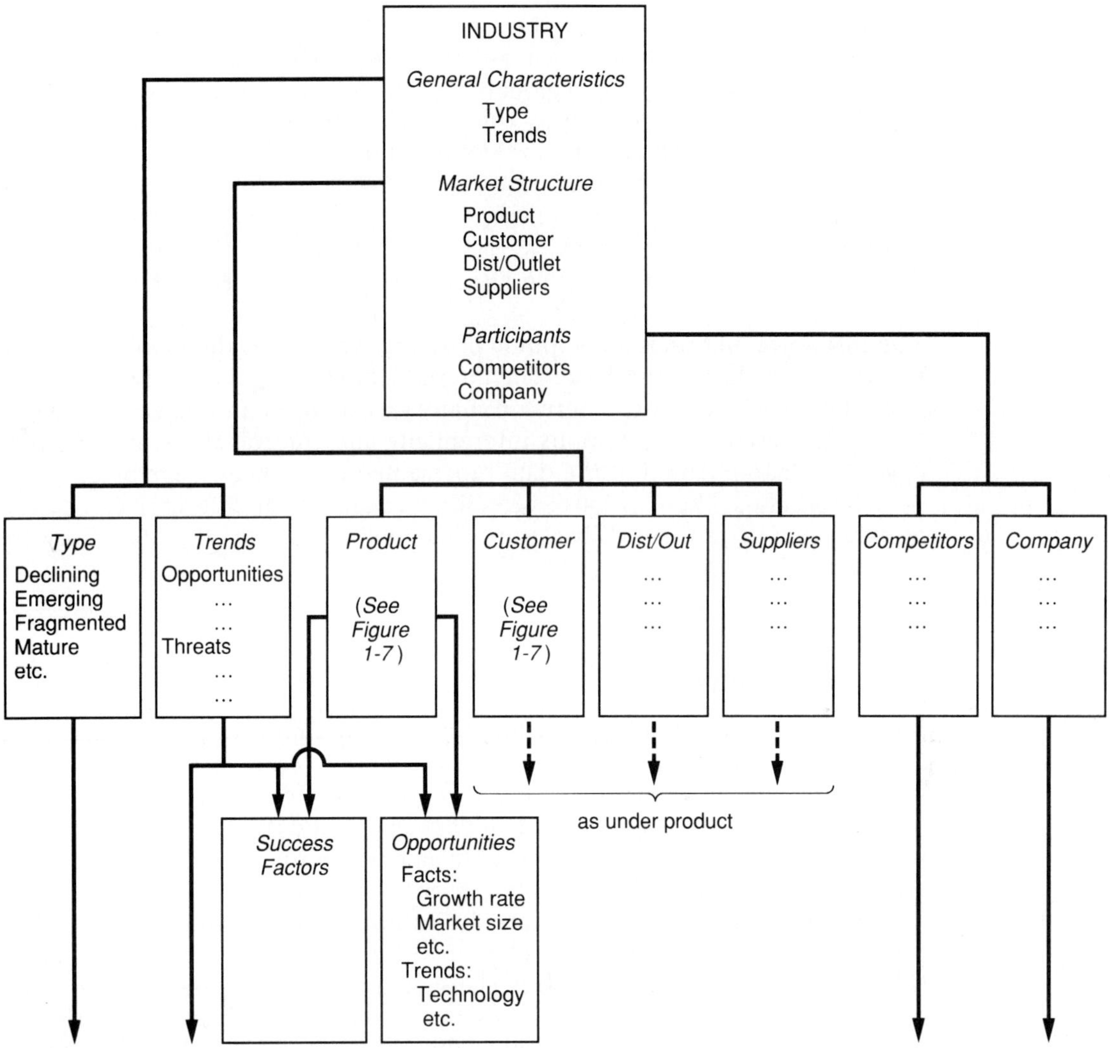

### Other Representations

Knowledge-based systems also use other forms of knowledge representation. One is called *logic representation.* The most familiar form of logic representation is *predicate logic* statements, such as "is-regional (company)." The statement literally means a company is regional. The answer can only be yes or no.

Logic statements, as well as rules, frames, frame hierarchies, and other knowledge representation tools, are discussed in more detail in Chapter 8.

## THE WAYS KBS "THINK" OR "REASON": THE INFERENCE ENGINE

The **inference engine** is a computer program that guides the manipulation of knowledge in a knowledge base. The inferential reasoning mechanism is distinct from the knowledge base. There are many ways that the inference engine in a knowledge-based system reasons inferentially and controls the reasoning processes and manipulation of the data represented in the knowledge base.

In deciding where to start a search for an answer, an inference engine can be either goal driven, called "backward chaining," or data driven, called "forward chaining."

### Backward Chaining

Backward chaining involves starting with one or more possible goals. In a rule-based system, for example, the inference engine tests each goal to see whether or not the IF clauses in the rule containing each possible goal are all true. It tests each rule in turn until an answer is found (that is, it finds a rule in which all the IF clauses are true), or until all possible rules are examined and no answer can be found.

Following the arrows in Figure 1–5 shows how this process works. The program begins its search for a solution with the goal it is seeking, a strategy (strategy-1). It seeks the first THEN clause in a rule in the knowledge base that contains the key word "strategy-1," as is indicated by the arrow line (A) on the left of Figure 1–5. The inference engine then "backward chains" to the first IF clause (or premise) within that rule and finds the key word "industry-type," as shown by the line (B) in the figure. The process continues in this way through the entire knowledge base until an answer is found. The answer is assumed found when:

- an answer is found for all of the IF clauses in a rule containing "strategy-1" in its THEN clause, or
- all the rules have been examined and the system determines an answer is not possible.

### Forward Chaining

Forward chaining involves reasoning from the other direction. It starts by examining the IF clauses and searches for a solution by working from the data toward a goal or a solution. When an answer is found to all of the IF clauses in a rule containing a goal word in its THEN clause (for example, "strategy-1"), it gives the user its recommended solution. It will report that no solution is possible if after an exhaustive search no answer is found.

Forward chaining searches can expand very rapidly, since a virtually unlimited number of rules may be examined. For this reason, controls are needed to set limits on the search process. In today's systems, therefore, forward chaining usually is combined with backward chaining, which sets limits on the number of goals examined, in order to reduce the time and computer capacity required for processing.

Forward and backward chaining and other search and reasoning techniques (for example, breadth and depth searches), reasoning with uncertainty, control mechanisms (which manage knowledge bases), explanation facilities, and natural language capabilities are all discussed at more length in Chapter 8.

## KNOWLEDGE-BASED SYSTEM PROGRAMMING LANGUAGES AND SHELLS

Knowledge-based systems were originally developed using programming languages such as LISP and PROLOG. Many other development tools and expert systems shells are available. They range from development versions of programming languages (such as OPS5 and INTERLISP) to larger shells (such as ART, ESE, and KEE) to more limited microcomputer shells (such as M.1 and VP-Expert).

Expert system "shells" contain such components as inference engine programs, programmed control mechanisms, programmed external software interface routines, and capabilities for storing and editing knowledge bases. A user of a shell is most often expected to create only the knowledge base. For these reasons, shells require very little, if any, programming expertise and so can be used to develop smaller KBS by nontechnical managers with minimal exposure to microcomputers. They are very useful to anyone just learning KBS development.

Some shells developed require the use of a mainframe computer. Some shells have been designed for use on LISP and other special-purpose (dedicated) symbolic processing machines. Many shells have been developed for personal computers. Brody (1989), Gevarter (1987), Finnie (1988), Rauch-Hindin ("Software," 1986), and Vedder (1989) provide detailed reviews of available expert system shells.

Microcomputer expert system shells are especially good for developing small systems which test the feasibility of proposed larger systems. Such test systems are called **prototype** systems. KBS developers almost always create a prototype of proposed larger systems. These prototypes are used to test the soundness of a system's design before undertaking expensive development efforts.

## THE ROLE AND IMPORTANCE OF PROTOTYPING

Since KBS are relatively new, and costly to develop, it is usually prudent to develop them in stages, starting with a small prototype of the actual system. This process is referred to as incremental prototyping; the actual prototypes can be called successive approximations.

At times, prototypes of an overall system are developed; these enable testing and refining the concept of a system. At other times, prototypes will be developed of different segments or modules of a system, as the overall system is developed in increments.

In developing prototypes, an effort is made to select only the most critical factors and to show only their most basic relationships, in order to test the underlying structure and concept of the system. For this reason, most prototype systems do not, and cannot be expected to, capture all the rich complexities involved in the actual situation. That is the function of later, more advanced versions of the system.

Although often crude first efforts—which is why they are sometimes called approximations—prototypes serve a useful purpose:

- They provide a preliminary analysis of the situation. Since they isolate the essence of the structure and concept of the system, they give a developer and users a chance to evaluate the overall approach before getting too deeply into the system development.
- They enable creating initial systems quickly. Producing a working system helps sustain the interest of experts at a high level, and whets the developer's appetite for expanding and enhancing a system.
- They encourage building a system in a modular, incremental way that is at the same time well coordinated. In larger projects, this enables using a development team, while still maintaining the integrity of the unified, overall system.
- Prototype system development is also oftentimes a useful tool for quickly eliciting knowledge from experts.

In addition to its practical value in actual business situations, prototype development is also an important learning and teaching tool, since it introduces a manager or potential manager to knowledge-based systems and to expert system shells in a very compact and efficient way.

## THE KBS DEVELOPMENT LIFE CYCLE

While the KBS development process, called the KBS development life cycle, is in many ways similar to the conventional computer information systems development life cycle, there are several substantial differences.

Figure 1–9 shows the conventional computer systems design process, as pictured in current systems analysis and design textbooks. It is only one of many approaches to this design work (Yen 1985). While the process may appear straightforward on first reading, some confusion can arise, especially in the system analysis segment. Part of the problem is that the word *system* is used ambiguously in the process description shown in the figure. In that figure

- in the phrase *system analysis,* the word *system* refers to the business situation being computerized
- in the phrase *system design,* the word *system* refers to the computer system

Further confusion arises from the fact that business situations being computerized can vary substantially. For example, Figure 1–10 shows several types of computerized systems.

- In data processing systems (DPS), the situation analyzed might be the existing computer system or the functional business tasks performed, or both.
- With management information systems (MIS), the situation analyzed involves the manager's business decision-making requirements and manual decision-supporting systems, as well as the existing computer databases, reports, and other information systems.

**Figure 1–9.** Conventional Computer Systems: The System Development Life Cycle

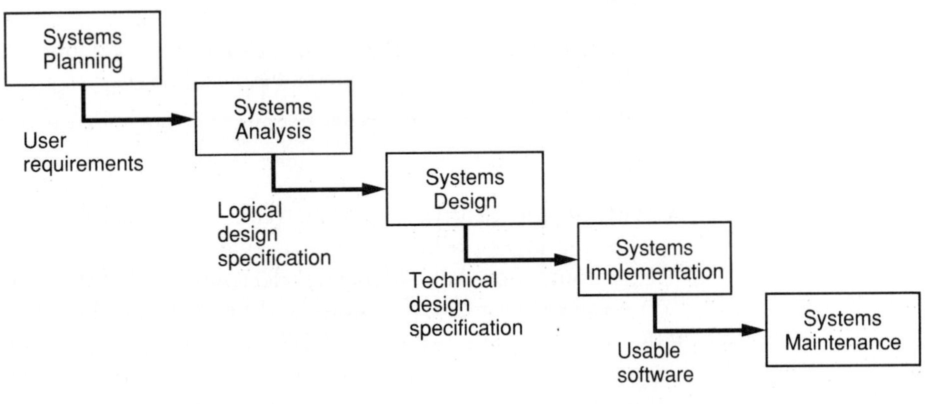

**Figure 1–10.** Major Types of Computer Systems: Situations Analyzed and Manager Participation

| System Type | Situation Analyzed | Participation in Analysis and Design by Manager-Executive/ Expert/User |
|---|---|---|
| Data processing systems (DPS) | Business functions and/or existing system | Not always mandatory: Definable functions and processes |
| Management information systems (MIS) | Existing reporting system and/or management needs | Some manager/user involvement |
| Decision support systems (DSS)—interactive conventional-procedural computer software | Management decision processes | High manager/user (decision maker) involvement |
| Knowledge-based systems (KBS) for operational knowledge areas—interactive knowledge-based software | Mainly how operations work or how lower level operating management decisions are made | Operational-level manager/user/expert involvement |
| Knowledge-based systems (KBS) for management decision making—interactive knowledge-based software | Manager/expert/user decision process (inside the head of a manager) | Manager/user/expert (decision maker) |
| Integratged DSS/KBS systems | Same range as the preceding three interactive systems described above | |

- With decision support systems (DSS), the situation involves interacting with managers while they are making a decision, and so requires examining not only managers' decision needs for information, but also the ways they make decisions and perform on the job.
- Knowledge-based systems (KBS) involve a range of different development situations. For example, with KBS for management decision making, the situation analysis always involves studying how a manager makes a decision, that is, the cognitive processes inside the head of a

manager. At other times, the situation might involve manufacturing operations situations.

As seen in Figure 1–10, the system analysis task shown in Figure 1–9 is in reality a *situation* analysis task in KBS development. For this reason, the term *situation analysis* will be used throughout this book to refer to the analysis involved in studying the situation to be replicated in a KBS.

An additional distinctive feature of the situation analysis involved in KBS development is that the situation analysis phase can involve both situation analysis and situation reformulation, two distinct tasks, which are shown in Figure 1–11 and discussed in detail in Chapter 2.

As for the system design phase, it can involve several primary tasks:

- the conceptual design, partially a nontechnical job—for example, creating a diagram model of the decision situation, such as the one shown in Figure 1–8
- system development, largely a system technician's job, which can involve software engineering and programming

Based on this review of the nature of KBS development tasks, better terms for *systems analysis* and *systems design* are *situation analysis/reformulation* and *system design/development.* These are, therefore, the terms used in Figure 1–11 and throughout this book.

Based on this more precise definition of the system development cycle as applied to knowledge-based system development, it would appear that considerably more management/expert involvement is required for knowledge-based system development. It would also appear that in many KBS development situations it is more a management decision-making task, *situation* analysis, than a computer information system technician task, *system* analysis.

Several major conclusions follow from any objective study of the KBS development life cycle—to name but a few, the more complex a knowledge domain is in larger, widely-deployed systems, the more likely that:

- a knowledge engineer familiar with the expert domain being put onto computer is needed for a successful development effort
- cognitive (thinking) skills, especially those associated with *flexible modelling*, are a requirement for success
- greater levels of interpersonal skills will be needed to extract information from experts
- less control of the development effort should be given to computer information systems technical personnel
- user-interface considerations will be important to success
- management, as opposed to technical, skills will influence the success of the effort

The revised systems development life cycle outlined in Figure 1–11 is an effort to incorporate the importance of situation analysis and reformulation tasks

**Figure 1–11.** Knowledge-Based Systems Development Life Cycle

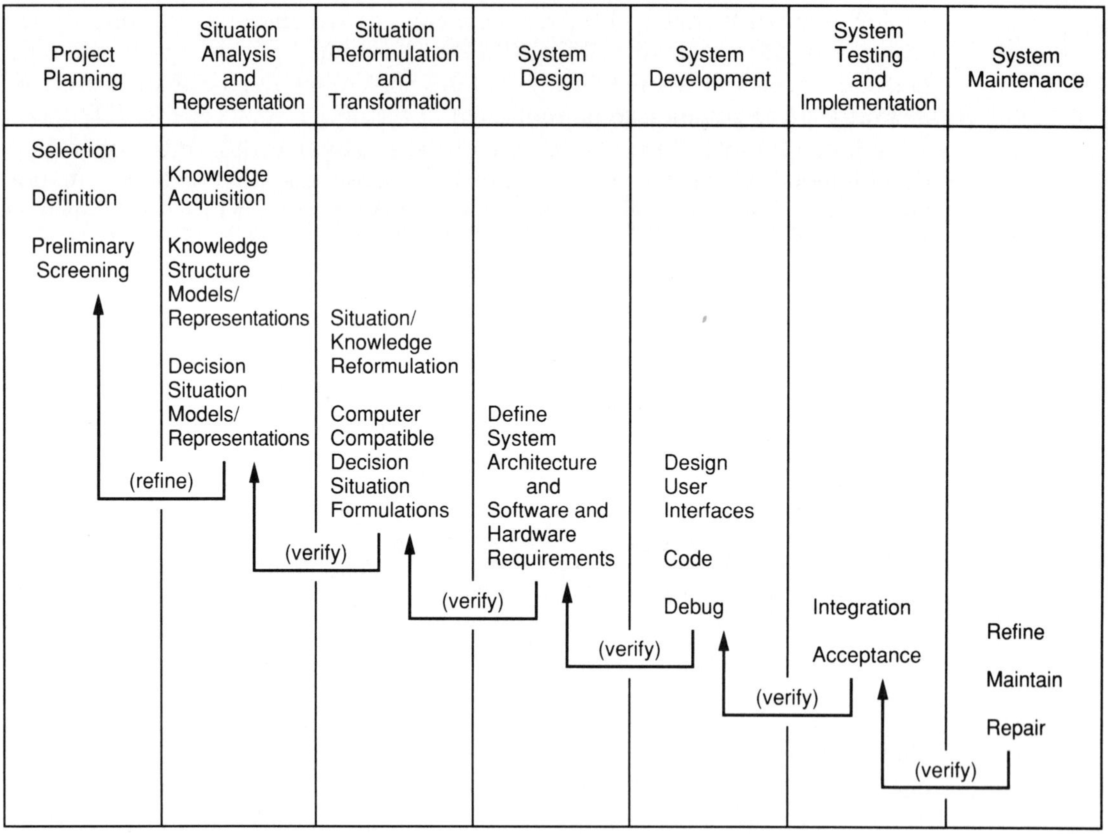


in KBS development. It also indicates some of the back-and-forth studying needed to refine, recheck, and retest all the way through the cycle. While Figure 1–11 may appear to indicate that the cycle is a sequential series of steps or phases, it is not. Rather, the cycle involves the interaction of a variety of decision-making and system-development processes and tasks (Weitzel 1989).

This life cycle process is the essence of the KBS development job. The cycle is discussed in some detail in the following chapter in this Part and in the chapters in Part Two.

## SKILLS USEFUL IN KBS DEVELOPMENT

A variety of cognitive (thinking) skills, individual interpersonal and organizational skills, and computer expertise skills are needed in developing KBS.

## Cognitive Skills

The cognitive (thinking) processes have a significant impact on success in developing KBS, especially when analyzing and modelling knowledge-domain situations and when transforming domain-knowledge representations into representations useful for computerization. This is particularly true in management decision-making situations, where the situation analysis and reformulating tasks can be very demanding.

For over fifty years, cognitive studies have provided insight into and definition of decision-making processes (see, for example, Dewey 1938; Einstein and Infeld 1938). Much of the current work on management decision making grows out of work done at Carnegie Mellon University and Massachusetts Institute of Technology by such people as Simon, Cyert, and Licklider (Keen and Morton 1978, p. viii; Morton 1971; Simon 1960, 1969, 1976, and 1979) and other early researchers (Brightman 1980).

In areas more directly related to KBS development, the capabilities and experiences of management decision makers have long been an interest of physiologists and psychologists (Miller 1967; Newell and Simon 1972). More recently, studies have been done on psychological types and their relationship to situational problem formulation (Brightman and Elrod 1986; Nutt 1986; Ramaprasad 1984). Studies are even being done of specific analytical and synthetic cognitive processes and their impact on situation reformulation/modelling (Abelson 1981; Lyles 1981; Madni 1988; Tversky and Kahneman 1974). Cognitive studies have also attempted to define and reconcile conceptual modelling differences between an expert's thinking patterns and the formal thinking-pattern representations used in computer inferential reasoning (for example: Davis 1986; Goul 1985; Gruber and Cohen 1987; Linden 1988; Pollack 1987; Sanger 1987; Schank 1977, 1984). These studies provide major insights into the cognitive processes of interest to knowledge engineering.

In addition to the familiar basic analytical, evaluative, and synthesizing cognitive processes, there are many specific cognitive skills important to successful KBS development. The following are some of the major ones.

***Conceptualization.*** Conceptualization (often referred to as abstraction) involves grouping specifics into "kind of" categories. Conceptualization skills are needed to reformulate knowledge during its acquisition, analysis, and representation. These skills are also needed to identify new relationships during the knowledge-transformation phase and to develop alternatives during the solution-finding or synthesis phase. The models given in Figures 1–8 and 1–11 are examples of conceptualizing management decision situations.

***Inferential Reasoning.*** An activity such as planning for KBS development requires drawing inferences or implications from facts, events, or almost anything perceived to be relevant by a decision maker. Inferential reasoning skills are necessary, for example, to:

- determine key success factors when developing personnel requirements to guide KBS development staff selection
- assign likelihoods to the possible occurrence of future events when estimating the riskiness of a proposed KBS development project

***Hypothesis Development and Testing.*** Hypotheses are supposed or proposed ideas about such things as possible anticipated key success factors, the likelihood of events occurring, or the possibilities of projects succeeding or failing.

***Associative and Intuitive Reasoning.*** Associative reasoning works on several levels. For example, **associative reasoning** is needed to create the rules linking the two related or associated frames shown in Figure 1–7 when making decisions about which products to sell to which customer groups. In many situations, such associations are *intuitive*, that is, they involve reasoning processes that after many years of managerial experience are no longer explicit. Intuitive skills can, therefore, contribute significantly to effective KBS development.

***Developing Heuristics.*** Heuristics are rules of thumb that experts use to help them solve problems and make decisions. A manager is constantly developing rules of thumb—which are represented by IF-THEN rules in KBS—to guide and assist in decision making. These guidelines are often built on situational premises: if certain conditions prevail in a situation (I haven't any money on hand), then one type of solution may, in all likelihood, be a good one (I stay home and watch television). Rules of thumb are the basis of the rules used in many existing KBS today.

***Cognitive Flexibility.*** In KBS development situations involving complex organizational settings and relatively unstructured decisions (for example, enterprise-wide strategic planning decisions), **cognitive flexibility** is needed. For example, it is needed to develop diagram representations or models which both accurately replicate the situation under study and at the same time lend themselves to transformation into the coded formulations needed for the computer software used.

### Individual Interpersonal and Organizational Behavior Skills

Two relevant aspects of behavioral science useful in KBS development are individual human behavior factors and organizational behavior factors.

***Individual Human Behavior Factors.*** Individual human behavioral factors are especially important during the KBS development phases involving acquiring knowledge from experts/users, staffing and directing a development effort, and dealing with users while implementing a system.

The human-behavior research literature is rich in useful studies of interviewing, communication, leadership, motivation, and other relevant areas (Argyris 1962; Bennis 1985; Brule 1986; Davis 1989; Fiedler 1967; McGregor 1966; Parham 1988; Rowe 1987). Studies of these factors have explored a variety of interpersonal skills helpful in defining expert decision processes, translating those thought processes into computer compatible models, and extracting expertise from the expert (for example: Evanson 1988; Garber, Johnson and Zualkernan 1987; Hart 1986; Hoffman 1987; LaFrance 1987; McGraw 1989; Mitchell 1987; Mockler 1989; Olson and Reuter 1987; Prerau 1987).

Of particular importance to effective KBS development are:

- *Interviewing skills.* These are needed by knowledge engineers when acquiring knowledge directly from experts and in creating user-effective systems. The kinds of interviewing approaches and skills needed will depend on the kind and complexity of the situation under study, the organizational setting and people involved, and the phase of the KBS development cycle (Stewart 1985).
- *Communication skills.* These skills are needed in all phases of managing KBS development and will affect success in many ways. For example, a considerable amount of skillful questioning is often needed to learn how an expert makes decisions and how users use systems. This questioning might be done when observing experts while they are working, or while they are explaining their handling of a typical, specific situation presented them, or while they are discussing how they or potential users do their job. Each of these approaches to questioning and interviewing an expert yields different kinds of information from different people in different kinds of jobs (Grabowski 1988).
- *Skills in overcoming emotional and psychological barriers.* Knowledge-based systems, like many new technologies, can create resistance among individuals. To get through these barriers and acquire the needed knowledge and cooperation from both knowledge-domain experts and from potential system users, skills in understanding individuals and in performing other interpersonal tasks are needed (Dologite 1989).
- *Leadership skills.* In many KBS development situations, a balance has to be maintained between the technical requirements and individual human requirements. Since this balance has to be maintained over a period of time, the leadership style used may have to be multifaceted, varying from authoritative to rational to participative to supportive management styles at different times throughout the development cycle. Skills are needed not only to determine the situationally appropriate style at each phase in a specific development project life cycle, but also to use that style effectively in a particular situation.

The nature of the KBS development job often requires team decision making and decision execution, involving both operating managers and technical personnel. In addition, in these situations there are often blurred lines of authority. Coordination, integration, and other related leadership skills are therefore especially important in successfully managing cooperative work situations (Kotter 1988; Manz 1988; Sayles 1979; Yukl 1981).

- *Motivation skills.* These involve understanding what motivates individuals, such as needs, job satisfaction, and rewards, and developing approaches which best meet specific individual KBS development project requirements.

***Organizational Behavior Skills.*** Organizational behavior factors can also impact on the successful outcome of KBS development projects. They are involved in understanding and defining (modelling) the organizational environment of expert and user in which the systems development is being done, in order to anticipate the impact of this new technology on an organization. These factors are also involved in developing organizational structures to facilitate successful development and use of the KBS. Considerable basic organizational-behavior research has been done in these areas (Costley 1987; DuBrin 1989; Etzioni 1961; French 1985; Huber 1986; Lawrence 1958; Lyles and Mitroff 1980; March and Simon 1958; Volkema 1983), especially in relation to managing technological change (Benjamin and Morton 1986; Bennis 1961; Buchanan and Boddy 1982; Dyer 1984; Kirkpatrick 1985; Munson 1984; Stone and Klemmerer 1984; Twiss 1986; Volkema 1983).

In carrying out large KBS development projects, organizational settings are studied when planning strategies for managing a project. Models of the existing organization can provide a definition of the requirements which must be met (Leonard-Barton 1987 and 1988).

Several critical organization skills have an impact on success. These include:

- identifying the locus of power
- understanding and using corporate culture
- developing organization structures
- staffing
- managing technological change

The organizational factors affecting KBS development, as well as the interpersonal and organizational skills useful in meeting their requirements, are discussed in Chapters 11, 13, and 14.

### Computer Expertise Skills

Extensive computer expertise is not always critical in all phases of KBS development or in many kinds of KBS development situations. For example, where managers are developing small systems on their own using an expert system shell, very little computer expertise may be needed to create a working knowledge-based system. On average, over 80 percent of the work is not computer related. Cognitive skills are always needed in any KBS development situation, however, and interpersonal skills have a major impact on a large portion of KBS development projects.

It is clear that the KBS development life cycle requires heavy emphasis on situation definition, analysis, and representation. The logic of the actual KBS development job, then, explains why primary emphasis is placed on cognitive skills and tasks in the discussion in this section, and why technical skills and tasks are discussed last.

This order of the discussion here may seem strange to many readers with computer information systems or software engineering backgrounds, because KBS in particular and AI in general are generally considered to be highly technical subjects. But the order followed here is logical when viewed in light of the analysis of the KBS development cycle presented earlier in this chapter.

This ordering of the discussion is not meant to diminish the importance of computer expertise in a wide range of KBS development situations. Computer expertise is very important in all types of development efforts, especially larger system development projects. For this reason, the technical aspects of KBS development are treated in great detail in the five chapters in Part Three, where there are extensive discussions of computer technology in a variety of KBS development areas.

## THE SITUATIONAL DECISION-MAKING ORIENTATION OF THE BOOK

The purpose of this book is to provide readers—who may be individuals working on their own or with systems developers, knowledge engineers working with experts or users or with systems engineers, or KBS development project managers working in more complex organizational environments—with guidance in developing KBS and managing KBS development projects. The situational decision-making orientation of this book is not dictated only by the situational nature of the KBS development life cycle and the situational orientation necessary for managing KBS projects. It is also dictated by the wide range of both nontechnical and technical readers for whom the book is written, each of whom has different learning requirements and levels of computer literacy.

As a result, there are no chapters on such subjects as PROLOG and LISP, logic and deduction, internal computer-representation formalisms, indexes and pointers, and other technical subjects in the book. Software engineering books are written for detailed treatments of these KBS related subjects.

## REVIEW QUESTIONS

1. Define *artificial intelligence* and its major branches.
2. The designation "expert system" has caused considerable confusion. Discuss the ways in which the term *expert* is used in relation to knowledge-based systems. Why is it best to consider it a relative, not an absolute, concept here?
3. What is a knowledge base? What is a knowledge-based system?
4. Describe the different ways to classify knowledge-based systems. Give examples of each.
5. Discuss the major applications of today's knowledge-based systems technology.
6. Describe the distinguishing characteristics of knowledge-based systems.
7. What are the major ways to represent knowledge in a knowledge base? Describe IF-THEN rules.
8. Define *inference engine* as related to knowledge-based systems. Distinguish different kinds of inferencing found in knowledge-based systems.
9. What are expert system shells? How do they work? What is their impact on knowledge-based system development?
10. Why do expert system shells make it possible for nontechnical managers to develop knowledge-based systems?
11. Why is it easier to modify knowledge-based systems than conventional computer systems?
12. What are prototype systems and why are they important in knowledge-based system development?
13. Why does the nature of knowledge-based systems dictate that a situational approach be used in their development?
14. How does a nontechnical manager participate in knowledge-based system development?
15. Describe the KBS development life cycle and its differences from conventional computer system development life cycles.
16. Identify the skills involved in performing and managing KBS development and discuss their importance in different types of development situations.

## EXERCISES

1. The disks accompanying this book contain a number of KBS. Following the directions accompanying the disks for using the M.1 expert system shell, run a consultation of the system with the file name CAREER.REV. This system is

designed to assist a user in deciding whether he or she would make a successful entrepreneur. The knowledge base for this system is stored as a text (sometimes called an ASCII) file, using the word processor Volkswriter. Print out the knowledge base using your own word processor, and study its rules and questions. A description of this system is given in Chapter 16 of this book.

2. Read through recent issues of KBS periodicals referred to in the references section at the end of the chapter, or through other related periodicals of your choice, and find a detailed description of a knowledge-based system. Write a brief report comparing one of those systems to the one you consulted in Exercise 1. If you feel it would be helpful, first print out the knowledge base of the system you consulted in Exercise 1, following the directions given to print a text (sometimes called an ASCII) file with your own word processor.

## REFERENCES


Abelson, R. P. "Psychological Status of the Script Concept." *American Psychologist,* 1981, 36, pp. 715–29.

Aiken, Milam W., and Olivia R. Liu Sheng. "Nexpert Object," *Expert Systems,* February 1990, pp. 54–57.

Argyris, Chris. *Interpersonal Competence and Organizational Effectiveness.* Homewood, IL: Dorsey, 1962.

Barker, Don, and Scott Shoemaker. "AI in Manufacturing." *PC AI,* March/April 1989, pp. 28–31.

Benjamin, Robert I., and Michael S. Scott Morton. *Information Technology, Integration, and Organizational Change.* CISR Working Paper #134, Center for Information Systems Research, Sloan School of Management, Cambridge, MA: MIT, April 1986.

Bennis, Warren, et. al. *The Planning of Change: Readings in the Applied Behavioral Sciences.* New York: Holt, 1961.

Bennis, Warren, and Burt Nanus. *Leaders, the Strategy for Taking Charge.* New York: Harper & Row, 1985.

Bonnett, Kendra R. "From Grassroots to Grand Plan." *AI Expert,* August 1989, pp. 54–60.

Bowerman, Robert G., and David E. Glover. *Putting Expert Systems into Practice.* New York: Van Nostrand Reinhold, 1988.

Brightman, H. J. *Problem Solving: A Logical and Creative Approach.* Atlanta, GA: Business Publications Division, Georgia State University, 1980.

Brightman, H. J., and R. Elrod. "The Use of Jung's Psychological Types for Developing Decision Aids for the Intelligence Phase of Problem Solving." In *Proceedings of the Annual Meeting of the Decision Sciences Institute,* Hawaii, 1986.

Brody, Alan. "The Experts." *Infoworld,* June 19, 1989.

Brule, J. F., *The Application of Systemic Family Therapy to Knowledge Acquisition.* Woburn, MA: Systems Designers Software, Inc., May 1986.

Buchanan, David A., and David Boddy. "Advanced Technology and the Quality of Working Life: The Effects of Word Processing on Video Typists." *The Journal of Psychology,* 1982, 55, pp. 1–11.

Bulkeley, William M. "Bright Outlook for Artificial Intelligence Yields to Slow Growth and Big Cutbacks." *The Wall Street Journal,* July 5, 1990, pp. B1, B3.

Chapnick, Philip. "MIS Is Not the Enemy." *AI Expert,* April 1988, pp. 5–6.

Charniack E., and D. McDermott. *Artificial Intelligence,* Reading, MA: Addison-Wesley, 1985.

Costley, Dan L., and Ralph Todd. *Human Relations in Organizations.* St. Paul, MN: West Publishing, 1987.

Davis, Bob. "Road to Reasoning: Superfast Computers Mimic the Structure of the Human Brain." *Wall Street Journal,* February 18, 1986, p. 1.

Davis, Keith, and John W. Newstrom. *Human Behavior at Work,* New York: McGraw-Hill, 1989.

Dewey, J. *Logic: The Structure of Inquiry.* New York: G.P. Putnam, 1938.

Dologite, D. G., and Robert J. Mockler. "Developing Effective Knowledge-Based Systems: Overcoming Cognitive, Organizational and Individual Behavioral Barriers." *Information Resource Management Journal,* Spring 1989.

DuBrin, Andrew, R. Duane Ireland, and J. Clifton Williams. *Management and Organization.* Cincinnati, OH: South-Western, 1989.

Dyer, William G. *Strategies for Managing Change.* Reading, MA.: Addison-Wesley, 1984.

Einstein, A., and L. Infeld. *The Evolution of Physics.* New York: Simon & Schuster, 1938.

Etzioni, Amitai. *A Comparative Analysis of Complex Organizations.* New York, Free Press, 1961.

Evanson, Steven E. "How to Talk to an Expert." *AI Expert,* February 1988, pp. 36–42.

"Expert Systems—Applications in Finance." *Financial Management,* Autumn 1988, pp. 12–86.

Feigenbaum, Edward, Pamela McCorduck, and H. Penny Nii. *The Rise of the Expert Company.* New York: Times Books, 1988.

Fiedler, Fred E. *A Theory of Leadership Effectiveness.* New York: McGraw-Hill, 1967.

Finnie, J. Scot. "Artificial Intelligence: Sudden Shower Enriches MIS Turf." *Computerworld,* October 17, 1988, pp. 77–96.

French, Wendell, Fremont E. Kast, James E. Rosenzweig. *Understanding Human Relations in Organizations.* New York: Harper & Row, 1985.

Garber, Sharon, Paul E. Johnson, and Imran Zualkernan. "Specification of Expertise." *International Journal of Man-Machine Studies,* 1987, 26, pp. 161–81.

Gevarter, William B. "The Nature and Evaluation of Commercial Expert Systems Building Tools." *Computer,* May 1987, pp. 24–41.

Goul, Kenneth Michael. *The Inclusion of Expertise in a Decision Support System for Strategic Decision Making.* Doctoral Thesis, Corvallis, OR: Oregon State University, 1985.

Grabowski, Martha. "Knowledge Acquisition Methodologies: Survey and Empirical Assessment." *Proceedings of the Ninth International Conference on Information Systems.* Minneapolis, MN: SIM, IMS and ACM, December 1988.

Gruber, Thomas R., and Paul R. Cohen. "Design for Acquisition: Principles of Knowledge-System Design to Facilitate Knowledge Acquisition." *International Journal of Man-Machine Studies,* 1987, 26, pp. 143–59.

Harmon, Paul, and Brian Sawyer. *Creating Expert Systems for Business and Industry,* New York: Wiley, 1990.

Hart, Anna. *Knowledge Acquisition for Expert Systems.* New York: McGraw-Hill, 1986.

Hoffman, Robert R. "The Problem of Extracting the Knowledge of Experts from the Perspective of Experimental Psychology." *AI Magazine,* Summer 1987, pp. 53–67.

Huber, George P., and J. Clifton Williams. *Human Behavior in Organizations.* 3d ed. Cincinatti, OH: South-Western, 1986.

Humpert, Benedikt, and Patrick Holley. "Expert Systems in Financial Planning." *Expert Systems,* May 1988, pp. 78–100.

Keen, Peter G. W., and Michael S. Scott Morton. *Decision Support Systems: An Organizational Perspective.* Reading, MA: Addison-Wesley, 1978.

Kirkpatrick, Donald L. *How to Manage Change Effectively.* San Francisco: Jossey-Bass, 1985.

Kotter, John P. *The Leadership Factor.* New York: Free Press, 1988.

LaFrance, Marianne. "The Knowledge Acquisition Grid: A Method for Training Knowledge Engineers." *International Journal of Man-Machine Studies,* 1987, 26, pp. 245–55.

Lawrence, Paul. *The Changing Organizational Behavior Patterns.* Boston: Harvard Business School, 1958.

Leaman, Claire M. "Rule-Based Structural Design in C." *AI Expert,* May 1989, pp. 28–35.

Leonard-Barton, Dorothy. "Technology Implementation as Integrative Innovation: The Case of an Expert System." *Sloan Management Review,* October-November 1987, pp. 84–109.

Leonard-Barton, Dorothy, and John Sviokla. "Putting Expert Systems to Work." *Harvard Business Review,* March-April 1988, 91–98.

Liebowitz, Jay, and Daniel DeSalvo. *Expert Systems for Business and Management.* Englewood Cliffs, NJ: Prentice Hall, 1990.

Linden, Eugene. "Putting Knowledge to Work." *Time,* March 28, 1988, pp. 60–63.

Lyles, M. A. "Formulating Strategic Problems: Empirical Analysis and Model Development." *Strategic Management Journal,* 1981, 2, pp. 61–75.

Lyles, M. A., and I. I. Mitroff. "Organizational Problem Formulation: An Empirical Study." *Administrative Science Quarterly,* 1980, 25, pp. 102–19.

Madni, Azad. "The Role of Human Factors in Expert System Design and Acceptance." *Human Factors,* 1988, 30 (4), pp. 395–414.

Manz, C., and H. Sims. *Superleadership.* Englewood Cliffs, NJ: Prentice Hall, 1988.

March, James G., and Herbert Simon. *Organizations.* New York: Wiley, 1958.

Martin, James, and Steven Oxman. *Building Expert Systems.* Englewood Cliffs, NJ: Prentice-Hall, 1988.

McGraw, Karen L., and Karan Harbison-Briggs. *Knowledge Acquisition.* Englewood Cliffs, NJ: Prentice Hall, 1989.

McGregor, Douglas. *Leadership and Motivation.* Edited by Warren Bennis et al. Cambridge, MA: MIT Press, 1966.

Miller, G. "The Magical Number Seven, Plus or Minus Two: Some Limits on Our Capacity for Processing Information." In G. Miller, ed., *The Psychology of Communication: Seven Essays.* New York: Basic Books, 1967.

Mitchell, Andrew A. "The Use of Alternative Knowledge-Acquisition Procedures in the Development of a Knowledge-Based Media Planning System." *International Journal of Man-Machine Studies,* 1987 (26), pp. 399–411.

Mockler, Robert J. *Knowledge-Based Systems for Management Decisions.* Englewood Cliffs, NJ: Prentice-Hall, 1989.

Morton, Michael S. Scott. *Management Decision Systems: Computer-Based Support for Decision Making.* Cambridge, MA: Division of Research, Harvard Business School, 1971.

Munson, Vernell K. "Automation Defined: Teaching Old Companies New Tricks." *The Office,* February 1984, pp. 19–22, 31.

Newell, A., and H. A. Simon. *Human Problem Solving.* Englewood Cliffs, NJ: Prentice-Hall, 1972.

Nutt, P. C. "Decision Style and Strategic Decisions of Top Executives." *Technological Forecasting of Social Change,* 1986, 30 (1), pp. 39–62.

O'Brien, John, Wayne P. Johnson, and Richard Woodhead. "The Ford Motor Company DLMS." *AI Expert,* August 1989, pp. 42–53.

Olson, J. R., and H. H. Reuter. "Extracting Expertise From Experts: Methods for Knowledge Acquisition." *Expert Systems,* August 1987, pp. 152–68.

Parham, A. Christine. *Psychology: Studying the Behavior of People.* 2d ed. Cincinnati, OH: South-Western, 1988.

Patterson, Dan W. *Introduction to Artificial Intelligence and Expert Systems.* Englewood Cliffs, NJ: Prentice Hall, 1990.

Pollack, Andrew. "More Human Than Ever, Computer Is Learning to Learn." *New York Times,* September 15, 1987, Section C, p. 1.

Prerau, David. "Knowledge Acquisition in the Development of a Large Expert System." *AI Magazine,* Summer 1987, pp. 43–51.

Ramaprasad, A., and I. I. Mitroff. "On Formulating Strategic Problems." *Academy of Management Review,* 1984, 9 (4), pp. 597–605.

Rauch-Hindin, Wendy B. "Software Integrates AI, Standard Systems." *Mini-Micro Systems,* October 1986, pp. 69ff.

Rogers, Ted. "Artificial Intelligence: Application in Taxation, IRS AI Program." *Expert Systems Review for Business and Accounting,* September 1988, pp. 8–10.

Rowan, Duncan A. "On-Line Expert Systems in Process Industries." *AI Expert,* August 1989, pp. 30–41.

Rowe, Alan, and James O. Mason. *Managing with Style.* San Francisco: Jossey-Bass, 1987.

Sanger, David E. "A Computer Full of Surprises." *New York Times,* May 8, 1987, Section D, p. 1.

Sayles, Leonard. *Leadership.* New York: McGraw-Hill, 1979.

Schank, Roger C., and Robert Abelson. *Scripts, Plans, Goals and Understanding: An Inquiry Into Human Knowledge Structure.* Hillsdale, NJ: Erlbaum, 1977.

Schank, Roger C., with Peter G. Childers. *The Cognitive Computer: On Language, Learning and Artificial Intelligence.* Reading, MA: Addison-Wesley, 1984.

Schorr, Herbert, and Alain Rappaport. *Innovative Applications of Artificial Intelligence.* Menlo Park, CA: AAAI Press, 1989.

Schur, Stephen. "The Intelligent Database." *AI Expert,* January 1988, pp. 26–34.

Simon, H. A. "Information Processing Models of Cognition." *Annual Review of Psychology,* 1979, 30, pp. 363–96.

Simon, H. A. *The New Science of Management Decision.* New York: Harper & Row, 1960.

Simon, H. A. *The Science of the Artificial.* Cambridge, MA: MIT Press, 1969.

Simon, H. A., and S. K. Reed. "Modelling Strategy Shifts in a Problem-Solving Task." In *Cognitive Psychology,* 8, 1976, pp. 86–97.

Stewart, Charles J., and William B. Cash. *Interviewing: Principles and Practices.* 4th ed. Dubuque, IA: Wm. C. Brown, 1985.

Stone, Dianna L., and Barbara Klemmerer. "Relationship Between Rigidity, Self-Esteem, and Attitudes about Computer-Based Information Systems." *Psychological Reports,* December 1984, pp. 991–98.

Turban, Efraim. *Decision Support and Expert Systems.* 2d ed. New York: Macmillan, 1990.

Tversky, A., and D. Kahneman. "Judgement under Uncertainty: Heuristics and Biases." *Science,* 1974, 185, pp. 1124–31.

Twiss, Brian. *Managing Technological Innovation.* 3d ed. White Plains, NY: Longman, 1986.

Vedder, Richard G. "PC-Based Expert System Shells: Some Desirable and Less Desirable Characteristics." *Expert Systems,* February 1989, pp. 28–42.

Volkema, R. "Problem Formulation in Planning and Design." *Management Science,* 1983, 29 (6), pp. 639–52.

Weitzel, John R., and Larry Kerselberg. "Developing Knowledge-based Systems: Reorganizing the System Development Lifecycle." *Communications of the ACM,* April 1989, pp. 482–87.

Yen, Chi-Chung. *Design of a Decision Support System Using Expert Systems Techniques.* Doctoral dissertation, Graduate College of the University of Nebraska, Lincoln, NE: 1985.

Yukl, Gary A. *Leadership in Organizations.* Englewood Cliffs, NJ: Prentice-Hall, 1981.

# 2

# Developing Knowledge-Based Systems: The Basic Knowledge Engineering Process

The objective of Chapter 2 is to provide an introduction on how to develop a small KBS using an expert system development shell. All of the topics presented here are covered in greater detail in Chapters 3 through 11.

The areas discussed in this chapter are

- The knowledge engineering job
- The KBS development cycle: a situational management process
- How to select a decision, problem, or task for KBS development
- Basic KBS development activities
- Some complexities of the development process
- Putting the system onto computer
- Some special problems in knowledge acquisition

## KNOWLEDGE ENGINEERING

In general, the tasks described in Chapters 2 through 11 fall under the heading **knowledge engineering,** a term that is used to describe the KBS development jobs of situation analysis and representation, and computer system design and implementation.

The exact nature of the knowledge engineering job will vary from situation to situation. For example, when experts are developing their own system using an expert system development shell, one person might perform all the knowledge engineering jobs: acquiring and defining knowledge (situation analysis); formulating and representing knowledge (situation representation and system design); and engineering and programming software (system design and development).

In more complex situations, knowledge engineers work with experts and system users, and so perform additional planning and managing tasks. In these situations, knowledge engineering can involve interpersonal tasks, such as interviewing, as well as the many other tasks involved in coordinating experts, users, and the various technical people that can be required for developing the actual system.

In larger system development situations, a **project manager** is often required to manage the multiple components of the project over longer periods of time. In these situations, the project management job can be distinct from the knowledge engineering job, and the knowledge engineering job for that particular project may involve only the early phases of the KBS development cycle (McGraw 1989, pp. 5–7).

## THE KBS DEVELOPMENT CYCLE: A SITUATIONAL MANAGEMENT PROCESS

In the KBS development process, which is often referred to as the KBS development life cycle, considerable emphasis is given to situation analysis—unlike the case in many conventional computer system development projects. This is because KBS replicate expert reasoning processes, which are often difficult to structure. As seen in Figure 2–1, the major phases of the KBS development life cycle are:

- project selection and definition
- knowledge acquisition, analysis, and representation for the situation under study
- knowledge reformulation and transformation for the situation under study
- system design
- system development
- system testing, implementation, and maintenance

At each major phase in the life cycle, decision alternatives are developed and evaluated, and decisions made and implemented, based on specific individual situation requirements. The life cycle is, therefore, as much an integrated set of decisions, as it is a series of sequential steps or stages or phases. The arrows at the bottom of the figure are designed to give a feeling for this dynamic integrated interaction.

The following sections discuss the basic knowledge engineering process involved in developing a KBS. In order to focus on the basic development

**Figure 2–1.** Knowledge-Based Systems Development Life Cycle

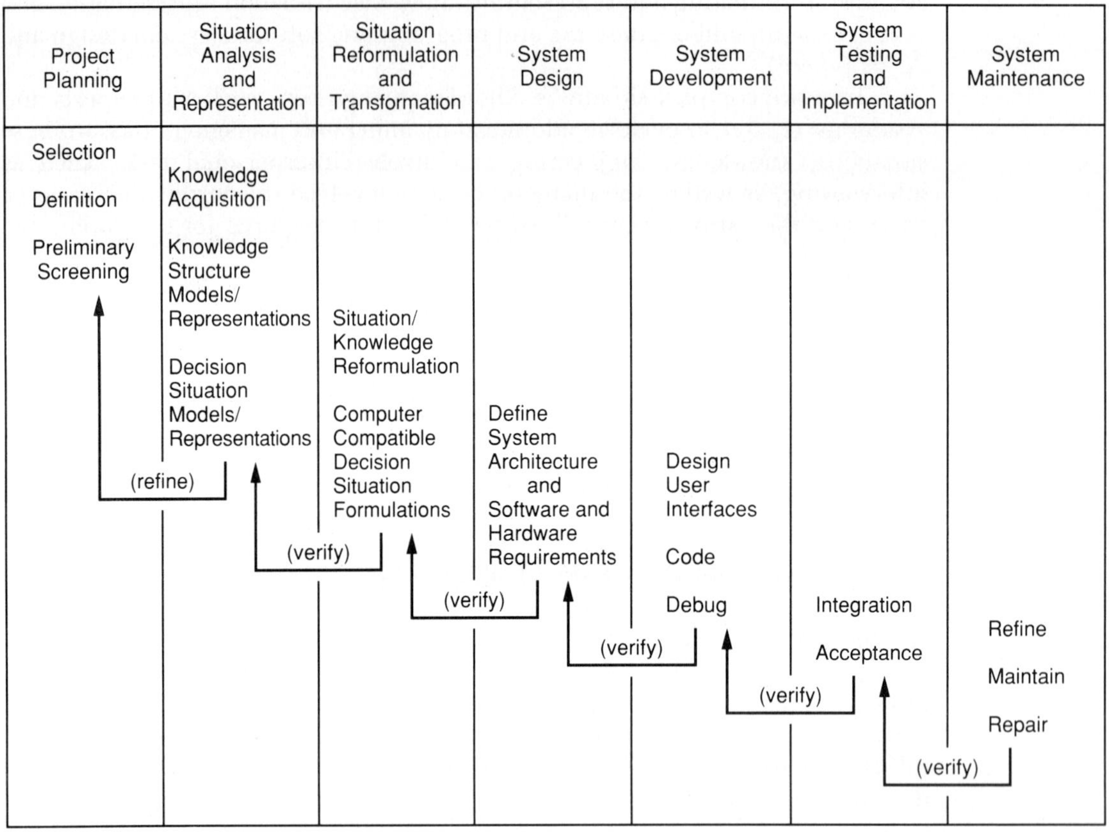


processes, the initial situation studied is limited to one in which an expert is creating his or her own system, that is, an *expert-driven* development effort.

## SELECTING A DECISION, PROBLEM, OR TASK FOR KBS DEVELOPMENT

Sometimes selecting a business decision, problem, or task for system development can be easy. For example, a consultant may be hired to do a specific system development project, such as creating a system to guide customer-service representatives in handling customer complaints.

At other times, a consultant (or company personnel themselves) experienced in knowledge-based systems development may be asked to review company operations to see where KBS development tools might be of help. This can initially involve a study ranging across many company operating areas. Eventually an area to be worked on would be selected from those examined.

The situation could also involve an individual operating manager with some computer training selecting a problem from among the many faced daily. For example, one manager faced a problem concerning poor performance in the telephone screening of auto insurance applicants. In this situation, there was a shortage of trained people available at a reasonable salary level. High turnover and poor performance had resulted.

> The problem situation examined was how to guide each phone operator through the applicant screening process and have a KBS make recommendations about whether or not to approve the application.

The solution to reconciling performance requirements and budget constraints was for the manager to spend several weekends developing a knowledge-based system on his own. The manager who developed and introduced the system in this situation was able to substantially increase performance consistency. In addition, the system reduced training time and cut training costs by a third.

More and more frequently, younger managers are taking the initiative in this way to solve their immediate problems. Often, the effort results in recognition, promotions, and raises.

Since the KBS discussed in this book are used to support business needs, the selection process first calls for examining business needs. For example:

- Is the human expertise that is needed for a particular task about to be lost?
- Is human expertise scarce?
- Is human expertise expensive in relation to a job's value to the company?
- Is the expertise needed in a variety of locations?
- Is the expertise needed in a hostile environment?
- Do the job requirements (such as speed and precision) exceed the capacity of normally available experts?

Such overall business-needs studies are being done frequently today at most large companies.

In addition to considering the business need, one determines whether or not a knowledge-based system is feasible and appropriate in the situation. In order to consider developing a knowledge-based system, the answer should be "yes" to most of the following:

- Do recognized experts exist?
- Can experts do the task better than amateurs and can their skills be taught to others?

- Do different experts agree on solutions?
- Does the task require reason and informed judgments, as opposed to mere common sense?
- Is the task well understood?
- Can the experts articulate their methods?
- Is the task of manageable size?
- Are typical example cases or situations readily available?

A major consideration frequently encountered is deciding whether or not to use a conventional computer application instead of a knowledge-based application for the problem, decision, or task under study. For example, if a task has a high quantitative or procedural content/structure, then one might consider using a more conventional computer tool, such as a spreadsheet or database management tool, and *not* using a knowledge-based system application.

Another consideration is whether or not the benefits or payoffs from introducing a KBS justify the costs of developing it. For example, where a situation involves a task that is encountered only a few times a year, then it is probably best handled by a human expert. Some kind of formal or informal cost/benefit analysis is usually needed during this preliminary planning phase.

Selecting a problem, decision, or task area for expert knowledge-based system development, then, involves studying:

- the business need (is a new system really needed to maintain or improve business operations?)
- the feasibility of it (is a KBS the most effective solution?)
- the benefits versus the costs (is it worth it?)

KBS designed to assist a knowledge engineer in doing these preliminary screenings in different kinds of development situations are described in Chapters 12 and 15 and in Mockler (1990).

## BASIC KBS DEVELOPMENT ACTIVITIES

Knowledge-based systems are developed by:

- analyzing, or decomposing, the situation under study and evaluating relationships
- reformulating or reconceptualizing the model or representation of the decision situation under study in order to put it into a computer usable format
- putting the decision onto the computer

The *analysis phase* requires breaking down the decision situation into its smallest components, once the situation has been selected and defined and the knowledge has been acquired. For example, even with a seemingly simple decision like whether or not to proceed with a small knowledge-based system development project, considerable imaginative thinking may be required (Ruth 1988) in order to recreate the actual future circumstances that might be encountered. Some *evaluation* is also required during this and the following phases in order to determine the relationships among the various situation factors and their relative importance.

For someone not trained or naturally skilled in this kind of forward thinking, it is often difficult to specify:

- every step involved in making a decision
- each piece of information needed
- all the many alternative decision paths the mind pursues in the decision process

It has been said that a good journalist or story writer is best trained for this analysis and evaluation phase of a knowledge-based system's development, since in a sense one is writing an accurate "story" or *scenario* of how a situation works.

As the situation is analyzed and evaluated, diagrams are often constructed to get a more precise picture of how the decision under study is made or the task under study is carried out. This is variously called the *situation reconceptualization* or *representation phase.* Figure 2–2 gives an example of such a diagram. The decision situation represented in the figure concerns a preliminary review of the potential appropriateness of a project proposed for knowledge-based development. The decision involves estimating the level of risk or chances of success for the proposed KBS development project.

This example is from an early development phase of the small concept-testing prototype KBS described in more detail in Chapter 15. It is called "concept testing" because during the reconceptualization phase one is often not sure if the initial situation diagram model, such as the one shown in Figure 2–2, is an accurate representation of the actual business situation under study. This approach is often called **incremental prototyping,** since it involves successive approximations of the actual decision situation.

This block diagram represents a definition of the knowledge needed to decide whether to proceed with a KBS development project. Such a diagram is referred to as a **decision situation diagram,** or model, in this book. Most often the initial versions of these diagrams are incomplete, as in Figure 2–2, since they do not specify and follow all the reasoning paths followed by the decision maker in dealing with a problem.

For example, in the model outlined in Figure 2–2, a number of decision rules, or rules-of-thumb (called heuristics), are used. These can be stated in IF-THEN form, as is shown at the top of Figure 2–3, where a few plain English examples are given.

As the study of the situation continues, questions are also developed about information the decision maker needs to have about the situation under study. Plain English examples of these are shown at the top of Figure 2–4.

As the study of the decision processes involved continues, more information is gathered about how the expert makes decisions. Based on this further

**Figure 2–2.** Decision Situation Diagram: Estimating KBS Project Proposal Level of Risk (Initial Prototype Phase)

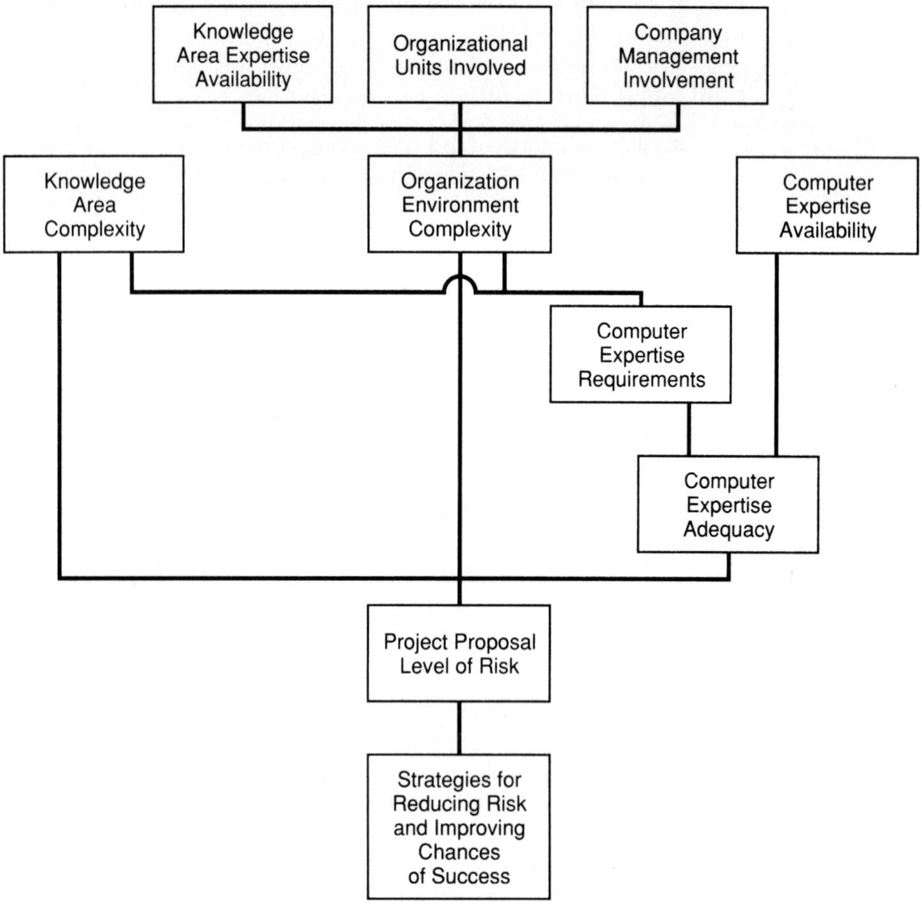


study, it is possible to expand the initial decision situation diagram in Figure 2–2 to give a stronger sense of how the decision is made. Figure 2–5 shows such an expanded decision situation diagram. It includes some indication of the reasoning paths, interim values, and possible recommendations. It should be noted that developing such an expanded decision situation diagram is not usually so simple a step in practice. Normally there is considerable alternative model development. During this process a number of different versions of the situation model are developed and evaluated. This alternative model development process is described in the following section.

**Figure 2–3.** Decision Situation under Study: Estimating KBS Project Proposal Level of Risk— Knowledge Base Rules, Three Forms (Initial Prototype Phase)

---

<u>Plain English Version</u>

```
rule-1-1:
if the knowledge area's level of complexity is simple and
if the organization's environment is favorable and
if the computer expertice adequacy is good or
if the computer expertise adequacy is okay
then the project has a low level of risk and a high
potential for success

rule-2-1:
if the reasoning and heuristics used in the area are simple and
if the factual knowledge of the area is simple
then the knowledge of the area's level of complexity is simple
```

<u>M.1 Condensed Version</u>

```
rule-1-1:
if the knowledge-area-complexity = simple and
   org-environment-complexity = favorable and
   computer-expertise-adequacy = ok or
   computer-expertise-adequacy = good and
      display ([nl,nl,nl,nl,nl,nl,nl,nl,nl,nl,nl,nl,nl,nl,nl'
Based on the answers you have given, the project you have
proposed has a low level of risk and a high potential for success
',nl,nl,nl,nl,nl])
      then phase-over = done1.

rule-2-1:
if reasoning-heuristics = simple and
   factual-knowledge = simple
then knowledge-area-complexity = simple
```

<u>VP-Expert Condensed Version</u>

```
Rule 1-1

If knowledge-area-complexity = simple and
   org-environment-complexity = favorable and
   computer-expertise-adequacy = ok or
   computer-expertise-adequacy = good and
then level_of_risk = low
CLS
DISPLAY" Based on the answers you have given, the project you
have proposed has a low level of risk and a high potential for
success";

Rule 2-1
if reasoning-heuristics = simple and
   factual-knowledge = simple
then knowledge-area-complexity = simple;
```

---

**Figure 2–4.** Decision Situation under Study: Estimating KBS Project Proposal Level of Risk—Knowledge Base Questions, Three Forms (Initial Prototype Phase)

```
Plain English Version
What level of management initiated the proposed project?

What is the highest level of management which has expressed
interest in and support for the project?

M.1 Version

question(initiated-by) =
[nl,nl,nl,nl,nl,nl,nl,nl,nl,nl,nl,nl,nl,nl,nl,nl,nl,nl,nl,nl,'
What level of management initiated the proposed project?

',nl,nl,nl,nl,nl,nl,nl].

legalvals(initiated-by) = [top-company-management,
operating-management, user/expert, outside-company].

question(supported-by) =
[nl,nl,nl,nl,nl,nl,nl,nl,nl,nl,nl,nl,nl,nl,nl,nl,nl,nl,nl,nl,'
What is the highest level of management which has expressed
interest in and support of the project?
',nl,nl,nl,nl,nl,nl,nl].

legalvals(supported-by) = [top-company-management,
operating-management].

VP-Expert Condensed Version

ASK initiated-by: "What level of management initiated the
proposed project?";

CHOICES initiated-by: top-company-management, operating-management,
user_or_expert, outside-company;

ASK supported-by: "What is the highest level of management
which has expressed interest in and support for the project?";

CHOICES supported-by: top-company-management, operating-management;
```

The next phase is to create models of the computer system, the actual software application. An example is given in Figure 2–6. Moving through the modelling phases described in Figures 2–2 to 2–6 is often referred to as the *transformation* or *reformulation* of the situation representation (model) into a computer-compatible formulation or model. In the examples shown in Figures 2–2 to 2–6, the transformation steps from initial decision situation diagram

**Figure 2–5.** Decision Situation Diagram: Estimating KBS Project Proposal Level of Risk (Initial Prototype Phase)

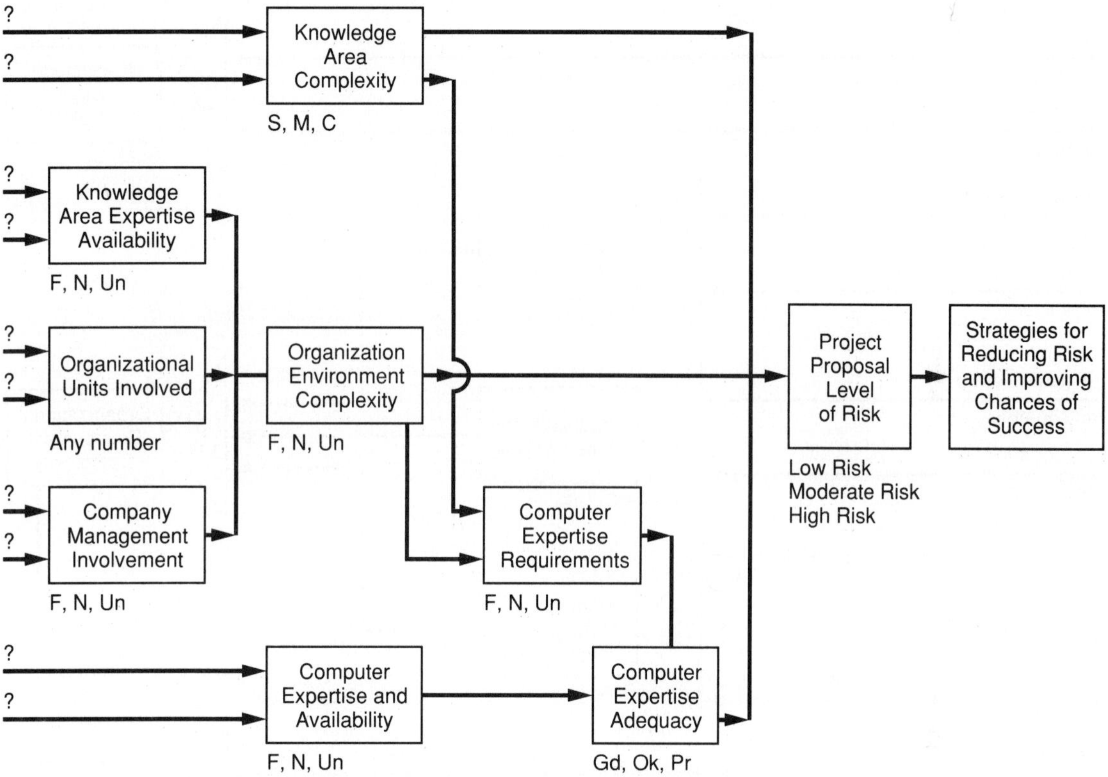


Key:

F = Favorable
N = Neutral
Un = Unfavorable

Gd = Good
Pr = Poor
Ok = Okay

S = Simple
M = Moderate
C = Complex

showing knowledge segments (Figure 2–2) to expanded, more detailed decision situation diagram (Figure 2–5) to a dependency diagram of the prototype knowledge-based computer system (Figure 2–6) have been greatly simplified to show the basic steps in the process. In practice, as is seen in the discussion that follows, transformation/reformulation is usually a much more complex process.

Diagrams such as the one shown in Figure 2–6 are called **dependency diagrams** in this book. Such diagrams are outlines of the computerized version of the decision situation under study. Ideally they are incremental extensions of the decision situation diagrams. Creating these dependency diagrams, together

**Figure 2–6.** Dependency (SYSTEM) Diagram: Estimating KBS Project Proposal Level of Risk (Initial Prototype Phase)

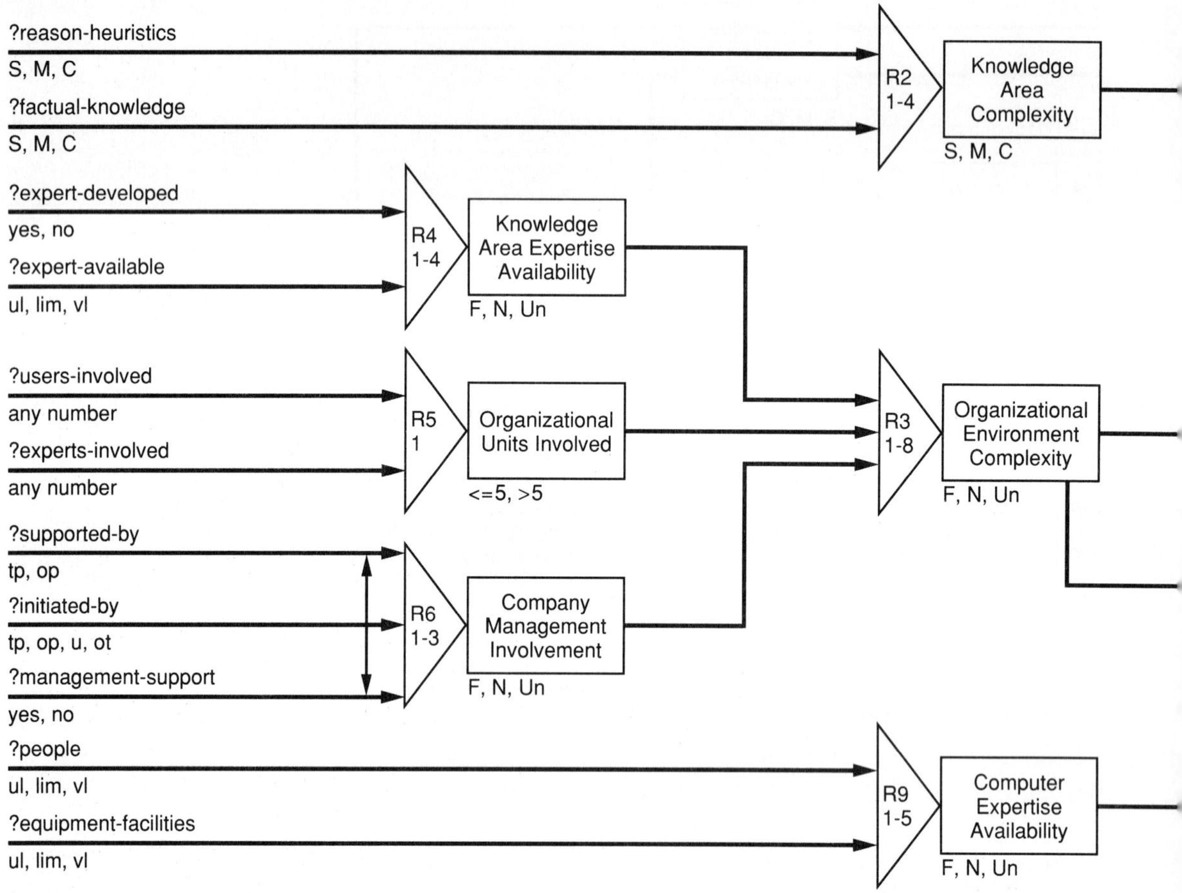


Key:

| | | | | | |
|---|---|---|---|---|---|
| F = Favorable | Gd = Good | S = Simple | op = operating mgt. | ul = unlimited | vl = very limited |
| N = Neutral | Ok = Okay | M = Moderate | u = user/expert | lim = limited | |
| Un = Unfavorable | Pr = Poor | C = Complex | tp = top company mgt. | ot = outside-company | |

with related tables and statements of rules and questions, is generally referred to as the *system design and documentation phase* of KBS development.

The preceding discussion describes, in very simplified form, the process involved in creating a knowledge-based system—excluding the final stage, putting it onto the computer. This final *implementation phase* in the process is described later in this chapter and in Chapters 3, 4, 5, and 6.

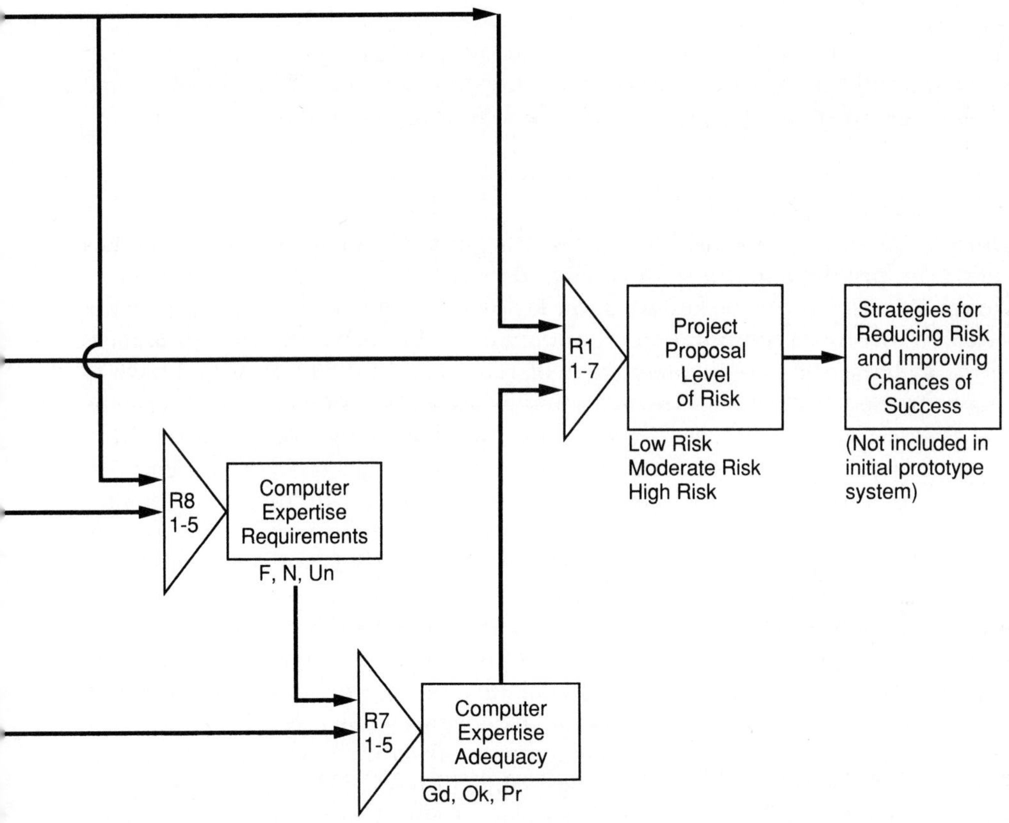


The basic KBS development activities described so far in this section involve:

- understanding and articulating how the decision or task works in very precise, detailed terms
- transforming that decision or task in stages into a representation format or model that a computer can work with

Because these activities mainly involve nontechnical situation structuring, they are within the capabilities of all competent managers skilled in management decision making, no matter what their level of technical computer expertise.

## SOME COMPLEXITIES OF THE DEVELOPMENT PROCESS

A lot more is normally involved in knowledge-based system development than was covered in the brief introductory discussion in the preceding section. Some of these complexities are discussed in the following paragraphs.

### Analyzing and Evaluating the Knowledge Domain

During the early phases of the process, the situation under study, sometimes called the **problem space** or **knowledge domain,** is explored from a variety of viewpoints. Key terms or key situation factors are defined. For example, if the situation involves a computer-configuration decision, such terms as *configuration, computer, components, central processing unit, connectors,* and the like would have to be understood and defined. In an automotive-diagnostic situation, such terms as *fuel injector, carburetor, spark plug,* and the like would be defined. In a marketing-management decision situation, such terms as *customer demographics, market mix, media,* and the like would need defining. In the development-planning situation described in Figures 2–2 through 2–6, much of the information defining knowledge-based systems is given in Chapter 1 of this book. As the situation-analysis phase continues, some sense of the structure of the knowledge segments within the area of expertise under study, including the type of situation, depth, and breadth of the knowledge area or area of expertise, would begin to emerge. In addition, some idea of the level or kinds of experts, users, and management involved would also begin to emerge.

There are a variety of ways to diagram or structure a decision situation, or knowledge domain. For example, a flow chart instead of the tree-type diagram shown in Figure 2–2 might be used (Kearney 1990). Finding the *best* modelling format is not the goal. Finding a reasonably good one that makes subsequent modelling phases easier is the goal, providing the model used is an accurate representation of the actual situation under study.

The type and structure of the reasoning processes are gradually defined in greater and greater detail, as system development proceeds. This process involves studying the relationships among the key situation components. It is an extension of the initial study of knowledge structures within the decision situation being replicated.

This restructuring requires developing a variety of scenarios of expert decisions or tasks being studied. Generally speaking, *it is best to focus on the most typical situations during these early phases of the study* and *to avoid the exceptional cases,* until reasonably good diagrams or models of the situation have been structured. Trying to incorporate all the nuances of the task into these early models very often impedes progress. The initial prototype systems will generally be designed to handle only the most typical situations.

For example, when creating the diagram model shown in Figure 2–6, a system developer might first write a scenario for estimating the level of risk involved in a small expert-developed KBS project. Additional scenarios might then be developed for more complex projects involving several experts, more complex decisions, and larger resource allocations, to determine just how much each element increases the chances of project failure or success. One might find, for instance, after examining a number of projects, that generally systems initiated by outsiders who do not work for the company for which the KBS is being developed have a high probability of failing (Cullen 1988). This information would then be incorporated into a revised situation diagram.

As part of this development process, one also defines the possible recommendations or actions that might be made or taken by the expert in the types of situations under study. For example, for the initial prototype system one might use three general levels of risk: low, moderate, and high, as in Figure 2–6. In addition, one might also go further and define possible recommendations about how to reduce risk and improve chances of success, such as through knowledge engineer training in interpersonal skills or greater involvement of experts in the development process.

Based on the study of typical situations, the structure of a decision situation begins to emerge. The early ideas of the decision structure can be fairly rough, as is evident in the decision situation diagrams in this chapter and the next. The diagrams shown in these chapters are not to be taken as examples of good models. They are examples of rough and imperfect early diagrams and are given here to illustrate how the more fully developed models, such as the versions shown in Appendix H, evolve later from very rough beginnings. It is an example of incremental prototyping, or of developing successive approximations of decision situations.

The process of structuring the situation in a way useful for knowledge-based systems development is a continuing, evolving one that calls for:

- reviewing typical decisions made, and developing typical scenarios of the expert at work
- specifying the recommendations possible in these typical decision situations, as well as the three or four factors that will affect the recommendation, as well as situation questions that need answering about these factors
- drawing initial block diagrams of the typical decisions, which serve as the beginning of the conceptualization or model-formulation phase
- reviewing additional test-case examples and revising or reformulating the block diagrams, as often as is needed or as time permits

This analysis and evaluation phase, like the subsequent phases, is not completed once and for all at the end of the phase. As is indicated by the arrows at the bottom of Figure 2–1, this analytical and evaluation phase continues throughout the development process. As the situation is studied in greater detail and more information about it is obtained, the system model is developed and refined.

### Reformulating and Reconceptualizing the Decision Situation

As indicated in Figure 2–1, developing and refining diagrammatic models or representations of the knowledge domain and reasoning processes can occur throughout the KBS development life cycle.

The following account traces some of the revisions and reformulations made in developing the models presented in Figures 2–2 and 2–6. The reader should keep in mind that this introductory discussion is designed only to illustrate some basic reformulation patterns. This phase can often be very difficult in practice.

The following discussion illustrates several essential reconceptualization steps which can occur at almost any stage in KBS development:

- the initial concept or general structure of the model is often reformulated, as decision reasoning paths and relationships are studied in more detail
- more detail is added, both expanding the depth and breadth or scope of the model
- the initial recommendations are revised or amplified, which may lead to further changes in the structure, scope, and depth of the model

Figures 2–7a through 2–7f give examples of some reconceptualizations which can occur during knowledge-based system development. The examples have been simplified to illustrate key points. Figure 2–7a shows an initial concept of the system. As the study of the decision situation progressed, several changes were made. First, it was decided to amplify the organization environment segment (Figure 2–7b).

Next, the questions explored by an expert in making these decisions were refined and amplified. For example, as shown in Figure 2–7c, if and only if the project was initiated by someone outside the company, would someone explore the question, "Though the system was initiated by someone outside the company, has management expressed significant interest in and support for the system development project?"

Amplifications and integrations (reconceiving and reformulating) are common during the model development process. For example, further study seemed to indicate that the availability of expertise in the knowledge area was related to other organization factors when estimating risks associated with a proposed project, and so it was integrated into the organization complexity segment, as shown in Figure 2–7d.

In Figure 2–7e, an additional relationship refinement was introduced into the decision situation diagram. The addition shows how the computer expertise required in a situation is determined by examining organization and knowledge-

**Figure 2–7.** Decision Situation under Study: Estimating KBS Project Proposal Risk—Reformulation of the Situation Representation, Knowledge Domain Model (Initial Prototype Phase)

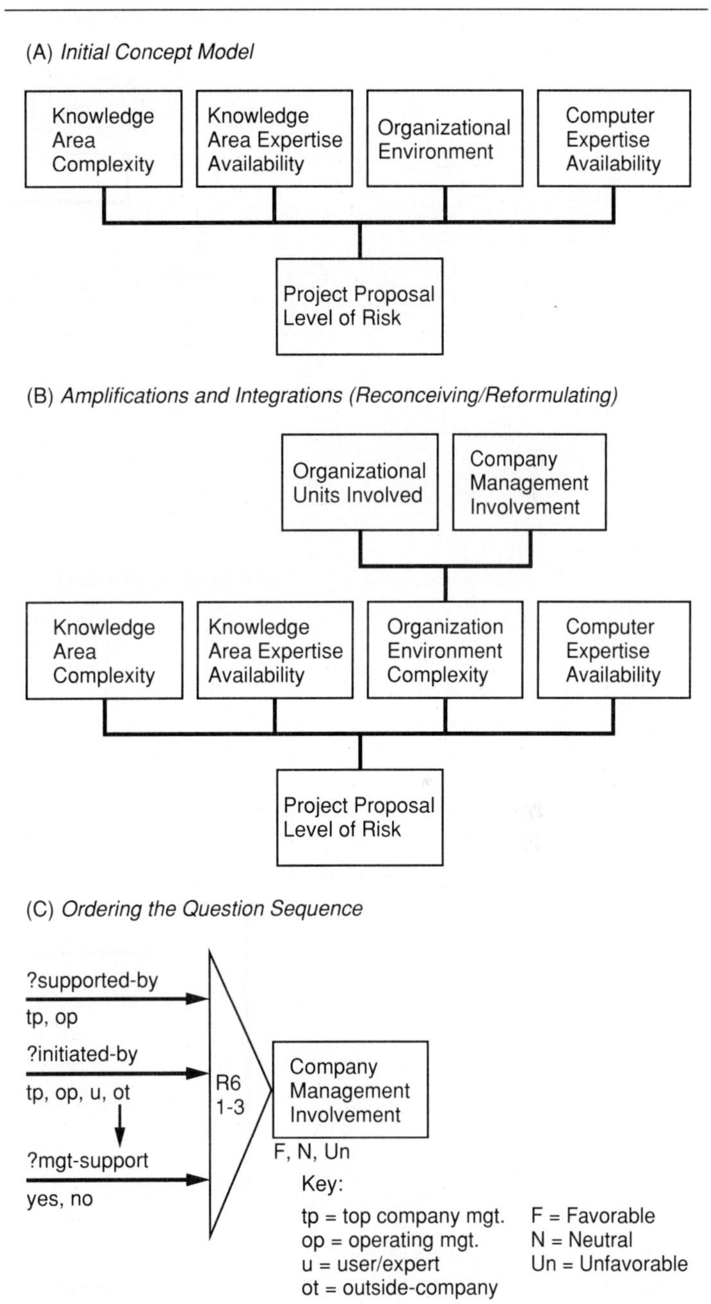

**Figure 2–7** *continued*

(D) *Further Reformulation*

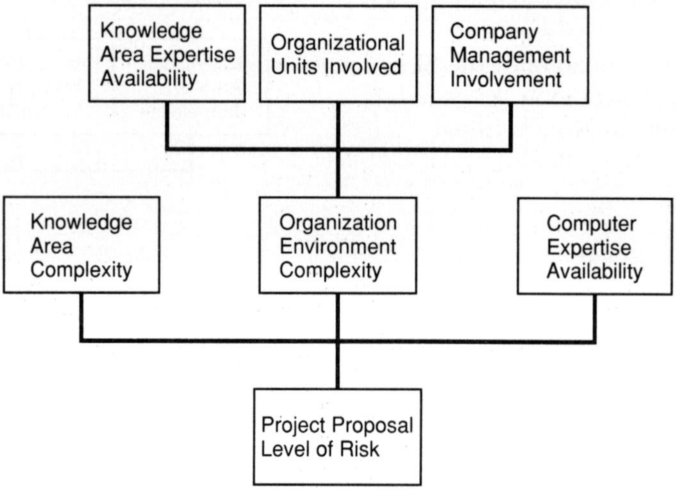


(E) *Further Reformulation*

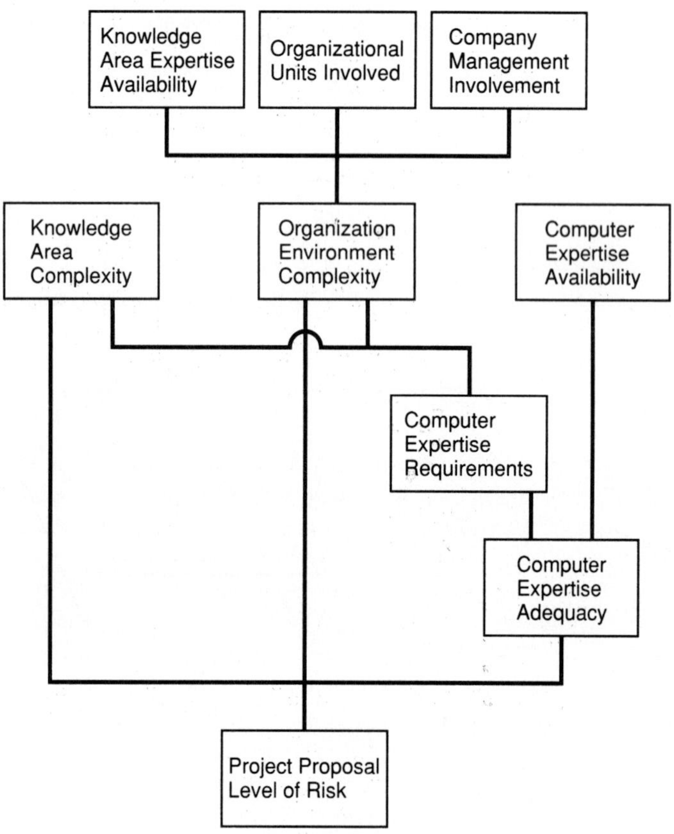

**Figure 2–7** *continued*

(F) *Amplification of Recommendations*

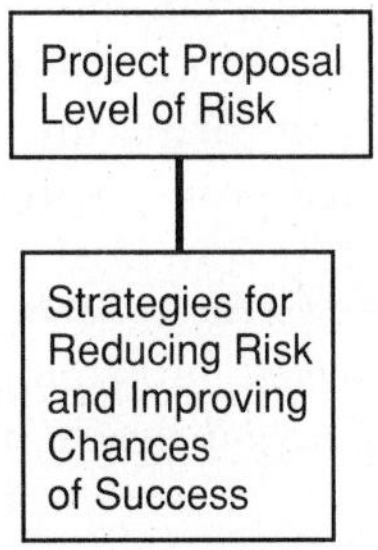


(G) *The Formulation and Reformulation of a KBS*

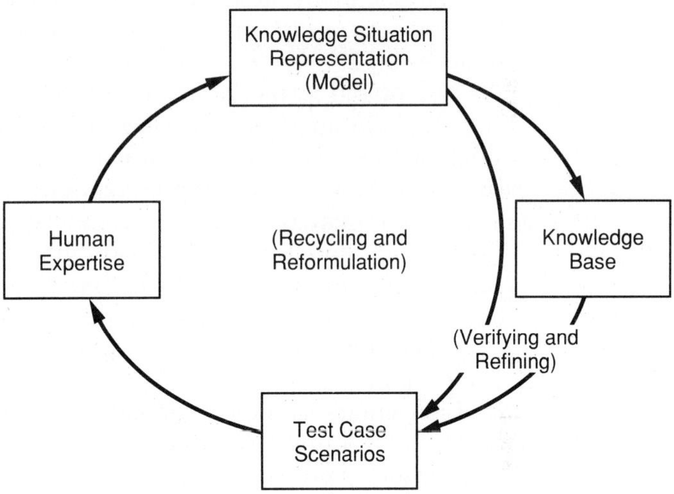


domain complexity factors. These requirements are then matched against available resources to determine whether the computer expertise available is adequate for the project.

In Figure 2–7f, the scope of the situation under study was extended beyond estimating the inherent risks in the proposed project to include recommending strategies to help ensure the project's successful implementation. In practice, one often changes the scope of a project as study of the situation progresses, or when identifying segments of the situation that can be prototyped.

Other studies have been made which define in more detail the process of model refinement, even going so far as to develop an automated tool for doing this refinement (Motta 1990). Many of these studies are discussed in Chapters 7 and 8 later in this book.

Figures 2–5 and 2–6 show the phases of modelling during which a decision situation diagram, such as the one shown in Figure 2–7, is transformed into a computer system dependency diagram.

The reference point through all of these revisions, as shown in Figure 2–7g, is *how the situation actually works*. Developing and then studying scenarios of typical decisions and specifying the recommendations made, the key factors, and specific information affecting those recommendations helps to keep this reference point in mind throughout the process.

*Test-case scenario writing has proved in practice to be the single most useful method for keeping knowledge-based systems true replications or emulations of actual experts at work.*

Further refinements and reformulations may be made through subsequently developing other, different typical decision situation scenarios and going through the model adjustment process again to make the model applicable to a wider variety of tasks, problems, or decisions. This sort of scenario analysis was done during the situation studies which led to the expansion and development of the system and its models diagrammed in Figures 2–2 through 2–7.

Keep in mind that the diagrams (or models) of decision, problem, or task situations exactly duplicate human reasoning processes only in very simple situations. Most of these representations only replicate, imitate, or approximate aspects of human thinking. They rarely duplicate the exact way an expert's mind moves back and forth continually among the different blocks or frames of knowledge—even after many revisions. Management decision situations generally are not that easy to represent graphically.

The reformulation of a situation, therefore, is always an imperfect compromise that tries to strike a balance. For example, in many management decision situations the reformulation is not necessarily a *prescription* for the best way to solve a problem or make a decision. Nor is it merely a *description* of how one person, a presumed expert, does it.

Rather, in management decision situations *the objective is often to replicate or emulate a composite description of how one pretty good expert might make a decision reasonably well.* In major systems this replication often is arrived at through a compromise, based on the judgments of a variety of experts in the field, after considering:

- the ways different experts actually work
- the best way to do the task or make the decision theoretically
- the limitations inherent in graphic representation techniques
- the technical limitations inherent in the expert system shells used to computerize the system

In general this phase, as illustrated in Figures 2–2 through 2–7, is referred to as the **reconceptualization** or **transformation phase,** since it involves transforming early rough situation models by gradual steps into computer-compatible situation diagrams, which in turn become dependency diagrams or some other form of computer formalization. It is clear from examining the process that it is a fluid one, requiring considerable flexibility in thinking in order to do it well.

Since knowledge-based systems are relatively new and costly to develop, it is usually prudent to develop them in stages, incrementally, starting with small prototype approximations of the actual system. This enables testing the basic structure and concept of the system, as well as specific parts of the system, before committing substantial resources to its development. It also enables developers to become familiar with knowledge-based system technology before undertaking larger, more costly systems. Additionally, it often leads to smaller working systems which are immediately useful on the job.

To do this in a way that enables using this smaller system development to build larger systems, one first has to study and model the overall system to be eventually developed. For example, Figure 2–8 gives an example of a decision situation diagram involving a strategic planning decision: developing a strategy at a large pharmaceutical company for a new product introduction at a local foreign affiliate. In developing Figure 2–8, the total decision area under study was first outlined, as shown in part in Figure 2–9, and then reexamined in depth. Specific smaller systems were then developed for segments of the overall system, such as the one shown in Figure 2–8.

Such an approach enables building a large system incrementally, adding modules or segments to it as they are developed, while at the same time building immediately useful smaller systems.

An outline for a report that might be made about the structured situation analysis and reformulation described so far in this chapter is given in Figure 2–10. Such a report, which can be prepared by the system developer (the knowledge engineer or expert), is a useful training tool in executive and college KBS development programs.

## PUTTING THE SYSTEM ONTO COMPUTER

The discussion in this section focuses on the system design and documentation required to develop smaller prototype systems designed for implementation with expert system shells. This initial work does not require programming experience or expertise.

Several formal steps are necessary to adequately design and document even a small prototype system. These steps can include:

- creating system proposals
- describing the system
- developing dependency diagrams
- developing decision charts
- designing and constructing the knowledge base
- some special considerations when putting the system on computer

**Figure 2–8.** Decision Situation under Study: New Product Strategy for Local Country Product Proposal—Decision Diagram (Initial Prototype Phase)

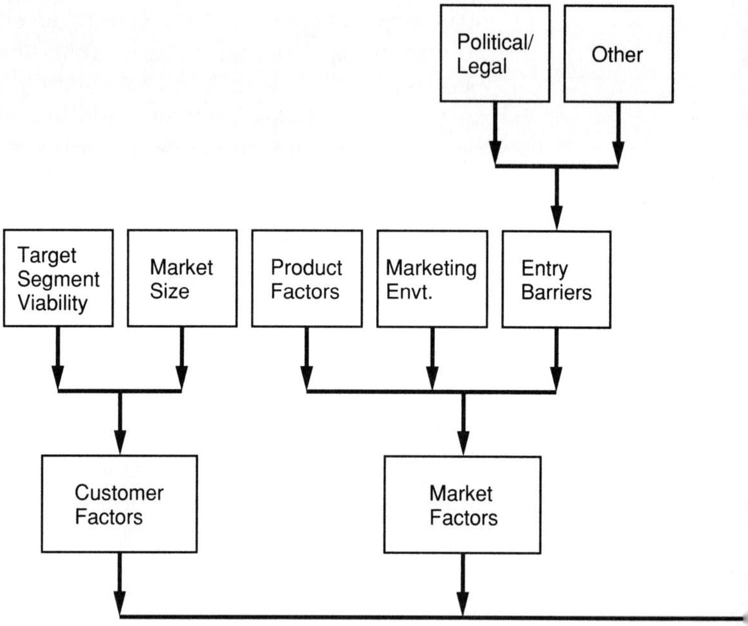


## System Proposals

Even when creating a system for one's own personal use, it is a good idea for documentation and reference purposes to define in a few sentences exactly what is to be accomplished and the resources required. Where it is necessary to convince a client or an employer or company management to support the undertaking of a system development project, such a system proposal is mandatory.

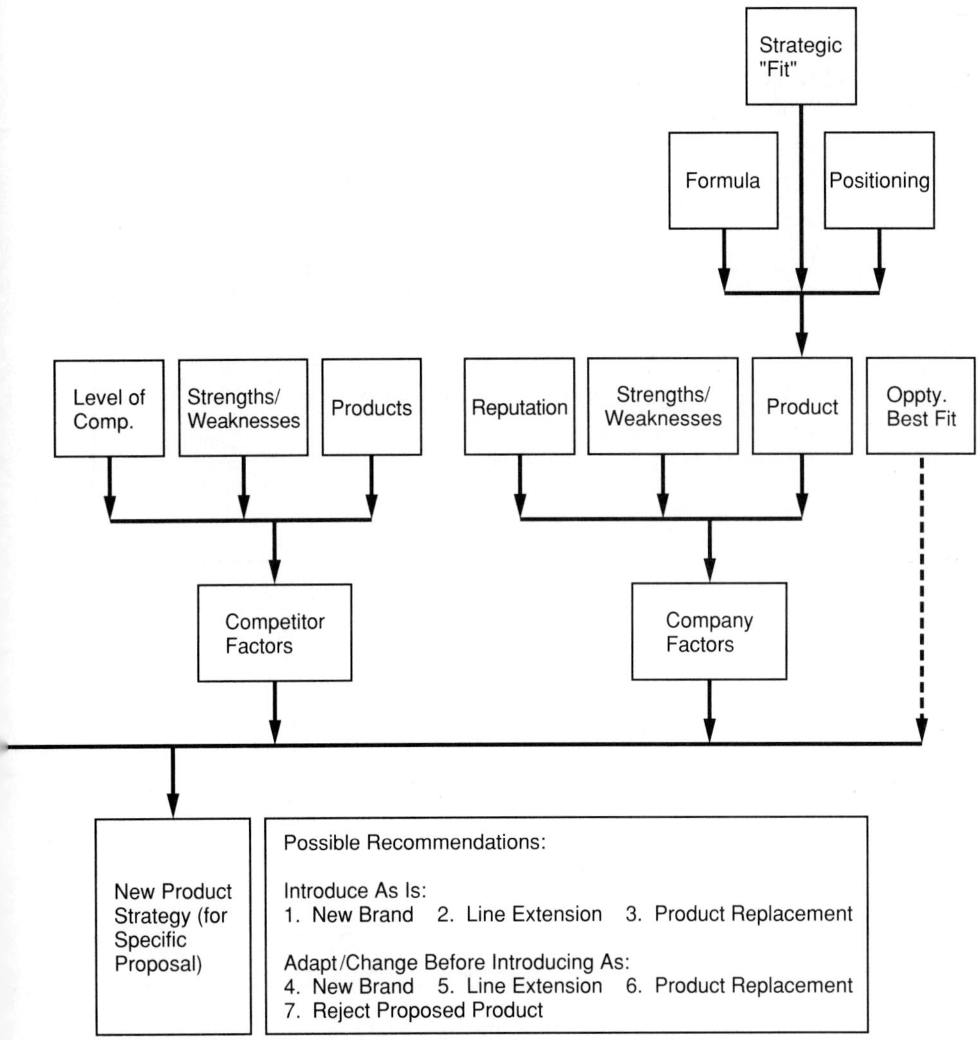


The following are some of the areas such a **system proposal** might cover:

- nature and purpose of the system
- why it is needed
- who will use it
- benefits to be derived from the system and problems if it is not developed
- cost to develop the system
- how long it will take to develop the system

**Figure 2–9.** Decision Situation under Study: Overall Marketing Strategy Development—Overview Diagram (Initial Prototype Phase)

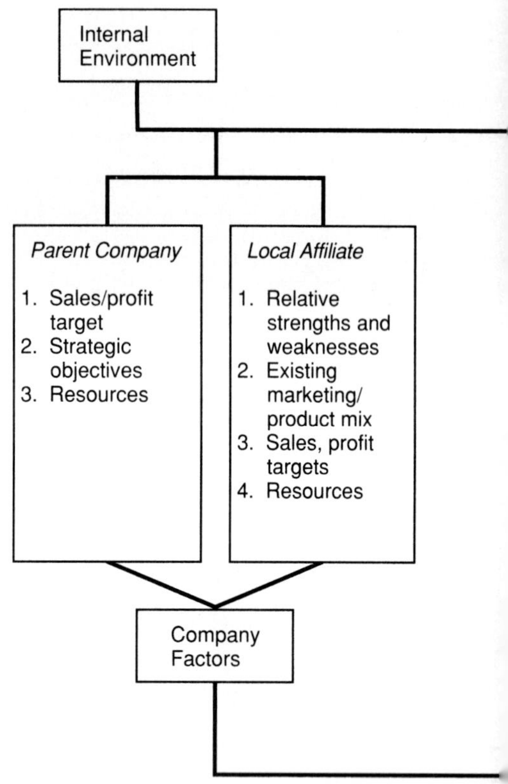


- who will develop the system and to what extent others will be involved
- knowledge sources to be used
- additional resources which must be acquired
- what controls there will be for monitoring progress of the project
- potential problems

This list might be expanded or condensed, and the proposal itself might vary in length and detail, depending on the actual situation under study. The proposal for a small prototype system might be only a few paragraphs, while extensive two- or three-year projects costing several millions of dollars, such as Digital Equipment Corporation's XSEL system, which is described later in this book, might require several volumes.

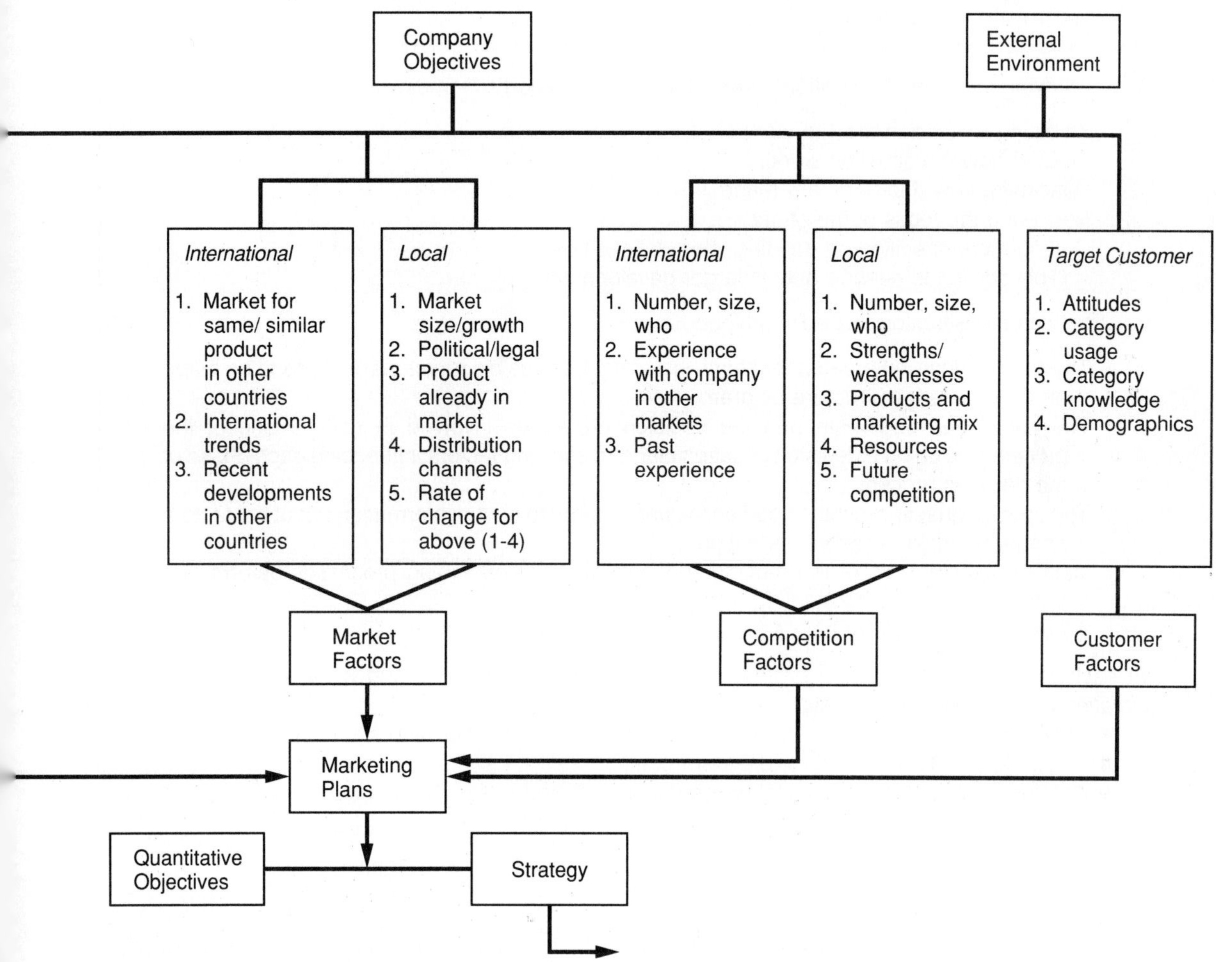


## Description of the System

A system description covers such topics as:

- system overview and objective
- nature of the user interface
- recommendations to be made by the system
- description of the knowledge structure and reasoning processes

Like the system proposal, the system description will vary in length and detail, depending on the decision, problem, or task situation under study. This very simple description was initially written for the system developed in Figure 2–6:

**Figure 2–10.** Topic Outline for a Report Summarizing the Situation Analysis and Reformulation for a Proposed KBS

A. Studying the Overall Situation: Understanding the Expert's Domain

Selecting a decision area to work on
Probing how the situation works
Describing how decisions are made
Narrowing the focus of the study
Getting more specific and defining interrelationships
(This section is needed only in larger development projects)

B. Studying the Situation to Be Prototyped

The precise decision area under study, including the possible recommendations to be made and a knowledge structure diagram
The knowledge segments and the decision processes involved in each phase of the process, including a decision situation diagram showing factors influencing each phase of the decision process
The specific questions which need answering in order to obtain information about the factors needed to make a recommendation
Detailed explanations of the recommendations and the reasoning processes determining them
An example scenario of how a typical decision is made

At each of these phases, *when probing, when getting more specific,* and *when studying the situation to be prototyped,* always

- Write and review a specific example (scenario) of a typical decision situation
- Draw a generalized model (or diagram) of it
- Review additional test or typical cases (scenarios) and revise the diagrams

- This is a knowledge-based system designed to help a user evaluate the risks anticipated in proposed knowledge-based system development projects. It is a concept-testing prototype of a larger, more comprehensive KBS designed to assist KBS project managers involved in developing large systems.
- The system would ask the user a number of questions about such things as the type, breadth, and depth of the knowledge domain for which a KBS is proposed.
- The recommendations would categorize projects as low-risk, moderately risky, or high-risk, and suggest ways to reduce risks.
- The recommendations are based on three critical factors: the knowledge domain, organizational environment, and computer expertise.
- IF-THEN rules and backward chaining inferencing are used to determine the intermediate decision values and make recommendations.

### Dependency Diagrams of the System

As mentioned earlier, dependency diagrams graphically model a knowledge-based system, showing the knowledge segments and their interrelationships. They also indicate some of the basic reasoning processes by which the knowledge is manipulated. They are a powerful tool for understanding a knowledge-based system and guiding its development, since they give a complete and accurate picture of the entire system or system component they represent. Figure 2–6 gives an example of one.

These *system* diagrams evolve from and are based on structured decision *situation* diagrams or models, such as the one shown in Figure 2–2, and are often developed and revised simultaneously before final versions are settled on.

Because the example is a small one, the relationship between the decision situation diagram in Figure 2–2 and the system dependency diagram in Figure 2–6 is very easy to see—they are almost the same. This is an ideal which is normally achieved only in small prototype system projects.

*The more focused, detailed, and structured the situation analysis is, the more likely the decision situation diagram and the system dependency diagram are to be similar and the easier the actual system development will be.*

In addition to showing the knowledge segments, the dependency diagram in Figure 2–6 shows exactly where each knowledge segment is manipulated in coming to a decision. It also indicates the reasoning paths followed through a knowledge hierarchy to arrive at a final decision or recommendation.

The following summarizes the basic components of these full system dependency diagrams:

- The triangles contain numbers that refer to the rules in the knowledge base which manipulate the knowledge segments adjacent to the triangles—there will be a decision chart for every triangle.
- The boxes and arrows adjacent to a triangle show the name of the knowledge segments to which they are related and which they manipulate.
- The question marks indicate questions asked by the system in order to get information input from users into the system. The subject of the questions is also given.
- Acceptable values for each phase in the process are given under the input arrows and boxes.
- The recommendations to be made by the system during a consultation are named under the final decision box in the diagram.

This document, or one like it, serves as a complete reference outline for understanding, controlling, and coordinating a knowledge-based system and its development effort. Such diagrams are mandatory for any well-planned and well-executed system development effort.

**Figure 2–11.** Decision Situation under Study: New Venture Using Franchising—Overview Dependency Diagram (Initial Prototype Phase)

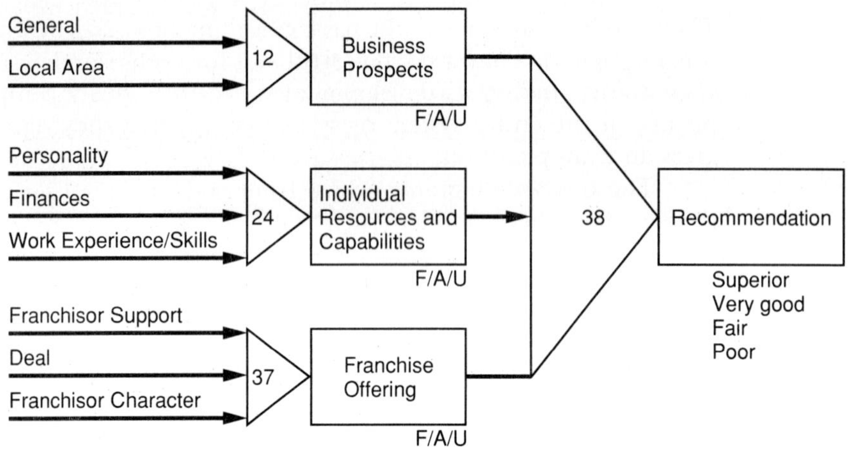


*Key: For Figures 2-11 through 2-15*

| | |
|---|---|
| S = Strong | Y = Yes |
| M = Medium | N = No |
| W = Weak | H = High |
| F = Favorable | L = Low |
| U = Unfavorable | A = Average |

Diagrams, such as the one shown in Figure 2–6, are clearly not the only kind of decision process models. Many systems are simply too large to enable creating such a detailed picture of them in a single document. Figures 2–11 through 2–14 show the dependency diagrams from a franchise-selection prototype system. In this case, there is an overview diagram of the system (Figure 2–11), followed by detailed diagrams of specific segments (Figures 2–12 to 2–14).

## Decision Charts or Tables

**Decision charts** should be prepared for every rule-set triangle in the dependency diagram. They are another graphic way to represent the knowledge segments and reasoning contained in the rule-based prototype systems discussed in this book.

A decision chart for the KBS development example described earlier is given in Figure 2–15. It represents the final rule set of the system (condensed version, rules 1-1 to 1-7), which is part of the knowledge base for the system in Figure 2–17, where the English version of the rules shown in the chart is given.

**Figure 2–12.** Decision Situation under Study: New Venture Using Franchising—Individual Resources and Capabilities Segment, Dependency Diagram (Initial Prototype Phase)

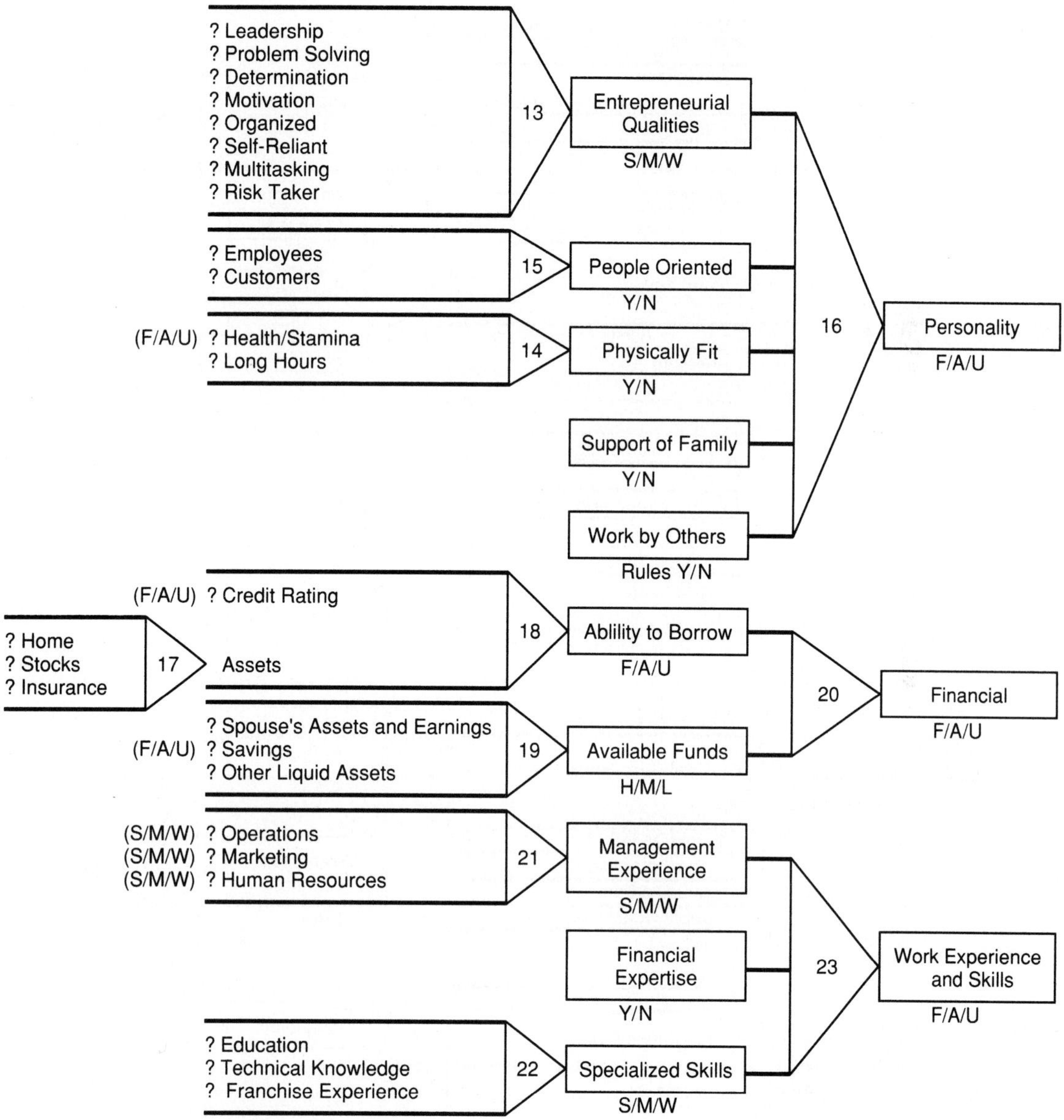


Note: All answers to questions are yes or no except where indicated.

**Figure 2–13.** Decision Situation under Study: New Venture Using Franchising—Franchise Offering Segment, Dependency Diagram (Initial Prototype Phase)

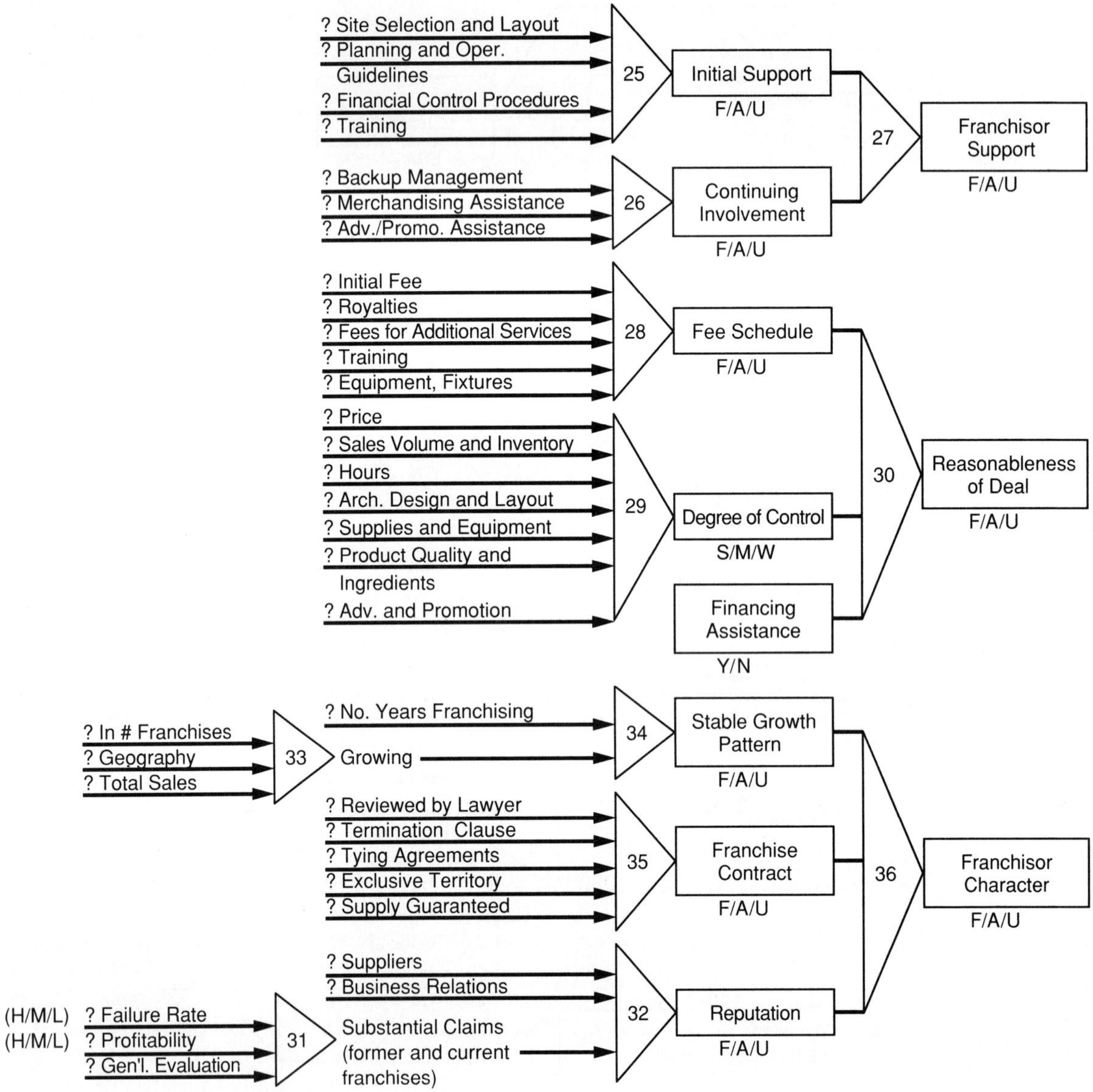


Note: All answers to questions are yes or no except where indicated.

**Figure 2–14.** Decision Situation under Study: New Venture Using Franchising—Business Prospects Segment, Dependency Diagram (Initial Prototype Phase)

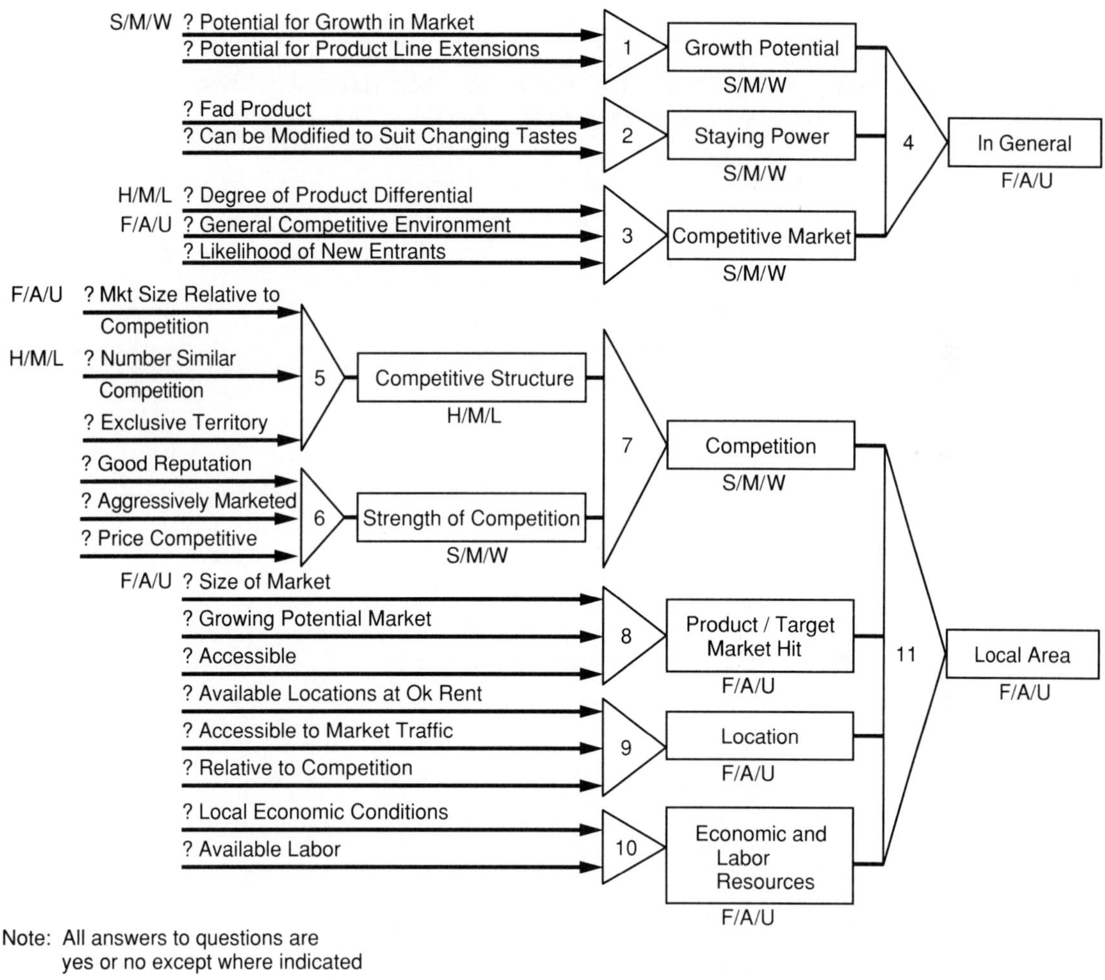


Another example of a decision chart or table is given in Figure 2–16. It involves the prototype knowledge-based system for franchise selection which is illustrated in Figures 2–11 to 2–14.

The timing of when the decision charts are developed, as well as their design, depends both on the situation and on the preferences of the system developer. For example, the decision charts may be prepared *after* the major rules are written. In this way the charts are used to check out the variations on

**Figure 2–15.** Decision Situation under Study: Estimating KBS Project Proposal Risk—Decision Chart, Final Rule Set (Initial Prototype Phase)

(A) *Initial Version*

| Rule # 1- | 1 | 2 | 3 | 4 | 5 | 6 | 7 | 8 | 9 | 10 | 11 | 12 | 13 |
|---|---|---|---|---|---|---|---|---|---|---|---|---|---|
| if knowledge-area-complexity | S | S | S/M | C | C | # | S | S | M/C | M | M/C | M | M |
| if org-environment-complexity | F | F/N | F | U | # | U | N | N/U | F | F | N | N/U | N |
| if computer-expertise-adequacy | G/O | G | G | # | P | P | O/P | O | O | O/P | G | G | O |
| then Level of Risk = | | | | | | | | | | | | | |
| low risk | X | X | X | | | | | | | | | | |
| moderate risk | | | | | | | X | X | X | X | X | X | X |
| high risk | | | | X | X | X | | | | | | | |

S = simple M = moderate C = complex
F = favorable N = neutral U = unfavorable
G = good O = okay P = poor
/ = or # = any answer

(B) *Final Condensed Version*

| Rule # 1- | 1 | 2 | 3 | 4 | 5 | 6 | 7 |
|---|---|---|---|---|---|---|---|
| if knowledge-area-complexity | S | S | S/M | C | C | # | # |
| if org-environment-complexity | F | F/N | F | U | # | U | # |
| if computer-expertise-adequacy | G/O | G | G | # | P | P | # |
| then Level of Risk : | | | | | | | |
| low risk | X | X | X | | | | |
| moderate risk | | | | | | | X |
| high risk | | | | X | X | X | |

S = simple M = moderate C = complex
F = favorable N = neutral U = unfavorable
G = good O = okay P = poor
/ = or # = any answer

Note for (B): Since rules are fired in sequence, Rule 7 functions as a default rule where Rule 1 through 6 have not yielded an answer.

each rule and to make sure nothing is missed. Alternately, decision charts can be prepared before the rules are written.

Usually, however, the development process is not so structured. Rather, the decision charts, dependency diagrams, and knowledge base rules and questions are compared, restudied, and revised in a variety of different ways continually during the course of the development process. The process even includes

**Figure 2–16.** Decision Situation under Study: New Venture Using Franchising—Sample Decision Chart (Initial Prototype Phase)

| | Rules | 108-110 | 111-113 | 114-116 | 117-119 | 120-122 | 123-125 | 126-128 | 129-131 | 132-134 |
|---|---|---|---|---|---|---|---|---|---|---|
| IF | BUSINESS | FFF | AAA | UUU | FFF | AAA | UUU | FFF | AAA | UUU |
| | RES-CAP | FFF | FFF | FFF | AAA | AAA | AAA | UUU | UUU | UUU |
| | OFFERING | FAU | FAU | FAU | FAU | FAU | FAU | FAU | FAU | FAU |
| THEN | SUPERIOR | X | | | X | | | | | |
| | VERY GOOD | X | X | | | | | | | |
| | FAIR | | X X | | X X | X X | | | | |
| | POOR | X | | X X X | | X | X X X | X X X | X X X | X X X |

*Key:*
F—Favorable
A—Average
U—Very good
S—Strong
V—Very weak
FA—Fair
P—Poor

referring back to the written typical expert decision scenarios, as well as the situation diagrams, and revising them. The development process is basically a fluid, evolutionary one and requires flexible conceptual modelling skills.

However used, decision charts provide important documentation for use in later stages of system development, when layers of complexities have been introduced. They are a good way to verify that modifications of the system are consistent and accurate. They are absolutely necessary to determine the completeness of rule sets. They are also useful during the rule condensation and reduction phase—all of which are discussed later in the chapters in Part Two.

### Designing and Constructing the Knowledge Base

Designing and constructing a knowledge base involves:

- selecting a representation form to be used
- writing out the knowledge for the knowledge base
- putting that knowledge into a form acceptable to the expert system shell or computer language chosen

***Selecting a Representation Form.*** The kind of decision, problem, or task situation can dictate whether a rule-based system or object-based (also called frame-based) representation form is used. These two types of knowledge representation were discussed in Chapter 1. Either one or the other, or some combination of the two (also called hybrid), may be selected. A rule-based structure is used in the system illustrated in Figures 2–2 through 2–6, since it suits the reasoning processes involved in the example situations, is easier for the nontechnician to follow, and is the representation form used in most expert system shells.

For illustrative purposes, the examples of knowledge bases given are designed for use on M.1 and VP-Expert. These shells were chosen because they are easy to use. For example, Cimflex Teknowledge's expert system shell, M.1, uses conventional English and simple syntax, and so is easy for the nontechnician to read and work with. Rules and questions can be written for M.1 on any conventional word processor. For these reasons, M.1 is a convenient expert system shell for developing smaller systems, especially prototypes. VP-Expert, in addition to being easy to use, can integrate with database management and spreadsheet applications, as is shown in the discussions of it in Chapters 3, 4, 5, and 6.

Both the VP-Expert and M.1 versions of the small risk-evaluation prototype KBS described in this chapter are given on the disks accompanying this book.

***Writing the Knowledge Base.*** Figures 2–17 and 2–18 show two versions (for M.1 and VP-Expert) of the knowledge base written for the system described in this chapter and outlined in the dependency diagram in Figure 2–6. In developing this knowledge base, the first phase was to specify the objective (decide on the degree of risk inherent in the proposed project), what values of recommendations the system will make (a low-risk project, a moderately risky project, a high-risk project), and what the structure of the final rule set will look like. Additional rules were then developed all the way back through the decision or reasoning paths until the questions were specified.

A knowledge base is developed with continuing reference to the decision charts and dependency diagrams, as well as to the typical sample decision scenarios and to the decision situation diagrams.

***Putting the Knowledge Base into Computer-Acceptable Form.*** In situations where an expert system shell is used, as in the prototype systems described in the figures in this chapter, this might involve such steps as changing the plain English statements into a computer readable format so that the knowledge base can be loaded with the shell to be used for running a consultation. Figure 2–3 gives an example of how plain English rules were rewritten in a condensed computer-compatible form, both for M.1 and VP-Expert, which are microcomputer expert system shells. The exact final form of the rules will depend on the development shell or programming language used.

This process is often referred to as the **encoding** phase. Examples of user questions rewritten for a computer shell are shown in Figure 2–4. These are also written for M.1 and VP-Expert.

**Figure 2–17.** Decision Situation under Study: Evaluating a KBS Development Project's Risk—Knowledge Base, M.1 Version (Initial Prototype, filename KBS-EVAL.M1)

```
goal = level-of-risk.

initialdata = intro-over.

   if display([nl,nl,nl,nl,nl,nl,nl,nl,nl,nl,'

                          WELCOME TO THE
                     RISK EVALUATION ASSISTANT

                  Copyright (c) 1992 by R.J. Mockler
                          All rights reserved

',nl,nl,nl]) and
      need-intro-1 = yes and
      display([nl,nl,nl,nl,nl,nl,nl,nl,nl,nl,nl,nl,nl,'

               This system is designed to help  you  evaluate
               the risks inherent in your proposed  knowledge
               based system project. Based on your replies to
               the questions  asked  about:
                 . the  organization environment
                 . the  knowledge area complexity
                 . the computer expertise adequacy
               you will be given an estimate of the project"s
               chances of success.

',nl,nl,nl]) and
      need-intro-2 = yes
      then intro-over.

      question(need-intro-1) = '
    Type "1" and press the ENTER key to continue.'.

      legalvals(need-intro-1) = [yes].

      question(need-intro-2) = '
    Type "1" and press the ENTER key to continue.'.

            legalvals(need-intro-2) = [yes].


      automaticmenu(ALL).
      enumeratedanswers(ALL).

/*      Level of Risk                    */
```

**Figure 2–17** *continued*

```
rule-1-1:
if knowledge-area-complexity = simple and
   org-environment-complexity = favorable and
   computer-expertise-adequacy = ok or
   computer-expertise-adequacy = good and
        display([nl,nl,nl,nl,nl,nl,nl,nl,nl,nl,nl,nl,nl,nl,nl,'
    Based on the answers you have given, the project you have
    proposed has a low level of risk and a high potential for success.
',nl,nl,nl,nl,nl,nl,nl,nl,nl,nl])
        then level-of-risk = low.

rule-1-2:
if knowledge-area-complexity = simple or
   knowledge-area-complexity = moderate and
   org-environment-complexity = favorable and
   computer-expertise-adequacy = good and
        display([nl,nl,nl,nl,nl,nl,nl,nl,nl,nl,nl,nl,nl,nl,nl,'
    Based on the answers you have given, the project you have
    proposed has a low level of risk and a high potential for success.
',nl,nl,nl,nl,nl,nl,nl,nl,nl,nl])
        then level-of-risk = low.

rule-1-3:
if knowledge-area-complexity = simple and
   org-environment-complexity = neutral or
   org-environment-complexity = favorable and
   computer-expertise-adequacy = good and
        display([nl,nl,nl,nl,nl,nl,nl,nl,nl,nl,nl,nl,nl,nl,nl,'
    Based on the answers you have given, the project you have
    proposed has a low level of risk and a high potential for success.
',nl,nl,nl,nl,nl,nl,nl,nl,nl,nl])
        then level-of-risk = low.

rule-1-4:
if knowledge-area-complexity = complex and
   org-environment-complexity = unfavorable or
   computer-expertise-adequacy = poor and
        display([nl,nl,nl,nl,nl,nl,nl,nl,nl,nl,nl,nl,nl,nl,nl,'
     Based on the answers you have given,
     the project you have proposed is a high risk project.
',nl,nl,nl,nl,nl,nl,nl,nl,nl,nl])
        then level-of-risk = high.

rule-1-5:
if org-environment-complexity = unfavorable and
   knowledge-area-complexity = complex or
   computer-expertise-adequacy = poor and
        display([nl,nl,nl,nl,nl,nl,nl,nl,nl,nl,nl,nl,nl,nl,nl,'
     Based on the answers you have given,
     the project you have proposed is a high risk project.
',nl,nl,nl,nl,nl,nl,nl,nl,nl,nl])
        then level-of-risk = high.
```

```
rule-1-6:
if computer-expertise-adequacy = poor and
   knowledge-area-complexity = complex or
   org-environment-complexity = unfavorable and
        display([nl,nl,nl,nl,nl,nl,nl,nl,nl,nl,nl,nl,nl,nl,nl,'
    Based on the answers you have given,
    the project you have proposed is a high risk project.
',nl,nl,nl,nl,nl,nl,nl,nl,nl,nl])
        then level-of-risk = high.

rule-1-7:
if knowledge-area-complexity = ANY1 and
   org-environment-complexity = ANY2 and
   computer-expertise-availability = ANY4 and
        display([nl,nl,nl,nl,nl,nl,nl,nl,nl,nl,nl,nl,nl,nl,nl,'
    Based on the answers you have given, the project you
    have proposed is a moderately risky one, which must be
    carefully planned. The specific areas to be re-examined and
    detailed plans for reducing the risk found in the project
    will be identified in more advanced versions of this system.

',nl,nl,nl,nl,nl,nl,nl])
        then level-of-risk = moderate.
/*   knowledge area complexity   */

rule-2-1:
if factual-knowledge = simple and
   reasoning-heuristics = simple
then knowledge-area-complexity = simple.

rule-2-2:
if reasoning-heuristics = complex and
   factual-knowledge = moderate or
   factual-knowledge = complex
then knowledge-area-complexity = complex.

rule-2-3:
if factual-knowledge = complex and
   reasoning-heuristics = complex or
   reasoning-heuristics = moderate
then knowledge-area-complexity = complex.

rule-2-4:
if reasoning-heuristics = ANY1 and
   factual-knowledge = ANY2
then knowledge-area-complexity = moderate.

question(reasoning-heuristics) =
[nl,nl,nl,nl,nl,nl,nl,nl,nl,nl,nl,nl,nl,nl,nl,nl,nl,nl,nl,nl,'
    For the proposed knowledge based system, would you describe
    the reasoning processes involved as simple,
moderately-complex
    or complex?

',nl,nl,nl,nl,nl,nl].

legalvals(reasoning-heuristics) = [simple, moderate, complex].
```

**Figure 2–17** *continued*

```
question(factual-knowledge) =
[nl,nl,nl,nl,nl,nl,nl,nl,nl,nl,nl,nl,nl,nl,nl,nl,nl,nl,nl,nl,'
    For the proposed knowledge based system, would you describe
    the factual knowledge covered in the area as straight-forward
    and simple (for example, how an electric motor works),
    moderately complex (for example, insurance claims processing)
    or complex (for example, international corporate tax planning
    and auditing)?

',nl,nl,nl].

legalvals(factual-knowledge) = [simple, moderate, complex].

/*   organization environment complexity   */

rule-3-1:
if knowledge-area-expertise-avail = favorable and
   organization_units_involved = A + B and
   A + B <= 5 and
   company-management-involvement = favorable or
   company-management-involvement = neutral
then org-environment-complexity = favorable.

rule-3-2:
if knowledge-area-expertise-avail = favorable or
   knowledge-area-expertise-avail = neutral and
   organization_units_involved = A + B and
   A + B <= 5 and
   company-management-involvement = favorable
then org-environment-complexity = favorable.

rule-3-3:
if knowledge-area-expertise-avail = neutral and
   organization_units_involved = A + B and
   A + B <= 5 and
   company-management-involvement = neutral
then org-environment-complexity = neutral.

rule-3-4:
if knowledge-area-expertise-avail = favorable and
   organization_units_involved = A + B and
   A + B <=5 and
   company-management-involvement = unfavorable
then org-environment-complexity = neutral.

rule-3-5:
if knowledge-area-expertise-avail = unfavorable and
   organization_units_involved = A + B and
   A + B <= 5 and
   company-management-involvement = favorable
then org-environment-complexity = neutral.

rule-3-6:
if knowledge-area-expertise-avail = favorable and
   organization_units_involved = A + B and
   A + B > 5 and
   company-management-involvement = favorable or
   company-management-involvement = neutral
then org-environment-complexity = neutral.
```

```
rule-3-7:
if knowledge-area-expertise-avail = favorable or
   knowledge-area-expertise-avail = neutral and
   organization_units_involved = A + B and
   A + B > 5 and
   company-management-involvement = favorable
then org-environment-complexity = neutral.

rule-3-8:
if knowledge-area-expertise-avail = Any2 and
   organization_units_involved = Any3 and
   company-management-involvement = Any1
then org-environment-complexity = unfavorable.

/*     knowledge area expertise availability     */

rule-4-1:
if expert-developed = yes
then knowledge-area-expertise-avail = favorable.

rule-4-2:
if expert-developed = no and
   expert-availability = unlimited
then knowledge-area-expertise-avail = favorable.

rule-4-3:
if expert-developed = no and
   expert-availability = limited
then knowledge-area-expertise-avail = neutral.

rule-4-4:
if expert-developed = no and
   expert-availability = very-limited
then knowledge-area-expertise-avail = unfavorable.

question(expert-developed) =
[nl,nl,nl,nl,nl,nl,nl,nl,nl,nl,nl,nl,nl,nl,nl,nl,nl,nl,nl,nl,'
     Will the system be developed by the expert whose knowledge
     is being replicated in the system?

',nl,nl,nl,nl,nl,nl,nl,nl].

legalvals(expert-developed) = [yes, no].

question(expert-availability) =
[nl,nl,nl,nl,nl,nl,nl,nl,nl,nl,nl,nl,nl,nl,nl,nl,nl,nl,nl,nl,'
     Where the system is not being developed by the expert(s)
     whose knowledge is being replicated in the system, how
     available will the expert(s) be who are involved in the
     project?

',nl,nl,nl,nl,nl].

legalvals(expert-availability) = [unlimited, limited,
very-limited].

/*     organizational units involved       */
```

**Figure 2–17** *continued*

```
rule-5-1:
if users-involved = A and
   experts-involved = B
then organization_units_involved = A + B.

question(users-involved) =
[nl,nl,nl,nl,nl,nl,nl,nl,nl,nl,nl,nl,nl,nl,nl,nl,nl,nl,nl,nl,'
     How many people are expected to use the proposed system on a
     regular basis? Type in any number.

',nl,nl,nl,nl,nl,nl,nl,nl,nl].

legalvals(users-involved) = number.

question(experts-involved) =
[nl,nl,nl,nl,nl,nl,nl,nl,nl,nl,nl,nl,nl,nl,nl,nl,nl,nl,nl,nl,'
     How many experts will be involved in the development of the
     system? Type in any number.

',nl,nl,nl,nl,nl,nl,nl,nl,nl].

legalvals(experts-involved) = number.

/*    company management involvement    */

rule-6-1:
if initiated-by = top-company-management or
   initiated-by = operating-management or
   initiated-by = user/expert and
   supported-by = top-company-management
then company-management-involvement = favorable.

rule-6-2:
if initiated-by = outside-company and
   management-support = no
then company-management-involvement = unfavorable.

rule-6-3:
if initiated-by = ANY and
   supported-by = ANY1
then company-management-involvement = neutral.

question(initiated-by) =
[nl,nl,nl,nl,nl,nl,nl,nl,nl,nl,nl,nl,nl,nl,nl,nl,nl,nl,nl,nl,'
     Who initiated the proposed project?

',nl,nl,nl,nl,nl,nl,nl].

legalvals(initiated-by) = [top-company-management,
operating-management, user/expert, outside-company].

question(supported-by) =
[nl,nl,nl,nl,nl,nl,nl,nl,nl,nl,nl,nl,nl,nl,nl,nl,nl,nl,nl,nl,'
     What is the highest level of management which has expressed
     interest in and support for the project?

',nl,nl,nl,nl,nl,nl,nl,nl].
```

```
legalvals(supported-by) = [top-company-management,
operating-management].

question(management-support) =
[nl,nl,nl,nl,nl,nl,nl,nl,nl,nl,nl,nl,nl,nl,nl,nl,nl,nl,nl,nl,'
     Though the system was initiated by someone outside the
     company, has management expressed interest in and support
     for the project?

',nl,nl,nl,nl,nl,nl,nl].

legalvals(management-support) = [yes, no].

/*   computer expertise adequacy      */

rule-7-1:
if computer-expertise-requirements = favorable and
   computer-expertise-availability = favorable or
   computer-expertise-availability = neutral
then computer-expertise-adequacy = good.

rule-7-2:
if computer-expertise-requirements = favorable or
   computer-expertise-requirements = neutral and
   computer-expertise-availability = favorable
then computer-expertise-adequacy = good.

rule-7-3:
if computer-expertise-requirements = unfavorable and
   computer-expertise-availability = unfavorable or
   computer-expertise-availability = neutral
then computer-expertise-adequacy = poor.

rule-7-4:
if computer-expertise-requirements = unfavorable or
   computer-expertise-requirements = neutral and
   computer-expertise-availability = unfavorable
then computer-expertise-adequacy = poor.

rule-7-5:
if computer-expertise-requirements = Any1 and
   computer-expertise-availability = Any2
then computer-expertise-adequacy = ok.

/*   computer expertise requirements     */

rule-8-1:
if knowledge-area-complexity = simple or
   knowledge-area-complexity = moderate and
   org-environment-complexity = favorable
then computer-expertise-requirements = favorable.

rule-8-2:
if knowledge-area-complexity = simple and
   org-environment-complexity = favorable or
   org-environment-complexity = neutral
then computer-expertise-requirements = favorable.
```

**Figure 2–17** *continued*

```
rule-8-3:
if knowledge-area-complexity = complex or
   knowledge-area-complexity = moderate and
   org-environment-complexity = unfavorable
then computer-expertise-requirements = unfavorable.

rule-8-4:
if knowledge-area-complexity = complex and
   org-environment-complexity = unfavorable or
   org-environment-complexity = neutral
then computer-expertise-requirements = unfavorable.

rule-8-5:
if knowledge-area-complexity = ANY1 and
   knowledge-area-complexity = ANY2 and
   org-environment-complexity = ANY3
then computer-expertise-requirements = neutral.

/*     computer expertise availability        */

rule-9-1:
if people = unlimited and
   equipment-facilities = limited or
   equipment-facilities = unlimited
then computer-expertise-availability = favorable.

rule-9-2:
if people = unlimited or
   people = limited and
   equipment-facilities = unlimited
then computer-expertise-availability = favorable.

rule-9-3:
if people = very-limited and
   equipment-facilities = limited or
   equipment-facilities = very-limited
then computer-expertise-availability = unfavorable.

rule-9-4:
if people = very-limited or
   people = limited and
   equipment-facilities = very-limited
then computer-expertise-availability = unfavorable.

rule-9-5:
if people = Any1 and
   equipment-facilities = Any2
then computer-expertise-availability = neutral.

question(people) =
[nl,nl,nl,nl,nl,nl,nl,nl,nl,nl,nl,nl,nl,nl,nl,nl,nl,nl,nl,nl,'
     To what degree will Computer Information System personnel,
     who are qualified to develop such a system, be made
     available to work on this project?

',nl,nl,nl,nl,nl,nl].
```

```
legalvals(people) = [unlimited, limited, very-limited].

question(equipment-facilities) =
[nl,nl,nl,nl,nl,nl,nl,nl,nl,nl,nl,nl,nl,nl,nl,nl,nl,nl,nl,nl,'
    To what degree will equipment and facilities needed to
    develop this proposed system be made available?

',nl,nl,nl,nl,nl,nl,nl].

legalvals(equipment-facilities) = [unlimited, limited,
very-limited].
```

## Some Special Consideratons When Putting the System on Computer

***Developing User-Questions.*** Developing user-effective questions can be more complex than the examples in Figure 2–4 indicate. For example, in the franchise-selection system described in Figures 2–11 to 2–14 the questions were used to guide the user to study the local market more carefully. To do this, questions are often rewritten and revised many times. For example,

> How appropriate or suitable is the market area under study for the proposed franchise?

was rewritten as follows:

> After identifying the target market for the franchise product and analyzing the demographics of the population in the area selected for the proposed store, how would you rate the appropriateness of the franchise for the market area under study?

First, the rewording avoids talking down to the user by ordering him or her to "go do something (such as analyze the market, turn on the computer, or carry out some other order)." Rather, the wording "after analyzing" carries the implication that the user is bright and competent. It seems to be more user friendly.

Second, for the purposes of the prototype system the new question wording guides the user's information search more than did the first version of the question. In later versions of the system, a series of questions was developed to guide the study of the local market in a more specific and detailed way.

As is suggested by the above discussion, the computer is often of secondary importance during the initial prototype concept-testing phases of knowledge-based system development. This is especially true in situations where an expert system shell, such as M.1 or VP-Expert, is used.

***Technical Considerations.*** Technical computer considerations are not emphasized in this chapter because it concentrates on basic KBS prototype-development processes. Technical considerations are nonetheless very important in knowledge-based system development. First, they are needed to make a system

**Figure 2–18.** Decision Situation under Study: Evaluating a KBS Development Project's Risk—Knowledge Base, VP-Expert Version (Initial Prototype, filename RISK.KBS)

```
RUNTIME;
ACTIONS
! PRINTON
DISPLAY"
                 ┌──────────────────────────────────────────────┐
                 │              WELCOME TO THE                  │
                 │         RISK EVALUATION ASSISTANT            │
                 │                                              │
                 │    Copyright (c) 1992 by R.J. Mockler        │
                 │           All rights reserved                │
                 └──────────────────────────────────────────────┘

      Press any key to continue.~"
      CLS

DISPLAY"
                 ┌──────────────────────────────────────────────┐
                 │ This system is designed to help  you  evaluate │
                 │ the risks inherent in your proposed  knowledge │
                 │ based system project. Based on your replies to │
                 │ the questions  asked  about:                   │
                 │    . the  organization environment             │
                 │    . the  knowledge  area  complexity          │
                 │    . the computer expertise adequacy           │
                 │ you will be given an estimate of the project's │
                 │ chances of success.                            │
                 └──────────────────────────────────────────────┘

          Press any key to continue~"
          CLS

FIND level_of_risk;


!    Level of Risk

Rule 1-1
if knowledge-area-complexity = simple and
   org-environment-complexity = favorable and
   computer-expertise-adequacy = ok or
   computer-expertise-adequacy = good
then level_of_risk = low
CLS
DISPLAY"
Based on the answers you have given, the project you have
proposed has a low level of risk and a high potential for
success";
```

```
Rule 1-2
if knowledge-area-complexity = simple or
   knowledge-area-complexity = moderate and
   org-environment-complexity = favorable and
   computer-expertise-adequacy = good
then level_of_risk = low
CLS
DISPLAY"
Based on the answers you have given, the project you have
proposed has a low level of risk and a high potential for
success";

Rule 1-3
if knowledge-area-complexity = simple and
   org-environment-complexity = neutral or
   org-environment-complexity = favorable and
   computer-expertise-adequacy = good
then level_of_risk = low
CLS
DISPLAY"
Based on the answers you have given, the project you have
proposed has a low level of risk and a high potential for
success";

Rule 1-4
if knowledge-area-complexity = complex and
   org-environment-complexity = unfavorable or
   computer-expertise-adequacy = poor
   then level_of_risk = high_risk
CLS
DISPLAY"
Based on the answers you have given,
the project you have proposed is a high risk project";

Rule 1-5
if org-environment-complexity = unfavorable and
   knowledge-area-complexity = complex or
   computer-expertise-adequacy = poor
   then level_of_risk = high_risk
CLS
DISPLAY"
 Based on the answers you have given,
 the project you have proposed is a high risk project";

Rule 1-6
if computer-expertise-adequacy = poor and
   knowledge-area-complexity = complex or
   org-environment-complexity = unfavorable
   then level_of_risk = high_risk
CLS
DISPLAY"
 Based on the answers you have given,
 the project you have proposed is a high risk project";
```

**Figure 2–18** *continued*

```
Rule 1-7
if level_of_risk = UNKNOWN
then level_of_risk = moderate
CLS
DISPLAY"
      Based on the answers you have given, the project you have
proposed is a moderately risky one, which must be carefully
planned. The specific areas that must be re-examined and detailed
plans for reducing the risk found in the project will be
identified in more advanced versions of this system";

!   knowledge area complexity   */

Rule 2-1
if factual-knowledge = simple and
   reasoning-heuristics = simple
then knowledge-area-complexity = simple;

Rule 2-2
if reasoning-heuristics = complex and
   factual-knowledge = moderate or
   factual-knowledge = complex
then knowledge-area-complexity = complex;

Rule 2-3
if factual-knowledge = complex and
   reasoning-heuristics = complex or
   reasoning-heuristics = moderate
then knowledge-area-complexity = complex;

Rule 2-4
if knowledge-area-complexity = UNKNOWN
then knowledge-area-complexity = moderate;

ASK reasoning-heuristics:" For the proposed knowledge based
system, would you describe the reasoning processes involved as
simple, moderately-complex or complex?";

CHOICES reasoning-heuristics: simple, moderate, complex;

ASK factual-knowledge:" For the proposed knowledge based
system, would you describe the factual knowledge covered in the
area as straight-forward and simple (for example, how an electric
motor works), moderately complex (for example, insurance claims
processing) or complex (for example, international corporate tax
planning and auditing)?";

CHOICES factual-knowledge: simple, moderate, complex;

!   organization environment complexity   */

Rule 3-1
if knowledge-area-expertise-avail = favorable and
   organization_units_involved <=5 and
   company-management-involvement = favorable or
   company-management-involvement = neutral
then org-environment-complexity = favorable;
```

```
Rule 3-2
if knowledge-area-expertise-avail = favorable or
   knowledge-area-expertise-avail = neutral and
   organization_units_involved <= 5 and
   company-management-involvement = favorable
then org-environment-complexity = favorable;

Rule 3-3
if knowledge-area-expertise-avail = neutral and
   organization_units_involved <= 5 and
   company-management-involvement = neutral
then org-environment-complexity = neutral;

Rule 3-4
if knowledge-area-expertise-avail = favorable and
   organization_units_involved <= 5 and
   company-management-involvement = unfavorable
then org-environment-complexity = neutral;

Rule 3-5
if knowledge-area-expertise-avail = unfavorable and
   organization_units_involved <=5 and
   company-management-involvement = favorable
then org-environment-complexity = neutral;

Rule 3-6
if knowledge-area-expertise-avail = favorable and
   organization_units_involved > 5 and
   company-management-involvement = favorable or
   company-management-involvement = neutral
then org-environment-complexity = neutral;

Rule 3-7
if knowledge-area-expertise-avail = favorable or
   knowledge-area-expertise-avail = neutral and
   organization_units_involved >5 and
   company-management-involvement = favorable
then org-environment-complexity = neutral;

Rule 3-8
if org-environment-complexity = UNKNOWN
then org-environment-complexity = unfavorable;

!     knowledge area expertise availability     */

Rule 4-1
if expert-developed = yes
then knowledge-area-expertise-avail = favorable;

Rule 4-2
if expert-developed = no and
   expert-availability = unlimited
then knowledge-area-expertise-avail = favorable;

Rule 4-3
if expert-developed = no and
   expert-availability = limited
then knowledge-area-expertise-avail = neutral;
```

**Figure 2–18** *continued*

```
Rule 4-4
if expert-developed = no and
   expert-availability = very-limited
then knowledge-area-expertise-avail = unfavorable;

ASK expert-developed:" Will the system be developed by the
expert whose knowledge is being replicated in the system?";

CHOICES expert-developed: yes, no;

 ASK expert-availability:" Where the system is not being
developed by the expert(s) whose knowledge is being replicated in
the system, how available will the expert(s) be who are involved
in the project?";

CHOICES expert-availability: unlimited, limited,
very-limited;

!     organizational units involved        */

Rule 5-1
if users_involved > -1 and
   experts_involved > -1
then organization_units_involved =
(users_involved+experts_involved);

ASK users_involved:" How many people are expected to use the
proposed system on a regular basis? Type in any number.";

ASK experts_involved:" How many experts will be involved in
the development of the system? Type in any number.";

!    company management involvement   */

Rule 6-1
if initiated-by = top-company-management or
   initiated-by = operating-management or
   initiated-by = user-or-expert and
   supported-by = top-company-management
then company-management-involvement = favorable;

Rule 6-2
if initiated-by = outside-company and
   management-support = no
then company-management-involvement = unfavorable;

Rule 6-3
if supported-by = top-company-management and
   initiated-by = outside-company and
   management-support = yes
then company-management-involvement = neutral;

Rule 6-4
if company-management-involvement = UNKNOWN
then company-management-involvement = neutral;
```

```
ASK initiated-by:" Who initiated the proposed project?";

CHOICES initiated-by: top-company-management,
operating-management, user-or-expert, outside-company;

ASK supported-by:" What is the highest level of management
which has expressed interest in and support for the project?";

CHOICES supported-by: top-company-management,
operating-management;

ASK management-support:" Though the system was initiated by
someone outside the company, has management expressed interest in
and support for the project?";

CHOICES management-support: yes, no;

!   computer expertise adequacy      */

Rule 7-1
if computer-expertise-requirements = favorable and
   computer-expertise-availability = favorable or
   computer-expertise-availability = neutral
then computer-expertise-adequacy = good;

Rule 7-2
if computer-expertise-requirements = favorable or
   computer-expertise-requirements = neutral and
   computer-expertise-availability = favorable
then computer-expertise-adequacy = good;

Rule 7-3
if computer-expertise-requirements = unfavorable and
   computer-expertise-availability = unfavorable or
   computer-expertise-availability = neutral
then computer-expertise-adequacy = poor;

Rule 7-4
if computer-expertise-requirements = unfavorable or
   computer-expertise-requirements = neutral and
   computer-expertise-availability = unfavorable
then computer-expertise-adequacy = poor;

Rule 7-5
if computer-expertise-adequacy = UNKNOWN
then computer-expertise-adequacy = ok;

!   computer expertise requirements      */

Rule 8-1
if knowledge-area-complexity = simple or
   knowledge-area-complexity = moderate and
   org-environment-complexity = favorable
then computer-expertise-requirements = favorable;

Rule 8-2
if knowledge-area-complexity = simple and
   org-environment-complexity = favorable or
   org-environment-complexity = neutral
then computer-expertise-requirements = favorable;
```

**Figure 2–18** *continued*

```
Rule 8-3
if knowledge-area-complexity = complex or
   knowledge-area-complexity = moderate and
   org-environment-complexity = unfavorable
then computer-expertise-requirements = unfavorable;

Rule 8-4
if knowledge-area-complexity = complex and
   org-environment-complexity = unfavorable or
   org-environment-complexity = neutral
then computer-expertise-requirements = unfavorable;

rule 8-5
if computer-expertise-requirements = UNKNOWN
then computer-expertise-requirements = neutral;


!     computer expertise availability        */

Rule 9-1
if people = unlimited and
   equipment-facilities = limited or
   equipment-facilities = unlimited
then computer-expertise-availability = favorable;

Rule 9-2
if people = unlimited or
   people = limited and
   equipment-facilities = unlimited
then computer-expertise-availibility = favorable;

Rule 9-3
if people = very-limited and
   equipment-facilities = limited or
   equipment-facilities = very-limited
then computer-expertise-availability = unfavorable;

Rule 9-4
if people = very-limited or
   people = limited and
   equipment-facilities = very-limited
then computer-expertise-availability = unfavorable;

Rule 9-5
if computer-expertise-availablity= UNKNOWN
then computer-expertise-availability = neutral;

ASK people:" To what degree will Computer Information System
personnel, who are qualified to develop such a system, be made
available to work on this project?";

CHOICES people: unlimited, limited, very-limited;

ASK equipment-facilities:" To what degree will equipment and
facilities needed to develop this proposed system be made
available?";

CHOICES equipment-facilities: unlimited, limited, very-limited;
```

run at all. Second, they determine how the system runs, which in turn has an impact on user acceptance and general usefulness of the system. Third, they affect the cost efficiency of a system.

Some familiarity with the technical computer aspects of knowledge-based development is needed to shape the initial prototype system. A great deal more is needed to develop an effective and efficient larger operating knowledge-based system.

***Balancing Technical and Nontechnical Requirements.*** Knowledge-based systems represent a balanced reconciliation of many factors:

- different ways different experts make decisions
- the theoretical "best" way to do it
- limitations of the available computer development tools
- time and money constraints
- special user characteristics and requirements

A classic conflict between the technician concerned with computer optimization and an expert concerned with the way the situation works can arise during system development. When the technician distorts the actual expert situation to accommodate technical computer limitations, the system can become what is called a **technician's toy.** In other words, it may be very useful in the lab, but of no use on the job. Constant reference to the situation scenarios and the expert are needed to keep this from happening. This can raise the cost of system development, but it is necessary to produce a good system.

In addition, as seen in the rewording earlier of the user question about appropriateness of proposed franchises for a local market, many problems can arise when trying to make a system easier for a person to use. It takes time to make a system more accessible and friendly for the user. Surveys show that it takes some 40 percent of the system development time on average to introduce user accommodating refinements. In other words, it can almost double the cost of system development. If one does not allow for the time and expense needed to make a system that accommodates the user, that is, makes it user-friendly or user-effective, then one risks having a system that it not accepted and used.

At the same time, technical considerations cannot be ignored. Computer storage costs and running time and other limitations of available software and hardware all can effect KBS development.

***Compromises Are Necessary.*** As in almost every system development project, in order to create the rules and questions in the sample KBS described in this chapter, some compromises were needed. They were needed to reconcile the way an expert thinks with the way a computer works. Developing effective compromises when building a knowledge base is very hard to learn to do, especially in management decision situations. Nontechnical managers just starting out in knowledge-based systems development are often frustrated by the fact that there is rarely "one best way" to diagram a decision. They feel that since several ways may be equally good, the selection process is arbitrary and unscientific. They want a more rigid approach to representing decisions.

This can be unproductive. In life, there is rarely one perfect way to make every management decision. Consequently, there will rarely be one perfect way to represent a decision. The goal is to develop a reasonably good way to do it that works.

The final form of a knowledge-based system will only be a reasonable replication of the way competent people would or could do a task or make a decision. In simple diagnostic situations, there may be "one best way," because that is the only way the *actual situation may work.* However, if in an actual situation, a management decision situation for example, there are several good ways to reason to a solution, then any expert knowledge-based system for that situation could have several best ways to represent the actual situation. To insist on one best way in such situations would be naive and unrealistic. Interestingly, at times the expert knowledge-based system is an improvement over the way many experts do go about solving a specific problem consistently over an extended period of time.

System engineering can seem an endless process. There always seems to be a way to make a system technically more efficient, more user-effective, and more accommodating to the nontechnician. The systems shown in this book are still being improved. The rule representations can almost always be made more condensed and more efficient. The questions can always be made more accommodating. The user interface can always be improved.

All these considerations are not as important for prototype system development, however, where the objective is to get a system up and running quickly. For this reason, technical refinements not related to the situational accuracy of the system, while recognized as important in system engineering, are beyond the scope of this chapter.

## SOME SPECIAL PROBLEMS IN KNOWLEDGE ACQUISITION

The discussion so far in this chapter has dealt largely with the complexities of the intellectual processes involved in developing knowledge-based systems. Not all knowledge-based systems are small expert-driven systems, that is, knowledge-based systems that have been developed by the experts themselves. As studies by Cullen (1988) indicate, most knowledge-based systems development situations involve the interaction of knowledge engineers and other computer-information system and technical personnel. This is in addition to interaction with the experts whose expertise is being replicated and with the users of the systems.

For example, Figure 2–19 shows one experienced knowledge engineer's outline of the knowledge-acquisition and system-refinement process in situations involving a knowledge engineer and expert. In the outline, the situation analysis phase has been broken down into four steps: expert observation, problem

**Figure 2–19.** Knowledge-Based System Development Process

| | |
|---|---|
| ■ Expert observation | Watch the expert solving real problems at work. |
| ■ Problem analysis | Explore the kinds of data, knowledge, and procedures needed to solve problems in the expert's area. |
| ■ Problem description | Have the expert describe a typical problem for each category of solution in the expert's area. |
| ■ Problem refinement | Present the expert with a series of realistic problems to solve, probing for the rationale behind the reasoning steps. |
| ■ System development and refinement | Once a description of how the expert works has been developed, have the expert give you a series of problems to solve using the rules acquired from the interviews. |
| ■ System testing | Have the expert examine and critique a prototype system's rules and control structure as well as the results of a prototype system consultation. |
| ■ System validation | Present the cases solved by both the expert and the prototype system to other outside experts. |

analysis, problem description, and problem refinement. At each of these phases, an interaction occurs between the knowledge engineer and the expert. Where the users are different from the experts, even more interaction is required. The different personalities of each participant in the project can also affect the outcome.

Since success here depends on the effectiveness of that interaction, an analysis is needed of such factors as:

- the personalities of the individuals involved
- the time available for the interaction
- the complexity of the expertise to be replicated
- the familiarity of the knowledge engineer with the expert's area
- other related factors

There is also an emotional context which must be examined. For instance, does the expert feel threatened by the system and is the knowledge engineer socially-oriented enough to overcome such emotional and psychological barriers? The solutions to these interpersonal problems and their impact on success are dictated both by the special circumstances involved in each situation and by the effectiveness of the knowledge engineer in dealing with the interpersonal problems.

Further complexities are introduced where the expert and the user are not the same individual. In these situations, the users and their task environment also have to be examined, if an effective delivery system is to be developed.

In general, it is to be expected that the complexity of the knowledge-based system development job will escalate as the size and complexity of the system, as well as the organizational environment in which it is developed and used, increases.

Before going on to a discussion of those complexities in Part Three, Chapters 3, 4, 5, and 6 give a more detailed tutorial for creating small knowledge-based systems such as those described in this chapter.

## REVIEW QUESTIONS

1. Define the knowledge engineering job.
2. Describe the steps involved in the KBS development life cycle.
3. What is involved in reformulation of decision situation diagrams?
4. What is a decision situation diagram?
5. Describe what takes place when transforming situation diagrams into system diagrams.
6. In addition to leading to the creation of a knowledge-based system, describe some of the other benefits of participating in the knowledge-based system development process.
7. What areas should be covered in a knowledge-based system development proposal?
8. Describe the major features of a knowledge-based system dependency diagram. Discuss the function of a dependency diagram in the knowledge-based system development process.
9. Discuss the ways in which typical decision situation scenarios can function to make the system a better replication of reality. In what development situations are they especially useful?
10. The objective of knowledge-based systems is often to "replicate how several pretty good experts work." Why can it be naive and unrealistic to insist on "one best way" in certain management decision situations?
11. Describe the ways in which decision situation analysis and documenting a knowledge-based system can be considered one continuous flowing process, and not two separate processes.
12. What are decision situation diagrams? Describe their role in the design of knowledge-based systems. At what point in the process are they developed?
13. Describe some of the problems that can arise when writing the plain English language version of a knowledge base. Discuss some of the ways to resolve these problems.
14. Discuss some of the dangers which can arise from over-attention to the technical aspects of system development.

15. Describe some of the inefficiencies and costs which can result from over-attention to the nontechnician viewpoint in system development.
16. Discuss some of the problems encountered when attempting to reconcile the technician's and nontechnician's viewpoints during system development.

## EXERCISES

1. The disks accompanying this book contain both a VP-Expert and M.1 version of the small risk-evaluation KBS described in this chapter. They are named RISK.KBS (VP-Expert version) and KBS-EVAL.M1 (M.1 version) in the disk files. Following the directions accompanying the disks for using M.1 and the instructions for running VP-Expert in Figure 4–2 of this book ("Procedure for Running a Consultation"), run a consultation using both systems. While doing this, refer to the knowledge bases for both systems given in Figures 2–17 and 2–18.
2. Develop a small knowledge base for a system of your own. First, write a scenario of how a typical decision is made. Second, list the major recommendations which might be made, three or four critical factors affecting the recommendation, and the major questions which need answering in order to obtain the information about the factors needed to make the recommendations. Third, use the information collected in the first and second steps to develop a block decision situation diagram that replicates or models the decision area to be converted into a KBS. Consult the M.1 KBS on the disks accompanying this book entitled SCREEN.PRE for guidance on how to do this. You may also want to review the description of that KBS, which is designed to help individuals construct their own systems, given in Chapter 15.
3. A more advanced version of the risk-evaluation system described in this chapter is also given on the disks accompanying this book. The system was built using the M.1 expert system shell and has the filename RISK.EVAL. You may also want to run this system to see how smaller systems are expanded during KBS development projects. A full description of this system is given in Mockler (1990).

## REFERENCES

Cullen, J., and A. Bryman. "The Knowledge Acquisition Bottleneck." *Expert Systems*, August 1988, pp. 216–25.

Kearney, Michele. "Making Knowledge Engineering Productive." *AI Expert*, July 1990, pp. 46–51.

McGraw, Karen, and Karan Harbison-Briggs. *Knowledge Acquisition,* Englewood Cliffs, NJ: Prentice Hall, 1989.

Mockler, Robert J. "Using Knowledge-Based Systems for Estimating Risks Inherent in a Proposed KBS Project." *Expert Systems,* February 1990, pp. 27–41.

Motta, E., T. Rajan, and M. Eisenstadt. "Knowledge Acquisition as a Process of Model Refinement." *Knowledge Acquisition,* 2, 1990, pp. 1–19.

Ruth, Stephen, and Christopher Carlson. "Shell-Based Expert Systems in Business: A Return on Investment Perspective." *Proceedings of the Ninth International Conference on Information Systems,* Minneapolis, MN: SIM, IMS, and ACM, December 1988.

# Part Two

## DEVELOPING A KBS USING VP-EXPERT

# 3

# Developing a First Knowledge-Based System

This chapter and the next three are designed to be a tutorial on developing a first knowledge-based system (KBS). The chapters walk through the entire development process, which includes using an expert system shell development tool to put the system on the computer.

This chapter provides an overview of the basic knowledge base design and development process. It covers

- The general business area selected for KBS development
- The development environment
- Steps to develop a first KBS
- Step 1—Isolate the area for KBS development
- Step 2—Target a decision to be prototyped
- Step 3—Create a dependency diagram
- Step 4—Create decision tables
- Step 5—Write IF-THEN rules
- Step 6—Construct the user interface
- Structure of a knowledge base

The general topics covered in the remaining chapters of this tutorial are

- Entering the first knowledge base into the computer
- Database, spreadsheet, and other knowledge base development techniques

- User-interface improvements to the knowledge base and summary reference guide

## THE GENERAL BUSINESS AREA SELECTED FOR KBS DEVELOPMENT

The general area selected for KBS development in this tutorial is health maintenance. The rapid escalation in health-care costs, combined with the increasing competition in the health-care industry, has generated a substantial interest in alternative methods for financing and delivering health-care services. Many forms of delivering medical services have developed to address the rising cost problem. Some are group practices that work on a prepaid, rather than a fee-for-service, basis.

One prominent variation on prepaid service is the health maintenance organization (HMO). HMOs provide medical service to members in return for a prepaid fee. In order for them to operate profitably, however, they must contain costs.

Generally, HMO organizations have been successful in providing a continuum of care based on their members' needs. These organizations have achieved lower costs through hospitalization rates that are lower than those in the fee-for-service sector. In order to contain costs further, however, HMOs must ration the availability of ambulatory service. It is this form of care that is used more frequently in prepaid plans than in fee-for-service health plans.

To achieve the goal of assuring that serious health problems obtain priority access to treatment over lower priority cases, the health-care manager, in this example, has arranged to have a KBS assist personnel who make screening decisions. In each situation, the pertinent criteria for qualification for treatment can be incorporated into the KBS. Personnel doing the screening can then quickly run through the approval-checking procedure by answering questions posed by the KBS. The system, in turn, asks follow-up questions based on the answers it receives. In a fully developed system, it would cover all the generalized standards for establishing the appropriate level of service support given the apparent seriousness of an individual's condition.

This screening problem is one which is similar to that faced by other organizations. For example, KBS have been built to successfully support decisions involving screening customer requests for bank loans as well as screening employee requests for factory-maintenance services. While all screening problems are similar in some fundamental ways, screening HMO service requests has unique requirements, since health- and even life-threatening factors may arise.

The application of KBS technology to the HMO problem provides the following potential benefits:

- The KBS provides for a consistent level of screening service to be delivered, regardless of who is on duty.

- The KBS makes possible decision making by personnel who were previously unauthorized to make decisions.
- The KBS ensures that screening decisions are always made using the same set of criteria. The possibility of inappropriate concerns (for example, a client's race, sex, political affiliation) are eliminated, and, in the event of a dispute, the criteria by which a particular decision was made can be proven.
- The KBS can be used to train screening personnel, which frees more experienced staff for other duties.
- The KBS can be replicated and used wherever members are serviced, assuring the organization of a consistent level of service.
- The KBS can easily be changed to reflect new or revised screening policies and then quickly be replicated and distributed to implement the change uniformly throughout the organization without incurring personnel retraining expenses.

These benefits are similar to those claimed by most organizations where KBS technology has been successfully applied to solve business problems.

## THE DEVELOPMENT ENVIRONMENT

For this development exercise, no previous reader background on computer system design or development is assumed.

The VP-Expert shell, or software development tool, is used in this tutorial. It is a rule-based expert system shell that runs on an IBM Personal Computer or compatible machine. A general familiarity with this IBM-PC microcomputer and its DOS operating system is assumed.

The software links with Lotus 1-2-3 spreadsheet files and dBASE III Plus database files. A working familiarity with this other software is assumed in the later sections of this tutorial. Such linkage features are commonplace on modern shell development tools. They enable users to build knowledge-based systems that add value to already developed computer-based files and systems. These enhanced systems are frequently called **integrated systems.** This tutorial will incrementally develop an "integrated" system from one that begins as a "stand-alone" system. While the shell used is VP-Expert, the design methodology can be applied to whatever shell is used.

The educational version of the VP-Expert shell is included on a disk that accompanies this book. Also included on the disk are all the knowledge base files created in this tutorial, plus other files used for exercises. Exercises are given at the end of Chapters 3, 4, 5, and 6.

Instruction for installing the VP-Expert shell software on a computer is provided in the summary reference guide of Chapter 6. Also provided there is a

**Figure 3–1**

**Steps to Develop a First KBS**

| Steps | Action |
|---|---|
| 1 | Create a block diagram of the area under study. It should indicate the sub-area selected for initial KBS prototype development. (See example in Figure 3–2) |
| 2 | Create a block diagram of the exact decision situation to be prototyped. It should indicate the critical factors necessary to make a recommendation. (See example in Figure 3–3) |
| 3 | Convert the final block diagram into a dependency diagram. It should indicate all input questions, rules, values, and recommendations made by the KBS prototype. (See example in Figure 3–4) |
| 4 | Create decision tables for all triangles on the dependency diagram. (See examples in Figures 3–5, 3–7, 3–9) |
| 5 | Convert the reduced decision table to IF-THEN rules. (See examples in Figures 3–6, 3–8, 3–10) |
| 6 | Construct the user interface segments of the KBS. These are the parts a user sees when running a consultation. It usually consists of the opening and closing messages for the consultation session, as well as the questions asked during the session. (See example in Figure 3–15) |
| 7 | Using a word processor or an expert system shell "editor," type the elements that constitute the "knowledge base" into a computer file. (See example in Figure 3–15) |
| 8 | Run a trial consultation. (See example in Figure 3–14) If errors prevent a smooth run, "debug" the errors using the editor. (See procedure in Figure 4–8) This "debugging" process often takes several iterations to rid the file of all latent "bugs." This is normal. |

summary of all the software keywords and other features discussed in this four-chapter tutorial.

The following sections describe how a concept-testing initial KBS prototype for one segment of an HMO service-screening assistant is developed.

## STEPS TO DEVELOP A FIRST KBS

The procedure to develop a first KBS is given in Figure 3–1.

The example given in Figure 3–2 is a block diagram for a hypothetical health maintenance organization (HMO). As is evident from the figure, the focus for the prototype is the HMO facility-management service function.

**Figure 3–2.** (a) Block Diagram of the Area under Study; (b) Focus of "Concept-Testing" Initial Prototype, Knowledge-Based System

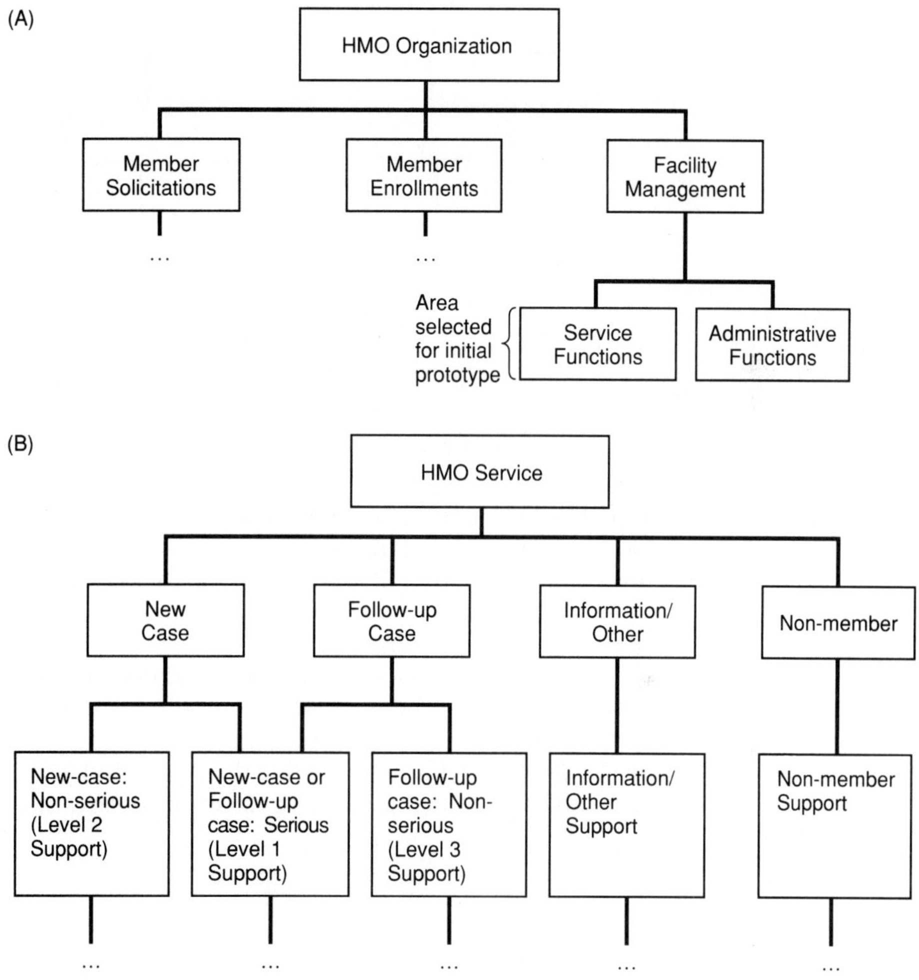


## STEP 1—ISOLATE THE AREA FOR KBS DEVELOPMENT

Although the block diagram of the area under study for this tutorial is compacted into the single Figure 3–2, many actual development cases require several layers of graphic description to move from a broad industry perspective to isolate the functional area selected for prototype development.

Many opportunities for KBS development exist in most organizations. Usually, one area will be isolated for an initial concept-testing, or prototyping,

**Figure 3–3.** Block Diagram of the Decision Situation to Be Prototyped: HMO Service Screening Assistant (Initial Prototype)

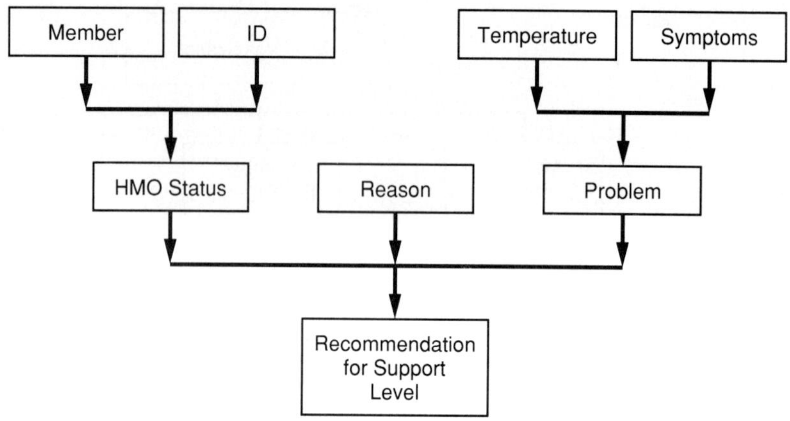


phase. In the HMO example, the member service function is selected for study because of its strategic importance to the success of the organization.

In the sample case, the KBS solution developed will be concerned more with illustrating concepts in an incremental learning process than with providing a comprehensive solution to any real problem. For this reason, selected features of the system are isolated for examination while others are intentionally ignored, although they would not be treated so in a fully developed actual case. Nonetheless, the potential of the sample KBS to evolve into a more comprehensive system that further helps to streamline the service function through a link to the member database, as well as a link to a service-control spreadsheet, will be covered.

## STEP 2—TARGET A DECISION TO BE PROTOTYPED

Once an area, such as HMO service, is isolated for study, then the precise opportunity or problem in the area is targeted for the KBS application. In the sample case, the initial intent is to build a stand-alone KBS to assist personnel who screen clients on entering the HMO facility. Clients routinely require medical support for new cases or follow-up cases. While some clients require information or other services, nonmembers are prime candidates for HMO membership solicitation.

The block diagram in Figure 3–3 is created to help define the critical factors in the target decision area to be prototyped. The three critical screening factors selected for this first-effort KBS are the following:

- *HMO status*—Is the client entitled to member service? Two items influence the answer: a client's declaration of membership followed by a verification check of the member's identification number in a control book. (Later, an automatic link to the HMO member database file will make the manual phase obsolete.)
- *Reason*—What is the reason for coming to the HMO facility? Is this a new case, a follow-up case, information-seeking, or "other" visit?
- *Problem*—How serious is the client's current condition? Two items can influence the answer. Are an abnormal temperature or other symptoms present which would require primary-care service?

Depending on the answers received, the client would be offered service as follows:

- level 1 support—for members with serious cases
- level 2 support—for members with non-serious new cases
- level 3 support—for members with non-serious follow-up cases
- information or "other" services support for members
- non-member support services

The requirements of this sample case are necessarily simplified to allow focusing on situations that help to illustrate features of the software development shell.

## STEP 3—CREATE A DEPENDENCY DIAGRAM

Step 3 in the KBS development process is the transformation of the block diagram from Step 2 into a dependency diagram, as shown in Figure 3–4. A dependency diagram indicates the relationships (dependencies) among critical factors, input questions, rules, values, and recommendations made by the KBS prototype. It is a complete graphical statement of the KBS. It serves as the paper model for how to write or code the actual knowledge base.

To begin creating the dependency diagram, it helps to turn the final Step 2 block diagram horizontally. This makes the relation between the block diagram prepared in Step 2 and the result desired in Step 3 apparent. To create the Step 3 diagram, begin by drawing boxes with triangles appended for any critical factors identified in Step 2. In the sample case, these factors are member status, reason, and problem. Because "reason" feeds directly into the final recommendation, the intermediate box can be deleted from the dependency diagram. Then on straight lines coming into the triangles, write a word or phrase that best describes the item that will influence the outcome of the critical factor. This item will be called a "variable." Under the line write all the possible values that the variable can have. Also, write names for the values that the critical factor itself can have under each box that represents a critical factor. Do the same for the recommendation box.

**Figure 3–4.** Dependency Diagram

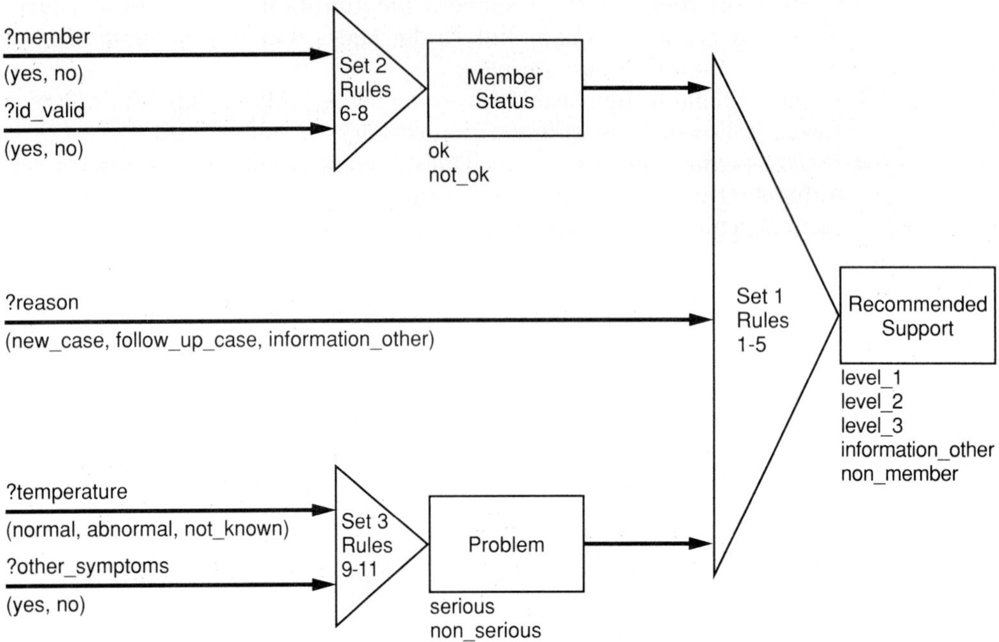


At this point, it is customary to label the triangles from right to left with numbers to identify their future status as KBS rule sets. Begin with the one final large triangle that links all the input lines at the concluding recommendation box (see Figure 3–4).

It is this seemingly mundane modelling that forces an evaluation of each piece of the KBS puzzle. The evaluation often causes the modelling process to be repeated over several iterations (with journeys back to Step 2) to model a correct solution. This is normal. The act of putting lines and words on paper and seeing the result causes the critical and creative processes to flow. Usually after several passes, a credible dependency diagram evolves.

In actual practice, there usually is a hierarchically linked set of dependency diagrams. The one shown in Figure 3–4 would merely represent the highest-level diagram.

## STEP 4—CREATE DECISION TABLES

Creating a decision table, such as the one shown in Figure 3–5, for each triangle on the dependency diagram is the final major modelling step. The decision table is necessary to show the interrelationships of values to the outcome of any intermediate phase or final recommendation of the KBS.

Preparing a decision table is a straightforward process, as is evident from comparing Figures 3–5, 3–7, and 3–9. The process begins by planning the number of rows necessary for the table. This can be determined by listing all the factors, now called *conditions*, that come into the triangle under consideration. In Figure 3–5, the decision table plan is for the final rule set which concerns three conditions, each of which can take a number of different values. Member status, the first condition, can take only two values; it is either ok or not ok. Such information comes from the dependency diagram and is easily mapped onto the decision table plan.

After all the conditions and values are listed, the number of rows for the decision table can be determined. In this case, there will be twelve rows: two possibilities for "member status," times three possibilities for "reason," times two possibilities for "problem." This calculated number represents all the possible combinations of conditions that can occur at this decision point in the KBS.

The twelve rows are arranged as shown in the completed decision table of Figure 3–5. Creating this table begins by drawing an empty table shell consisting only of row numbers, which will become rule numbers in the knowledge base, and column labels. Column labels are the condition names and a heading is added for an extra column to identify the possible outcome of each combination of values. This modelling approach allows all combinations of the values of different conditions to be evaluated.

To simplify filling the values into each cell of the table, it helps to draw horizontal dividing lines between rows. The place to draw a dividing line is determined by the number of values from the earlier planning stage. For example, the first condition, member status, has only two possible values. So the first dividing line splits the rows in half (a *2 cut*) between rows 6 and 7. Each half is now a separate whole to be taken into consideration when dividing the rows for the second condition.

The second condition, reason, has three possible values, so a *3 cut* division is appropriate. This 3 cut must now be done twice, once over the top half of rows and once again over the bottom half of rows.

The final condition, problem, requires a 2 cut and calls for treating each of six subdivisions as a whole. So the last horizontal lines split each pair of rows.

Values are next placed into this divided shell of empty cells. As evident from the member status column, the value "ok" is repeated over half the cells and "not ok" is repeated over the other half. Moving right one column, the three values for the second condition are repeated over both halves of the originally divided table. Moving right one more column, it remains to iterate the two values associated with the last condition over each pair of rows.

With all the cells filled in, it now remains to evaluate each combination of values and write the outcome value in the last column. There is no easy formula for doing this. It requires scrutinizing each row, or example case, evaluating all the values listed, and having an expert determine what would be concluded from the evidence given. An evaluation of the first four rows could be read as follows:

1. If member status is ok and reason is a new case, and the problem is serious, then the person should be assigned level 1 support (level 1 is for members with serious problems.)
2. If member status is ok and reason is a new case, and the problem is non-serious, then the person should be assigned level 2 support (level 2 is for members with new cases who do not have serious problems.)
3. If member status is ok and reason is a follow-up case, and the problem is serious, then the person should be assigned level 1 support (level 1 is for members with serious problems.)
4. If member status is ok and reason is a follow-up case, and the problem is non-serious, then the person should be assigned level 3 support (level 3 is for members with follow-up cases who do not have serious problems.)

### Reducing a Decision Table

To continue an evaluation of the next row, it quickly becomes obvious that some conditions are meaningless in certain contexts. This is cause for reducing the completed decision table.

In row A5, the case evaluated is a member who requires information or other nonmedical service. There is no reason to consider whether there is a medical problem, or its seriousness. In this case, an **indifference symbol,** the hyphen, can be used to indicate that the condition does not have any bearing on the evaluation. Its effect is to collapse rules A5 and A6 into the single rule B5.

Likewise, once it is determined that a case involves a non-member, nothing else is relevant. All non-members are assigned to a special non-member support category. The result is that rules A7 to A12 can be collapsed into the single rule B6.

The final reduced decision table appears at the bottom of Figure 3–5. Figures 3–7 and 3–9 should be examined to see how the same pattern just described is applied to different situations that map dependency diagram triangles into final reduced decision tables.

The decision table format used here is a variation of traditional decision table structure and is adapted to facilitate rule-based modelling. In a traditional decision table, rules would be defined by the columns.

## STEP 5—WRITE IF-THEN RULES

Writing rules for the knowledge base is an easy exercise at this point in the development process. Usually, every rule in the reduced decision table is converted into an IF-THEN rule, as shown in Figures 3–6, 3–8, and 3–10.

The structure and syntax of a rule is given in Figure 3–11. Basically, a rule begins with the keyword IF followed by the conditions evaluated. A series of conditions can be linked by the logical operators AND and OR. AND means that conditions on both sides of the AND must be true in order for the rule to pass or "fire." OR means that one or both conditions must be true.

The first rule in Figure 3–6 illustrates the use of both AND and OR. The use of OR allows combining rules B1 and B3, which explains why the reduced decision table calls for six rules and the conversion process yielded only five rules for the first rule set. A similar use of OR in Rule 11, shown in Figure 3–10, explains why the four-rule reduced decision table in Figure 3–9 yielded only three rules.

If all the conditions in a rule are true, the THEN clause, or conclusion, of a rule is fired. It causes the variable named on the left side of the equal sign in the THEN clause to be assigned the value of the variable on the right side of the equal sign.

For example, look at this simple rule:

```
RULE 6
     IF member = yes and
        valid_id = yes
     THEN member_status = ok;
```

This rule says, in effect, "IF, during a consultation, the value of the variable 'member' is found to be 'yes,' AND the value of the variable 'valid_id' is found to be 'yes,' THEN the variable 'member_status' should be assigned the value 'ok.'"

Rules for naming variables and values, as well as the rule name itself, are identified in Figure 3–12. Because it is not permissible to use keywords as variable or rule names, a list of keywords is given in Figure 3–13 for reference purposes.

Following the THEN conclusion, the ELSE keyword and alternate conclusions can optionally be added to a rule. When present in a rule it says, in effect, "If the premise stated in the rule is known *not* to be true, do this." For example, consider this rule:

```
RULE to_avoid
     IF member = yes and
        valid_id = yes
     THEN member_status = ok
     ELSE member_status = not_ok;
```

It can be observed that this rule suffices to express the entire reduced decision table in Figure 3–7. The rule states that IF a person is a member with a valid ID number, THEN this person's member status is good, otherwise it is not. This is a form of default reasoning provided by the ELSE clause. One reason ELSE is rarely used in this tutorial is that it makes the conditions for the alternative

**Figure 3–5.** Decision Table for Final Rule Set

**Step 1: Plan**

| | | Number of Values |
|---|---|---|
| Conditions: | Member_status (ok, not_ok) | = 2 |
| | Reason (new_case, follow_up_case, information_other) | = 3 |
| | Problem (serious, non_serious) | = 2 |

Row = 2 × 3 × 2 = 12 ←

**Step 2: Completed Decision Table**

| Rule | Member Status | Reason | Problem | Concluding Recommendation for Support Level |
|---|---|---|---|---|
| A 1 | ok | new_case | serious | level_1 |
| A 2 | ok | new_case | non_serious | level_2 |
| A 3 | ok | follow_up_case | serious | level_1 |
| A 4 | ok | follow_up_case | non_serious | level_3 |
| A 5 | ok | information_other | serious | information_other |
| A 6 | ok | information_other | non_serious | information_other |
| A 7 | not_ok | new_case | serious | non_member |
| A 8 | not_ok | new_case | non_serious | non_member |
| A 9 | not_ok | follow_up_case | serious | non_member |
| A 10 | not_ok | follow_up_case | non_serious | non_member |
| A 11 | not_ok | information_other | serious | non_member |
| A 12 | not_ok | information_other | non_serious | non_member |
| | ↑ 2 cut | ↑ 3 cut | ↑ 2 cut | |

Step 3: Reduced Decision Table

| Rule | Member Status | Reason | Problem | Concluding Recommendation for Support Level |
|---|---|---|---|---|
| B 1 | ok | new_case | serious | level_1 |
| B 2 | ok | new_case | non_serious | level_2 |
| B 3 | ok | follow_up_case | serious | level_1 |
| B 4 | ok | follow_up_case | non_serious | level_3 |
| B 5 | ok | information_other | — | information_other |
| B 6 | not_ok | — | — | non_member |

**Figure 3–6.** Convert Decision Table to Rules—Final Rule Set

```
RULE 1
     IF member_status = ok and
        reason = new_case or
        reason = follow_up_case and
        problem = serious
     THEN support = level_1;

RULE 2
     IF member_status = ok and
        reason = new_case and
        problem = non_serious
     THEN support = level_2;

RULE 3
     IF member_status = ok and
        reason = follow_up_case and
        problem = non_serious
     THEN support = level_3;

RULE 4
     IF member_status = ok and
        reason = information_other
     THEN support = information_other;

RULE 5
     IF member_status = not_ok
     THEN support = non_member;
```

**Figure 3–7.** Decision Table for Rule Set 2

**Step 1: Plan**

| | | Number of Values |
|---|---|---|
| Conditions: | Member (yes, no) | = 2 |
| | Valid_ID (yes, no) | = 2 |

Rows = 2 × 2 = 4 ←

**Step 2: Completed Decision Table**

| Rule | Member | Valid_ID | Member Status |
|---|---|---|---|
| A 1 | yes | yes | ok |
| A 2 | yes | no | not_ok |
| A 3 | no | yes | not_ok |
| A 4 | no | no | not_ok |

↑ 2 cut (Member) ↑ 2 cut (Valid_ID)

**Step 3: Reduced Decision Table**

| Rule | Member | Valid_ID | Member Status |
|---|---|---|---|
| B 1 | yes | yes | ok |
| B 2 | — | no | not_ok |
| B 3 | no | — | not_ok |

conclusion implicit rather than explicit. Another reason is that it may cause an illogical questioning sequence in a user consultation.

For example, the above rule conditions are tested in sequential order, and in this case, assume that a user is screening a person who is not an HMO member. Since the rule does not conclude after a "no" response to member, it continues to evaluate the next condition and asks if the same person has a valid

**Figure 3–8.** Convert Decision Table to Rules—Rule Set 2

```
RULE 6
     IF member = yes and
        valid_id = yes
     THEN member_status = ok;

RULE 7
     IF member = yes and
        valid_id = no
     THEN member_status = not_ok;

RULE 8
     IF member = no
     THEN member_status = not_ok;
```

ID number! The only way to avoid this illogical situation is to make the negative condition explicit with a separate rule, for example:

```
RULE 8
     IF member = no
     THEN member_status = not_ok;
```

Because this negative condition is handled in a separate rule, it requires that Rules 6 and 7 be explicit, as shown in Figure 3–8.

A good rule-of-thumb for a first KBS effort is to write one rule for every row on the reduced decision table. As experience is gained, shortcuts can be explored for increasing the efficiency of writing rules and running a knowledge base consultation.

## STEP 6—CONSTRUCT THE USER INTERFACE

Once the IF-THEN rules are written, the **user interface** elements of the knowledge base need to be constructed, as identified in Figure 3–14. In this case, the user interface refers to all the parts a user actually will see and interface with when running the KBS in a consultation session. At a minimum, this consists of the opening and closing messages and the questions posed during the consultation session.

Human factor considerations come into play as the KBS developer constructs appropriate questions for each question mark on the dependency diagram. There is a fine art to posing questions in a way that elicits the input desired. Often questions are rewritten several times until they seem right. Even after they seem right, they must be tested in live consultation sessions.

**Figure 3–9.** Decision Table for Rule Set 3

Step 1: Plan

| | | Number of Values |
|---|---|---|
| Conditions: | Temperature (normal, abnormal, not_known) | = 3 |
| | Other_symptoms (yes, no) | = 2 |

Rows = 3 × 2 = 6 ←

Step 2: Completed Decision Table

| Rule | Temperature | Other Symptoms | Problem |
|---|---|---|---|
| A 1 | normal | yes | serious |
| A 2 | normal | no | non_serious |
| A 3 | abnormal | yes | serious |
| A 4 | abnormal | no | serious |
| A 5 | not_known | yes | serious |
| A 6 | not_known | no | serious |

↑ 3 cut ↑ 2 cut

Step 3: Reduced Decision Table

| Rule | Temperature | Other Symptoms | Problem |
|---|---|---|---|
| B 1 | normal | yes | serious |
| B 2 | normal | no | non_serious |
| B 3 | abnormal | — | serious |
| B 4 | not_known | — | serious |

Writing the actual questions on paper often crystalizes one's thinking about the overall design of the KBS. It is not unusual to find some questions superfluous and others missing. This sends the developer back to earlier steps in the development process to rethink and retool the KBS design. Designing and

**Figure 3–10.** Convert Decision Table to Rules—Rule Set 3

```
RULE 9
     IF temperature = normal and
        other_symptoms = yes
     THEN problem = serious;

RULE 10
     IF temperature = normal and
        other_symptoms = no
     THEN problem = non_serious;

RULE 11
     IF temperature = abnormal or
        temperature = not_ known
     THEN problem = serious;
```

**Figure 3–11**

**Rule Structure for VP-Expert**

| | |
|---|---|
| **RULE** label | The keyword RULE followed by a label. |
| **IF** | Identifies the beginning of the RULE condition(s). |
| **THEN** | Identifies the beginning of the RULE conclusion. |
| **ELSE** | Used optionally to identify the beginning of an alternative conclusion of a RULE. |
| **BECAUSE** | Used optionally to offer an explanation of the meaning of the premise, conclusions, and alternate conclusions of the RULE. |

A RULE must end with a semicolon.
Conditions can be combined in rules using the logical operators:

| | |
|---|---|
| **AND** | Both conditions must be met for the rule to be "true" and, therefore, "pass." Up to 20 conditions using AND can be combined in one rule. |
| **OR** | One or both conditions must be true. Using OR with AND in a rule limits the number of conditions that can be combined to 10. |

developing a KBS is essentially an iterative process. The developer moves back and forth among the various steps in the development process to incrementally improve the design. The design is the creative part of the job. Converting the design to knowledge base code is mechanical.

For example, consider the question "What is the reason for coming to the HMO facility?" The developer tested the term *purpose* in place of *reason,* and tried

**Figure 3–12**

## Variable and Rule Names in VP-Expert

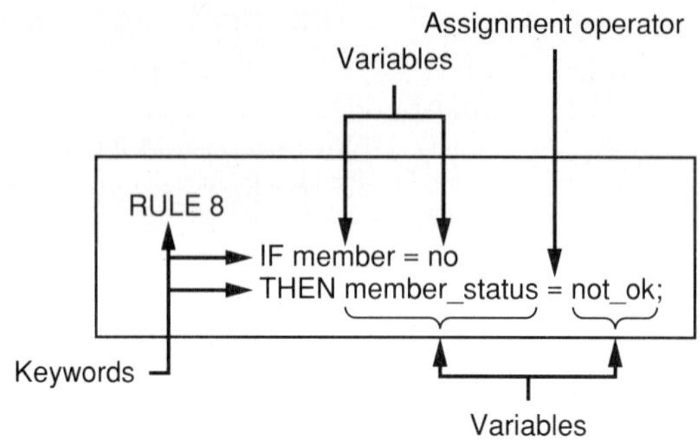


### Variable Names

- Variable names must begin with a letter.
- Each variable name must be unique.
- Variable names and values are restricted to 40 characters, which can include letters (upper or lower case), numbers, and the following special characters: _ $ ^ ¦ %
- Spaces are not allowed in variable names or values. Instead of spaces, use the underline character (for example, member_status).
- Keywords cannot be used as variable names. If they are, errors may occur when the consultation is executed. Keywords can, however, be included within variable names. For example, color cannot be used as a variable name, because COLOR is a keyword. But the_color is a perfectly legal variable name. A complete list of keywords is provided in Figure 3–13.
- Most variables can be assigned values of no more than 40 characters.

### Rule Names

- Rule names (or labels) generally follow the same naming conventions as variables (given above), except that a rule name can begin with a number.
- Each rule name must be unique.

variations such as "What is the reason the person came to the HMO facility?" Often there is no guidance for what works in a given situation except trial and error.

Coding the questions into the knowledge base requires using two new keywords:

- ASK, which is used to query the user for values to be assigned to a variable when there are no value assignments in the rules

**Figure 3–13.** Knowledge Base Keywords

*Note:* Keywords are used in the construction of a knowledge base. They include the words that begin every line (clause or statement), special words used in rule construction, and other words reserved for special use in the knowledge base.

**Keywords**

| | | | | | |
|---|---|---|---|---|---|
| @ABS | BUTTON | ENDOFF | HYPERTEXT | PLURAL | *THEN |
| @ACOS | CALL | EXECUTE | *IF | POP | TMODE |
| @ASIN | CCALL | FDISPLAY | INDEX | PRINTOFF | TRACK |
| @ATAN | CHAIN | FILL | LBUTTON | PRINTON | TRUTHTHRESH |
| @COS | *CHOICES | *FIND | LENGTH | PSET | UNKNOWN |
| @EXP | CHR | FIXED | LINETO | PUT | VGAUGE |
| @LOG | CLOSE | FOR | LOADFACTS | PWKS | WCLOSE |
| @SIN | CLROFF | FORMAT | LOCATE | RECEIVE | WFORMAT |
| @SQRT | CLRON | FORMFIELD | MENU | RECORD_NUM | WHENEVER |
| @TAN | CLS | GBCOLOR | MENU_SIZE | RECTANGLE | WHILEKNOWN |
| *ACTIONS | COLOR | GCLS | METER | REPORT | WHILETRUE |
| ACTIVE | COLUMN | GCOLOR | MOUSEOFF | RESET | WKS |
| ALL | COUNT | GDISPLAY | MOUSEON | ROW | WOPEN |
| *AND | CURR | GET | MOUSEX | *RULE | WORKON |
| APPEND | DBFORM | GETCH | MOUSEY | RUNTIME | WORKSHEET |
| *ASK | *DISPLAY | GETMOUSE | MOVETO | SAVEFACTS | |
| AUTOQUERY | EJECT | GLOCATE | MRESET | SCI | |
| BCALL | ELLIPSE | GMODE | NAMED | SHIP | |
| BECAUSE | ELSE | HGAUGE | *OR | SHOWTEXT | |
| BKCOLOR | END | HOTREGION | PDISPLAY | SORT | |

*The most critical VP-Expert keywords are discussed in this chapter.

**Figure 3–14.** Example of How a User Interfaces with a KBS During a Consultation Session

User interface elements

Opening message →

Questions with answer choices

Closing message →

```
Welcome to the HMO Service Screening Assistant
Is the person an HMO member?
 yes◄                     no

Does the person have a valid HMO 'id' number?
 yes◄                     no

What is the reason for coming to the HMO facility?
 new case◄                follow up case          information other

What is the person's temperature?
 normal◄                  abnormal                not known

Does the person claim other symptoms?
 yes◄                     no

Recommended support: level 1.

 1Help    2Go      3WhatIf  4Variable 5Rule     6Set      7Edit     8Quit
 1Help 2How? 3Why? 4Slow 5Fast 6Quit
```

**Figure 3–15.** Structure of a Knowledge Base and Printout of the Complete First Knowledge Base File

Structure of a Knowledge Base

Note: the name of this knowledge base file on the Sample Files disk is HMO.KBS or HMORUN. KBS

ACTIONS block

```
ACTIONS
     DISPLAY "Welcome to the HMO Service Screening Assistant"
     FIND support
     DISPLAY "Recommended support: {support}."
;
```

RULES block

```
RULE 1
     IF member_status = ok and
        reason = new_case or
        reason = follow_up_case and
        problem = serious
     THEN support = level_1;

RULE 2
     IF member_status = ok and
        reason = new_case and
        problem = non_serious
     THEN support = level_2;

RULE 3
     IF member_status = ok and
        reason = follow_up_case and
        problem = non_serious
     THEN support = level_3;

RULE 4
     IF member_status = ok and
        reason = information_other
     THEN support = information_other;

RULE 5
     IF member_status = not_ok
     THEN support = non_member;

RULE 6
     IF member = yes and
        valid_id = yes
     THEN member_status = ok;
```

- CHOICES, which is used in conjunction with the ASK keyword to present a number of allowable values that can be assigned to the requested variable

Examples of how the ASK and CHOICES keywords are used with questions in the knowledge base can be found in Figure 3–15. Typically the user questions

```
RULE 7
     IF member = yes and
        valid_id = no
     THEN member_status = not_ok;

RULE 8
     IF member = no
     THEN member_status = not_ok;

RULE 9
     IF temperature = normal and
        other_symptoms = yes
     THEN problem = serious;

RULE 10
     IF temperature = normal and
        other_symptoms = no
     THEN problem = non_serious;

RULE 11
     IF temperatue = abnormal or
        temperature = not_known
     THEN problem = serious;

ASK member: "Is the person an HMO member?";
CHOICES member: yes, no;

ASK valid_id: "Does the person have a valid HMO `id' number?";
CHOICES valid_id: yes, no;

ASK reason: "What is the reason for coming to the HMO facility?";
CHOICES reason: new_case, follow_up_case, information_other;

ASK temperature: "What is the person's temperature?";
CHOICES temperature: normal, abnormal, not_known;

ASK other_symptoms:  "Does the person claim other symptoms?";
CHOICES other_symptoms: yes, no;
```

QUESTIONS block

are found at the end of the knowledge base in a separate Questions Block.

The last user interface element to be considered appears in the Actions Block, which is located at the beginning of the knowledge base. For this example, it consists of a line that serves as an opening message and another line that concludes the consultation. The keyword DISPLAY causes these messages to appear on the user's screen during a consultation. The text of the concluding message includes the variable name "support" surrounded by curly brackets. The curly brackets are symbols that cause replacement of the enclosed variable name with its value whenever the accompanying text is displayed. Such a replacement is illustrated in Figure 3–14, where level 1 is the support recommended for the person screened.

Much can be done to improve this user interface. Such improvements will be the main topic of Chapter 6.

## STRUCTURE OF A KNOWLEDGE BASE

Figure 3–15 shows the overall structure of a knowledge base which consists of three basic parts:

- Actions Block
- Rules Block
- Questions Block

The keyword ACTIONS identifies the beginning of an **Actions Block.** It sets the agenda for a consultation. In this case, it DISPLAYS the opening message, then sets out to FIND a value for the goal variable in this consultation, and concludes by reporting to the user what it finds in a concluding message. This set of only three procedural instructions drives the entire consultation. It says, in effect, "First do this, then do this, then do this," and so on sequentially through each line in the Actions Block.

An Actions Block typically contains at least one FIND keyword. It is the critical keyword in this KBS because it causes control to be transferred to the rules block during the consultation. The expertise contained in the Rules and Questions Block of the knowledge base then is used to solve the problem of the consultation. In this case, it is to find an appropriate level of support to recommend for the person being screened.

Once a value is known for the variable "support," control is returned to the Actions Block. When the final instruction in the Actions Block has been executed to completion, the consultation is finished.

## REVIEW QUESTIONS

1. What are the eight major steps in developing a KBS?
2. What occurs during Steps 1 and 2?
3. How does one progress from Step 2 to Step 3?
4. What is the reason for creating dependency diagrams?
5. Why are decision tables created?

6. What occurs during the preparation phase of Step 4, creating decision tables?
7. How is the decision table actually laid out?
8. How is the decision table actually filled in?
9. Why is it that frequently there are fewer IF-THEN rules than combinations of outcomes in the decision table?
10. What are the major considerations in completing Step 6, constructing the user interface?
11. Describe the structure of a knowledge base.

## EXERCISES

1. This exercise concerns the mechanics of running a consultation. Run a consultation with the knowledge base HMORUN.KBS from the Sample Files disk.
   a. Use the "Procedure for Running a Consultation," given in Figure 4–2, to run the consultation.
   b. Use Figure 3–14 as a guide for response entries, which should be as follows:

| *Response* | *Keys to Press to Indicate Response* |
|---|---|
| yes | (Enter, End) |
| yes | (Enter, End) |
| new case | (Enter, End) |
| normal | (Enter, End) |
| yes | (Enter, End) |

   c. Run another consultation and enter different responses.
   d. Compare and record the results observed from the two consultations.
2. This exercise continues to explore the mechanics of running a KBS. Run a consultation with the knowledge base TAXGUIDE.KBS from the Sample Files disk.
   a. Use the "Procedure for Running a Consultation," given in Figure 4–2, to run the consultation.
   b. Run another consultation entering different responses.
   c. Compare and record the results observed from the two consultations.
3. This exercise looks at an "industrial strength" KBS. Run a consultation with the knowledge base DEPENDEN.KBS from the Sample Files disk.
   a. Because this knowledge base exceeds the limits of the educational version of VP-Expert, it is stored in a special file DEPENDEN.KMP. It has a special .KMP (versus a .KBS) filename extension. To run this knowledge base,

start at the DOS prompt. For example, if your Sample Files disk is in the A drive, type

```
A>VPXRUN DEPENDEN
```

Notice that the filename extension is *not* entered.

**b.** Run another consultation entering different responses.

**c.** Compare and record the results observed from the two consultations.

**d.** Examine this knowledge base by getting a printout from the normal .KBS file (DEPENDEN.KBS which is also on the Sample Files disk). Follow the instructions for "Printing the Sample Files," found in the summary reference guide in Chapter 6.

**4.** For this exercise concerning the mechanics of diagramming, assume that four (instead of three) critical factors determine the recommendation made in the HMO Service-Screening Assistant KBS.

**a.** Redraw Figure 3–3 and position a blank box to indicate the influence of a fourth critical factor on the recommendation made.

**b.** Assume that two items influence the outcome of the fourth critical factor. Refine the above block diagram to illustrate this hierarchical linkage.

**c.** Redraw the dependency diagram in Figure 3–4 to position the addition of the fourth critical factor.

**d.** Revise Step 1 in Figure 3–5, "Decision Table for Final Rule Set," to show the influence of a fourth critical factor with two values.

**e.** Revise Step 2 in Figure 3–5, the "Completed Decision Table," to show the influence of a fourth critical factor with two values. Label the actual data elements Value 1 and Value 2 for the fourth critical factor in your decision table. Leave the recommendation area blank.

**5.** This exercise concerns the mechanics of creating a decision table. Prepare a decision table for one rule set of a knowledge base that determines pricing from two conditions:

- Quantity ordered is greater than the discount quantity (yes, no)
- Customer is a wholesaler (yes, no)

A discount is given only to wholesalers who order in quantities greater than the discount quantity. Use Figure 3–5 as a guide for doing the three steps of this exercise to plan, complete, and reduce the decision table.

**6.** This exercise concerns the conversion of a decision table into rules. Convert the reduced decision table from Exercise 5 into rules. Use Figures 3–11 and 3–12 for guidance concerning rule structure and naming conventions.

**7.** This exercise explores the construction of the user-interface questions. Write the questions and answer choices that would be appropriate for the scenario given in Exercise 5.

**8.** Build a knowledge-based system of your own design that progressively develops through Steps 1–6 described in Figure 3–1. Expect to throw out and redo the work from one or more steps. This is normal, because development involves an iterative process of backing up one or more steps, improving your design, and then moving ahead again.

# 4

# Entering the First Knowledge Base into the Computer

This chapter discusses the concluding steps and related background material in the basic knowledge base design and development process that began in Chapter 3.

After all elements of the knowledge base are defined, the knowledge base must be entered, or typed, into the computer and saved as a knowledge base file on a disk. This working disk file is then available for use as often as desired for consultation sessions.

The chapter covers these areas:

- Step 7—Enter the knowledge base into the computer
- Step 8—Run a trial consultation
- How the inference engine works
- An example of backward chaining
- Using the Editor
- The basics of debugging
- The developer's toolkit—more on debugging
- The user's options—more on running a consultation

## STEP 7—ENTER THE KNOWLEDGE BASE INTO THE COMPUTER

To type the knowledge base into the computer, a developer can use a favorite word processor. Alternatively, a developer can type the knowledge base into the

**Figure 4–1.** Expert System Shell Components

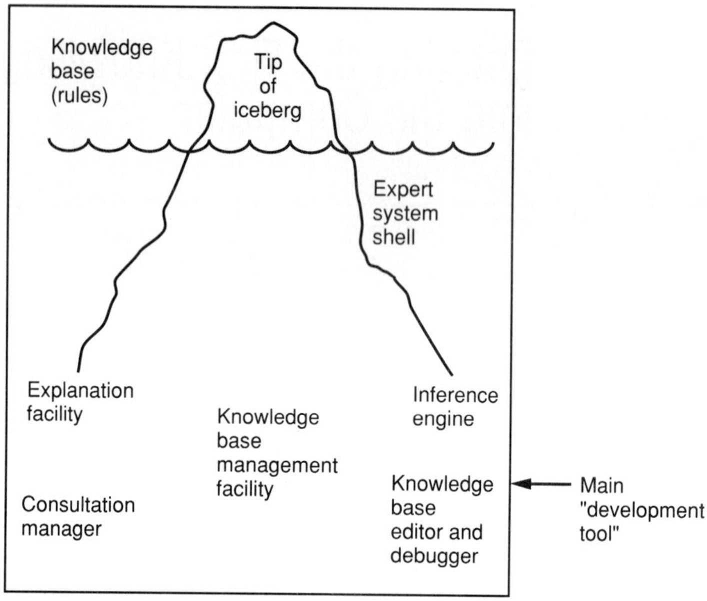


**Source:** Adapted from Bruce G. Buchanan. From a presentation made at the First Artificial Intelligence Satellite Symposium, sponsored by Texas Instruments, Nov. 23, 1985.

computer using the word processor built into the expert system shell software. The built-in word processor is called an *Editor* or *Editor and Debugger.*

Figure 4–1 identifies the Editor as one of several components in the expert system shell software. Usually it is the main component used to develop a new KBS.

The procedure for entering the knowledge base into the computer is:

1. Type the knowledge base into a computer file using the Editor.
2. Run a trial consultation. It is normal to expect errors or "bugs" because of typing mistakes or logic errors.
3. Return to the Editor to correct the errors. This process is called *debugging* the file or system.
4. Run another trial consultation.
5. Repeat Steps 3 and 4 until a clean consultation run is achieved.

Learning to use the Editor of any shell, like learning to use a new word processor, is a tedious, time-consuming task. But it usually is necessary in order to facilitate the debugging process. A brief tutorial for using the VP-Expert Editor is presented later in this chapter.

## STEP 8—RUN A TRIAL CONSULTATION

Running a trial consultation, such as the example given in Figure 3–14, is a normal part of the KBS development process. It is often repeated many times in order to completely debug a new knowledge base.

New KBS developers find that understanding knowledge-based systems is aided by running consultations with preexisting KBS. Since the KBS shown in Figure 3–15 is available on the samples disk that accompanies this book, the reader may want to explore how a consultation works first-hand. The procedure for doing this is available in Figure 4–2.

(It is highly recommended that a duplicate working copy be made of all original disks supplied with this book. The originals should be stored safely and the working copies used for all exercise purposes. This way, if an exercise disk or file is somehow destroyed, the original is always available to begin again.)

New developers also benefit from an understanding of how the inference engine works during a consultation. The inference engine is the shell component that directs the path or search strategy through the Rules Block of the knowledge base. It is quite different from the sequential process explored earlier for the Actions Block.

## HOW THE INFERENCE ENGINE WORKS

The process the inference engine in VP-Expert uses to manipulate the rules during a consultation session is called *backward chaining*. (For a fuller discussion of backward chaining, see Chapters 2 and 8.) The concept is diagrammed in Figure 4–3, using an abbreviated version of the HMO sample system.

It starts by knowing the goal variable for which the consultation session must determine a value. The first rule found with the goal in its conclusion causes the conditions of that rule to become sub-goals. All the sub-goals must be determined or known for the THEN part of the rule to fire the goal variable and pass control back to the Actions Block. If at any point a sub-goal cannot be satisfied with another sub-goal in another rule, the inference engine looks for an ASK statement in the Questions Block to obtain the value from the user. If this alternative does not work, the search fails and the consultation aborts.

Backward chaining is characteristic of many rule-based systems as well as artificial intelligence techniques in general. In particular, the rules in the rule base are not processed in a purely sequential order, but rather are selected based on their relevance to the unique problem at hand.

## AN EXAMPLE OF BACKWARD CHAINING

Tracing each step the inference engine takes to satisfy a goal helps to understand how backward chaining works. It also helps show why questions are displayed in a given sequence during a consultation session.

**Figure 4–2**

**Procedure for Running a Consultation**

The following instructions are written to guide a user who is sitting at a microcomputer, to run the HMO Service Screening Assistant sample system. (Computer set-up requirements are available in Chapter 6, "Summary Reference Guide".)

1. Load the expert shell program from the C:>, A:> or other system prompt by typing VPX and pressing the Enter key.

   An opening copyright screen appears with the following Main Menu at the bottom of the screen.

Main Menu (first line)

Lightbar over the "Consult" menu option

```
1Help  2Induce  3Edit  4Consult  5Tree  6FileName  7Path  8Quit
1Help  2Go  3WhatIf  4Variable  5Rule  7Set  8Edit  9Quit
```

Submenu for the item highlighted on the first line ("Consult" in this example)

2. Use the right arrow key to move the lightbar to Path and press Enter. A message appears on the screen asking "What is the pathname?" If your Samples Disk (or other working disk) is in drive A, type A: or if it is in drive B, type B:. Press Enter. (Note: This step is normally done only once at the start of a session.)

3. Use the right arrow key to move the lightbar to FileName and press Enter. A message appears on the screen asking "What is the name of the knowledge base you want to use?" A list of existing knowledge base files is presented. To choose from this list, move the lightbar to a desired filename (using the arrow keys) and press Enter. To run the first sample system, select the HMORUN.KBS filename. The Main Menu reappears. (Note: This step has to be done only once if repeated consultations are desired using the same knowledge base file.)

This section will walk through the step-by-step process the inference engine uses to satisfy the goal variable in Figure 4–3.

The inference engine begins by knowing that the goal variable to be satisfied is "support." It then searches for the first rule showing "support" in its THEN conclusion. In the example, it is Rule 1. The value of the variable is "level_1," but it is not yet known. For it to be known, all the IF conditions of Rule 1 also have to be known.

The inference engine backs up to examine all the IF conditions in Rule 1. When it goes to the first IF condition, it finds the variable "member_status" is unknown. So it establishes "member_status" as a sub-goal.

Note: There are four ways to make a menu selection:

- Use the right and left arrow keys to move the lightbar to a desired choice, then press Enter.
- Press the number associated with a desired choice
- Press the first letter of a desired choice.
- Press the function key corresponding to the menu number (for example, for menu choice 1, press F1).

4. Press Enter to select Consult from the Main Menu. The message "Loading File..." appears on a blank screen. If you are running the consultation shown in Figure 3-14, the message "a:/hmorun.kbs loaded" appears at the upper left corner of the consultation screen, and the following Consult Menu appears at the bottom of the screen:

Consult Menu

```
1Help  2Go     3WhatIf  4Variable   5Rule  6Set  7Edit  8Quit
1Help  2How?  3Why?  4Slow   5Fast  6Quit
```

Using one of the menu selection methods described in the accompanying box, choose Go the begin the consultation. (Because the lightbar is already on Go, simply press Enter.)

For the example case, the top of the consultation window should look like Figure 3-14. The lightbar rests over the first answer to the first question.

5. Pressing Enter chooses the highlighted option and automatically places a triangle next to the chosen item. The arrow keys are used to move the lightbar among answer choices. Pressing the End key on the numeric keypad signals the end of an answer.

   Note: To cancel a selection before pressing End, presss the Del key while the lightbar is over the item you wish to "unchoose."

   Use this procedure to answer each question. After the last question, the consultation ends with a recommendation.

6. Select Quit to return to the Main Menu, or Go to run another consultation.

Then the inference engine looks for the first available rule that has the sub-goal "member_status" in its THEN conclusion. In this example, it finds "member_status" in the conclusion to Rule 2. Again, the value of the sub-goal "member_status" is not yet known.

The inference engine must now try to solve or test all the open IF conditions in Rule 2 in order to fire the rule. To do this, it backs up to examine the first IF condition, "member." Once again, it finds "member" has never been tested. It is an unknown variable which must be set up as a new sub-goal and be resolved before resuming. In this case, although the inference engine first looks for a rule with "member" in its THEN conclusion, it finds none in the example

**Figure 4–3.** A Backward Chaining Example

This is the "goal" variable (it starts the problem-solving process called "backward chaining")

```
ACTIONS
  DISPLAY "Welcome to the HMO Client Screening Assistant"
  FIND support
  DISPLAY "Recommended support: {support}."
;

RULE 1
  IF member_status = ok and
    reason = new_case
  THEN support = level_1;

RULE 2
  IF member = yes and
    valid_id = yes
  THEN member_status = ok;

ASK member:  "Is the person an HMO member?";
CHOICES member: yes, no;

ASK valid_id: "Does the person have a valid HMO `id' number";
CHOICES valid_id: yes, no;

ASK reason:  "What is the reason for coming to the HMO facility?";
CHOICES reason: new_case, follow_up_case, information_other;
```

(A) (B) (C) (D)

system. At this point its problem-solving strategy is to see if this variable can be found through direct user input. In other words, it looks for an ASK statement, which it finds. So the solution to the IF condition is simply to ask the user consulting the expert system for a direct keyboarded response to a prepared question attached to the variable "member." Once the user inputs a response, "member" becomes the first known sub-goal.

In this example, the inference engine continues to pursue the task of resolving the most recent sub-goal, which is "member_status," by examining the next IF condition in Rule 2. "Valid_id" is not found in the THEN conclusion of any rule. The strategy is, as before, to locate an ASK statement and seek direct user input. Once a user response is obtained to "valid_id," all IF conditions are known and Rule 2 can fire. The inference engine assigns the value "ok" to "member_status" only if the user answers "yes" to both Rule 2 IF conditions. A more complete example would have other rules to handle "no" responses (see Rules 7 and 8 in Figure 3–15).

With the sub-goal "member_status" solved, the inference engine chains back to resolve the second IF condition in Rule 1. The sub-goal "reason" is established and no rule is found that has "reason" in its THEN clause. So the inference engine checks and finds an ASK statement.

Once the user inputs a response, "support" becomes known because all IF conditions in Rule 1 are tested. It then is appropriate to fire the THEN conclusion to Rule 1. The inference engine assigns the value "level_1" to the primary goal variable "support" only if "reason" is "new_case" and "member_status" is "ok."

With a value found for the goal variable, the inference engine returns control to the Actions Block, which continues sequentially through its instructions. In the example, the next instruction generates a screen display of a concluding message, which terminates the user session.

## USING THE EDITOR

Using the Editor built into an expert system shell is like using a crude word processor. It has fewer features than a good word processor and can seem awkward at times. Nonetheless, it is important to learn how to use it, especially for debugging purposes.

There is an alternative, but it requires an undesirable tradeoff. It is possible to link VP-Expert to a favorite word processor for entering and debugging a knowledge base. The tradeoff is that if a bug is detected during a trial consultation, no error message is provided about where the error occurred. This rates as a debugging nightmare.

On the other hand, when using the built-in Editor, bugs are identified and located during a consultation. Simply pressing the Enter key switches from the Consult to the Edit mode with the cursor placed in the approximate vicinity of the error that needs fixing. This feature alone seems justification enough to learn how to use the built-in Editor.

A good way to learn the built-in Editor is to enter a first knowledge base that is bug-free and known to run or execute correctly, such as the sample in Figure 3–15. A step-by-step procedure for getting into the Editor to enter the sample, or any other knowledge base, is given in Figure 4–4.

Initially the Editor's screen is blank, but after some typing it should resemble the one shown in Figure 4–5. Typing the knowledge base is very much like typing with a word processor. The basic editing keys, identified in Figure 4–6, are the same.

The knowledge base can be typed in all lowercase letters, including keywords, to simplify typing. It may be desirable to type the knowledge base in all lowercase letters, since it is often much easier to read than all uppercase letters. The reason the figures in this text have keywords in uppercase letters is for emphasis and to support learning. Only DISPLAY text requires careful

**Figure 4–4**

Procedure for Entering (or Editing) a Knowledge Base

The following instructions are written to guide a user, who is sitting at a microcomputer, to enter the HMO Service Screening Assistant sample system. (System set-up requirements are available in Chapter 6, "Summary Reference Guide".)

1. Load the program from the C:>, A:> or other system prompt by typing VPX and pressing the Enter key. An opening copyright screen appears with the following Main Menu at the bottom of the screen.

Main Menu (first line)　Lightbar over the "Consult" menu option

```
1Help 2Induce 3Edit 4Consult  5Tree  6FileName 7Path 8Quit
1Help 2Go 3WhatIf 4Variable 5Rule 7Set 8Edit 9Quit
```

Submenu for the item highlighted on the first line ("Consult" in this example)

2. Use the right arrow key to move the lightbar to Path and press Enter. A message appears on the screen asking "What is the new pathname?" If your Samples disk (or other working disk) is in drive A, type A: or if it is in drive B, type B:. Press Enter. (Note: This step is normally done only once at the start of a session.)

3. Use the right arrow key to move the lightbar to Edit and press Enter. A message appears on the screen . "Choose a file:" with the cursor positioned after the colon. Type a new filename of your choice, such as XHMO, and press Enter. Alternately, use the arrow key to move the lightbar over any existing filename that appears on the screen and press Enter to select it.

4. This opens the Editor, which has a blank screen and a distinctive bottom panel that looks similar to the one in Figure 4-5. The blank screen has the new filename in the upper right corner. A .kbs extension has automatically been added to the filemname. If an existing file is selected, it will appear on the screen and look similar to Figure 4-5.

attention to mixed upper- and lowercase. DISPLAY text normally is designed to resemble normal text.

The upper right corner of the screen identifies the filename, and the bottom of the screen presents a menu of options. The menu options change when the Alt, Ctrl, or Shift keys are pressed. Some of the more useful key combinations, as well as other editing keys, are listed in Figure 4–7.

5. Type the knowledge base into the computer. As it is typed, it appears on the screen (see Figure 4-5), just as it would if using a word processor. All the basic editing keys on the computer keyboard (see Figure 4-6) work exactly as they do with a word processor. Other useful editing keys (seeFigure 4-7), have to be mastered as needed.

   Note:
   The knowledge base can be typed in all upper, lower, or mixed-case characters. A left-pointing triangle, called a hard carriage return symbol, automatically appears at the end of each line and the beginning of blank lines.

6. After completely typing the knowledge base, check it for errors. Then save it by pressing the Alt key and the F6 function key together. At the prompt, "Save as XHMO.KBS (Y or N)?," type Y.

7. When returned to the Main Menu, choose Consult to run a trial consultation. On the top of the three-window consultation screen, similar to the one in Figure 4-9, the message "Loading File..." and "file Loaded" appear. At the bottom of the screen, the lightbar is over Go. Press Enter to select Go.

8. If no errors are present in the knowledge base, it is possible to run a consultation following the "Procedure for Running a Consultation" given in Figure 4-2. If errors are detected, the knowledge base must be "debugged." To debug a knowledge base, follow the "Procedure for Debugging a Knowledge Base" given in figure 4-8. (Note: During a consultation, compound variables such as "level_1" or "follow_up_case" apperar on the screen without the underscore connectives. The underscore connectives always appear during editing sessions.)

After the knowledge base is completely typed, it should be checked visually for errors. Some common errors to look for are

- missing semicolons
- misspelled keywords
- illegal characters in rule labels, variable names, or values
- keywords mistakenly used as variable names

**Figure 4–5.** Using the Editor

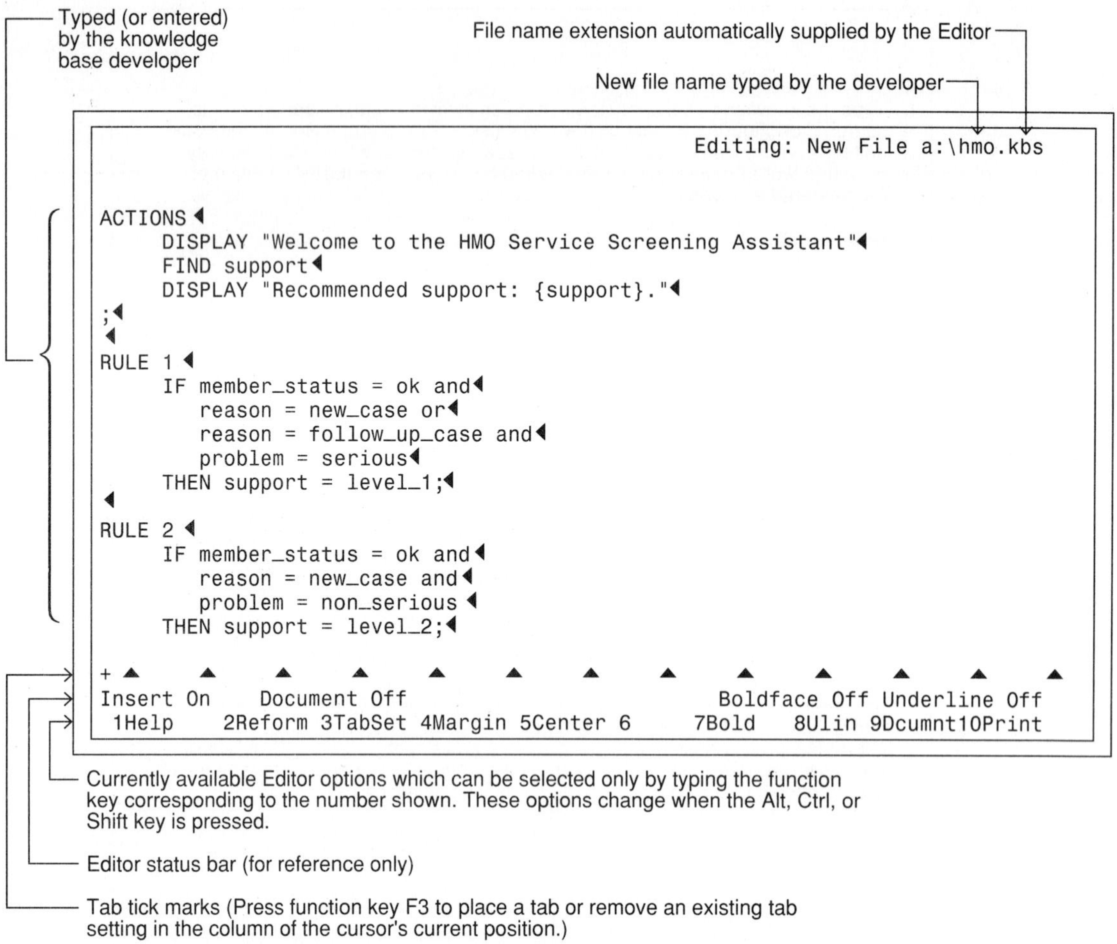


If there appears to be no errors, the knowledge base is ready to be saved according to the instructions found in the procedure for entering (or editing) a knowledge base in Figure 4–4. After the file is saved, the Editor returns control to the Main Menu.

The normal procedure at this point is to see if the file works. This requires running a trial consultation. Generally the file does not work during the first trial consultation due to commonly overlooked errors.

## THE BASICS OF DEBUGGING

Cleaning up the errors at this point is commonly called "debugging" the file. A procedure for debugging a knowledge base file is given in Figure 4–8.

**Figure 4–6**

**Main Editing Keys**

The following keys work just as they would in most word processors.

| Key | Action |
|---|---|
| ←(Backspace) | Deletes character left of cursor |
| Del | Deletes character at cursor |
| ↵ (Enter) | At the end of a line, or any entry, creates a hard carriage return. |
| Esc | Cancels incomplete operations |
| Ins | Toggles insert mode on and off (for character inserts at the cursor). Inserted text pushes existing text to the right. |
| ↑ ↓<br>←<br>→ | Arrow keys move the cursor around the screen in the direction of the arrow. |
| PgDn | Moves cursor to next screen |
| PgUp | Moves cursor to previous screen |
| PrtSc | Prints the contents of the screen when pressed with the Shift key |
| Tab | Moves cursor forward one tab stop |

When the knowledge base hasn't been edited correctly, the developer is confronted with error messages that appear on the screen. They either pinpoint the problem, such as "Missing;" or generalize the problem, such as "Syntax error." The message also includes "Error in line (number)," even though the knowledge base has no line numbers! In most cases, this is not a problem, because by pressing any key, the developer is returned to the Editor with the cursor placed on, or near, the line with the problem.

Frequently, the real cause of an error is one or more lines above the line the cursor rests on when the Editor returns from an error message. The shell program only makes assumptions about which line contains the error. For example, if the semicolon is missing from the end of the Actions Block, the program may assume that the Actions Block continues past where it should end. It may not recognize the mistake until it finds the first keyword RULE in the Rules Block.

If the knowledge base is edited correctly, a consultation screen will appear much like the one in Figure 3–14 or 4–9. During development, the consultation screen is usually a three-window screen as shown in Figure 4–9. The screen consists of a reduced consultation window, as compared to the full user-version

**Figure 4–7**

## Other Important Editing Keys

| Action Desired | Key(s) to use |
|---|---|
| Help | F1 |
| Tab set | F3 |
| Insert a line | Ctrl—Enter |
| Delete entire line | Ctrl—Y |
| Cursor moves—special: | |
| Move cursor to the beginning of the line | Home |
| Move cursor to the end of the line | End |
| Move cursor to the top of the file | Ctrl—PgUp |
| Move cursor to the bottom of the file | Ctrl—PgDn |
| Move cursor left one word | Ctrl—← |
| Move cursor right one word | Ctrl—→ |
| Block text | |
| Start block | Ctrl—F3 |
| End block | Ctrl—F4 |
| Copy block | Ctrl—F7 |
| Delete block | Ctrl—F8 |
| Cancel block (Use this after Copy block) | Ctrl—F5 |
| Move block | Ctrl—F6 |
| Recall block | Ctrl—F10 |
| Files | |
| Save file and leave Editor* The previously saved version automatically becomes a backup file (with a filename extension .BAK). | Alt—F6 |
| Update file without leaving Editor | Alt—F5 |
| Insert existing file, which can be another .KBS or .TXT or other type of file, at the location of the cursor | Alt—F4 |
| Abandon file without saving or changing | Alt—F8 |
| Print file Pressing F10 calls the Print Menu screen. Press the END key to print the file with the current setting, or change settings and then press END. | F10 |

*Note: If you save an edited file under a *new* name, always include the drive and path prefix. This avoids saving files on the hard drive that are intended for the floppy disk drive. Also, to make a backup file the first time requires going into DOS to do a, for example, "COPY a: filename b:filename." This establishes the filename on the backup disk. Future saves to the backup disk then can be made using Alt—F6.

**Figure 4–8**

## Procedure for Debugging a Knowledge Base

1. Run a trial consultation by selecting Consult from the Main Menu and Go from the Consult Menu. Alternatively, follow the appropriate steps in "Procedure for Running a Consultation" given in Figure 4–2. This causes the file to be loaded and checked for errors.
2. If there are any mistakes, a message appears that might look something like this:

   Missing ';'
   (Press any key to go on)
   Error in line 20

   This particular message would indicate that line 20 of the knowledge base is missing a semicolon. If such a message appears, press any key to automatically return to the knowledge base in the Editor. The cursor will be placed on (or near) the offending line (which has no line reference number!). If there appears to be no problem with the line the cursor is on, look at the "Quick Checklist" below to see if that helps.

   Note: VP-Expert only makes assumptions about which line contains an error. For example, if a semicolon is omitted at the end of a rule, it may assume that the rule continues past where it should end and not recognize the mistake until it finds a semicolon several lines later. If an error is reported in a line that looks all right, check previous lines for errors. Frequently, the real cause of an error is one or more lines above the line identified with the error message.
3. If the knowledge base is edited correctly, the consultation begins immediately.

### Quick Checklist

- Do the Actions Block, each rule, and each statement in the Questions Block end with a semicolon? Are there any additional semicolons out of place? The only place—besides the end of a rule, statement, or Actions Block—that a semicolon can be used is inside the double quotes that surround display text (for example, the text in an ASK statement, DISPLAY clause, etc.)
- Are all keywords spelled correctly (see Figure 3–13)?
- Are there any illegal characters (see Figure 3–12) in rule labels, variable names, or values?
- Are any keywords (see Figure 3–13) mistakenly used as variable names?

of the consultation screen shown in Figure 3–14, and the "Rules" and "Facts" windows.

For the developer, the Rules window is a viewport into the inference engine's search strategy. It is a live scrolling record of how the inference engine performs its search strategy and what the inference engine is currently doing. Its

**Figure 4–9.** Consultation Screen for Developers

```
 yes◀                     no

What is the reason for coming to the HMO facility?
 new_case ◀               follow_up_case             information_other

What is the person's temperature?
 normal◀                  abnormal                   not_known

Does the person claim other symptoms?
[yes]                      no

----------- [ RULES ] ------------    ----------- [ FACTS ] -----------
Testing 9                             member = yes CNF 100
RULE 9 IF                             valid_id = yes CNF 100
temperature = normal and              member_status = ok CNF 100
other_symptoms = yes                  reason = new_case CNF 100
THEN                                  temperature = normal CNF 100 <-
problem = serious CNF 100
Finding temperature
Finding other_symptoms <-

↑↓→←Enter to select   END to complete   /Q to Quit   ? for Unkown
```

Viewport into the inference engine's most recently established (known) fact

Viewport into the inference engine's current task

path of reasoning is made transparent for the developer to observe while a consultation is actually in progress.

The Facts window is a viewport into the system's **working memory** (sometimes called the cache). It identifies the values, both intermediate and final, derived during the course of the consultation. They are expressed in equations like "member = yes CNF 100." A confidence factor of 100 (CNF 100) is given to indicate the degree of certainty, or "confidence," that a particular conclusion is valid. More will be said about confidence factors in Chapters 5 and 8.

Placing the RUNTIME keyword in a KBS eliminates the two bottom windows. This is usually done before a KBS is delivered to a user.

## THE DEVELOPER'S TOOLKIT—MORE ON DEBUGGING

Expert system shells generally make a variety of tools available to assist in developing and debugging a knowledge base. Most of those discussed here are available as options selected from various menus. Figure 4–10 illustrates the

**Figure 4–10.** VP-Expert Menu Tree

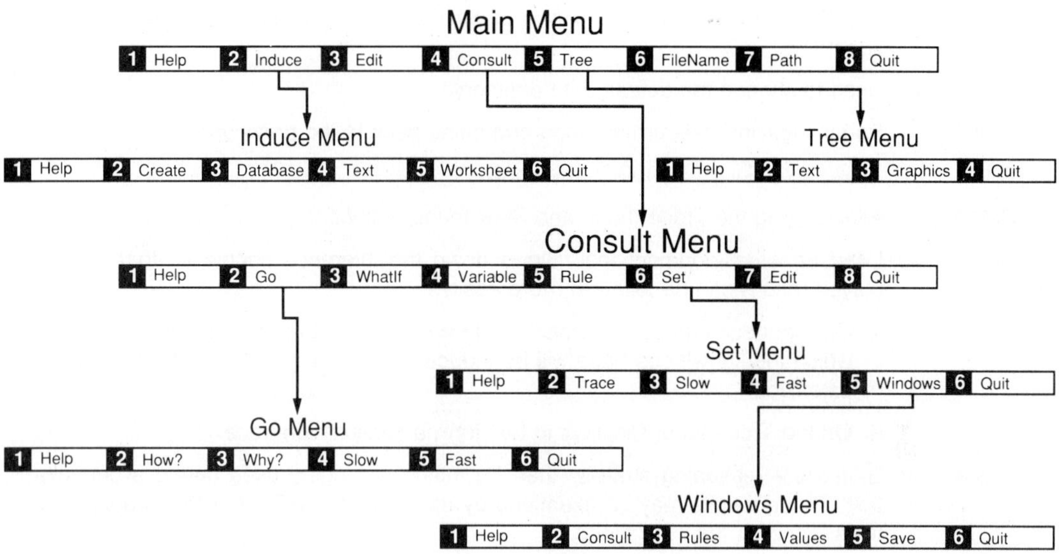


**Selecting Menu Options**

Menu options can be selected in any one of the following ways:

Type the first letter of the option.

Type the number of the menu option selected or, alternatively, the identically numbered Function Key.

Use the arrow keys to move the lightbar to a menu option and press Enter.

**Menu Options Reference**

| | |
|---|---|
| Consult | Permits getting into the Consult submenu in order to begin a consultation. |
| Create | Brings up the Editor in order to create or edit an induction table. The extension .TBL is assumed. |
| Edit | Brings up the Editor. |
| Fast | Undoes the Slow option. |
| Filename | Loads a knowledge base for consultation or editing. |
| Go | Begins a consultation. |
| Graphics | Displays a consultation Trace in tree form. |
| Help | Allows getting information on menu options. |
| How? | Used during a consultation to find how a variable value was assigned. |

**Figure 4–10** *continued*

| | |
|---|---|
| Induce | Creates a knowledge base from a table of examples, a database file, or a worksheet file. |
| Path | Used to change the default data directory. |
| Quit | Permits leaving the current menu and going back to the previous menu. |
| Rule | Allows examining any rule in the knowledge base. |
| Set | Allows using the Trace, Fast, and Slow menu options. |
| Slow | Used as a development tool. Slows down the inference engine so that the displayed results can be followed more easily. |
| Text | 1. On the Induce menu: Informs the inference engine that the induction table from which the knowledge base will be induced is contained in a text file with a TBL extension. |
| | 2. On the Tree menu: Displays in text form a consultation trace. |
| Trace | Stores the reasoning strategy that the inference engine uses during a consultation. These results may be examined by using either the Text or the Graphics options found on the Tree menu. |
| Tree | Enables examining the results of a consultation Trace in either Text or Graphic form. |
| Variable | Allows examining the values and confidence factors assigned to a variable as a result of a consultation. |
| WhatIf | Allows seeing the effect of a change in the value of a variable on the results of a consultation. |
| Why? | Used during a consultation to find out why a particular question is being asked. |
| Windows | Allows moving or re-sizing the consultation window. |

hierarchy or tree of menus in VP-Expert and describes toolkit features in more detail.

The Slow option on the Set Menu, as an example, slows down the execution of the knowledge base so that a developer can more easily follow the activity in the Rules and Facts windows visually during a consultation. Figure 4–11 outlines the procedure to follow to explore this and other options available for developers.

Frequently, a developer has to deal with the problem of a knowledge base that runs, or executes, but seems to contain some logical errors. An aid in this situation is to perform a "trace" on the consultation to see what's going on behind the scenes. The procedure to perform a trace is given in Figure 4–11.

A trace saves the search pattern used by the inference engine to a file with the same name as the knowledge base, but with a TRC file extension. This file

**Figure 4–11**

## Procedures to Explore Options Useful to Developers

### Slow Down a Consultation

1. Choose Consult from the Main Menu, then choose Set to display the Set Menu.
2. Select Slow. Note: Slow affects some computers more than others. If Slow does not slow a consultation enough, repeatedly press the F3 function key. This has a cumulative effect.
3. Choose Quit to return to the Consult Menu.
4. Select Go to begin the consultation. The activity in the Rules and Facts windows should now be slow enough to follow.
5. To return to normal speed, type a slash (/) and choose Fast from the Go Menu. Note: Slow and Fast options appear on the Go Menu as well as the Set Menu. This allows altering consultation speed both prior to and during a consultation.

### Trace a Consultation

1. Choose Consult from the Main Menu, then choose Set to display the Set Menu.
2. Select Trace. This displays the message, "The trace is on," indicating that the subsequent consultation will be recorded and sent to a disk file.
3. Choose Quit to return to the Consult Menu.
4. Select Go to begin the consultation.
   After the consultation concludes, to see the result of the Trace:
5. Choose Quit from the Consult Menu, then choose Tree from the Main Menu.
6. Choose Text. This displays a text representation, similar to the one in Figure 4–12, of the previous consultation on the Editor screen.
7. Press Alt and function key F8 to quit the Editor.
   If the computer being used has graphics capability (a CGA, EGA, Hercules monochrome, or compatible graphics board):
8. Choose Graphics from the Tree Menu. A graphics tree appears in the upper left corner of the screen in a highlighted box.
9. Press the spacebar to enlarge the area inside the box, making that portion of the display legible, similar to the example shown in Figure 4–13. Use the arrow keys or the PgUp and PgDn keys to zoom in on other areas of the tree. Press the spacebar again to return to the box on the previous display. Alternatively, the box can be moved with the arrow keys or the PgUp and PgDn keys. By moving in box-size steps, and pressing the spacebar, it is possible to zoom in on any section of the graphic tree for closer examination.
10. Pressing ESC at the first graphics screen with the highlighted box causes a return to the Tree Menu.

#### Learn "Why?" a Question Is Asked or "How?" a Value Was Assigned to a Variable

1. Choose Go from the Consult Menu and after any question is displayed, type the backslash (/) key.
2. Move the lightbar to Why? and press Enter. The appropriate response is displayed.
3. Press any key to escape. Resume the consultation and answer one or more questions.

**Figure 4–11** *continued*

4. Type the backslash (/) key.
5. Move the lightbar to How? and press Enter. Make a selection by using the arrow keys to highlight a variable choice. Press Enter. A response identifying how the variable was set is displayed.
6. Press any key to escape.

**Explore Alternatives ("WhatIf") or Examine a Rule or Variable**

1. Choose WhatIf from the Consult Menu.
2. Choose a variable from the list of variable names presented and press Enter. The appropriate question appears for answering.
3. Select an answer. This may, in some circumstances, cause the consultation to restart. In some cases, the inference engine has all the information it needs to draw a new conclusion. In other cases, the new answer might cause the inference engine to take a new logic path through the rules. This may generate new questions.
4. At the Consult Menu, choose Rule or Variable. Make a selection from the list of rules or variables presented. A response identifying the variable with its value(s) or the rule chosen is displayed.
5. Press any key to escape.

can be viewed two ways: as a *text tree* or as a *graphics tree.* Examples of both are shown in Figures 4–12 and 4–13.

The following three options may also help a developer during a debugging session:

- *How?*—describes how a value was assigned to a variable which a developer selects from a list of choices. Responses are because "You said so," or because "Rule X fired," or even "There are no values for that variable."
- *Rule*—allows examining any rules (selected from a list of choices) in the knowledge base.
- *Variable*—allows examining the value(s) and confidence factors assigned to any variable (selected from a list of choices) as a result of a consultation.

The procedure to use these options is described in Figure 4–11. When these options are used, they all appear in pop-up windows that resemble the examples in Figures 4–14 and 4–15.

## THE USER'S OPTIONS—MORE ON RUNNING A CONSULTATION

Two menu options benefit users who run a consultation as much as they benefit developers. These are the *Why?* and *What If* options.

**Figure 4–12.** Text Trace of a Consultation Session

Goal variable.

The word "Testing" followed by a rule label means the rule is being tried.

The name of a variable indicates that its value is being sought at that point in the consultation.

Text in parentheses shows that a value has been assigned to the variable (determined by following up the column of exclamation marks located to the left of the value).

```
Testing a:\HMO.kbs
(= yes CNF 0 )
!   support
!   !   Testing 1
!   !   !   member_status
!   !   !   !   Testing 6
!   !   !   !   !   member
!   !   !   !   !   !   (= yes CNF 100 )
!   !   !   !   !   valid_id
!   !   !   !   !   !   (= yes CNF 100 )
!   !   !   !   (= ok CNF 100 )
!   !   !   reason
!   !   !   !   (= new_case CNF 100 )
!   !   !   problem
!   !   !   !   Testing 9
!   !   !   !   !   temperature
!   !   !   !   !   !   (= normal CNF 100 )
!   !   !   !   !   other_symptoms
!   !   !   !   !   !   (= yes CNF 100 )
!   !   !   !   (= serious CNF 100 )
!   !   (= level_1 CNF 100 )
```

One of the features of a KBS compared to a conventional computer system is its ability to explain. This feature allows a user, or developer, to stop a consultation anywhere and ask why a question is being asked. Figure 4–11 provides the procedure for exploring this feature. Figure 4–14 illustrates an example of using the Why? feature.

Especially with a KBS designed to assist in managerial decision-making tasks, users often consider it essential to be able to examine and critique how a decision is determined. The built-in Why? feature enables this kind of probing. Chapter 6 discusses a way to improve this explanation facility with the use of the BECAUSE keyword.

Also, if a decision maker is using a KBS to explore various scenarios, as in a strategy-planning KBS, it is valuable to be able to change a variable to see how that change could affect a solution. The What If feature answers questions such

**Figure 4–13.** Graphic Trace of a Consultation Session

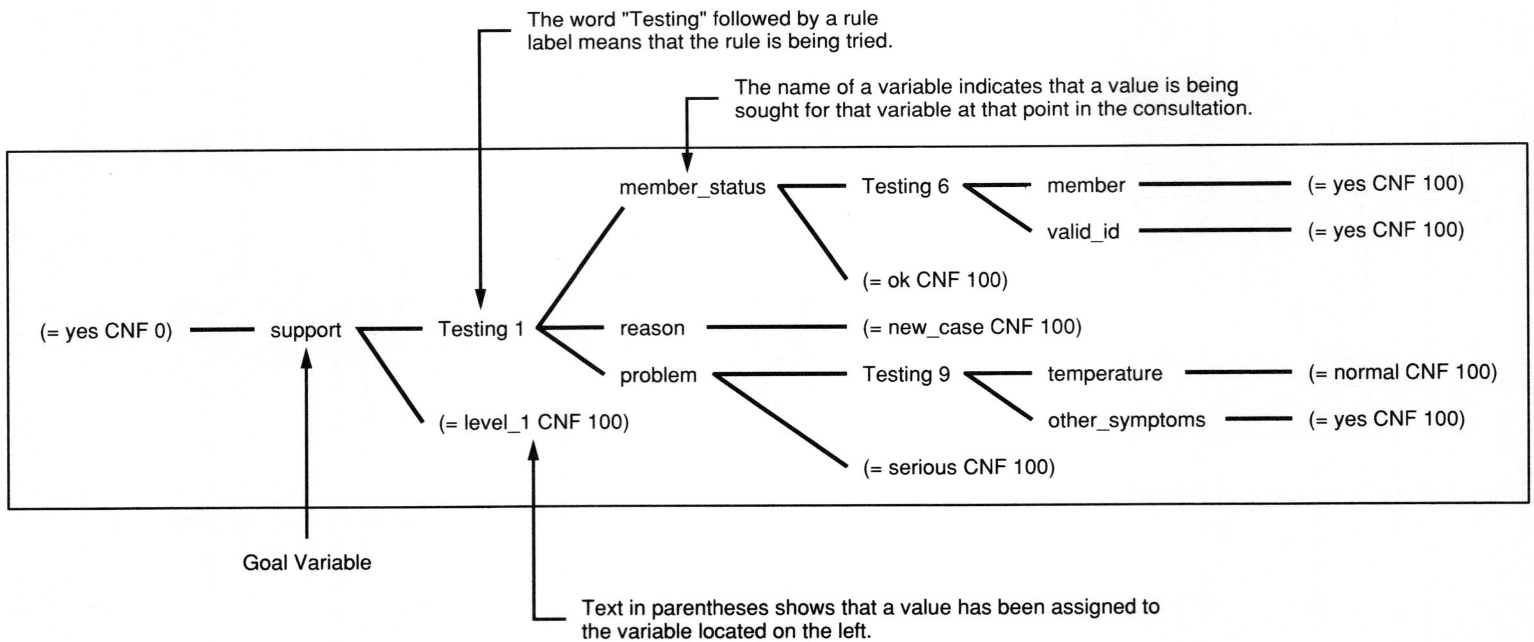

**Figure 4–14.** The "Why" Explanation Feature

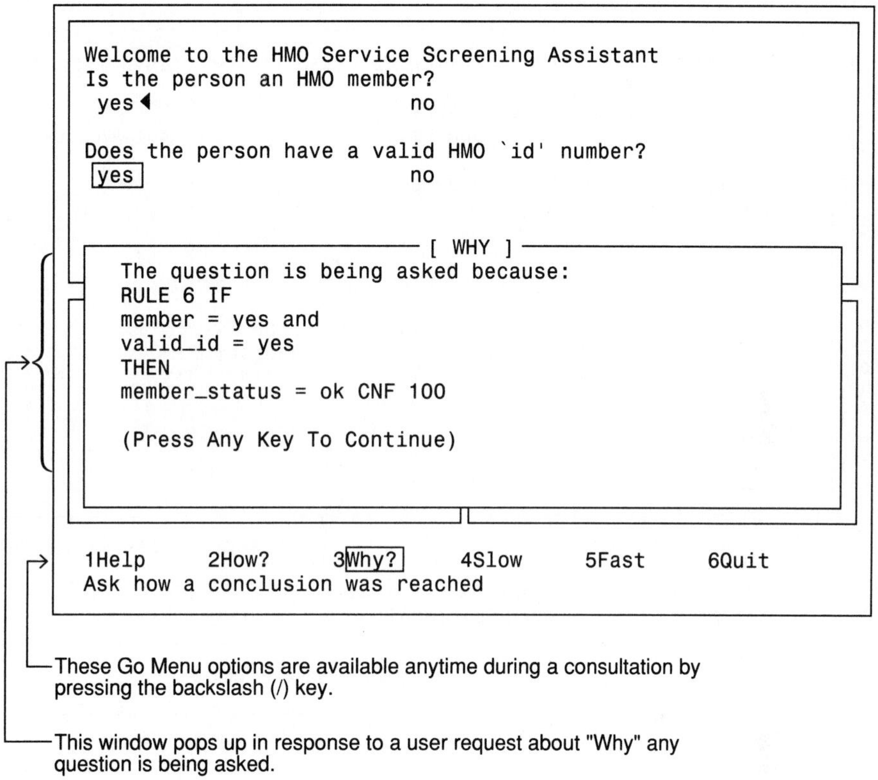


as, "What if I had chosen 'No' instead of 'Yes' at the last prompt?" The procedure to use the What If feature is given in Figure 4–11 and illustrated in Figure 4–15.

The options discussed should be sufficient for completing and debugging the sample systems in this tutorial. Detailed documentation is provided in the *VP-Expert Manual*.

**Figure 4–15.** Examining "What If" Alternatives

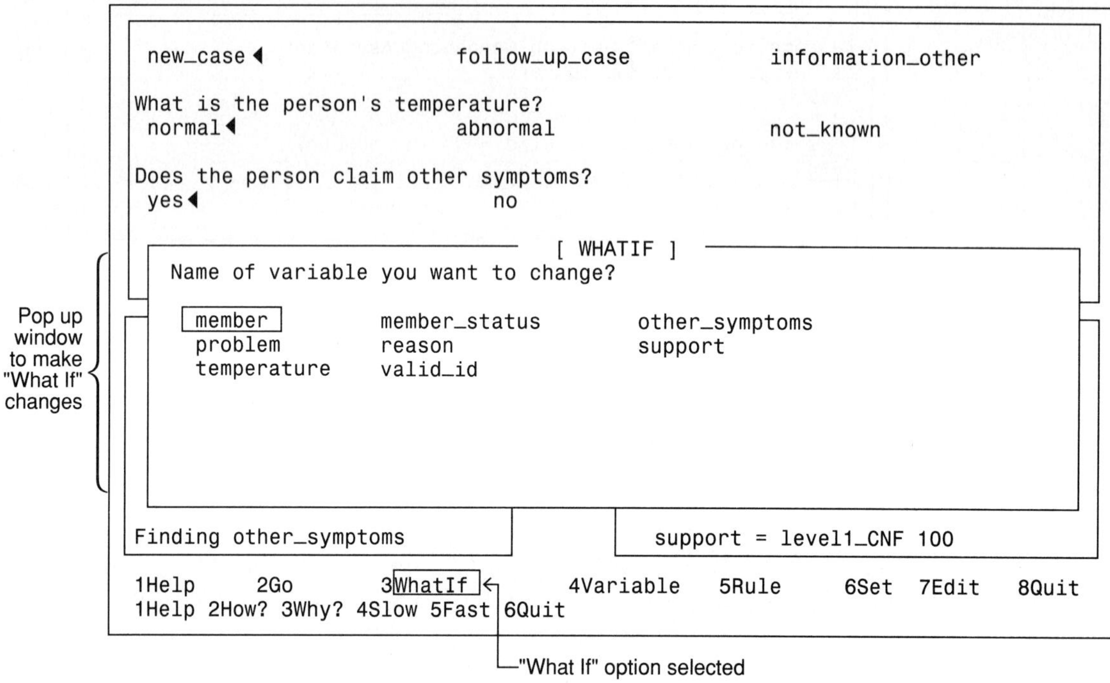


## REVIEW QUESTIONS

1. How does the inference engine work?
2. What generalizations can be made concerning backward chaining?
3. How does the Editor function in an expert system shell?
4. What are the basics of debugging a knowledge base?
5. What kinds of errors commonly occur in KBS programs?
6. Why does the configuration of the consultation screen sometimes vary between the development and delivery phases?
7. What are the benefits of the Why? and What If options in an expert system shell?
8. What are the reasons for using the How? or Variable options in an expert system shell?

## EXERCISES

1. This exercise contrasts the user's and the developer's view of a KBS. Run a consultation with the knowledge base HMORUN.KBS from the Sample Files disk.
   a. Use the "Procedure for Running a Consultation," given in Figure 4–2, to run the consultation.
   b. Run a consultation using the knowledge base HMO.KBS from the Sample Files disk.
   c. Compare and record the results observed from the two consultations. Why are they different?
2. To explore working with the Editor, enter the knowledge base from Figure 4–3 into the computer. When asked to "choose a file," enter any 8-digit or less filename, such as MYHMO. Use your own personal disk to save this exercise, which will be referenced as your "Exercise" disk in future exercises. (It is highly recommended that you have two "Exercise" disks. One should be the "Master" disk and the second a duplicate "Backup" safety disk.)
   a. Use the "Procedure for Entering (or Editing) a Knowledge Base," given in Figure 4–4, to key the code into the computer.
   b. Run a trial consultation and record the results. Use the "Procedure for Running a Consultation," given in Figure 4–2, to run the consultation.
   c. If errors are present, use the "Procedure for Debugging a Knowledge Base," given in Figure 4–8, to make corrections.
   d. Repeat Steps b and c until the knowledge base is completely debugged, or error free.
   e. Test all possible paths through the knowledge base. Record each test attempted and the result of each.
3. This exercise continues to explore working with the Editor. Make the following changes to the knowledge base created in Exercise 2.
   a. Insert a blank line above the keyword ACTIONS and type the keyword RUNTIME; (include the semicolon) on the new first line. Run a trial consultation. Record the results observed.
   b. Delete the first line (RUNTIME;). Block all of Rule 2 and move it above Rule 1. Renumber the rules. Run a trial consultation. Record the results observed. Does switching the rules make a difference as to how the knowledge base executes?
   c. Print a copy of the knowledge base file. Follow the "Print file" instructions in Figure 4–7.
4. Explore other kinds of options available to developers. Follow the "Procedures to Explore Options Useful to Developers," given in Figure 4–11.
   a. Use the knowledge base created in Exercise 2 for exploring options. Record the results observed.
   b. Use the HMO.KBS knowledge base from the Sample Files disk. Record the results observed.

5. Use a word processor or the Editor to enter a knowledge base of your own design into the computer file.
   a. Run a trial consultation.
   b. Debug any errors using the Editor and make another trial run. Repeat this procedure until your new knowledge base is completely debugged.

# 5

# Database, Spreadsheet, and Other Knowledge Base Development Techniques

This chapter continues the tutorial that began in Chapter 3 on developing a first knowledge-based system (KBS). This chapter moves beyond the basics to cover

- Database integration
- Spreadsheet integration
- Using induction to create a knowledge base
- Confidence factors

To focus learning, each new theme begins by going back to the original simplified knowledge base presented in Figure 3–15. Then incremental changes are discussed as applied to that basic knowledge base.

For examples presented in this chapter, the recommended learning process involves these steps:

1. Run the new knowledge base using the file on the samples disk to see how it works. Use the "Procedure for Running a Consultation" (given in Figure 4–2) to do this.
2. Go back to copy the original simplified knowledge base (HMO.KBS shown in Figure 3–15) and make the incremental changes to it that you will be learning about in this chapter. Use the "Procedure for Entering (or Editing) a Knowledge Base" (given in Figure 4–4) to do this. Match your finished knowledge base with the one on the Sample Files disk.

There should be no differences between them. This method always starts with a model that is known to be correct. It provides a goal to aim for during the early phase of learning how to develop a KBS.

If you follow this learning plan, it is ideal to have two blank formatted disks labelled as

1. KBS Exercises—Master
2. KBS Exercises—Backup

The Backup is a safety disk that is a copy of the Master disk. The Master should be "backed up" frequently during and after each development session at the computer. This is always good computing practice in order to protect against inadvertently erased or damaged disks.

As mentioned earlier, while the software development tool used is the VP-Expert system shell, the themes discussed are applicable to whatever shell is used. Also, only selected keywords and features are covered in this tutorial. It is advisable to consult the *VP-Expert Manual* for additional detail.

## DATABASE INTEGRATION

One of the powerful features of today's expert system shells is their ability to integrate with existing database and spreadsheet files. Such files store a vast amount of information that represents, for many organizations, a substantial corporate asset.

Often a KBS can help to leverage use of the information contained in the files. For example, in the HMO case, database information can be imported at the start of the consultation to replace the tedious manual ID-verification task otherwise performed by an HMO service representative.

The first example of this chapter explores *database integration.* Here, the HMO KBS integrates with a MEMBER database file to verify that a client is, in fact, a valid HMO member. This automated check:

- spares the HMO service representative from having to consult a large computer printout of current members
- makes the operation more efficient and accurate
- reduces the total time needed to service the HMO client

This KBS application takes the HMO client's "ID" number from the MEMBER database, processes it, and converts it into specific action recommendations. If the client is a valid member, the service representative is informed and prompted to proceed with screening the client. If the client is not validated, the KBS informs the service representative and recommends further action as a "non-member" client. This application is characterized by taking database output as its input, making judgments based on it, and then presenting specific suggestions to the user.

But the application also captures information during processing and updates the database in order to support management decision-making. For example, decisions on how much to charge HMO members for services is based on historical records of services rendered to clients. To automate the maintenance of these important historical records, the KBS updates a member's record each time the screening process results in a validated request for service.

### Member Database File

Assume for this example that the HMO organization has a computerized database of member information that includes, among other items, the following:

- member ID or identification number
- full name and address
- type of plan (example: family, individual, co-payment, etc.)
- plan payor (example: private, company, etc.)
- original date of membership
- date of current membership expiration
- annual service charge
- payment schedule (example: yearly, monthly, etc.)
- payment status (example: good, delinquent, etc.)
- number of requests for service during current year
- number of requests for service previous year

This administrative information is in addition to detailed billing and medical history files.

Figure 5–1 shows an extract of this database information and presents it as the MEMBER file. Both the record structure and test records for this file are given. It is on the samples disk as a dBASE file with the .DBF filename extension (MEMBER.DBF).

### KBS Link to Database

The knowledge base that links into the MEMBER file to automate member validation is given in Figure 5–2. When the HMO service representative runs a consultation with it, the screen looks like the example in Figure 5–3.

The database link has little effect on the screen that the service representative sees. This is evident from a comparison of Figures 5–3 and 3–14. Formerly, the service representative had to get a client's ID, then walk over to a centrally located computer-printed listing of member information. The result of this manual verification of member status was keyboarded into the KBS. Consultation resumed in cases where a valid ID was found, and terminated if the client was found to be invalid.

The new KBS version asks for the client's ID number and instantly returns the message "Member status is "ok" or "not ok" as appropriate. The status is

**Figure 5–1.** MEMBER Database File

Structure for Each Record
in the MEMBER Database File

| Field Name | Width | Field Type (Character or Numeric) | Field Description |
|---|---|---|---|
| ID | 3 | N | ID |
| P_TYPE | 10 | C | PlanType(FAM=family; COPAY=co-payment; IND=individual) |
| LNAME | 15 | C | Last Name |
| FNAME | 15 | C | First Name |
| REQUESTS | 3 | N | Requests for service this year |

Test Records
(9 test records exist
in the MEMBER database file)

| Record Number | ID | P_TYPE | LNAME | FNAME | REQUESTS |
|---|---|---|---|---|---|
| 1 | 111 | fam | Jones | Irene | 12 |
| 2 | 222 | ind | Tyson | Christopher | 2 |
| 3 | 333 | copay | Wong | Swee | 4 |
| 4 | 444 | fam | Malone | John | 10 |
| 5 | 555 | copay | Mendez | Nick | 7 |
| 6 | 666 | copay | Dietz | Elizabeth | 1 |
| 7 | 777 | ind | Lacy | MaryBeth | 5 |
| 8 | 888 | fam | Tillman | Bradford | 5 |
| 9 | 999 | fam | Gilmore | Matthew | 2 |

determined from a database search by the KBS for a record with a matching ID number.

A successful match causes additional database processing that remains invisible to the KBS user. The member record that causes the match is automatically updated to reflect an addition to the number of requests for HMO service in the current year. In a more sophisticated system, this update would be more refined to reflect the specific type of service rendered. It could also allow for matching on either ID number or last name.

### The GET Keyword

Figure 5–4 provides a summary of GET and other selected keywords used to integrate a KBS with a database file. Figure 5–2 shows how the GET and PUT database keywords are used in practice. In the example, they are used as enhancements to the original KBS which appears in Figure 3–15.

Rule 6 in Figure 5–2 uses the GET keyword to search ALL the records in the MEMBER file for a record whose ID matches the one just entered. The entry of the current ID is caused by the FIND keyword instruction which precedes the GET instruction. FIND is used here simply to force the "ASK id_number" statement to solicit keyboarded input.

Figure 5–5 identifies the meaning of each parameter associated with the GET keyword. The first parameter specifies either that ALL records are to be selected, or only those records that match one or more conditions specified. In the example shown, the first parameter is "id_number = id." This specifies the condition for which a record is to be selected from the database file. The consultation screen in Figure 5–3 shows 666 is the "id_number" entered, so a match is expected with record number 6 in the file of test records shown in Figure 5–1.

The second GET parameter identifies the name of the database file to be searched. In this case it is the MEMBER file. It must be a file with a .DBF filename extension. However, the extension must not be explicitly provided, or a syntax error will result. If necessary, a DOS pathname can also be specified with the filename.

The third and final parameter indicates which fields in a record are of interest. Either ALL or one field can be specified. In the example, ALL fields are identified, which is the normal case.

The final instruction in Rule 6 uses the RESET keyword, which automatically changes the value of any variable named to UNKNOWN. In the example, it is necessary to change the variable "member_status" to UNKNOWN in order to return the inference engine to its normal search path.

The inference engine originally arrived at Rule 6 searching for "member_status" because the first IF condition in Rule 1 sent it there. Rule 6 is the first rule in the knowledge base that has "member_status" in its THEN clause, so the inference engine stops to evaluate all IF conditions in Rule 6 first. The IF part of the rule has only one condition and it requires a keyboarded response to indicate whether or not a client is an HMO "member." If the response is yes, the inference engine needs to do a database check. In order to do this, it is necessary to "skip over" the first THEN clause and get on to the second and third clauses. This is easily done by temporarily filling "member_status" with a "dummy" value. In this case, "member_status" is temporarily set to "check_valid," but could just as well be any other value desired.

Such a temporary procedure forces the inference engine to execute all the instructions after the THEN clause. Once these instructions are executed, it is appropriate to restore the "member_status" variable to UNKNOWN, because it forces further searching to establish its correct value in Rule 7, 8, or 9.

It is interesting to compare the position of rules in Figures 3–15 and 5–2. A comparison highlights the importance of rule placement, or position, in a knowledge base. For example, in Figure 3–15 both "member = yes" conditions

**Figure 5–2.** A Knowledge Base with a Link to a Database File

Notes:
. The name of this knowledge base file on the Sample Files disk is HMO.KBS and MEMBER. DBF is the database file.
. The blocked areas indicate changes to the original HMO.KBS file (see Figure 3-15).

```
RUNTIME;
ACTIONS
  DISPLAY "Welcome to the HMO Service Screening Assistant"
  FIND support
  DISPLAY "Recommended support: {support}."
;

RULE 1
      IF member_status = ok and
         reason = new_case or
         reason = follow_up_case and
         problem = serious
      THEN support = level_1;

RULE 2
      IF member_status = ok and
         reason = new_case and
         problem = non_serious
      THEN support = level_2;

RULE 3
      IF member_status = ok and
         reason = follow_up_case and
         problem = non_serious
      THEN support = level_3;

RULE 4
      IF member_status = ok and
         reason = information_other
      THEN support = information_other;

RULE 5
      IF member_status = not_ok
      THEN support = non_member;

RULE 6
      IF member = yes
      THEN member_status = check_valid
         FIND id_number                         !ASK for direct user input
         GET id_number = id, member, ALL !look in database for a match
         RESET member_status;
```

```
RULE 7
     IF member = no
     THEN member_status = not_ok;

RULE 8
     IF id_number = (id)
     THEN member_status = ok
        DISPLAY "Member status is ok"
        requests = (requests + 1)                  !increment requests
        PUT member;                          !update the database record

RULE 9
     IF id_number <> (id)
     THEN member_status = not_ok
        DISPLAY "Member status is not valid.";

RULE 10
     IF temperature = normal and
        other_symptoms = yes
     THEN problem = serious;

RULE 11
     IF temperature = normal and
        other_symptoms = no
     THEN problem = non_serious;

RULE 12
     IF temperature = abnormal or
        temperature = not_known
     THEN problem = serious;

ASK member: "Is the person an HMO member?";
CHOICES member: yes, no;

ASK id_number: "What is the 'id' number?";

ASK reason: "What is the reason for coming to the HMO facility?";
CHOICES reason: new_case, follow_up_case, information_other;

ASK temperature: "What is the person's temperature?";
CHOICES temperature: normal, abnormal, not_known;

ASK other_symptoms:  "Does the person claim other symptoms?";
CHOICES other_symptoms: yes, no;
```

**Figure 5–3.** Using GET and PUT Keywords to Retrieve and Update a Database Record

This number is used by the GET keyword (in RULE 6) to look for a match in the MEMBER database file. →

This message verifies that a matching record is found (see RULE 8). It causes an automatic update of the database record with the PUT keyword (which is not visible to the user). The update adds one to the number of service "requests" in the member's record. →

```
Welcome to the HMO Service Screening Assistant
Is the person an HMO member?
[yes] ◄                     no

What is the `id' number?
[666]

Member status is ok
What is the reason for coming to the HMO facility?
[new case] ◄               follow up case            information other

What is the person's temperature?
[normal] ◄                 abnormal                  not known


Does the person claim other symptoms?
[yes] ◄                    no


Recommended support: level 1.
```

appear in Rules 6 and 7 before the single "member = no" condition (Rule 8). Following this pattern, it would seem instinctively right in Figure 5–2 to position Rules 8 and 9, which are logical follow-up questions to "member = yes," right after Rule 6. In practice, however, this placement causes an illogical request for a member's ID, even if the client is not a member! To correct this requires bumping the "member = no" rule to a higher position in the sequential rule order.

Every KBS developer creates techniques to expedite coding a knowledge base. There are usually several solutions that would work equally well to solve any single coding challenge.

To help document new additions to the knowledge base, comments are added to the right of selected program lines. Comments begin with an exclamation mark (!) and may appear anywhere in the knowledge base. The inference engine ignores all text after an exclamation mark.

### The PUT Keyword

Rule 8 in Figure 5–2 demonstrates the use of the PUT keyword to update an existing record in a database file. (The term *update* is used interchangeably with *edit, change,* or *revise.*) In this case, the update concerns incrementing by one the number in the REQUESTS field of the member's record. Management policy

**Figure 5–4.** Database Access Keywords

**Selected Database Keywords**

| Keyword | Description |
|---|---|
| ALL | Used with GET and MENU keywords to indicate that no special condition needs to be met when selecting a record. |
| GET | Used to retrieve values from a database file. |
| MENU | Used in conjunction with the ASK statement to generate a menu of allowable values that can be assigned to a variable based on the field values of a database file. |
| PUT | Used to update or change a record in a database file. |

**Other Related Keywords**

| Keyword | Description |
|---|---|
| END | Signals the end of a WHILEKNOWN–END loop. END is the last word of a WHILEKNOWN-END loop. |
| RESET | Removes any values assigned to the named variable and returns it to the value UNKNOWN. The most frequent use of the RESET keyword is in a WHILEKNOWN–END loop where a variable's value is being repeatedly sought, but where the value must be returned to UNKNOWN before each iteration of the FIND clause. |
| WHILEKNOWN | All lines appearing between the WHILEKNOWN keyword and the END keyword are repeatedly executed in loop fashion so long as the value of the variable named in the WHILEKNOWN clause has a known value. Once the value of the variable becomes UNKNOWN, the lines contained inside the loop are executed one final time. (A loop can begin with the WHILEKNOWN variable set to UNKNOWN. If the variable is not set to some other value before the END key is reached, however, the loop will terminate.) This WHILEKNOWN-END loop is frequently used with the GET keyword to access records in a database file. (Nested, or loop-within-a-loop, techniques are not supported. Only one WHILEKNOWN-END loop can be active at a time.) |

decisions are based on the data provided by this field, which is a running tally of the number of times a member solicits HMO services in the current year. The PUT instruction that actually causes the HMO member's record to be updated in the database file is straightforward. It includes only two elements: the keyword PUT and the name of the database file. To verify that the update has taken place, it is necessary to go into the dBASE program and check the record in the MEMBER.DBF file.

**Figure 5–5.** Database Access Examples

### GET (retrieve) Information from a Database File

The first parameter in a GET instruction is either the keyword ALL (for all records) or an expression specifying one or more conditions by which a record will be selected from the database file. (Up to twenty conditions, linked by ANDs or ORs, are permitted.)

The third parameter is either the keyword ALL or the name of a single field. It indicates which values of the record should be transferred to knowledge base variables.

```
GET id_number = id, member, ALL
```

The second parameter must be the name of an existing database file with a .DBF extension. However, the extension must not be explicitly provided, or a syntax error will result. If necessary, a pathname can also be specified.

The GET keyword is used to retrieve values from a database file.

### PUT (Write) Information to a Database File

The PUT keyword is used to edit (update, change, or revise) an existing record.

```
PUT member
```

The only parameter in a PUT instruction is the name of an existing database file with a .DBF extension. However, the extension must not be explicitly provided, or a syntax error will result. If necessary, a pathname can also be specified.

### Generate a MENU of Options to Accompany an ASK Question

The first parameter is the name of a knowledge base variable.

The third parameter must be the name of an existing database file with a .DBF extension. However, the extension must not be explicitly provided, or a syntax error will result. If necessary, a pathname can also be specified.

```
Menu plan_type, ALL, member, p_type
```

The fourth parameter is a field name from the database file. The contents of this field will be used for the menu choices. The field name used must correspond to a field name in the database file specified.

The second parameter is either the keyword ALL, or an expression (see the GET example), specifying one or more conditions by which records in the database file will be selected.

The MENU keyword generates a menu of options to accompany a question displayed by a corresponding ASK statement. It is similar to the CHOICES keyword, but, unlike CHOICES, it takes its options from the field values of a given database file. The MENU instruction must be placed where it will be executed before the corresponding ASK statement is executed (though it need not be immediately before).

Before the update takes place, the IF condition in Rule 8 acts as a filter. It allows only certain cases to pass through. The ID number entered must match an ID number in the database.

## INDIRECT ADDRESSING

The ID number in the IF clause of Rule 8 is surrounded by parentheses. They indicate to the inference engine that the enclosed item is a variable name whose value must replace the name. To replace the variable name with its value, the inference engine goes into its working memory and makes the replacement itself. Programmers call this *indirect addressing*. It is a technique where a variable name is used as an indirect way of addressing its value.

This technique is always useful, for example, to display the results of a consultation. This is evident in the last line of the Actions Block in Figure 5–2. There the value of the variable "support" is displayed when a consultation session terminates.

Figure 5–6 provides examples to show the various ways indirect addressing is useful in knowledge base development. Example 4 is taken from Rule 8 in Figure 5–2. It shows its use in math operations. In this case, the value of the REQUESTS field is incremented by one. After this operation occurs on the right side of the "equal" sign, the result is assigned to the variable named on the left of the "equal" sign. In this case, it is the same variable. REQUESTS ends up containing the result of the addition.

Once the addition is done, the updated record is ready to be returned to the MEMBER database file.

### Other Applications of Database Linkage

This update example only begins to tap the surface of the potential use of linking a database with a KBS. To extend the present example, assume management wants to know when something is about to go wrong. It would like to embed intelligence in the KBS to flag cases, for example, of members who have an "individual" policy and who exceed, say, five requests for service this year. The KBS could have a rule that watches in the background and when it finds such a case, it could, for example:

- Automatically create a new record of the exception in a special file created for this purpose. (The APPEND command, not covered here, provides for adding records to a database file.)
- Automatically display or print a message about any special processing required. Chapter 6 describes how a message could be printed, or alternatively, a warning could be displayed in a pop-up window.

**Figure 5–6.** Indirect Addressing or Referencing the Value of a Variable

The method of indirectly accessing a value by means of a variable name is called "indirect addressing."

Example 1

```
DISPLAY "Recommended support: {support}."
```

```
Assume:  support = level_1
The displayed result is:
Recommended support:  level 1.
```

Curly brackets mean that the "value" of the named variable should be shown. (Curly brackets are used for indirect addressing in a DISPLAY instruction).

Example 2

```
IF id_number = (id)
```

Parentheses mean that the "value" of the named variable should be evaluated. (Normal parentheses are used for indirect addressing in a rule.) (Note: VP-Expert will not find the value of a variable on the right-hand side of the IF condition.)

```
Assume:  id = 666
And:  id_number = 666
The rule is evaluated as true
because 666 = 666.

If id_number = 555, the rule
would be evaluated as false.
```

Example 3

```
FIND month
best_month = (month)
```

Parentheses around a variable name are used to "assign" the value of one variable to another variable. The expression:

variable = (variable)

assigns the value of the variable named in parentheses to the variable named on the left (the variable on the left cannot be enclosed in parentheses).

```
Assume:  month = June
After the above
assignment:
best_month = June
```

Example 4

```
requests = (requests + 1)
```

Parentheses always enclose math operations that specify the value of one or more variables.

```
Assume:  requests = 6

After the above assignment,
requests will have a value of 7.
```

This extra embedded intelligence makes the KBS a low-cost diagnostic tool that can make a major contribution to operational control.

## ARITHMETIC AND RELATIONAL SYMBOLS

Rules 8 and 9 introduce new arithmetic and relational symbols, which are identified in Figure 5–7. These symbols, also called operators, are the same as those used in almost every modern program coding language.

In the HMO example, the plus sign represents the add operation required in "requests = (requests + 1)." Any arithmetic operation that specifies using the value of one or more variables must be enclosed in parentheses, as the example demonstrates.

The IF condition in Rule 9 illustrates the use of the "not equal to" (<>) relational symbol. It consists of placing a less than (<) symbol next to a greater than (>) symbol.

Rule 9 filters out any case where the database file has no record for a client who claims to be a member. IF the "id number" that the client gives is "not equal to" an ID in the database, then the "member_status" is set to "not_ok." A message is immediately displayed to tell the HMO service representative that the member status is not valid. In this example case, all clients with a "member_status" of "not_ok" are automatically recommended for non-member support.

**Figure 5–7.** Arithmetic and Relational Symbols (Operators)

**Arithmetic Symbols**

| Symbol | Meaning |
|---|---|
| + | Used for addition of numbers. |
| – | Used for subtraction of numbers. |
| * | Used for multiplication of numbers. |
| / | Used for division of numbers. |

**Relational Symbols**

| Symbol | Meaning |
|---|---|
| = | Used as the equal-to relation. |
| > | Used as the greater-than relation. |
| < | Used as the less-than relation. |
| >= | Used as the greater-than-or-equal-to relation. |
| <= | Used as the less-than-or-equal-to relation. |
| <> | Used as the not-equal-to relation. |

## RUNTIME KEYWORD

The knowledge base in Figure 5–2 begins with the RUNTIME keyword. Placing this keyword in the KBS eliminates the two bottom windows, shown in Figure 4–9, that appear during a consultation. Instead, the consultation window occupies the full screen, as shown in Figure 3–14. This improves the appearance of the system which the user sees.

The RUNTIME keyword should be added to a knowledge base when development is finished and the knowledge base is ready for user, or "runtime," consultations.

## THE MENU KEYWORD

Another keyword used exclusively for database access is MENU. The example in Figure 5–8, which is created only for illustration purposes, demonstrates how MENU is used in practice. This keyword is used in conjunction with the ASK statement to generate a menu of allowable values that can be assigned to a variable. The assignable values are extracted from those found in the actual database records.

In the example, the database variable of interest is "p_type." Figure 5–1 shows that the MEMBER database file has three unique values repeatedly used in the "p_type" field, which are:

| *Value* | *Meaning* |
|---|---|
| fam | Family plan |
| ind | Individual plan |
| copay | Co-pay plan |

In the example, a user selects from this list of plan types to trigger a selective retrieval of database records.

The MENU keyword, in the Actions Block of Figure 5–8, sets up the menu of values that will be called into action when needed. Its three parameters, generally identified in Figure 5–8, are:

| *Parameter* | *Meaning* |
|---|---|
| plan_type | the knowledge base variable that will accept all the values from the database variable of interest |
| plan_type = p_type<br>cut_off < requests | conditions to preselect records |
| MEMBER | the name of the database file |
| p_type | the field name that contains the values of interest |

The next keyword in the Actions Block, after MENU, is "FIND plan_type." Since no rule has "plan_type" in its conclusion, the inference engine automati-

**Figure 5–8.** Using the MENU Keyword and a WHILEKNOWN-END Loop

Note: the name of this knowledge base file on the Sample Files disk is HMODB1.KBS or HMODB1R.KBS and MEMBER.DBF is the database file.

```
ACTIONS
     DISPLAY "This example assists your interrogation of the"
     DISPLAY "MEMBER database file."
     MENU plan_type, ALL, member, p_type
     FIND plan_type
     FIND cut_off
     DISPLAY "The following database records meet your criteria:"
     WHILEKNOWN p_type
          GET plan_type = p_type and cut_off < requests, member, ALL
          RESET message
          FIND message
     END
;

RULE 1
     IF p_type <> unknown
     THEN message = displayed
          DISPLAY "{id}, {p_type}, {lname}, {fname}, {requests}"
     ELSE message = displayed
          DISPLAY "End of file";

ASK plan_type: "What plan type do you want to check?";

ASK cut_off: "If you want only those records with `requests'
above a certain number, please enter the number (or zero).";
```

This knowledge file created this consultation screen:

These are selections generated by the MENU keyword from using information in the "p_type" field of the MEMBER database file.

```
This example assists your interrogation of the
MEMBER database file.
What HMO plan type do you want to check?
 [fam]◄                        ind                        copay

If you want only those records with `requests' above
a certain number, please enter the number (or zero).
[5]

The following database records meet your criteria:
111, fam, Jones, Irene, 12
444, fam, Malone, John, 10
End of file
```

Each record displayed here is the result of a separate cycle through the WHILEKNOWN-END loop.

cally looks for user input. The "ASK plan_type" question is not, however, followed by a CHOICES keyword. Instead, the ASK and MENU keywords are linked by their common variable "plan_type." So the MENU keyword provides the choices this time.

The second FIND keyword in the Actions Block similarly causes the second ASK statement to be activated. The user is asked if database record retrieval should be based on the number of times a member has requested service in the current year. Because a typed response is expected, no CHOICES statement is appropriate here.

## LOOPING OR ITERATIVE PROCESSING

The HMO example in Figure 5–2 works on the assumption that only one database record meets the selection criteria. But what if an application, like the one in Figure 5–8, anticipates several records meeting the selection criteria?

The solution is to use looping or iterative processing. This is accomplished with the combination of the WHILEKNOWN and END keywords. They mark the beginning and end, respectively, of a loop that is processed repetitively until some exit condition is reached.

The main reason a loop is required is because the GET keyword retrieves only one database record at a time. In order to retrieve other records, the GET must be reactivated. Reactivation is normally done inside a WHILEKNOWN-END loop.

The example in Figure 5–8 retrieves decision-making information from the MEMBER database file. It first asks a user what type of plan is of interest. Available member plan types are displayed. After the user makes a selection, an option is presented. The KBS is to select records where members have requested service more than a specific number of times. A list follows of database records that meet the selection criteria entered.

### WHILEKNOWN-END Loops

In the example, the WHILEKNOWN-END loop occurs in the Actions Block. Looping can also occur, if an application requires it, in the THEN part of a rule. A limitation is that only one WHILEKNOWN-END loop can be active at a time.

The variable after the keyword WHILEKNOWN performs a role similar to a guard at a gate who checks a pass to see if entry should be allowed. Entry is allowed under two conditions:

- The first time through the loop, no entry variable is checked. This is normal because the first GET call to the database occurs after initial entry to the loop. Once the first record is retrieved, the "entry" variable, which is "p_plan," is a "known variable."
- All other times, entry into the loop is allowed only if the entry variable has a known value. This will be true until the last database record is reached. After the last record is reached, "p_plan" is automatically set to "unknown." The loop logically terminates only after one final pass through the loop after the exit variable is set to "unknown."

Comparing the consultation screen in Figure 5–8 with the MEMBER database records in Figure 5–1 helps to demonstrate how looping works in practice. In the first pass through the loop, the WHILEKNOWN variable is ignored. Then the following sequence occurs:

- GET retrieves the first "Jones" record. It is a "fam" family type, and so matches the entered selection criteria (plan_type = p_type).
- The GET instruction requires a match on another condition. That is, the entered "cut_off" value, 5 in this example, must be less than the value in the requests field of the record. In the Jones case, 5 is less than the number in the requests field, which is 12. The second criteria matches, so the first record passes the GET rule.
- "RESET message" in the WHILEKNOWN-END pair clears the goal variable and "FIND message" activates a jump to the only rule in this example.
- RULE 1 first checks to be sure the end of the file is not reached. The variable "p_type" will be automatically set to "unknown" after the last record is processed.
- If it is not the last record, the "THEN message" is fired. It causes the display of all the values in the Jones record.
- After the display, the inference engine returns to the WHILEKNOWN loop to find the END keyword. Control returns to the top of the loop and the process begins again.

Since only the first record has been processed, there still is a value in "p_type" so the loop begins again. The second time through the loop, the GET statement finds no match of its conditions with record number 2 or 3. Their "p_type" are different. But record number 4 matches the "p_type" as well as the cut_off conditions. So the record is retrieved and the loop repeats, as before.

Recycling occurs with no further successful matches. Although records 8 and 9 pass on the "p_type" condition, they fail on the cut_off criteria. Record 8 has a value of 5 for "requests," which is equal to the cut_off point, not above it, as required. So it is rejected. The AND condition requires both premises to pass.

After the last record, "p_type" automatically becomes "unknown." The loop executes one final time from beginning to end. When the FIND message clause sends the inference engine to RULE 1, the IF condition fails. Finally, "p_type" does, indeed, equal "unknown." This causes the alternate ELSE conclusion to fire. It causes "End of file" to display. It also causes the session to end.

Figure 5–9 illustrates, in skeleton outline form, another WHILEKNOWN-END loop. The only difference between this example and the one in Figure 5–8 is in the GET first parameter. In Figure 5–8, a selection criterion occurs in the first parameter of the GET instruction. In Figure 5–9, by contrast, ALL records are retrieved. But a similar selection process occurs in RULE 11. This comparison illustrates alternative ways to accomplish the same thing. The

**Figure 5–9.** Looping or Iteration Using the WHILEKNOWN-END Keywords

```
Example:

   .
   .
   .
WHILEKNOWN stock_name
  GET all, stock, ALL
  RESET response
  FIND response
END
   .
   .
   .
RULE 11
  IF stock_price > (buy_price) and
   stock_price < (10_wk_average)
  THEN response = sell
   .
   .
   .


Sample STOCK Database File:

STOCK NAME     STOCK PRICE   BUY PRICE    10 WK AVERAGE  : Loop Results
                                                         :
   AAA            28.16        24.68          31.14      :<—sell (first loop)
   BBB            16.11        17.24          16.79      :(skip) (second loop)
   CCC            43.62        35.91          45.44      :<—sell (third loop)
                                                         :    end (fourth loop)
```

creative developer can find many alternatives, among the options offered, to produce effective applications.

### Other Database Applications and Considerations

Figure 5–9 illustrates how a WHILEKNOWN-END loop is the focus of another database-oriented application. It is part of a commodities advisory system that recommends when it is appropriate to sell stock based on "buy-price" and other factors stored in a database. Database information comes from financial data services that transfer the data over communication lines.

Another database-oriented application contains information about factors that go into a decision of whether or not to grant a customer credit. For each factor in the decision, the file contains a list of all possible values. A numeric weight is stored with each value to indicate its significance in the overall decision-making process. Although this information could have been stored in the form of rules, it was stored in a database file to make the system more efficient and easier to maintain.

In another system, a travel-advisory KBS at a foreign consulate office in the United States, the system's recommendations are stored in a database file. The file contains information about hotels, restaurants, and other facilities in the country, arranged by categories such as luxury, budget, and so forth. Once the KBS evaluates the category of travel desired, along with other preferences, it displays or prints its recommendations of services available. Having the list of hotels and restaurants in a database file enormously simplifies the KBS program. It also allows the consulate to easily add, change, or delete records to keep the KBS's recommendations current. This way updates never require a single change to a KBS rule.

Many developers can take similar advantage of using database files to enhance KBS projects. In particular, many designs can benefit from narrowing a conclusion to a category or type. This classification can then be used to retrieve more specific detail from records stored in a database file.

## SPREADSHEET INTEGRATION

Similar to database integration, spreadsheet integration includes transferring data back and forth between a spreadsheet and a knowledge base. Most modern expert system shells provide links to integrate a knowledge base file with a spreadsheet file. As an example, the VP-Expert shell transfers data with the Lotus 1-2-3, VP-Planner, and Symphony spreadsheet programs.

To explore how spreadsheet integration works, assume that the director of the HMO service facility wants to keep a daily running total of how many clients are serviced, by service type. She wants to be able to look at a simple spreadsheet, such as the one in Figure 5–10, at the end of each day, or at random times throughout the day, to check on case volume. The up-to-the-minute figures enable her to make adjustments in personnel to avoid potential service bottlenecks and to maintain a high level of member-service responsiveness.

Changes would have to be made to the original knowledge base presented in Figure 3–15 to satisfy the director's need for current decision-making information. Figure 5–11 shows the revised knowledge base that integrates with the spreadsheet shown in Figure 5–10. The spreadsheet was prepared using Lotus 1-2-3.

When the knowledge base is run, the user consultation screen remains unchanged from Figure 3–14. The spreadsheet is updated in the background with processing that remains hidden from the user's view. The user will, however, experience a longer delay in processing on some slower computers.

Processing requires that the spreadsheet template is already prepared and ready for update when the knowledge base system is running. A fresh copy of

**Figure 5–10.** Sample Spreadsheet SSHMO.WKS

```
        A             B       C              D
1    HMO Service Screening Control 3/11/9X
2
3    Service_Type            No_Cases
4
5    level_1                       34
5    level_2                       65
7    level_3                      104
8    information_other             41
9    non_member                    17
10
11
12
```

the spreadsheet template, with cells B5 to B9 set to an initial value of zero, is always prepared at the end of one work day in readiness for the next day's processing.

During processing, each time a consultation results in firing a rule that establishes a value for "support," it also triggers a spreadsheet update. The update adds one to the number already accumulated in the spreadsheet cell that corresponds to the "support" type. This immediate updating provides the director with control figures, whenever desired, that are as current as the last update.

### The WKS Keyword

As evident from Figure 5–11, the WKS keyword retrieves data from a spreadsheet. It is only one of several keywords, as identified in Figure 5–12, used to access a spreadsheet from the knowledge base.

When the WKS keyword is used, it requires three parameters. They are identified in detail in Figure 5–13. The first is the name of any knowledge base variable which receives the value or values being transferred from the spreadsheet. The second parameter identifies the location of the values in the spreadsheet. The final parameter identifies the spreadsheet filename.

Figure 5–14 shows only two of many variations that the "second," or location parameter, can take. The first example comes from the knowledge base given in Figure 5–11. It shows the WKS keyword used to transfer the value 34 from the single spreadsheet cell, B5, into the knowledge-base variable "old-number." This is the simplest transfer of all.

**Figure 5–11.** Knowledge Base File with a Link to a Spreadsheet

Notes:
. The name of this knowledge base file on the Sample Files disk is HMOSS.KBS and SSHMO. WKS is the spreadsheet file.
. The blocked areas indicate changes to the original HMO.KBS file (see Figure 3-15).

```
RUNTIME;
ACTIONS
     DISPLAY "Welcome to the HMO Service Screening Assistant"
     WFORMAT fixed, 0            !format PWKS values without decimal places
     FIND support
     DISPLAY "Recommended support: {support}."
;

RULE 1
     IF member_status = ok and
        reason = new_case or
        reason = follow_up_case and
        problem = serious
     THEN support = level_1
        WKS old_number, B5, SSHMO        !transfer the value of spreadsheet
                                     !cell B5 into the variable "old_number"
        new_number = (old_number + 1)               !add 1 to the old number
        PWKS new_number, B5, SSHMO;                 !put the new number back

RULE 2
     IF member_status = ok and
        reason = new_case and
        problem = non_serious
     THEN support = level_2
        WKS old_number, B6, SSHMO
        new_number = (old_number + 1)
        PWKS new_number, B6, SSHMO;

RULE 3
     IF member_status = ok and
     reason = follow_up_case and
     problem = non_serious
     THEN support = level_3
     WKS old_number, B7, SSHMO
     new_number = (old_number + 1)
     PWKS new_number, B7, SSHMO;

RULE 4
     IF member_status = ok and
        reason = information_other
     THEN support = information_other
        WKS old_number, B8, SSHMO
        new_number = (old_number + 1)
        PWKS new_number, B8, SSHMO;
```

**Figure 5–11** *continued*

```
RULE 5
     IF member_status = not_ok
     THEN support = non_member
        WKS old_number, B9, SSHMO
        new_number = (old_number + 1)
        PWKS new_number, B9, SSHMO;

RULE 6
     IF member = yes and
        valid_id = yes
     THEN member_status = ok;

RULE 7
     IF member = yes and
        valid_id = no
     THEN member_status = not_ok;

RULE 8
     IF member = no
     THEN member_status = not_ok;

RULE 9
     IF temperature = normal and
        other_symptoms = yes
     THEN problem = serious;

RULE 10
     IF temperature = normal and
        other_symptoms = no
     THEN problem = non_serious;

RULE 11
     IF temperature = abnormal or
        temperature = not_known
     THEN problem = serious;

ASK member: "Is the person an HMO member?";
CHOICES member: yes, no;

ASK valid_id: "Does the person have a valid HMO `id' number?";
CHOICES valid_id: yes, no;

ASK reason: "What is the reason for coming to the HMO facility?";
CHOICES reason: new_case, follow_up_case, information_other;

ASK temperature: "What is the person's temperature?";
CHOICES temperature: normal, abnormal, not_known;

ASK other_symptoms:  "Does the person claim other symptoms?";
CHOICES other_symptoms: yes, no;
```

**Figure 5–12.** Selected Spreadsheet Access Keywords

**Selected Spreadsheet Keywords**

| Keyword | Description |
|---|---|
| COLUMN | Used with the WKS or PWKS keywords to identify a column location in a spreadsheet. |
| NAMED | Used with the WKS or PWKS keywords to identify a cell range in a spreadsheet. |
| PWKS | Used to transfer values from a knowledge base variable into a spreadsheet. |
| ROW | Used with the WKS or PWKS keywords to identify a row location in a spreadsheet. |
| WFORMAT | Defines the cell format for numeric values that will be transferred to a spreadsheet with the PWKS keyword. |
| WKS | Used to transfer values from a spreadsheet into a knowledge base variable. |

**Figure 5–13.** WKS and PWKS Keywords for Spreadsheet Access

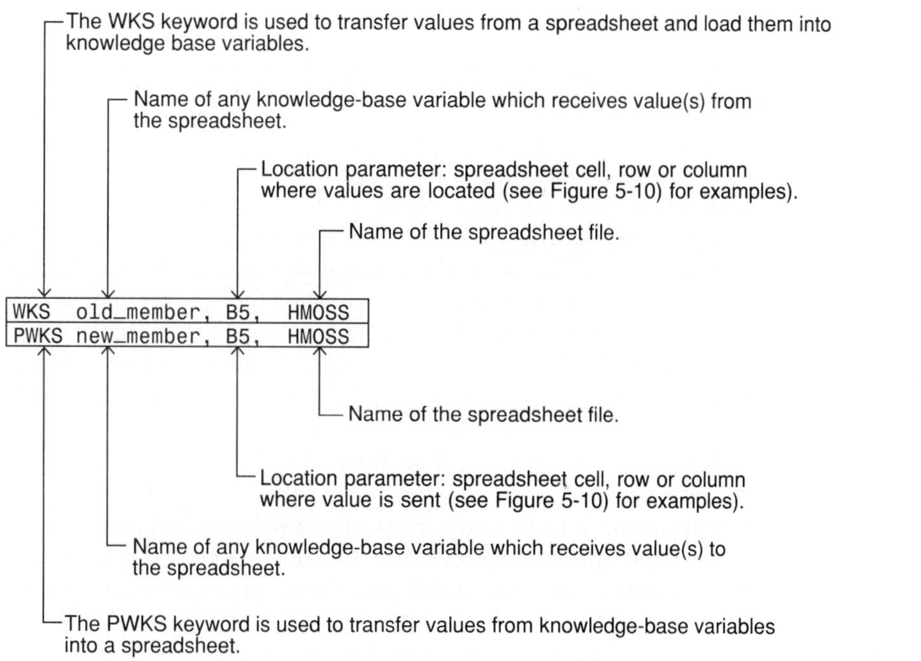

**Figure 5–14.** The Location Parameter in WKS and PWKS Keywords

When the WKS or PWKS keywords are used, the second parameter is a location parameter. It can reference a spreadsheet cell, row, column, or range. Examples of reference to both a single cell and a column follow:

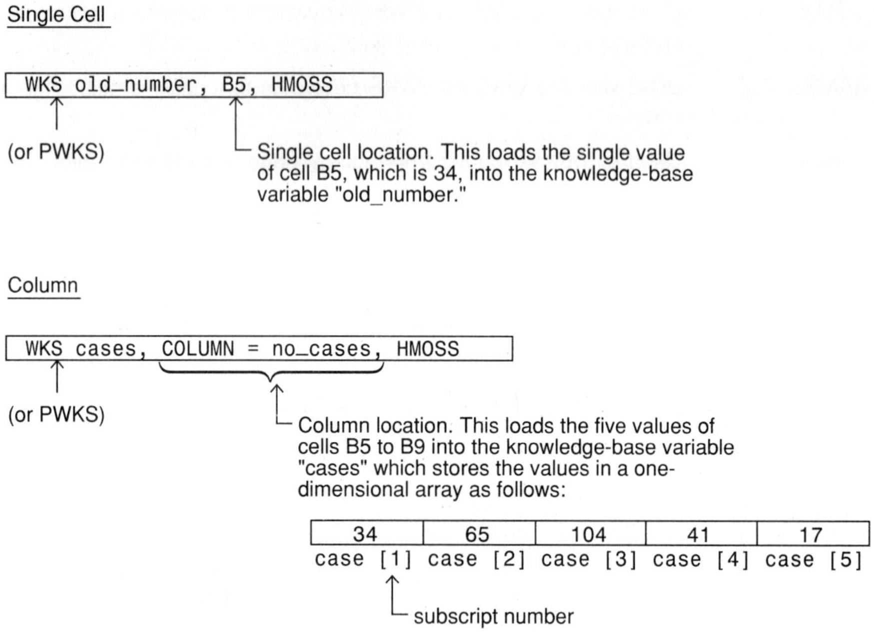


The second example is for illustration purposes. It shows the WKS keyword used for a more complex transfer of values. In this case, an entire column of values is being transferred from the spreadsheet into the knowledge base variable "cases." Because the column contains five values, the inference engine automatically provides five slots to hold all the values. In order to keep each value unique, it assigns a so-called "subscript" number to each.

When the WKS keyword retrieves data from more than one cell, such as from a column, range, or row, the values are stored in a so-called "subscripted" or "dimensioned" variable. The programming required to manipulate such a variable is more complex than for one that contains a single value.

In the example in Figure 5–11, after Rule 1 fires, the THEN part of the rule has several tasks to do. First, the WKS keyword activates the transfer of the value from spreadsheet cell B5. It is loaded into the knowledge-base variable "old_number." Next, a calculation must be performed. It involves adding one to the value in the variable "old_number." Since the old value is 34, the addition sums to 35. This result is assigned to the variable "new_number." In this case, the "equal" sign is read as an "assignment" symbol. It assigns the value on the right of the equal sign to the variable on the left side. Any arithmetic operation is always performed before an assignment takes place.

After the arithmetic, the next step is to transfer the new number back to the spreadsheet.

### The PWKS Keyword

The PWKS keyword does the job of transferring the value 35 from the knowledge base to the spreadsheet. The PWKS keyword requires the same three parameters as the WKS keyword. In this HMO example, the PWKS parameters attached to Rule 1 have the following meaning:

1. "New_number" is the knowledge base variable that contains the value 35.
2. "B5" is the spreadsheet cell where the value stored in "new_number" will be sent.
3. "HMOSS" is the name of the spreadsheet file.

The PWKS instruction ends the three-part sequence added to the conclusion of Rules 1 to 5. The sequence consists of:

- First, retrieve a value from the spreadsheet cell where the "service type" corresponds to the "support" type in the knowledge base rule.
- Second, add one to the value just retrieved.
- Third, replace or update the value in the same spreadsheet cell with the new incremented value.

### The WFORMAT Keyword

The WFORMAT keyword defines the format for numeric values that are transferred to target cells in a spreadsheet with the PWKS keyword. In the HMO example, the WFORMAT keyword appears in the Actions Block, where it defines the format desired, before rule processing begins. WFORMAT can appear, however, anywhere in a knowledge base before the PWKS instruction.

The WFORMAT keyword requires two parameters. The first parameter defines the data format that will be assigned to values transferred to the spreadsheet. There are three possible numeric formats, which are:

| *Numeric Data Format* | *Meaning* |
|---|---|
| FIXED | fixed decimal point format |
| CURR | currency format |
| SCI | scientific format |

The second parameter indicates the number of places behind the decimal point. Two examples of its use are:

| *Example* | *Stored in Spreadsheet* |
|---|---|
| WFORMAT FIXED, 0 | 35 |
| WFORMAT CURR, 2 | $35.00 |

To examine spreadsheet updates made by a knowledge base, it is necessary to

- Activate the spreadsheet program, such as Lotus 1-2-3
- Retrieve the spreadsheet, such as SSHMO.WKS

The SSHMO.WKS spreadsheet should have an accurate count of any consultations processed.

### Spreadsheet Considerations

Spreadsheet integration includes several considerations that can make it more problematical than database integration.

For example, VP-Expert supports the older Lotus 1-2-3 Version 1A spreadsheet WKS filename extension. Later Lotus versions have a WK1 filename extension. In order to be useable, WK1 filename extensions must be renamed (during a spreadsheet /File, Save operation, or with the DOS rename command). It is possible to retrieve and view or check the renamed file, however, with the later Lotus version programs.

Some other considerations are:

- The "at" symbol (@) must be used for indirectly addressing. For example:

  ```
  cell = B5
  WKS new_number, @call, SSHMO
  ```

  This technique could be used to develop a more streamlined code in the HMO example.
- Blank spreadsheet cells can cause potential assignment errors in the knowledge base. For example, if columns are being read and one column has a blank cell while the other columns contain values, the values would not end up in the correct relationship. Cells can be given a value of zero or the value of a space, but they must have a value.

Other considerations apply to importing and exporting more than one spreadsheet value at a time. Information on this and other spreadsheet uses are contained in the *VP-Expert Manual.*

## USING INDUCTION TO CREATE A KNOWLEDGE BASE

One simple way of constructing a small knowledge-based system is to represent the expert's knowledge in a table of examples, much like the one shown in Figure 5–15. The example cases can come from a text, database, or spreadsheet file.

**Figure 5–15.** Creating an Induction Table

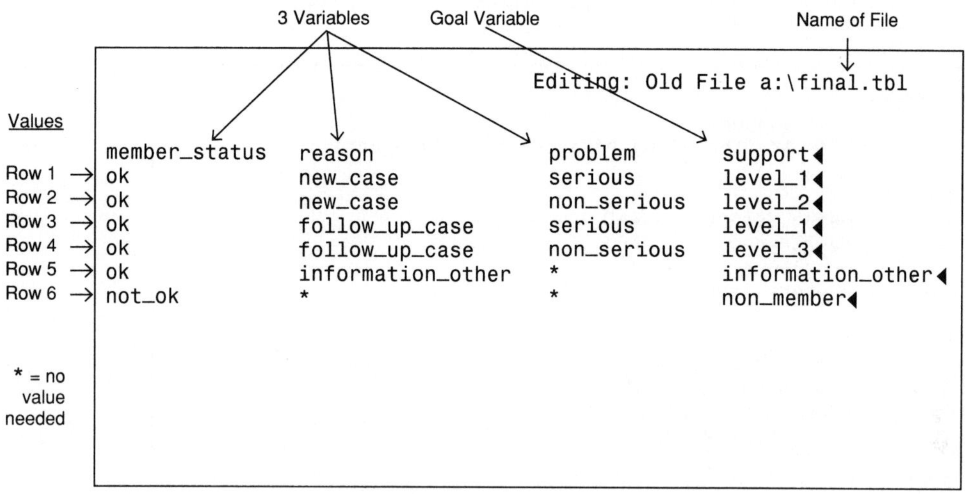


Note: the name of this file on the Sample Files disk is FINAL.TBL.

Once the example cases are recorded in a file, the file can be processed through a so-called "induction algorithm." This processing automatically converts the examples into a working minimal knowledge base.

Absolutely no program coding is required to get results such as the knowledge base shown in Figure 5–16.

Usually, a consultation session with an "induced" knowledge base is very crude, or user "unfriendly," as the example in Figure 5–17 demonstrates.

Some expert system shells, such as 1st CLASS, are optimized induction systems. They are designed to take a file of examples and produce a working knowledge base from the file without any programming.

A file of examples consists of rows, similar to those in Figure 5–15. Each row is one example case with the outcome at the end of the row. The case in each row is described by values that are carefully aligned under column headings.

After inducing a knowledge base from the example cases, a shell like 1st CLASS might ignore some columns determined to be unnecessary to reach a conclusion. This kind of optimization may mean that only two questions are necessary to determine a solution, instead of three or more. Also, the columns of values might be reordered into a different sequence determined to be the most efficient to reach a specific recommendation. Such an "induction" system or shell is an ideal KBS prototyping tool.

### The Induce Option

In a less robust way, the Induce option in the VP-Expert system shell can induce a simple knowledge base from a table of examples. Since no optimization occurs,

**Figure 5–16.** A Minimal "Induced" Knowledge Base (No Programming)

Comparisons with the FINAL.TBL file in Figure 5-15

Notes:
. The name of this knowledge base file on the Sample Files disk is HMOIND.KBS.
. This KBS file was created without programming using the FINAL.TBL file and the "Induce" Main Menu option.

```
                ACTIONS
Goal variable {         FIND support
                        DISPLAY "The value of support is {support}";

Row 1 →         RULE 0
                IF      member_status=ok AND
                        reason=new_case AND
                        problem=serious
                THEN    support=level_1;

Row 2 →         RULE 1
                IF      member_status=ok AND
                        reason=new_case AND
                        problem=non_serious
                THEN    support=level_2;

Row 3 →         RULE 2
                IF      member_status=ok AND
                        reason=new_case AND
                        problem=serious
                THEN    support=level_1;

Row 4 →         RULE 3
                IF      member_status=ok AND
                        reason=new_case AND
                        problem=non_serious
                THEN    support=level_3;

Row 5 →         RULE 4
                IF      member_status=ok AND
                        reason=information_other
                THEN    support=information_other;

Row 6 →         RULE 5
                IF      member_status=not_ok
                THEN    support=non_member;

Variable 1 →    ASK member_status: "What is the value of member_status?";
                CHOICES member_status: ok,not_ok;

Variable 2 →    ASK reason: "What is the value of reason?";
                CHOICES reason: new_case,follow_up_case,information_other;

Variable 3 →    ASK problem: "What is the value of problem?";
                CHOICES problem: serious,non_serious;
```

**Figure 5–17.** Consultation Screen from Induced Knowledge Base

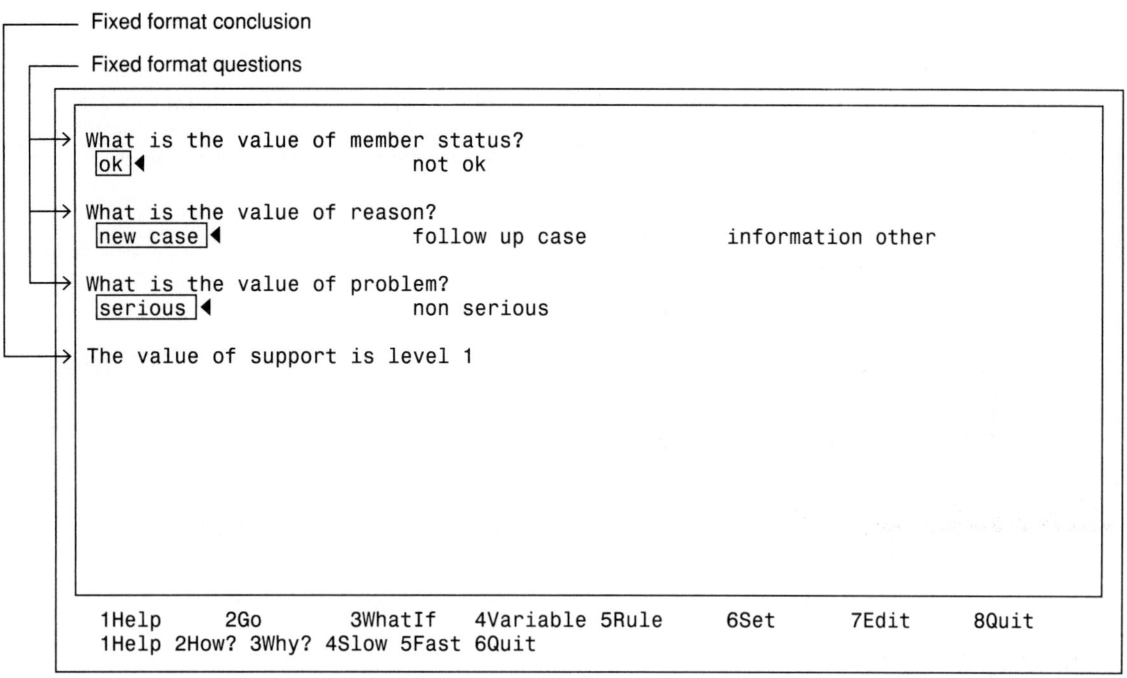


all columns of values remain in the order given and every row becomes one rule in the knowledge base. In effect, the result is more realistically approached as a syntactic transformation of a set of examples into a set of rules. A one-for-one conversion of rows to rules takes place. The procedure to follow to use the induce option in VP-Expert is given in Figure 5–18.

Once a KBS problem has been modeled using decision tables, such as the HMO example in Figure 3–5, it can be converted into rules in a straightforward fashion using the Induce option on VP-Expert's Main Menu. This is one use of the Induce option, since a one-for-one syntactic transformation of the decision table into rules is required.

Even though the HMO example consists of three decision tables (Figures 3–5, 3–7, and 3–9), for the sake of demonstrating use of the Induce option, it temporarily will be assumed to consist of only one decision table. That will be the decision table in Figure 3–5.

***Step 1: Create an Induction Table or File.*** The decision table in Figure 3–5 first must be entered into an induction table or file with a .TBL extension. The detailed procedure for doing this is given in Figure 4–4. Essentially, it consists of

**Figure 5–18**

**Procedure to Create a Table File and "Induce" a Knowledge Base**

The following instructions are written to guide a user, who is sitting at a microcomputer, to create a table file and use it to "induce" a minimal knowledge base. The example aims to create the table file (FINAL) shown in Figure 5–15, and the knowledge base (HMOIND) shown in Figure 5–16.

| Keystrokes | Action |
|---|---|
| i | To select Induce from the Main Menu |
| c | To select Create from the Induce Menu |
| FINAL | To enter the table filename |
| | A blank editing screen appears with the filename in the upper right corner. Type the table columns as shown in Figure 5–15. |
| Alt-F6 | To save the completed table file as FINAL.TBL |
| y | Yes, to confirm. This returns the Induce Menu. |
| t | To indicate a "text" file will be used to induce a knowledge base file |
| Enter | To select the filename FINAL.TBL (which will be under the lightbar) |
| HMOIND | To enter the filename for the knowledge base when asked to "Choose a file:" |
| | The knowledge base is created instantly and invisibly in the background and the Induce Menu appears again. |
| q | To "quit" the Induce Menu and return to the Main Menu |
| e | To enter the "edit" screen to view the "induced" knowledge base file |
| Alt-F8 | To exit the edit screen |
| y | Yes, to confirm the exit without saving the file (it is already saved) and to return to the Main Menu |
| c | To select "consult" to run a consultation |
| g | To select "go" |

going into the Editor, or any word processor that outputs an ASCII text file, and typing the table with the following considerations:

- The top row will become the variable names in the resulting knowledge base.
- The last column will become the conclusion for each rule.
- A star or asterisk symbol (*) represents a "don't care" situation where no specific value is needed.

The completed table should look like the example in Figure 5–15.

From a review of the Induce Menu options in Figure 4–10, it is evident that three kinds of files are acceptable. This HMO example uses the "text" option to create a file with a .TBL extension from scratch. Other options allow inducing a knowledge base from

- a database file with a .DBF filename extension
- a spreadsheet file with a .WKS filename extension

Many organizations have database and spreadsheet files that contain information used for decision making. Sales information, customer information, employee data, and similar kinds of information traditionally are stored in such files. With the Induce feature, files can easily be transformed into knowledge bases that can leverage their decision-making value.

To use the records and fields of an existing database as an induction table, several changes must typically be made, such as:

1. Fields that are not relevant in decision making must be eliminated from the database.
2. A column will usually have to be added at the extreme right of the file. This column contains data representing the conclusion or decision indicated for each row of "decision making" data.
3. Fields containing additional relevant data may need to be added.

Similar changes are necessary to make a spreadsheet file useable as an induction table. Tables created with spreadsheets also have a few restrictions that do not apply to text or database tables, such as:

1. A spreadsheet must contain a blank row under the column headings.
2. There can be no blank cells in columns.
3. There can be no blank rows above or to the left of the table.

Any knowledge base created from any induction table is only as good as the data from which it was induced. In other words, if crucial decision-making factors are absent from the induction table, then the resulting knowledge base will be of questionable value.

***Step 2: Induce the Knowledge Base File.*** After the "induction table" is available in a file, the second step is simple. It requires providing a name for the new knowledge base file. The knowledge base is created instantly and invisibly in the background. In the HMO case, the induced knowledge base file will look like the one in Figure 5–16.

The transformation that occurs can be made visible by viewing the induced knowledge base file using the Editor. The screen shows

- The heading of the last table column is taken as the goal variable used for the FIND keyword in the Actions Block. It is also used to display a message at the end of the consultation session.
- Each table row becomes one rule. Rules start with zero and appear slightly different from the style conventions used for other knowledge bases in this tutorial.
- An ASK statement is generated for all IF condition variables. The values in the corresponding CHOICES statements come from reading down the columns with the appropriate heading.

This "induction" technique creates a minimal rule base, which usually must be modified for appearance or functionality. The consultation screen as shown in Figure 5–17, for example, could use upgrading to appear more user friendly. The fixed format questions and concluding display are minimally acceptable. In addition, the known rules for determining "member_status" and "problem" must be added, and the ASK/CHOICES statements for these variables removed. This rule base then would be functionally equivalent to the one shown in Figure 3–15.

***Limitations of the Induce Option.*** Caution is urged in using the Induce feature. It may not be as useful as it may appear on first glance. One limitation is that it can generate rules only from a single decision table. Since most realistic applications are more complicated than this, other rules need to be added manually to the generated rule base. Once the generated rule base has been modified to add other rules or to change the ASK statements, it cannot be regenerated in its upgraded format from the simpler original decision table.

## CONFIDENCE FACTORS

A method normally used to deal with uncertain data in a knowledge base is to use confidence factors. In Figure 5–19, as an example, the THEN clauses of Rules 9, 10, and 11 use confidence factors. They demonstrate varying levels of confidence that the expert has concerning these conclusions.

A confidence factor is a number attached to a value that indicates the developer/expert's or user's degree of certainty in the value. In VP-Expert, zero indicates no confidence and 100 indicates total confidence or trust in the value. Other development shells may use different scales, such as $-1$ to $+1$ or $-100$ to $+100$, among other possibilities.

A confidence factor is not a statistical probability, although it often is referred to as a percentage. It may be based on subjective intuition or objective criteria to represent how sure one is that a value is correct. It can be compared with other confidence factors and used as a guide. If no confidence factor is expressed, the default value of 100 is normally assumed.

The knowledge base in Figure 5–19 gives an example of how confidence factors are used by a developer or expert. By examining the THEN clauses for Rules 9, 10, and 11, it is evident that the developer/expert has varying degrees of confidence in the conclusions reached. On the one hand, an HMO client who claims to have a normal temperature and no other symptoms is considered, with 99 percent confidence (see Rule 10), to be a non-serious case. On the other hand, the developer/expert is less certain that a client who claims to have a normal temperature and other symptoms is a serious case (see Rule 9). The numbers preceded by CNF express the reliability attached to these conclusions.

Figure 5–20 demonstrates the effect on a consultation of these confidence factors, an effect which is mainly invisible to a user. In this case, the HMO service representative indicates that a client reports a normal temperature and the presence of other symptoms. These conditions cause Rule 9 to fire. The conclusion of Rule 9 automatically assigns the "problem" variable a value of "serious" along with a confidence factor (CNF) of 80. This fact is displayed in the lower-right FACTS window in Figure 5–20.

**Figure 5–19.** A Knowledge Base with Confidence Factors

Notes:
. The name of this knowledge base file on the Sample Files disk is HMOCNF.KBS.
. The blocked areas indicate changes to the original HMO.KBS file (see Figure 3-15).

```
ACTIONS
     DISPLAY "Welcome to the HMO Service Screening Assistant"
     TRUTHTHRESH = 60
     FIND support
     DISPLAY "Recommended support: {# support}."
;

RULE 1
     IF member_status = ok and
        reason = new_case or
        reason = follow_up_case and
        problem = serious
     THEN support = level_1;

RULE 2
     IF member_status = ok and
        reason = new_case and
        problem = non_serious
     THEN support = level_2;

RULE 3
     IF member_status = ok and
        reason = follow_up_case and
        problem = non_serious
     THEN support = level_3;

RULE 4
     IF member_status = ok and
        reason = information_other
     THEN support = information_other;

RULE 5
     IF member_status = not_ok
     THEN support = non_member;

RULE 6
     IF member = yes and
        valid_id = yes
     THEN member_status = ok;
```

**Figure 5–19** *continued*

```
RULE 7
     IF member = yes and
        valid_id = no
     THEN member_status = not_ok;

RULE 8
     IF member = no
     THEN member_status = not_ok;

RULE 9
     IF temperature = normal and
        other_symptoms = yes
     THEN problem = serious cnf 80;

RULE 10
     IF temperature = normal and
        other_symptoms = no
     THEN problem = non_serious cnf 99;

RULE 11
     IF temperature = abnormal or
        temperature = not_known
     THEN problem = serious cnf 90;

ASK member: "Is the person an HMO member?";
CHOICES member: yes, no;

ASK valid_id: "Does the person have a valid HMO `id' number?";
CHOICES valid_id: yes, no;

ASK reason: "What is the reason for coming to the HMO facility?";
CHOICES reason: new_case, follow_up_case, information_other;

ASK temperature: "What is the person's temperature?";
CHOICES temperature: normal, abnormal, not_known;

ASK other_symptoms:  "Does the person claim other symptoms?";
CHOICES other_symptoms: yes, no;
```

The FACTS window shows another item of interest. The CNF from the firing of Rule 9 has a ripple effect. It changes the CNF value for the "support" variable found in Rule 1. Recall that Rule 1 exerts the driving force that causes Rule 9 to fire. Once Rule 9 fires, the final unknown IF condition in Rule 1 is satisfied. The way is then clear to fire Rule 1 itself.

For the purpose of this example, the final recommendation is displayed with a confidence factor. Mechanically this requires including a pound sign (#) inside the curly brackets of the display message, as shown in Figure 5–19.

**Figure 5–20.** Displaying a Confidence Factor with a Recommendation

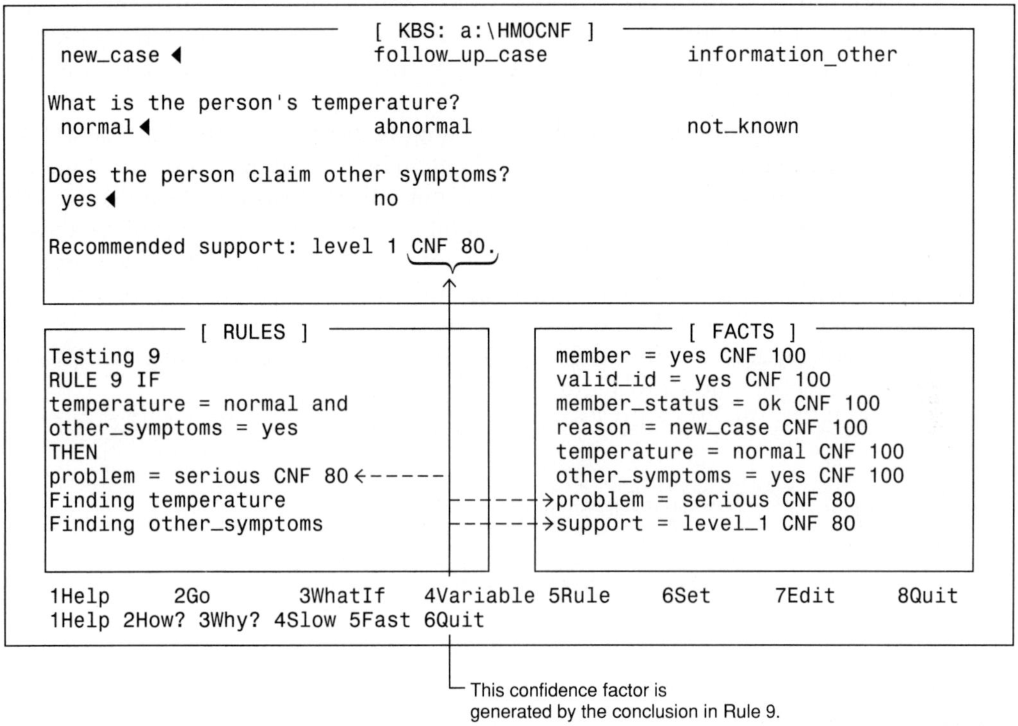


## How Confidence Factors Are Calculated

It is necessary to understand something about how confidence factors are combined and calculated to see how Rule 1 concluded with "support = level 1 CNF 80." For example, reconsider the simpler Rule 9 again. It contains two IF conditions. When one or more AND connectives are used in a rule, the confidence factor is calculated by multiplying the *lowest* confidence factor assigned to the conditions being tested times the confidence factor of the rule conclusion. When Rule 9 is evaluated, the so-called Final-CNF is 1.00 (the lowest default condition CNF) times .80 (the conclusion CNF), or 80 percent.

From this example, it is possible to see how Rule 1 concludes with a CNF of 80. Only one of its conditions has a specific CNF assigned during a consultation. It is "problem = serious CNF 80." All other conditions are assigned the default CNF 100 value. So when Rule 1 fires, the so-called Final-CNF is .80 (the lowest condition CNF) times 1.00 (the default conclusion CNF), or 80 percent.

Confidence factor calculations remain the same when users choose, or are invited to enter, confidence factors for any or all CHOICES selections. For example, consider the consultation shown in the second example in Figure 5–21. The procedure used by the HMO service representative to dynamically enter the "user" confidence factors during a consultation is given at the bottom of Figure 5–21. This procedure can be used to experiment not only with the HMOCNF knowledge base, but also with any other knowledge base on the Samples Files disk.

In the hypothetical case shown in Figure 5–21, assume that the HMO service representative learns from a client that he is almost positive, with 90 percent certainty, that his temperature is normal. He also reports he is only 75 percent certain that he has other symptoms, because an allergy problem always seems to interfere with his well-being. These percentages, entered by a user as confidence factors, affect the calculation of the CNF attached to the recommendation made in Figure 5–21.

Both Figures 5–20 and 5–21 were produced using the same HMOCNF knowledge base (shown in Figure 5–19).

**Figure 5–21.** User Entry of Confidence Factors

```
                         [ KBS: a:\HMOCNF ]
 new_case ◄               follow_up_case            information_other

What is the person's temperature?
→normal  90 ◄             abnormal                  not_known

Does the person claim other symptoms?
→yes 75◄                  no

Recommended support: level 1 CNF 60.

          [ RULES ]                         [ FACTS ]
Testing 9                          member = yes CNF 100
RULE 9 IF                          valid_id = yes CNF 100
temperature = normal and           member_status = ok CNF 100
other_symptoms = yes               reason = new_case CNF 100
THEN                               temperature = normal CNF 90
problem = serious CNF 80           other_symptoms = yes CNF 75
Finding temperature                problem = serious CNF 60
Finding other_symptoms             support = level_1 CNF 60

1Help    2Go      3WhatIf   4Variable  5Rule    6Set     7Edit     8Quit
1Help 2How? 3Why 4Slow 5Fast 6Quit
```

Procedure to enter a confidence factor in response to a question:
1. Move the lightbar ot the desired response.
2. Press the HOME key, then type the confidence factor value.
3. Press the ENTER key to continue.

The calculation to arrive at "problem = serious CNF 60" in Figure 5–21 is straightforward. It involves a rule with two conditions connected by AND. The lowest condition CNF entered is 75. So the Final-CNF is .75 (the lowest condition CNF) times .80 (the conclusion CNF), or 60 percent.

If Rule 9 had an OR connector, and both conditions tested true, a "multiple path formula" would apply as follows:

$$\underset{(CNF1)}{(\text{Condition 1 CNF}} + \underset{(CNF2)}{\text{Condition 2 CNF})} - \underset{(CNF1)}{(\text{Condition 1 CNF}} \times \underset{(CNF2)}{\text{Condition 2 CNF})}$$

Then this condition CNF result would be multiplied by the conclusion CNF to get a Final-CNF. The actual calculation would be as follows:

$$\begin{aligned}
\text{Step 1: Condition CNF} &= (\text{CNF1} + \text{CNF2}) - (\text{CNF1} \times \text{CNF2}) \\
&= (.90 + .75) - (.90 \times .75) \\
&= 1.65 - .68 \\
&= .97 \\
\text{Step 2: Conclusion CNF} &= .80 \\
\text{Step 3: Final-CNF} &= \text{Condition CNF} \times \text{Conclusion CNF} \\
&= .97 \times .80 \\
&= .77
\end{aligned}$$

By contrast, Rule 1 has an OR in it but it is not calculated with the OR "multiple path rule." The reason is that only one of its OR conditions tests true. Rule 1, therefore, is treated as having only AND connectives.

More complex combinations are possible which result in more complex calculations. The *VP-Expert Manual* contains more information on this.

### Truth Threshold

Another method of dealing with uncertain data in a KBS is to set a truth threshold. This is a number, supplied by the developer, to determine the minimum confidence factor required for a rule condition to be considered true.

Each expert system shell sets its own default truth threshold. In VP-Expert it is published in various sources as 40 or 50, while the educational version actually tested at 20! In any case, the developer can control the cutoff point with the keyword TRUTHTHRESH. An example of use is the clause "TRUTHTHRESH = 60" shown in the Actions Block in Figure 5–19.

To experiment with its use, try running a trial consultation with the HMOCNF knowledge base. Enter a confidence factor of 50 for the question about temperature, after selecting "normal." Use the procedure found in Figure 5–21 to enter the confidence factor during the consultation. Since 50 is below the boundary that divides a true from a false condition, Rule 9 fails and the consultation aborts. In order for the rule to pass, both conditions must be true.

New rules would be necessary to handle exceptions gracefully and avoid the abrupt termination of the session.

It is also possible to reset TRUTHTHRESH anywhere after the THEN clause within the KBS rules. Such a setting would affect everything that occurs after the rule passes, until another TRUTHTHRESH clause is encountered.

TRUTHTHRESH in no way affects the conclusion of a rule (the THEN or ELSE parts); it only concerns rule conditions or premises (the IF part). Should the confidence factor of a conclusion CNF value fall below the "truth threshold," the rule will not be prevented from passing.

### Practical Considerations

Using confidence factors should be approached with caution. Unless carefully planned and tested, they can produce unpredictable results. Also, they often become far more complicated to manage than expected.

In practice, confidence factors are reserved for use in special cases or small segments of larger systems. Rarely are they used throughout a full production KBS.

Interestingly, since no approach has been established as a standard, there are various methods of calculating confidence values. It is up to a developer to determine if the approach used by one expert system shell, as opposed to another, best fits a KBS development project.

## REVIEW QUESTIONS

1. What is the importance of database integration with a knowledge-based system?
2. How does a database become mechanically integrated with a KBS?
3. How does a KBS transfer data to a database?
4. What is the purpose of indirect addressing?
5. How is looping, or iterative processing, accomplished?
6. Why is it important to be able to integrate a spreadsheet with a knowledge-based system?
7. How is a spreadsheet mechanically integrated with a KBS?
8. How does a KBS transfer data to a spreadsheet?
9. How are numeric formats handled when transferring data from a KBS to a spreadsheet?
10. How does one use induction to create a knowledge base?
11. What is the meaning of a confidence factor?

## EXERCISES

**1.** This exercise explores KBS and database integration. Run a consultation with the knowledge-base HMODB.KBS from the Sample Files disk. This KBS uses the MEMBER.DBF database file from the Sample Files disk. Enter the following responses:

| *Response* | *Keys to Press to Indicate Response* |
|---|---|
| yes | (Enter, End) |
| 666 | (Enter) |
| new case | (Enter, End) |
| normal | (Enter, End) |
| yes | (Enter, End) |

**a.** Run a second consultation using 123 as the ID (second) entry.
**b.** Compare and record the results observed from the two consultations.
**c.** If possible, use dBase III Plus or dBase IV to add a new record to the MEMBER.DBF database file:

| *Field* | *Entry* |
|---|---|
| ID | 123 |
| P_TYPE | ind |
| LNAME | Ward |
| FNAME | Kim |
| REQUESTS | 9 |

Then repeat Steps 1a and 1b above.
**d.** Obtain a printout of HMODB.KBS. Identify the code that links HMODB.KBS to the MEMBER database file.
**e.** Use the printout of HMODB.KBS and identify all examples of

- indirect addressing
- arithmetic symbols
- relational symbols

**2.** This exercise explores loop processing. Run a consultation with HMODB1.KBS from the Sample Files disk and enter the following responses

| | |
|---|---|
| fam | (Enter, End) |
| 5 | (Enter) |

**a.** Run a second consultation using 0 (numeric zero) as the second entry.
**b.** Compare and record the results observed from the two consultations.
**c.** Obtain a printout of HMODB1.KBS. Identify the code that processes each database record through a loop.

3. This exercise explores KBS and spreadsheet integration. Run a consultation with the knowledge base HMOSS.KBS from the Sample Files disk. This KBS uses the SSHMO.WKS spreadsheet file from the Sample Files disk.
   a. Observe and record the "support" level recommended.
   b. If possible, use Lotus 1-2-3 to view the spreadsheet SSHMO.WKS. Get a "screen dump" of the screen on paper. To do this, first make sure the printer is turned on. While the spreadsheet is displayed on the screen, press the Shift key and Prt Sc key together. Note: Since the file is already saved, it is important to exit the spreadsheet without resaving the file. If it is necessary to save the file, it must be saved with a .WKS (not a .WK1) filename extension.
   c. Run a consultation with HMOSS.KBS. Observe and record the "support" level recommended.
   d. Use Lotus 1-2-3 to view the spreadsheet SSHMO.WKS. Compare the current screen with the earlier "screen dump" and record the difference observed.
   e. Obtain a printout of HMOSS.KBS. Identify the code that links HMOSS.KBS to the SSHMO.WKS spreadsheet file.
4. This exercise examines induction. Use the instructions given in Figure 5–18 (Procedure to Create a Table File and "Induce" a Knowledge Base) to:
   a. Enter the table from Figure 5–15 with the Editor. Save the completed file as MYFINAL.TBL on your exercise disk. When asked to "Choose a file," enter the filename MYIND. Run a consultation using MYIND.
   b. Run a consultation with the knowledge base HMO.KBS. Compare and record the results observed from the consultations with MYIND.KBS and HMO.KBS.
   c. Get printouts of MYIND.KBS and HMO.KBS. Compare and record the differences observed.
   d. Use the instructions given in Figure 5–18 to enter a table of your own design and "induce" a knowledge base.
5. This exercise explores confidence factors. Run a consultation with the knowledge base HMOCNF.KBS from the Sample Files disk.
   a. Enter the following responses:

| *Response* | *Keys to Press to Indicate Response* |
|---|---|
| yes | (Enter, End) |
| new case | (Enter, End) |
| normal | (Enter, End) |
| yes | (Enter, End) |

   b. Observe and record the recommendation made as well as the CNF values displayed in the FACTS window.
   c. Write an explanation of how the final confidence factor was calculated.
   d. Run a consultation with the knowledge base HMO.KBS. Repeat Steps 5a and 5b above.

**e.** Compare and record the differences observed in the two consultations.
**f.** Obtain a printout of HMOCNF.KBS. Identify the code that

- produces the display of the final recommendation CNF value
- gives a CNF value to a rule conclusion

**6.** This exercise continues to explore confidence factors. Run a consultation with the knowledge base HMOCNF.KBS from the Sample Files disk.
**a.** Use the instructions given at the bottom of Figure 5–21 to enter the confidence factors shown in the same figure.
**b.** Write an explanation as to how the final confidence factor was calculated. Write another explanation of how the final confidence factor would be calculated if Rule 9 separated its IF conditions with an OR instead of an AND, and both conditions tested true.
**c.** Copy HMOCNF.KBS to your exercise disk as MYCNF.KBS. Then use MYCNF.KBS and the Editor to change the AND in Rule 9 to an OR. Repeat Step 6a above. Then compare the Final-CNF with the one calculated in 6b above and record the result.

**7.** This exercise explores truth threshold. Run a consultation with the knowledge base HMOCNF.KBS from the Sample Files disk.
**a.** Enter a confidence factor of 50 after "normal" for the question about temperature. Use the instructions found in Figure 5–21 to enter this. Provide an explanation for the results observed in the FACTS window and in the main consultation window.
**b.** Run another consultation and enter a confidence factor of 70 after "normal." Provide an explanation for the results observed in the FACTS window and in the main consultation window.
**c.** Copy HMOCNF.KBS to your exercise disk as MYCNF1.KBS. Then use MYCNF1.KBS and the Editor to change the TRUTHTHRESH value in the Actions Block. Run trial consultations to observe and record the results of the changes on the Final-CNF.

**8.** Develop or enhance a knowledge base of your own design that incorporates one or more of the following features:

- Integration with a database
- Integration with a spreadsheet
- Confidence factors

# 6

# User Interface Improvements to the Knowledge Base and Summary Reference Guide

This chapter concludes the tutorial that began in Chapter 3. Its main focus is on

- Ways to improve the dialogue between the knowledge-based system (KBS) and the user of the system
- Ways to chain a series of knowledge base files together
- A summary of features covered in the entire tutorial

The quality of the user interface, or dialogue between the computer and user during a consultation, can make the difference between whether or not a KBS is actually used in a real-world situation. In many instances, a developer or KBS researcher becomes enamored of the technical capability of the system being developed. Little attention is given to the user-interface requirements of the system. This situation is the main cause, some researchers believe, that some KBS never make the transition from the research or development laboratory to the real world.

In this chapter the basic knowledge base file from Chapter 3 (Figure 3–15) is taken through two levels of user interface improvements. First, screen display enhancements are covered, then, print enhancements. The final result incorporates some design and layout improvements that begin to be representative of more "industrial-strength" KBS.

Since working, sophisticated KBS are often designed in modules, then linked together, chaining knowledge base files is also covered.

The chapter concludes with a section that serves two purposes. First, it serves as a summary of all the important keywords and features discussed in the entire four-chapter tutorial. Second, because all this summary information is consolidated in one place, it can be used as a single-source "reference guide." It will be useful to anyone using this tutorial to construct a KBS.

The recommended learning process for the example incrementally developed in this chapter is:

1. Run the new knowledge base using the file on the samples disk to see how it works. Use the "Procedure for Running a Consultation" (given in Figure 4–2) to do this.
2. Make a copy of the original knowledge base file HMO.KBS (see Figure 3–15), but give it a new knowledge base filename with an "X" or number or other unique identifier.
3. Make incremental changes to the "X" file until it runs or executes exactly like the finished model file. Use the "Procedure for Entering (or Editing) a Knowledge Base" (given in Figure 4–4) to do this.

As mentioned earlier, while the software development tool used is the VP-Expert system shell, the themes discussed are applicable to whatever shell is used. Also, only selected keywords and features are covered in this tutorial. It is advisable to consult the *VP-Expert Manual* for additional information.

## IMPROVING THE USER INTERFACE

Building the user interface of a KBS takes almost as much effort as building the main part of the system. Studies show that developing the user interface for a KBS approximately doubles the resources and time committed to a project. It also increases the coding necessary in the KBS file. This is evident in Figure 6–1. Although the base file is unchanged from Figure 3–15, the additional user interface considerations are responsible for all the added new code.

The crude user interface built into the first KBS effort from Chapter 3 offers many opportunities for improvements. Figure 6–1 is a printout of the revised knowledge base that incorporates user-interface improvements. The improvements include

- a new opening screen (see Figure 6–2)
- a new instructions window (see Figure 6–3)
- a new closing screen (see Figure 6–4)

### Opening Screen

Figure 6–2 shows the improvements made beginning to appear as soon as a user starts a consultation. The new opening screen is colored with a light blue background that has a visually attractive frame around the opening message.

The message now does four things:

- It describes the objective of the consultation.
- It describes how the consultation will work.
- It indicates what kind of closure to expect.
- It puts the user in control to activate the consultation.

These are the kinds of things that a human factors practitioner or researcher would recommend be part of any well-designed application of KBS technology.

The opening screen was created with the code, shown in Figure 6–1, that begins with the first WOPEN keyword and concludes with the first WCLOSE keyword. As explained in Figure 6–5, the WOPEN keyword creates a window on the consultation screen. Each number following the WOPEN keyword has a special meaning. The numbers are called parameters and their purpose is as follows:

| *Parameter Number* | *Parameter Purpose* |
|---|---|
| 1 | The number of the window being opened |
| 2 & 3 | The row and column coordinates of the upper left-hand corner of the window |
| 4 | The number of rows the window occupies (a number from 2 to 77) |
| 5 | The number of columns the window should occupy (a number from 2 to 77) |
| 6 | The color for the background of the window (a number from 0 to 7—see Figure 6–6) |

Although WOPEN defines a consultation window, it does not activate it. The keyword ACTIVE (along with a window number) is required to actually place the window image on the screen.

All following DISPLAY text appears in the activated window. Some trial-and-error is required to discover the best placement of text within a window. Even if the LOCATE keyword is used (see the bottom of the Actions Block in Figure 4–1) to specify row and column placement for text within a window, some experimentation is needed to arrive at a visually pleasing window arrangement.

The tilde character (˜) at the end of the DISPLAY message causes the message to pause until the user presses any key. Any number of tildes can be used in the DISPLAY clause.

### Instructions Window

Figure 6–3 shows that the user interface design improvements include an "instructions" window. It has a uniquely colored background to set it apart from

**Figure 6–1.** First Knowledge Base with an Improved User Interface

Notes:
. The name of this knowledge base file on the Sample Files disk file is HMOUSER.KBS.
. Blocked areas indicate new additions (to HMO.KBS)

```
! HMO Service Screening Assistant
! with an improved user interface
! Saved as HMOUSER.KBS
!*************************************************************************
BKCOLOR = 3;                    !set screen background color to light blue
RUNTIME;                                !eliminate rules and facts windows
ENDOFF;                        !eliminate need to press END after a choice

!=============================== Actions Block ===========================
ACTIONS
     WOPEN 1,3,10,13,60,7                          !define opening window 1
     ACTIVE 1                                            !activate window 1
     DISPLAY "

              HMO Service Screening Assistant

  This consultation assists you to screen a person who
  enters an HMO facility.  It asks a series of questions
  about the person, then recommends a level of support
  appropriate to the person's needs.

  Please press any key to begin the consultation.~

       "
    WCLOSE 1                                               !remove window 1
    WOPEN 1,1,1,5,77,2                              !define instructions w
    ACTIVE 1                                             !activate window 1
    DISPLAY "                         Instructions
         Use the arrow keys to move the lightbar to a desired
         answer choice then press the Enter key."
    WOPEN 2,7,1,14,77,3                       !define consultation window 2
    ACTIVE 2                                             !activate window 2
    FIND support
    WCLOSE 1                                               !remove window 1
    WCLOSE 2                                               !remove window 2
    WOPEN 1,5,13,9,48,7          !define concluding recommendation window 1
    WOPEN 2,6,14,7,46,7               !define window 2 (nested in window 1)
```

**Figure 6–1** *continued*

```
     ACTIVE 2                                                 !activate window 2
     LOCATE 1,9                            !specify row and column for next display
     DISPLAY "Based on the answers given,
         the recommended support is:
                  {support}.
(Press any key to conclude the consultation.)~"
;
!============================== Rules Block ==============================

RULE 1
     IF member_status = ok and
        reason = new_case or
        reason = follow_up_case and
        problem = serious
     THEN support = level_1;

RULE 2
     IF member_status = ok and
        reason = new_case and
        problem = non_serious
     THEN support = level_2;

RULE 3
     IF member_status = ok and
        reason = follow_up_case and
        problem = non_serious
     THEN support = level_3;

RULE 4
     IF member_status = ok and
        reason = information_other
     THEN support = information_other;

RULE 5
     IF member_status = not_ok
     THEN support = non_member;

RULE 6
     IF member = yes and
        valid_id = yes
     THEN member_status = ok
     BECAUSE "Validated members are provided with medical support, while
     non-members are provided with other appropriate support.";

RULE 7
     IF member = yes and
        valid_id = no
     THEN member_status = not_ok;
```

```
RULE 8
     IF member = no
     THEN member_status = not_ok;

RULE 9
     IF temperature = normal and
        other_symptoms = yes
     THEN problem = serious
     BECAUSE "The presence of an abnormal temperature or other symptoms
     indicate a serious problem that requires immediate attention.";

RULE 10
     IF temperature = normal and
        other_symptoms = no
     THEN problem = non_serious;

RULE 11
     IF temperature = abnormal or
        temperature = not_known
     THEN problem = serious;

!=============================== Questions Block =========================

ASK member: "Is the person an HMO member?";
CHOICES member: yes, no;

ASK valid_id: "Does the person have a valid HMO `id' number?";
CHOICES valid_id: yes, no;

ASK reason: "What is the reason for coming to the HMO facility?";
CHOICES reason: new_case, follow_up_case, information_other;

ASK temperature: "What is the person's temperature?";
CHOICES temperature: normal, abnormal, not_known;

ASK other_symptoms:  "Does the person claim other symptoms?";
CHOICES other_symptoms: yes, no;
```

the main consultation window. This design has the instructions window remain on the screen during the entire consultation.

The instructions convey precise directions to anyone consulting the KBS. Such detailed keystroke-by-keystroke instruction is helpful especially to non-technically-oriented computer users. Some users are afraid of making a mistake and freeze over a computer keyboard. Simple, clear operating instructions go a long way toward improving a user's comfort level at the computer and with the software.

**Figure 6–2.** User Interface Improvements—Opening Screen

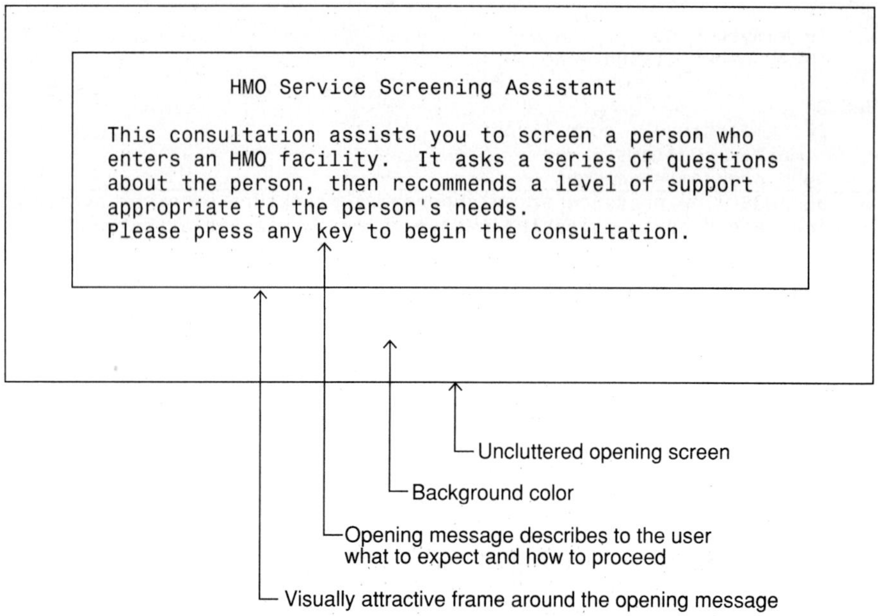


The instructions window is defined by the second WOPEN keyword in the knowledge base printout shown in Figure 6–1. It is activated just before the full consultation window, which is defined by the third WOPEN keyword on the printout.

During a user session, if questioning continues beyond the window space available, information scrolls off the top edge of the consultation window section and disappears from the screen. This scrolling technique is common in modern software design.

Another improvement that could be evident to a user during a consultation appears in the Rules Block. It is the addition of BECAUSE text to Rules 7 and 10. BECAUSE is used to provide explanatory text in response to the Why? command given by a user during a consultation. When BECAUSE text is not provided, and a user issues the Why? command, an appropriate IF-THEN rule is displayed. This is far less user-friendly than providing a logical explanation in idiom that the user understands.

Frequently, developers use the BECAUSE keyword to document the source or reference for a rule. In a KBS that assists tax auditors, for example, a feature similar to BECAUSE is used to document sections of the tax law that influence the expertise in the rule or its conclusion.

**Figure 6–3.** Instructions Window

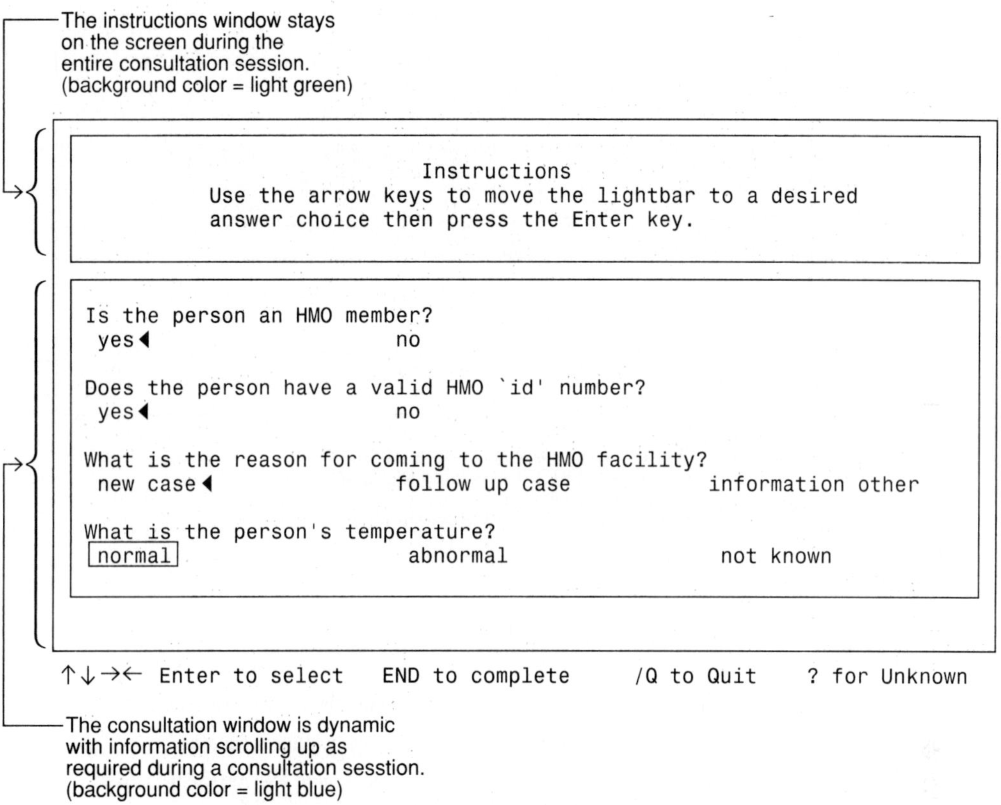


## Closing Screen

The consultation ends with a simple message in a double frame on an uncluttered screen, as shown in Figure 6–4. The message states that the user's input, or responses, played the key role in arriving at a recommendation. The recommendation itself is highlighted by its presence on a line by itself. Finally, control is returned to the user in the request to "Press any key to conclude the consultation."

The fourth and fifth WOPEN statements in the listing in Figure 6–1 created the double-frame, or nested, windows shown in Figure 6–4. Only the last-defined window, number 2, is activated to DISPLAY the text that follows.

Text is placed inside the display space with the help of the LOCATE keyword. Its parameters are the starting row and column coordinates where text is to be placed inside the window.

**Figure 6–4.** A Nested Window Example—Closing Screen

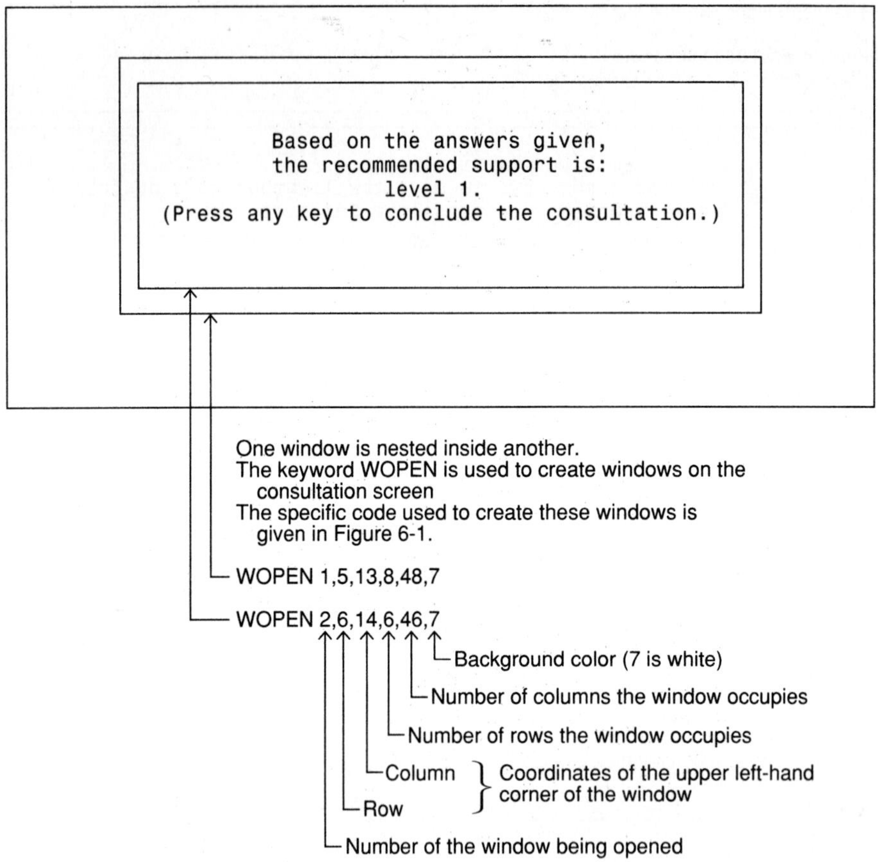


### Other Improvements

Three other improvements are not as obvious as the windows. They are features introduced with the addition of new keywords:

| *Keyword* | *Action* |
|---|---|
| BKCOLOR | Used to set the background color of the consultation screen. |
| RUNTIME | Eliminates the Rules and Facts windows from the consultation screen. |
| ENDOFF | Eliminates the need to hit the End key when finished choosing answers to a question. |

**Figure 6–5**

### Creating a Window

WOPEN is used to create a window on the consultation screen. (Note: A knowledge base can contain a maximum of 9 WOPEN windows). It requires six parameters. The meaning of these parameters is as follows:

| Parameter Number | Parameter Purpose |
|---|---|
| 1 | The number of the window being opened (a number from 1 to 9) |
| 2 & 3 | The row and column coordinates of the upper left-hand corner of the window |
| 4 | The number of rows the window should occupy (a number from 2 to 77) |
| 5 | The number of columns the window should occupy (a number from 2 to 77) |
| 6 | The color for the background of the window (a number from 0 to 7) |

Each parameter must be typed in the sequence noted, followed by a comma only (no space), as in the following example:

WOPEN 1,5,13,8,48,7

**Related Keywords**

ACTIVE is used to activate a window. The keyword ACTIVE is followed by a single number from 0 to 9. This is the number of the window inside which the following DISPLAY text is to appear. This number will be the same as the first parameter of the corresponding WOPEN clause, except for the number zero. ACTIVE 0 will cause the text to be DISPLAYed on the default, or regular, Consult (three-window) screen.

LOCATE is used to specify where in the active text window the next executed DISPLAY text should begin. The keyword LOCATE is followed by two number parameters. These are the row and column coordinates inside the designated ACTIVE window where the next DISPLAY text is to begin. (Note: Trial runs are frequently necessary to place text accurately in a window.)

WCLOSE is used to remove text windows created using the WOPEN clause. When a window is removed, the contents of the text window are erased as well. The keyword WCLOSE is followed by a single integer to specify the window number in a previously executed WOPEN instruction.

These keywords normally appear grouped together at the beginning of a knowledge base. Figure 6–7 shows this order in its "Suggested Structure for a Knowledge Base."

During debugging, it is often helpful to disable the RUNTIME feature. The simplest way to do this is to put an exclamation point in front of the keyword. The inference engine ignores any text after an exclamation point. Such text is regarded as comment or "memo" items.

**Figure 6–6.** Color Choices

For Background (BKCOLOR keyword)

| Number | Color Represented |
|---|---|
| 0 | Black |
| 1 | Blue |
| 2 | Green |
| 3 | Light Blue |
| 4 | Red |
| 5 | Magenta |
| 6 | Brown |
| 7 | White |

For Text (COLOR keyword)

| Number for Normal | Color Represented | Number for Blinking |
|---|---|---|
| 0 | Black | 16 |
| 1 | Blue | 17 |
| 2 | Green | 18 |
| 3 | Cyan | 19 |
| 4 | Red | 20 |
| 5 | Magenta | 21 |
| 6 | Brown | 22 |
| 7 | White | 23 |
| 8 | Gray | 24 |
| 9 | Light Blue | 25 |
| 10 | Light Green | 26 |
| 11 | Light Cyan | 27 |
| 12 | Light Red | 28 |
| 13 | Light Magenta | 29 |
| 14 | Yellow | 30 |
| 15 | Bright White | 31 |

Typically, any text preceded by an exclamation point is a comment by the KBS developer to document what is going on in the knowledge base. The comments are sometimes called **remarks** or **in-program documentation** or internal documentation. These comments help anyone, such as another developer or a user, to understand the knowledge base. They are especially valuable if a KBS prototype is passed on to other developers for full production. Also, they help users or others who have the continuing responsibility to maintain or revitalize the knowledge base once it is released from development.

**Figure 6–7.** Suggested Structure for a Knowledge Base

Capitalized words are the most common keywords used in the construction of a knowledge base.

```
                         EXECUTE;
User                     BKCOLOR = <number>;
Consultation             RUNTIME;
Considerations           ENDOFF;

                         ACTIONS
                         <keyword instruction1>
                         <keyword instruction2>
Actions to Be Followed             .
                                   .
                                   .
                         ;

                         RULE <label1>
                               IF  AND/OR
                               THEN
                               ELSE
The Rule Base                  BECAUSE "__________";

                         RULE <label2>
                                   .
                                   .
                                   .;

Questions and Information  ASK <variable>: "<text>";
about Variables            CHOICES <variable>: <value>;
                           PLURAL <variable>;
```

In addition to the comments, physical layout considerations also make the knowledge base easier to understand. All the lines inside the Actions Block are evenly indented, except for DISPLAY text which breaks out of the alignment due to actual screen alignment considerations. Also, horizontal lines separate major segments of the knowledge base. This facilitates focusing on one segment of the knowledge base as a single problem distinct from the rest during debugging sessions.

## ADDITIONAL ENHANCEMENTS AND KEYWORDS

As a knowledge base is incrementally improved, physical layout considerations become more important to help keep track of the increasingly refined logic. Consider, for instance, the example in Figure 6–8. The main improvement here

**Figure 6–8.** Enhancing the Knowledge Base with Customized Conclusions

Notes:
. The name of this knowledge base file on the Sample Files disk is HMOADD1.KBS.
. Blocked areas indicate new additions (to HMOUSER.KBS)

```
! HMO Service Screening Assistant
! with additional enhancements: customized conclusions
! Saved as HMOADD1.KBS

!**************************************************************************
                                     !set screen background color to light blue
BKCOLOR = 3;                                !eliminate rules and facts windows
RUNTIME;

!============================ Actions Block ============================

ACTIONS
     WOPEN 1,3,10,13,60,7                             !define opening window 1
     ACTIVE 1                                               !activate window 1
     DISPLAY "

              HMO Service Screening Assistant

   This consultation assists you to screen a person who
   enters an HMO facility.  It asks a series of questions
   about the person, then recommends a level of support
   appropriate to the person's needs.

   Please press any key to begin the consultation.~

      "
     WCLOSE 1                                                 !remove window 1
     COLOR = 20                      !set following text color to blinking red
     DISPLAY "          CAUTION!"
     COLOR = 4                         !set following text to non-blinking red
     DISPLAY "Please make sure your printer in ON."
     DISPLAY "Press any key to continue.~"
     CLS                                                    !clear the screen
     COLOR = 0                             !set following text to normal black
     WOPEN 1,1,1,6,77,2                         !define instructions window 1
     ACTIVE 1                                              !activate window 1
     DISPLAY "                           Instructions
          Use the arrow keys to move the lightbar to a desired
          answer choice then press Enter key.
          Press the End key to move to the next question."
     WOPEN 2,8,1,13,77,2                        !define consultation window 2
     ACTIVE 2                                              !activate window 2
     FIND support
     FIND message                          !set sub-goal to customize messages
     DISPLAY "Press any key to conclude this consultation.~"
```

```
;
!============================ Rules Block ===============================

!-------------------- Rule Set 1: Recommendations -----------------------

RULE 1_1                                   !number rules to correspond to rule set
     IF member_status = ok and
        reason = new_case or
        reason = follow_up_case and
        problem = serious
     THEN support = level_1
             room = room 201;                        !assign a value to a variable

RULE 1_2
     IF member_status = ok and
        reason = new_case and
        problem = non_serious
     THEN support = level_2
             room = room_202;                        !assign a value to a variable

RULE 1_3
     IF member_status = ok and
        reason = follow_up_case and
        problem = non_serious
     THEN support = level_3
             room = room 203;                        !assign a value to a variable

RULE 1_4
     IF member_status = ok and
        reason = information_other
     THEN support = information_other;

RULE 1_5
     IF member_status = not_ok
     THEN support = non_member;

!-------------------- Rule Set 2: Member Status -------------------------

RULE 2_1
     IF member = yes and
        valid_id = yes
     THEN member_status = ok
        FIND id_number                                      !get direct user input
     BECAUSE "Validated members are provided with medical support,
     while non-members are provided with other appropriate support.";

RULE 2_2
     IF member = yes and
        valid_id = no
     THEN member_status = not_ok;

RULE 2_3
     IF member = no
     THEN member_status = not_ok;
```

**Figure 6–8** *continued*

```
!----------- Rule Set 3: Problem (Determine seriousness) -------------------

RULE 3_1
     IF temperature = normal and
        other_symptoms = yes
     THEN problem = serious
     BECAUSE "The presence of an abnormal temperature or other symptoms
     indicate a serious problem that requires immediate attention.";

RULE 3_2
     IF temperature = normal and
        other_symptoms = no
     THEN problem = non_serious;

RULE 3_3
     IF temperature = abnormal or
        temperature = not_known and
        other_symptoms = yes
     THEN problem = serious
     BECAUSE "The presence of an abnormal temperature or other symptoms
     indicate a serious problem that requires immediate attention.";
```

```
!--------------------- Rule Set 4: Concluding Messages --------------------

RULE message_level123                  !use a meaningful name for a rule label
     IF support = level_1 or
        support = level_2 or
        support = level_3
     THEN message = print_form
        PRINTON                      !send display text to screen and printer
        DISPLAY "Authorization Form For Service - {support}"
        DISPLAY "ID: {id_number}"
        DISPLAY "Reason: {reason}"
        DISPLAY "Self-reported: temperature - {temperature}"
        DISPLAY "                symptoms - {other_symptoms}"
        PRINTOFF                                         !disable printon
        PDISPLAY "Kindly go to {room} for service."       !send text only
                                                              !to printer
        FIND co_pay                  !set sub-goal to determine co-pay charges
        EJECT                          !move printer paper to top of next page
        DISPLAY ""                                   !display one blank line
        DISPLAY "Please tear the Authorization Form off the printer.";

        RULE check_co_pay            !single rule to determine co-pay charges
             IF id_number > 999999
             THEN co_pay = yes
                  PDISPLAY"(Co-Payment charge of $8.00 made for service.)";

RULE message_non_member
     IF support = non_member
     THEN message = station_Z
        DISPLAY "Appropriate service is available at {message}.";
```

```
RULE message_info
     IF support = information_other
     THEN message = station_X
         DISPLAY "Appropriate service is available at {message}.";

!============================ Questions Block =============================

ASK member: "Is the person an HMO member?";
CHOICES member: yes, no;

ASK valid_id: "Does the person have a valid HMO `id' number?";
CHOICES valid_id: yes, no;

ask id_number: "What is the `id' number?";

ASK reason: "What is the reason for coming to the HMO facility?";
CHOICES reason: new_case, follow_up_case, information_other;

ASK temperature: "What is the person's temperature?";
CHOICES temperature: normal, abnormal, not_known;

ASK other_symptoms:  "Does the person claim other symptoms?";
CHOICES other_symptoms: yes, no;
```

is to customize the recommendations made by the HMO Service Screening Assistant. Figure 6–9 illustrates the main changes made.

An "Authorization Form for Service" is printed on the spot to give to the HMO client. The form contains the available client information, including three new items of interest:

- The client's ID number is used to make an automatic determination of whether or not the client participates in a co-payment plan and is charged a nominal fee for service. Any HMO member with an ID number greater than 999999, for this example case, is assessed a fixed co-payment fee.
- A specific room-location number tells the client where the required support is administered. There is a different room for each level of service support offered.
- If appropriate, a reminder is printed on the "Authorization Form" that a co-payment charge is to be collected for service.

The blocked areas of the knowledge base printout, shown in Figure 6–8, indicate the exact changes made to implement the improvements. A new rule set

**Figure 6–9.** Using the PRINTON and PDISPLAY Keywords

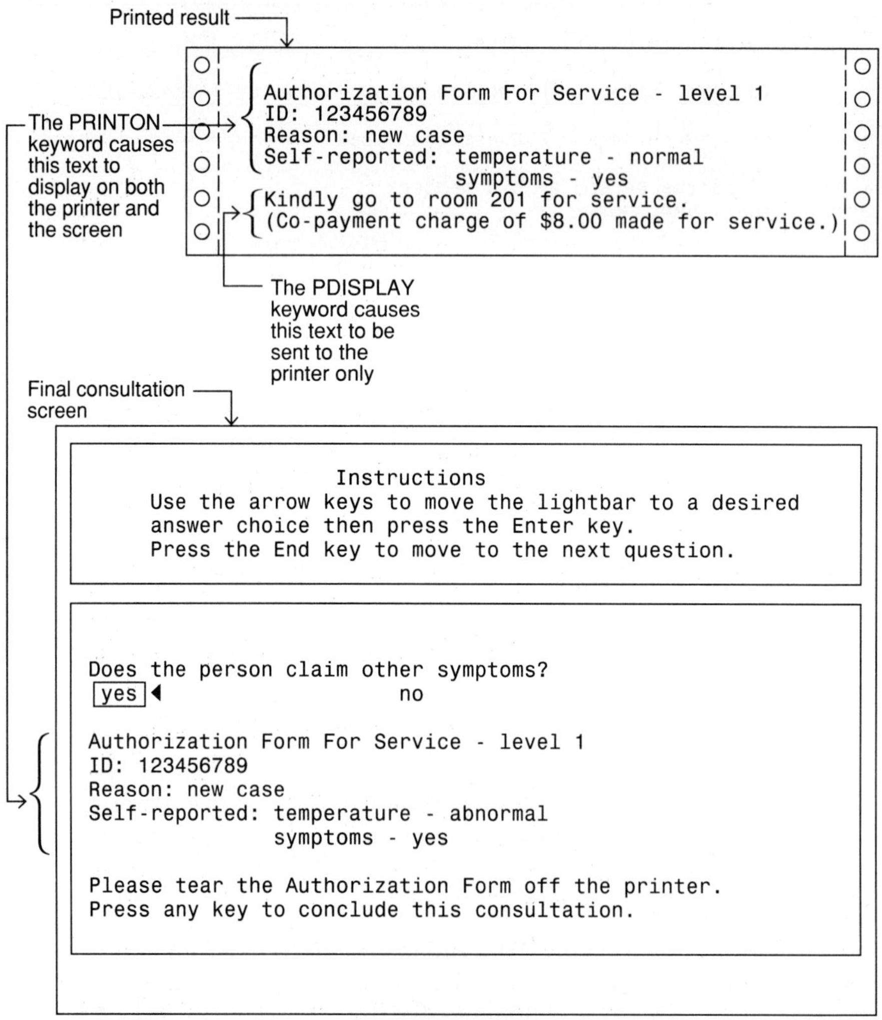


is added to customize the concluding messages. Each of the changes is discussed more fully in the following sections.

To make the growing knowledge base easier to follow, the physical layout has been improved, as has the in-program documentation. For example:

- Rule sets are labeled and separated from each other with horizontal lines. Rule sets one to three contain the same eleven rules shown earlier in Figures 3–15 and 6–1.

- Rule labels have meaningful names or numbers that easily relate a rule to a rule set.
- All instructions that relate to a rule are either: (a) subordinated under the rule that controls execution (see the THEN part of rule message_level123), or (b) set apart in a separate rule set (see Rule Set 4: Concluding Messages).

It is recommended that the reader run a consultation using the file HMOADD1.KBS on the samples disk to examine how the design enhancements described in this section work.

The best way to learn how to use the keywords and features described in this section is to upgrade the base file HMOUSER.KBS to include the enhancements made to HMOADD1.KBS. To do this:

1. Start with the base file, which is HMOUSER.KBS. Make a copy of it and name the copy XHMOADD1.KBS. An example of how this can be done at the DOS prompt is: copy B:HMOUSER.KBS B:XHMOADD1.KBS/V <Enter>.
2. Use the new file (XHMOADD1.KBS) and incrementally add changes until the file runs or executes exactly as the HMOADD1.KBS model.

This procedure is highly recommended to learn each incremental upgrade in this tutorial.

## Color Text

The first enhancement shown in the Actions Block of Figure 6–8 is DISPLAY text that not only is differently colored, but also is set to blinking. Figure 6–10 illustrates the effect of this change on the user's consultation screen.

Blinking red text (COLOR = 20), used for the word "CAUTION," alerts a user to the importance of the message that follows. Figure 6–6 shows that the keyword COLOR can be assigned up to 32 numbers (0–31) that give text either normal or blinking color attributes.

**Figure 6–10.** Using the COLOR Keyword

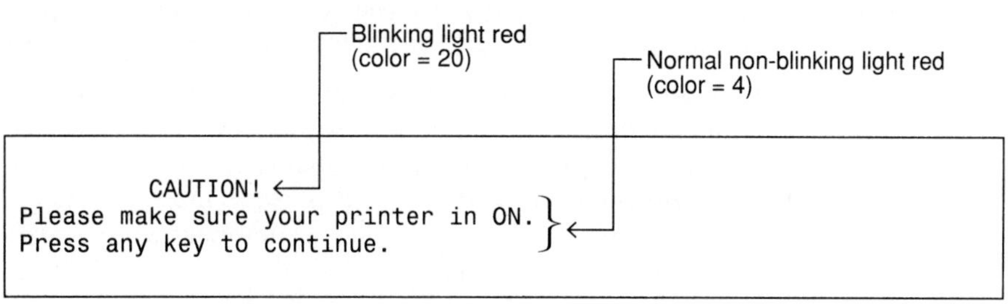

After the blinking text, normal red text (COLOR = 4) is used for instructions that tell the user to make sure the printer is turned on and to signal the program to continue. Unlike previously displayed messages, this one repeatedly uses the DISPLAY keyword for each line of text displayed. This alternative way of displaying text often makes it easier to control text placement on the screen. If the printer is not turned on, displays that are directed to the printer will instead be sent to the screen.

Once the user signals the program to continue, the keyword CLS clears the screen. Text is restored to normal black (COLOR = 0).

### Multiple FIND Goals

The Actions Block now has two FIND goals. The first one, FIND support, works exactly as it did in the original HMO example in Figure 3–15. The new one, FIND message, is used to return control to the Rules Block in order to customize the recommendation from a consultation session. The added "Rule Set 4: Concluding Messages" provides solutions (in the THEN part of the rules) for the goal FIND message. Once these rules serve to customize a conclusion, by either printing or displaying a message, control returns to the Actions Block and the session terminates.

An overview of the three main rules that make up this new rule set follows:

- Rule message_level123 prints the "Authorization Form for Service" shown in Figure 6–9. Only sessions that conclude with a support level of 1, 2, or 3 end with a printed form. The THEN part of the rule uses a dummy word, in this case "print_form," which serves only to send the inference engine to execute all of the remaining instructions below THEN. Technically, the THEN part of the rule does not conclude until the semicolon after the word "printer," about 13 lines below the THEN keyword.

  As evident from the instructions shown, the expanded THEN portion of the rule resembles the type of instructions formerly associated with the Actions Block. This example demonstrates how convenient it is to execute procedural tasks right in the THEN portion of a rule, if appropriate.

  Observe that the THEN portion of this rule also sets up its own sub-goal, FIND co-pay. Since the sub-goal is solved with only one rule, that rule is included and indented right under the controlling rule.
- Rule message_non_member displays a screen message that indicates where appropriate service is available for non-members.
- Rule message_info displays a screen message that indicates where appropriate service is available for members who require information or other non-member services.

Another FIND keyword appears after the THEN clause in Rule 2–1. In this case, FIND is used only to get a direct user response to the new ASK question

"What is the 'id' number?" Any number the user enters during the consultation is assigned to the variable "id_number." Because an entry is expected, the ASK question is not followed by a CHOICES keyword.

The ID number is used in "rule check_co_pay" to determine if an HMO member owes a fixed nominal co-payment fee for services. Only members with ID numbers greater than (indicated by the > symbol) 999999 are assessed the fee.

### Print Options

The "rule message_level123" uses two print options that are illustrated in Figure 6–9. The first is PRINTON which is used to send text to both the screen and the printer. All DISPLAY messages following PRINTON go to both devices until a PRINTOFF keyword disables the feature.

In the example, the first five lines of the "Authorization Form" are sent to both the screen and the printer. They include customized data supplied by values in the following variables:

- support
- id number
- reason
- temperature
- other-symptoms

A sixth line is sent only to the printer by using the PDISPLAY keyword. The line includes the room number where the HMO client is to go for appropriate service support. The room number is set with a variable assignment appended to Rules 1–1, 1–2, and 1–3.

The PDISPLAY keyword is also used to print a seventh optional line. It alerts a member that a co-payment charge for service is made. Only members who have the co-pay plan see this printed message.

After all information is printed on the "Authorization Form," the EJECT keyword moves the printed paper to the top of the next page. The HMO service representative then sees a reminder message on the screen to tear the form off the printer. The form is given to the HMO client as a formal document to receive the type of service indicated at the location specified. In a real situation, the form would be printed on multi-part paper. One part would serve as a receipt for payment of the service fee. It would include the name and address of the HMO organization, as well as other pertinent information.

## WHENEVER: FORWARD CHAINING

Even though backward chaining is the control strategy used by VP-Expert, a WHENEVER rule provides a means for performing forward chaining. (For a full discussion of forward chaining, see Chapters 2 and 8.) Consider the following example:

```
WHENEVER message_non_member
IF support = non_member
THEN DISPLAY "Appropriate service is available at
station Z.";
```

This rule is automatically checked any time the value of the variable named in the IF statement, in this case "support," changes.

This WHENEVER rule provides what is known in artificial intelligence programming as a **demon.** It watches the variable(s) referenced by its IF condition(s) and executes each time the condition(s) evaluates as true. This causes the inference engine to jump out of its backward chaining search strategy and, instead, leap forward to execute the appropriate WHENEVER rule, wherever it appears in the knowledge base. In the example in Figure 6–8, the WHENEVER rule would cause an immediate forward chain to itself the moment the variable "support" is set to "non_member" in Rule 1–5.

One restriction is that a WHENEVER rule cannot have a FIND keyword in its conclusion. This eliminates using it for the first rule in "Rule Set 4: Concluding Messages." It could, however, have been used for the last rule, message_info, of the same rule set.

Unlike standard rules, the WHENEVER rule does not require a typical THEN conclusion of assigning a value to a variable. As the example demonstrates, it is possible to follow the THEN keyword with another keyword. In the example, the DISPLAY keyword follows the THEN clause. The example is saved on the samples disk as filename HMOADD1F.KBS.

## PLURAL VARIABLES

The PLURAL keyword identifies "plural variables," or variables that can be assigned multiple values during a consultation, as shown in Figure 6–11. When the inference engine sets out to find values for PLURAL variables, it "assigns" to them as many values as it possibly can before ending the search.

Figure 6–12 illustrates additions to the HMO Service Screening Assistant that show how the PLURAL keyword is used. The example is saved on the samples disk as HMOADD2.KBS. The extension concerns a consultation where the HMO client requires "information" or "other" services. In this case, the system asks "What kind(s) of information is (are) desired?" The service representative could indicate that the client requires information on one or more of the following:

- individual plan
- family plan
- co-pay plan
- other

**Figure 6–11.** Using the PLURAL Keyword

Two PLURAL variables: (1) interest_areas (makes multiple answers possible)
(2) info_help (makes multiple conclusions possible)

```
What is the reason for coming to the HMO facility?
 new case                  follow up case          information other

What kind(s) of information is (are) desired?
 individual plan         family plan            co pay plan
 other

Service is available for plan type / at: co pay other station Z
family station Y
individual station X
Press any key to conclude this consultation.
```

Based on the items selected, the system displays where the requested information or service is available. As evident from Figure 6–11, the display of PLURAL variables is limited and somewhat awkward without more extensive programming.

Figure 6–12 shows one FIND keyword added to "rule message_info" that is used to get direct user input about what kind of information is desired. This requires the addition of an ASK question to the Questions Block to get a member's "interest_areas." Because one or more CHOICES items can be selected to answer the question, the "interest_areas" variable is declared to be PLURAL. This is done in the last line of code in the knowledge base.

To select more than one item, the user must move the lightbar over a selection and hit the Enter key. After all selections are made, the End key must be pressed. The reminder to press the End key, even after single-valued variables, is coded in the second box in Figure 6–8. This reminder is necessary because the keyword ENDOFF is deleted from this knowledge base. Its absence allows a user to make mistakes or change answers without penalty. Changes are made with the DEL delete key. In some cases, the extra step of having a user hit both the Enter and End keys to record a choice is desirable. In other cases, it can be an annoyance.

A second variable name, "info_help," also appears in the PLURAL statement at the end of the knowledge base. It identifies the PLURAL nature of the FIND sub-goal in "rule message_info." Any or all of the three rules in Rule Set 5 can satisfy the sub-goal "info_help" through THEN clauses. As evident from Figure 6–11, all these rules can fire for a single consultation, if appropriate.

**Figure 6–12.** Additions to Explore PLURAL Variables

Notes:
. The name of this knowledge base file on the Sample Files disk is HMOADD2.KBS.
. Blocked areas indicate new additions to HMOADD1.KBS. See Figure 6-8 for the parts of this file not shown here.

```
RULE message_info
     IF support = information_other
     THEN message = display_service
        FIND interest_areas                          !get direct user input
        FIND info_help                   !set sub-goal to customize messages
        DISPLAY "Service is available for plan type / at: {info_help}";

!------------------- Rule Set 5: Information Help Messages ---------------

RULE 5-1
     IF interest_areas = individual_plan
     THEN info_help = individual_station_X;

RULE 5-2
     IF interest_areas = family_plan
     THEN info_help = family_station_Y;

RULE 5-3
     IF interest_areas = co_pay_plan or
        interest_areas = other
     THEN info_help = co_pay_other_station_Z;
 .
 .
 .

ASK interest_areas: "What kind(s) of information is (are) desired?";
CHOICES interest_areas: individual_plan, family_plan, co_pay_plan, other;

PLURAL: interest_areas, info_help;
```

Figure 6–13 shows an expanded dependency diagram that summarizes all the current changes to the HMO Service Screening Assistant. It shows the "fan in" to a recommendation and the "fan-out" to a customized conclusion. All information comes from old data, except "interest_areas." Since "interest_areas" comes from direct user input, it is shown with the conventional initial question mark.

## CHAINING KNOWLEDGE BASES

If a knowledge base file becomes too large, it runs slowly or not at all when a computer does not have enough memory. One solution is to divide the large file into two or more smaller files. The CHAIN, SAVEFACTS, and LOADFACTS keywords, described in Figure 6–14, enable a KBS developer to "chain" together two or more knowledge bases for use in a single consultation.

The chaining feature encourages the modular development of very large KBS. Each module remains a smaller independent subset of the whole KBS. This enables each subset to be designed, coded, and maintained more easily and—if necessary—by different developers.

The educational version of VP-Expert used for this tutorial allows the chaining of only three 16-Kbyte knowledge base files. The regular version is not limited in the size or number of files that can be chained.

In some cases, it may be practical to chain two knowledge bases together to obtain information not available from each knowledge base alone. For example, one investment advisory knowledge base may determine that a client should consider investing in bonds. Another knowledge base may advise a client about which bonds are best to consider. The chained knowledge bases offer a more comprehensive system than either stand-alone KBS.

### A Chaining Example

To examine how chaining works, the HMOADD2.KBS file is separated into two modules. Each module is a smaller logical segment of the larger KBS. The two modules roughly concern the following logic:

| *Logic Segment* | *Sequence* | *Filename* |
|---|---|---|
| FIND support<br>This is the original kernel of the HMO Service Screening Assistant | 1 | MODULE1.KBS |
| FIND message<br>This is the added module that customizes the concluding messages | 2 | MODULE2.KBS |

For the sake of this example, assume that the two logic segments were created by different developers and it is decided to CHAIN the finished modules together.

As evident in Figure 6–15, the logic embodied in MODULE1.KBS is the opening message and main "FIND support" goal. Most of this code is not shown because it duplicates that shown in Figure 6–8, except for Rule Set 4.

To a user, this KBS produces screens during a consultation that are similar to those in Figures 6–2 and 6–3.

Once a "support" level is known, there is a pause and a screen message indicates "Loading file..." This message is automatically generated by the CHAIN keyword. CHAIN causes the MODULE2 knowledge base file to be loaded for continuing the rest of the consultation. (Although the example does not show it, a path name can prefix any filename used in the knowledge base. No filename extension is allowed.)

**Figure 6–13.** Expanded Dependency Diagram

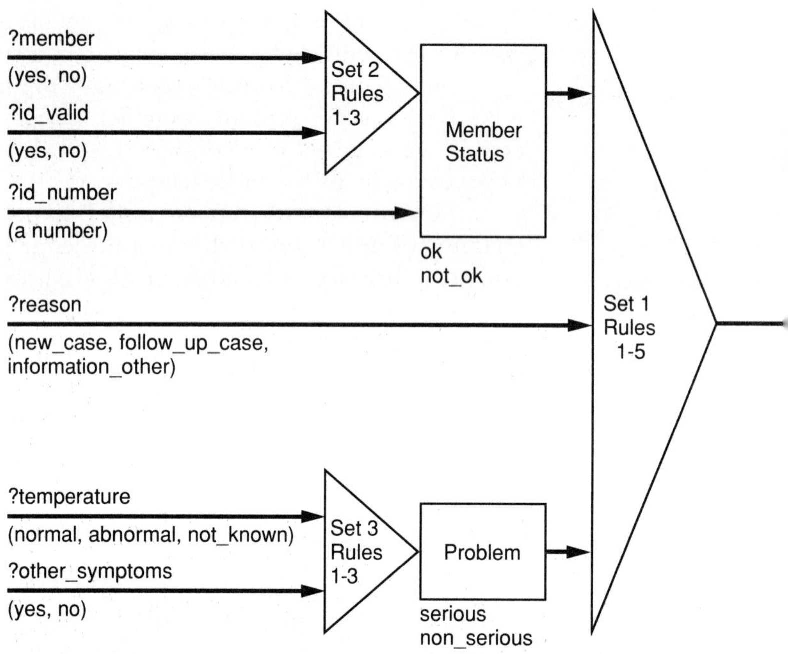


Just before the link occurs, the SAVEFACTS keyword stores all known variable values in a temporary file called TEMPDATA. A developer can give the SAVEFACTS file any name desired, as long as it remains within file-naming constraints.

Figure 6–16 gives the listing for the second file, MODULE2.KBS. Its purpose is to produce a concluding message customized by "support" level. To a user, this KBS generates screens during a consultation that are similar to those in Figures 6–9 and 6–11.

As evident from Figure 6–16, the LOADFACTS keyword is used to load into memory all variable names and values stored in the temporary file TEMPDATA. Although only one value, for "support," is relevant to MODULE2.KBS, all variables whose values are known and saved at the time the SAVEFACTS keyword is executed are loaded.

In this example, after an appropriate message is displayed or printed, the knowledge base chains back to MODULE1.KBS. This creates a looping action to enable a user to begin another consultation session, if desired. Since the educational version of VP-Expert permits only three links, after the second consultation a warning message appears. It declares that the limits of this version are exceeded, then proceeds to terminate at the DOS prompt. By contrast, a full

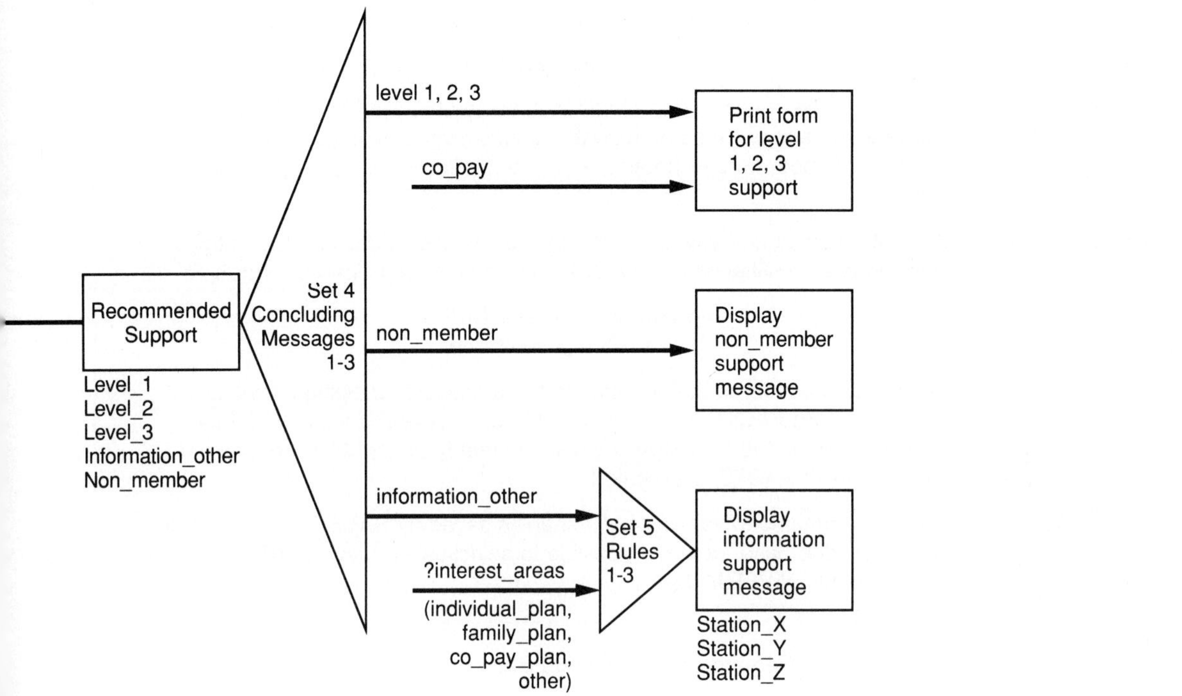


version of VP-Expert would cycle through the two-part KBS session as often as desired.

Because MODULE2.KBS is an independent module, rule set numbers and rule numbers are changed as appropriate. Rule Sets 1 and 2, for example, were Rule Sets 4 and 5 in the original single HMOADD2.KBS.

### Practical Considerations

Chained segments can be linked in the THEN part of a rule as well as in the Actions Block. Consider the following example:

```
IF advice = invest and
   investment = bonds
THEN type = bonds
     CHAIN B:BONDS
```

The THEN part of this rule links directly to the KBS that determines bond investments. If necessary, a SAVEFACTS statement could have captured all known variables before chaining.

**Figure 6–14**

### Chaining Keywords

| Keyword | Description |
|---|---|
| CHAIN | Permits the use of knowledge bases that would otherwise be too large to be contained in memory. Also permits the modularization of knowledge bases which makes both troubleshooting and writing effective knowledge bases easier. |
| SAVEFACTS | Stores the names and values of *all* variables whose values are presently known in the consultation to an ASCII text file with the following format:<br>variable1 = value1 CNF n<br>variable2 = value2 CNF n<br>SAVEFACTS usually is the first step in the process of chaining knowledge base files. SAVEFACTS cannot be used to save *selected* variables. If the text file named in the SAVEFACTS clause already exists, it will be overwritten when SAVEFACTS is executed. |
| LOADFACTS | Loads the names and values of *all* variables saved by SAVEFACTS into the new knowledge base. (It is not possible to selectively retrieve values from a file created by SAVEFACTS.) |

#### Basic Steps Required in Knowledge Base Chaining

- Use SAVEFACTS to save the known values (facts) from the current consultation. (It is not always necessary to pass information from one knowledge base to another.)
- Use CHAIN to name a new knowledge base file. (The old knowledge base file will be closed, and this file will take its place in the current consultation.)
- Use LOADFACTS to load the values saved by SAVEFACTS into the new knowledge base.

SAVEFACTS and CHAIN should occur in the first knowledge base file. LOADFACTS occurs in the second knowledge base file.

An example of the syntax normally used in transferring knowledge and execution from the first knowledge base is:

```
SAVEFACTS B:tempdata
CHAIN B:module2.kbs
```

The syntax of the second knowledge base is:

```
LOADFACTS B:tempdata
```

## Figure 6–15. First of Two Chained Knowledge Bases

Notes:
. The name of this knowledge base file on the Sample Files disk is MODULE1.KBS.
. Blocked areas indicate changes from HMOADD2.KBS.
. The part of the knowledge base file after the "Rules Block" line is not shown here. It matches a similar part already given in Figure 6-8. The only difference is that Rule Set 4 does not appear in this MODULE1.KBS.

```
! HMO Service Screening Assistant
! Chaining Example: This is the first of two linked knowledge base files.
!                   It is saved as MODULE1.KBS.
!                   It saves all names and values of variables in
!                   a SAVEFACTS file called TEMPDATA.
!                   (It links to MODULE2.KBS)

!**************************************************************************

!EXECUTE;                                        !start consultation immediately
     !use exclamation point temporarily to disable execute while debugging
BKCOLOR = 3;                             !set screen background color to light blue
RUNTIME;                                        !eliminate rules and facts windows

!============================== Actions Block ============================

ACTIONS
     WOPEN 1,3,10,13,60,7                              !define opening window 1
     ACTIVE 1                                                !activate window 1
     DISPLAY "

              HMO Service Screening Assistant

   This consultation assists you to screen a person who
   enters an HMO facility.  It asks a series of questions
   about the person, then recommends a level of support
   appropriate to the person's needs.

   Please press any key to begin the consultation.~

     "
     wclose 1                                                  !remove window 1
     COLOR = 20                           !set following text color to blinking red
     DISPLAY "          CAUTION!"
     COLOR = 4                              !set following text to non-blinking red
     DISPLAY "Please make sure your printer in ON."
     DISPLAY "Press any key to continue.~"
     CLS                                                       !clear the screen
     COLOR = 0                                  !set following text to normal black
     WOPEN 1,1,1,6,77,2                             !define instructions window 1
     ACTIVE 1                                                !activate window 1
     DISPLAY "                            Instructions
          Use the arrow keys to move the lightbar to a desired
          answer choice then press the Enter key.
          Press the End key to move to the next question."
     WOPEN 2,8,1,13,77,3                            !define consultation window 2
     ACTIVE 2                                                !activate window 2
     FIND support
     SAVEFACTS tempdata                     !save all variable names and values in a
                                                    !temporary text file called TEMPDATA
     CHAIN module2                         !link to another .KBS file called MODULE2

;
!============================== Rules Block ==============================
```

(See Figure 6-8 for the code following the Rules Block)

**Figure 6–16.** Second of Two Chained Knowledge Bases

Notes:
. The name of this knowledge base file on the Sample Files disk is MODULE2.KBS.
. Blocked areas indicate changes from HMOADD2.KBS. In addition, Rule Set numbers are changed.

```
! HMO Service Screening Assistant
! Chaining Example: This is the second of two linked knowledge base files.
!                   It is saved as MODULE2.KBS.
!                   It does not have any variables.
!                   (It links back to MODULE1.KBS.)

!*************************************************************************

!EXECUTE;                                   !start consultation immediately
      !use exclamation point temporarily to disable execute while debugging
BKCOLOR = 3;                        !set screen background color to light blue
RUNTIME;                                 !eliminate rules and facts windows

!============================== Actions Block ==============================

ACTIONS
     LOADFACTS tempdata     !load into memory all variable names and values
                              !stored in the temporary file called TEMPDATA
     COLOR = 0                               !set following text to normal black
     WOPEN 1,1,1,6,77,2                          !define instructions window 1
     ACTIVE 1                                              !activate window 1
     DISPLAY "                           Instructions
          Use the arrow keys to move the lightbar to a desired
          answer choice then press the Enter key.
          Press the End key to move to the next question."
     WOPEN 2,8,1,13,77,3                         !define consultation window 2
     ACTIVE 2                                              !activate window 2
     FIND message                           !set goal to customize messages
     DISPLAY "Press any key to conclude this consultation.~"
     CHAIN module1          !link back to the original MODULE1.KBS to begin
                                  !another consultation session, if desired
;
!============================== Rules Block ==============================

!-------------------- Rule Set 1: Concluding Messages --------------------

RULE message_level123                !use a meaningful name for a rule label
     IF support = level_1 or
        support = level_2 or
        support = level_3
     THEN message = print_form
        PRINTON                          !send display text to screen and printer
        DISPLAY "Authorization Form For Service - {support}"
        DISPLAY "ID: {id_number}"
        DISPLAY "Reason: {reason}"
        DISPLAY "Self-reported: temperature - {temperature}"
        DISPLAY "                  symptoms - {other_symptoms}"!disable printon
        PRINTOFF                                              !send text only
        PDISPLAY "Kindly go to {room} for service."             !to printer
                                  !set sub-goal to determine co-pay charges
        FIND co_pay                      !move printer paper to top of next page
        EJECT                                           !display one blank line
        DISPLAY ""
        DISPLAY "Please tear the Authorization Form off the printer.";
```

```
        RULE get_co_pay              !single rule to determine co-pay charges
        IF id_number > 999999
        THEN co_pay = yes
             PDISPLAY"(Co-payment charge of $8.00 made for service.)";

RULE message_non_member
     IF support = non_member
     THEN message = station_Z
        DISPLAY "Appropriate service is available at {message}.";

RULE message_info
     IF support = information_other
     THEN message = display_service
        FIND interest_areas                           get direct user input
        FIND info_help                   !set sub-goal to customize messages
        DISPLAY "Service is available for plan type / at: {info_help}";

!------------------- Rule Set 2: Information Help Messages ---------------

RULE 2-1
     IF interest_areas = individual_plan
     THEN info_help = individual_station_X;

RULE 2-2
     IF interest_areas = family_plan
     THEN info_help = family_station_Y;

RULE 2-3
     IF interest_areas = co_pay_plan or
        interest_areas = other
     THEN info_help = co_pay_other_station_Z;

!=========================== Questions Block ============================

ASK interest_areas: "What kind(s) of information is (are) desired?";
CHOICES interest_areas: individual_plan, family_plan, co_pay_plan, other;

PLURAL: interest_areas, info_help;
```

It is not necessary in all cases to pass information from one knowledge base to another. An example is given in Figure 6–16. After the end of the consultation session, the CHAIN keyword in the Actions Block returns control to MODULE1.KBS to begin another session, if desired. In this case, there is no need to pass data, so CHAIN is not preceded by a SAVEFACTS keyword.

It is recommended that the EXECUTE keyword be the first keyword in a file so as to achieve a smooth transition when chaining from one knowledge base to another. But use of this keyword causes a consultation to terminate a session at the DOS prompt, which is very inconvenient when debugging a KBS. Putting an exclamation point in front of EXECUTE conveniently disables it for debugging sessions. The chained KBS files will seem to function just as well with EXECUTE disabled.

Finally, some debugging tips for working with chained KBS files follow:

- First, make a chained module or KBS work independently of all linkages.
- During independent module tests, set up dummy variables and values in the Actions Block, if necessary, to simulate imported SAVEFACTS data.
- Create extra DISPLAY messages that serve as an audit trail to track the progress of execution through difficult or problem code.
- Use the exclamation point to deactivate dummy variables and the EXECUTE keyword during live tests of linkages. Remember to delete dummy variables, extra DISPLAYS, and any exclamation points used only to support debugging sessions after the chained KBS works smoothly.

## SUMMARY REFERENCE GUIDE

The remaining sections of this chapter are designed to be a summary, as well as a reference guide, to the keywords and features covered in the tutorial Chapters 3, 4, 5, and the first part of 6. This section provides a single reference source to supplement information contained in these four chapters.

In addition, this summary reference guide covers new material of interest to KBS developers, including:

- instructions to install VP-Expert
- error messages

Additional information is provided in the *VP-Expert Manual*.

### System Requirements

VP-Expert runs on an IBM Personal Computer and compatible (clone) computers with:

- 512K or more RAM
- DOS version 2.0 or higher

In order to use the graphics features, an IBM CGA, EGA, or VGA, a Hercules monochrome graphics adapter, or a compatible video adapter (graphics card) is required.

The software may not run with certain co-resident (terminate and stay-ready "TSR") programs.

### Educational Version Limitations

1. The size of the knowledge base is limited to 16 Kbytes.
2. The maximum number of knowledge base files which can be chained together is 3.
3. The maximum number of database file records which can be read is 150.

### Installation

It is strongly recommended that the reader make a duplicate back-up copy of the disks accompanying this book. Save the originals in a safe place and use the back-up, or working copy, of the disks to install the programs onto diskettes or a hard drive. (*Note:* The distribution disks contain so-called zipped or compressed files. Files first must be unzipped, accomplished by running the Install program. Specific instructions follow.)

In this summary, the DOS prompt that is displayed on the screen is underlined. For instance, in A:\>INSTALL <Enter>, the A:\> is displayed by the computer on the screen. You would type in only INSTALL and then press Enter.

### For a Diskette-Drive Only Computer (No Hard Drive)

If your system does not have a hard drive, place Disk #1 in drive A, change to an A> prompt, and issue this command:

```
A:>install
```

At the first menu, choose option 2—Install Programs to Diskette. This assumes that you have two high-density disk drives and three formatted high-density diskettes ready to accept the unzipped files. Follow the instructions displayed. (*Note:* Option 2 also makes separate diskettes for the M.1 and ObjectCraft files. They are used in later chapters of this book.)

The reader is advised to make a duplicate (back-up) copy of the (unzipped) VP–Expert diskette. This is the diskette that is referred to as the "Sample Files" disk in this book. The back-up should be used as a working copy to do the exercises in the chapters. Before doing the exercises a second or third time, make a fresh backup disk from the unzipped VP–Expert diskette to ensure that the correct sample files are used.

To start the program, insert the VP–Expert diskette into the A: or B: drive and type VPX <Enter>.

### For a Hard-Disk-Drive Computer

Because the diskettes accompanying this book are designed to copy in one operation all the software that comes with the book, there must be at least 6 megabytes of hard disk storage space available to complete the installation. To check available hard disk storage space, log onto the hard disk (assumed to be the C: drive; if your hard disk is not the C: drive, substitute your hard disk identifier where you see C:) and enter the following command:

```
C:\>CHKDSK <Enter>
```

The amount of available disk space in bytes will be given.

It is helpful if the DOS prompt displays the path to the current subdirectory. This can be done by issuing this command:

```
C:\>prompt $p$g <Enter>
```

This installation is designed to begin at the root directory of the hard drive. If you are in the root directory, the prompt should display C:\>.

If you are in a subdirectory, for example, a subdirectory called WP, you can return to the root directory by entering the following command:

```
C:\WP>cd\
```

The prompt should now read C:\>.

Now place Disk #1 in the A: drive. Change to the A: prompt by typing the following command:

```
C:\>A: <Enter>
```

Begin the install program by typing the following command:

```
A:>install <Enter>
```

On the opening menu of the install procedure, choose option 1—Install Programs to Hard Disk. Follow the instructions displayed to install the programs.

Once the installation is completed, change to the VP–Expert subdirectory by issuing the following command:

```
C:\>cd\KBSBOOK\VPEXPERT
```

The VP–Expert program is started by issuing the command vpx at the prompt. The screen should look like this:

```
C:\KBSBOOK\VPX>vpx <Enter>
```

### Printing the Sample Files

Some users may wish to have a printed copy of the knowledge bases provided on the Sample Files disk. This is easily accomplished using the DOS print utility (PRINT.COM), the DOS COPY command or a word processor. To use PRINT.COM, issue the command below after DOS has been loaded into your computer's memory:

```
print <filename>.kbs
```

The computer will respond with the message

```
Name of list device (PRN):
```

If your printer is LPT1, press Enter to continue. If your printer is LPT2 or COM1, enter that information and then press Enter.

To use the DOS COPY command, enter the following:

```
COPY <filename>.kbs lpt1
```

The sample knowledge base files are ASCII text files. To use your word processor to print the .KBS files, follow your system's instructions for DOS or ASCII text files.

### Obtaining Help

From anywhere in VP-Expert, you can press F1 to receive immediate help on the screen. Once in the Help subsystem, press the Escape key to bring up the Topics Menu. Page through it for the keyword of interest. To get a printout of any material of interest from the Help subsystem:

- Have the desired information displayed on the screen
- Check to see that your printer is ON
- Press P

The Help subsystem is not available while a consultation session is in progress.

### General Keywords Summary

| *Keyword* | *Description* |
|---|---|
| ACTIONS | Must begin the ACTIONS block, which controls the action of a consultation. |
| ACTIVE | Causes subsequent display text to appear in the specified window defined by a WOPEN keyword. |
| ASK | Used to query the user for values to be assigned to a variable when the inference engine fails to find any values in the rules. |

| | |
|---|---|
| AUTOQUERY | In the absence of an appropriate ASK statement, this statement automatically generates a generic question asking the user for a value to be assigned to the required variable. |
| BKCOLOR | Used to set the background color of the consultation screen. |
| CHAIN | Permits the use of knowledge bases that would otherwise be too large to be contained in memory. Also, permits the modularization of knowledge bases which makes both troubleshooting and writing effective knowledge bases easier. |
| CHOICES | Used in conjunction with the ASK or AUTOQUERY statement to present a menu of allowable values that can be assigned to the requested variable. A CHOICES keyword may be followed by no more than 10 variables. |
| CLS | Used to clear the consultation window. |
| COLOR | Used to set text color to be displayed. |
| DISPLAY | Displays text and values in the consultation window. |
| EJECT | Ejects the remainder of a page from the printer. |
| END | The last word of a WHILEKNOWN-END loop. |
| ENDOFF | Eliminates the need to hit the End key when finished choosing from a CHOICES menu. |
| EXECUTE | Used to initiate a consultation automatically when Consult is chosen from the Main Menu. It eliminates the extra step of having to select Go from the Consult Menu before the consultation starts. |
| FIND | Used in a consultation to find goals. |
| LOADFACTS | Loads the names and values of all variables saved by SAVEFACTS into a CHAINed knowledge base. |
| PDISPLAY | Prints text and values on the printer only. Text can contain a maximum of 1,000 characters including spaces. |
| PLURAL | Used to declare a variable as one that may be assigned more than one value in a consultation. A PLURAL keyword may be followed by no more than 10 variables. |
| PRINTOFF | Disables PRINTON. |

| | |
|---|---|
| PRINTON | Prints text and values to both the screen and the printer. |
| RESET | Reinitializes a variable to the value UNKNOWN. |
| RULE | Used to represent the expert knowledge in a knowledge base. |
| RUNTIME | Eliminates the Rules and Facts windows from the consultation screen. Usually added after a system has been completely developed. |
| SAVEFACTS | Stores the names and values of *all* variables whose values are presently known in the consultation to an ASCII text file. |
| TRUTHTHRESH | Sets the minimum confidence value required to fire a RULE. |
| WHILEKNOWN | First word of a WHILEKNOWN-END loop. A WHILEKNOWN-END loop executes all clauses contained between the keywords WHILEKNOWN and END, provided that the variable used to control the loop has a value other than UNKNOWN whenever END is reached. Only one WHILEKNOWN-END loop can be active at one time. |
| WOPEN | Used with a corresponding ACTIVE keyword to generate a window around text displays during a consultation. A knowledge base can contain a maximum of 9 WOPEN keywords. |

### Database Keywords Summary

| *Keyword* | *Description* |
|---|---|
| ALL | Used with GET and MENU keywords to indicate that no special condition needs to be met when selecting a record. |
| GET | Used to retrieve values from a database file. |
| MENU | Used in conjunction with the ASK statement to generate a menu of allowable values that can be assigned to a variable based on the field values of a database file. |
| PUT | Used to update or change a record in a database file. |

### Spreadsheet Keywords Summary

| *Keyword* | *Description* |
|---|---|
| COLUMN | Used with the WKS or PWKS keywords to identify a column location in a spreadsheet. |

| | |
|---|---|
| NAMED | Used with the WKS or PWKS keywords to identify a cell range in a spreadsheet. |
| PWKS | Used to transfer values from a knowledge base variable into a spreadsheet. |
| ROW | Used with the WKS or PWKS keywords to identify a row location in a spreadsheet. |
| WFORMAT | Defines the cell format for numeric values that will be transferred to a spreadsheet with the PWKS keyword. |
| WKS | Used to transfer values from a spreadsheet into a knowledge base variable. |

### Structure of a Rule

| | |
|---|---|
| RULE label | The keyword RULE followed by a label. |
| IF | Identifies the beginning of the RULE condition(s). |
| THEN | Identifies the beginning of the RULE conclusion. |
| ELSE | Used optionally to identify the beginning of an alternative conclusion of a RULE. |
| BECAUSE | Used optionally to offer an explanation of the premise, conclusion, and alternate conclusion of the RULE. |

A rule must end with a semicolon. Conditions can be combined in rules using the logical operators:

| | |
|---|---|
| AND | Both conditions must be met for the rule to be "true" and, therefore, "pass." Up to 20 conditions using AND can be combined in one rule. |
| OR | One or both conditions must be true. When both AND and OR are used in a rule, OR takes precedence over AND. It is as though parentheses surround the expressions connected by OR. Using OR with AND in a rule limits the number of conditions that can be combined to 10. |

### Arithmetic Symbols (Operators)

| | |
|---|---|
| + | Used for addition of numbers. |
| − | Used for subtraction of numbers. |
| * | Used for multiplication of numbers. |
| / | Used for division of numbers. |

### Relational Symbols (Operators)

| | |
|---|---|
| = | Used as the equal-to relation. |
| > | Used as the greater-than relation. |

| | |
|---|---|
| < | Used as the less-than relation. |
| >= | Used as the greater-than-or-equal-to relation. |
| <= | Used as the less-than-or-equal-to relation. |
| <> | Used as the not-equal-to relation. |

### Assignment Operator

| | |
|---|---|
| = | Used to assign values to variables. |

### Special Symbols

| | |
|---|---|
| ! | Used to identify comments. |
| ? | Used as a shorthand for the special value unknown. |
| * | ("Wildcard") used in an induction table column to indicate that a value is not required for the corresponding (asterisk) variable. |
| ~ | (Tilde) used in text to initiate a pause until the user presses any key. |
| # | Used to display the confidence factor associated with the value of the variable which follows the pound sign. |
| { } | Used to display the value of a variable. |
| ( ) | Used in: 1) all math calculations. 2) assigning values to variables by indirect addressing. |
| ; | Used at the end of Actions Block, each rule, and each statement in the Questions Block. |
| [ ] | Used for indexing dimensioned variables. |
| " | Used to identify text in ASK, BECAUSE, DISPLAY, and PDISPLAY statements. |
| UNKNOWN | The initial value of a variable. |
| CNF | Used to assign confidence factors. |

### Text Color

The keyword COLOR is used to change the color of the text when displayed on a color monitor and also to display blinking text. COLOR can be used to alter text color and text blinking as often as desired during a consultation. COLOR is followed by =, then a number from 0 to 31.

| *Number to Use for Normal Text* | *Color* | *Number to Use for Blinking Text* |
|---|---|---|
| 0 | Black | 16 |
| 1 | Blue | 17 |
| 2 | Green | 18 |
| 3 | Cyan | 19 |
| 4 | Red | 20 |
| 5 | Magenta | 21 |
| 6 | Brown | 22 |
| 7 | White | 23 |
| 8 | Gray | 24 |
| 9 | Light Blue | 25 |
| 10 | Light Green | 26 |
| 11 | Light Cyan | 27 |
| 12 | Light Red | 28 |
| 13 | Light Magenta | 29 |
| 14 | Yellow | 30 |
| 15 | Bright White | 31 |

### Background Color

BKCOLOR sets the background color of the screen for a consultation. BKCOLOR is followed by = and then a number from 0 to 7. BKCOLOR may not be used to change the background color during a consultation. If more than one BKCOLOR statement is present in a program, only the last one will be used. (Note: On a monochrome monitor the numbers 0–6 display a black background.)

| *Number to Use* | *Background Color* |
|---|---|
| 0 | Black |
| 1 | Blue |
| 2 | Green |
| 3 | Light Blue |
| 4 | Red |
| 5 | Magenta |
| 6 | Brown |
| 7 | White |

### Error Messages

This listing of some common error messages includes a short explanation of the message and some possible ways to correct the error situation.

| | |
|---|---|
| Error in END clause | Each WHILEKNOWN clause in the knowledge base must contain an END clause. |
| Error in math | Illegal math expression, usually due to unbalanced parentheses, illegal numerical formats or values, illegal functions, etc. |
| Illegal color | Text color values range from 0 to 15; blinking text colors from 16 to 31. Background color values range from 0 to 7. Check assigned values. |
| Illegal confidence factor | Confidence factor values must range from 0 to 100 (use 0 for absolutely false and 100 for absolutely true). Check assigned values. |
| Illegal statement | Statement is not correct, usually due to a syntax or spelling error. |
| Illegal truth threshold | Truth threshold values must range from 0 to 100. Check assigned values. |
| Math expression too long | The limit is 256 characters. |
| Missing comma | Variable names must be separated by commas in ASK, CHOICES, and PLURAL statements. |
| Out of memory error | Memory limit has been exceeded. Try dividing the knowledge base into smaller units and chaining them together. |
| Premature end of the file | Usually occurs because of missing final semicolon in the knowledge base. |
| Recursion too deep | The limit is ten sub-goal levels when using backward chaining. |
| Syntax error | Check spelling and usage. |
| Text string too long | The limit is 1,000 characters in ASK, BECAUSE, DISPLAY, and PDISPLAY text. |
| Too many columns | The limit is eleven columns in an induction table. |
| Too many examples | The limit is 120 rows in an induction table. |
| Trace file not present | The Tree Menu's Text and Graphics options require the existence of a .tbl file with the same file name as the current knowledge base. Use the Set Menu to create a trace file. |
| Trace file too big | The limit is 500 lines when using a tree. |
| Word too long | The limit is 40 characters for RULE labels and also for most variable names. |

## REVIEW QUESTIONS

1. How much effort and time must be allotted to user interface building?
2. What is the importance of the opening message?
3. What is the function of the BECAUSE text in a rule?
4. What is the definition and function of a comment in a knowledge base file?
5. How does the physical layout of the knowledge base assist in understanding the KBS?
6. What is the function of a WHENEVER rule in a backward-chaining KBS?
7. What is the purpose of chaining knowledge bases together in an expert system?
8. How would you print a copy of the knowledge base provided on the Sample Files disk?
9. What is the structure of a rule?
10. What are the arithmetic and relational symbols normally used in KBS development?
11. Identify what the assignment operator and some of the other special symbols are used for in the construction of a KBS file.
12. What are some common error messages that can occur during KBS development?

## EXERCISES

1. The object of this exercise is to examine how a KBS's user interface can be improved. Run a consultation with the knowledge base HMOUSER.KBS from the Sample Files disk. Then run a consultation with HMORUN.KBS.
   a. Compare and record the differences observed.
   b. When the question appears "Is the person an HMO member?" type the backslash (/) key, move the lightbar to "Why?" and press Enter. Record the response observed. Press the Escape key to resume the consultation.
2. The goal of this exercise is to explore how to create windows to enhance a KBS's user interface. Copy HMOUSER.KBS from the Sample Files disk to your Exercise disk with

   ```
   A>COPY HMOUSER.KBS  B:MYUSER.KBS
   ```

   a. Use the Editor to create changes that produce a double framed window around the opening message of MYUSER.KBS.
   b. Change the background color for the opening message to another color of your choice.

3. This exercise demonstrates how selected changes to a "plain vanilla" KBS can make it more user friendly. Copy HMORUN.KBS from the Sample Files disk to your Exercise disk with

```
A>COPY HMORUN.KBS  B:XMYUSER.KBS
```

Use the Editor to enter into XMYUSER.KBS the new additions shown in the blocked areas of Figure 6–1. Your completely debugged knowledge base should run just like the model HMOUSER.KBS on the Sample Files disk.
4. This exercise explores printing and other enhancement options. Run a consultation with the knowledge base HMOADD1.KBS from the Sample Files disk. Compare and record the differences between it and HMOUSER.KBS.
5. This exercise demonstrates how to handle a multiple-response question. Run a consultation with the knowledge base HMOADD2.KBS from the Sample Files disk using the following responses:

| *Response* | *Keys to Press to Indicate Response* |
|---|---|
| yes | (Enter, End) |
| yes | (Enter, End) |
| 99999 | (Enter) |
| information other | (Enter, End) |
| family plan | (Enter) |
| co-pay plan | (Enter, End) |

   a. Record the results observed.
   b. Compare your observations with Figure 6–12 and identify which lines of code produced which part of the results observed.
6. This exercise demonstrates the use of chained or linked KBS modules. Run a consultation with the knowledge base MODULE1.KBS from the Sample Files disk. This file will automatically call and use MODULE2.KBS from the Sample Files disk. During the consultation, a temporary file called TEMPDATA is created.
   a. Observe and record the results observed during the transition from MODULE1 to MODULE2.
   b. Obtain a printout of MODULE1.KBS and MODULE2.KBS. Identify the code that processes the linkages.
7. Improve the user interface for a knowledge base of your own design with these features:
   a. An opening message that
      - describes the objective of the consultation
      - describes how the consultation will work
      - indicates what kind of closure to expect
      - puts the user in control to activate the consultation

   **b.** An "instructions" window.

**8.** If you have an EGA or VGA graphics adapter and mouse, run CARPICT.KBS from the Sample Files disk. It demonstrates the graphic capabilities of VP-Expert.
   **a.** Record the results observed.
   **b.** Obtain a printout of the code and identify the new keywords introduced.
   **c.** Use the Help subsystem (F1 key) to obtain a printout of new keyword descriptions.
   **d.** Run several consultations with CARPICT and study the printout of the code during the consultation. Studying it in this manner can be very informative.
   **e.** Consider using the new capabilities to enhance a knowledge-based system of your own design.

**9.** If you have an EGA or VGA graphics adapter and mouse, run FORMDEMO.KBS from the Sample Files disk. It demonstrates how to create entry systems based on "intelligent" forms. Repeat the step-by-step instructions for Exercise 8.

**10.** File README.KBS on the Sample Files disk demonstrates the use of hypertext. During a consultation, it uses the README.TXT file. Run a consultation using README.KBS.

# Part Three

## KBS DEVELOPMENT: THE BASIC KNOWLEDGE ENGINEERING JOB

# 7

# Knowledge Acquisition and Representation

This chapter discusses knowledge acquisition and representation, an early phase of the situation analysis and representation task in the knowledge-based system (KBS) development life cycle shown in Figure 7–1.

The objective of this chapter is to enable readers to understand:

- The nature of knowledge acquisition and representation
- General knowledge acquisition strategies
- General knowledge acquisition techniques and tools
- An approach to making decisions in specific situations
- Applying this general approach to making decisions about which observation techniques to use

The chapter concludes with:

- A description of a KBS for assisting in making these decisions
- A discussion of the varying importance of domain knowledge

## KBS DEVELOPMENT: KNOWLEDGE ACQUISITION AND REPRESENTATION

Knowledge acquisition and representation is the knowledge engineering job of acquiring and organizing the knowledge needed to develop a knowledge-based

**Figure 7–1.** Knowledge-Based Systems Development Life Cycle

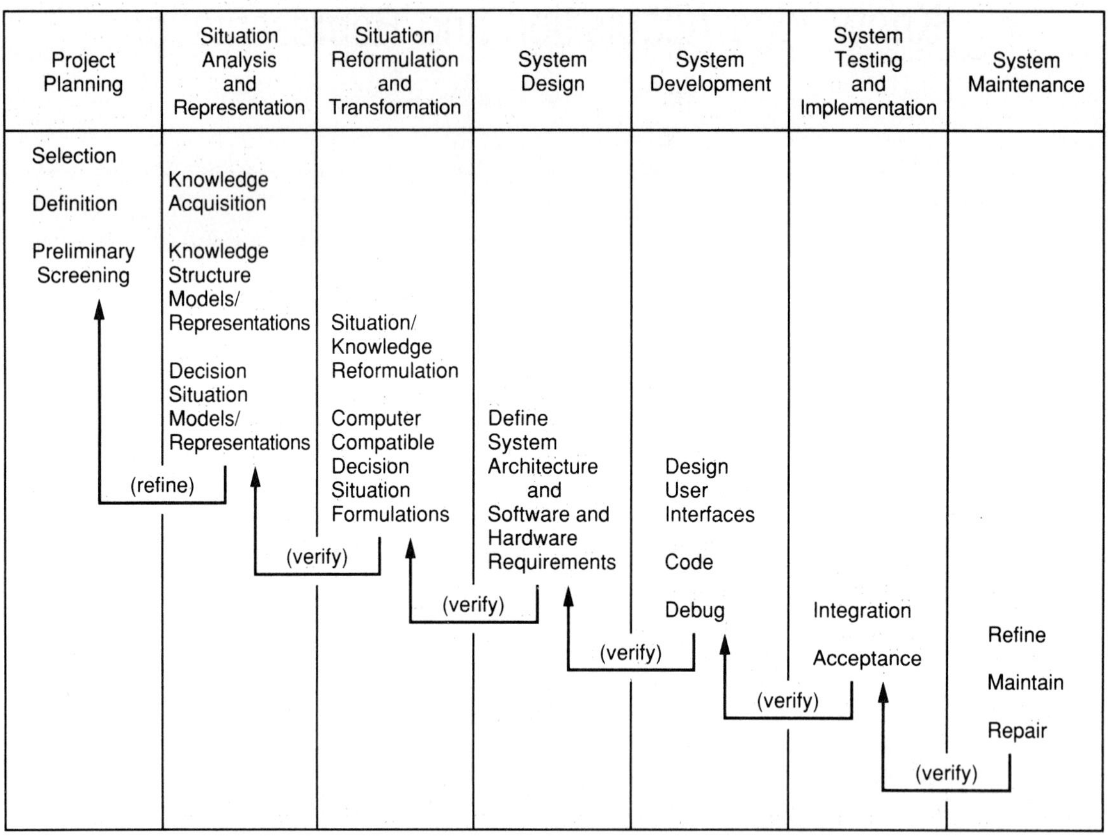


system. The term *knowledge* refers to the fact or condition of knowing something with familiarity gained through experience or association—the integration of a collection of facts, beliefs, heuristic rules, and relationships. The job of acquiring and representing knowledge involves:

- acquiring the knowledge to be replicated in the system
- organizing and representing the knowledge in a way that ensures an accurate replication of the knowledge and the decision situation under study in a form useful for transferring the knowledge to a computer system
- augmenting and reformulating the knowledge, refining the heuristics, and correcting errors over a period of time during the system development life cycle

The goal of knowledge acquisition and representation is the transfer and transformation of problem-solving and decision-making expertise from some knowledge source into a form useful for developing a knowledge-based system. Knowledge acquisition and representation can be a very time-consuming and costly process in the KBS development life cycle (Rothman 1988, p. 28). In fact, it has often been referred to by experts as a "bottleneck" (Hoffman 1987, p. 53).

In practice, like the knowledge-based system development life cycle shown in Figure 7–1, the process involved in acquiring and representing knowledge, which is shown in Figure 7–2 and discussed in this chapter, is a continuing one. It is not a step-by-step procedure, but a group of iterative, dynamically overlapping, integrated subprocesses.

The knowledge acquisition and representation job in many complex KBS development situations can in fact continue throughout the KBS development life cycle. No matter what the phase in the KBS development cycle, knowledge engineers—individuals who design and build knowledge-based systems by helping problem-domain experts map information into a form from which to build a system that other individuals may later use to get advice—can find themselves continually exploring such questions as:

- Is the definition of final recommendations incomplete or inaccurate?
- Is more clarification or specific information needed about any fact or reasoning area in the knowledge domain?
- Is the domain conceptualization adequate or efficient?
- Is the domain framework appropriate?
- Is the background knowledge (e.g., concepts, terminology) incomplete?

A **domain expert** is an individual who is widely recognized as having the knowledge and know-how necessary to solve a problem or make a decision in the domain in which the KBS is being developed. A knowledge domain is a field of knowledge which can be defined by scope, range, depth, or breadth.

In theory a knowledge engineer would like to have the knowledge domain and its heuristics fully and completely defined and structured before going on to subsequent systems development phases of the KBS development cycle. In practice, this is frequently impossible.

An effective knowledge engineer makes use of many specific knowledge acquisition strategies and techniques in carrying out the knowledge acquisition job. The actual techniques used will depend on the phase of knowledge acquisition and representation, on the type or level of knowledge to be acquired during each phase, and on the complexity of the interrelationships of factors within the situation under study. Specific situation requirements have a significant impact on knowledge acquisition strategy and technique selection.

## GENERAL KNOWLEDGE ACQUISITION STRATEGIES

Two overall strategic aspects of knowledge acquisition, as shown in Figure 7–3, are the nature of the interaction between the knowledge engineer and

**Figure 7–2.** The Tasks Involved in Acquiring and Representing Knowledge

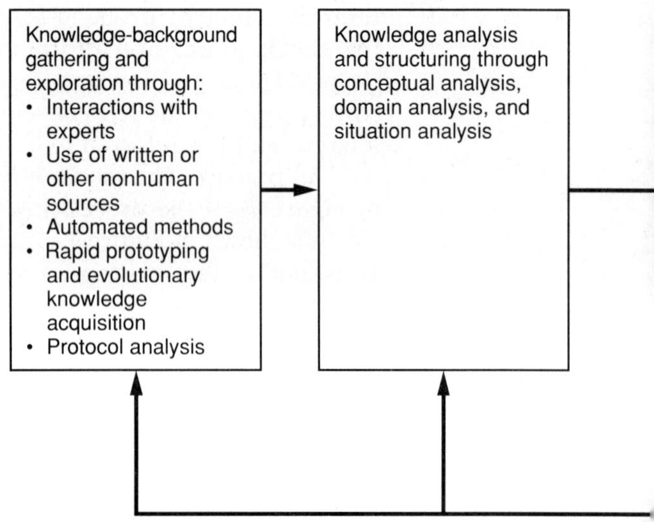


knowledge source during knowledge acquisition, and the time frame of the knowledge acquisition.

### The Nature of the Interaction

Three basic types of possible interactions during knowledge acquisition can be identified:

- A knowledge engineer interacting with a domain expert
- A knowledge engineer interacting with written and other knowledge sources
- A machine interacting with knowledge sources

***A Knowledge Engineer Interacting with an Expert.*** This type of interaction may involve unstructured interviews, structured interviews, and observation of the expert.

*An unstructured interview* is used to start many knowledge acquisition tasks, since it can be effective in exploring the background knowledge involved in a situation. During an unstructured interview, a knowledge engineer actively questions the expert, for example, by asking spontaneous questions as an expert is performing a task (Hoffman 1987, p. 54). Through this questioning it is hoped that the expert will amplify how he or she goes about making the decision or doing the task under study. The disadvantages of this type of knowledge acquisition include lack of

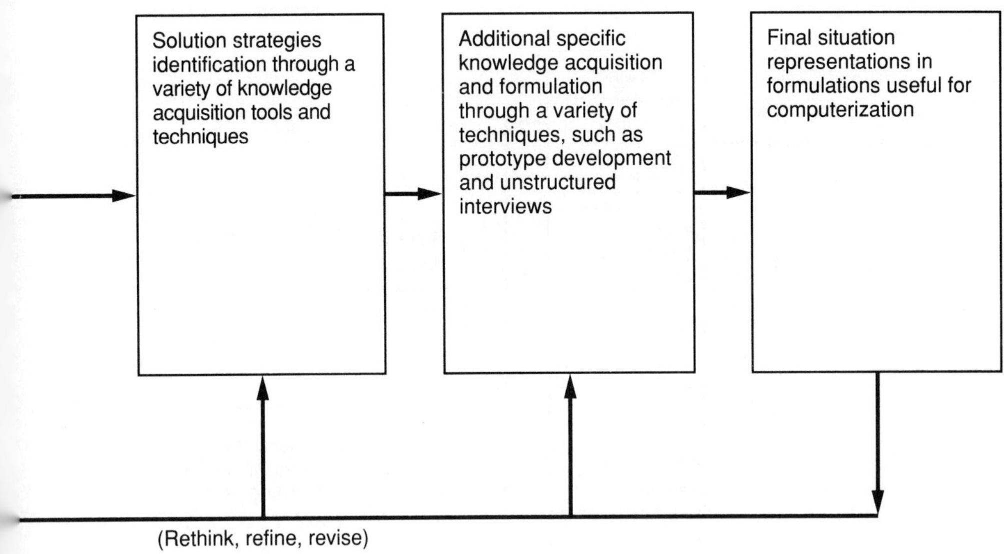


focus, dependence upon the domain expert's ability to "teach," and the possibility of not using the expert's time efficiently (McGraw, 1989, p. 73).

*Structured interviews* normally take place after the knowledge engineer has become familiar with the expertise under study. During structured interviews with an expert, a knowledge engineer pursues specific goals and asks questions designed to elicit more and more specific information. This type of interview generally takes place after the initial knowledge base has been established, and is used to refine the knowledge base (Grabowski 1988, p. 48; Agarwal and Tannira, 1990).

*Observation of the expert* involves the knowledge engineer observing domain experts as they:

- perform a familiar task, solve a problem, or make a decision
- deal with a simulated situation, case study, or real-world problem
- describe possible decision situation scenarios that might be encountered on the job

***A Knowledge Engineer Interacting with Written and Other Knowledge Sources.*** This type of contact includes using sources such as documents, technical manuals, videotapes, audio tapes, and databases. The techniques used in acquiring knowledge in each of these instances will vary with the specific source; they do not require the use of interpersonal skills. The availability of an expert is not a concern if these knowledge sources are present and considered adequate.

**Figure 7–3.** Knowledge Acquisition Strategies

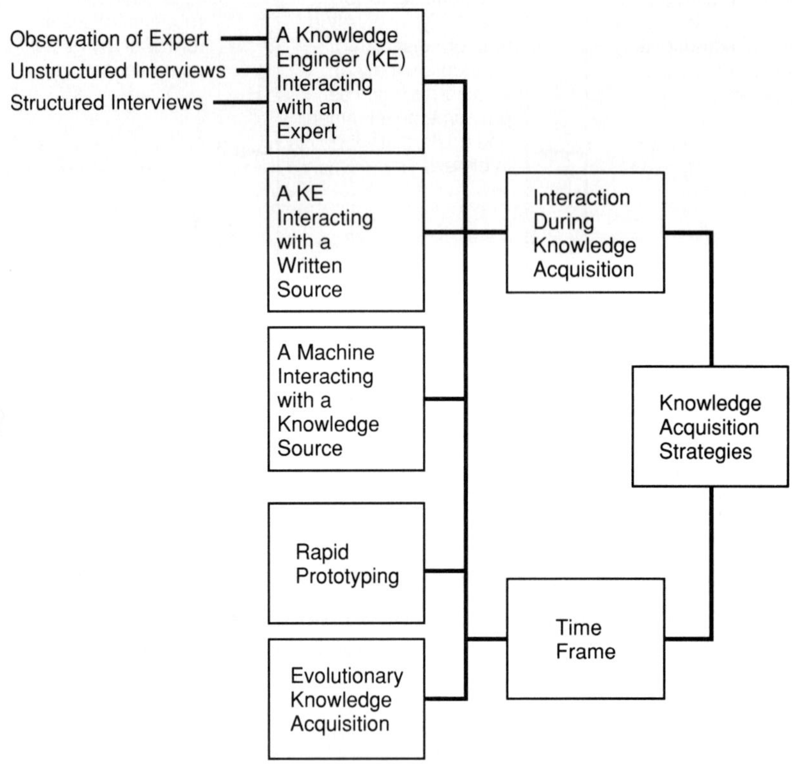


***A Machine Interacting with Knowledge Sources.*** This type of acquisition may occur with or without the presence of a knowledge engineer. It involves a machine interacting with a domain expert, written documents, or with computerized databases or other sources of input knowledge, such as sensors. Several automated knowledge acquisition tools are discussed later in this chapter.

## The Time Frame of Knowledge Acquisition

The time frame available for knowledge acquisition determines whether a rapid prototyping or an evolutionary knowledge acquisition strategy is used, as shown in Figure 7–3.

***Rapid Prototyping.*** This strategy involves quickly creating computer prototypes or paper models of small segments or overall concepts of the proposed system. The term *concept*, as used here, refers to a representation of an object or an event which is based on its characteristics or its relationships to other objects or events.

Dependency diagram models of KBS, for example, are paper-model conceptualizations of actual systems.

Once initial design and knowledge base decisions have been made, a computer prototype is developed very rapidly to assess the initial design and determine whether or not (or how much and what kind of) refinement or additional knowledge is necessary. This strategy is typically used over a short span of time very early in the knowledge acquisition process.

***Evolutionary Knowledge Acquisition.*** This strategy is generally used in a large system development project, and usually occurs over a prolonged period of time. This strategy involves the iterative development of design models and knowledge bases and may include structured and unstructured interviews with an expert, as well as use of other knowledge sources. Computerized prototypes may be developed early in the process. However, the main vehicle for knowledge acquisition and system design using this strategy normally consists of media such as paper models, not computer prototypes. These models or prototypes are often referred to as successive approximations.

### Incremental Approach

An incremental, or modular, method of expert system design has been described by Edmund Payne (1991). This method advocates the ease of testing, maintenance, and expansion when multiple discreet knowledge modules are used. This allows numerous possibilities for planning and diagnosis rather than the single initial prototype.

## KNOWLEDGE ACQUISITION TECHNIQUES AND TOOLS

There are many knowledge acquisition techniques and tools available to a knowledge engineer (Boose 1988; Boose 1989). Some of the more commonly used tools and techniques are described in this section, including:

- techniques for observing experts, sometimes referred to as process tracing
- protocol analysis
- other tools and techniques used in gathering data
- other tools and techniques for acquiring and formulating knowledge: manual and automated
- prototyping

### Techniques for Observing Experts (Process Tracing)

In observing an expert, a number of general **process tracing** techniques are used that allow a knowledge engineer to follow a domain expert's train of thought or reasoning as he or she completes a task. These techniques, which are outlined in Figure 7–4, are discussed in this section.

***Direct Observation of Familiar Tasks.*** A knowledge engineer may observe domain experts performing their usual tasks. This enables a knowledge engineer to observe what information is important to the domain expert in performing a job, as well as to identify the critical situational factors affecting the expert's job performance. Where possible, several tasks familiar to the expert are observed. An analysis of these observations, supplemented where possible by an analysis of available texts and technical manuals describing the tasks, can be used to generate a "first pass" at a knowledge base and sometimes enable developing of an initial prototype system (Grabowski 1988, p. 48; Hoffman 1987, p. 54).

One disadvantage to this knowledge acquisition technique is that it is very time consuming both from the point of view of the expert and of the knowledge engineer. In addition, experts in many situations do not have the time while doing a task to describe exactly how they are making the decisions.

***Recollections of Past Experiences.*** This technique involves asking experts how they arrived at a solution to a problem in the past, and how the various aspects of the situation affected their decision. In essence, experts are simply asked to talk about their jobs, in the course of which they often draw analogies with other similar experiences to illustrate points. This enables them to more fully explain the tasks and reasoning processes involved than while being observed doing their job. Using such a technique often produces more detailed models of the expert's reasoning processes (Grabowski 1988, p. 51).

**Figure 7–4.** Tools and Techniques for Observing Experts—Process Tracing

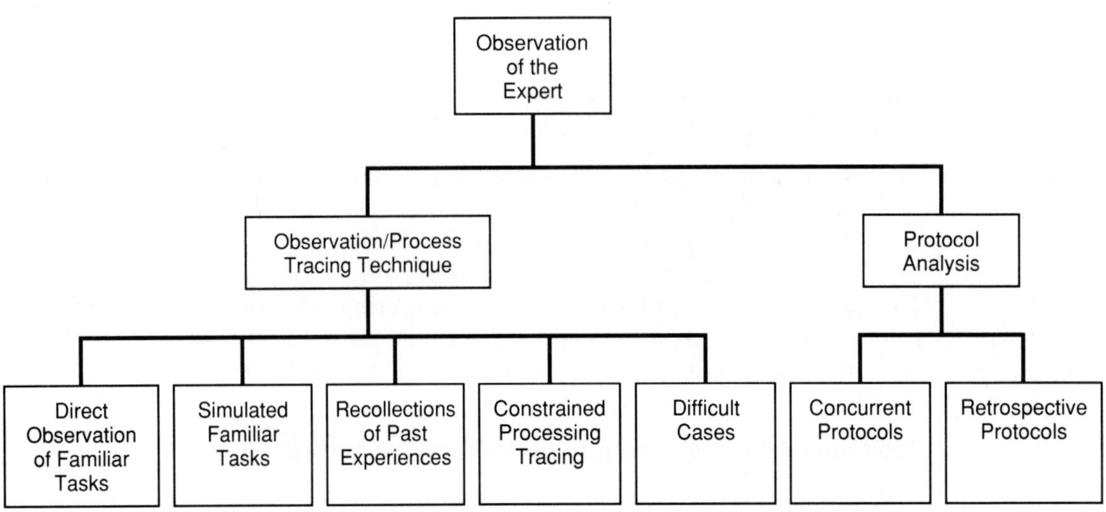

***Simulated Familiar Tasks.*** This technique uses information accumulated from past observation, interviews, and searches of the written material available. It allows an expert to simulate the performance of a familiar task using a case study (Grabowski, p. 48). The availability of archival data is a prerequisite for using this technique (Hoffman 1987, p. 57). Having been given an actual case, the expert would talk aloud about how to solve the problem simulated in the case study. By using such simulated scenarios the expert is forced to concentrate on specific aspects of a case or problem, which helps to produce a more detailed operational picture of how the expert goes about the task. The expert also has time to discuss some of the reasoning involved in performing the job, since there is no pressure of actual events. Where a variety of familiar tasks are involved and time is limited, simulating familiar tasks is a very useful knowledge acquisition technique. Its disadvantage is that at times real world events, factors, and unremembered expert thought processes are omitted.

***Constrained Process Tracing.*** This technique involves having an expert perform a familiar task or discuss a simulated or recollected task, but under a time or information constraint, or both. Where the information-constraint technique is used, contextual information is withheld, forcing the expert to rely heavily upon his or her knowledge and reasoning skills (Hoffman 1987, p. 56). Where a time-constraint technique is used, a time limit is set for completing a task or making a decision. Both time and information constraints can be tailored to extract information on selected sub-domains of knowledge, or on the domain expert's reasoning strategies. This technique clearly only works in very well-focused situations and can create anxieties which might distort the expert's reasoning processes. In addition, the expert may feel uncomfortable and become hesitant to make judgments.

***Difficult Cases.*** This technique involves observing an expert dealing with a case that has unusual, unfamiliar, or challenging features. This technique is usually used in the later stages of knowledge acquisition, in order to refine the reasoning behind a decision and to expand the applicability of a system to a wider range of situations. This technique is often used to get evidence about the subtle or refined aspects of the expert's reasoning (Hoffman 1987, p. 57).

### Protocol Analysis

During observations of the expert, **protocol analysis** is used to analyze, organize, and represent a domain expert's overall decision-making approaches and the specific methods used to move from one knowledge state to another (Grabowski 1988, p. 48). Protocol analysis is the process of translating "thinking aloud" verbalizations into more accessible and meaningful representations, such as the decision scenarios described in Chapter 2 and the many tools and techniques described later in this chapter (Bouwman 1978; Ericcson 1980). In using this technique, a knowledge engineer is able to formulate a sequenced map of the expert's decision-making thoughts. **Verbal protocols** are verbalizations of an expert thinking aloud, which can be tape-recorded, transcribed, or otherwise recorded. There are two different types of verbal protocols, concurrent and retrospective.

**Concurrent protocols** are obtained by recording an expert's verbalization of thoughts and reasoning processes while solving a problem. One advantage to this type of protocol analysis is that it requires little equipment. In addition, the knowledge engineer may not have to be present at the time that the expert encounters a tough case in a real world situation. Using this technique, the expert is equipped with a small tape recorder and for instances where the knowledge engineer is not to be present is instructed in how to make a verbal protocol of personal observations when encountering, for example, a tough case (Hoffman 1987, p. 57). One disadvantage of this technique is that the expert's simultaneous performance of a task while thinking aloud may interfere with the expert's performance of the activity. In addition, the act of voicing one's thoughts can interfere with or inhibit trains of thought for some individuals. In select situations, a video recorder may be used to record concurrent protocols.

**Retrospective protocols** are protocols obtained by asking a domain expert to review audio, video, or transcription records of the expert's previous verbalizations after the task is completed. The expert is then questioned about decision-making criteria he or she used at certain points in the recorded session. Retrospective protocols are often used when concurrent protocols are suspected to adversely affect the expert's task performance, or when task performance is suspected to interfere with the expert's ability to offer a coherent protocol (Wright and Ayton 1987, p. 26). Also, when a team of domain experts is used, retrospective protocols would be recommended in conjunction with group discussions. The disadvantage of this approach is that experts do not always recall all the reasoning steps, since mental processes are difficult to recall and verbalize (Nisbett 1977).

### Other Tools and Techniques Used in Gathering Data

Gathering data for the development of a knowledge-based system generally requires the formation of a written knowledge handbook, dictionary, or other kind of database which contains initial project information and continually updated knowledge:

***Initial Project Information.*** This would include:

1. a description of the general problem
2. the context of the knowledge domain, covering both:
    - the broader context of the problem domain
    - related domains

3. a list of experts available for the study
4. a list of users of the system and their expectations for the system
5. staff, software, computer, and other resource availability
6. a more detailed description of the domain involved in the development project
7. objectives of the initial and ultimate phases of the project
8. limitations of the project
9. a bibliography of reference sources

***Continually Updated Knowledge.*** This would include:

1. listings and definitions of key terms, phrases, acronyms, concepts, and other factual data
2. descriptions of typical reasoning scenarios
3. descriptions of the key tasks involved in the decision under study
4. descriptions of the factors affecting the different decisions made or possible outcomes of the task
5. notes on the derivation of the rules guiding a domain expert's decisions or actions
6. listings of the possible recommendations to be made by the system
7. descriptions of the heuristics involved in making these recommendations in typical situations
8. descriptions of tough or unusual problem situations
9. interview and other meeting sessions records

The media chosen for these records could vary from manual, such as knowledge acquisition forms and questionnaires, to computer records (knowledge databases), to audio tapes and video recordings.

### Other Tools and Techniques for Acquiring and Formulating Knowledge: Manual and Automated

Manual and automated tools and techniques are used in knowledge acquisition. They help to identify knowledge-domain concepts and define structure and decision-making *heuristics*—rules of thumb or other strategies used in problem solving and decision making. The following section describes the commonly used manual and automated tools which are identified in Figure 7–5.

***Manual Tools and Techniques.*** The discussion in this section, which focuses mainly on manual diagramming techniques, covers four types of tools and techniques.

*Diagramming techniques* are used extensively in knowledge acquisition and representation to record and represent domain information. In many situations, knowledge diagrams consist of hierarchical, top-down descriptions of events, linkages between events, primitive events, and objects. Each level of the diagrams

**Figure 7–5.** Tools and Techniques for Acquiring and Formulating Knowledge

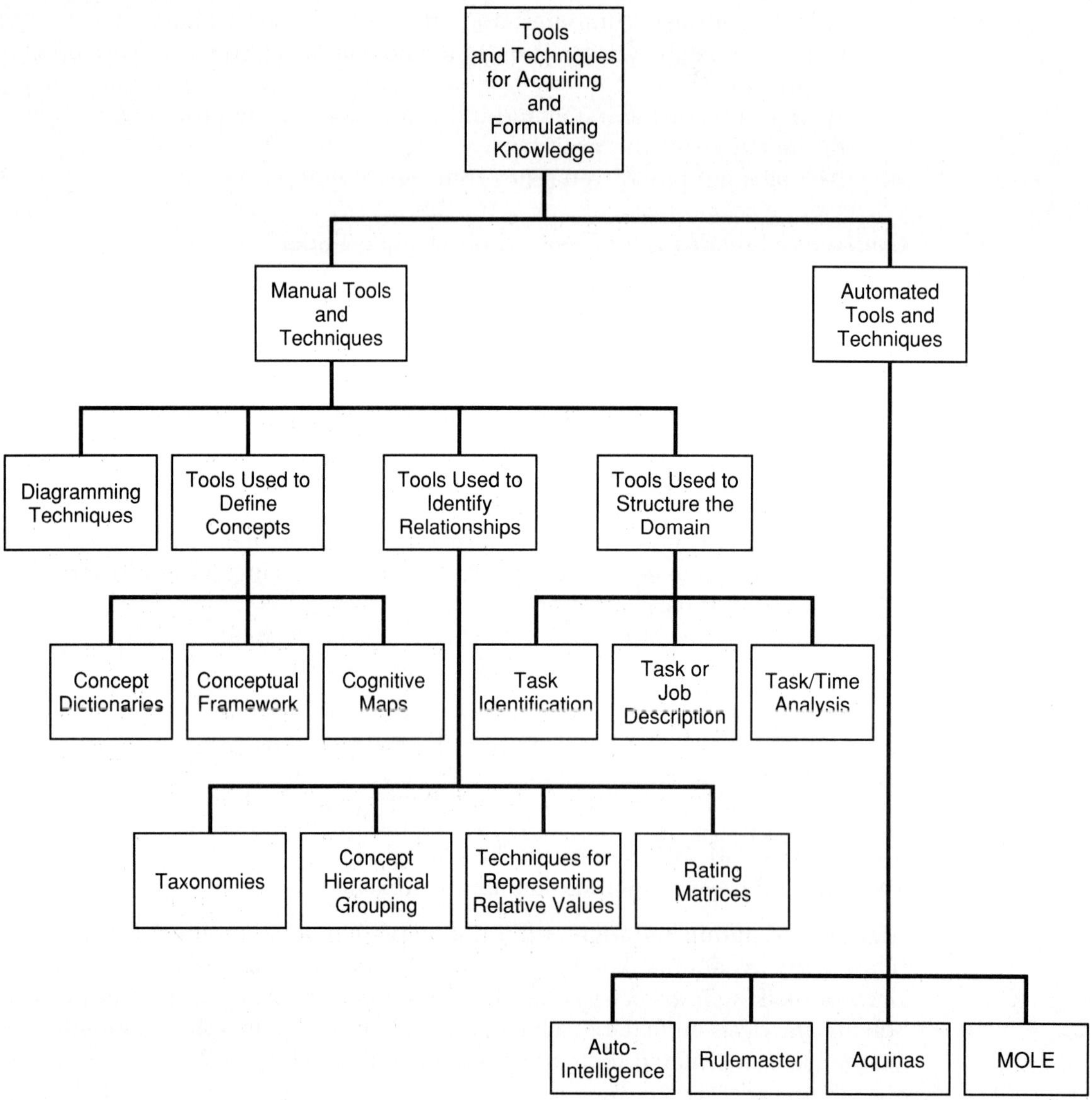

provides a partitioned view of events and objects. Events are decomposed into lower-level events until, at the lowest level, primitive events and objects are described. As knowledge is acquired, the diagrams support the analysis and planning of subsequent acquisition activities which aid in the generation of knowledge bases (Hillman 1988, p. 38). Examples of diagramming techniques include decision charts, hierarchy knowledge-domain diagrams, and diagrams of reasoning processes, such as those shown in Chapter 2. Dependency diagrams, such as the one shown in Figure 7–6, are also examples of these kinds of diagrams. More detailed examples of such hierarchical diagramming techniques are shown in the dependency diagrams for the systems described in Figures 2–7 a through f in Chapter 2.

**Figure 7–6.** Decision Situation Diagram: Estimating KBS Project Proposal Level of Risk (Initial Prototype Phase)

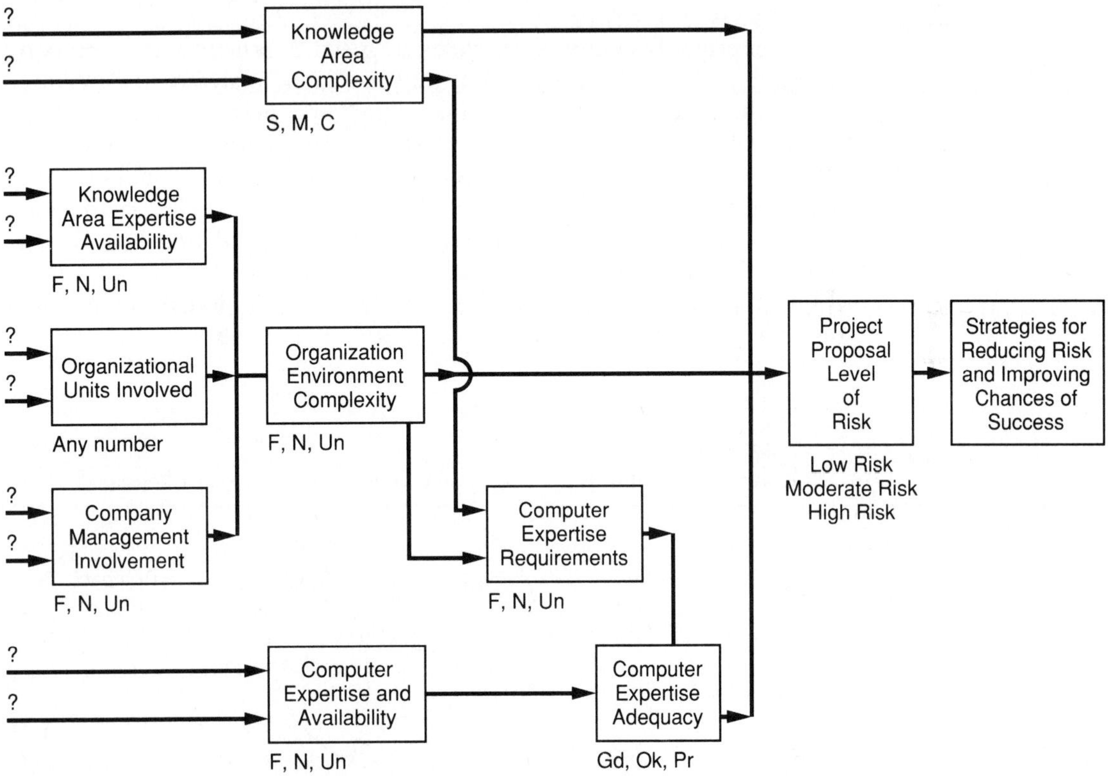


Key:

F = Favorable
N = Neutral
Un = Unfavorable

Gd = Good
Pr = Poor
Ok = Okay

S = Simple
M = Moderate
C = Complex

A wide range of diagramming techniques are being used today. A sampling of some of the ones more currently used in the early 1990s are given in Goodman (1990), Woodward (1990), Lirov (1990), and Kearney (1990).

*Tools used to define situation concepts in general* include: concept dictionaries, conceptual frameworks, and cognitive maps.

- A **concept dictionary** provides a reference mechanism for recording and understanding the primary concepts in a domain and the terminology used to label them. In order to create such a dictionary, a knowledge engineer must have working knowledge of the domain and appropriate terms must be selected and agreed upon with the expert. For example, the definitions of basic terms such as *knowledge domain*, *domain expert*, and *knowledge base* given elsewhere in this chapter might be included in an initial segment of a concept dictionary prepared as part of the system development project described at the end of this chapter. Concept dictionaries sometimes contain diagrams such as the one shown in Figure 7–7 (McGraw 1989, p. 136).
- A **conceptual framework** provides a specific structure for depicting categories of critical information that are later analyzed to determine how an individual drew conclusions. The conceptual framework allows the knowledge engineer to abstract key information from the interviews or observations to determine the concepts, attributes, and values that are important in the subset of the domain under scrutiny. The classification of "Tools and Techniques for Acquiring and Formulating Knowledge" (Figure 7–5) given at the beginning of this section is an example of a conceptual framework. Structure is created for the domain by dividing the topic into "Manual Tools" and "Automated Tools".

**Figure 7–7.** An Example of Designs Included in a Concept Dictionary

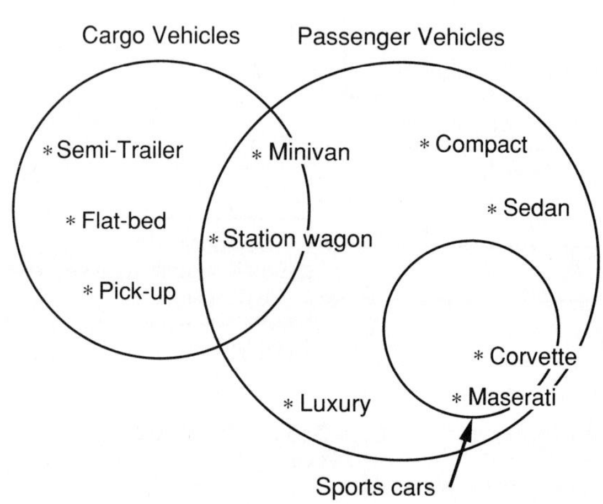

- **Cognitive maps** represent in very general terms a domain expert's ideas about primary relationships and concepts in a domain. They allow a knowledge engineer to become familiar with major concepts and relationships in the domain and can be used to organize later knowledge acquisition sessions. The primary disadvantage is that they are based on the domain expert's perception and are subject to inaccuracies. They are often no more than initial rough diagrams of an expert's view of the domain or decision situation during the early phases of knowledge acquisition. The semantic network shown in Figure 8–5 is one kind of cognitive map.

*Tools used to identify relationships more specifically* include: taxonomies, concept hierarchical groupings, techniques for representing relative values, and rating matrices.

- **Taxonomies** are basic classification systems that are more detailed versions of the conceptual frameworks described above. They enable designers or knowledge engineers to describe conceptual identifications and dependencies. Figure 7–8 shows elements grouped together in a taxonomy. The construction of a taxonomy involves identifying, defining, comparing, and grouping elements. Taxonomies are most useful in the organization of declarative knowledge, such as that replicated in diagnostic knowledge-based systems.
- **Concept hierarchies** or groupings are a psychological technique which involves constructing a "tree" of related concepts. An example of a concept hierarchy is shown in Figure 7–9. These hierarchical groupings

**Figure 7–8.** An Example of a Taxonomy

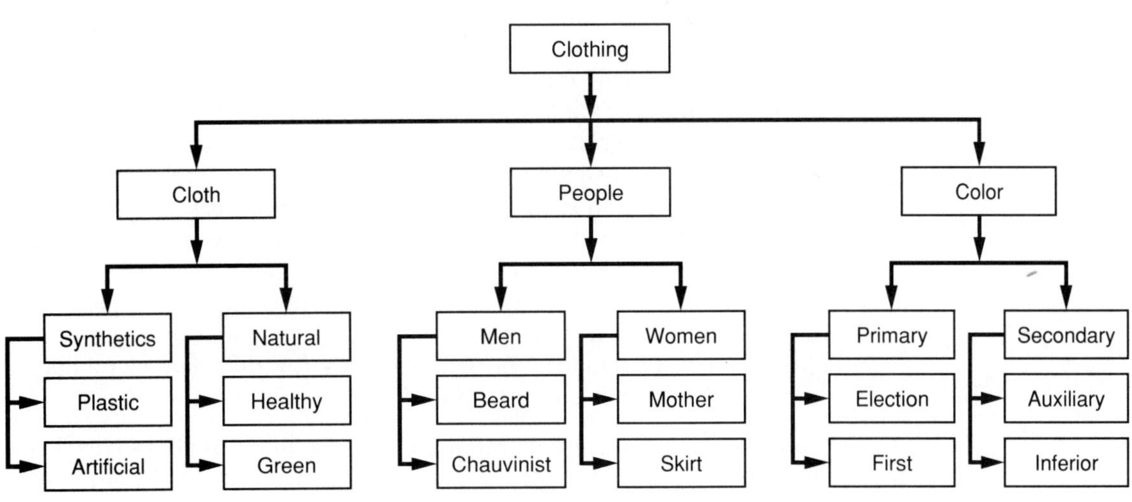

**Figure 7–9.** Concept Hierarchy

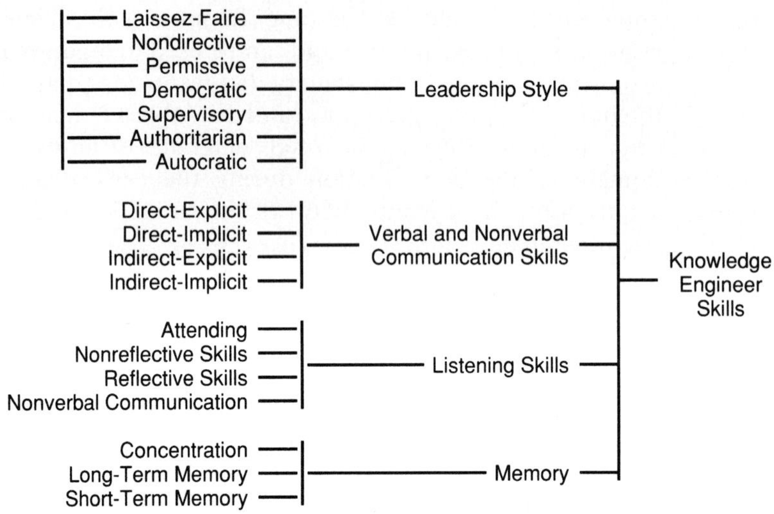


facilitate the comprehension of the expert's personal domain organization and visualization of its subsystems. This leads to more structure within the subgroups than with taxonomies. These conceptual groupings are often provided numerical values, as shown in Figure 7–10.

- **Techniques for representing relative values** are another way to compare and analyze knowledge. An example of a rating scale is shown in Figure 7–11. Such an approach allows a knowledge engineer to rank the strength of relationships among concepts according to how different experts compare and rank the same objects and concepts. For example, the strong–weak scale might be used to record and measure ratings of a knowledge engineer's interpersonal skills in handling interactions with coworkers and supervisors. The flexible–inflexible scale might be used for specifying a knowledge engineer's capabilities in handling unusual knowledge acquisition situations. Rating techniques have the advantage of being less introspective and offering more formal, as well as objective, means of acquiring knowledge.
- **Rating matrices** are representations of an expert's view of a particular problem using a matrix or grid form, such as in the example given in Figure 7–12. The matrix provides ratings for different elements or components of a situation under study.

*Tools used to structure the domain* are used after the initial analyses have been completed in order to describe in even greater detail the tasks a human expert performs. This is necessary to determine specific knowledge acquisition require-

**Figure 7–10.** Conceptual Groupings with Numerical Values

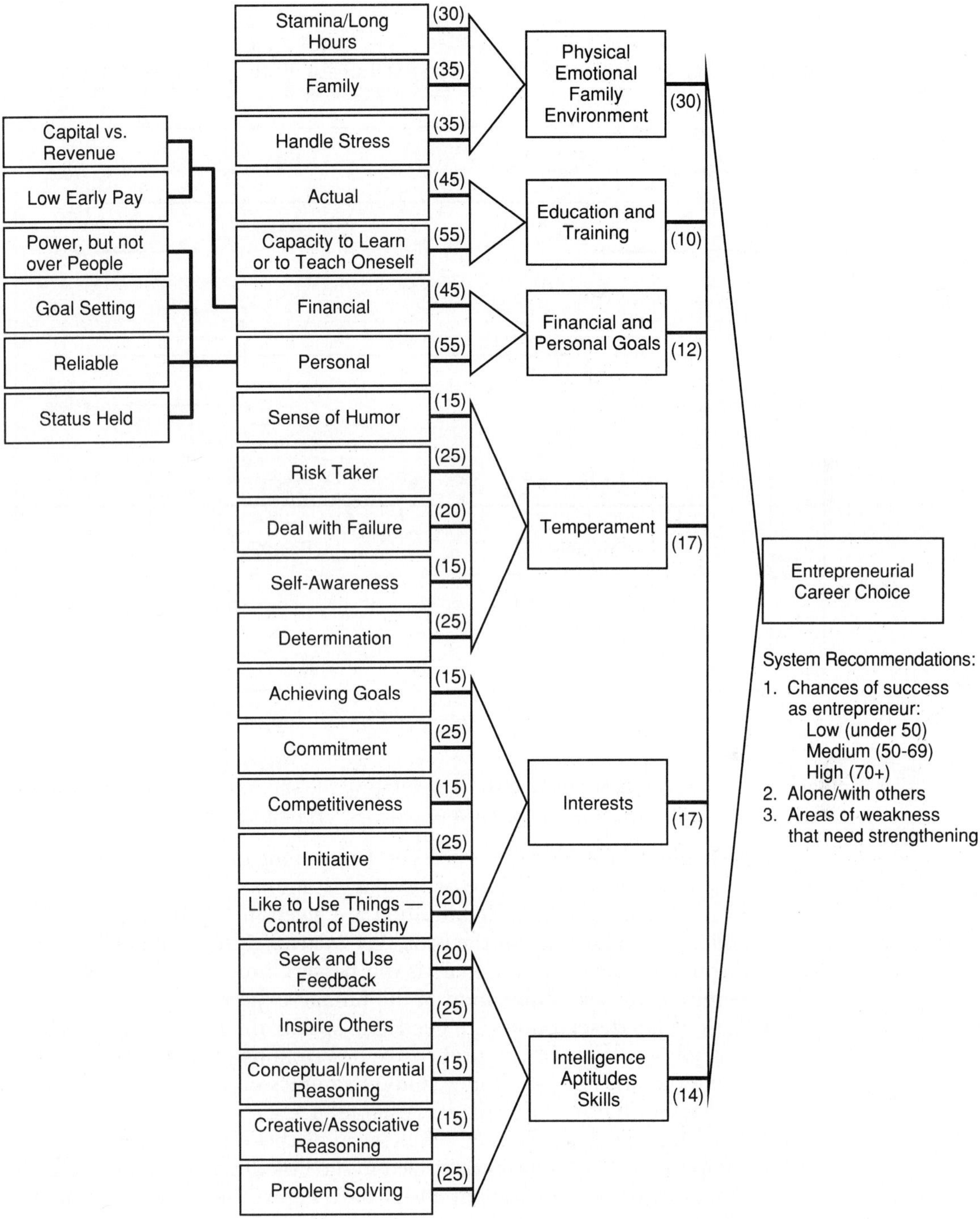

**Figure 7–11.** Examples of Three Approaches for Rating Relative Values

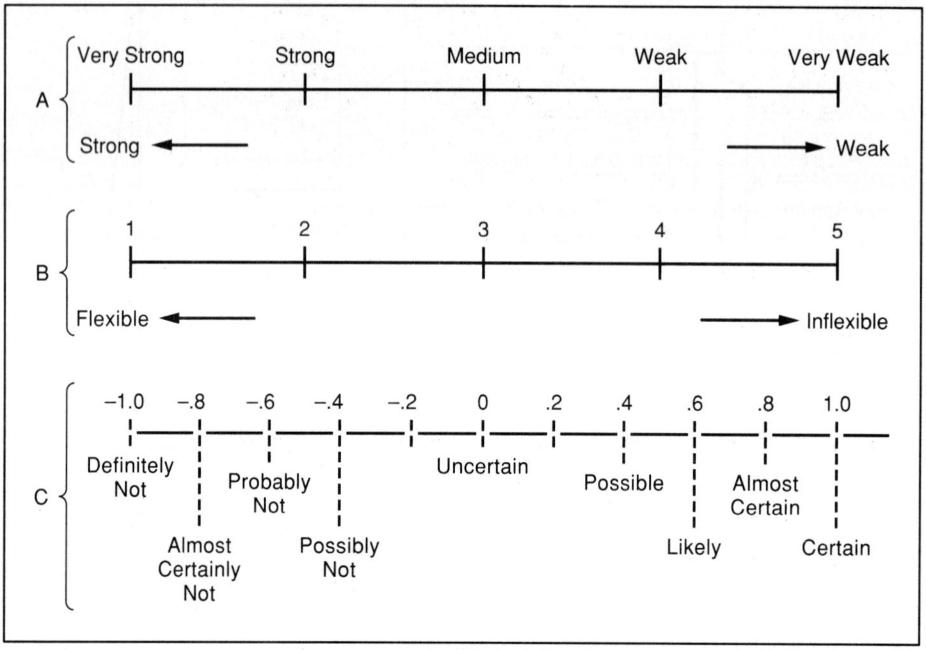


ments for the actual detailed system development. Included are: task identification, task or job description, task/time analysis, and checks for expert biases.

- **Task identification** is the process of determining or describing the nature of a task, job, or procedure by breaking it into its essential components. Examples of basic task identification are given in Figures 7–1 and 7–2 and in the discussions of the prototype systems developed in Chapters 2 through 6. Detailed task analysis can be very time consuming and may require extensive observation of the human expert.
- **Task or job descriptions** are needed to specify the major responsibilities of a job and include comprehensive descriptions of what is involved in doing the tasks or jobs under study. Examples of job analyses are given in detail in the staffing chapter, Chapter 14.
- **Task/time analysis** is used to determine the effect of time on task completion. The subtasks described in the task descriptions are assigned times for completion and put into a chart. Figure 7–13 shows a task/time analysis for knowledge acquisition.
- **Bias checks and debiasing** involves strategies and procedures for reviewing knowledge structures to eliminate the normal biases some experts have when approaching a decision (Silverman 1990).

**Figure 7–12.** Sample Rating Matrices Decision Situation under Study: Estimating KBS Project Proposal Level of Risk—Decision Chart, Final Rule Set (Initial Prototype Phase)

(A) *Initial Version*

| Rule #1– | 1 | 2 | 3 | 4 | 5 | 6 | 7 | 8 | 9 | 10 | 11 | 12 | 13 |
|---|---|---|---|---|---|---|---|---|---|---|---|---|---|
| if knowledge-area-complexity | S | S | S/M | C | C | * | S | S | M/C | M | M/C | M | M |
| if org-environment-complexity | F | F/H | F | U | * | U | M | M/U | F | F | N | N/U | N |
| if computer-expertise-adequacy | G/O | G | G | * | P | P | O/P | O | O | O/P | G | G | O |
| then Level of Risk = | | | | | | | | | | | | | |
| low risk | X | X | X | | | | | | | | | | |
| moderate risk | | | | | | | X | X | X | X | X | X | X |
| high risk | | | | X | X | X | | | | | | | |

S = simple M = moderate C = complex
F = favorable N = neutral U = unfavorable
G = good O = okay P = poor
/ = or * = any answer

(B) *Final Condensed Version*

| Rule #1– | 1 | 2 | 3 | 4 | 5 | 6 | 7 |
|---|---|---|---|---|---|---|---|
| if knowledge-area-complexity | S | S | S/M | C | C | * | * |
| if org-environment-complexity | F | F/N | F | U | * | U | * |
| if computer-expertise-adequacy | G/O | G | G | * | P | P | * |
| then Level of Risk = | | | | | | | |
| low risk | X | X | X | | | | |
| moderate risk | | | | | | | X |
| high risk | | | | X | X | X | |

S = simple M = moderate C = complex
F = favorable N = neutral U = unfavorable
G = good O = okay P = poor
/ = or * = any answer

***Automated Tools for Acquiring and Formulating Knowledge.*** Considerable research is being done to develop knowledge acquisition software (Boose and Gaines 1988; di Piazza 1990; McGraw 1989, p. 283). In order to give an idea of these tools and how they work, this section describes two of them, Auto-Intelligence and Aquinas.

One of the better known and earliest commercially available automated tools for knowledge acquisition and structuring is *Auto-Intelligence.* Auto-Intelligence consists of five main modules (Parsaye, pp. 58–59):

**Figure 7–13.** A Sample Task/Time Analysis of Knowledge Acquisition Tasks for a Specific Project

| Step | Knowledge Acquisition Tasks | Purpose | Time Required to Complete |
|---|---|---|---|
| 1 | Analysis of Familiar Tasks | Familiarizes the knowledge engineer with the expert's domain. Yields some information for the initial concept-testing knowledge base. | Three weeks |
| 2 | Unstructured Interview | Further familiarizes the knowledge engineer with the expert's domain. Provides information for the initial concept-testing knowledge base. Helps in determining/identifying user requirements and general design of system. | Two to Three Weeks |
| 3 | Preparation of Initial Concept-Testing Knowledge Base | Initial prototype system development—first pass. | One Month |
| 4 | Observation of Expert at Work | Further helps knowledge engineer become familiar with the expert's domain. Provides information for the initial prototype knowledge base. Helps in identifying user requirements and developing the design of the system. | Three to Four Weeks |
| 5 | Structured Interviews | Provides information for the initial knowledge base. | One to Two Weeks |
| 6 | Review with Expert | Further helps knowledge engineer with the expert domain. Provides information for the initial prototype knowledge base. Helps in determining/identifying user requirements and design of the system. | Three Weeks or More |

- *Interview Manager* is responsible for interacting with the expert and capturing knowledge. It manages interaction with the expert dynamically by selecting a suitable interview style.
- *Structure Discovery System* captures the structure of the knowledge and helps identify key components used by the expert in making decisions. The information provided by the expert is analyzed for redundancy and inconsistency, often helping the expert explicitly discover knowledge previously unknown in explicit form.
- *Example Manager* keeps track of data and examples and helps the expert in performing record-keeping tasks.
- *Induction System* both classifies and generalizes data and examples provided by the expert. Classification results in rules that capture the example set and nothing more. Induction produces much more general rules that go beyond the logic of the examples.
- *Expert System Generator* generates a working expert system that may be either readily executed with an inference engine or incorporated into and modified with an expert system shell.

The expert system shell 1st-Class also makes effective use of an induction table to provide a means of quickly constructing a knowledge base and prototype KBS built upon it. So does VP-Expert. An example of how to use an induction table for organizing knowledge acquired is given in Chapter 5.

*Aquinas* is an automated knowledge acquisition tool that combines ideas from psychology and knowledge-based systems research to support knowledge acquisition tasks. Aquinas interviews experts and helps them analyze, test, and refine the knowledge base. Expertise from multiple experts and other knowledge sources can be represented and used separately or in combination. Because it contains many tools for knowledge acquisition, it is useful in rapidly initiating prototypes and serving as a testbed for complex knowledge-based systems (Boose & Gaines v.2 1988, p. 39).

Automated tools are still in the early stages of development (for examples, Motta 1990). Many are not yet easy to use. Until they are made accessible to a wider range of knowledge engineers, their use will be very limited.

## Prototyping

Prototyping is one of the major techniques used to structure and represent knowledge and is used throughout the KBS development process. With prototyping, a knowledge engineer and an expert work together to quickly identify basic information requirements and build a prototype expert system quickly.

Once an initial prototype knowledge-based system is constructed, both the knowledge engineer and the expert have a common base of reference from which to develop and refine the system (Menzies 1989). Since the prototype uses the same terminology that the expert uses to solve problems in the domain, the knowledge engineer should have an easier time correcting and modifying the system's rules and relationships. Use of the prototype also rejuvenates expert enthusiasm, which often decreases in later stages of expert system development work (Grabowski, p. 49).

Examples of prototype knowledge-based systems are found throughout this book.

## AN APPROACH TO MAKING DECISIONS IN SPECIFIC SITUATIONS

The preceding sections described how the knowledge acquisition and representation situation works, as well as some strategies and techniques useful in carrying out knowledge acquisition and representation tasks. This section describes how decisions are made when selecting knowledge acquisition and representation techniques and tools to use in individual reader KBS development situations—that is, situations you yourself might encounter.

The overall decision-making process involved is shown in Figure 7–14. As seen in that figure, a variety of decisions are possible in this area:

- selecting a general process-tracing strategy for observing an expert
- the type of interview strategy to use
- whether to use rapid prototyping or evolutionary knowledge acquisition strategies
- choosing protocol analysis techniques and equipment
- selecting a concept, domain, or task-analysis technique

This section first describes how specific knowledge-domain, organizational, and available-resource factors are analyzed and structured. It then covers how these factors are used in making decisions about which knowledge acquisition and representation strategies to use in different kinds of KBS development situations.

A wide range of KBS development situations can be involved when making these decisions: situations vary from large and diverse KBS development projects involving hundreds of nontechnical users working in widely dispersed and potentially dangerous locations to situations involving financial analysts and corporate executives working in quiet corporate offices on Wall Street.

Because of this wide range of possible decisions and decision situations, the approach described in this section is necessarily a general one, which is intended to give only an overview introduction to the approach. Specific applications of this general approach are described in the final sections of this chapter.

The following sections discuss:

- critical factors that affect decisions concerning knowledge acquisition and representation
- making decisions based on these critical situation factors

**Figure 7–14.** Overall Decision Situation—Knowledge Acquisition and Representation Strategy and Technique Selection

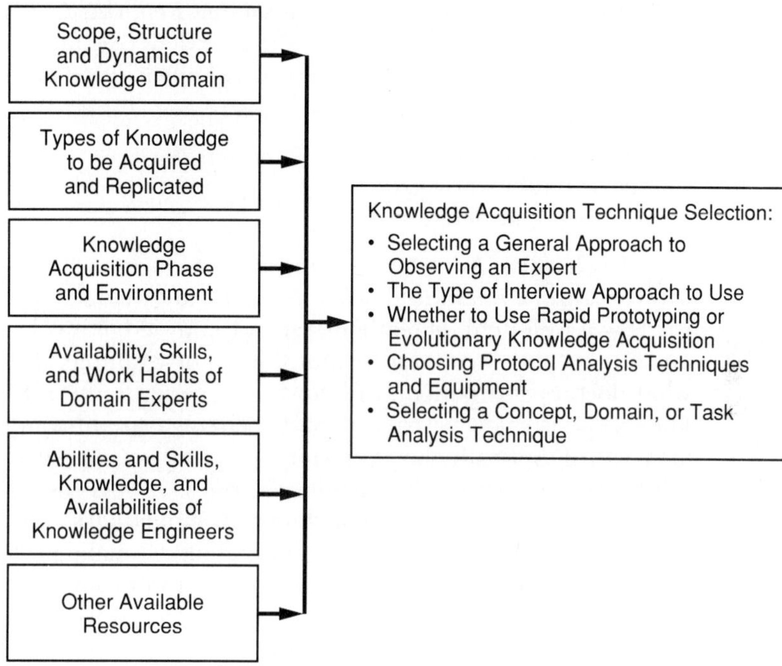


### Critical Factors Affecting Decisions in This Area

This chapter discusses the six critical factor areas shown in Figure 7–14.

***Scope, Structure, and Dynamics of a Knowledge Domain.*** These factors can affect both the kind and amount of knowledge acquisition strategies and techniques used. For example, the broader the knowledge domain, the greater will be the number of factors affecting the decision and so the more likely the need for different interviewing strategies and uses of prototyping. The more complex the domain, the more sophisticated and numerous will be the cognitive tools needed to analyze, formulate, and represent the domain. One also considers how static or dynamic the domain is—whether the knowledge domain has changed due to recent developments or is subject to frequent change—since this might, for example, affect the usefulness of domain experts' recollections of past experience as a knowledge acquisition technique.

Obviously, in a simple knowledge domain, such as the screening of insurance applications, the decision as to which knowledge acquisition strategies to use is considerably less complex than when dealing with a complicated computer-configuration knowledge domain.

***The Types of Knowledge to Be Acquired and Replicated.*** The type of knowledge sought will have a great effect on the knowledge acquisition and representation process. For situation analysis purposes, knowledge types can be categorized as:

- declarative knowledge
- procedural knowledge
- semantic knowledge
- metaknowledge

**Declarative knowledge** represents surface-level information that experts can verbalize. Declarative knowledge is the knowledge one has about the external world—a well-defined textbook type of knowledge involving facts about objects and events and their interrelationships. For example, it includes knowledge of what doctors and patients are, and their general interrelationships. Declarative knowledge is easily verbalized, and is characterized by an expert's being able to articulate specifically the characteristics of objects and events. It is useful in the initial stages of knowledge acquisition but is of less value in later stages.

**Procedural knowledge** includes an individual's capabilities in performing such routine tasks as driving an automobile or dialing a telephone. Procedural knowledge is relatively well defined, but often not easily verbalized by an expert. It is sometimes called *performance knowledge*. Since prolonged and frequent performance often tends to make the knowledge intuitive and reflex—often the completion of one task triggers the beginning of another—the expert may be aware of what has to be done, but not always why.

**Semantic knowledge** is the deep-level knowledge that involves structure, organization, and representation of cognitive or thinking processes. It is of primary importance in the building of expert systems because it includes concepts and relationships among factors that are used when domain experts make decisions. Semantic knowledge includes mostly decision-making heuristics, such as those described in the risk-estimating decisions covered in Chapters 2 and 12.

**Metaknowledge** is knowledge or awareness of facts, heuristics, and/or rules, and the context in which they are used and manipulated. An example would include the recognition of the limits of one's own knowledge. For instance, knowing that one's knowledge of car repair is limited to American cars and that there is a broader knowledge area of car repair, including repairing all makes of cars worldwide, is an example of metaknowledge.

Different types of knowledge can require different knowledge acquisition strategies and techniques.

***Knowledge Acquisition Phase and Environment Involved.*** For analysis purposes, knowledge acquisition can be segmented into three distinct knowledge acquisition phases.

Phase I involves the knowledge gathering and exploration that provides a foundation for subsequent knowledge gathering and representation steps. Important tasks to be completed during this phase include developing a knowledge dictionary of domain terms and concepts. In this phase, techniques such as unstructured interviews, cognitive mapping, and task/time analysis may be appropriate.

Phase II involves knowledge structuring and identifying solution strategies. Here, the information sought becomes more specific and requires observing the expert at work, process tracing, structured interviewing, rating matrices, and task and job analysis. A great deal of the domain expert's time will be required during this phase in more complex situations. The additional input required by the expert ensures effective development and refinement of a prototype system during this and the next phase.

Phase III involves more specific knowledge acquisition and representation. This is the refinement stage, during which prototyping is almost always used, if it has not been already. System prototypes are needed at this point since refining and developing the system requires the expert to verify the accuracy of the knowledge replicated. Review of prototypes has proven to be an effective way to do this. The knowledge engineer is most likely to use recollections of past experiences, constrained processing tasks, or difficult case observations as knowledge acquisition techniques during this phase.

Obviously the environment may also affect the strategy and techniques used. For example, the techniques used in observing a tugboat or airplane pilot will differ from those used in observing lawyers and accountants at work in an office, or from those used to observe manufacturing operations on the factory floor.

***The Availability, Skills, and Work Habits of the Domain Experts.*** These factors affect decisions about knowledge acquisition strategies. For example, at Coopers & Lybrand there was a problem with observing tax experts directly—they said they couldn't work well with clients while being closely observed. As a result, the observations were made through a partition that seemed opaque to the experts (a one-way mirror) but through which the knowledge engineers could observe and record the experts' actions. The ability of experts to verbalize their thoughts and define their reasoning processes will also affect the kinds and number of task analyses, conceptual hierarchies, and prototypes that may have to be developed and used.

One of the most commonly encountered problems is the limited availability of experts, who normally have regular full-time jobs to do.

***The Ability, Skills, Knowledge, and Availability of Knowledge Engineers.*** The skills of the knowledge engineers involved in the project also can have an impact on which knowledge acquisition and representation techniques are most likely to be useful. For example, novice knowledge engineers often do not have extensive training in cognitive mapping, task analysis, and other knowledge acquisition techniques, which would discourage reliance on these techniques in situations where they are involved. Other knowledge engineers lack good interpersonal skills, which may limit the use of more sophisticated interviewing techniques. A knowledge engineer already familiar with the knowledge domain under study might use different acquisition techniques from those used by a knowledge engineer unfamiliar with it. Constraints on the number, availability, or mobility of the knowledge engineers in specific situations can also affect the knowledge acquisition techniques used.

***Other Available Resources.*** Time and money constraints have to be considered in any business situation. In addition, the availability of equipment, facilities, computers, automated knowledge acquisition software, and other resources, such as expert system shells for prototyping, will also make an impact on the techniques that can be used in a given situation.

### Making Decisions Based on These Critical Situation Factors

Many decisions are made during the knowledge acquisition and representation phase within the context of critical situation factors and their related requirements. Since these decisions, which are listed in Figure 7–14, are made in light of factors particular to each specific situation, the strategies and techniques used can vary by situation.

For example, as for the first decision listed in Figure 7–14—selecting a general strategy for process tracing, that is, selecting a strategy for observing an expert at work as he or she makes decisions and performs tasks—the direct observation of a familiar task method would be recommended if:

- the knowledge domain has a simple structure
- the type of knowledge the knowledge engineer wants to acquire is *not* complex, deep, or semantic
- the domain expert's skills are strong
- the domain expert's availability is high
- the environment of the acquisition session is favorable

On the other hand, recollections of past experience might be recommended if the knowledge domain is not simple, if the type of knowledge to be acquired is not procedural, if the later phases of the knowledge acquisition process are involved, if the domain expert's skills are strong, and if the domain expert's availability is good.

As for selecting general knowledge acquisition strategies, the third decision listed in Figure 7–14, in small development projects where declarative knowledge is involved and the domain is not complex, such as in many mechanical diagnostic trouble-shooting situations, and where the knowledge engineer is familiar with the domain, rapid prototyping would be the preferred method, especially for the early stages of the development effort.

When choosing protocol analysis techniques and equipment, the fourth decision listed in Figure 7–14, a retrospective protocol using video tape would be used if the type of knowledge to be acquired is metaknowledge, the domain experts would be disrupted in performing the task by a concurrent protocol, the environment the task is performed in is hostile, the knowledge engineers are not very experienced in the domain, the domain is complex, and video tape resources are available.

Obviously there is more to making these decisions than is covered in these brief summaries. In order to explore in more depth the processes involved in making such decisions, the following section discusses in detail the approach to making decisions involving the selection of observation techniques to use.

## APPLYING THIS GENERAL APPROACH TO MAKING DECISIONS ON WHICH OBSERVATION TECHNIQUES TO USE

The decision situation under study in this section involves selecting the most appropriate alternative(s) from among the five following observation or process-tracing techniques:

- direct observation of familiar tasks
- recollections of past experiences
- simulated familiar tasks
- constrained processing tasks
- using difficult cases

The discussion in this section covers:

- critical factors affecting the decision
- possible recommendations and how they are made

The discussion follows the decision situation outline shown in Figure 7–15. The structured situation analysis done here is designed to provide the basis for developing a KBS replicating this knowledge. Such a KBS is described at the end of this chapter.

### Critical Factors Affecting the Decision

Once the decision has been made that expert observation is the knowledge acquisition method to use in the KBS situation under study, the following critical factors are considered:

- experts' work environment
- knowledge acquisition phase
- skills and qualifications of the experts

**Figure 7–15.** Process-Tracing Selection Decision—Decision Diagram

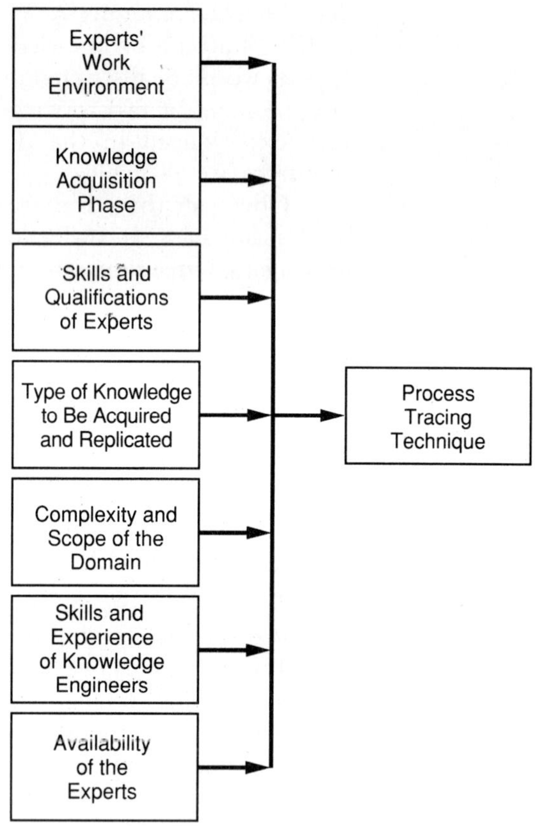


- type of knowledge to be acquired and replicated
- complexity and scope of the knowledge domain
- skills and experience level of the knowledge engineer
- availability of the experts

While possible techniques are mentioned in each section of the following discussions of critical factors, such recommendations are only tentative suggestions of alternatives to explore. Any final recommendation usually requires balancing many different, and often conflicting, factors.

***The Experts' Work Environment.*** Analyzing the experts' work environment involves answering such questions as:

- Does the environment in which the expert works present a constraint because it is difficult to control or may be considered unsafe?

- Is it likely that the domain expert will be interrupted (by co-workers, phone calls, etc.) more than five times an hour during knowledge acquisition sessions in the work environment?

If either of these questions is answered yes, the experts' work environment would be considered unfavorable, and direct observation would in all likelihood be ruled out as a potential process-tracing method in most situations.

***Knowledge Acquisition Phase.*** The knowledge acquisition phase would have an effect on the type of knowledge to be acquired. The following questions would help to determine which knowledge acquisition phase the project is in:

- To what extent has all the required background information on the KBS topic been collected and documented, such as by compiling a concept dictionary?
- To what extent have the basic concepts and interrelationships of the various factors been defined, such as by conceptual frameworks, cognitive maps, and hierarchical groupings?
- Whether or not a prototype has already been developed, would you agree that there is enough information to develop a prototype so that the knowledge acquired thus far can be tested and refined?

Phase I, remember, involves acquiring general background knowledge. Direct observation of familiar tasks and recollections of past experiences are frequently good methods to employ during this phase. Phase II refers to the phase when background knowledge has been collected but all aspects of the domain have not yet been explored. In many situations, simulated familiar tasks would be an effective method to consider using during this phase. Phase III is the refinement phase. Constrained processing and using difficult cases are more likely to be used during this phase, other factors permitting.

***The Skills and Qualifications of the Experts.*** The evaluation of experts' skills and qualifications is based on the answers to such questions as:

- How do management and co-workers of the experts rate the experts' conceptual skills?
- Based on input from management and the co-workers of the experts, how would you rate the experts' willingness and ability to verbalize and communicate thoughts, ideas, concepts, and reasoning patterns?
- Is the experts' experience in the knowledge domain as a trainer, a doer, or both?
- Does the expert become anxious under time constriants or limited-information constraints?
- How would you rate the expert's ability to remember and describe past cases and the reasoning processes which were utilized to make past decisions?

As expert skills and qualifications decrease, a technique such as simulated familiar tasks is more appropriate because it puts less pressure on the expert.

***Type of Knowledge to Be Acquired and Replicated.*** Whether the domain knowledge being acquired and replicated is declarative, procedural, semantic, metaknowledge, or a combination of these will have an effect on the observation technique selected. Such questions as the following help determine what type of knowledge is to be acquired:

- Based on your experience in and review of the knowledge domain (for example, manuals, initial interviews, etc.) to what extent do you consider the knowledge that is to be acquired well defined, in terms of its structure and dimensions?
- To what extent can the knowledge to be acquired be adequately described in a manual or text, as opposed to something that could only be described or known by a human expert?
- How would you rate the degree of awareness or cognizance that the expert has of his or her decisions and reasoning processes, in regard to the relationships among the factors of the knowledge domain?
- To what extent can the experts describe the reasoning behind their decisions and actions only while they are performing and making them?
- To what extent is the knowledge to be acquired learned on the job and from past experiences, as opposed to the type acquired through formal classroom training or from a text?

Declarative knowledge is most easily acquired through direct observation of familiar tasks and recollections of past experiences. Procedural knowledge is best acquired through direct observation of familiar tasks, simulated familiar tasks, and constrained processing tasks. Semantic knowledge is best acquired through simulated familiar tasks, constrained processing tasks, and using difficult cases. Metaknowledge is best acquired through direct observation of familiar tasks, simulated familiar tasks, and recollections of past experiences.

***Complexity and Scope of the Knowledge Domain.*** The complexity and scope of the knowledge domain can be determined by answering such questions as:

- How would you rate the depth and breadth of the knowledge domain? Consider the number of modules and sub-domains that the domain can be segmented into, as well as the number of possible recommendations.
- Are the intermediate decision-making steps involved in the task or decision obviously sequential, or are they more discrete with the steps seeming to overlap?
- How would you rank the dynamics of the knowledge domain? Is it very dynamic with important factors changing quickly over time, somewhat dynamic displaying less rapid change, or somewhat stagnant with a relative absence of change?

- How would you rate the availability of other sources of knowledge and archival cases which may exist in forms such as written material, audio tapes, video tapes, or databases?

If the scope of the knowledge domain is very large, it is often better not to use familiar tasks as an observation technique, because it would be too time consuming to collect all the information. Also, if the knowledge domain is dynamic, this would often exclude the choice of recollections of past experiences as an observation technique because they may no longer be relevant.

***The Skills and Experience of the Knowledge Engineer.*** This includes the knowledge engineer's availability, communication and interpersonal skills, and domain knowledge. The answers to the following questions would be used to explore these areas:

- How would you rate the knowledge engineer's familiarity with the domain and knowledge to be replicated in the KBS?
- Based on what you know about the background of the knowledge engineer, how would you rate the knowledge engineer's communication and interpersonal skills?
- How would you describe the amount of time the knowledge engineer has to devote to this KBS project?

If the knowledge engineer is familiar with the domain, then simulated familiar tasks and recollections of past experiences would not need to be used. If the interpersonal skills and availability of the knowledge engineer are low, direct observation and recollections of past experiences would be less appropriate.

***The Availability of the Experts.*** Although databases and written material are often available as knowledge sources, in many KBS development situations at least one expert has to be consulted at some point during the KBS development cycle. The evaluation of expert availability is based on the answers to such questions as:

- How many experts will be needed and available to work on the KBS?
- How would you describe each expert's time availability for this project?
- How would you rate the enthusiasm of the experts involved in the project?
- Have the experts involved, and their managers, been informed of and have they agreed to the amount of time necessary for the knowledge acquisition sessions?

As expert availability and enthusiasm decreases, knowledge acquisition sessions with them should be more focused to best utilize their limited time. These sessions can also be held while the expert is performing typical tasks, so that the experts can work while knowledge is being acquired. Techniques such as direct observation of familiar tasks, constrained processing tasks, and using difficult cases are most appropriate when expert availability is low.

### Possible Recommendations and How They Are Made

Five possible recommendations for observing an expert at a particular phase in the development of a KBS are available in most situations. They include:

- direct observation of familiar tasks
- recollections of past experiences
- simulated familiar tasks
- constrained processing tasks
- using difficult cases

*Direct observation of familiar tasks* would be recommended if the experts' work environment is favorable, the knowledge acquisition phase is Phase I, the skills and qualifications of the experts are medium, the type of knowledge to be acquired is declarative, the complexity and scope of the domain are low or medium, the skills and experience of the knowledge engineer are low or medium, and availability of the experts ranges from high to low.

*Recollections of past experience* would be recommended if the knowledge acquisition phase is Phase I, the skills and qualifications of the experts are medium to high, the type of knowledge to be acquired is declarative or metaknowledge, the complexity and scope of the domain are low or medium, the skills and experience of the knowledge engineer are low or medium, and the availability of the experts is high.

*Simulated familiar tasks* would be recommended if the knowledge acquisition phase is Phase II, the skills and qualifications of the experts are medium to low, the type of knowledge to be acquired is *not* declarative, the complexity and scope of the domain are low or medium, the skills and experience of the knowledge engineer are low or medium, and the availability of the experts is high or medium.

*Constrained processing tasks* would be recommended if the knowledge acquisition phase is Phase II or III, the skills and qualifications of the experts are medium to high, the type of knowledge to be acquired is *not* declarative, the complexity and scope of the domain are high or medium, the skills and experience of the knowledge engineer are high or medium, and the availability of the experts is low or medium.

*Using difficult cases* would be recommended if the knowledge acquisition phase is Phase II or III, the skills and qualifications of the experts are medium to high, the type of knowledge to be acquired is semantic, the complexity and scope of the domain are high or medium, the skills and experience of the knowledge engineer are high or medium, and the availability of the experts is low or medium.

**Figure 7–16.** Process Tracing Selection Decision—Dependency Diagram (Initial Prototype)

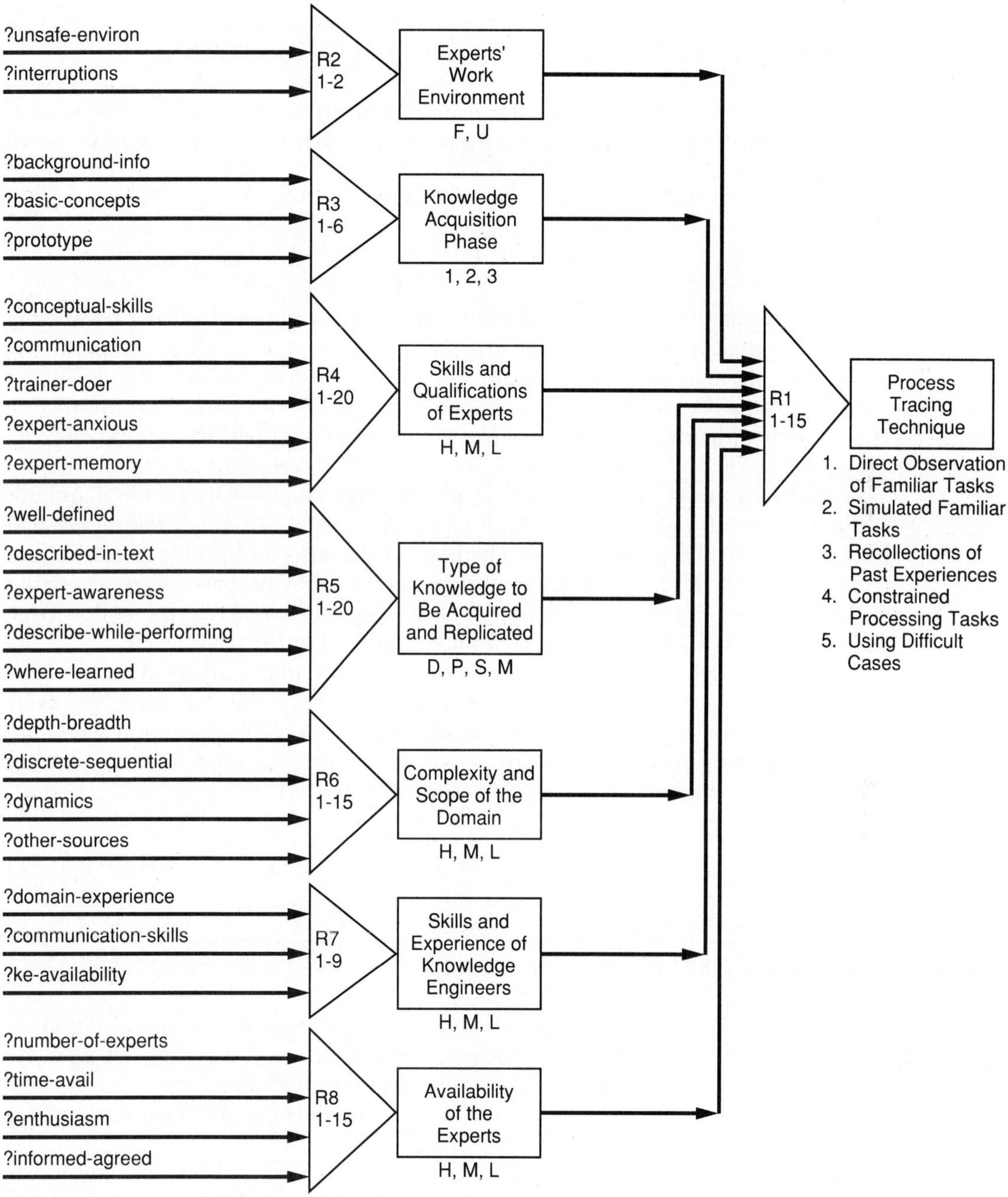


Key:

F = favorable U = unfavorable H = high L = low M = medium
D = declarative P = procedural S = semantic M = metaknowledge

## A KBS FOR ASSISTING IN MAKING THESE DECISIONS

A knowledge-based system has been developed to assist in making the type of decision described in the preceding section. The initial prototype of that system is diagrammed in Figure 7–16.

## THE VARYING IMPORTANCE OF DOMAIN KNOWLEDGE

There are many situations in highly technical areas where acquiring knowledge of the domain may be a major obstacle in developing an effective KBS. For example, in one KBS development situation described by Rose (1988) involving dam leakage diagnosis/trouble-shooting for a utility company, two knowledge engineers with advanced degrees in computer science apparently spent two years and $300,000 learning dam fault diagnosis and developing an 80-rule system which was apparently never used. If a knowledge engineer trained in dam fault diagnosis or an expert in dam fault diagnosis trained in KBS development had been used for the project, it is likely many of the costs and problems could have been avoided. In many situations studied, severe problems have arisen where the knowledge engineering job is staffed with computer science trained knowledge engineers unfamiliar with the area under study (Tuhrim 1988).

Knowledge domain expertise is not always that critical in every KBS development situation, however. For example, where the domain is relatively simple or easy to learn and understand, such as in credit-application screening KBS, knowledge domain expertise is not that important a criteria when selecting a knowledge engineer for a KBS development project.

## REVIEW QUESTIONS

1. Describe the tasks involved in knowledge acquisition and representation.
2. Define *domain expert, knowledge, knowledge domain,* and *knowledge engineer.*
3. Identify the major overall knowledge acquisition strategies.
4. Identify the five major techniques used in observing domain experts making decisions.
5. Define *protocol analysis* and describe different ways to go about doing it.
6. Describe some of the diagramming techniques and tools used to define concepts. Cite examples of these techniques used in earlier chapters in this book.
7. Describe the role of prototyping in knowledge acquisition and representation.

8. Identify the major critical-situation factors analyzed when making decisions about what knowledge acquisition strategies and techniques to use in specific KBS development situations.
9. Identify categories of knowledge sought during knowledge acquisition and the phases identified with knowledge acquisition.
10. Point out the differences between structured and unstructured interviewing and different situations in which they can be useful knowledge acquisition techniques.

## EXERCISES

1. After reviewing the decision situation and dependency diagram outlines in Figures 7–14, 7–15, and 7–16, and the discussion in the two chapter sections entitled "An Approach to Making Decisions in Specific Situations" and "Applying This General Approach to Making Decisions on Which Observation Techniques to Use," develop a small KBS to assist in any of the decisions discussed in this chapter. Follow the directions in either Chapter 2, or in Chapters 3 through 6, when developing the system.
2. Read through recent issues of KBS periodicals listed in the references section of this chapter, and through other related artificial intelligence and user interface books and periodicals, and find discussions of the main topics covered in this chapter. Write a brief report describing how this reading provided you with insights and guidance when developing your KBS for Exercise 1.

## REFERENCES

Agarwal, Rita, and Mohan R. Tannira, "Knowledge Acquisition Using Structure Interviewing: An Empirical Investigation." *Journal of Management Information Systems,* Summer 1990, p. 123.

Boose, John H. "A Survey of Knowledge Acquisition Techniques and Tools." *Knowledge Acquisition*, March 1989, pp. 3–36.

Boose, John H., and Brian R. Gaines. *Knowledge Acquisition for Knowledge-Based Systems.* 2 vols., San Diego, CA: Academic Press, 1988.

Bouwman, M. "Financial Diagnosis: A Cognitive Model of the Processes Involved." Unpublished Ph.D. thesis, Pittsburgh, PA: Carnegie-Mellon, 1978.

di Piazza, Joseph S., and Frederick A. Helsabeck. "LAPS: Cases to Models to Complete Expert Systems. *AI Magazine*, Fall 1990, pp. 80–107.

Ericcson, K., and H. Simon. "Verbal Reports on Data." *Psychological Review*, 87:3 (1980), pp. 215–51.

Goodman, R. M., and P. Smyth. "Decision Tree Design Using Information Theory." *Knowledge Acquisition*, 2 (1990), pp. 1–19.

Grabowski, Martha. "Knowledge Acquisition Methodologies: Survey and Empirical Assessment." *Proceedings of the Ninth International Conference on Information Systems*, Minneapolis MN: SIM, IMS and ACM, December 1988.

Hillman, David. "Bridging Acquisition and Representation." *AI Expert*, November 1988, pp. 38–46.

Hoffman, Robert R. "The Problem of Extracting the Knowledge of Experts from the Perspective of Experimental Psychology." *AI Magazine*, Summer 1987, pp. 53–67.

Kearney, Michele. "Making Knowledge Engineering Productive." *AI Expert*, July 1990, pp. 46–51.

Lirov, Yuval. "Systematic Invention for Knowledge Engineering." *AI Expert*, July 1990, pp. 28–33.

McGraw, K., and K. Harbison-Briggs. *Knowledge Acquisition.* Englewood Cliffs, NJ: Prentice Hall, 1989.

Menzies, Tom. "Domain-Specific Knowledge Representation." *AI Expert*, June 1989, pp. 36–45.

Motta, E., T. Rajan, and M. Eisenstadt. "Knowledge Acquisition as a Process of Model Refinement." *Knowledge Acquisition*, 2 (1990), pp. 21–49.

Nisbett, R., and T. Wilson. "Telling More Than We Can Know: Verbal Reports on Mental Processes." *Psychological Review*, 84:3 (1977), pp. 231–59.

Parsaye, Kamroan. "Acquisition and Verifying Knowledge Automatically." *AI Expert*, May 1988, pp. 48–63.

Payne, Edmund C. "A Modular Knowledge Model." *AI Expert,* May 1991, pp. 36–41.

Rose, Frederick. "An 'Electronic Clone' of a Skilled Engineer Is Very Hard to Create." *The Wall Street Journal*, August 12, 1988, pp. l and 14.

Rothman, David. "Knowledge Transformation." *AI Expert*, November 1988, pp. 28–35.

Silverman, Barry. "Critiquing Human Judgment Using Knowledge-Acquisition Systems." *AI Magazine*, Fall 1990, pp. 60–79.

Tuhrim, Stanley, James A. Riggia, and Michael R. Widk. "A Method for Evaluating Candidate Expert Systems Applications." *AI Magazine*, Winter 1988, pp. 45–53.

Woodward, R. "Knowledge Acquisition at the Front End: Defining the Domain." *Knowledge Acquisition*, 2 (1990), pp. 73–94.

Wright, A. and P. Ayton. "Eliciting and Modelling Expert Knowledge." *Decision Support Systems*, 3(1987), pp. 13–26.

# 8

# Knowledge Transformation: Knowledge Reformulation and System Design

This chapter deals with the next phase of the KBS development life cycle shown in Figure 8–1. *Knowledge transformation* is reformulating and remodelling the knowledge to be replicated into representations useful for system design. These representations replicate as closely as possible the way an expert works in the situation under study. At the same time they are designed to make the transfer of the replication to a computer system as efficient and effective as possible.

The objective of this chapter is to help readers understand:

- The nature of the reformulation involved in knowledge transformation and system design
- Knowledge representation needed for system design
- Inference mechanism models needed for system design
- How to make basic system design strategy decisions

As in other chapters, the final section introduces readers to a KBS for making these decisions.

## KNOWLEDGE TRANSFORMATION: KNOWLEDGE REFORMULATION AND SYSTEM DESIGN

As KBS development progresses, a knowledge engineer moves from developing the initial situation representations to transforming or reformulating these

**Figure 8–1.** Knowledge Base Systems Development Life Cycle

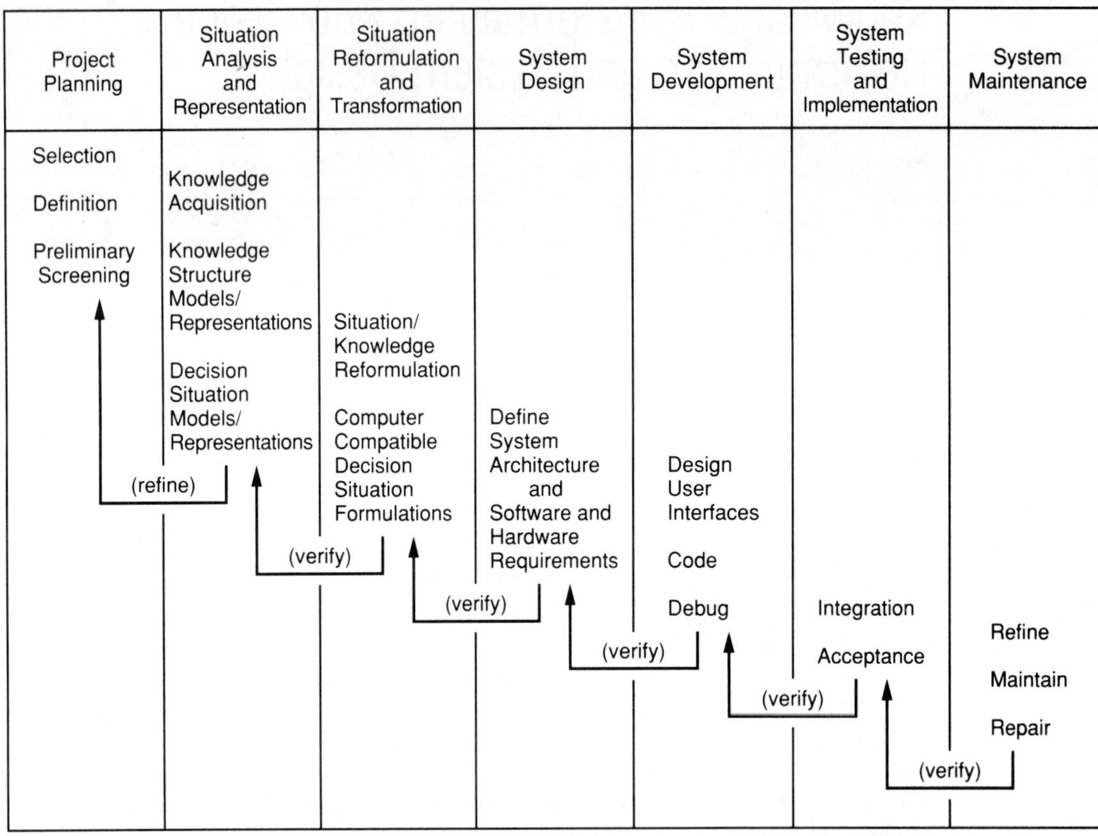


representations into *system representations* or *overall system design formulations*. The tasks described in this chapter lead to the development of some form of initial or prototype system. The process continues through as many prototype systems or other system development phases as are needed to develop, test, and refine the basic concept and structure of the system from two viewpoints:

- the accuracy of its replication of the expert situation
- its effective and efficient functioning on computer

Clearly, as shown in Figure 8–1 and elsewhere in this book, the KBS development life cycle involves continual iterative recycling through all phases or tasks involved in the process. Therefore, while this knowledge transformation phase is discussed in this chapter as a discrete step in the life cycle, it can be a part of all segments of the entire process.

## Knowledge/Decision Situation Representation and Reformulation

In smaller KBS development situations where a rule-based expert system shell is used, the transformation to computer is relatively easy to visualize. The process was described in Chapters 2, 3, 4, 5, and 6.

Where appropriate, situation diagrams or models are used to elicit and organize knowledge from experts. This can be accomplished through a series of reformulations or reconceptualizations of a diagram of the situation. In stages, a transformation is made from a *situation* diagram to a *system design* diagram. An example of such a situation diagram is shown in Figure 8–2. It was discussed in Chapter 2 and illustrated step by step in Figures 2–7a through 2–7g. Extensive additional examples of how situation diagrams are developed and transformed into system diagrams are given in the chapters describing actual prototype systems, Chapters 3, 4, 5, 6, 12, and 14, and all the chapters in Part Five.

Three types of situation diagrams or models commonly used to replicate and structure knowledge in a way that helps in developing a system design are problem reduction representations, state-space representations, and semantic networks.

***Problem Reduction Representations.*** Problem reduction representation models reduce or segment a particular problem or situation into subproblems. These are conceptual hierarchical groupings which identify the tasks to be done in the situation. Each subproblem is continually broken down and segmented until an answer or solution can be found directly and no further subdivision is necessary (Wolfgram 1987, p. 72).

Figure 8–2, and the related diagrams in Figures 2–7a through 2–7g, are examples of problem reduction representations. (They are read from bottom to top.) In Figure 8–2, assessing the level of risk in a proposed KBS project is the problem to be solved in general. It is segmented or broken down into several subproblems, including "Organization Environment Complexity" which is segmented into three subproblems, including "Company Management Involvement." Such segmentation or reduction can facilitate knowledge reformulation and system design.

***State-Space Representation.*** A state-space represents all of the possible states of a given situation. It involves looking at particular states, or snapshots, of various conditions at one moment in time. It is one kind of task description. Two examples of these are given in Figures 8–3 and 8–4.

As seen in Figures 8–3 and 8–4, a state can be transformed into another state through the use of *operators*. Operators are used to transform an *initial state* into the subsequent states ending with the *goal state*. For example, in Figure 8–3 the initial state of a project's risk level may be high. The goal of the project manager is to reduce the project's risk in order to increase its chances of success to an acceptable level. Different operators (such as increasing the time and

**Figure 8–2.** Decision Situation Diagram—Estimating KBS Project Proposal Level of Risk (Initial Prototype Phase)

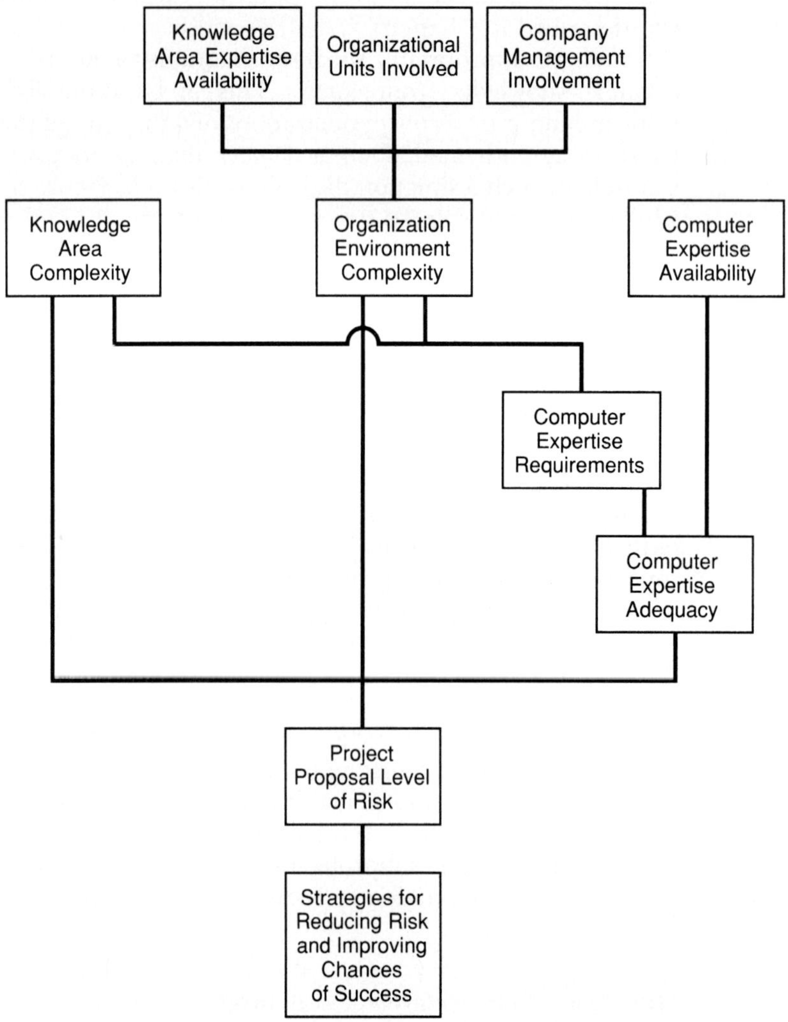


money for the project) can be used to manipulate the initial state (high project risk) to bring about the goal state (reduced risk). State-space representation models can be used to identify the various alternatives to a problem and the different paths that can be used to reach the goal state.

***Semantic Networks.*** Semantic networks are very general representation structures that are used by some knowledge engineers as a basis for building other

**Figure 8–3.** State-Space Representation

| Initial State | Operators | Goal State |
|---|---|---|
| ■ High-Risk Project | ■ Increase time, money<br>■ Provide more/better: knowledge engineers, experts, users<br>■ Increase management support<br>■ Take steps to reassure the experts of their importance<br>■ Take steps to facilitate organizational change | ■ Low- to Moderate-Risk Project |

types of representations. They are rarely used by themselves to model and represent expert knowledge for actual system design. They are concept diagrams which show interrelationships in the knowledge domain under study. A semantic network consists of a group of objects, concepts, or situations that are called nodes. The various relationships that may exist between these nodes are expressed through the use of arcs or arrows with descriptive text. An example of a semantic network is shown in Figure 8–5. The ovals in Figure 8–5 represent nodes and the lines with arrows represent arcs.

These three modelling tools (problem reduction representation, state-space representation, and semantic networks) are only a few of the many available knowledge acquisition tools, such as those already described in Chapter 7, that can help in representing and gradually reformulating knowledge in a situation under study.

Figure 8–6 shows an example from Chapter 2 of a *system diagram* (called a dependency diagram) developed from the situation diagram shown in Figure 8–2. Figures 8–7 and 8–8 show the specific transformation or encoding of questions and rules into formulations compatible with two expert system development shells, M.1 and VP-Expert, that are discussed in Chapters 2, 3, 4, 5, and 6. Decision charts, as shown in Figure 8–9, are also an effective tool that can be used to capture, represent, and refine knowledge. They are used in all of the systems described in Part Five of this book.

Since the basic approach to knowledge/decision situation reformulation is covered in Chapters 2, 3, 4, 5, and 6, this chapter will focus on introducing the reader to system design.

## System Design

It is not enough that situation models or representations accurately replicate the situation under study. These representations have to take into account the

**Figure 8–4.** Alternative State-Space Representation Example

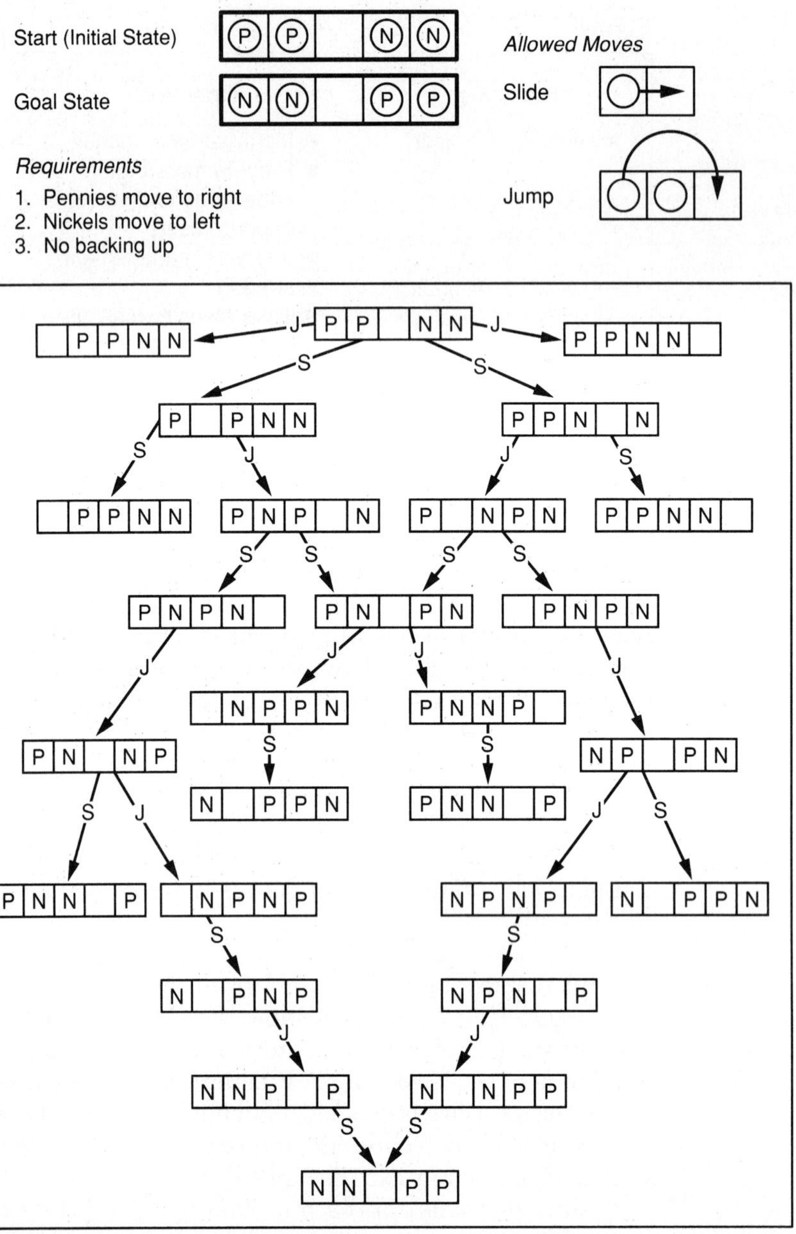


**Source:** Adapted from Paul Harmon and Brian Sawyer, *Creating Expert Systems for Business and Industry,* John Wiley and Sons: New York, 1990.

**Figure 8–5.** Knowledge Representation Using a Semantic Network

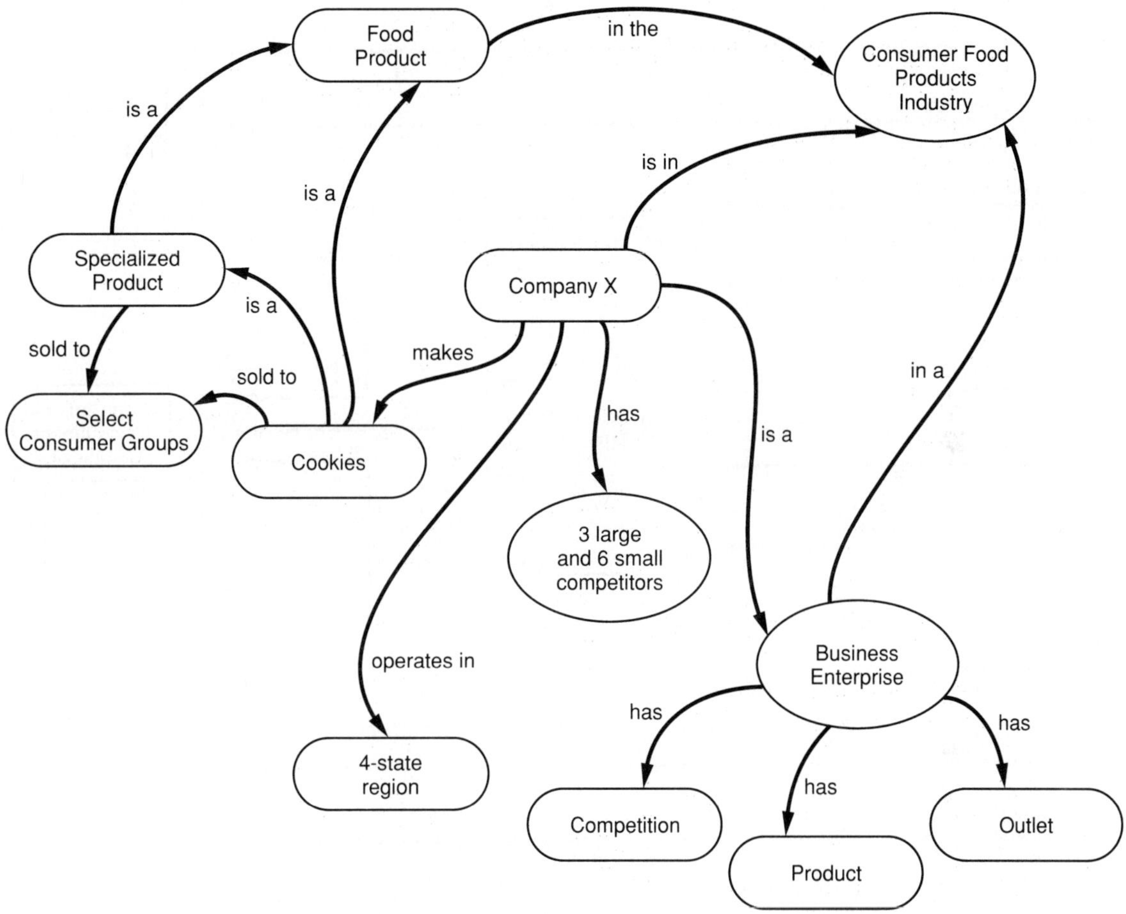


technical limitations of available computers and computer software. This requires studying the software design and architecture alternatives available.

Figure 8–10 shows the components of a knowledge-based system. Two aspects of it are discussed in this chapter: the knowledge base and the representations of it, and the inferencing mechanisms or general problem-solving strategies.

The objective of a knowledge engineer is to select or develop a knowledge-based formulation or representation model and an inference mechanism that most closely mimics the way the expert situation actually works and at the same time enables putting the replication as effectively and efficiently as possible onto

**Figure 8–6.** Decision Situation under Study: Estimating KBS Project Proposal Level of Risk—Dependency (System) Diagram (Initial Prototype Phase)

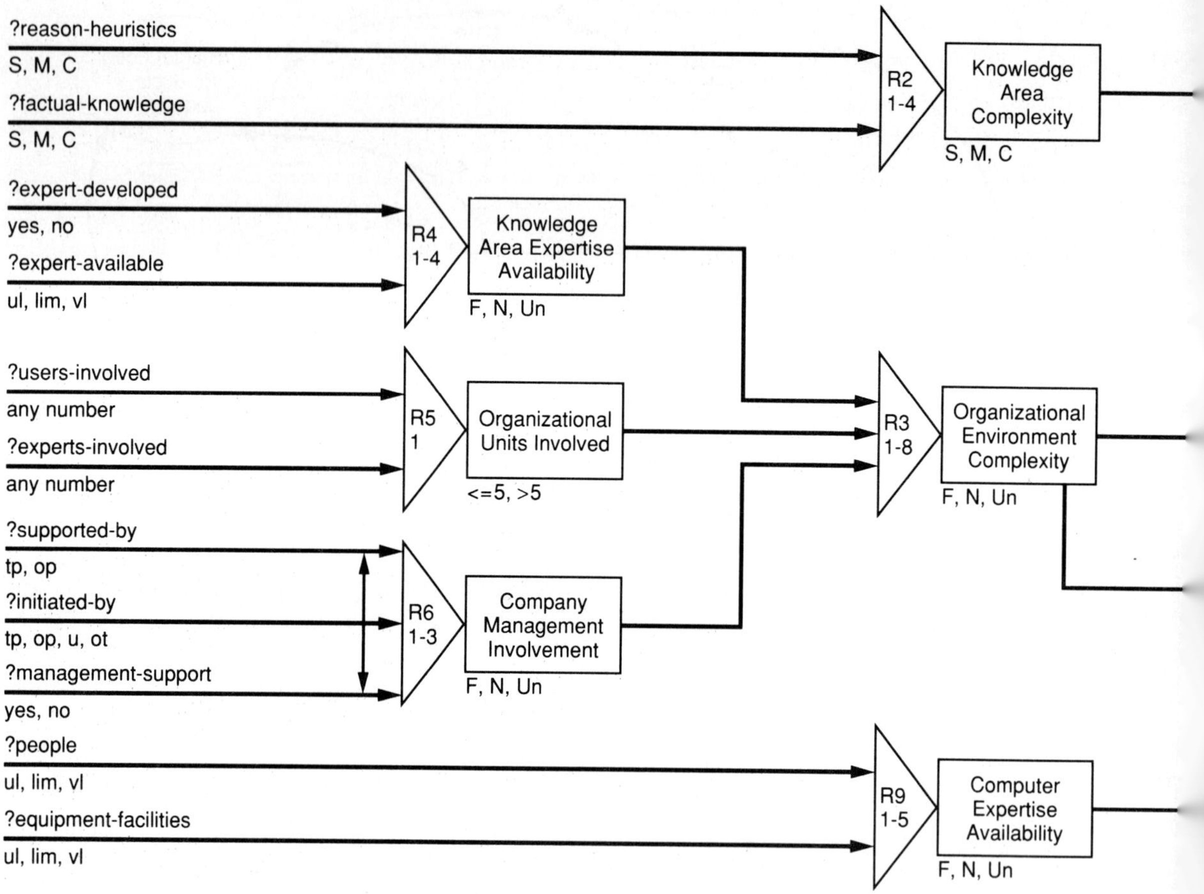


Key:

F = Favorable
N = Neutral
Un = Unfavorable

Gd = Good
Ok = Okay
Pr = Poor

S = Simple
M = Moderate
C = Complex

op = operating mgt.
u = user/expert
tp = top company mgt.

ul = unlimited
lim = limited
ot = outside-company

vl = very limited

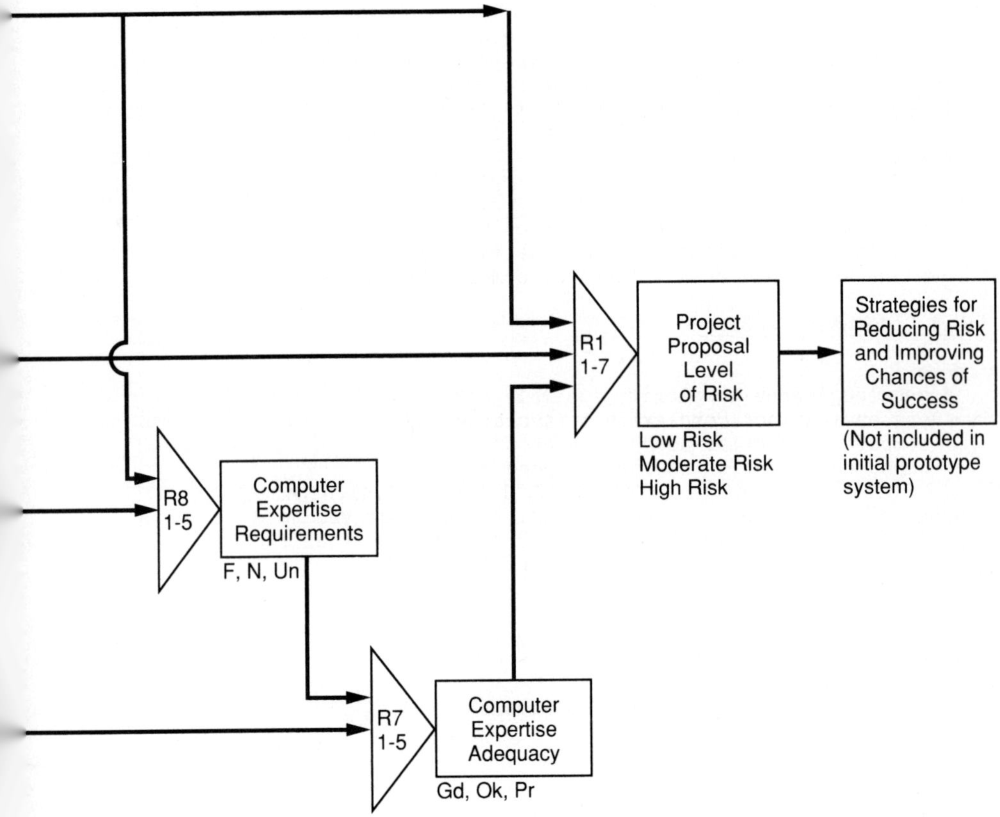
R1
1-7
Project
Proposal
Level
of Risk
Low Risk
Moderate Risk
High Risk
Strategies for
Reducing Risk
and Improving
Chances of
Success
(Not included in
initial prototype
system)
R8
1-5
Computer
Expertise
Requirements
F, N, Un
R7
1-5
Computer
Expertise
Adequacy
Gd, Ok, Pr

**Figure 8–7.** Decision Situation under Study: Estimating KBS Project Proposal Level of Risk—Rules, Three Forms (Initial Prototype Phase)

Plain English Version

```
rule-1-1:
if the knowledge area's level of complexity is simple and
if the organization's environment is favorable and
if the computer expertise adequacy is good or
if the computer expertise adequacy is okay
then the project has a low level of risk and a high
potential for success

rule-2-1:
if the reasoning and heuristics used in the area are simple and
if the factual knowledge of the area is simple
then the knowledge area's level of complexity is simple
```

M.1 Condensed Version

```
rule-1-1:
if knowledge-area-complexity = simple and
   org-environment-complexity = favorable and
   computer-expertise-adequacy = ok or
   computer-expertise-adequacy = good and
      display([nl,nl,nl,nl,nl,nl,nl,nl,nl,nl,nl,nl,nl,nl,nl,'
Based on the answers you have given, the project you have
proposed has a low level of risk and a high potential for
success. ',nl,nl,nl,nl,nl,nl,nl,nl,nl,nl])
            then phase-over = done1.

rule-2-1:
if reasoning-heuristics = simple
   factual-knowledge = simple
then knowledge-area-complexity = simple.
```

VP-Expert Condensed Version

```
Rule 1-1

if knowledge-area-complexity = simple and
   org-environment-complexity = favorable and
   computer-expertise-adequacy = ok or
   computer-expertise-adequacy = good and
then level_of_risk = low
CLS
DISPLAY" Based on the answers you have given, the project you
have proposed has a low level of risk and a high potential for
success";

Rule 2-1
if reasoning-heuristics = simple and
   factual-knowledge = simple
then knowledge-area-complexity = simple;
```

**Figure 8–8.** Decision Situation under Study: Estimating KBS Project Proposal Level of Risk—Questions, Three Forms (Initial Prototype Phase)

Plain English Version

What level of management initiated the proposed project?

What is the highest level of management which has expressed interest in and support for the project?

M.1 Version

```
question(initiated-by) =
[nl,nl,nl,nl,nl,nl,nl,nl,nl,nl,nl,nl,nl,nl,nl,nl,nl,nl,nl,nl,'
What level of management initiated the proposed project?

',nl,nl,nl,nl,nl,nl,nl].

legalvals(initiated-by) = [top-company-management,
operating-management, user/expert, outside-company].

question(supported-by) =
[nl,nl,nl,nl,nl,nl,nl,nl,nl,nl,nl,nl,nl,nl,nl,nl,nl,nl,nl,nl,'
What is the highest level of management which has expressed
interest in and support for the project?

',nl,nl,nl,nl,nl,nl,nl,nl].

legalvals(supported-by) = [top-company-management,
operating-management].
```

VP-Expert Condensed Version

```
ASK initiated-by:  "What level of management initiated the
proposed project?";

CHOICES initiated-by: top-company-management, operating
management, user_or_expert, outside-company;

ASK supported by:  "What is the highest level of management
which has expressed interest in and support for the project?";

CHOICES supported by:  top-company-management,
operating-management;
```

**Figure 8–9.** Decision Situation under Study: Estimating KBS Project Proposal Level of Risk—Decision Chart, Final Rule Set (Initial Prototype Phase)

(A) *Initial Version*

| Rule #1 | 1 | 2 | 3 | 4 | 5 | 6 | 7 | 8 | 9 | 10 | 11 | 12 | 13 |
|---|---|---|---|---|---|---|---|---|---|---|---|---|---|
| if knowledge-area-complexity | S | S | S/M | C | C | * | S | S | M/C | M | M/C | M | M |
| if org-environment-complexity | F | F/N | F | U | * | U | N | N/U | F | F | N | N/U | N |
| if computer-expertise-adequacy | G/O | G | G | * | P | P | O/P | O | O | O/P | G | G | O |
| then Level of Risk = | | | | | | | | | | | | | |
| low risk | X | X | X | | | | | | | | | | |
| moderate risk | | | | | | | X | X | X | X | X | X | X |
| high risk | | | | X | X | X | | | | | | | |

S = simple  M = moderate  C = complex
F = favorable  N = neutral  U = unfavorable
G = good  O = okay  P = poor
/ = or  * = any answer

(B) *Final Condensed Version*

| Rule #1 | 1 | 2 | 3 | 4 | 5 | 6 | 7 |
|---|---|---|---|---|---|---|---|
| if knowledge-area-complexity | S | S | S/M | C | C | * | * |
| if org-environment-complexity | F | F/N | F | U | * | U | * |
| if computer-expertise-adequacy | G/O | G | G | * | P | P | * |
| then Level of Risk = | | | | | | | |
| low risk | X | X | X | | | | |
| moderate risk | | | | | | | X |
| high risk | | | | X | X | X | |

S = simple  M = moderage  C = complex
F = favorable  N = neutral  U = unfavorable
G = good  O = okay  P = poor
/ = or  * = any answer

computer. To be able to make these decisions successfully, it is first necessary to understand what strategies and techniques are commonly available. The following sections describe commonly used strategies and techniques in this area.

Since this is an introductory chapter, the discussion is designed only to give a selective overview of the area. More detailed discussions can be found in the books listed in the reference section at the end of this chapter. In addition, further discussions of the chapter topics, including both rule-based and frame- or object-based systems, are found throughout this book.

**Figure 8–10.** Essential Components of a Knowledge-Based System

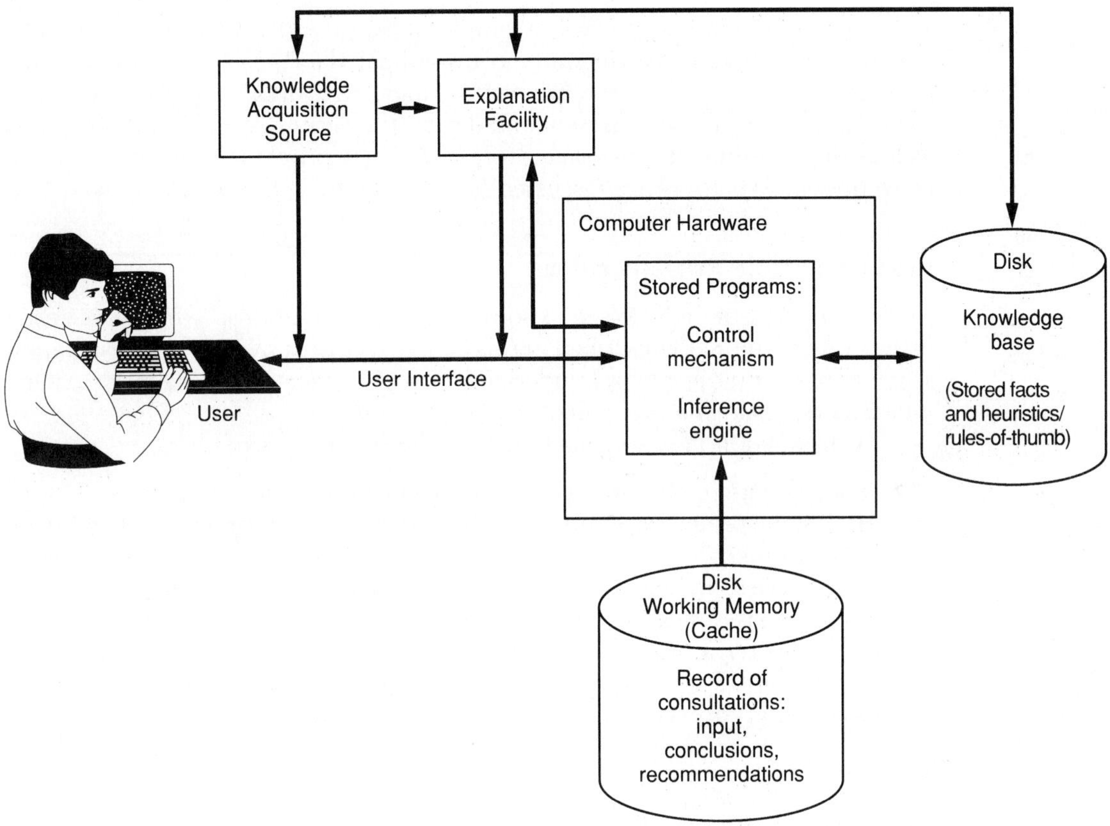


## SYSTEM DESIGN: KNOWLEDGE REPRESENTATION

Knowledge representations used for system design are the *architecture* or *formalisms* used to model and represent the knowledge in a way that enables the knowledge to be processed by a computer system. This section covers the following different approaches to knowledge representation commonly used today, as well as several related topics:

- production rules
- predicate calculus
- objects/frames
- hybrids
- dealing with uncertainty

- working memory
- neural networks

The different approaches are in some ways extensions of various data structures in current use in more conventional data processing systems, for example, lists, tables, hierarchies, sets, rings, networks, and matrices. The formalisms necessary to represent and denote the entities, events, and objects, as well as the relationships, associated with KBS that supplement or extend these conventional structures are discussed here.

### Production Rule Representations

*Production rule* or rule-based knowledge representations, which are used extensively in the KBS described in this book, refer to knowledge representation schemes based on the general underlying idea of *condition-action* pairs, also called *if-then* pairs, *situation-action* pairs, or *production rules*.

A production rule system consists of the following parts:

- a rule base composed of a set of production rules
- an interpreter or control mechanism to determine the actions to be performed
- databases, or context data structures, which contain information relevant to the task under study
- a short-term or working memory file that holds the current context data under study for a particular consultation, and whose contents grow as questions are answered and action clauses are activated

***Production Rules.*** The following is an example of a production rule:

```
if grass = tall and
   weather = good and
   ability = yes
then recommendation = cut-the-grass
else recommendation = do-not-cut-the-grass;
```

In these conditional IF-THEN or IF-THEN-ELSE descriptions of a given situation or problem context, the IF clause describes an object, situation, or position. If the IF clauses are found to be true, the THEN clause of the rule is activated. If the rule contains an ELSE clause and the IF clauses are found to be false, the ELSE clause of the rule is activated. The IF clause is called the premise; the THEN and ELSE clauses are called the action. Not all rules necessarily contain an ELSE clause.

***The Control Mechanism.*** The control mechanism for production rule systems operates through a three-part cycle, comprised of matching, conflict resolution, and action.

*Matching* involves testing conditions of various rules with the other rules or facts stored in the knowledge base. For example, as seen in Figure 8–11, the condition of a rule, "if job-demands are high" is matched or compared to the particular situation under study through the use of a question "question(job-demands) = 'How would you describe the demands placed on your time by your job? high, average, or low?'." *Conflict resolution* is involved since there are three rules that can be executed, instantiated, or called, and a conflict arises as to which one to activate. *Action* refers to the actual execution of a rule or set of rules, including the sequence in which the rules are executed, or "fired."

***Context Databases and Structures.*** Many rule-based systems provide for a set of situation facts or conditions to be entered which are used during a consultation. For example, *context data structures* are composed of information in the knowledge base which influences how rules are used during a consultation—that is, structures which dictate that not all rules will be fired all of the time, but only when dictated by particular situational circumstances. For instance, when deciding how to invest one's money, buying an apartment building may not be within the context of the specific decision under study: if a person does not have the money or credit to buy an apartment building, such a large investment would not be within the context of their particular decision although it might be a valid investment vehicle in other situations. A KBS designed to help people make investment decisions would not direct the consultation towards such irrelevant questions as whether or not to consider buying an entire apartment building once it is known that an individual's resources are limited. *Context databases*, on the other hand, are databases from which information is automatically drawn during a consultation so that the system does not have to ask the user for the

**Figure 8–11.** Matching Rules and Questions: An Example

```
rule-1: if job-demands = high
        then time-constraints = significant.

rule-2: if job-demands = average
        then time-constraints = moderate.

rule-3: if job-demands = few
        then time-constraints = low.

question (job-demands) = 'How would you describe the
demands placed on your time by your job? high,
average, or low?'
```

information. For example, the fact that an employee is entitled to certain benefits due to seniority may be entered and used during any part of a consultation, without any need to ask the user for input.

***Working Memory.*** Since working memory—that part of a KBS that holds information and knowledge which is dynamic and may change from one consultation of the KBS to the next—is used in all types of representations, it is discussed later in this section.

Production rule systems have several advantages. They are modular and allow for ease of modification. Rules can be added, deleted, or changed without influencing the other rules in the system. This modularity also allows for the incremental building and expansion of systems over time to encompass ever increasing portions of an expert's domain.

They represent knowledge in a uniform manner. Rules always start with an IF clause which is followed by a THEN clause, and sometimes by an ELSE clause. This makes the information and knowledge contained in the rules relatively easy for people to see, follow, and understand. They are one of the natural ways in which experts express particular kinds of knowledge, and so often replicate the kind of reasoning used by experts to make numerous different decisions.

Production rule systems have several disadvantages. They are inefficient in their execution because the three-part cycle of matching, conflict resolution, and action is inefficient compared to other programming methods. They are also limited in the manner in which they represent knowledge.

IF-THEN-ELSE statements cannot always adequately represent an expert's knowledge and reasoning processes. The situations in which production rules are best used are:

- In domains of diffused knowledge that cover a broad scope and contain numerous facts that may not be well defined, as, for example, in a system for predicting economic growth for a particular region. Production rules are also useful in situations where factors that are most important—and how these factors interrelate—are not well known or defined.
- In domains where the knowledge can be easily segmented into different modules or segments, as, for example, in the situation modeled in Figure 8–2.

### Predicate Calculus

*Predicate calculus* is a way of mathematically representing and manipulating logical thought and knowledge. It can be used to derive new knowledge from old, through mathematical deduction (Schutzer 1987, p. 18).

Predicate calculus and first-order logic, an extension of predicate calculus, are two of the most commonly used mathematical logic systems. They are based on the truth of statements, and the rules of inferences. In predicate calculus a properly formed statement must be either "true" or "false."

Using these formalisms it can be concluded that a new statement is true by proving that it follows from statements already known to be true (Schutzer, pp. 18–19; Wolfgram, p. 64). For example, if the statement "All utilities are regulated by the government through a commission that sets rates charged to consumers to limit the utility's profit" is known to be true, and the statement "Con Edison is a utility" is known to be true, then it can be concluded that "Con Edison is regulated by a government commission that sets their rates and limits their profits."

To reason to conclusions, predicate calculus uses rules of inference, proof by refutation, and resolution theorem proving. Various logical operators, including "and," "or," "not," "implies," and "equivalent," can be added to the truth of various statements to expand the logic and represent the knowledge.

Predicates can be considered verbs and be applied to any number of arguments or variables. In the following example, "IS-UTILITY" is an argument, "X" is a variable that in this instance refers to "Con Edison," and the statements on the right side of the equivalent sign (≡) consist of predicates, connectives, and qualifiers.

```
IS-UTILITY(X, Con Edison) ≡ is (X, regulated by govt.)
                            and rates (X, set by
                            commission) and
                        not rates (X, set by monopoly
                            power) and profit is (X,
                            limited)
```

The above example can be interpreted to mean that in order for an object "X," in this case Con Edison, to be known as a utility, it must be regulated by the government, have its rates set by a commission, not have its rates set through monopoly power, and have a limit put on its profits. If any of these things are not true for "X," "X" is not a utility.

Predicate calculus has several advantages. It is precise, since it is based on logic and standard methods of determining the meaning of expressions. Like production rules, it is modular, since statements can be added, deleted, or changed independently of each other. This modularity also allows for the incremental growth of a system.

Predicate calculus also has several disadvantages. It can easily become unwieldy. As the number of facts in the knowledge base grows, the number of ways to combine facts and information and infer consequences grows exponentially.

The disadvantages of predicate calculus also include the inability to express uncertain and approximate knowledge, as well as its processing inefficiency.

Predicate calculus is best used in domains of concise knowledge that cover a narrow scope and contain well-defined facts and heuristics. For example, a predicate calculus-based knowledge representation scheme would be appropriate for a system for diagnosing computer malfunctions because of its limited scope and the well-defined interaction of components. It also would be appropriate for a system representing knowledge about chemical interactions.

### Objects/Frames

Objects and frames are a kind of template for holding related clusters of data, facts, rules, hypotheses, or any other knowledge in a single conceptual unit. *Object* is the term used to define the programming concept, a computer system entity that includes facts, rules, pointers, and procedures; *frame* is the term used in general to describe the clusters of knowledge themselves (Harmon 1990, p. 41). Figures 8–12 and 8–13 are examples of an object and a frame hierarchy.

Objects use slots to hold information about the attributes and values of an item, an object or class of objects, a situation, an action, or an event. Slots may also contain procedures and pointers for getting facts from other objects in the knowledge base. Slots can also contain rules and questions as well as text to be displayed to users. They may also contain declarative knowledge, such as default values, which are values assumed if no other values are available or contradictory evidence is not found. An example of such slots is found in the object shown in Figure 8–12.

A frame can be linked with other frames to form a frame hierarchy. This can be done through the use of procedural knowledge, pointers, or links that direct the system to search other frames for related data when executed. For example, as seen in Figure 8–13, the slot "Member" under "Joe's Food Service" specifies "Fast Food Industry." This slot links the frame, in this case "Joe's Food Service," with another frame, in this case the frame for the fast-food industry. Through this linkage, Joe's Food Service inherits all of the properties of the frame "Fast Food Industry." The frame "Fast Food Industry" may include slots describing it as having low prices, fast service, and no waiters or waitresses. The frame for "Joe's Food Service" can then inherit these characteristics, as well as the characteristics for the "Prepared Food Service Industry," from other segments of the hierarchy. It is not necessary to repeat all of the attributes of the fast food industry when describing Joe's food service because of this hierarchical frame linkage.

There are several advantages of frame-based representations. They are efficient in their execution and use of processing resources to achieve goals and solve problems because of the frames' structure. They represent one of the typical ways an expert may reason, or think, and manipulate information.

The disadvantage of frame-based representations is that the performance of a frame-based system is very sensitive to the organization of the structure and frames. Considerable time is required to ensure that the frames are well designed.

**Figure 8–12.** Segment of Product/Customer Matching Objects—Marketing Planning System (Initial Prototype)

```
                                PRODUCT

Characteristics - Type:  High Quality Skis
                  Name:  Brand X
                  Specifications: Low volume, high margins; rapidly changing,
                                  high-tech; specialty/fashionable sports;
                                  short selling season; etc.

Factors Affecting Success:  Familiarity with latest technology and fashions to
                            maintain up-to-date, high quality image; ability to
                            adapt to rapid changes; not especially price
                            sensitive; ability to obtain outlets and
                            endorsements of champions/winners; etc.

Opportunities: Growing customer market, with rapidly expanding disposable
               income, etc.

Interconnecting-       Rule-6-1, etc.
  Procedures-Pointers
Rules:                 Rule-5-1, Rule-9-1, etc.
Questions:             Question (....), etc.
```

```
                                CUSTOMER

Category:  Young Adult

Attributes:    (age) 22-29
               (income) $36,000 - 52,000
               (education) 16 years + etc.

Controlling
   Concepts:  Experimental, growing, changeable, high disposable income, well
              educated, etc.

Product
  Implications: Fashionable and current; image of high quality; price is not
                barrier, image of new, up to date, technology, etc.
Interconnecting-              Rule-6-1, etc.
  Procedures-Pointers
Rules:                        Rule-9-1, Rule-5-1, etc.
Questions:                    Question (....), etc.
```

**Figure 8–13.** Prepared Food Service Industry Frame Hierarchy

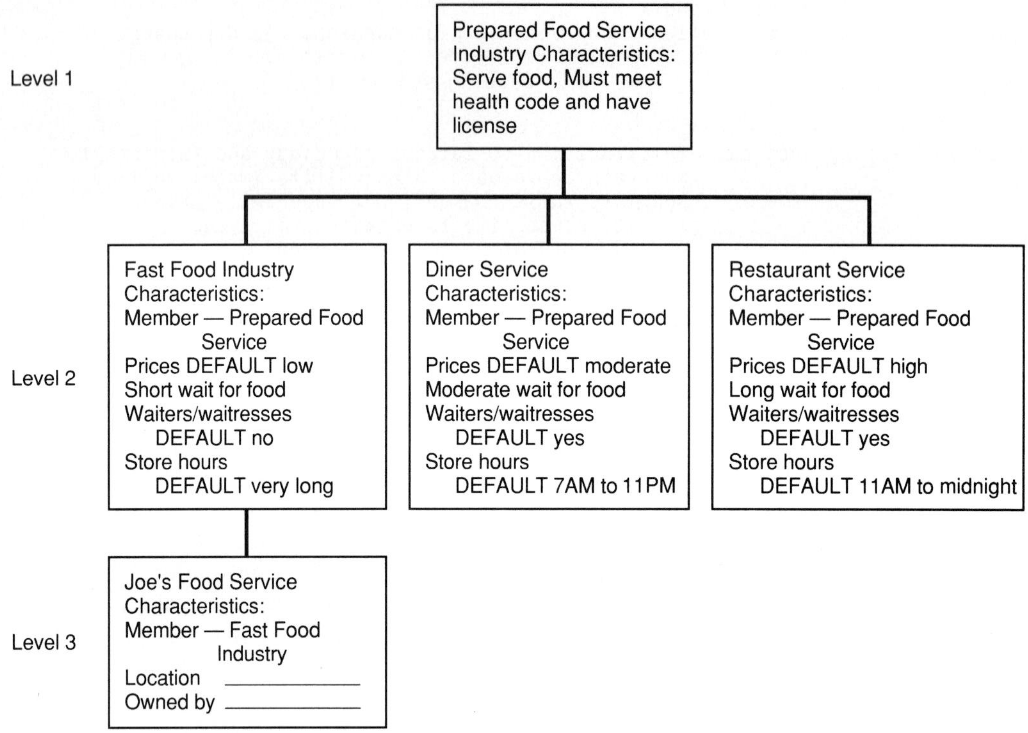


Frame-based representations are best used in situations where:

- The knowledge and relationships of the various factors in the knowledge domain are well defined.
- The knowledge domain covers a narrow scope.
- There is context dependence or a hierarchical structure to the knowledge involved.
- Representations and control strategies are combined, or the knowledge of what to do is combined with how to do it. For example, in Figure 8–13 all the frames on level 2 are linked to level 1 and so inherit the characteristics of level 1. That is, they serve food, must meet the health code, and have a license.

Whether objects or rules are used in a system will often depend on the involved expert's way of thinking in the situation under study.

It is important to note that almost any collection of rules can be converted to a set of objects and rules. For example, in the situation pictured in Figure 8–13, instead of frames one might say "if Joe's Food Service is a Fast Food restaurant, then Joe's has the attributes of the Fast Food Industry (low prices, short wait for food, no waitresses/waiters, and very long store hours)."

Frame- or object-based KBS are discussed in more detail in Chapter 21.

### Hybrids

Hybrids are knowledge representation models for system design that may include some combination of rules, objects, and predicate calculus. Hybrids are used when the limitations of using any one particular representation model preclude adequate replication of the expertise/knowledge involved. Judging by the systems being developed in the early 1990s, the majority of KBS will most likely be hybrid systems. In these situations the knowledge to be replicated in the system is so diverse that multiple knowledge representation methods are required. Hybrids are especially evident in the frame type of architecture, as illustrated in Figure 8–12, where rules and predicate calculus are often found within the object/frame-based KBS (Thuraisingham 1989).

### Dealing with Uncertainty

Often, facts are not known with absolute completeness and the knowledge and reasoning processes in a particular area may involve uncertainty as to conclusions. The major ways to represent uncertainty of facts and conclusions include probabilities, as well as certainty and confidence factors.

A *probability* represents the chances of a particular event or conclusion occurring or being true. A probability can be represented by a probability factor that may range from 0 to 100. A value of 100 implies the maximum probability of 100 percent that a statement or assertion will be true or occur. A value of 0 implies the minimum probability of 0 percent that a statement or assertion will be true or occur. For example, a factory's foreman may know, based on past data, that when a particular machine operates for more than 500 hours without maintenance, 40 percent of the time the machine gets jammed and requires a major overhaul. Thus there is a 40 percent chance or probability that the machine will get jammed and require a major overhaul and a 60 percent chance or probability that the machine will not get jammed and require the overhaul after 500 hours of operating without maintenance. This probability estimate is based on mathematical calculations of past data.

*Certainty and confidence factors* are informal estimates that a particular fact or conclusion is true. These estimates are usually based on less quantifiable experiences, as opposed to data. They are made under the assumption that a statement or an assertion may be either true or false to some degree. They also imply the strength or weakness of a statement or assertion. For example, in expert system development shells, such as VP-Expert and GURU, if a statement or assertion is absolutely known to be true, then it is given a value of 100; if it is known to be false, it is given a value of 0. It can also be given any value between 0 and 100. As the value moves from 0 to 100 for a statement or assertion, the statement's truth, or certainty of being right, increases. Any value greater than 0 means that the statement is true to some degree. A value of 0 means that a statement is known to be false. Certainty and confidence factors are discussed in greater detail later in this chapter.

### Working Memory

Working memory is the part of a KBS that holds information and knowledge which is dynamic and may change from one consultation of the KBS to the next. It is often referred to as the *cache* or *cache file*. It represents information and knowledge that is unique to a particular case. This information and knowledge may include user's answers to questions, and conclusions to rules that have fired (were found to be true). This information and knowledge is often held in a cache or temporary storage file in rule-based systems. Figure 8–14 is an example of a printout of such a cache file from a consultation with the Risk Evaluation Assistant prototype KBS described in Chapter 2. The contents of the cache grow as each question is answered and conclusions are reached and rules are triggered and succeed, that is, as all the IF clauses of a particular rule are found to be true.

All of the knowledge representations use working memory. Filling of slots that do not contain permanent knowledge in frame-based systems, and the theorem proving and/or proof by refutation needed to arrive at conclusions in predicate calculus-based systems, are analogous to the compilations in a cache in rule-based systems.

**Figure 8–14.** Contents of Working Memory—Example of M.1 Cache File

```
need-intro-1 = yes cf 100 because 'you said so'.
need-intro-2 = yes cf 100 because 'you said so'.
intro-over = yes cf 100 because kb-3.
factual-knowledge = simple cf 100 because 'you said so'.
reasoning-heuristics = simple cf 100 because 'you said so'.
knowledge-area-complexity = simple cf 100 because rule-2-1.
expert-developed = yes cf 100 because 'you said so'.
knowledge-area-expertise-avail = favorable cf 100 because rule-4-1.
users-involved = 2 cf 100 because 'you said so'
experts-involved = 1 cf 100 because 'you said so'.
organization_units_involved = 2+1 cf 100 because rule-5-1.
initiated-by = user/expert cf 100 because 'you said so'.
supported-by = top-company-management cf 100 because 'you said so'.
company-management-involvement = favorable cf 100 because rule-6-1.
org-environment-complexity = favorable cf 100 because rule-3-1.
computer-expertise-requirements = favorable cf 100 because rule-8-1.
people = unlimited cf 100 because 'you said so'.
equipment-facilities = unlimited cf 100 because 'you said so'.
computer-expertise-availability = favorable cf 100 because rule-9-1.
computer-expertise-adequacy = good cf 100 because rule-7-1.
level-of-risk = low cf 100 because rule-1-1.

cf = confidence factor, a degree of certainty about the factor
```

### Neural Networks

The work currently being done in using neural networks for KBS development, a fairly recent development at the time this book was written, is discussed in Chapter 22.

## SYSTEM DESIGN: INFERENCING MECHANISMS FOR PROBLEM SOLVING

Inferencing mechanisms used to solve problems are the ways in which knowledge is manipulated, controlled, or reasoned about. They can include the paths, actions, or steps taken to move from one part of a knowledge base to another. This is the part of the KBS where the reasoning actually takes place. This section describes the following reasoning strategies commonly used in inference engines of knowledge-based systems:

- formal reasoning
- general search strategies: blind and heuristic
- specific inferencing strategies: forward chaining, backward chaining, bi-directional, and means-end
- reasoning with uncertainty

### Formal Reasoning

*Formal reasoning* is based on the ideas developed in the study of mathematical theorem-proving, and is usually associated with predicate calculus. For instance, a theorem can be represented conceptually as a statement in which an assertion can be made that a certain premise implies a given conclusion. Take for example the statement, "If it is raining then the grass is wet." One can either prove this theorem true or assume the negative of the theorem is true. If one cannot prove that the negative of the theorem ("If it is raining then the grass is not wet") is true, it is concluded that the theorem is true. When dealing with a logical assumption, proving a theorem (statement) equates to deriving new facts from a given set of facts.

### General Search Strategies

General search strategies are the solution paths followed to reach conclusions and the decision's ultimate goal. They can be described as either blind searches or heuristic searches.

***Blind Searches.*** Blind searches refer to general search strategies in which domain-specific relationships and situational variables do not influence the search path. Blind searches are considered "weak" searches because they do not utilize specific information to direct the search.

One type of blind-search strategy is the *breadth-first* search, where the first part of all the available reasoning paths is examined. If this does not yield an answer, the second part of each path is investigated. The subsequent steps in each path are searched in this manner until an answer is found.

For example, the breadth-first strategy might be used to help someone find a blue scarf which is somewhere in the bedroom dresser. Using the breadth-first strategy, a search for the blue scarf would begin by opening one dresser drawer and checking only the first layer of clothes. If the scarf is not on the top layer, the search would move to the next drawer. Using the breadth-first strategy, only the top layer of each drawer would be searched. If the scarf was not found on the top layer of clothes in any of the drawers, the second layer of each would be searched, and then the third until the scarf was found. This type of search is illustrated in Figure 8–15.

Another type of blind search strategy is the *depth-first* search, where one particular path is searched exclusively until an answer is found or a dead end is reached. Applying this method to the search for the blue scarf one would look through the entire contents of each drawer one drawer at a time until the scarf was found. This type of search is also illustrated in Figure 8–15.

In this situation, the depth-first strategy would clearly be the most efficient way of doing a random search for the blue scarf. In the same way, different kinds of knowledge-domain situations require different search strategies.

***Heuristic Searches.*** Heuristic searches are referred to as "strong" searches because they use domain-specific and situational information to reach a goal. One type of heuristic search is called *hill climbing*, where the first path chosen is the one closest to the goal. If the first path is not successful, the next closest path to the goal is tested. The process continues by taking the next shortest path to the

**Figure 8–15** Creating Forward Chaining Systems

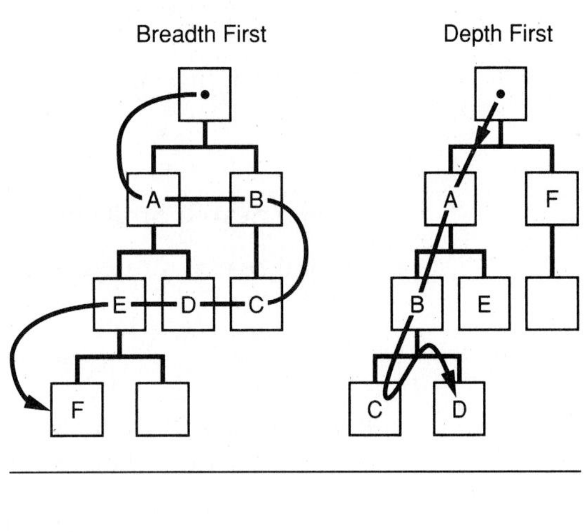

goal until an answer is found. Applying this method to the search for the scarf, the first drawer searched would be the one with the fewest clothes. The drawer with the next fewest clothes in it would be searched next, until the scarf was found.

Another type of heuristic search is known as a *best-first search*, where heuristic knowledge is used to select a search path. A particular path is chosen based on experience with, or knowledge of, past experiences. Utilizing the best-first search strategy to find the blue scarf, one would use knowledge about where the scarf is usually stored to direct the path of the search—such as usually in the bottom drawer or usually with the other winter clothes.

Other heuristic search methods include:

1. *Branch and bound searches*, which are similar to hill climbing, but once the first path is exhausted, the next path chosen is the shortest one to the goal after considering the area already covered in previous searches
2. *Generate and test*, which is described by the following steps:
    - Add a specification criteria.
    - Try a path that satisfies the specification.
    - Determine whether the path is plausible, and "prune" that path if it's not plausible—that is, do not follow that particular path of solutions. If pruning paths successfully reduces the solution space, it is a good, strong search method; if pruning paths fails to reduce the solution space, it becomes a blind search (Wolfgram, 1987, pp. 76–82).
    - Move to the next path.
    - When complete, check to see if all specifications have been met. If not, add the next specification criterion and go through the above steps again. If all specifications have been met, then the process is complete.

### Specific Inferencing Strategies

Inferencing strategies refer to the specific techniques used to manipulate knowledge. These strategies are used to decide what to do next in the reasoning process. They involve the process or method used in reasoning to a solution to a problem. Knaus has developed a fairly brief, easy-to-follow explanation of how to build a very basic inference engine (1990).

Types of inferencing strategies include:

- backward chaining
- forward chaining
- bi-directional
- means-end

***Backward Chaining.*** Backward chaining is a goal-directed search that works backward from the goal or hypothesis to the facts or evidence. In a rule-based system, the backward chaining process is initiated by a goal. The system attempts to find a value for the goal by testing or firing a rule that has a value for the goal in its THEN clause. The system then backs up to the IF clauses of the rule and tries to determine if they are true. This, in turn, leads the system to consider other rules that might confirm the IF clauses. In this way, the system backs into its rules, and eventually, each backward chaining sequence ends when a question is asked or a previously stored result is found. This process continues until a goal or hypothesis value is found (Rosenberg 1986, p. 15). This process is illustrated in Figure 1–5 and described in Chapter 1 as well as in Chapter 4.

Backward chaining provides a greater focus than forward chaining in that backward chaining follows specific paths and avoids the firing of unnecessary rules and performance of unnecessary inferences.

A disadvantage of backward chaining is that it replicates only one fairly limited type of expert reasoning. Also, as the amount of sub-goals and rules increases, the system may become excessively large, which increases processing time.

Common backward chaining applications include diagnostic, monitoring, and controlling situations (Wolfgram 1987, p. 83). Backward chaining is the most common inferencing mechanism found in KBS development shells.

***Forward Chaining.*** Forward chaining starts with the initial given conditions and then searches forward through the knowledge base towards a solution. For example, in a rule-based system, the inference engine starts with the data, examines the IF clauses, and searches for a solution by working from the data toward a goal. Using this reasoning process, the system builds its case working from data toward a solution. When an answer is found to all of the IF clauses in a rule containing a goal word in its THEN clause, it gives the user its recommended solution (Mockler, 1989, pp. 113–14). This method works from facts to conclusion, and is also referred to as a *data-driven*, or *event-driven*, search.

Forward chaining is best used to mimic deductive reasoning or "what if" scenarios. Typical applications include designing, forecasting, predicting, and planning (Wolfgram 1987, p. 83).

Forward chaining searches can expand very rapidly, since a virtually unlimited number of rules may be examined. For this reason, forward chaining often involves overly extensive searches. Forward chaining systems tend to discover all the logical consequences of the set of facts whether they are needed or not. Also, since facts can trigger many diverse applicable rules, the conflict resolution problem can get unwieldy. For this reason, controls are usually set to limit the search process (Schutzer 1987, p. 53).

Because of the characteristics of forward and backward chaining, as shown in Figure 8–16, forward chaining is more likely to be used where the facts or initial data are limited, and where the possible solutions are numerous. Backward chaining, on the other hand, is more likely to be used where the recommendations are limited in number.

**Figure 8–16.** Use of Forward and Backward Chaining

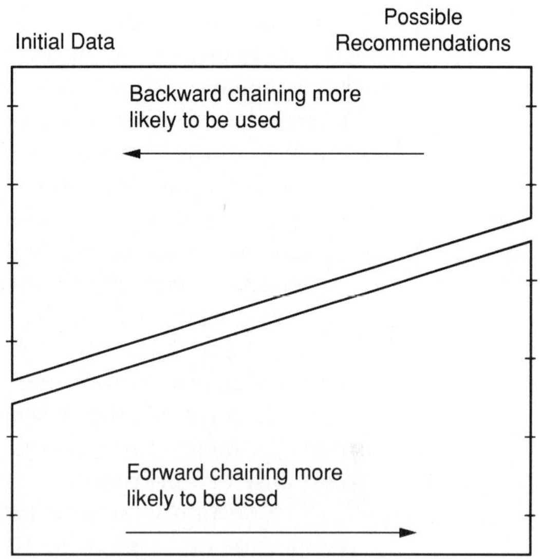


***Bi-directional.*** Bi-directional reasoning is a combination of forward and backward chaining techniques, and integrates the data-driven and goal-driven characteristics of those two methods with an attempt to minimize the weaknesses associated with each. The inference engine may be directed to use either forward or backward chaining to solve a particular aspect of the problem. Bi-directional reasoning is best implemented in hybrid systems that contain frames, production rules, and predicate calculus.

***Means-End.*** Means-end reasoning is a type of bi-directional method in which the inference engine performs both backward and forward chaining at the same time. When the two paths followed by the different reasoning techniques meet, an answer can be found and the goal can be reached. Such systems are not widespread, because ensuring the connection of forward and backward chaining paths can be very difficult (Schutzer, p. 56).

### Reasoning with Uncertainty

Reasoning with uncertainty is supported with the use of certainty factors. As described earlier in this chapter, a certainty factor is an informal measure or expression of certainty that a piece of evidence is true. Certainty factors are also called confidence factors, and abbreviated as CF or CNF. They deal with uncertain or unknown information.

The question of certainty almost always comes up in management decision situations, especially those involving planning. For example, one may estimate the likelihood of a proposed project being suitable for KBS development based on estimates of the relative complexity of the organization environment and the knowledge domain, and on the adequacy of resources. During the situation analysis, these estimates or certainties are very often couched in qualitative terms, for example, "pretty good," or "bad," because this is the vocabulary of nontechnical experts. The quantification of these values occurs during transformation into systems representations. Where the expert feels comfortable with qualitative terms, quantitative estimates can of course be used much earlier, for example, when asking the expert questions. However, experience shows that trying to obtain quantitative estimates from nontechnical managers can skew the knowledge acquisition process and create psychological barriers.

Because of the uncertainties often encountered in business decision making, most expert system shells have ways to handle or represent degrees of certainty or uncertainty.

A certainty factor is represented by a number within some predetermined range: for example, 0 to 100 in VP-Expert and GURU, and −100 to +100 in M.1. In VP-Expert and GURU, a certainty factor of 100 is the highest possible certainty, while a 0 certainty factor represents the lowest possible certainty. In M.1, +100 represents the highest certainty, 0 represents neutrality, and −100 means that the value is definitely ruled out. If no CF is given, 100 percent certainty is assumed in both systems.

Some development shells use still other ways to represent certainty factors. Ranges such as −1 to +1 are used, as well as other systems, among them Bayesian probabilities, Dempster Shaafer belief-theory parameters, and fuzzy possibilities. Discussions of these are available in other sources, such as the Charniack and McDermott (1984, Chapter 8) and Hunt (1986) books in the reference list for this chapter.

Certainty factors can be assigned to the value of a variable in premises, in answers to questions, or in conclusions. There are many ways to calculate and assign certainty factors. The following discusses some common ways that certainty factors are handled in the most popular rule-based KBS system shells.

**1.** *User input information.* A user may not be certain about a piece of information requested by a knowledge-based system during a consultation. For example, a system may ask a user:

```
"How likely do you think the economy is to remain
strong over the next two years?"
```

A user may answer:

```
"Pretty sure" or "Strong CF70"
```

This answer indicates that the user is only 70 percent confident (that is, only "pretty sure") about the answer turning out to be true.

**2.** *A premise CF value can give a CF value to the THEN clause.* CF values in premises can create CF values in THEN clauses in a variety of ways:

**a.** Where a premise is given a CF value, for example, in a rule which reads:

```
"IF over the next two years the economy is
      expected to be strong,
  THEN the likelihood of inflation is strong."
```

If a user answers "strong CF70" when questioned about the "economy" during a consultation, the conclusion about "inflation" would also carry a value of strong CF70.

**b.** Where there is more than one premise and the premises are connected by an AND, there are two commonly used ways to handle certainty factors. First, the THEN clause value could become the *lowest CF value*. For example, a knowledge-based system might contain the following rule:

```
"IF over the next two years the economy is
      expected to be strong AND
      the availability of investment capital is
      expected to be low,
  THEN the likelihood of inflation = strong."
```

If during a consultation a user is asked questions about the first two premises and a user answers "strong CF80" about the "economy" and "low CF60" about the "availability of investment capital," the conclusion about "inflation" would carry a CF value of "strong CF60," since the default CF value of rules in the example is 100. In this example, the confidence factor is calculated by multiplying the *lowest* confidence factor (60) assigned to the conditions being tested *by* the confidence factor of the rule conclusion (100).

Second, if a system developer feels the actual situation warrants it, the developer might choose to use *joint certainty* in this situation, by multiplying 80 times 60 (divided by 100, since the figures represent a percent), to give a "likelihood of inflation" of "strong CF48."

**c.** Where there is more than one premise and the premises are connected by an OR, there are again two common ways to handle certainty factors. First, the THEN clause value could be given the *highest CF value*. For example,

```
"IF over the next two years the growth outlook
      for the economy is poor OR
      the unemployment outlook is poor,
  THEN the economic outlook is poor."
```

If during a consultation a user is asked questions about the first two premises and a user answers "poor CF70" about the "growth outlook" and "poor CF60" about the "employment outlook," the conclusion about "economic outlook" would carry a CF value of "poor CF70."

Second, a system developer may choose to *combine* the values in these premises, if the developer feels that it better represents the situation and the expert system shell allows it to be done. For example, in the rule above for "economic outlook" the certainties could be combined using the formula: the sum of the certainty factors minus the product of the certainty factors (over 100) equals the combined certainty, or in this case:

$$60 + 70 - \frac{60 \times 70}{100} = 130 - 42 = \text{CF88}$$

**3.** *A knowledge-based system may be developed with a CF factor built into the THEN clauses.* For example, a rule may be written:

```
"IF over the next two years the economy is
     expected to be strong,
 THEN the likelihood of inflation is strong CF40."
```

If during a consultation a user is asked a question about the first premise and a user answers "strong CF70" about the "economy," the conclusion about the "likelihood of inflation" would carry a CF value of strong CF28 (40 times 70 divided by 100 = 28).

**4.** *Some systems allow for setting a minimum acceptable CF value.* For example, a system may allow the developer to set a minimum acceptable CF value, for example 30, so that any resulting CF value in a THEN clause below 30 would yield a failed or negative answer, as in the rule in the example above.

**5.** *Incremental certainty through rule firing.* In the same way that premises can be combined to increase the certainty of a conclusion, THEN clauses may also be combined to yield a gradually increasing certainty for a goal conclusion. For example, in some systems each time a THEN clause fires with a CF factor, the ultimate goal becomes more certain. For instance if two different rules give the "likelihood of inflation" at CF28 and CF40 for different reasons, then the combined "likelihood of inflation" CF would be:

$$28 + 40 - \frac{28 \times 40}{100} = 68 - 11.2 = \text{CF56.8}$$

Here, as elsewhere, a developer would use the type of certainty factor calculation which best suited the real world situation that was being replicated in the KBS.

**6.** *Fuzzy variables.* At times in decision situations, variables can have more than one value. For example, two experts may have different ideas on the economic outlook: one may see growth ahead, another recession. Even the same expert can have differing ideas: for example, an expert may estimate that the economy over the next two years (the economic outlook) will be strong with a confidence factor of 70 and weak with a confidence factor of 40.

These are called "fuzzy variables" in an expert knowledge-based system. Most expert system shells are capable of simultaneously keeping track of different values for the same variable.

In M.1, for example, a system developer can give instructions to treat a variable as a fuzzy variable by writing "multivalued(...)", as in "multivalued (eoutlook)." in the knowledge base. With this instruction, when a user consults the system, the inference engine won't stop seeking other values for "eoutlook" after it finds the first value for it. The inference engine will simultaneously keep track of different values (for example, strong CF70 and weak CF40 for "eoutlook"), and independently carry out the subsequent inference for a fuzzy variable's different values.

There are a variety of other ways that CF factors can be used in knowledge-based systems and expert system shells. The above discussion is designed only to give a brief introduction to this knowledge-based system design tool.

An example of the use of confidence factors is given in Chapter 5, in the VP-Expert tutorial.

## MAKING BASIC SYSTEM DESIGN STRATEGY DECISIONS IN SPECIFIC SITUATIONS

The discussion in the earlier sections of this chapter described commonly used approaches and techniques for knowledge-based representation and inferencing mechanisms. Any one or any combination of these approaches and techniques may be useful to the developer, depending on the KBS development situation he or she faces.

The overall approach to making strategy decisions about system design is shown in Figure 8–17. This section describes how specific knowledge-domain structure, degree of domain-knowledge heuristic definition, scope of the knowledge domain, reasoning methods in the domain, and type of situation problem or decision are analyzed and structured. It also examines how this information is then used in making decisions about which system design strategies and techniques to use in different kinds of situations.

As seen from the discussions in the preceding chapters, a wide range of KBS development situations can be involved when making these decisions. These situations can range from large and diverse KBS development projects for

**Figure 8–17.** System Representation Decision Diagram

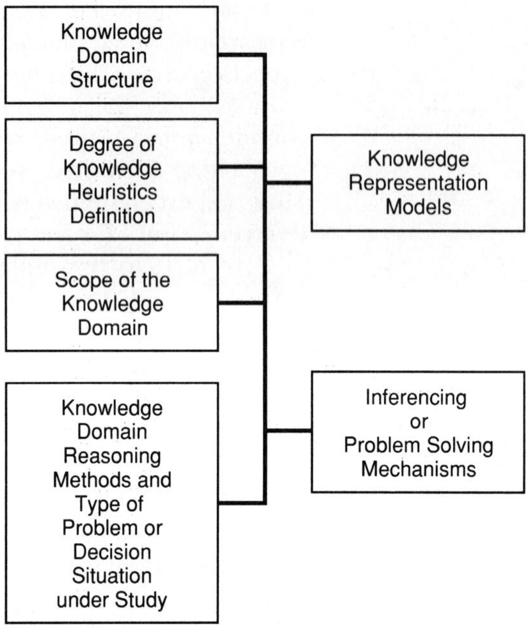


multi-divisional companies to small systems developed by the intended manager/user of the system.

Because of this wide range of possible decisions and decision situations, the approach described here is necessarily a general one, which is intended to give only an overview introduction to the approach. Specific applications of this approach are described in the final sections of this chapter.

### Critical Factors Affecting Decisions in This Area

As shown in Figure 8–17, when making system representation decisions about choosing a knowledge representation architecture and inferencing or problem-solving mechanism, several key factors are considered, including the:

- knowledge-domain structure
- degree of domain-knowledge heuristic definition
- scope of the knowledge domain
- knowledge-domain reasoning methods and type of problem or decision situation under study

***Knowledge-Domain Structure.*** The knowledge-domain structure refers to the relationships of the various bits of knowledge and other factors that will be contained in the KBS. These relationships may be hierarchical, that is, linked with inheritability and dependent upon one another, or they may be separated into independent modular chunks.

The structure of a knowledge domain is considered hierarchical, or *dependent*, if different factors inherit attributes because they belong to a particular group or class. An example of this hierarchical relationship was shown in Figure 8–12 where "Joe's Food Service" inherited the characteristics of the "Fast Food Industry" and the "Prepared Food Industry."

The structure of the knowledge domain is considered independent if attributes of the various factors are not based on their membership in a particular class of objects, and the various factors can be separated and represented in distinct modules. An example of this is shown in Figure 8–6 where the attributes (such as "favorable," "neutral," or "unfavorable") of the different factors are not based on the class of objects the factors belong to, and the different factors (such as "knowledge area complexity," "company management involvement," and "computer expertise availability") have been broken down into separate and distinct segments.

***The Degree of Domain-Knowledge Heuristics Definition.*** This area involves identifying how well defined the heuristics in the domain are.

Well-defined knowledge is usually found in mechanical diagnostic systems. For example, when an expert auto mechanic fixes a carburetor, just what parts are involved and how they should work and interact is known to a very high degree.

Ill-defined knowledge is often found in planning and prediction systems. For example, when an expert economist wants to forecast the economic growth for a particular city or state, there are numerous different factors that impact on the forecast. These factors are not easily identified and their relationships are in a dynamic environment, which further complicates the forecasting process. Such less well-defined knowledge often requires the use of confidence or certainty factors.

***Scope of the Knowledge Domain.*** The scope of the domain refers to the size of the situation to be prototyped. The scope can be evaluated in terms of both breadth and depth.

In situations where the depth of the knowledge is deep and the breadth is wide, a project's scope can be considered large. It may cover a wide range of knowledge and cover a particular area that contains many different facts in great depth, such as making economic forecasts or choosing new markets to enter.

In situations where the depth of the knowledge is shallow and the breadth is narrow, a project's scope can be considered small. It may cover a narrow range of expertise and a very limited number of facts, such as choosing a monitor for a personal computer where the choice of monitors is limited, or trouble-shooting a carburetor where there are a limited number of parts to be examined.

***Knowledge-Domain Reasoning Methods and Type of Problem or Decision Situation under Study.*** The reasoning methods used in the domain and the type of situation are also examined when choosing an inferencing and knowledge representation strategy. For example, the reasoning methods used by domain experts may most closely resemble backward chaining, forward chaining, bi-directional, or means-end inferencing schemes and methods.

Decision situations such as forecasting, predicting, designing, and planning are usually best suited to forward chaining because forward chaining most closely resembles the type of reasoning involved in those decision situations. Situations involving diagnostic, monitoring, and controlling decisions are usually best suited to backward chaining because backward chaining most closely resembles the type of reasoning involved in those types of situations. Bi-directional and means-end are often used when the application requires a hybrid type of inferencing method.

### Making Decisions Based on These Critical Situation Factors

Many knowledge transformation and design decisions are made within the context of these critical situation requirements. Two key decisions involve choosing a knowledge representation model and choosing an inferencing mechanism to manipulate the knowledge base.

In these decision areas, knowledge representation models can be chosen from production rules, predicate calculus, frames, and hybrids. An inferencing mechanism can be chosen from forward chaining, backward chaining, bi-directional, and means-end. In choosing system design strategies, decisions have to be made about which of the above knowledge base representation architectures and inferential mechanisms to use in a particular development situation.

For example, for decisions about choosing inferencing mechanisms, if the knowledge-domain structure is independent and modular, the degree of domain-knowledge definition is only somewhat defined or ill defined, the scope of the knowledge domain is large, and the knowledge-domain reasoning methods and type of problem or decision under study are either diagnostic, monitoring, or controlling, *backward chaining* should be explored as a likely approach to use.

As another example, in choosing knowledge base representation architectures (models), if the knowledge-domain structure is independent and modular, the degree of domain-knowledge definition is only somewhat or ill defined, and the knowledge-domain reasoning methods and type of problem or decision under study point toward the use of forward *or* backward chaining, then *production rules* should be used.

Obviously there is more to making system design strategy decisions than is covered in these brief summaries. For example, while in many situations it is possible to initially select a general representation approach, such as production rules or predicate calculus, considerable refinement is often needed. In addition, in many situations the most appropriate representation model is not always apparent, or several may be appropriate.

In order to explore in more depth the processes involved in making system design decisions, the following section discusses in detail one of these decisions, choosing a knowledge representation model.

## APPLYING THIS GENERAL APPROACH TO MAKING KNOWLEDGE REPRESENTATION STRATEGY DECISIONS

This section describes how decisions can be made in choosing a knowledge representation model from among production rules, predicate calculus, frames, and hybrids. This situation study was in turn used to develop an initial concept-testing prototype system for such decisions. For this reason, the decision has been simplified considerably. It is recognized that in most KBS development situations the actual knowledge representation decision is usually much more complicated than the one described here. A much larger and more complex series of KBS is under development in this area, as it is in the other areas discussed in the chapters in Part Three of this book.

The discussion in this section covers factors affecting the decision as well as recommendations and how they are made.

### Factors Affecting the Decision

The different factors affecting the situation, as shown in Figure 8–18, include the knowledge structure of the domain, degree of knowledge heuristics definition, and the scope of the domain.

***Knowledge Structure of the Domain.*** In determining the degree to which the knowledge structure is hierarchical and dependent or independent and modular, questions such as the following are asked:

- Are there any common characteristics or attributes shared by the various objects or categories in the knowledge domain?
- Can the characteristics of one object be assumed to be characteristics of another object?
- Can the knowledge be segmented into distinct modular chunks with values being found for each individual segment?

If there are any common characteristics shared by the various facts/objects in the knowledge situation, it indicates that the knowledge might be dependent. If the characteristics of one object in the knowledge domain can be assumed to be characteristics of another object, then the knowledge is considered dependent. If there are no common characteristics shared by the various facts/objects in the knowledge domain, and the knowledge can be segmented into distinct sections, the knowledge is considered independent.

Figure 8–18. Making Decisions—Choosing a Knowledge Representation Model

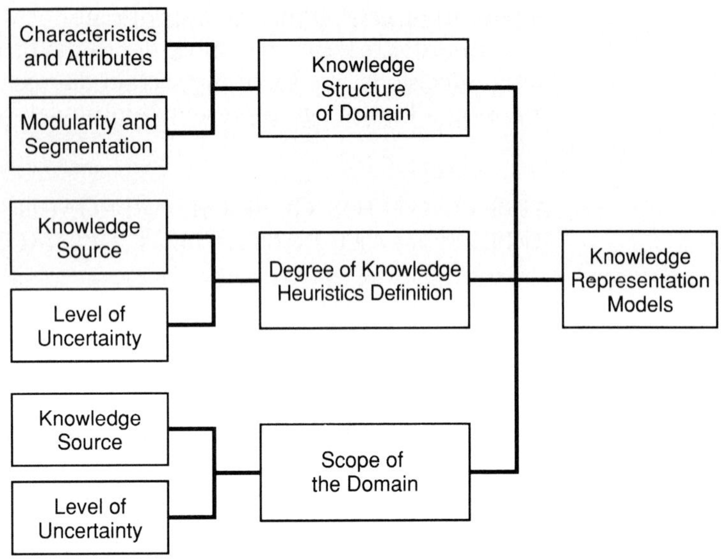


***Degree of Knowledge Heuristics Definition.*** In determining whether the knowledge-domain heuristics definition is well defined, somewhat defined, or ill defined, two areas are examined, the knowledge source and the level of uncertainty.

The *knowledge source* is evaluated through the following questions:

- To what extent is the knowledge to be replicated in the system available from written documents (books, manuals, etc.) that clearly describe what to do in detail?
- To what extent do different experts agree as to how the various factors of the knowledge domain interrelate?
- To what extent is the decision situation well understood by the experts?

If the knowledge to be replicated is available in written form, experts agree completely as to how the various decision factors interrelate, and the decision is well understood by the experts, the knowledge source is considered favorable. If the knowledge to be replicated is not available in written form, the experts do not agree as to how the various factors interrelate, and the decision is not well understood by the experts, the knowledge source is considered unfavorable.

The *level of uncertainty* is evaluated through the following questions:

- To what degree is the expert confident about the certainty of conclusions being drawn?
- To what extent is the available data and information reliable, consistent, and accurate?

The more confidence experts have about the certainty of their conclusions, and as reliability, accuracy, and consistency of the information increase, the more the level of uncertainty decreases.

***Scope of the Domain.*** In evaluating whether the scope of the knowledge domain is large or small, the following questions are asked:

- Does the knowledge to be replicated in the KBS cover multiple areas of expertise or one narrow area?
- Does the knowledge to be replicated in the KBS entail a large amount of facts and heuristics or a small amount?

If the knowledge to be replicated covers multiple areas of expertise or it entails a large amount of facts and heuristics, the scope of the domain is considered large. Otherwise it is considered small.

**Possible Recommendations and How They Are Made**

For the initial prototype, the four possible recommendations for a knowledge representation model were limited to:

- Production rules should be used to represent the knowledge;
- Predicate calculus should be used to represent the knowledge;
- Frames should be used to represent the knowledge;
- A hybrid, or some combination of production rules, predicate calculus, or frames should be used to represent the knowledge;

These recommendations are made by evaluating the knowledge structure of the domain, its degree of knowledge heuristics definition, and the scope of the domain that will be replicated by the KBS.

*Production rules* would be recommended to represent the knowledge if: the knowledge structure of the domain is independent and modular; the degree of knowledge heuristics definition is somewhat defined or ill defined; and, the scope of the domain to be replicated in the KBS is large or small. Production rules would also be recommended if: the knowledge structure of the domain is independent and modular; the degree of knowledge heuristics definition is well defined; and the scope of the domain to be replicated in the KBS is large.

*Predicate calculus* would be recommended to represent the knowledge if: the knowledge structure of the domain is independent and modular; the degree of knowledge heuristics definition is well defined; and the scope of the domain to be replicated in the KBS is small.

*Frames* would be recommended to represent the knowledge if: the knowledge structure of the domain is hierarchical and dependent; the degree of knowledge heuristics definition is well-defined, and the scope of the domain to be replicated in the KBS is small.

*A hybrid* or some combination of production rules, predicate calculus, or frames is recommended to represent the knowledge if: the structure of the knowledge domain is hierarchical and dependent; the knowledge is somewhat or ill-defined; and the scope of the domain is large or small.

## A KBS FOR ASSISTING IN MAKING THESE DECISIONS

A knowledge-based system has been developed to assist in making the type of decision described in the preceding section. The initial prototype of that system is shown in Figure 8–19.

**Figure 8–19.** Dependency Diagram—Choosing a Knowledge Representation Model

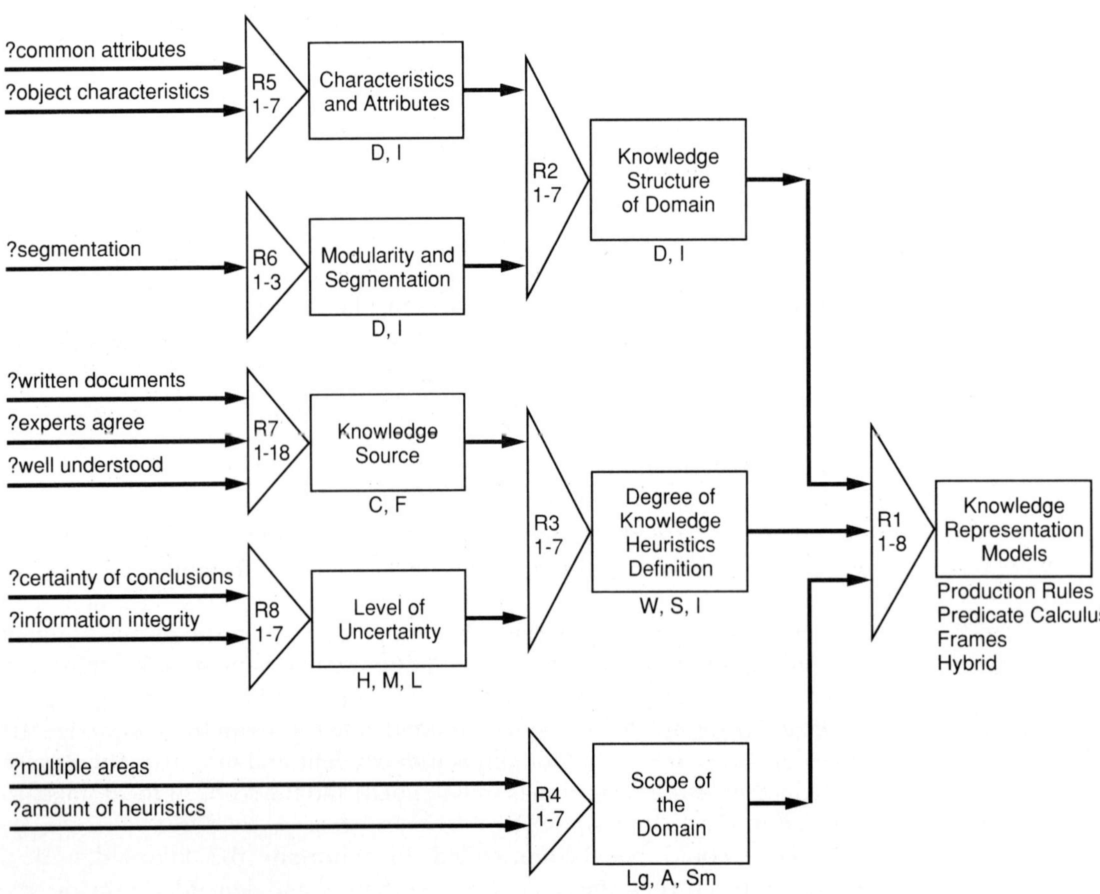


Key:

D = Dependent I = Independent C = Clear F = Fuzzy H = High
M = Medium L = Low W = Well-defined S = Somewhat-defined
I = Ill-defined Lg = Large A = Average Sm = Small

## REVIEW QUESTIONS

1. What is knowledge transformation in KBS development?
2. Identify three ways to replicate and structure knowledge which are especially useful for system design purposes.
3. Describe four of the more commonly used knowledge base representation methods in KBS development.
4. Discuss the advantages of frames or objects and identify situations where they are best used.
5. Describe working memory and how it is used in KBS.
6. Describe certainty factors and why they are used in KBS.
7. Describe some of the more common inferencing strategies used in KBS development.
8. Describe the situations in which the different inferencing alternatives can most effectively be used, either singly or in combination.
9. Describe some of the key factors which affect the system design decisions discussed in this chapter.

## EXERCISES

1. After reviewing the decision situation and dependency diagram outlines in Figures 8–17, 8–18, and 8–19, and the discussion in the two chapter sections entitled "Making Basic System Design Strategy Decisions in Specific Situations" and "Applying This General Approach to Making Knowledge Representation Strategy Decisions," develop a small KBS to assist in any of the system design decisions discussed in this chapter. Follow the directions in either Chapter 2 or in Chapters 3 through 6 when developing the system.
2. Read through recent issues of KBS periodicals listed in the references section of this chapter, and through other related artificial intelligence and user interface books and periodicals, and find discussions of the main topics covered in this chapter. Write a brief report describing how this reading provided you with insights and guidance when developing your KBS for Exercise 1.

## REFERENCES


Bowerman, Robert G., and David E. Glover. *Putting Expert Systems into Practice.* New York: Van Nostrand Reinhold, 1988.

Charniack E., and D. McDermott. *Artificial Intelligence,* Reading, MA: Addison-Wesley, 1986.

Feigenbaum, Edward, Pamela McCorduck, and H. Penny Nii. *The Rise of the Expert Company.* New York: Times Book, 1988.

Harmon, Paul, and Brian Sawyer. *Creating Expert Systems.* New York: Wiley, 1990.

Hart, Anna. *Knowledge Acquisition for Expert Systems.* New York: McGraw-Hill, 1986.

Hunt, V. Daniel. *Artificial Intelligence and Expert Systems Sourcebook.* New York, Chapman and Hall, 1986.

Knaus, Rodger. "A Portable Inference Engine." *AI Expert,* January 1990, pp. 17–20.

Liebowitz, Jay, and Daniel DeSalvo. *Expert Systems for Business and Management.* Englewood Cliffs, NJ: Prentice Hall, l990.

Martin, James, and Steven Oxman. *Building Expert Systems.* Englewood Cliffs, NJ: Prentice-Hall, 1988.

Mockler, Robert J. *Knowledge-Based Systems for Management Decisions.* Englewood Cliffs, NJ: Prentice-Hall, 1989.

Patterson, Dan W. *Introduction to Artificial Intelligence and Expert Systems.* Englewood Cliffs, NJ: Prentice-Hall, 1990.

Roew, Neil. *Artificial Intelligence Through Prolog.* Englewood Cliffs, NJ: Prentice Hall, 1988.

Rosenberg, Jerry M. *Dictionary of Artificial Intelligence and Robotics.* New York: Wiley, 1986.

Schutzer, Daniel. *Artificial Intelligence.* New York: Van Nostrand Zeinhold, 1987.

Thuraisingham, Bhavani. "From Rules to Frames and Frames to Rules." *AI Expert,* October 1989, pp. 31–39.

Waterman, Donald A. *A Guide to Expert Systems.* Reading, MA: Addison-Wesley, 1986.

Wolfgram, D., T. Dear, and C. Galbraith. *Expert System for the Technical Professional.* New York: Wiley, 1987.

# 9

# System Design and Development: Software and Hardware Selection

System design and development, as shown in Figure 9–1, involves defining KBS architecture; in this stage software and hardware development and selection decisions, as well as decisions about user interfaces, are made.

The objective of this chapter is to help the reader understand the nature of KBS hardware and software and understand how knowledge engineers make decisions in this area of the KBS development life cycle. The discussion covers:

1. KBS software:
   - The differences between conventional and knowledge-based applications
   - General purpose AI languages, such as LISP and PROLOG
   - Experts system shells and other development tools
   - Commercial knowledge-based systems
2. An approach to making software selection decisions in specific situations
3. KBS hardware:
   - Computer architecture: symbolic processing machines and conventional computing machines
   - Computer size
   - Computer components
   - Vendors

**Figure 9–1.** Knowledge-Based Systems Development Life Cycle

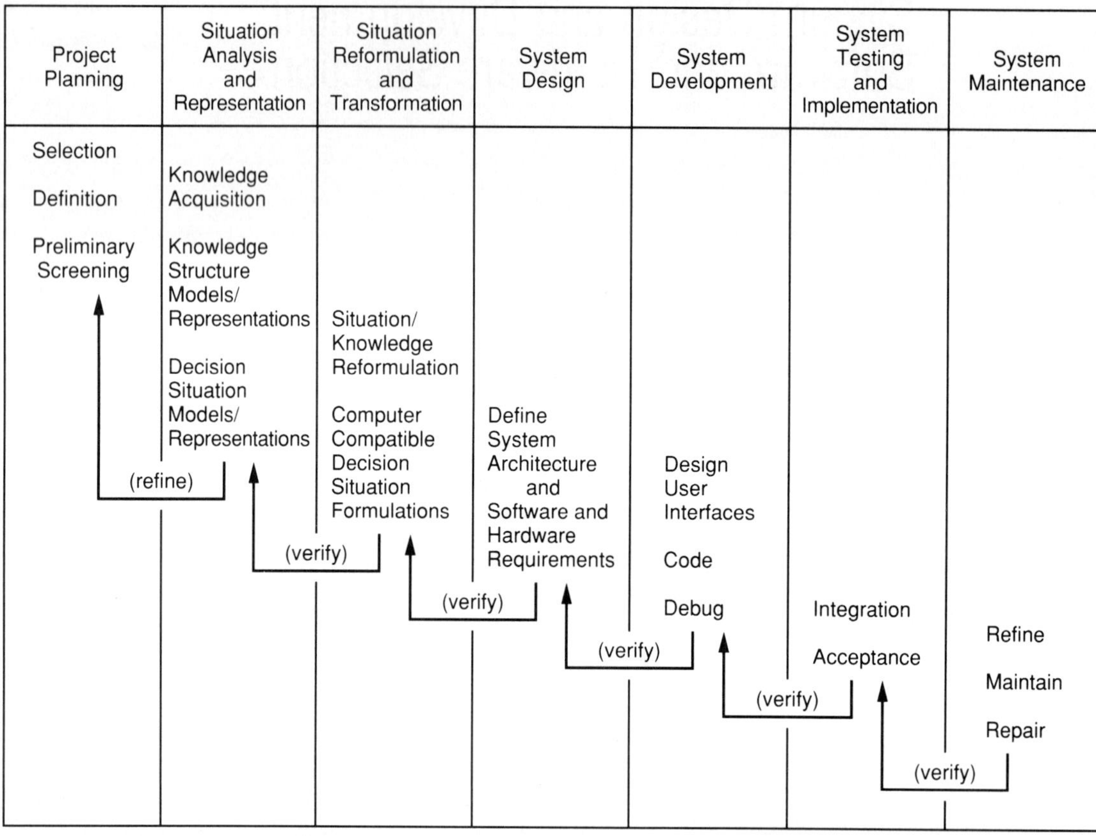


**4.** Varying levels of computer expertise needed

In the discussion of each area, basic decision-making strategies, as well as the techniques and tools commonly available today, are discussed.

The focus of this chapter is on making the software and hardware selection decisions within the context of specific KBS development situation requirements. Since the selection decision criteria for software and hardware differ in several key ways, the two are covered separately in the following discussions.

## KBS SOFTWARE

Four aspects of knowledge-based system software are discussed in this section: the differences between conventional and knowledge-based applications; expert system shells and other development tools; general-purpose AI languages, such as LISP and PROLOG; and commercial KB systems.

### The Differences Between Conventional and Knowledge-Based Applications

Several key differences are apparent between conventional data processing and the knowledge processing discussed in this book.

The most critical difference between knowledge-based systems software and conventional systems software is that in knowledge processing systems the knowledge base is separate from the inferencing or procedural segments of the system. This enables easier and quicker manipulation of the knowledge base and permits adaptation of the system to changing conditions more quickly. It also enables easier and quicker manipulation and understanding of the knowledge base by managers with little computer training, as well as much easier incremental prototype building.

Other differences are:

- Conventional data processing software mainly uses algorithms (for example, mathematical equations). Knowledge processing uses both algorithms and heuristics (rules of thumb).
- Conventional data processing software represents and manipulates data, such as tax rates, employee monthly pay, and hours worked. Knowledge processing software systems represent and manipulate knowledge, such as the rules of thumb and inferences described in the tutorial systems in Chapters 2 through 6.
- Conventional data processing software uses repetitive processes. Knowledge processing software uses inferential processes. One of the major advantages of conventional software is that it can reliably and accurately repeat a process throughout a specific task, for example, calculating tax rates for individual employees and calculating net pay after deductions for each employee. When adjustments have to be made for a variety of exceptions according to different rules of thumb because of situational factors, such as when evaluating auto accident insurance claims, then it is more likely that knowledge processing software will be more useful.

In many situations, systems replicating expert processes and knowledge can be programmed using either conventional data processing or knowledge processing software. The choice hinges on which type of software is more efficient, best replicates the processes or knowledge, and is the more easily developed, maintained, and updated as required by the specific application under study. Each type has its strengths and weaknesses, its advantages and disadvantages. For example, a system involving many repetitive calculations, such as one which enables the simulation of financial results based on different sales level projections, is usually best done on conventional spreadsheet software or in a conventional programming language. On the other hand, the more judgmental decision support knowledge-based systems described in this book are for the most part, at least in their advanced versions, more efficiently and effectively done with expert system development shells or in AI programming languages.

Knowledge-based systems have critical advantages in situations where continuing changes are expected, since they are easier to update than conventional systems. They are also more appropriate in situations where nontechnical people have to review and understand the reasoning in a system in order to help create and update it, and in situations where the reasoning needs to be explained relatively frequently. For example, Leaman (1989) describes a system developed to do structural design work for an architectural firm: a knowledge-based system was used because frequent building code changes had to be incorporated quickly into the system and because nontechnical managers (architects) could more easily consult and help refine the knowledge base.

They are also useful in the early stages of system development, since they allow for building system segments quickly and so facilitate incremental prototype system development.

### Expert System Shells and Other Development Tools

A variety of expert system shells were developed during the 1980s. As shown in Figure 4–1 (which is reproduced in Figure 9–2), they contain such components as inference engine programs, programmed control mechanisms for managing the knowledge base, facilities for explaining how and why a conclusion was reached, and capabilities for storing and editing knowledge bases. They also contain: programmed external software interface routines that enable them to integrate with external databases and spreadsheets; performance tools for testing and debugging during development, graphics/windowing features for studying relationships and switching environments; and integrity checks to eliminate duplication and uncover missing information. For these reasons, expert system shells can be easier and quicker to use than programming languages.

Because of their built-in capabilities, the less expensive basic shells require very little, if any, programming experience. A user is expected to create only the knowledge base. Nontechnical managers with minimal exposure to microcomputers and programming can, therefore, use these smaller shells to develop small KBS and prototypes of larger systems.

Shells have limitations, however, so they cannot be used in all situations. The major disadvantages of shells are the limitations related to the inferencing mechanism built into the shell. For example, many of the original PC-based shells were rule-based, as are many of the lower priced ones in use today. This limits potential applications to those decisions that can be replicated using only IF-THEN rules. This limitation is especially restrictive in the management decision-making area.

Some shells require the use of a mainframe computer. Some have been designed for use on LISP and other special purpose (dedicated) symbolic

**Figure 9–2.** An Expert System Shell's Underlying Components

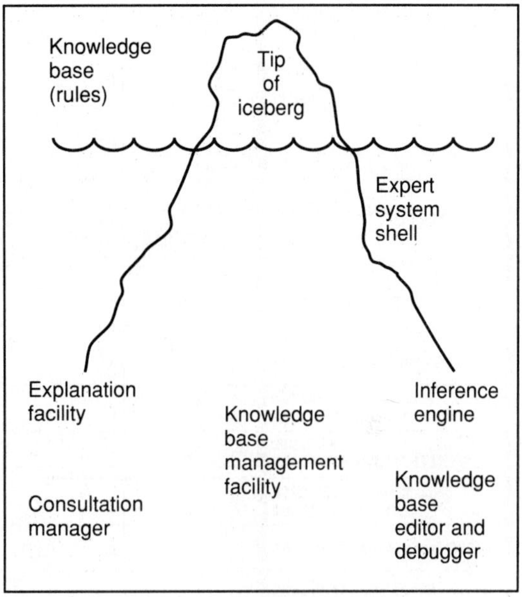


**Source:** Adapted from Bruce G. Buchanan. From a presentation made at the First Artificial Intelligence Satellite Symposium, sponsored by Texas Instruments, Nov. 23, 1985.

computers. Many shells have also been developed for personal computers. PC expert system shells range from very simple, limited, and inexpensive shells (such as ESIE) that foster creation of knowledge bases in plain English, to expensive shells with object-oriented capabilities, such as KAPPA, and those based on neural nets, such as NeuroShell, NeuralWorks, and BrainMaker (covered in Chapters 21 and 22 of this book). Several articles list and describe major available shells and their distinguishing characteristics (Brody 1989, Citrenbaum 1987, Coffee 1990, Finnie 1988, Gevarter 1987, Rauch-Hindin 1986, Richer 1987, Vedder 1989, and Williamson 1986). Figure 9–3 reproduces the summary chart of expert system shells and their capabilities and costs given by Finnie (1988). The most current review of expert system shells available at the time of publication is Enrado's "Expert System Resource Guide" (1991).

The discussion in this section covers both micro-based shells and the larger shells designed for symbolic processing machines or mainframe computers, as well as other software development tools.

***Microcomputer Shells.*** The expert system shells of greatest interest to this study are those written for microcomputers.

# Figure 9–3. Expert System Shells

| COMPANY | PRODUCT | HARDWARE PLATFORM | LANGUAGE USED | KNOWLEDGE REPRESENTATION | TYPES OF CONTROL STRUCTURES | INCLUDES CERTAINTY FACTORS | INCLUDES EDITING TOOLS | INCLUDES TRACE AND DEBUG FACILITIES | INCLUDES EXPLANATION FACILITY | EXPLAINS CONCLUSION REACHED | EXPLAINS INFORMATION REQUESTS | SAVES DATA FOR TESTING | SOFTWARE INTERFACES | TYPES OF USER INTERFACE | INCLUDES SEPARATE RUNTIME MODULE | PRICE |
|---|---|---|---|---|---|---|---|---|---|---|---|---|---|---|---|---|
| Alcorp, Inc. (617) 890-8400 | KBMS | IBM 370, 4300, 3000 and compatibles | C | Object-oriented | Inferencing | No | Yes | Yes | Yes | Yes | Yes | Yes | DB2, SQL/DS, VSAM, Adabas, IMS, IDMS, KDB | Menu, graphics, natural language | Yes | $90,000-$225,000 |
| Aion Corp. (415) 328-9595 | Aion Development System | Any IBM 370 architecture under VM and MVS, IBM PC, PS/2 | Pascal, C, Cobol, assembler | Rules, object-definition structure | Forward and backward chaining, procedural control | Yes | Yes | Yes | Yes | Yes | Yes | Yes | DL/1, DB2, SQL/DS, VSAM, QSAM, Teradata, Dbase III, Rbase 5000 | Menu, graphics, text, window | Yes | $7,000-$60,000 |
| | Aion Execution System | Any IBM with 370 architecture under VM and MVS, IBM PC, PS/2 | Pascal, C, Cobol, assembler | Rules, object-definition structure | Forward and backward chaining, procedural control | Yes | Yes | Yes | Yes | Yes | Yes | Yes | DL/1, DB2, SQL/DS, VSAM, QSAM, Teredata, Dbase III, Rbase 5000 | Menu, graphics, text, window | Yes | $250-$25,000 |
| Arity Corp. (508) 371-1243 | Expert | IBM PC, XT, AT and compatibles | Prolog | Frame- and rule-based | Backward chaining | Yes | Yes | Yes | Yes | Yes | Yes | Yes | C, Pascal, Fortran, assembler, Dbase III, 1-2-3 | Graphics, windows | Yes | $295 |
| Automated Reasoning Corp. (516) 484-6254 | I-CAT Troubleshooting System, Automatic Test Development System | Macintosh II, all Unix-based computers running X Windows | C | Rules | Procedural control logic- | Yes | Yes | Yes | Yes | Yes | Yes | Yes | Any ASCII files | Menu | No | $15,000 |
| Battelle Columbus Division (614) 424-3747 | DSPL | Xerox | LISP | Objects, plans, rules | Plan selection, constraint-directed redesign | No | Yes | Yes | Yes | Yes | No | Yes | NP | Graphics, text, tables | No | $9,500 |
| | CSRL | Microvax, Sun, Apollo, Xerox | LISP | Objects, rules | Establish, refine | Yes | Yes | Yes | Yes | Yes | No | Yes | C | Graphics, text, tables | Yes | $4,500 |
| BBN Software Products Corp. (617) 873-5000 | RS series Expert System Shell | IBM VM/370, PC XT, AT and compatibles; HP 9000 Series 300, Sun, DEC VAX | C, RPL | Rules, decision tree | Forward chaining, inference engine | No | Yes | Yes | Yes | No | Yes | Yes | Any via custom interfaces | Menu | Yes | NP |
| Berkshire Software Corp. (516) 593-8019 | Turbo Shell | IBM PC, XT, AT and compatibles | Prolog | Rules, frames | Backward chaining | Yes | Yes | Yes | Yes | Yes | Yes | No | 1-2-3, Dbase III | Menu | No | $89 |
| Califorina Intelligence (415) 391-4846 | Xsys | IBM PC, XT, AT and compatibles; VAX/VMS, any running Unix | LISP, C | Rules, frames | Forward and backward chaining | Yes | Yes | Yes | Yes | Yes | Yes | Yes | Symphony, Dbase III, any program with EXE or COM extension | Menu, variable questions, graphics, icons | Yes | $395 |
| Carleton Corp. (617) 272-4310 | CQS-AET | IBM 4300 series and up | Cobol | Logical rules | Forward chaining | Yes | Yes | Yes | Yes | Yes | No | Yes | VSAM, BDAM, IMS/DL1, IDMS/R, Datacom/DB, Adabas, Total/Supra, DB2 | Menu | Yes | $9,500 |
| Carnegie Group, Inc. (412) 642-6900 | Knowledge Craft | Microvax, VAX; Sun-3, Sun-4, TI Explorer | LISP | Frames, logic, rules | Forward, backward chaining | No | Yes | Yes | No | No | No | Yes | C, SQL | Graphics, text | No | NP |
| | Test Bench | IBM PC, AT and compatibles; TI Explorer | LISP, C | Frames | Forward, backward chaining | No | Yes | Yes | Yes | No | Yes | Yes | None | Graphics, text | Yes | NP |

| | | | | | | | | | | | | | | | | |
|---|---|---|---|---|---|---|---|---|---|---|---|---|---|---|---|---|
| **Computer Software Management and Information Center (Cosmic) (404) 542-3265** | C Language Integrated Production System (CLIPS) V 4.2 | IBM PC and compatibles, Macintosh, VAX | C | Symbolic facts | Forward chaining | Yes | Yes | Yes | Yes | No | No | No | C, Fortran, Ada | Window, command line | Yes | $250 |
| **Control Data Corp. (800) 553-2215** | KES | Cyber mainframes | C | Rules, demons, classes | KES control language | Yes | No | Yes | Yes | Yes | Yes | Yes | C applications | Terminals | Yes | $4,000-$20,000 |
| **Coyne Kalajian, Inc. (703) 522-7026** | ExpertR | Wang VS | C | Rules | Forward and backward chaining, combined chaining | Yes | Yes | Yes | Yes | Yes | Yes | Yes | Wang WP, WP+, ResponseR, WIIS and any DBMS on the VS | Menu, PF-key-driven, Strategy Language (proprietary) | Yes | $20,000-$40,000 |
| **Cullinet Software, Inc. (617) 329-7700** | Application Expert | IBM mainframe running MVS, DOS, VM, OS/2, VAX | Expert language (proprietary) | Rules | Forward, backward chaining | Yes | Yes | Yes | Yes | Yes | Yes | No | MVS/CICS, MVS,IDMS, VM/IDMS, DOS/CICS, DC/UCF, DC/UCF, VAX/VMS | Intelligent dialogue, smart forms | Yes | $3,000-$60,000 |
| **Data General Corp. (508) 870-6763** | Gold Works | Dasher 286, Dasher 386, Eclipse MV | LISP | Frames, rules, object representation | Forward, backward chaining, demons, sponsors, agendas, pattern matching | Yes | Yes | Yes | Yes | Yes | NP | NP | CEO, Infos II, 1-2-3, Dbase III | Line, menu, why, how, Help | Yes | $1,520-$24,370 |
| **Digital Equipment Corp. (800) 344-4285** | VAX Decision Expert | VAX family, Vaxstation, | C | If-then rule tables, decision trees, trees | Forward chaining, goal-directed reasoning | No | Yes | Yes | Yes | Yes | Yes | Yes | VAX languages, applications, databases | Menus, Decwindows | Yes | NP |
| **Drasch Computer Software (203) 429-3817** | CLisp, CRules | NA — runs with C | C | Rules | Production system | No | No | Yes | No | No | No | No | None | C | No | $268 |
| **Dynacomp, Inc. (716) 265-4040** | Hansen-Predict | IBM PC, XT, AT and compatibles | C | Rules | NP | No | Yes | Yes | Yes | Yes | Yes | Yes | 1-2-3, Symphony | Menu | No | $100 |
| **Envos Corp. (415) 966-6200** | Loops | Sun3, Sun4 | LISP | Object hierarchies | Forward chaining, active values | No | Yes | Yes | Yes | Yes | No | Yes | Document and graphics editors | Graphics | No | $7,000 |
| **Expertelligence, Inc. (805) 967-1797** | Experfacts | Macintosh 512, Plus, SE | Experlisp 1.5 | Knowledge | Forward, backward chaining, meta rules, asking justification, caching | No | Yes | Yes | Yes | Yes | Yes | No | None | Mac Toolbox | No | $495 |
| | ExperOPS5-Plus | Macintosh 512, Plus, SE | Expercommon LISP | Rules | Forward chaining | No | Yes | Yes | No | Yes | No | No | None | Mac Toolbox | No | $495 |
| | Expercommon OPS5 | Macintosh 512, Plus, SE | Expercommon LISP | Rules | Forward chaining | No | Yes | Yes | No | Yes | No | No | None | Mac Toolbox | No | $625 |
| **Expert Systems International (215) 735-8510** | ESP Advisor | IBM PC, XT, AT and compatibles, VAX | Prolog | Rules | Backward chaining | No | Yes | Yes | Yes | Yes | Yes | Yes | None | Prolog 2 | Yes | $895 |
| | ESP Frame-Engine | IBM PC, XT, AT and compatibles | Prolog | Rules, frames | Forward, backward chaining | No | Yes | Yes | Yes | Yes | Yes | Yes | None | Prolog 2 | Yes | $895 |
| **Exsys, Inc. (505) 256-8356** | Exsys | IBM PC, XT, AT, Compaq, VAX/VMS, Unix machines | C | Rules | Forward and backward chaining | Yes | Yes | Yes | Yes | Yes | Yes | Yes | Any running under host operating system | Menu | Yes | From $395 |

The companies included in this chart responded to a recent telephone survey conducted by *Computerworld.* When a vendor is unable to provide specific information about its product, the abbreviation NP (not provided) is used. When a question does not apply to a vendor's product, the abbreviation NA (not applicable) is used. Further product information is available from the vendors.

**Figure 9–3** *continued*

| COMPANY | PRODUCT | HARDWARE PLATFORM | LANGUAGE USED | KNOWLEDGE REPRESENTATION | TYPES OF CONTROL STRUCTURES | INCLUDES CERTAINTY FACTORS | INCLUDES EDITING TOOLS | INCLUDES TRACE AND DEBUG FACILITIES | INCLUDES EXPLANATION FACILITY | EXPLAINS CONCLUSION REACHED | EXPLAINS INFORMATION REQUESTS | SAVES DATA FOR TESTING | SOFTWARE INTERFACES | TYPES OF USER INTERFACE | INCLUDES SEPARATE RUNTIME MODULE | PRICE |
|---|---|---|---|---|---|---|---|---|---|---|---|---|---|---|---|---|
| Exsys, Inc. (505) 256-8356 | Expert System Development Package | IBM PC, XT, AT, Compaq, VAX/VMS, Unix machines | C | Rules | Forward and backward chaining | Yes | Yes | Yes | Yes | Yes | Yes | Yes | Any running under host operating system | Menu | Yes | From $395 |
| 1st Class Expert Systems, Inc. (508) 385-7722 | 1st Class Fusion | IBM PC, XT, AT, PS/2 and compatibles | Pascal, assembler | Examples, rules | Forward and backward chaining | Yes | Yes | Yes | Yes | Yes | Yes | Yes | 1-2-3, Dbase III, any ASCII file | Menu, graphics | Yes | $1,295 |
| General Research Corp. (703) 893-5900 | The Intelligent Machine Model (TIMM) | IBM PC XT, AT and compatibles, IBM mainframes, VAX, Prime | Fortran 77 | CASE-based in a multidimensional space | Forward, backward chaining | Yes | Yes | Yes | No | Yes | Yes | Yes | User-defined via custom interfaces | User-defined | Yes | $1,900 (PC) $19,000 (mainframe) |
| Gensym Corp. (617) 547-9606 | G2 Real-Time Expert System | DEC, HP, Sun, TI, Symbolics | Common LISP | Rules | Meta controls, inference engine, real-time scheduler with priorities, demons | Yes | Yes | Yes | Yes | Yes | Yes | Yes | Fortran, C, | Structured natural language, direct graphical manipulation, animation | Yes | $18,000-$36,000 |
| Gold Hill Computers, Inc. (617) 621-3300 | Goldworks II | IBM PC, AT, Macintosh II, Sun workstations | Allegro Common LISP, Golden Common LISP, Sun Common LISP | Multiple inheritance frame-based lattice | Forward, backward, bidirectional chaining, rules, sponsors, object-oriented programming, rule sets, handlers | Yes | Yes | Yes | Yes | Yes | Yes | Yes | Dbase, 1-2-3, Hypercard, Window Draw, DDE | Menu, developer's interface, functional LISP environment | Yes | $3,995-$7,500 |
| Human Intellect Systems/Mindsoft (800) 522-5939 | Instant-Expert | Macintosh | Modula-2 | Rules | Forward, backward chaining, combination | Yes | Yes | Yes | Yes | Yes | Yes | Yes | None | Menu, Q&A | Yes | $49.95 |
| | Instant Expert Plus | Macintosh, IBM PC with 640K | Modula-2 | Rules | Forward, backward chaining, depth first search, probability, certainty | Yes | Yes | Yes | Yes | Yes | Yes | Yes | Graphic, Pict and Pict-2 | Graphic, Q&A, menu, mouse | Yes | $498 |
| | Nexus | IBM PC with 640K | Modula-2 | Rules | Forward, backward chaining, combination, depth first search, probability, certainty | Yes | Yes | Yes | Yes | Yes | Yes | Yes | User-defined with full language included | Mouse, menu | No | $4,800 |
| IBM (617) 576-5301 | IBM Knowledgetool | 370 | PL/I | Object attribute value, arrays, single variables, rules | Forward chaining, pattern matching, conflict resolution, procedural block structure | No | No | Yes | No | No | Yes | Yes | DB2, SPL/DS, DL/1, VSAM, Cobol, PL/I, assembler, Fortran, Pascal, ISPF, GDDM | Menu-driven, windows, commands | Yes | $9,205-$105,880 |
| | Expert System Environment | 370, PS/2, PC, XT, AT | Pascal | Single- and multiple-valued parameters, rules focus control blocks, rule-selection strategies | Forward, backward chaining | Yes | Yes | Yes | Yes | Yes | Yes | Yes | DB2, SQL/DS, Files, DL/1 VSAM, Cobol, PL/I, Fortran, assembler, Pascal, Rexx | Menu-driven, commands | Yes | $515-$57,570 |

| | | | | | | | | | | | | | | | | |
|---|---|---|---|---|---|---|---|---|---|---|---|---|---|---|---|---|
| | KEE | 370 | IBM Common LISP | Frames, demons, methods, multiple words, rules, rule classes, rule hierarchies | Forward and backward chaining, pattern matching, agenda, hypothetical reasoning, truth maintenance, object-oriented | No | Yes | Yes | Yes | Yes | Yes | Yes | DB2, Fortran, assembler, other languages via LISP | Menu-, mouse-driven commands, windows | Yes | $98,000 |
| | Enhanced Common LISP Production System | 370 | IBM Common LISP for MVS | Rules, rule groups, working memory elements, on-change demons, all Common LISP flavors | Forward chaining, pattern-matching, rule sequencing control, MEA, LEX, FIFO queuing | No | No | Yes | No | No | No | No | LISP | ISPF panels, PC windows | No | $5,000 |
| **Inference Corp.** **(213) 417-7997** | Automated Reasoning Tool | Apollo DN3000, DN4000, HP 9000, Symbolics, Sun-3, Sun-4, VAX, TI Explorer I, II, Microexplorer | LISP | Rules, facts, relationships schema; integrated forward, backward chaining | Pattern matching, viewpoints | Yes | Yes | Yes | Yes | Yes | Yes | Yes | Custom interfaces for Oracle, Ingres, IMS, CICS | Graphics | Yes | $22,500-$45,000 |
| | Automated Reasoning Tool for Information Management | IBM AT, PS/2 and compatibles, IBM mainframes running MVS | C | Rules, facts, relations schema, pattern matching | Forward chaining, truth maintenace | Yes | Yes | Yes | Yes | Yes | Yes | Yes | ISPF, IMS, VSAM, Dbase | ISPF, MF | Yes | $7,000-$8,000 (PC), $60,000-$70,000 (mainframe) |
| **Information Access Systems, Inc.** **(303) 442-6224** | Intelligent Text Management System | VAX/VMS, CDC 910/Unix | C | Judgment space | NA | Yes | Yes | Yes | Yes | No | No | Yes | NP | User definable | Yes | $5,000-$155,000 |
| **Information Builders, Inc.** **(800) 444-4303** | Level 5 | IBM PC, XT, AT, PS/2, Macintosh Plus, SE, II, VAX/VMS, IBM mainframe | Pascal, C, assembler | Rules | Goal outlining, procedural rules | Yes | Yes | Yes | Yes | Yes | Yes | Yes | Dbase, Excel, Focus, RS/1, Datatrieve, RDB, CDC | PF-key driven, windowing, mouse, menu | Yes | $685-$36,000 |
| **Intellicorp, Inc.** **(415) 956-5500** | Knowledge Engineering Environment (KEE) | Sun workstations, VAX, Vaxstation, IBM mainframe, Apollo, Macintosh II, HP, IBM RT, 80386-based machines | LISP, C | Frames, rules, object-oriented | Forward, backward chaining, mixed initiative, attached procedural, message passing | No | Yes | Yes | Yes | Yes | Yes | Yes | C integration tool kit, common windows | Graphics | Yes | $9,000-$98,000 |
| **Intelligenceware, Inc.** **(213) 417-8896** | IXL: The Machine Learning System | IBM PC, AT | C | Discovery rules | Forward, backward chaining | Yes | No | No | Yes | Yes | Yes | Yes | NP | Menus, graphics | Yes | $490 |
| | Intelligence/ Compiler | IBM PC, AT; VAX | C | Frames, rules, procedures | Forward, backward, inexact chaining | Yes | Yes | Yes | Yes | Yes | Yes | Yes | NP | Menus, graphics | Yes | $490 |
| | Auto-Intelligence | IBM PC, AT | C | Rules, interviews | Forward, backward, inexact chaining | Yes | Yes | No | Yes | Yes | Yes | Yes | NP | Menus, graphics | Yes | $490 |
| **Intelligent Controlsystem Corp.** **(508) 458-6029** | Picon System | Explorer II LX | LISP | Frame-, rule-based | Forward, backward chaining | Yes | Yes | Yes | Yes | Yes | No | Yes | Major distributed control systems | Menu | Yes | $120,000 (includes hardware) |
| **Intelligent Environments, Inc.** **(508) 256-6412** | Crystal | IBM PCs and compatibles with 350K of RAM | C | Rules, variables | User-defined | Yes | Yes | Yes | Yes | Yes | Yes | Yes | 1-2-3, Symphony, Dbase III, DOS, any ASCII, C | Menus, forms, graphics, multifield forms, flip-flop menus, reports, induction | Yes | $995 (MS-DOS), $1,995 (OS/2) |
| **Jeffrey Perrone & Associates, Inc.** **(415) 431-9562** | Expert Ease | IBM PCs except AT, PS/2 | Pascal | Examples | Inductive inference | No | Yes | Yes | Yes | Yes | Optional | Yes | None | Menus, graphics | Yes | $695 |
| | Expert Edge | IBM AT and compatibles | Pascal | Rules | Forward, backward chaining | Yes | Yes | Ltd | Yes | Yes | Yes | Yes | 1-2-3, Visicalc, Dbase III, any ASCII | Menu | Yes | $1,495 |
| **KDS Corp.** **(312) 251-2621** | KDS3.3 | IBM PC, XT, AT, PS/2 and compatibles | Assembler | Rules, frames, facts, objects | Forward, backward chaining, mixed chaining, blackboard | Yes | Yes | Yes | Yes | Yes | Yes | Optional | 1-2-3, Dbase III, ASCII files | Text, graphics | Yes | $1,495 |

 Figure 9–3 *continued*

| COMPANY | PRODUCT | HARDWARE PLATFORM | LANGUAGE USED | KNOWLEDGE REPRESENTATION | TYPES OF CONTROL STRUCTURES | INCLUDES CERTAINTY FACTORS | INCLUDES EDITING TOOLS | INCLUDES TRACE AND DEBUG FACILITIES | INCLUDES EXPLANATION FACILITY | EXPLAINS CONCLUSION REACHED | EXPLAINS INFORMATION REQUESTS | SAVES DATA FOR TESTING | SOFTWARE INTERFACES | TYPES OF USER INTERFACE | INCLUDES SEPARATE RUNTIME MODULE | PRICE |
|---|---|---|---|---|---|---|---|---|---|---|---|---|---|---|---|---|
| **Kemp-Carraway Heart Institute (205) 226-6697** | Flops | IBM PC, AT, PS/2 with MS- or PC-DOS | C | Rules | Clipboard, rules, block control | Yes | NP | Yes | No | No | No | No | C, DOS programs | Line interface | No | $495 |
| **Lightwave, Inc. (813) 988-5033** | Expert System Inference Engine (ESIE) | IBM PCs running MS-DOS | Pascal | If-then rule structure | Backward chaining, inference engine | No | Yes | Yes | Yes | Yes | Yes | Yes | None | Menus, graphics | Yes | $145 |
| **Logicware, Inc. (416) 672-0300** | Twaice | IBM MVS/TSO, VM/CMS, VAX, all Sun, Silicon Graphics 4D, all Apollo, Integrated Solutions, Tektronix, HP 386, CDC, Cyber | MProlog | Frames, rules | Forward, backward chaining | Yes | Yes | Yes | Yes | Yes | Yes | Yes | Fortran, Cobol, C, assembler | NP | Yes | $48,900 |
| | MProlog | IBM MVS/TSO, VM/CMS, VAX, Sun, Apollo, IDT, Tektronix, HP 386, Silicon Graphics 4D, Integrated Solutions, Cyber, CDC | C | Frames, rules | Forward, backward chaining | Yes | Yes | Yes | Yes | Yes | Yes | Yes | Fortran, Cobol, C, assembler | NP | Yes | $48,900 |
| **Machine Intelligence Corp. (516) 589-1676** | Mice | IBM PC, XT, AT and compatibles | C | Semantic net, frames | Forward, backward chaining, confidence factors, flow control | Yes | Yes | Yes | Yes | Yes | Yes | Yes | None | Menu, graphics | Yes | $1,750 |
| **MDBS, Inc. (800) 344-5832** | Guru | IBM PC XT, AT, PS/2 and compatibles, VAX/VMS, Sun Unix | C | Rules | Forward, backward chaining | Yes | Yes | Yes | Yes | Yes | Yes | Yes | Dbase III+, MDBS III, Knowledgeman/2, 1-2-3 | Menu, natural language, command language | Yes | $6,500 |
| **Miller Microcomputer Services (508) 653-6136** | Expert-2 in MMSForth | IBM PC, XT, AT, PS/2, Tandy TRS-80 1, 2, 4 | MMSForth | Rule-based | Backward chaining | Optional | Yes | Yes | Yes | Yes | Yes | No | MMSForth editor extension word sets | Menu, graphics, natural language | No | $250-$1,250 (including MMSForth) |
| **Mind Path Technologies (214) 233-9296** | Intelliform | IBM PC, XT, AT, PS/2 and compatibles | C | Rules | Forward, backward chaining | Yes | Yes | No | No | Yes | Yes | Yes | ASCII files | Forms, pop-up windows | Yes | $495 |
| **Mountain View Press, Inc. (415) 961-4103** | Expert 2 | IBM PC, Apple II | Forth | Rules | Backward chaining | No | Yes | No | Yes | Yes | No | Yes | NP | NP | Yes | $150 |
| **Mystech Associates, Inc. (203) 572-9571** | Aurora | Xerox 1100, IBM PC, VAX | Interlisp, Common LISP, C | Production rule | Forward, backward chaining | Yes | Yes | Yes | Yes | Yes | Yes | NP | LISP, Common LISP, C | Keyboard, mouse | No | $1,500-$8,000 |
| **Neuron Data (415) 321-4488** | Nexpert Object | IBM AT, PS/2, Macintosh SE, II, DEC VAX, Vaxstations under VMS and Ultrix, Sun, HP, Apollo workstations, IBM RT under AIX, IBM mainframes under VM | C | Rules, objects | Forward, backward chaining | No | Yes | Yes | Yes | Yes | Yes | Yes | Excel, 1-2-3, Ease-Plus, Hypercard, Oracle, Sybase, Ingres, DEC RDB, Dbase III, Data Views | Graphics | Yes | $3,650-$8,000 |
| **Paperback Software International (415) 644-2116** | VP-Expert | IBM PC, XT, AT, PS/2 and compatibles | C | Rules | Forward, backward chaining | Yes | Yes | Yes | Yes | Yes | Yes | Yes | Any DOS-executable file | Text, dynamic graphics, windows, pull-down menus, mouse | No | $249 |

| | | | | | | | | | | | | | | | | |
|---|---|---|---|---|---|---|---|---|---|---|---|---|---|---|---|---|
| **Prediction Systems, Inc. (201) 223-5000** | General Simulation Systems | Microvax | PSI simulation language | Expert system, database | Hierarchical | Yes | Yes | Yes | Yes | Yes | Yes | Yes | NP | Menu, graphics | Yes | $19,000 |
| **Production Systems Technologies (412) 683-4000** | OPS83 | Apollo, AT&T 3B, AT&T 6386, HP 9000/300, Masscomp, Stratus, Sun, VAX, MS-DOS, OS/2 | C | Rules | Any | No | No | Yes | No | No | No | No | C | NP | Yes | $2,000-$20,000 |
| **Quantum Inknowvations Corp. (408) 496-6933** | Pro Genesis | IBM AT, PS/2 Model 50 and higher, 286, 386 compatibles | C | Objects, rules, variables, models | Forward, backward chaining | No | Yes | Yes | Yes | No | No | Yes | SQL to Oracle, DB2, Informix, C | Windows, forms, speadsheets | Yes | $4,995 |
| **Radin Corp. (512) 454-4797** | Rulemaster 3 | IBM PC, XT, AT, 3000 | C | Rules, examples | Forward, backward chaining | Yes | Yes | Yes | Yes | Yes | Yes | Yes | Any ASCII file, files that can be called from C | Menu, window | Yes | $495 |
| | Rulemaster 2 | Cyber 860, 990, 205, VAX, HP 9000, Apollo, Sun workstations, Masscomp, Unisys XE/550 | C | Rules, examples | Forward, backward chaining | Yes | Yes | Yes | Yes | Yes | Yes | Yes | Any ASCII file, files that can be called from C | Menu | Yes | $7,500-$28,000 |
| **Smart Communications, Inc. (212) 486-1894** | Smart Expert Editor-Smart Translators | IBM PS/2, VAX, Unix workstations | C | Lexical tokens | Rule base linked to databases | Yes | Yes | Yes | Yes | No | Yes | Yes | ANSI C, Unix SVID, VMS VM/CMS | None | Yes | $12,500 (with expert editor package) |
| **Softsync, Inc. (212) 685-2080** | Superexpert | IBM PC, XT, AT, Macintosh, Macintosh Plus, SE, II | Pascal, Forth | Examples | Forward, backward chaining | Yes | Yes | No | Yes | Yes | Yes | Yes | Any ASCII file | Menu | No | $199 |
| **Software Architecture and Engineering, Inc. (703) 276-7910** | Knowledge Engineering System | IBM mainframes, PCs and compatibles, Apollo, HP, Silicon Graphics workstations, VAX under VMS and Unix, Gould Powernodes, any Unisys, CDC Cyber | C | Rules, descriptions, classes | Forward and backward chaining | Yes | No | Yes | Yes | Yes | Yes | Yes | Anyu file that can be called from C | Menu-driven text queries, graphics optional | Yes | $4,000-$60,000 |
| **Sourceview Software International (415) 685-3635** | Micro Mind Knowledge Engineering Tool | IBM PCs | IQ LISP | Rules | Forward, backward chaining | Yes | Yes | Yes | Yes | Yes | Yes | Yes | 1-2-3, Dbase | Menu, graphics | Yes | $9,995 |
| **Symbolics, Inc. (617) 621-7500** | Joshua | Symbolics 3600 | Symbolics Common LISP | Statement-oriented language, object-oriented | Forward, backward chaining | No | Yes | Yes | Yes | Yes | NP | NP | Symbolics Software System | Genera user interface | No | $15,000-$60,000 |
| **Teknowledge, Inc. (415) 424-0500** | M.1 | IBM PC and compatibles with 512K | C | Rules | Backward chaining, pattern matching | Yes | Yes | Yes | Yes | Yes | Yes | Yes | C files | Menus, application can substitute own interface | No | $2,000 |
| | S.1 | VAX, Microvax, NCR Tower, HP 9000-300, Apollo Domain IX, Aegis, Sun-3, IBM AT and compatibles | C | Rules | Backward chaining, attached procedures, explicit procedure calling | Yes | Yes | Yes | Yes | Yes | Yes | Yes | C files | Menus, application can substitute own interface | Yes | $15,000 (PC), $20,000 (mainframe) |
| | Copernicus | VAX, Microvax, Sun, Apollo/Domain IX, Aegis | C | Rules | Forward, backward chaining, attached procedures, explicit procedure calling | Yes | Yes | Yes | Yes | Yes | Yes | Yes | C files | Menus, application can substitute own interface | No | $30,000 |
| **Texas Instruments, Inc. (800) 527-3500** | Personal Consultant Easy | IBM XT, AT, PS/2 and compatibles with 512K | Scheme LISP | Frames, rules | Forward, backward chaining | Yes | Yes | Yes | Yes | Yes | Yes | Yes | 1-2-3, Dbase, any DOS.EXE programs | Menu, graphics | Yes | $495 |

**Figure 9–3** *continued*

| COMPANY | PRODUCT | HARDWARE PLATFORM | LANGUAGE USED | KNOWLEDGE REPRESENTATION | TYPES OF CONTROL STRUCTURES | INCLUDES CERTAINTY FACTORS | INCLUDES EDITING TOOLS | INCLUDES TRACE AND DEBUG FACILITIES | INCLUDES EXPLANATION FACILITY | EXPLAINS CONCLUSION REACHED | EXPLAINS INFORMATION REQUESTS | SAVES DATA FOR TESTING | SOFTWARE INTERFACES | TYPES OF USER INTERFACE | INCLUDES SEPARATE RUNTIME MODULE | PRICE |
|---|---|---|---|---|---|---|---|---|---|---|---|---|---|---|---|---|
| **Texas Instruments, Inc. (800) 527-3500** | Personal Consultant Plus | IBM 286-, 386-based micros and compatibles | Scheme LISP, C | Frames, rules | Forward, backward chaining | Yes | Yes | Yes | Yes | Yes | Yes | Yes | Any DOS program and external language interface, 1-2-3, Dbase | Menu, graphics | Yes | $2,950 |
| | Procedure Consultant | IBM AT, PS/2, TI Professional and Business Pro | PC Scheme, C | Tree structure | Fault tree | No | Yes | No | Yes | Yes | Yes | Yes | 1-2-3, Dbase | Q&A, graphics, windows | Yes | $495 |
| **Thunderstone/EPI, Inc. (216) 449-6104** | Metamorph | Minis, micros | C, assembler | Rules frames | Forward, backward chaining | Yes | Yes | Yes | Yes | Yes | Yes | Yes | Unltd | Natural-language protocols | Yes | $5,000 (site license) |
| **Transpower Corp. (215) 495-6362** | Expert Thinker | IBM PC XT, AT and compatibles, PS/2 | Compile Arity Prolog, Turbo Prolog | Logic | Backward chaining | No | Yes | Yes | Yes | No | Yes | Yes | Any ASCII text file | Menu, graphics | No | $149 |
| **Unisys Corp. (313) 972-7000** | KES II | IBM PC, AT, Unisys B series workstations, Unix systems | C | Rules, frames | Forward and backward chaining, procedural control | Yes | No | Yes | Yes | Yes | Yes | Yes | C, Pascal | Windows | Yes | $50-$10,000 |
| | KEE | Explorer, Explorer II, U5000/50 | LISP | Rules, frames | Forward, backward chaining, active values, methods, truth maintenance system, keywords | No | Yes | Yes | Yes | Yes | Yes | Yes | LISP, C | Windows | No | $30,000 |

VP-Expert, for example, one of the higher rated and least expensive ones (Brody 1989), is used in constructing the sample system described in Chapters 3 through 6. M.1, one of the original expert system shells, is used in other examples throughout the book despite its limitations because it enables developing systems in a language very close to plain English and so is useful in working with nontechnical managers.

Many of the newer PC shells have substantial object capabilities. For example, LEVEL5 OBJECT (included in this book) and KAPPA, like the earlier Nexpert, all fall into this category. Several of these are described in Chapter 21. Since they are more complex and harder to use, these shells are often referred to as development environments. Shells for developing artificial neural networks are described in Chapter 22.

Expert system shells are used exclusively for the sample prototype systems described in this book. Tutorials for using a PC-based expert system shell (or development tools, as they are sometimes called) are given in Chapters 2 through 6 and in Chapters 21 and 22.

***Larger Shells.*** Four large expert system development shells are discussed here:

- Knowledge Engineering Environment (KEE) from IntelliCorp
- Automated Reasoning Tool (ART) from Inference Corp.
- Knowledge Craft from Carnegie Group Inc.
- S.1 from Teknowledge Inc.

As seen from Figure 9–3, these shells were originally designed for use on mainframe, mini, and symbolic computers and related workstations.

KEE supports both rules and frames for knowledge representation, backward and forward chaining, object-oriented programming, an active-values mechanism, and viewpoints, which are called "worlds."

KEE's active-values mechanism provides a way to attach procedures to frame slots so that when these slots are accessed or changed, specified procedures are executed. For example, if the temperature represented in a frame slot is increased, a procedure can be triggered that activates a thermostat or causes the temperature in an image of a thermometer to change accordingly.

Another KEE feature, "worlds," allows users to hypothesize various situations and reason about them in parallel. This enables the generation and evaluation of alternatives in such situations as determining alternate truck routes under varying dispatch conditions.

Babcock & Wilcox has used KEE to build a factory welding scheduler. Lawrence Livermore Laboratories has used it to build an intelligent interface to instrumentation. The Electrical Power Research Institute has used KEE to build a crisis-management system for a nuclear power plant. Of the tools that support multiple knowledge representation and inferencing models (for example, rule-based and object-oriented), KEE is one of the simplest to use.

*ART,* in the past, was considered a higher level—and more difficult to use—tool than KEE. ART's capabilities have been demonstrated through its use for developing the Hughes Radar Systems Group's circuit-board-diagnosis system, Composition System's electronic-typesetting and editorial-layout knowledge-based software, and Eastman Kodak's knowledge-based document management and updating system for the F-14 aircraft documentation.

ART supports rules, frames, integrated backward and forward chaining, viewpoints for reasoning about hypothetical worlds, and object-oriented programming capabilities.

In object-oriented programming, procedures are called methods, and ART's version of methods is called "multimethods." Multimethods allows users to send a message—a procedure to be executed—to a generalized group of closely linked objects instead of to only a single object. This, in turn, allows for fewer procedures to be written because each one handles more objects.

For example, a factory system might be divided into machines. During production, certain groups of machines, such as a feeder, a milling machine, and a transporter, must be periodically synchronized. With multimethods, a single generic synchronization procedure can be written for these machines. The message "synchronize" is then sent to the generalized class that contains the machines to be synchronized. A microcomputer version of ART is available.

*Knowledge Craft* is an outgrowth of Schema Representation Language (SRL), a tool developed at Carnegie-Mellon University (CMU). In its precommercial days, Knowledge Craft was used to build ISIS—a CMU-Westinghouse Electric Company factory-scheduling system—and various other planning, factory-management, and monitoring systems for Westinghouse, Digital Equipment Corp., the US Air Force, and Alcoa.

Knowledge Craft features rules and frames for representing knowledge. It supports three languages: OPS5, Prolog, and a frame-based language called CRL. Another feature, an agenda mechanism, tracks multiple queues of events and manages scheduling of the events for execution. It is also useful for such applications as simulation. Moreover, the agenda mechanism can track multiple contexts—subdivisions of a problem—sprouted by rules, in effect creating a viewpoint mechanism.

A unique attraction of Knowledge Craft, as well as KMBS, another development shell, is a natural-language interface. It allows these systems to obtain natural-language input. The ultimate goal is to allow knowledge engineers to use natural language to acquire domain knowledge and develop knowledge systems.

S.1, of these four tools, is the simplest to learn and use. It is primarily a rule-based, backward-chaining tool that also features a block-structure language. It has sometimes been accused of being limited in techniques and being useful only for diagnostic applications, but S.1 users have revealed in interviews that they were never at a loss. Delco Products used S.1 to build its design systems for DC motor components. (M.1 is, to a very limited degree, a microcomputer version of S.1.)

***Other Expert System Development Tools.*** In addition to expert system shells, there are numerous programming and development tools which have varying preprogrammed functions and routines useful in developing KBS. These include OPS5, INTERLISP, Objective C, and C++. In terms of difficulty for the nontechnical manager to use, these development tools would be ranked somewhere between the PC expert systems shells described earlier and the programming languages discussed in the following section.

So far this book has concentrated on rule-based systems because they are easy to understand, have wide applicability in prototyping simpler management decision-making situations, are easier to construct, and are widely used. In addition, most microcomputer expert system shells in common use today have rule-based capabilities.

Many experts in the field believe that object-oriented systems have great potential in developing larger, more advanced management decision-making and production systems. However, these shells and development environments are for the most part designed for people with high levels of computer literacy, and so are difficult to use when explaining and teaching basic expert knowledge-based systems concepts. Object-oriented systems and shells are discussed in Chapter 21.

### General Purpose AI Languages: LISP and PROLOG

The two most commonly used programming languages for knowledge-based system development are LISP and PROLOG. Because languages do not have as many preprogrammed (built-in) routines as do expert system shells, languages are more flexible and so can handle more demanding problems. At the same time, they are more difficult to use than expert system shells, because the system developer is usually required to design from scratch both the knowledge base and the inference mechanism which accesses it. For this reason, using a programming language normally takes longer and is more expensive. At the same time, however, its use will very often lead to a system that will better match the specific requirements of the situation under study.

***PROLOG.*** PROLOG (which stands for PROgramming language for LOGic) was initially developed in 1972 by A. Colmerauer and P. Roussel at the University of Marseilles. PROLOG is a programming language that utilizes a simplified version of predicate calculus and is thus a true logical language.

PROLOG, like LISP, is designed for symbolic (word) manipulation, rather than simply numerical computation. PROLOG is very efficient at processing lists, such as lists of rules that are matched during processing. PROLOG is an interpreted language and so responds to any query by attempting to return an answer immediately, as is seen in the example below.

To program in PROLOG requires:

1. Specifying some facts about objects and their relationships;
2. Specifying rules about objects and their relationships.

For example, the facts might be:

Mary likes chocolates;
Piquant is a well-known brand of chocolates;

These facts are entered in PROLOG as follows:

```
likes(mary, chocolates).
is(piquant, chocolates).
```

The format in which such statements are written is called a language's "syntax." Therefore, each sentence, or line, in this example follows a formal structure dictated by the PROLOG language.

To ask the question "Does Mary like Piquant chocolates?" in PROLOG, the following form could be used:

```
?-likes(mary, piquant).
```

PROLOG would respond to this question or query by printing: `yes`

In this small example, the word "likes" is the predicate that indicates that such a *relationship* exists between one *object,* Mary, and a second *object,* Piquant chocolates. The question, in effect, asks PROLOG to say whether it can establish the truth of the assertion that "Mary likes Piquant chocolates." In this case PROLOG says that it can, based on the facts it has been given.

A word starting with an upper case letter is used to create a variable in PROLOG. For example, if asked the question:

```
?-likes(mary,X).
```

PROLOG would answer:

```
X = chocolates.
```

That is, Mary likes chocolates.

The symbol for if, ":-", is used to establish an IF-THEN rule in PROLOG. The rule in this case might read:

```
buys(mary, piquant):- is(piquant, chocolates).
```

Using the principles outlined so far, one can construct a simple prototype of a market product/customer matching system in PROLOG, such as the one given in Figure 9–4. The system took someone not very familiar with computers less than an hour to construct, and so is admittedly trivial. But it illustrates how a PROLOG knowledge base looks and works. For example, a user might ask the system outlined in Figure 9–4 the question "Is there a good chance the young-urban-professional (young adult) market would accept and buy Piquant chocolates?" in the following way:

```
?-likely_to_buy(young_urban_professionals, piquant).
```

**Figure 9–4.** Prolog Knowledge Base: Product/Market Compatibility

Facts:

```
product(piquant_chocolates).
product_kind(chocolate_candy).
is(piquant_chocolates, chocolate_candy).
is_high_priced(piquant_chocolates).
is_high_quality (piquant_chocolates).
has_great_brand_image(piquant_chocolates).
market(young_urban_professionals).
is_well_educated(young_urban_professionals).
is_young_adult(young_urban_professionals).
is_affluent(young_urban_professionals).
likes(young_urban_professionals,chocolate_candy).
```

Rule-1:

```
likely_to_buy(B,G)  :-
market(B),
product(G),
product_kind(A),
is(G,A),
is_well_educated(B),
is_young_adult(B),
is_affluent(B),
likes(B,A),
is_high_priced(G),
has_great_brand_image(G).
```

Note: Uppercase letters are the variables.

From the facts, it is known that:

A = chocolate candy
B = young urban professionals
G = piquant chocolates

The characteristics of B and G are also known from the facts. When all the facts are inserted into the rule variables, all of the IF clauses prove to be true, that is, the rule fires. The answer to this consultation, therefore, is "yes," that is, young urban professionals are good prospects for piquant chocolates.

PROLOG would answer "yes," based on the facts and Rule 1 in the knowledge base in Figure 9–4. In the figure, the variables are:

A = chocolates

B = young urban professionals

G = Piquant chocolates

This is known from the facts stated in the figure. Further, the fact statements give the characteristics of both B and G. When these facts are inserted in the rule variables, all the IF clauses are true, so that the rule fires, that is, gives the answer "Young urban professionals are a good potential market for Piquant chocolates."

Computation in PROLOG is controlled logical deduction. A decision maker first states the rules or relationships used to make a decision. These rules are programmed into the system. At some subsequent time, as shown in Figure 9–4, someone asks the system to make a decision by stating a set of situation facts. PROLOG is prepared, when asked, to say whether or not any specific conclusion can be deduced from those facts, based on the rules originally placed in the system.

***LISP.*** LISP (which stands for LISt Processing language) was created by John McCarthy in 1958. Of the major languages still in use, only FORTRAN is older than LISP. Until recently LISP was the major artificial intelligence language in the United States.

There are many reasons for LISP's widespread popularity:

- easy and flexible symbol manipulation
- automatic memory management
- sophisticated editing and debugging aids
- uniform treatment of program code and data, which means a LISP program can modify its own program code as easily as its data. This last feature lends itself to writing programs that learn new rules or modify existing ones in the knowledge base.

In LISP, relations between objects are often represented as lists containing a relation followed by objects that the relation links. For example, "the target market for Piquant chocolates is affluent young people" might be written in LISP-like notation as:

```
(MARKET(PIQUANT CHOCOLATES)(AFFLUENT YOUNG PEOPLE))
```

The term MARKET is a link that indicates a relation between the first argument (PIQUANT CHOCOLATES) and the second argument (AFFLUENT YOUNG PEOPLE). Using this same scheme one might write rules such as "IF the target market for Piquant chocolates is high income people, THEN explore selling to young urban professions (YUPPIES)" as follows:

```
(IF(MARKET CHOCOLATES AFFLUENT)
THEN(EXPLORE SELLING-YUPS))
```

It would be necessary to write the inference engine that would be capable of using rules such as the above to process data or fact expressions, such as those given in the example involving young urban professionals.

The "strings" between parentheses may contain many combinations of characters, and they are very often alphanumeric. Mathematical functions, predicate logic, and list manipulation can be applied to these lists or strings.

Using LISP requires a developer to translate rules and facts into lists, such as those shown above between the parentheses. LISP then makes use of a variety of list processing functions. These functions enable information manipulation similar to that described in the PROLOG example.

The LISP notations shown above are not necessarily the best way of representing the information in these situations. The illustrations are designed merely to give the reader a quick feeling for LISP and how its syntax differs from PROLOG's.

### Commercial Knowledge-Based Systems

Prepackaged software systems also exist which can be purchased from vendors or obtained from the United States government. Harmon, for example, lists 139 commercial knowledge-based systems in use in 1988, of which 47 were available for purchase or on request (in Feigenbaum 1988, pp. 273–315). A number of those described by Harmon are summarized in Figure 9–5.

## AN APPROACH TO MAKING SOFTWARE SELECTION DECISIONS IN SPECIFIC SITUATIONS

This section discusses how specific knowledge-domain, organizational, system, company, and other available resource factors are analyzed in making the many decisions involved in software selection. An approach to making these decisions is shown in Figure 9–6.

A wide range of decisions can be encountered in this area. These decision situations can range from ones involving expert-driven systems developed by the experts who will be using the system themselves to ones involving KBS development efforts involving hundreds of users, experts, and system developers working in widely dispersed and potentially dangerous locations.

Because of the wide range of possible decisions and the even wider range of possible situations in which these decisions may be made, the approach described in this section is necessarily a general one, which is intended to give only an overview of the process.

### Critical Factors Affecting Decisions in This Area

As seen in Figure 9–6, software selection decisions are dictated by system and situation requirements. These include:

- knowledge-domain and task factors
- system factors
- internal company factors
- hardware factors
- vendor factors

**Figure 9–5.** Sampling of Prepackaged Software Applications Available Commercially

**Ace** (AT&T Bell Laboratories). This system is an equipment diagnosis and preventive maintenance planning system. Its purpose is to help telephone operating companies reduce the incidence of phone cable failures.

**Chart and Map Expert System** (Human Technology, Inc.). This system provides guidelines to cartographers for compiling features on nautical maps and charts.

**Client Profiling** (Applied Expert Systems). This system is designed to assist field sales representatives of insurance companies, banks, and other financial institutions to tailor packages of financial products for middle-income clients.

**COCOMO1** (Level Five Research). This system helps engineers and managers schedule and staff software development projects. The system predicts the labor, cost, and time involved in projects.

**Management Advisor** [formerly called Financial Advisor] (Palladian Software). This system is designed to assist senior managers who are faced with the evaluation of complex business proposals. Using this system, a manager can consider alternative approaches to new product development proposals, evaluate major strategic investments, and consider the consequences of cost-reduction plans and buying and leasing equipment.

**Foreign Exchange Options Advisory System** (Athena Group). This system assists in the development of strategies for trading foreign-currency options.

**Grain Marketing Advisor** (Purdue University). Based on its analysis of the future markets, this system helps farmers choose marketing or storage strategies for their grain crops.

**Information Engineering Workbench** (Knowledgeware). This system assists systems analysts in the planning, analysis, design, and construction of management information systems. Use of the systems eliminates the bottleneck caused by slower production of manually drawn diagrams.

**PlanPower** [Applied Expert System (APEX)]. This system assists specialists in financial organizations and independent financial consultants in the preparation of financial plans for high-income clients.

**Press Line-Up Advisor** (Rockwell International Corp.). This system analyzes newspaper formats and suggests a configuration for placement of printing plates for the press.

**More** (Persoft, Inc.). More is an expert system that identifies the most profitable prospects on large-scale mailing lists.

**Technical Specifications Advisor** (Stone & Webster Engineering). This system provides information regarding the safety and regulatory related consequences of proposed equipment maintenance and operator actions in manufacturing plants, power plants, and chemical plants.

**Thermal Information Program** (General Physics). This system monitors high exit gas temperatures in electric-power generating plants and recommends steps to reduce waste heat, which would increase the efficiency and profitability of the power plant.

**Underwriter** (General Data Systems). This system performs risk analysis and problem solving formerly done by senior underwriters. This system is used for both commercial and personal lines of insurance.

**Welder Qualification Test Selection System** (Stone & Webster Engineering). This system saves time and money by helping managers pick the appropriate qualification tests for welders hired on major construction projects.

**Figure 9–6.** Overview of KBS Software Selection Decision

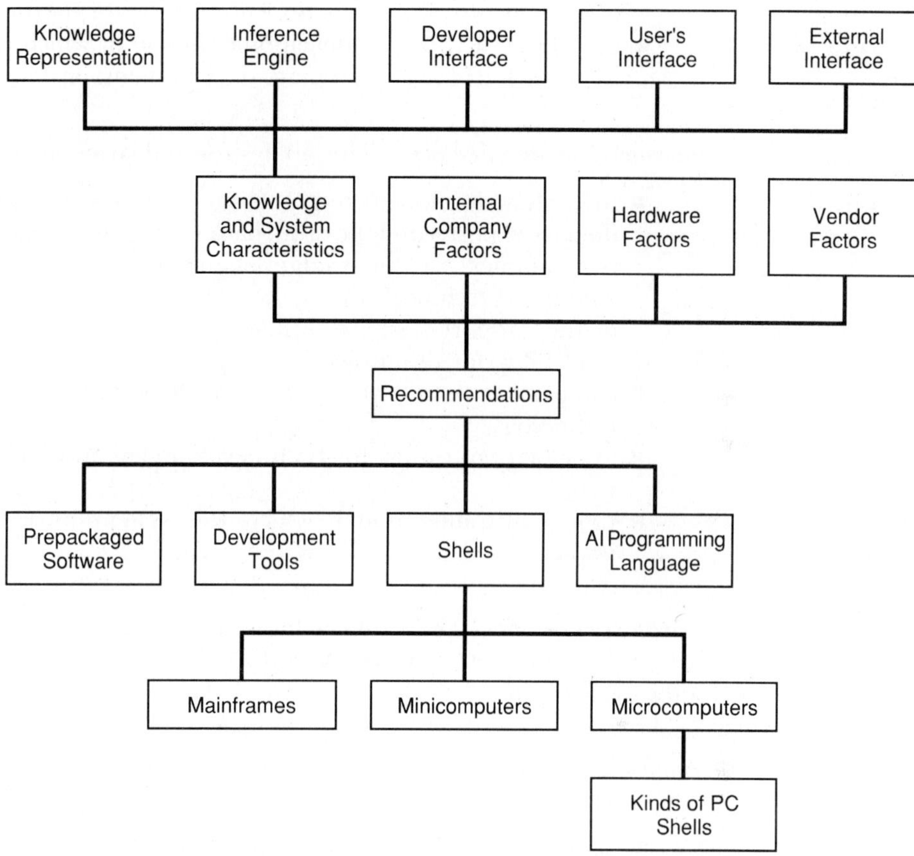


***Knowledge-Domain and Task Factors.*** This analysis considers the size of the system, as well as the following:

- primary knowledge representation methods needed in the system, such as frames, rules, or a hybrid
- secondary knowledge representation methods needed in the system, such as representing uncertainty, use of variables or wildcards, multivalued or plural expressions, fact strings, and mathematical calculations
- inferencing approach needed in the system, such as forward or backward chaining, bi-directional, means-end, and reasoning with uncertainty

***System Factors.*** This analysis covers such items as:

- user considerations, such as how many users there will be, what their skill levels are, what type of interface is required, what time restraints they will

be working under, and what type of environment they will be working in
- required interfaces with external systems, such as spreadsheets, databases, or word processors on various types of hardware
- the phase of the KBS development cycle in which the software will be used, such as the prototyping, development, or delivery phase

***Internal Company Factors.*** This analysis would cover such items as:

- the system developer's requirements, such as who the developer will be (a domain expert with little or no background in computers, an experienced programmer, or knowledge engineer, or some combination), what amount of technical support is available to the developers, and the level of the support staff's computer skills and experience, as well as their availability for the project
- company policies and objectives, such as future plans for the use of AI technology
- availability of funds, for both development and acquisition and maintenance
- time constraints under which the system must be developed and implemented

***Hardware Factors.*** The available hardware alternatives, including architecture, size, and components, covered in the following hardware section, also impact on software selection.

***Vendor Factors.*** In addition to considering the above situation constraints, other technical factors are considered, such as:

- product reliability (Is it a proven product?)
- vendor reliability (Does the company that developed the language, development tool, or shell still support and maintain it?)

### Making Decisions Based on These Critical Situation Factors

As seen in Figure 9–6, the critical situation factors described in the preceding section are analyzed and used in making a variety of software selection decisions, including:

- selecting a general type of knowledge processing software—programming language, shell, development tool, or prepackaged commercial KBS
- choosing the specific programming language to be used
- choosing a specific "off-the-shelf" prepackaged commercial system to be purchased
- choosing a particular expert system shell

The choice of which general type of knowledge processing software to use is dictated by the situation factors. For example, if extensive forward chaining thought processes are involved in actually making a decision, as in many strategic planning situations (Mockler, *Strategic Planning,* 1989), a large number of users will be involved in the system delivery/production environment, and the knowledge base is large and complex, one of the programming languages would probably be needed. The selection of development software may also be influenced by the phase of the development process in which it is to be used. For example, it is possible that the prototype system can be developed on a small shell to get it out quickly and facilitate the knowledge acquisition process, while the final system may have to be developed with a more robust development tool.

The *programming language* used may depend on knowledge-domain and task factors as well as the experience of the available staff and ability to find skilled personnel. It can also be influenced by any required interaction with other systems. For example, the KBS may be developed in a "C" compatible version of LISP so that it can interact with other systems written in "C."

Purchasing an "off-the-shelf" prepackaged commercial KBS depends on whether or not a commercial KBS exists that meets the requirements of the situation and whether or not the company wants to hire personnel with KBS development experience or train company personnel in KBS development skills.

When choosing a particular shell the type or types of hardware on which the KBS will be developed and delivered at the company are considered. Also, if the decision situation makes little use of heuristics involving IF-THEN rules, such as those situations involving strategic planning in larger competitive environments (Hiddings 1989), then expert system shells based on IF-THEN rules would not be appropriate. A shell with object-frame capabilities would be needed, even for incremental prototyping. Further discussion of this type of decision, and a KBS to assist in making such decisions, is given in Robert J. Mockler, *Developing Knowledge-Based Systems Using an Expert System Shell,* published by Macmillan (1992).

## KBS HARDWARE

This section and the next discuss the other aspect of system development covered in this chapter, computer hardware selection decisions.

Computer hardware, as the name implies, refers to all the computer equipment required to develop, deliver, and use a knowledge-based system, including computers and their components, as well as such peripheral equipment as printers and monitors.

The areas covered in this discussion include:

- computer architecture: symbolic and conventional computing machines
- computer size
- computer components
- vendors

### Computer Architecture: Symbolic Processing Machines and Conventional Computer Machines

Computer architecture refers to the basic design of a computer. Computers of different architectures are by their nature incompatible, just as the two formats of video cassette recorders (Beta and VHS) are incompatible.

Computer hardware for KBS development can be divided into two general categories of architecture: specialized machines—referred to as "symbolic processors"—and conventional computing machines.

***Symbolic Processing Machines.*** **Symbolic processors** are designed specifically for use in knowledge-based system development. Because of this, they are often referred to as "dedicated" machines. A "symbol" is something that refers to an object, or idea. For example, the word "chair" refers to the piece of furniture that is used for sitting. The word "several" refers to the concept of a quantity. Both these words are symbols referring to an object or an idea—a chair, a quantity.

Symbolic processors get their name from their ability to manipulate complex symbols and relationships, as well as to do the more limited numbers and text symbol manipulation done by conventional computers. Symbolic computers are ideally suited to supporting programming languages such as LISP (Schutzer 1987, p. 124). As such, in many KBS development situations a symbolic computer can significantly decrease the time required to develop a KBS, as well as the time needed to run and consult a KBS once a system has been developed.

***Conventional Computers.*** Conventional computers are more versatile general-purpose machines that can support a greater variety of processing applications than symbolic computers. In addition, conventional computers offer the advantage of a greater availability of skilled users, attractive price/performance ratios due to the greater competition among vendors, and greater availability of maintenance and support.

***Major Differences.*** Several primary design differences between symbolic and conventional computer systems can be identified:

*Data Types.* Data types refer to the form of information a computer can manipulate. The letter "T" is an example of "text" data. A "2" is "numeric" data. A circle is "symbolic" data. A computer that cannot support symbolic data could represent a circle as a series of numbers that mathematically define a circle.

Symbolic machines have the ability to manipulate numbers, text, and symbols, as well as relationships between them. As such, it is in many instances easier to program a symbolic computer to draw inferences and make deductions, such as those found in KBS, than it is to do so with a conventional computer.

Conventional machines are designed to work with numbers and text only. In conventional computer systems, text and numbers are not easily mixed. For example, the date 10/09/91 would be a text data type because of the alphanumeric character (/) it contains. If the computer needed to add two months to this date, it would first have to convert the first two "characters" ("10") to a computer-readable numeric value. Essentially, this means that more effort is needed to program a conventional system to do what a symbolic system can do directly.

This difference between symbolic and conventional machines is analogous to a person's vocabulary. The individual with a larger vocabulary (like the symbolic processor) will find it easier to express thoughts and concepts than a person with a more limited vocabulary (conventional processor).

*Users.* Symbolic processing machines and conventional microcomputers were initially designed to support only one user. However, both these types of computers can now be networked together to serve more than one user. Recent advances in technology also give these computers the ability to run several applications at the same time. Conventional minicomputers can easily support from one to several hundred users. Mainframes have the potential to support thousands of users, since mainframe networks can bring together a vast number of users from around the world.

*Memory.* Computers require places to permanently store computer programs and places to temporarily store data while executing or working with program applications. Examples of two types of **permanent storage,** a hard disk and a diskette, are shown in Figure 9–7. In addition to these two types of physical computer memory, there is another type called virtual memory. **Virtual memory** is a technique or capability, not a physical computer storage component, that allows the computer to use permanent storage space for working memory, which is temporary storage. Using virtual memory allows a system to run programs that are so large that they will not physically fit into the computer's existing working memory space. Symbolic machines have extensive virtual memory capabilities, as do mainframes and minicomputers. Such techniques are limited on older microcomputers. This situation is rapidly changing with the newer microcomputer technology advances.

*Memory Allocation.* KBS generally make substantial demands on a computer's memory resources. For this reason, symbolic machines use various techniques (such as virtual memory) to make the most effective use of these resources. Another of these techniques is known as **garbage collection.** This facility allows the system to reclaim for other use memory that is no longer needed by the application. While this technique is an integral feature that is effectively used in symbolic machines, it is poorly implemented in conventional machines.

*Incremental Compilation.* The **compilation** process is how the computer translates the programmer's instructions into **machine language**—the language

**Figure 9–7.** Computer Disk Examples

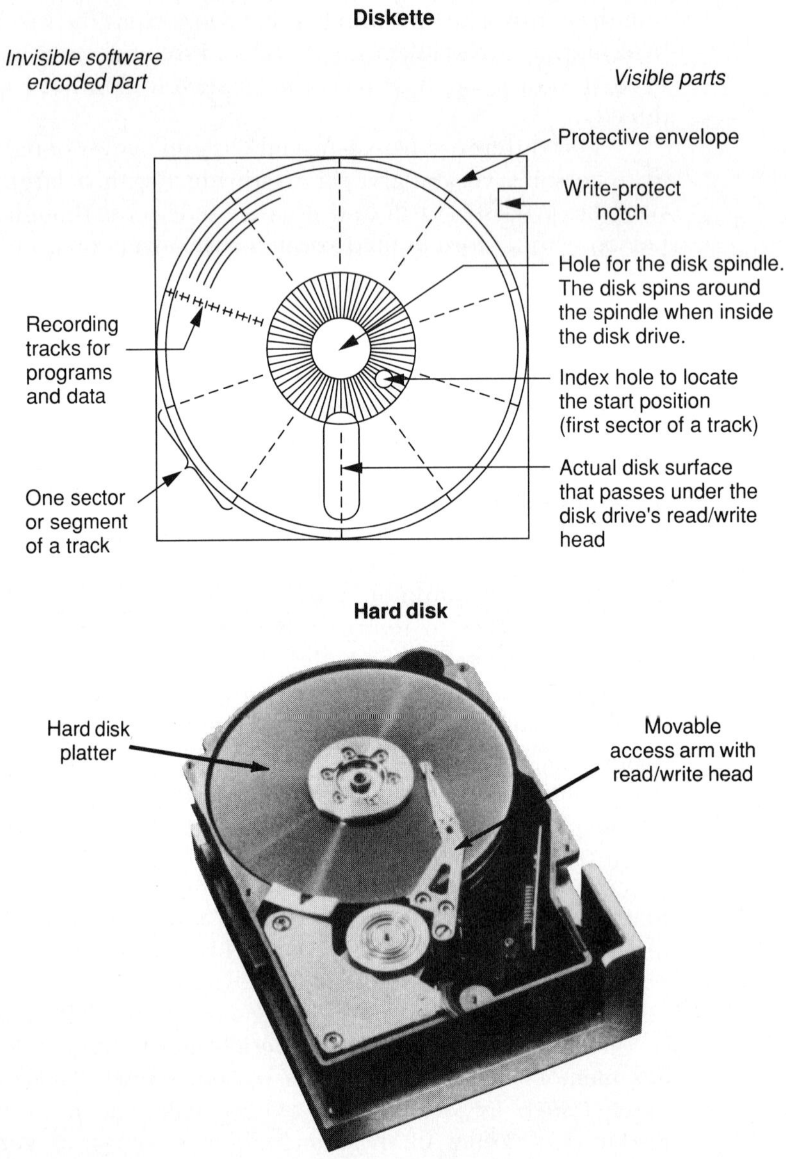


**Source:** Hard disk courtesy Microscience International.

the computer actually understands. A symbolic processing computer allows the programmer to easily test small changes without requiring the entire system to be compiled. This feature significantly speeds up the system development process. On conventional machines, it is up to the programmer to write the program as a series of separate pieces in order to speed up the development process. If done well, incremental or partial compilation may be possible. If poorly done, then even the most minor modification will require the entire program to be recompiled.

In sum, all the design differences between symbolic and conventional processors lead to one overall advantage for symbolic systems for KBS: speed—both in the development process and in the actual use of completed systems. The disadvantages of symbolic systems are higher-cost dedicated hardware, greater difficulty in finding personnel with appropriate experience, and their inability to run the vast amount of software that exists for conventional processors.

### Computer Size

In general, computers can be grouped into three size categories: microcomputers, minicomputers, and mainframe computers. The differences in the categories are analogous to the differences between a car, a pickup truck, and a tractor trailer. All are vehicles of transportation, but each is better suited to different types of uses.

While conventional computers are found in each of these categories, symbolic systems are generally only available in the first two, the very powerful microcomputer and minicomputer categories. With advances in technology and in the ability to almost endlessly upgrade an existing system, the differences between the three size categories are becoming blurred. Examples of microcomputers and mainframes are shown in Figures 9–8 and 9–9.

The major differences in the three computer sizes are their costs and their processing power.

***Cost.*** The prices of microcomputers range up to about $20,000. Minicomputers and symbolic processing machines generally start at between $30,000 to $50,000 and can run up to several hundred thousand dollars for complete systems, including workstations. Mainframe computers come at costs that often start at several million dollars.

***Processing Power.*** Microcomputers generally are well suited for applications such as word processing, spreadsheets, and small databases, such as those found in mailing list maintenance situations. The most advanced micro systems have begun to approach the processing speeds of some minicomputer and even mainframe systems. Initially, symbolic processing machines had significant processing power advantages over microcomputers; with the advances in

**Figure 9–8.** Microcomputer Hardware

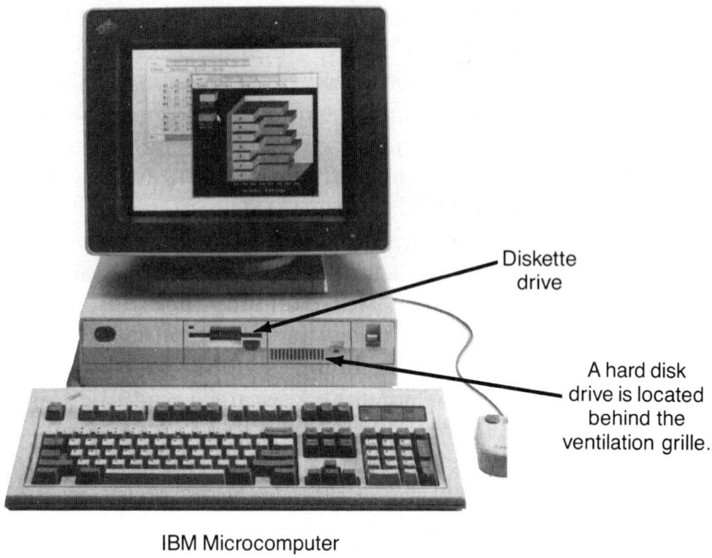


**Source:** Courtesy International Business Machines.

**Figure 9–9.** Mainframe Computer Hardware

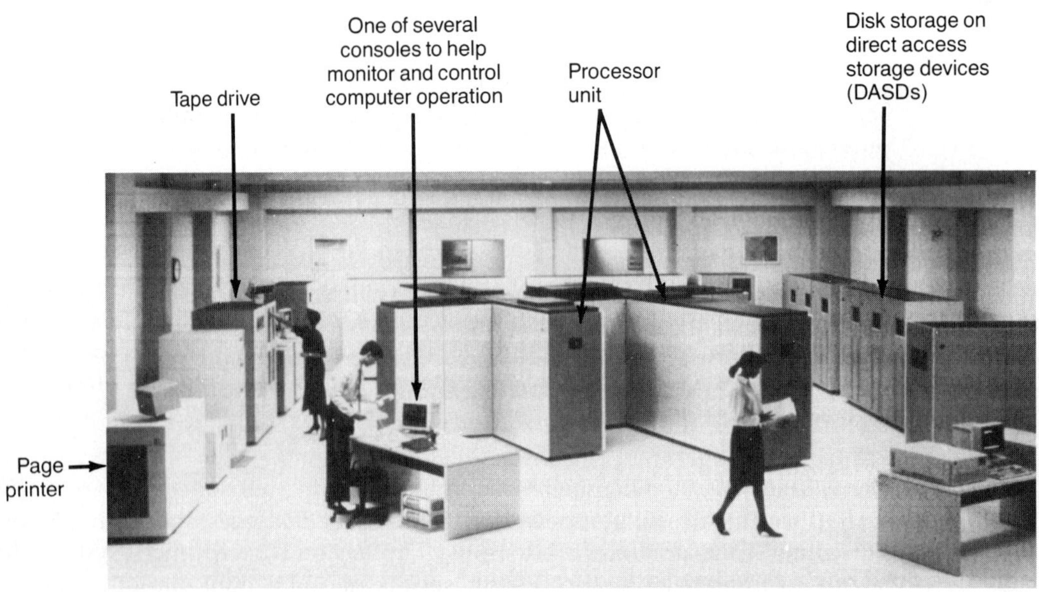


**Source:** Courtesy International Business Machines.

microcomputer power this is no longer the case. Minicomputers are generally used by small- to medium-sized companies for applications such as inventory, payroll, accounting, and personnel. Mainframes have the power to handle requirements exceeding that of the peak hourly volumes of activity on the New York Stock Exchange.

### Computer Hardware Components

The major components described in this section are:

- central processing unit (CPU)
- memory
- disk space

The combination of selected components is referred to as the **computer configuration** or **computer system.** Figures 9–8 and 9–9 illustrate these components in micro and mainframe computers.

***Central Processing Unit (CPU).*** The **CPU** can be thought of as the "controller" of the overall computer system. The CPU processes the instructions that the computer is given—such as those from a software package or from a user's keyboard input. It also performs the necessary math and logic required to run the software. Less obvious, but equally important, the CPU controls the other components (memory and disks) and all the auxiliary devices, or **peripheral equipment**—such as printers and video displays—that is part of a total computer system. The CPU in essence functions as the clearinghouse in accepting input from the keyboard, displaying output on the screen or printer, storing and retrieving data, and performing calculations. In these capacities, the CPU plays a critical role in determining the overall performance, that is, speed, of the computer system.

The choice of CPU is the most critical component of a mainframe and minicomputer hardware configuration. Not only does it determine performance, but once selected, it will limit the choices for other components. For example, a CPU can only run the programs that were designed for that family of CPUs. Because great product differences can exist among manufacturers of minis and mainframes, the CPU decision is closely linked to the manufacturer decision. As a result, the choice of manufacturer for the CPU may force the same manufacturer to be used for the memory and disk space components, to insure compatibility.

The choice of a CPU for microcomputers (PCs) usually dictates the type of PC selected. The choice of PC CPU is not as dependent on a specific CPU manufacturer. The speed and such other factors as the amount of memory required by a PC application will result in the choice of a machine or machines with a specific chip. These chips in order of increasing power include the '086, '286, '386, and '486 chips made by INTEL.

***Memory.*** As discussed earlier, when a computer is operating, it requires space to store the instructions of the program being executed. The program in turn requires space to store the information it is processing. Both types of space are generically referred to as memory. In general, a computer with more memory will be able to execute larger applications and execute programs faster than a computer with less memory. There are three types of memory that can be used (Somsel 1988, p. 38): static memory, dynamic or working memory, and virtual memory.

*Static Memory.* **Static memory** is the fastest memory available. Since retrieving information from static memory is much faster than retrieval from other kinds of memory, it is desirable to have as much static memory as possible. However, this speed comes at a high cost. Because of this, most computers have only a small amount of static memory so that the most frequently used instructions and data can be accessed quickly.

Most manufacturers consider static memory to go hand-in-hand with the CPU. For this reason, they will prepackage the CPU and static memory together. As such, static memory is usually only available with certain CPUs and is not an "add-on" option the user can request.

*Dynamic or Working Memory.* **Dynamic memory** is the most commonly used type of memory. This sort of memory is frequently referred to as **RAM** (*R*andom *A*ccess *M*emory). RAM is very fast, though not as fast as static memory, and is very affordable. Like disk space, memory size is measured in bytes. A personal computer might have 640,000 bytes of RAM, while a large mainframe might have 32,000,000 bytes. As computer programs have become more sophisticated, they have required the use of more and more working memory. It is becoming more common to find micros configured with several million bytes of working memory.

In some cases, the user will not only have a selection of how much memory to use, but how fast the memory operates. The instances where this choice is offered is limited, and very closely related to the CPU and any prepackaging of memory the manufacturer may offer.

Usually each CPU will have a specific range of memory with which it can operate. The need for very large amounts may force a reevaluation of the CPU selection, to find one that will operate with the determined memory requirements.

*Virtual Memory.* The slowest type of memory is known as **virtual memory**. However, it is a different type of memory from that of static or dynamic memory. While static and dynamic memory are physical components, virtual memory is a technique used by the CPU that allows the system to use another hardware component—disk space, which is usually needed for long term storage of programs and data—as dynamic memory. The primary advantage to this technique is that disk space is usually readily available and very inexpensive. On the down side, accessing data from the disk can be very slow. Nevertheless, virtual memory is sometimes the only realistic way of satisfying an application's memory requirements.

On mainframes and minicomputers, virtual memory techniques are usually built into the operating system (OP). The **OP** is the program that defines how the CPU interacts with the other parts of the system: memory, disk, printer, screen, and the like. On microcomputers, virtual memory techniques must be built into each software application that needs to use virtual memory. However, recent advances in microcomputer OP, such as OS/2, have begun to take on this burden (Linnell 1989, p. 46).

***Disk Space.*** Disk space is a magnetic surface that the computer uses to store and retrieve information. Hard disk space is very similar in function to memory in that it is used to store programs and data. However, while memory is used for short-term storage (working memory is usually erased when a program terminates execution, or the computer is turned off), hard disk space is used for long-term storage of programs and data. For example, a word processing document is stored on a disk so that the information contained in the document is not lost when the computer is turned off. A diskette can be used for this but is much slower, and has substantially less capacity. Figure 9–7 shows examples of a diskette and a hard disk.

A word processing application that is used to create the documents can also be stored on the hard disk so that it can easily be accessed each time the computer is used. Disk space is usually measured in "bytes." One byte is equal to one alphabetic character, or space, such as: "," "t," "1," "%," and "7." A personal computer can have a disk capacity in excess of 100 million bytes. A large mainframe computer would easily have a disk capacity of tens or hundreds of billions of bytes.

On a microcomputer system, most of the hard disk space is usually occupied by application software, such as accounting or word processing software packages. On a large mainframe, the lion's share of the disk is usually occupied by data files such as personnel and accounting records, and the application programs make up only a small percentage of the stored files.

In making the computer configuration decision, a system developer will keep certain overriding concerns in mind: cost, expandability, trends in the industry, and reliability. For example, if the ideal system for immediate needs is one that offers no capability to grow or expand, it would not make a sensible choice. Similarly, it would not be wise to select an obsolete system simply because it is the most cost effective.

### Vendor

In many situations, not only must one decide which computer manufacturer to use, but also who to purchase the computer from. This is especially true for microcomputers which are generally sold through retailers. When individuals decide to buy an IBM PC, for example, they must also decide which retailer to purchase from. With mini and mainframe computers, a purchase directly from the manufacturer is much more likely. However, it is possible to purchase a mini or mainframe computer through a third party who is performing an added service by supplying not only all the hardware, but all the software and the support services.

The combination of manufacturer and retailer decisions is referred to as the vendor selection.

Some of the factors considered when buying a car also apply to buying computer hardware:

- vendor's experience in the business
- vendor's relationship with manufacturer
- availability of support facilities (remote versus on-site service)
- cost of maintenance
- vendor guarantees concerning up time and loaner equipment
- size of vendor's customer base
- age of the product line
- other customers' satisfaction with their choice of vendor
- vendor's ability to accommodate upgrades, as judged from the breadth and depth of its product line
- availability of customer references
- soundness of vendor's business enterprise
- vendor's future plans for the product line under study

If the decision has been made to use a microcomputer, there is quite a bit more flexibility when deciding about vendors. Microcomputers have become so popular that there are literally hundreds of manufacturers, distributors, and retailers. Due to the highly competitive nature of this industry segment, technology is advancing very fast, causing existing equipment to become rapidly obsolete. In general, many of the components for a microcomputer can be ordered by calling a toll-free number and charging the purchase to a personal credit card. In the microcomputer world, it is common to mix components from several different vendors in a single configuration.

If the decision has been made to use either a mini or mainframe computer, the choice of vendors may be limited to just a handful. Furthermore, it is highly likely that a component from one vendor will be incompatible with a component from another vendor. For minicomputer and mainframe systems, the vendor will usually be able to offer a variety of purchase, lease, and rental options.

## VARYING LEVELS OF COMPUTER EXPERTISE NEEDED

While it is often possible for a manager with little computer knowledge to make a decision about which PC expert system development shell to use, selecting the hardware or expert system shell or programming language is a more complex technical job in most situations involving mini and mainframe computers.

This does not mean that a general business manager cannot understand the kinds of decisions made in the software and hardware area. It simply means that a considerable amount of technical computer information and expertise is needed as background in order to recognize the alternatives available, to understand the technical aspects of the selection criteria, and to be able to properly evaluate the decision from a technical viewpoint.

As for the other situational factors, a nontechnical manager can in some situations provide a broader perspective on the business context within which the decision is being made. In some instances, these broader business considerations will outweigh the technical factors.

## REVIEW QUESTIONS

1. Describe the differences between conventional and knowledge-based computer systems, as they relate to computer software application development and selection.
2. Describe expert system development shells, situations where they are useful, and their limitations.
3. Describe some prepackaged applications that are commercially available.
4. Describe general purpose AI languages and discuss their advantages and disadvantages.
5. Describe the general approach to software selection decisions and discuss some of the critical factors that can affect these decisions.
6. Describe the different computer architectures available for KBS development and deployment and discuss the advantages of each.
7. Describe the key differences between conventional and symbolic computer systems.
8. Describe the different measures of computer size.
9. What are some of the factors considered when choosing a computer vendor?

## EXERCISES

1. After reviewing the decision situation outline in Figure 9–6 and the discussion of it in this chapter in the section "An Approach to Making Software Selection Decisions in Specific Situations," develop a small KBS to

assist in selecting a shell from among four or five that are listed in Figure 9–3. The characteristics of the shell listed there should be used, along with whatever other information your own research can uncover. For example, the article by Richard Vedder included in the references section that follows will be useful in developing your KBS. Follow the directions in either Chapter 2, or in Chapters 3 through 6, when developing the system.

2. Read through the recent issues of KBS periodicals listed in the references section of this chapter, or through other related artificial intelligence publications, and find descriptions of specific types of computer hardware useful in developing and deploying KBS. Write a brief report describing some of this hardware and ways in which it might be useful in different knowledge engineering areas.

## REFERENCES

Brody, Alan. "The Experts." *Infoworld,* June 18, 1989, pp. 59ff.

Citrenbaum, Ronald, James R. Geissman, and Roger Schultz. "Selecting a Shell." *AI Expert,* September 1987, pp. 30–39.

Coffee, Peter, et al. "AI Tools for PCs Tackle App Development." *PC Week,* February 26, 1990, pp. 86–88, 127–28.

Enrado, Patty. "Expert System Resource Guide." *AI Expert,* May 1991, pp. 52–53.

Feigenbaum, Edward, Pamela McCorduck, and H. Penny Nii. *The Rise of the Expert Company.* New York: Times Books, 1988.

Finnie, J. Scot. "Sudden Shower Enriches MIS Turf." *Computerworld,* October 17, 1988, pp. 77–96.

Gevarter, William B. "The Nature and Evaluation of Commercial Expert System Building Tools." *Computer,* May 1987, pp. 25–41.

Hiddings, G. "KBS for Strategic Planning at Coopers and Lybrand." Presented at the *Decision Sciences Institute Seminar,* New Orleans, LA, November 22, 1989.

Leaman, Claire M. "Rule-Based Structural Design in C." *AI Expert,* May 1989, pp. 28–35.

Linnell, Dennis. "The OS/2 Puzzle Takes Shape." *PC Tech Journal,* February 1989, pp. 45–48.

Mockler, Robert J. *Knowledge-Based Systems for Strategic Planning.* Englewood Cliffs, NJ: Prentice-Hall, 1989.

Rauch-Hindin, Wendy B. *Artificial Intelligence in Business, Science and Industry (Volume II—Applications),* Englewood Cliffs, NJ: Prentice-Hall, 1985.

Richer, Mark H. "An Evaluation of Expert System Development Tools." *Expert Systems,* July 1986, pp. 166–83.

Schutzer, Daniel, *Artificial Intelligence,* New York: Van Nostrand Reinhold, 1987.

Somsel, Joe. "AI on Your Personal Computer." *AI Expert,* December 1988, pp. 36–41.

Vedder, Richard G. "PC-Based Expert System Shells: Some Desirable and Less Desirable Characteristics." *Expert Systems,* February 1989, pp. 28–42.

Williamson, Mickey. "Expert System Shells." *Computerworld,* July 14, 1986, pp. 51ff.

# 10

# System Development and Implementation: User Interfaces

This chapter concerns selecting and designing user interfaces for knowledge-based systems.

The major focus of the discussion so far in Part Two has been on the domain expert and on developing systems that both function well on a computer, that is, run efficiently, and at the same time adequately replicate the expert situation under study. The focus in this chapter and in Chapter 11 is on the user requirements and on the interpersonal tasks involved in implementing a KBS development effort and in delivering a KBS in the work environment.

The objective of this chapter is to enable readers to make strategy decisions in this KBS development area. The topics covered are:

- User interfaces
- KBS development and implementation: developing user interfaces
- Primary interaction styles and strategies
- Specific user-interface techniques, tools, and tasks
- Some general guidelines for developing effective user interfaces
- An approach to making decisions in specific situations
- Applying this general approach to decisions involving primary interaction styles
- A KBS designed to assist in making primary interaction style decisions

KBS development has grown rapidly in recent years in part because of the introduction of expert system shells. These shells essentially make it possible for managers with little computer training to develop KBS, because they have reduced technical system development requirements.

The same principle is at work when a KBS is developed and delivered to users in an organization. The easier it is for people to *use* a system and the less threatening the computer technology barrier, the more widely and frequently these systems are likely to be used.

Because of this, considerable attention is now being paid to making KBS and other computer systems more user friendly and user effective. In a sense, computer technology has outstripped usage, and now attention is being paid to making the technology that already exists more widely used.

User problems are especially important in KBS development, because KBS are highly interactive systems, and so require effective integration with user work habits, attitudes, perceptions, and skill and education levels.

## USER INTERFACES

User interfaces can be defined as the point where users in a business department, such as sales or accounting, interact with a computer system. For example, if a user department has terminals, these terminals provide the "link" to the system. The user interface, an example of which is shown in Figure 10–1, is what users see when they access a system on a computer terminal. It is the mechanism through which a user passes information to a system and through which the system communicates with a user. A well-designed interface can attract new users, while a poorly designed one can turn them away (Edmunds 1985, p. 469; Houghton 1986, p. 56). Knowledge-based systems will be increasingly incorporated into the business environment only as obstacles associated with user interfaces are surmounted (Potter 1988, p. 28).

Frustration and anxiety are often a part of daily life for many users of knowledge-based systems. Users encounter such serious cases of computer confusion, network neurosis, or terminal terror that they avoid using the system. Cures for these diseases are effective user interfaces. Some of the problems caused by ineffective user interfaces are:

- inconsistent command language
- confusing operation sequences
- chaotic display formats
- inconsistent terminology
- incomplete instructions
- misleading or threatening error messages

These problems arise because a systems developer often assumes many technical aspects to be trivial and easily understandable. However, the user

**Figure 10–1.** The User Interface

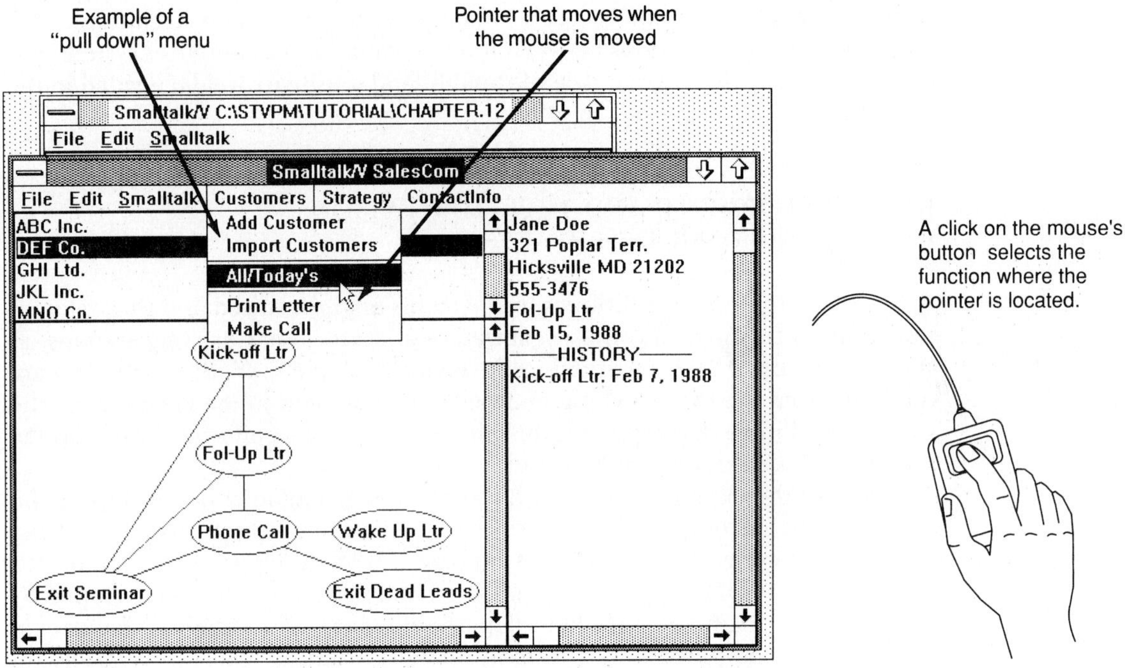


**Software:** SmallTalk V/Windows, courtesy Digitalk Inc.

sitting alone at a terminal with an instruction manual may find the instructions unclear and even be horrified by the complexity of the system. This can be frustrating to the user, such as a manager, whose goal is to access information quickly and easily in order to use the particular system as a tool in his or her job.

The best way to prevent these problems and diminish user avoidance of KBS is to build effective user interfaces into a system from the start. Although the need for effective user interfaces is widely recognized throughout the computer systems engineering field, advanced computer systems such as KBS present special problems requiring new techniques and guidelines for user-interface development.

KBS communicate with the user by:

- asking questions
- presenting a number of action choices
- providing feedback about what has occurred in the system
- explaining reasoning processes
- providing supporting information
- asking for additional information

These are all fundamentally human transactional activities. Considerable finesse is often required in such transactions, even when they are taking place between people who know each other well. In designing techniques for facilitating such interactions between human beings and a computer system, it is even more likely that a great deal of thought and sensitivity will be needed in the process.

## KBS DEVELOPMENT AND IMPLEMENTATION: DEVELOPING USER INTERFACES

As system development continues, refinements are introduced and the system is tested and integrated into the organization and into other existing systems, as shown in Figure 10–2. In situations involving multiple users of a KBS who are different from the expert whose knowledge is replicated in the system and who was involved in its development, this phase can have a significant impact on the success of a KBS development effort.

Where the expert working with the knowledge engineer in developing the system will be the only user, very little work may be needed for this phase of the development cycle. At the DuPont Company's KBS development program, for example, initially the systems involved were small ones, very often developed by managers for their own or their department's use. In addition, the people involved were computer literate. Clearly, in these instances where the systems are small and are developed by users for themselves or for a small, controlled group of computer literate individuals, user interface requirements are often minimal (Bailey 1987).

At Digital Equipment Company, on the other hand, where the users were several hundred salespersons, many of whom did not have extensive computer training and were not involved in the development project and so were unfamiliar with the system, developing user interfaces and delivery systems turned out to be almost as time consuming as developing the system itself. In these kinds of situations, the effectiveness of the user interface and delivery systems are critical to the successful implementation and use of the system (Leonard-Barton 1987).

In a recent project undertaken by the authors, several strategic planning systems were developed and run to the satisfaction of the computer information systems technicians involved in their development. Since these systems were to be used by upper-level managers, a second stage of design and development was required to create effective user interfaces that would make the systems easy for busy non-computer managers to use. These steps involved more than just redesigning the screens and menus. In some instances, they involved redesigning the way the system processed knowledge. In all it took just about as much time and money to develop a truly user-effective version of the system as it did to develop the original version, which had performed the planning job reasonably well (Dologite 1990).

**Figure 10–2.** Knowledge-Based Systems Development Life Cycle

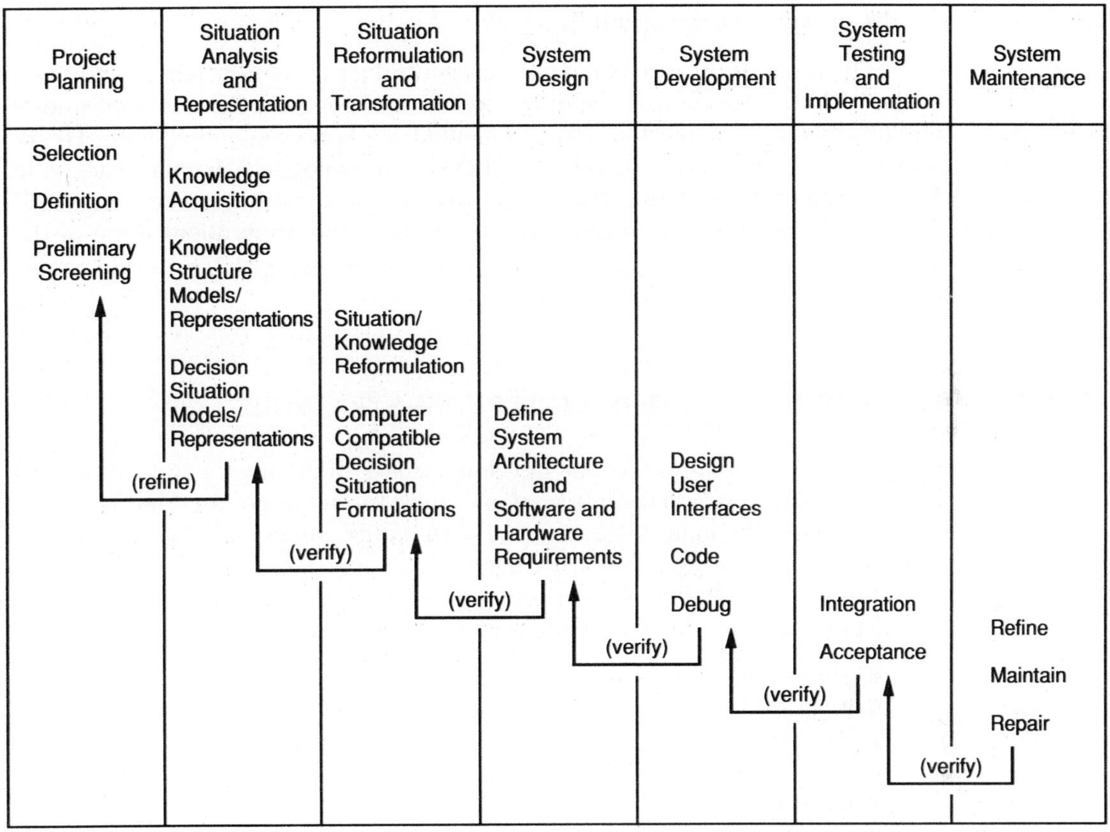


During this phase of the KBS development effort, what is important to system design is how a KBS communicates with the user. For too long, analysis of the human-machine interaction was neglected. This neglect of user needs in the design process is one of the many reasons that relatively few knowledge-based systems were being effectively used in the business world during the mid-1980s. Some experts have gone so far as to recommend that user interfaces be developed prior to the reasoning part of the KBS and be planned for and built into the earlier phases of the KBS design and development cycle (Gordon 1988, p. 55).

More and more system designers are using field studies and collecting performance data from users, and even inviting users to participate in design teams, to support organizational decision making for interface design (Schneiderman, 1987, pp. v & vi).

The following discussion of user interfaces covers:

- primary interaction styles
- other user-interface techniques and tools

The focus of the discussion is on user-interface design for KBS. In addition to the authors' experiences, the discussion draws upon such KBS-focused studies as Wexelblat's "On Interface Requirements for Expert Systems: (1989), Hendler's *Expert Systems: The User Interface* (1988), and Dologite's "Human Factors in Expert Systems: Designing the User Interface for a Strategic Planning KBS" (1990). It also draws upon the body of research and applications done in the user-interface area related to conventional computer systems (for example, Schneiderman 1987; Gality 1989).

## PRIMARY INTERACTION STYLES AND STRATEGIES

In designing systems, a system developer most often uses a mix of several interaction styles, especially in situations where the required tasks and users are diverse (Schneiderman 1987, pp. 57–60). This discussion focuses on the individual merits of each primary interaction or interface style or method.

When a KBS designer is designing an actual system, there are five primary interaction styles for the user interface (Schneiderman 1987, pp. 59–60):

- menu selection
- form fill-in
- command language
- direct manipulation
- natural language

### Menu Selection

This interaction style provides the user with a list of items. Users select the one most appropriate to the task, indicate the selection, confirm the choice, initiate the action, and observe the effect. As seen in Figure 10–3, menus enable users to select categories such as what level of assistance is desired. If the terminology and meaning of the items are understandable and distinct, then the users can accomplish tasks with little learning or memorization and few keystrokes. This interaction style is appropriate for novice and intermittent users and can be appealing to frequent users if the display and selection mechanisms are very rapid. They are useful in situations where choices are well defined and limited. In situations where there is a wide range of choices and flexibility is needed, menus are not as effective and other interaction styles would be considered.

For designers, menu selection systems require careful task analysis to ensure that all functions are supported conveniently and that terminology is chosen carefully and used consistently.

**Figure 10–3.** Primary Interaction Style: Menu Selection

A. Keystroke-entry example

```
For the following question, please type the number of your
answer choice and then press the RETURN key, unless directed
otherwise.

How important to success is a sales force?
   1-very important
   2-moderately important
   3-not important
>>2

How capital-intensive is the area under study?
   1-very capital-intensive
   2-moderately capital-intensive
   3-not capital-intensive
>>1

Assess the degree to which government regulation impacts
success in your industry.
TYPE A PERCENTAGE  (0 to 100) AND PRESS RETURN
>>93
```

B. Touch-screen example

```
TYPE OF ASSISTANCE REQUIRED:

[      ]  Entry-level example
[      ]  Moderately complex example
[      ]  Advanced example

   Touch only one item.

       [ DONE ]
```

*Note:* The "Done" hot-button is included to allow users to change their minds before going on. In some situations, it may be considered redundant and eliminated.

### Form Fill-In

When data entry is required, menu selection usually becomes cumbersome and form fill-in (also called fill-in-the-blanks) is an appropriate alternative to consider. As seen in Figure 10–4, users see a display of related fields, move a cursor among the fields, and enter data where desired. Shafer describes the procedure for creating form fill-in front ends with two popular expert system development shells, VP-Expert and KnowledgePro (1989). With the form fill-in interaction style, the users must understand the field labels, know the permissible values and the data entry method, and be capable of responding to error messages. Frequently, instructions for filling out the forms and the permissible values which can be entered are included on the screen, presented on a separate "Instructions" screen, also shown in Figure 10–4, or are made available through pressing a "Help" key. Since some knowledge of the keyboard, the labels, data entry procedures, and permissible values is required, some training may be necessary. This interaction style, therefore, is most appropriate for knowledgeable intermittent or frequent users.

### Command Language

Command languages are another familiar primary interaction style. They provide frequent users with a strong feeling of control and initiative. Command languages, which originated with operating systems commands, are distinguished by their immediacy: users issue a command and watch what happens. If the result is correct, the next command is issued; if not, another command is used. As can be seen in Figure 10–5, which lists commands from one particular system, commands are most often brief and their existence is transitory. The users learn the syntax and can often express complex instructions without having to read distracting instructions (known as prompts). However, error rates are typically high, considerable training is often necessary, and retention can be poor. Error messages and online assistance are hard to provide because of the diversity of possible errors. Command languages are best for frequent users who have mastered the semantics and syntax of the system.

### Direct Manipulation

When a system designer can create a visual representation of the world of action, the users' tasks can be greatly simplified by allowing direct manipulation of the object of interest. As seen in Figure 10–6, by pointing at visual representations of objects and actions, users can rapidly carry out tasks and immediately observe the results. In direct manipulation, keyboard entry of commands, menu choices, and form fill-in are replaced by cursor motion devices to select from a visible set of objects and actions. The mouse used with Macintosh computers or the lightpen used in other systems are two familiar direct manipulation devices.

**Figure 10–4.** Primary Interactive Style: Form Fill-In

A. Form-filling example screen

COMPARE KEY-TO SUCCESS FACTORS

| Key-to-Success Factors | My Co. | AAA | BBB | CCC | #4 | #5 |
|---|---|---|---|---|---|---|
| | | ---------------- Competitor Strength ---------------- | | | | |
| sales-force | 5 | 8 | 8 | 7 | 0 | 0 |
| distribution-channels | 5 | 8 | 7 | 7 | 0 | 0 |
| R&D | 8 | 5 | 5 | 5 | 0 | 0 |
| labor-intensive | 7 | 3 | 4 | 4 | 0 | 0 |
| major-competitors | 8 | 6 | 6 | 6 | 0 | 0 |
| price-sensitivity | 4 | 4 | 4 | 4 | 0 | 0 |
| capital-intensive | 3 | 3 | 3 | 0 | 0 | 0 |

When done, press F10 key.

*Note:* Blocked area indicates the information to be filled in by the user. During input, cursor automatically moves from column to column.

B. "Instructions" screen that preceded the above screen

INSTRUCTIONS

In the following screen you will be asked to rate your company's and competitors' relative strength in relation to the most important key-to-success factors. Use a scale of 1 (weak) to 10 (strong). As a general guideline, 1 to 3 is weak, 4 to 7 is average, and 8 to 10 is strong.

–– Press any key to continue ––

Direct manipulation is appealing to novices, easy to remember for intermittent users, and with careful design it can be a rapid interaction style for frequent users. Two methods of direct manipulation are shown in Figure 10–6. The top of the figure shows a touch sensitive display, where the user enters commands or instructions by touching the screen. The bottom of the figure shows the familiar mouse, used in many computer systems today.

**Figure 10–5.** Primary Interaction Style: Command Language

**Function Keys—Text Editor Commands**

| | |
|---|---|
| <F1> | Help key. Context-sensitive help can be retrieved from any screen. Pressing <F1> a second time restores the current screen. |
| <F2> | Print the current document (rule base) from the position of the cursor through the end of the file. |
| <F3> | Marks the beginning and end of a block of text. |
| <F4> | Copies the currently marked block of text to the cursor position. |
| <F5> | Moves the currently marked block of text to the cursor position. |
| <F6> | Displays the currently active rule being sought. |
| <F7> | Saves the current file. |
| <F8> | Moves cursor to top of current file. |
| <F9> | Moves cursor to end of current file. |
| <F10> | Exit the text editor. |

**Special Keys and Words**

| | |
|---|---|
| RUN | Starts a knowledge base directly from the compiler. |
| PG/DOWN | Advances to the next screen (page). |
| PG/UP | Returns to the previous screen (page). |
| NEW | Opens a new file. |
| RPRT | Begins the Reports Menu from the Report Subsystem. |
| ? | Indicates that a question in a consultation cannot be answered. |
| * | Resumes a knowledge base execution. |
| @ | Deletes a designated fact or file. |

## Natural Language

Natural language interface is a more complex form of interface that requires the computer to translate English language words into specific procedures required for the computer to perform the user instructions. This can be done by developing a database consisting of English words with their corresponding computer-understandable translations. When a sentence is entered into the system via the interface, the interface or another subprogram would attempt to find the keywords in the sentence or a reasonable facsimile thereof in the database and send the translated instructions to the computer processor. This

**Figure 10–6.** Primary Interaction Style: Direct Manipulation

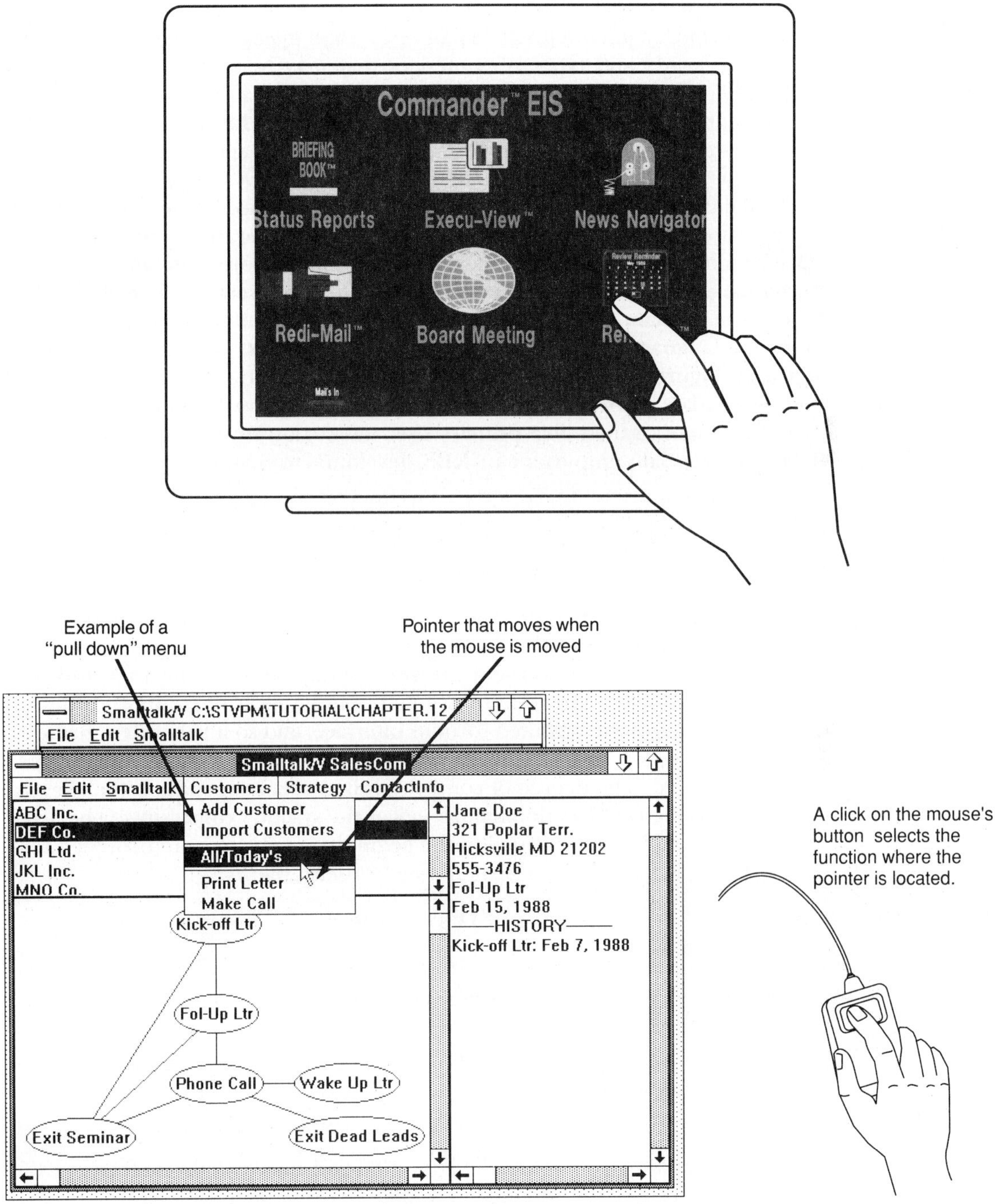


**Source:**(Top) Courtesy Comshare. (Bottom) Software: SmallTalk V/Windows, courtesy Digitalk Inc.

type of interface requires a great deal of research in the expert field to determine all possible words and types of sentences that may be input. The degree of complexity can range from very simple one-word commands to intricate English sentences. In either case, the database would be searched for the keywords input.

One way to simplify natural language interface is to specify to the user a list of words or commands that are acceptable. This, however, would greatly limit the flexibility of a natural language system and in essence become a command language interface. In addition, natural language interaction often requires "clarification dialog," and so may be slower and more cumbersome than alternative primary interaction systems. Still, where users are knowledgeable about a task domain whose scope is limited and where intermittent use inhibits command language training, there exist opportunities for natural language interfaces. Figure 10–7 gives two examples of how natural language computer systems translate plain English instructions into computer language.

In addition to these five primary user interaction strategies, there are two which are especially important in KBS development: controlled dialogue and speech.

### Controlled Question and Answer Dialogue

This interaction style is used in a wide range of KBS, as has been seen in the KBS described elsewhere in this book. Dialogue control is a socratic form of user interface. It involves question and answer sessions between the user and the system, which usually offer the user limited options and some opportunities to interrupt. It is a relatively limited form of interface, and so it very often includes the ability to explain the reasoning process and allow the user to redirect this process, if desired. The degree of control given to users depends on their levels of expertise in the problem domain, as well as the system's constraints. The level of expertise should be ascertained in the beginning of the session through a few key questions. For example, a session may begin as follows:

```
Question: Is this your first time at a terminal?
Answer:   No.

Question: Are you an expert or novice?
Answer:   Expert.

Question: Would you like to skip the explanatory
          section?
Answer:   Yes.
```

Another example of a controlled question and answer dialogue from a KBS example was given earlier in Figure 10–3a.

Dialogue techniques are also used to support other interaction styles, such as when asking users about what type of items they want to select from a menu.

**Figure 10–7.** Primary Interaction Style: Natural Language

**A.**

Let me see the top 5 electronic firms in terms of income/assets. ← This is the request as the user types it

0.131 ELECTRONICS GENERAL
0.128 NATIONAL ELECTRIC
0.125 GENERAL ELECTRIC SUPPLIES
0.122 HARRY & SONS INC.
0.119 NATIONAL APPLIANCES

NEXT REQUEST.

PRINT A TOP 5 OF COMPANY NAME IN TERMS OF (1988 INCOME / 1988 ASSETS) OF ALL COMPANIES WITH INDUSTRY = ELECTRONICS. ← This is how the natural language software interprets the user's request.

**B.**

Show their 10 year average return. Order by growth rate. ← This is the request as the user types it

| GROWTH RATE | COMPANY NAME | 10 YEAR LONG TERM RETURN |
|---|---|---|
| N/A | HARRY & SONS INC. | N/A |
| 8.8 | ELECTRONICS GENERAL | 2.26 |
| 9.4 | NATIONAL ELECTRIC | 1.10– |
| 9.9 | GENERAL ELECTRIC SUPPLIES | 4.23 |
| 10.7 | NATIONAL APPLIANCES | 13.92 |

NEXT REQUEST.

PRINT THE COMPANY NAME AND LONG TERM RETURN SORTED BY 199X GROWTH RATE OF ALL COMPANIES IN THE PREVIOUS GROUP. ← This is how the natural language software interprets the user's request.

Work is being done in reducing the rigidity of such exchanges through the use of natural languages.

## Speech Input/Output

This type of user interface is relatively new. It is being used and tested in many advanced KBS, especially in the area of robotics and their supporting KBS systems. Speech input/output usually requires close work with the user to train the computer to "understand" the user's voice. Speech input/output interfaces are practical, and have been developed, for systems that are used in:

- an environment where the user is in constant motion and cannot sit at a terminal, such as a hospital operating room or a battlefield (Perspectives 1990)
- any situation where the user is unable to either see the keyboard or terminal, or is unable to use it due to a handicap (Perspectives 1990)
- an awkward environment such as an airplane cockpit, where the use of a keyboard is difficult (Harmon 1990, p. 98)

This type of interface is still in the process of development (Alexander 1990; Perspectives 1990). One problem is that the computer may not accurately interpret the user's voice if that voice deviates from the originally-coded voice due to user stress, illness, or change of mood. In addition, this type of interface is usually limited to understanding only a specified set of words, though in some systems this limit is being expanded to several thousand words.

## SPECIFIC USER-INTERFACE TECHNIQUES, TOOLS, AND TASKS

In addition to selecting a primary interaction style, there are a variety of other tasks, as well as tools and techniques, available to a system developer when designing and selecting user interfaces. A number of these, several of which concern screen design, are covered in this section, including:

- graphics
- windows
- animation, color, and other screen design techniques
- online help
- response time and display rate considerations
- testing and evaluating user requirements

### Graphics

Advanced development tools, like ART and KEE, enable a developer to incorporate graphics into the user interface, as shown in Figure 10–8. This capability is becoming increasingly available in all levels of PC expert system shells, such as VP-Expert. In most situations, a developer is required to learn a special set of program codes to create the graphics. Integrated expert system shells, such as GURU, also have a graphics capability, for example, to link spreadsheets with pie or bar charts.

The graphics designer would have to be able to graphically visualize complex situations within the knowledge domain and present them clearly and simply in the interface. Graphics can be used to draw a conceptual model of the

**Figure 10–8.** An Example of the Graphics Capabilities of KEE: Display of a Thermoactuator, a Class of Activeimages

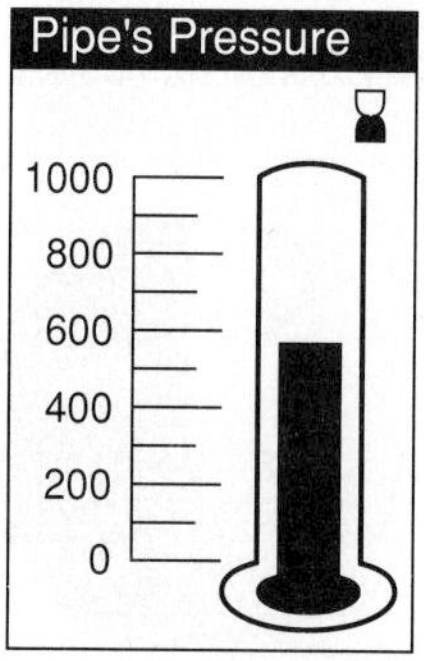


**Source:** Marilyn Stelzner and Michael D. Williams, "The Evolution of Interface Requirements for Expert Systems," in Hendler (Editor), *Expert Systems: The User Interface,* Norwood, NJ: Ablex Publishing Company, 1989. Reprinted with permission of the publisher.

user's mental model of the domain problem in a variety of ways, as shown in Figure 10–9. Since a picture can be worth a thousand words, the use of graphics can help the user understand the problem area without going through a lot of text.

### Windows

Windows are meaningful groups of information that can be displayed on a screen simultaneously with standard text. Where sections of the screen are devoted to specific fields such as title, error messages, instructions, and online help, windows can enhance the functionality of a KBS and can be very useful when independent tasks are being carried out simultaneously.

Since multiple windows can be seen on one screen while performing a particular task, a KBS user can pop-up a new window, take care of another task, and return to the main task without losing context or restarting the work. An example of this is given in Figure 10–10. Expert system development tools, such as ART and KEE, as well as shells such as GURU and VP-Expert, enable a developer to create windows in a KBS application.

In designing windows, a system designer should ensure that any additional effort required to open, move, size, and delete windows will not be a distraction from the user's primary task.

### Animation, Color, and Other Screen Design Techniques

Animation and color also play important roles in user interfaces. Although users generally prefer to see little movement on the screen, some form of animation may be warranted, depending on the user and the domain application.

## Figure 10–9. A Graphics Example

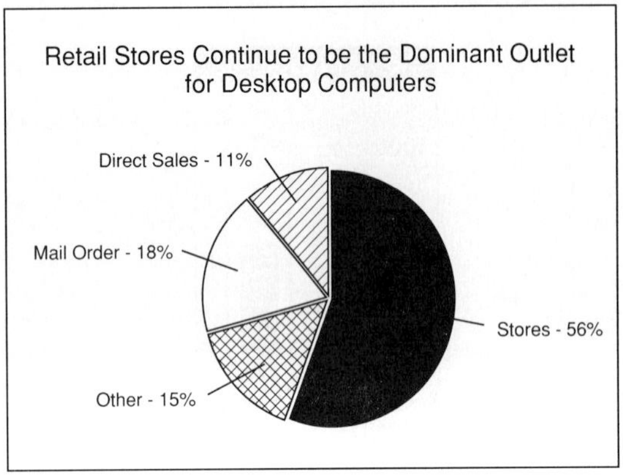


Pie

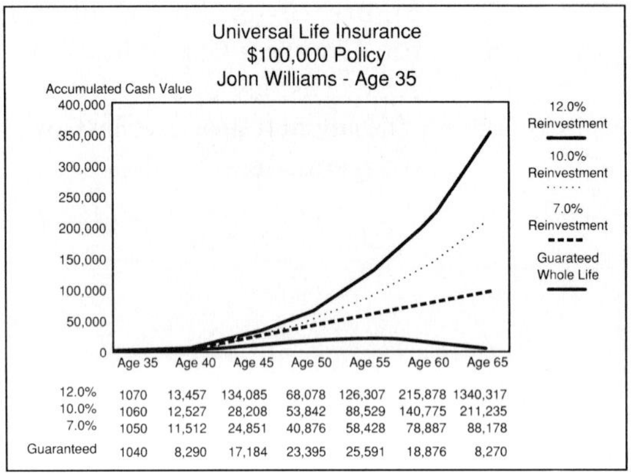


Line-table

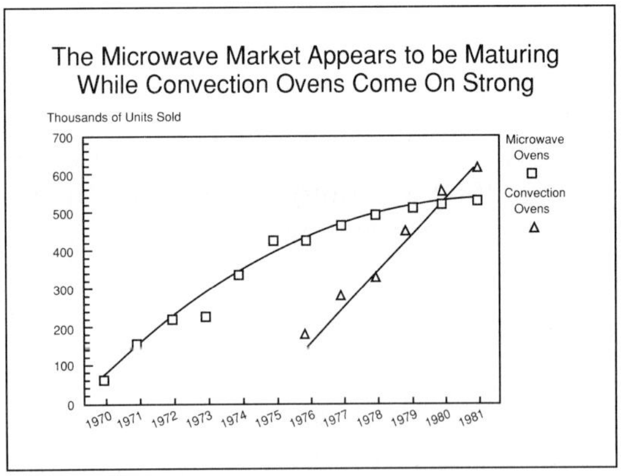


Scatter

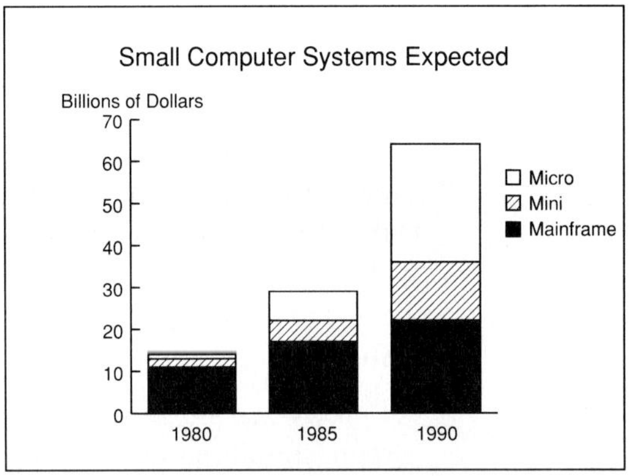


Segmented bars

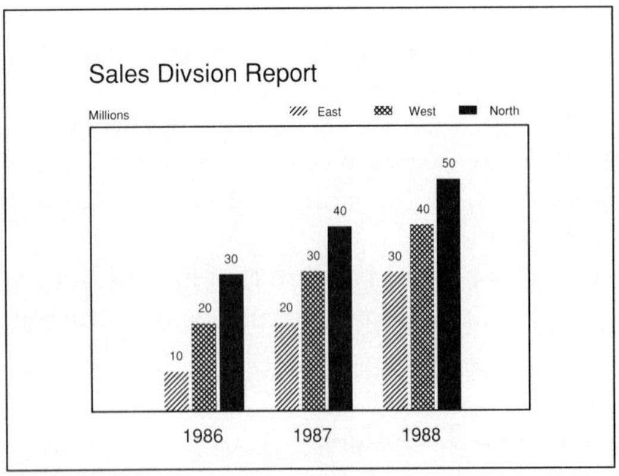


Clustered bars

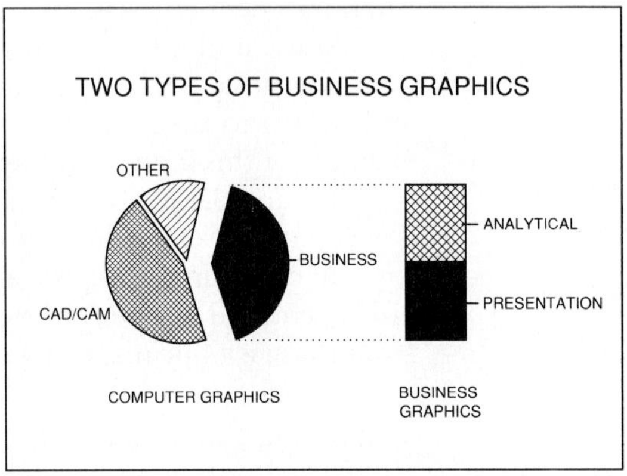


Pie-bar combination

**Figure 10–10.** Diagnostic Screen for Tomoscan Diagnosis KBS: An Example of Windows

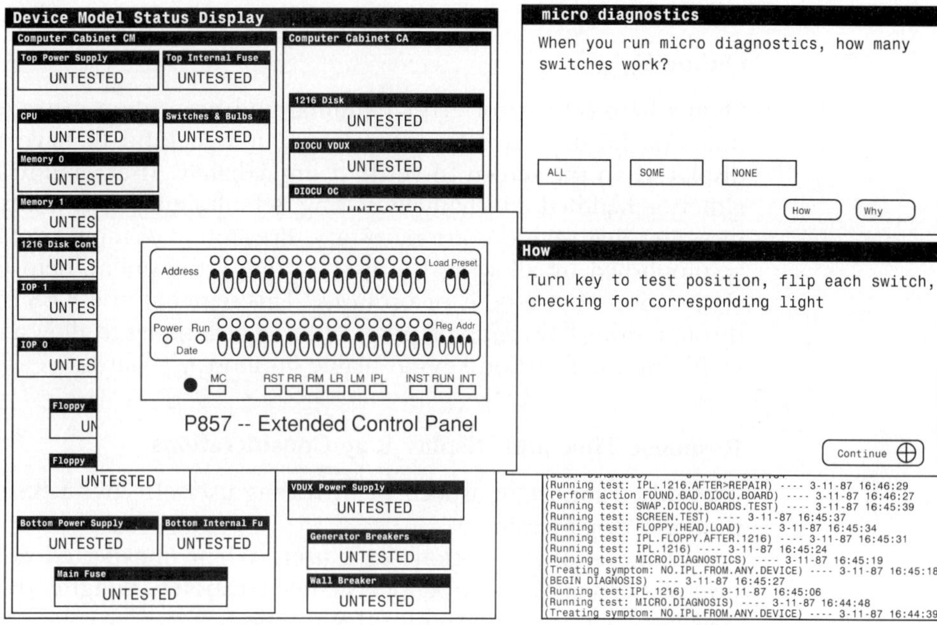


**Source:** Richard L. Wexelblat, "On Interface Requirements for Expert Systems," *AI Magazine.* Fall 1989, 10(3), p. 69. Reprinted with permission of AAAI Press.

Since the job of the interface is to make the system a valuable tool for users, the more the users can concentrate on the subject they are exploring rather than on the computer, the more effective the system will be. One way to accomplish this is through color. The *Presentation Manager* software graphics design package, for example, which is available commercially, uses a dull gray background and pastel menu bars to allow the user to focus on the application rather than on the background.

Color displays are attractive to KBS users and can often improve task performance. Color displays can be soothing or striking to the eye. Color can also add accents to uninteresting displays or emphasize the logical organization of information. However, there are dangers from misuse, where color is used for its own sake and so distracts from the primary task at hand.

The size and layout of the screen is another possible decision that a KBS designer will have to face. For most interactive systems, screen displays are a key component of successful design. Decisions regarding screen size and layout are influenced by the particular tasks involved in the KBS. Effective screen design must provide all the necessary data in the proper sequence to carry out the task.

To account for limited screen sizes, displays can be organized into pages. Meaningful groupings of items and consistent sequencing of groups will enhance the screen layouts.

### Online Help

Online help consists of error handling and prevention messages and information. As the user keys in information, it is helpful to have the information displayed on the screen to verify it immediately. If errors are found, they can either be handled internally by setting default limits or by notifying the user via messages that revisions are necessary. Prevention of input problems can also be accomplished by allowing the user to query the online help facility to obtain clarification of questions or prompts. This segment of a KBS can be developed through using conventional programming techniques to allow a user to seek help by hitting the function keys available on most keyboards.

### Response Time and Display Rate Considerations

Two other important aspects of providing user-effective KBS involve response time and display rate.

Time is often precious to a user. When unexpected delays impede the progress of a task, many people become frustrated. Lengthy response times and slow display rates can produce this reaction.

Response time is the number of seconds it takes from the moment a user initiates an activity until the computer begins to present results on the screen or printer. Display rate is the speed in characters per second at which characters appear for the user to read. If a lot of data is to be displayed and the text is only scanned, then fast display rates may produce a powerful advantage in task completion times and user satisfaction.

### Testing and Evaluating User Requirements

It is not always easy to anticipate user requirements. For this reason, time has to be allowed in many KBS development situations for exploring, testing, and evaluating user requirements. It is very difficult for computer information systems technicians who are familiar with a system to guess what the reactions and requirements of nontechnical users will be.

There are many productive avenues for assessing user requirements. Where development situations permit it, the best way is to have users participate in the KBS development effort from the start. Surveys and interviews are helpful in other situations. Pilot and acceptance tests, especially those using well thought out early prototype KBS, have also proven effective, not only for system development, but later in system acceptance by users—a problem some developers encounter in larger projects (Leonard-Barton 1987). In addition, by testing and evaluating the KBS as it is being developed, the system designer will ensure not only that the system is effective and accepted, but that the system replicates the expertise more accurately. For these reasons, testing and evaluating user requirements will very often save time and money in the long run.

In the short run, however, such studies can at times lead to abandoning a project. For example, in many situations, system developers initially do not recognize the substantial costs involved in developing effective user interfaces. These costs are often at least as much as the cost of the basic KBS itself. Only in the later stages of development do these inexperienced system developers finally realize these requirements. To avoid this problem, Gordon (1988, p. 55) recommends doing preliminary user-interface design studies prior to developing the knowledge base of the KBS.

## SOME GENERAL GUIDELINES FOR DEVELOPING EFFECTIVE USER INTERFACES

Two areas in which human/computer dialogue can be improved are examined in this section, screen design and user interaction (Brown 1988; Molich 1990; Rubin 1988; Lamberti and Wallace, 1990).

### Screen Design

In designing computer screens, strive to:

- Minimize text, maximize spacing. Preferably design a screen where less than 25 percent of the space is used, so that it is uncluttered, with plenty of blank space.
- Avoid paragraphs of text, if possible. Aim to give highlights, not full paragraphs.
- Vary use of upper- and lowercase in any lengthy text.
- Use consistent terminology, wording, icons, and placing of instructions.
- Use color and graphics where appropriate to create interest and relieve boredom.
- Limit menu selection items, preferably to no more than seven.

### User Interaction

In planning for user interaction, strive to:

- Incorporate the user's language. Try to avoid technical words and phrases.
- Try to avoid extraneous material; make both language and the order of statements used in dialogue as natural as possible.
- Provide feedback and on-line help. Keep users informed about what is happening by providing them with appropriate feedback within a reasonable time.

- Allow for atypical users and users of different levels of expertise, providing shortcuts for more experienced users.
- Allow for error correction, give clear instructions for correcting errors, and do not criticize the user in error messages.
- Build quick response time into the system. Avoid blank screens for any extended period of time, by explaining to the user what is going on.
- Provide users clear guidance through the system. Allow the user to review prior steps where possible and appropriate.
- Minimize what the user has to remember. Make prior instructions retrievable, or repeat them where necessary.

## AN APPROACH TO MAKING DECISIONS IN SPECIFIC SITUATIONS

The approach to making decisions about designing and selecting user interfaces is shown in Figure 10–11.

This section discusses how specific knowledge-domain, system, user, organizational, delivery-environment, and computer and other resource factors are analyzed and structured, and then used in making such decisions as selecting:

- primary interaction style
- screen layout
- color and window
- input device
- type of graphics

A wide range of situations can be involved when making these decisions, from large and diverse KBS development projects involving hundreds of nontechnical users working in widely dispersed and potentially dangerous locations to small systems developed by the manager whose department will be using the system.

Because of this wide range of possible decisions and decision situations, the approach described in this section is necessarily a general one, intended to give only an overview of the approach. Specific applications of this general approach are given in the final sections of this chapter.

### Critical Factors Affecting Decisions in This Area

As shown in Figure 10–11, a variety of factors are analyzed in making decisions regarding user interface design, including:

- the purpose, nature, complexity, and frequency of use of the knowledge domain and the system replicating it
- user characteristics
- user/delivery environment
- available resources and other requirements

**Figure 10–11.** User-Interface Decision—Decision Situation Diagram

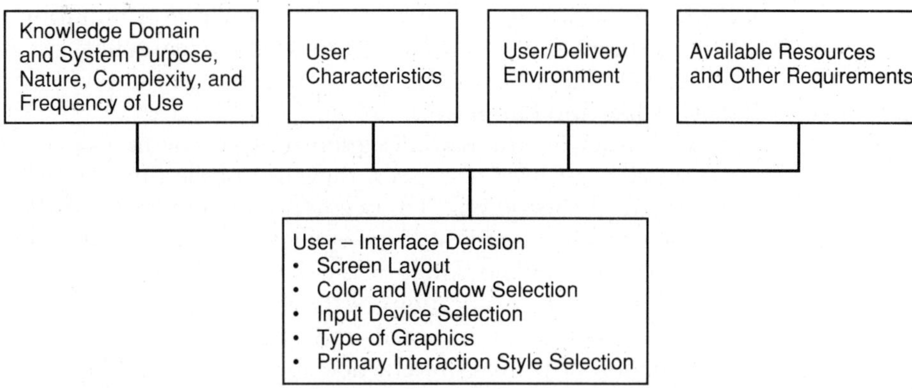


***The Purpose, Nature, Complexity, and Frequency of Use of the Knowledge Domain and the System Replicating It.*** In order for the KBS designers to make the necessary decisions regarding the selection of user interfaces, the *purpose of the system* to be designed is identified. For example, it is important for a systems developer to know, based on a system's requirements analysis, whether a system is to be used in life and death situations or to assist the user in other kinds of task performance, or if it is to be a training system, or if it is to be used to actually make business decisions. A system would be designed differently for life-critical situations such as air traffic, medical care, or military operations than for industrial/commercial or office uses, or for home or entertainment or exploratory creative purposes.

A system that serves a tutorial function, for example, one that is used to train novice marketing managers, is likely to have an interface that contains more text and online help facilities than an advisory system. On the other hand, a second-opinion application used by managers to check on their own analysis can probably assume that the user is fairly knowledgeable in the field and is more interested in getting to the bottom line as quickly as possible. This type of system would require fewer explanatory facilities (Dologite 1990).

The designer also needs information about the *nature of the knowledge*, to determine the kind of interface strategy to use. A financial consulting system, for example, may require interfaces that are rather structured, using charts and other standard financial forms that are common in the financial area. This could be accomplished by combining in the interface spreadsheet programs and packages with other "front-end" communicators—programs that prompt the user for information and pass the data to the software packages which are connected to the inference engine that does the processing.

On the other hand, a domain that is more text-oriented—as in the small KBS described in Chapter 2 or in the tutorial KBS described in Chapter

15—may not require the use of graphics or direct manipulation in the interface, but may communicate best through a menu, or dialogue-controlled interface. Graphics may be more suitable for an application requiring economic advice, such as forecasting or analyzing the effects of particular variables on the Gross National Product. This type of system could get its point across through such tools as line and bar graphs.

In order for the KBS designers to make the necessary decisions regarding the selection of user interfaces, they also probe the *complexity of the task domain* replicated in the system. To ascertain the complexity of the task domain, the designer would identify its terminology, structure, and scope. If the domain's nature (facts, concepts, kinds of decisions) is complex, its structure (the routines, procedures, and classifications of the knowledge) is complex, and its scope (the breadth and depth) is broad and deep, then the designer would need a combination of primary interaction styles that would be sufficiently complex to handle this particular system.

The *frequency or degree of usage* is also an important consideration. A system that is accessed daily may be awkward and time consuming if it has a rigid menu interface that requires the user to go through a tedious procedure every time the system needs to be run. Building some flexibility and override options into the interface will make the system more user-effective in these situations.

***User Characteristics.*** User-interface design decisions have to focus on the user. If users do not find an expert system easy to learn, communicate with, and get information from within a satisfactory amount of time, they will not be inclined to use it. Knowing the user, therefore, is essential to efficient interface design.

The job of the interface is to allow the user to communicate with a KBS. The communication is two-way: the KBS prompts the user for information via the interface, processes it, allows the user to make inquiries and revisions which it then processes, and provides the user with valuable advice or recommendations. The user may also require the option of seeing the reasoning process that the KBS used to arrive at the conclusions.

In order to be useful, this interaction must be at a level the user understands. Knowing the users' profile—age, computer training and competence, and educational background—is therefore useful in many situations. Users' work habits and ways of solving problems, expectations for the system, number and diversity, location, and biases and organizational pressures are also useful pieces of information that can help make user interfaces more effective in many situations.

Where situations permit and warrant it, some sort of user profile can be done, whether the user consists of one individual or a group. If there is sufficient time available, a psychological profile is also helpful in some situations. This would involve analyzing the user or user community to identify the following characteristics (Schneiderman 1987, pp. 24–25):

- risk taking/risk avoidance
- reflective/impulsive (action-oriented)

- high/low anxiety
- high/low tolerance for stress
- assertive/passive
- left/right brain orientation

Human perceptual abilities could also be examined. These would be flicker sensitivity, contrast sensitivity, motion sensitivity, and depth perception (Schneiderman 1987, pp. 19–20).

One effective way to obtain user information is to have the user involved in the design of the knowledge-based system as it is being developed. By having users participate in the system design and by other methods such as personal interviews and surveys, the KBS designer will be able to obtain information about users' general education and training levels, computer competence and experience, trainability, work habits, patterns of thinking, psychological and emotional profiles, and familiarity with the knowledge domain replicated in the KBS.

Many sophisticated systems being designed today have the ability to adapt to the level of the user through an interactive process. As the user gains expertise in running the system, the simplified levels of interface can be bypassed. In an interface that uses menus, for example, there is an option on the first screen that allows the user to jump to a specific section of the interface or the system.

***Delivery Environments.*** The KBS must be designed to match the office or workplace of the systems' users. In order to make decisions regarding the KBS, the designer will identify by interview, or preferably through first hand experience, the users' access to the system, the times they have to use it, and the compatibility of the expert system with other interfaces the users interact with in their work environment. For example, the KBS designer would want to know if the system requires unusually quick response time or if the environment is a potentially dangerous one, such as a nuclear power plant (Hendler 1988, p. 4). Too often, these factors are not taken into account.

As another example, Grabowski (1988) describes the special problems arising from a KBS she developed for tugboat captains aboard ships in New York Harbor. The users' main focus of attention in this situation was piloting the boat, a situation similar to that of airline pilots, where interaction with the computer is possible only through specially designed input and speech-recognition interfaces.

The computer equipment used for delivering the system can also affect the type of interface chosen, as well as the tools used to develop the interfaces. A graphics interface, for example, may not be practical in a mainframe-based KBS that services users at terminals that are character-oriented. A similar condition exists on PCs where target users may still have character-oriented monitors.

Where complex graphics are required, developers sometimes create the KBS with an advanced development tool, such as KEE or ART, using powerful graphics workstations or PCs. Then, when the application is ready for delivery to users, it is ported down to a less powerful machine. Porting software is possible because only the KBS and inference engine need to be delivered to the user's machine. All the power-hungry development-aiding software, like KBS file editors, debuggers, tracers, drawing tools, and the like, can be removed from the final delivered, or "run-time," system.

***Available Resources and Other Requirements.*** Depending on the situation, a variety of other factors can affect user-interface development. For example, money may be a factor—the system situation simply may not justify the amount of money needed to develop the most effective user interface, such as a speech recognition subsystem for KBS supporting tugboat captains. Or, money may not be available for the software packages or computer hardware needed to design and deliver sophisticated graphic interfaces for a system under study.

Available development time may be another factor, as may anticipated technological developments and obsolescence. In many situations, such factors can lead to abandoning a project under development, once the very real costs of developing user interfaces are finally recognized.

### Making Decisions Based on These Critical Situation Factors

As seen in Figure 10–11, the critical situation factors described in the preceding sections are analyzed and used in making a variety of user-interface decisions, such as:

- whether to use graphics, and if so, what kind
- primary interaction style selection
- input device selection
- screen design, layout, color, and windows

For example, the use of graphics would be recommended in situations where:

- the knowledge domain involves financial forecasting,
- the system is designed to provide higher management with summary information,
- a considerable amount of data needs to be summarized,
- professional financial analysts are using the system,
- the system will be used in an office environment, and appropriate software is available.

On the other hand, graphics are not that important in many of the systems described in this book.

As for selecting the primary interaction style, in situations where

- the type of system is entertainment,
- the user has little computer training,
- the system's task domain is not complex, and
- the system is to be used frequently,

then direct manipulation would be the best option, since it is easy to learn, encourages exploration, and has high subjective satisfaction.

A keyboard input device would be selected in other situations where:

- the purpose of the system is to assist professional personnel in a moderately complex knowledge domain, on a relatively frequent basis,
- the domain does not require the users to draw pictures,
- the users are relatively homogeneous, and familiar and comfortable when working with computers,
- an office is the delivery environment, and
- adequate resources and other requirements are available.

Obviously more is involved in making these decisions than is covered in these brief summaries. The following sections describe one type of user-interface decision in more detail, that is, the selection of primary interaction styles, and also present a KBS designed to assist in making such decisions.

## APPLYING THIS GENERAL APPROACH TO DECISIONS INVOLVING PRIMARY INTERACTION STYLES

The specific decision situation under study in this section is the selection of primary interaction styles for a KBS. The possible recommendations are:

- menu selection
- form fill-in
- command languages
- direct manipulation
- natural language
- controlled dialog
- speech input/output

The discussion in this section covers:

- factors affecting the decision
- possible recommendations and how they are made

### Factors Affecting the Decision

As shown in Figure 10–12, deciding on what specific type or types of interaction style(s) to select for a KBS is influenced by many factors, including:

- user/delivery environment
- system purpose
- system use
- knowledge domain
- user characteristics
- available resources and other requirements

**Figure 10–12.** Primary Interaction Decision—Decision Situation Diagram

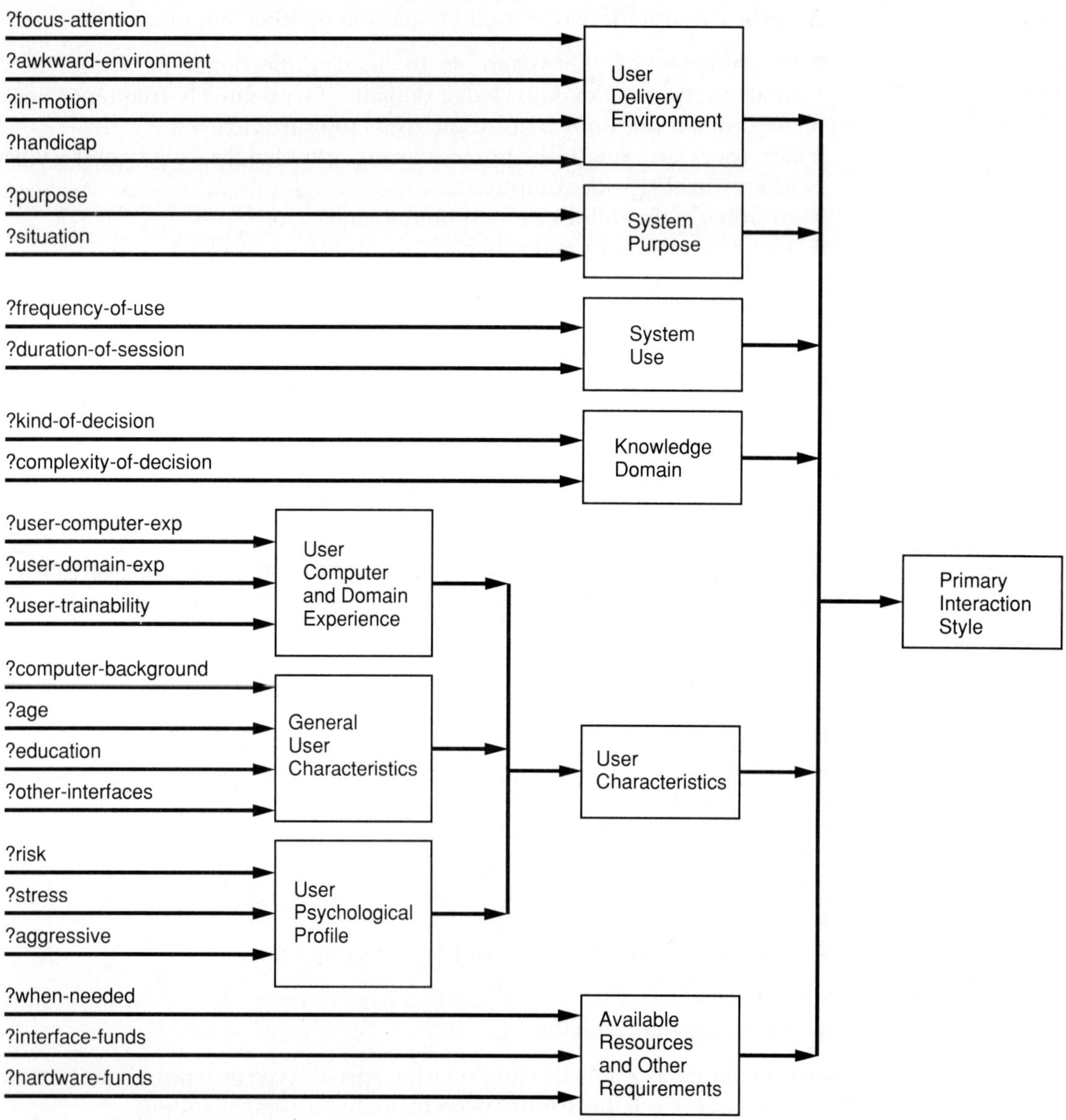

The above factors are used to select primary interaction styles in two ways: by weeding out styles that are inappropriate for the situation, and by suggesting an appropriate style to consider for a particular situation.

***User Delivery Environment.*** Analyzing the user delivery environment involves answering such questions as:

- Will the system be used in an environment where the users must focus their attention on the task at hand and not focus it on a computer screen or keyboard, such as on a tugboat moving through the water?
- Will the system be used in an awkward environment such as an airplane cockpit where the use of a keyboard is extremely difficult?
- Will the system be used in an environment where the user is in constant motion and cannot sit at a terminal, such as in a hospital operating room or a battlefield?
- Will the system be used in any situation where the user is unable either to see the keyboard or terminal or is unable to use it due to a handicap?

If all of the above questions are answered no, then the user delivery environment would be considered typical, and speech input/output would be ruled out as a possible interface to consider. If the answer to any of the above questions is yes, then user/delivery environment would be considered unusually demanding, restrictive, dangerous, or even hazardous or hostile.

***System Purpose.*** Analyzing the system purpose requires answering such questions as:

- What is the purpose of the KBS? Will it be used for training, tutoring, assisting/aiding, data entry, or entertainment?
- Is the KBS to be used in life-critical situations, such as medicine, air traffic control, or military operations?

***System Use.*** Analyzing system use requires investigating the following:

- How frequently will the KBS be used—many times a day, daily, weekly, bi-weekly, monthly?
- How long is the typical session—less than 15 minutes, between 15 and 30 minutes, between 30 and 60 minutes, more than 60 minutes?

If the system is used daily and the typical session length is between 30 and 60 minutes, then system use would be considered heavy.

***Knowledge Domain.*** Analyzing the knowledge domain factors requires answering such questions as:

- What kind of decision situation is the KBS to be used in—production, robotics control, financial or marketing decision making, inventory control, insurance claims processing, applicant screening, course selection, product configuration, making staffing decisions, giving customer advice, or some other area?

- How would you estimate the complexity of the knowledge domain under study, based on a study of the breadth and depth of the knowledge and on the complexity of the processes involved?

If the KBS will be used, for example, for applicant screening situations, and the depth and breadth of the knowledge domain to be replicated by the KBS is relatively easy to define and model, then the domain factors would be considered uncomplex.

***User Characteristics.*** As shown in Figure 10–12, a number of user characteristics are analyzed, including:

- computer and domain experience
- general characteristics
- psychological profiles

Analyzing user computer and domain experience involves answering such questions as:

- How would you describe the users' level of computer training, experience, and competence?
- What is the users' general level of experience in the knowledge domain?
- How would you describe the users' trainability in both the knowledge domain and the use of computers?

These questions provide insight about the level of interface complexity that the users can adapt to easily. For example, if the users' level of computer training and competence is moderate, their experience in the knowledge domain is above average, and their trainability is above average, then the user computer and domain experience factors would be considered favorable because the users could easily adapt to any interface style, depending upon the particular situation.

Analyzing general user characteristics involves answering such questions as:

- Is the user group homogeneous, or are there many different types of users with widely varying computer backgrounds?
- Are the typical users young (below age 45)?
- What is the highest level of education that most of the users have completed?
- What types of primary interaction styles does the user group have experience with and currently use with other systems?

These questions provide insight about the types of interfaces that the users will accept and use. If the user group consists of individuals with similar computer backgrounds, who are young, and most of whom have completed college, then the general user characteristics would be considered favorable.

Analyzing user psychological profiles involves answering such questions as:

- Do the users like to take risks or avoid them?
- Do the users have a high, moderate, or low tolerance for stress and anxiety?
- Are the users assertive or passive?

These questions provide insight about the types of interfaces that the users will be most comfortable with, based on their psychological attitudes. If the users prefer to take risks, have a moderate tolerance for stress and anxiety, and tend to be assertive, then the user psychological profiles would be considered aggressive.

If the user computer and domain experience factors were considered favorable, the general user characteristics were considered favorable, and user psychological profiles were aggressive, then the user characteristics would be considered favorable.

***Available Resources and Other Requirements.*** Available resources and other factors are also analyzed. This process calls for answering such questions as:

- How quickly is the system needed?
- Are funds available to develop a speech recognition or natural language interface?
- Are funds available to acquire expensive hardware and software for both development and delivery of the system?

These questions are only asked if answers to previous questions indicate that a speech input/output or natural language interface is the preferred primary interaction style. If that is the situation, if the system is not needed quickly, and if the resources are available, then available resources and other requirements would be considered adequate.

### Possible Recommendations and How They Are Made

Based on the above situation analysis, a KBS developer would be able to make some preliminary decisions about what primary style or styles might be most effective for the system under study.

A KBS designer will select a primary interaction style based on information obtained regarding such factors as the user/delivery environment, system purpose, knowledge domain, system use, user characteristics, and available resources and other requirements. The potential primary interaction styles, once again, include:

- menu selection
- form fill-in
- command language

- direct manipulation
- natural language
- controlled dialog
- speech input/output

Recommendations for selecting primary interaction styles are made in two ways: by weeding out styles that are inappropriate for the situation, and by highlighting the most appropriate style for a particular situation. It is possible in many situations to recommend multiple styles for a system.

***Recommendation to Use Menu Selection.*** For example, in a situation where the user/delivery environment is normally stable and without major problems, the purpose of the system is training, system use is infrequent, the knowledge domain is simple, and users are moderately competent workers, then menu selection would be the best option, since it shortens learning, structures decision making, and easily supports error handling.

***Recommendation to Use Form Fill-In.*** In a situation having similar characteristics to the one described in the preceding paragraph, with the exception that the system's purpose is data entry instead of training and the system use is intermittent instead of infrequent, then form fill-in would be an option to consider, since it requires modest training, assistance can be conveniently provided, and data entry is simplified.

***Recommendation to Use Command Language.*** In a situation where the user/delivery environment is normally (but not always) stable and has reasonably good working conditions, where the system purpose is assisting/aiding, where the system use is frequent, where the knowledge domain is complex, where users are fairly well trained and above average workers, and where available resources are favorable, then command language would be an option to consider, since it is flexible, supports user initiative, and appeals to frequent users.

***Recommendation to Use Direct Manipulation.*** In a situation where the user/delivery environment is reasonably favorable, the system purpose is entertainment, the system use is frequent, the knowledge domain is simple, and users are not necessarily computer literate or well-educated, then direct manipulation would be the best option since it is easy to learn, encourages exploration, and has high subjective satisfaction.

***Recommendation to Use Natural Language.*** In a situation where the user/delivery environment is reasonably favorable, the system purpose is life-critical, system use is frequent, the knowledge domain is simple, users are intelligent and well-trained, and available resources and other requirements are adequate, then natural language would be an option to consider, since it appeals to infrequent users and to users who are knowledgeable about a task domain which has a limited scope.

**Figure 10–13.** Dependency Diagram—Primary Interaction Style for a KBS (Initial Prototype Phase)

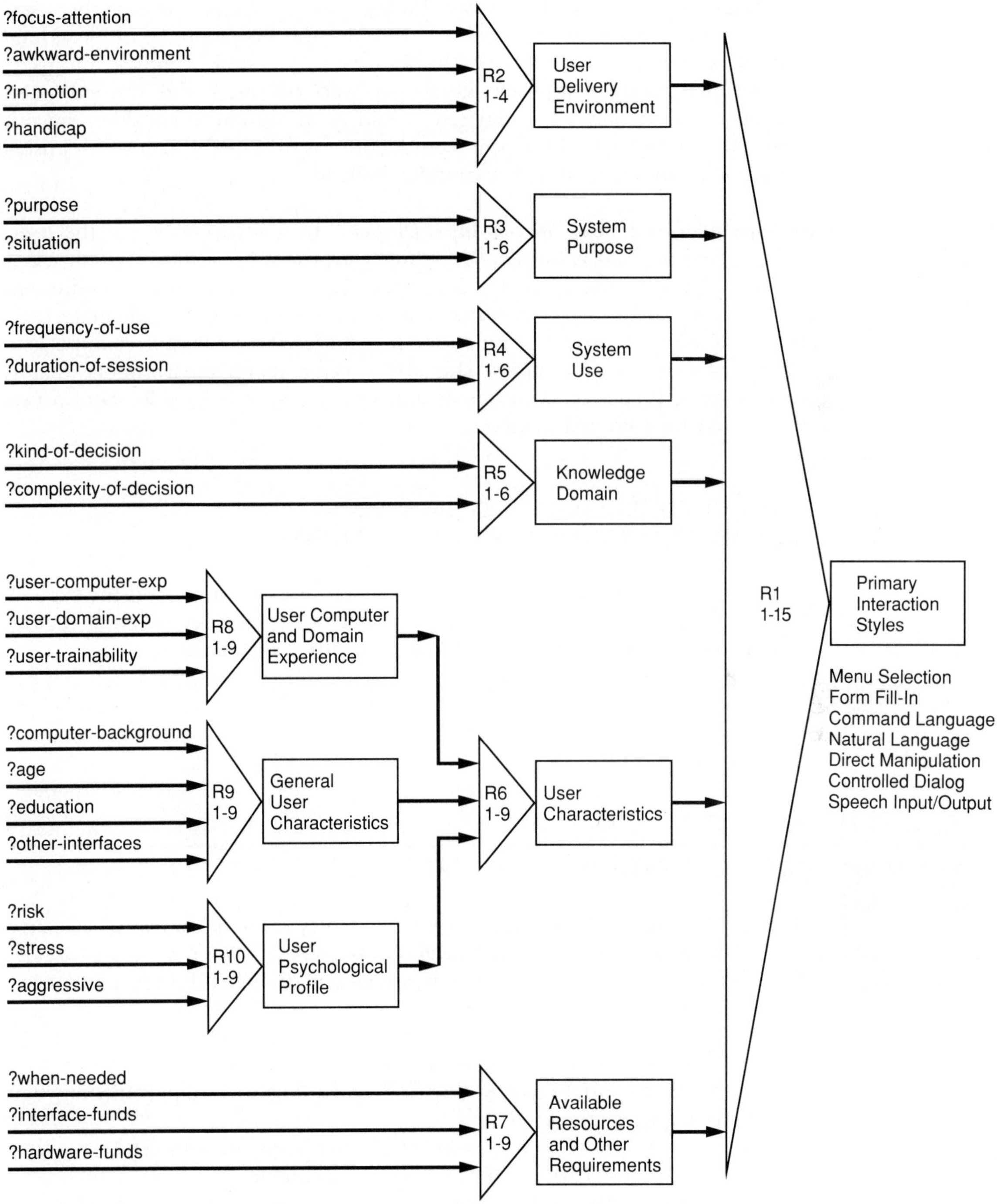

***Recommendation to Use Controlled Dialog.*** In a situation where the user/delivery environment is reasonably favorable, the system purpose is aiding/assisting, system use is infrequent, the knowledge domain is complex, and users are not necessarily computer literate or well educated and trained, then controlled natural language dialogue would be an option to consider, since it allows the computer to direct the consultation for infrequent or low-level users dealing with subject matter in a complex domain.

***Recommendation to Use Speech Input/Output.*** In a situation where the user/delivery environment is hostile, the system purpose is life-critical, system use is frequent, the knowledge domain is simple, users are reasonably well-educated and trainable, and available resources and other requirements are adequate, then speech input/output would be an option to consider. This is because it appeals to infrequent users and to users who are working in an environment that is demanding, difficult, or even hostile and who are knowledgeable about a task domain having a limited scope.

## A KBS DESIGNED TO ASSIST IN MAKING PRIMARY INTERACTION STYLE DECISIONS

A knowledge-based system has been developed to assist in making the type of decision described in the preceding section. The dependency diagram for the initial prototype of that system is shown in Figure 10–13.

## REVIEW QUESTIONS

1. Describe what user interfaces are and discuss the importance of effective user interfaces to successful KBS development.
2. Describe the five primary interaction styles and discuss different situations in which they are useful.
3. Discuss the ways in which graphics, color, windows, and color screen design techniques are useful in designing effective user interfaces.
4. Discuss the importance of testing and evaluating user requirements when developing user interfaces.
5. Discuss why some experts recommend identifying user interface requirements during the early stages of KBS development.
6. Identify some general guidelines for developing effective user interfaces.

7. Describe the critical factors that are analyzed in making user interface decisions.
8. Give an example of a situation in which the user environment had an impact on the kind of user interface used.
9. Describe some of the user characteristics that affect interface design and selection.
10. Discuss the ways in which available resources can affect user interface design and selection decisions.

## EXERCISES

1. After reviewing the decision situation and dependency diagram outlines in Figures 10–11, 10–12, and 10–13, and the discussion in the two chapter sections entitled "An Approach to Making Decisions in Specific Situations" and "Applying This General Approach to Decisions Involving Primary Interaction Styles," develop a small KBS to assist in any of the user-interface decisions discussed in this chapter. Follow the directions in either Chapter 2, or in Chapters 3 through 6, when developing the system.
2. Read through recent issues of KBS periodicals listed in the references section of this chapter, and through other related artificial intelligence and user interface books and periodicals, and find discussions of the main topics covered in this chapter. Write a brief report describing how this reading provided you with insights and guidance when developing your KBS for Exercise 1.

## REFERENCES

Alexander, Michael. "Edging Down the Road to Voice Recognition." *Computerworld*, January 15, 1990, p. 17.

Bailey, Jennifer Jo. *Economic Evaluation of Knowledge-Based Systems*. Master of Science Paper, Boston, MA: Massachusetts Institute of Technology, 1987.

Brown, G. B. *Human-Computer Interface Guidelines*. Norwood, NJ: Ablex Publishing, 1988.

Dologite, D. G. "Human Factors in Expert Systems: Designing the User Interface for a Strategy Planning KBS." Unpublished manuscript, 1990.

Edmunds, R. *The Prentice-Hall Standard Glossary of Computer Terminology*. Englewood Cliffs, NJ: Prentice-Hall, 1985.

Gality, Wilbert O. *Handbook of Screen Design*, 3d ed. Wellesley, MA: QED Information Sciences Inc., 1989.

Gordon, Sallie E. "The Human Factor in Expert Systems." *AI Expert*, January, 1988, pp. 55–59.

Grabowski, Martha. "Knowledge Acquisition Methodologies." *Proceedings of the Ninth International Conference on Information Systems*. Minneapolis, MN: SIM, IMS, and ACM, December 1988.

Harmon, Paul, and Brian Sawyer. *Creating Expert Systems*. New York: Wiley, 1990.

Hendler, James, ed. *Expert Systems: The User Interface*. Norwood, NJ: Ablex Publishing Corp., 1988.

Houghton, Raymond C., "Designing User Interfaces: A Key to Success", *Journal of Information Systems Management*, Summer, 1986, pp. 56–61.

Lamberti, Donna M., and William A. Wallace. "Intelligent Interface Design: An Empirical Assessment of Knowledge Presentation in Expert Systems." *MIS Quarterly,* September 1990.

Leonard-Barton, Dorothy. "The Case for Integrative Innovation: An Expert System at Digital." *Sloan Management Review*, Fall 1987, pp. 7–19.

Molich, Rolf, and Jacob Nielsen. "Improving a Human-Computer Dialogue." *Communications of the ACM*, March 1990, pp. 338–48.

Perspectives. "Voice Recognition: Still a Long Way to Go." *InfoWorld*, March 26, 1990, pp. 43, 46, 48.

Potter, Andrew. "Direct Manipulation Interfaces." *AI Expert*, October 1988, pp. 28–35.

Rubin, T. *User Interface Design For Computer Systems*. New York: Wiley (Halsted Press), 1988.

Schneiderman, B. *Designing The User Interface: Strategies For Effective Human-Computer Interaction*. Reading, MA: Addison-Wesley, 1987.

Shafer, Dan. "Focus on Entry Techniques for Expert Systems." *PC AI*, September-October 1989, pp. 55–58.

Wexelblat, Richard L. "On Interface Requirements for Expert Systems." *AI Magazine*, Fall 1989, pp. 66–78.

# 11

# System Implementation

This chapter concerns another critical aspect of the KBS development cycle, the interpersonal interaction and other integrating tasks involved in developing and implementing a KBS. The objective of this chapter is to help readers understand:

- The overall strategies, as well as tasks, techniques, and tools, involving interpersonal interaction during KBS development and implementation
- How to make interpersonal interaction decisions in specific situations
- The special problems involved in system installation, testing and validation/verification, documentation, introduction, evaluation, and maintenance
- Integration of KBS with conventional computer systems
- The impact of KBS and their development on the management information systems area

## INTERPERSONAL INTERACTION IN KBS DEVELOPMENT AND IMPLEMENTATION

In non-expert-driven KBS development and implementation situations, a knowledge engineer can be involved with many kinds of interpersonal interactions when dealing with:

- users
- experts
- senior managers
- computer information systems and system engineering technicians
- other company personnel

This interaction can occur throughout the KBS development life cycle shown in Figure 11–1, especially during

- knowledge elicitation, acquisition, representation, and reformulation
- user-interface development and integration of KBS with conventional computer systems
- delivery of the system into the user environment
- system testing, validation, and evaluation

**Figure 11–1.** Knowledge-Based Systems Development Life Cycle

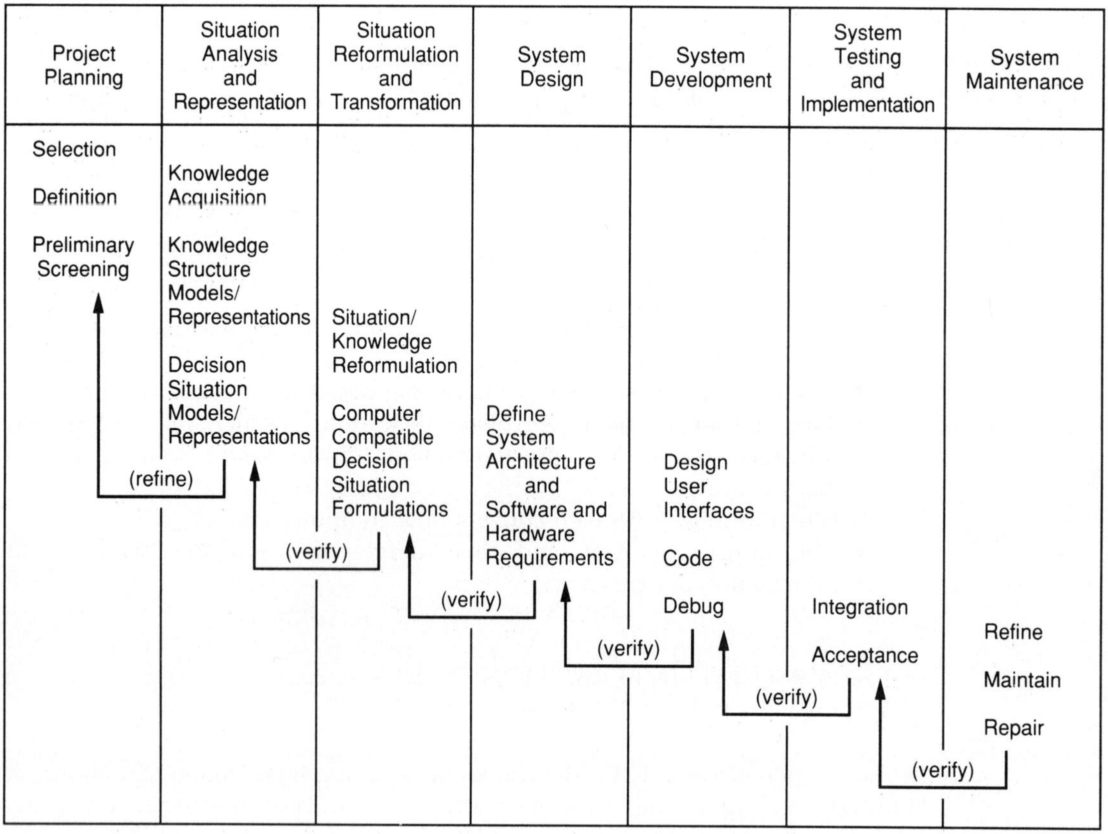

In all these situations, this interpersonal interaction is a major factor in getting the KBS development job done and getting the KBS used effectively in the work environment.

## OVERALL STRATEGIES

The nature of the KBS development job and the variety of development situations encountered requires a knowledge engineer to perform several different roles during the KBS development cycle, including: manager and director, facilitator, coordinator and integrator, and listener (McGraw 1989, pp. 109–15).

As *manager* of the knowledge acquisition process, a knowledge engineer needs to maintain an effective relationship with an expert in order to obtain useful information during knowledge acquisition sessions. The leadership styles used can range from supportive to authoritative. For example, during a knowledge acquisition session with an expert, an effective knowledge engineer establishes certain objectives and performs certain tasks in order to maintain the relationship with the expert and to increase the effectiveness of a knowledge acquisition session, including:

- Establishing active leadership upon greeting the domain expert. This can be done either explicitly or implicitly. Explicit leadership control includes welcoming the expert, introducing the session, presenting the agenda, and keeping the interview on the most productive track. Implicit control involves such techniques as body language and seating arrangements.
- Seating the expert in a position that allows her or him to be as productive as possible.
- Positioning the knowledge engineer near the lights, videotape equipment, and other elements of control.
- Guiding the expert through the knowledge acquisition session, following the agenda as much as possible. An effective knowledge engineer communicates to the expert what the agenda will be before the session starts. If the engineer follows the agenda, it will communicate to the expert that the session has been well thought out and organized to make the best use of everyone's time.
- Focusing the expert on the appropriate points. For instance, an effective knowledge engineer knows what type of information is to be obtained during the session. If the expert does not answer a question fully, follow-up and clarification are needed if the engineer is to get the information wanted.

While managing the knowledge acquisition session, knowledge engineers also act as *facilitators*. For example, an effective knowledge engineer uses both nonverbal and verbal behavior to help meet session goals. This behavior includes:

- Stimulating discussions.
- Balancing the discussion if there is more than one expert so that more than one view is addressed.
- Reconciling controversies.
- Actively summarizing the knowledge acquisition session for the expert at the close of the session. An effective knowledge engineer will not just allow a session to end, but will recap the session with the expert, focusing on accomplishments, pointing out new areas to explore, and letting the expert know what to expect as a follow-up.

As *coordinator or integrator,* in addition to domain experts a knowledge engineer will also interact with users, senior managers, computer information systems technicians, system engineering technicians, and other company personnel in many situations. A knowledge engineer has to be able to deal with different individuals at their own level.

There are three main groups that the knowledge engineer interacts with: senior management, technical personnel and domain experts, and the user group.

When dealing with senior management, an effective knowledge engineer realizes that they may be as concerned with the technical aspects of the KBS as with the overall status of the project. Therefore an effective knowledge engineer not only briefs senior management on the highlights of where the project is currently and where it is going, but also tries to anticipate the needs of senior management for technical information, and fulfill those needs with *as little technical jargon as possible.* Bridging this technological gap while integrating the perspectives of nontechnical managers during a KBS development project is a major function of a knowledge engineer. The need to do this kind of integrating task is what often leads to staffing the knowledge engineer job with someone trained in psychology or sociology.

When dealing with technical and domain experts, an effective knowledge engineer assumes that the other experts have varying degrees of understanding of the project. The knowledge engineer will deal with these professionals on a level that is comfortable for both parties and suited to each person's understanding of what is involved in the project. This requires knowing enough about computer technology to deal effectively with computer technicians, learning enough about the knowledge domain to deal with the domain experts, and having the skills to bridge the gaps sometimes existing between the two groups.

If the KBS under development is to assist operating and clerical people who will be using the system to perform specific tasks, the knowledge engineer will spend whatever time is required with the user group, learning how their jobs are performed, and what is needed to enhance them. This will be a very intense one-on-one interaction exploring user needs *in user terms, not in technical terms.*

An effective knowledge engineer recognizes the different types of interaction necessary for different situations, and will let the situation dictate interaction strategies. Generally, while facilitating, coordinating, and integrating, a knowledge engineer functions to bridge the gaps between the technology and technicians and the domain experts and users, who are often nontechnical. In such situations, the job of the knowledge engineer is to *translate the technical aspects of a system into a language understandable to the nontechnicians involved.* The inability of many computer-trained knowledge engineers to do this job has caused computer information systems personnel to have diminished roles in KBS development in many companies (Mockler 1991).

Being an effective *listener* is also crucial during knowledge acquisition, as it is during other phases of the KBS development cycle. Good listening requires that the engineer minimize distractions, pay attention, establish and maintain eye contact, and use positive body language. Some of the skills involved in effective listening are:

- being silent when a team member is speaking
- keeping one's responses to a minimum
- clarifying any misunderstanding
- interpreting facial expressions
- interpreting posture and position

## TASKS, TECHNIQUES, AND TOOLS INVOLVED

In addition to the overall strategies, there are a wide range of interpersonal tasks, techniques, and tools involved in handling interpersonal interaction effectively during KBS development and implementation, including:

- selecting knowledge experts and determining how to handle and work with them
- briefing and orienting participants
- creating an effective interview environment
- interviewing techniques
- developing and maintaining rapport with experts, users, management, and development personnel
- overcoming emotional and psychological barriers and handling special behavioral problems
- communicating with users, management, and other development personnel

### Selecting Experts and Determining How to Handle and Work with Them

Two typical situations are discussed here:

- where a knowledge engineer has a choice of expert(s)
- where a knowledge engineer does not have a choice of expert(s)

***Where a Knowledge Engineer Has a Choice of Expert(s).*** When a knowledge engineer has not been given an expert to work with, it is up to the knowledge engineer to select one or more. Several factors are good measures of domain experts' potential for effective KBS development participation (McGraw 1989, p. 97; Keller 1987, pp. 30–32):

1. domain background
2. level of expertise: experience, training, education
3. past performance
4. acceptance of candidate's expertise by others involved in the system
5. availability
6. personal characteristics and attitudes, including:

   - sense of humor
   - listening skills
   - sense of commitment
   - patience
   - ability to communicate ideas and concepts
   - willingness to prepare for the session
   - honesty with self and others
   - persistence
   - interest in the KBS

After reviewing the backgrounds of the experts under consideration, a knowledge engineer will talk with them to gather information in the above areas. In addition, a knowledge engineer will talk with those who have used the services of the expert in business to determine the expert's effectiveness in getting actual jobs done.

As for personality fit, a knowledge engineer and an expert can have a great deal of personal interaction during the knowledge acquisition and representation process. This is why personal attitudes and characteristics also need to be identified.

A knowledge engineer also checks with the people the candidate expert works for, to determine just how available the expert will be. Some development situations can require up to 25 percent of the expert's time during peak development periods. This can require a major commitment from the organization, especially in situations where the expert is also expected to make major contributions to ongoing company operations during the period the KBS is being developed. Without that commitment many knowledge engineers will not undertake a project (Edwards 1987). A knowledge engineer also checks an expert's personal commitment to the project to see if the expert will have the level of enthusiasm needed to carry the project through to completion.

***When the Knowledge Engineer Does Not Have a Choice of Expert(s).*** When a knowledge engineer has been given an expert to work with, and so is not able to choose the expert involved, there can be different problems. For example, the expert may be uncooperative, unavailable, or have other attributes the knowledge engineer feels would hamper an effective KBS development effort. Taking specific steps to overcome resistance to change and to overcome any emotional and psychological barriers, such as those described later in this chapter and in Chapter 14, therefore, is a key contribution to success in many KBS development situations.

### Briefing and Orienting Participants

The kind and amount of briefing and orientation needed will depend on the situation. A knowledge engineer always checks to see how familiar the team members are with the knowledge-based system being developed. Team members, who can include users, domain experts, senior managers, CS and system engineering personnel, and other company personnel, are instructed on how the sessions will work, what is to be accomplished, and the role that each person will play in relation to the entire KBS project.

For example, orientation techniques used by a senior knowledge engineer in helping other knowledge engineers in a KBS development team include presenting the following (McGraw 1989, pp. 86–89):

- background on the current project (information from the proposal, statement of work, contract)
- prerequisite domain background (domain training materials, videotapes, terminology)
- introduction to knowledge acquisition procedures (sample forms, checklists for procedures)
- training in specific knowledge acquisition techniques

The first three types of background can be presented either through training sessions or through written documents that are distributed to all knowledge engineers working on a project. The fourth area can be handled by the use of mock interviews during training sessions. The knowledge engineers review and evaluate videotapes of selected techniques used by themselves and others, such as those covered in Chapter 7 of this book. Reviewing the videotaped delivery of selected knowledge acquisition techniques allows knowledge engineers to refine their delivery and become more comfortable with each technique before working with the expert.

The orientation with domain experts, on the other hand, would cover:

- general introduction to expert systems, where needed
- project background and goals
- the domain expert's role
- an overview of knowledge acquisition procedures and techniques

At DuPont, where managers were initially encouraged to develop systems on their own for their operations, Ed Mahler ran two- and three-day sessions during which each participant actually developed a small KBS (Mahler 1986; Bailey 1987).

Senior managers are frequently briefed on a one-on-one basis. Briefing users who are not domain experts occurs somewhat later in the development effort and is discussed in later sections of this chapter.

### Creating an Effective Interview Environment

The environment in which the information needed for developing a KBS is obtained from a domain expert can also be critical in many situations. Some of the environmental factors affecting interpersonal interaction during knowledge acquisition sessions to be considered are:

- room size
- room arrangement
- room cleanliness
- room temperature
- proximity to rest rooms and drinking fountains
- seating arrangements

Environmental factors can influence how long a knowledge acquisition session will last, an expert's attitude toward the knowledge acquisition session, and the effectiveness of the interpersonal interaction.

Room size should not appear to be too large or the expert may feel lost and intimidated. On the other hand, it should not appear to be too small or the expert may feel confined and unprofessional. Room arrangements require considering such factors as the number, size, and shape of areas or tables, proximity to writing boards and projection tools, and the placement of taping equipment. Temperature should be moderate and should allow the expert to remain in the room for the duration of the typical session, about one hour, without getting tired. Proximity to rest rooms and drinking fountains further improves the comfort factor.

The planned length of the knowledge acquisition session will be determined by the knowledge engineer before the session starts. An accepted guideline is that the session normally last no more than one hour, with 90 minutes being the absolute maximum. As sessions get longer, experts and knowledge engineers often suffer attention-span problems, increasing the likelihood of information being lost. If, during subsequent sessions, a knowledge engineer finds that an hour is too long, the sessions can be shortened and their number increased. As with any such general guidelines, however, there are always exceptions. On several occasions, for example, the authors have participated in knowledge acquisition sessions lasting half a working day because of the high levels of interest exhibited by the domain experts.

Seating arrangements help create a favorable interview environment. Circular arrangements can stimulate integrated interaction and lessen the likelihood of dominance by a single individual. In situations where there are multiple experts, seating arrangements can be used to help establish the knowledge engineer's position of control and leadership.

At special times the situation may dictate having special seating arrangements. For example, Shpilberg (1986) describes a situation at Coopers & Lybrand where it became necessary to have the knowledge engineers observe experts at work through a two-way mirror. This was required because the presence of a knowledge engineer inhibited the experts working on a problem using normal work routines.

### Interviewing Techniques

The interpersonal interaction at work in interviews between experts and the knowledge engineer can have a critical impact on the success of a KBS development effort (Stewart 1985).

Knowledge engineers employ several different techniques in order to acquire the expert knowledge needed, as was described in Chapter 7. Knowledge engineers have to decide which techniques will help ensure that the knowledge being acquired is accurate. Techniques should be chosen that will help the knowledge engineer to:

- select and conduct the appropriate type of interview, according to the knowledge acquisition goals
- determine the appropriate record-keeping technique for a knowledge acquisition session
- recognize and produce specific types and levels of questions
- select the most appropriate question phrasing, based on terminology, level, and complexity of the expertise

There are two types of interviews: unstructured and structured. In unstructured interviews, a knowledge engineer talks to the expert about the tasks that the expert performs, asking spontaneous questions and initially exploring an issue almost randomly. A structured interview is more formal. It is goal-oriented, trying to get specific answers to specific questions.

Unstructured interviews can be effective at the beginning of the process, where the knowledge engineer is trying to develop a rapport with the expert, in order to put the expert at ease. They are useful in gaining general knowledge of the domain area under study. A structured interview is effective when the knowledge engineer is trying to write the knowledge base. This is a very detailed process to which the structured interview lends itself very well. Interview techniques were discussed in detail in Chapter 7.

Before a knowledge acquisition interview session starts, the knowledge engineer determines which of three types of record-keeping are to be used. Each method—manual note taking, audiotaping, and videotaping—can have varying degrees of impact on interpersonal interaction.

Manual note taking is controlled by the knowledge engineer. The knowledge engineer takes notes during the session which determine what information will be saved, reducing the cost in equipment and time. A disadvantage of this technique is that the knowledge engineer is now performing two tasks during the session, taking notes and managing the interview, and decreasing the attention given to each. While concentrating on taking notes, the knowledge engineer may miss something the expert is trying to convey and may never be able to recover that piece of information.

Audiotaping allows the knowledge engineer to focus on the expert, that is, on managing the session, without being distracted by note taking. After the session, the engineer can review the tape for any information not absorbed during the session. The tape can also be shared with other knowledge engineers to help avoid their duplicating questions in later sessions with the same experts. It is also a good source for documenting the knowledge acquired.

Videotaping has advantages over audiotaping. Audiotapes may not be able to identify speakers if multiple experts are used. Videotaping also shows any nonverbal interaction going on between the expert and the knowledge engineer, and thus often allows the engineer to determine an expert's degree of certainty on a particular answer. A disadvantage of videotaping is that it may have an adverse effect on experts, making them nervous, embarrassed, and reluctant to answer questions. Another disadvantage of both audiotape and videotape is cost. The knowledge engineer must also deal with the preparation of the tapes before the session, and with any mechanical difficulties that may arise during the session.

Questions asked during interviews can be categorized as open and closed. **Open questions** are general and place very few limits on the expert. They do not seek a specific answer; they encourage a free-flowing response. **Closed questions** set limits on the type, level, and amount of information an expert provides.

The disadvantage of open questions is that they may reveal very little information at the level required for KBS development. They may also lead to uncertainties when actually writing the KBS. On the other hand, closed questions may lead to receiving too little information, therefore requiring more sessions. Also, experts may not volunteer valuable information if the knowledge engineer does not ask specific questions touching on it. In addition, if a knowledge engineer uses the wrong term in asking a closed question, the response may be incorrect.

There are two levels of questions: primary and secondary. **Primary questions** are used to introduce topic areas or to move to another area. These are questions usually asked during the first session. **Secondary questions** are probing questions. Their purpose is to get more information in response to a primary or a preceding secondary question; they are follow-up questions, requesting more specific information.

After selecting the type and level of the questions, the knowledge engineer determines how to phrase them. There are three factors to be considered: terminology, level, and complexity.

Knowledge engineers who use the correct terminology will cause the expert to spend less time translating questions and more time providing the correct answers. By using the correct terminology, the engineer can effectively use the time allotted in the session.

What is the level of expertise of the expert? What type of knowledge will the expert have? If the knowledge engineer knows the answers to these questions, the correct questions will be asked. If questions are asked above the level of the expert, this may cause embarrassment, reluctance, and a lack of honesty. Questions that are asked below the level of the expert may cause the expert to feel that time is being wasted and this may lead to a less-than-adequate answer.

While trying to ask specific questions, a knowledge engineer may also ask questions that are too complex to answer. This can also cause the expert to respond incorrectly, or not to answer the actual question asked.

### Developing and Maintaining Rapport with Experts, Users, Management, and Development Personnel

One of the major tasks faced by the knowledge engineer is how to develop and maintain a rapport with all of the different team members during the KBS development.

Once all of the team members have been briefed and oriented, an effective knowledge engineer will try to motivate the team towards the successful implementation of the KBS. There are several approaches a knowledge engineer can use, including (Herzberg 1987):

- stress the benefits that the KBS will bring to the company and to the team members
- stress the recognition that the team members will receive upon successful implementation of the KBS
- stress the responsibility that the team members have accepted and how important it is to the KBS
- stress the possibility of personal advancement upon successful implementation of the KBS
- stress the potential growth and learning benefits individual team members will receive during the development of the KBS

An effective knowledge engineer tries to build up team members, reminding them of their importance to the KBS. Stating that no team member is more important than another can help motivate the team to try and work more cohesively together, which will aid in the successful implementation of the KBS.

### Overcoming Emotional and Psychological Barriers and Handling Special Behavioral Problems

Planning for and managing the impact of KBS technology on individuals' attitudes and perceptions is a major factor affecting the success of a KBS development project. This is due to the fact that knowledge acquisition involves *individual* experts and knowledge engineers and because successful implementation involves getting *individuals* to use a system.

The following are some of the common individual psychological and emotional problems (and their solutions) that have been encountered by the authors when helping business managers during the development of over one hundred knowledge-based systems (Chau 1990; Dologite 1989).

**1.** *It is hard to write down concisely and precisely how we do something or make decisions.* The better managers are at doing a job, the harder it often is to describe how they do the job. They often can see all the nuances, exceptions, and ramifications of various aspects of a problem, decision, or task. They also often make decisions intuitively, and are no longer conscious of how they go about doing it. This can make writing a simple scenario model or diagram of how a problem is solved or decision made very difficult. That is why it is often better to have a third party, like a knowledge engineer, help to do it, or actually do it.

*Solution:* Focus on a typical specific situation. Ignore exceptions until later. Settle at first for a diagram and written *scenario* which covers only the most typical situations. This is done whether experts are developing systems on their own, or a knowledge engineer is working with an expert to develop a system (see, for example, Garber, Johnson, and Zualkernan 1987; LaFrance 1987; and Mockler and Dologite 1990).

As part of this focusing process, it helps to write a list of the specific recommendations the expert might possibly make, given the possible circumstances in the type of decision, problem, or task situation under study.

Such simplifications enable identifying more quickly what Evanson and others refer to as an expert's basic "information processing strategy" (Evanson 1988, p. 40). Such a focused approach also enables a knowledge engineer, where one is involved, to become familiar with the vocabulary or language of an expert in a shorter period of time. Language (reference) barriers have been identified as stumbling blocks in many studies (for example, Buchanan 1983, pp. 133 ff).

**2.** *It is a bothersome job that seems pointless.* Competent experts know how to do their jobs. So initially, experts have trouble seeing the necessity of writing down how they work. For most people, writing it down is a hard, nasty, dumb job. This is especially true for managers who are doers—that is, managers who are good at getting things done in a pressured work environment. *It also takes a lot of time,* something which busy people are short of. It can appear to be an intellectual exercise with no point.

The problem is that without extensive and active participation by experts, the system probably won't be effective.

*Solution:* Emphasize the benefits, while acknowledging the drawbacks, as discussed in the following paragraphs. If the expert will not participate sufficiently, there is a high probability the project will fail. In fact, the authors have come to the conclusion that unless the expert, and sometimes the user, is willing to actually develop or participate in developing at least a small initial prototype on their own, using an expert system development shell, with the knowledge engineer's assistance where needed, it is not worthwhile to proceed with the development project (also see, for example, Edwards 1987, p. 99).

**3.** *There appears to be no payoff.* Initially, this very often appears to be true to the expert involved. The *solution* is to review the KBS' actual benefits. The benefits of the proposed KBS can include:

- providing a quick reference point or reminder guide for any manager who has multiple jobs to perform under time pressure
- functioning as an effective training tool for others
- enabling more consistent performance

One major payoff, then, can be self-interest: many experts find that KBS development helps them know and do their jobs better.

**4.** *Even when recognized, the benefits rarely seem to justify the effort and costs.* The costs can be enormous, since they involve not only time spent but also potential damage to ego perceptions. Some of these costs are:

- Once the expert has written down how the task, problem, or decision is handled, the magic is gone, and with it the ego satisfactions. Part of the power and satisfaction in a job is the magic: "Nobody can do it like ol' George." In reality, many jobs in business are not that complicated, and require no truly superior competence. In addition, when written down they can seem even less complex than they actually are, since only the most typical situations are usually replicated in the system.

  *Solution:* Emphasize the fact that the professional expert will still be needed to handle the tough exceptional problems, and probably even have more fun and satisfaction without having to do the routine tasks.
- *They won't need you anymore.* This problem is related to the fear of automation. If you help create the system, then you assume the system will be able to do your job and you will not be needed. This is probably true in a general sense, since not as many people may be needed and the less competent ones may be replaced. This fear, therefore, is well founded. While truly competent professionals will always be needed and probably have an even stronger position, there may be fewer of them.

  *Solution:* Only work with the better, stronger professionals when developing knowledge-based systems. Fearful, insecure, less-than-competent experts are highly likely to sabotage the system development effort.

**5.** *Even for the seasoned professionals, there will be a hard-to-resolve conflict of professional instincts.* On the one hand, if an individual expert refuses to participate in a knowledge-based system development effort, his or her professionalism may be called into question—it might be assumed she or he cannot do the job and so is not really competent. On the other hand, if the individual expert does participate, enormous time is involved and the end result may be to create a system which replaces or makes the expert obsolete. So, enormous costs and risks are present.

*Solution:* The first step towards a solution is to appreciate the conflict, the dilemma, and how emotionally charged this conflict is for an individual. If one wishes to use a particular expert to develop a knowledge-based system and one's business needs that expert over the long run, then provide sufficient rewards and satisfactions, both real and psychic, for the expert who is expected to help build the system and get the system used. That is the only long-term, effective way to solve this last problem.

The most effective organizational way to do this is to involve the expert, and where needed the user, in the system development in a way that promotes a proprietary interest in the system. This strategy is being used by many companies today. The way it is implemented can vary considerably, however, as is suggested by the company studies in Chapter 14, because of the individual situational requirements.

### Communicating with Users, Managers, and Other Development Personnel

If team members do not communicate well, responsibilities may be duplicated or ignored completely. Problems may not be resolved for extended periods of time, undermining the successful implementation of the KBS. An effective knowledge engineer will be able to break any communication barriers among team members. Some of the factors and techniques an effective knowledge engineer may use to improve team communications include (D'Aprix 1982; Rogers and Roethlisberger 1952):

- face-to-face meetings, as opposed to large meetings and memos
- electronic networks, allowing team members to communicate with each other in different geographic regions
- regularly scheduled meetings to discuss any problems arising during the project
- giving feedback to team members very quickly
- trying to develop mutual communication, which tends to be pointed toward solving a problem rather than attacking a person or group

Communications decisions can involve not only choosing oral and written communications approaches and the most effective ways of providing feedback, but can also involve technical areas, such as the use of electronic mail and communication and conferencing software (Keen 1986, 1988, and 1989). In considering expert systems development Earl Sacerdoti stresses an overall awareness of the project as it progresses. He warns against over-using expert systems, losing perspective on the project and overestimating its importance, taking excessive risks, and losing confidence in the project (Sacerdoti 1991).

## AN APPROACH TO MAKING INTERPERSONAL INTERACTION DECISIONS IN SPECIFIC SITUATIONS

The discussion to this point in the chapter has covered interpersonal strategies, tasks, skills, and techniques which are important aspects of the interpersonal interaction that is involved in KBS development and implementation. All are part of a knowledge engineer's job.

This section focuses on an approach to making decisions related to interpersonal interaction in a KBS development project. That approach is diagramed in Figure 11–2.

The discussion in this section explores how specific knowledge-based system, knowledge engineer, expert, user, organizational, and other resource factors are analyzed and structured, and then used in making key decisions involving interpersonal strategies, skills, tasks, and techniques.

A wide range of situations can be involved when making these decisions—from large and diverse KBS development projects involving hundreds of experts, knowledge engineers, and nontechnical users, such as Digital Equipment Corporation's XSEL system project, to situations involving a group of professionals working on a highly technical KBS.

Because of the wide range of possible decisions and decision situations, the approach described in this section is necessarily a general one, which is intended only to give an overview of the approach. Specific applications of this general approach are given in the final sections of the chapter.

Two key topics are discussed in this section:

- critical factors affecting decisions in this area
- making decisions based on these critical situation factors

### Critical Factors Affecting Decisions in This Area

Interpersonal interaction decisions are based on a variety of situational factors, as shown in Figure 11–2, including:

- purpose, nature, size, and complexity of the KBS
- types, number, and qualifications of knowledge engineers
- types of experts needed and available
- type of users involved and the impact of the KBS on their work routine
- organization factors

***The Nature, Purpose, Size, and Complexity of the KBS.*** These factors can affect the degree and kinds of interpersonal strategies, skills, and techniques needed in a KBS development effort in several ways. For example, if the purpose of a KBS is to assist a large number of computer sales personnel in a complex and dynamic domain, such as Digital Equipment's XSEL project (which is described in detail in Chapter 14), the interpersonal skills required to both acquire the knowledge

**Figure 11–2.** Knowledge Engineer Interpersonal Interaction—Overall Decision Situation Diagram

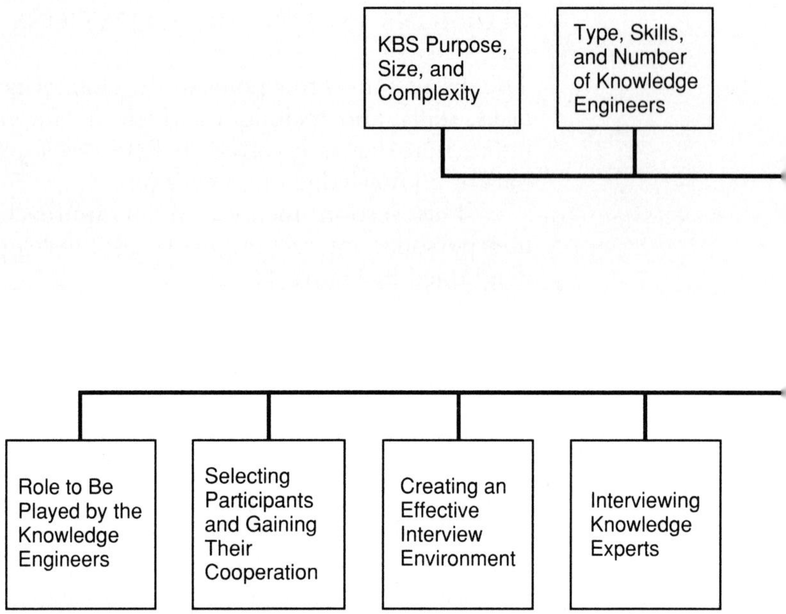


from the experts and to develop a KBS that the sales personnel can and will utilize would be considerable. At the other end of the spectrum, if a KBS is developed by an expert for personal use, that is, it is expert-driven, interpersonal considerations are of little consequence.

***Knowledge Engineers.*** The type, number, and qualifications of knowledge engineers also will impact on interpersonal interaction decisions. For instance, as the domain knowledge of a knowledge engineer increases, fewer general interpersonal skills may be required because the knowledge engineer can interact with, and understand the jargon of, experts in the domain more easily. This can lead to fewer interruptions to clarify terms, thinking processes, and basic concepts. If the knowledge engineer has a technical computer background and is unfamiliar with the knowledge domain, greater interpersonal skills may be needed. As more knowledge engineers are assigned to a project, interpersonal skill requirements will also often increase, since the more people involved, the greater the communication requirements often are.

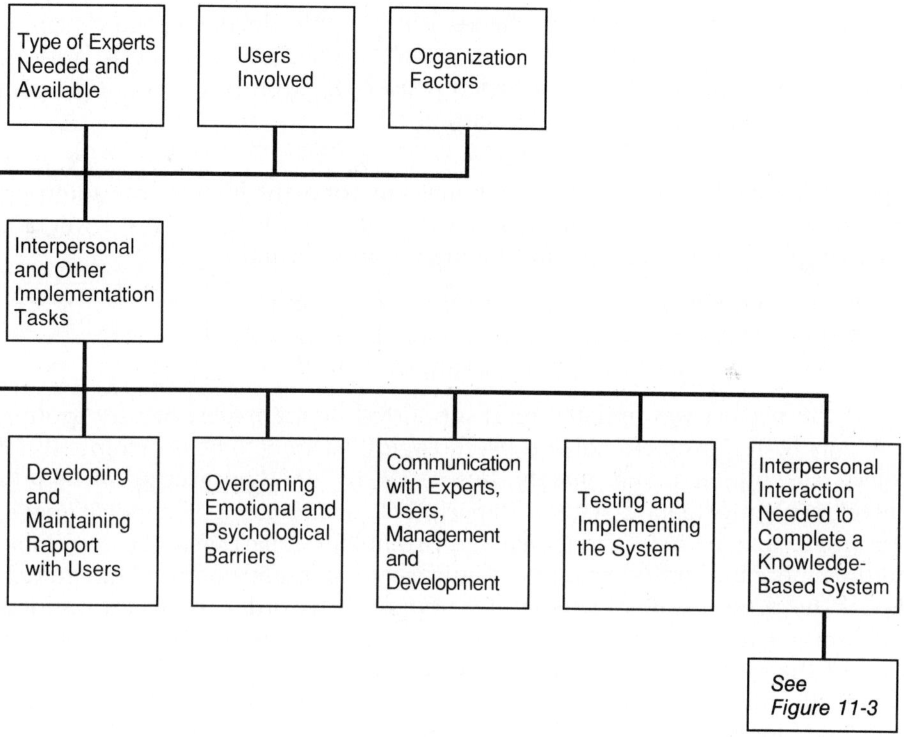


***Type of Experts Needed and Available.*** The type of experts to be used in the development of the KBS will also help determine which interpersonal strategies and techniques can be employed, and the interpersonal skills that will be needed. For example, secure experts may require less reassurance than insecure experts, who are more likely to feel their jobs are threatened. However, their time may be more valuable (to themselves and their firm) than that of other less secure experts and they may require that the benefits to be gained be made crystal clear. Also, as expert availability becomes more limited, audiotaping may be chosen as the record-keeping technique so that using the expert's time to clarify or restate information is minimized.

***Type of Users Involved and the Impact of the KBS on Their Work Routine.*** The type of users involved and the impact of the project on their work routine also helps determine which interpersonal strategies and techniques can be employed and the interpersonal skills that will be needed. If the KBS performs the major functions of a user's job, system users will require reassurance that it will help them perform their jobs better or more easily, and not replace them, as well as explanations of how their job will change with the introduction of the system. If the users will rely on the KBS for some aspect of their job, special care must be taken to ensure that the KBS is sufficiently user-effective. If it is not, it may not be used as intended, or may not be used at all.

***Organization Factors.*** The organizational environment impacts the interpersonal interaction in a variety of ways. An effective knowledge engineer will take into account several factors within the organization including:

- who initiated and is supporting the project, and why
- the number and kind of organizational units involved
- the geographic locations of the units involved

If the project was initiated or is supported by the expert or user groups, there may be fewer emotional and psychological barriers to be overcome. If the project was initiated and mainly supported by another group, such as a management information systems department, or members of upper management, there may be more emotional and psychological barriers to be overcome, and thus more and different types of interpersonal interaction will be required. Also, if the project was initiated and is supported in order to meet a business need and not just to test KBS technology, it will be easier to communicate the worth of the system to the people involved.

As the number and kind of organizational units involved increases and their geographic locations become more dispersed, stronger interpersonal skills are needed to deal with the increasing types and numbers of people involved. A knowledge engineer may have to communicate effectively with both highly technical experts and clerical staff. This communication challenge may be expanded if people are located in dispersed geographic locations and face-to-face communication is limited.

### Making Decisions Based on These Critical Situation Factors

The critical situation factors described in the preceding section are analyzed and used in making a variety of interpersonal interaction decisions, such as:

- determining the knowledge engineer's overall role
- selecting domain experts and determining how to deal with them
- orienting participants and gaining their cooperation
- creating an effective interview environment
- choosing interview techniques for use with domain experts
- developing and maintaining rapport with experts, users, management, and development personnel
- handling situations involving multiple experts and how to resolve any conflicts among them

- overcoming emotional and psychological barriers and handling special behavioral problems
- choosing ways to communicate with experts, users, management, and other development personnel
- identifying the level of interpersonal interaction needed in a knowledge-based system development effort

For example, the *role to be played by the knowledge engineer,* as mentioned earlier, can vary and include:

- manager and director
- facilitator
- coordinator and integrator
- listener

In deciding which role will be most effective in the situation under study, and in the phase of the KBS development cycle under study, several factors are considered. If the KBS to be developed is a large one, with multiple experts and users involved from different organizational units, the knowledge engineer may be more of a manager and coordinator. In smaller projects, the primary knowledge engineering interpersonal skill requirement may just be that of a good listener.

*How the experts are selected* and are dealt with may be influenced by their availability and their expected commitment to the project. The experts who are chosen should have as high a commitment to the project as possible, and preferably a proprietary interest. They should not be intimidated or feel threatened by the project, and should feel free to divulge all of their expertise. Achieving these goals, and making the compromises necessary, requires adapting ideal approaches to the situation constraints.

*Orienting participants and gaining their cooperation* may involve holding large staff meetings to stress the importance and goals of a project and its goals to the individuals involved and to the organization. It may involve showing each individual what is to be gained from the project. It may also be necessary to provide background information about KBS technology in general to those unfamiliar with it. The approaches used will vary with the situation factors identified.

*Creating an effective interview environment* will depend to a great extent on the characteristics of the individuals being interviewed and the environment in which they work. For example, if the work environment is an off-shore oil rig, the knowledge engineer and the expert may be too self-conscious about their safety to have an effective interview. Also, if the individuals are very self-conscious, audio- and videotaping may intimidate them. If this is the case, note taking should be used, and a nonthreatening, familiar environment should be chosen for the interview location. However, if video- or audiotaping is still required, the individuals being interviewed should be told well in advance of the taping so they can get used to the idea. It should also be anticipated that the individual will be very self-conscious during the first few tapings and that this may lessen as the process becomes more familiar.

The *interview techniques* used with domain experts will depend on the availability and commitment of the experts, the type of knowledge to be acquired, and the phase the project is in. As expert availability and commitment to the project increases, and where the type of knowledge to be acquired is less well defined and the project is in its earlier phases, more unstructured interview techniques can be used and may be needed. As expert availability and commitment to the project decreases, and where the type of knowledge to be acquired is better defined and the project is in its later phases, more structured interview techniques can be used and may be needed.

*How rapport with experts, users, management, and systems development personnel is created and maintained* is influenced by the purpose, nature, size, and complexity of the KBS, as well as by the types of individuals involved. If it is anticipated that the purpose of the KBS may threaten the position or prestige of a group or several groups involved in the project, specific steps appropriate to situation factors must be taken to develop rapport with each group that will enable the knowledge engineer to communicate with, and influence, the involved parties.

When *handling situations involving multiple experts and resolving any conflicts among them,* the purpose and benefits of the KBS should be stressed as well as the need for a team effort. If experts disagree as to how decisions should be made, either a consensus can be reached or the opinions of the more experienced experts may be used. In any case, the input of all the experts should still be acknowledged so that they will continue to provide needed input. As in other decision areas, the people involved, as well as other situation characteristics, dictate the approaches used.

*Overcoming emotional and psychological barriers and handling special behavioral problems* may be a particular problem if the developed KBS will substantially alter the regular tasks of the individuals involved. This may also result if the individuals are intimidated or feel threatened by the project and its goals. Selecting the approaches to use will depend on the situation factors identified.

*Choosing effective ways to communicate with experts, users, management, and other systems development personnel* will depend to a large extent on the size of the project, its complexity, who must be communicated with, and where they are located. Written documentation may be the main form of communication with units or groups located in dispersed geographic areas. The larger the project is, the more likely it is that different groups will require communication of the project's status and its progress in meeting its goals. Communication with management may be particularly important to ensure that adequate resources are provided, while communication with experts, users, and other personnel may be critical in gaining and keeping their support and cooperation, depending on situation requirements.

*The level of interpersonal interaction needed* in a knowledge-based system development effort depends on its purpose, nature, size, and complexity, as well as the number and types of knowledge engineers, experts, users, management, and other personnel involved.

The above discussion is clearly only a brief summary of all that is involved in making these decisions, since it is designed only to introduce the subject. A number of experimental KBS prototypes have been developed in the area of KBS implementation, which define in much greater detail the way situation factors influence each of these decisions. For example, Figures 11–3, 11–4, 11–5, and 11–6 give the decision situation diagrams for a prototype system used to determine how much personal interaction is needed in a KBS development effort. Figure 11–7 gives the dependency diagram of the KBS based on these decision situation models.

## KBS IMPLEMENTATION: SPECIAL PROBLEMS IN SYSTEM INSTALLATION, TESTING AND VALIDATION/VERIFICATION, DOCUMENTATION, INTRODUCTION, EVALUATION, AND MAINTENANCE

The following sections cover several additional important aspects of system implementation.

**Figure 11–3.** Amount of Knowledge Engineer Interpersonal Interaction Needed When Dealing with Experts: Overall Decision Situation Diagram

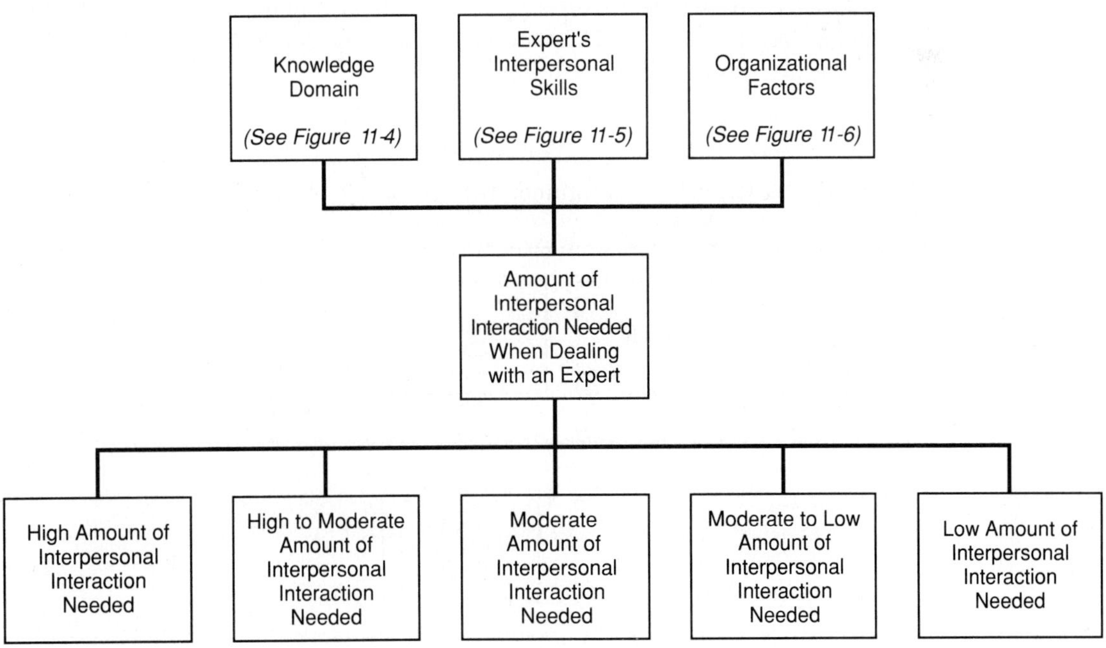

**Figure 11–4.** Knowledge Engineer Interpersonal Interaction Decision Situation: Knowledge Domain Factors

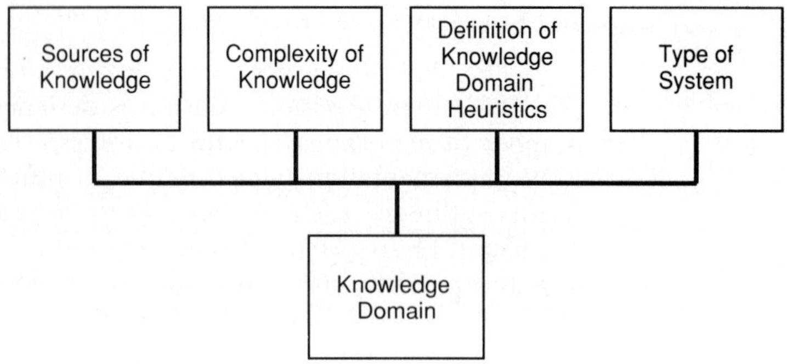


### System Installation

The substantial user involvement in many KBS development projects usually means that some preparations for the installation and use of the system have been going on throughout the development cycle.

As the time for installing the system nears, more formal steps are often needed. These steps may involve integrating the system with other systems and operations, which in turn might involve changing work routines and introducing new users to the system. At other times, the introduction may have been built up to gradually, so that the transition to the final system creates only minimal problems. Several aspects of system installation in a variety of KBS development situations are discussed in the following sections.

**Figure 11–5.** Knowledge Engineer Interpersonal Interaction Decision Situation: Expert Factors

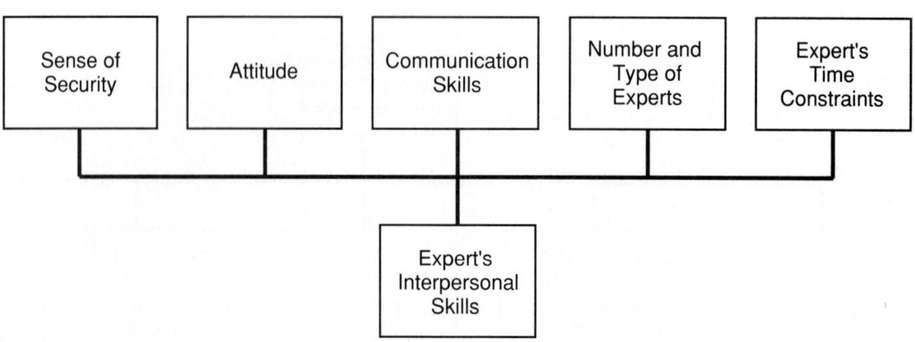

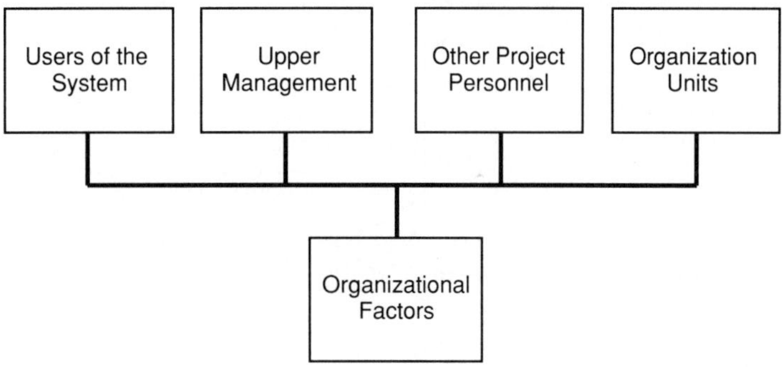


**Figure 11–6.** Knowledge Engineer Interpersonal Interaction Decision Situation: Organizational Factors

### System Testing and Validation/Verification

Clearly, if a system does not work as promised, it will not succeed. That is why this phase is so critical. Systems validation/verification, which most often includes beta testing or field testing the system, involves testing the system from a number of viewpoints:

- System performance—does it accurately represent an expert's knowledge in a particular problem domain and does it do what it was intended to do (O'Leary 1990)?
- Peak load performance—can it handle all situations?
- Human engineering—is it suitable for users?
- Methods and procedures—are the procedures and methods for using the system in day-to-day operations adequate?
- Back up and recovery—can the operation function during times when the primary system is down?

During the 1990s, considerable work was being done in formulating ways to validate and verify KBS. Validation usually refers to the system's mechanical compliance to technical requirements, and verification to the system's fulfillment of its purposes and user requirements (Landauer 1990, p. 293). The following discussion reviews some of the highlights of this emerging research area.

Testing systems can involve searching for what are referred to as static errors—for example, spelling errors, use of reserved words, rules that do not link with the rest of the knowledge base, and other technical problems. Many of these can be detected by a careful reading of the knowledge base or by using an interactive tool such as Validator (Kang 1990) or EVA (Chang 1990), by following formal validation/verification procedures drawn from conventional programming disciplines (O'Keefe 1990; Wood 1990; Oxman 1991), or by using one of several newly emerging KBS testing techniques and models (Barrett 1990;

**Figure 11–7.** Knowledge Engineer Interpersonal Interaction Decision System—Dependency Diagram (Initial Prototype)

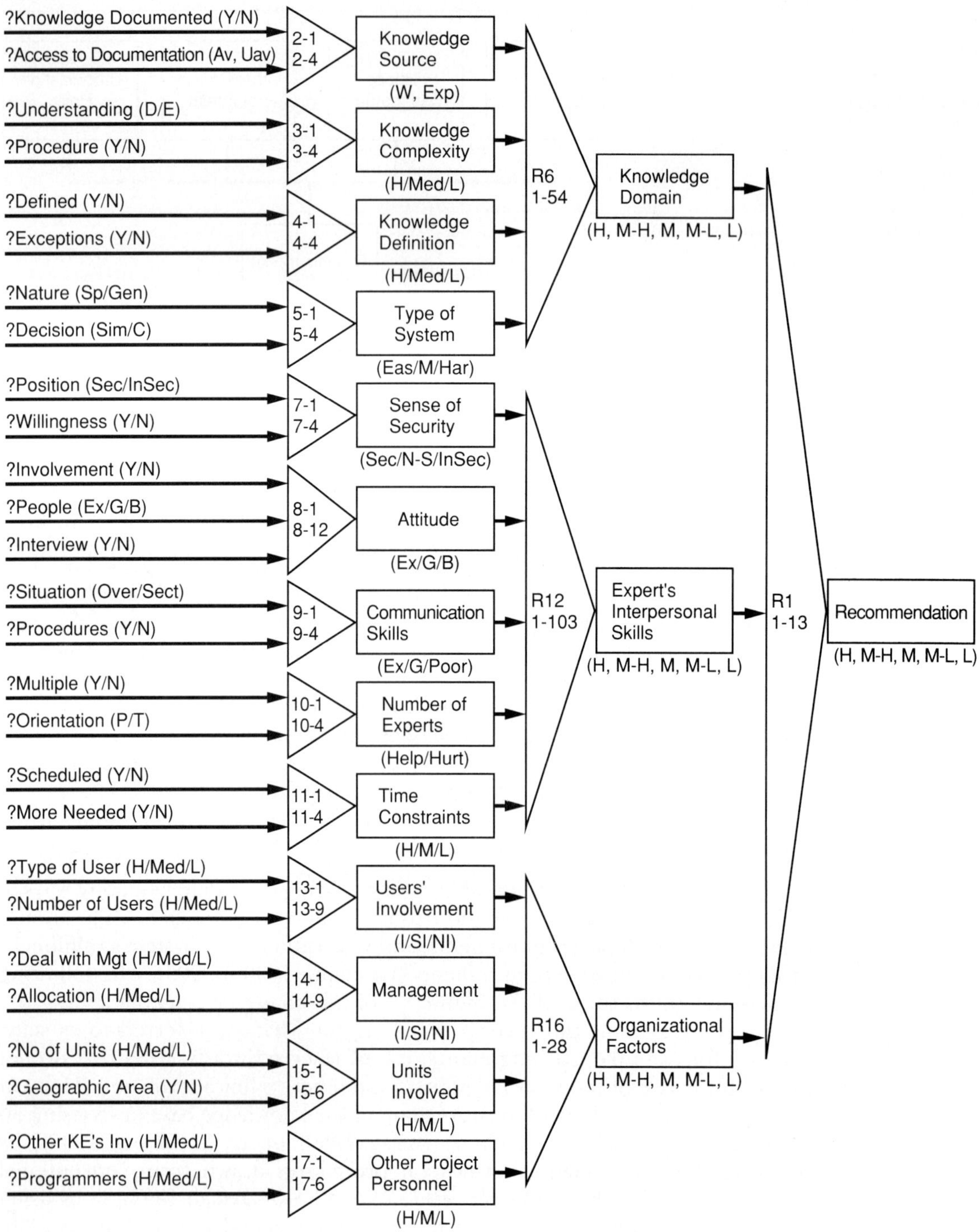

*Key*

| | | | |
|---|---|---|---|
| Y = Yes | Sec = Secure | P = People | Har = Hardest |
| N = No | N–S = Not Sure | T = Technical | Help = Help |
| Av = Available | InSec = Insecure | H = High | Hurt = Hurt |
| Uav = Unavailable | Ex = Excellent | M–H = Moderate to High | I = Involved |
| D = Difficult | G = Good | M = Moderate | SI = Semi-Involved |
| E = Easy | B = Bad | M–L = Moderate to Low | NI = Not Involved |
| Sp = Specific | Poor = Poor | L = Low | |
| Gen = General | Over = Overall | Med = Medium | |
| Sim = Simple | Sect = Sections | W = Written | |
| C = Complex | | Exp = Expert | |
| | | Eas = Easiest | |

Constantine 1990; Linden 1990; Miller 1990; Ribar 1991). Techniques have also been developed for testing the accuracy of the knowledge-domain models (Bellman 1990).

Testing KBS always involves the time-consuming process of running test cases. These test cases involve expert-generated tests, such as having the expert use the system for a variety of actual decisions and having a printout trace the line of reasoning. The typical decision scenarios discussed in Chapter 2 and in several of the chapters in Part Five are examples of this procedure (O'Leary 1990).

Test cases can also be created by the knowledge engineer and system designer, and be used to test the efficiency and accuracy of the system design. Test cases from a user's viewpoint are also needed. All three critical viewpoints, expert, user, and system designer, need to be tested and evaluated during the validation/verification phase (Kang 1990).

A problem the knowledge engineer may encounter during the testing and implementation is the reconciliation of viewpoints of the technical personnel, experts, and users. In larger KBS projects, if the system is not completely debugged, which is very often the case, technical system design and development personnel will have to get involved in this phase.

The knowledge engineer often, therefore, has to act as the buffer between computer information systems technicians and experts and users. Here the problem is not only satisfying user needs within the technical limitations of computer systems. It is also translating user needs into technical frames of reference, and translating technical terminology into a vocabulary that a user can understand.

### Introduction of the System into the User Environment

The same attention to planning and managing interpersonal interactions is needed in delivering the system into the user environment and in getting it used effectively, as is needed in designing and developing the system.

In many situations, the system introduction may have to be planned and carried out in stages, because of limited personnel, wide geographic dispersion of users, or other similar problems. This was the case at Coopers & Lybrand when introducing their ExperTAX KBS in the mid-1980s. The program they used is described in Chapter 13 and in Appendix B.

This phase can include creating user manuals that are clear and easy to follow. This can require specialized help, since technical manual writing is becoming an art form.

User training programs may also have to be established. In larger projects, this may involve decisions about who will do the training, how long it will last, the training methods to be used, location of the training, and other key aspects of formal training program planning and implementation.

Since the users are the ones who are going to actually employ the system, in order for the KBS to be considered effective it will have to *suit user needs* and *be accepted by users.* For these reasons, an effective knowledge engineer will listen to any criticism that the users may have of the system during all phases of development, and if at all possible a knowledge engineer will try to integrate the expressed needs of the users into the system. In this way, the users will feel more a part of the implementation process and be more receptive to using it. In addition, the system will be more user-effective.

Techniques useful in building effective user interfaces were discussed in Chapter 10. Incorporating these techniques into the design of the system involves including users in the KBS development process during its early phases. In addition, it involves using the same interpersonal techniques described earlier for dealing with domain experts—when selecting users to participate in the KBS development, briefing them, creating effective interview environments, interviewing, developing and maintaining rapport, overcoming psychological and emotional barriers, and communicating with them in appropriate ways, as required by the situation.

### System Evaluation

Thompson and Feinstein (1990) describe an approach to estimating the value of a KBS during the proposal stages:

- describe the project
- measure the benefits
- estimate the cost
- provide a summary cost/benefit analysis

A sample of such a cost/benefit analysis, based upon an analysis of the perceived benefits of a project and its estimated costs, is given in Figure 11–8.

Such initial evaluations provide a framework for evaluating a KBS after it has been installed and used. These post-installation evaluations are important, in order to provide a more objective basis for planning future KBS development

**Figure 11–8.** KBS Cost/Benefit Analysis Worksheet

| OUT-OF-POCKET COSTS | | RISK | NET | ONE-TIME | ONGOING | |
|---|---|---|---|---|---|---|
| Software | ($2,000) | 1.0 | ($2,000) | ($2,000) | | |
| Hardware | ($12,000) | 1.0 | ($12,000) | ($12,000) | | |
| Training | ($3,000) | 1.0 | ($3,000) | ($3,000) | | |
| Licensing | ($1,200) | 1.0 | ($1,200) | ($1,200) | | |
| Documentation | ($800) | 1.0 | ($800) | ($800) | | |
| Consulting | ($6,000) | 1.0 | ($6,000) | ($6,000) | | |
| Total out-of-pocket costs | | | | ($25,000) | | |
| **LABOR COSTS** | | **RISK** | **NET** | **ONE-TIME** | **ONGOING** | |
| Expert time | ($2,000) | 1.4 | ($2,800) | ($2,800) | ($750) | |
| Knowledge Eng. | ($4,000) | 1.6 | ($6,400) | ($6,400) | | |
| Programming | ($6,000) | 1.2 | ($7,200) | ($7,200) | ($1,250) | |
| Training | ($2,000) | 1.0 | ($2,000) | ($2,000) | ($500) | |
| Testing | ($1,000) | 1.1 | ($1,100) | ($1,100) | ($500) | |
| Validation | ($1,500) | 1.0 | ($1,500) | ($1,500) | ($500) | |
| QA | ($1,500) | 1.2 | ($1,800) | ($1,800) | ($500) | |
| Evaluation | ($1,500) | 1.0 | ($1,500) | ($1,500) | | |
| Maintenance | ($3,000) | 1.2 | ($3,600) | | ($3,600) | |
| Operation | ($2,000) | 1.1 | ($2,200) | | ($2,200) | |
| Total labor costs | | | | ($24,300) | ($9,800) | |
| | | | | | × 2 years | |
| COST GRAND TOTAL | | | | ($49,300) | ($19,600) | |
| **BENEFITS** | | **RISK** | **NET** | **ONE-TIME** | **ONGOING** | ($68,900) |
| Time saved | $5,000 | 0.8 | | $4,000 | $12,000 | |
| Productivity | $4,000 | 0.9 | | $3,600 | $7,000 | |
| Loss reduction | $3,000 | 0.6 | | $1,800 | $4,000 | |
| Less rework | $1,500 | 0.6 | | $900 | $1,500 | |
| Accuracy | $1,000 | 0.9 | | $900 | $12,000 | |
| Total tangible benefits | | | | $11,200 | $36,500 | |
| Strategic | $6,000 | 0.6 | | $3,600 | $3,000 | |
| Opportunities | $5,000 | 0.6 | | $3,000 | $5,000 | |
| Loyalty | $2,000 | 0.5 | | $1,000 | $1,000 | |
| Service | $2,000 | 0.7 | | $1,400 | $1,000 | |
| Knowledge | $6,000 | 0.8 | | $4,800 | $2,000 | |
| Total intangible benefits | | | | $13,800 | $12,000 | |
| Total Benefits | | | | $25,000 | $48,500 | × 2 |
| | | | | | × 2 years | $122,000 |
| NET BENEFITS | | | | $25,000 | $97,000 | $53,100 |

projects, and to encourage additional investment by company management in these systems.

A survey of company experiences reported by Ruth (1989) indicates that system evaluations show very promising returns on many investments in KBS. At DuPont, for example, a typical application developed during the late 1980s (the company did hundreds) cost about $20,000 and paid back ten to twenty times the investment. Similar results have been experienced at large accounting firms and automobile manufacturers. American Express also experienced high returns from implementing expert systems in their credit-approval operations. In situations where the KBS development has been carefully planned, improvements in annual return on investment from KBS projects in many instances seem to far exceed the percentage returns from investments in traditional MIS applications.

### System Documentation

System documentation—documentation of how the system was designed and of how it was designed to operate—are necessary for both system development and system maintenance.

Adequate documentation—in the form of knowledge handbooks or dictionaries or other media—is important especially in larger systems during the development phases, since many people will work on such projects over a span of time and new team members need to know the reasoning behind what has been done by others, if they are to be effective.

The same principle holds true for KBS of any size. While knowledge bases may be available, often explanations of the reasoning behind them is not. During development, adequate records are indispensable in anticipation of the day when others not familiar with these earlier phases may need them to do further development or modifications of the system, or to simply maintain the system.

Frequently, there is some reluctance to adequately document the entire system. The authors' experience has been that conventional computer systems developers very often have trouble understanding the major role that nontechnical experts and users can have in developing and in maintaining a KBS. Hence they resist or neglect providing the depth of explanations and other documentation that is needed during later system development and maintenance phases.

For example, in reviewing the several hundred systems development projects the authors have been involved in, where nontechnical managers were involved in the development, system documentation understandable to experts and users was almost always available. This enabled the systems to continue to grow and evolve over time.

On the other hand, in almost every situation where system technicians played a major role, the documentation was rarely adequate unless considerable pressure was brought to bear on the system personnel. Those systems lacking adequate documentation understandable to nontechnical managers almost always died eventually from lack of expert and user involvement, since most KBS exist in a dynamic business environment. KBS are normally used instead of conventional computer systems because they are easily updated, and adaptable to dynamic, changing situation requirements. Adequate documentation therefore is essential to effective system maintenance.

### System Maintenance

Maintenance is especially important in KBS, as pointed out in the preceding section, because KBS are usually built on the premise that they are replicating a dynamic situation and therefore change can be expected.

This usually means allocating time and personnel to, and developing procedures for, continuing "postimplementation" reviews of a system. These reviews are done to:

- evaluate the system to determine its operational effectiveness and its cost effectiveness, and to reverify its actual cost savings
- evaluate user satisfaction
- identify ways to improve or modify the system
- identify ways to improve general system development practices
- help train new users and new system development personnel (Kumar 1990)

As an example, a technique has been developed for tracing the utilization of rules in KBS during use (Madeo 1990). This analytical tool facilitates identifying overused rules (so that they may be refined) and unnecessary or underused rules (which may be edited or eliminated).

Some generally applicable maintenance lessons learned at GTE Laboratories when developing the KBS COMPASS cover the following areas (Prerau 1990):

- *Software modularity and task assignment.* The modularity of an expert system cannot be defined solely in a way that is convenient for software development.

  *Problem.* Designing an expert system's top level modularity. The system must roughly follow the modularity of an expert's knowledge. As a result, separate parts of the system may be more interdependent than is desirable for software engineering reasons. Yet the system must be modularized in such a way that each developer can work on a module without depending too much on other developers.

  *Solution.* Divide the program into several knowledge bases, some corresponding to a recognizable subtask of the expert task, and some providing necessary abstractions.
- *Style.* Different parts of COMPASS written by different people were sometimes written in different styles.

  *Problem.* Ensuring that the COMPASS software had a uniform "look" to aid in use and maintainability.

  *Solution.* Adopt programming conventions.

- *The maintainability of knowledge.* When a choice of programming paradigms exists, one major factor in selection should be the resulting program's maintainability.
  *Problem.* Representing knowledge in the system to make it as easy as possible for non-CS personnel to maintain.
  *Solution.* Use rules or frame structures rather than programming language code wherever possible.
- *Configuration management and control.* Expert system development environments provide access to multiple generic AI paradigms. Tool developers concentrate on these characteristics and thus provide few system management tools.
  *Problem.* Providing system management tools to facilitate development and maintenance.
  *Solution.* Develop a configuration control facility for maintenance.
- *Data access.* If data access requirements and data access paths are not clear (as is often true in systems with multiple knowledge bases and data-activated procedures), maintenance becomes much more difficult.
  *Problem.* Clarifying and standardizing dataflow.
  *Solution.* Adopt a set of conventions and use a generic mechanism for inter-knowledge-base data access.
- *Control flow.* Complex expert system programs often have complex flow paths, not just within routines but also between knowledge bases and objects.
  *Problem.* Clarifying how the flow is controlled—flow control in an object-oriented programming system is often unclear, which causes problems for maintainers.
  *Solution.* Develop a top-level knowledge base that defines the control flow, and adopt a set of conventions for initiating action within a knowledge base.
- *Input and output.* Providing structured formalisms for input and output can aid maintainability.
  *Problem.* Improving the maintainability and flexibility of input and output. Large systems often contain a scattering of input and output statements written for a specific terminal.
  *Solution.* Develop a knowledge base to serve as a central clearinghouse for input and output.

## INTEGRATION WITH CONVENTIONAL COMPUTER SYSTEMS

One of the fastest growing uses of KBS technology in business is in conjunction with conventional computer systems. Knowledge-based systems may be **embedded** within and/or integrated with conventional computer systems in a variety of ways. As one example, they are now found as so-called "front ends" of database management systems (Gralla 1988; Schur 1988). As Chapnick (1988) points out, while there will always be a need for some true stand-alone knowledge-based systems, most of these systems in the future must be prepared to integrate in some way with conventional systems and processes already in place and in use.

American Express, for instance, has developed a system that enables its telephone operators to check multiple databases when approving credit purchases. This in turn has enabled the company to operate without advertised credit limits, and given them a competitive advantage in the credit card market. This system would be classified as an integrated front end for their existing customer files and systems (Alper 1987). A considerable amount of work is being done in developing so-called intelligent databases (Harmon 1990; Schur 1988). A detailed example of the integration of KBS with a database is given in Chapter 5.

Integration with spreadsheets, such as Lotus 1-2-3, is also becoming fairly common. For example, GURU, an expert systems development shell, has a built-in spreadsheet for integrated applications. A detailed example of the integration of KBS with a spreadsheet is given in the tutorial in Chapter 5. Other examples of the integration and embedding of AI technology with Lotus 1-2-3 are given by Hintz (1989) and Johnston (1990).

The commercial loan screening KBS outlined in Figure 11–9 has three integrated or embedded KBS within a system that uses conventional spreadsheet analysis and databases. The first checks for the loan's compliance with corporate strategic objectives, the second helps evaluate the management of the company seeking the loan, and the third focuses on studying the company's strategic or long-term prospects (Mockler 1989). A much larger version of such an integrated system with embedded KBS segments, Lending Advisor, is sold by Syntelligence.

Lance Eliot (1989) has described several "mass market" expert system applications which combine KBS with conventional computer system technology. These are still available in the early 1990s. These applications range in price from under $100 to $500. They include:

- determining sample sizes for statistical studies
- technical stock trading
- pediatric advice

Integration is also being done in the financial area (Freundlich 1990), as well as in a variety of DSS/KBS areas (Eliot 1990).

Stone & Webster has developed a number of integrated systems in the manufacturing area (Stone 1990). For example, Stone & Webster's Production Scheduling Advisor integrates a commercial expert systems shell with interactive graphics, optimizers, and spreadsheets. The user controls the Advisor through a proprietary interactive graphics module. The graphics illustrate the production schedule, together with constraints in the form of a bar chart, or Gantt chart. Production cycles can be manually added, deleted, stretched, or moved with an electronic mouse. The spreadsheets contain product demand data which is

**Figure 11–9.** Overall Dependency Diagram: Commercial Loan Screening System (Initial Prototype)

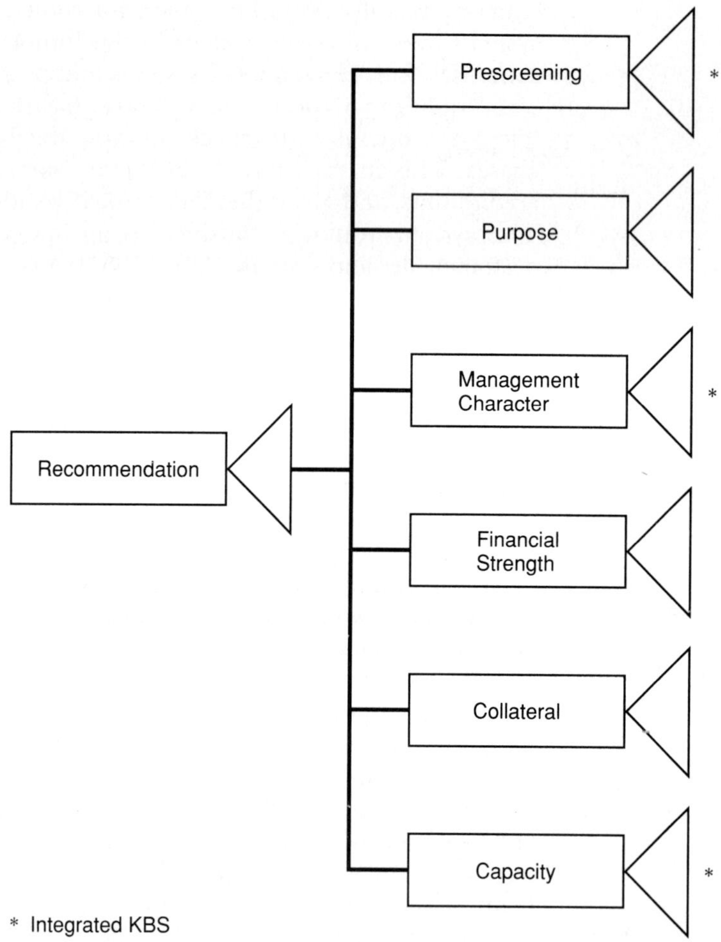


entered either manually or directly from a corporate sales and order system. The spreadsheets also model the production parameters such as physical constraints, rates, and unit availabilities.

Typically, the scheduler works with the most recent schedule. After updating the Advisor with latest product-demand requirements, an optimizer, a commercial linear programming package, is called from the Gantt chart. The optimizer adjusts production starting dates and durations for each product to satisfy as many inventory and other constraints as possible. The expert system is called from the Gantt chart to help diagnose schedule problems that the optimizer cannot solve. It identifies problems and makes recommendations. The expert system also checks feasibilities of meeting demands and suggest a sequence for the scheduling of units and products. In order to facilitate such interaction and integration, Stone & Webster has developed a blackboard tool which links commercially available graphics and other conventional software with three expert system development shells, EXSYS, LEVEL5, and NEXPERT.

## IMPACT OF KBS AND THEIR DEVELOPMENT ON THE MANAGEMENT INFORMATION SYSTEMS AREA

It is clear that new systems technologies involving DSS and KBS have both initiated and reinforced the development of many current trends in MIS in the 1990s. These include:

- Encouraging more frequent use of prototyping, to improve MIS development accuracy and efficiency, to foster more user involvement in the MIS development process, to give users more proprietary interest in the MIS, and to generate more excitement and general enthusiasm for the MIS being developed (Foss 1990)
- Helping system development personnel become more sensitive to user-department needs and spend more time on investigating user requirements (Pastore 1989)
- Encouraging more user involvement in MIS development
- Fostering system development flexibility and forcing MIS to more frequently adapt to and accommodate user needs, rather than requiring users to adapt to MIS technological requirements
- Fostering more "downsizing" of computer operations, that is, placing them more under the control of user departments (Radding 1989)
- Creating more "end user computing" groups within traditional MIS departments (Carr 1988)
- Increasing the importance of nontechnical training, skills, and experience among systems analysts of the 1990s (Israel 1990)

## REVIEW QUESTIONS

1. Describe the role of interpersonal interaction both in developing and implementing KBS.
2. Describe the varying roles played by a knowledge engineer during the KBS development cycle.
3. Describe two typical situations that demonstrate a range of interpersonal tasks involved in KBS implementation.

4. Discuss some of the steps that can be taken to effectively orient development project participants and gain their cooperation.
5. Describe some of the ways that a knowledge engineer might go about handling interviews in order to make them more effective and efficient during knowledge acquisition and when introducing KBS into the user environment.
6. Identify some of the psychological and emotional problems that may be encountered in carrying out a KBS development project and describe ways in which they can be overcome.
7. Discuss some of the steps that can be taken to improve team communications.
8. Describe the critical factors that are considered when making decisions about, and handling, interpersonal interactions during KBS development and implementation.
9. The critical factors identified in the previous answer are analyzed and used in making a variety of interpersonal interaction decisions. Identify some of them.
10. Discuss the importance of system testing and validation to successful implementation of KBS.
11. Describe why ongoing system maintenance is especially important in KBS projects and discuss the role of documentation in promoting effective maintenance.
12. Discuss why evaluation is important in the post-implementation phases of KBS development.

## EXERCISES

1. After reviewing the decision situation and dependency diagram outlines in Figures 11–2 through 11–7 and the discussion in the chapter section entitled "An Approach to Making Interpersonal Interaction Decisions in Specific Situations," develop a small KBS to assist in making any of the implementation strategy decisions discussed in this chapter. Follow the directions in either Chapter 2, or in Chapters 3 through 6, when developing the system.
2. Read through recent issues of KBS periodicals, and through other related artificial intelligence and KBS implementation periodicals and books, and find discussion of the main topics covered in this chapter. Write a brief report describing how this reading provided you with insights and guidance when developing your KBS for Exercise 1.

## REFERENCES

Alper, Alan. "Expert System Versus Credit Fraud." *Computerworld,* April 13, 1987, pp. 25, 30.

Bailey, Jennifer Jo. *Economic Evaluation of Knowledge-Based Systems.* Master of Science Paper, Boston, MA: Massachusetts Institute of Technology, 1987.

Barrett, Britt W. "A Hypothetical Application of the Statistical Modelling and Estimation of Reliability Functions for Software (SMERFS) to Knowledge-Based Systems (KBSs)." *Expert Systems With Applications,* 1(3), Fall 1990, pp. 281–89.

Bellman, Kirstie L. "The Modelling Issues Inherent in Testing and Evaluating Knowledge-Based Systems." *Expert Systems With Applications.* 1 (3), Fall 1990, pp. 199–215.

Buchanan, Bruce G., et al. "Constructing an Expert System." In *Building Expert Systems.* eds. Frederick Hayes-Roth et al. Reading, MA.: Addison-Wesley, 1983, pp. 127–68.

Carr, Houston H. *Managing End User Computing.* Englewood Cliffs, NJ: Prentice Hall, 1988.

Chang, C. L., J. B. Combs, and R. A Stachowitz. "A Report on the Expert Systems Validation Associate (EVA)." *Expert Systems With Applications.* 1 (3), Fall 1990, pp. 217–30.

Chapnick, Philip. "MIS Is Not the Enemy." *AI Expert.* April 1988, pp. 5–6.

Chau, Patrick Y. K. "Non-Technical Barriers to Successful Expert Systems: Sources and Ways to Overcome Them." *Information Executive,* Winter 1990, pp. 51–53.

Constantine, Monica M., and Jacob W. Ulvila. "Testing Knowledge-Based Systems: The State of the Practice and Suggestions for Improvement." *Expert Systems With Applications.* Volume 1 (3), Fall 1990, pp. 237–48.

D'Aprix, Roger. "The Oldest (and Best) Way to Communicate with Employees." *Harvard Business Review,* September-October 1982, pp. 30ff.

Dologite, D. G. and Robert J. Mockler. "Developing Effective Knowledge-Based Systems: Overcoming Cognitive, Organizational and Individual Behavioral Barriers." *Information Resources Management Journal,* Winter 1989, pp. 27–40.

Edwards, Alex. "What is the Answer? In That Case, What is the Question?" *Accountancy,* August 1987, pp. 97–99.

Eliot, Lance B. "Decision Analysis and Expert Systems." *Decision Line,* December/January 1990, p. 7.

Eliot, Lance B. " Mass Market Applications: They're Here." *AI Expert,* December 1989, pp. 9–14.

Evanson, Steven E. "How to Talk to an Expert." *AI Expert,* February 1988, pp. 36–42.

Foss, W. Burry. "Early Wins Are Key to System Success." *Datamation,* January 15, 1990, pp. 79–82.

Freundlich, Yehudah. "Transfer Pricing: Integrating Expert Systems in MIS Environments." *IEEE Expert,* February 1990, pp. 54–64.

Garber, Sharon, Paul E. Johnson, and Imran Zualkernan, "Specification of Expertise." *International Journal of Man-Machine Studies,* 26, 1987, pp. 161–81.

Gralla, Preston. "Embedded AI: The Look of Things to Come." *PC Week,* April 19, 1988, pp. 106–07.

Harmon, Paul, and Brian Sawyer. *Creating Expert Systems.* New York: Wiley, 1990.

Herzberg, Frederich. "How Do You Motivate Employees?" *Harvard Business Review,* September-October 1987, pp. 109ff.

Hintz, Richard. "If/Then . . . The Hands-On Introduction to Artificial Intelligence Using Lotus 1-2-3." *PC AI,* September/October 1989, pp. 50–51.

Israel, Burt. "Hiring Systems Analysts for the 1990s." *Information Executive,* Winter 1990, pp. 35–36.

Johnston, Stuart J. "AI Technology Hides in Traditional Software." *Infoworld,* March 5, 1990, pp. 15–16.

Kang, Yue, and A. Terry Bahill. "A Tool for Detecting Expert System Errors." *AI Expert,* February 1990, pp. 46–51.

Keen, Peter G. W. *Business Without Bounds: Telecommunications and Business Strategy.* Cambridge, MA: Ballinger Publishing, 1986.

Keen, Peter G. W. *Computing in Time: Using Telecommunications For Competitive Advantage.* Cambridge, MA: Ballinger Publishing, 1988.

Keen, Peter G. W. "Interview." *Information Management Review,* Winter 1989, pp. 65–75.

Keller, Robert. *Expert System Technology: Development and Applications.* New York: Yourdon Press, 1987.

Kumar, Kuldeep. "Post Implementation Evaluation of Computer-Based Information Systems: Current Practices." *Communications of the ACM,* February 1990, pp. 203–12.

LaFrance, Marianne. "The Knowledge Acquisition Grid: A Method for Training Knowledge Engineers." *International Journal of Man-Machine Studies,* 26, 1987, pp. 245–55.

Landauer, Christopher. "Correctness Principles for Rule-Based Expert Systems." *Expert Systems With Applications,* 1 (3), Fall, 1990, pp 291–316.

Linden, Theodore A. "A Meta-Level Software Development Model That Supports V&V for AI Software." *Expert Systems With Applications,* 1 (3), Fall 1990, pp. 271–79.

Madeo, Lawrence A., and Reuven R. Levary. "On Maintaining and Updating Expert Systems." *Expert Systems,* May 1990, pp. 121–23.

Mahler, Ed. "Developing Expert Systems at DuPont." *Expert Systems: Getting Business Results From Applied AI.* Randall Davis Seminar, New York, NY: Decision Support Technology, October 26–28, 1987.

McGraw, K., and K. Harbison-Briggs. *Knowledge Acquisition,* Englewood Cliffs, NJ: Prentice-Hall, 1989.

Miller, Lance A. "Dynamic Testing of Knowledge Bases Using the Heuristic Testing Approach." *Expert Systems With Applications,* 1 (3), Fall 1990, pp. 249–69.

Mockler, Robert J. *Knowledge-Based Systems for Strategic Planning.* Englewood Cliffs, NJ: Prentice-Hall, 1989.

Mockler, R. J. "Non-Technical Managers' Modelling of Management Decision Situations." *Journal of Systems Management,* May 1990, pp. 7–13.

Mockler, Robert J. "Strategies for Transferring Information Systems Tasks to Managers: The Changing Knowledge Engineering Role." Accepted for publication in *The Review of Business Studies,* Fall 1991.

O'Keefe, Robert M., and Sunro Lee. "An Integrative Model of Expert System Verification and Validation." *Expert Systems With Applications,* 1 (3), Fall 1990, pp. 231–48.

O'Leary, Timothy, Michael Goul, Kathleen E. Moffett, and E. Essam Radivam. "Validating Expert Systems." *IEEE Expert,* June 1990, pp. 51–58.

Oxman, Steven W. "Reporting Chemical Spills: An Expert Solution." *AI Expert,* May 1991, pp. 50–51.

Pastore, Richard. "Shhh! Don't Talk Tech at Cadbury." *Computerworld,* September 25, 1989, pp. 65–66.

Prerau, David A., Alan S. Genderson, Robert E. Reinke, and Mark R. Adler. "Maintainability Techniques in Developing Large Expert Systems." *IEEE Expert,* June 1990, pp. 71–80.

Radding, Alan. "Technology Issues in Downsizing." *Computerworld,* June 12, 1989, pp. 69–78.

Ribar, Gary, Frank Arcoleo, and Denise Hollo. "Loan Probe: Testing a Big Expert System." *AI Expert,* May 1991, pp. 43–49.

Rogers, Carl R., and F. J. Roethlisberger. "Barriers and Gateways to Communication." *Harvard Business Review,* July-August 1952, pp. 46ff.

Ruth, Stephen R. "Expert Systems For Competitive Advantage: A Bottom Line Perspective." *Proceedings: 10th International Conference on Information Systems.* Boston, MA: Society for Information Management, December 4–6, 1989, p. 396.

Sacerdoti, Earl D. "Managing Expert System Development." *AI Expert,* May 1991, pp. 26–33.

Schur, Stephen. "The Intelligent Database." *AI Expert,* January 1988, pp. 26–34.

Shpilberg, David, Lynford E. Graham, and Harry Schatz, "ExperTAX: An Expert System for Corporate Tax Planning." *Expert Systems,* July 1986, pp. 136–51.

Stewart, Charles J., and William B. Case. *Interviewing: Principles and Practices,* 4th ed. Dubuque, IA: William C. Brown Publisher, 1985.

Stone & Webster. "Integrated Expert Systems for Manufacturing." *AI Review,* July/August 1990, pp. 43–46.

Thompson, Donna M., and Jerald L. Feinstein. "Cost Justifying Expert Systems." In *Managing Artificial Intelligence and Expert Systems,* edited by Daniel A. De Salvo and Jay Liebowitz. Englewood, Cliffs, NJ: Yourdon Press, 1990.

Wood, William T., and Elaine N. Frankowski. "Verification of Rule-Based Expert Systems." *Expert Systems With Applications,* 1 (3), Fall 1990, pp. 317–22.

# Part Four

## MANAGING KBS DEVELOPMENT EFFORTS

# 12

# Planning for KBS Development Efforts: The Preliminary or Feasibility Studies

As more complex KBS development efforts are undertaken, the management requirements increase proportionately. This chapter discusses some of the overall management tasks involved in many KBS development efforts. It also describes an approach to doing preliminary planning and feasibility studies for individual KBS development projects.

The discussion in this chapter covers:

- The KBS development project management job
- Planning for KBS development efforts
- The nature of preliminary planning and feasibility studies for individual projects
- An integrated approach to formal feasibility studies in specific situations
- Applying the approach in different KBS development situations
- A KBS to assist in doing preliminary screenings
- Manual approaches

## THE KBS DEVELOPMENT PROJECT MANAGEMENT JOB

Classical management theory has identified five management functions:

- planning
- organization

- direction
- control
- human resources management: staffing

Since management does not exist in a vacuum, there is an additional, sixth management job that is not always mentioned in management textbooks:

- knowing the business area being managed

The management area under study here, knowledge-based systems and their development, is described in Chapters 1 through 11. This chapter and the two others in Part Four extend that discussion into task areas critical to successful *management* of KBS development efforts in general, and of individual KBS projects in particular.

While planning is listed as a separate function or task, in reality it occurs throughout KBS development and implementation management. For example, Chapters 7 through 11 describe both planning *and* doing five different KBS development tasks. In the same way, both planning and implementation are described in each of the KBS project management functions described in Chapters 12 through 14.

## PLANNING FOR KBS DEVELOPMENT EFFORTS

Several kinds of planning done when managing KBS development efforts are discussed in this section, including overall strategic planning, operational planning, and strategic planning for individual efforts.

### Overall Strategic Planning

Just as overall strategic planning is needed for computer information systems in general in a company (Mockler 1991, Chapter 12), overall strategic planning is needed for the AI technologies area, especially KBS development.

Companies are beginning to do this type of planning and writing about it. For example, in his article *Strategic Planning for Expert Systems*, Bernard Moullin (1990) describes the overall strategic planning done at La Laurentienne, a billion dollar Canadian insurance company. The following is a summary outline of that strategic master plan:

*Executive Summary*

1. Objectives and limits of the plan
2. How the plan was developed
3. General description of La Laurentienne, Mutuelle d'Assurance (the company)
    - Introduction
    - The distribution function

- The production function
- Departments selected for the study

4. General presentation of expert system technology
   - The various system categories in organizations
   - Expert and knowledge-based systems
   - Typical applications of expert systems technology
   - Applications in insurance and financial services
5. Action plan
   - Proposal for an expert systems strategy
   - Summary of potential applications for selected departments, using expert systems technology
   - Summary of potential expert system applications for which several departments should be involved
6. Potential applications synthesis, development priorities, and proposal regarding expert systems development tools
7. Recommendations

Such overall strategic planning has been and is being done at many U.S. companies with major commitments to AI technology, including Lockheed, General Motors, Digital Equipment Corporation, DuPont, Boeing, FMC Corporation, Metropolitan Life Insurance Company, and Chase Manhattan Bank. As seen in the descriptions of these planning efforts in Chapter 13, each company approaches overall strategic planning differently and organizes in ways that are unique to the requirements of their particular company's business situation.

Two key overall strategic planning decisions considered at these companies were:

1. *The type of KBS to be developed*:
   - small KBS designed to function as intelligent job aids and to be delivered on PCs or Macintoshes
   - mid-size KBS designed to serve as advisors and to be delivered on PCs or workstations
   - mid-size KBS designed to serve as advisors and to be delivered on mainframes
   - largely strategic systems generally developed in LISP and delivered on either LISP machines or on workstations running in LISP
   - embedded KBS to enhance the development or maintenance of existing or planned conventional computer systems
2. *The overall organization of the KBS effort in general:* whether it is to be carried out by existing company personnel within existing departments, by newly hired people in a newly formed department, by outside consultants working with company experts or with company CS personnel, or by some combination of these strategic approaches.

The situations in which each of these overall strategies can be useful, as well as an approach to developing overall strategies for planning, organizing, implementing, controlling and staffing KBS development efforts, are discussed in Chapters 13 and 14.

### Operational Planning

Operational planning in five critical KBS development task areas was discussed in Part Three. This operational planning is an important part of KBS development project management, since it defines the functional plans needed to carry out the KBS development life cycle. For example, knowledge engineers will plan details such as the most effective ways to obtain knowledge from experts, even to the point of planning the length of interview sessions and room layouts. A wide range of these kinds of operating plans was discussed throughout Part Three.

### Strategic Planning for Individual Projects

Planning for KBS development also involves strategic planning for individual projects. The discussion in this chapter concentrates on the specific strategic planning and feasibility studies done at the outset of individual KBS development projects. Such studies focus on the question of whether or not the KBS proposed is the kind of project that should be undertaken—that is, whether or not to allocate resources to the specific kind of proposed KBS under study. This is a strategic planning question which arises in individual project management.

## THE NATURE OF PRELIMINARY PLANNING AND FEASIBILITY STUDIES FOR INDIVIDUAL PROJECTS

A project is a one-time, specific, finite task, as opposed to a company's ongoing everyday operations. A project can be described as a single task or a group of tasks, such as might be involved in building a new factory, marketing a new product, or developing a new computer system (Meredith 1989).

When a specific KBS project is proposed, studies are needed to determine whether or not to proceed with it. Such studies can be done once at the outset of a project. More commonly, they occur at various stages during a project, when decisions are made about whether or not to continue a project.

The preliminary planning phase is often more difficult in KBS development projects than in conventional computer system development projects, because of the relative newness of KBS technology. A project manager does not always have a history of experiences with prior projects to use as a planning projection base. This can create problems.

For example, computer information personnel unfamiliar with KBS development often do not realize the amount of time needed and the difficulties encountered in acquiring knowledge. As a result of this inexperience and the newness of the technology, they often do not plan for or budget enough time, personnel, and money for knowledge acquisition in their initial preliminary plans.

This lack of experience and other potential pitfalls leads some project managers to approach project planning incrementally. They will develop initial plans, and then do some small prototype development projects, in order to test concepts and to gain experience, before doing more formal plans and feasibility studies.

For these reasons, KBS development project planning may pass through many stages. Final **feasibility judgements** may not be made until much later in a project, after several initial prototype systems have been developed. In addition, there are often enormous situational variations in how this planning phase is carried out because of the wide range of kinds and sizes of KBS that can be developed.

This is the reason a variety of preliminary feasibility studies are described in this book. This chapter describes an initial feasibility study which might be done in business. Chapter 15 describes one that might be done by students taking a KBS development course in school.

There is also some confusion about the use of the word *feasibility* in business practice. "Feasibility" is not a study in the strictest sense of the word, but a judgment based on a planning analysis study. For example, in determining feasibility, a project manager decides whether or not a project should proceed based on a structured situation analysis and the planning requirements defined during that analysis. A feasibility study, then, is the investigative study done to help determine if a KBS project can be successful.

In business practice, the term *feasibility* is used to describe a wide range of studies done in the computer area. In this discussion, the term will be used to describe only planning studies whose purpose is to determine a KBS project's chances of being successfully developed and implemented in an organization.

## AN INTEGRATED APPROACH TO FORMAL FEASIBILITY STUDIES IN SPECIFIC SITUATIONS

The discussion in this section covers the general approach to making formal **feasibility** or **investigative studies** in situations involving more complex knowledge-based systems. The approach to preliminary planning and formal feasibility studies described in this chapter is outlined in Figure 12–1.

This section describes how specific critical situation factors listed in Figure 12–1 are analyzed and structured, and then used in making decisions about a KBS development project's feasibility. Many kinds of decisions are involved here,

**Figure 12–1.** Decision Situation under Study: Feasibility or Investigative Studies—Decision Domain Diagram

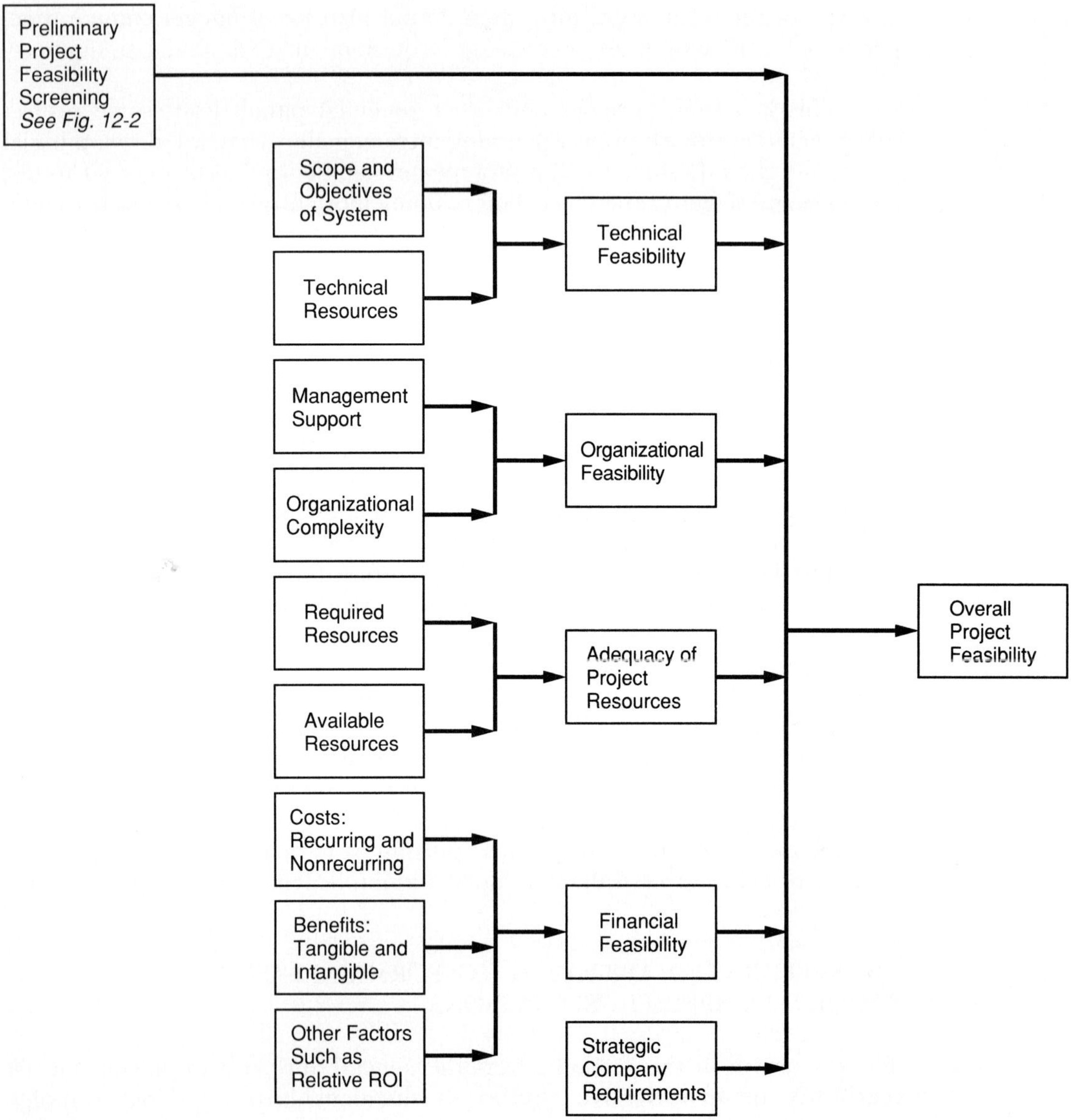

from deciding on operational and financial feasibility to deciding on the risks inherent in a proposed KBS development project and how those risks might be reduced.

In addition, the kinds of situations encountered can vary considerably, from large-company, large-project situations, to those encountered at DuPont, a large company creating a program for developing a wide range of smaller KBS throughout its many divisions, to small KBS developed for personal use by only one expert.

Because of this wide range of possible decisions and situations, the approach described in this section is necessarily a general one, which is intended to give only an overview of the approach. Specific applications of this general approach are described in the final sections of this chapter, Chapter 15, and Mockler (1990).

The following sections discuss:

- critical factors affecting decisions in this area
- how decisions are made based on these critical factors
- different kinds of situations

### Critical Factors Affecting Decisions in This Area

Determining a KBS development project's feasibility, as shown in Figure 12–1, involves

- a preliminary screening,

as well as in-depth studies covering:

- technical feasibility
- organizational feasibility
- the adequacy of project resources
- financial feasibility
- strategic requirements of the company

A proposed KBS project is usually subjected to a **preliminary screening** to get an idea of its feasibility. The type of preliminary screening done will depend on the particular situation. This preliminary screening may suffice as the total or overall feasibility study for smaller projects. Later in this chapter, a KBS for doing a preliminary screening is described in detail.

If, after the preliminary screening is completed, the proposed project seems worthwhile, more in-depth, comprehensive studies are conducted for larger projects. These more comprehensive formal feasibility studies build upon and go beyond the areas covered in the preliminary screening.

*Technical feasibility* refers to the ability of available technology (both hardware and software) and other resources to meet the objectives of the proposed KBS.

The complexity of the scope and objectives of the proposed KBS are influenced by factors such as the type of situation, the source of the knowledge, its structure (breadth and depth), and the types of reasoning processes and recommendations involved in the expertise to be computerized.

When investigating the adequacy of the technical resources, a project manager, knowledge engineer, or systems analyst starts by finding out whether existing software and hardware resources already in use can be added to or upgraded to meet the need in question. If existing systems cannot be expanded or altered to effectively meet the need, the next question investigated is whether other hardware and software can be acquired and/or developed to meet the scope and objectives of the system. Whether or not the technology to be employed is unproven or proven (and to what degree) is also explored. This includes assessing the availability of off-the-shelf software, the need for custom software, and the existence of similar systems. These questions can be answered through a project manager's research, contacts with vendors, and past experiences.

*Organizational feasibility* refers to the study of whether the system will be used as intended by the targeted users, as well as whether the system will operate as required when installed. Organizational feasibility depends on two key factors:

- the degree of management support of the project needed to ensure that sufficient resources will be allocated to the project
- organizational complexity

Factors influencing the management support level include: who initiated the project and why, who supports the project and to what extent, and whether and to what extent there is an effective champion.

Organizational complexity depends upon the amount and types of experts, users, and developers who will be involved in developing and using the system and their perceptions of it. In addition, the geographic locations, structures, and cultures of the different organizational units involved in the system's development and use influence organizational complexity.

*Adequacy of project resources* has to do with the study of project resource requirements in relation to available project resources. These resources include the different types and numbers of people needed (users, experts, knowledge engineers, software programmers) and their levels of cognitive and interpersonal skills. It also includes the hardware and software required to develop and use the KBS.

*Financial feasibility* deals with the study of the available financial resources of the organization, as well as with cost-benefit analyses. Clearly, if the company does not have the financial resources to develop and deliver a proposed project, or cannot get the funds needed, the project is not financially feasible even if the system could be very profitable. Even when funds are available, the question of whether or not the project is truly worth the cost also must be studied.

Costs can be described as either recurring or nonrecurring. *Nonrecurring costs* are one-time expenditures, such as consultants, hardware, and software. Other nonrecurring costs may cover training, documentation, conversion, and site preparation. *Recurring costs* are costs that are generated on a regular basis as a result of operating the new system. These costs include the wages and salaries arising from the operation and management of the system, and items such as maintenance and repair of software, hardware, facilities, and other equipment, as well as electricity, insurance, paper, and any other supplies, equipment, and people required on a regular basis.

Once the costs are determined, they can be compared to the project's benefits. The benefits can be described as either tangible or intangible. *Tangible benefits* include lower costs, increased cash flow and profits, reduced need for fixed assets, less staffing required, and better accuracy and reliability. *Intangible benefits* may include improved customer satisfaction, more efficient use of personnel, and improved worker satisfaction and work environment. These intangible benefits, such as better motivated workers, may lead to tangible benefits, such as less sick leave and lower medical insurance costs, that are difficult to link directly to the system's introduction.

Even if the project's benefits are significantly greater than the costs, it still may not be financially feasible. This is because companies usually have multiple projects to invest in but limited financial and management resources. For instance, if two projects have equal levels of risk and are both expected to be profitable but the company only has enough resources to pursue one of them, the project with the highest return on investment (ROI) will usually be chosen. This is often based on a comparison of the net present value and internal rate of return of the two projects (Van Horne 1986).

Financial feasibility can also be influenced by other factors. For example, on occasion a project with a lower return may be chosen if it meets a strategic goal of the company which outweighs other considerations.

*Strategic company requirements* for a KBS may arise from competitive pressures, strategic business areas that a company wants to get into, or from some need to strengthen links with key customers or augment other services provided to them.

Companies like American Express and United Airlines, for example, have experienced competitive pressures which led them to proceed with computer information systems development projects in order to remain competitive or increase their competitive position (Mazer 1988, Mockler 1989, Newquist 1987, Wiseman 1988). For instance, American Express has a KBS that enables telephone operators to check through many customer databases in a few seconds to authorize purchases. This helps American Express to operate without the credit limits found at other credit card companies and helps minimize credit losses, and so has helped give the company a competitive edge.

Questions are also raised about the company's general strategy for its KBS development effort, such as how it will be staffed and organized in general, and what its relation will be to other company organizational units, especially other MIS and computer organization units.

### How Decisions Are Made Based on These Critical Factors

After evaluating the above criteria, a report is made that outlines the study's findings and offers recommendations. The possible recommendations that can result from the study include:

- *Do not proceed with the project*—this would be recommended if the project's technical, organizational, or financial feasibility are very doubtful, or the adequacy of project resources is insufficient.
- *Postpone development*—this would be recommended if resources, such as people and cash, are not now available but may become available in the future, or if the project is not technically feasible, but recent research indicates it soon may be.
- *Continue the investigation further*—this would be recommended if the project manager or person performing the feasibility study is not yet able to access needed information, or if new developments occur within the investigation area after information has been collected.
- *Develop the system with some modifications*—this would be recommended if certain areas can be changed to make the project feasible or increase its chances of success.
- *Develop the system as is*—this would be recommended if the system is feasible and any improvements are not substantial.

### Different Kinds of Situations

While the preceding sections give a general idea of how feasibility studies are carried out, the specifics will depend on each individual's situation requirements.

For example, a feasibility study may involve a situation where an expert-driven KBS project is being done by an individual with little experience with KBS technology or with structuring decisions. This situation may require that the individual be assisted in finding, selecting, and defining an area for development. Such a study might also include evaluating the project's appropriateness for KBS technology, technical feasibility, and its usefulness to the individual involved.

In another type of situation, a feasibility study for a KBS development project may involve investigating the business need for the system, the appropriateness of KBS technology to meet the need, its mechanical feasibility, and its operational feasibility.

A feasibility study for a large development project spanning different organizational units in dispersed geographic locations may require a preliminary feasibility screening and subsequent, more comprehensive, overall feasibility studies. Once these are completed, the formal study might look at: technical feasibility, to see if a KBS can meet the need; organizational feasibility, to see if the KBS can be effective in the organization; the adequacy of project resources, to see if the organization has or can get the resources required to develop the system; financial feasibility and strategic company requirements, to see if the KBS is worthwhile for the company to develop.

To illustrate how a reader might adapt the general approach to his or her own specific KBS development situation, the following section describes doing a feasibility study for a small KBS development project involving investigating the business need for the system, the appropriateness of KBS technology to meet the need, its mechanical feasibility, and its operational feasibility. Such a study can also be used as a preliminary screening for larger projects. This chapter concludes with a description of a KBS to assist the reader in doing this kind of feasibility study.

Additional applications of this general approach to feasibility studies for KBS projects to other specific kinds of situations are given in Chapter 15 and Mockler (1990).

## APPLYING THIS GENERAL APPROACH IN DIFFERENT SITUATIONS

The situation described in this chapter involves a preliminary screening that individual managers working on their own, knowledge engineers, or project managers might use to make a preliminary estimate of the feasibility of a proposed KBS project. In addition, this screening involves finding ways in which the project's chances for success might be improved. A screening such as this may also serve as an overall feasibility study for smaller development projects.

The diagram in Figure 12–2 outlines the key decisions made in these kinds of situations. The discussion in this section closely follows the decision situation outlined in Figure 12–2. The discussion is divided into two sections:

- factors affecting the decision
- recommendations and how they are determined

### Factors Affecting the Decision

The critical factors affecting decisions in these situations can be grouped into four categories:

- the business needs served by the proposed KBS
- the appropriateness of the project for KBS technology
- the mechanical feasibility given the nature of the expertise involved
- the operational feasibility

Throughout this discussion it is assumed that the system under study is the kind of system the company has decided in general it strategically wants to develop.

**Figure 12–2.** Decision Situation under Study: Preliminary Feasibility Screening—Decision Domain Diagram

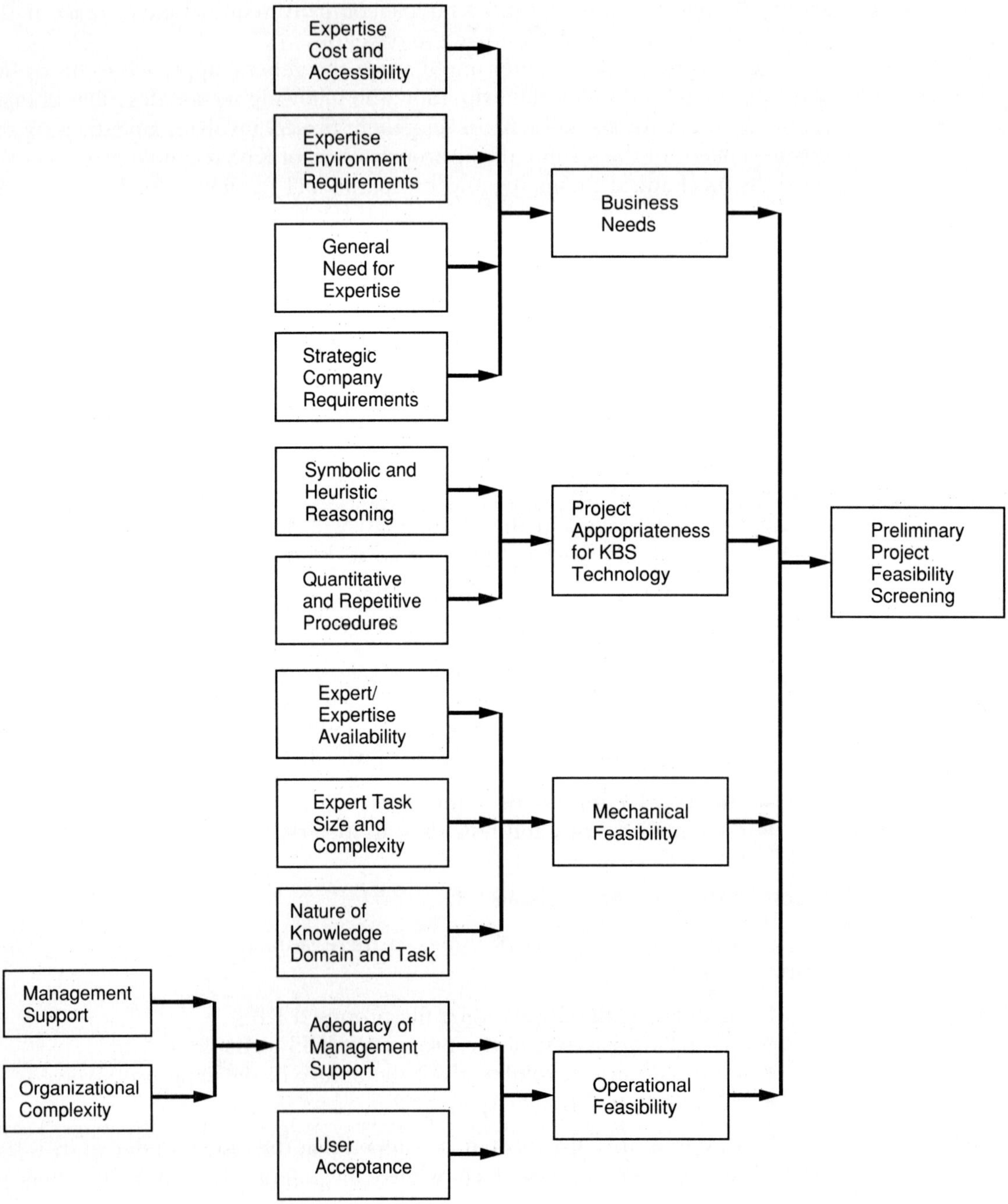

***Business Needs Served by the Proposed KBS.*** A business's need for a KBS can be determined by examining four key factors:

- cost and accessibility of expertise
- environment requirements of expertise
- the general need for expertise
- strategic company requirements

Determining the *cost and accessibility* of the expertise to be replicated in the KBS involves answering such questions as:

- Is human expertise about to be lost?
- How scarce is human expertise?
- How expensive is human expertise?

If the cost of the expertise is high and/or accessibility to it is low, developing a KBS to replicate the knowledge or expertise is usually worthwhile. For example, NASA has turned to KBS development because many of its top scientists and engineers will soon be eligible for retirement. The knowledge possessed by these experts stems from years of education and experience in the space program. NASA is relying on KBS to help fill this potential experience shortage (Broad 1989).

At Corning Glass, only a few skilled operators could manage the process involved in controlling the rate of change of temperatures as glass tubes are fired and then cooled in large gas ovens; very precise and quickly calculated measurements in an environment of widely changing temperatures are required. Corning developed an expert system to do this work (Barber 1989).

Digital Equipment developed a KBS called XSEL (Leonard-Barton 1987) to assist its sales force in configuring computer systems, a task that requires significant technical expertise. Since sales expertise is less scarce and less costly than technical computer expertise, and sales people with both selling skills and technical expertise are hard to find, this was an opportunity for cost reduction and for improved operational effectiveness.

Determining the *expertise environment requirements* involves answering such questions as:

- Is the expertise needed in a variety of locations?
- Is the expertise needed in an environment hostile to people?
- Do the job requirements, such as speed or precision, or dealing with large numbers of variables under time constraints, exceed the capacity of normally available experts?

For example, MCI has developed a commercial products advisor for use by its 1000 sales and marketing personnel around the country (Newquist 1989). Sanders Associates has developed a KBS which simulates the actions and reactions of an enemy submarine commander for anti-submarine warfare training (Newquist 1989). In addition, NASA is planning to develop a KBS to identify the nature of a problem in a few seconds, if a countdown automatically stops when launching the space shuttle. KBS development is being considered because in many situations people are not as good as KBS at keeping track of and interpreting rapidly changing situations that cover large amounts of information (Broad 1989).

Determining the *general need for the expertise* involves answering such questions as:

- Has the decision or task for which you are considering developing a KBS been previously identified as a problem area?
- Is the expertise being replicated in the proposed KBS needed often and on a regular basis—more than once a week on average, for example?
- To what extent can your proposed KBS be used to help repair and service products?
- To what extent can your proposed KBS be used to give sales assistance to customers?
- To what extent can your proposed KBS be used to help train or retrain employees?
- To what extent does your proposed KBS have some other practical use at work?
- Does your proposed KBS have some practical use in a possible new venture your company is considering?
- Is the main purpose of the system to test KBS technology?

In addition to the systems mentioned above which fulfilled a general business need, the following are examples of KBS targeted at fulfilling specific needs.

- Navistar International (formerly International Harvester) has a system to help estimate production costs for truck parts.
- An expert system has been developed to advise lawyers on the Latent Damages Act in England and Wales (Applications 1989).

If, based on an the evaluation of these three critical factors—expertise cost and accessibility, expertise environment requirements, and the general need for expertise—sufficient business need does *not* exist, the screening ends and the KBS project is not pursued further, unless there is an overriding strategic business need for the system.

*Strategic company requirements* for a KBS may arise from competitive pressures or from the requirements of strategic business areas a company wants to get into. This sort of need was seen in the American Express example discussed earlier. Strategic requirements may also include developing a KBS to strengthen links with important customers or augment other services provided to them. These needs for information systems can override short-term operational and cost considerations of KBS development.

Companies may also choose to develop KBS to expand the services they provide. For example, accounting firms have developed KBS to help them perform tax-planning services (Shpilberg 1986). They have then used the experience gained in developing in-house KBS to expand the services offered to their clients to include KBS development services. This strategic move has increased their product line, attracted new clients, and strengthened ties with existing clients.

Companies may also develop KBS to maintain the level of service provided to customers. For example, one major reason Digital's XSEL system was developed was a shift in the sales force from people with technical experience and training to people with general sales skills. The development of XSEL allowed for the expansion of the sales force and increased sales, while maintaining adequate control of the technical aspects of system configuration.

***The Appropriateness of a Project for KBS Technology.*** Determining a project's appropriateness for KBS technology requires looking at the kind of reasoning processes involved to see if they are:

- quantitative, with repetitive procedures, or
- heuristic and symbolic, with inferential procedures

The nature of reasoning processes are quantitative, with repetitive procedures, if they can be reduced to a mathematical formula. For example, if a decision relies mainly on mathematical computations, such as when to reorder a particular product for inventory or when and how much to bill a customer, the reasoning or decision-making involved is quantitative. Quantitative reasoning involves manipulating numbers as opposed to concepts. Decision situations which are largely quantitative with repetitive procedures are usually best suited for conventional computer systems.

For a project proposal to be appropriate for KBS development, a significant portion of the reasoning involved in the task or decision should be heuristic and symbolic, that is, **knowledge intensive** in nature, not process intensive or quantitative. Knowledge intensive refers to inferential reasoning or the knowledge of how different factors interrelate to arrive at some conclusion. Heuristic and symbolic reasoning processes are appropriate for KBS technology because they are suitable to the reasoning process patterns built into KBS system development shells and languages.

Heuristics are rules of thumb that experts use to help them solve problems. For example, an expert baseball manager might know that when a particular pitcher's fastball rises more than usual the pitcher is getting tired. This is an example of just one of the many heuristics that a manager may use when evaluating players throughout the league.

Heuristic knowledge is judgmental in nature. The rules of thumb that it is based on do not always guarantee a single best solution. The IF-THEN rules described later in this chapter are one way to represent heuristic knowledge in a KBS.

**Symbolic reasoning** involves manipulating symbols that represent concepts. Symbolic reasoning is based on using strategies and heuristics to manipulate symbols representing problem concepts. **Syllogisms** are examples of symbolic reasoning. Syllogisms are arguments consisting of at least three propositions, as in:

> The students in BA 224 are studying business.
> Carol is a student in BA 224.
> Therefore, Carol is studying business.

The first two propositions are called premises and have one term (symbol) in common (students in BA 224) which furnishes a logical connection between the two other terms (studying business, and Carol), which are then linked in the third proposition, or conclusion.

Questions such as the following are asked to determine a project's appropriateness for KBS technology. The answers to the first two questions should be "significant," while the next two should be answered "limited" in order for KBS technology to be judged appropriate for the project.

- To what degree does the reasoning process involved in your proposed project require symbolic manipulation?
- To what degree does the reasoning involved in your proposed project require using rules of thumb or heuristics?
- To what degree does your proposed project only involve giving yes or no answers to questions?
- To what degree is the decision or task involved in your proposed project quantitative enough that you could make a version of it work on a spreadsheet system?

In addition, if the reasoning process involved in the proposed project just requires common sense, such as whether or not to take an umbrella with you if it is raining, or whether or not to take your passport with you if you are traveling to Europe, or the reasoning involves mostly a procedural process that can be reduced to a single sheet of instructions, the scope of the system is too small and is thus inappropriate for KBS or any kind of systems development.

Also, since KBS technology allows for easier postimplementation modification than conventional computer technology, if the project covers an area that changes often, such as tax laws, KBS technology may be useful. For example, one of the reasons that Digital Equipment chose KBS technology to develop XSEL was because different components were often added and sometimes deleted from the company's product line, and conventional computer systems could not easily be altered to reflect these changes (Rauch-Hindin 1985).

***Mechanical Feasibility.*** A project's mechanical feasibility depends on such critical factors as:

- expert/expertise availability
- expert task size and complexity
- the nature of the knowledge domain and task

Determining the *expert/expertise availability* involves answering such questions as:

- To what extent do recognized experts or sources of expertise exist?
- To what extent do you have or can you get adequate access to these sources of knowledge and/or expertise?
- To what extent can experts do the task better than amateurs?
- To what extent can expert skills be taught to others?
- How well can the available experts articulate the general methods that they use to reach conclusions and make decisions?
- How cooperative and committed to the project do you expect the available experts to be?
- How would you describe the chances that the experts used to build the system will feel threatened or intimidated by it?

These questions are asked to determine that true expertise or specialized knowledge exists, and that those developing the system have access to the expertise. In NASA's situation, recognized experts exist to a significant extent. It is the fear of losing these experts and their expertise that is a prime motivation for KBS development. NASA presently employs the experts, and can use them for KBS development projects if it wishes, thus providing significant sources of expertise.

In another situation, the development of a computer hardware breakdown diagnosis system for the St. Louis public school system, recognized experts were available in the form of three technicians and two PC experts who supported the hardware, and service manuals and records were also available (Williamson 1989). The developer had ample access to this expertise, and the experts did the job better than amateurs. In addition, the experts' reasoning methods could be articulated and taught to others. The experts involved were expected to be cooperative if approached correctly. They did not seem to feel threatened by the KBS because there were only five experts servicing 2,000 PCs at 160 locations, and the KBS would cover the more mundane problems.

Also, much of the expertise required for the KBS is in written form. This makes it easy for the KBS developer to acquire and model the expert knowledge. As expertise becomes more complicated and spans different areas, such as international tax planning, and where written knowledge sources are not available, the risks involved with acquiring the expertise increase.

Evaluating the *expert task size and complexity* requires the project evaluator to imagine how the proposed system would look on computer. This involves examining and consulting sample systems, if the evaluator is not familiar with KBS technology, and then answering the following questions:

- Is the task for which you are considering developing a KBS of manageable size? Does it seem that the amount of rules, questions, and other things involved will work using available KBS technology?

- Have similar KBS been built before?
- How many questions need to be answered about the area involved when making/performing the decision/task?
- How long, in minutes, does it take an expert in the area to make the decision, solve the problem, or do the task under study once all of the required information has been gathered?
- How many different rules of thumb or heuristics would you estimate are used by the expert when performing the task or making the decision?
- How many different major factors do you estimate are evaluated by the expert when performing the task or making the decision?
- Will the proposed system require that information be gathered from a spreadsheet or database?
- How many recommendations do you estimate there will be in the system?

These questions are asked to get an idea of the size and complexity of the KBS and whether or not the expert knowledge involved can be put into a KBS, given available technology. For example, a KBS that requires fewer than 100 rules, has 4 or 5 possible recommendations, 15 user questions, and performs a task usually done by an expert in 10 to 15 minutes, is likely not to be very complex. This size task can probably be replicated using widely available KBS expert system shell technology. As these factors increase, so does the KBS development project's level of complexity.

Determining the *nature of the knowledge domain and task* involves answering such questions as:

- Can the reasoning process involved in the proposed project be identified and defined?
- Do different experts usually agree on the solutions to typical problems?
- To what extent is the task well understood by the experts?
- Are typical test cases or example situations readily available?
- Does the decision or task require extensive natural language capabilities, such as an unstructured conversational give and take, as opposed to asking and answering questions and displaying information?
- What type of skills are used by the expert, cognitive (thinking) or physical?
- Do experts need to use creativity to solve typical problems?

These questions are asked to determine the nature of the knowledge domain and the experts' task. If the nature of the knowledge domain is such that the reasoning involved is ill-defined or the skills required are not cognitive ones, the feasibility of KBS development is doubtful. To increase the KBS project's chances of being successfully developed and reduce risk, the reasoning process involved in the expert's domain should be identifiable and well understood by the experts. This is often the case if different experts usually agree on solutions to typical problems (Cullen 1988). This can be tested by using typical test cases or example situations. Also, if test cases are readily available, there is a higher probability that the area is well defined. KBS can only replicate cognitive or reasoning skills and do not have the ability to interact with users in an unstructured manner.

***Operational Feasibility.*** Determining a KBS project's operational feasibility involves examining two areas: adequacy of management support and user acceptance.

*Adequacy of management support* is determined by looking at the organizational complexity and the level of management support. Specifically, the adequacy of management support is based on a comparison of the organizational complexity and the level of management support. As the organizational complexity involved in the situation increases, so does the need for management support (Davenport 1989). For small, expert-driven projects, very little management support may be needed. For larger projects that involve multiple organizational units and numerous experts and users, significant support is usually needed.

Analyzing *organizational complexity* involves asking such questions as:

- Are the user, expert, and developer functions all performed by the same person, with only minor assistance from others?
- How many different organizational units or departments will be involved in the system's development and use?
- How many different geographic locations will the system be used in?
- How many different people will use the system on a regular basis?
- How would you describe the diversity of user types, or the levels of assistance required from the system by the different types of people who will use the KBS on a regular basis?
- How many different experts will be needed to develop the system?
- How many different specialized areas of knowledge requiring different experts will be replicated in the KBS?

A substantial commitment from *management* to *support* a KBS project is desirable, and often critical to the success of larger development projects spanning different organizational units (Cupello 1988). This support can be gauged or measured in terms of the resources that management is willing to commit to the project. A preliminary measure of the expected level of management support for a project can be gathered through answering the following questions:

- Who initiated the proposed project?
- What is the highest level of management that has expressed interest in and support for the project?
- Has management been educated in the strengths and weaknesses of KBS technology and does it have realistic expectations of the system?

- During the development phase, to what extent is management willing to provide the time of the various typical users of the KBS to help test and develop it?
- To what extent is management willing to provide the time of the various required experts to test and develop the KBS?
- To what extent is management willing to provide the time of the various knowledge engineers and/or software programmers required to test and develop the KBS?
- To what extent is management willing to see the KBS project through to its end?

*User acceptance* of a KBS project is a critical factor in the project's success because if the KBS is not used as intended it may be worthless. A preliminary measure of the expected level of user acceptance or resistance can be gathered through the following questions:

- Will users perceive the KBS as a helpful tool to accomplish work or as a threat to their jobs?
- To what extent can the KBS be smoothly integrated into the workplace?
- To what extent will the users' work routine be upset and changed?
- To what degree will typical users be available to test versions of the system and provide feedback?
- Do the users have realistic expectations of the system's scope and limitations?
- To what extent can the KBS clearly explain its actions, reasoning, and solutions to the users?
- To what extent can the KBS intelligently question the users, asking the most relevant questions first and avoiding unnecessary questions?

Users of the KBS should perceive it as a tool to help them with their work, not as a potential threat to replace them and take over their jobs (Leonard-Barton 1987). If they feel threatened by the KBS, they may reject or even sabotage it (Dologite 1989). Resistance to the KBS may also increase as disruption to the users' work routine increases. This is especially true if the change in the routine is not adequately planned for and managed and the users are not prepared for the change.

As the ability of the KBS to explain its reasoning processes and its recommendations to users increases, so do the chances of user acceptance of the system. Also, if the system asks questions that are obviously pertinent from the users' point of view, they are more likely to use and accept the KBS.

### Recommendations and How They Are Determined

In situations involving a feasibility study for smaller systems, or the preliminary screening of a KBS project proposal by an individual manager working on his or her own, or a knowledge engineer or a project manager who is trying to determine if a large proposed KBS should be developed for a particular decision or task, three basic recommendations can be made:

- Proceed with the proposed KBS project as it is.
- Do not proceed at all with the proposed KBS project—reject it.
- Modify some aspect of the proposed KBS project to increase its chances of being successfully developed and used, and proceed only if you can make the required modifications.

One would proceed with the proposed KBS project without any modifications if:

- the business needs are significant or sufficient, and
- the proposed project's appropriateness for KBS technology is significant or moderate, and
- the proposed project's mechanical feasibility is high or probable, and
- the proposed project's operational feasibility is significant or moderate.

The KBS project would be rejected outright if:

- the business needs are limited, or
- the proposed project's appropriateness for KBS technology is limited, or
- the proposed project's mechanical feasibility is very doubtful, or
- the proposed project's operational feasibility is doubtful.

Under certain circumstances one would proceed with the proposed KBS project if modifications to the project could be made. For example, if the project's operational feasibility was questionable because of uncertain management support, the project might be able to proceed if the size and scope of the project were reduced, or an articulate corporate sponsor or project champion could be found.

These modifications would only be suggested if:

- the business needs are significant or sufficient, and
- the proposed project's appropriateness for KBS technology is significant or moderate, and
- the proposed project's mechanical feasibility is high or probable.

## A KBS TO ASSIST IN DOING PRELIMINARY SCREENINGS

This section describes a KBS developed for doing the feasibility (preliminary screening) study described in the preceding section.

The discussion covers the:

- system proposal
- description of the prototype system
- dependency diagrams
- designing and constructing of the knowledge base

### System Proposal

The objective of the project is to develop a KBS that will assist an individual manager, a knowledge engineer, or a project manager in estimating the feasibility of a proposed KBS project.

The system was developed by business managers and computer information systems technicians familiar with the process of evaluating the feasibility of proposed KBS projects. Published sources were also used. The system yields two major benefits: it will enable inexperienced developers to work more independently, quickly, and efficiently; and it will serve as a prototype for more comprehensive feasibility evaluation systems.

### Description of the System

***System Overview and Objective.*** The prototype system being developed during the first phase of the project is designed to help users do a preliminary screening of a proposed KBS project. It may also serve as an overall feasibility study for smaller projects. It does this by evaluating four major areas: business need, appropriateness for KBS technology, mechanical feasibility, and operational feasibility. The system uses IF-THEN rules and backward chaining to guide the user and reach recommendations.

***Recommendations To Be Made by the System.*** The recommendations made by the system include:

1. Proceed with the proposed KBS project as it is.
2. Do not proceed at all with the proposed KBS project —reject it.
3. Modify the proposed KBS project, where:
   - The project's operational feasibility is questionable. To increase its chances of success, proceed with the project only if its scope can be narrowed, so that little management support is needed, or find an effective champion or sponsor for the project who can build support for it.
   - The project's mechanical feasibility is questionable because the experts to be employed in the project either cannot articulate their methods, are not expected to be cooperative and committed to the project, or feel threatened by it. To increase its chances of success, proceed with the project only if you can employ experts who will not have these problems.
   - The project's mechanical feasibility is questionable because the task or decision to be replicated by the KBS is not well understood by the experts. To increase its chances of success, proceed with the project only if you can reduce its scope to an area that is well understood by the experts.

- The project's mechanical feasibility is questionable because the typical test cases or example situations are not readily available. To increase its chances of success, proceed with the project only if you can find typical test cases or example situations.

***Nature of the User Interface.*** The typical user dialogue covers four major areas:

- *Business needs.* This information is obtained from questions about the cost and accessibility of the expertise, expertise environment requirements, general need for the expertise, and strategic company requirements.
- *Appropriateness for KBS technology.* This information is obtained from questions about the reasoning processes involved in the decision to see if they are quantitative with repetitive procedures, or heuristic and symbolic with inferential procedures.
- *Mechanical feasibility.* This information is based upon questions about expert availability, the expert's task size and complexity, and the nature of the knowledge domain.
- *Operational feasibility.* This information is obtained from questions about the adequacy of management support and user acceptance.

### Dependency Diagrams

Figures 12–3a through 12–3e show the dependency diagrams for the preliminary feasibility screening KBS. The diagrams present a summary outline of all the questions, rules, knowledge segments and their interrelationships, values, and recommendations in the system.

### Decision Charts

Figure 12–4 shows a sample of a decision chart for the prototype system developed.

### Designing and Constructing the Knowledge Base

Rules, questions, and examples to be shown to the user were developed based upon the situation study.

A segment of the prototype system's knowledge base is shown in Figure 12–5. The expert system shell used is M.1. It was chosen because it allows rule writing in plain English, had the capability of handling a system of this size, and had a reasonably efficient and friendly user interface. The IF-THEN rules were written to reflect the relationships shown in the dependency diagram and match those specified in the decision charts.

This prototype feasibility KBS is given on the disks accompanying this book.

**Figure 12–3.** Preliminary Project Feasibility Screening—Dependency Diagrams (Initial Prototype Phase)

*(A) Overview*

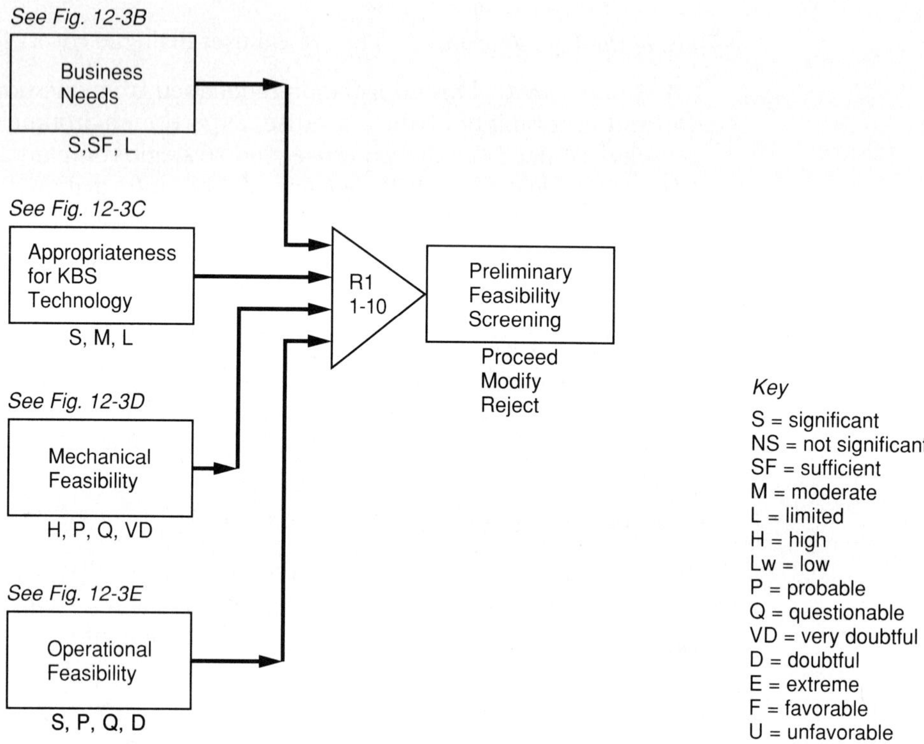

(*B*) *Business Needs*

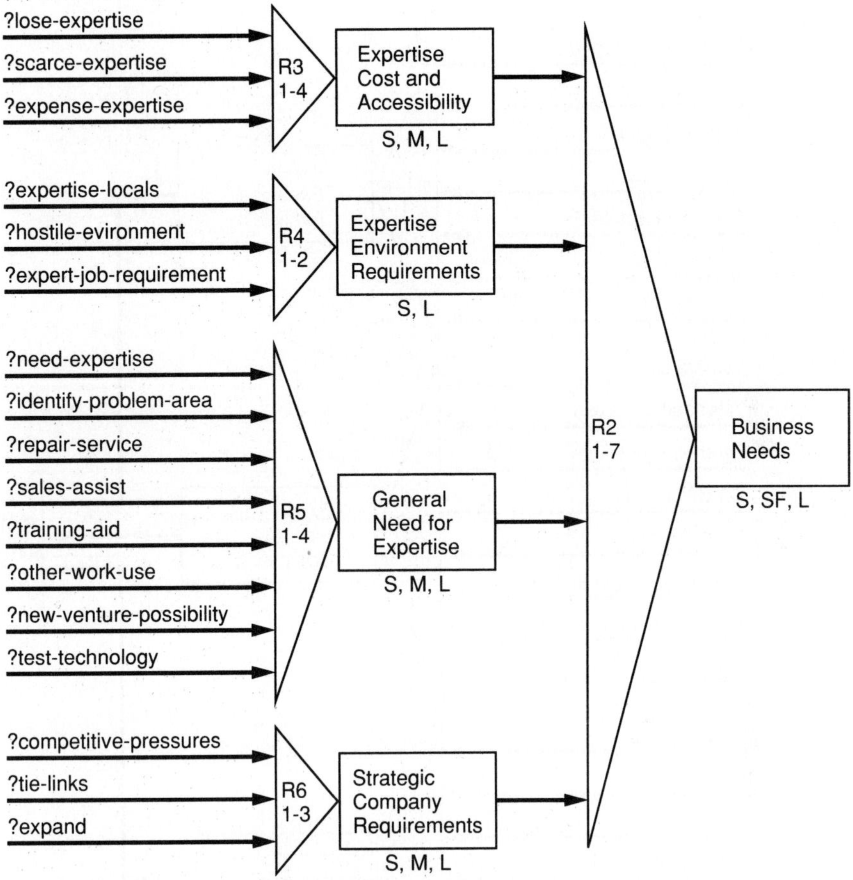


(*C*) *Appropriateness for KBS Technology*

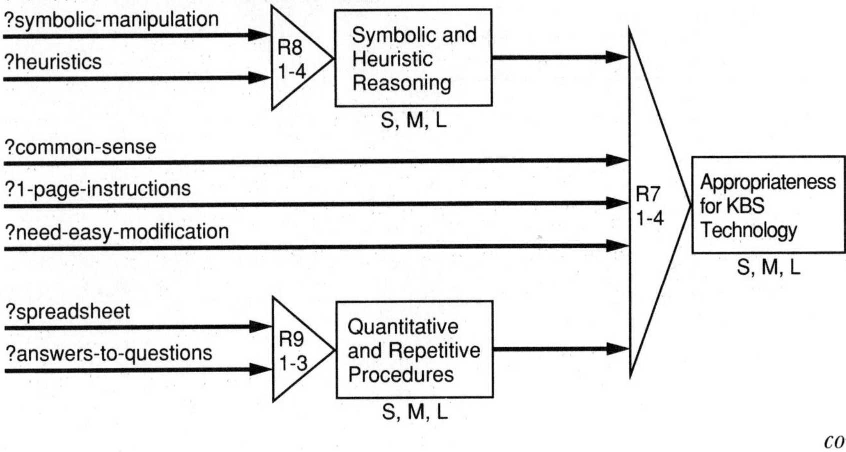


*continued*

**Figure 12–3** *continued*

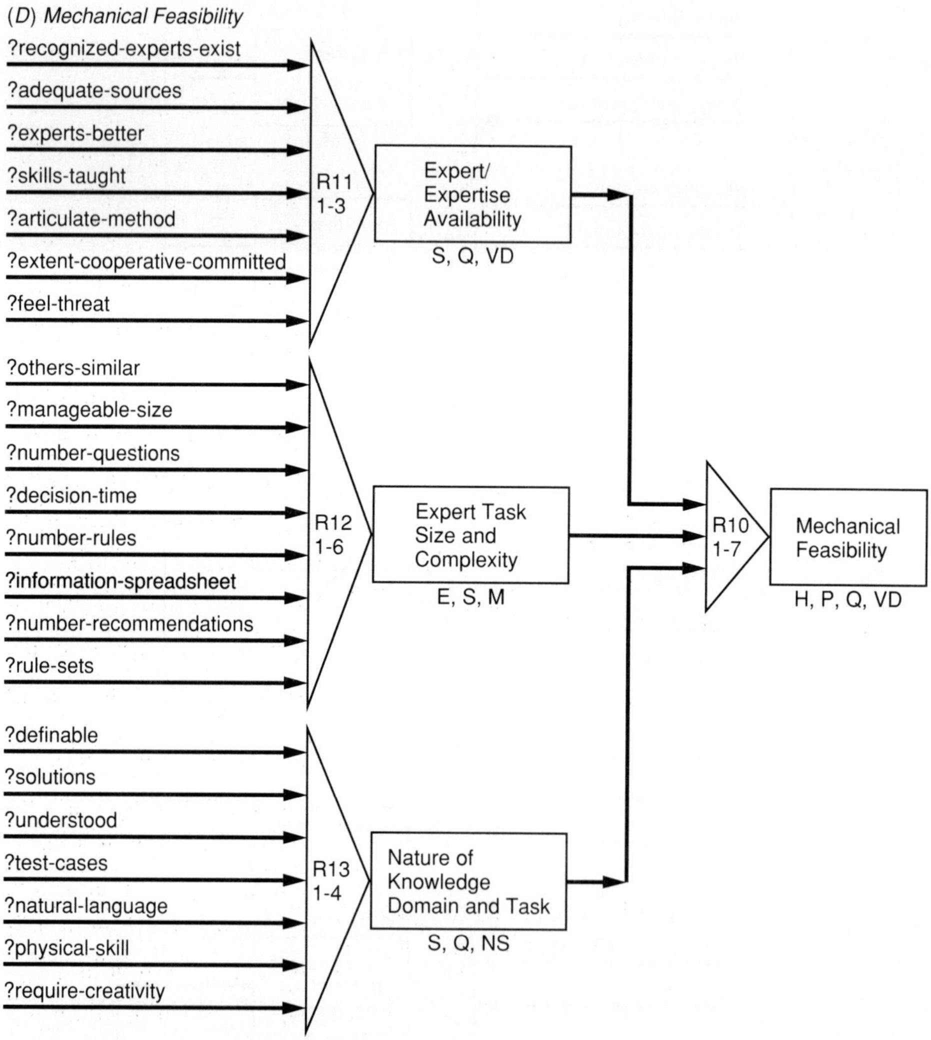

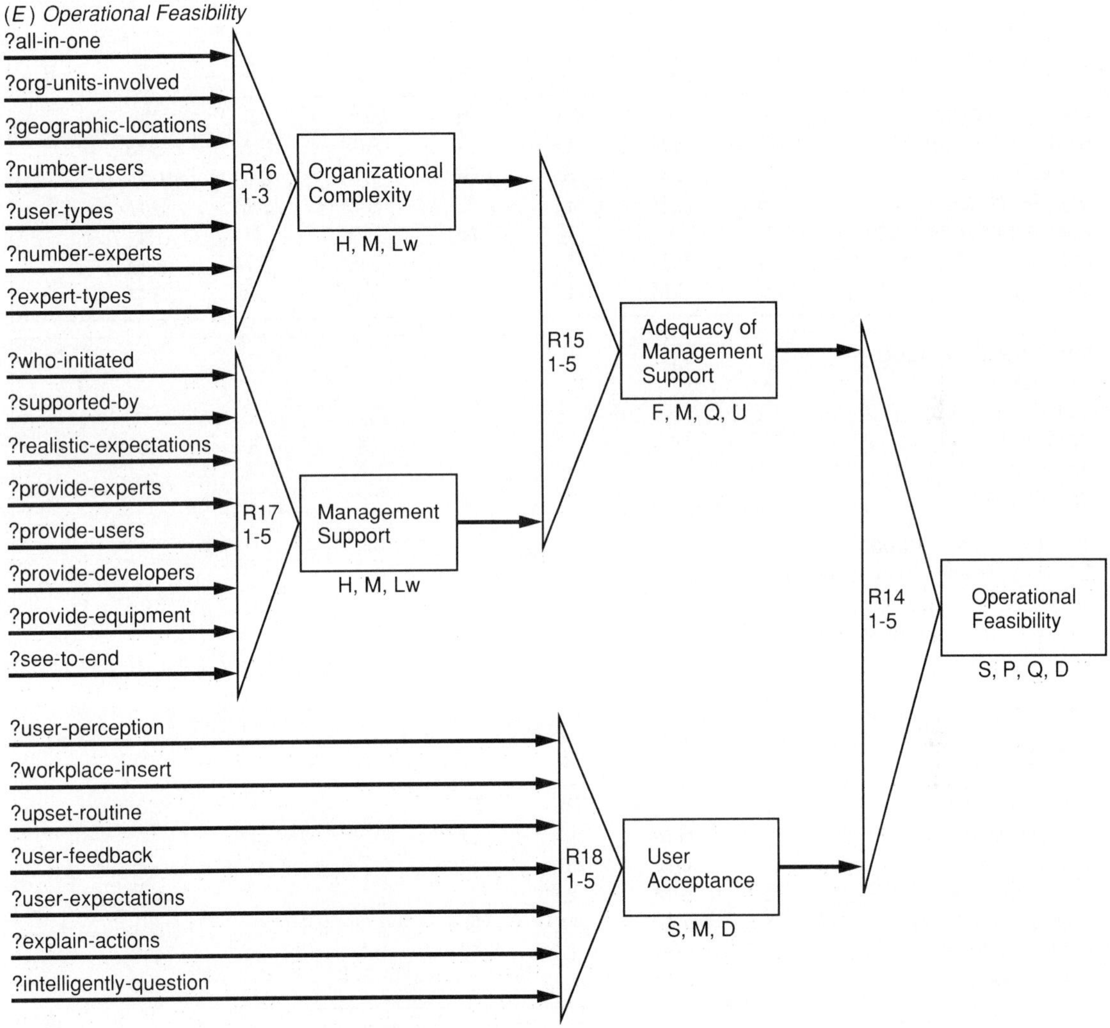
(E) Operational Feasibility
?all-in-one
?org-units-involved
?geographic-locations
?number-users
?user-types
?number-experts
?expert-types
R16
1-3
Organizational Complexity
H, M, Lw
?who-initiated
?supported-by
?realistic-expectations
?provide-experts
?provide-users
?provide-developers
?provide-equipment
?see-to-end
R17
1-5
Management Support
H, M, Lw
R15
1-5
Adequacy of Management Support
F, M, Q, U
?user-perception
?workplace-insert
?upset-routine
?user-feedback
?user-expectations
?explain-actions
?intelligently-question
R18
1-5
User Acceptance
S, M, D
R14
1-5
Operational Feasibility
S, P, Q, D

**Figure 12–4.** Project Feasibility Screening System—Decision Chart: User Acceptance (Initial Prototype Phase)

*(A) Initial Version*

| Rule Set 18 – | 1 | 2 | 3 | 4 | 5 | 6 | 7 | 8 |
|---|---|---|---|---|---|---|---|---|
| user-perception | T | T | Th/ | Th/ | Th | T | Th | * |
| workplace-insert | S | S/M | L | L/ | S/M | S/M | S/M | * |
| upset-routine | L | L/M | S/ | S/ | L/M | L/M | L/M | * |
| user-feedback | S | S/M | L | L | S/M | S/M | S/M | * |
| user-expectations | Y | Y | N | N/ | Y | N | N | * |
| explain-actions | S | S/M | L | L/ | S/M | S/M | S/M | * |
| intell-question | S | S/M | L | L | S/M | S/M | S/M | * |
| then user-acceptance = | | | | | | | | |
| significant | X | | | | | | | |
| significant cf 80 | | X | | | | | | |
| moderate | | | | | X | X | X | X |
| doubtful | | | X | | | | | |
| doubtful cf 80 | | | | X | | | | |

T = tool  Th = threat
S = significant  M = moderate  L = limited
Y = yes  N = no
/ = or  * = any answer

*(B) Condensed Version*

| Rule Set 18 – | 1 | 2 | 3 | 4 | 5 |
|---|---|---|---|---|---|
| user-perception | T | T | Th/ | Th/ | * |
| workplace-insert | S | S/M | L | L/ | * |
| upset-routine | L | L/M | S/ | S/ | * |
| user-feedback | S | S/M | L | L | * |
| user-expectations | Y | Y | N | N/ | * |
| explain-actions | S | S/M | L | L/ | * |
| intell-question | S | S/M | L | L | * |
| then user-acceptance = | | | | | |
| significant | X | | | | |
| significant cf 80 | | X | | | |
| moderate | | | | | X |
| doubtful | | | X | | |
| doubtful cf 80 | | | | X | |

T = tool  Th = threat
S = significant  M = moderate  L = limited
Y = yes  N = no
/ = or  * = any answer

## FURTHER STUDIES

The feasibility study replicated in this KBS is only one of many that might be done. This chapter has described an initial feasibility study which might be done in business. Chapter 15 describes one that might be done by students taking a KBS development course in school. A more detailed subsequent feasibility study which might be done for any size of proposed KBS project is described in Mockler (1990).

## MANUAL APPROACHES

Manual approaches have also been developed to do this kind of screening of proposed projects. For example, Figure 12–6 gives one such approach. Such forms can provide useful information-gathering mechanisms for obtaining the information needed to provide the input necessary for the screening KBS described in this chapter, as well as for doing a cursory initial screening.

**Figure 12–5.** Project Feasibility Screening System—Knowledge Base: User Acceptance (Initial Prototype Phase)

```
/*      User Acceptance    */

rule-18-1:
if user-perception = tool and
   workplace-insert = significant and
   upset-routine = limited and
   user-feedback = significant and
   user-expectations = yes and
   explain-actions = significant and
   intell-question = significant
then user-acceptance = significant.

rule-18-2:
if user-perception = tool and
   workplace-insert = significant or
   workplace-insert = moderate and
   upset-routine = limited or
   upset-routine = moderate and
   user-feedback = moderate or
   user-feedback = significant and
   user-expectations = yes and
   explain-actions = moderate or
   explain-actions = significant and
   intell-question = moderate or
   intell-question = significant
then user-acceptance = significant cf 80.

rule-18-3:
if user-perception = threat or
   workplace-insert = limited and
   upset-routine = significant or
   user-feedback = limited and
   user-expectations = no and
   explain-actions = limited and
   intell-question = limited
then user-acceptance = doubtful.

rule-18-4:
if user-perception = threat or
   workplace-insert = limited or
   upset-routine = significant or
   user-feedback = limited and
   user-expectations = no or
   explain-actions = limited or
   intell-question = limited
then user-acceptance = doubtful cf 80.

rule-18-5:
if user-perception = ANY1 and
   workplace-insert = ANY2 and
   upset-routine = ANY3 and
   user-feedback = ANY4 and
   user-expectations = ANY and
   explain-actions = ANY5 and
   intell-question = ANY6
then user-acceptance = moderate.

question(user-perception) =
    [nl,nl,nl,nl,nl,nl,nl,nl,nl,nl,nl,'
    Will users perceive the KBS as a helpful tool to
    accomplish work or as a threat to their job?
```

```
',nl,nl,nl,nl,nl,nl].

legalvals(user-perception) = [tool, threat].

question(workplace-insert) =
    [nl,nl,nl,nl,nl,nl,nl,nl,nl,nl,nl,'
    To what extent can the KBS be smoothly inserted into the
    workplace?


',nl,nl,nl,nl,nl,nl].

legalvals(workplace-insert) = [significant, moderate, limited].

question(upset-routine) =
    [nl,nl,nl,nl,nl,nl,nl,nl,nl,nl,nl,'
    To what extent will the user''s work routine be upset and
    changed?


',nl,nl,nl,nl,nl,nl].

legalvals(upset-routine) = [significant, moderate, limited].

question(user-feedback) =
    [nl,nl,nl,nl,nl,nl,nl,nl,nl,nl,nl,'
    To what extent will typical users be available to test
    versions of the system and provide feedback?

',nl,nl,nl,nl,nl,nl].

legalvals(user-feedback) = [significant, moderate, limited].

question(user-expectations) =
    [nl,nl,nl,nl,nl,nl,nl,nl,nl,nl,nl,'
    Do the users have realistic expectations of the system''s
    scope and limitations?


',nl,nl,nl,nl,nl,nl].

legalvals(user-expectations) = [yes, no].

question(explain-actions) =
    [nl,nl,nl,nl,nl,nl,nl,nl,nl,nl,nl,'
    To what extent can the KBS clearly explain its actions,
    reasoning, and solutions to the users?


',nl,nl,nl,nl,nl,nl].

legalvals(explain-actions) = [significant, moderate, limited].

question(intell-question) =
    [nl,nl,nl,nl,nl,nl,nl,nl,nl,nl,nl,'
    To what extent can the KBS intelligently question the users,
    asking the most relevant questions first and avoiding
    unnecessary questions?

',nl,nl,nl,nl,nl,nl].

legalvals(intell-question) = [significant, moderate, limited].
```

**Figure 12–6.** Application Analysis Worksheet

| APPLICATION ANALYSIS WORKSHEET (Page 1) | |
|---|---|
| Name ______ <br> Date ______ | |
| Overall Strategy: ☐ Embedded ☐ PC-based ☐ Mainframe-based ☐ PC/Workstation-based | |
| **Considerations** | **Potential Application** |
| Overall Task Description | |
| How Is Task Currently Accomplished? Ex: User Input--- Analysis--- Recommendation | |
| How Will Task Be Accomplished with an Expert System? | |
| Key Criteria: ☐ Human Expert Availability ☐ Narrow, Well-defined Task ☐ Structured Analysis Task ☐ Procedural Task ☐ Verbal Knowledge ☐ Sample Decision Descriptions Available ☐ Hardware/Software Availability ☐ Other | |
| Avoid Tasks Involving: ☐ Common Sense ☐ Reasoning by Analogy ☐ Uncertain Changing Expertise ☐ Expert Disagreement ☐ Perceptual Expertise ☐ Complex Causal Relations ☐ Complex Geometric or Spatial Reasoning | |

| Considerations | Potential Application (Page 2) |
|---|---|
| Cognitive Structure of Problem: ☐ Procedural ☐ Diagnostic ☐ Monitoring ☐ Interpretation ☐ Repair ☐ Design ☐ Planning and Scheduling ☐ Forward Chaining ☐ Backward Chaining | |
| User Concerns: ☐ Perceived Need ☐ Motivation of User ☐ Training of Users ☐ Explanation Required ☐ System Speed ☐ Accuracy Required | |
| Management Concerns: ☐ Senior Management Spurns ☐ Cultural Impact ☐ High/Low Profile | |
| Value of System: ☐ Internal Cost Savings ☐ Improves Quality and Consistency of Decision Making ☐ Speeds Up Work ☐ Creates New Products or Services ☐ Captures Valuable, Existing Company Information for: ☐ Sales ☐ Distribution ☐ Training | |
| ☐ Estimated Rate of Interest | |

**Source:** Adapted from Jim Carnes, "Expert Systems Program Manager's Guide," paper delivered at the Forum on Artificial Intelligence in Acquisition Management conference, May 14-17,1990.

## REVIEW QUESTIONS

1. Identify the management functions defined by classical management theory that are involved in managing a KBS project.
2. Discuss what is involved in strategic planning for KBS development projects.
3. Describe formal preliminary planning and feasibility studies.
4. Discuss different kinds of preliminary planning and feasibility studies done in different KBS development project situations.
5. Discuss some of the special problems involved in KBS development project planning that are not encountered as often in conventional project planning situations.
6. Describe the critical factors examined during a structured situation analysis when doing formal in-depth feasibility studies.
7. Discuss some of the specific steps involved in determining a project's operational feasibility.
8. Describe some of the situations in which it might be preferable to use conventional computer systems tools rather than KBS tools for system development.

## EXERCISES

1. The disks accompanying this book contain the prototype KBS described at the end of this chapter. Following the directions accompanying the disks for using the M.1 expert system shell, run a consultation using the system, which has the file name FEASIBLE. If you wish, you might also print out the knowledge base and study it while you are running the system and restudying this chapter.
2. Use the system described in Exercise 1 to study the feasibility of one of the systems you developed as part of the exercises in Chapters 2 through 6.

## REFERENCES

"Applications." *Expert Systems*, February 1989, pp. 48–49.

Barber, Dan, and Scott Shoemaker. "AI in Manufacturing." *PC AI*, March-April 1989, pp. 28–30.

Broad, William, J. " 'Smart' Machines Ready to Assume Many NASA Duties." *New York Times*, March 6, 1989, pp. A1, B9.

Cullen, J., and A. Bryman. "The Knowledge Acquisition Bottleneck: Time for Reassessment?" *Expert Systems* 5 (3), August 1988, pp. 216–25.

Cupello, James M., and David J. Mishelevicksy. "Managing Prototype Knowledge/Expert System Projects." *Communications of the ACM*, May 1988, pp. 534–41.

Davenport, Thomas. "The Case of the Soft Software Proposal." *Harvard Business Review*, May-June 1989, pp. 12–24.

Dologite, D.G., and Robert J. Mockler, "Developing Effective Knowledge-Based Systems: Overcoming Organizational and Individual Behavior Barriers." *Information Resources Journal*, Winter 1989, pp. 27–39.

Leonard-Barton, D. "The Case for Innovative Integration: An Expert System at Digital." *Sloan Management Review*, Fall 1987, pp. 7–9.

Martin, James, and Steven Oxman. *Building Expert Systems*, Englewood Cliffs, NJ: Prentice-Hall, 1988.

Mazer, Linda. *Artificial Intelligence/Expert Systems at Covia*. A PC EXPO Presentation, Rosemont, IL: Covia Co. (a wholly owned subsidiary of United Airlines), July 22, 1988.

Meredith, Jack R., and Samuel J. Mantel. *Project Management*, 2d ed., New York: Wiley, 1989.

Mockler, Robert J., "Using Knowledge-Based Systems for Estimating Risks Inherent in a Proposed KBS Project." *Expert Systems*, February 1990, pp. 27-41.

Mockler, Robert J. *Knowledge-Based Systems for Management Decisions*. Englewood Cliffs, NJ: Prentice-Hall, 1989.

Moullin, Bernard. "Strategic Planning for Expert Systems." *IEEE Expert*, April 1990, pp. 69–75.

Newquist, Harvey P., III. "American Express and AI: Don't Leave Home Without Them." *AI Expert*, April 1987, pp. 63–65.

Newquist, Harvey P., III. "Expert Systems Invade Main Stream." *AI Expert*, April 1989, pp. 71–73.

Rauch-Hindin, Wendy B. *Artificial Intelligence in Business, Science and Industry (Volume II—Applications)*, Englewood Cliffs, NJ: Prentice-Hall, 1985.

Shpilberg, David, Lynford E. Graham, and Harry Schatz. "ExperTAX: An Expert System for Corporate Tax Planning." *Expert Systems*, July 1986, pp. 136–51.

Van Horne, James C. *Financial Management and Policy*. Englewood Cliffs, NJ: Prentice-Hall, 1986.

Williamson, Mickey. "User-developed Expert Systems." *PC AI*, March-April 1989, pp. 11–15.

Wiseman, George. *Strategic Information Systems*. Chicago: Irwin, 1988.

# 13

# Organizing and Implementing

The objective of this chapter is to enable readers to understand how to organize, direct, and control KBS development efforts. The discussion covers:

- Organizing and implementing KBS development efforts
- General strategies for organizing and implementing KBS development efforts
- Techniques and tools
- Large-systems efforts at large companies
- Small-systems efforts at large companies
- Other types of KBS development management situations
- An approach to decision making in specific situations

The discussion begins with a brief overview of the area under study: KBS development effort organization and implementation. The discussion then covers different organization planning and implementation strategies, as well as tasks and techniques used in different kinds of KBS development situations. The chapter also provides extensive examples of how companies made organization decisions in actual working situations, and the lessons learned from these experiences. The chapter closes with a discussion of approaches used in making decisions in this area and of a KBS designed to assist in making these decisions.

## ORGANIZING AND IMPLEMENTING KBS DEVELOPMENT EFFORTS

In addition to the overall planning jobs already discussed, strategies and implementation plans and actions are also needed to organize, direct, and control the development effort. Planning the organization of the development group and implementation of the development effort involves studying the tasks to be done and the people and company organization involved, grouping activities into logical segments, delineating authority and responsibility within these groups, establishing working relationships among the groups that will satisfy both people and job requirements, establishing controls, and directing the KBS development effort.

These are key KBS development management functions, which can have a major impact on the effectiveness of the development effort. Several aspects of planning, staffing, directing, organizing and controlling the KBS development effort have been discussed in Chapters 11 and 12. This chapter continues those discussions, while focusing mainly on broader organization and implementation aspects of larger KBS development efforts.

## GENERAL STRATEGIES FOR ORGANIZING AND IMPLEMENTING KBS DEVELOPMENT EFFORTS

Once a decision has been made to develop a KBS, several overall organizing decisions are made, such as:

- Whether to do the KBS development using existing personnel or departments, hire new people, have an outside consulting or software development service firm do it, or use some combination of these resources
- What the formal organizational relationships of KBS development groups will be
- Whether the development effort should be treated as a continuing effort or as a one-time project
- How the project should be structured—the tasks to be done, the groupings of tasks, and the interrelationships of tasks within the development group
- Whether or not to create and/or use development support groups
- Who will head the development effort and to whom she/he/they report

The exact combination of organizational structure and implementation strategies will depend on the type of KBS development situation under study. As is seen in the sections that follow, for example, the structures used in large companies and small companies and for large and small systems efforts can vary considerably. The nature and complexity of the KBS being developed will also affect the organization and staffing in KBS development situations.

In addition, general strategies may differ for the different phases of a KBS development effort, for example, for the system development phase and for the system delivery (or use) phase. In these situations, a collaborative development team of experienced domain experts working with a knowledge engineer may be the core of the system *development* organization. The phase involving the *delivery* of the system may consist of a team of technical support people, operating managers, users, and knowledge engineers.

Organizational planning and administration skills are needed to shape structures that balance technical and business operating requirements in a way appropriate to the specific situation under study (Davis 1989; DuBrin 1989; Huber 1986; Luconi 1984; Szilagyi 1987).

Because of the wide range of possible KBS development environments and the wide range of possible KBS organization decisions, the following discussions cover several different types of situations, including:

- large-system efforts at large companies
- small-system efforts at large companies
- other types of KBS development situations

The following sections discuss both the general approaches to and techniques used in developing, directing, and controlling organizations in these different kinds of KBS development situations. These sections offer examples of how specific companies went about organizing their efforts and the lessons learned from their experiences. These lessons provide guidelines not only as to the advantages and disadvantages of different approaches and techniques, but also as to the situations in which each are likely to be most effective.

## LARGE-COMPANY, LARGE-SYSTEM EFFORTS

Dorothy Leonard-Barton (1987 and 1988) describes in some detail the development of the XSEL expert system at Digital Equipment Corporation. This system was designed to support field sales personnel in originating computer configuration designs to meet customer needs.

### Description of the Situation

The Digital Equipment Corporation develops computer systems. These systems can be built or configured using various types of central processors and other hardware components. The various hardware components are not all compatible with each other, so every system that is built or configured must be checked for compatibility. In the early 1980s, Digital developed an expert knowledge-based system called XCON to check the compatibility and accuracy of completed computer system configurations. It was one of the earliest fully functioning knowledge-based systems in business.

Systems were configured by sales representatives to meet the particular needs of each customer. It became apparent that it would be beneficial to configure systems correctly from the start, not just check the configurations after they are completed. It was decided to build another expert system, called XSEL, to do just that.

The purpose of XSEL was to guide and check the hardware configuration designs of sales representatives. The need for the system arose out of the increasing number of possible configurations which resulted from the growth of the product line to over 50 types of central processors and more than 400 core options. This provided for millions of design possibilities that would increase exponentially as new options were developed. Also, the sales force was shifting from people with technical experience and training to people with general sales skills.

The critical situation characteristics could be summarized as:

- Development of a large and complex system for a large technological corporation by highly trained computer technicians using sophisticated computer hardware and software
- Use of the system by sales personnel at widely diversified geographic locations; the sales people had a wide range of experience in selling, from very little to over twenty years, and an equally wide range of computer literacy levels
- A long development and introduction time span—measured in years
- Need for sophisticated computer hardware and software support designed specifically for users of the system after it was in place

Based on the situation analysis, initially it appeared that the following needed to be done for the system to succeed:

- Cultivate users as co-developers, in a situation where users ranged widely in skills and interests, and where user turnover was expected to be frequent over the development period
- Take steps to sell the system during development by creating a network of supporters among the management and operating personnel involved
- Design a delivery and support environment which accommodated the specific needs of the personnel and organization involved

These organizational steps were all in addition to satisfying technical system requirements.

### Development of XSEL

The development of XSEL began in the spring of 1981. The first fully functioning version was distributed in the summer of 1984. The following discussion summarizes what was done in the three task areas defined initially.

***Cultivating Users as Co-developers.*** Participative design was used in the development of XSEL to cultivate users as co-developers. This entailed actively getting end-users of the system involved in its shaping and development. This helped give users a sense of proprietorship from the start, allowed them to impact the design of the system, and helped reduce unrealistic expectations by exposing them to the limitations of the technology. It was also done to help educate knowledge engineers in the area of expertise and the environment into which the new system would be introduced.

The concept of participative design was implemented through a User Design Group. The User Design Group (UDG) was comprised of those who heard about the development effort through word of mouth and expressed interest in participating in it.

While the UDG generally accomplished its participative design objective, several problems arose in using this group to cultivate users as developers. Of the twenty or so original members of the group, only about four to five senior sales representatives worked on the system until its implementation. It was difficult to incorporate new less-skilled sales representatives into the group because they were intimidated by the highly experienced and vocal senior sales representatives. For this reason, the majority of the user input into the design of the system came from experts, not typical users. This created a bias that was difficult to overcome. For example, the experts became impatient with XSEL's initial prompts and questions because they did not need help in these areas due to their experience and expertise. This led to the construction of a "mini-XSEL" which bypassed preliminary questions. The resources used to construct the mini-XSEL amounted to two person-months. By building the mini-XSEL, the needs of the UDG were being met at the expense of typical users who needed assistance with hardware configurations from the start.

***Selling the System During Its Development.*** Various steps were taken to sell XSEL during its development by creating a network of supporters among management and the operating personnel involved.

One of the first visible advocates for XSEL in the sales management group was a vice president who was impressed with an early prototype. In September of 1982 he challenged the development team to have XSEL on the desk of every sales representative as a Christmas present. The development team reluctantly agreed to try to meet the deadline. Due to the V.P.'s interest, the sales organization also agreed to supply a computer dedicated to running XSEL in each sales region before Christmas. However, it took until the fall of 1983 before the initial system was sent to the field.

The management support was welcome, but not well timed, because it raised expectations that could not be met for a couple of years. As one team member described the situation, "It was as if we had been sloughing off, when really, there was no way we could have met that deadline." Also, the V.P.'s support was short lived because he shortly moved on to another position in the company.

The first release of XSEL was not ready to go to the field until nine months after the dedicated computer hardware for it was in place. This created a major obstacle to introducing the system. During that nine-month interval, space on the dedicated hardware was usurped to run other software. This hardware was in seven regional areas under control of each region's systems manager. Sales representatives who wanted to run XSEL applied to their system manager. The amount of space allotted to XSEL depended on the systems manager's skill and willingness to move other programs around to make room. The systems managers' support was also critical in that they were the most available trainers for sales personnel in the use of the system. Thus the seven regional systems managers who regulated usage and space allotments on these machines became especially critical to the dissemination of XSEL.

The systems managers, especially the skeptical ones, had to be properly educated about XSEL if its implementation was to be successful. In order to enlist their support, several meetings were held to inform them about the technology, prepare them to train users in their area, and to encourage their support of XSEL.

One systems manager at first criticized XSEL and had discouraged users in his geographic region from even trying the innovative new software. He concluded initially that XSEL was inefficient, because when he viewed the rules being invoked they were activated in random patterns rather than the orderly progression of a traditional COBOL or BASIC program. Later he learned that this supposedly sloppy programming was characteristic of a heuristic rule-based system. The meetings with the systems managers were successful in eliminating this resistance based on ignorance of the technology and in increasing awareness of the increased productivity that XSEL would generate.

Problems in building the support network arose in part because of the separation of the development group (which was part of the manufacturing division) from the system's intended users in the sales department. As a result, the sales department's management had to be "sold" on XSEL's viability and worth in order to overcome this obstacle.

The User Design Group's (UDG) support was instrumental in gaining acceptance for XSEL by the sales division's top management. Because XSEL's first release had so many problems, it was recalled to work out major bugs, making the system even harder to sell. A new corrected version was released, but few people were aware of its improvements and the program seemed in danger of being cancelled. At this point the UDG met with top management of the sales department to describe the value of the system. The UDG's credibility contributed to the official agreement to move ahead.

***Designing a Delivery and Support Environment.*** An effective delivery and support environment for XSEL was not in place when the software was first distributed, but evolved as XSEL was used. Sales representatives' using XSEL cited slowness as its key weakness. This slowness was the result of overlyburdened hardware and communication lines. The slow response time discouraged

XSEL's use by those who were exposed to the system and created "innovation assassins" who advised people not to use the system. The hardware limitation was finally overcome in 1986 when powerful VAX machines were purchased to support XSEL in the field, increasing its response time.

Support for users of XSEL developed gradually. After the initial system was introduced late in 1983, several steps were taken to increase support to users and boost usage of the system. For example, in 1984 the internal service hotline for Digital software packages agreed to support XSEL, and in 1985 XSEL was introduced into the orientation and training courses for new sales representatives. The software was also improved throughout this period. With the proper support and delivery mechanisms in place, efforts were focused on advertising the system's improvements, especially to dissatisfied past users.

Digital's experience with XSEL also showed that technological innovations are not always used as their developers originally intend or foresee. As different groups use a system, adjustments may have to be made to the delivery and support environment. For example, in Europe, XSEL was used to increase the productivity of technical editors who manually checked configurations rather than as a tool for sales representatives. As another example, a valuable prototyping exercise is presently underway in Europe where three different methods of configuration are being used. They are: manual configuration of a system by a technical specialist, configuration of a system by a technical specialist using XSEL, and configuration of a system by a sales representative using XSEL. Depending on the group or groups that eventually use XSEL, adjustments may have to be made to the delivery and support environment.

### Situational Guidelines

It is clear from the study that actions could have been taken earlier in the effort to relieve some of the problems which occurred. The following is a list of steps that could have been or were taken to effectively plan the organization of the KBS development at Digital from the outset of the development effort.

- When developing a large system for use at numerous locations it is important to find good experts *interested* in, *committed* to, and *enthusiastic* about working on the system development. This helps build effective systems and gives them credibility from the start. In the case of XSEL, this was done through the User Design Group. The UDG was comprised of those users (in the sales department) who heard about the project by word of mouth. Those not truly interested in development of the system would not be expected to volunteer where their services were so informally requested.
- When developing large systems to be distributed to a diverse group of users and throughout various locations, systems such as XSEL can benefit by having *recognized* experts or high performers in the systems domain (in this case sales of computer systems) advocate the system's use and value.

In the case of XSEL this was done through the User Design Group which was composed of experienced and successful salespeople.

- Use the experts who helped build the system, in this case the UDG, as important advocates of the system. This is especially important for large systems that will be used by a large number of people not involved in the system's development. The UDG members were used to help sell XSEL to top management in the sales division. Having multiple experts supporting a system adds credibility to it before its value is proven in the field. This also enables superior knowledge to be built into the system, creating a better product.
- Use the experts involved in system development to sell it to the end users, especially when the system's performance is not directly tied to the end users' performance. In the XSEL case, the system was believed to have improved the accuracy of the sales representatives' configurations, but this would not result in an immediate or obvious increase in sales or customer satisfaction.
- When the majority of the end users do not participate in a system's development, test the system to ensure that it meets the needs of all the intended end users, not just the needs of the experts primarily involved in developing it. This can be done by involving a wide range of end users in the system's development. The system should handle the problems that may seem simple (mundane) to experts but are challenges to those who are less experienced.
- Develop prototype systems frequently along the way as a means of obtaining feedback from experts/users. They must be working systems, and must be promoted only for what they are: tools for obtaining feedback.
- Don't distribute early prototypes with numerous bugs to be worked out to the general user population. Premature distribution may prejudice users against the finished product when they receive it. It will create doubt in the minds of the future users as to the worth and effectiveness of the system. They don't realize it is an early prototype used to further refine the knowledge represented in the system.
- The process of designing a delivery and support environment which accommodates the specific needs of the personnel and organization involved (organizational prototyping) may span the development, implementation, and postimplementation of the system. This process also looks at who the actual users of the system are, how they use the system, and the actual value of the system to the company and how it should be measured. XSEL was used primarily by the sales representatives to verify a configuration designed manually (62 percent) with others using it to complete a partial configuration started manually (21 percent), and the rest (17 percent) using it to guide the configuration from the beginning.
- Adequate delivery systems, such as the proper hardware, should be available to users from the beginning of a system's introduction. If it is

not, it may encourage innovation assassins—those who have negative experiences using the system and advise other people not to use it. This may hamper integration of the system into work routines. It can be avoided by having sufficient hardware dedicated to the new system.

- Realistic time frames should be developed for the widespread use of the new system. The system development team should not be rushed into distributing the system by managers enamored of the technology's potential but not involved in the particular system's development.
- Don't oversell or raise extremely high expectations for the system. If one doesn't deliver a properly functioning system as advertised and/or when expected it will create skepticism about the system's value.

These management guidelines are situational guidelines for the organization and implementation of large systems for use by multiple users at different locations in large companies. They are not necessarily all applicable to other types of situations.

### Lessons Learned from Similar Studies

Major studies relevant to KBS development effort organization have been done in the decision support system area. Several key lessons can be learned from them.

A review of the literature shows a variety of studies have been done, especially at MIT, on organizing and carrying out DSS and related executive information and support systems (EIS and ESS) development efforts. These include:

- Alloway and Quillard, *User Managers' Systems Needs* (1982)
- Benjamin and Scott Morton, *Information Technology, Integration, and Organizational Change* (1986)
- DeLong and Rockart, *A Survey of Current Trends in the Use of Executive Support Systems* (1984)
- Keen and Scott Morton, *Decision Support Systems: An Organizational Perspective* (1978)
- Lee and Treacy, *Information Technology Impacts on Power and Influence* (1987)
- Rockart, *The Changing Role of the Information Systems Executive: A Critical Success Factors Perspective* (1982)
- Rockart and Crescnezi, *Engaging Top Management in Information Systems Planning and Development: A Case Study* (1984)

The study by DeLong and Rockart (1986) typifies these studies in discussing eight key considerations which should be addressed in carrying out any DSS development effort, and the strategies relevant to each area, including:

- *A committed and informed executive sponsor.* There must be an executive who has a realistic understanding of DSS capabilities and limitations, and who really wants the system so badly that she or he is willing to devote considerable time and energy to seeing that a system gets developed.

- *An operating sponsor.* Because an executive sponsor usually lacks sufficient time, it appears very worthwhile to have an "operating sponsor" designated to manage the details of implementation from the user's side. This person would be a trusted subordinate or executive assistant who is very familiar with the sponsor's work style and way of thinking.

The conclusion of this and related studies is that managers/users should have control of the systems development effort, with CIS personnel playing an important but subordinate role. For example, the results of one of these studies, which is summarized in Figure 13–1, show that most DSS developed at the companies studied were created by managers using the system or by staff analysts working for those managers (Keen 1981). Such a transfer of systems development tasks arose from manager/user needs and was apparently made possible by the wider availability of PC technology and newer, easier-to-use software.

Leonard-Barton's study recommends a larger role for managers/users in KBS development, as co-developers and internal "salesmen" of the system, while leaving ultimate control with CS personnel. Other studies of KBS development have reached conclusions similar to those in the DSS studies cited in Figure 13–1. For example, Cupello (1988) found that because user champions are so important to success, as many user advocates as computer technicians should be included in the KBS development effort. In addition, because senior management and user support is so important, they recommend the user advocate head the development team and report directly to the senior management of the user operation. These conclusions are confirmed by Cullen (1988) and by the authors' studies of such organizations as the IRS and a major auto company described later in the chapter, as well as by others (Bailey 1987; Cullen 1988; Leonard-Barton 1988; Luconi and Malone 1984; Martin 1988, Chapter 13; Prerau 1987; Shpilberg 1986; Sumner 1987).

Whatever the final organization in a specific situation, these studies emphasize that in organizing KBS development efforts the expert/user viewpoint always be given as much, if not more, emphasis as technical computer AI

**Figure 13–1.** Managers' Dominant Role in Decision Support System (DSS) Development and Use (42-Company Survey)

| | Data Processing | Staff Analyst | Middle Management | Top Management |
|---|---|---|---|---|
| Who requested the application | 0 | 4 | 30 | 66 |
| Who built it | 3 | 53 | 22 | 22 |
| Who uses the terminal | 0 | 70 | 21 | 9 |
| Who uses the output | 0 | 6 | 42 | 52 |

competence and that business managers rather than technical computer managers have overall responsibility for system development.

## LARGE-COMPANY, SMALL-SYSTEM EFFORTS

Other types of development situations require different variations of the general approach to KBS development organization described earlier. For example, during the late 1980s DuPont focused their development effort on creating hundreds of small systems each year.

In their KBS development program, the company encourages operating managers to originate and participate in the design of the systems. To this end, the company provides training and PC expert system shells to enable the managers to do prototyping and, where appropriate, actual system development. The technical computer support organization is intended to function mainly to support the operating managers in the development effort, since it is clear that the major beneficiaries of the systems, the operating managers, are often expected to be the major initiators and developers of the systems.

The kind of approach used at DuPont differed considerably from that used in developing XSEL at Digital, because the situational needs differed considerably. The following discussion is based on the author's interviews with Dr. Edward Mahler and on Jennifer Bailey's study (1987) of the company.

Ed Mahler, the man in charge of introducing AI technology into operations at DuPont, approached his task with some innate, down-home strategic thinking. He had worked many years at DuPont, in manufacturing, strategic planning, and research. His training in computers was limited: he was spreadsheet literate, but not a programmer. As he often has said, he knows there is a difference between a bit and a byte; he just isn't sure what that difference is. His approach had to be designed to take advantage of his own strengths and weaknesses, as well as those of DuPont.

In examining those factors at DuPont that would impact on his task, very early on he noted that DuPont had very dispersed, and also very diversified, manufacturing facilities. This meant that the knowledge was not only widely dispersed, but also (and this was important) highly localized because of the different business at each location. While the operating managers were in general computer literate (30,000 are considered to be what is called "Lotus literate"), only about 10 percent of that number could be considered technologically literate (that is, programmers plus) in computers.

Another key strategic planning factor that influenced Mahler was imbedded in the corporate culture. It was widely believed at the operating level that anything that came from corporate headquarters had to be wrong, and so should be ignored. It was believed that if the operating managers were just left alone, the company would be better off. At the corporate level, while there was strong support for the KBS effort, there were still pockets of uncertainty about just what, when, and how much this new technology could help operations, and eventually profits.

Certain characteristics of the task itself also influenced his approach. First, knowledge-based systems required much more user involvement than did conventional computer system development. This is confirmed by other studies (Tuhrim 1988). They also involved considerably more user interest in the system to ensure the system's use after it was introduced. Second, the technology was new and in some ways more complex and sophisticated than conventional computer system technology.

In a way, Ed Mahler was as worried about what he didn't know as about what he did know. This meant allowing for an uncertain learning curve, since the risk of mistakes was high.

An initial strategy for organizing and introducing the KBS effort at DuPont began to emerge from this situational analysis.

- As for the timing, it appeared that early efforts should be treated as learning experiments (the technology was developing, there were limited benchmark experiences) and the capital investment initially kept low (the risk of mistakes was high in an uncertain environment).
- As for the systems, the operational organization (dispersed *and* localized knowledge) seemed to indicate that small systems would be appropriate and useful.
- As for the mechanism for computerization, expert system development and application PC shells were being introduced that would enable computer-literate, but nonprogrammer, managers to create their own systems, and require low capital outlay, reducing the cost of mistakes, whose likelihood was high.
- As for the organization of the system development effort, it was basically cooperative, since a major part of it would have to be done by the operating managers (the users), both for corporate culture reasons and because it was needed to give users a proprietary interest in the systems and so ensure their involvement in development and their interest in using the final system.
- As for the balance between computer technicians and operating manager (user) viewpoints in the organization and implementation of the development effort, the computer technicians would have to function in a support role for the most part, their primary role being to help (cooperate with) the managers who do the system development.
- As for the manager's role, it was perceived as user, knowledge engineer, and system developer—and initiator—in most instances, so that control remained with the expert/manager.
- As for the way it would be presented, because of corporate culture factors, the effort would have to be allowed to grow from the ground up, rather than being initiated and run from the top down, because of

corporate culture factors, so as to allow time for an informal support network and good working relationships to develop (Foss 1990).

Carrying out the above strategy was not easy, but the situation factors dictated that something along those lines be tried and that it would have a reasonable chance of success, if executed well.

The development effort was helped greatly by the personality of Ed Mahler, a veteran of many years at the company, who genuinely believed in his subordinate supportive role. This belief was matched by an equally genial and cooperative personal style.

There are several examples of how this strategy was executed. It was necessary to create training programs for operating managers on how to develop systems. Classes were to be small (fewer than twenty persons) and strictly voluntary. The first one was promoted for no more than it was—the first. Feedback from participants was taken daily (and still is) and the course was adjusted in many ways to meet expressed needs. For example, early courses were only about 30 percent hands-on exercises, while later courses were close to 70 percent.

Some compromises were necessary. The objective of the training (which generally lasts two days) was to have as many participants as possible have a working prototype system by the end of the session. On average about five do, another ten have the sketch of a system, and about five find they are not interested or can find no suitable applications in their job or work area. This meant gradually reducing the amount of time devoted to AI theory in the course. Books on theory were provided, but acquiring the theory was the burden of the participant outside the course. Some complained of this, but it was required by the practical orientation of the course.

A variety of expert system shells were made available to the operating managers. Considerable assistance was provided by the twelve or so technical people on Ed Mahler's staff after the managers finished the course and were back on the job. The cost of the shell and the assistance was billed to the division only after some results were achieved. The division had the option to pay the bill, or to write a one page letter describing why they found the project unsatisfactory and so would not pay the bill. The training course itself could be conducted on site or at headquarters, and was billed to the division.

The developing of systems followed a similar pattern, with the amount and kind of assistance required varying greatly from individual to individual.

A major lesson learned from this experience was that a situational approach was needed. Ed Mahler listened to the situation, heard what it told him, and developed a strategy with those situational influencing factors in mind. At the same time, he used some techniques drawn from his own experiences, as well as from system theory, AI technology, and situational and organization theory. Ed Mahler's experience reflects a growing trend among companies to "downsize" computer systems, that is, placing their development and use further "down" into an organization, preferably at the level where they have the most immediate use and payoff (Radding 1989).

## OTHER TYPES OF KBS DEVELOPMENT MANAGEMENT SITUATIONS

This section reviews a number of other companies' experiences in organizing and implementing knowledge-based systems development efforts.

### Coopers & Lybrand: ExperTAX

At Coopers & Lybrand, Dr. David Shpilberg was hired in 1983 to develop decision support systems for the company. In June 1985, after working with a task force of C & L managers in various accounting and tax areas and developing a list of potential computer systems projects, funds were allocated to develop a "proof-of-concept" prototype of what was to eventually become C & L's ExperTAX knowledge-based system. This system is described in Appendix B of this book. The prototype was developed by a team of two people experienced in accounting, computer software development, statistics, and cognitive science, working with Dr. Shpilberg (Sviolka 1988).

In this situation, the development team was brought in from the software engineering field, and so were outsiders to the accounting firm. They were, however, essentially "Renaissance" men, since they were people of very broad backgrounds with considerable experience in and familiarity with a wide range of business areas. Although essentially outsiders, they worked closely in all phases of the system's development with existing operating experts and other personnel at the company who would be using the system. The new system work was also strongly supported by higher management.

After almost a year of field testing and development, during which the scope and direction of the effort evolved and changed dramatically, the system was developed. It focused on a single universally-applicable tax planning function. Two people from the company's marketing department at this point were assigned the job of developing a plan to "market" the new system to its prospective users at the company. Here, in Sviolka's words, are the final phases of that "marketing" plan:

> The campaign included step-by-step instructions, training aids, and promotional materials (such as pennants in the various practice offices). Late in 1986, the roll-out began in earnest. Fifty regional coordinators were brought to Chicago for a "Train the Trainers session." At this event, everyone was given a marketing kit for ExperTAX which included a videotape, a slide show, and other supporting material for presentation at their own offices. Each

> individual was responsible for presenting the product to each of the offices in his or her geographic area during the following quarter. During 1986–1987, each local office's audit and tax partner was given the job of putting at least one client through the ExperTAX system because the paper-based system used up to that time would be phased out. (Sviolka 1988)

Subsequently, policies were developed for updating and maintaining the system. Throughout the development and installation of the ExperTAX system, extremely strong top management support was given to it.

### Boeing Computer Services (BCS)

BCS was a subsidiary of the Boeing Company that provided computing services to both Boeing and outside customers. It had 13,000 employees and $800 million of equipment in 1986 (Gogan 1986).

During 1983, one of the fourteen new technologies that Boeing management identified as important strategic technologies of the future was artificial intelligence (AI). Because of this, AI was made a major priority of the BCS division.

The AI Center of Excellence, as it was called, first undertook to set up a training program for Boeing employees, since there seemed to be a shortage of AI personnel at that time. The program created was to last one year, require participants to not only learn theory but also to create working "proof-of-concept" prototypes, and was staffed by new employees and part-time personnel from universities.

In 1986 about two-thirds of the fifty-eight faculty members at Boeing's AI Center of Excellence had PhDs in AI or related fields, and many had taught before joining the faculty. Janusz Kowalik headed the faculty. He had a PhD from the Polish Academy of Science, had taught in Norway, Australia, and Canada, and was a professor at Washington State University.

By February 1986, twenty-two individuals had completed the one-year program. All of them were Boeing employees prior to coming to the program, and had been required to propose a KBS application in their area of work at Boeing before being admitted to the program. They were on one-year leaves of absence from their jobs while in the program.

Problems were encountered in the program, the main one being that graduates who returned to their original division rarely worked on AI programs, the initial major thrust of the program. In addition, many of them returned to other divisions where they also did not work on AI-related projects.

The lesson learned at Boeing during the initial phases of the program appeared to be that divisions which sent promising people to the year-long training program apparently were not required to make a major commitment to using AI technology. Simply having a person from that division on leave for a year made the project seem to originate from outside the division.

The approach was considerably different from the one pursued by DuPont, where the transfer of AI technology was more effectively handled through more involvement by the division, quicker initial results, initiation of projects by operating personnel on the job, short periods of training, and lower levels of expectations.

### FMC Corporation

FMC is an international conglomerate with manufacturing and mining facilities worldwide, agricultural equipment and chemical concerns, and defense equipment and development activities.

Based on work in vision and autonomous control during the early 1980s, in 1984 the CEO and the President and Chief Operations Director of FMC decided to make a major investment in AI as strategic technologies. FMC decided initially to develop a central group for applied AI research and development. The Artificial Intelligence Center (AIC) was funded as part of the Electronics, Engineering and Computer Sciences Laboratories in FMC's Central Engineering Laboratories in Santa Clara, California (Melaragno and Allen 1989).

The AIC's objective was to be a leader in the application of AI in industry and defense. The emphasis was on immediate and repeating application needs. Further, FMC selected a subset of AI technologies as applicable to computing between then (1984) and the year 2000. The selected technologies were vision, knowledge-based planning and configurations systems, structured selection and data interpretation, intelligent human/machine interface, and computer-based training. Other objectives were to develop the technical "integration" skills—both cultural and electronic—to successfully transfer the technology to the divisions, and to leverage internal capabilities through affiliations with local universities (for example, Stanford University) and companies (FMC purchased 10 percent of Teknowledge, an expert systems tool vendor).

Since 1984, the organization and management of AI technology at FMC has evolved through several phases to meet the ever-changing needs of its business. Initially, the AIC was funded through division- and corporate-sponsored work. Research and development and capability development were budgeted; operating divisions and government contracts paid for applications development. Personnel were trained for internal development of the AIC and not for technology transfer to operating divisions or dissemination of the technologies. The plan was to recruit talent for the center by offering an exceptionally attractive environment. Divisions were responsible for life-cycle support of applications. The AIC transferred development technologies and integration skills to the divisions in the course of applications development.

By 1987, the AIC had about forty professionals, 80 percent of whom held advanced degrees, half of which were PhDs. In February 1989, the AIC was broken into subgroups: an AI Department tasked with applied research and applications development; a Software Engineering Group combining knowledge engineers and conventional software programmers; and a Signal Processing, Vision and Electronics Group, which handles vision technology needs. All were located in the Electronics Engineering and Computer Sciences Laboratories. The AIC no longer trained new personnel; it now considered itself fully staffed.

An additional model for technology dissemination among the divisions was also being implemented in 1989–90. FMC began distributing expert systems tools throughout the divisions in an attempt to disperse the expertise broadly. The Central Engineering Laboratories conduct regular seminars for division personnel; AI topics are included. It also conducts a monthly 5-day KBS course in conjunction with the distribution of low-end tools. Of the 70 or 80 total applications through early 1990, an estimated 25 had been fielded (including defense demonstration application prototypes built under contract).

Evaluation of payback is informal. Historically, no postproject audits were performed; hence, no corporate-wide figures are available. Projects have succeeded in capturing vanishing expertise from retiring personnel, and anecdotal stories tell of increased performance and financial returns.

### Lockheed Corporation

Lockheed's Artificial Intelligence Center (AIC) is in the Research and Development Division of Lockheed Missiles and Space Company, Inc., which is one of the five major groups comprising Lockheed Corporation (Melaragno and Allen 1989). In late 1985, a Lockheed corporate AI task force determined a need and made the recommendation for an AIC. Within six months, an AIC manager had been assigned to the Research and Development Division. The first task of the AIC was to survey Lockheed's organizations and make a situational assessment.

The AIC's charter covers three major areas: research and technology development, technology transfer, and education and training. The AIC is organized into nine sections. The seven sections working on research and technology development are: the Validation of Knowledge Bases Section, the Human Interface Section, the Real Time Symbolic Systems Section, the Image Understanding Section, and the Autonomous Planning Section. The two remaining sections are the Technology Transfer Section and the Training and Education Section.

In addition to research in the particular areas, the sections develop, test, verify, and support AI tools, some in-house and some commercial. The AIC supports university research projects and has connections with Stanford University. The AIC also has affiliations with commercial organizations (for example, Inference Corporation and SRI International) to help leverage AI technologies. In addition, the sections conduct externally funded research.

The Technology Transfer Section is tasked with establishing technology transfer interfaces with Lockheed's product divisions. It conducts the AIC's technical consulting with product divisions, acts as the conduit to integrate the AIC's AI research into the product divisions, and maintains the corporate AI applications database.

The Training and Education Section conducts one- to two-week courses in implementation skills and holds one-day and one-week courses for executives; those courses include an overview of AI technologies and AI development effort management techniques. The Training and Education Section also has a six-month residency program. In that program, a product division nominates a candidate, approves a project, and submits a proposal to the AIC. The resident attends twelve weeks of classroom and laboratory course work and then is assigned an AIC mentor. For the next twelve weeks, the resident and the mentor team work on the application. The resident, now a graduate from the AIC's residency program, returns to the product division with a completed project.

### A Major Automobile Company

A major automobile company undertook a development effort to create a KBS to assist design engineers in specifying types of metal to be used in developing automobile prototype models. Two areas of expertise were involved, advanced metallurgy and purchasing.

In examining the situation, the depth and breadth of the major knowledge area, metallurgy, was considered a major decision factor by the KBS development manager. It appeared that it would be far more difficult to train a knowledge engineer in metallurgy than to train a metallurgist in KBS technology. In addition, it was felt that knowledge acquisition would be greatly facilitated by having a metallurgist doing the interviewing of other professional experts in the field. It would help reinforce the cooperative nature of the KBS development effort organization, since it created an atmosphere of professionals working together.

Two key organization steps were taken to fill the technological gap left by having a metallurgist function as knowledge engineer. First, an outside software engineering firm was engaged to support the effort. Such a move is sometimes referred to as "outsourcing" (Caldwell 1989). In this situation, the knowledge engineer was given direct authority and control over the outside firm, that is, a hierarchical arrangement. This avoided the kind of internal political conflict which can arise at a large company where a technical support group, such as computer information systems, is assigned to work with a less technically qualified line manager who has no direct control over the group. Second, the metallurgist who was to function as the knowledge engineer was sent to extended KBS training programs before undertaking the job.

### Other Company Experiences

Such an approach was not used at a major utility described by Rose (1988). There recent doctoral graduates from computer science programs working for outside consultants served as knowledge engineers on a project involving diagnosis of dam faults and failures. The expertise involved knowledge acquired over many years and decisions made at a very intuitive level. As a result it was very difficult and time consuming for CS-trained personnel to learn how the area worked. After two years an 80-rule system had been developed at a cost of $300,000, but the system was not used. It appeared that outsiders, without knowledge of the expert domain, could not overcome either the knowledge acquisition barriers or organizational resistance barriers, given the way the KBS development effort was staffed and organized.

In contrast, the IRS has chosen to send their own systems personnel experienced in tax accounting and auditing to school for two years to learn artificial intelligence and KBS development. This was done to enable them to create their own internal KBS development department which was familiar with the specific knowledge domains of the IRS. Such a training and staffing strategy provided a means of balancing technical and domain-expert interests in future KBS development efforts (Brown 1988).

## AN APPROACH TO DECISION MAKING IN SPECIFIC SITUATIONS

The discussion in the preceding section covered the area under study, planning and managing the organization of the KBS development effort. Any of the organization strategies, techniques, and tools discussed there may or may not be useful to the reader, depending on the KBS development situation under study.

As seen in the preceding discussions of company experiences, determining which organization strategies, tools, and techniques to use requires analyzing the specific situation under study.

The general approach to making decisions about organization design for KBS development efforts is shown in Figure 13–2.

This section describes how specific knowledge domain, existing organization situation and people, and available resource factors are analyzed and structured, and then used in making decisions about organizational design in different kinds of reader situations.

As seen from the preceding discussions a wide range of decisions can be involved in this area, including:

- The overall organization mix strategy—whether to use existing personnel or departments, hire new people, have an outside consulting or software development service firm do it, or use some combination of these resources
- The formal organization relationships of KBS development groups
- How the effort should be structured—the tasks to be done, finding personnel with the mix of skills to perform the tasks, interrelationships of the tasks within the development effort structure
- Creation and/or use of development support groups
- Who will head the effort and to whom they will report

**Figure 13–2.** An Overall Approach to Making KBS Development Organization Decisions

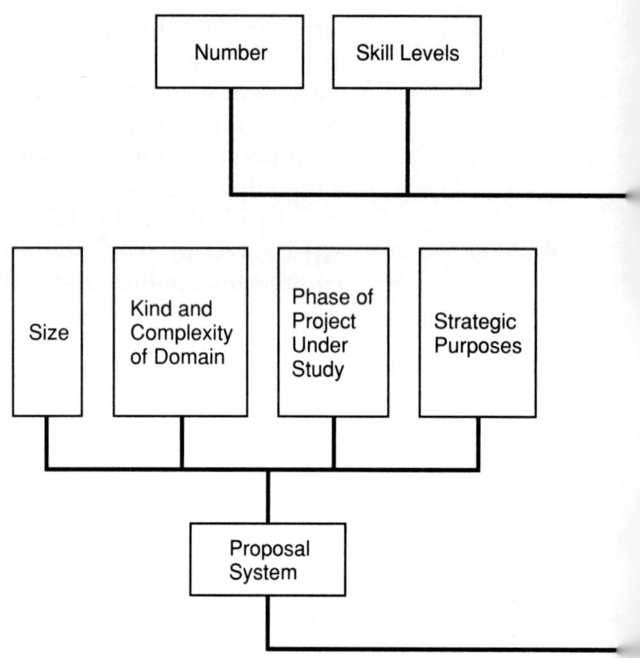


In addition, the kinds of situations can vary considerably, as is seen from the range of large and small company projects discussed so far in this chapter.

Because of this wide range of possible decisions and decision situations, the approach described in this section is necessarily a general one, which is intended to give only an overview of the approach.

The following sections discuss:

- critical factors affecting decisions in this area
- how decisions are made based on these critical factors

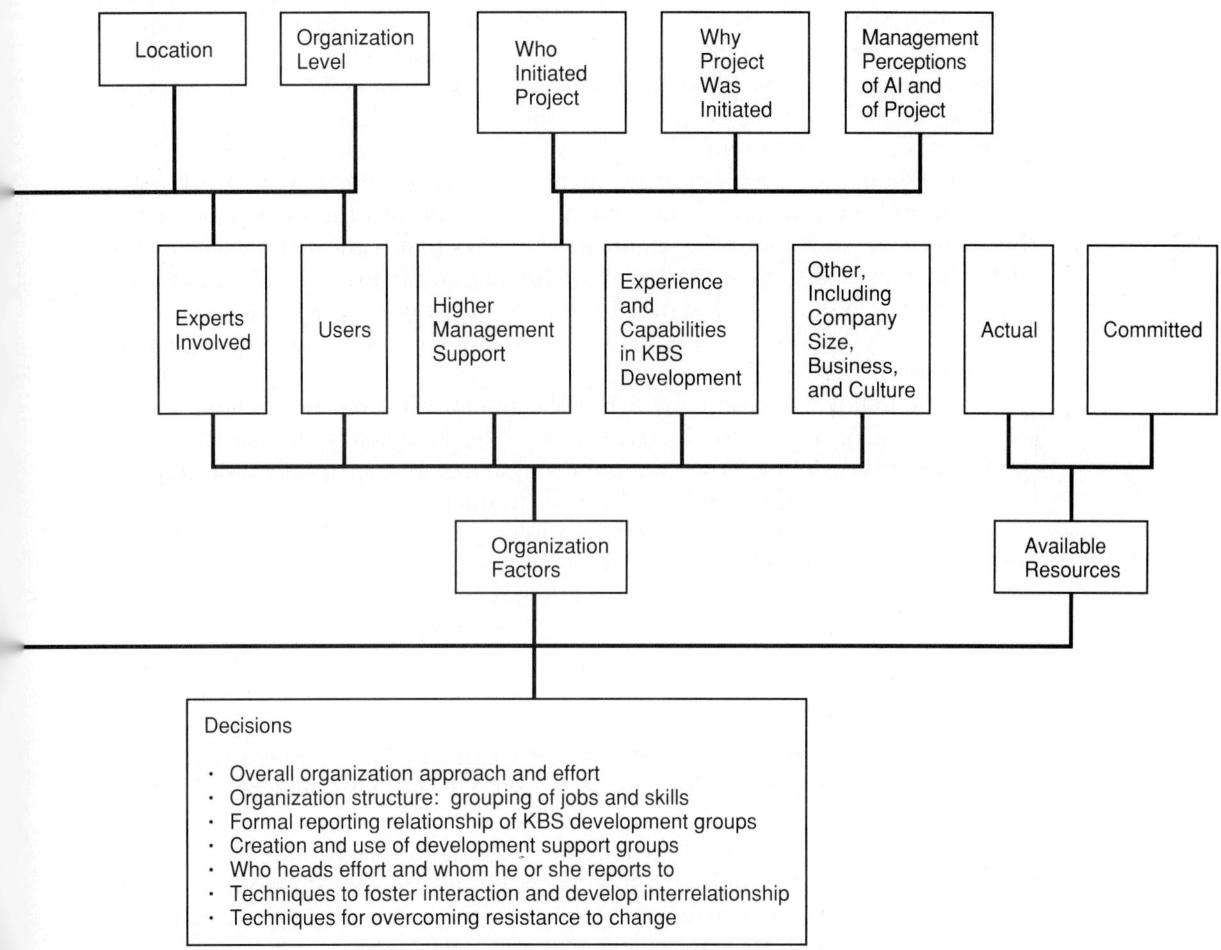


### Critical Factors Affecting Decisions in This Area

As seen from Figure 13–2 and from the discussions of company experiences, several kinds of critical factors are studied:

- nature of the system to be developed
- the organization factors
- the available resources

***Nature of the System To Be Developed.*** The size of the system, the kind and complexity of the domain replicated, the phase of the project under study, and the strategic purposes of the system all can affect organization decisions.

For example, at DuPont, based on a study of the company situation, it was determined that small systems, with limited domains, were to be developed during the initial years of the program. The purpose of the initial KBS development effort was to be to produce a large number of smaller working systems, both to obtain a more immediate payout and also to help the organization adapt more quickly and easily to the new technology.

At Digital, the XSEL system was to be much larger, the domain much more complex, and the purpose of the system to be to support the sales effort across the entire company, both to extend the benefits that came from their earlier XCON system and to give the company further competitive advantages in the field. The new system was designed to provide better customer service, speed up the delivery cycle, and cut production costs, and so had a strategic impact on several business areas.

At the major auto company, while the system itself was not as large as the one at Digital, it was a good-sized system. The knowledge domain was very specialized and complex, however, and the system was strategically important to the degree that it could speed up the new product design process.

The phase of the system effort under study can also impact on the organization decision. In some situations, for example, the system development requirements can differ from the system deployment and delivery requirements. For instance, at Digital the User Design Group was an integral part of the development process. Technical support services, on the other hand, were needed to integrate the system into the work environment and ensure its effective use.

The strategic importance of the KBS can also vary from situation to situation. For example, at Coopers & Lybrand ExperTAX was perceived by management as having both an immediate impact on tax advisory services rendered by the company as part of its ongoing business, and as having a longer-term impact through creating a new money-making division providing artificial intelligence client consulting services, as well as through creating an image of the company as being a leader in new technologies (Sviolka 1988).

Each of these systems' factors can impact on the way that the company organizes its development effort, as seen in the earlier discussions. Each reader in the same way would examine his or her own proposed system's characteristics in these three areas to provide a basis for selecting and designing an organizational strategy appropriate to the specific situation.

***Organization Factors.*** The factors covered under this heading include the experts (their number, skills, geographic location, and organizational level), organizational characteristics (the number, skills, geographic location, and organizational level of users and user units involved), higher management support anticipated, the experience and skills of company personnel in KBS development and related computer information systems areas, and other considerations (company business, culture, size, and diversity).

For example, at Digital the experts were salespeople with diverse computer skills and sales experience, who were located in widely dispersed geographic areas. Experts and users were part of the same sales group and numbered over 200. Higher management supported the project in general but lacked an organizationally effective means for demonstrating that support initially. While the company was large, it was well focused in the computer area.

At DuPont, on the other hand, while the company was much larger and more diversified, the systems were to be developed by the domain experts for use in their own areas at their geographically-dispersed division locations. The experts and users were, therefore, very familiar with their domains. While many experts and users were involved in the entire project, each individual system development effort was limited to a very small number of experts and users, in some cases a single person. Company management was very supportive of the project, but only to the degree that operating personnel were willing to accept it and demonstrate its usefulness.

At the major auto company, the experts involved were a well-defined group of highly specialized professionals, metallurgists, and company purchasing agents. The experts were part of the user group, and both were located in fairly circumscribed geographic areas. The company was huge and very supportive of the project.

The experience of a company in KBS development can also influence organization decisions. For example, it can influence the amount of outside support used in the development effort, as well as the amount of training (and so time) needed to make it possible to use existing personnel in the development organization.

Higher management support is probably the most critical factor affecting KBS development success. This support can to some degree be measured by who initiates a project and why it was initiated. For example, at Coopers & Lybrand the project had top management support from the beginning, since top management appears to have initiated the project for strategic, as well as operating, reasons. Where an academic or outsider initiates the project, the project needs to be organized in a way that obtains maximum support from top management, since—as with most new technologies—it can take time for top management to realize its benefits (Davenport 1989) and organizations are reluctant to support outside KBS development initiatives without top management support (Cullen 1988).

***Available Resources.*** These factors include not only the people, hardware, software, and financial resources available within the company, but also the amount of resources that are allocated to a project, based on the perception of its value to the company under study.

Available resources can affect a project organization in terms of the people available to sponsor and supervise an effort, since this affects the number of reporting relationships possible, as well as the possible groupings of different individuals of varying skills. For example, at Digital the change in management personnel affected the hierarchical reporting relationships and so sponsorship of the effort by higher management. In addition, the availability and willingness to participate affected the composition of the User Design Group at Digital.

The cooperative work groupings in DuPont's KBS development effort, and the success of the technical systems support group in cooperatively working with the individual system developers in the operating groups, depended in large measure on the personality of the project's leader, Ed Mahler, since it was through his leadership that the project was able to function so well as a collaboratively organized project.

Even in situations where resources are available, there can at times be a question of how much of available resources higher management is willing to commit to ventures such as KBS development efforts, since their value is often hard to measure (Davenport 1989).

### How Decisions Are Made in Light of These Critical Factors

A wide range of decisions are made in light of these key factors. The following briefly traces some of the more general conclusions that are drawn from key factor analysis, based on the discussions of company experiences in the preceding sections.

The *overall organization mix strategy* decision involves decisions about the degree the project is to be done by external or internal personnel. A project manager might consider using only internal personnel if the size of the system was small, the complexity of the system was moderate to complex, the company has experience in KBS development, internal staff with KBS experience and domain expertise are available, the organization is receptive to new technology, resources are available for acquiring KBS development equipment and facilities, and internally developing KBS serve strategic purposes of the organization.

As for *formal organization relationships* of KBS development groups within the company, the larger and more strategically important the systems are, the larger the number of operating managers and personnel who are affected by them, and the greater the resources made available for the project, the more important it is to have higher management sponsor and oversee the project. However, if multiple small KBS are to be developed, a more decentralized reporting and management structure, with operational management's support and oversight, would be an appropriate alternative to consider.

*How the effort itself should be structured* involves determining the internal organization of the KBS development effort. This involves deciding on the organizational roles and interrelationships of experts, users, operating management, and technical support groups within the KBS development effort. For example, if the knowledge domain becomes more complex, the level of user skill that is needed increases. If the KBS development effort is smaller, more control of the development effort by the operating area for whom the system is being developed is needed, and the technical group is more able to function as a support group. On the other hand, the less deep and complex the knowledge domain is, the lower the level of user skills required, and the larger the system, the more control technical personnel can have of the development effort—provided adequate participation by user groups is built into the project organization. In situations involving nontechnical managers who are involved in the development effort, additional training and support groupings will also be needed, often at the operating manager's work location. Available resources also must be considered. For example, if PCs or access to easily learned KBS development software is not widely available to expert/user developers, more support may be required from technical personnel.

*As for the creation and/or use of development support groups*, the more diverse the skills and background that expected users of the system have and the greater their numbers, the greater the need for formal user groups with a wide range of skill levels to be integral parts of the development effort. Also, the deeper the knowledge domain and the less uniform the expert judgements, the greater the need for formal representative expert groups to be integral parts of the development effort. The ability to form these groups will be controlled to a large degree by their availability and by the degree of top management support of the effort.

Obviously, a great deal more is involved in making organization decisions in KBS development situations than is covered in this brief discussion of the general approach to decision making in this area. This discussion should, however, provide a general introduction to basic concepts and approaches involved in making key decisions in this phase of KBS project management.

In addition, the above discussion provides a basis for more specific cognitive modelling of the decision processes involved in organizing and carrying out KBS development efforts and for developing KBS based on these underlying cognitive models.

## REVIEW QUESTIONS

1. Describe some of the general strategies used in organizing KBS development efforts.
2. Describe the different specific situation factors at Digital that influenced the way the KBS development project could be most effectively organized.
3. Describe the User Development Group at Digital and its function. Discuss some of the ways in which it helped further the development effort and some of the ways in which, as it was originally set up, it impeded the development effort's effectiveness.

4. Describe the role of supporters or champions in KBS development efforts and discuss the various ways (both effective and ineffective) that champions were provided in the organization of the KBS development effort at Digital.
5. Describe some of the ways in which the system delivery environment at Digital was modified during the development of their XSEL system to encourage more users to make greater use of the system.
6. Describe some of the lessons learned from Digital's experiences with XSEL about effectively organizing KBS development efforts.
7. Describe the situational factors at DuPont affecting organization of their KBS development effort and discuss the way it differed from Digital.
8. Describe how the organization of DuPont's KBS development effort was dictated by situational factors.
9. What major lessons can be learned from the DuPont experience about organizing KBS development efforts?
10. Identify the key situational factors examined when making decisions about organizational strategies for KBS development efforts and discuss the ways in which these factors affect strategy development in different kinds of situations.

## EXERCISES

1. Read through recent issues of KBS periodicals listed in the references section of this chapter, and through other related artificial intelligence and systems management books and periodicals, and find discussions of the main topics covered in this book. Pay special attention to descriptions of how companies went about organizing their KBS development efforts. Write a report on how you would go about organizing a development effort for one of the companies you read about, or a report on what you learned about situational approaches to organizing KBS development efforts from your reading.
2. After reviewing the decision situation outline in Figure 13–2 and the discussion of it in the chapter in the section "An Approach to Decision Making in Specific Situations," develop a small KBS to assist in one of the strategy decisions listed at the bottom of the figure. Follow the directions in either Chapter 2, or in Chapters 3 through 6, when developing the system.
3. Based on the research reading done for Exercise 1 above, write a brief report on how that reading helped you in developing your system in Exercise 2.

## REFERENCES

Alloway, Robert M., and Judith A. Quillard. *User Managers' Systems Needs.* CISR Working Paper #86, Center for Information Systems Research, Sloan School of Management, Cambridge, MA: MIT, April 1982.

Bailey, Jennifer Jo. *Economic Evaluation of Knowledge-Based Systems.* Master of Science Paper, Boston, MA: Massachusetts Institute of Technology, 1987.

Benjamin, Robert I., and Michael S. Scott Morton. *Information Technology, Integration, and Organizational Change.* CISR Working Paper #134, Center for Information Systems Research, Sloan School of Management, Cambridge, MA: MIT, April 1986.

Brown, Carol, ed. "Artificial Intelligence: Application in Taxation." *Expert Systems Review*, September 1988, pp. 3–16.

Caldwell, Bruce. "Is Outsourcing a Good Move?" *Information WEEK*, September 25, 1989, pp. 42–47.

Cullen, J., and A. Bryman. "The Knowledge Acquisition Bottleneck." *Expert Systems,* August 1988, pp. 216–25.

Cupello, James M., and David J. Mishelevicksy. "Managing Prototype Knowledge/Expert System Projects." *Communications of the ACM,* May 1988, pp. 534–41.

Davenport, Thomas H. "The Case of the Soft Software Proposal." *Harvard Business Review*, May–June 1989, pp. 12–24.

Davis, Bob. "Road to Reasoning: Superfast Computers Mimic the Structure of the Human Brain." *Wall Street Journal*, February 18, 1986, p. l.

DeLong, David W., and John F. Rockart. *A Survey of Current Trends in the Use of Executive Support Systems.* CISR Working Paper #121, Center for Information Systems Research, Sloan School of Management, Cambridge, MA: MIT, November 1984.

DuBrin, Andrew, R. Duane Ireland, and J. Clifton Williams. *Management and Organization.* Cincinnati, OH: South-Western, 1989.

Foss, W. Burry. "Early Wins Are Key to System Success." *Datamation*, January 15, 1990, pp. 79–82.

Gogan, Janis. *Boeing Computer Services: The AI Research Center.* Boston, MA: Publishing Division, Harvard Business School, 1986.

Huber, George P., and J. Clifton Williams. *Human Behavior in Organizations,* 3d ed., Cincinnati, OH: South-Western, 1986.

Keen, Peter G. W. "Value Analysis: Justifying Decision Support Systems." *MIS Quarterly,* March 1981, pp. 1–15.

Keen, Peter G. W., and Michael S. Scott Morton. *Decision Support Systems: An Organizational Perspective.* Reading, MA: Addison-Wesley, 1978.

Lee, Soonchul, and Michael Treacy. *Information Technology Impacts on Power and Influence.* CISR Working Paper #l56, Center for Information Systems Research, Sloan School of Management, Cambridge, MA: MIT, April 1987.

Leonard-Barton, Dorothy. "Technology Implementation as Integrative Innovation: The Case of an Expert System." *Sloan Management Review,* October-November 1987, pp. 84–109.

Leonard-Barton, Dorothy, and John Sviolka. "Putting Expert Systems to Work." *Harvard Business Review,* March–April 1988, pp. 91–98.

Luconi, Fred L., Thomas W. Malone, and Michael S. Scott Morton. *Expert Systems and Expert Support Systems:/ The Next Challenge for Management."* CISR Working Paper

#122, Center for Information Systems Research, Sloan School of Management, Cambridge, MA: MIT, December 1984.

Martin, James, and Steven Oxman. *Building Expert Systems.* Englewood Cliffs, NJ: Prentice-Hall, 1988.

Melaragno, Jeffrey, and Mary Kay Alen. *A Plan for the Application of Artificial Intelligence to DoD Logistics.* Report PL816R1, Bethesda, MD: Logistics Management Institute, October 1989.

Prerau, David. "Knowledge Acquisition in the Development of a Large Expert System." *AI Magazine,* Summer 1987, pp. 43–51.

Radding, Alan. "Technology Issues in Downsizing." *Computerworld,* June 12, 1989, pp. 69–78.

Rockart, John F. *The Changing Role of the Information Systems Executive: A Critical Success Factors Perspective.* CISR Working Paper #85, Center for Information System Research, Sloan School of Management, Cambridge, MA: MIT, April 1982.

Rockart, John F., and Adam D. Crescnezi. *Engaging Top Management in Information Systems Planning and Development: A Case Study.* CISR Working Paper #115, Center of Information Systems Research, Sloan School of Management, Cambridge, MA: MIT, July 1984.

Rose, Frederick. "An 'Electronic Clone' of a Skilled Engineer Is Very Hard to Create." *Wall Street Journal,* August 12, 1988, pp. 1 and 14.

Shpilberg, David, Lynford E. Graham, and Harry Schatz. "ExperTAX: An Expert System for Corporate Tax Planning." *Expert Systems,* July 1986, pp. 136–51.

Sumner, Mary, and R. Klepper. "Information Systems Strategy and End-User Application Development." *Data Base,* Summer 1987, pp. 19–30.

Sviolka, John. *ExperTAX: Coopers & Lybrand's Tax Accrual and Tax Planning Expert System.* Boston, MA: Publishing Division, Harvard Business School, 1988.

Szilagyi, Andrew, and Marc Wallace. *Organizational Behavior and Performance,* 4th ed. Glenview, IL: Scott Foresman, 1987.

Tuhrim, Stanley, James A. Riggia, and Marianne Floor. "Expert Systems Development: Letting the Domain Specialist Directly Author Knowledge Bases." In *Expert Systems: The User Interface* (pp. 37–56), ed. by James A. Hendler. Norwood, NJ: Ablex Publishing, 1988.

# 14

# Staffing

The objective of this chapter is to enable readers to understand the nature of KBS development effort staffing in general, as well as how to make knowledge engineer assignment decisions for specific KBS projects. The topics covered include:

- Human resources management
- General strategic approaches for staffing KBS development efforts
- Specific staffing tasks
- An approach to making knowledge engineer assignment decisions
- A KBS designed to assist in assigning knowledge engineers to KBS development projects

## HUMAN RESOURCES MANAGEMENT

Managing human resources is "the use, development, assessment, reward, and management of individual organizational members of worker groups. It includes the design and implementation of systems for planning, staffing, developing employees, managing careers, evaluating performance, compensating workers, and smoothing labor relations" (Gordon 1986, p. 5).

This chapter deals with the staffing job. Staffing involves many tasks, including: job analysis; forecasting personnel needs; recruiting, screening, and selecting from among job applicants; training and development of personnel; evaluating personnel performance; and employee compensation and benefits.

This chapter focuses on the screening and selection decisions made when staffing knowledge engineer positions, and on the job analysis required to make these decisions.

## GENERAL STRATEGIC APPROACHES TO STAFFING KBS DEVELOPMENT EFFORTS

Several kinds of critical strategic decisions are made in the staffing area in KBS development situations. For example, in staffing a KBS project, many companies consider several alternative strategies: training their existing MIS and operating personnel in KBS and related AI technology, hiring new people, or using outside consultants.

The IRS, for instance, trained its own people in KBS and AI technology—often a useful strategy when a knowledge domain area is very specialized and deep. The theory behind this strategy is that it is often easier to train knowledgeable, bright, domain-experienced personnel in KBS technology than to train technical personnel in a complex business area for which systems are to be developed (Bredin 1990, p. 123). In keeping with this policy, the IRS pays to have a large number of its own people take a two-year graduate AI program.

A hybrid strategy, which is fairly common today, is to engage consultants to work with company MIS personnel in developing systems. These consultants may be either domain experts or AI technology experts, depending on the situation needs. This strategy can serve two purposes: to train company MIS development personnel in KBS and AI technology; and/or to fill temporary knowledge and technical gaps that are not expected to be encountered on a continuing basis.

Another strategy which has been successful is to hire domain specialists, train them in KBS technology, and then use outside software engineers to assist in the development phase. This is a useful strategy in situations where the domain knowledge is deep and broad, such as in the metallurgy or international tax planning areas.

A strategy which uses consultants trained in KBS technology but not in the knowledge domain area under study can at times be a prescription for failure. Rose (1988) describes one company's experiences, where computer science technicians employed by a consulting firm developed a system for dam fault diagnosis for a major utility company. The consultants, who were recently graduated PhDs, worked with the company expert in dam diagnosis, a job which requires considerable experience and expertise. More than two years and $300,000 was spent to develop an 80-rule system that was not used. In this instance, it probably would have been wiser and cheaper to train the company engineer who did the dam diagnoses in KBS technology, rather than expect inexperienced computer scientists to acquire dam fault diagnosis expertise.

A large brokerage firm also chose to hire computer science personnel to staff its KBS development operation. The proposed KBS development effort involved options trading. Unfortunately, the domain in this case was so complex that the technicians were unable to learn it well enough to create effective systems. This project also failed.

This chapter continues the discussion in Chapter 13 in exploring a number of organization and staffing strategies useful in KBS project management and the situations in which they might be used effectively.

## SPECIFIC STAFFING TASKS

One of the critical factors affecting the success of a KBS development effort is the qualifications and skills of the staff members who work on it. This is true whether the effort involves a small expert-driven KBS or a large KBS with multiple project members, domain experts, and users. Screening applicants and selecting staff, therefore, is an important KBS development effort management job.

In order to effectively screen and select staff, a careful situation analysis is needed to determine the specific staffing requirements for the KBS development situation under study. This situation analysis begins with job analysis.

Job analysis involves defining the skills required to perform a particular job. It is "the process of obtaining information about jobs by determining what the duties, tasks, or activities of particular jobs are" (Chruden 1988, p. 100–101). The perception of the jobs of both a KBS development effort manager and of a knowledge engineer has been changing. As mentioned earlier, there is an emerging perception that cognitive, interpersonal, and management skills may be as important as, if not more important than, technical computer skills to the successful performance of these jobs.

A knowledge engineer designs and builds systems that involve knowledge in a particular area of expertise. The knowledge engineering job usually includes such duties and tasks as interviewing experts, and structuring the knowledge acquired from the experts and other sources in a way that adequately replicates the knowledge and that can be put into computer-compatible form.

Extracting and formalizing knowledge in such a way that it can be used in KBS is generally considered a difficult task. The knowledge engineer's role in performing this task can vary. For example, if a specific KBS development project is expert-driven, then the knowledge engineer is also the knowledge expert and no interaction with other experts is required to acquire knowledge. On the other hand, if a specific KBS development project is not expert-driven, then the interaction with experts to acquire knowledge can be considerable (Bernold 1986 pp. 133–36). This chapter presents an approach which can be adapted to staffing in such a wide range of situations.

As shown in the discussions in Chapters 2 through 11, knowledge engineering work generally requires the ability to acquire domain knowledge, as well as requiring a variety of cognitive, interpersonal, and technical computer skills.

Several studies point out the need for cognitive skills. For example, according to Cullen's study (1988), the major cause for failure in KBS development efforts are shortcomings in such cognitive tasks as:

- systematically analyzing the knowledge domain to determine its characteristics (breadth, depth, complexity, structure of knowledge, reasoning processes involved, and the like)
- reformulating the situation in knowledge representation structures that are appropriate to the situation and compatible with computer representation capabilities
- selecting a decision situation appropriate to available resources
- selecting development tools appropriate to the situation

These conclusions are further substantiated by Hoffman (1987), Prerau (1987), and Volkema (1988). Cognitive skills are especially important in complex less-defined judgmental situations, such as management planning and decision-making situations; they are not as important in operational or procedural KBS situations. This is evident from the analyses summarized in Figure 14–1, which indicate the increasing importance of decision-making tasks in more advanced KBS.

In addition, in knowledge engineering, knowledge is needed about the expert or user domain. The key facts and reasoning strategies relevant to the decision under study need to be identified before final reformulation of the decision expertise can be done, since system development cannot begin without detailed knowledge of the expert domain. Such knowledge can be acquired from a human expert (requiring cognitive and interpersonal skills), from written sources, or from experience if a manager/expert/user is developing her or his own system. A knowledge engineer who has experience in the knowledge domain or a related field can spend more time developing the KBS and less time learning the domain; it is also more likely that the decision situation will be more accurately replicated. A knowledge engineer with knowledge of and experience in the domain is often a prerequisite for success in KBS development situations involving a complex domain.

In situations where a knowledge engineer—not the expert/user—is designing the system, interpersonal skills, including interviewing, motivational, and communication skills, are needed (Cullen 1988; Hart 1986; Hayes-Roth 1983). However, several studies point out that while having these skills is relevant in performing the knowledge engineering job (human resistance was a problem in 37 percent of the projects in one study), possessing them is generally not the most crucial success factor (Berry 1986; Cullen 1988).

Significantly, technical computer skills have become considerably less important to successful knowledge engineering in a wide range of DSS and KBS

**Figure 14–1.** Major Types of Computer Systems: Situations Analyzed and Manager Participation

| System Type | Situation Analyzed | Participation in Analysis and Design of Manager-Executive Expert/User |
|---|---|---|
| Data processing systems (DPS) | Business functions and/or existing system | Not always mandatory: Definable functions and processes |
| Management information systems (MIS) | Existing reporting system and/or management needs | Some manager/user |
| Decision support systems (DSS)—interactive conventional procedural computer software | Management decision processes | High manager/user (decision maker) |
| Knowledge-based systems (KBS) for narrow, factual, operational knowledge areas—Interactive knowledge-based software | Mainly lower level, operating decisions | Lower-level manager/user |
| Knowledge-based systems (KBS) for management decision making | Manager/expert/user decision process (inside the head of a manager) | Very high manager/user/expert (decision maker) |
| Integrated DSS/KBS systems | Same range as the preceding three interactive systems described above | |

development situations, especially in judgmental management decision-making situations and where expert system shells are used. However, technical computer skills, or access to these skills, are nonetheless key requirements for knowledge engineers in most situations.

Initially, CS personnel were sought to fill the knowledge engineering job because KBS development was perceived as being part of a high-tech area (artificial intelligence) and so seemed to require computer technicians to do it. This perception is no longer generally accepted (Bredin 1990; Furno 1990).

For example, Couger's studies (1978, 1987, 1988) point out that computer/technical personnel (programmer/analyst, software engineer, or computer-oriented knowledge engineer) do not rate high on average in social need, and so are less likely to seek out needed *interpersonal interactions* with users and experts. In addition, it is unrealistic to expect that CS technicians will generally be able to acquire in-depth expertise in a wide variety of different knowledge domains.

Further evidence exists that CS technical personnel are less likely to have the needed *cognitive flexibility* (Fellers 1988). For example, CS personnel:

- work with applying fairly restrictive mathematical and computer models, not necessarily with flexibly creating models for relatively unstructured decisions—something decision makers have to do

- are necessarily technique oriented, not situationally oriented, the way management decision makers are
- are often used to dealing more with the concrete reality of computers than with the abstractions of management decision making

The new requirements and the problems they cause, and the apparent lack of skills of the people initially selected to do the job of bridging the gap between manager/expert/user and CS technician, have led to a search for new strategies for dealing with the job structure and with selecting people to fill the job. While it is certain that many CS personnel have the competencies or can be trained to bridge this new, emerging gap, it may also be necessary to transfer many information systems development tasks to managers (Mockler 1991).

Knowledge-based systems—such as the ones described in this chapter—and the studies on which they are based, are designed to provide an objective means of finding and selecting personnel for the knowledge engineering job. Such an approach can help project managers ignore preconceptions based on past experience which may bias and distort their selection decisions.

Job analysis of the knowledge engineering tasks to be performed in a specific KBS development situation is required in many different types of staffing, screening, and selecting decision situations, including:

- *Assignment* decisions, when a KBS development manager or company executive is selecting someone to do a specific KBS development project
- *Hiring* decisions, when a company is hiring staff for the artificial intelligence or KBS section of its system development group
- *Training* decisions, when a company is looking to upgrade the skills of individuals who possess the general skills required of knowledge engineers

The following section describes an approach to selecting knowledge engineers to staff KBS development efforts.

## AN APPROACH TO MAKING KNOWLEDGE ENGINEER ASSIGNMENT DECISIONS IN KBS DEVELOPMENT EFFORTS

This section concerns making staffing decisions for the knowledge engineering job. For prototype development purposes, it focuses on a common staffing decision faced in KBS development efforts, the assignment of an individual from a company's available personnel to a particular KBS development project. When assigning a knowledge engineer to a project, a project manager (or whoever is making the assignment decision) compares the skills of the available individuals to the skills required for the particular project, as well as considering other strategic factors which will affect the decision. The project manager then assigns to the project the individual knowledge engineer who has the best mix of skills required to meet the situation requirements.

When making these assignment decisions, the needs of the particular KBS development project will influence the relative importance of the required knowledge engineering skills. For example, in some situations domain knowledge and interpersonal skills are very important, while cognitive and technical computer skills may be less important. In other situations, the opposite might be true. The individual assigned to the project would be the one whose qualifications most closely match the particular situation requirements, provided that strategic factors do not dictate another course of action.

If no one individual has the required level of skills (or if the project is sufficiently large), multiple knowledge engineers who have the required skills in the aggregate may be assigned to the project. For instance, a project requiring a high level of knowledge-domain, cognitive, and computer skills may be staffed by one knowledge engineer with the required domain and cognitive skills and another with the required computer skills. As more people (knowledge engineers, experts, users, and software personnel) become involved in the project, interpersonal skill requirements usually increase. In the above situation, for instance, the two knowledge engineers must of course be able to interact effectively with each other, as well as with the domain experts and users.

In some situations training may be recommended for the knowledge engineer whose skills most closely match those required by the project, or training may be recommended for the most trainable knowledge engineer. Trainability is important because in many complex projects no individual usually has a high level of proficiency in all the required skill areas. An individual's level of trainability is also often an indication of that individual's level of cognitive flexibility.

In other situations, based on strategic situational factors, it would be recommended that a knowledge engineer from outside the company be hired, or that the company use an outside consultant for the KBS project.

The decision to be prototyped in this study involves the assignment of a knowledge engineer from a company's available personnel to a KBS development project. This assignment decision involves *analyzing* and *evaluating* the individuals and the specific KBS development project to find the person or persons with the mix of skills best suited to it. If knowledge engineers within the company have weak skills in key areas, recommendations may be made for training the candidate knowledge engineer, rejecting the candidate knowledge engineer and studying others inside the company, looking outside the company to hire a knowledge engineer with the required skills, or engaging the services of an outside consulting firm.

While all available candidates for the knowledge engineering assignment are considered, for clarity's sake this discussion treats the evaluation of the different individuals as discrete steps and discusses only one candidate at a time. The investigation of the following factors would be repeated for each candidate considered. When all of the evaluations are completed, a comparative evaluation would be made of all candidates.

The discussion in this section covers:

- critical factors affecting the situation
- possible initial recommendations and how they are made
- other critical factors that may affect the situation
- other possible recommendations and how they are made

### Critical Factors Affecting the Situation

Assigning a knowledge engineer to a KBS development project involves evaluating and comparing the skills required by the particular project with the skills of the individual knowledge engineer. A project manager evaluates the skills of all the individual knowledge engineers based upon their experience, past performance, education, and any available tests of the required skills. As seen in Figure 14–2, knowledge engineer assignment decisions are based on the following critical factors:

- knowledge domain: knowledge domain complexity and the individual's domain knowledge
- cognitive skills: project requirements and the individual's skills
- interpersonal skills: project requirements and the individual's skills
- technical computer skills: project requirements and the individual's skills

***Knowledge Domain.*** As seen in Figure 14–3, the knowledge domain analysis and evaluation compares the project's knowledge domain complexity to an individual's knowledge of the domain.

**Figure 14–2.** Knowledge Engineer Assignment Decision

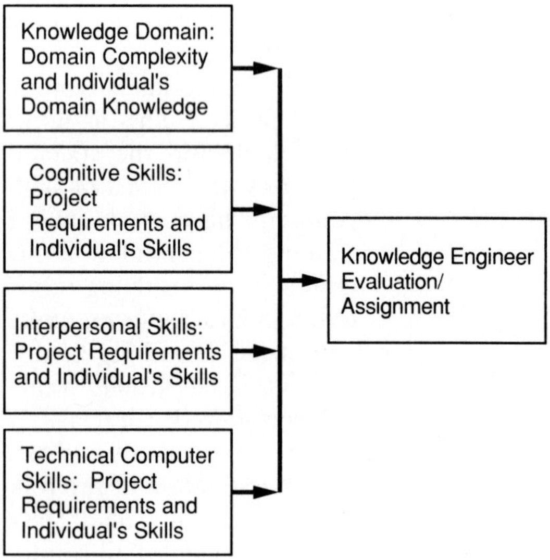

**Figure 14–3.** Knowledge Engineer Evaluation/ Assignment: Knowledge Domain—Decision Diagram

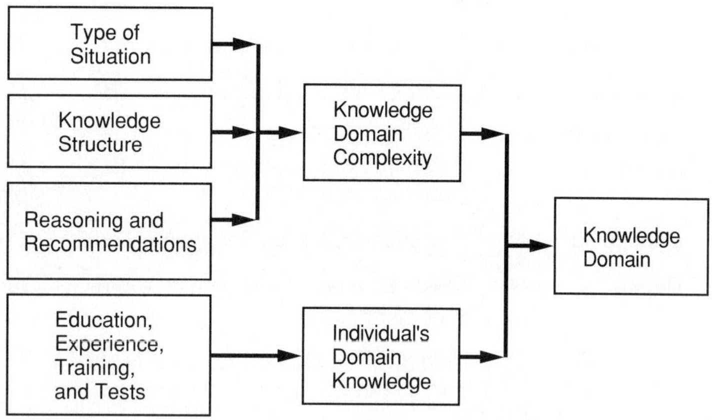


*Knowledge Domain: Knowledge Domain Complexity.* The analysis and evaluation of a project's knowledge domain complexity is based on such factors as:

- type of situation
- knowledge structure
- reasoning processes and recommendations

The evaluation of the domain's knowledge structure and reasoning processes and recommendations focuses only on the part or parts of the knowledge domain that will be replicated by the KBS, not the entire knowledge domain. A KBS development project may be in a domain with a complex structure, but the knowledge structure for the particular project may be moderate if only segments of the knowledge domain will be involved.

The *type of situation* involved in a KBS development project can provide insight into the complexity of the knowledge domain. The type of situation or decision may vary from one where the knowledge involved is used for diagnosis, monitoring, repair, instruction, prediction, design, planning, selection, scheduling, or classification, as shown in Figure 14–4.

The expertise or knowledge involved in diagnostic and monitoring situations tends to be explicit and well documented. Such situations, therefore, do not usually require knowledge engineers with high levels of domain or cognitive skills. For example, the expertise needed to develop a diagnostic system to identify causes of machine failure in a production plant will often be well defined and documented in the machinery's operation and repair manuals. While the knowledge engineer must be able to understand and interpret the manuals, the important pieces of knowledge and how they interact should have already been spelled out in the manuals.

As the decision situation becomes less defined or more general, such as planning, design, and prediction, the complexity of the domain tends to increase.

**Figure 14–4.** Generic Categories of KBS Applications

| Category | Problem Addressed | Types of Systems |
|---|---|---|
| Diagnosis | Infers system malfunctions from observations | Medical, electronic, financial analysis, auditing, machine repair |
| Monitoring | Compares observations in order to plan vulnerabilities | Management control, nuclear power plant regulation |
| Debugging | Prescribes remedies for malfunctions | Computer software |
| Repair | Executes a plan to administer a prescribed remedy | Automobile, computer, telephone |
| Instruction | Diagnoses, debugs, and corrects student behavior | Tutorial, remedial |
| Control | Interprets, predicts, repairs, and monitors system behaviors | Air traffic control, battle management, manufacturing process control |
| Prediction | Infers likely consequences of given situations | Weather forecasting, crop estimation, financial forecasting |
| Interpretation | Infers situation descriptions from sensor data | Speech understanding, image analysis, surveillance, mapping |
| Design | Configures objects within situation constraints | Circuit layout, budgeting, automatic program generation |
| Planning | Develops guidelines for action | Strategic planning, process scheduling, military planning |

This is because the expertise and knowledge involved tends to be less well-defined and documented, in terms of both what data is important and how it is manipulated. These situations, which might involve such areas as capital investment, options trading, and marketing planning, tend to require knowledge engineers with high levels of both domain and cognitive skills.

When evaluating the complexity of the *knowledge structure*, such items as the depth and breadth of the knowledge to be replicated in the KBS under development are considered. The breadth of the knowledge included in a fault diagnosis situation can be relatively narrow, for example, where it involves a telephone call switching system. However, at the same time the technical expertise involved in analyzing maintenance messages may be relatively deep if the switching system is a complex one, such as a GTE electronic automatic exchange that can interconnect up to 400,000 telephone lines (Prerau 1987).

The decision maker or individual who performs the task to be replicated by the KBS is also considered when determining the complexity of the knowledge structure. If a KBS being developed covered either a broad or deep knowledge domain and the decision being replicated was usually made by upper management, the knowledge structure would be considered very complex. However, if the knowledge domain was narrow and shallow and the decision being replicated was usually made by operating personnel, the complexity of the knowledge structure would be considered low.

When evaluating the *reasoning processes and recommendations* involved in a knowledge domain, how well defined the reasoning and knowledge to be replicated by the KBS is can be an important consideration. Whether the reasoning involved is primarily rule-based and heuristic or object-based is also considered, as is the degree to which models exist of how the knowledge to be replicated in the KBS is manipulated to reach conclusions. The types of recommendations that will be made by the KBS are also considered, such as whether there are a limited number of specific and predefined typical recommendations, as in the KBS described in Chapters 2 through 6, or the recommendations are open ended, such as when recommending a new business area to enter.

If the reasoning and knowledge to be replicated by the KBS is well defined and is primarily rule-based and heuristic, if models of how decisions should be made exist, and if the typical recommendations to be made are limited and/or easily predefined, then the reasoning processes and recommendations involved in the domain would be considered less complex.

As the reasoning processes and recommendations become less well defined, rely more on object-based reasoning, lack preexisting models of how the knowledge is manipulated, and have multiple open-ended recommendations—such as in strategic planning situations—the knowledge domain becomes more complex.

*Knowledge Domain: Individual's Domain Knowledge.* This analysis and evaluation is based upon such factors as the individual's education, training, and work experience in the knowledge domain for which the KBS is being developed. If available, tests may be administered to measure an individual's knowledge of the domain to be replicated by the KBS. However, in most situations a supervisor or colleague's evaluation of the individual's skills and prior work is the best source of information in this area.

As the knowledge to be replicated in a KBS development project becomes more complex, a greater degree of preexisting domain knowledge is desirable. As the knowledge to be replicated in a KBS development project becomes less complex, and thus easier to learn, or as the experts involved are better at explaining the workings of the domain, a lower degree of preexisting domain knowledge is required of the knowledge engineer.

The appropriateness or match of the individual's domain knowledge to the knowledge domain complexity is considered *good* if both are rated the same, that is, both are either high, moderate, or low. The match is *acceptable* if the individual's domain knowledge is high and the knowledge domain complexity is moderate, or if the individual's domain knowledge is moderate and the knowledge domain complexity is low. Individuals are *overqualified* if their domain knowledge is high and the knowledge domain complexity is low. If individuals' domain knowledge is low and the knowledge domain complexity is high, their domain knowledge is considered to be *insufficient.* If individuals' domain knowledge is moderate and the knowledge domain complexity is high, or if their domain knowledge is low and the knowledge domain complexity is moderate, their domain knowledge would be *poor and training should be considered.*

***Cognitive Skills.*** As seen in Figure 14–5, the cognitive skills analysis and evaluation compares an individual's cognitive skills to the cognitive skills required by the project.

*Cognitive Skills: Project Requirements.* This analysis and evaluation is based upon:

- knowledge domain complexity
- expert types and communication and domain skills
- existence of decision models

The *knowledge domain complexity,* as discussed previously, is determined by the type of situation, knowledge structure, and reasoning processes and recommendations. As the complexity of the project knowledge domain increases, so do the cognitive skills required by the project. For example, as the type of situation moves from diagnostic to planning, increased cognitive skills are required for a knowledge engineer to be effective. This is also the case as the availability of existing models of the domain's knowledge structure decreases, and as the reasoning processes and recommendations involved rely less on rule-based heuristics and become more dependent on object-based reasoning.

When evaluating *expert types,* and their *communication and domain skills,* the level of domain expertise possessed by the experts who will work on the KBS development project is considered, as is the experts' ability to describe and clearly articulate relevant concepts in the knowledge domain. The involvement of more articulate experts in the project may lessen the need for knowledge engineers with high cognitive skills. However, if the experts are less articulate in explaining the intricacies of their knowledge domain, considerable cognitive skills on the part of knowledge engineers may be required. Also, if multiple experts are involved in the project and they solve typical problems using different methods, the knowledge engineer will need superior cognitive skills to select the best method or to synthesize the differing approaches.

The *existence of decision models* for a KBS development project influences the cognitive skills required of a knowledge engineer. If preexisting models of the structure of the knowledge to be replicated in the KBS are available, fewer cognitive skills are required. However, considerable cognitive skills may be required to structure the knowledge in a domain where existing models are not available.

**Figure 14–5.** Knowledge Engineer Evaluation/Assignment: Cognitive Skills—Decision Diagram

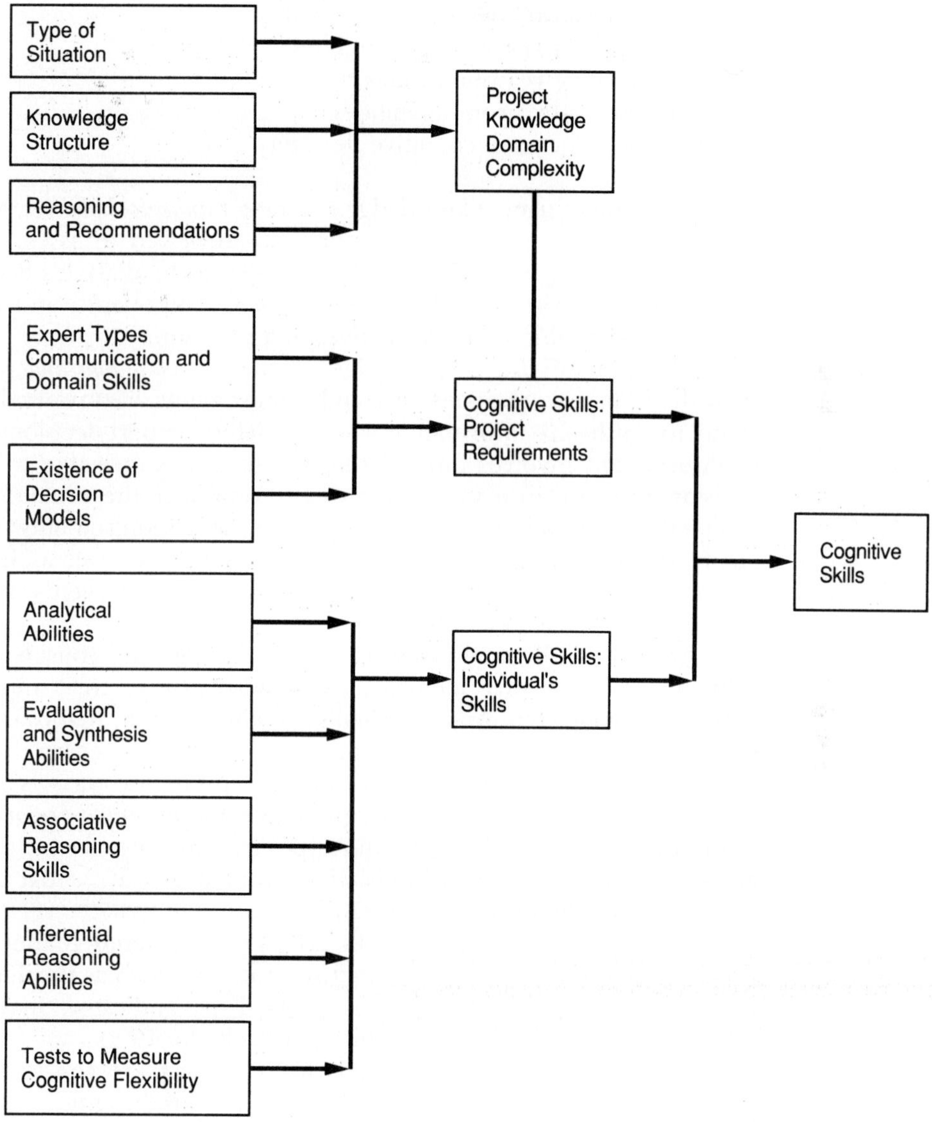

*Cognitive Skills: Individual's Skills.* This analysis and evaluation is based upon the individual's:

- analytical abilities
- evaluation and synthesis abilities
- associative reasoning skills
- inferential reasoning abilities
- tests to measure cognitive flexibility

When measuring a knowledge engineer's *analytical abilities,* the individuals' past experiences and accomplishments are reviewed to assess their ability to comprehend complex decision-making processes, to analyze a decision situation by breaking the situation down into smaller components, and to identify the various opportunities and alternatives in a situation.

When identifying a knowledge engineer's *evaluation and synthesis abilities,* individuals' past work experience and achievements are reviewed to assess their ability to synthesize information when modelling expert decisions. The synthesis of information involves interrelating the diverse knowledge components of a decision situation in a way which validly replicates the situation under study, while taking into account the technical computer requirements. An individual's ability to use heuristics and develop hypotheses, as well as her or his conceptualization skills—the ability to group specific events into "kind of" categories—are also identified.

Also, the individual's *associative reasoning skills* are considered. Associative reasoning skills involve identifying a pattern in one area, and applying that pattern in a new area. An individual's *cognitive flexibility,* that is, the ability to use different problem-solving and modelling techniques based on the requirements of the situation or the ability to see old problems in new ways, is also considered.

When examining a knowledge engineer's *inferential reasoning abilities,* an individual's observed past work and experience are reviewed to assess his or her ability to draw inferences or implications from diverse areas that are perceived to be relevant by the decision maker.

*Tests to measure cognitive skills* are also considered if they are available. Preliminary research has shown that several tests, such as the Thurston Test of Mental Alertness and the Myers-Briggs Type Indicator, may be useful in indicating potential strength in this area (Dologite 1991).

An individual's cognitive skills for a project are considered *good* if the individual's cognitive skills and the project's required cognitive skills match, that is, both are either high, moderate, or low. The match is considered *acceptable* if the individual's skills are high and the required skills are moderate, or if the individual's skills are moderate and the required skills are low. Individuals are considered *overqualified* if their skills are high and the required skills are low. Based on situational factors, cognitive skills would be considered *insufficient* if the individual's skills are low and the required skills are high or moderate, or if the individual's skills are moderate and the required skills are high.

***Interpersonal Skills.*** As seen in Figure 14–6, the analysis and evaluation of interpersonal skills compares an individual's interpersonal skills to the interpersonal skills required by the project.

*Interpersonal Skills: Project Requirements.* This analysis and evaluation is based upon the:

- knowledge source
- nature and amount of interaction with domain experts based on the complexity of the knowledge domain
- types and numbers of users, experts, and other personnel involved
- expert's communication and domain skills

The *knowledge source* for a KBS development project can have a significant impact on the interpersonal skills required. The extent to which the knowledge or expertise being replicated in the KBS is available in written form or from

**Figure 14–6** Knowledge Engineer Evaluation/ Assignment: Interpersonal Skills—Decision Diagram

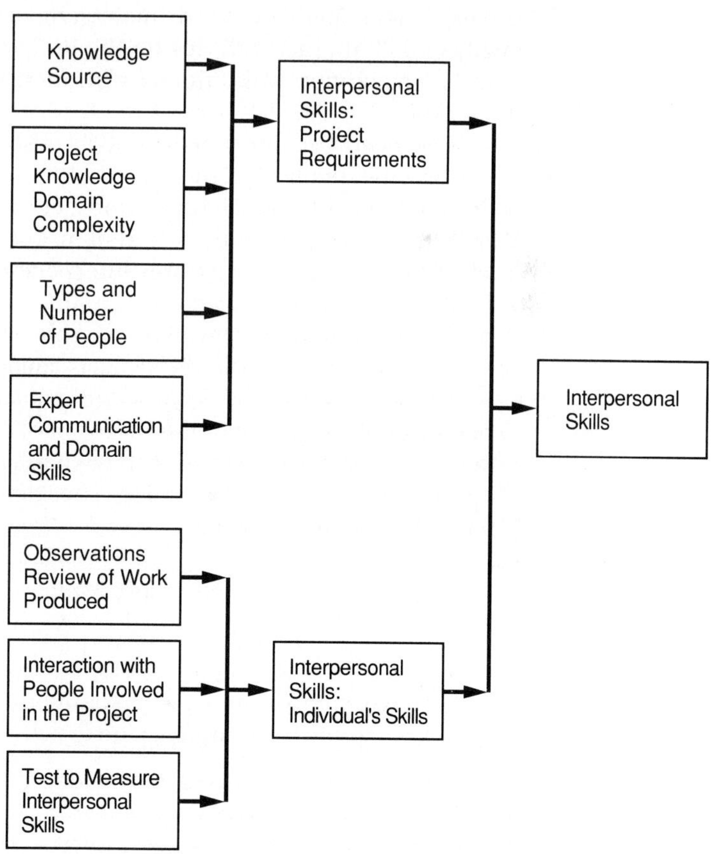

human experts is analyzed. In situations where most of the knowledge is available in written sources, lower levels of interpersonal skills are needed. When human experts are the main source of knowledge and expertise, high levels of interpersonal skills are usually required.

The *nature and amount of interaction with domain experts* can vary considerably based on the *complexity of the knowledge domain*. For example, in situations where the domain is less complex and existing models of how decisions are made are available, interaction with experts would tend to be aimed at confirming the validity of the existing models and making adjustments to meet the needs of the particular situation. In situations where models of how decisions are made do not yet exist, more interaction between the knowledge engineer and the experts is needed because the nature of their meetings is to elicit and structure knowledge from scratch.

When evaluating the *numbers and types of users, experts, and other personnel involved,* the number of users that the knowledge engineer will interact with during the course of the project is analyzed, as is the number of experts and other people—such as systems personnel, other knowledge engineers, and other project team members and management personnel—that the knowledge engineer will interact with during the project. As the number of people that the knowledge engineer will interact with increases, so does the need for interpersonal skills.

The need for interpersonal skills also increases as people with different needs become involved in the project. When the knowledge engineer must work with people of different backgrounds, such as experts with varying degrees of knowledge and users with different needs from the system—including user interface requirements—greater interpersonal skills are needed.

When evaluating *expert communication and domain skills* the level of domain expertise possessed by the experts who will work on the KBS development project is considered, as is the experts' ability to describe and clearly articulate relevant concepts of the knowledge domain. The involvement of articulate experts in the project may lessen the need for knowledge engineers with high interpersonal skills. However, if the experts are not very articulate in explaining the intricacies of their knowledge, considerable knowledge engineer interpersonal skills may be required.

*Interpersonal Skills: Individual's Skills.* This analysis and evaluation is based upon:

- past observations and a review of work produced
- actual interaction with personnel involved in the project
- tests to measure interpersonal skills

Interpersonal skills of a knowledge engineer can be gauged through *past observations and a review of work produced.* For example, a project manager may know that an individual has good interpersonal skills because he has witnessed them at work in the past, or has seen the results of completed projects that the individual worked on which required interpersonal skills. Individuals' education, past experiences, and accomplishments are also evaluated to determine their ability to communicate with and get along with the types of experts and users involved in the project, as well as their ability to elicit knowledge and feedback from the types of experts and users involved in the project.

An individual's interpersonal skills can also be measured through witnessing *actual interaction with personnel involved in the project.* This technique can be used on large projects with multiple experts/users and multiple knowledge engineers. The project manager can observe the knowledge engineers interview the experts/users and assign those individuals who work well together to subsequent segments or phases of the project.

*Tests to measure interpersonal skills,* such as those developed by Couger (1978, 1987, 1988), are also considered, if appropriate, in the situation under study.

The appropriateness of an individual's interpersonal skills for the project under study is considered *good* if the individual's interpersonal skills and the interpersonal skills required by the project are the same, that is, both are either high, moderate, or low. The individual is considered *acceptable* if her or his skills are high and the required skills are moderate, or if her or his skills are moderate and the required skills are low. The individual is considered *overqualified* if the personal skills are high and the required skills are low. Individuals are considered to have *insufficient skills* if their skills are low and the required skills are high or moderate, or if their skills are moderate and the required skills are high.

***Technical Computer Skills.*** As seen in Figure 14–7, the technical computer skills analysis and evaluation compares the technical computer skills required by the project to an individual's level and kind of technical computer skills.

*Technical Computer Skills: Project Requirements.* This analysis and evaluation is based upon the:

- project's knowledge domain complexity
- development and delivery requirements
- available assistance from other personnel

The *project's knowledge domain complexity* influences the computer skills required in a KBS development project in that complex domains tend to have complex reasoning methods that require high levels of computer skills to put them into a form that can be manipulated by a computer.

The *development and delivery requirements* are influenced by the environment in which the KBS will be developed and delivered. The hardware and software chosen must meet these requirements. If the users are dispersed throughout a building and need access to a common database, the installation of appropriate hardware and software may require considerable technical computer skills.

The technical computer skills required of the knowledge engineer may also vary, depending on whether developing the KBS will require the writing of an

**Figure 14–7.** Knowledge Engineer Evaluation/Assignment: Technical Computer Skills—Decision Diagram

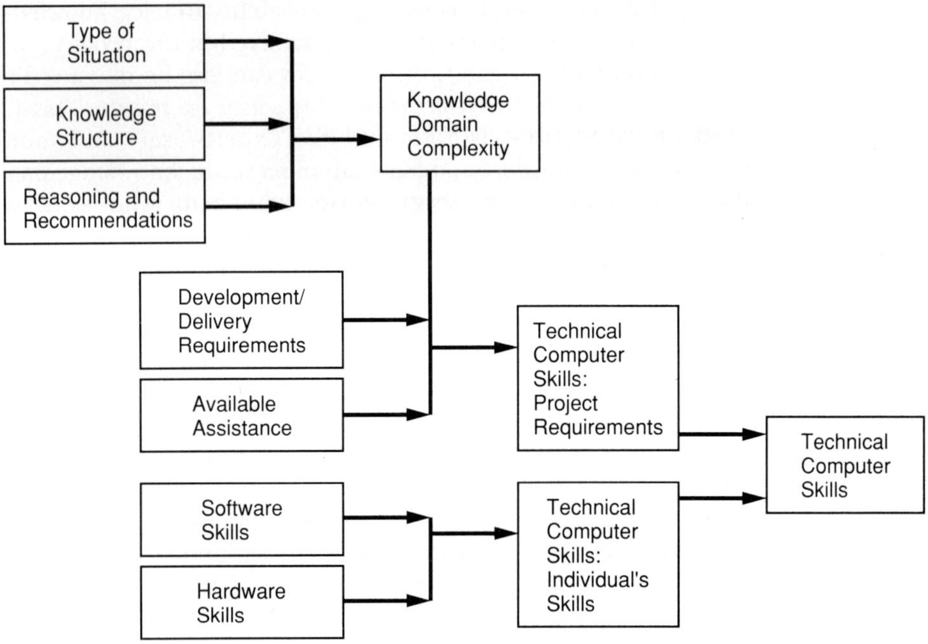


inference engine, the use of an AI language such as LISP or PROLOG, or the use of a complex expert system shell or a simple expert system shell.

In situations where the KBS must interface with other existing or planned computer systems or the type of user interface planned or required for the KBS is a complex one, considerable technical computer skills usually are required of the knowledge engineer. The hardware platform or platforms on which the KBS will be developed/delivered (mainframe, minicomputer, workstations network, PC network, PCs) is also considered.

The *available assistance from other personnel* can have a major impact on the technical computer skills required of a knowledge engineer. Consideration is given to who will be responsible for technical tasks, such as programming and hardware configuration. Such tasks may be the primary responsibility of the knowledge engineer or of other personnel. Also, the number of other technically skilled programmers, analysts, or knowledge engineers that will be assigned to the project to handle technical tasks is considered, as is whether they will be assigned on a full-time, part-time, or as-needed basis. The less help the knowledge engineer is expected to receive, the greater the need for technical computer skills in most situations.

*Technical Computer Skills: Individual's Skills.* This analysis and evaluation is based upon the individual's:

- software skills
- hardware skills

The individual should have a working knowledge of the computer tools that will be used in the development of a KBS. Software tools can range from PC expert system shells characterized by low-level languages to more difficult AI languages, such as LISP. Hardware tools can range from relatively inexpensive PCs to expensive mainframes. Individuals' skills can be determined by evaluating their education, experience, and training in these areas.

When evaluating an individual's *software skills*, education, training, experience, and capability with the type of software which will be used to develop and/or deliver the KBS is considered. The candidate's experience with and capability in developing the type of user interface planned for the KBS is considered, as is her or his experience, training, and capabilities in interfacing and connecting different computer systems if this is applicable to the situation.

When evaluating individuals' *hardware skills*, their education and training with the hardware which will be used to develop/deliver the KBS and their general capabilities in installing and configuring the hardware is considered, as is their experience and training in interfacing and connecting different computer systems if applicable to the situation.

The appropriateness of individuals' technical computer skills for the project under study is considered *good* if their computer skills and the required computer skills are the same, that is, both are high, moderate, or low. Individuals' skills are considered *acceptable* if their computer skills are high and the required computer skills are moderate, or if their skills are moderate and the required skills are low. Individuals are considered *overqualified* if their computer skills are high and the required computer skills are low. Individuals are considered to have *insufficient skills* if their computer skills are low and the required computer skills are high. The appropriateness of individuals' skills would be *poor and training should be considered* if their computer skills are moderate and the required computer skills are high, or if their skills are low and the required computer skills are moderate.

### Possible Initial Recommendations and How They Are Made

The recommendations made when evaluating a knowledge engineer for assignment to a particular KBS development project include the following:

- An individual knowledge engineer evaluated is a *good* choice and *acceptable* for the KBS development project if her or his domain knowledge, cognitive skill level, interpersonal skill level, and technical computer skill level are all good or acceptable.
- An individual knowledge engineer evaluated is a *weak* choice and should be *rejected* for the KBS development project if he or she has insufficient

qualifications for the particular project in any of the four critical areas: domain knowledge, cognitive skills, interpersonal skills, or technical computer skills.

- An individual knowledge engineer evaluated is an *acceptable* choice but is *overqualified* for the KBS development project if she or he is overqualified in any one of the four critical factor areas, and his or her skills are either good or acceptable in the other three areas.
- An individual knowledge engineer evaluated is a *questionable* choice if his or her domain knowledge is poor but training may be helpful, while his or her cognitive skills, interpersonal skills, and technical computer skills rate as good, okay, or overqualified.
- An individual knowledge engineer evaluated is a *questionable* choice if technical computer skills are poor but training may be helpful, while cognitive skills, domain knowledge, and interpersonal skills rate as good, okay, or overqualified.

### Other Critical Factors That May Affect the Situation

Other critical factors that may affect the knowledge engineer evaluation/assignment decision for specific projects include:

- trainability
- strategic company factors

These factors are considered if an individual's skills were questionable or if the above recommendation is to reject all of the individuals who were considered.

***Trainability.*** Trainability is a major consideration when assigning a knowledge engineer to a KBS development project only if all the available knowledge engineers considered are deficient in knowledge domain expertise, technical computer skills, or interpersonal skills. Also, cognitive skills are not so much taught as developed, so it is assumed that they cannot be sufficiently developed or acquired through a short training session for one particular project.

***Strategic Company Factors.*** Strategic company factors can also affect knowledge engineer evaluation/assignment decisions for specific KBS projects. In situations where existing company personnel do not have the required skills and are not sufficiently trainable, a decision must be made whether to hire a knowledge engineer with the needed skills, hire outside consultants to develop the KBS, or abandon the project.

Factors considered when making such decisions include whether future KBS development projects require skills similar to the skills needed for the present KBS project but lacking in present personnel. Whether the company plans to develop or expand a knowledge engineering group to take advantage of KBS technology or to support KBS development in order to gain a competitive advantage or to survive in its industry is also considered. Also, whether most of the future KBS developed by the company will be primarily expert-driven—that is, developed by the domain experts themselves rather than by computer programmers—is considered.

### Other Possible Recommendations and How They Are Made

Recommendations made after the evaluation of the skills match include the following:

- The knowledge engineer's skills are deficient in domain knowledge (or technical computer or interpersonal skills), but the candidate does not seem to be trainable. Reject the candidate.
- The knowledge engineer's skills are deficient in domain knowledge (or technical computer or interpersonal skills), but the candidate seems to be trainable. Provide the candidate with training, evaluate her or his progress, and assign him or her as the required skills are developed or improve sufficiently.
- Multiple knowledge engineers should be assigned to the project, if such an allocation of resources is warranted, because the project requires skills that are possessed by them in aggregate.
- None of the knowledge engineers have adequate skills, but KBS development is of strategic (long-term) importance to the company. Hire a knowledge engineer who possesses the required skills.
- None of the knowledge engineers have adequate skills, and KBS development is of average importance to the company. Consider engaging an outside consulting firm to develop the KBS.
- None of the knowledge engineers have adequate skills, and KBS development is of minor importance to the company. Consider reducing the scope of the project.
- None of the knowledge engineers have adequate skills, and KBS development is of minor importance to the company. Do not proceed with the KBS development project.

## A KBS DESIGNED TO ASSIST IN ASSIGNING KNOWLEDGE ENGINEERS TO KBS DEVELOPMENT PROJECTS

The discussion in this section covers:

- system overview and objective
- recommendations to be made by the prototype KBS
- typical user dialog
- system documentation: dependency diagrams and decision charts
- designing and constructing the knowledge base

### System Overview and Objective

This prototype system was developed to evaluate a knowledge engineer's skills in relation to the skills required in a specific KBS development project. This evaluation is used to assist a project manager when making knowledge engineer assignment decisions.

### Recommendations To Be Made by the Prototype KBS

The recommendations made by the prototype system include:

- The candidate knowledge engineer is a good choice for the KBS development project because his or her level of domain knowledge, cognitive skills, interpersonal skills, and technical computer skills are either good or okay.
- The candidate knowledge engineer is an acceptable choice for the KBS development project because, while he or she is overqualified in one or more of the four critical factor areas, in areas where not overqualified his or her skill level is either good or okay for the project under study.
- The candidate knowledge engineer is a questionable choice for the KBS development project because the level of domain knowledge and of interpersonal and technical computer skills are poor, while the cognitive level is overqualified, good, or okay. In this case, training would be considered.
- The candidate knowledge engineer is a questionable choice for the KBS development project because the level of domain knowledge is poor, while the cognitive, interpersonal, and technical computer skills levels are either good, overqualified, or okay. Training would also be considered in this case.
- The candidate knowledge engineer is a questionable choice for the KBS development project because, while the technical computer skills level is poor in relation to the level required by the project, the cognitive and interpersonal skills and domain knowledge levels are overqualified, good, or okay. Training would be recommended in this case.
- The candidate knowledge engineer is a poor choice for the KBS development project because the technical computer, cognitive, and interpersonal skills, or domain knowledge level, indicates insufficient skills.

### Typical User Dialog

The typical user dialog covers four major areas shown in Figure 14–8:

- domain knowledge
- cognitive skills
- interpersonal skills
- technical computer skills

**Figure 14–8.** Knowledge Engineer Evaluation/Assignment KBS—Dependency Diagrams (Initial Prototype Phase)

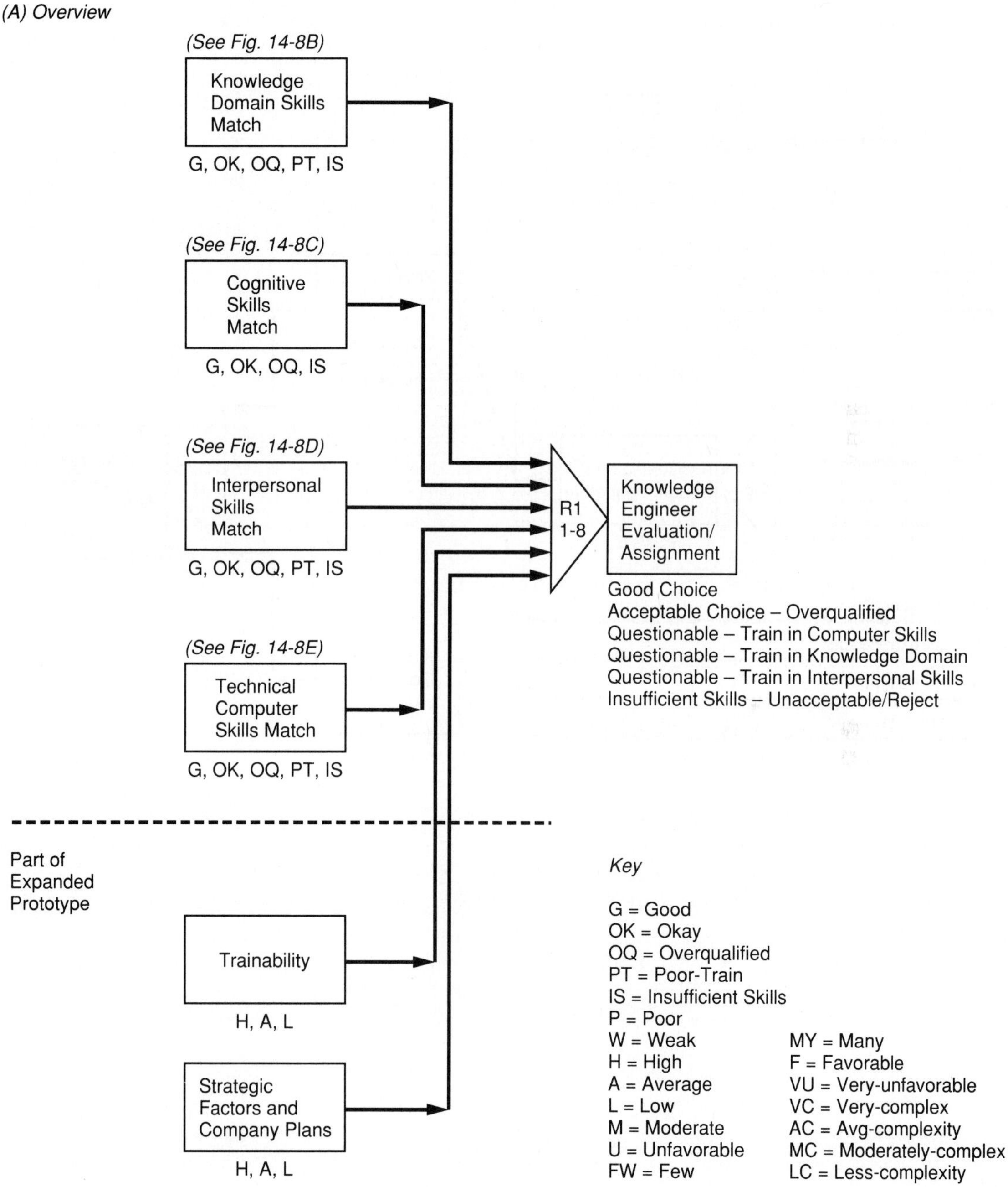


*continued*

**Figure 14–8** *continued*

(*B*) *Knowledge Domain Skills Match*

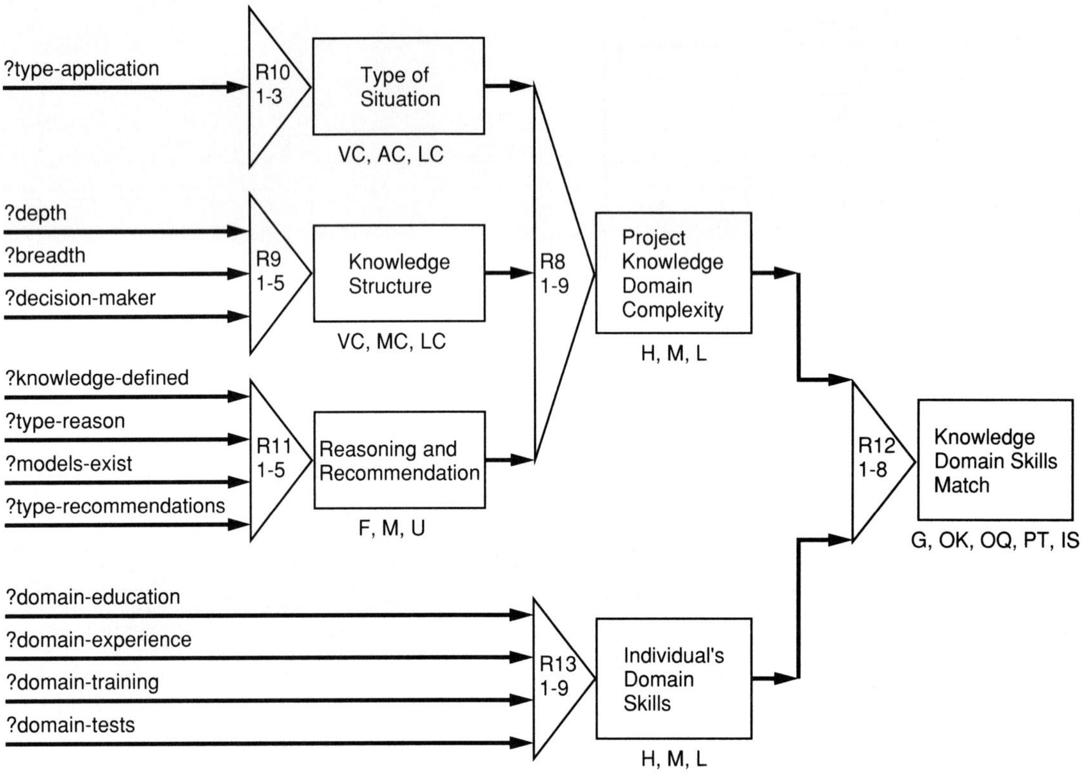

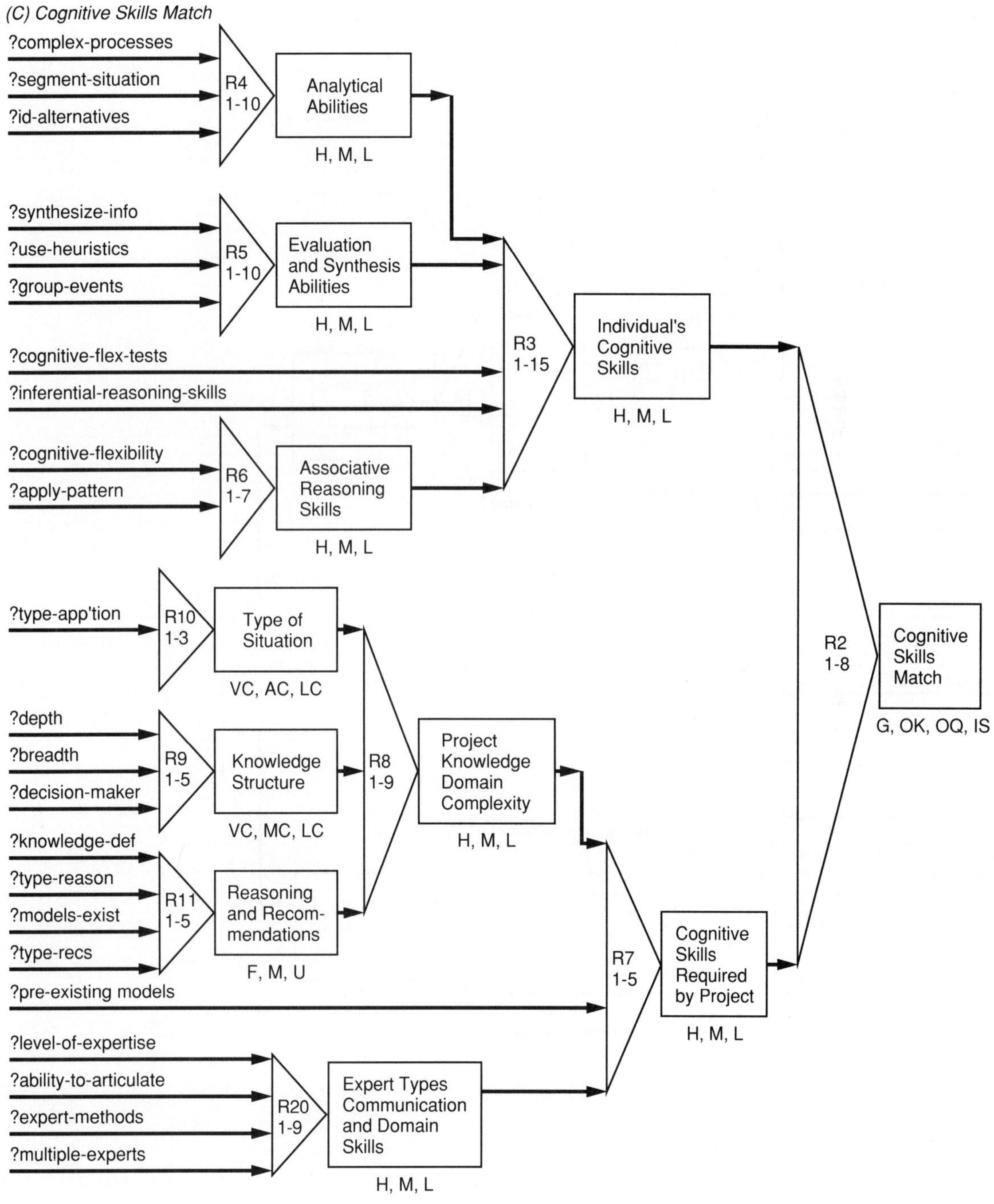
(C) Cognitive Skills Match
?complex-processes
?segment-situation
?id-alternatives
R4
1-10
Analytical Abilities
H, M, L
?synthesize-info
?use-heuristics
?group-events
R5
1-10
Evaluation and Synthesis Abilities
H, M, L
?cognitive-flex-tests
?inferential-reasoning-skills
R3
1-15
Individual's Cognitive Skills
H, M, L
?cognitive-flexibility
?apply-pattern
R6
1-7
Associative Reasoning Skills
H, M, L
?type-app'tion
R10
1-3
Type of Situation
VC, AC, LC
?depth
?breadth
?decision-maker
R9
1-5
Knowledge Structure
VC, MC, LC
R8
1-9
Project Knowledge Domain Complexity
H, M, L
?knowledge-def
?type-reason
?models-exist
?type-recs
R11
1-5
Reasoning and Recom-mendations
F, M, U
?pre-existing models
R7
1-5
Cognitive Skills Required by Project
H, M, L
R2
1-8
Cognitive Skills Match
G, OK, OQ, IS
?level-of-expertise
?ability-to-articulate
?expert-methods
?multiple-experts
R20
1-9
Expert Types Communication and Domain Skills
H, M, L

*continued*

**Figure 14–8** *continued*

*(D) Interpersonal Skills Match*

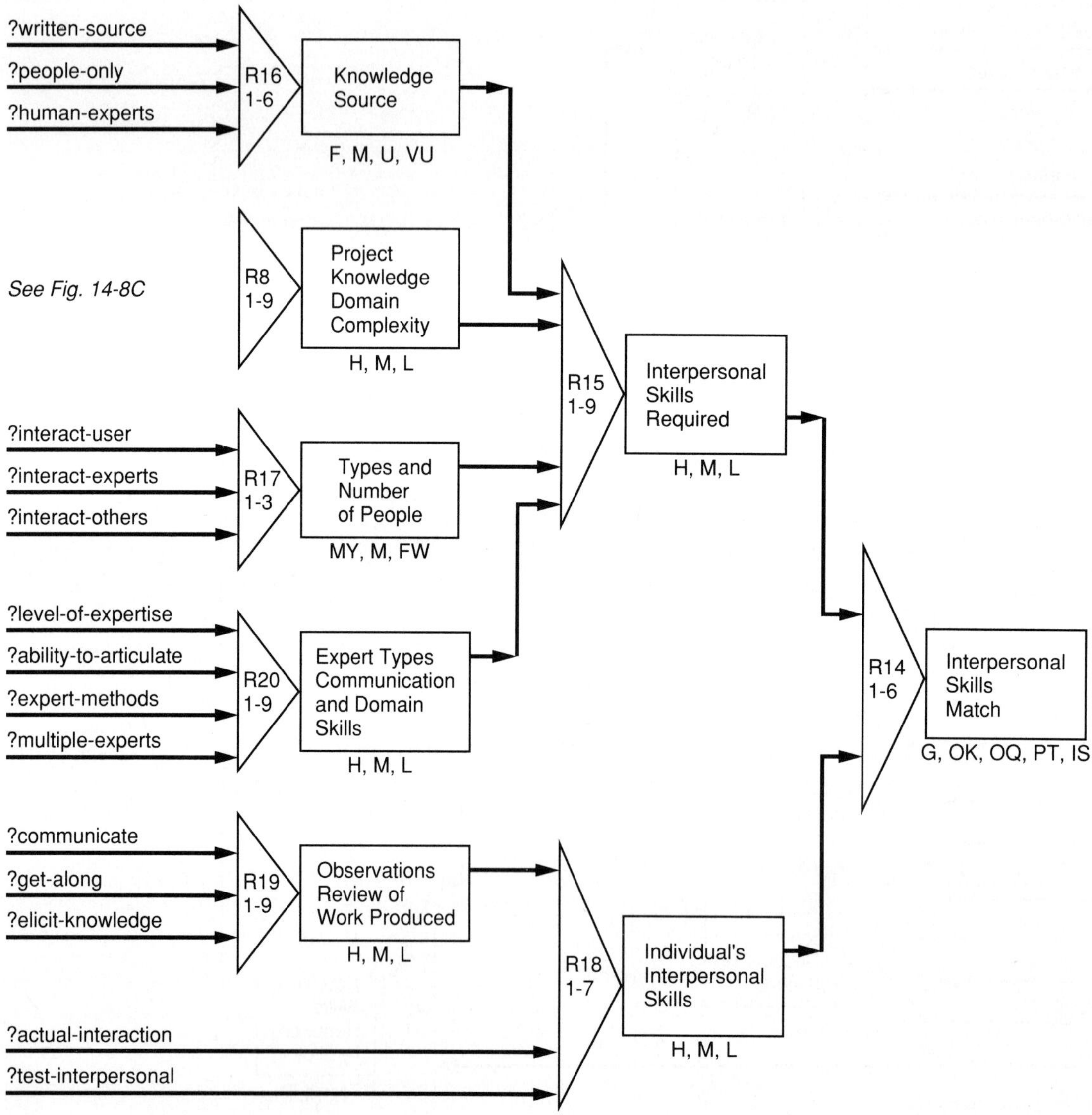

(*E*) *Technical Computer Skills Match*

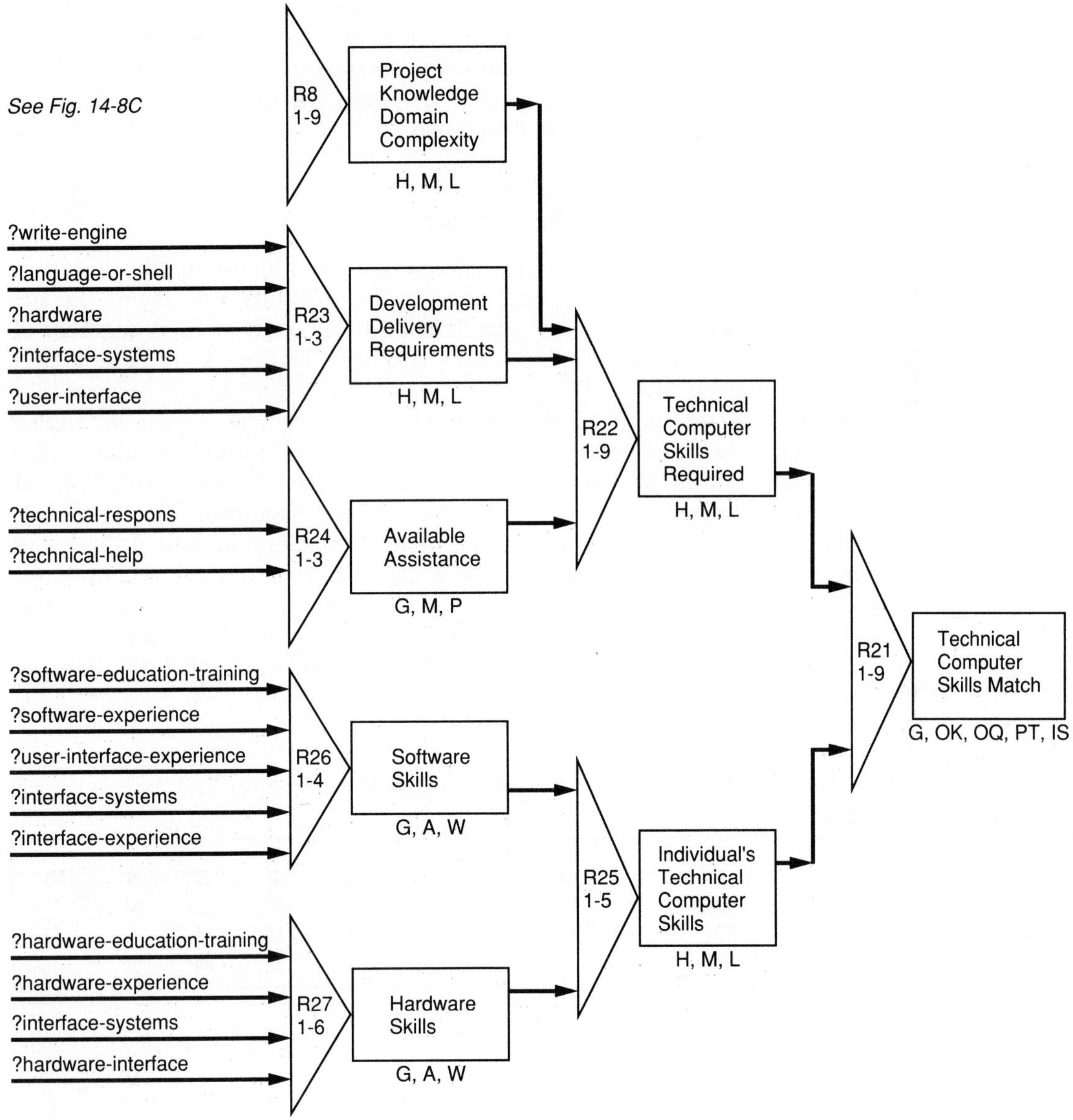

### System Documentation: Dependency Diagrams and Decision Charts

Figures 14–8a through 14–8e show the dependency diagrams of the prototype Knowledge Engineer Evaluation/Assignment KBS. The diagrams present a summary outline of all the knowledge segments and their interrelationships, including questions, rules, facts, values, and recommendations in the system.

Figure 14–9 shows a sample decision chart for the "analytical abilities" segment of the prototype system developed.

### Designing and Constructing the Knowledge Base

Rules and questions were developed based on the situation study described earlier in this chapter. That structured situation study was based on the developer's experience and the research listed in the references. A segment of the prototype system's knowledge base is shown in Figure 14–10. The expert system shell used is M.1.

The three questions in the knowledge-base segment shown in Figure 14–10 each have three potential answers; this yields 27 possible combinations. Through the use of the logical operator OR and M.1 "variables" (the capital letters) only 10 rules are needed to cover the 27 combinations.

The values on the right hand side of the equal sign in Rule 4–1 are all identical and all capital letters. The THEN clause of this rule will be considered "true" if the answers to all three questions are identical. For example, if the answers to "complex-processes," "segment-situation," and "id-alternatives" were all "high," analytical-abilities would receive a value of "high." If all three

**Figure 14–9.** Knowledge Engineer Evaluation/Assignment KBS—Decision Chart (Initial Prototype)

| Rule Set 4 | 1 | 2 | 3 | 4 | 5 | 6 | 7 | 8 | 9 | 10 |
|---|---|---|---|---|---|---|---|---|---|---|
| complex-processes | HML | H | H | M | L | L/ | M | L | M | * |
| segment-situation | HML | H | M | H | L/ | L | M | M | L | * |
| id-alternatives | HML | M | H | H | L | L | L | M | M | * |
| then analytical-abilities = | | | | | | | | | | |
| high | X | X | X | X | | | | | | |
| low | X | | | | X | X | X | X | X | |
| moderate | X | | | | | | | | | X |

H = High
M = Moderate
L = Low
/ = or
* = any answer

questions were answered "moderate," "analytical-abilities" would be considered moderate, and if all three questions were answered "low," "analytical-abilities" would be considered low. This one rule, Rule 4–1, covers three combinations.

Rule 4–5 covers 5 combinations through the use of the logical operator OR. If "complex-processes" and "segment-situation" are answered "low," "id-alternatives" can be answered in any of the three possible ways and the rule would still "succeed." Also, if "complex-processes" and "id-alternatives" are answered "low," "segment-situation" can be answered in any of the three possible ways and the rule would still "succeed." Together, Rules 4–5 and 4–6 ensure that if any of the two factors are answered "low," "analytical-abilities" will have a value of low.

Rule 4–10 is used as a "default" rule. This rule will "succeed" whenever all of the previous rules with "analytical-abilities" in their THEN clause "fail" or their IF statements are not found to be "true."

**Figure 14–10.** Knowledge Engineer Evaluation/Assignment KBS—"Analytical Abilities" Segment of Knowledge Base

```
/* Analytical Abilities */

rule-4-1:
 if complex-processes = HML and
    segment-situation = HML and
    id-alternatives = HML
then analytical-abilities = HML.

rule-4-2:
 if complex-processes = high and
    segment-situation = high and
    id-alternatives = moderate
then analytical-abilities = high.

rule-4-3:
 if complex-processes = high and
    segment-situation = moderate and
    id-alternatives = high
then analytical-abilities = high.

rule-4-4:
 if complex-processes = moderate and
    segment-situation = high and
    id-alternatives = high
then analytical-abilities = high.

rule-4-5:
 if complex-processes = low and
    segment-situation = low or
    id-alternatives = low
then analytical-abilities = low.

rule-4-6:
 if segment-situation = low and
    complex-processes = low or
    id-alternatives = low
then analytical-abilities = low.

rule-4-7:
 if id-alternatives = low and
    complex-processes = moderate and
    segment-situation = moderate
then analytical-abilities = low.
```

```
rule-4-8:
 if complex-processes = low and
    segment-situation = moderate and
    id-alternatives = moderate
then analytical-abilities = low.

rule-4-9:
 if segment-situation = low and
    complex-processes = moderate and
    id-alternatives = moderate
then analytical-abilities = low.

rule-4-10:
 if segment-situation = A and
    complex-processes = B and
    id-alternatives = C
then analytical-abilities = moderate.


/* Analytical Abilities (questions) */

    question(complex-processes) = [nl,nl,nl,nl,nl,nl,nl,nl,nl,nl,'
    Based on the individual''s past experience and
    accomplishments, how would you characterize their ability to
    comprehend complex decision making processes?
    ',nl,nl,nl,nl,nl,nl,nl].

    legalvals(complex-processes) = [high, moderate, low].

    question(segment-situation) = [nl,nl,nl,nl,nl,nl,nl,nl,nl,nl,'
    Based on the individual''s past experience and
    accomplishments, how would you characterize their ability
    to analyze a decision situation by breaking the situation
    down into various smaller components?',nl,nl,nl,nl,nl,nl,nl].

    legalvals(segment-situation) = [high, moderate, low].

    question(id-alternatives) = [nl,nl,nl,nl,nl,nl,nl,nl,nl,nl,'
    Based on the individual''s past experience and
    accomplishments, how would you characterize their ability
    to evaluate information to identify the various
    opportunities and alternatives in a situation?',nl,nl,nl,nl,nl,nl,nl].

    legalvals(id-alternatives) = [high, moderate, low].
```

## REVIEW QUESTIONS

1. Define *human resources management* and *staffing* in general.
2. Describe some of the general strategies used in staffing KBS development efforts and the situations in which they might be useful.
3. Discuss the role of job analysis in making staffing decisions involved in managing KBS development efforts.
4. Discuss how the perception of the knowledge engineering job has been changing and how this has led to changes in the skills requirement definition.
5. Describe an approach to making knowledge engineer assignment decisions in KBS development efforts.
6. Discuss the ways in which the knowledge domain analysis and evaluation case impact the assignment decision.
7. Discuss the ways in which cognitive skills can impact the assignment decision.
8. Discuss the ways in which interpersonal skills can impact the assignment decision.
9. Discuss the ways in which technical skills can impact the assignment decision.
10. Describe ways in which overall strategic company factors might affect the staffing decision in some situations.
11. Discuss the ways in which training can be used in the assignment decision.

## EXERCISES

1. The disks accompanying this book contain the prototype KBS described in the second half of this chapter. Following the directions accompanying the disks for using the M.1 expert system shell, run a consultation using the system, which has the file name STAFFING. If you wish, you might also print out the knowledge base and study it while you are running the system and restudying this chapter.
2. After reviewing the situation outlines in the chapter figures for the decision involving assigning a knowledge engineer to a KBS development project, and the discussion of them in the section "An Approach to Making Knowledge Engineer Assignment Decisions for KBS Development Projects," develop a small KBS to assist in making a strategy decision in some other staffing area described in the chapter, for example hiring instead of assigning. Follow the

directions in either Chapter 2, or in Chapters 3 through 6, when developing the system.

**3.** Read through recent issues of KBS periodicals listed in the references section of this chapter, and through other related artificial intelligence and systems management books and periodicals, and find discussions of the main topics covered in this chapter. Pay special attention to descriptions of how companies went about staffing their KBS development efforts. Write a report on what you learned about situational approaches to staffing KBS development efforts in general, or specific individual KBS development projects, from your reading.

## REFERENCES


Bernold, Thomas. *Expert Systems and Knowledge Engineering.* New York; Elsevier Science Publishers, B.V., 1986.

Berry, D. C., and D. E. Broadbent. "Expert Systems and the Man-machine Interface." *Expert Systems,* October 1986, pp. 228–31.

Bredin, Alice. "AI: Techies Need Not Apply." *Computerworld,* February 19, 1990, p. 123.

Chruden, Herbert J., Arthur W. Sherman, and George W. Bolhlander. *Managing Human Resources,* 8th ed. Cincinnati, OH: South-Western Publishing, 1988.

Couger, Daniel J. "Motivating IS Personnel." *Datamation,* September 15, 1988, pp. 59–64.

Couger, Daniel J., and Scott C. McIntyre. "Motivation Norms of Knowledge Engineers Compared to Those of Software Engineers." *Journal of Systems Management,* Winter 1987-88, pp. 82–93.

Couger, Daniel J., and Robert A. Zawacki. "What Motivates DP Professionals." *Datamation,* September 1978, pp. 82–93.

Cullen, J., and A. Bryman. "The Knowledge Acquisition Bottleneck: Time for Reassessment?" *Expert Systems,* 5 (3), August 1988, pp. 216–25.

Dologite, Dorothy G. "Knowledge-based Systems: A Study of End-User Developers." In publication—review article based on an original research study.

Fellers, Jack W. "An Exploratory Investigation of Critical Success Factors for Knowledge Acquisition in Expert Systems Development." *Conference on the Impact of Artificial Intelligence on Business and Industry,* Denton TX: The Information Systems Research Center, University of Texas, October 9–11, 1988.

Furno, Daryl J. "Staffing Your New AI Groups." In *Managing Artificial Intelligence & Expert Systems,* eds. Daniel A. DeSalvo and Jay Liebowitz. Englewood Cliffs, NJ: Prentice Hall/Yourdon Press, 1990, pp. 1–20.

Gordon, Judith R. *Human Resource Management: A Practical Approach.* Boston, Allyn and Bacon, 1986.

Hart, Anna. *Knowledge Acquisition for Expert Systems.* New York: McGraw-Hill, 1986.

Hayes-Roth, F., D. A. Waterman, and D. B Lenat. *Building Expert Systems.* Reading, MA: Addison-Wesley, 1983.

Hoffman, Robert R. "The Problem of Extracting the Knowledge of Experts from the Perspective of Experimental Psychology." *AI Magazine,* Summer 1987, pp. 53–67.

Mockler, Robert J. *Knowledge Based Systems for Management Decisions,* Englewood Cliffs, NJ. Prentice-Hall, 1989.

Mockler, Robert J. "Strategies for Transferring Information Systems Tasks to Managers: The Changing Knowledge Engineering Role," *The Review of Business Studies,* accepted for publication, Fall 1991.

Prerau, David, "Knowledge Acquisition in the Development of a Large Expert System." *AI Magazine,* Summer 1987, pp. 43–51.

Rose, Frederick. "An 'Electronic Clone' of a Skilled Engineer Is Very Hard to Create." *Wall Street Journal,* August 12, 1988, pp. 1 and 14.

Volkema, Roger J. "Problem Complexity and the Formulation Process in Planning and Design." *Behavioral Science,* October 1988, pp. 292–300.

# Part Five

## SAMPLE PROTOTYPE KBS

# 15

# Initial Screening for an Expert-Driven KBS Project

This chapter discusses the preliminary project screening done in decision situations involving an individual (student or manager) working on his or her own who:

- Has little or no computer training,
- Is doing a relatively small system or concept-testing prototype system, and
- Is in a business school program, or taking an executive seminar, or working in business.

This screening is part of the project planning phase of the KBS development life cycle shown in Figure 15–1.

Figure 15–2 outlines the decision situation under study. Before an individual attempts such a preliminary screening of a proposed KBS development project, he or she should review what knowledge-based systems are and what they can do, which can be done by reviewing Chapters 1 and 2 of this book.

The recommendations made in such situations include:

- proceed with the project as it is,
- do not proceed with the project at all, or
- modify some aspect of the project.

**Figure 15–1.** Knowledge-Based Systems Development Life Cycle

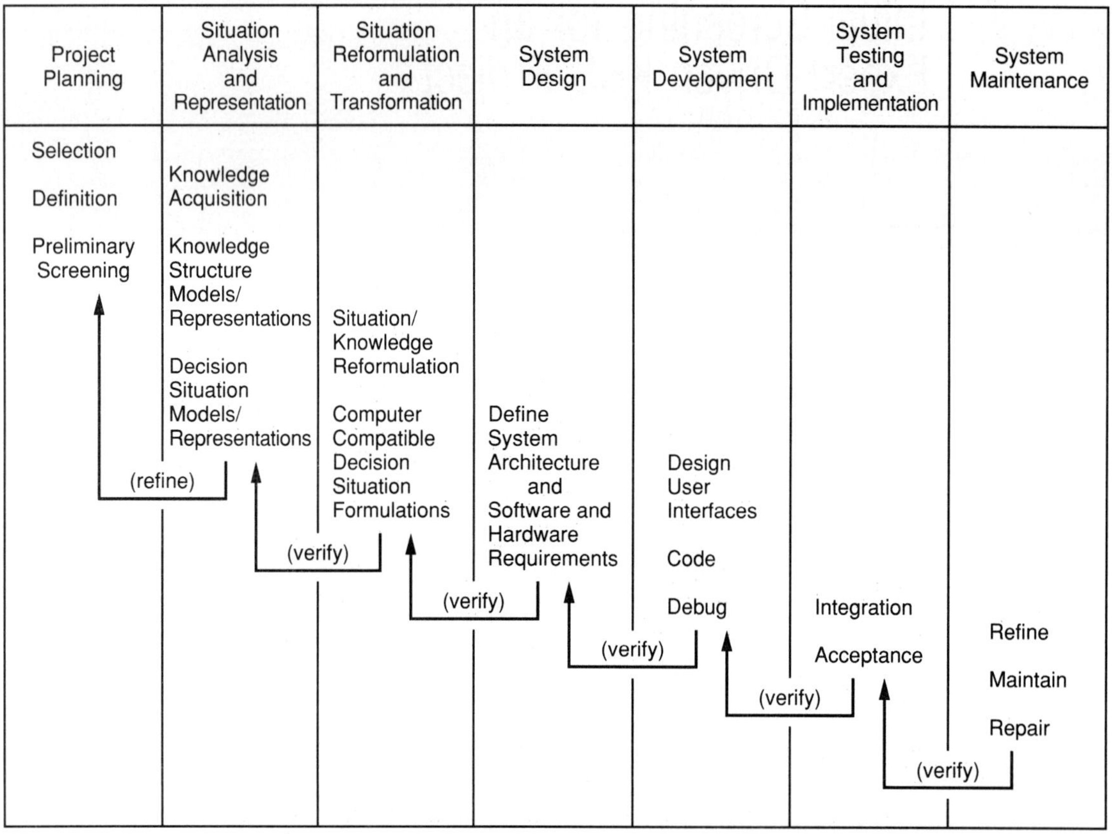


While the KBS in this chapter in some way recalls the KBS described in Chapter 12, which also involves screenings of project feasibility, it is different. The KBS here focuses on projects of fairly limited scope, and on KBS developers who do not necessarily have any technical background or training.

The following discussion of the decision situation, and the KBS developed to replicate it, covers:

- the situation to be prototyped
- documenting the system and putting it onto computer

## THE DECISION SITUATION TO BE PROTOTYPED

The decision situation involves a preliminary screening and evaluation of a KBS project proposal. It also involves any necessary guidance or assistance that an

**Figure 15–2.** Decision Situation under Study: Preliminary Screening of a Small Individual Project Proposal—Decision Domain Diagram

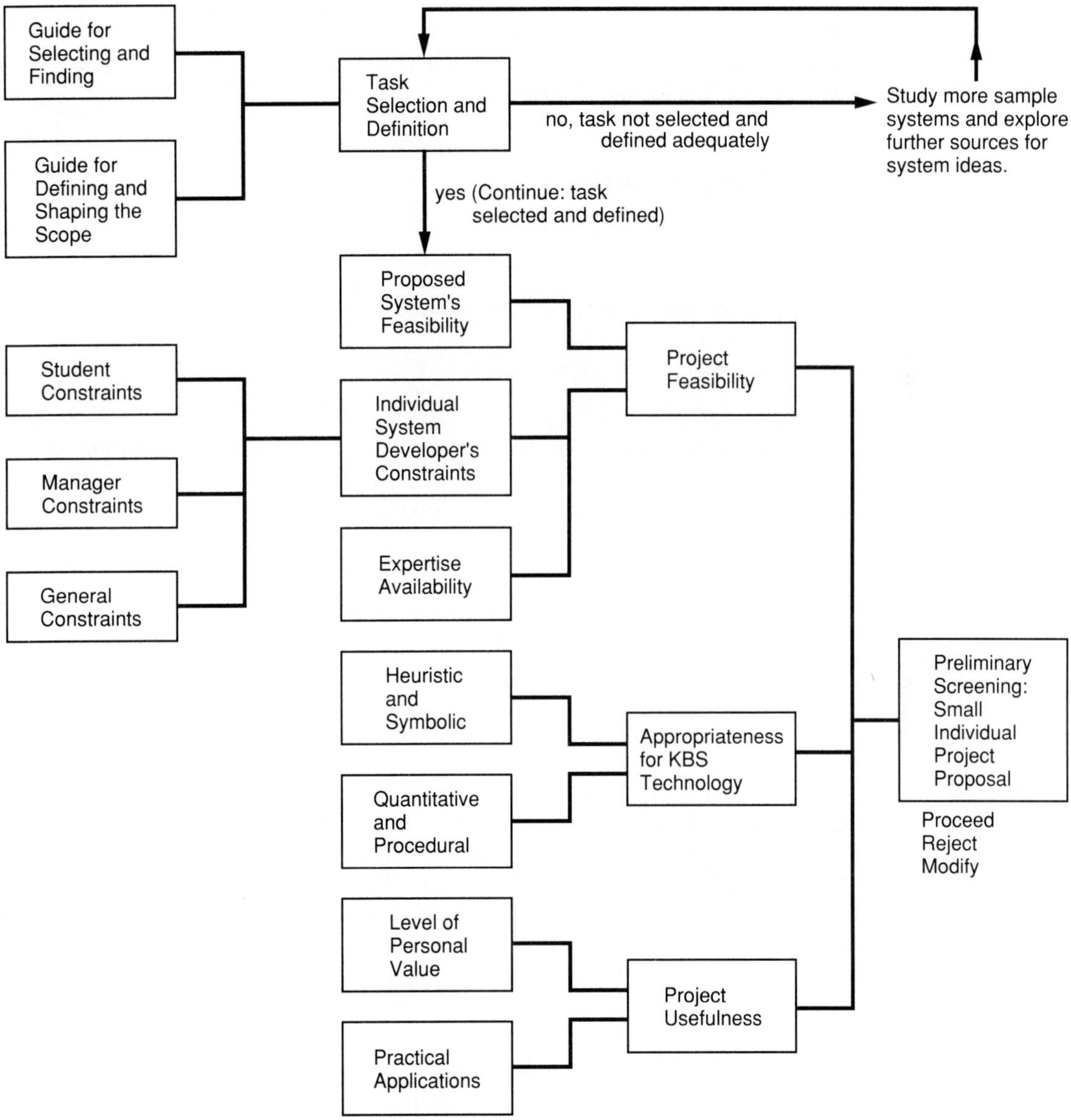

individual student or manager might require in finding, selecting, and defining a project for class or for work.

The discussion is divided into three sections:

- factors affecting the decision
- recommendations and how they are arrived at
- a typical decision scenario

### Factors Affecting the Decision

The critical factors affecting decisions in these situations can be grouped into three categories, as shown in Figure 15–2:

- appropriateness of proposed project for KBS technology
- KBS project feasibility
- KBS project usefulness

In all the preliminary screening situations described in this section, it is assumed that an initial decision has been made that for reasons of career or job development, or personal growth, the project is considered a worthwhile investment of time by the individual involved in the study.

The study of the above factors in situations involving people inexperienced in either knowledge-based system development or management decision making may also include providing help for those who are:

- having trouble finding a suitable decision, problem, or task for KBS development, or
- having trouble defining and shaping an interesting potential decision, problem, or task

A good starting point in understanding KBS development is to review some of the knowledge-based systems described in Chapters 1, 2, 3, Part Five, and the Appendices in this book. Examining sample systems will give the individual insight into applications of KBS technology (for example: Agnew 1988; Bramer 1988; "Expert Systems" 1988; Humpert 1988; "Inanimate Analysts" 1987; Lasher 1988; Mockler 1989; Rauch-Hindin 1985; "Robots Are Coming" 1988). It will also give an idea of the structure, type of reasoning, and effort involved in building a KBS. Running some of the sample systems on the disk accompanying this book will also be helpful.

For some, such a study will suggest ideas for KBS development projects. However, often individual students or managers may need further guidance in finding an area for a KBS development project. If this is the case, in order to assist them with this decision it is useful to know their amount and level of work experience and schooling. For example, one might be:

- a full-time undergraduate student with little or no work experience
- a full- or part-time graduate student with some managerial experience

- a person with some work experience at the managerial level but with little experience in KBS development or formal problem definition

To help guide individuals in finding and selecting a KBS project that is feasible, is appropriate for KBS technology, and has a high level of usefulness (personal value and/or practical applications), individuals would be directed to consider the following as a possible source for a KBS development project:

- A decision or task they presently perform either at school or at work
- Hobbies or interests that they may have a strong curiosity about
- A decision or task that their superiors or co-workers make or perform that they are interested in learning more about and for which they have or can get access to the expertise involved
- A specific area in which they might want to start a new business
- Any other job-related decision or task that they are interested in and would like to understand better, or be able to perform just to satisfy their own curiosity or meet their goals

The key here is to start with an area in which there is a very high level of interest and potential long-term benefits to the individual involved.

Based on individuals' situations and preferences, they would be shown further examples of systems previously developed by people in similar situations in order to help stimulate their thinking. For example, an undergraduate student might be shown Examples A and B in Figure 15–3, graduate students might be shown Examples B, C, and D, while working managers might be shown sample systems similar to Examples C, D, and E.

Once a general decision, problem, or task area has been selected for KBS development, it is usually necessary to define the decision, problem, or task more precisely. This phase is often referred to as *refining* and *defining* the scope of the project. The examples in Figure 15–3 include brief examples of the initial phases of refining and defining.

This phase sometimes requires broadening the scope of the project and sometimes narrowing it.

In order to determine that the breadth and depth (scope) of a KBS project are not too great, the following steps can be helpful:

- Write a very detailed scenario (story) of how the task or decision under study is carried out in a specific situation, including such specifics as time, place, people involved, and other actual events which would occur on a given day in a real situation.
- Identify the recommendations which can be made in the kind of situation under study, limiting the answer to no more than four or five basic ones.
- Specify the three or four critical factors which are considered in making these recommendations and describe how these factors affect which recommendation is made.
- List ten or twelve specific questions which need answering in order to obtain information about the factors needed to make a recommendation.

**Figure 15–3.** KBS Project Descriptions

**Example A:** A "PC Expert System Shell Selection System" developed by an undergraduate student for part of a software review course.

The general area under study was software selection. This involves evaluating the capabilities of different types of software and matching them against user needs and abilities, technical computer capabilities, and situation needs to select the best software package. Software may be selected from the many different word processing, expert system shell, spreadsheet, desktop publishing, graphics, database, and integrated packages available.

The area selected for further study was selection of a PC expert system shell for use in a class project. The scope of the initial prototype system to be developed was narrowed further to the five shells available at the school's computer lab.

**Example B:** A "Horse Race Betting System," which was developed based on a manager's hobby.

The general area under study was horse racing, one of the sporting events in the United States where money can be wagered legally. This money-making aspect combined with the expert decision making (handicapping) that goes into placing a wager makes horse race betting a good candidate for the application of KBS technology.

There are different types of horse races, for example, thoroughbred and harness racing. The scope of the prototype system to be developed was narrowed to handicapping thoroughbred horse races run on a fast dirt track and limited to claiming races.

**Example C:** An "Auto Stock Analyst System" developed by a graduate student who wanted to acquire a better understanding of the area.

The general area under study was financial planning and analysis. Financial planning and analysis encompasses a very broad range of areas including personal investment planning, cash management, merger and acquisition analysis, and individual company analysis. Individual company analysis was chosen for study from these areas.

The scope of the prototype system to be developed was narrowed to regular and periodic fundamental analysis of the common stock of the three major auto companies. The scope was narrowed so that the breadth covered by the system was of manageable size and so that the system could cover the chosen area in sufficient depth.

**Example D:** A "Franchise Selection System," which was developed by a consultant with considerable work experience in the area under study.

The general area under study was entrepreneurial new-venture planning. This area covers such decisions as:

- whether or not to be an entrepreneur
- whether to go into business alone or with partners
- choosing the type of venture to undertake
- whether or not to use franchising
- whether or not to accept a specific new venture deal offered

Of all the possible entrepreneurial decision areas, franchise selection was chosen for further study. Franchise selection decisions are frequently faced by individual entrepreneurs, both because of the individuals' lack of capital and because of their unfamiliarity with the demands of running a business.

The focus of the study was further limited to the fast food and specialty food areas. Of the many possible retail ventures considered, fast food and specialty food stores are recognized as strong opportunity areas, both because of population demographics (an increase in the number of working mothers who depend on convenience foods; an increase in working teenagers and young, affluent, childless couples; geographic population shifts; and shifts in shopping and eating habits) and local conditions (large groups of these people are concentrated in selected areas).

The situation to be prototyped assumed that the individual involved had already made the decision to be an entrepreneur, and to go into business on his or her own.

The prototype system covers the critical knowledge areas examined in making these decisions. They are: (1) the general and local business prospects, including opportunities, success factors, and general market structure; (2) the individual's resources and capabilities to meet success criteria; and (3) the franchisor's offering.

**Example E:** A "Commercial Loan Approval System," which was developed by two loan officers at a large metropolitan bank.

The general area under study was financial planning and analysis. Many areas of financial planning lend themselves to KBS development, including personal investment planning, capital investment planning, cash management, merger and acquisition analysis, individual company analysis, and commercial and personal loan application analysis.

The business or commercial loan application analysis area was selected for prototype development for several reasons, including

- there are recognized experts in the field
- expert decision skills are needed to do the job
- it requires informed judgement
- the task is well understood
- the decisions have a high payoff and practical value
- the system developer was familiar with the area

Within the commercial credit screening area, several types of companies and loans were identified for possible prototype development including:

- loans to new businesses, under three years old, with no record of past performance
- loans to existing businesses
- loans of varying amounts

The scope of the system was narrowed to commercial loan requests between $250,000 and $2.5 million from businesses in existence for at least three years and not in violation of a bank's policies regarding target markets.

The focus of the study was also further narrowed to nonfinancial considerations, such as the future prospects of the company applying for the loan, the character of its management, and the fit of a proposed loan with the bank's strategic guidelines, since these considerations involve nonquantitative, more subjective and more strategic factors, and thus are more appropriate for KBS development.

- If you are dealing with a diagnostic situation, reduce it to a technical manual outline and describe alternative ways this manual might be used to answer three or four specific questions or problems.
- Reexamine samples of existing KBS.

To help guide an individual in doing these steps, examples would be given of how each of these steps were carried out for a particular decision, task, or problem and how a KBS was developed in this way. Examples of some of the steps in this process for the "Franchise Selection" and the "Shell Selection" KBS are shown in Figure 15–4.

It is also possible for the scope of the decision, task, or problem area to be too narrow. Several questions are explored in determining if a KBS project proposal is (or has become) too narrow. These questions include:

- Does the situation involve just common sense, for example, whether or not to wear a coat on a sub-zero winter day?
- Are the final recommendations simply yes or no?
- Does the reasoning involve mostly a procedural process that can be reduced to a single sheet of instructions or a check list of criteria which dictate a specific solution?

If the answer to these questions is "yes," then the project proposal (situation definition) is probably too narrow and needs to be broadened. In such a case, it is necessary to reexamine the situation and study existing sample systems.

A commonly encountered narrow proposal definition involves evaluating only one option: for example, a decision as to whether or not to purchase a specific expert system shell, such as VP-Expert. Such a decision is too narrow mainly because of its limited usefulness and its simplicity. Such a system could be broadened very simply by redefining it as:

> A decision involving selecting the expert system shell (from the major ones available on the market) which best meets the needs of the individual (who could be anyone in any type of business) who is considering making such a purchase.

Only after an individual has *found* and *selected* an area, task, or decision for KBS development and adequately *defined its scope*, is it worthwhile to examine the critical factors affecting the evaluation of the proposed KBS project. These critical factors can be grouped into three categories:

- appropriateness of the proposed project for KBS technology
- KBS project feasibility
- KBS project usefulness

***Appropriateness for KBS Technology.*** Determining a project's appropriateness for KBS technology requires looking at the nature of the reasoning processes involved to see if they are:

- quantitative, with repetitive procedures, or
- heuristic and symbolic with inferential procedures

**Figure 15–4.** Examples of Steps Taken to Define a Proposed KBS Project

**Example A: A Franchise Selection System**

*Note:* This system is an early prototype of a KBS being developed for a company with 100 locations which sells franchising advisory services for a fee to prospective entrepreneurs.

To help determine the adequacy of the scope of your KBS project proposal you should:

1. *Identify the recommendations which can be made in the kinds of task situations under study, limiting your answer to no more than four or five basic recommendations.*

Typical recommendations made when evaluating franchise offerings include:

- *Superior*—Actively pursue the offering;
- *Very good*—Pursue the offering, but commit to it only after further analyses and evaluations are completed of such factors as local business prospects, and especially the competition;
- *Fair*—If the local business prospects are weak, examine a similar proposal in another location; if the franchise offering is the weak factor, look for another offering with a similar product and location, but through a different franchisor;
- *Poor*—Abandon the proposal.

2. *Specify the three or four critical factors which are considered in making these recommendations and how these factors can affect which recommendation is made.*

The critical factors considered when evaluating franchise offerings include:

- The business prospects, both general and local;
- Individual resources and capabilities, such as personality, financial position, and work experience and skills;
- The franchise contract covering franchisor support, the reasonableness of the deal, and the franchisor character.

A franchise offering would be considered *superior* if both the business prospects and the franchise contract were favorable and the individual's resources were favorable or average.

A franchise offering would be considered *very good* if both the business prospects and the individual's resources were favorable and the franchise contract was only average. It would also be considered *good* if the business prospects were average and both the franchise contract and the individual's resources were favorable.

A franchise offering would be considered *fair* if both the business prospects and the individual's resources were average and the franchise contract was average or favorable.

A franchise offering would be considered *poor* if any of the critical factors were considered unfavorable.

3. *List ten or twelve specific questions which need answering in order to obtain information about the factors needed to make a recommendation.*

Some of the questions asked when evaluating franchise offerings include:

For Business Prospects:

"After examining demographic characteristics such as age, income, and size of the target market, what is your estimate of the potential growth in the market in general?"

*continued*

**Figure 15–4** *continued*

For the Individual's Resources and Capabilities:

"What amount of money are you able to borrow?"

For the Franchise Offering:

"What is the average failure rate of former franchisees in the past?"

"Has the general evaluation of the franchisor by former and current franchisees been favorable?"

**4.** *Write a detailed scenario of how the task or decision under study is carried out, including such situation specifics as time, place, people involved, and other actual events which would occur on a given day in a real situation. The scenario will probably not be complete after a first draft but will grow as you investigate how the situation and decision work.*

Robert London, age forty-two, is a single male interested in a retail fast food franchise. He has worked in investment banking for the last ten years, and prior to that, worked in a branch of a suburban bank. He holds a bachelor's and master's degree in business and lives in a rented apartment in a middle class suburban area near a major city. Rob engaged a consultant (expert) in the field to help in deciding whether or not to purchase a Burger King franchise near his home.

The consultant first collected background information. In terms of general business prospects, the product was examined for growth potential and staying power. Since fast food products are common products consumed by many segments of the general population, ample demographic and market studies were available that showed the overall growth prospects for the fast food market were generally favorable. However, analysis of the local area revealed several weak points. The consultant found that the location Rob was looking at was already saturated with competition, including a McDonald's, a Wendy's, and a Roy Rogers, all within a mile radius of each other. In addition, the franchise Rob was interested in would be located near an exit ramp to a major highway, but would be the last eating place that travelers would reach coming off the highway exit.

Although the demographic profile of the local area matched the franchise's target market, the market area was not expected to grow significantly in the future. The consultant talked with small business owners in the area and found that general indicators called for only modest overall growth. Although the other franchises in the area seemed busy, the consultant's research indicated that competitors' sales had been fairly flat over the prior three years.

The consultant interviewed Rob to see if he was cut out to be an entrepreneur. Based on experiences Rob described from his past, he seemed capable of taking charge, organizing and handling multiple jobs, and dealing effectively with people. He had demonstrated determination and self-reliance to a high degree. Rob generally seemed competent enough to run his own business but lacked the willingness to take big risks.

Next, the consultant examined the franchise offering. Burger King provides substantial initial assistance at no additional cost in the areas of operations, equipment maintenance, and training. However, they have a relatively high annual franchise payment, provide no assistance with financing, and subject franchisees to a wide variety of controls. Burger King, in business since 1954, has maintained excellent relations with its franchisees and business contacts. The company is predicted to increase its 3,000 units substantially in the next decade. Although a very reputable franchisor, Burger King's contract gives no guarantee of exclusivity of territory, and contains some tie-in purchasing agreements with suppliers.

The consultant summarized his evaluation as follows:

- *Business prospects.* The general prospects were favorable. However, because of a stagnating local market and poor location, the local business prospects were considered unfavorable. The business prospects were, therefore, rated unfavorable overall.
- *Individual resources and capabilities.* Because Rob had favorable personal, financial, and business skills, the overall rating was favorable.
- *Franchisor offering.* Franchisor support was very favorable. However, due to the lack of financial assistance and only fair fee schedule, the reasonableness of the deal was rated average. Although Burger King's reputation is excellent, lack of exclusivity of territory and tie-in agreements yielded an average rating for the contract. The overall rating for the franchise offering was average.

Based on this analysis and evaluation, the consultant's overall rating of the venture was only fair. Knowing that the local area was not well suited to the particular franchise because of heavy competition, and that Rob would need assistance with some financing, the expert recommended looking for a more generously financed offering, with a similar product but in a better location.

5. *To help determine the adequacy of the scope of your KBS project proposal you should compare it to existing sample systems in the textbook.*

**Example B: A PC Expert System Shell Selection System**

To help determine the adequacy of the scope of your KBS project proposal you should:

1. *Identify the recommendations which can be made in the kinds of task situations under study, limiting your answer to no more than four or five basic ones.*

Typical recommendations made when selecting from among the five available shells in a computer lab include:

- Use VP-Expert
- Use M.1
- Use GURU
- Use ESIE
- Use Level 5

2. *Specify the three or four critical factors which are considered in making these recommendations and how these factors can affect which recommendation is made.*

The critical factors considered when choosing an expert system shell include:

- System developer's computer experience
- Size and kind of system to be developed
- Required links or interfaces with other software
- Special required user interface and environment requirements
- Special reasoning (for example, backward vs. forward chaining) requirements

*continued*

**Figure 15–4** *continued*

*ESIE* would only be recommended for situations in which the developer did not have much computer experience, the size of the system to be developed was very small, there were no required software links or interfaces, user interface requirements were limited, and there was need for backward chaining only.

*VP-Expert* would be recommended for situations in which developer's computer experience ranged from low to high, the size of the system to be developed ranged from small to large, software interface with Lotus 1-2-3 or dBase was required, user interface requirements were not of paramount importance, and there was the need for either backward or forward chaining.

*M.1* would be recommended for situations in which developer's computer experience ranged from low to average, the size of the system to be developed ranged from small to large, software interface with Lotus 1-2-3 or dBase was not required, user interface requirements were important, and there was the need for mainly backward chaining.

*GURU* would be recommended for situations in which developer's computer experience was high, the size of the system to be developed was large, software interface with a spreadsheet and a database application was needed, user interface requirements were of paramount importance, and there was the need for either backward or forward chaining.

*Level 5* would be recommended for situations in which the developer's computer experience ranged from average to high, the size of the system to be developed ranged from small to large, software interface with dBase was required, user interface requirements were not of paramount importance, and there was the need for mainly backward chaining.

3. *List as many specific questions as you can that need answering in order to obtain information about the factors needed to make a recommendation.*

Some of the questions asked when selecting an expert system shell include:

- "What is the developer's level of computer skills?"
- "Will the system require interfacing with a spreadsheet or database?"
- "How many questions, rules, and rule sets do you estimate will be in the system?"
- "How many different types of recommendations can the system make?"
- "Does the user interface require more than just answering questions? Does it require that the user be shown large amounts of text, or graphs and charts?"
- "Does the reasoning involved in your system require backward chaining, forward chaining, or both?"

4. *Write a detailed scenario of how the task or decision under study is carried out, including such situation specifics as time, place, people involved, and other actual events which would occur on a given day in a real situation. The scenario will probably not be complete after a first draft but will grow as you investigate how the situation and decision work.*

Cindy Conlon is an undergraduate student taking a course on KBS development. She has to develop a KBS as part of a class project, and can use one of the five shells available at the school's computer lab. The five shells are ESIE, M.1, VP-Expert, Level 5, and GURU. She has chosen a marketing "media selection" decision as her topic for KBS development.

The size of the system Cindy planned to develop was relatively large (it was expected to be about 200 rules), software interface with Lotus 1-2-3 or dBase was not required, user interface requirements were important because messages and questions had to be displayed to the user and sent to the printer, and the reasoning involved required mainly backward chaining. Cindy's computer experience was average.

After reviewing these factors and the capabilities of the five shells with a lab assistant familiar with them, Cindy decided that:

ESIE would not be the best choice because it could not use condensed rules and it could not meet user interface requirements.

VP-Expert did not meet her user interface requirements and its logic debugging facilities were not sufficiently user-friendly.

GURU required a higher degree of computer expertise than she had, and she did not need the full extent of its features.

Level 5 would not be the best choice because M.1 met her user interface needs better and she did not require its ability to interface with other software.

M.1 was the best choice because it met her development needs better than the other four available shells. It could provide for adequate user interface and had an easily usable "trace" capability to help her debug logic problems.

5. *To help determine the adequacy of the scope of your KBS project proposal you should compare it to existing sample systems in the course textbook, with the system reports on file in the library, with the systems on the floppy disks on file in the lab, and on the hard disk of the computer devoted to the course in the computer lab.*

Reasoning processes are classified as quantitative if they can be reduced to a mathematical formula. For example, if a decision relies mainly on mathematical computations, such as when to reorder a particular product for inventory or when and how much to bill a customer, the reasoning or decision making involved is quantitative. Quantitative reasoning involves manipulating numbers as opposed to concepts. Decision situations which are largely quantitative are usually best suited for conventional computer systems, not for knowledge-based systems.

For a project proposal to be appropriate for KBS development, the reasoning involved in the task or decision should be heuristic and symbolic, that is, knowledge intensive in nature, not procedure intensive or quantitative. *Knowledge intensive* refers to information or knowledge of how different decision factors are interrelated in arriving at some conclusion. An example can be seen in Figure 15–4, section 2 in both Examples A and B.

Heuristics are rules of thumb that experts use to help them solve problems. For example, an expert mail order marketing manager may know from experience that orders per thousand are higher in general in January than during the summer. This is an example of just one of the many heuristics that a mail order marketing manager may use when scheduling major catalog or special-product-offer mailings for the coming year. Heuristic knowledge is judgmental in nature. It is not intended to guarantee a single best solution, but to allow one to make a reasonably good decision.

Symbolic reasoning involves manipulating symbols that represent concepts. Syllogisms, which are arguments consisting of at least three propositions, are examples of symbolic reasoning. For example:

All the accountants in a company are CPAs.
Betty is an accountant in the company.
Therefore, Betty is a CPA.

The first two propositions are called premises and have one term (symbol) in common (accountants in a company) which furnishes a logical connection between the two other terms (CPA and Betty), which are then linked to arrive at the third proposition or conclusion.

Decision situations involving heuristics and symbolic reasoning are appropriate for KBS development.

Questions such as the following are asked to find a project's appropriateness for KBS technology. The answers to the first two questions should be "significant"; the next two should be answered "limited."

- To what degree does the reasoning process involved in the proposed project require symbolic manipulation?
- To what degree does the reasoning involved in the proposed project require using rules of thumb or heuristics?
- To what degree does the proposed project only involve giving yes or no answers to questions?
- To what degree is the decision or task involved in the proposed project quantitative enough that one could make a version of it work on Lotus 1-2-3 or some other spreadsheet system?

In addition, KBS technology allows for easier modification than conventional computer technology. For this reason, if a project covers an area that changes often, such as tax laws or building codes, KBS technology may be superior. For example, one of the reasons that Digital Equipment chose KBS technology to develop XCON, an expert computer configuration system, was because different components were often added and sometimes deleted from the company's product line, and conventional computer systems could not easily be altered to reflect these changes (Rauch-Hindin 1985).

Another measure of KBS technology appropriateness is the amount of interaction with nontechnical managers its development and use involves. Since the knowledge base in KBS is separate from the inferencing procedures and the knowledge base is often written in nontechnical terms at least during the early development stages, the knowledge base can be studied, understood, modified, and manipulated more easily by nontechnical managers.

An example of an appropriate type of application for KBS technology is diagnosis. The reasoning process used in diagnosing computer hardware problems, for example, is symbolic and relies significantly on heuristics, as in the rule "If the keyboard is not working, first check to see that it is plugged in." In light of the multitude of both simple and complex hardware problems that might possibly be encountered, it is clear that in many situations the decision to be replicated by the KBS could not be done with a spreadsheet type application and relies on much more than common sense.

***Project Feasibility.*** A project's feasibility depends on three major factors:

- expertise availability
- the proposed system's feasibility
- the individual system developer's constraints

A project's feasibility depends first upon the *expertise availability*. Expertise availability refers to the availability of sources of expertise that can be used to develop the system. This may include the expert or experts who can be used as sources of knowledge, as well as books, manuals, and any other expertise or knowledge sources.

Determining the expert/expertise availability involves answering such questions as:

- Can the reasoning process be identified and defined?
- Do recognized experts or sources of expertise exist?
- Can experts do the task better than amateurs, and can their skills be taught to others?
- Can the available experts articulate the general methods that they use to reach conclusions and make decisions?
- Do you have, or can you get, adequate sources of the knowledge and/or expertise to develop the KBS?

Unless the answers to all of these questions are positive, sufficient expertise is not available for the project and it is *not* feasible. If all of these questions are answered satisfactorily, the evaluation of the proposed KBS would continue.

Determining the *proposed system's feasibility* requires the individual to imagine how the proposed system would look on computer. To do this, it is usually necessary to develop several scenarios of how typical decisions are made, problems are solved, or tasks are performed in the situation which is to be replicated in the KBS. It also involves examining and consulting sample systems and then answering the following questions about the decision situation under study and the system proposed to replicate it. Samples of these questions are given in Figure 15–4.

- Approximately how many questions need to be answered about the area involved when making/performing the decision/task?
- How long do you estimate that it takes an expert in the area to make the decision, solve the problem, or do the task under study?
- How many major factors influencing the final decision do you estimate there are?

- Will the proposed system require that information be gathered from a spreadsheet or database?
- How many recommendations do you estimate there will be in the system?

The above review of the situation should be repeated until a fairly detailed picture is formulated of how the decision, task, or problem situation is structured.

A project's feasibility also depends upon the *individual system developer's constraints.* Individual system developer constraints can vary considerably, depending on the situation. Typical situations include:

- systems developed as part of an undergraduate or graduate course
- systems developed throughout an entire course
- systems developed by fulltime managers for use at work
- systems developed as part of a business seminar

The different constraints arising from these situations can be broken down into three categories:

- student constraints, if the developer is a student
- manager constraints, if the developer is a manager
- general constraints, that apply to all types of situations

Students' constraints cover such questions as:

- the number of other courses taken
- the year of school they are in
- whether they are undergraduate or graduate students
- their other obligations, such as work, family, and special circumstances

Managers' constraints fall into such areas as:

- job demands
- their other obligations, such as family, school, or other special circumstances

General constraints cover such areas as:

- the amount of time and energy that can be devoted to the project
- individuals' knowledge of the areas to be prototyped
- their background in computers
- their general competency in the cognitive skills area

For managers in a training seminar, in addition to the information gathered from the above questions, the duration of the training program would be a factor in evaluating time constraints.

The level of difficulty of a proposed KBS is likely to increase with each added level of situation complexity—from an undergraduate course up to a seminar for experienced executives working on relatively complex systems to support their jobs at work.

Assuming the expertise is available, the individual system developer constraints are matched against the proposed system's feasibility to determine the overall *project feasibility*.

For example, the situation may involve a project that is part of a marketing course in which the KBS development project is designed to support the learning of advertising techniques. In this instance, the project might be a relatively small system for choosing the most effective radio stations to advertise on for a specific product, for instance, blue jeans. While this particular project might be part of a larger media-choice decision that would also include television and print advertising, the actual prototype system would be fairly small. For instance, such a system might include 10 to 12 questions, 20 to 40 rules, 6 or 7 factors, and only 3 recommendations, with no database or spreadsheet interfaces. It might replicate a decision which would take an experienced media buyer 7 or 8 minutes to make.

Adjustments or modifications are often made to increase the likelihood of developing a worthwhile KBS in a given situation. These modifications usually involve altering the scope or adjusting the amount of time and resources that the individual devotes to the project. As more time or expertise is made available, larger, more difficult projects can be undertaken.

If individual developers knew nothing about media selection and their time was very limited and they could not allocate more of their time to the project, they might narrow the scope to replicate a decision made in 5 minutes or less by an expert.

In another situation, if the entire course were devoted to developing a KBS, the individual developer had extra time and was interested in the area, or two individuals were working together on the project, the project might be expanded to include 50 to 150 rules, 4 to 6 recommendations, and both database and spreadsheet interfaces. It might replicate a decision which would take an experienced media buyer 10 to 12 minutes to make.

***Project Usefulness.*** Determining a project's usefulness involves examining such factors as:

- the practical applications of the system
- its level of personal value to the individual developer

Practical applications of a system may include helping people make decisions in their jobs. Or, a system may contain personal value to the developer if the individual is interested in learning more about the area involved or if it helps one's career.

In measuring the *practical business applications* of the system, an individual answers such questions as:

- Is the expertise replicated in the proposed KBS needed often and on a regular basis at work—for example, more than once a week on average?

- To what extent can the proposed KBS be used to help repair and service products?
- To what extent can the proposed KBS be used to give sales assistance to customers?
- To what extent can the proposed KBS be used to help train or retrain employees?
- Does the proposed KBS have some other practical use at work?
- Does the proposed KBS have some practical use in a possible new venture under consideration?
- Is the main purpose of the system to test KBS technology?

In measuring the *personal value* of a decision, task, or area selected for KBS development, an individual answers such questions as:

- Did you choose to develop a KBS in this particular area, or was the project assigned to you?
- How would you describe the extent to which your KBS will help you at school, in your job, or elsewhere?
- Would learning how to perform the task or make the decision involved in the KBS provide personal satisfaction?
- Does the proposed KBS deal with your hobbies or interests?
- How would you describe the chances of your project helping you get a new job, a promotion, a raise, or job security?
- Will developing this system impress your boss?
- How would you describe the feeling or sense of accomplishment that you expect to get from developing this system?
- Are you being paid to develop this system?

The KBS project proposal's *usefulness* is based upon the answers given to the above sets of questions. For example, if the system will have a practical application at work, such as training employees who work for the KBS developer, the project's usefulness is significant. If the individual developer is assigned to develop a particular system as a class project or its main purpose is to test KBS technology at the company where the individual works, the project's usefulness would be limited.

### Recommendations and How They Are Arrived At

Three basic recommendations can be identified in these preliminary screening situations:

- Proceed with the proposed KBS project as it is.
- Do not proceed at all with the proposed KBS project.
- Modify some aspect of the proposed KBS project to increase its chances of being successfully developed and used, and proceed only if you can make the required modification.

One would proceed with the KBS project as proposed without any modifications if:

- the project feasibility is acceptable, that is, expertise is available and the amount of time the individual has to work on the proposed project is sufficient to handle a project of its scope and the scope is sufficiently large, and
- the proposed project is significantly or moderately appropriate for KBS technology, and
- the proposed system is significantly or moderately useful.

The KBS project would be rejected outright if:

- expertise is not available, or, given the scope of the project, the amount of time the individual has to work on it is insufficient and the scope cannot be narrowed further or more time cannot be made available, or
- the project is not appropriate for KBS technology, or
- its usefulness is very limited.

Under certain circumstances one would proceed with the KBS project proposal only if modifications could be made. For example:

- if an individual has very little time available, he or she should narrow the scope of the proposed project
- if the project's scope is large, more time should be made available or the scope should be narrowed

Under other circumstances, an individual may want to make other kinds of modifications to the project proposal. For example:

- if the individual has lots of time available he or she may want to increase the scope of the project and develop a larger system
- if the area of the KBS project proposal has a high degree of personal value, then the individual may want to develop a more complex system and devote more time to it

These modifications would only be suggested if:

- adequate expertise is available, and
- the proposed project is significantly or moderately appropriate for KBS technology, and
- the proposed system is significantly or moderately useful.

### A Typical Decision Scenario

The following account describes a sample decision faced by someone involved in a preliminary screening for an individually developed KBS project.

Kate Moore, a part-time MBA student who works part time as a market researcher and has had some managerial experience, is searching for an area, task, or decision for prototype KBS development. The system is being developed for a graduate course in strategic planning, the only course she is taking. Half of the course time will be devoted to developing the system.

Kate started by looking at and consulting sample existing KBS to get an idea about the structure, type of reasoning, and effort involved in developing a KBS.

To help stimulate her thinking about *finding* and *selecting* a topic for KBS development, she met with the instructor to discuss ways in which she might go about examining different aspects of her work experience and hobby interests in a search for ideas. Together, they examined such areas as:

- a decision or task that she presently makes or performs, or is familiar with either at school or at work
- a decision or task that her boss or co-worker makes or performs that she is interested in learning more about and for which the expertise is accessible
- any other job-related decision or task that she is interested in and would like to understand better or be able to perform in order to satisfy her own curiosity or meet her own goals
- hobbies or interests that she may have a very strong curiosity about

Kate was then provided with a large number of sample systems with complete documentation, abbreviated versions of which are shown in Figures 15–3 and 15–4. After studying these examples over one weekend, she found an idea for KBS development: international marketing strategy decisions for an international health care company. She chose this area because she presently worked part-time for a major international health care company as a market researcher and wanted to get a job in international marketing management with the company after graduation. The people she knew at the company who were familiar with the area agreed to help her and so serve as a source of expertise.

(If, after seeing the KBS examples and exploring her background and interests, she still had no idea for a KBS project, she would have been directed to look at additional sample systems and continue to search for an idea.)

To help narrow the scope of this area and *define* the decision more precisely, Kate did the following:

- wrote a detailed scenario of how the decision was made, including such situation specifics as time, place, people involved, and other actual events which would occur on a given day in a real situation
- identified the three or four recommendations which could be made in the situation under study
- specified the three or four critical factors which are considered in making these recommendations and described how these factors affected which recommendation is made

- listed ten or twelve specific questions which need answering in order to obtain information about the factors needed to make a recommendation
- examined samples of existing systems

Through this process, which is illustrated in Figure 15–4, the scope was narrowed to making strategic decisions about a product's market potential in specific local (national) markets of foreign affiliates (subsidiaries) of the company.

Kate found that her project was very *appropriate for KBS technology* because it required the use of judgmental rules of thumb to reach conclusions about the major factors involved. The decision could be made with little reliance on mathematical formulas.

Next, Kate's *proposed system feasibility* was determined by identifying the amount of time it took an expert to make such a decision, as well as the number of questions, rules, and recommendations that the system would contain. She did this by questioning two friends at work, who made similar decisions. She also spent time researching the area at the campus and company libraries. In addition, she found another student in class who was from Venezuela and had worked there, who wanted to work with her on the project.

Kate and her co-developer found through this research that the decision would require about 60 questions, 200 rules, and had 5 critical factors, and 4 recommendations, with several sub-recommendations. A proposed system of this size is feasible for KBS technology.

After describing and evaluating the area further, they decided that it was too large for the time available so the scope was narrowed again to the introduction of only new, nonprescription drug products in different national markets in smaller developing countries.

This was still a project covering a considerable scope, but Kate's *individual constraints* were few. For example, she had extra time available, could devote half her free time to the project, had few other obligations, and enjoyed using and learning about computers. She also had few job demands because her job was only part-time and she was extremely interested in the area. The same was true for her co-developer.

Based on their available time and the proposed system's scope, the match or correspondence of the proposed system's feasibility with their individual situation constraints made the *project's feasibility* acceptable. This is because the two students had the time to develop a system with the scope and size of the one selected.

Developing the KBS project proposal would be very *useful* to Kate because she is extremely interested in the area and she hopes the project will help her get a job in the area at her company. Her co-developer intended to return to Venezuela after graduation and work for an international company doing business there.

They then proceeded to develop this system because it was appropriate for KBS technology, a feasible project, and significantly useful to them.

## DOCUMENTING THE PROTOTYPE SYSTEM AND PUTTING IT ON COMPUTER

The following discussion covers:

- description of the Project Proposal Evaluator prototype system
- dependency diagrams
- designing and constructing the knowledge base

### Description of the System

***System Overview and Objective.*** The prototype system developed is designed to help users evaluate a proposed KBS project. It also assists in finding, selecting, and defining an area for KBS development if the user needs such assistance. The system uses IF-THEN rules and backward chaining to guide the user and reach recommendations.

Typical users include graduate and advanced undergraduate students, as well as business managers inexperienced in KBS development.

The system was developed by educators, managers, and CS technicians with experience in assisting people with such decisions. Published sources of expertise were also used. The system yields two key benefits: it enables inexperienced developers to work more independently, quickly, and efficiently; it reduces the amount of course time needed for learning and doing KBS development.

***Recommendations To Be Made by the System.*** The recommendations made by the system include:

- Look at more sample systems. This is made to people who still have not found, selected, and defined a decision for KBS development.
- Proceed with the proposed KBS project as it is.
- Proceed with the proposed KBS project with the option of increasing the scope.
- Do not proceed at all with the proposed KBS project—reject it.
- Modify the proposed KBS project by either narrowing its scope or committing more time to it.
- Modify the proposed KBS project by increasing its scope and committing more time to it.
- Modify the proposed KBS project by increasing its scope.
- Modify the proposed KBS project by committing more time to it.

***Typical User Dialogue.*** This covers five major areas:

- *Guide for finding and selecting.* If assistance is needed, the assistance provided is based on the type of developer, for example, student, graduate student, or manager, since different examples are shown to different types of people.

- *Guide for defining and shaping*. If assistance is needed in this area, it is also based upon the type of developer, with different examples shown to different types of developers.
- *Appropriateness for KBS technology*. This information is obtained from answering questions about the reasoning processes involved in the decision, to see if they are quantitative, or heuristic and symbolic.
- *Project feasibility*. This information is based on answering questions about expertise availability, the proposed system's feasibility, as well as the individual's situation and individual developer constraints.
- *Project Usefulness*. This information is based on answering questions about practical applications of the system, as well as its level of personal value to the developer.

### Dependency Diagrams

Figures 15–5a through 15–5e show the dependency diagrams for the prototype KBS. The diagrams present a summary outline of all the questions, rules, and knowledge segments and their interrelationships, values, and recommendations in the system.

### Decision Charts

Figure 15–6 shows a sample of a decision chart for the system.

### Designing and Constructing the Knowledge Base

Rules, questions, and examples to be shown to the user were developed based on the situation study. They were largely based on the developers' experiences in helping different kinds of people make selection decisions and define and structure the area that they selected.

A segment of the prototype system's knowledge base is shown in Figure 15–7. The expert system shell used is M.1. It was chosen because it allows rule writing in plain English, has the capability of handling a system of this size, and has a reasonably efficient and user-friendly interface. The IF-THEN rules were written to reflect the relationships shown in the dependency diagram and match those specified in the decision charts.

The prototype KBS described in this chapter is given on the disks accompanying this book.

## FURTHER SCREENINGS

Subsequent to the initial project evaluation described in this chapter, more business-oriented preliminary screenings are performed. The KBS that assists KBS developers in doing these subsequent screenings are described in Chapter 12 and Mockler (1990).

**Figure 15–5.** Project Proposal Evaluator System—Dependency Diagram (Initial Prototype)

*(A) Overview*

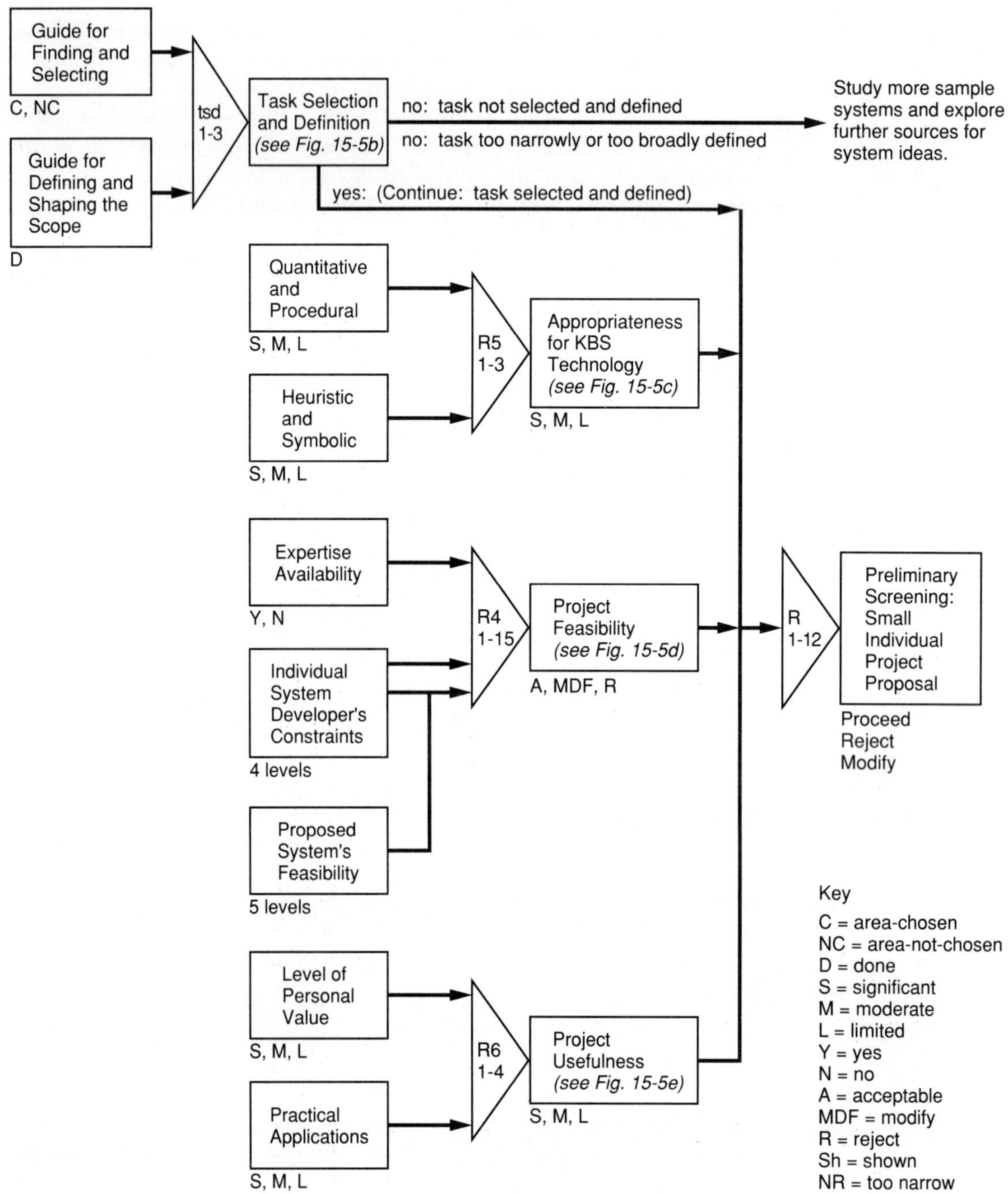

(*B*) *Task Selection and Definition*

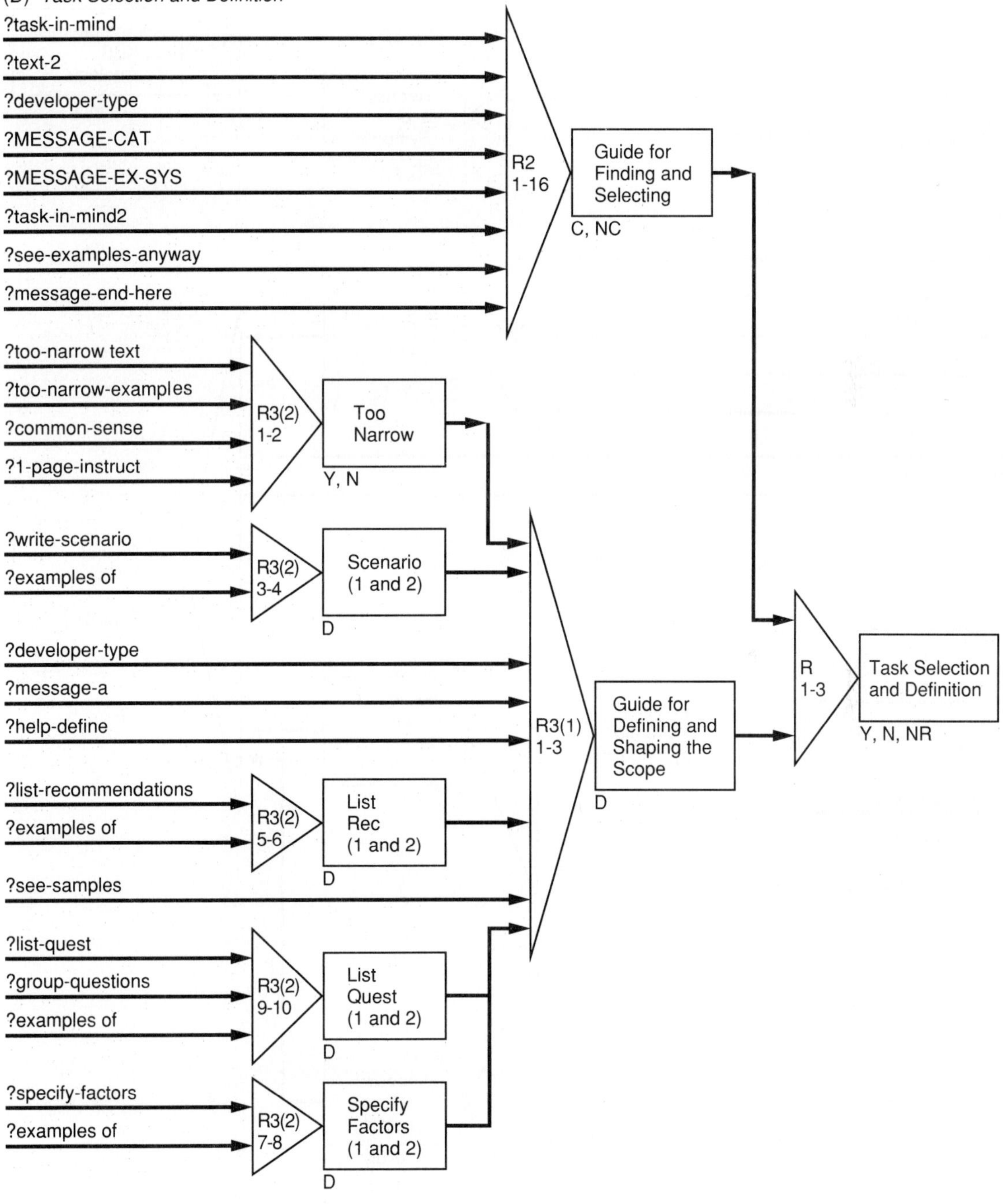


*continued*

**Figure 15–5** *continued*

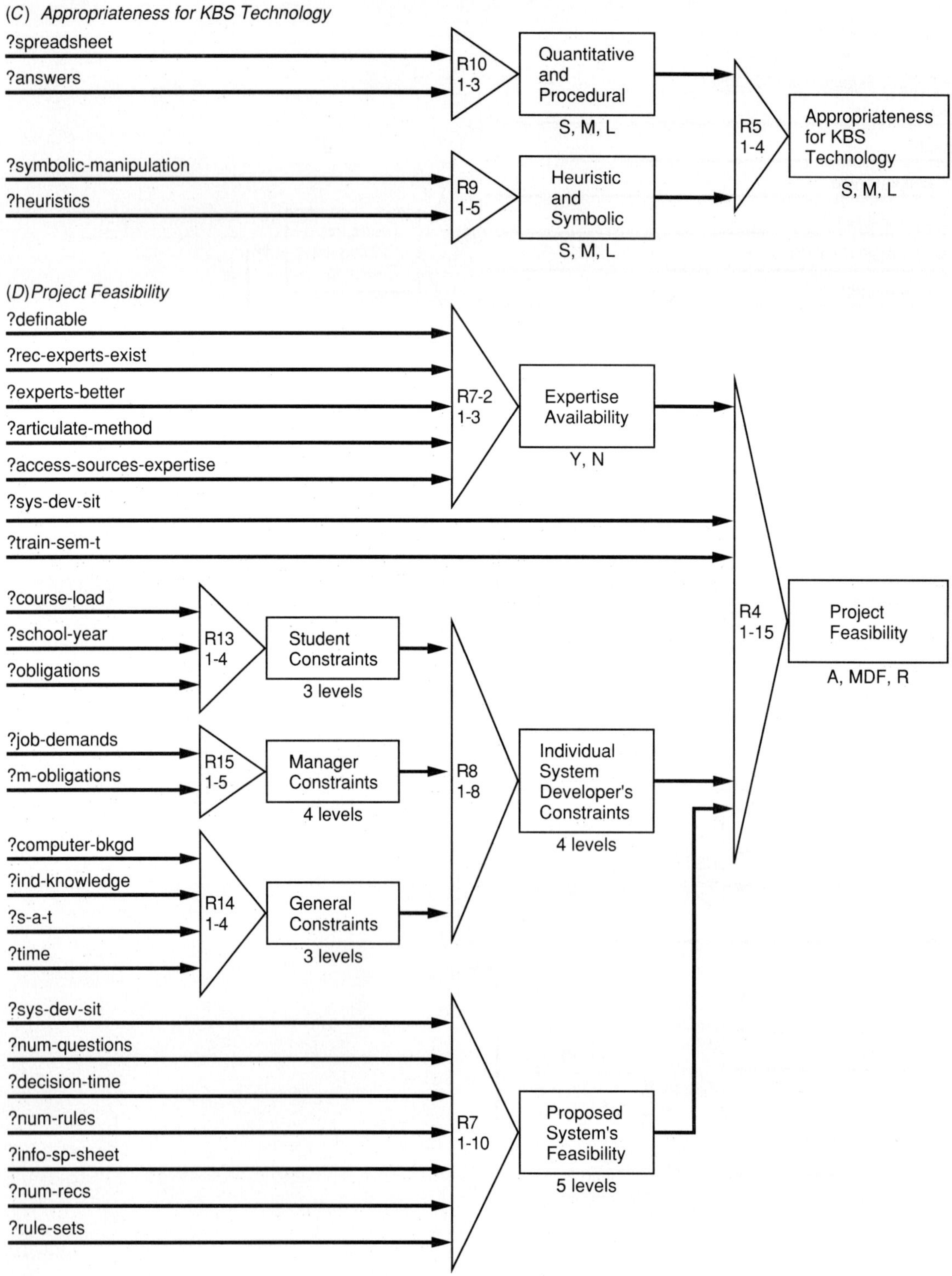

(*E*) *Project Usefulness*

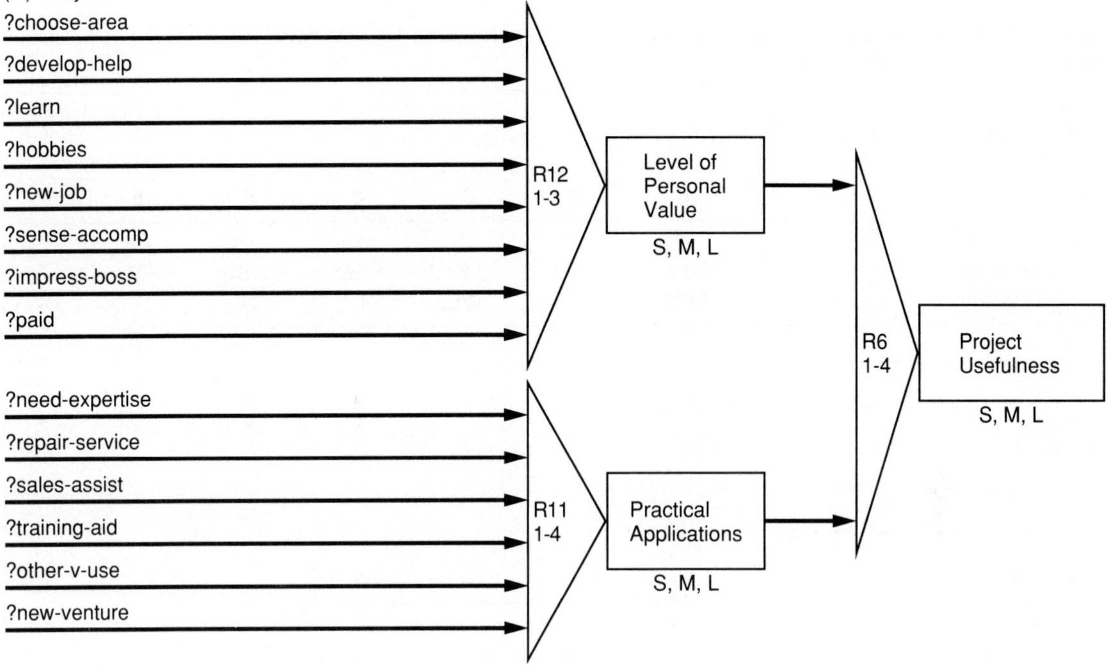

**Figure 15–6.** Project Proposal Evaluator System—Decision Chart: Student Constraints (Initial Prototype)

*(A) Initial Version*

| **Rule # 13-** | **1** | **2** | **3** | **4** | **5** | **6** | **7** |
|---|---|---|---|---|---|---|---|
| if course-load | >5 | 5 | <5 | >5 | >5 | <5 | * |
| if school-year | F/Sp | J/Sp | J/Sr | F/Sp | J/Sr | F/Sp | * |
| if obligations | M/S | M/L | M/L | L | S | * | * |
| then st-constraints = | | | | | | | |
| level-1 | X | | | | | | |
| level-2 | | X | | X | X | X | X |
| level-3 | | | X | | | | |

*(B) Final Condensed Version*

| **Rule # 13-** | **1** | **2** | **3** | **4** |
|---|---|---|---|---|
| if course-load | >5 | 5 | <5 | * |
| if school-year | F/Sp | J/Sp | J/Sr | * |
| if obligations | M/S | M/L | M/L | * |
| then st-constraints = | | | | |
| level-1 | X | | | |
| level-2 | | X | | X |
| level-3 | | | X | |

S = significant M = moderate L = limited
F = freshman Sp = sophomore J = junior Sr = senior
/ = or * = any answer

**Figure 15–7.** Project Proposal Evaluator System—Knowledge Base Sample: Rules and Questions from Student Constraints Segment (Initial Prototype)

```
/*  Student Developer Constraints   */

rule-13-1:
if course-load = A and
   A > 5 and
   school-year = freshman or
   school-year = sophomore and
   obligations = moderate or
   obligations = significant
then st-constraints = 1.

rule-13-2:
if course-load = A and
   A = 5 and
   school-year = junior or
   school-year = sophomore and
   obligations = moderate or
   obligations = limited
then st-constraints = 2.

rule-13-3:
if course-load = A and
   A < 5 and
   school-year = junior or
   school-year = senior and
   obligations = moderate or
   obligations = limited
then st-constraints = 3.

rule-13-4:
if course-load = A and
   school-year = B and
   obligations = C
then st-constraints = 2.

/* Student Questions   */

question(course-load) = [nl,nl,nl,nl,nl,nl,nl,nl,nl,nl,nl,nl,'
    How many courses are you taking this semester?

    Type in a number such as "5" and press "ENTER".

',nl,nl,nl,nl,nl,nl,nl]. legalvals(course-load)= number

question(school-year) = [nl,nl,nl,nl,nl,nl,nl,nl,nl,nl,nl,nl,'
    What year of school are you in?

',nl,nl,nl,nl,nl,nl,nl,nl,nl]. legalvals(school-year)=
[freshman, sophomore, junior, senior].

question(obligations) = [nl,nl,nl,nl,nl,nl,nl,nl,nl,nl,nl,nl,'
    How would you describe demands placed on your time by
    obligations such as work, your family and friends, or other
    circumstances?

',nl,nl,nl,nl,nl,nl,nl,nl,nl].

legalvals(obligations)= [significant, moderate, limited].
```

## EXERCISE

The disks accompanying this book contain the prototype KBS described at the end of this chapter. Following the directions accompanying the disks for using the M.1 expert system shell, run a consultation using the system, which has the file name SCREEN.PRE. If you wish, you might also print out the knowledge base and study it while you are running the system and restudying this chapter.

## REFERENCES

Agnew, Joe. "Artificial Intelligence With a Marketing Use." *Marketing News*, September 25, 1988, pp. 3,6.

Bramer, Max. "Expert Systems in Business: A British Perspective." *Expert Systems*, May 1988, pp. 104–17.

"Expert Systems—Applications in Finance." *Financial Management,* Journal of the Financial Management Association, Autumn 1988, pp. 12–86.

Humpert, Benedikt, and Patrick Holley. "Expert Systems in Financial Planning." *Expert Systems,* May 1988, pp. 78–100.

"Inanimate Analysts: Expert Systems for Marketing." *Marketing*, September 3, 1987, p. 21.

Lasher, Elaine. "An Expert System for Logistics Management." *AI Expert*, September 1988, pp. 46–53.

Mockler, Robert J. *Knowledge-Based Systems for Management Decisions*. Englewood-Cliffs, NJ: Prentice-Hall, 1989.

Mockler, Robert J. "Using Knowledge-Based Systems for Estimating Risks Inherent in a Proposed KBS Project." *Expert Systems*, February 1990, pp. 27–41.

Rauch-Hindin, Wendy B. *Artificial Intelligence in Business, Science and Industry (Volumes I & II)*. Englewood Cliffs, NJ: Prentice-Hall, 1985.

"Robots Are Coming: Use of AI and Expert Systems in Marketing." *Marketing*, February 25, 1988, p. 3.

# 16

# Career Planning Decision: Entrepreneurial New Ventures

This chapter describes the development of a knowledge-based system to assist in career planning decisions concerning becoming an entrepreneur and taking on new ventures. The discussion is divided into three sections:

- Studying the situation to be prototyped
- Documenting the system
- System refinements

## STUDYING THE SITUATION TO BE PROTOTYPED

Fundamental to any decision involved in new venture planning is the decision an individual makes as to whether or not he or she wants to be an entrepreneur, and if so, the kind of new venture preferred. This section discusses how one might go about making such decisions, focusing specifically on two areas:

- how likely an individual is to be a successful entrepreneur
- steps that can be taken to improve one's chances of success as an entrepreneur

The discussion, which follows the outline shown in Figure 16–1, is in two parts:

**Figure 16–1.** Decision Situation Under Study: Career Choice: Entrepreneurial New Ventures—Rough Overview Sketch

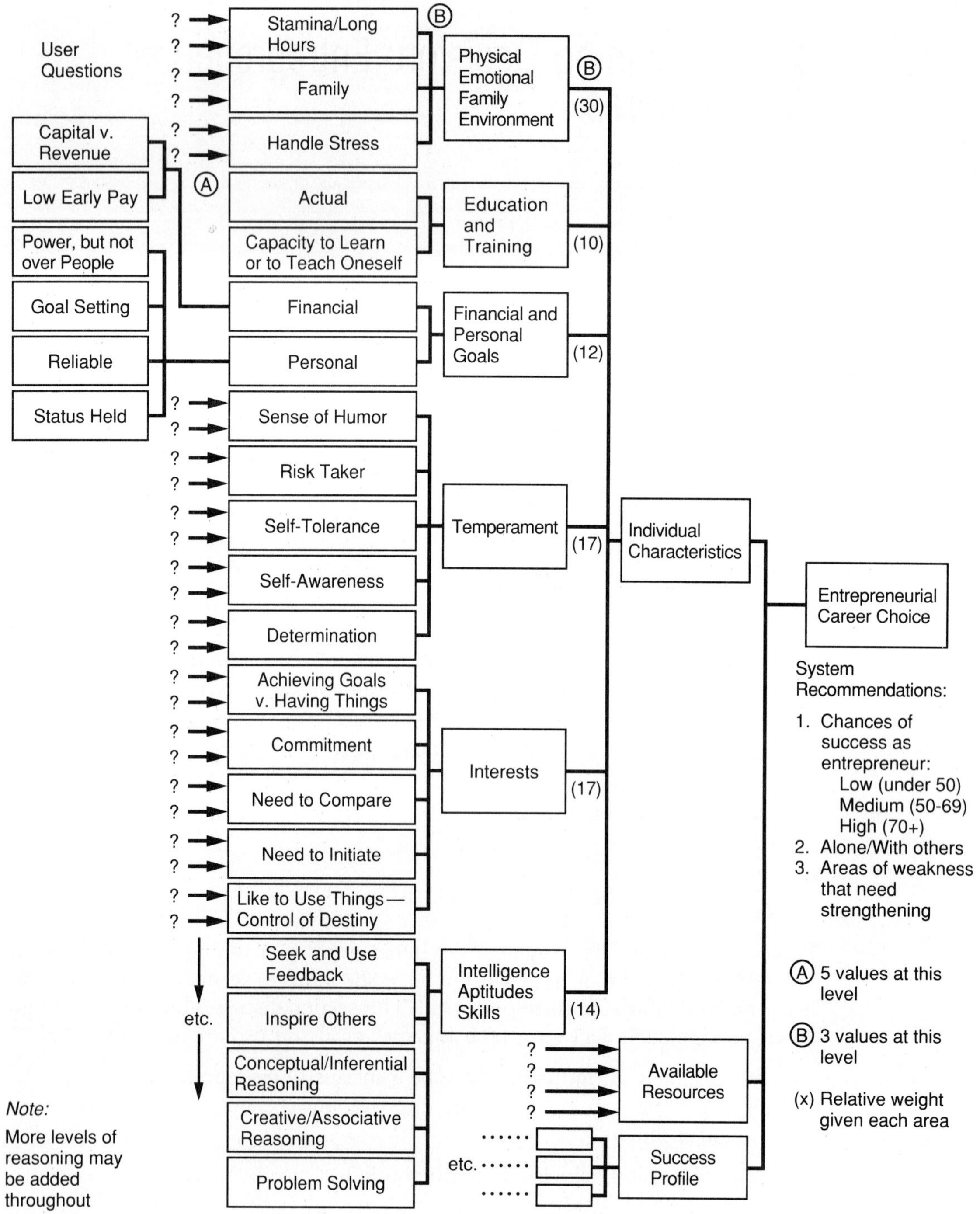

- critical factors affecting the decision
- making decisions

### Critical Factors Affecting the Decision

***Determining Individual Characteristics.*** As seen in Figure 16–1, questions about an individual's personality are explored in a variety of areas, including:

- physical and emotional characteristics, and family environment
- education and training
- financial and personal goals
- temperament
- interests
- intelligence, aptitudes, and skills

Some of the questions will be easy to answer, such as questions about one's education and training. Unfortunately, not all of the questions are easy to answer. Consider the following:

- Just what kinds of conceptual skills do you have?
- How good a problem solver are you?
- What kinds of problems do you like to solve, or do you solve well?
- How effective are you under pressure?

Such questions do not always have precise answers.

For someone with considerable work experience, the answers to these questions can be based on actual experiences and what was learned from them. Answering these questions is more difficult, though, for younger people who have not had much work experience. One way to help such individuals find these answers is through a *related incident* approach. This involves making and then analyzing a list of

- things you have done well
- things you enjoy doing
- things you get great satisfaction from doing, if different from the above

Using this approach involves searching your memory for actual events, and writing down their outcomes. You then assess what in particular about each event made you like it or what caused it to turn out the way it did.

The first advantage of this approach is that it starts an individual thinking about concrete events, rather than abstractions. You focus on things you did. Second, it forces an individual to think in terms of outcomes—did an event turn out well or poorly? Third, it requires evaluation or assessment, since you have to determine what led to good or bad outcomes, and what led to your likes, dislikes, or satisfaction.

It is also helpful to know what tasks we performed poorly or didn't like to do, though this only helps eliminate occupations. In the long run, it is more important to focus on events with successful outcomes.

Very quickly one can begin to isolate specific characteristics. You may handle people very well, but only in certain situations. Define these situations precisely. For example, you may find that you can deal effectively with customers or people on a daily basis, as do salespeople. Or you realize that you can deal effectively with people at meetings and occasionally in a work environment, but prefer for the most part to work alone, as a market researcher might have to do.

In the area of intelligence, aptitudes, and skills, everybody is smart or good at something. Logic problems may intrigue you. Computations with precise figures, however, may bore you. Manipulating shapes and forms, as required in architecture, may have kept you up long into the night in the past. You may like to design information systems, but hate to program them, or vice-versa. Anything to do with abstractions or concepts may make you uncomfortable, or you may prefer dealing with such theoretical concerns.

With a little effort and discipline, it is possible to identify *patterns* about yourself, "profiles" of the kinds of things you like to do and do well. Such an incident approach is needed because it doesn't work to simply ask a person such general questions as "Are you good with people?" or "Are you a good problem solver?" People's answers would be clouded with ego perceptions. The information has to be gotten indirectly in most instances, through studying reactions to incidents. It is a rare individual who has the capacity to identify his or her own character traits objectively, in terms which make it easy to match them with job and career requirements.

This segment of the analysis also leads to an initial definition of some of the personal *preferences* an individual has for the kind of new venture to be considered. These preferences are revised as an individual gains more experience with new ventures and so gains a better understanding of what is involved in being an entrepreneur.

***Available Resources.*** In decision situations involving a career strategy, financial resources often play a secondary role for younger people, since the choice is made essentially based on personal factors. In some situations, however, where an individual has major family obligations, including high mortgage payments, the lack of personal financial resources or borrowing capacity can severely limit career choices, especially those involved in becoming an entrepreneur.

***Analyzing the New Venture Situation Requirements: An Entrepreneur Success Profile.*** In situations involving a decision about whether or not to become an entrepreneur, a number of analyses have been done as to what it takes to be an effective entrepreneur *in general* (for example, Timmons 1985; Kuratko 1989). These success profiles have been generated by analyzing the kinds of situations an entrepreneur has to deal with. For example, individual entrepreneurs on their own do not have the organizational support that those working for existing companies have. When you are on your own, you have to establish working relationships with auditors, banks, suppliers, lawyers, distributors—everyone affecting your business. An existing company provides these. Operating without these existing company support services requires a lot of determination, perseverance, drive, and initiative. It requires those qualities normally associated with the term "self-starter."

Since there are no bosses to please or displease when on your own, the measure of success shifts from a promotion or a raise to things like increased sales, more satisfied customers, meeting payrolls, and the like. An entrepreneur would, therefore, seem to have to be more goal- or opportunity-oriented.

On your own, there is also no organization to hide behind when things don't work out. On the other hand, when things do work out, it is pretty clear who should get the credit—you. An entrepreneur would seem to have to like being the one responsible for performance and outcomes of performance, whether successes or failures.

Things can get pretty hectic at times when you are on your own. There is never enough time to do things right; there is always too much to do. These circumstances require a person who likes to solve problems quickly, not at a leisurely pace. Also, that person would have to be someone who can tolerate ambiguity, stress, uncertainty, and in many instances the lack of perfection.

When on your own, there is great reliance on performance—meeting deadlines, keeping promises and commitments, avoiding shoddy services and products—in order to establish strong links with customers. Because of this, entrepreneurs tend to believe they are responsible for outcomes, and not the victim of circumstances gone wrong, or bad luck.

Since you are not just a worker doing a job in an organization, there is no boss to ask "How can I do better?" So an entrepreneur seeks out other means of feedback—actual performance, other people, advisors. Failure is another source of learning feedback. Interestingly, entrepreneurs seem to look upon failure as the price of risk taking, a step along the way, something that can be learned from. They expect some failures and so are not discouraged by them. Being keenly aware of the consequences of success and failure, entrepreneurs are good risk takers. They are not gamblers. They seem to know not only how to measure the odds, but more important how to create more favorable odds. They take steps to reduce risks, rather than avoid risks entirely.

Since working on your own requires balancing many forces, entrepreneurs are usually good negotiators and have a sense of humor. They are also realistic about their own limitations and the limitations of others. They may be persistent, but they seem to know when to move away from unresolvable problems.

The ability to resolve contradictions is another characteristic of successful entrepreneurs. They are able to resolve paradoxes, find new solutions, balance many conflicting factors in a situation, and negotiate for pragmatic solutions. They are above all realists. Their creative solutions are done within the limits of available resources.

Where the situation involves new ventures with partners, an entrepreneur needs to be able to share—not only risks, but also responsibilities, credit, decision making, and rewards.

While entrepreneurs appear driven by a desire for control over their own destinies, they do not seem driven by a need for control and power over others. They do not primarily seek status symbols as the ends of their efforts, but just as by-products of their entrepreneurial activity. They are interested in a greater degree of control over their own future than can be provided by a company owned by someone else.

Unfortunately, one of the major negative byproducts of entrepreneurial pressures is a too-consuming dedication to the venture. This can often damage or even destroy personal relationships. For someone looking ahead to being an entrepreneur, this factor can set limits on how the venture will be formed and structured.

From this analysis of the types of situations within which entrepreneurs operate, it is possible to develop a *structure* or *success profile* of individual requirements for being a successful entrepreneur. These individual requirements can be summarized as follows:

- determination, commitment, perseverance, and initiative
- great desire to grow and achieve something, but little desire for status
- goal or opportunity orientation
- responsibility for performance and outcome of performance
- ability to solve problems quickly
- reliability of performance
- belief that outcomes are not based on luck or circumstances, but on one's own performance
- seeking out and using feedback
- good negotiating skills, a sense of humor, and a realistic assessment of one's weaknesses
- good risk-taking skills and temperament
- ability to reconcile conflicts and differences
- capacity to share and work with a team
- little interest in status or power over others
- ability to balance family commitments and commitments to work
- tolerance for stress and ambiguity
- belief that failure is a learning experience

In addition to these learnable attributes, there are several not-so-learnable ones which seem to characterize entrepreneurs. These include:

- intelligence, at least of a pragmatic kind
- excellent conceptual and inferential reasoning skills
- good associative reasoning skills and related creative skills

In addition, two other characteristics seem to be needed:

- good health and high energy level
- capacity to get others to work for you

The reader should keep in mind that this is not a prescription for what it takes to be a good entrepreneur. It is just a review of some of the characteristics found in many successful entrepreneurs by people who have studied the area. The ultimate test of an entrepreneur is whether their make-up is suited to the specific new venture situation they have decided to undertake. As with other areas discussed in this book, the final decision is ultimately a situational one.

**Making Decisions**

Once an individual's characteristics are identified, the new venture decision involves *pattern matching*. This involves comparing one's individual characteristics, personality, preferences, and resources with the requirements for being a successful entrepreneur. The correlations will rarely be 100 percent, but more often an estimate of chances of success. Hopefully, the answer will also contain some specifics about weaknesses that will need to be addressed.

Much more is involved in actually starting and running a new venture. What has been isolated here, through a selective situation analysis, is a number of aspects which are relevant to assessing an individual's qualifications for undertaking a new venture (a kind of preliminary screening), as well as some of the steps that can be taken to improve the chances of success.

This decision, which was chosen for prototype knowledge-based system development, was initially broken down into three parts:

- Deciding about going into business for oneself. The answer here would be in terms of the chances of success as an entrepreneur, rated as high, medium, or low.
- Recommending steps to improve chances of success. At this point such steps involve modifications in behavior, expectations, or any other aspect of the six areas studied involving the individual.
- Deciding on the scope and objective of the venture, that is, modifying the shape of the new venture to better match the character and personality of the individual. Relevant here are such questions as whether the individual should work alone or involve others in the venture.

This kind of decision range seems consistent with the general behavioral research done on matching an individual to a situation to obtain effective outcomes (a review of this research is given by Chatman 1989). Behavioral studies appear to suggest that the approach to matching an individual to a situation is three-pronged:

- Use individual traits to select the kinds of situations whose requirements come closest to matching an individual's traits.
- Where possible, look for ways to modify individual behavior to better meet situation requirements.
- Where possible, make changes in the situation to better suit an individual's traits, for example through modifying contracts during

negotiations, through the selection of the people to work with, and the like.

## DOCUMENTING THE SYSTEM

The discussion in this section covers:

- system overview and objective
- system documentation

### System Overview and Objective

The general objective of the project is to develop a knowledge-based system that gives an individual advice about deciding on a career. The prototype system is designed to help users determine how suited they are to a career as an entrepreneur, and what they might do to increase their chances of succeeding as entrepreneurs. Since the system will not only assess the likelihood of success, but also advise on steps to take to improve the chances of success, it should be of benefit to anyone considering such a career choice.

The prototype system developed during the first phase of the project is limited to a narrow range of options, in order to test the feasibility of developing a larger knowledge-based system for career strategy selection. The system uses IF-THEN rules and backward chaining to reason about the information given by a user, in order to reach its recommendations.

### System Documentation

***Dependency Diagrams.*** Figure 16–2 gives an abbreviated dependency diagram for the entire prototype system. Figure 16–3 gives one of the detailed dependency diagrams of one segment of the system. The figures provide complete summary outlines of all the questions, rules, knowledge segments and their interrelationships, values, and recommendations within the system.

***Recommendations To Be Made by the System.*** The initial prototype system is limited to making three kinds of recommendations:

- how suitable an entrepreneurial career is for the user
- areas of weaknesses that need strengthening
- if a new venture is undertaken, whether the user might be better off going it alone or with others

***Nature of the User Interface.*** The typical user dialogue covers six key knowledge areas:

- *Interests.* In exploring a user's capabilities in this area, sample questions which might be asked include: "When you are playing a game, such as

**Figure 16–2.** Career Strategy Decision System: Entrepreneurial New Venture—Overall Dependency Diagram (Initial Prototype System)

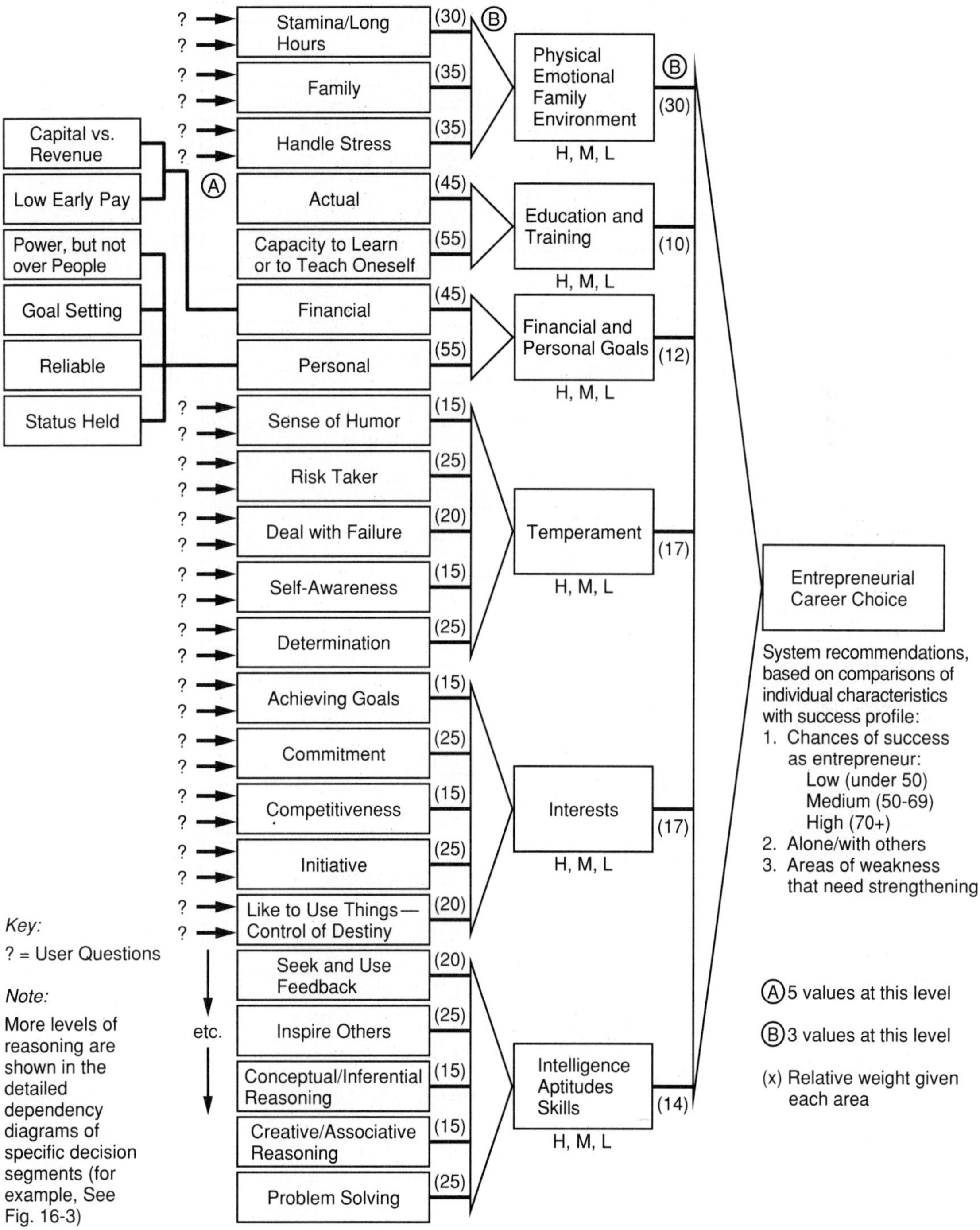

**Figure 16–3.** Career Strategy Decision System: Entrepreneurial New Venture—Interests Segment (Initial Prototype System)

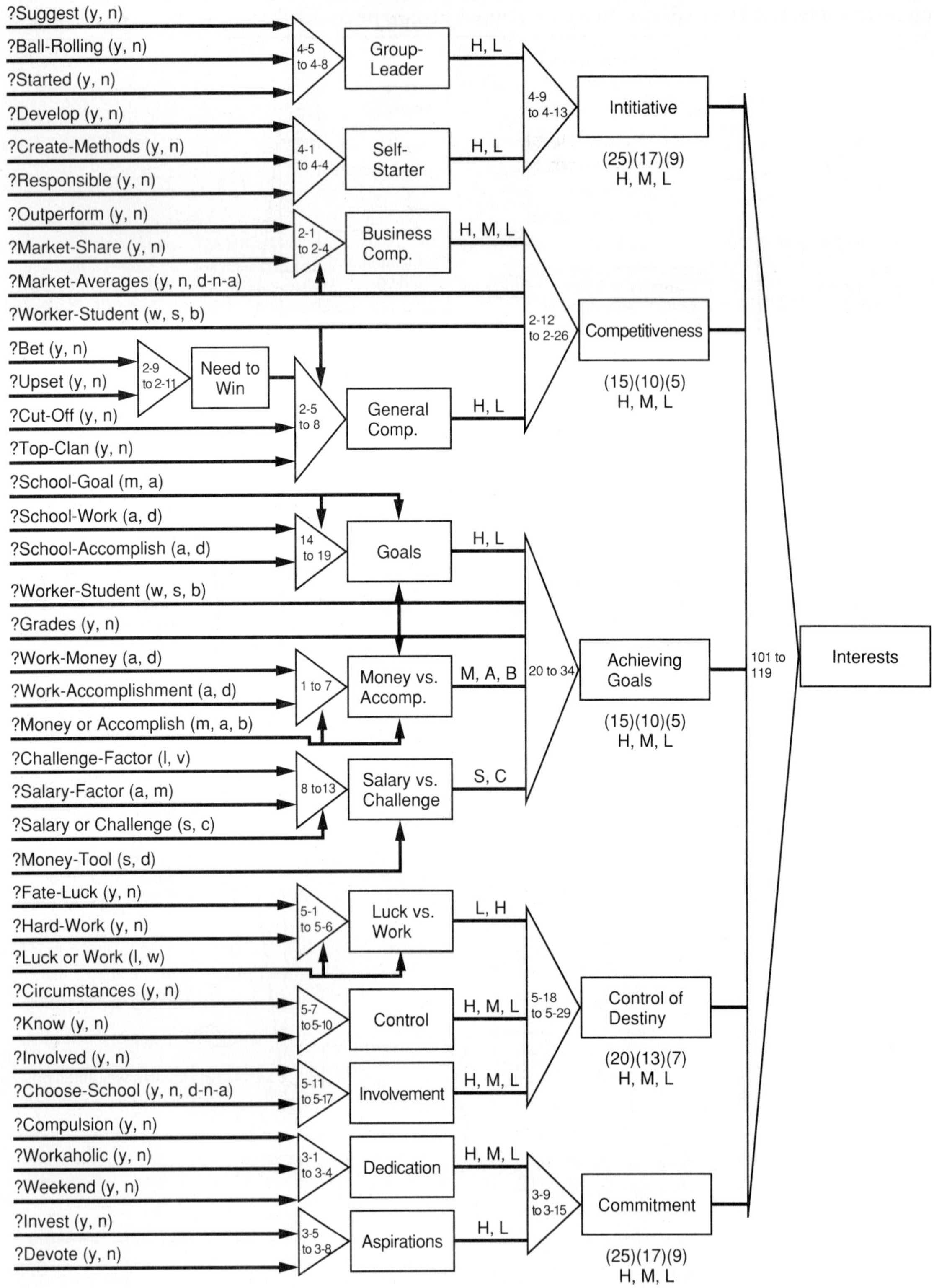

football, tennis, or monopoly, do you get upset if the game is well-played on all sides, but you or your team loses?" And, if the answer to that question is negative, "Would you be upset if you had placed a bet on the game?"

- *Temperament.* In exploring a user's capabilities in this area, sample questions which might be asked include: "Do you generally avoid taking on a job you are pretty sure you cannot handle?" or "Late at night when there is no traffic, does it bother you if the driver of the car you are in goes through a red light?"
- *Intelligence, aptitudes, and skills.* In exploring a user's capabilities in this area, sample questions which might be asked include: "How frequently do you approach co-workers or fellow students to get their opinions of your ideas or work performance?" or "When you work with others, how often does the interaction of your group lead to creative solutions to problems, that no individual alone would have developed?"
- *Financial and personal goals.* In exploring a user's capabilities in this area, sample questions which might be asked include: "Is it more fun to make money than to spend it?" or "Would you be willing or able to have an irregular paycheck, or no paycheck at all, until your new venture gets off the ground?" or "When you tell a friend or business associate you will do something by a certain time, do you do it as promised?"
- *Education and training.* In exploring a user's capabilities in this area, sample questions which might be asked include: "Do you possess any valuable special training such as CPA certification, technical training, or unique job experience?" or "How often do you teach yourself how to do something new by doing it, making mistakes, yet sticking to it until you get it right?"
- *Physical, emotional, and family environment.* In exploring a user's capabilities in this area, sample questions which might be asked include: "Would you be willing to work long hours and on weekends on a regular basis for several years to make a go of your own new venture?" or "Do you have family responsibilities that require you to have a steady work income?"

While some general questions are asked, a great number of the questions involve an individual's reaction to specific incidents, or so-called "test cases."

***Description of the Knowledge Structure and Reasoning Process.*** The recommendations made by the prototype system are based on six critical factors: intelligence, aptitudes, and skills; interests; temperament; financial and personal goals; education and training; and the physical, emotional, and family environment.

In turn, the values for each of these factors is based on a number of other factors:

- *Interests* are determined by the degree of competitiveness, commitment, need to initiate and control one's destiny, and kind of goal orientation.

- *Temperament* is determined by self-awareness, how one handles failure, ability to take risks, sense of humor, and strength of determination.
- *Intelligence, aptitudes, and skills* are determined by such factors as creative, conceptual, and problem-solving abilities, and inferential and associative reasoning skills, as well as the capability to use feedback and inspire others.
- *Financial and personal goals* are determined by such factors as available financial resources, family obligations, and personal values.
- *Education and training* are determined by the user's actual formal training and education, and by his or her capacity to learn.
- *Physical, emotional, and family environment* are determined by health, family situation, and ability to handle stress.

Samples of additional influencing factors are given in the dependency diagrams cited below.

IF-THEN rules are used to determine the values at each stage. The inference engine uses backward chaining. The values are measured for each of the factors in the reasoning chain as: high, medium, low; disagree, agree; salary-size, challenge-goal; sometimes, usually, always; money, accomplishment; yes, no, agree, disagree; certainty factors; and a variety of similar values.

***Decision Charts.*** Figure 16–4 shows a sample decision chart from the prototype knowledge-based system. There is a decision chart for every rule-set triangle in the dependency diagram.

### Designing and Constructing the Knowledge Base

Rules and questions were developed from the situation study. They were based on the system developer's analysis of how expert career planners actually go about giving advice in such decisions.

A segment of the prototype system's knowledge base is given in Figure 16–5. The expert system shell used is M.1.

Two very simple introductory and concluding panels (screens) were created for the prototype system to help the user understand and use the system during a consultation.

The IF-THEN rules in the knowledge base in Figure 16–5 match those specified in the decision charts shown in Figure 16–4. They were written to reflect the relationships shown in the dependency diagram in Figure 16–3; they use the values shown there and in the decision charts. The questions in the knowledge base (Figure 16–5) are those indicated in the dependency diagram.

## SYSTEM REFINEMENTS

The prototype system included several refinements found throughout other systems described in this book.

**Figure 16–4.** Career Strategy Decision System: Entrepreneurial New Venture—Decision Charts (Initial Prototype System)

| | | Rules 1 | 2 | 3 | 4 | 5 | 6 | 7 |
|---|---|---|---|---|---|---|---|---|
| **MONEY-V-ACCOMPLISHMENT** | | | | | | | | |
| If: | Work-money | Agree | Disagree | Agree | Disagree | | | |
| | Work-accomplishment | Agree | Disagree | Disagree | Agree | | | |
| | Contradiction | | | | | True | True | True |
| | Money-or-Accomplishment | | | | | Money | Accomp-lishment | Both-same |
| Then: | Contradiction | True | True | | | | | |
| | Accomplishment | | | | X | | X | |
| | Money | | | X | | X | | |
| | Both-about-same | | | | | | | X |

| | | Rules 14 | 15 | 16 | 17 | 18 | 19 |
|---|---|---|---|---|---|---|---|
| **GOALS** | | | | | | | |
| If: | Schoolwork | Agree | Disagree | Agree | Disagree | Agree | Disagree |
| | School-accomplishment | Agree | Disagree | Disagree | Agree | Agree | Disagree |
| | School-goal | Money | Accomp. | | | Accomp. | Money |
| Then: | Goals = High | | X | | X | X | |
| | Goals = Low | X | | X | | | X |

1. *Testing for accuracy of input information.* Multiple questions are often asked, for example, about a character trait such as self-awareness, to verify the accuracy of a user's general initial self-assessments. The verification usually is in the form of asking for reactions to specific test situations.
2. *Resolving contradictions.* Where contradictions are found, in stating personal goals, for example, additional questions are generated by the system to resolve the conflict.
3. *Alternate reasoning paths.* In many other instances, alternate lines of reasoning (and series of questions) will be followed depending on information provided by a user or conclusions drawn at different points

**Figure 16–5.** Career Strategy Decision System: Entrepreneurial New Venture—Segment of Knowledge Base (Initial Prototype System)

```
/*------------------INTERESTS--------------------*/

/*----------------Achieving Goals----------------*/
automaticmenu(ALL).
enumeratedanswers(ALL).

question(worker-student) = 'Do you consider yourself a member of
the work force, a student, or both?'.

legalvals(worker-student) = [work-force,student,both].

question(work-money) = 'You work hard primarily for money and
what it brings.'.

legalvals(work-money) = [disagree,agree].

question(work-accomplishment) = 'You work hard primarily for the
sense of accomplishment it brings.'.

legalvals(work-accomplishment) = [disagree,agree].

question(money-tool) = 'Money is a tool to measure your success
(keep score) and judge your performance compared to others.' .

legalvals(money-tool) = [disagree,agree].

question(salary-factor) = 'When you accepted your most recent job
offers, of all the factors you considered in your decision to
take the job, how important a factor was the size of the salary?'

legalvals(salary-factor) = [of-average-importance,
the-most-important-factor].

question(challenge-factor) = 'When you accepted your most recent
job offers, in your decision to take the job, how important a
factor was the challenge of achieving new goals?' .

legalvals(challenge-factor) = [little-importance,very-important].

question(money-or-accomplishment) = 'Do you work hard mainly for
the money, or do you work hard mainly for the sense of
accomplishment and the goals you achieve?' .

legalvals(money-or-accomplishment) = [money,both-about-same,accomplishment].

question(salary-or-challenge) = 'When you accepted your most
recent job offers, what factor, the size of the salary or the
challenge of achieving new goals, was most important in your
decision to take the job?' .

legalvals(salary-or-challenge) = [salary-size,challenge-goals].

question(schoolwork) = 'You work hard at your schoolwork
primarily to get good grades so you can make money when you
graduate' .
```

```
legalvals(schoolwork) = [disagree,agree].

question(school-accomplishment) = 'You work hard at your
schoolwork primarily for the sense of accomplishment it brings' .

legalvals(school-accomplishment) = [disagree,agree].

question(grades) = 'Do you often aim to get an "a" in courses you
are taking, and do you meet your goal of getting them?' .

legalvals(grades) = [yes,no].

question(school-goal) = ' Do you work hard at your schoolwork
primarily to get good grades so you can make money when you
graduate or for the sense of accomplishment it brings?' .

legalvals(school-goal) = [money,accomplishment].



/*----------Rules-Money-v-Accomplishment---------*/

rule-1:  if work-money = agree and
            work-accomplishment = agree
         then contradiction = true.

rule-2:  if work-money = disagree and
            work-accomplishment = disagree
         then contradiction = true.

rule-3:  if work-money = agree and
            work-accomplishment = disagree
         then money-v-accomplishment = money.

rule-4:  if work-accomplishment = agree and
            work-money = disagree
         then money-v-accomplishment = accomplishment.

rule-5:  if contradiction = true and
         money-or-accomplishment = money
         then money-v-accomplishment = money cf 80.

rule-6:  if contradiction = true and
            money-or-accomplishment = accomplishment
         then money-v-accomplishment = accomplishment cf 80.

rule-7:  if contradiction = true and
            money-or-accomplishment = both-same
         then money-v-accomplishment = both-about-same.

/*---------Rule-Salary-v-Challenge---------*/

rule-8:  if salary-factor = of-average-importance and
            challenge-factor = little-importance
         then contradiction-b = true.
```

*continued*

**Figure 16.5** *continued*

```
rule-9:  if salary-factor = the-most-important-factor and
            challenge-factor = very-important
         then contradiction-b = true.

rule-10: if contradiction-b = true and
            salary-or-challenge = salary-size
         then salary-v-challenge = salary cf 80.

rule-11: if contradiction-b = true and
            salary-or-challenge = challenge-goals
         then salary-v-challenge = challenge cf 80.

rule-12: if salary-factor = of-average-importance and
            challenge-factor = very important
         then salary-v-challenge = challenge.

rule-13: if challenge-factor = little-importance and
            salary-v-challenge = the-most-important-factor
         then salary-v-challenge = salary.


/*-------------------goals----------------------*/

rule-14: if schoolwork = agree and
            school-accomplishment = agree and
            school-goal = money
         then goals = low.

rule-15: if schoolwork = disagree and
            school-accomplishment = disagree and
            school-goal = accomplishment
         then goals = high.

rule-16: if schoolwork = agree and
            school-accomplishment = disagree
         then goals = low.

rule-17: if schoolwork = disagree and
            school-accomplishment = agree
         then goals = high.

rule-18: if schoolwork = disagree and
            school-accomplishment = agree and
            school-goal = accomplishment
         then goals = high.

rule-19: if schoolwork = disagree and
            school-accomplishment = disagree and
            school-goal = money
         then goals = low.
```

in the inferential reasoning chain. For example, at times different questions are asked of professionals and of students.

4. *Confidence factors.* These are used in later versions of the system to replace value sets such as high-medium-low.
5. *Relative impact of different factors.* Since not all factors affect the assessment as to entrepreneurial potential, different weights are given different character traits.
6. *Reducing the Risks.* Identifying one's weaknesses in relation to the demands of an undertaking serves to reduce risks:

   - It pinpoints strategic choices to avoid. If we lack critical resources required to make a strategy work, we can decide not to pursue it.
   - It pinpoints steps which should be taken to make a strategic plan work. If we lack critical resources required to make a strategy work, we can decide to get those resources, if the strategy is otherwise desirable.

   Either way, the risk of failure is reduced. Identifying weaknesses is an enormous help in building a strategic plan. It indicates where additional resources will be needed to succeed. It enables taking anticipatory action to avoid problems and increase the chances of success. Providing a knowledge-based system with the capability to recommend risk-reducing steps to consider is another step towards introducing ways of taking advantage of the judgmental capabilities of knowledge-based systems.

## EXERCISE

The disks accompanying this book contain the prototype KBS described at the end of this chapter. Following the directions accompanying the disks for using the M.1 expert system shell, run a consultation using the system, which has the file name CAREER.REV. If you wish, you might also print out the knowledge base and study it while you are running the system and restudying this chapter.

## REFERENCES

Chatman, Jennifer. "Improving Interactional Organizational Research: A Model of Person-Organization Fit." *Academy of Management Journal*, July 1989, pp. 333–49.

Kuratko, Donald, and Richard Hodgetts. *Entrepreneurship.* New York: Dryden Press, 1989.

Timmons, Jeffrey A. *New Venture Creation*, 2d ed., Homewood, IL: Irwin, 1985.

# 17

# IRS Income Tax Auditing

This chapter describes the development of a knowledge-based system designed to assist federal IRS income tax auditors in uncovering unreported income and in determining how an audit of an annual tax return should be closed.

The discussion covers

- the situation to be prototyped
- documenting the prototype system

## THE SITUATION TO BE PROTOTYPED

The general area under study is Internal Revenue Service income tax audits. As seen in Figure 17–1, there are many types of audits, ranging from those involving individual taxpayers or individuals operating sole proprietor businesses, to corporations of all sizes, tax shelters, estates, and not-for-profit organizations. These audits may be performed at the IRS office by an office auditor or by a field agent or other specialized IRS agent at the taxpayer's place of business or another location.

Many knowledge-based systems are presently under development in the auditing field. Such systems are being developed to reduce the need for "on-the-job instructors" within the IRS, which hopefully will result in substantial cost

**Figure 17–1.** The Examination Division of the Internal Revenue Service (Categories of Audits)

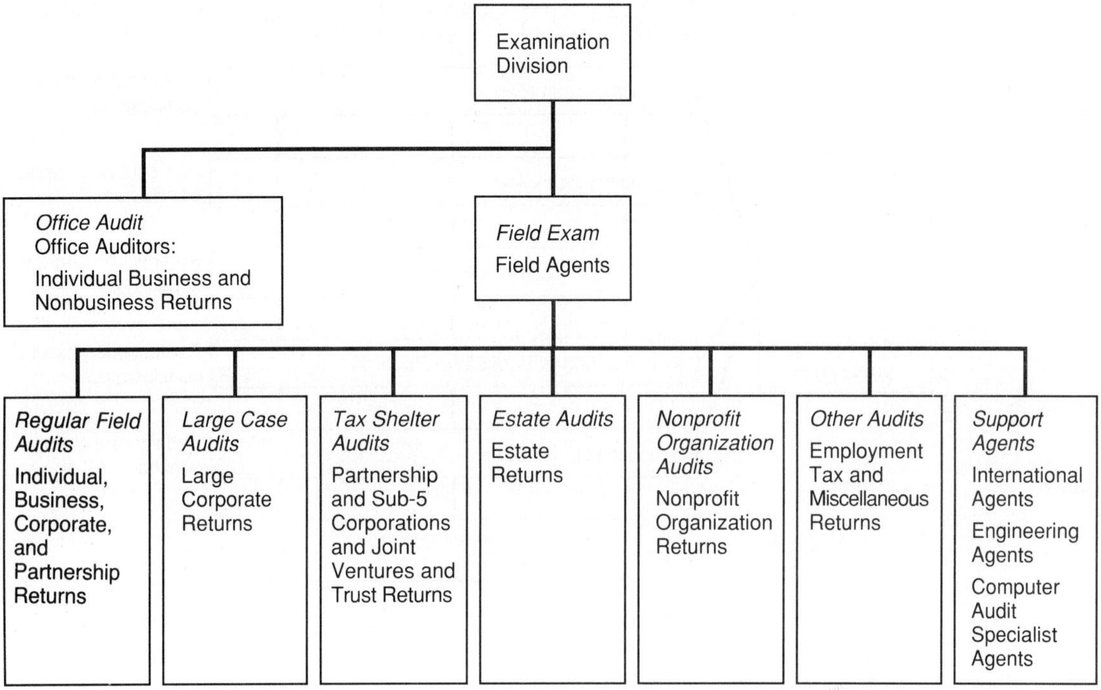


savings and improved tax collections. Because of these potential benefits, this chapter focuses on a KBS designed to guide inexperienced IRS auditors from the start through the completion of an audit.

The focus of the initial prototype was narrowed to finding unreported income during audits of sole proprietorships, which are performed at the taxpayer's place of business by a field agent. Closing the audit is also included in the prototype.

As shown in Figure 17–2, each field audit of a sole proprietorship can be divided into five audit segments:

1. *Pre-Audit Plan*—the agent reviews the tax return and any information forwarded with the return to decide if the return is worthy of audit. If it is, the agent decides which issues to review in depth.
2. *Initial Interview*—the agent interviews the taxpayer or his or her representative for general background information and to possibly resolve any obviously questionable items noted on the return during the pre-audit plan.

**Figure 17–2.** The Auditing Process (a Rough Diagram)

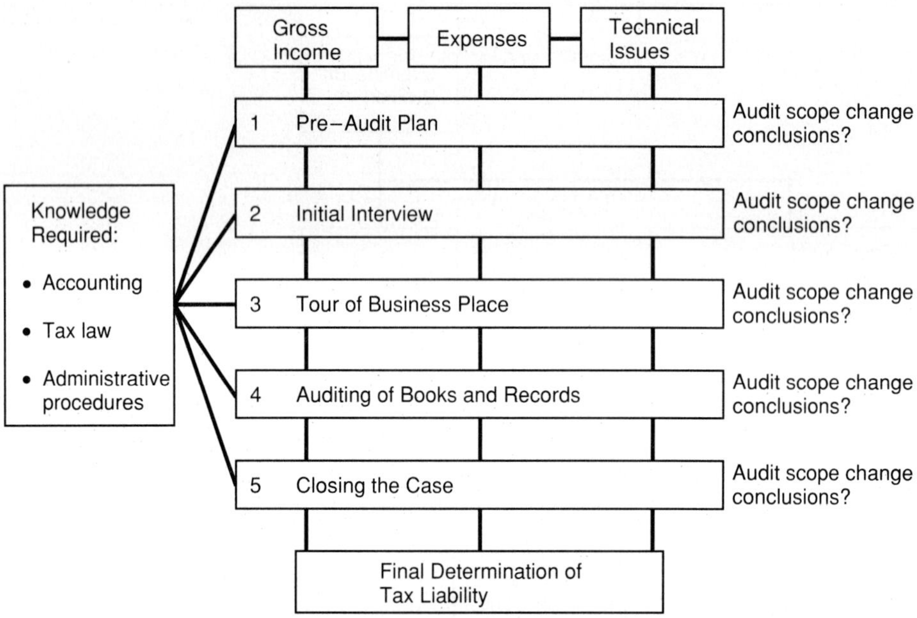


3. *Tour of the Place of Business*—the taxpayer or his or her representative gives the agent a tour of the taxpayer's place of business to acquaint the agent with the taxpayer's operations.
4. *Auditing of Books and Records*—the agent reviews the taxpayer's books and records, any relevant substantiation, related tax returns, bank accounts, and the like. The agent also gives the taxpayer or his or her representative a chance to explain any questionable items. If the agent feels there is significant evidence of unreported income, the agent will expand the audit to include a more thorough probe of unreported income. If, on completion of the probe, the agent feels the taxpayer has committed a fraudulent act, the audit is turned over to the Criminal Investigation Division of the Internal Revenue Service.
5. *Closing the Case*—the agent proposes any necessary tax liability adjustments to the taxpayer or his or her representative during the closing conference. The agent decides on the proper disposal of the audit depending upon the taxpayer concurrence and other relevant information.

For initial prototype purposes, the initial KBS system was further narrowed to cover only Segments 4 and 5, the decisions made when auditing books and records and closing the case. The factors on which those decisions are based are outlined in Figures 17–3 and 17–4.

During audit Segment 4, Auditing of Books and Records, all clues to unreported income noted during the previous audit segments are analyzed in detail. Any information uncovered will be the factors the agent considers in further probing for unreported income. As seen in Figure 17–3, these factors cover:

1. *Prior Audit Segments*. Information from prior audit segments includes all information gathered in any of the previous three audit segments, and can also include information from the closing conference if new relevant information is introduced during that conference.

**Figure 17–3.** Audit Segment 4, "Auditing of Books and Records"—Factors Affecting the Decisions

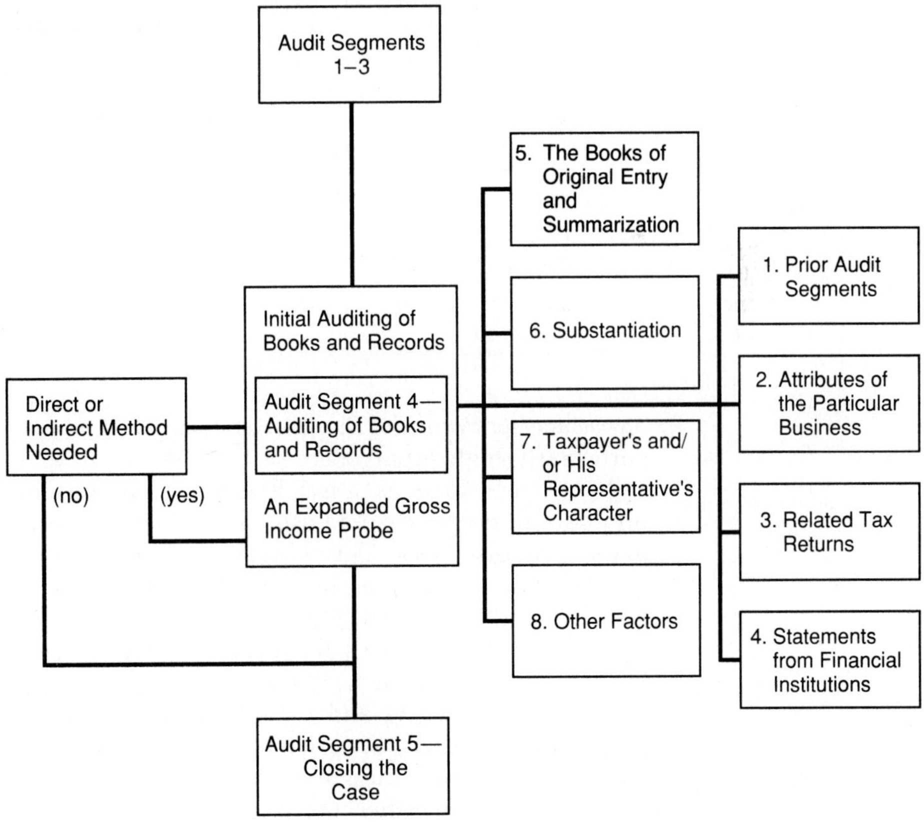

**Figure 17–4.** Audit Segment 5, "Closing the Case"—Factors Affecting the Decision

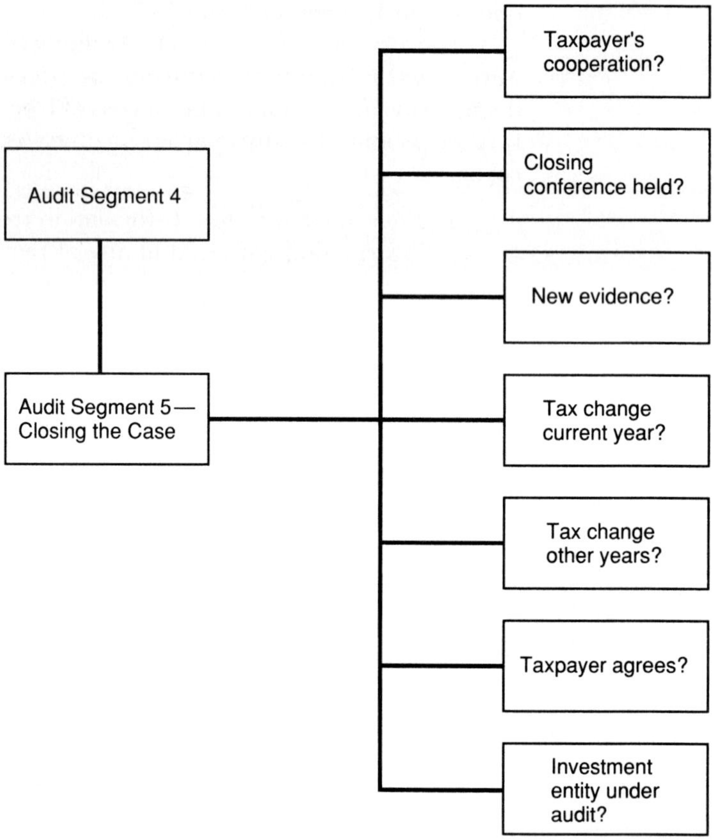


2. *Attributes of the Particular Business.* The nature of some businesses leads to particularly high occurrences of unreported income. For example, a cash business such as a small candy store is more likely to have unreported income than a business in which income is usually received in the form of a check. This is because cash transactions leave a minimal record trail and also because the sole proprietor receiving the cash actually handles the cash. These are very tempting circumstances. Other factors that would increase the likelihood of a particular type of business having unreported income include whether the type of business is favorable to bartering and if the merchandise sold can also be used personally by the sole proprietor.
3. *Related Tax Returns.* Clues and evidence of unreported income can also be obtained from other tax returns of the entity under audit. For example, a review of a prior year's income tax return could reveal a decrease in gross income in the current year, while expenses remained

the same. Such a situation could be due to increased expenses caused by inflation combined with a market for the merchandise sold by the sole proprietor that is not strong enough to absorb a price increase. However, such a situation also can be a sign of unreported income. Other clues of unreported income that can be obtained from reviewing the taxpayer's prior- and subsequent-year income tax returns include rises in net worth, operating expenses, living expenses, and interest expenses that are inconsistent with income. Gross income per the taxpayer's sales tax returns also should be reconciled to the taxpayer's income tax return. Employment tax returns should be reconciled to the taxpayer's books. The agent should also evaluate whether the number of employees reported on employment tax returns is consistent with the volume of work the taxpayer handles.

4. *Statements from Financial Institutions*. A review of statements from financial institutions, which includes a review of all of the taxpayer's bank and brokerage statements, usually gives the agent a fairly accurate picture of the taxpayer's financial health and the amount of care the taxpayer exercises in recording gross receipts. This review also includes a test check of cancelled checks and deposit slips, in which the agent traces the checks or deposit slips to the books in which the transactions involving the checks and deposit slips were originally recorded. Also, while scanning the cancelled checks, the agent determines if an excessive amount of checks were made to cash or to questionable payees. The agent determines if any checks were altered and if an excessive number of checks were cashed in geographical locations not in the vicinity of the taxpayer's or the taxpayer's suppliers' places of business. Such checks could be a sign of diverted income.

   Other factors revealed by statements from financial institutions include whether the taxpayer has a separate business account, deposits all receipts, or has many unexplained deposits. The agent must take into consideration whether the taxpayer was readily willing to allow the agent to review the taxpayer's statements from financial institutions, or whether the taxpayer made any attempts to conceal accounts. The agent must inquire about any accounts the taxpayer maintains outside of the taxpayer's residential and business locality. Such accounts can be clues of the taxpayer operating another business or owning property of which the agent was originally unaware.

5. *The Books of Original Entry and Summarization*. Information from the books of original entry and summarization is evidence obtained from the journals, ledgers, and any workpapers used by the taxpayer during the year as part of the accounting system. The review of the books includes reconciling ledger amounts to the tax return and reconciling journal amounts to their corresponding ledger postings. Substantial discrepancies noted while reconciling could be evidence of unreported income. Other evidence of unreported income could include a use of cash

inconsistent with the nature of the business. Excessive billing discounts or spoilage expense can also be signs of unreported income. Or, a test check of income and expense transactions for which the taxpayer must provide substantiation is also prepared.

6. *Substantiation*. Once substantiation is presented by the taxpayer for the test check of income and expenses, the agent traces each transaction from the original transaction document to the transaction journal entry. While tracing income transactions, the agent is looking for signs of missing transactions, such as invoices missing from a numerically sequenced system. The agent also notes any discrepancies between the original transaction document and the journal entry. While tracing expense items the agent determines if the expense was actually incurred and if it was incurred for a legitimate business purpose. The agent reconciles the invoices and cancelled checks to each other and to the corresponding journal entries, and reviews the cancelled checks and invoices, checking for signs of possible alteration or fictitious payees.
7. *Taxpayer's and His or Her Representative's Character*. Possible signs of unreported income can be inferred from the taxpayers' or their representative's character. Factors considered include whether they usually supply required information, cancel appointments, act in a belligerent manner, or appear overly eager to complete the audit. Other factors to consider include whether the taxpayer is a known racketeer, or if the taxpayer changes return preparers yearly. Also, the agent should determine whether the preparer has ever been barred from practicing before the IRS.
8. *Other Factors*. There are numerous other sources of information from which clues of possible unreported income can be uncovered. For example, an agent may be able to detect unreported income by using third party contacts to determine the taxpayer's unit volume of sales. Usually a number of third parties can be helpful in this regard. Contacting the taxpayer's customers to confirm the amount each customer paid to the taxpayer is the most direct way of determining the taxpayer's unit volume of sales. Also, the agent can attempt to compare the taxpayer's gross or net profit percentage to those of similar businesses. These percentages are sometimes published in governmental and trade magazines. The agent may uncover clues from various other sources which show the taxpayer had an unusual increase in assets or was living beyond his or her financial means.

After completing audit Segment 4, auditing of books and records, the agent proceeds with audit Segment 5, Closing the Case. If audit Segment 4 has been prematurely terminated due to a lack of taxpayer cooperation, an agent closes the case to tax court. If the audit segment has been fully completed, an agent holds a closing conference with the taxpayer and/or the taxpayer's representative. During the closing conference the agent proposes any adjustments to the tax return the agent feels to be warranted. Any new information presented by the taxpayer is considered. The agent then adjusts the audit findings, or refutes the new information. If the new information will take a substantial amount of time to evaluate, the audit reverts back to Segment 4, Auditing of Books and Records.

Once the agent arrives at a final determination of tax liability, the case is closed based on whether the agent is accepting the return as filed, proposing a change which will affect tax liability in the year under audit, or proposing a change which will affect the tax liability of another year, as seen in Figure 17–4. The agent must also consider whether the taxpayer agrees to the audit findings and whether the taxpayer is an investor in any other tax entities under audit. Such entities could include partnerships, subchapter S corporations, or joint ventures.

### Recommendations

One of the most important decisions an agent makes during Segment 4 is determining whether income can be established by a direct approach. A direct approach involves recalculating a taxpayer's income by adding together specific income transactions of the taxpayer. If feasible, this method should be used whenever an agent suspects there is substantial underreported income. However, an indirect method, which relies on circumstantial evidence, must be used when the taxpayer's income cannot be accurately calculated using a direct approach. An indirect method should also be used as a secondary means of determining income when a direct method is used as the primary method. In such instances, as seen in Figure 17–5, an agent would choose from the following five basic indirect methods.

1. *Bank Deposit Method*. The bank deposit method is based on the theory that income can either be deposited or spent as cash. This method is

**Figure 17–5.** The Five Basic Indirect Methods of Determining Income

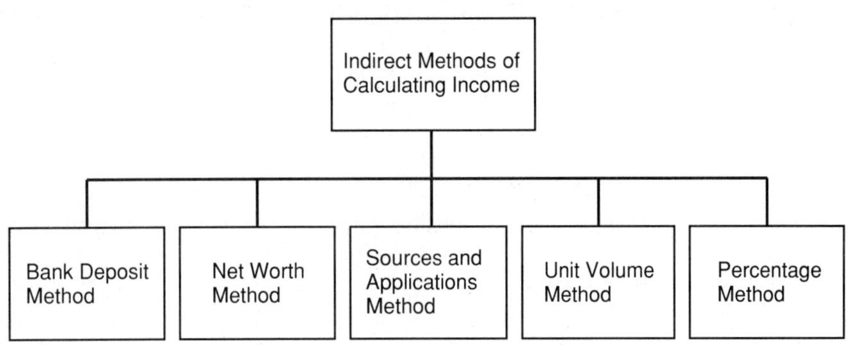

usually the best choice when it appears that most of the taxpayer's income has been deposited.

2. *Net Worth Method*. The net worth method is based on the theory that increases or decreases in a person's net worth during a specific period, adjusted for living expenses, are the result of a taxpayer's net income. The net worth method is used when several of the taxpayer's assets or liabilities have changed substantially during the period under audit, and a significant amount of income does not appear to have been deposited.
3. *Sources and Applications*. The sources and applications method is based on the theory that if a taxpayer's expenditures for a specific time period exceed reported income, the difference must be unreported income. This method is used when it appears that significant amounts of income have not been deposited, and the taxpayer has spent income on lavish living rather than on the accumulation of capital assets.
4. *Unit Volume Method*. The unit volume method is based on the theory that if the number of units handled by the taxpayer and the price charged per unit by the taxpayer can be determined, income can be determined by multiplying price per unit by the number of units handled. This method is used when one of the three previously mentioned methods are inappropriate, and the business involved handles only a few items with little variation in services performed.
5. *The Percentage Method*. The percentage method is based on the theory that if the gross income or net profit percent of the taxpayer's particular type of business and the correct amount of expenses the taxpayer incurred can be determined, the taxpayer's income can be "backed into." The percentage method is used when the other indirect methods are inappropriate and a reliable gross or net profit percentage can be determined.

During this audit segment the agent would also decide whether control of the audit should be given to the Criminal Investigation Division of the Internal Revenue Service. Agents will only propose turning the case over if they feel they can prove a fraudulent act has been committed. Agents must also prove that the act was deliberate and voluntary, and the taxpayer was aware of the illegality of the act. Assuming Segment 4 is completed without control of the case being turned over to the Criminal Investigation Division of the IRS, an agent can close the audit in one of several ways, as seen in Figure 17–6.

1. *Statutory Notice of Deficiency*. The case is sent directly to tax court because the taxpayer has been completely uncooperative. An agent will disallow all expenses and attempt to arrive at as accurate a gross income figure as possible.
2. *No Change*. The return is accepted as filed.
3. *Change/No Change*. A change in the tax return has been agreed to by the taxpayer which does not affect the tax liability of the year in question but could affect the tax liability of a prior or future year.

**Figure 17–6.** Audit Segment 5, "Closing the Case"—The Possible Ways to Close a Case (Audit)

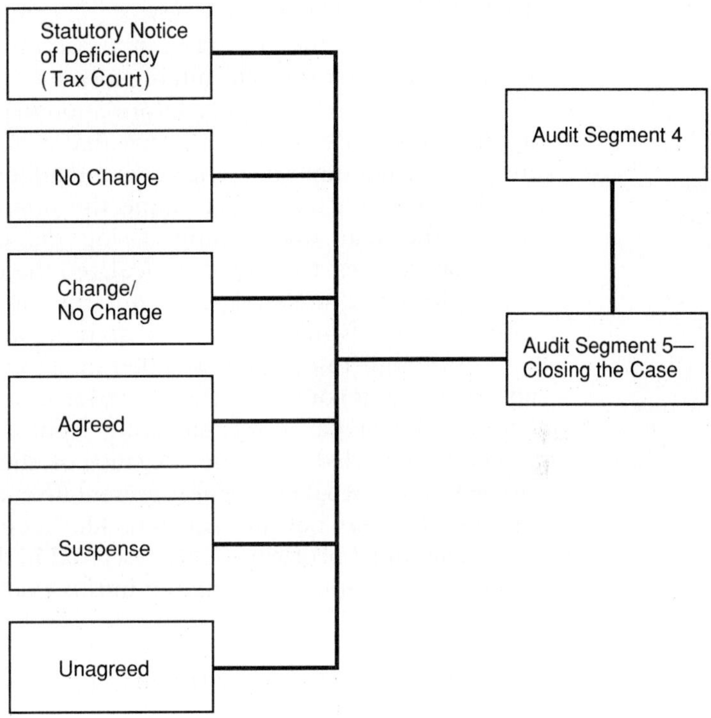


4. *Agreed*. A change in the tax return which affects the tax liability of the year in question has been agreed to by the taxpayer.
5. *Suspense*. The return is sent to partnership suspense because the taxpayer under audit is an investor in a partnership, subchapter S corporation, joint venture, or other flow-through entity that is currently under audit.
6. *Unagreed*. The taxpayer does not agree to the audit findings, therefore, the case is transferred to the appellate level within the Internal Revenue Service.

## A Typical Decision Scenario

The following is an example of how an audit decision-making situation was handled in an actual test-case scenario.

During the pre-audit planning segment, the initial interview, and the tour of the place of business of the owner/operator of a greeting card store, the revenue agent uncovered no clues of unreported income. While reviewing the taxpayer's bank statements, the agent reconciled total deposits to the income figure reported on the taxpayer's 1040, and found no discrepancies. However, although the taxpayer reported a similar gross income amount on his prior year 1040, his cost of goods sold was significantly larger in the year under audit. Considering that the taxpayer ran a cash business, the agent decided to use an indirect approach for determining income.

Unable to find adequate information to perform a net worth or sources and applications analysis, and believing that a substantial portion of the taxpayer's income was not deposited, the agent attempted a unit volume analysis. Hallmark Cards was contacted to determine the number of cards the store purchased during the year under audit. Using the taxpayer's beginning and ending inventory figures, the agent recalculated the number of cards sold by the store. Using the taxpayer's oral testimony, the sale price per card multiplied by the number of cards sold was used to arrive at a gross income figure.

Although uncovering $25,000 in unreported income, the agent decided against turning control of the case over to the Criminal Investigation Division because the taxpayer was suffering from Alzheimer's disease and therefore intent or knowledge of the illegality of the taxpayer's actions could not be proven. The taxpayer's legal representative agreed to the agent's findings and did not offer any new information. The agent closed the case *agreed*.

The initial prototype KBS described in the next section replicates the kind of decision situation encountered in this example.

## DOCUMENTING THE PROTOTYPE SYSTEM

The following discussion covers:

- description of the prototype system
- decision charts
- designing and constructing the knowledge base

### Description of the Prototype System

***System Overview and Objective.*** The specific objective of the prototype system is to provide new Internal Revenue agents with assistance in probing for unreported income while auditing books and records during Segment 4 of an income tax field audit of a sole proprietorship. It also assists these agents in determining the proper disposal of a completed audit in Segment 5. The system asks the user questions to determine if the use of an indirect method is warranted and to recommend the best indirect method to use in the particular situation. The system also helps determine how the audit should be closed, if it is completed. Although one of the recommendations the system makes is to turn control of the audit over to the Criminal Investigation Division for a fraud investigation, the system does not determine this, but rather only provides information useful to the user in making that decision. The area of fraud investigation should be a system in itself. This system does not attempt to resolve technical issues of law.

***Recommendations To Be Made by the System.*** The recommendations the system makes for Segment 4, Auditing of Books and Records, are as follows:

1. Use the bank deposit method.
2. Use the net worth method.
3. Use the sources and applications method.
4. Use the unit volume method.
5. Use the net or gross profit percentage method.
6. An indirect method is not needed.
7. Refer the case to the Criminal Investigation Division.

The recommendations the system can make for Segment 5, Closing the Case, are as follows:

8. Send the case to tax court.
9. Hold a closing conference.
10. Evaluate new information.
11. Close the case no change.
12. Close the case change/no change.
13. Close the case agreed.
14. Close the case to suspense.
15. Close the case unagreed.

***Nature of the User Interface, Including a Typical User Dialogue.*** The user is asked a series of questions to determine if an indirect method of auditing books and records is necessary, which indirect method would be applicable to the situation, and whether or not a referral to the Criminal Investigation Division is warranted. If all the above have been resolved, the user is asked questions to determine if and how the audit should be closed. The questions are structured to provide the user with guidelines to follow while performing a gross income probe during the type of audit under study. For example:

System: How would you describe any discrepancies noted while reconciling the taxpayer's income tax return with his sales tax return?
User: Substantial

***Description of the Knowledge Structure and Reasoning Processes.*** The recommendations made by the system are based on the user responses to questions related to the two audit segments involved. IF-THEN rules and backward chaining are used.

**Figure 17–7.** Data Dependency Diagram of the System (Overview)

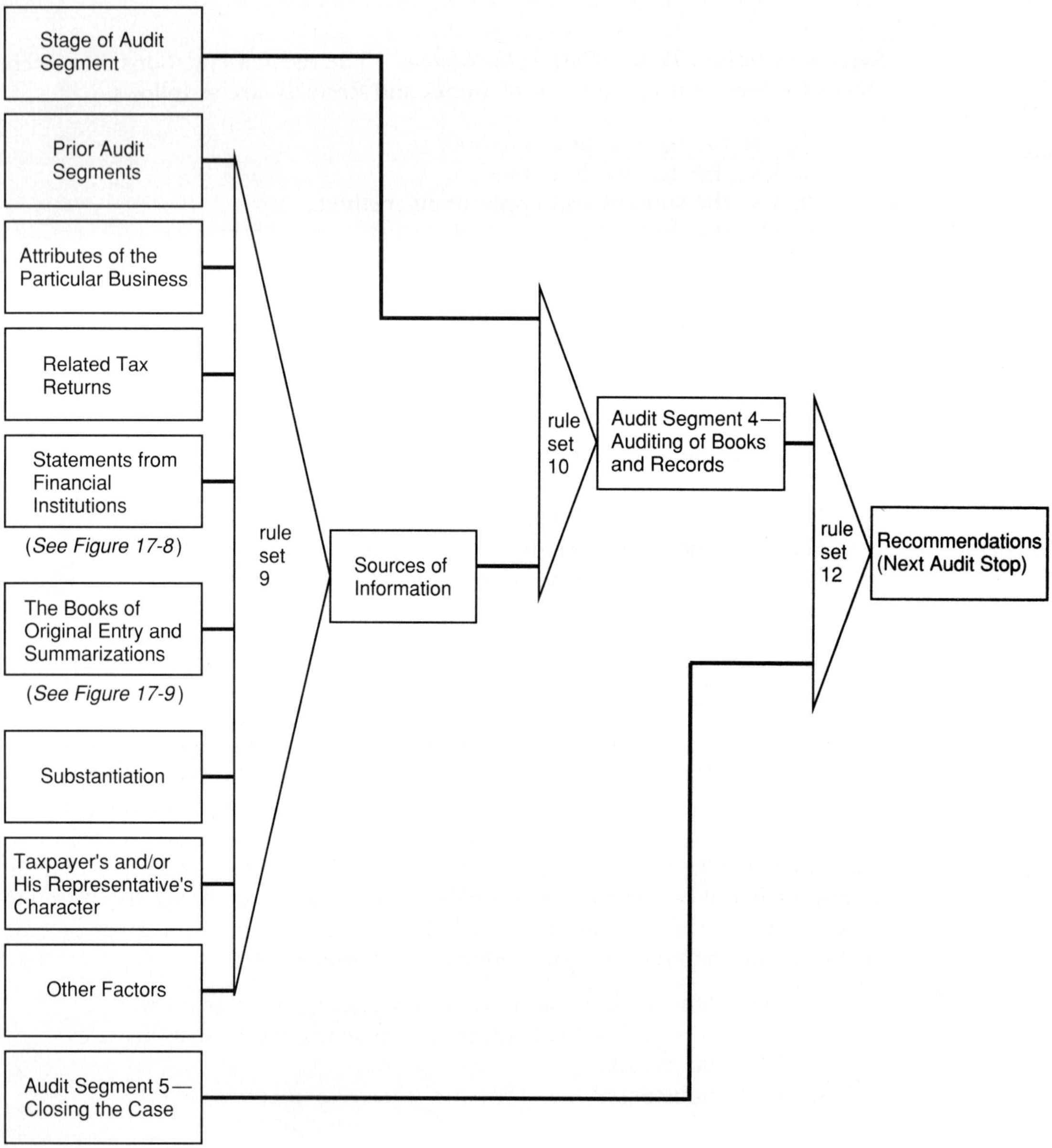

## Dependency Diagrams

The dependency diagrams show the decision-making process of the system in detail. Figure 17–7 is an overall dependency diagram, while Figures 17–8 and 17–9 give the details of two of the individual segments of the overall decision: Statements from Financial Institutions, and Books of Original Entry and Summarization. Similarly, all of the other individual segments shown in Figure 17–7 also have corresponding dependency diagrams.

**Figure 17–8.** Statements from Financial Institutions—Data Dependency Diagram

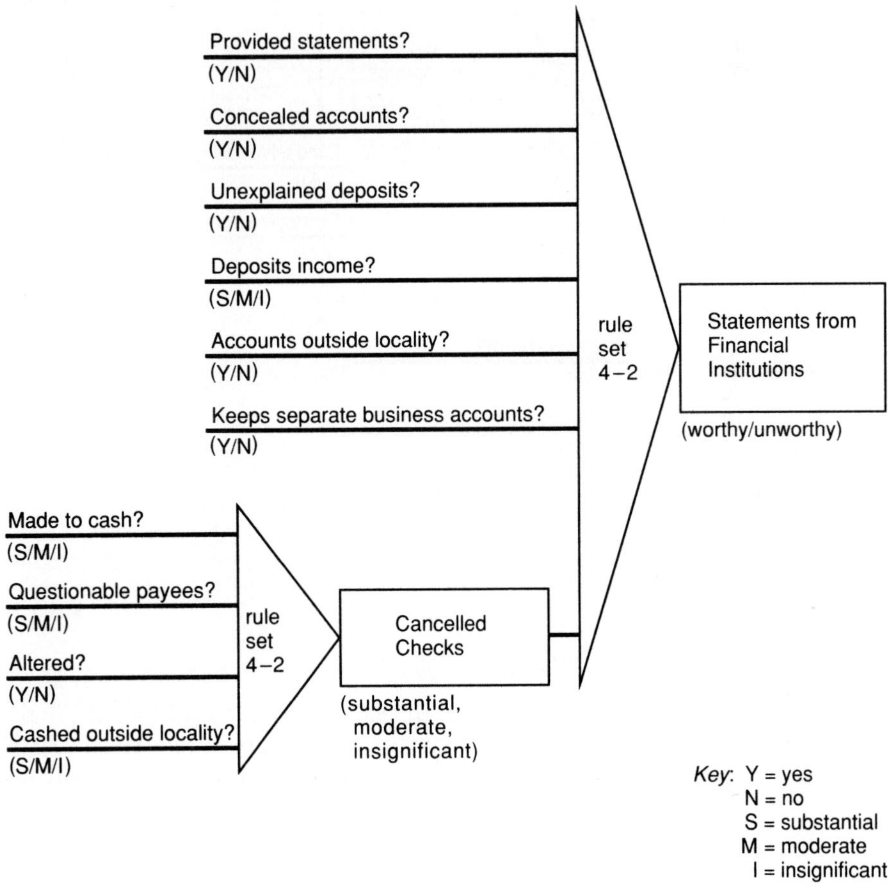

**Figure 17–9.** Books of Original Entry and Summarization—Data Dependency Diagram

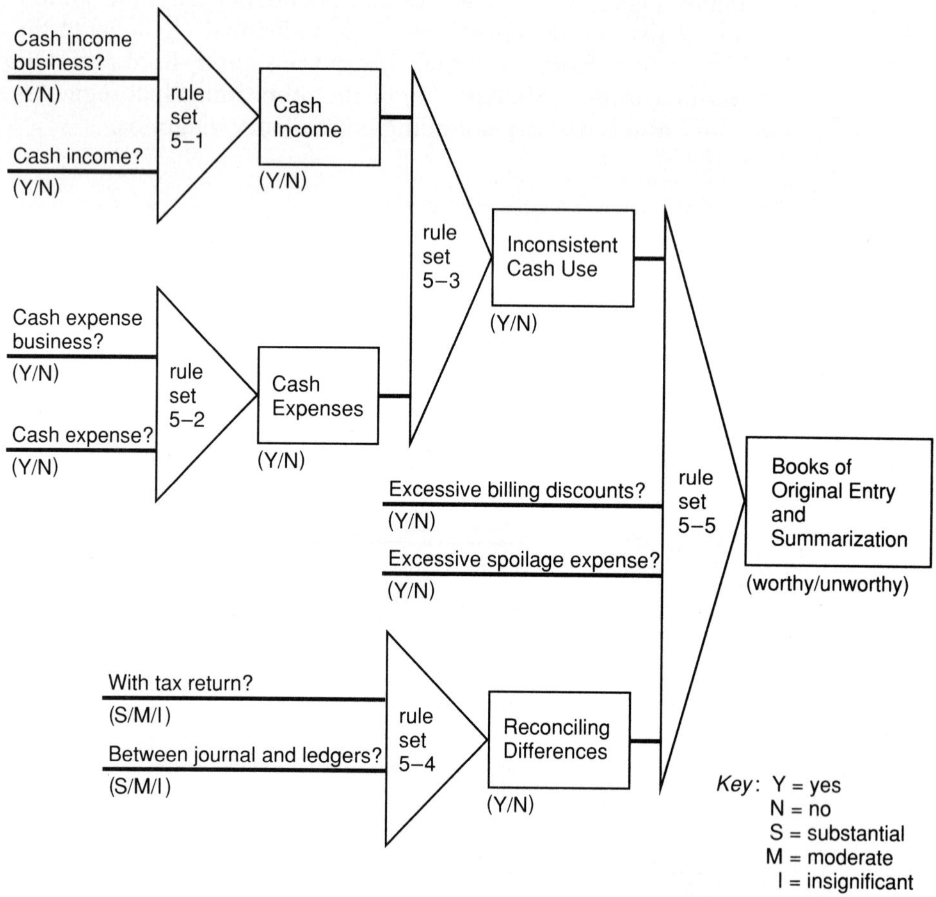


## Decision Charts

A decision chart has been developed for each rule set of the prototype KBS. The decision chart for the final rule set appears in Figure 17–10. Decision charts are one of the tools used to document the reasoning process involved in constructing the KBS.

## Designing and Constructing the Knowledge Base

Questions and rules were developed from the situation under study. They are based on the steps an experienced revenue agent might use during the type of

**Figure 17–10.** Decision Chart for the Final Decision Rule

| rule set 12 | 1 | 2 | 3 | 4 | 5 | 6 | 7 | 8 | 9 | 10 | 11 | 12 | 13 | 14 | 15 |
|---|---|---|---|---|---|---|---|---|---|---|---|---|---|---|---|
| If "audit-books-records" = | r | bd | nw | sa | uv | pp | un | c | c | c | c | c | c | c | c |
| And "close-case" = | | | | | | | | tc | cc | ei | nc | c/c | a | ps | ap |
| Then "next-step" = | | | | | | | | | | | | | | | |
| refer-to-cid | X | | | | | | | | | | | | | | |
| bank-deposit | | X | | | | | | | | | | | | | |
| net-worth | | | X | | | | | | | | | | | | |
| sources-and-applications | | | | X | | | | | | | | | | | |
| unit-volume | | | | | X | | | | | | | | | | |
| profit-percentage | | | | | | X | | | | | | | | | |
| indirect-method-unnecessary | | | | | | | X | | | | | | | | |
| close-to-tax-court | | | | | | | | X | | | | | | | |
| hold-closing-conference | | | | | | | | | X | | | | | | |
| evaluate-new-information | | | | | | | | | | X | | | | | |
| close-no-change | | | | | | | | | | | X | | | | |
| close-change-no-change | | | | | | | | | | | | X | | | |
| close-agreed | | | | | | | | | | | | | X | | |
| close-to-partnership-suspense | | | | | | | | | | | | | | X | |
| close-to-appeals | | | | | | | | | | | | | | | X |

key:

r = refer-to-cid
bd = bank-deposit-needed
nw = net-worth-needed
sa = sources-and-apps-needed
uv = unit-volume-needed
pp = profit-percentage-needed
un = unworthy
c = complete
tc = tax-court
cc = closing-conference
ei = evaluate-new-information
nc = no-change
c/c = change-no-change
a = agreed
ps = to-partnership-suspense
ap = to-appeals

audit described. The knowledge sources used to develop the prototype system included:

- an experienced IRS agent who participated in the KBS development
- interviews with other experts in the field
- published material and internal IRS documents

A partial rule base from the system is shown in Figure 17–11. The expert system shell used is M.1. The IF-THEN rules in the knowledge base in Figure 17–11 are written to reflect the relationships in the dependency diagrams. They use the values shown in the dependency diagrams and decision charts.

**Figure 17–11.** Sample Rule Set 7–1 (Partial)

The rule set below determines if the taxpayer is exhibiting a lack of cooperation. Taxpayers sometimes do not cooperate with the auditor in an attempt to prevent the auditor from uncovering unreported income.

```
7-1-1:
     if supplies-info = rarely or
        belligerent = yes or
        does-not-keep-apts = often
     then cooperation = no.

7-1-2:
     if supplies-info = sometimes and
        overly-eager-to-complete = yes and
        does-not-keep-apts = sometimes
     then cooperation = no.

7-1-3:
     if supplies-info = sometimes and
        belligerent = no and
        overly-eager-to-complete = yes and
        does-not-keep-apts = rarely
     then cooperation = yes.

7-1-4:
     if supplies-info = often and
        belligerent = no and
        overly-eager-to-complete = yes and
        does-not-keep-apts = sometimes
     then cooperation = yes.

7-1-5:
     if supplies-info = often and
        belligerent = no and
        overly-eager-to-complete = yes and
        does-not-keep-apts = rarely
     then cooperation = yes.

7-1-6:
     if supplies-info = often and
        belligerent = no and
        overly-eager-to-complete = no and
        does-not-keep-apts = sometimes
     then cooperation = yes.

7-1-7:
     if supplies-info = often and
        belligerent = no and
        overly-eager-to-complete = no and
        does-not-keep-apts = rarely
     then cooperation = yes.
```

The prototype KBS described in this chapter is given on the disks accompanying this book.

## EXERCISE

The disks accompanying this book contain the prototype KBS described at the end of this chapter. Following the directions accompanying the disks for using the M.1 expert system shell, run a consultation using the system, which has the file name AUDITING.IRS. If you wish, you might also print out the knowledge base and study it while you are running the system and restudying this chapter.

# 18

# Analyzing Power Plant Turbine/Condenser Performance

This chapter discusses decision situations involving analysis of steam turbine/generator performance in a conventional fossil-fuel-fired power plant.

As the electric utilities are a highly regulated industry, their production costs must be strictly controlled. Inefficiencies in the operation of equipment results in higher operating costs and eventually increased electric rates. To help plant personnel analyze these inefficiencies and reduce operating costs, a knowledge-based system was developed. This system was designed to identify the root causes of these inefficiencies and make recommendations for improvements.

The discussion of this system and its development covers:

- the overall situation under study: understanding the expert's field
- the situation to be prototyped
- documenting the prototype system

The early sections of the discussion describe the overall situation within which the system is being developed. The initial situation to be prototyped, one aspect of turbine performance, is then described. The final section describes the development of the prototype system within the framework of the overall decision situation. A selected glossary of terms used is given at the end of this chapter.

## OVERALL SITUATION UNDER STUDY: UNDERSTANDING THE EXPERT'S FIELD

The discussion in this section covers:

- selecting a decision area to work on
- probing how the situation works and how decisions are made in general
- narrowing the focus

### Selecting a Decision Area to Work On

The study of turbine/condenser performance was the area selected for prototype knowledge-based system development, because the problems which develop in this area are repetitive in nature, can lead to losses that are extremely costly to the plant, and require prompt decision making to correct.

The KBS is feasible for the following reasons:

- Experts of condenser technology exist throughout the industry.
- The tasks are well understood.
- Many examples are available.
- The scope is applicable to knowledge-based system technology.

The task requires reasoning and judgement, as various situational factors are analyzed to determine the root cause of condenser inefficiency. This analysis is the basis for determining corrective action.

Knowledge required for the system development was first acquired through reviewing test procedures, condenser repairs manuals, journals, and operating data to obtain sufficient background for questioning the experts. Company experts were then interviewed, and test cases were reviewed to determine typical condenser inefficiencies and their causes. Following this, the experts examined the prototype of the knowledge-based system and applied it to real cases for verification and refinement. The developer was one of those experts.

### Probing How the Situation Works

The decision situation under study involves analysis of turbine/condenser performance in a fossil-fuel power plant in a major public utility in a large metropolitan area. At each power plant, standards of equipment performance are set by plant management based on equipment design and operating conditions.

As in any conventional power plant, water is pumped from a holding tank called a hotwell through a series of feedwater heaters which preheat the water before it enters the boiler. A schematic diagram of this power plant cycle is shown in Figure 18–1. As fuel is burned in the boiler, water is converted to steam at high temperature and pressure. This steam is forwarded to the high-pressure

**Figure 18–1.** Typical Power Plant Cycle

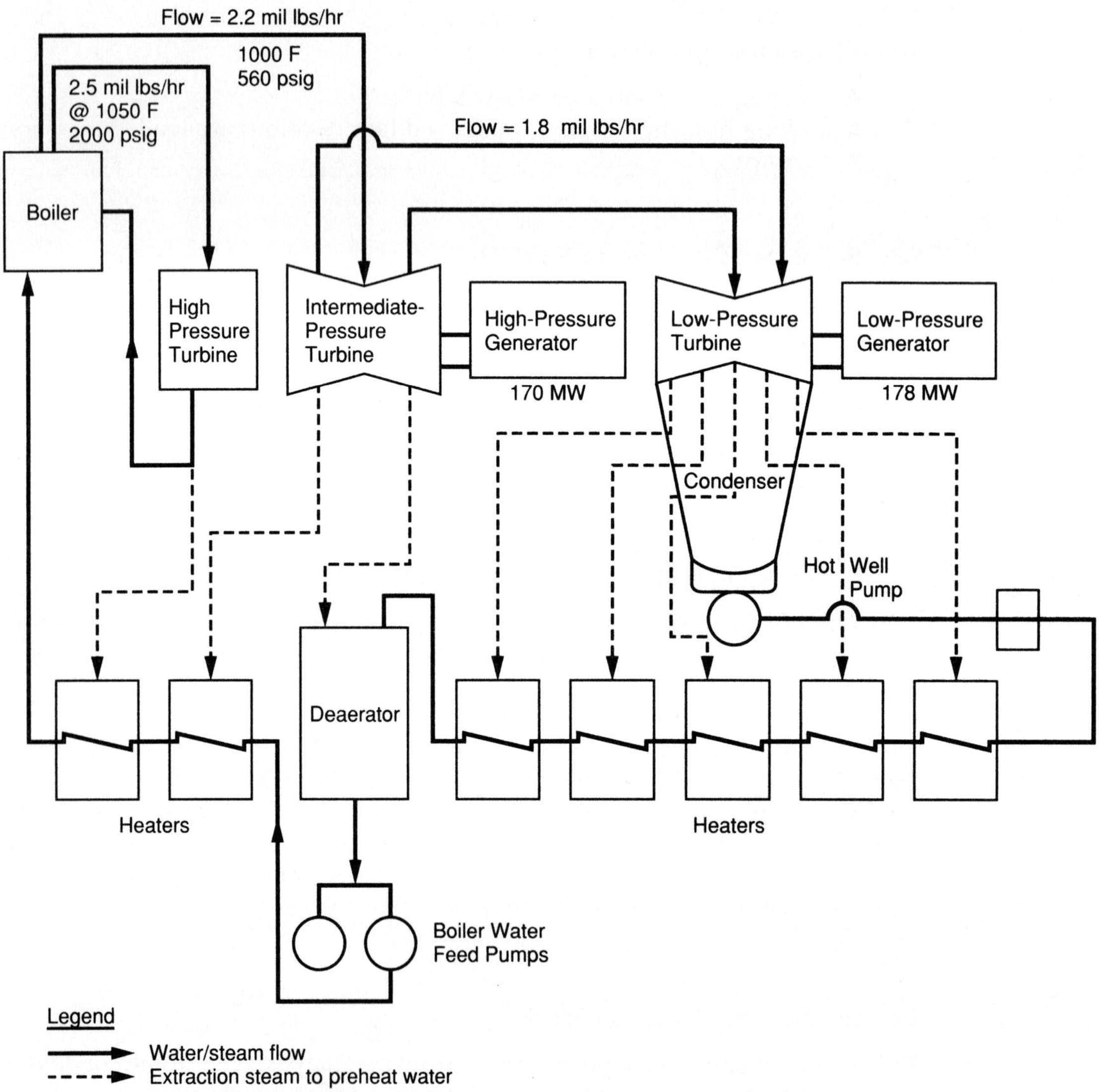


turbine which extracts energy from the steam as it expands, causing the turbine to turn or rotate at high speeds.

After the steam passes through the high-pressure turbine, it is returned to the boiler to increase its temperature (and thus energy). Following the increase in temperature, the steam flows to the intermediate-pressure turbine, where it expands further converting the energy in the steam to rotational energy. Finally, steam is directed to the low-pressure turbine, where its remaining energy is removed. During this process, a portion of steam is directed from each turbine to the individual feedwater heaters to preheat fresh water just entering the cycle. In simple terms, this process is analogous to steam produced in a teapot which, when exposed to a pinwheel, will turn it.

The high-pressure and intermediate-pressure turbines are connected to the high-pressure generator through a drive shaft. Likewise, the low-pressure turbine is coupled to the low-pressure generator. The rotation of each turbine transmits energy, otherwise called work, to the generator via the drive shaft. This shaft is a rotating magnet which produces magnetic fields, which in turn produce alternating current or electricity within the generator.

As for turbine performance, steam is introduced into a turbine at a rated high pressure and temperature. The steam flow (expressed in lbs/hr, or pounds per hour) which enters the turbine determines the amount of electricity (called "load") that can be generated. The steam turns the rotating elements of the turbine, converting pressure energy into rotational energy as it expands through each stage of the turbine.

As the steam moves through the low-pressure turbine outlet (or exhaust), river water is used to cool and condense the steam to the lowest vacuum and temperature possible to remove the most energy in the steam to do useful work. This process produces maximum turbine performance. The process of cooling uses water flowing through tubes of a heat exchanger (called a condenser), where steam will be condensed on the outside of the tubes to produce water which drops into a collecting tank called a hotwell. A simplified diagram of the process is shown in Figure 18–2.

In order to supply water to cool the steam, water is pumped from the river using high-volume circulating pumps. This water passes through trash rakes which filter large debris such as plastic, wood, and so forth. Then the water passes through rotating screens which filter out smaller pieces of debris. The water continues into a tunnel to the plant proper. It enters the condenser salt water inlet box via an inlet valve and flows through tubes (several thousand of which are separated from the steam side of the turbine by a partition called a tubesheet) and discharges into the condenser outlet box, returning to the river. The condenser box is designed to allow all tubes to be supplied by water (and thus ensure full cooling flow and efficiency) unless a leak develops in either the inlet or outlet boxes, which collapses the level of water in the condenser. In this case, water may be prevented from reaching the upper tubes.

In order to fill the boxes on startup of the circulating pumps, the boxes are designed with syphons, which are devices to lift the level of water in the box and remove trapped air.

The entire process of converting energy in the fuel released in the boiler into electrical energy is only 35 percent efficient. Other losses besides turbine/condenser inefficiency include extra heat that is generated to be rejected to the stack. However, turbine/condenser inefficiency is the largest single loss (that is controllable by an operator) in the entire power plant cycle and is therefore the

**Figure 18–2.** Typical Turbine/Condenser Design

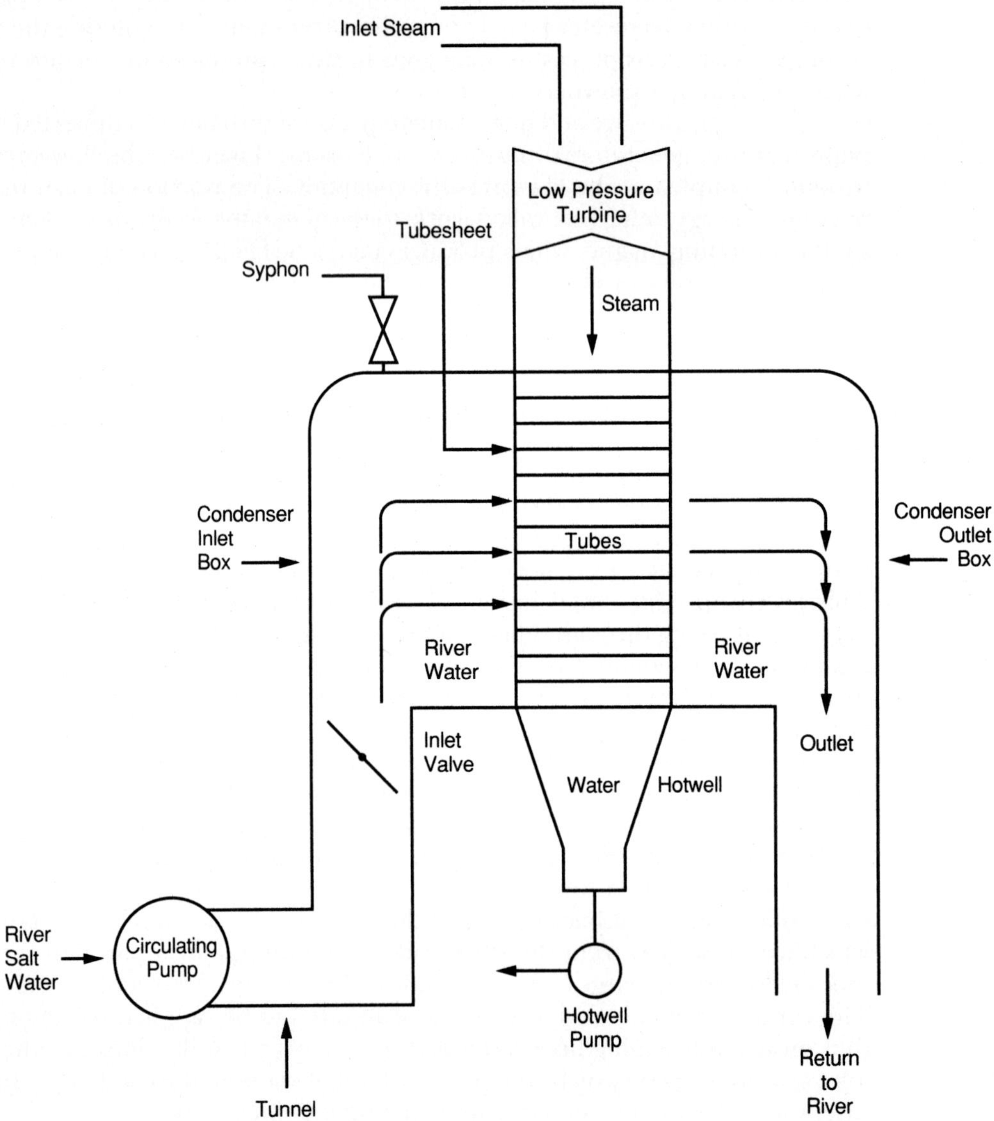

most important factor that plant management addresses on a daily basis. Causes of this turbine inefficiency are shown in Figure 18–3 and discussed in the following paragraphs.

In the course of operating, the turbine is subject to wear or failure of its rotating and stationary parts (called blades and diaphragms). This allows steam to bypass each rotating section and reduces the amount of steam to turn the turbine and convert pressure energy into rotational energy. This is called turbine deterioration. This is directly related to: the number of equipment startup and shutdown cycles that the turbine experiences; improper maintenance during overhaul of the turbine; and, changes in steam conditions while the turbine operates (due to changes in temperature, vibration, pressure, and percent of moisture). In addition, the turbine may be coated or fouled with chemicals that are carried in the steam from the boiler. This may be due to improper chemical control in the boiler or failure of boiler steam separators. The end result is reduced transfer of rotational energy in the turbine. This is known as turbine fouling, and usually occurs during transition periods such as unit startups.

To regulate the amount of steam flow and the load generated, the turbine is equipped with valves called control valves. The turbine also has valves called stop valves that isolate the turbine from steam flow. If mechanical failures of these valves develop, the steam delivered to the turbine may vary from expected flow, temperature, or pressure conditions, thus affecting turbine performance. Likewise, inadequate control to maintain required temperature and pressure of the steam to the turbine will reduce efficiency. This can be caused by malfunctioning controllers and/or improper boiler conditions. Finally, deterioration in the performance of the condenser may reduce the amount of work produced by the turbine by reducing the amount of vacuum and temperature that the steam may condense to. Condenser inefficiency may be attributed to two major causes:

1. *Terminal difference* (TD)—defined as the temperature difference between the steam leaving the turbine exhaust and the river water outlet temperature.
2. *Circulating water temperature rise* (CWTR)—defined as the temperature rise between the river water leaving the condenser and the river water entering the condenser.

Terminal difference may be caused by several factors including:

1. Insufficient air removal capacity. Air present in the turbine exhaust must be removed, since air acts as an insulator around the tubes preventing steam from condensing and thus reducing turbine efficiency. Air-removal problems result from defects in air-removal equipment (called evactors or vacuum pumps) or air leakage into the low-pressure turbine. Air leaks into the turbine, as the turbine is under high vacuum.
2. Condenser tube fouling (either internal or external to the tubes). Fouling is coating of the condenser tubes caused by either deposits from

**Figure 18–3.** Cause of Turbine Inefficiency

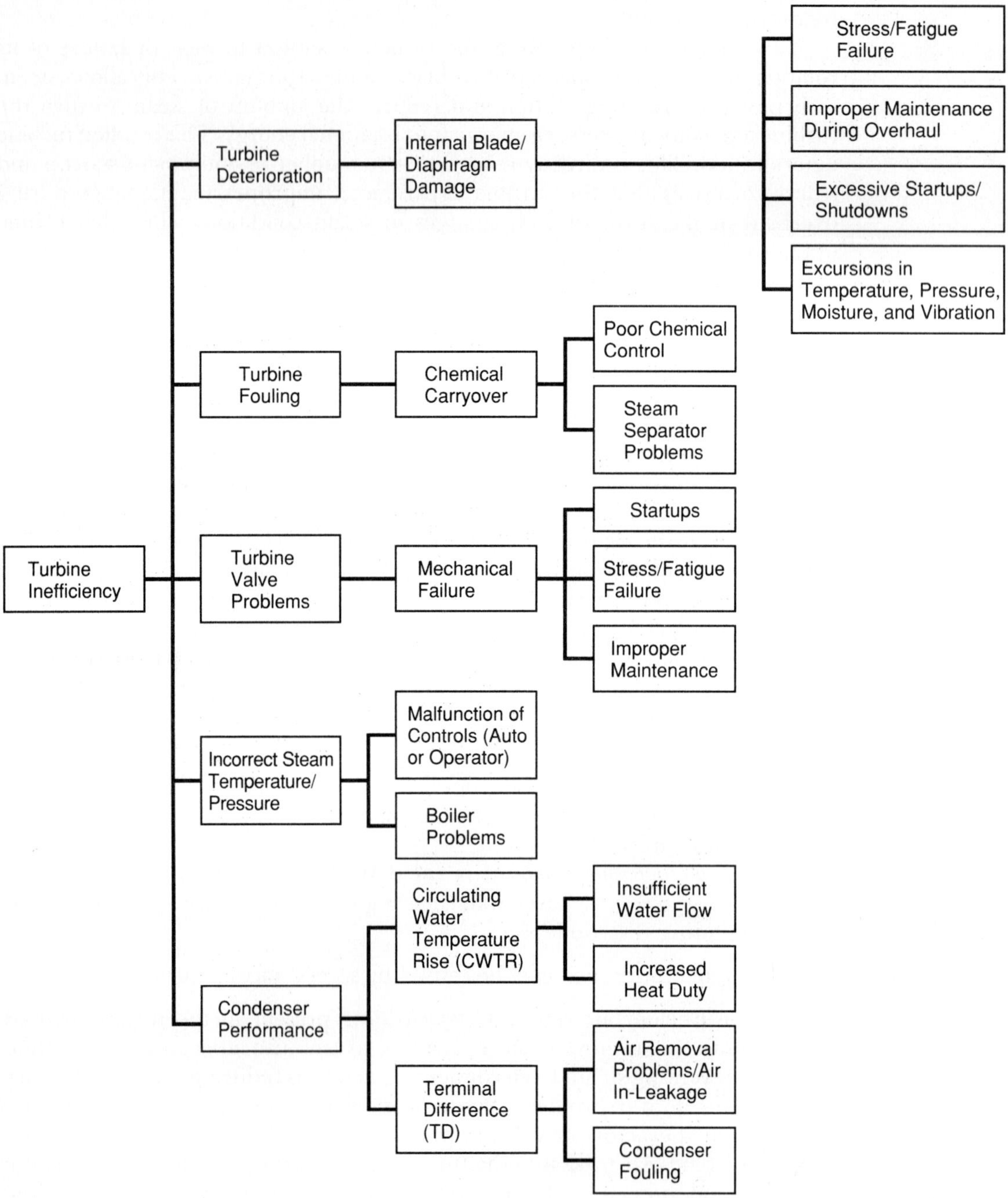

the steam (external to the tubes), river algae formation, or river silt accumulation on the inside of the tubes. Fouling acts as an insulator, preventing proper heat transfer for the steam to condense.

The second factor which impacts on condenser inefficiency is circulating water temperature rise (CWTR), which is primarily caused by one of two factors:

1. Insufficient river water flow to cool the steam at the steam exhaust. This includes blockage in the bays or tunnels from the river where the circulating pumps draw water into the condenser inlet box. This may be caused by silt accumulation or barges in front of the plant. It may also be due to low tide level or restrictions in the condenser inlet box valve. CWTR may also be attributed to blockage problems of the rotating screens or trash rakes, preventing sufficient water flow to the condenser. Reduction in circulating water pump output may also reduce the amount of water available for cooling purposes.

   Condenser waterbox problems are the most likely cause of insufficient water flow. These can be caused by debris carryover from the screens into the condenser inlet box, which causes tubesheet pluggage, which in turn reduces flow through the tubes. This is characterized by high circulating pump motor current. In addition, leakage in either condenser box or syphons decreases the height of water in the box and reduces the level of water in the tubes.
2. Increased heat within the turbine exhaust. As a power plant cycle is designed to recover as much heat and steam as possible, drains from the power plant cycle are returned to the turbine exhaust. However, failure of these drains may increase the amount of heat returned to the turbine. As the turbine is designed to handle only a given amount of steam, the extra heat is rejected to the river. Excess steam is commonly due to open drains or failure of internal steam lines within the turbine. These internal steam lines extract steam from the turbine to preheat water entering the boiler.

### Narrowing the Focus

The analysis of causes of turbine inefficiency can be extremely complex and require much research over long periods of time. For example, turbine inefficiency caused by internal damage to rotating sections may occur slowly over time, and years may pass before plant operators detect that problems exist.

However, deterioration in condenser performance is readily detected and controlled by plant operators. Condenser problems are repeatable, well understood, and easily corrected.

As heat rejected to the river via the condenser is the problem bringing about the largest loss in the plant cycle, it is, therefore, most logical to narrow the focus of this prototype development to analysis of condenser performance. In this way an operations manager or engineer may better evaluate probable root causes of condenser inefficiency, in order to reach well-reasoned decisions for corrective action. Through use of this analysis, a reduction in operating costs of up to $500,000 per year can be realized.

## STUDYING THE SITUATION TO BE PROTOTYPED

This section first describes the analysis of deterioration in condenser performance. Then an overall decision-process model is presented which explains and determines all potential sources of inefficiency, ranging from the easiest to detect to more complex analysis. As the decision model includes approximately forty rule sets, an example will be used to demonstrate how the process works and its application to a real situation. Finally, possible recommendations for corrective action to address each potential problem will be made.

Upon initial installation, the turbine manufacturer provides expected performance curves of the unit at given steam flow (or load), temperature, pressure, and river water conditions. This is called the turbine heat rate curve. Heat rate refers to the amount of fuel burned to deliver energy into the turbine per amount of electricity produced (in million BTU per net kilowatt hour produced). This curve is represented in Figure 18–4 and depicts expected turbine exhaust pressure for given conditions of load (in megawatts or MW) at specific river water temperatures.

To determine deviations from these standards using these curves, plant management measures the difference between the actual exhaust pressure and the expected one for the given load and river temperature. When this deviation from standard exceeds .1 BTU/NTKWHr, testing to determine the condition of the turbine/condenser is performed. This deviation from standard or bogey is called deviation from bogey, or DFB.

These tests attempt to determine if condenser inefficiency is primarily due to terminal difference or due to circulating water temperature rise. These tests measure the following parameters: air leakage into the condenser; difference in level of water and temperature between the salt water inlet boxes and the salt water outlet boxes; steam pressure and temperature at the low pressure turbine exhaust; pressure and temperature of water exiting the hotwell. To ensure accurate and repeatable data, the instrumentation is checked for proper calibration.

When terminal difference (TD) exceeds 50 percent of total DFB, efforts are then made to narrow down to probable cause. First, if air leakage exceeds 10 cubic feet/minute (above capacity of air removal equipment), it is anticipated that air leakage is directly affecting back pressure. With this in mind, the steam seals along the turbine shaft (which are designed to keep steam within the turbine and keep air out) will be checked to ensure proper pressure for positive sealing. If the seals are satisfactory, next all of the drains returning to the condenser will be taken out of service one at a time to isolate (and repair) the system creating high air inleakage. If this is unsuccessful, surveys using a tracer gas sprayed in areas of potential air inleakage will be conducted to pinpoint a source. In this way,

**Figure 18–4.** Station B Condenser No. 3 Turbine Heat Rate Curve

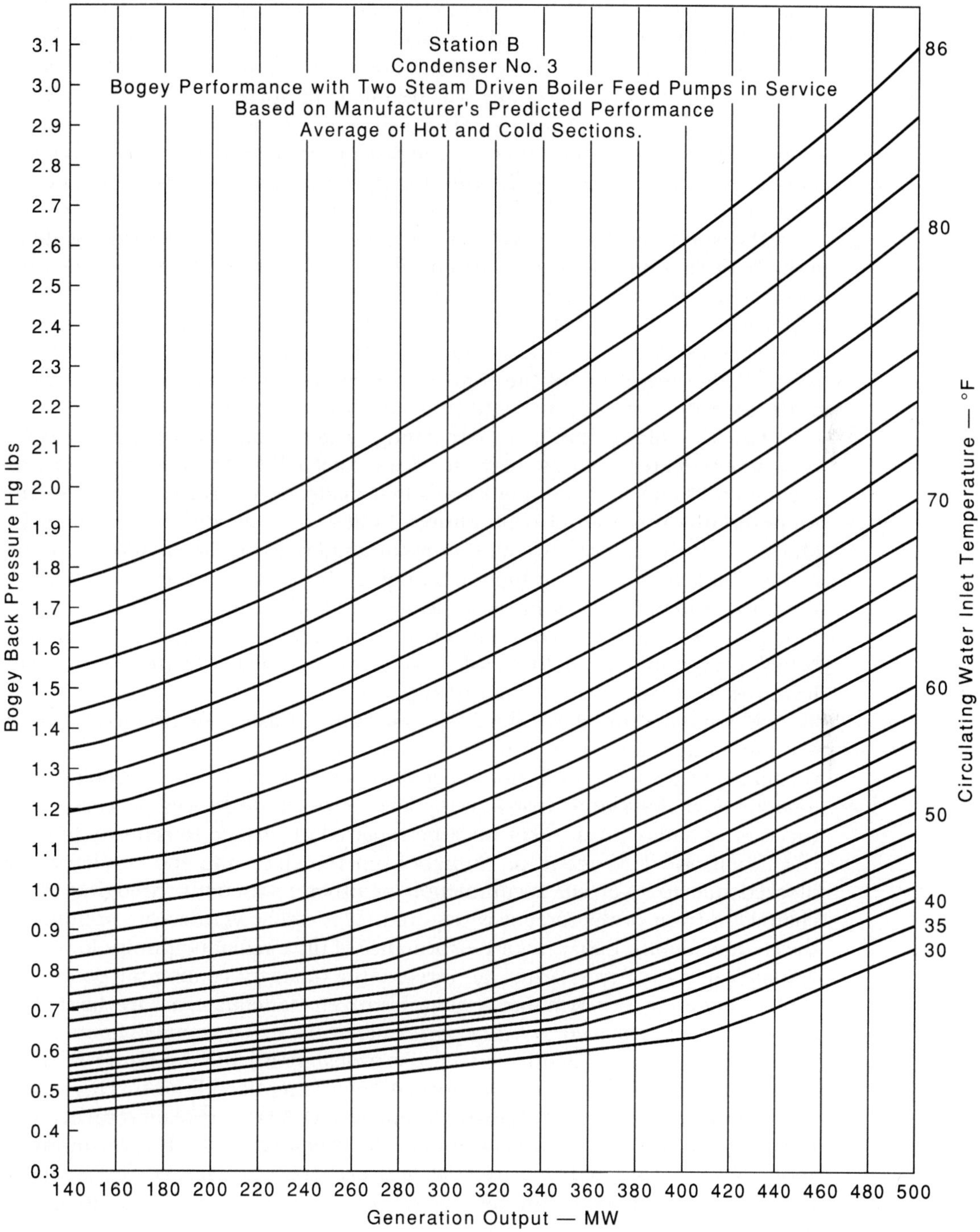

repairs can be performed as soon as possible to stop leakage. However, if air removal equipment such as the evactors or vacuum pumps appear to be functioning inadequately, the loop seals and traps will be checked to ensure the loops are full. If not, the loops will be filled. Performance testing of the air removal equipment can then be performed. This can help identify which nozzle on the evactor is not operating or in the case of the vacuum pumps which piston valves are not functioning. In this way, repairs can be performed and the condenser retested to assess effects of these repairs.

If inspection of the condenser salt water boxes during cleaning of debris indicate fouling due to algae growth or silt inside the tubes, cleaning of the tubes using high pressure water shot with small brushes is warranted. This can be supplemented with use of a chemical called hypochlorite which chlorinates the water, killing off the bacterial sludge and hence allowing heat transfer across the tubes. If the steam side of the condenser tubes is coated, flushes with water or acids can reduce the deposits and thus improve efficiency.

On the other hand, if circulating water temperature rise (CWTR) represents greater than 50 percent of the total DFB, the following steps are warranted. A check of the tide level is first made. If tide is low, the circulating water pumps cannot supply full volume of water to the condenser, thus reducing efficiency. If the tide is normal, the motor amperage on the circulating pumps can be checked. If these are high or swinging, there is an indication of a blocked tubesheet due to debris; it must be cleaned. The same phenomena occurs when water-box or syphon leaks develop and drop the level in the condenser salt water boxes, preventing full delivery of cooling water available to the tubes. These leaks can be identified, and then repaired.

Along with the above items, screen and/or trash rake problems may be causing insufficient river water flow. Due to mechanical failure or severe pluggage, these devices will not adequately pass sufficient water through them. This is evident by a large drop in water level across these devices. To correct this, the screens and/or trash rakes must be repaired or flushed to remove debris.

Similarly, if the bays or tunnels from the river into the condenser are blocked due to river silt accumulation or other restrictions, dredging of the channel in front of the screens is required. This can be verified by soundings of the channel depth. Lastly, poor performance of the circulating pumps lowers the volume capacity of river water delivered to the tubes for cooling purposes. This can be verified by performance testing. If proven inadequate, an overhaul of the pump can be performed to bring performance back to acceptable limits.

Finally, if CWTR is still evident, it is probable that the condenser is subject to increased heat due to above normal "operating" conditions. This can be caused by unnecessary and excessive drainage of cycle water/steam returned back to the condenser. This can be identified by checking all the return drains for heat. Another cause of excessive heat returned to the condenser can be failures of internal steam lines within the condenser (such as feedwater heater expansion joints or steam seals). This can be checked by conducting feedwater heater tests to determine change in performance of heaters. In this way, the problem can be pinpointed and repairs made when the unit is out of service for maintenance repair.

Figure 18–5 outlines the process and the questions that an expert uses to determine the root causes of condenser inefficiency, based upon condenser test information. This outline will serve as the model for developing the knowledge-based system to assist with test analysis.

As the model uses approximately forty rule sets, Figure 18–6 will be used to show an example of how the process is applied to a real situation. The shaded areas show the logic that an expert uses in determining causes of inefficiency and providing recommendations.

The following discussion traces the analysis of high DFB from the determination of root cause to the corrective action, using an example from condenser test information.

Condenser testing performed on a 360 MW turbine/generator on January 23, 1992 indicated total DFB = 0.25 as shown in Figure 18–7. The instrumentation was recalibrated and confirmed the original test data. The condenser test showed that the total DFB was divided as follows:

0.17 of total DFB was due to terminal difference
0.08 of total DFB was due to circulating water temperature rise

The steps followed by the expert as shown in Figure 18–6 are as follows:

Step 1: The expert first compares the DFB due to terminal difference and DFB due to circulating water temperature rise. In this case, terminal difference exceeds 50 percent of total DFB and therefore the answer is yes to TD greater than CWTR.

Step 2: Next, the amount of air inleakage into the turbine is compared to an accepted value equal to 10 $ft^3/min$. If the air leakage exceeds the air removal equipment capacity, high exhaust pressure and low performance may result. Since air inleakage exceeds this value, the answer is yes.

Step 3: The process proceeds to ask if the turbine steam seal pressure exceeds 5 psig. The steam seal system provides sealing steam along the turbine shaft and is designed to maintain steam within the turbine as well as keep air out. Since the steam seal pressure is 6.8 psig. the answer is yes.

Step 4: The next question asks if the unit is equipped with either vacuum pumps or evactors for air removal capability. Vacuum pumps are generally piston-type, which extract air from the condenser then exhaust it to the atmosphere during each cycle. On the other hand, an evactor uses steam at high pressure to remove air at a lower pressure and discharge to atmosphere. The plant in question is equipped with evactors.

**Figure 18–5.** Overall Decision Process Model—Example of a Logic Trace

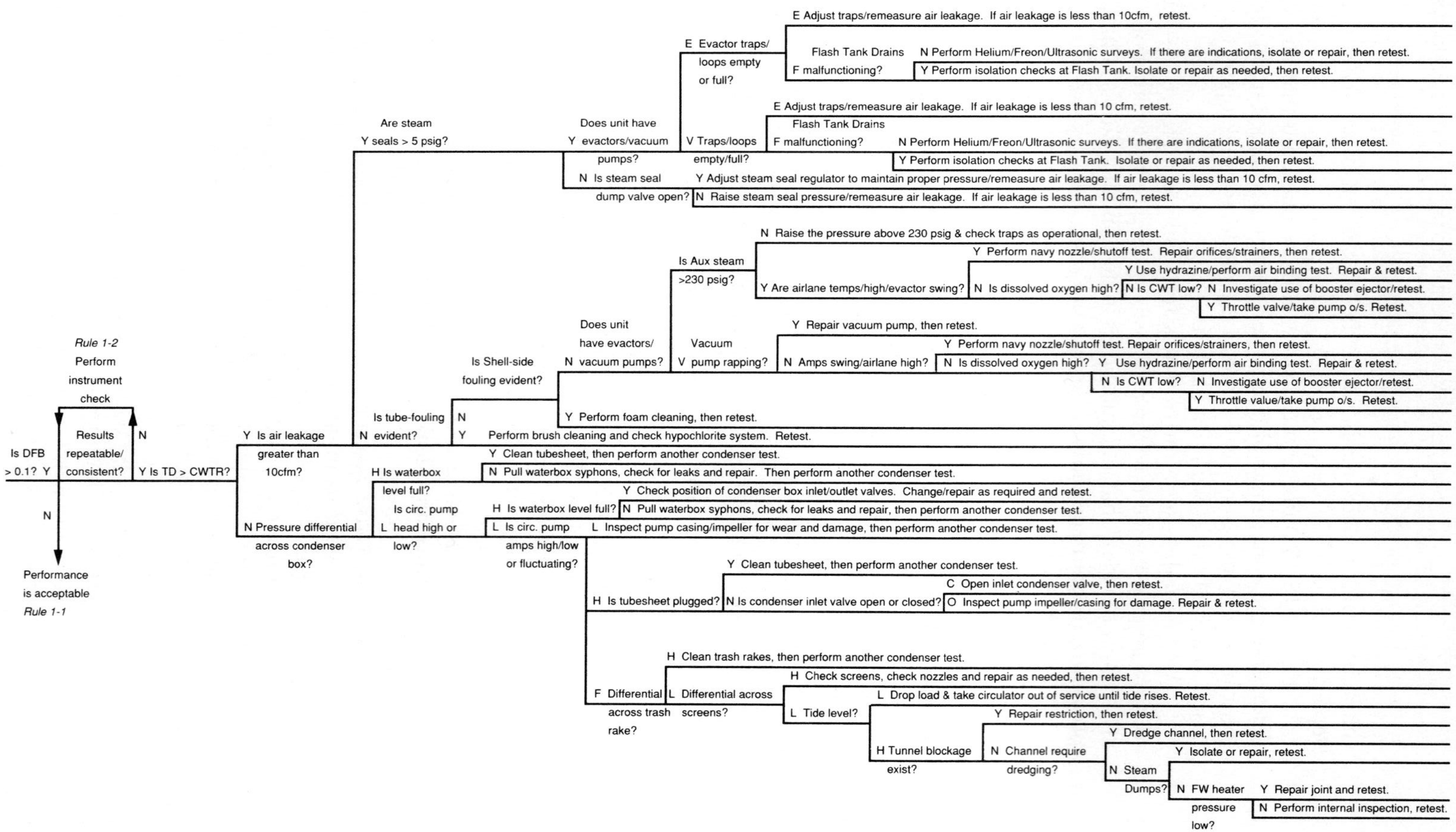

**Figure 18–6.** Overall Decision Process Model

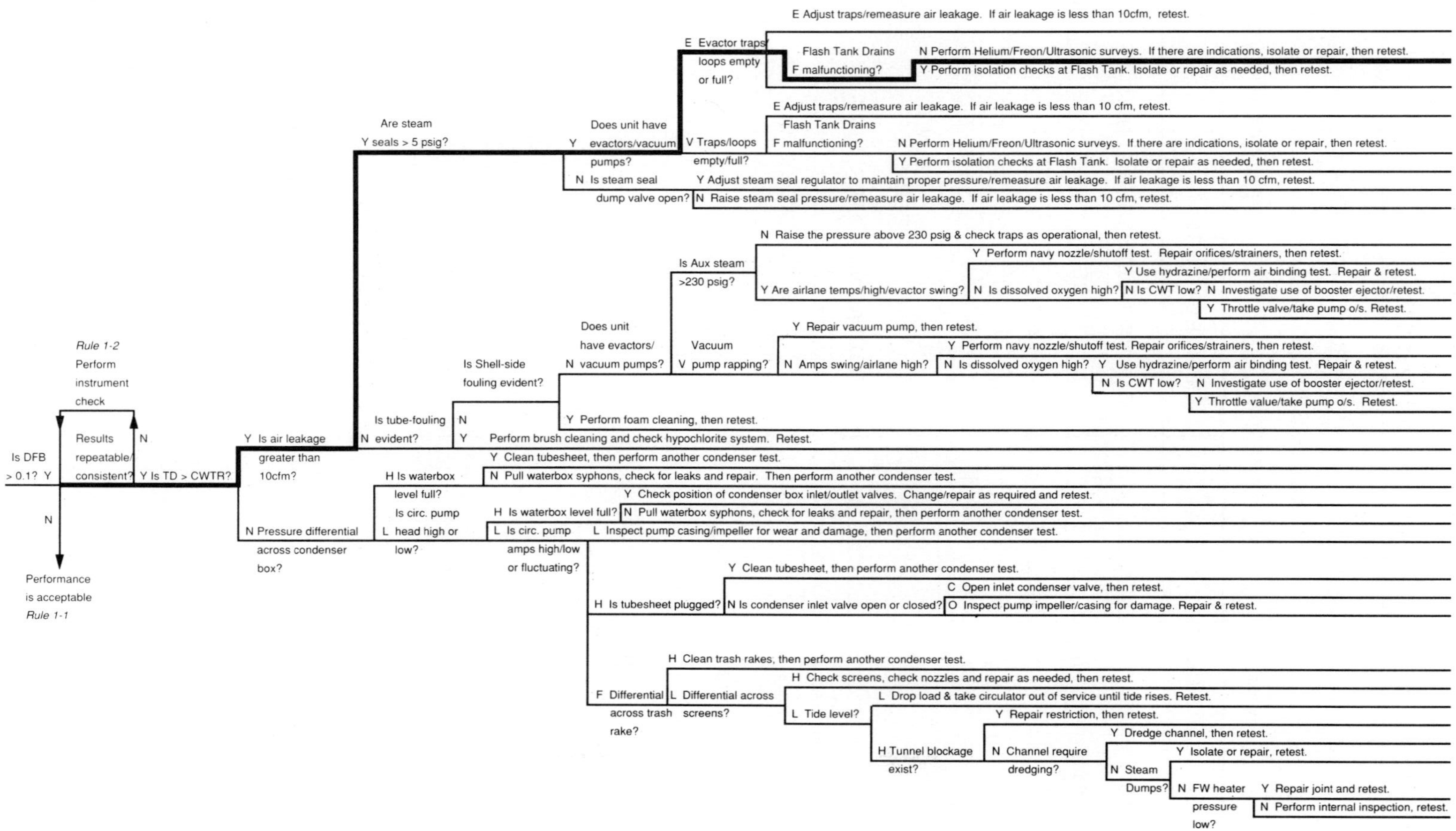

**Figure 18–7.** Station B Unit No. 4 Condenser Test 248

STATION B
UNIT NO. 4
CONDENSER TEST

DATE 1-23-92
TIME 1 AM (PM)

TEST NO. 248

READINGS TAKEN BY: JGS / PDQ

| CONTROL BOARD READINGS | FIELD READINGS |
|---|---|

**CONTROL BOARD READINGS**

| | | |
|---|---|---|
| MW LOAD | | 310 |
| EXH. PRESS. | N | .98 |
| | S | .95 |
| | AVG. | .91 |
| C.W.T. INLET | | 41.2 |
| CIRC. AMPS | (21) | 1.08 N |
| | (22) | 0.98 S |
| AIR LEAKAGE | N | 0 |
| | S | 0 |
| | TOTAL | 5 |
| STM SEAL PRESS. | | 6.8 |
| S/B PRESS. | S/H | 240/# (#3) |
| | R/H | 65/# |

AMERTAPS I/S ( ) O/S ( ✓ )

VAC. PUMP TIE OP(✓) CL (✓)

VACUUM TIES TO B.F.P (AK3)
OPEN (/) CLOSED (/)

COMMENTS:
TEST CUT SHORT:
S.O.NEEDED UNIT
UNABLE TO GET
WATER BOX DROPS.

8/85 J.A.
R9/87 J.A.

**FIELD READINGS**

EXHAUST PRESSURE "Hg ZIMM. #____

| | NE | NW | SE | SW | AVG |
|---|---|---|---|---|---|
| 1 | 1.24 | 1.10 | 1.11 | 0.97 | |
| 2 | 1.24 | 1.09 | 1.10 | 0.97 | |
| AVG | 1.24 | 1.10 | 1.11 | 0.97 | 1.11 |
| BOGEY | 0.86 | 0.86 | 0.86 | 0.86 | 0.86 |
| D.F.B. | 0.38 | 0.24 | 0.25 | 0.11 | [0.25] |

D.F.B. DUE TO:

| | | |
|---|---|---|
| C.W.T | 32 % | [0.08] |
| TERM.DIFF | 68 % | [0.17] |

CIRCULATING WATER TEMP.

| | 21 *EAST | 22 *WEST | 23 — | 24 — | AVG — |
|---|---|---|---|---|---|
| OUTLET | 54.6 | 53.1 | 52.3 | 55.7 | 53.9 |
| INLET | 40.8 | 41.0 | 40.8 | 41.0 | 40.9 |
| RISE | 13.8 | 12.1 | 11.5 | 14.7 | 13.0 |
| BOGEY | 10.7 | 10.7 | 10.7 | 10.7 | 10.7 |
| D.F.B. | 3.1 | 1.4 | 0.8 | 4.0 | [2.3] |

| | | | |
|---|---|---|---|
| SAT. TEMP | 82.3 | FLOW FACTOR | 82% |
| HOTWELL TEMP. | 78.5 | | |
| HOTWELL DEPT. | 3.8 | TERM. DIFF. | 28.4 |
| COND. CLN. FACT. | | BOGEY | 23.0 |
| | | D.F.B. | 5.4 |

WATER BOX DROPS:

| | INLET LL/RL | INLET DIFF. | OUTLET LL/RL | OUTLET DIFF. | TOTAL |
|---|---|---|---|---|---|
| 21 | | | | | |
| E/23 | | N/A | | | |
| 22 | | | | | |
| W/24 | | | | | |

AIR LEAKAGE

| | LL/RL | DIFF. | ORIF. | C.F.M. | |
|---|---|---|---|---|---|
| N | 0/0 | 0 | --- | 0 | TOTAL |
| S | 19.5/ 10.0 | 9.5 | .740 | 23.0 | [237] |

| | | | |
|---|---|---|---|
| 1 54.9 | 2 54.3 | 3 53.2 | 4 52.9 |
| 1 53.2 | 2 51.4 | 3 56.3 | 4 55.4 |

–10.8/40.8 INLET 78.5/78.5 H

Step 5: The evactor discharge steam traps and loop seals are checked for water level. These traps and loop seals are designed to maintain proper condensing of the steam in the evactor and proper return of this condensate back to the turbine exhaust. As the traps are found to be functioning properly and not empty, the answer is full.

Step 6: Next, the drains to the condenser from the power plant cycle which return to the condenser are checked to see if any are malfunctioning. This can be determined by detecting drain lines as cold, or as open when they should be closed. This may be a source of air inleakage to the condenser when drains are not pressurized. In this case, all drains are functioning properly and therefore the answer is no.

Step 7: As air inleakage is determined to be the root cause of the problem, the process now requires performing surveys using a tracer gas such as helium. This gas is sprayed in all potential areas of air inleakage to the turbine. An instrument to detect this gas is placed at the evactor exhaust. If a leak exists in an area while spraying, it will be detected downstream by a monitor. In this case, a loose access plate at the hotwell is found to be causing air inleakage to the condenser.

Step 8: As the leak is identified, efforts are now made to repair it by tightening and resealing the plate.

Step 9: The final recommendation is to perform a retest of the condenser to determine if condenser performance is now acceptable. In this case, the air inleakage dropped to 6.3 cfm, and the turbine exhaust pressure DFB is .09 as shown in Figure 18–8 and 18–9. This is considered acceptable performance and no further repairs are required.

In order to summarize all possible outcomes and simplify the decision paths, the following section briefly describes the recommendations which can be made based on the analysis model diagrammed in Figure 18–5.

**Possible Recommendation**

Recommendation 1: If air removal equipment is malfunctioning, test individual components to identify repair. Then retest following completion of required repairs.

Recommendation 2: If air inleakage is high, verify turbine steam seals are correct and perform surveys to

**Figure 18–8.** Station B Unit No. 4 Condenser Test 249

STATION B
UNIT NO. 4
CONDENSER TEST

DATE 1-30-92
TIME 10:00 (AM)/PM

TEST NO. 249

READINGS TAKEN BY: JGS / PDQ

| CONTROL BOARD READINGS | FIELD READINGS |
|---|---|

**CONTROL BOARD READINGS**

MW LOAD ________

EXH. PRESS. N ________

S ________

AVG. ________

C.W.T. INLET ________

CIRC. AMPS 21 ________ N

22 ________ S

AIR LEAKAGE N ________

S ________

TOTAL ________

STM SEAL PRESS ________

S/B PRESS. S/H ________ (#3)

R/H ________

AMERTAPS I/S (   ) O/S (   )

VAC. PUMP TIE OP(   ) CL (   )

VACUUM TIES TO B.F.P (AK3)
OPEN (   ) CLOSED (   )

COMMENTS:

________
________
________
________

8/85 J.A.
R9/87 J.A.

**FIELD READINGS**

EXHAUST PRESSURE "Hg ZIMM. #____

| | NE | NW | SE | SW | AVG |
|---|---|---|---|---|---|
| 1 | | | | | |
| 2 | | | | | |
| AVG | | | | | |
| BOGEY | | | | | |
| D.F.B. | | | | | [ ] |

D.F.B. DUE TO:

C.W.T ___% [ ]
TERM.DIFF ___% [ ]

CIRCULATING WATER TEMP.

| | 21 *EAST | 22 *WEST | 23 -- | 24 -- | AVG -- |
|---|---|---|---|---|---|
| OUTLET | 54.3 | 53.7 | 54.4 | 55.6 | 54.5 |
| INLET | 41.8 | 42.6 | 40.8 | 42.6 | 42.0 |
| RISE | 12.5 | 11.1 | 13.6 | 13.0 | 12.5 |
| BOGEY | 10.9 | 10.9 | 10.9 | 10.9 | 10.9 |
| D.F.B. | 1.6 | 0.2 | 2.7 | 2.1 | [1.6] |

SAT. TEMP 78.1 FLOW FACTOR 87.2%
HOTWELL TEMP. 74.0
HOTWELL DEPR. +4.1 TERM. DIFF. 23.6
COND CLN FACT ______ BOGEY 22.3
D.F.B 1.3

WATER BOX DROPS:

| W.L. | | INLET LL/RL | INLET DIFF | OUTLET LL/RL | OUTLET DIFF | TOTAL |
|---|---|---|---|---|---|---|
| +3.5 | 21 | | −2.5 " Hg | | −9.0 " Hg | −10.0 |
| +3.5 | E/23 | | −3.0 " Hg | | −9.0 " Hg | −9.5 |
| +3.0 | 22 | | −2.0 " Hg | | −9.0 " Hg | −10.0 |
| +3.0 | W/24 | | −3.0 " Hg | | −9.0 " Hg | −9.0 |

AIR LEAKAGE

| | LL/RL | DIFF. | ORIF. | C.F.M. | TOTAL |
|---|---|---|---|---|---|
| N | 14.2/15.8 | 1.6 | .3125 | 1.6 | TOTAL |
| S | 7.2/8.8 | 1.6 | .525 | 4.7 | [6.3] |

*EAST 1 54.3 2 54.3 3 53.8 4 53.6
*WEST 1 53.5 2 55.2 3 55.7 4 54.4

HW 74.1/73.8 INLET TEMP. 21 . 42., 22 . 41.

**Figure 18–9.** Station B Unit No. 4 Condenser Retest 249

STATION B
UNIT NO. 4
CONDENSER TEST

DATE 1-30-92
TIME 10:15 (AM) PM

TEST NO. 249

READINGS TAKEN BY: JGS / PDQ

| CONTROL BOARD READINGS | FIELD READINGS |
|---|---|

**CONTROL BOARD READINGS**

MW LOAD 318

EXH. PRESS. N .90 (1.06)

S .87 (0.89)

AVG. .89 (0.98)

C.W.T. INLET 41.9 (0.09)

CIRC. AMPS 21 1.08 N Kamps

22 0.95 S Kamps

AIR LEAKAGE N ____

S ____

TOTAL ____

STM SEAL PRESS 6.9

S/B PRESS. S/H 260 (#3)

R/H 20

AMERTAPS I/S ( ) O/S ( )

VAC. PUMP TIE OP( ) CL ( )

VACUUM TIES TO B.F.P (AK3)
OPEN ( ) CLOSED ( )

COMMENTS:

8/85 J.A.
R9/87 J.A.

**FIELD READINGS**

EXHAUST PRESSURE "Hg ZIMM. #____

| | NE | NW | SE | SW | AVG |
|---|---|---|---|---|---|
| 1 | 1.12 | 0.97 | 0.92 | 0.82 | 0.96 |
| 2 | 1.12 | 1.00 | 0.98 | 0.83 | 0.98 |
| AVG | 1.12 | 0.99 | 0.95 | 0.83 | 0.97 |
| BOGEY | 0.88 | 0.88 | 0.88 | 0.88 | 0.88 |
| D.F.B. | 0.24 | 0.11 | 0.07 | -0.05 | [0.09] |

D.F.B. DUE TO:

C.W.T. 56 % [0.05]
TERM.DIFF. 44 % [0.04]

CIRCULATING WATER TEMP.

| | 21 *EAST | 22 *WEST | 23 -- | 24 -- | AVG -- |
|---|---|---|---|---|---|
| OUTLET | | | | | |
| INLET | | | | | |
| RISE | | | | | |
| BOGEY | | | | | |
| D.F.B. | | | | | [ ] |

SAT. TEMP. 78.1 FLOW FACTOR 87.2%
HOTWELL TEMP. 74.0
HOTWELL DEPR. +4.1 TERM. DIFF. 23.6
COND. CLN. FACT. ---
BOGEY 22.3
D.F.B 1.3

WATER BOX DROPS:

| | INLET LL/RL | INLET DIFF. | OUTLET LL/RL | OUTLET DIFF. | TOTAL |
|---|---|---|---|---|---|
| 21 | | | | | "Hg |
| E/23 | | | | | "Hg |
| 22 | | | | | "Hg |
| W/24 | | | | | "Hg |

AIR LEAKAGE

| | LL/RL | DIFF. | ORIF. | C.F.M. | TOTAL |
|---|---|---|---|---|---|
| N | | | | | |
| S | | | | | [6.3] |

*EAST 1 ____ 2 ____ 3 ____ 4 ____
*WEST 1 ____ 2 ____ 3 ____ 4 ____

| | |
|---|---|
| | locate leaks. Following this, perform repairs, then retest. |
| Recommendation 3: | If condenser fouling is high, perform brush cleaning or foam cleaning, then retest. |
| Recommendation 4: | If heat duty is high, test extraction lines of feedwater heaters to detect excessive steam dumps, check that all drains to condenser are set properly and perform internal inspection. Repair as needed, then retest. |
| Recommendation 5: | If tunnel blockage occurs, dredge channel to remove silt or correct restriction in inlet valves, then retest. |
| Recommendation 6: | If screen or trash rake problems exist, repair screens, clean condensers, then retest. |
| Recommendation 7: | If a circulating pump problem is suspected, verify by testing, then perform overhaul. Retest again. |
| Recommendation 8: | If tubesheet is plugged, clean, then retest. |
| Recommendation 9: | If the water box or syphon is leaking, repair, then retest. |

## DOCUMENTING THE SYSTEM

The following discussion covers:

- system overview and objective
- recommendations to be made by the system
- nature of the user interface
- description of the knowledge structure and learning processes
- dependency diagram and decision table
- definitions of key terms

### System Overview and Objectives

The general objective of the project is to develop a knowledge-based system that assists an operating manager/engineer in determining the corrective action to take in reducing turbine/condenser inefficiency for a conventional steam condensing turbine. The initial prototype deals with just condenser inefficiency.

The system asks on-screen questions about conditions affecting condenser performance (such as river water temperature, air leakage, etc.) to guide an operator through analysis.

The system uses IF-THEN rules and backward chaining to reason about the information given by a user to reach a conclusion and issue a recommendation.

The benefits of this project are:

- Improved capability of analyzing deterioration of condenser performance at many major plants within the utility.
- Prompt corrective action due to improved analysis. This will lead to major reductions in operating costs.
- Use as a training tool for operators. As operators observe the steps and logic of this system, they will also be gaining the knowledge necessary to make the correct decision themselves.

Information needed to develop this system was obtained from:

- experts in turbine/condenser analysis
- condenser design data
- test procedures and manuals
- industry journals
- previous test data

### Recommendations To Be Made by the System

1. If air removal equipment is malfunctioning, repair.
2. If air inleakage is high, perform surveys to locate sources.
3. If heat duty is high, check drainage for problems.
4. If condenser is fouled, perform brush cleaning.
5. If flow restriction is present, dredge channel and/or correct restriction.
6. If screen/trash rakes are malfunctioning, repair.
7. If pump exhibits problems, repair.
8. If tubesheet is plugged, clean condenser boxes.
9. If water box problems exist, repair.

### Nature of User Interface

The knowledge-based system that has been developed is designed for users with knowledge of power plant cycles and terminology, turbine/condenser design, and related operating problems. Using the results of condenser testing and operating conditions, the operations manager/engineer is guided through a series of questions that are designed to narrow the high deviation from bogey (DFB) problem to a particular root cause (under the main categories of terminal difference or circulating water temperature rise).

Typical user dialogue includes questions such as:

```
"What is the terminal difference deviation from bogey?
Type in a number (such as 0.12) times 1000."
"Is the condenser air leakage greater than 10 cfm?"
(Yes or No)
"Is the pressure differential across the box high or
low?" (High or Low)
```

## Description of the Knowledge Structure and Reasoning Process

The recommendations made by the prototype system are based on the determination first of the root cause for the high deviation from bogey through the process of elimination. Once the root cause has been identified (by answering a series of questions based on operating conditions) the recommendations become a direct output to solve the problem.

IF-THEN rules are used to determine recommendations at each stage. The inference engine uses backward chaining to determine these recommendations.

## Dependency Diagram and Decision Table

Figure 18–10 gives a widespread dependency diagram for the system. Figure 18–11 gives the decision table. Figure 18–12 gives sample rules and questions.

The prototype KBS described in this chapter is given on the disks accompanying this book.

## Definitions of Terms Used in the Overall Study

*Deviation from bogey (DFB)*—A deviation from a standard design condition for a turbine/condenser for a given load and river water temperature.
*Terminal difference (TD)*—The temperature difference between the steam leaving the turbine exhaust and river water outlet temperature.
*Circulating water temperature rise (CWTR)*—The temperature rise between the river water leaving the condenser and the river water entering the condenser.
*Condenser air leakage*—Amount of air entering the condenser which is under vacuum (measured in $ft^3$/min.)
*Steam seals*—Located at the ends of the turbine shaft and designed to keep steam within the turbine while keeping air out.
*Evactor*—Condenser air removal device that uses high pressure (or auxiliary) steam to evacuate the air.
*Vacuum pump*—Condenser air removal device that uses pistons under high compression to evacuate the air.
*Steam seal dump valve or regulator*—Valves used to regulate the pressure on the steam seal system.
*Flash tank*—A tank designed to allow high pressure and temperature drains from the power plant cycle to "flash" before condensing in the hotwell. (A heat/water recovery system.)
*Helium/freon/ultrasonic surveys*—Use of tracer gas or ultrasonics to pinpoint sources of condenser air leakage.
*Tube-fouling*—Fouling of the internal surfaces of the condenser tubes due to river algae, silt.
*Hypochlorite*—Chemical injected to kill river algae inside condenser tubes.

**Figure 18–10.** Condenser Inefficiency Diagnosis KBS—Dependency Diagram (Initial Prototype System)

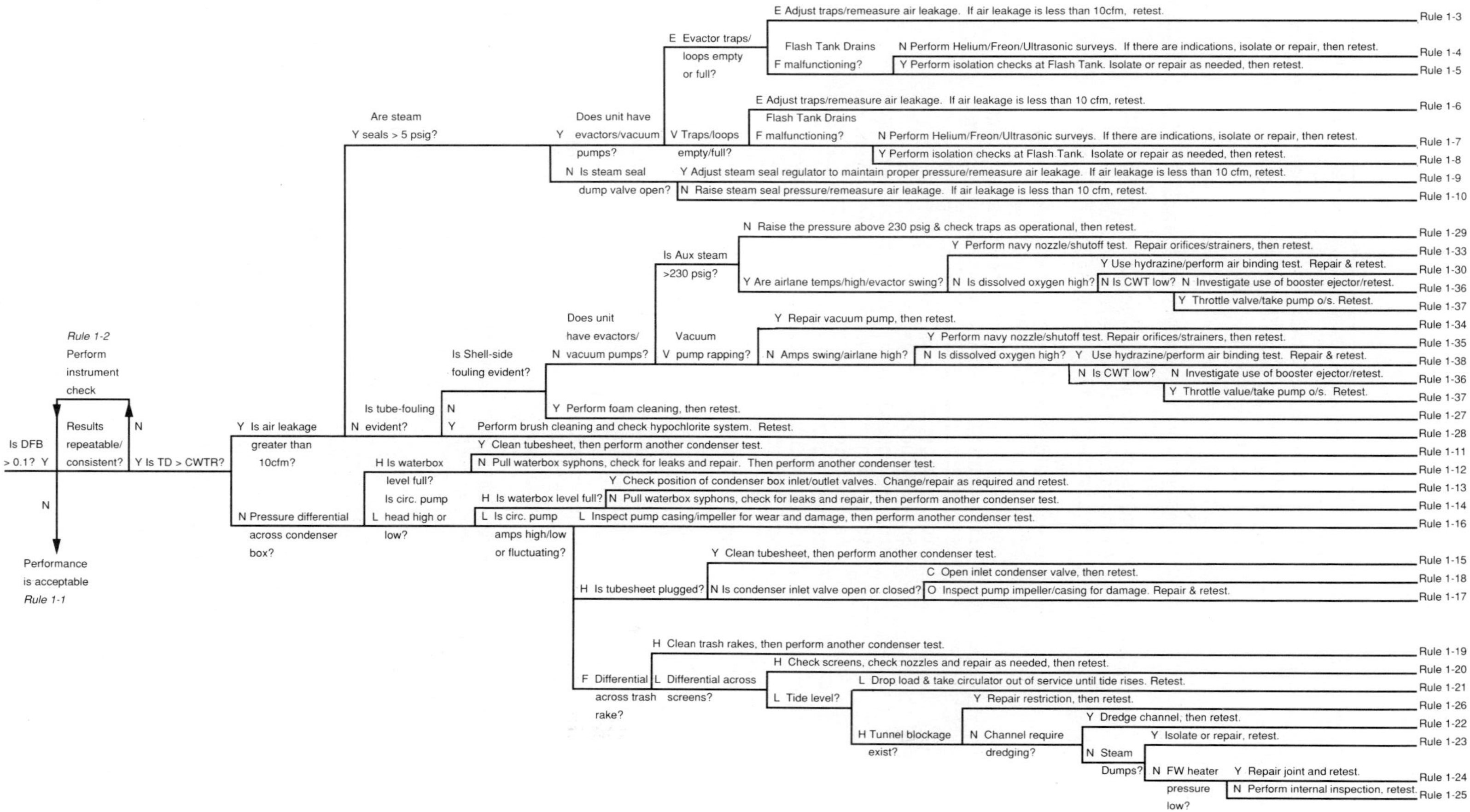

**Figure 18–11.** Condenser Inefficiency Diagnosis KBS—Decision Table (Initial Prototype System)

```
Based on the answers you have given, we recommend that an
internal turbine steam space inspection be performed, followed
by repairs and another condenser test.'
,nl,nl,nl,nl,nl,nl])
then recommendation = shown-25.

rule-1-26:
if deviation-from-bogey = X and
X >= 1000 and
results-repeatable = yes and
terminal-difference-dfb = Z and
circulating-water-temperature-rise-dfb = Y and
Y > Z and
pressure-differential-across-box = low and
circulating-pump-head = low and
circulating-pump-amps = fluctuating and
differential-across-trash-rake = low and
differential-across-screens = low and
tide = high and
tunnel-blockage = yes and
display([nl,nl,nl,nl,nl,nl,nl,nl,nl,'
Based upon the answers you have given, we recommend repairing
the restriction at the tunnel then performing
another condenser test.'
,nl,nl,nl,nl,nl,nl])
then recommendation = shown-26.

question(tube-fouling) = '
Is fouling on the tube side of the condenser evident?'.
legalvals(tube-fouling) = [yes,no].
question(shell-side-fouling) = '
Is fouling on the shell side of the condenser evident?'.
legalvals(shell-side-fouling) = [yes,no].
question(auxiliary-steam) = '
Is the auxiliary steam pressure greater than 230psig?'.
legalvals(auxiliary-steam) = [yes,no].
question(air-lane-temp-or-evactor-swing) = '
Are the air lane temperatures high or the evactor swinging?'.
legalvals(air-lane-temp-or-evactor-swing) = [yes,no].
question(dissolved-oxygen) = '
Is the dissolved oxygen in the hotwell high?'.
legalvals(dissolved-oxygen) = [yes,no].
question(circulating-water-temperature) = '
Is the circulating water temperature lower than 40F?'.
legalvals(circulating-water-temperature) = [yes,no].
question(vacuum-pump-rapping) = '
Is the vacuum pump rapping?'.
legalvals(vacuum-pump-rapping) = [yes,no].
question(vacuum-pump-amps) = '
Are the vacuum pump amps swinging or low or the air lane
temperatures high?'.
legalvals(vacuum-pump-amps) = [yes,no].
```

**Figure 18–12.** Sample: Rules and Questions

```
Based on the answers you have given, we recommend that an internal
turbine steam space inspection be performed, followed by repairs
and another condenser test.'
,nl,nl,nl,nl,nl,nl])
then recommendation = shown-25.

rule-1-26:
if deviation-from-bogey = X and
X >= 1000 and
results-repeatable = yes and
terminal-difference-dfb = Z and
circulating-water-temperature-rise-dfb = Y and
Y > Z and
pressure-differential-across-box = low and
circulating-pump-head = low and
circulating-pump-amps = fluctuating and
differential-across-trash-rake = low and
differential-across-screens = low and
tide = high and
tunnel-blockage = yes and
display ([nl,nl,nl,nl,nl,nl,nl,nl,nl,'
Based upon the answers you have given, we recommend repairing
the restriction at the tunnel then performing
another condenser test.'
,nl,nl,nl,nl,nl,nl])
then recommendation = shown-26.

question(tube-fouling) = '
Is fouling on the tube side of the condenser evident?'.
legalvals(tube-fouling) = [yes,no].
question(shell-side-fouling) = '
Is fouling on the shell side of the condenser evident?'.
legalvals(shell-side-fouling) = [yes,no].
question(auxiliary-steam) = '
Is the auxiliary steam pressure greater than 230psig?'.
legalvals(auxiliary-steam) = [yes,no].
question(air-lane-temp-or-evactor-swing) = '
Are the air lane temperatures high or the evactor swinging?'.
legalvals(air-lane-temp-or-evactor-swing  = [yes,no].
question(dissolved-oxygen) = '
Is the dissolved oxygen in the hotwell high?'.
```

*continued*

**Figure 18–12** *continued*

```
legalvals(dissolved-oxygen) = [yes,no].
question(circulating-water-temperature) = '
Is the circulating water temperature lower than 40F?'.
legalvals(circulating-water-temperature) = [yes,no].
question(vacuum-pump-rapping) = '
Is the vacuum pump rapping?'.
legalvals(vacuum-pump-rapping) = [yes,no].
question(vacuum-pump-amps) = '
Are the vacuum pump amps swinging or low or the air lane
temperatures high?'.
legalvals(vacuum-pump-amps) = [yes,no].
```

*Shell side fouling*—Fouling of the external surfaces of condenser tubes.
*Auxiliary steam*—High-pressure steam used for various plant purposes.
*Traps/loops*—Devices used to capture heat of vaporization.
*Air lanes*—Piping from condenser used to remove accumulated air.

## EXERCISE

The disks accompanying this book contain the prototype KBS described at the end of this chapter. Following the directions accompanying the disks for using the M.1 expert system shell, run a consultation using the system, which has the file name TURBINE. If you wish, you might also print out the knowledge base and study it while you are running the system and restudying this chapter.

# 19

# Logistics Planning

This chapter describes a knowledge-based system for use at a major international company to determine the suitability of a manufacturing country as a supplier of finished goods to a nonmanufacturing country.

The discussion of this system and its development covers:

- The situation to be prototyped
- Documenting the prototype system
- Enhancing the prototype system

## THE SITUATION TO BE PROTOTYPED

The general area under study is operations management. The main strategic goal of operations management in the situation studied is the management of materials, distribution, prices, and costs, both to serve the needs of overseas markets, and to ensure the judicious use of corporate resources.

In international companies, operations management is organized into several functional areas, as shown in Figure 19–1:

- *Production Planning and Inventory Control* involves determining strategic and operational needs and use of raw materials, bulks (semi-processed products), and finished goods.

**Figure 19–1.** Operations Management Overview

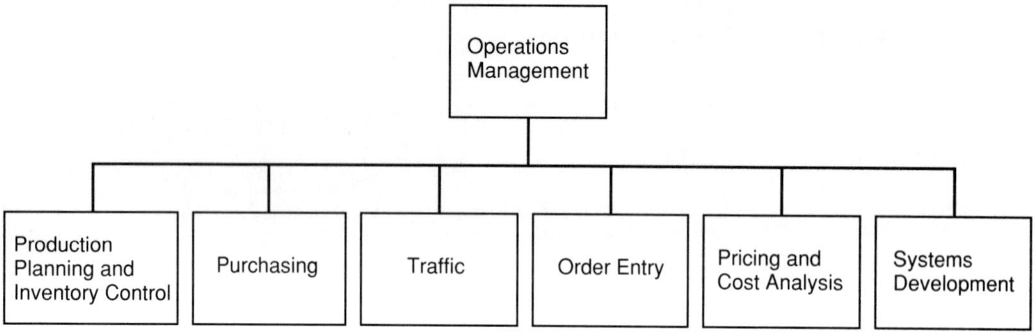


- *Purchasing* involves making strategic decisions when buying materials that are going to be used worldwide.
- *Traffic* involves strategic and operational decisions on how to move these materials from one country to another, making effective use of distribution channels.
- *Order Entry* involves placing overseas orders with either domestic or foreign plants.
- *Pricing and Cost Analysis* involves determining manufacturing costs and setting prices worldwide, based on costs and strategic positioning of the product(s) with respect to the competition.
- *Systems Development* involves developing computer and other types of systems useful in making operations decisions and managing operations.

The focus of this initial prototype of the decision-making area was narrowed to the Product Planning and Inventory Control (PPIC) area. The KBS prototype was further narrowed to one function of PPIC, the sourcing of finished goods. This initial prototype system is designed to help determine the best or optimum supply source of finished goods for a nonmanufacturing country, that is, a country in which the company does not have a manufacturing plant. The decision process involved in sourcing is outlined in Figure 19–2.

As illustrated in Figure 19–2, a decision situation arises when a nonmanufacturing market asks the PPIC department for direction about which manufacturing country to use as a source for, as an example, a new product that it wants to introduce. The finished products sourcing decision is usually handled by a materials analyst and involves the following steps:

1. The analyst first determines in what geographical area the requesting market is located. Once the area is determined, the analyst follows specific sourcing guidelines for that area.
2. Each area is normally supplied by a designated international warehouse (or Supply Point). The analyst reviews the inventory report for that

**Figure 19–2.** Overall Decision Area: Determining Source of Finished Goods, International Operations

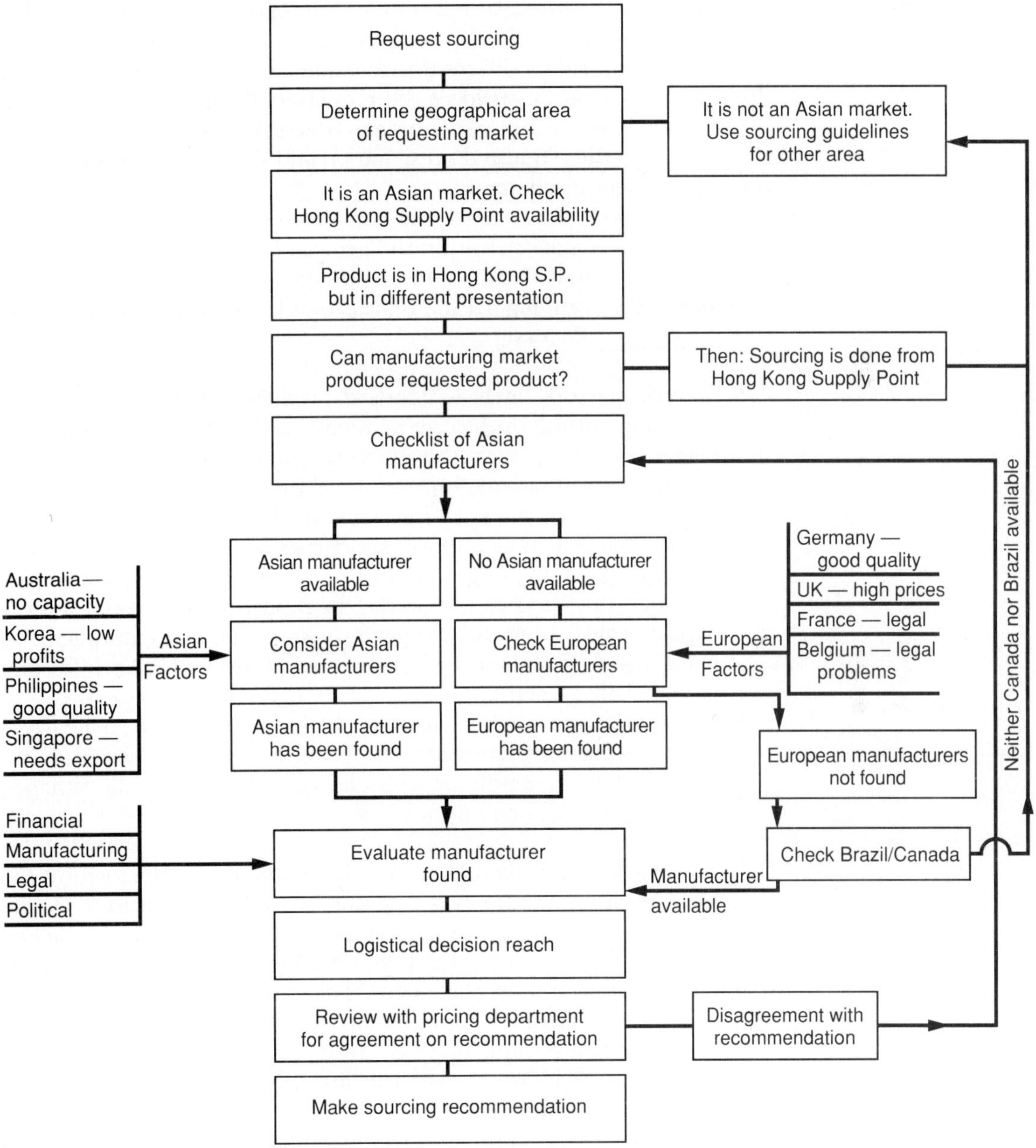

Supply Point to determine if it carries the requested product. If it does, the problem is resolved, since supplying from the Supply Point is always the first choice. If the Supply Point does not have the product, the analyst checks the forecast report to see if it is going to have that product when it is needed. Another option could be that the Supply Point has the requested product in a different presentation (for example, packaged as 20 units per carton, instead of the requested 15 units per carton). An effort is made to determine if the manufacturing country can package the product in the requested presentation and ship it to the Supply Point on time to meet the demand.

3. If all the above fails, then the analyst reviews a list of sourcing (manufacturing) markets within the geographical area, looking for one that either now manufactures the requested product or has the capacity to make it. If a sourcing area(s) is(are) found, then it is studied in light of the following factors:

    - financial factors, such as standard product cost, product markup, how much of the profits can be repatriated to the parent company, and taxes to be paid in the sourcing country
    - manufacturing factors, such as actual product cost, manufacturing quality, plant capacity, and availability of materials
    - legal factors, such as import/export laws (some countries set ratios of imports to exports), availability of foreign currency to buy material, the need of the market to export (based on the import/export ratios), and the ownership status of the manufacturing plant—some plants are wholly owned (100 percent), while some are partially owned
    - political factors, such as stability of the government (at peace or experiencing social unrest), the government's relations with the United States (friendly or unfriendly), and its economic situation (growing, stable, or in decline)

If several markets are manufacturing the requested product within the area, then each one of them is examined based on these four factors (financial, manufacturing, legal, and political). A decision is reached weighing all of these factors, with financial factors given the most weight, followed by the need-to-export factor. The market with the best profile, or qualifications, gets the assignment of "sourcing" the nonmanufacturing market. When several options are equal, telexes are sent to the competing sources to see if they can improve their bidding position, usually by reducing their markups.

When there is only one country manufacturing the needed product within the area, a decision is usually reached fairly quickly. If there are several manufacturers, then the Pricing/Costing department gets involved. After the decision is made based on the logistical part of the equation (PPIC), the outcome is given to the Pricing/Costing department to see if the sourcing country also satisfies its criteria. If the two departments agree, they report the results to the requesting market. If they do not agree, the Materials group reworks its sourcing methodology. If they still are in disagreement, a consensus is reached emphasizing the Pricing/Costing concerns. These steps are outlined in Figure 19–2.

4. If the search for a manufacturing country in the specific area/market fails, then the search begins again within the next closest geographical area, going back to Step 2 of this outline.
5. Another decision that can be made with respect to sourcing, in which the Materials Analyst is not involved, is to use a third party manufacturer, most likely one from the same country as the nonmanufacturing market. These decisions are made by upper management within Operations Services and by the requesting country manager.

In considering the large number of available market sources worldwide, the developers of this KBS decided that the prototype should be narrowed even further to consider only sourcing decisions for Asian countries. The Asian area was chosen for initial prototype development because:

- Asia has well-defined sourcing guidelines.
- There is always a need to make sourcing decisions for Asian markets, because most of them are nonmanufacturing divisions.
- The prototype is part of a larger system, and the reasoning involving decisions in Asia is similar to that in other sourcing decisions worldwide.
- A well-defined area, such as Asia, provides a good testing ground for the concept and structure of an overall system.

### A Typical Decision Scenario

The following is an example of how a sourcing situation is handled in an actual test case scenario. The process described here is outlined in Figure 19–3.

RXC in Malaysia sent a sourcing request to its headquarters for a pharmaceutical product: Feldene 25mg in bottles of 50 capsules, packaged in boxes of 100 bottles per box. RXC needed 100 boxes per month for 6 months, starting on September 1.

The Materials Analyst at headquarters first determines Malaysia's geographical area to be Asia. The Supply Point, according to the Asia Sourcing Guidelines, is located in Hong Kong. The analyst then determines if the requested product is available in the Hong Kong Supply Point.

Two reports are used to determine availability: the Hong Kong Supply Point Inventory Report and the Shipment Forecast report (from the manufacturing area). The Inventory Report is studied first, showing that Feldene 25 mg in bottles of 50 capsules is not in inventory. The next step is to determine if Feldene 25 mg, regardless of the number of capsules per bottle, is in inventory

**Figure 19–3.** Decision Area to be Prototyped: Logistics Planning—Determining Source of Finished Goods

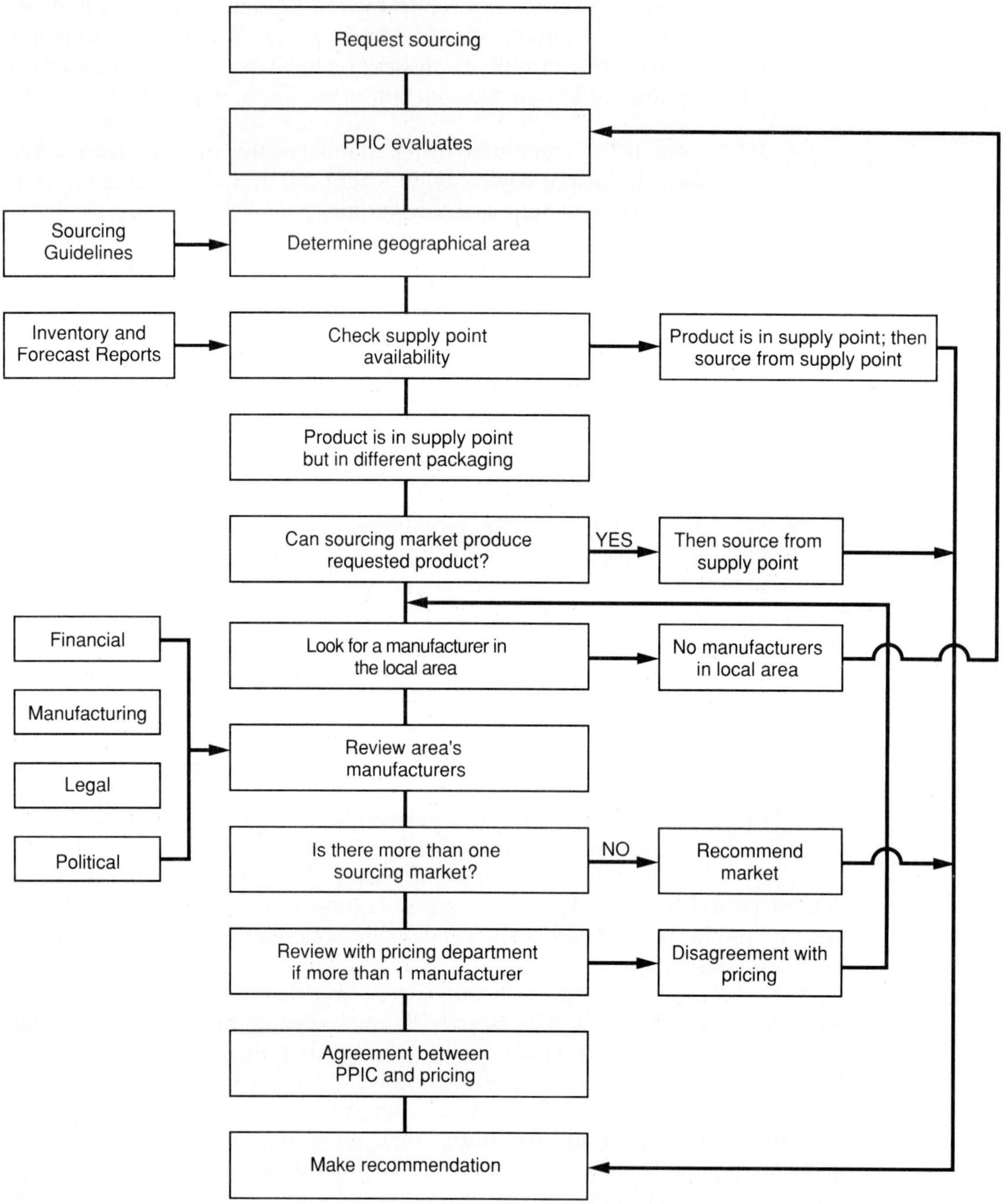

at all. If this were the case, the manufacturer could repackage Feldene 25 mg in bottles of 50 capsules as requested by Malaysia. In this scenario, there is no inventory for Feldene 25 mg in Hong Kong.

The Shipments Forecast report is studied next to verify if there are going to be future shipments to the Hong Kong Supply Point of Feldene 25 mg. A review reveals that there is no forecasted shipment of the product. At this point, the analyst concludes that the Hong Kong Supply Point cannot be used as a supplier of the requested product.

The analyst next determines what Asian manufacturers are producing Feldene 25 mg in bottles of 50 capsules. This search produces two prospective sources: Australia and the Philippines. The Sourcing Guidelines indicate that Australia has a capacity problem and is currently manufacturing Feldene 25 mg for domestic consumption only. Australia is therefore eliminated as a candidate for sourcing.

The Materials Analyst next examines the Philippines. The financial factors studied show that the standard product cost is average, it has a low markup on the product, and the percentage of profits that can be sent back to the parent company in the United States is high. Therefore, overall, the financial factors are favorable.

Study of manufacturing factors shows that actual product cost is average, product quality is high, plant capacity is good, and materials availability is also good. Overall manufacturing factors are also favorable.

Study of legal factors reveals that import laws are flexible (low), the need to export is high, and ownership status is high (the Phillipine manufacturer is wholly owned). Overall legal factors are therefore favorable.

Political factors analyzed show that the government is not stable (low), relations with the United States are good (high), and the economic situation is low. In this case, overall political factors are average.

At this point the Materials Analyst assesses the outcome of this evaluation of the Philippines Supply Point:

| | |
|---|---|
| Financial factors | = favorable |
| Manufacturing factors | = favorable |
| Legal factors | = favorable |
| Political factors | = average |

Based on the analysis, a recommendation is made to use the Philippines to supply Malaysia with Feldene 25 mg in bottles of 50 capsules. This decision is taken to the Pricing/Cost department. After a study of all the factors, they agree to use the Philippines as a source.

In this situation, an Asian manufacturer was found. There are, however, cases where there are no viable sourcing candidates in Asia. The analyst would then check European manufacturers. Germany is considered first because it has favorable export laws. The United Kingdom has excellent quality but its prices are high, while France and Belgium have too many import/export restrictions. If the search for a European source fails, Brazil is considered because it has excess capacity, followed by Canada, due to its high quality and reasonable prices. Once a country outside the Asian area is found, it is submitted to the same analysis of financial, manufacturing, legal, and political factors described in the preceding section.

The initial prototype KBS described in the following section replicates the kinds of logistical decisions made to determine a suitable finished-goods source for nonmanufacturing countries.

## DOCUMENTING THE PROTOTYPE SYSTEM

The discussion in this section covers:

- description of the system
- dependency diagrams
- decision charts
- designing and constructing the knowledge base

### Description of the System

***System Overview and Objective.*** The KBS prototype developed during the first phase of the project is designed to help a Materials Analyst in selecting a suitable source of finished goods for a nonmanufacturing country. A sourcing situation arises when a nonmanufacturing market requests direction on the sourcing of a finished good. The Materials Analyst uses this KBS to determine the availability of a supply source in terms of financial, manufacturing, legal, and political factors.

The first phase of the project is limited to a specific type of decision, selecting the source of finished goods in Asia. This phase is designed to help test and build concepts and structure for a larger system that will cover the sourcing of raw materials and semi-processed products, as well as finished goods, worldwide.

The prototype first questions the user about the availability of the Hong Kong Supply Point as a supplier of the requested product. If this search fails, it next asks questions about the availability of another prospective supplier country. Specific factors are examined to assess the candidate country's suitability. The KBS system assesses these factors and makes recommendations one country at a time. The Materials Management Analyst then makes the final decision about what country to use as a source of the requested product.

***Recommendations To Be Made by the System.*** For prototyping purposes, the system is limited to making these recommendations:

1. Whether the marketing country can be supplied from the area's Supply Point, or international warehouse. If the answer is "yes," then the recommendation is to ship from the Supply Point.

2. Whether some other manufacturing country can be used as a supplier of finished goods to the marketing country. If "yes," the system will qualify the supplier country as

   - optimum
   - favorable
   - average
   - unfavorable

***Nature of the User Interface, Including Typical User Dialogue.*** The typical user dialogue covers two key knowledge areas:

- *The international warehouse availability.* This information is obtained from a monthly inventory report. Some typical questions are: "Does the Hong Kong Supply Point carry this product?" and "Does the Supply Point carry the particular presentation (packaging) requested?".
- *The candidate(s) market.* This information is obtained from a variety of sources: the manufacturing group, cost factors, and pricing, tax, and legal factors. Some typical questions are: "What is the product markup?" "What is the ownership status of the manufacturing plant?" and "Are there any import/export restrictions?"

***Description of the Knowledge Structure and Reasoning Processes.*** The recommendations made by the system are based on two critical factors: availability of the requested product in the international warehouse and the suitability of a manufacturing country as a source of supply of finished goods. These two factors are further defined by the user's input:

1. *Availability of requested product in the Supply Point* is determined by the current available inventory in the warehouse and forecasted inventory for the next year. Consideration is also given to the existence of the product in a different packaging presentation.
2. *Suitability of a manufacturing country* is determined by manufacturing, financial, political, and legal factors.

   - *Manufacturing factors* are defined by the quality of the product, plant capacity, actual manufacturing costs, and materials availability to satisfy demand.
   - *Financial factors* are determined by standard manufacturing costs, the country's markup above manufacturing cost, and the percentage of profits that the parent company can repatriate.
   - *Legal factors* are determined by the manufacturing country's import/export laws, the ownership status of the manufacturing facilities, and the need of the sourcing country to export goods.
   - *Political factors* are determined by issues such as the stability of the government, its relations with the United States, the country's economy, and the like.

Boolean logic and IF-THEN rules are used to assign values to the user's input. Using backward chaining techniques, the prototype KBS system follows alternative questioning and reasoning paths to infer and make recommendations.

The recommendations made by the initial prototype system are based on two critical factors:

- Availability of the Hong Kong Supply Point as a supply source. If this is true, then the system always recommends to use the Supply Point as a source of finished goods.
- Suitability of a candidate market as a supply source. Candidate countries are evaluated based on financial, manufacturing, legal, and political

**Figure 19–4.** Dependency Diagram Logistics Planning: Determining Source of Finished Goods—(Initial Prototype)

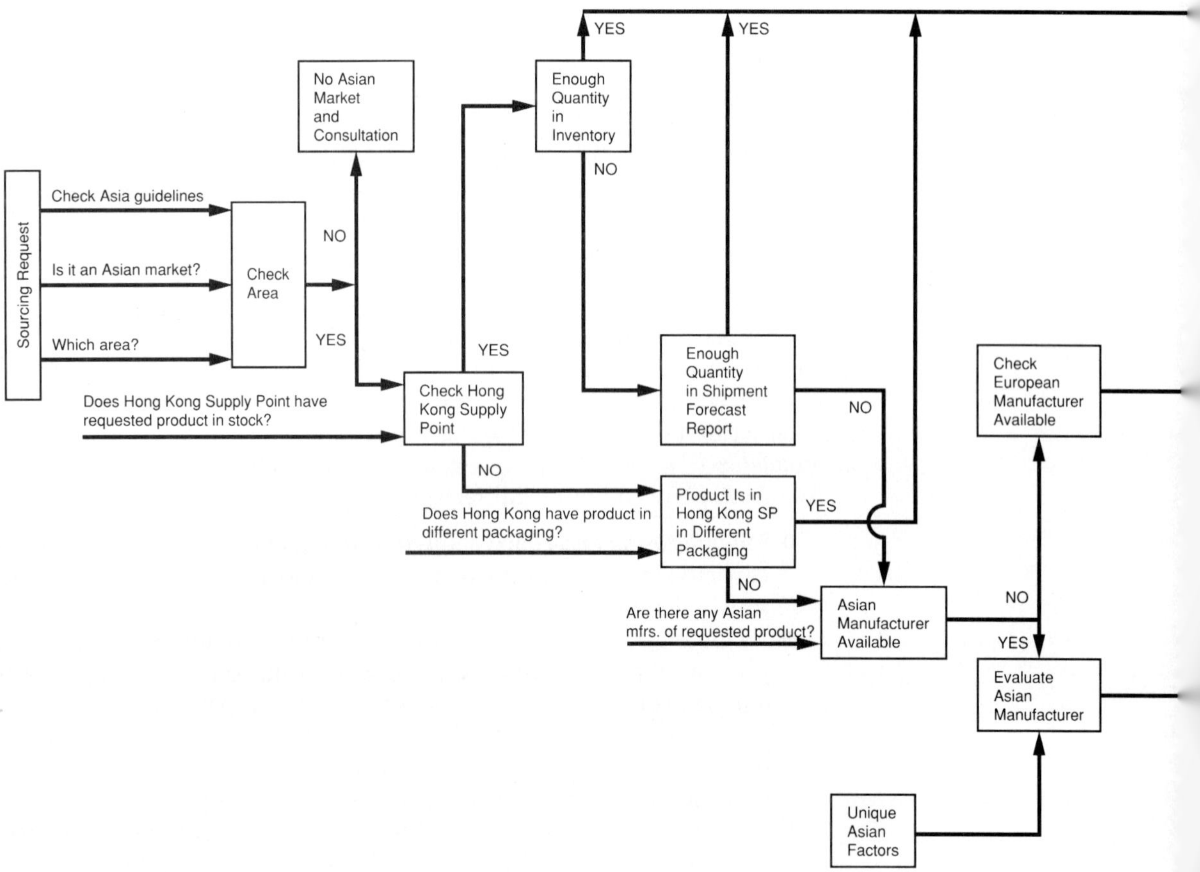

factors. Each of these factors can be either favorable, unfavorable, or average. These four factors are evaluated together, and the conclusion is either an optimum, favorable, average, or unfavorable candidate. Once an optimum or favorable conclusion is reached, the system stops examining candidate countries.

## Dependency Diagrams

Figure 19–4 shows the overall dependency diagram for the Sourcing of Finished Goods in Asia KBS prototype. It is a summary outline of the questions, rules, knowledge segments and their interrelationships, values, and recommendations within the system.

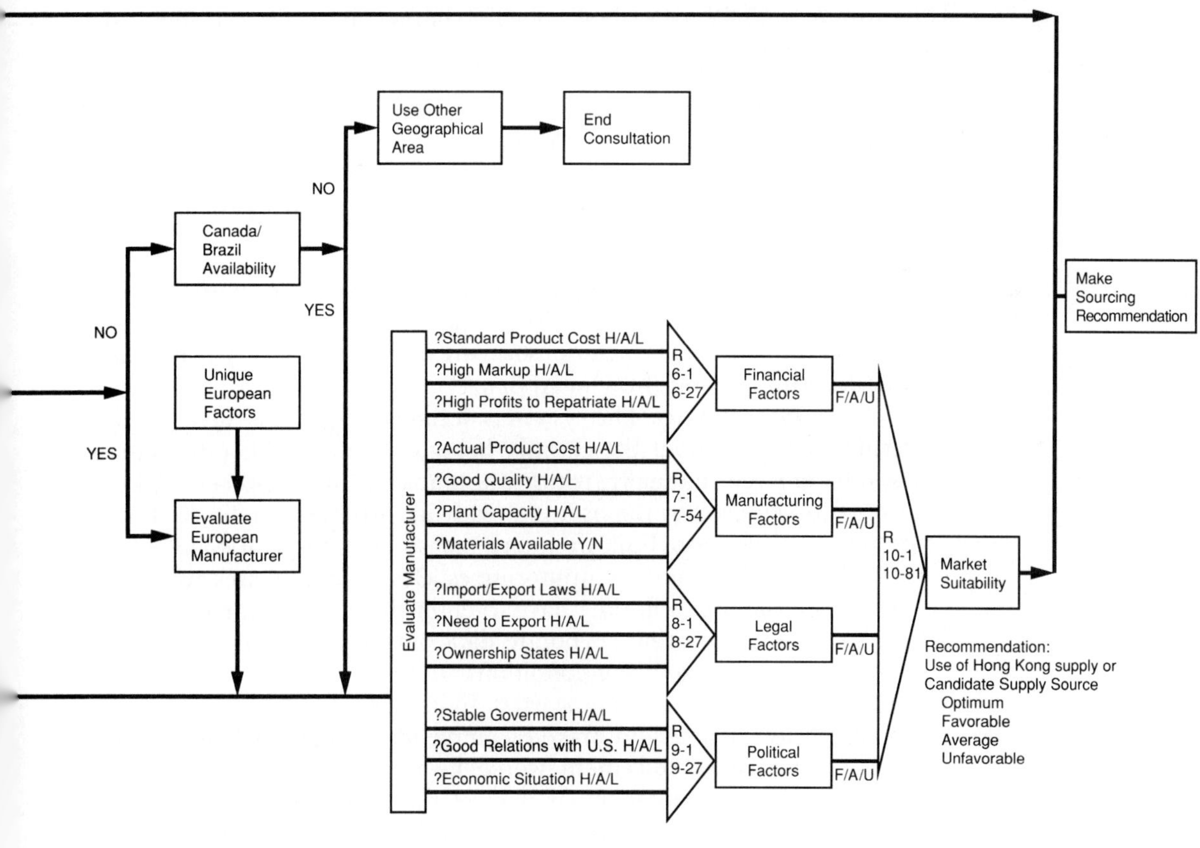

### Decision Charts

Figure 19–5 shows a sample decision chart from the final rule set of the Sourcing of Finished Goods in Asia KBS. Decision charts are one of the tools used to document the reasoning process involved in constructing the KBS. There is a decision chart for every rule set in the system.

### Designing and Constructing the Knowledge Base

Rules and questions were constructed from the situation under study. They were developed by examining the sourcing decision-making process of Material Analysts. Portions of the Sourcing Guidelines for Asia documentation, as well as other published references, were also used in developing this KBS prototype system.

A sample segment of the knowledge base from the prototype system is given in Figure 19–6. The expert system shell used to develop the system was M.1.

The prototype KBS described in this chapter is given on the disks accompanying this book.

## ENHANCING THE PROTOTYPE SYSTEM

Several areas have been identified by the developer for possible enhancements and extensions to this KBS prototype system:

- *Worldwide finished goods sourcing guidelines.* Only the Asian finished goods sourcing guidelines are built into the initial prototype system. The system could be expanded to include sourcing guidelines for Africa, Latin America, Europe, and the United States.
- *Use of corporate databases.* The system is designed to prompt the user with specific questions about the country being evaluated. This information has to be entered manually, which is a time-consuming process. All the information entered by the user is already in corporate databases. There are plans to develop built-in interfaces so that these databases are available to the KBS as data input sources. Once the databases are linked to the KBS, the user will only have to enter the country name, and the KBS will use the existing corporate databases to assess factors such as financial and manufacturing conditions.
- *Comparison of multiple candidate markets.* In its current form, the prototype is designed to evaluate and make recommendations on one country at a time. A valuable enhancement would be to enable the user to enter several countries simultaneously and let the system assess them using certainty factors. It would then rate each market in turn and make a recommendation about which country would be the best supply source.

**Figure 19–5.** Logistics Planning: Determining Source of Finished Goods—Sample Decision Charts (Initial Prototype)

| | FACTORS | 1 | 2 | 3 | 4 | 5 | 6 | 7 | 8 | 9 | 10 | 11 | 12 | 13 | 14 | 15 | 16 | 17 | 18 | 19 | 20 | 21 | 22 | 23 | 24 | 25 | 26 | 27 |
|---|---|---|---|---|---|---|---|---|---|---|---|---|---|---|---|---|---|---|---|---|---|---|---|---|---|---|---|---|
| IF | Financial | F | F | F | F | F | F | F | F | F | F | F | F | F | F | F | F | F | F | F | F | F | F | F | F | F | F | F |
| | Manufacturing | F | F | F | F | F | F | F | F | F | F | A | A | A | A | A | A | A | A | U | U | U | U | U | U | U | U | U |
| | Legal | F | F | F | A | A | A | U | U | U | F | F | F | A | A | A | U | U | U | F | F | F | A | A | A | U | U | U |
| | Political | F | A | U | F | A | U | F | A | U | F | A | U | F | A | U | F | A | U | F | A | U | F | A | U | F | A | U |
| THEN: | RECOMMENDATION | O | O | A | F | F | A | A | U | F | A | A | A | A | A | U | U | U | U | U | U | U | U | U | U | U | U | U |

| | | 28 | 29 | 30 | 31 | 32 | 33 | 34 | 35 | 36 | 37 | 38 | 39 | 40 | 41 | 42 | 43 | 44 | 45 | 46 | 47 | 48 | 49 | 50 | 51 | 52 | 53 | 54 |
|---|---|---|---|---|---|---|---|---|---|---|---|---|---|---|---|---|---|---|---|---|---|---|---|---|---|---|---|---|
| IF | Financial | A | A | A | A | A | A | A | A | A | A | A | A | A | A | A | A | A | A | A | A | A | A | A | A | A | A | A |
| | Manufacturing | F | F | F | F | F | F | F | F | F | A | A | A | A | A | A | A | A | A | U | U | U | U | U | U | U | U | U |
| | Legal | F | F | F | A | A | A | U | U | U | F | F | F | A | A | A | U | U | U | F | F | F | A | A | A | U | U | U |
| | Political | F | A | U | F | A | U | F | A | U | F | A | U | F | A | U | F | A | U | F | A | U | F | A | U | F | A | U |
| THEN: | RECOMMENDATION | F | F | A | A | A | A | U | U | U | A | A | A | A | A | A | U | U | U | U | U | U | U | U | U | U | U | U |

| | | 55 | 56 | 57 | 58 | 59 | 60 | 61 | 62 | 63 | 64 | 65 | 66 | 67 | 68 | 69 | 70 | 71 | 72 | 73 | 74 | 75 | 76 | 77 | 78 | 79 | 80 | 81 |
|---|---|---|---|---|---|---|---|---|---|---|---|---|---|---|---|---|---|---|---|---|---|---|---|---|---|---|---|---|
| IF | Financial | U | U | U | U | U | U | U | U | U | U | U | U | U | U | U | U | U | U | U | U | U | U | U | U | U | U | U |
| | Manufacturing | F | F | F | F | F | F | F | F | F | A | A | A | A | A | A | A | A | A | U | U | U | U | U | U | U | U | U |
| | Legal | F | F | F | A | A | A | U | U | U | F | F | F | A | A | A | U | U | U | F | F | F | A | A | A | U | U | U |
| | Political | F | A | U | F | A | U | F | A | U | F | A | U | F | A | U | F | A | U | F | A | U | F | A | U | F | A | U |
| THEN: | RECOMMENDATION | A | A | U | A | U | U | U | U | U | U | U | U | U | U | U | U | U | U | U | U | U | U | U | U | U | U | U |

**KEY** O = Optimum
F = Favorable
A = Average
U = Unfavorable

**Figure 19–6.** Logistics Planning: Determining Source of Finished Goods—Segment of Knowledge Base, Sample Rules (Initial Prototype)

```
/* RULE SET SIX :   VERIFY MARKETS FACTORS (FINANCIAL,
MANUFACTURING, LEGAL AND POLITICAL)  */
/* CHECK FINANCIAL FACTORS  */

rule-6-0-1:   if mkt-name2 = uk
            then markup = high.

rule-6-1:     if std-prod-cost = high and
                 markup = high and
                 profts-back = high
            then fincl-factor = average.

rule-6-2:     if std-prod-cost = high and
                 markup = high and
                 profts-back = avg
            then fincl-factor = average.

rule-6-3:     if std-prod-cost = high and
                 markup = high and
                 profts-back = low
            then fincl-factor = unfavor.

rule-6-4:     if std-prod-cost = high and
                 markup = avg and
                 profts-back = high
            then fincl-factor = favorable.

rule-6-5:     if std-prod-cost = high and
                 markup = avg and
                 profts-back = avg
            then fincl-factor = average.

rule-6-6:     if std-prod-cost = high and
                 markup = avg and
                 profts-back = low
            then fincl-factor = unfavor.

rule-6-7:     if std-prod-cost = high and
                 markup = low and
                 profts-back = high
            then fincl-factor = favorable.

rule-6-8:     if std-prod-cost = high and
                 markup = low and
                 profts-back = avg
            then fincl-factor = favorable.
```

This initial prototype for determining a suitable source for supplying finished goods to Asian markets is a useful tool in building a total system to cover all components of Production Planning and Inventory Control for international companies.

## EXERCISE

The disks accompanying this book contain the prototype KBS described at the end of this chapter. Following the directions accompanying the disks for using the M.1 expert system shell, run a consultation using the system, which has the file name SOURCING. If you wish, you might also print out the knowledge base and study it while you are running the system and restudying this chapter.

# 20

# Product Pricing Strategy in the Computer Industry

This chapter describes the development of a knowledge-based system to assist in creating pricing strategies in the computer manufacturing industry. The topics covered are

- The situation to be prototyped
- Documenting the prototype system

## THE SITUATION TO BE PROTOTYPED

The general area under study is the field of pricing and pricing strategies in the computer industry. This area is applicable to companies that manufacture computers and related products and to wholesalers and retailers who determine markups based on product costs.

As a new product passes through the development phase of the product life cycle, increasingly more specific cost estimates are developed. These costs take into consideration the research, marketing, general and administrative costs, and other fixed and variable costs of manufacturing and marketing a product. They are used as the base for determining a pricing strategy.

Pricing strategy, of which a key element is markup, also depends on the type of product to be priced. Computer products are often categorized into three groups:

- Hardware products include supercomputers, mainframes, minicomputers, and microcomputers. Also included in the category of computer hardware are storage devices, CRTs and monitors, printers, and other miscellaneous items, such as communication devices, mice, and so forth.
- Software is usually segmented into two areas: applications software, which enables computer users to solve specific problems and perform a wide range of tasks; and systems software, which provides the communication between the hardware and the application program.
- Other computer-related products include diskettes, cables, carrying cases, computer furniture, and so forth.

The amount of markup depends on the type of product because the characteristics and profit expectations are different for each category. For example, hardware products might be considered strategic, meaning that once a computer is sold, the customer is locked into certain types of software. There are also different competitor and consumer attitudes in each of the three product categories, which play a role in dictating prices.

Because the field of pricing is so broad and complex, the focus of this initial prototype is limited to *manufacturers of computer hardware products making pricing decisions on new product announcements*. Other pricing decisions, such as pricing for existing products and decisions involving wholesalers and retailers, are not within the scope of this initial prototype KBS.

This KBS is intended to guide a pricing manager in examining all the relevant factors affecting a pricing decision for a computer hardware product. The recommendations made by the initial prototype system are limited to five markup categories: at cost (no markup), low, moderate, high, and extremely high markup. The markup is then used to develop the list price announced for the product.

Figure 20–1 outlines the decision area to be prototyped. As shown in the figure, the recommended markup is determined by two sets of factors: primary and secondary.

The two primary factors, product characteristics and competition, help to determine the strengths of the new product being priced compared to the competitions' products, if any. In the prototype system, the result of this comparison yields a value ranging from "very weak" to "very strong," depending on the strength or weakness of the new product. The secondary factors, strategic and financial, must be evaluated in order to narrow the price range and determine the specific markup. The values for these factors range from "low" to "high."

## Primary Factors

***Product Characteristics.*** Figure 20–2 outlines the product characteristics studied. This area involves four product factors: type, function, effects on existing products, and outside sourcing from another manufacturer.

**Figure 20–1.** Diagram of Decision Area to be Prototyped—Pricing Strategy for Computer Hardware

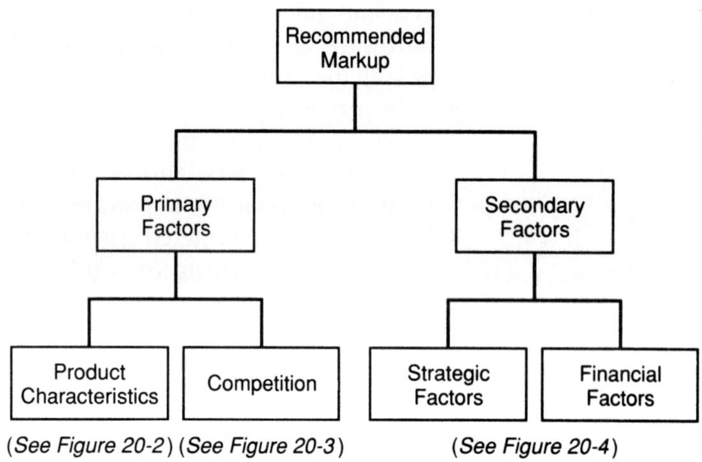


- Type of product is important to a pricing decision since different types of products command different markups. For example, a low markup might be appropriate for a strategic product, such as a new operating system, since a company could expect to "lock in" customers and profits from future product sales tied into that operating system. On the other hand, stand-alone products are major systems, such as microcomputers or mainframes, which generally carry higher markups.
- The function of the product affects markup because consumers are generally willing to pay higher prices for a product with more and improved functions, or one which complements existing products. The amount of functions (determined by the capabilities and expandability of the product), the degree of high-technology, how new the technology is, and product ease-of-use determine overall functionality on markup. These elements combine to determine a value for the function of the product, ranging from "low" to "high" in the initial prototype KBS.
- If a product is a follow-on to an existing product, or can be substituted for it, such as an upgraded personal computer, then a low price on the new product may force the inventory of the existing product to be scrapped. In this case, a higher markup, at least initially, may be preferable. The pricing manager must also find out the willingness of management to change the prices on existing products to help deplete inventories, should the new product have similar functions and price, and so can be substituted for the existing product.
- Generally speaking, the more outside sourcing, or amount of the product's components produced by outside vendors, the lower the markup that can be considered. This is true because vendors can sell the

**Figure 20–2.** Decision Diagram for Computer Hardware Pricing System—Product Characteristics

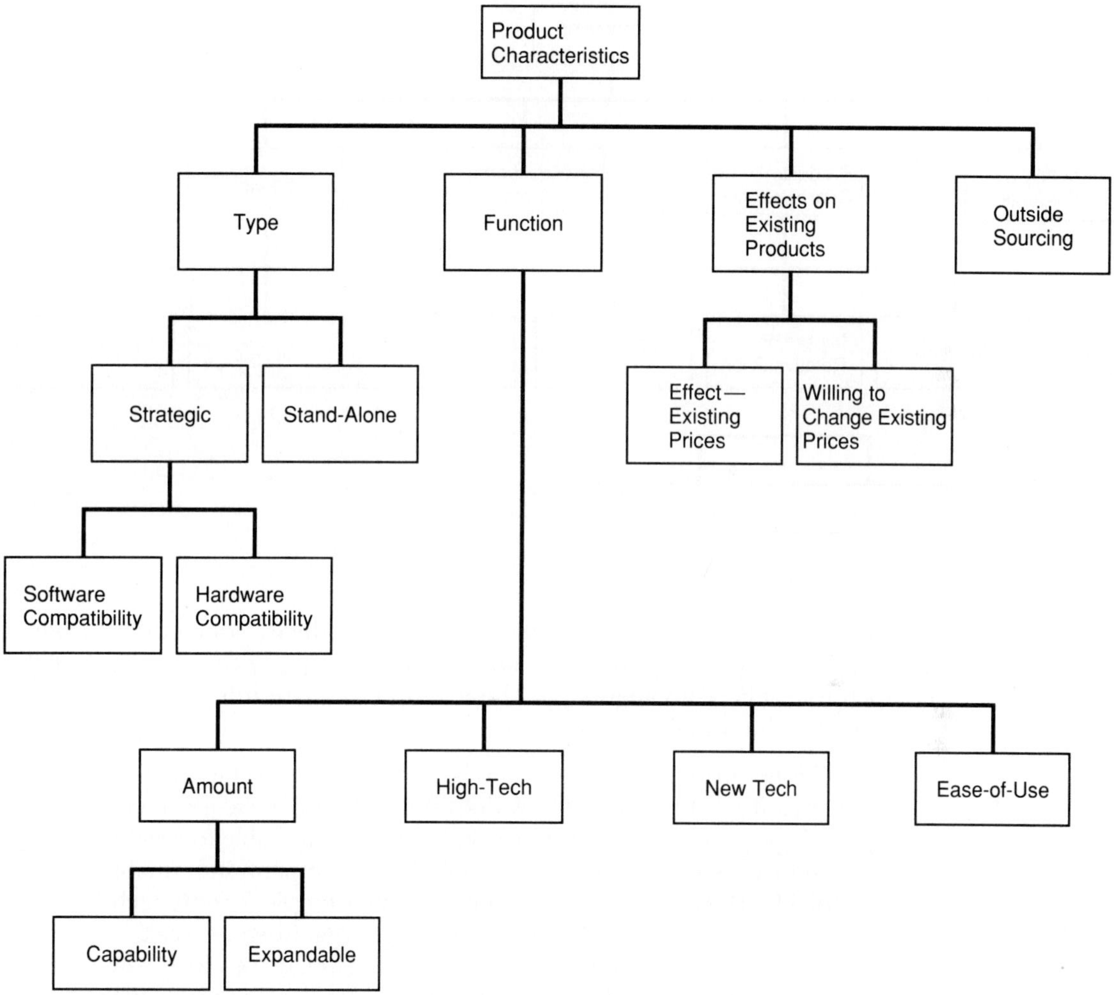


components to many manufacturers and so amortize fixed costs over a larger sales base.

For initial KBS purposes, the combination of these factors result in a value for the product characteristics section ranging from "weak" to "strong."

***Competition.*** Figure 20–3 outlines the factors affecting competition factor analysis. Four factors are examined to determine the strength of the competition

**Figure 20–3.** Decision Diagram for Computer Hardware Pricing System–Competition Characteristics

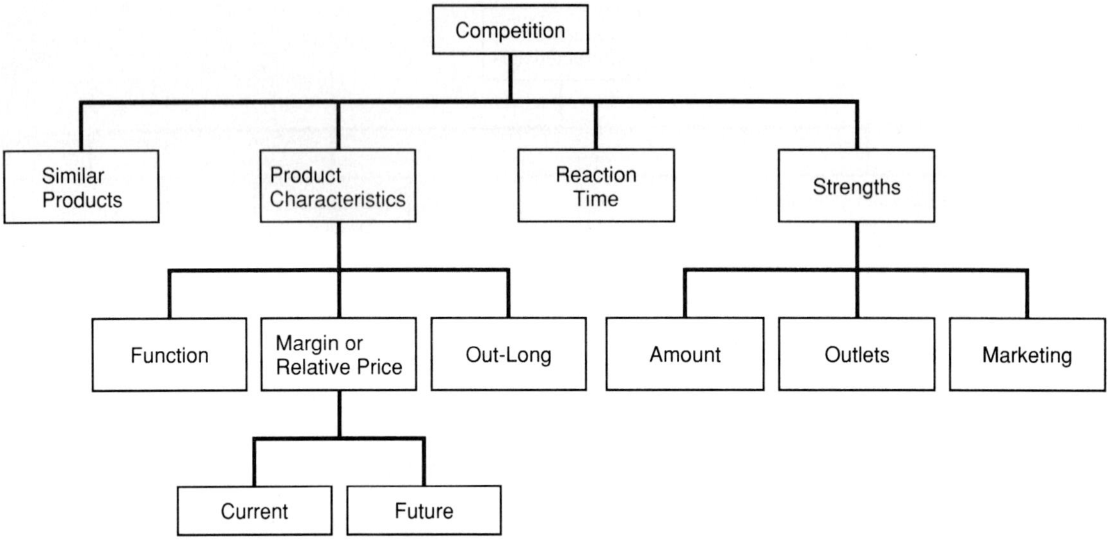


in relation to the company: similarity of the products, competitive product characteristics, the ability of the competition to react, and the strengths of the competition. The combination of these four factors results in a competition assessment value ranging from "weak" to "strong" in this prototype KBS.

- Whether or not the competition has a similar product is critical to pricing decisions. If the competition does not currently have a similar product, their position is considered weak, unless they are able to react quickly to produce a competitive new product. If the competition is unable to react quickly, possibly because the new product employs some technological breakthrough, then this value would again be rated as weak.
- Assuming competitors do not have a similar product, the pricing manager needs to estimate their ability to react, or to quickly develop and market a competing product. Another scenario is that the competition may be ready to announce a similar product. Determining the ability of the competition to react is based upon understanding the competitors' profiles, including past product announcements, recent technology used, product schedules, information from industry vendors and other industry sources, and the like.
- If competitors have a similar product, it is necessary to determine their product's characteristics. If the competition's products are better in terms of function, a lower markup may be considered. If they have a low

margin or relative price, or if the competition is likely to drop their prices, a lower markup may also be in order. The same low markup may be applicable if the competition's products have been out in the market for a long time.

- The strengths of the competition in relation to those of the company under study are also critical. Factors affecting these relative strengths are the number of competitors, the number of outlets they have, and the kind and amount of marketing they are capable of and expected to invest in.

### Secondary Factors

As seen in Figure 20–4, key secondary factors in pricing decisions are *strategic factors* and *financial factors*. A company about to announce a product may have a particular strategy (for example, to improve market share in relation to competitors, or maximize short-term profit) or a reputation which will influence pricing. Financial factors first consider sales forecasts, which are needed to determine the fixed costs allocated to each unit of sales, and so the market or price needed to cover costs and break even. Another factor, customer price sensitivity, helps to determine an upper limit to the price or markup a manufacturer can charge. Any potential substitutes for the product might limit the markup as well.

***Strategic Factors.*** There are two areas of strategic factors:

- The internal strategy of the company may be long-term, focusing on obtaining market share to lock in customers through lower prices. The opposite strategy, a short-term one, is to focus on obtaining maximum profits over the short run, until the competition forces lower prices.
- The reputation of the company, as compared to the competition's, also affects pricing strategy decisions. A company with a superior reputation may be able to command a higher markup on a product. The three measures of reputation are overall reputation, service, and quality.

***Financial Factors.*** There are two major components of financial factors:

- Product forecasts help a pricing manager determine how the product will affect profits. For example, if sales forecasts call for a great number of units to be sold, then the pricer can recommend a slightly lower markup and still achieve profit targets, since fixed costs can be spread over a larger unit sales base. As shown in Figure 20–4, both external and internal factors are examined in making these forecasts.

  External factors, such as size of the market and the competition, as well as the economic climate, affect how many units are sold. The economic climate is studied from both anticipated overall economic

**Figure 20–4.** Decision Diagram for Computer Hardware Pricing System—Secondary Factors

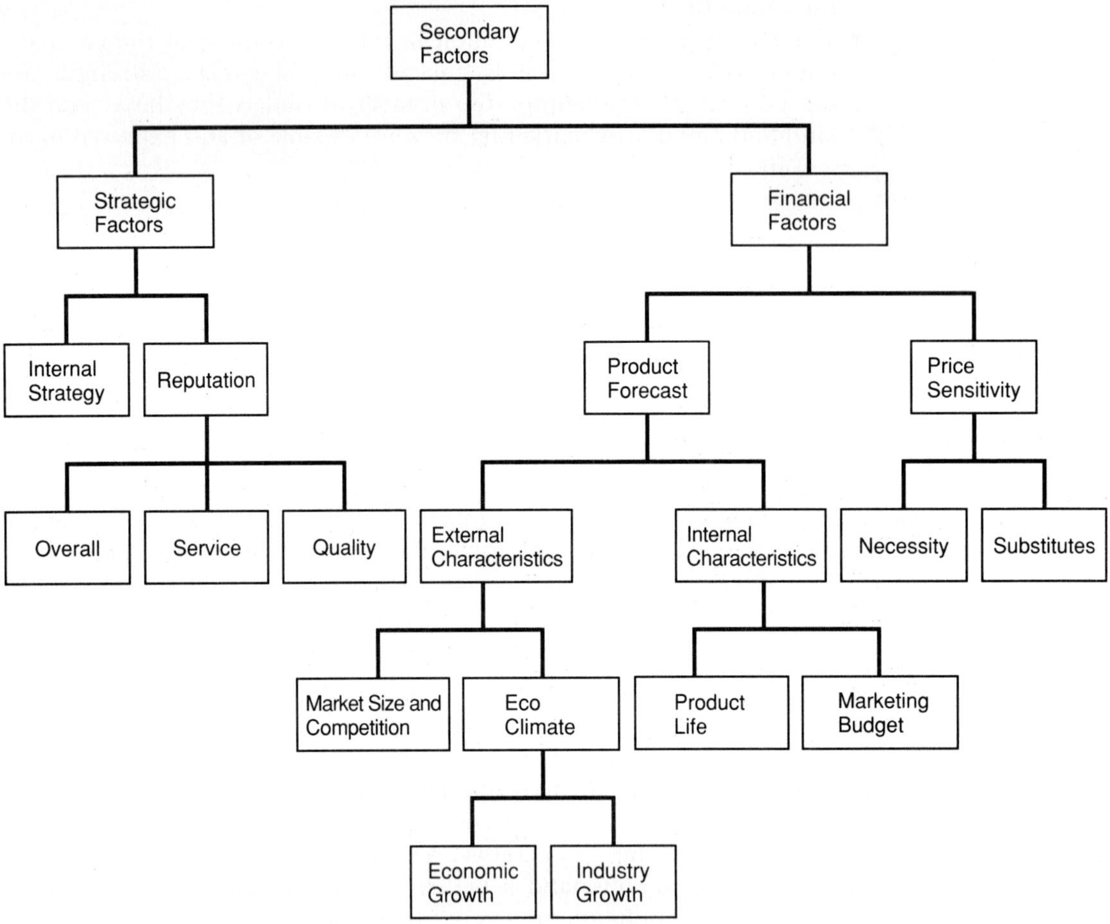


growth and industry growth viewpoints. Internal factors, such as the anticipated product life and the marketing budget allocated to the new product, also will affect the markup decision. The longer the product life and the larger the marketing budget, the higher the number of products likely to be sold, and thus the lower the markup required to meet profit targets.

- Lastly, the degree of customer price sensitivity affects pricing strategy decisions. The factors that determine sensitivity are whether or not the product is a necessity and whether or not any substitutes exist.

### Possible Recommendations and How They Are Made

After evaluating the impact of the above factors and underlying subfactors, five possible strategic recommendations were identified as possible markup recommendations to be made by the initial prototype KBS when introducing a new product:

1. *Introduce the product at cost.* This recommendation would be appropriate where the new product is weak, the competitions' products are strong, and secondary factors are low.
2. *Introduce the product at cost plus a low markup.* This would be appropriate where
   - the new product is weak, the competitors' products are strong, and secondary factors are neutral or high, or
   - the new product is worse than the competitions' and secondary factors are low or neutral, or
   - the new product is similar to the competitions' and secondary factors are low.
3. *Introduce the product at cost plus a moderate markup.* This would be appropriate where
   - the new product is worse than the competitions' but secondary factors are high, or
   - the new product is similar to the competitions' and secondary factors are neutral, or
   - the new product is better than the competitions' and secondary factors are low.
4. *Introduce the product at cost plus a high markup.* This would be appropriate where
   - the new product is stronger than the competitions' and secondary factors are neutral or high, or
   - the new product is much stronger than the competitions' and secondary factors are low or neutral.
5. *Introduce the product at cost plus a very high markup.* This would be appropriate where the new product is much stronger than the competitions' and secondary factors are high.

## DOCUMENTING THE SYSTEM

The discussion in this section covers:

- description of the prototype system
- dependency diagrams

- sample decision chart
- designing and constructing the knowledge base segment

## Description of the Prototype System

***System Overview and Objective.*** The KBS prototype system developed during the first phase of the project is designed to help managers recommend pricing strategies for new hardware products developed by computer manufacturing firms. The initial prototype system developed during the project's first phase described here focuses on a limited range of pricing options for a new computer hardware product in order to test the feasibility of developing a larger KBS for pricing strategy selection. The system was developed using the M.1 expert system shell, which employs IF-THEN rules and backward chaining to reason about the information given by a user (pricing manager) in order to reach its recommendations.

***Recommendations To Be Made by the System.*** The initial prototype system is limited to making five specific recommendations. These are to introduce the product at:

- cost
- cost plus a low markup
- cost plus a moderate markup
- cost plus a high markup
- cost plus an extremely high markup

***Nature of the User Interface.*** The typical user dialogue covers two key knowledge areas, primary and secondary factors:

- *Primary Factors.* Product characteristics, such as product type, function, effects on existing products, and outside sourcing, all play a role in determining the markup. Sample questions include: "Is this product considered to be a stand-alone product?" "Does the product require special software compatibility?," and "Are most of the product's components purchased from vendors?"

  Another major determinant of what a company can charge for a product is the nature of the competition. Sample questions are: "Is there a similar product on the market?" "How many competitors are there?" and "If the competition does not have a similar product, what is the likelihood of their developing one in the near future?"
- *Secondary Factors.* The two specific secondary factor areas examined in this initial KBS prototype are strategic factors and financial factors. Sample strategic factor questions include "How would you define your company's reputation as compared to the competition's?" and "Are there any substitutes for the product being priced that could be used in lieu of the product?" Sample financial factor questions are "How would you

**Figure 20–5.** Computer Hardware Pricing System—Overall Dependency Diagram (Initial Prototype)

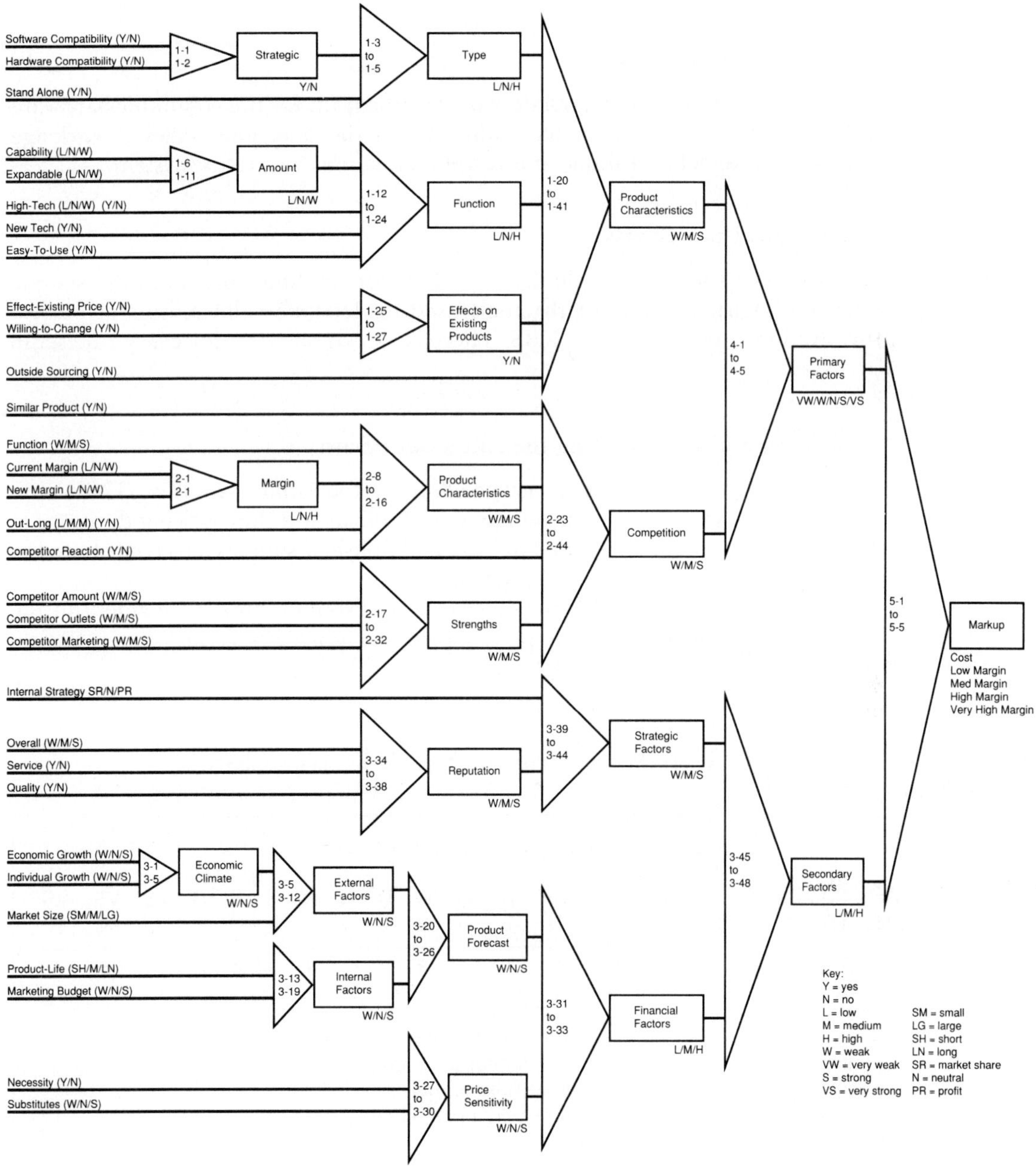

describe the anticipated expenditures and sales force effort that will be made in marketing the new product?" "How large is the market for this product?" and "What is the expected economic growth in the future?"

### Dependency Diagrams

Figure 20–5 shows the overall dependency diagram for the computer hardware pricing KBS. It is a summary outline of all the questions, rules, knowledge segments, interrelationships, and recommendations within the system.

### Sample Decision Charts

Figure 20–6 shows a sample decision chart for the final rule set in the system. Decision charts are one of the tools used to document the reasoning process involved in constructing the KBS. There is a decision chart for every rule set in the system.

### Designing and Constructing the Knowledge Base

Rules and questions were constructed from the situation study. They were developed from the expertise of managers familiar with how pricing decisions in the computer hardware market are made. Published sources also contributed to the expertise built into this KBS prototype.

A partial rule base for the Competitor's Product Strength segment of the hardware pricing KBS prototype is shown in Figure 20–7. The expert system shell used is M.1.

**Figure 20–6.** Computer Hardware Pricing System—Sample Decision Chart (Initial Prototype)

**Final Rule Set Rules—5–1 to 5–5**

| | | | | | | | | | | | | | | | | |
|---|---|---|---|---|---|---|---|---|---|---|---|---|---|---|---|---|
| If | PRIMARY FACTORS | VW | VW | VW | W | W | W | N | N | N | S | S | S | VS | VS | VS |
| | SECONDARY FACTORS | L | N | H | L | N | H | L | N | H | L | N | H | L | N | H |
| Then | RECOMMENDATION | 1 | 2 | 2 | 2 | 2 | 3 | 2 | 3 | 4 | 3 | 4 | 4 | 4 | 4 | 5 |

**Key:**
VW = very weak
W = weak
N = neutral
S = strong
VS = very strong
L = low
H = high

1 = Cost
2 = Low margin
3 = Moderate margin
4 = High margin
5 = Very high margin

**Figure 20–7.** Computer Hardware Pricing System—Segment of Knowledge Base: Sample Rules (Initial Prototype)

```
/*  Rules 2-8 to 2-16  -  C-PROD-STRENGTH  */

        rule-2-8:
             if similar = n and
                reaction = y
             then out-long = n.

        rule-2-9:
             if c-function = w and
                out-long = y
             then c-prod-strength = m.

        rule-2-10:
             if c-function = w and
                out-long = n and
                margin = l
             then c-prod-strength = m.

        rule-2-11:
             if c-function = w and
                out-long = n and
                (margin = m or
                margin = h)
             then c-prod-strength = w.

        rule-2-12:
             if c-function = m
                and out-long = y
             then c-prod-strength = s.

        rule-2-13:
             if c-function = m and
                out-long = n
             then c-prod-strength = m.

        rule-2-14:
             if c-function = s and
                out-long = y
             then c-prod-strength = s.

        rule-2-15:
             if c-function = s and
                out-long = n and
                (margin = l or
                margin = m)
             then c-prod-strength = s.

        rule-2-16:
             if c-function = s and
                out-long = n and
                margin = h
             then c-prod-strength = m.
```

The prototype KBS described in this chapter is given on the disks accompanying this book.

---

**EXERCISE**

The disks accompanying this book contain the prototype KBS described at the end of this chapter. Following the directions accompanying the disks for using the M.1 expert system shell, run a consultation using the system, which has the file name PRICING. If you wish, you might also print out the knowledge base and study it while you are running the system and restudying this chapter.

# Part Six

## SPECIAL TOPICS

# 21

# Object-Based Systems and Shells

This chapter extends earlier discussions of object-oriented systems and shells. The objective of this chapter is to help readers understand the nature of object-based KBS and learn how to develop an object-based KBS using the versions of two object-based development tools included on the disks accompanying this book: ObjectCraft and LEVEL5 OBJECT.

The discussion in this chapter covers:

- An overview of object orientation in computer technologies
- An example of the object-oriented development process
- A comparison of object-oriented with conventional systems
- A discussion of object-based KBS
- A review of object-based PC development shells
- An introduction to object-based development shells using ObjectCraft
- A tutorial to create an object-based KBS using LEVEL5 OBJECT.

## AN OVERVIEW OF OBJECT ORIENTATION

Many computer technologies appear to be—or claim to be —object oriented. There are object-oriented programming languages, operating systems and environments, databases, and development systems among the growing list of object-oriented associations.

Fundamental to all these is the concept of an object. From the viewpoint of object-oriented programming, commonly abbreviated as OOP, an **object** is a data structure which represents anything tangible or abstract. It encapsulates both data and procedures.

Figure 21–1 gives an example of three objects: order object, domestic order object, and foreign order object. The top order object contains three data items: price, number, and total. It also contains a procedure about how to calculate total whenever price and number are filled in:

$$\text{total} = \text{price} \times \text{number ordered}$$

Sometimes the terms "object" and "class" are used interchangeably. Each **class** can be thought of as a template that gives an object its specific structure and behavior characteristics. In the example, there are three classes: the order class, the domestic order class, and the foreign order class.

Class has analogies with a database record structure. A class declaration describes the object's data names, or attributes, which are analogous to field names in a database record. In the example, the attributes for the top class are "price," "number," and "total." Unlike databases, however, classes can contain information about how to obtain the values of their attributes.

Figure 21–1 also shows linkages representing an **inheritance** process by which one class (a parent class) transfers its structure and behavior to another class (a child class). Both the domestic order class and the foreign order class are children, or subclasses, of the parent, or order supraclass. Through inheritance, a child class receives all of the capabilities of its parent class.

Instances often occur at the bottom of an inheritance chain. An **instance** is an object that inherits its structure and behavior from its parent class, and it contains specific values. It is a specific occurrence of an object and is analogous to a database record with data in it. For example, Figure 21–2 shows three instances of the "Fast Food Industry" class. They are Joe's, Marie's, and Jane's Food Services. In an inheritance hierarchy, each instance class inherits all the features of its parent class. In this example, each instance also contains attributes unique to its subclass: "location" and "owned by."

These object-oriented concepts are not new. Work in this field by Douglas Englebart at SRI International was going on in the early 1960s. But the growing interest in object orientation today is caused in part by increasing technological and systems complexity. This concept that links data and procedures provides one way of dealing with this technological complexity in general and with increasing systems complexity in particular.

## DEVELOPMENT PROCESS

The following discussion walks through an example of the overall process involved in developing an object-oriented KBS application. The example is a small subset of a human asset-management application. It determines the

**Figure 21–1.** Object Structure for an Order Processing Application

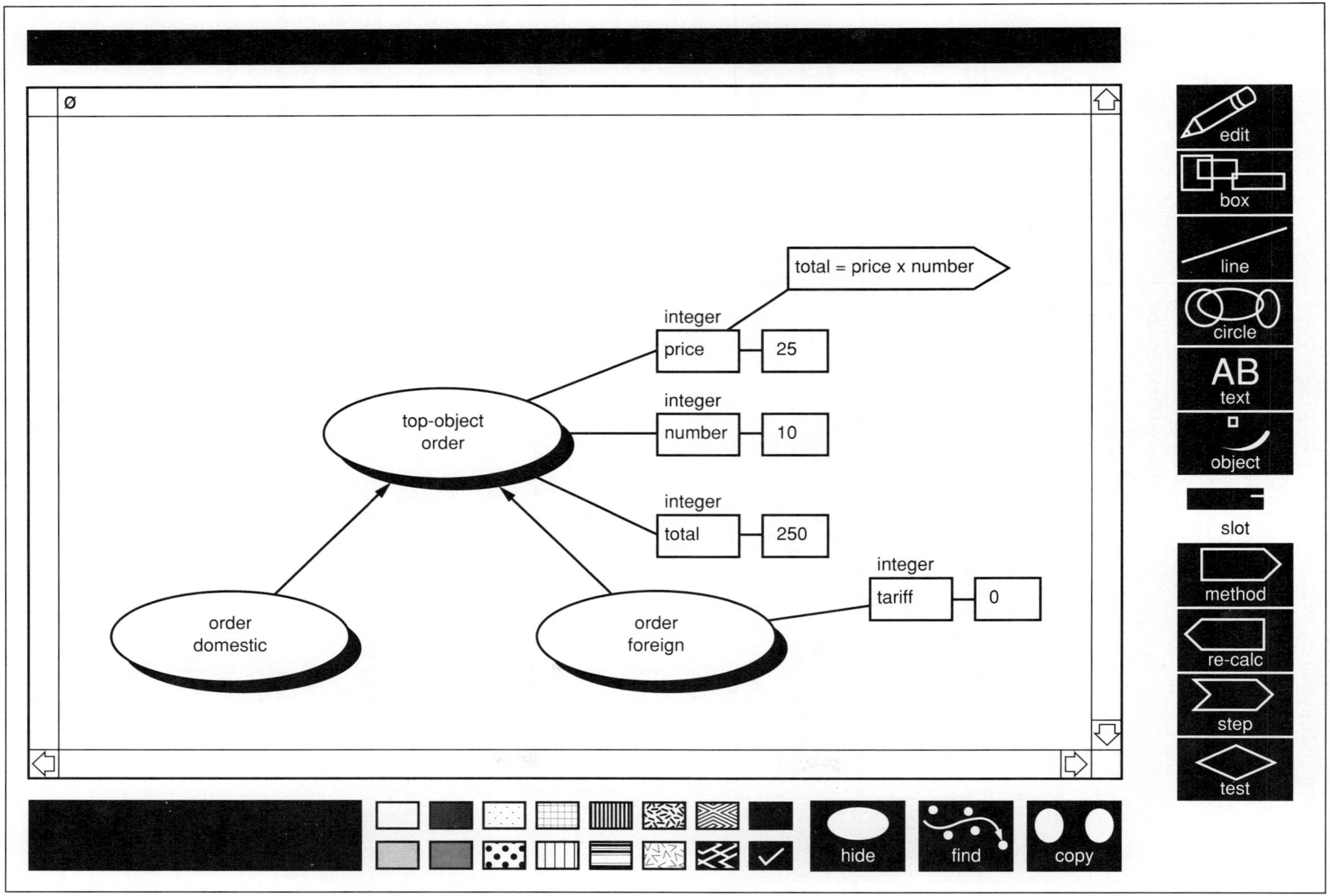

**Figure 21–2.** Prepared Food Service Industry Object Hierarchy

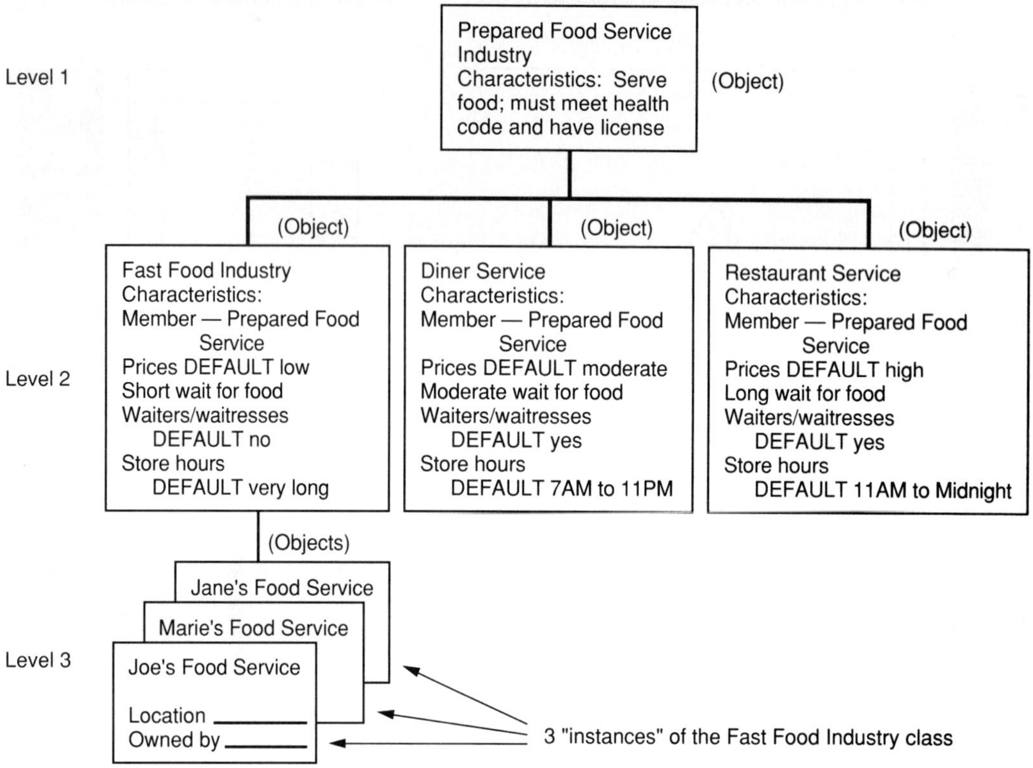


overhead cost of an employee and the employee's benefits. The example is the basis of the LEVEL5 OBJECT tutorial at the end of this chapter. The discussion introduces additional object-oriented concepts.

The overall development process for an object-oriented KBS is somewhat different from a rule-based KBS. With an object-oriented approach, development may proceed through the four following phases:

Phase 1—Define objects, and the relationships between them, or inheritance
Phase 2—Define the attributes of the objects
Phase 3—Define methods for each object
Phase 4—Define the interface

The present discussion will focus on the first three phases.

### Define Objects and Inheritance

Figure 21–3 shows the object structure for the employee example. The topmost class in the hierarchy is "person." Its attributes represent the basic information that is common to all people: name, age, and sex. The next class, "employee," also represents a person, so it inherits the attributes of the person class. The class "employee" is the child of its parent class, "person." In addition, an employee has the unique attributes "salary" and "overhead cost." So it is evident that while all employees are persons, the reverse is not true. All persons are not necessarily employees, and the attributes of "employee" are not inherited by the class person. This one-way hierarchy is an important characteristic of object inheritance. A class can inherit from more than one class, that is, have multiple parents, but a parent class cannot inherit from its child. A parent class can be a child of another, different parent class.

In this class network, an employee also belongs to a department. However, a department consists of a much different set of logically related characteristics, so it forms a separate class. Since an employee has a department, it inherits the department class and its attributes, "department name" and "cost factor."

The remaining class in the hierarchy, "benefits," represents another set of related items consisting of the type of benefits an employee may have. Again, since the benefits are related items, it was found useful to group them in a separate class. The employee class also inherits the "benefits" class.

**Figure 21–3.** Object Structure for the Employee Example

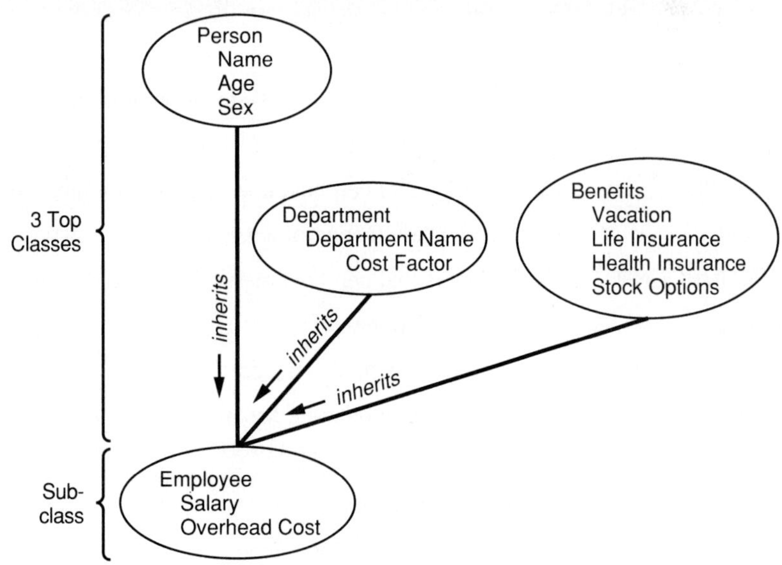

### Define Attributes

An **attribute** is the name of a data item and a specification of the type of data item. Some object-oriented development shells use the term **slots** in place of attributes. Figure 21–4 includes a list of the attribute types that are available to help define the data represented in a LEVEL5 OBJECT KBS.

**Figure 21–4.** Assigning Types to Class Attributes

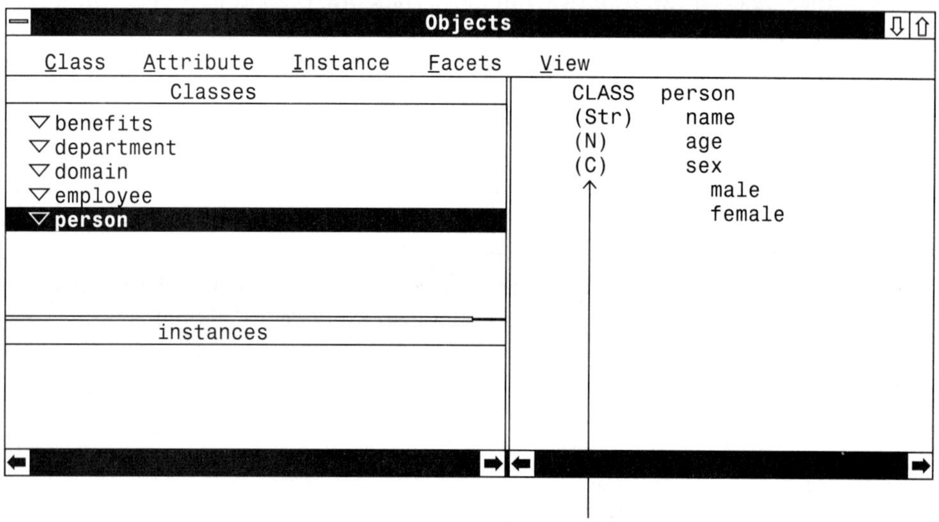


| Attribute Type | Data Represented |
|---|---|
| COLOR | For storing color values |
| COMPOUND | For attributes that can hold one value from a group of related values |
| INTERVAL | For representing a span of time |
| MULTICOMPOUND | For attributes that can hold many values from a group of related values |
| NUMERIC | For numeric information |
| PICTURE | For bit-mapped graphic images |
| RECTANGLE | For attributes that define a screen location |
| SIMPLE | For true/false data |
| STRING | For alphanumeric data |
| TIME | For representing a point in time |

The figure shows that for the person class, three attributes are defined as follows:

| *Attribute* | *Type* |
|---|---|
| name | string; for alphanumeric data |
| age | numeric |
| sex | compound; for attributes that can hold one value from a group of related values |

The specific values available for the compound attribute sex are also defined: male, female.

Also included in an attribute definition is information to the inference engine about how to process the attribute. This information generally fits into one of the following categories:

| *Attribute Information* | *Possible Specifications* |
|---|---|
| Inferencing | Search order... |
| | Exhaustive |
| | Breakpoint |
| User prompt | Query from... |
| | Text... |
| | Expand... |
| | Unknown value prompting |
| | Confidence prompting |
| Value | Initial value |
| | Reinitialized value |
| | Default value |

Inferencing information specifies where, and in what order, the backward chaining inference engine will try to obtain the attribute's value (Search order), whether the inference engine will pursue all possible rules that can conclude the attribute's value instead of stopping with the first successful rule (Exhaustive), and whether the inference engine will stop when the attribute is evaluated during a knowledge base session (Breakpoint).

Prompting information controls aspects of the query presented to the end-user when the attribute's value is asked for. It is possible to designate a specific display to query from (Query from), substitute text in the default query for the attribute (Text), provide a display of supplemental information (Expand), allow the user to answer "unknown" (Unknown prompting), or have the user indicate a confidence level in the value entered (Confidence prompting).

Value information provides specific values for the attribute. Initial values are set the first time the knowledge base is started, reinitialized values are set when the knowledge base is restarted by an inference engine cycle or started by a CHAIN command, and default values are set when they are evaluated as part of the attribute's search order.

### Define Methods

Attributes can have methods attached which need definition. A **method** is a procedure associated with an attribute that can determine the attribute's value or execute a series of procedures when the attribute's value changes. Methods are also called operators, procedures, functions, and other terms in various development systems.

The human assets application demonstrates the use of three methods as indicated in Figure 21–5. The development tool used in this example uses WHEN NEEDED methods to hold the information for determining the attribute's value.

WHEN CHANGED methods, on the other hand, are procedures that are executed whenever an attribute's value changes. These WHEN CHANGED methods are often called **demons** in object-oriented and forward chaining rule-based systems.

The goal of this sample application is to determine the overhead cost of an employee and the appropriate employee benefits. The procedure for determin-

**Figure 21–5.** Three "Methods" Determine Attribute Values

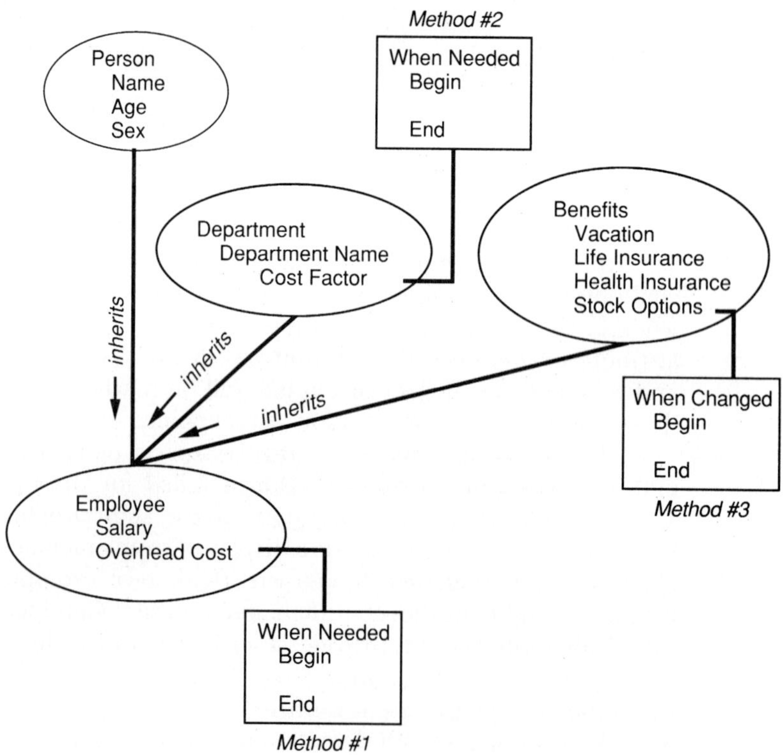

ing the overhead cost is encoded in two WHEN NEEDED methods, one for the calculation of the overhead cost of the employee and one to determine the appropriate department cost factor to use in the calculation. Since "employee" inherits the "department" class, the procedure for determining a cost factor can be stored as part of that class, distinct from the "employee" class. Once the overhead cost is calculated, a WHEN CHANGED method in the "benefits" class is used to assign the appropriate benefits to the employee.

An example of method grammar appears in Figure 21–6. Note that an attribute must be referred to by its attribute *and* its class, according to the following syntax: "attribute name OF class name."

The WHEN NEEDED method performs two functions. It first does a simple calculation to determine the value of "overhead cost." It then determines if the employee is eligible for the stock options benefit. Setting the value of stock options triggers the WHEN CHANGED method in the third example to set the remaining benefits for the employee.

Once a WHEN NEEDED method is created for an attribute, the search order is set to just WHEN NEEDED. Consequently, whenever the value of the attribute is needed, the shell runs the method.

Two values will have to be obtained in order to compute the overhead cost: the "salary OF employee" and the "cost factor OF employee." The salary is obtained by querying the end user at run-time. The value of "cost factor" is inherited from the "department" class.

The method for calculating "cost factor OF department" is shown in Example 2 of Figure 21–6. When this method requires the department name for the employee, the user will be asked to provide it.

The third method in Figure 21–6 is fired when the "stock options" value is set by the WHEN NEEDED method for "overhead cost OF employee." This WHEN CHANGED method assigns the life insurance and vacation benefits.

Like all components of an object, methods are inherited. Implicit in the idea of inheritance is that an object can specialize, or override, information that is inherited. In the example in Figure 21–7, for example, the version of method 1 attached to Object B has been specialized. Instance B-1 inherits the specialized version of the method from its immediate parent.

The employee application just discussed demonstrates three methods that form an interconnected set linked by chains of inheritance. Many object-oriented development shells, however, use a technique called **message passing** to interconnect methods that occur in different objects, or even in the same object. A **message** is a request from one method or object to another, or from a user. A message is not a procedure, but simply a name or symbol to which the object responds. When an object receives a message, it checks within its own data and procedures to determine how it should respond. Each object (or its parent or parents) must contain procedures that will decode, interpret, and act on any messages the object might receive. Its actions will typically include procedures that generate messages to other objects, methods, or to a user.

**Figure 21–6.** Examples of Three "Methods"

Method #1: Calculates the overhead cost of the employee

```
WHEN NEEDED
 BEGIN
  overhead cost OF employee :- salary OF employee * cost factor OF employee
   IF salary OF employee > 50000 THEN
     stock options OF employee :- TRUE
   ELSE
     stock options OF employee :- FALSE
 END
```

Method #2: Determines appropriate cost factor to use in Method #1

```
WHEN NEEDED
 BEGIN
       IF department name OF department IS technical staff
         OR department name OF department IS administration
THEN
         cost factor OF department :- 1.6
       ELSE
         cost factor OF department :- 1.4
 END
```

Method #3: Assigns the appropriate benefits to the employee

```
Rule/Demon/Method Editor
Methods   Edit   Select   Lists   View
Save   When Changed for: stock options OF benefits   Delete

  WHEN CHANGED
   BEGIN
     IF stock options OF benefits THEN
       BEGIN
         life insurance OF benefits :- salary of employee * 2
         vacation OF benefits IS four weeks :- TRUE
       END
     ELSE

       BEGIN
         life insurance OF benefits :- salary OF employee
         vacation OF benefits IS two weeks :- TRUE
       END
   END
```

**Figure 21–7.** Inheritance and Specialization

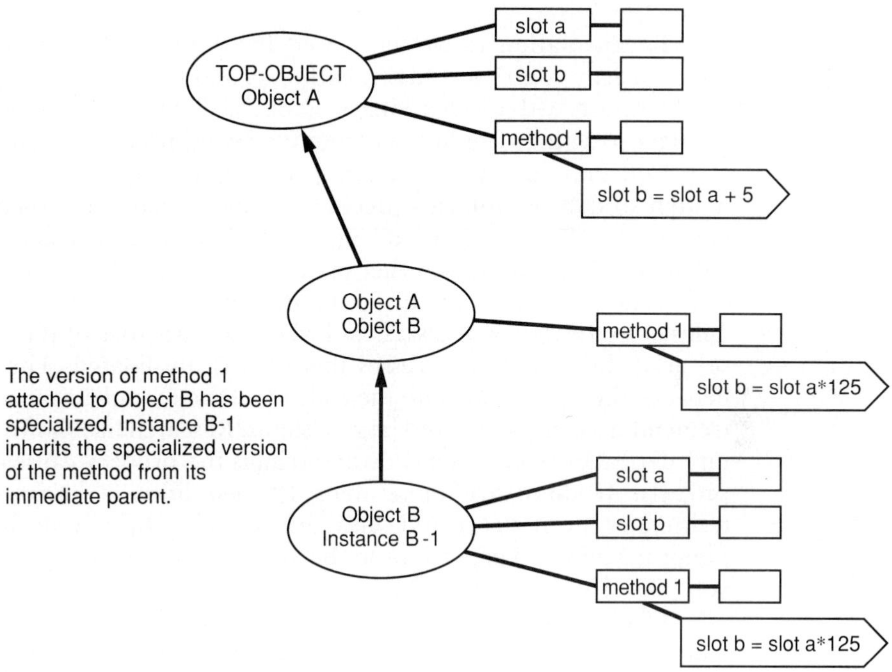


It is understood that the process of developing the employee application, to be complete, would include work on creating the user interface. This is included in the keystroke tutorial for this application, supplied at the end of this chapter.

## Object-Oriented Versus Conventional Systems

Why would a developer want to create an object-oriented rather than a conventional computer system? One reason is that object-oriented systems are a powerful way to modularize code so that it can be used with or without modification in different applications. Objects that handle the windowing functions for graphical user interfaces, as an example, are used without modification from application to application.

Another benefit is that a developer need know nothing about creating windows to use this feature. Using it only requires sending a message. Consider an example where a federal tax table object is to be used in conjunction with a payroll system to calculate such things as the dollar amount of withholding tax for a specific gross salary and exemption status. A developer need not know anything about the tax laws, the internal procedure and code of the object, or the format of its sorted data. The object in this case was simply bought from a software vendor and plugged into the existing payroll system. Compatibility was a non-issue because the data and code were bound tightly together, encapsulated within the object.

**Encapsulation** is the term used for the idea that an object should be a self-sufficient unit that contains both data and the methods to process that data. This contrasts with conventional systems, as diagrammed in Figure 21–8, where the data structures are distinct from the coded programs that operate on them.

Conventional system-building techniques require that program code be written so that it conforms precisely to the format and structure of the stored data that it will access. Record lengths, blocking factors, data types, key positions, database subschemas, and other parameters must all be specified in the program code. The problem with this is the data dependence it creates: code must be tailored to the data it accesses, and when the structure of the data changes, part or all of the code that accesses that data is invalidated. The interdependence between the sorted data and the code of all the modules that access it introduces tremendous complexity into large systems. Research has shown that this complex interdependence between code and data is the primary cause of failure in large projects. If there are more than 100,000 lines of program code, current techniques, even structured ones, are swamped by complexity, and seemingly minor patches and extensions to the system produce unexpected results that are very difficult to debug.

Object-oriented techniques do not just solve the data dependence problem. They completely eliminate it by binding data and code so tightly together within objects that the two become indistinguishable. The world of applications systems becomes one of autonomous objects passing messages back and forth, and eliminating the data dependence problem dramatically reduces the complexity of large systems.

To summarize the comparison, the concepts underlying object-oriented computer system development that make them different from existing procedural computer language concepts are:

- encapsulation of data and code within objects greatly simplifies the complexity of large systems by reducing interaction among modules;

**Figure 21–8.** Two Views of Code and Data

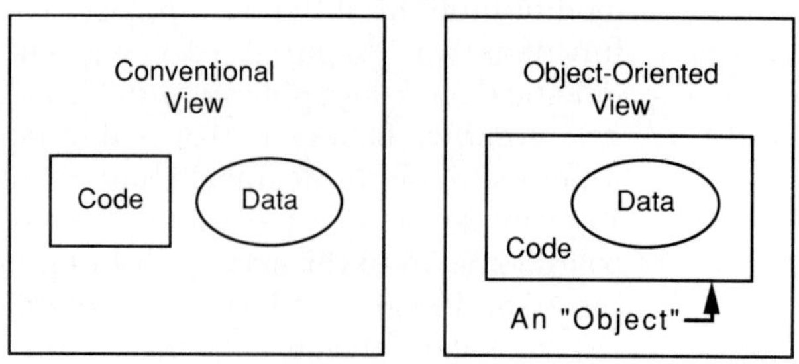

- hidden method code and the message approach to communication convert the programmer's job from a primarily procedural one to a primarily nonprocedural one; and
- inheritance helps to eliminate redundancy in systems.

The encapsulation and reusability capabilities of object-oriented systems are the key to their promise of quantum improvements in software development productivity.

## OBJECT-BASED KBS

Object-oriented systems are a much simpler and more natural way of clustering data and procedures than those used in rule-based KBS. One benefit of this approach is that it encourages a domain expert or knowledge engineer to organize domain knowledge in a hierarchical fashion, from high-level abstract concepts to lower-level specific entities. The structure makes it easier initially to collect, organize, and manage knowledge, and later to modify the knowledge base as new information is acquired.

Another benefit of object-oriented KBS is their ability to keep information about an object's characteristics and behavior within the object, rather than have it scattered throughout the knowledge base. This also makes the knowledge base more readable, since specific knowledge about objects does not have to be written into rules.

Because object hierarchies automatically model the relationships among objects, the need to explicitly define relationships in rules is eliminated. In some object-oriented KBS, rules exist only to define methods, as demonstrated in the LEVEL5 OBJECT example at the end of this chapter.

Many knowledge-based systems use objects. For example, in an investment advisory KBS, stocks are grouped by industry, such as banking, publishing, automobile, steel, prepared food, airline, and the like. These supraclass objects in turn are broken down into more specific subclasses, as shown in the example of the Prepared Food Industry KBS in Figure 21–2.

In a financial system, adding a new bank stock to the knowledge base no longer requires entering information about the banking industry in general each time a new bank is added. The inheritance capability of objects enables picking up general banking industry information automatically in object-based KBS. Even more important, specific stocks can be added fairly easily, without the major programming changes which might be required in a conventional procedural computer system.

In a strategy formulation system developed by Andersen Consulting, competitive markets are broken down by type, such as sportswear, and by subtype, such as retailers and manufacturers, within sportswear. Sub-subclasses within each subtype represent different competitive approaches to making money in the area. For example, in sportswear manufacturing there are subobjects for manufacturers who specialize in footwear for women in general and those who specialize in high-tech footwear for specific sports. These subobjects contain detailed information on what steps need to be taken to compete successfully in the area. This system enables a user to determine if a specific company under study has the marketing, manufacturing, and other programs needed to succeed in its competitive market, and to ask the system to recommend specific changes which will improve the chances of that company succeeding.

Object-based KBS can also be integrated with rule-based KBS to create hybrid KBS. Production scheduling and resource allocation decisions are two applications where object and rule-based approaches can be integrated effectively (Kowalski, 1990). For example, a rule-based component selects which machines to use for a particular production run, while the object-based segments control each individual machine's operations. These two components might also be integrated with a neural network component, such as the one described in Chapter 22. A neural net, for example, can be used to forecast production requirements for individual products during the period being planned for.

In Andersen Consulting's strategy formulation system, the rules guide the comparison of what the company under study is presently doing in distribution, manufacturing, advertising, and other functional areas, to what should be done to succeed in those areas (which is outlined in different KBS objects), in order to evaluate the company's existing strategies and recommend improvements.

Judicious use of each type of knowledge representation—object-based, rule-based, and neural net—can substantially improve the efficiency and effectiveness of the KBS being developed. In some KBS, for example, substituting objects for rules for some portions of the system improved processing and development time by between 30 and 50 percent.

## OBJECT-BASED PC DEVELOPMENT SHELLS

Nexpert Object is one of the more widely known object-oriented shells on the market. As early as 1987, it was called the most capable and full-featured shell for the PC on the market (Somsel 1987), and it continues to be upgraded and improved (Ferranti 1990). It is available from Neuron Data, 156 University Avenue, Palo Alto, CA 94301. The PC version cost $8000 as of April 1991.

LEVEL5 OBJECT is described by its developers as a hybrid application development tool that integrates, into one product, expert systems technologies, object-oriented programming, relational database models, hypertext capabilities, computer-assisted software engineering (CASE), and graphical development and debugging tools. It encompasses the scope of modern application development from rapid prototyping to large-scale systems development and maintenance.

A tutorial on building a simple object-oriented KBS using LEVEL5 OBJECT, included on the disks accompanying this book in a demonstration version, concludes this chapter. The shell may be obtained from Information

Builders, Inc., 1250 Broadway, New York, New York 10001. The PC version costs $495.

ObjectCraft, which was released in 1990, is a software tool for object-oriented programming. Its graphic environment uses mostly drawings rather than code to let even novice users explore the key concepts of object-oriented programming: classes, instances, methods, and inheritance through intuitive visual models.

ObjectCraft's graphic interface has many visual elements in common with established designs, such as Windows and the Macintosh, but retains an original look and feel that supports many visual effects. In particular, the 3-D View command creates the appearance of going "under" the display, showing the screen from an oblique perspective that reveals underlying layers of the program. Animated lines indicate links between visual interface objects and the object-programming model. This makes ObjectCraft a powerful learning tool. It is a far more visual approach than the text-based "browsers" of other object environments.

In addition to their value for rapid interactive development, ObjectCraft's graphics tools can create intuitive controls for finished applications. In one example furnished with the product, a simulation of water flowing between tanks lets the user flip the symbol of a valve open and shut, or select an indicator and enter a number to force the water level to a particular value.

The process of concealing the internals of an application is a logical extension of the object-oriented idea of encapsulation (or "information hiding"). In line with this idea, the ObjectCraft demo shows a small screw's-head icon to indicate that their objects can be opened for inspection; the developer can conceal these icons to make an application tamperproof.

ObjectCraft's procedural language, if needed, is straightforward for anyone capable of learning BASIC. The tricky parts of other object-oriented languages, such as declaring classes and defining their inheritance relationships, are handled in ObjectCraft entirely through the interactive graphics environment. The developer can then use the code-generation facilities of this shell to become familiar with the more complicated syntax of text-based object-oriented programming environments. ObjectCraft is available from ObjectCraft Inc., 2124 Kittredge Street, Suite 118, Berkeley, CA 94704. It costs $399 (Coffee 1990).

## AN INTRODUCTION TO OBJECT-BASED DEVELOPMENT SHELLS USING OBJECTCRAFT

For a visual introduction to object-based development shells, the disks accompanying this book contain a demonstration version of ObjectCraft.

ObjectCraft is a development tool for doing object-oriented programming visually, as well as a training tool to learn about object-oriented concepts. With this tool, a developer can "draw" the program's object structures, interface, flow, and even database connection, instead of writing code. Then the developer can have the diagram converted automatically to commented code in standard object-oriented programming languages, such as C++ or Turbo Pascal. Alternately, the diagram can be converted to code that runs under ObjectCraft itself.

Figure 21–9 illustrates an ObjectCraft diagram of an object, the fundamental unit of all diagramming done with the development tool.

The demonstration provided focuses on a simple example to build a system for processing orders of parts made by a manufacturing company. The object structure for this example is shown in Figure 21–1.

This example is a completely automated and animated demonstration that requires only a single keystroke to advance from one screen to the next. The demo requires the following hardware:

- an IBM PC or compatible
- a floppy disk drive
- 640 KB of memory
- an EGA or VGA graphics board and monitor
- mouse (optional)

To run the demo from a diskette drive, place the ObjectCraft diskette created during the install procedure into the disk drive. If necessary, change the DOS prompt to the drive containing the disk. (If the software was installed to a hard drive, at the C:> prompt, type CD\KBSBOOK\OBJECTC.) Type *demo* and press the Enter key. Follow the instructions that appear on the screen. They require pressing the Enter key, or clicking on the mouse, to advance from screen to screen.

To develop the sample application, an *order* object is created to represent the properties that all orders have in common. Then attributes, which are called

**Figure 21–9.** An ObjectCraft Diagram of an Object

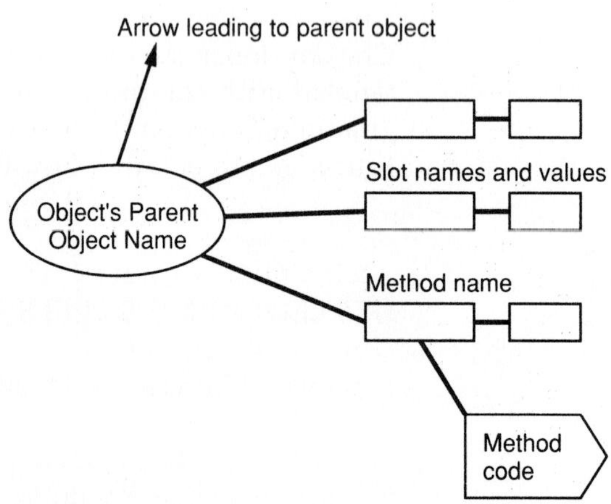

*slots* in ObjectCraft, are added to the order object. They specify the properties that every order has: a price, a number of units, and a total price.

Next, methods are created to specify how the object behaves. One method concerns the total price to charge for an order. The amount is equal to the price of the part being ordered, multiplied by the number of parts in the order. This formula is encoded as a method attached to the slot called "price." Once the method is created, the order object knows how to calculate "total" whenever "price" and "number" are filled in. For example, if the "number" slot is filled with 10 and the "price" slot with 25, when the method fires the "total" slot will automatically be set to 250.

Two "children" of the order object specify special kinds of orders: domestic and foreign. Lines connect them to the "parent" order object so that they inherit all the properties of the "order" object. These new objects can also have their own unique properties. For example, foreign orders might have an additional attribute slot called "tariff."

When finished creating objects, sub-objects, slots, and methods, ObjectCraft automatically creates the code, so that the developer can avoid that programming chore.

This small example is included on the disks solely to help a reader with little computer training to understand how a shell can be used to create objects and object-based systems.

## CREATING AN OBJECT-ORIENTED KBS USING LEVEL5 OBJECT

The following is a step-by-step tutorial on how to create an object-oriented KBS application. It is to be used in conjunction with the LEVEL5 OBJECT development system included on the disks accompanying this book. The version of LEVEL5 OBJECT system included on the disks can be used to develop and run full knowledge-based applications. Because this is a demonstration version of the product, it can save files created but cannot import the saved files to run them. The saved files can be run only on the full version of LEVEL5 OBJECT, although minor modifications may be necessary.

The goal of the sample application is to determine the overhead cost of an employee and the appropriate employee benefits. It is part of a larger human asset management application. A portion of the application has already been started and is on the LEVEL5 OBJECT disk as OBJECTS.KNB.

Figure 21–3 shows the object structure for the sample application. It consists entirely of objects and the methods shown in Figure 21–6. It demonstrates the inheritance of methods and how values are obtained through objects linked by chains of inheritance. An agenda with a single goal is used to initiate backward-chaining inferencing. The rest of the information concluded by the application is determined from the processing of methods and chains of inheritance linking objects.

The basic objectives of this example are:

- Create a new class. (Three of the objects have already been completed and are on the OBJECTS.KNB file. This example will create only the person object.)
- Establish the inheritance.
- Write methods to determine attribute values.
- Set a goal.
- Modify the conclusion display.
- Run the knowledge base.

### Installation and Start-up

To use LEVEL5 OBJECT requires:

- an IBM PC or 100 percent compatible with a 286 or 386 processor
- a hard disk drive
- at least 2MB of memory
- a VGA graphics board and monitor
- a mouse
- Microsoft Windows 3.0

With Disk #1 in the disk drive, be sure the DOS prompt refers to the drive containing the disk. Type *install* and press the Enter key. Follow the instructions that appear on the screen to complete the installation of the software that accompanies this book, LEVEL5 OBJECT will be installed in a subdirectory called L5DEMO.

To start this tutorial, follow these steps:

1. Be sure LEVEL5 OBJECT Demo and Windows are installed on the hard disk.
2. Change the drive and directory to the L5DEMO directory on the hard disk.
3. Type WIN L5DEMO and press the Enter key. The LEVEL5 OBJECT opening screen appears.
4. Click on the OK box. It is possible to run a selection of demonstration applications at this point. This tutorial, however, does not use them. Instead, it uses the application development environment, as follows.
5. Double-click on the "close" box in the upper-left corner of the window to close the session. (Ignore the animated logo symbol). Click "yes" when the Terminate Session dialog box appears.

### Create a New Class and Attributes

To begin developing the application, complete the object structure of the application and create the inheritance hierarchy. The topmost object in the hierarchy is the class "person," as shown in Figure 21–3. This class has not been created in the knowledge base yet, so start by creating it.

1. Select the "File" option on the menu bar and the "Open" option from the drop-down menu. Double-click on OBJECTS.KNB.
2. Select the "RuleTalk" option on the menu bar and the "Objects" option from the drop-down menu to open the Objects Editor.
3. Select the "Class" option on the menu bar and the "New" option from the drop-down menu.

The first component of a class is its class name. Class names must be unique. A class name cannot be used for any other item in a knowledge base. As evident on the screen, the new class has the default name "Untitled Object 23."

4. Type "person" over the default name in the Editor panel in the right of the screen. The class that is currently being edited always appears in the Editor panel. Press the Enter key to complete the entry.

The next step is to define the class attributes which define the information contained within the object.

5. Select "Add" from the Attribute Menu to create a new attribute. The "Select the Attribute Type" dialog box appears.
6. Since the first attribute is the name of the person, select "STRING" for the attribute type and click "OK." Other attribute types are listed in Figure 21–4.
7. LEVEL5 OBJECT gives the new attribute the default name "untitled attribute 1." Since this attribute is the person's name, type "name" over the default name. Press the Enter key to complete the entry.

Attribute names, unlike class names, do not have to be unique. Different classes may have attributes with the same name. As a result, whenever an attribute is referenced in a knowledge base, the class and attribute names must be specified.

Reference is made to attributes in this example in the format "attribute OF class."

8. The next attribute represents the person's age, so add a NUMERIC attribute (reference steps 5, 6, and 7), and name it "age."
9. Add the new attribute, "sex," to the "person" class (reference steps 5, 6 and 7). Since the value of this attribute can be one of two mutually exclusive items, male or female, create it as a COMPOUND attribute type.

The menu item "Add Compound Item" is now available. This menu item allows adding to the class definition the possible values that the compound attribute can assume.

10. Click on the word "sex," then click on the "Attribute" option from the menu bar. Select "Add Compound Item" from the drop-down menu and change the name of the item to "male." Click on the word "sex" then click on the "Attribute" option from the menu bar. Select "Add

Compound Item" from the drop-down menu and change the name of the item to "female" to complete the class structure. It should look like the example in Figure 21–4.

### Set the Class Inherit Property

In addition to its attributes, a class also has properties that specify its inheritance. The next steps use the Inherit property to build the chain of inheritance for the objects of this application.

**11.** Double-click on the "employee" class in the Classes list. The class and its attributes switch over to appear in the Editor panel on the right.

The employee class currently shows the attributes "salary" and "overhead cost." When the class' inheritance is defined, the class definition will include the attributes of the inherited classes.

**12.** Click on the word "person" in the upper left panel of the screen to highlight it. Select "Class" from the main menu bar and then "Inherit" from the drop-down menu.

A dialog box appears asking for verification that the "employee" class (shown in the Editor panel) is to inherit the "person" class.

**13.** Click "OK" to verify the inheritance. Now the class definition for "employee" reflects the inherited attributes. The inherited attributes appear in a different color in the Classes list. To see this, click on the triangle in front of the word employee. Immediately a list of attributes appears under the word employee. To see the full list of inherited items, repeatedly click on the down arrow that appears in the approximate center of the screen. The up arrow that appears above the down arrow can be clicked on repeatedly to reverse scrolling for viewing purposes. To collapse the list to its original form, again click on the triangle in front of employee. (Note that inherited attributes do not appear in the Editor panel to the right of the screen, because inherited attributes cannot be edited within a class.)

**14.** Complete the inheritance by adding the "benefits" and "department" classes to the "employee" class inheritance list as previously demonstrated for the "person" class. Then select "Show Inheritance" from the Class Menu.

All of the classes inherited by "employee" are shown as indicated in Figure 21–10. The complete list of attributes of the employee class now includes all of the inherited attributes.

**15.** Double-click on the "close" box to close the Inherits dialog box.

**Figure 21–10.** Verification of Class Inheritance by the Employee Class

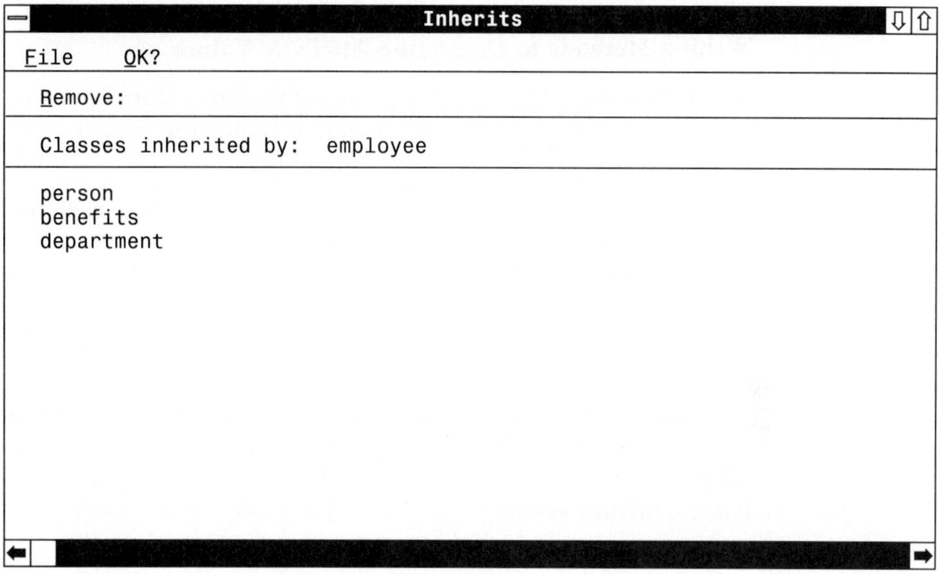


### Set the Initial Value of an Attribute

Attributes themselves can contain additional information other than their name and type. Methods, rules, demons, and facets are all linked to an attribute in LEVEL5 OBJECT.

16. Click on the Facets Menu to view the list of possible attribute facets. To close the list after viewing, click on the "Facets" option on the menu bar.

Facets provide information to the inference engine about how to process the attribute. There are three basic types of facets in LEVEL5 OBJECT: inference, prompt, and value.

For this example, set an initial value for the "name" and "age" attributes of the "person" class.

17. Double-click on the "person" class in the Classes panel and click on the "name" attribute in the Editor panel. Then select "Init Value" from the Facets Menu to open the String Initial Value Editor.
18. Type any name for the initial value of "name OF person" and double-click on the close box to close the String Initial Value Editor.
19. Click on the "age" attribute and select "Init Value" from the Facets Menu. The Numeric Initial Value Editor appears.
20. Type any number for the initial value of "age," then click "OK."

When the knowledge base is run, LEVEL5 OBJECT will set these values at the beginning of the session.

### Writing Methods to Determine Attribute Values

The next steps write methods to determine the values of some of the attributes of the employee class. In particular, it builds the first two methods shown in Figure 21–6.

**21.** To create method 1 in Figure 21–6, double-click on the "employee" class to place it in the Editor panel.
**22.** Click on the "overhead cost" attribute in the Editor panel and select "When Needed Method" from the Attributes Menu to open the Rule Editor for creating the method. An example of the Rule Editor screen is given in Figure 21–6.

The Rule Editor appears with the WHEN NEEDED method template for "overhead cost" in the Editor panel (containing only the four words WHEN NEEDED, BEGIN, and END). Method grammar follows a strictly procedural, block structure syntax.

**23.** Type method 1 as shown in Figure 21–6. Note that it is not necessary to enter the indentation shown. LEVEL5 OBJECT automatically reformats the method when it is completed.
**24.** To save method 1 and to create method 2 in Figure 21–6, select "Methods" from the menu bar and "New" from the drop-down menu. Click on Yes to save the previous method.
**25.** Click on the triangle in front of the department class to expand the list. Click on the "cost factor" attribute.
**26.** Choose "Select" on the menu bar and the "When Needed For" method from the drop-down menu. Type method 2 as shown in 21–6.
**27.** When method 2 is completely typed, select "Methods" from the menu bar and "New" from the drop-down menu. Click on Yes to save method 2.
**28.** To review method 3, which is already typed, click on the triangle in front of the "benefits" class, then click on "stock options."
**29.** From the Select Menu, choose "When Changed" method to review the method.

After reviewing the method, double-click on the "close" box to close the Method Editor, then close the Objects Editor by double-clicking on the "close" box.

The complete object hierarchy with its methods is shown in Figure 21–5.

### Set a Goal

The application is almost complete. It is now necessary to set a mechanism to initiate the inferencing process. Since the methods of the knowledge base are triggered when the value of the "cost overhead OF employee" attribute is needed, the most direct way to initiate the backward-chaining inference process is to make that attribute the goal of the knowledge base.

**30.** To set a goal, select "Agenda" from the RuleTalk Menu to open the Agenda Editor, as shown in Figure 21–11, then expand the "employee" class in the Classes panel by clicking on the triangle in front of the word employee. Double-click on the "overhead cost OF employee" attribute to make it the goal. Double-click on the close box to close the Agenda Editor.

### Modify the Conclusion Display

When this knowledge base is run, LEVEL5 OBJECT will present a conclusion display summarizing the values obtained and their source. The display is already built. However, it is necessary to modify it to show the initial values obtained earlier.

**31.** Select "Displays" from the RuleTalk Menu, and select the "Employee Data Summary Display" from the Select a Display dialog box, then click on "OK."

The display that appears, similar to the one in Figure 21–12, contains several value boxes that are attached to the attributes whose values are determined during the knowledge base session. Only the two valueboxes for name and age have not already been attached to their corresponding attributes.

**Figure 21–11.** Setting a Goal

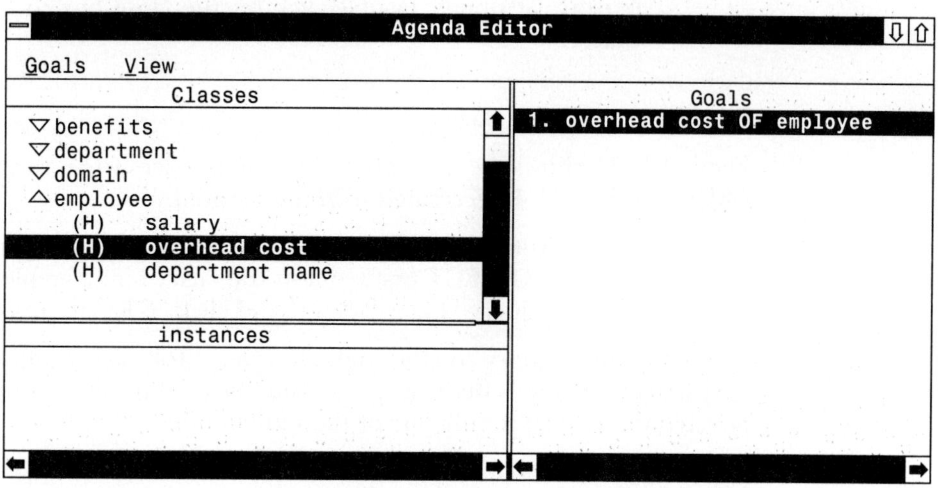

**Figure 21–12.** Sample Concluding Display

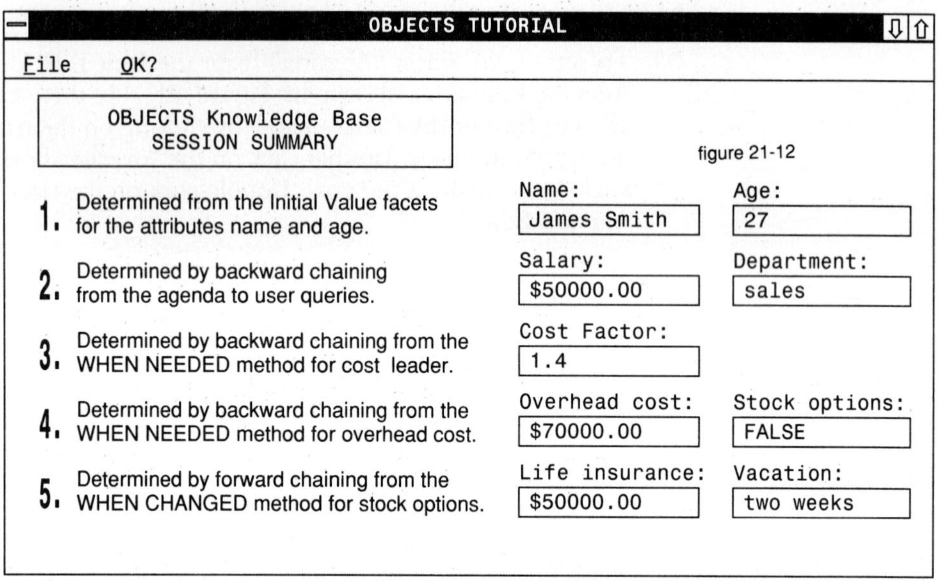


32. Click on the "name" valuebox to select it. Choose "Attribute Attachment" from the Attributes Menu.
33. Use the scroll boxes to locate the "person" class and double-click on the "name" attribute.
34. Repeat the above steps to attach the "age" valuebox to the "age OF person" attribute. Double-click on the close box to exit the Display Editor.

### Run the Knowledge Base

Figure 21–13 shows the main screens that a user sees when running the sample LEVEL5 OBJECT KBS created with this tutorial.

35. Select "Run" from the File option on the menu bar to open the session.
36. LEVEL5 OBJECT first requests the salary for an employee in a default numeric query. Type "50000" and click "OK!" to proceed.

The next query is the default query for the compound attribute, "department name." Because compound facts may only assume one of the possible values, select only one of the radiobuttons.

37. Click the radiobutton next to "Sales," then click "OK!"

**Figure 21–13.** User Views of a Consultation with the LEVEL5 KBS OBJECT

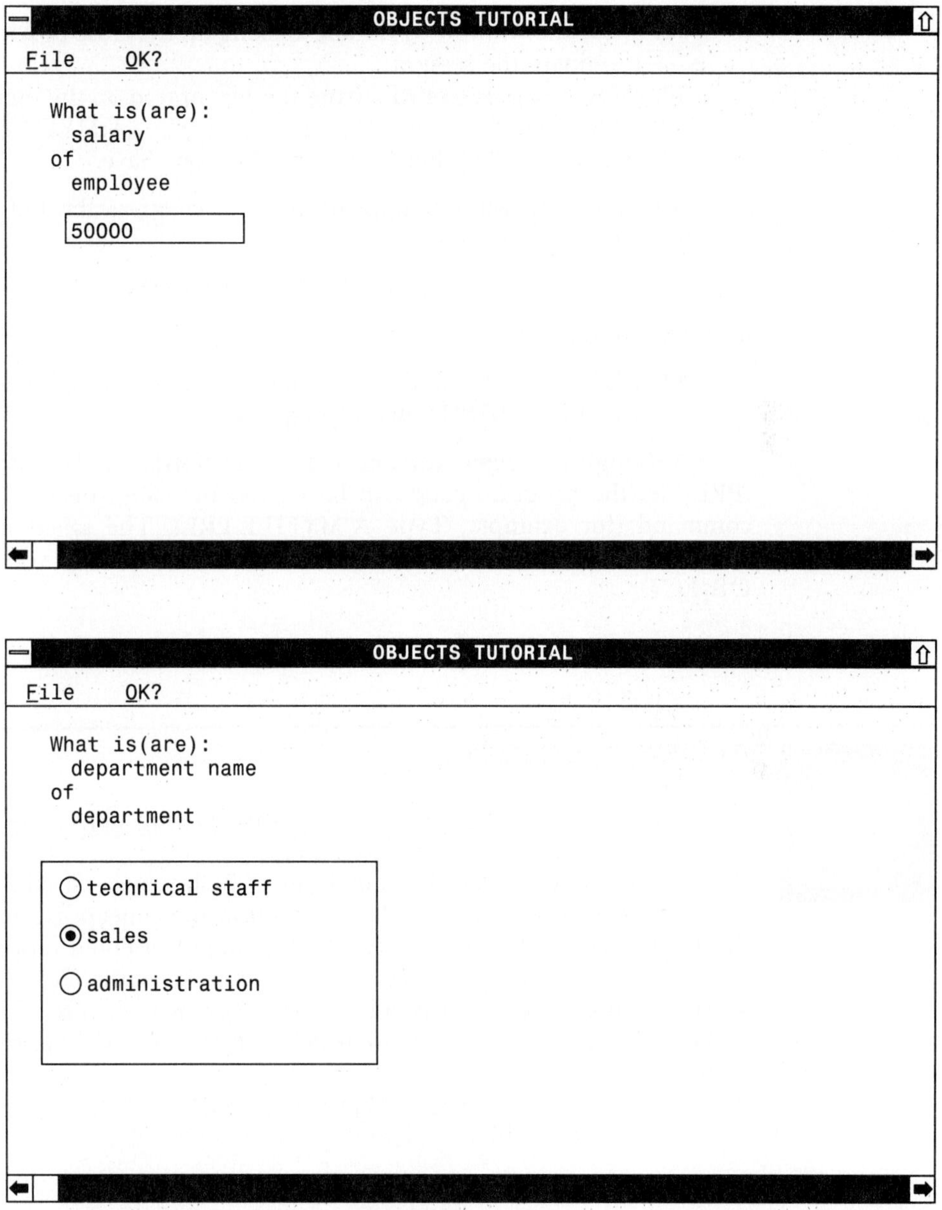

This brings up the conclusion display similar to the one in Figure 21–12, summarizing the values obtained.

**38.** Close the window by double-clicking on the close box. Click on "yes" to terminate the session.

**39.** Select "Export to PRL" from the File option on the menu bar. Type in a file name for saving the new file such as "A:MYFILE.PRL." Be sure to add the .PRL file extension. Click on "Save."

An Exporting window appears on the screen as the file is being saved. Finally a message that says

**EXPORT COMPLETED**

appears in the window

**40.** Click on "OK" and then double-click on the close box to exit the LEVEL5 OBJECT demo program.

Although the demo version of LEVEL5 OBJECT cannot import a saved .PRL file, the program code can be viewed by using the DOS Type or Print command (for example, Type A:MYFILE.PRL). The saved file can be run, although minor modifications may be necessary, on the full version of LEVEL5 OBJECT.

## REVIEW QUESTIONS

1. Identify and define the key concepts underlying object-based KBS: object, methods, message, and encapsulation.
2. Describe what is meant by "inheritance" in an object-based KBS.
3. Describe what is meant by classes and how the concept relates to objects.
4. Discuss the differences between the object-oriented approach and the conventional approach to computer system development.
5. Discuss the ways in which object-based systems make use of rules.
6. Discuss some of the ways in which rule-based and object-based KBS are integrated.
7. Describe some examples of object-based KBS.

## EXERCISES

1. To explore how object-oriented applications are developed, run the ObjectCraft demonstration supplied on the disks accompanying this book. Detailed instructions are available in the chapter section "An Introduction to Object-Based Development Shells Using ObjectCraft."
2. To explore how to create and run an object-oriented application using LEVEL5 OBJECT, follow the step-by-step tutorial available in the chapter section "Creating an Object-Oriented KBS Using LEVEL5 OBJECT."

## REFERENCES


Coffee, Peter. "ObjectCraft Gives Users a Hands-On Intro to OOP." *PC Week*, June 16, 1990, pp. 65, 71.

Ferranti, Marc. "Neuron Readies More Flexible Nexpert." *PC Week*, July 2, 1990, pp. 43, 48.

Helton, Thomas. "Object Orientation 5th-Generation Tool, Level5 Object." *AI Expert*, November 1990, pp. 61–63.

Henderson-Sellers, Brian, and Julian M. Edwards. "The Object-Oriented Systems Life Cycle." *Communciations of the ACM*, September 1990, pp. 142–60.

Howard, Geoffry S. "Object Oriented Programming Explained." *Journal of Systems Management*, July 1988, pp. 13–19.

Kleist, Ricki A. "KES at Work." *PC AI*, July/August 1990, pp. 18–19.

Korson, Tim, and John D. McGregor. "Understanding Object-Oriented: A Unifying Paradigm." *Communications of the ACM*, September 1990, pp. 40–60.

Kowalski, Bernadette, and Lori Stipp. "Object Processing for Knowledge-based Systems." *AI Expert*, October 1990, pp. 34–41.

Millikin, Michael D. "Object Orientation: What It Can Do For You." *Computerworld*, March 13, 1989, pp. 103–13.

Somsel, Joseph. "NEXPERT Object and HUMBLE: Object-Based Shells." *AI Expert*, November 1987, pp. 75–79.

Wirfs-Brock, Rebecca J., and Ralph E. Johnson. "Survey of Current Research in Object-Oriented Design." *Communications of the ACM*, September 1990, pp. 104–24.

# 22

# Artificial Neural Networks

The objective of this chapter is to enable readers to:

- Understand the nature of neural networks, existing and potential neural network KBS applications, and neural network development shells
- Build a prototype system with a neural network shell and integrate a neural network with other kinds of knowledge-based systems

Artificial neural networks, referred to simply as **neural networks** in this chapter, are computer systems. Like object-oriented and rule-based systems, they can be useful in replicating certain levels of expert decision-making processes. While often discussed as something separate from knowledge-based systems (Sherald 1989), neural networks can also be used in conjunction with rule-based and object-oriented systems to build effective integrated knowledge-based systems.

From the point of view of the user, neural networks are a trainable or learning program that can be used to induce or extract a pattern of information from a structured set of data. A typical business situation might use a set of examples and conclusions from historical business data available in a corporate database. A neural network is especially useful in situations where the numbers are vast and the relationships are often unclear or even hidden. A neural network can be used to glean information from patterns in the database in a way that is apparently similar to the human brain's.

Neural networks are generally effective in applications involving pattern matching. Such applications include identifying an object on a radar screen, such as a submarine, or spotting objects in the path of a robotically-controlled vehicle. In the business area, neural networks are being used in software applications to establish credit worthiness of commercial loans (Marose 1990), control production quality, predict stock market movements, diagnose diseases, select employees, analyze capital markets, and develop strategies (Humpert 1990).

## NEURAL NETWORK TECHNOLOGY

Neural network technology is often explained by reference to concepts found in biology and neurology, especially in studies of how neurons (small energy-producing elements in the brain) interact through interconnections (known as synapses) in normal brain and nervous system activity in the human body (Jorgensen 1986).

Computerized (artificial) neural networks are computer systems made up of many simple, highly interconnected processing elements, as shown in Figure 22–1. The processing elements—the artificial neural network equivalent of neurons—are generally simple devices that receive input signals and, based on those inputs, either generate a single output signal (fire) or do not. The output

**Figure 22–1.** Neural Network Processing Elements

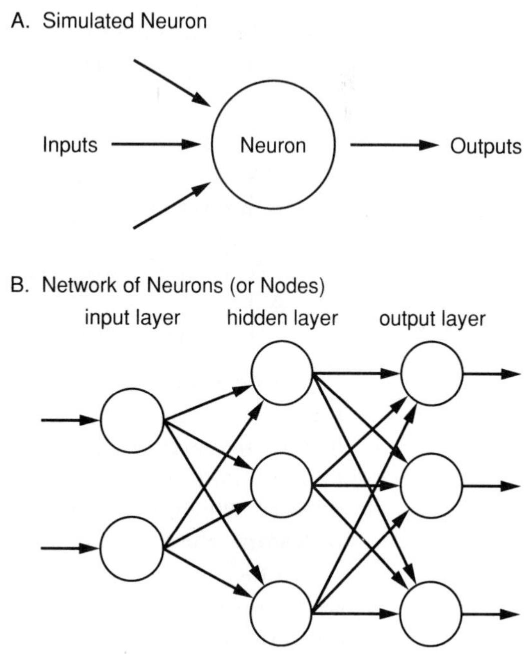

signal of an individual processing element is sent to many other processing elements (and possibly back to itself) as input signals via the programmed interconnections (called **"synaptic" connections**) between processing elements. A neuron typically does little more than calculate a weighted sum of all its inputs to derive its output (Caudill 1987 and Butler 1990).

While neural networks are often explained by reference to human neurological systems, such human systems in general are much more complex than existing artificial neural network computer systems. For example, one estimate is that existing artificial neural nets have the computing capacity of a cockroach and that it will be 120 years before neural network computer systems will come anywhere near being able to replicate the way people actually think [Lawrence 1990(A), p. 37].

The structure of the neural network is defined by:

- the interconnection architecture between the processing elements
- the rules that determine whether or not a processing element will fire (**the transfer function**)
- the rules governing changes in the relative importance of individual interconnections to a processing element's input

Neural network development shells have different kinds of built-in or predefined structures or **algorithms.** A developer can choose the one best suited to the problem under study. Software that defines these aspects of a neural network's structure and that can generate a network that solves a specific user problem is called *netware* (Caudill 1987 and Butler 1990).

A neural network system developer does not program the algorithm for executing each processing element, as the programmer of a more traditional computing system would. Instead, as is shown in the tutorial later in this chapter, the developer can specify:

- the input and output attributes of the problem and the attribute interrelationships (for example, in a hospital situation, attributes and their interrelationship can be the number of patients that need service each day of the week given the weather)
- historical sample cases (for example, the exact number of patients and the exact weather conditions for each day during selected past weeks)

The sample cases are used to "train" the network so that it can later recognize similar cases. The data set used for training can be obtained by using historical data in which the outcomes are known, or by creating sample problems and solutions with the help of experts. A menu selection starts the training process, which can take anywhere from a few seconds to days. Only a moving **milestone chart** alerts the developer that training is progressing.

Once a neural network has been "trained" a user can then use it to assist in decision making. For example, in the simple situation described in the preceding paragraphs, the user might apply inputs to the network such as the day under study—for instance tomorrow, which is Friday—and the weather conditions expected tomorrow, and then let the neural network do its calculations and predict the number of patients expected tomorrow given the anticipated weather conditions. If the network is correctly written and includes all appropriate attributes and interrelationships, which in this case would cover many more factors such as the season of the year, and if the training input was accurate, which can be tested by sample cases, the overall state of the network after it has reacted to the input will be a relatively accurate response (Caudill 1987 and Butler 1990).

In the training phase, neural network technology mimics some of the brain's own problem-solving processes. Just as humans apply knowledge gained from past experience to new problems or situations, a neural network takes previously solved examples to build a system of "neurons" that makes new decisions, classifications, and forecasts [Ward 1990(B)].

A typical network usually has three layers of neurons, as diagramed in Figure 22–1, each of which is connected to the neurons in the next layer. These connections are weights which are applied to values passed from one neuron to the next. Input values in the first layer are given weights and passed to the second (hidden) layer. Neurons in the hidden layer "fire" or produce outputs that are based upon the sum of weighted values passed to them. The hidden layer passes values to the output layer in the same fashion, and the output layer produces the desired results (predictions or classifications).

The neural network uses the **hidden layers** that lie between the input layers and output layers to create a network between the two. By finding points or **nodes** between the two layers, it effectively maps out a kind of internal map of the relationships between them. When the network has been fed sufficient data and has formed a network, a set of data—even an incomplete one—can be passed through it and it will give a conclusion based on the data it was trained with.

The network "learns" by constantly adjusting the interconnection weights. The answers (weighted outputs) the network produces are repeatedly compared with the sample case answers (outputs), and each time the connecting weights are adjusted slightly in the direction of the correct answers (outputs).

Eventually, if the problem has sufficient data that can be learned, a stable set of weights adaptively evolves and the network is said to be **trained**. A trained network then is able to produce good decisions or predictions (outputs) for all new inputs applied against its trained pattern. The real power of neural networks is evident when the trained network is able to produce good results for data which the network has never seen before.

## APPLYING THE TECHNOLOGY

To understand how the technology works, it helps to walk through an example—such as how one might set up an application to predict the stock market. This simple example was created with limited knowledge about the stock market and data obtained from a public library [Ward 1990(A)].

The first step in setting up an application is to decide what to predict or classify. In this case, next month's average Standard & Poor's Stock Price Index was chosen, although any number of other areas would have served just as well. Obviously, there are many other results that could be predicted, such as turning points, market direction, and the like.

The next step is to decide which input facts or parameters are necessary or useful for predicting the chosen result(s). For this problem assume that the stock price index this month is an important factor in predicting next month's index. Several other important factors include economic indicators available in current business news journals.

Next, the names of the input facts (defining characteristics) and corresponding output results (classifying characteristics) for the problem are entered into the neural network development shell. For the example, the names and related values that are entered are shown on the simulated screen in Figure 22–2.

The next step is to enter case histories or examples of previous results in order to train the network. These samples can be entered interactively or they can be obtained from a file. For this example, information for all the months in

**Figure 22–2.** Data Entry Screen to Set up a Neural Network Application Designed to Predict the Stock Market

Typed input values by a user

Input "defining" characteristics previously typed by a developer.

```
Identify Case Characteristics

 38.23  Retail sales not adjusted for seasonal variation (billions)
  7.76  Average 3 month Treasury bill rate
 79.84  Total US Government securities (billions)
 90.50  Index of Industrial production (relative, 1977 = 100)
129.70  New York Gold price
 54.59  Outstanding commercial paper and acceptances (billions)
 29.79  Value of Swiss Franc
 23.48  US Government receipts (billions)
 23.66  US Government Expenditures (billions)
 96.11  Monthly average Standard and Poor's stock price index
----------------------------------------------------------------------
 93.45  Standard and Poor's stock price index next month
```

"Output" classifying characteristic(s) (previously typed by a developer)

Output Value(s)

**Figure 22–3.** Main Steps to Develop and Use a Simple Neural Network Application

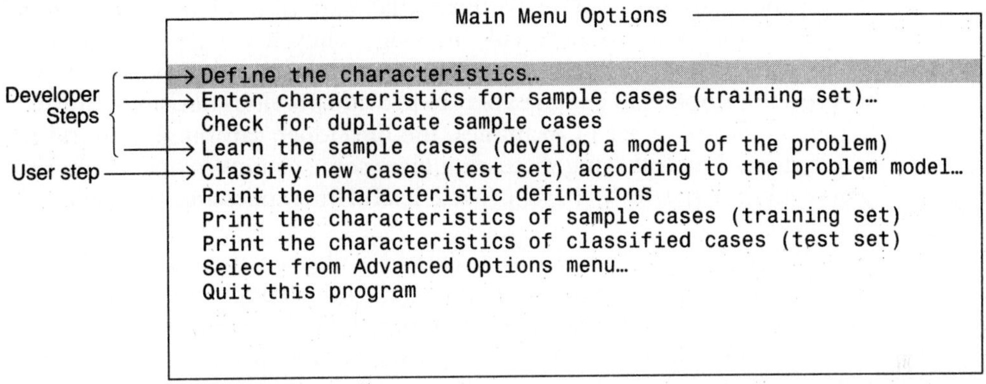


the years from 1974 through 1978 is entered. The goal was to see if the neural network could predict the stock market prices in 1980 after prices began rising from the 1970s levels.

After several silent hours of learning, the neural network is able to make predictions about 1980. For each month, it predicts the following month's stock price index. Comparing the results predicted by the neural network with the actual indexes, the neural network predicted the first 8 months with less than 3.2 percent average absolute error and the entire 12 months of 1980 with only 4 percent average error.

This unsophisticated approach can almost certainly be improved upon, at least during more stable periods, and with more knowledge of the stock market, superior networks are likely to be possible.

Interestingly, no programming, no configuring, no cryptic commands or symbols were necessary to create the sample application. The main menu for the simple neural network development shell used, shown in Figure 22–3, guided the sequential steps necessary to set up the application.

## NEURAL NETWORK APPLICATIONS

Since neural networks learn by example, handle fuzzy logic, can give tight data fits, and do not try to capture knowledge in rules, in many cases they are being used as an alternative to, and in conjunction with, rule-based systems [Ward 1990(A)].

When building rule-based systems, some find that trying to get all the rules from experts is frustrating. In dealing with many situations, experts do not always think in rules; they use judgment and intuition based on years of experience. Neural networks mimic the biological learning and decision-making process used in these situations by learning and recognizing patterns as the brain does. They can find subtle patterns that experts and other systems cannot because some patterns defy rule making. They learn from examples, not a complicated set of IF-THEN rules. In general, in certain kinds of situations where a developer can get an expert to provide previous decisions, or can get the expert to classify a set of examples, the developer can build a neural network application. The following discussion gives some examples of decision situations where neural networks have proved useful in replicating how experts make decisions.

While neural networks have existed and been used in research for over thirty years, as recently as 1988 very little information was available on their practical day-to-day use (Schorr 1989, p. xiv). This seems to be changing.

For example, Chase Manhattan Bank has a statistically-based hybrid neural network that is used to reduce losses on loans made to public corporations (Marose 1990). The neural network, called ADAM, uses historical financial data for strong and weak sample companies, and industry norms calculated using financial-statement data from companies in specific industries (obtained from COMPUSTAT). ADAM arranges financial variables in patterns and analyzes them to determine the optimal ones. ADAM is part of an expert knowledge-based system (called PCLM) which analyzes the financial information on a particular company, compares it to the most appropriate industry variables as developed by ADAM, and produces extensive reports on the credit worthiness (vulnerability) of the particular company under study.

Chase Manhattan has also developed a credit card fraud detection system using a neural network development shell (NeuralWorks). The system looks at information about the individual transaction, such as type and amount of purchase and the geographical area. This data becomes the inputs to the neural network. The output from the network is one of two variables —*high* means the transaction is potentially fraudulent, while *low* indicates that it is not. The bank then investigates suspect transactions to determine if a customer's card has been lost or stolen (Klimasauskas 1990).

Neural networks are used at airports in a machine developed to detect plastic explosives in sealed luggage. The system (called TNA) exposes luggage to radiation, and then classifies image patterns and analyzes them using a neural network. Each TNA system costs approximately $750,000 (Schwartz 1989).

Neural networks are being used by Raytheon in a computer system designed for submarine-seeking and tracking (Newquist 1990). Using NeuralWorks, Raytheon's system analyzes signal data collected from sonar and other signal-capturing equipment. The system attempts to recognize patterns or specific features in the signals. Over a continuous period of time, the network may analyze enough information to provide specific details about the monitored object: for example, whether the object is indeed a submarine, its location, and even its type or class (and so whether it is friend or foe). Neural nets are very useful in applications which have imprecise answers such as the "chances are that this is a submarine of a certain class." Neural nets can give a weighted average response to the likelihood of a conclusion being correct (Shafer 1990). This is similar to receiving a confidence factor response in a KBS.

In developing and using a neural network, the user needs to enter examples, such as samples of a person's signature or handwriting for check verification, features of a submarine for identification, or financial variables needed to predict a company's financial success. The neural network then "learns" these characteristics or features. Subsequently, new data is entered which the system matches to learned patterns and in this way gives output information about the match—in the opinion of many experts, such *pattern matching* or recognition is the single best area for the application of neural nets [Barker 1990(B)].

According to reports from the creators of the neural network shells NeuroShell and BrainMaker, as well as from others, there is a wide range of applications developed or being developed using neural nets. These include: screening travel vouchers, profiling security risks, assigning staff, spotting obstructions in a vehicle's path, predicting labor hours required for industrial processes, teaching problem solving, quality control, stock market predictions, sales prospect selection, competitive and capital market analysis, disease diagnosis, and fault tracing [Humpert 1990; Lawrence 1990(A); Ward Systems Group 1990(A)].

One of the major drawbacks of neural networks is that they do not give explanations, the way expert knowledge-based systems can be programmed to do. This drawback can be overcome, as in the Chase Manhattan financial system described above (PCLM), by integrating the neural network with a rule-based KBS.

Many applications of neural nets can also be handled by other computer approaches, such as induction tables and objects (Shafer 1989). The point is that neural nets are another approach which can be more effective and efficient in those situations where pattern recognition is critical, the degree of fuzziness and uncertainty is high, large numbers of examples are examined, and the decision factors can be quantified. The ultimate choice of approach used will depend both on the specific application under study and one's available resources.

During the late 1980s, there was some discussion of the advantages of neural networks versus rule-based and object-oriented KBS (Sherald 1990). As development of neural networks progresses, it is becoming clear that the future lies in integrated systems which combine conventional computer systems (for example, databases and spreadsheets), rule-based and object-based KBS, and neural nets [Barker 1990(A)].

Since this chapter is an introduction to the subject, the following discussion is limited to fairly simple decisions, developed using a neural net development shell. It is not intended to be a comprehensive technical treatment of the subject.

## NEURAL NETWORK SHELLS: NEUROSHELL; BRAINMAKER; NEURALWORKS

There are a large number of neural network shells available today (Eliot 1990; "Neural Networks" 1989). Three well-known ones are:

- NeuroShell, which was developed by Ward Systems Group, Inc, 228 W. Patrick Street, Frederick, MD 21701, is one of the least expensive shells discussed in this section and is relatively easy to learn to use. Its only version cost around $200 in 1991.
- BrainMaker, which was developed by California Scientific Software, 160 E. Montecito #E, Sierra Madre, CA 91024-9960, had two versions in 1991. Its lowest priced version cost around $200; its professional version around $800.
- NeuralWorks, which was developed by NeuralWare Inc., Penn Center West - Building IV, Suite 227, Pittsburgh, PA 15276, is a much more powerful and expensive neural network development tool (Klimasauskas 1990). It sold for around $2000 in 1991.

The following section describes the development of a small prototype KBS using NeuroShell. The choice was admittedly an arbitrary one, since all three shells mentioned above are good and all of their developers are known to provide excellent service and assistance.

## BUILDING AND CONSULTING A PROTOTYPE SYSTEM

As seen from examples discussed earlier in this chapter, neural nets are a trainable learning device that can be used to induce or extract a pattern from a set of examples—especially in a situation where the numbers are vast or the relationships are unclear. For example, a mortgage company might feed a neural net with several years worth of loan information describing the factors used to make a decision and the final outcome of the loans' repayments. The neural net would form a series of nodes that would indicate which factors had the most effect on the outcome (loan repayments) and which would be minimal or even irrelevant.

Another way to use a neural net is to have it monitor ongoing information flows and allow it to modify itself as conditions change. For example, a currency trader might create a series of factors that theoretically could affect the price of world currencies, such as national productivity rates, inflation, and unemployment. By keeping the neural net in a learn mode, the net could be examined periodically to see which factors appeared to be having the most important effect on a particular currency's value at a given time.

### Background for the Prototype System

Since neural nets are used to induce information from a set of data, they are also often used in place of statistics—particularly linear regression.

In KBS, an often useful function of neural nets is to help in dealing with fuzzy information that would be almost impossible to capture in a set of rules. For example, in a health care/hospital situation, it is often difficult to develop staffing plans for each day of the week. Some days will require heavy personnel support and other days less. Normally, weekends and holidays require larger staffs in the accident and trauma wards but far less in elective surgery, which is busy during midweek. In addition, the patient load in the emergency ward usually increases with bad weather.

The knowledge needed to make staffing decisions in these situations often resides in the heads of experienced administrators. For example, a hospital administrator who has many years experience might have a simple method for calculating how many more doctors are needed on a Friday night than on a weekday night. But these methods are inexact and are based on best guesses. With neural nets it is possible to build more precise rules of thumb by working with historical data. Assuming that data is good, it is possible to extract a far more accurate determination of the precise number of doctors needed for any given night of the week. In addition, it is possible for a neural net to keep learning and adjusting to data as it changes.

In this example, a neural network is used to predict patient loads accurately. This information is then sent to a rule-based KBS, which estimates the staffing needed to meet patient load requirements. Such systems have become more feasible, and so promise to become more widespread, with the introduction of low-cost neural network products, such as NeuroShell, and expert system development shells, such as VP-Expert, which can work together.

The following discussion shows how a neural network and a rule-based KBS can be integrated to make the staffing decision at the hospital. In the example, the user trains the neural network with a data set consisting of a random sample of days of the week, the weather on each sample day, and the patients received on each of the sample days. Once the neural network has been trained, it is linked to the KBS, which extracts the patient load predicted by the neural network to make a doctor staffing recommendation. An administrator, for example, can simply tell the integrated neural net/KBS system the day of the week and the weather expected on that day. First, the KBS accepts the input and delivers the information to the neural network, which classifies it, runs it through a trained neural network, and comes up with an expected number of patients for that day. The predicted number of patients is then sent back to the KBS, which applies a very simple rule set to recommend to the user how many doctors to schedule.

The example is, of course, overly simplified, in order to illustrate how this interaction works. The basic idea is, nonetheless, valid and extremely useful when building a more sophisticated KBS that integrates with a neural network.

### Creating the Neural Network Using NeuroShell

Building a prototype KBS using a neural network shell initially requires collecting the same type of information (knowledge) needed for building any rule-based or object-oriented system, or an induction table.

First, one identifies a decision objective: determine the need for staff at a hospital at different times during the week.

Second, one identifies what information factors are generally used by experts to reach the decision, perform the task, make the prediction, or solve the

**Figure 22–4.** Sample Learning Cases for Staff Planning Decision

| Case | Day of Week | Weather Conditions | Number of Patients |
|---|---|---|---|
| 1 | 1 | 1 | 66 |
| 2 | 1 | 1 | 64 |
| 3 | 1 | 2 | 70 |
| 4 | 1 | 2 | 71 |
| 5 | 1 | 3 | 75 |
| 6 | 1 | 3 | 76 |
| 7 | 1 | 4 | 80 |
| 8 | 1 | 4 | 82 |
| 9 | 2 | 1 | 35 |
| 10 | 2 | 1 | 37 |
| 11 | 2 | 2 | 40 |
| 12 | 2 | 2 | 41 |
| 13 | 2 | 3 | 45 |
| 14 | 2 | 3 | 46 |
| 15 | 2 | 4 | 50 |
| 16 | 2 | 4 | 51 |
| 17 | 3 | 1 | 37 |
| 18 | 3 | 1 | 34 |
| 19 | 3 | 2 | 40 |
| 20 | 3 | 2 | 41 |
| 21 | 3 | 3 | 45 |
| 22 | 3 | 3 | 46 |
| 23 | 3 | 4 | 49 |
| 24 | 3 | 4 | 50 |
| 25 | 4 | 1 | 42 |
| 26 | 4 | 1 | 39 |
| 27 | 4 | 2 | 45 |
| 28 | 4 | 2 | 46 |
| 29 | 4 | 3 | 50 |
| 30 | 4 | 3 | 51 |
| 31 | 4 | 4 | 55 |
| 32 | 4 | 4 | 56 |
| 33 | 5 | 1 | 50 |

problem. In the example chosen here, staffing a hospital trauma ward, one studies the factors affecting the inflow of patients: weather and the day of the week significantly affect the flow of patients in the accident and trauma wards, since accidents occur more often in bad weather and on Fridays and Saturdays—based on historical data.

Third, it is useful to construct some kind of table or matrix which summarizes the impact of these factors on the decision. Such a matrix is shown in Figure 22–4. The form of the table will depend on the development shell being used and the specific decision under study.

| Case | Day of Week | Weather Conditions | Number of Patients |
|---|---|---|---|
| 34 | 5 | 1 | 47 |
| 35 | 5 | 2 | 55 |
| 36 | 5 | 2 | 56 |
| 37 | 5 | 3 | 61 |
| 38 | 5 | 3 | 60 |
| 39 | 5 | 4 | 65 |
| 40 | 5 | 4 | 64 |
| 41 | 6 | 1 | 70 |
| 42 | 6 | 1 | 68 |
| 43 | 6 | 2 | 75 |
| 44 | 6 | 2 | 76 |
| 45 | 6 | 3 | 80 |
| 46 | 6 | 3 | 83 |
| 47 | 6 | 4 | 90 |
| 48 | 6 | 4 | 92 |
| 49 | 7 | 1 | 98 |
| 50 | 7 | 1 | 95 |
| 51 | 7 | 2 | 105 |
| 52 | 7 | 2 | 103 |
| 53 | 7 | 3 | 110 |
| 54 | 7 | 3 | 112 |
| 55 | 7 | 4 | 114 |
| 56 | 7 | 4 | 115 |

**Key:**

*Weather*
1 = clear
2 = cloudy
3 = rainy
4 = heavy rain, thunder

*Day of week*
1 = Sunday
2 = Monday
3 = Tuesday
4 = Wednesday
5 = Thursday
6 = Friday
7 = Saturday

Fourth, one selects the development tools to be used. In this example, the developer uses NeuroShell for the neural network development and consultation, and VP-Expert for the rule-based system development and consultation. The educational version of VP-Expert used to do the development work and the runtime version of NeuroShell (including the trained file named PATIENT.NET) used to run the consultation are given on the disks accompanying this book.

The decision selected in this example is part of a larger staff-planning decision.

The following is a walk-through of how the neural network portion of this KBS is entered, tested, and used to support the patient load decision-making task.

*Step 1*: After DOS is loaded and NeuroShell installed on the hard disk, or the NeuroShell disk inserted into the A drive of the computer, type in the word "analog" at the "A" prompt and then press the Enter (also called carriage return) key.

```
A>analog <Enter>
```

*Step 2*: When the first screen appears, type "Patient" (without the quotation marks) on the first line to identify the name of this example problem, and press Enter. A message will appear:

```
"No configuration file was found for this problem:
patient.fig. Characteristics will have to be defined
and entered".
```

Press the Escape key to continue.

*Step 3*: When the "Main Menu Options" screen appears, as shown in Figure 22–3, the selection bar will be on the "Define the Characteristics" option. Press the Enter key.

*Step 4*: When the "Define Characteristics" screen appears, there will be one blank line over the dash line. Press the "Insert" key once in order to create two blank lines above the dash line. This will leave room to insert the two characteristics shown in Figure 22–5.

*Step 5*: Press the Enter key to move the cursor to the top line of the screen. Type in the first characteristic "Day" of the week. Then press the Enter key. The characteristic will automatically appear on the first line above the dash line. Press the Enter key and type in the second characteristic "Weather."

*Step 6*: When the two characteristics "Day" and "Weather" have been entered, enter the output or conclusion, which is shown in Figure 22–5—"Patients." Type it in below the dash line, as the characteristics were typed in above the dash line.

Finish this setup section by changing the default minimum and maximum values. Pressing the left arrow key shows that the minimum values are already set

**Figure 22–5.** Entering Training Cases

Case number: 1

| Identify Case Characteristics |
|---|
| |
| 1.00 Day |
| 1.00 Weather |
| ---------------------------------------- |
| 66.00 Patients |
| |
| |
| |
| |
| |

Case number: 2

| Identify Case Characteristics |
|---|
| |
| 1.00 Day |
| 1.00 Weather |
| ---------------------------------------- |
| 64.00 Patients |
| |
| |
| |
| |
| |

to zero. Position the selection bar, using the up/down arrow keys, over the following items and enter these new minimum values:

1 Day
1 Weather
--------------------
30 Patients

Press the Enter key after each entry to change the value.

To change the maximum values, press the right arrow key twice. Use the same procedure as before to enter these new maximum values:

| | |
|---|---|
| 7 | Day |
| 4 | Weather |
| --------------------- | |
| 120 | Patients |

Press the Escape key when done.

*Step 7*: When the "Main Menu Options" screen appears, press the down arrow key to move the selection bar to the "Enter characteristics for sample cases (training set)" line. Press the Enter key.

*Step 8*: When the "Identify Case Characteristics" screen appears, type in the numeric values for each case shown in Figure 22–4. The first two sample cases are shown entered in Figure 22–5. Use the up and down arrow keys for moving the cursor to any characteristic (input) or conclusion (output) to type in the appropriate numeric values for the sample cases. Use the right arrow key to move from one case to the next case.

Press the Escape key when finished entering the values for the 56 sample "training set" cases.

*Step 9*: A small "test set" of data normally is selected from the full "training set" of data to test how well the neural net is "learning" to give good results. Because this problem is small, nearly all of the cases from the "training set" are used as the "test set." Test set cases can be randomly chosen from the training set as follows:

- From the Main Menu, choose "Select from Advanced Options menu," then choose "Transfer to NeuroShell Utility," then choose "Import, export, and manipulate problem files," then choose "Extract cases from .CHR file for a new .CLS file."
- Type a percent, such as 99, 50, or whatever is desired, in response to the prompt for the approximate percentage of cases to extract. Cases will automatically be extracted to serve as the "test set."
- Choose "Transfer to NeuroShell" to return to normal processing.

*Step 10*: When the "Main Menu Options" screen appears again, move the selection bar down to the line "Learn the sample cases (develop a neural model of the problem)" and press the Enter key. The neural network will now begin learning. This can take a varying amount of time that depends on the hardware used and the complexity of the patterns in the training set. For instance, the above example took about one and a half hours to learn on a microcomputer with an Intel 80386 microprocessor and math co-processor. The learning was frequently interrupted (using the Escape key) to check how the "test set" was doing. Once the "test set" showed results close to the same cases in the "training set," learning was stopped. The problem was considered "learned to the point where it gives the best answers for the test set."

NeuroShell recommends that a developer stop the learning process whenever good results are obtained on a "test set" of data. This procedure is recommended instead of allowing learning to continue until some arbitrary threshold is reached. NeuroShell claims that it is actually possible to "overlearn" and get poor generalizations on problems. (*Note to users of the regular version of NeuroShell:* This is a small example data set for this kind of problem and it works best with the following changes to the "Network Factors":

| *Change From:* | *To:* | *Network Factor:* |
|---|---|---|
| 0.50000 | 0.00000 | Output threshold |
| 0.00000 | 5.00000 | Hidden nodes |
| 0.60000 | 0.10000 | Learning rate |
| 0.90000 | 0.00000 | Momentum |
| 100.00000 | 60.00000 | Maximum cases in memory |
| 80.00000 | 5.00000 | Maximum characteristic definitions |
| 0.00000 | 1.00000 | Presentation |
| 5.00000 | 3.00000 | Characteristics: digits left of decimal |
| 2.0000 | 0.00000 | Characteristics: digits right of decimal |

During the entire "learning" process, a histogram appears on the screen indicating how many sample cases fall into any of nine error ranges. When all cases fall below .0001, learning is completed and the Main Menu automatically returns to the screen, unless learning is purposefully stopped sooner.

*Step 11*: When the neural network is through learning, it is ready to use.

The version of NeuroShell included on the disk accompanying this book is a runtime version only (program name: BANALOG), which does not permit the training described in this section. The results of the training are included on the disk in the file named PATIENT.NET. This file is used in the following example.

### Integrating the Neural Network with a KBS File

The KBS part of the program, as shown in Figure 22–6, acts as the interface and control program. It will be used to ask for the data on the day of the week and the weather forecast. It will then send the data over to the neural network in a text file. The neural network will be called up in "background mode" to process the data. It takes the day of the week and the weather forecast, and, based on its training, predicts how many patients will appear on that day. The number is written to a text file that is read by the KBS file. The KBS file uses the number and applies it to rules that determine how many doctors should be scheduled for that number of patients.

Conceptually, the rule structure is very simple. If it is day *A*, and the patient load is *B*, then the number of doctors required is *C*. If the number of doctors

**Figure 22–6.** KBS File That Integrates with a Neural Network

Note: The name of this knowledge-base filed on the Sample Files disk is DOCTORS.KBS.

```
ACTIONS
      BCALL Reset                    !Invokes RESET.BAT file which deletes
                                     !       previous consultation files
      FIND Day                       !Makes system look for 1st variable
      FIND Weather                   !Makes system look for 2nd variable
      SHIP Patient, Day              !Puts day of week in Patient file
      SHIP Patient, Weather          !Puts expected weather in Patient file
      BCALL Nuroshll                 !Invokes NUROSHLL.BAT file which
                                     !       manages the flow of information
                                     !       with the neural network
      RECEIVE Patient, Patients      !Reads value in Patient text file back
                                     !       into VP Expert
      FIND Doctors;                  !Fires rule set


Rule 1      IF  Patients <= 60
            AND Day < 6
            THEN Doctors = 8;

Rule 2      IF  Patients > 60
            AND Day < 6
            THEN Doctors = 12;

Rule 3      IF Patients <= 60
            AND Day > 5
            THEN Doctors = 14;

Rule 4      IF Patients > 60
            AND Day > 5
            THEN Doctors = 18;


ASK Day: "What day of the week is being planned for?
             1 = Sunday           5 = Thursday
             2 = Monday           6 = Friday
             3 = Tuesday          7 = Saturday
             4 = Wednesday";
CHOICES Day: 1, 2, 3, 4, 5, 6, 7;

ASK Weather: "Rate the weather expected using the following scale:
                     1 = Clear
                     2 = Cloudy
                     3 = Rainy
                     4 = Heavy rain, thunder";
CHOICES Weather: 1, 2, 3, 4;
```

required were dependent only on the day of the year, then it would be easy just to rely on expert system rules. The assumption, however, is that the fluctuation of the patient load is also dependent on a variable—the weather. The neural network can be used to mine historical data to determine how weather affects patient load on a given day.

It should be noted that the links are not flawless—for example, VP-Expert cannot directly integrate with NeuroShell. This results in the need to create an intermediate (.BAT or batch) file, shown in Figure 22–7. It facilitates the integration and is discussed later in this chapter.

Using VP-Expert, the rule programming structure is broken into three parts, as is evident in Figure 22–6. The first part is called the Actions Block, where much of the procedural code—including the goal sequence—is maintained. The second section contains the actual IF-THEN rules. The third section is the query interface—the queries that the KBS asks the user in order to make a decision. The reader can refer to the tutorial chapters of this book (Chapters 3 to 6) for specific instructions about VP-Expert use, programming, and related issues.

**Figure 22–7.** Service Files for the Neural Network Example

A. NUROSHLL.BAT file manages the flow of information with the neural network.

Note: The name of this ASCII text file on the Sample Files disk is NUROSHLL.BAT.

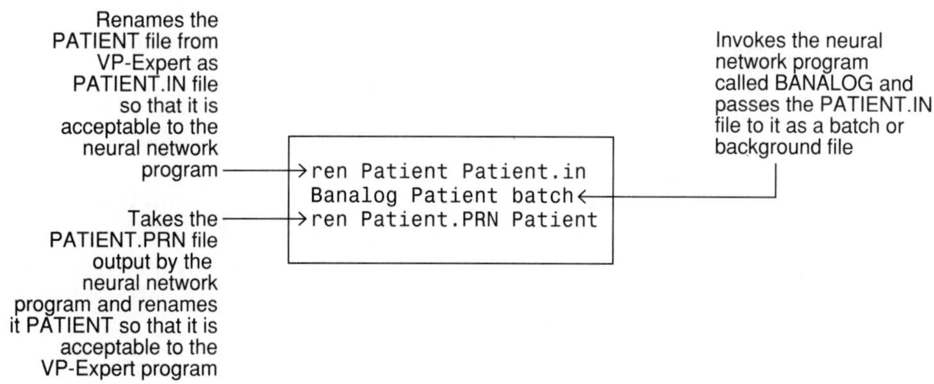


B. RESET.BAT file deletes previous consultation files (before starting a new consultation)

Note: The name of this ASCII text file on the Sample Files disk is RESET.BAT.

```
del Patient.in
del Patient
```

In order to simplify the KBS program code, this example assumes that all data and programs are in the same subdirectory. Obviously, if the program or data files are maintained in separate subdirectories, the appropriate PATH information will have to be added to .BAT file calls.

### Creating the KBS Program

To create the KBS program in Figure 22–6, the reader is advised to refer to Chapter 4 for a tutorial on entering programs with the VP-Expert development shell. The following step-by-step sequence provides only a generalized overview of the procedures which the tutorial covers in detail. The completed KBS program, called DOCTORS.KBS, however, does not have to be programmed from scratch. It is supplied on the disks that accompany this book, along with all other files and programs discussed in this chapter.

The following steps trace the procedure followed to create DOCTORS.KBS from scratch.

*Step 1*: From VP-Expert's opening bar menu, select 3 Edit. When asked for the name of the knowledge base desired, type DOCTORS.

*Step 2*: At the blank editing screen, begin typing the Actions Block exactly as it is shown in Figure 22–6. It is not necessary to type any of the exclamation marks or comments that follow the exclamation marks.

The Actions Block begins with the keyword BCALL to invoke the RESET.BAT file. This appears first in order to flush (delete) all the files used in interfacing with the neural network from the old consultation before starting a new consultation. Otherwise the neural network program aborts. The content of this file is shown in Figure 22–7.

The two FIND keywords are used to force the ASK questions at the end of the KBS file. The questions ask a user to input values representing the day of the week and the weather conditions.

At this stage, it is appropriate to have the values processed by NeuroShell. To do this requires creating a file to transfer the information. The first SHIP statement creates the PATIENT file and appends the value previously input for "day" of the week. The second SHIP statement only adds its value, about the weather, to the file.

Because file integration is not seamless, an extra step occurs here in the form of a call to a .BAT file. The BCALL keyword is used to invoke NUROSHLL.BAT. This file has the jobs shown in Figure 22–7, Part A:

- to smooth the way for the PATIENT file (by renaming it PATIENT.IN) to link to the neural network,
- to invoke the neural network program called BANALOG, alert it to the existence of the PATIENT file, and inform it that the processing will occur in the background, or "batch" mode, and
- to smooth the way for the PATIENT file to be received back by the KBS program. This requires removing the .PRN filename extension.

As apparent from Figure 22–6, the RECEIVE keyword actually reads the value which the neural network places in the PATIENT file. That value is the number of patients which the neural network estimates will demand service on the day in question, given the weather forecast.

To conclude the Actions Block, a FIND keyword this time functions in a goal statement to send the expert system shell into the Rules Block, the second major segment of the KBS file.

*Step 3*: The "doctor" rules in this very simplified example establish the number of doctors to be scheduled on the higher volume weekend days versus other days. The number of doctors is based on the number of patients estimated by the neural network. All IF clauses read the value for "Patients" received earlier from the PATIENT file.

Because this example is simplified for tutorial purposes, only one cut of patient load, above or below 60 patients, is shown in the rules. The rules obviously could multiply the cuts to refine the scheduling in any way desired.

Similarly, this simplified example shows only one cut through the days of the week. Clearly, this could be refined in a real situation as the need warrants.

The THEN clause in any rule fires only if all the conditions in the rule are true. In the example, when a rule fires, the user consultation session is complete. The expert system simply displays the number of patients and doctors concerned in the screen's lower right window.

*Step 4*: The user interface Questions Block is the area where the questions needed to solicit user input are structured with ASK and CHOICES keywords. Although they appear at the end of the KBS file, the questions are generated by the two FIND statements in the Actions Block, as soon as a consultation session begins.

*Step 5*: Finally, the two .BAT or batch files must be created. To do this, it is necessary to exit the expert system shell by typing:

Alt-F6 to exit the editing mode
Y to save the file
F8 to quit the program

Both the NUROSHLL.BAT and RESET.BAT files, as shown in Figure 22–7, can be created using any word processor or text editor. It just must be able to save a file as a so-called ASCII (text) file with a .BAT filename extension.

In the NUROSHLL.BAT file, the BANALOG name refers to the b(atch)analog version of the NeuroShell neural network program. This "batch" version circumvents the program's menu interface so that it works invisibly in the background. Except for a few interrupting screens that display the code in the batch file, a user is unaware of the neural network's part in the consultation's final recommendation.

The "ren" rename lines in the NUROSHLL.BAT file shown in Figure 22–7 serve to add or delete filename extensions. While NeuroShell works with filename extensions, VP-Expert does not. The rename statements resolve this incompatibility.

To review, the Patient file is renamed by NUROSHLL.BAT as PATIENT.IN so that it could be read in by NeuroShell. The information is then output in a file generated by NeuroShell called PATIENT.PRN. The NUROSHLL.BAT file renames the output file PATIENT so that it can be read back by VP-Expert.

The two data-passing files, PATIENT and PATIENT.IN, are deleted by the RESET.BAT program when the next consultation begins.

**Running a Consultation**

Once programming is complete, DOCTORS.KBS can be run. To enter VP-Expert from DOS requires typing VPX. This brings up the main menu where the #4 choice, Consult, is already highlighted. Simply hit the Enter Key to select Consult. When the system asks "What is the name of the knowledge base you want to use?" either type DOCTORS or use the cursor keys to move the highlight bar over DOCTORS and then press the Enter key. The system presents a screen with three windows. The top window displays the user queries. The bottom left window shows the rules being processed, and the bottom right window shows the conclusions, or fired rules.

On the menu bar at the bottom of the screen, the #2 choice, Go, will be highlighted. Press the Enter key and the program will load. First, the screen will temporarily blank out to run the two delete commands in the RESET.BAT file. Then, the standard screen with three windows will reappear with the first question at the top of the screen:

```
"What day of the week is being planned for?"
```

On the highlighted window at the lower left are the seven possible choices: 1, 2, 3, 4, 5, 6, 7. To answer, move the cursor to the number desired—the day of the week being planned for (1 = Sunday; 7 = Saturday), and then press the Enter key, as well as the End key (on the numeric keyboard).

Next, the KBS asks:

```
"Rate the weather expected using the following scale:
1 = Clear
2 = Cloudy
3 = Rainy
4 = Heavy rain, thunder"
```

Use the same keystroke sequence described above to enter an answer.

As soon as the two questions are answered, the KBS traces its activities in the lower right window (Day is ..., weather is ..., Patients = Patients, and in each case gives a CNF—certainty factor—of 100). Then the BCALL NUROSHLL. BAT command is invoked and the screen momentarily blanks, as data is passed through NeuroShell.

When done, a VP-Expert screen appears with the twin conclusions in the lower right window:

```
Patients = ... CNF 100
Doctors = ... CNF 100
```

(In all cases, since none of the VP-Expert uncertainty features are used here, the conclusions will show a certainty factor of 100.)

The end result is a seamless combination of an expert system that gathers data and automatically passes it to a pretrained neural network. The network processes the data and, in this case, returns a prediction. It is passed back to the expert system to be processed according to the programmed rules. All the user had to do was answer the two questions about day being planned for and weather expected on that day.

With the data transfer features of VP-Expert, the final recommendation could as easily have been passed on to another program like a database, a calendar, or electronic mail system that could have informed the staff of their schedule.

In the future, as batch processing powers of products like NeuroShell evolve, they will also be able to retrain while in use so as to keep abreast of changing data patterns. This simple example of integrating a neural network with a rule-based expert system is an indication of the compelling applications that are possible when combining these intelligence processing approaches.

## CONCLUSION

There are a growing number of KBS development and replication tools. The number and sophistication of these tools and related techniques are expected to continue to grow throughout the 1990s.

This chapter describes one such development tool, artificial computer neural networks. These clearly have their limitations, and so one must be careful not to overpromise their usefulness. They do, however, have distinctive characteristics which can be of use in many KBS replication situations and as such are another useful tool for the KBS developer to put to work in those situations where appropriate.

## REVIEW QUESTIONS

1. Define what an artificial neural network is, and the ways in which it is similar to and different from human neural networks.
2. Describe how an artificial neural network works.
3. Describe how an artificial neural network is developed.
4. Describe some artificial neural networks that have been developed.

5. Describe why artificial neural networks can be used as an alternative to rule-based systems.
6. Give an example of neural network and rule-based KBS integration.
7. Discuss some of the limitations of artificial neural networks.

## EXERCISES

1. This exercise explores KBS integration with a neural network program (called BANALOG). It uses the DOCTORS.KBS file and a trained neural net called PATIENT.NET. This integration occurs in the background and is largely invisible to a user.
   a. Run a consultation with the knowledge base DOCTORS.KBS from the Sample Files disk. Use the "Procedure for Running a Consultation," given in Chapter 4, Figure 4–2, to run the consultation. Make any responses desired to the questions asked.
   b. Run another consultation entering different responses.
   c. Compare and record the results observed from the two consultations.
2. Explore the mechanics of how the knowledge base integrates with the neural network.
   a. What happens to the consultation screen when the KBS turns control over to the neural network program?
   b. What happens to the consultation screen after the neural network program returns control to the KBS?
   c. What happens to the consultation screen at the start of a session? Explain the reason for the phenomenon observed.
3. Use Figure 22–6 and identify the KBS code that
   a. Creates a file of data for transfer to the neural network program. What data is actually transferred? What is the filename of the transfer file?
   b. Receives a file of data back into the KBS. What data is actually received?
4. Make your own changes to a copy of the DOCTORS.KBS file (name your copy something else to preserve the original) to explore their impact on a consultation. Chapter 4 provides tutorial guidance for editing a KBS file. Suggested changes to the rules are:
   a. Change the cut of "patients" from <=60 or > 60 to another value(s).
   b. Change the cut of "day" to another value(s).

## REFERENCES


Barker, Don. "Analyzing Financial Health: Integrating Neural Networks and Expert Systems." *PC AI*, May/June 1990(A), pp. 24–27, 62–64.

Barker, Don, and Chia-Ling. "NeuroShell: Common Sense Applied to Decision Making." *PC AI*, March/April 1990(B), pp. 48–52.

Berg, Eric N. "At Fuller Brush, New Ways to Get Foot in Door." *The New York Times*, May 18, 1989, pp. D1, D2.

Butler, Charles, and Maureen Caudill. *Naturally Intelligent Systems*. Cambridge, MA: MIT Press, 1990.

Caudill, Maureen. "Neural Networks Primer, Part I." *AI Expert*, December 1987, pp. 46–50.

Eliot, Lance. "Neural Network Applications." *FAIM Conference*, Monterey, CA: Naval Post Graduate School, May 14–17, 1990.

Engel, Charles W., and Margaret Cran. "Pattern Classification: A Neural Network Competes with Humans." *PC AI*, May/June 1990, pp. 20–61.

Feder, Barnaby J. "Hanson Coup: Smith Corona Offer." *New York Times*, June 6, 1989, pp. D1, D9.

Hamermesh, Richard G. *Making Strategy Work*. New York: Wiley, 1986.

Hiddings, Gezinus. "Expert Systems and the Competitive Spectrum Model." Center for Strategic Techology Research, Andersen Consulting, *Seminar*, New Orleans, LA: Decision Sciences Institute, November 22, 1989.

Humpert, Benedikt. "Using Neural Networks." *FAIM Conference*, Monterey, CA: Naval Post Graduate School, May 14–17, 1990.

Jorgensen, Chuck, and Chris Matheus. "Catching Knowledge in Neural Nets." *AI Expert*, December 1986, pp. 30–41.

Klimasauskas, Casey and Jane, founders of NeuralWare. "Interview." *PC AI*, May/June 1990, pp. 38–41.

Lawrence, Mark. "BrainMaker." *PC AI*, May/June 1990(A), pp. 34–37, 59.

Lawrence, Mark, Al Petterson, and Jon Hartzberg. *BrainMaker Version 2 User's Guide*, 4th ed. Sierra Madre, CA: California Software, 1990(B).

Marose, Robert A. "A Financial Neural-Network Application." *AI Expert*, May 1990, pp. 50–53.

Mockler, Robert J. *Knowledge-Based Systems for Strategic Planning*. Englewood Cliffs, NJ: Prentice-Hall, 1989.

"Neural Networks: Theory and Practice." *Byte*, August 1989, pp. 244–45.

Newquist, Harvey P. "Neural Networks That Work." *AI Expert*, May 1990, pp. 67–69.

Porter, Michael E. *Competitive Advantage*. New York: The Free Press, 1985.

Porter, Michael E. *Competitive Strategy*. New York: The Free Press, 1980.

Schorr, Herbert, and Alain Rappaport, eds. *Innovative Applications of Artificial Intelligence*. Cambridge, MA: MIT Press, 1989.

Schwartz, Tom J. "8 Parables of Neural Networks." *AI Expert*, December 1989, pp. 54–61.

Shafer, Dan. "Comparing Expert Systems and Neural Nets for Applications." *PC AI*, November/December 1989, pp. 40, 49.

Sherald, Marge. "Neural Networks Versus Expert Systems: Is There Room for Both?" *PC AI*, July/August 1989, pp. 10–15.

Stanley, Jeanette. *Introduction to Neural Networks*. Sierra Madre, CA: California Scientific Software, 1989.

Ward Systems Group. *101 Ways to Use NeuroShell*. Frederick, MD: Ward Systems, 1990(A).

Ward Systems Group. *User Guide*. Frederick, MD: Ward Systems, 1990(B).

# Appendices

## READINGS

| | |
|---|---|
| Appendix A | Expert Systems for Configuration at Digital: XCON and Beyond |
| Appendix B | ExperTAX$^{sm}$: An Expert System for Corporate Tax Planning |
| Appendix C | The Ford Motor Company Direct Labor Management System |
| Appendix D | On-Line Expert Systems in Process Industries |
| Appendix E | Rule-Based Structural Design in C |
| Appendix F | User-Developed Expert Systems |

# APPENDIX A

## Expert Systems for Configuration at Digital: XCON and Beyond

*Members of Digital Equipment Corporation's team of expert system experts reflect and recount a decade's worth of lessons learned in designing and building a core of configuration systems*

The XCON configuration system at Digital Equipment Corporation was the first expert system in daily production use in industry [2, 10, 11]. It is the cornerstone of Digital's knowledge network vision: a number of expert systems embedded in both the company's order process cycle and its new product introduction cycle [4]. Today, Digital is continuing to extend the knowledge network, as well as using expert systems technology in many additional aspects of the company's business. In fact, XCON is only one of several expert systems dealing with hardware and software configuration which are currently in use or under development at Digital. The configuration systems "family" includes four expert systems in production use. Several additional configuration expert systems are in the research, advanced development, or prototype stage of development.

The development of these expert systems has spanned nearly 10 years; Digital's Configuration Systems Development Group (CSDG) has thereby gained considerable understanding of all phases of the life-cycle of production quality expert systems: design, development, production, and ongoing support. In this article we highlight some of the key lessons we have learned:

- Building a successful expert system involves much more than simply putting rules into a knowledge base. Rather, to successfully develop and provide ongoing support for expert systems and to integrate them into the fabric of one's business, as has been done at Digital, one must attend to the needs of the business and to human resource and organizational issues as well as to technical issues.
- Although many software engineering practices carry over to the engineering of expert systems, we have nonetheless needed to be creative in developing practices specifically tuned to this relatively new, and still evolving, technology.

While the accompanying article by Bachant and Soloway focuses specifically on the technical issues underlying XCON and the other configuration systems, we take a more holistic, integrative approach in this article and attempt to put the aforementioned concerns into a coherent perspective.

## CONFIGURATIONS SYSTEMS AT DIGITAL TODAY

The Digital Configuration Systems Timeline (p. 693) shows, for each of the configuration systems, key stage-of-life milestones, including initial production use where appropriate.

XCON is used to validate the technical correctness (configurability) of customer orders and to guide the actual assembly of these orders. It provides the following functionality:

- Configures CPUS, memory, boxes, backplanes, cabinets, and power supplies, disks, tapes, HSC/CI, printers, etc.
- Diagrams complete system configuration (Figure 1 overlays selected pages of a sample XCON diagram)
- Checks marketing restrictions, system building block menus, and prerequisites
- Assigns addresses/vectors and determines box power status
- Partitions multiple-cpu orders and cluster systems
- Determines and lists cabling information
- Lists components ordered with configuration-related comments
- Generates warning messages on issues affecting technical validity.

XSEL [7, 9] is used interactively to assist in the selection of saleable parts which make up a customer order. It provides the following functionality:

- Allows interactive selection by generic component name, partial or full model number
- Performs completeness checking, adding and suggesting required parts
- Checks software compatibility, prerequisites, license and media completeness
- Checks standard and system building block menus, marketing and engineering restrictions
- Provides computer room environmental data and requirements
- Links to Automated Quotation System.

XFL is used to diagram a computer room floor layout for the configuration(s) under consideration. It provides the following functionality:

- Provides "minimum footprint" floor layout of components
- Allows custom rooms (user-specified dimensions and placement)
- Can include several configurations or a cluster in one site layout.

XCLUSTER is used to assist in configuring clusters. It provides the following functionality:

- Clusters multiple-node configurations for validation
- Specifies device quantity for dual porting
- Upgrades appropriate clusterable tapes.

In addition to these four systems currently in production use, two other configuration systems are under development:

XNET is an expert system which will be used to design local area networks, to select appropriate components for such networks, and to validate the technical correctness of the resultant network configurations.

SIZER is a research effort addressing the need for tools to assist in the sizing of computing resources required for any of a wide variety of uses in various types of organizations.

To support the ongoing development of the configuration systems in production use and to enable us to more effectively build new configuration systems, we have developed a software engineering methodology, called RIME [1, 12, 13], expressly for expert systems. Because RIME provides substantial insight into the engineering issues that require particular attention in building expert systems, it is discussed at some length in "The Engineering of XCON."

## SCOPE AND USAGE

The configuration systems provide full product coverage for Digital's current product set. This product set today consists of 42 different families of central processor types and their supporting peripherals and software. In order to be useful business tools, released versions of these systems must include configuration knowledge of Digital's newest products by the time of product an-

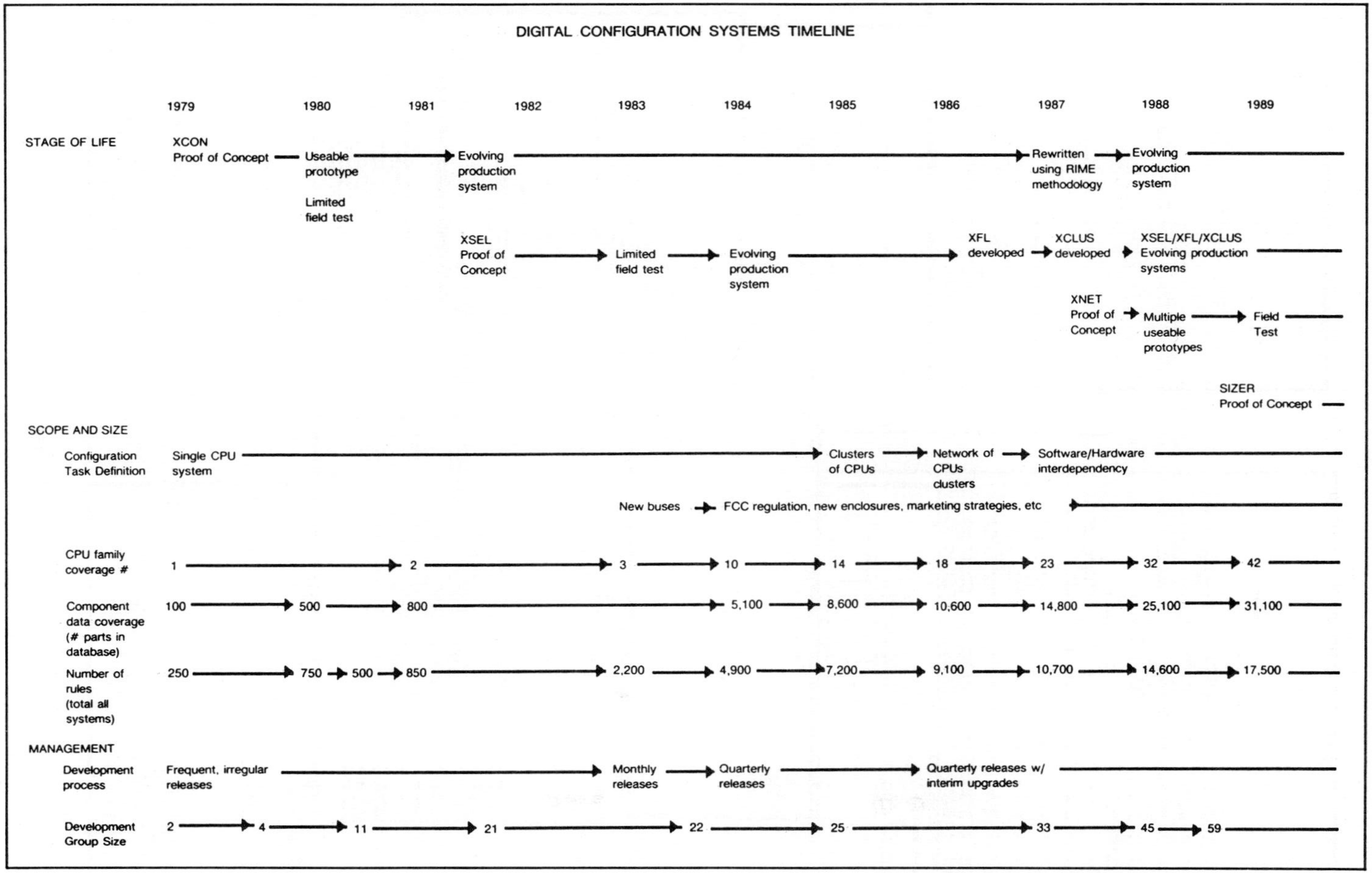
DIGITAL CONFIGURATION SYSTEMS TIMELINE
1979
1980
1981
1982
1983
1984
1985
1986
1987
1988
1989
STAGE OF LIFE
XCON
Proof of Concept
Useable prototype
Limited field test
Evolving production system
Rewritten using RIME methodology
Evolving production system
XSEL
Proof of Concept
Limited field test
Evolving production system
XFL developed
XCLUS developed
XSEL/XFL/XCLUS
Evolving production systems
XNET
Proof of Concept
Multiple useable prototypes
Field Test
SIZER
Proof of Concept
SCOPE AND SIZE
Configuration Task Definition
Single CPU system
Clusters of CPUs
Network of CPUs clusters
Software/Hardware interdependency
New buses
FCC regulation, new enclosures, marketing strategies, etc
CPU family coverage #
1
2
3
10
14
18
23
32
42
Component data coverage (# parts in database)
100
500
800
5,100
8,600
10,600
14,800
25,100
31,100
Number of rules (total all systems)
250
750
500
850
2,200
4,900
7,200
9,100
10,700
14,600
17,500
MANAGEMENT
Development process
Frequent, irregular releases
Monthly releases
Quarterly releases
Quarterly releases w/ interim upgrades
Development Group Size
2
4
11
21
22
25
33
45
59

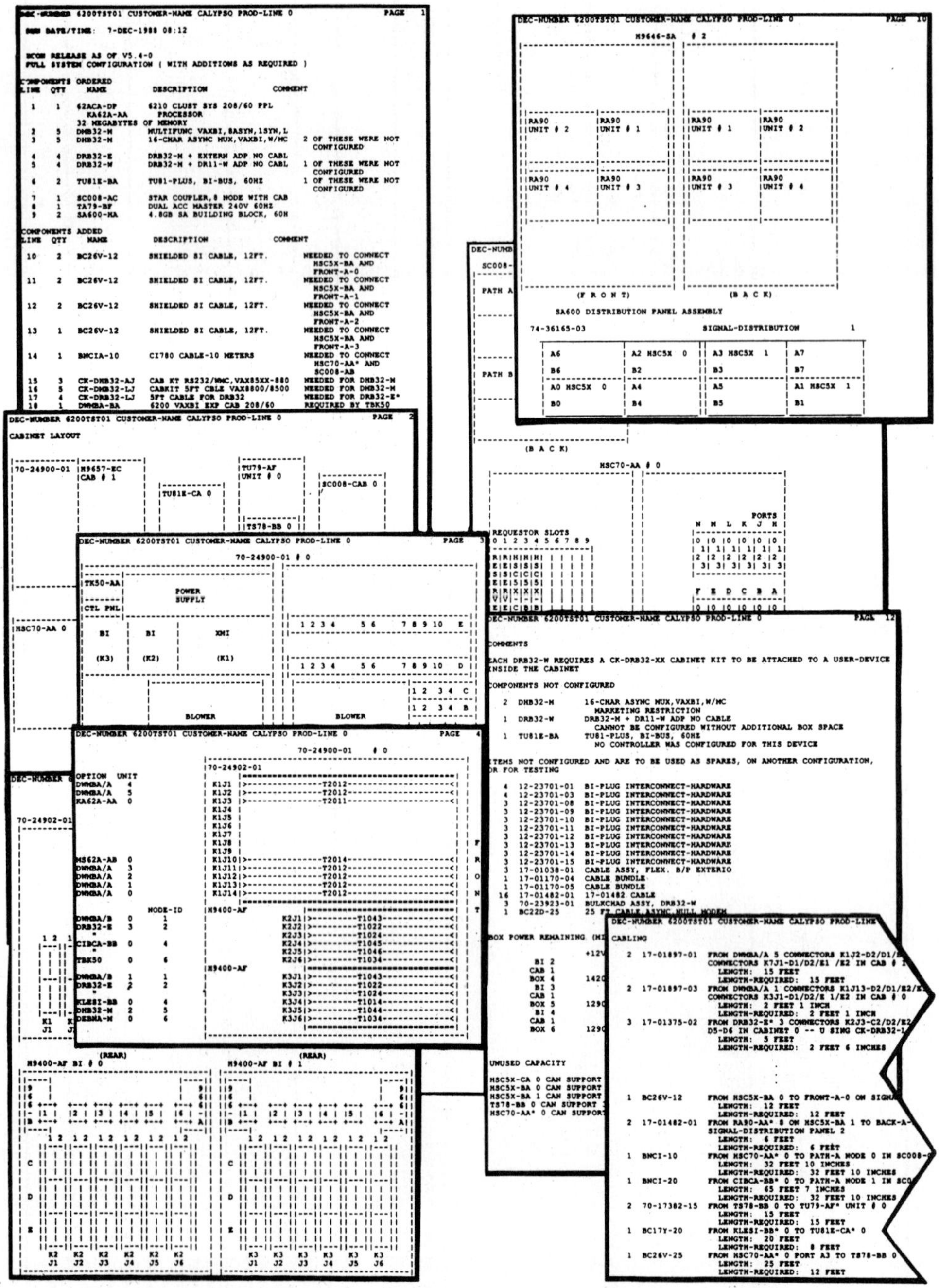

**FIGURE 1. Selected Pages from a Sample XCON Diagram**

nouncement. In practice, this means that CSDG provides major releases of these systems once each quarter, with at least one interim upgrade to insure adherence to the time-of-announcement requirement.

Hardware and software configuration is at the core of Digital's business. The configuration systems are used worldwide, throughout the corporation, by a broad set of users across the company's major functions: sales, manufacturing, field service, and engineering. The users of these systems perform functions which span Digital's complete order flow and manufacturing cycle, and, thus, are involved with many different business processes. This is a large and varied constituency to support—each has different needs and takes a different perspective on the configuration information provided:

- Sales uses the configuration systems as an integral part of the automated process to generate quotations for customers, and to insure that every order is technically valid.
- Manufacturing uses the information to verify buildability of all incoming orders, to understand physical partitioning of an order into various sub-assemblies to determine which plants should build which segments of an order, to guide the assembly of all orders, to determine the optimal set of diagnostics to run on each order.
- Field service has the perspective of consolidation and assembly of the order in the customer's unique environment and possibly with existing equipment already installed.
- Manufacturing and engineering benefit from the configuration systems' focus on system integration, as analysis of product knowledge for inclusion in the configuration systems identifies potential problems in system-level design and manufacturability.

This user profile has expanded dramatically over the years (see timeline). For example, the initial purpose of XCON was to assist manufacturing plant personnel in validating the technical correctness of system orders about to be built. Since then, this technical validation function has changed in response to business needs and is now performed in the field as well. In addition, the technicians in the plants who build the computers now use XCON diagrams to see how to put the systems together, and they include those diagrams in the shipment to the customer for use by field service installers at the customer site. XSEL was originally designed for use by sales representatives, and is now used by our OEM customers as well. Implementation of XNET will add specialized field support personnel to the user list in the near future. There are additional "indirect" users of these systems through automated linkages to other software systems (both traditional and expert systems) which depend on the configuration information supplied.

The configuration systems user base not only represents over 10 distinct business functions, but is also spread across the world, and has varied geography-specific needs. Overall, CSDG supports over 50 production installation sites, and the number is growing. In sum, then, the configuration systems are firmly embedded in Digital's most critical business processes. The existence of these expert systems has significantly improved these processes and continues to provide insight into opportunities for the future.

**BENEFITS**

Only a modest amount of attention has been given to documenting the benefits of applying expert systems technology [3, 8]. The configuration systems are a success and there is a major dependency on them within the corporation, worldwide. They benefit Digital in a number of ways, contributing to customer satisfaction, lower costs, and higher productivity. These systems are recognized as a critical factor in Digital's ability to maintain its highly successful *a la carte,* build-to-order marketing strategy (customized configurations to fit each customer's specific needs); this is one of the company's key competitive advantages. Some of the benefits are difficult to quantify, but overall the net return to Digital is estimated to be in excess of $40 million per year.

The use of the configuration systems insures that complete, consistently configured systems are shipped to the customer. Incomplete orders do not get through the process. In addition, XCON generates configurations which optimize system performance, so customers consistently get the best view of our products. Before the configuration systems, we would often ship the same parts configured differently. (There are multiple ways to configure the same set of parts to create a working system.) This was a major source of customer complaints and confusion, especially for OEM's who order large numbers of the same system and in turn reconfigure them all in the same way as part of their market-specific value added process.

The process of new product introduction is enhanced greatly by the focus on configuration information provided by the configuration systems. The existence of a single source of configuration information by the time of product announcement for use on initial customer orders simplifies field and manufacturing training needs and avoids confusion about new products which can delay time-to-market significantly. This is of critical importance given the volume of new products Digital continues to introduce each year. This single source of configuration information also increases manufacturing's flexibility by enabling product manufacture (and the knowledge of how it is done) to be moved from one plant to another without costly training or disruptive re-assignment of people. The use of XCON has facilitated this re-alignment of manufacturing capacity several times.

The use of the configuration systems has significantly increased the technical accuracy of orders entering manufacturing. Straightening out problem orders is a costly and time-consuming activity which disrupts the normal processes and increases order cycle time (i.e., delays order shipment). Overall, the additional discipline of both field and manufacturing use of these systems has shortened cycle times, contributed to more flexible, smoother-running processes, and lowered the number of people who would otherwise be needed for a given volume of orders.

XCON is seen as a critical component of Digital's current process of shipping segments of an order from various component plants, to consolidation points, and from there to the customer site. The use of XCON throughout the manufacturing process assures that when the components of the order come together for the first time at the customer site the system will work. Before the use of XCON, there were special manufacturing plants where every customer order was completely assembled, tested, disassembled, and repacked prior to shipping in order to insure the system would work when installed at the customer site. The elimination of this step in the manufacturing process (called Final Assembly and Test) has had a major positive impact on cycle times, inventory levels, and manufacturing costs, especially in light of Digital's four-fold increase in systems product volume since 1980.

Thus, the configuration systems are key in Digital's ability to handle the product complexity that technology advances are enabling and that our customers are demanding.

## THE CONFIGURATION SYSTEMS EXPERIENCE

At Digital, we believe that our success in the application of expert systems technology is attributable to a conscious recognition of and careful balance among three important perspectives: strategic/business, technical, and human resource/organizational.

## STRATEGIC/BUSINESS ISSUES

Digital has reaped and continues to reap enormous benefits from the configuration systems. It was, of course, an experimental effort at first but it was nurtured and allowed to progress and turned out to be a resounding success. Now Digital considers its use of expert systems technology a strategic investment.

What are the characteristics of an appropriate business problem for this type of strategic investment in a new technology? The problem must be real and systemic to the enterprise to justify the right kind of nurturing and supportive business environment. The solution will probably impact multiple organizations or functions and, hopefully, will bring about significant and positive changes in the way the enterprise operates. The configuration problem at Digital certainly qualifies. Digital's strategy of selling customized solutions is one of its critical competitive advantages, and gives rise to an indefinite number of valid configurations of its product set. In the 1970s, problems with handling this were starting to surface, and it was understood that automated support would be critically important as sales volumes increased and products became more varied and complex.

One of the main challenges we have encountered in developing systems which support strategic, cross-functional business needs is sorting out how the technologists connect with the business. As with any software development effort, it is necessary to form a solid partnership with the business being supported. Usually, that means with the end users and their immediate, operational management. In the case of strategic, cross-functional systems, we have discovered that the development effort must also be tightly connected at a more strategic level of management. This is simply a reflection of the fact that the problem being addressed has strategic impact and the solution may include and/or provide opportunities for far-reaching changes in the business [6] of which the tactically focused end user groups may be unaware.

CSDG is tapped into business planning at several levels to insure adequate awareness and connectivity and support. This has been and continues to be of critical importance to the ongoing success of the configuration effort at Digital. Much of the strategic connectivity over the years has been informal for the configuration systems effort: based on personal relationships with key individuals. Recently, we have initiated some efforts to formalize some of these processes. For example, we have set up a Configuration Systems Steering Committee made up of strategically focused managers representing our various business constituencies. This forum provides guidance on planning and priority-setting for the configuration systems in the context of a cross-functional vision looking out several years. In addition, a more formal corporate-level focus on system integration issues is evolving, which should provide formal long-term direction.

One of the most important factors in our success has been the existence of an enabling business/development environment for the introduction of new technologies like expert systems. During the early 1980s, Digital's manufacturing operations were open to embracing new ideas and technologies that would help them change the way work was done, affording higher productivity and shorter cycle times in response to customer requirements. Further, it was believed that this expert system technology could help shape the way Digital did business, allow the company functions to manage complexity, preserve the knowledge of its experts, and provide an approach to exception management more consistent with its growth demands. An environment has been provided which has nurtured the emerging technology and recognized that the people involved are managing change, evolution, and significant learning. It is understood that there will be new and changing operating norms and success criteria over time. Thus, at Digital there has been real management commitment to helping the technology succeed in helping the business progress.

## TECHNICAL ISSUES

Technologies develop iteratively through a number of phases:

- Investigation and experimentation,
- Stabilization with limitations,
- Identification of opportunities for optimization, and
- Maturity.

No aspects of expert systems technology have really reached maturity yet. This need not be an impediment to its successful use, but it must be understood and proper expectations must be set. In a new and emerging technology, there are many opportunities for technical creativity as new discoveries and capabilities surface. There is also the likelihood that a serious application development effort will push at the limits of what the technology has to offer at a particular point in time, and in so doing, can contribute greatly to the further development of that technology.

### Technology Challenges

The main challenges stemming from the emerging nature of this technology are:

1. Dealing creatively with the current limitations of the specialized languages and tools, and
2. Formulating an appropriate software engineering methodology (this is the thrust of the RIME development effort)

to produce efficient, maintainable, extensible expert systems.

Today's expert systems languages (and shells) offer varied but somewhat limited functionality. Most do not provide true extensibility to a production environment. There are very few knowledge engineering productivity tools available as yet on the market. The OPS5 language was originally chosen for the development of R1, the forebearer of XCON. As XCON and the other configuration systems have evolved using VAX OPS5,* its strong pattern-matching capability and its speed have maintained it as our language of choice over all others on the market today. CSDG has directly influenced the development of VAX OPS5, based on our experience, and continues to do so.

Bachant and Soloway introduce a software engineering methodology appropriate for the development of expert systems. They make two primary points: (1) A task such as XCON's, where thousands of highly context-dependent decisions must be made in order to correctly configure a system, can take advantage of a language, like OPS5, that presupposes "situation recognition" rather than "algorithmic" control. (2) But, as the number of alternatives that an expert system must decide among becomes large, there is strong motivation to augment situation recognition with other kinds of control mechanisms. RIME, a software engineering methodology developed within CSDG, identifies three mechanisms that an OPS5, program can use to determine what to do and when to do it. This methodology, which was first used to reimplement XCON, has proven beneficial in the management of complexity and facilitation of change.

Testing, by traditional standards, is a major problem for expert systems. Can you test an expert system the way you evaluate a human expert? Since the understanding of the business problem is often enhanced over time by the use of the expert system, how can you define a set of tests that are sure to be relevant from one release to the next? Since there are, typically, an indeterminate number of paths through an expert system, it is not possible to exhaustively test all scenarios. What is correctness? Consider the relationship between the optimal solution and an accurate solution. An error can be difficult to distinguish from a wish-list item. The expert system may come up with the right answer, but for the wrong reasons. What about the cases where the experts disagree? There are other related testing issues as well, all of which cry out for new views of design-for-testability and new testing concepts, methods, and tools. This is assuredly

*VAX OPS5 is a registered trademark of Digital Equipment Corporation.

**Application Challenges**

There are three application characteristics which are major contributors to the challenges faced in expert systems development:

1. Volatile subject domain,
2. Expanding functional scope, and
3. Large system size and complexity.

These are primary characteristics of the configuration systems, and have presented us with our toughest challenges over the years: (1) computer configuration is a dynamic subject domain; (2) once the systems were viewed as successful business support tools, users have wanted more and more from them; and (3) the configuration systems have become very large and are dealing with increasingly complex information relationships. Success has come only from our ability to respond to these challenges without disrupting or degrading the accuracy of the systems or our predictability in providing regular production releases.

***Volatility***

Each year, about 40 percent of the rules in the configuration systems knowledge base change (this includes rule additions and deletions, as well as rule modifications). This rate of change in the engineering, manufacturing, and marketing rules is due to a number of factors. Digital offers several hundred major new products and many more "minor" ones each year. Configuration information about them all must be included in the configuration systems knowledge base. In addition, sometimes knowledge about how to configure existing products must be changed to incorporate their configurability with new ones. Also, existing products are often re-packaged, as dictated by engineering, marketing, or government regulation. And, finally, CSDG periodically re-writes focused sets of rules as more is learned about the configuration of a particular product set and how to represent the knowledge more effectively.

There is another dimension of volatility in the configuration domain: the scope of the configuration task itself has changed significantly. The complexity and flexibility of Digital's product strategies has increased steadily since XCON was first designed. A single computer system can no longer be configured in isolation, but must be considered in relation to its role in a cluster or network. Clusters and networks offer multiple ways of configuring computers and connecting devices. Cluster and network connections are coming to be thought of as the main bus, with systems and devices providing functionality for one large "solution system." Moreover, distinctions between systems and devices are becoming less clear. The configuration-related interdependencies between hardware and software are much more numerous and complex today. In summary, the basic concepts and components of the configuration domain are being redefined continuously.

***Expansion***

The configuration systems we have noted serve increasingly varied user groups from different business functions and geographies. New types of users with new perspectives generate new requirements which frequently enlarge the functional scope of the systems. For example, when the plant technicians began to use the XCON diagram as the official document from which to construct the computer, a whole new set of requirements was generated. CSDG made an architectural change to the system in order to support these needs (altering some of the knowledge representation, transitioning functionality between the OPS5 rules and non-OPS5 code to create the diagrams, and developing a specialized database).

As their businesses change, existing users have discovered new and different ways to use the configuration systems. For example, as order volumes have increased and the technical validation function has changed, those users want to interact with the tool in different ways and need different kinds of information from the systems. They have asked for more streamlined ways to access the XCON results, as their processes have changed to preclude the need for steps previously performed and reflected in the XCON menu access scheme.

When XCON started feeding information to other systems, there have been instances where the rules have had to be changed to accommodate a new perspective on the configuration information. For example, there is another expert system used in manufacturing which helps judge how to split the construction of the order across several plants which specialize in certain subassemblies [4]. This system needs information from XCON on the physical partitioning of the order and what parts are used in what subassembly. XCON rules had to be changed to be able to explicitly provide this information at an intermediate point in XCON's overall process.

We learned that once we were successful, our users expected more. Users have higher expectations of a successful, operational system. Scrutiny has shifted from the accuracy of the knowledge base to things like ease of use, seamless integration with other software systems, etc. CSDG is in the process of re-designing the user interface across the full family of configuration systems, to make it more flexible and less cumbersome for users. Part of this effort includes a new interface architecture which will also respond to the increasing demand for more flexible, straightforward interfaces to other software systems. Also, various system functions previously considered luxuries, now become requirements. This can be anything from cosmetic features to customized output for different manufacturing plants.

**Size and Complexity**

The configuration systems are large and technically complex. We will discuss this from the perspective of the rule bases, the databases, and the traditional software programs and routines which make up the systems. It is hoped that this will give some perspective on the dimensions along which an expert system must be managed technically. Figure 2 gives a simplified view of the current configuration systems architecture (i.e., the systems' functional components and their interrelationships), focusing only on the systems in production use.

RULE BASES: The configuration systems rule bases are written in VAX OPS5. The specific rule counts (as of September, 1988) for each expert system are as follows:

| | |
|---|---|
| XCON | 10129 |
| XSEL | 3629 |
| XFL | 1808 |
| XCLUSTER | 243 |
| XNET (prototype) | 1700 |

Rule count alone is an inadequate characterization of a rule-based expert system. Representational complexity is another important dimension and can be summarized for the configuration systems as follows:

- Average number of condition elements per rule (the "if" portion of a rule, must be satisfied for the rule to activate) 6
- Average number of attributes per condition element (tests, pattern dimensions, a mea-

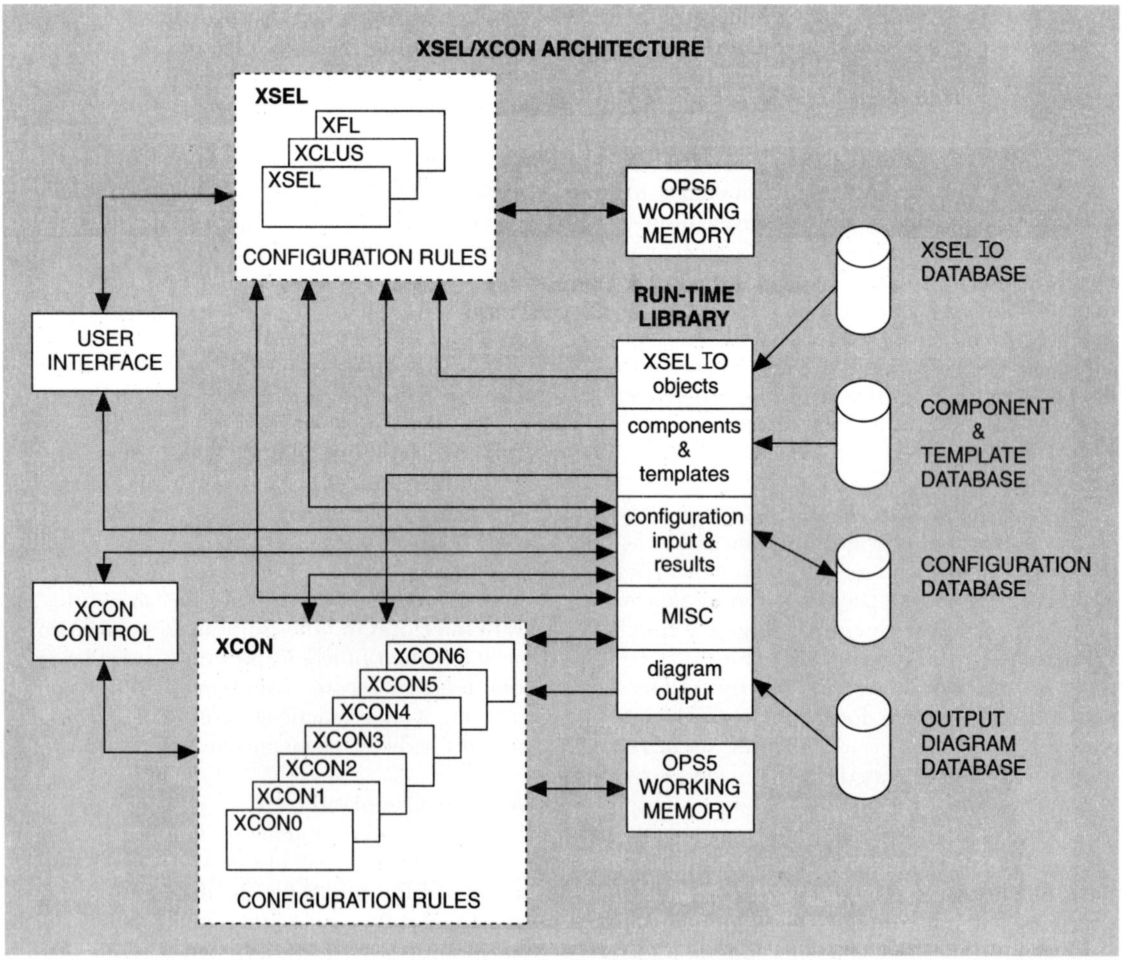


**FIGURE 2. XSEL/XCON Architecture**

sure of the amount of detail in each condition element) 5

- Average number of action elements per rule (the "then" portion of a rule, actions to be taken when rule is activated) 4

Thus, on average, the number of tests that each rule must make on each cycle to determine whether it is applicable is $6 \times 5 = 30$.

DATABASES: The configuration systems include five databases.

The component database contains configuration information on over 30,000 parts. There are from 25 to 125 attributes per part, with an average of about 40, depending on the type of part. There are over 40 types of parts; for example, cabinets, cables, controllers, disks, processors, tapes. This is a compiled database, memory-resident, compressed, with multiple indices.

The container-template database contains information on certain types of parts (e.g., backplanes) which describes their containership characteristics (e.g., number and size slots). There are over 725 such templates. This database is technically structured in the same way as the component database.

The diagram-template database contains over 1,200 graphical representations of the major types of parts (e.g., cabinets, boxes, backplanes), for use in the XCON output diagrams. This database is a combination of an application-specific file system and text libraries.

The question-template database contains over 1,000 questions used by XSEL, XFL, and XCLUSTER when interacting with the user. The following examples used in XSEL are illustrative:

- This configuration is not complete without media for your VMS license. If you already have media on another system, you do not have to add it here. Do you have another system with appropriate media?
- How many of your terminals will be connected locally to a communication device or terminal server?

This database is made up of an application-specific file system.

The configuration database holds the user input (e.g., line items) and system output (e.g., XCON diagrams) on each configuration or order entered into the system for processing. The content and number of these databases varies by production installation site. This is a VAX DBMS* database structured according to the CODASYL network model.

TRADITIONAL SOFTWARE: A significant portion of the configuration systems (over 350 programs/routines and over 50,000 lines of code) are written in traditional languages best suited for the specific input, output, file handling, etc. tasks being performed. This is summarized as:

| | |
|---|---|
| BASIC | User interface and related mechanisms |
| C | Component database access |
| BLISS | Component database access and creation |
| PASCAL | XCON batch control |
| MACRO | Transfer vectors |
| SCAN | Pre-specified systems selection |

In addition, a number of routines written in traditional languages are called from OPS5 to perform a variety of tasks such as counting, sorting, and various numeric conversions.

### Managerial Implications

In managing the configuration systems development effort, we have found it important to pay particular attention to several key areas impacted by the various technical challenges previously discussed.

We have learned that it is imperative that the development effort be in the context of a stated overall system architecture (such as that in Figure 2) at any point in time. From that we have an explicit understanding of what parts of the systems use expert system technology and what parts do not; of how those different parts must interact and how that interaction will be controlled; of what kinds of databases are needed and how they integrate; of performance implications of the architecture; etc. These are basic software engineering norms which we believe do apply to expert systems work. In the early years, we did not have an explicit architecture; the sys-

*VAX DBMS is a registered trademark of Digital Equipment Corporation.

tems were considered fluid and evolving and to some degree everything was experimental. But we quickly discovered that without the context and discipline which an architecture provides, there is no way to insure that growth in system size and complexity can be managed successfully. Indeed, we have changed and are still changing the configuration systems architecture, sometimes significantly, to reflect their ongoing evolution. As our experience grows, we gain more insight into the relative importance of different design principles.

We are always concerned about maintainability. Only with a great deal of effort and the utilization of periodic relevant advances in the technology, have we been able to keep the configuration systems viable. The learning curve for new developers in CSDG has been as high as 12 months. People we hire are typically not experienced in OPS5, do not know the computer configuration task, and have no technical knowledge of the configuration systems. It takes a long time for even an experienced software engineer to become adept enough in all three of these areas of expertise to have a net positive impact on the group (i.e., for their contribution to outweigh the drain on others of training them). We are shrinking this learning curve by using Digital's two-month AI Training Program, by providing specialized configuration training of our own, and by using a fairly structured, step-wise approach to integrating new developers. The RIME methodology is expected to have a major impact on the developer learning curve, by making it much easier to become familiar with the systems through the explicit representational structure it provides. In addition, the RIME methodology reduces the problems of system changes having unexpected impacts and facilitates catching certain kinds of bugs.

Maintainability is also affected by the allowable cycle time from acquiring new knowledge to releasing the systems; the dynamic nature of Digital's product set makes it difficult to optimize the frequency of our releases. Our users need access to configuration information as soon as new products are announced. Time-to-market is getting shorter and shorter in the computer industry, and Digital announces a large number of new products each year. This leaves CSDG with very little time to gather and incorporate product configuration knowledge into the configuration systems. CSDG currently provides quarterly releases with interim upgrades as needed to incorporate major new products by the time they are announced.

For expert systems, we believe that tool development must go hand-in-hand with the development of the application programs to insure success with systems in production use—where operating efficiency, reliability, and productivity are so important. We have come to realize the need for home-grown developers tools if what is needed is not otherwise available, and that there is a support cost involved for such tools. Over the years, CSDG has developed or influenced the development of tools to provide the following:

- OPS5 workstation environment,
- Code (including rules) management,
- Rule compilation,
- Rule checking,
- Specialized database management,
- Automatic testing, and
- On-line user problem reporting and feedback.

These tools have been critical to the success of the configuration systems and a major factor for us in enhancing both maintainability and developer productivity.

CSDG is constantly balancing short-term and long-term tradeoffs. Is the development effort a testbed for research breakthroughs, new tools, new language releases, new engineering methodologies? Or is it a production "shop," requiring consistent levels of quality, predictability, timeliness, and reliability? For us, it is very definitely both. We constantly work at maintaining a manageable balance. This is an art, not a science, and we believe it is one of the most critical factors in succeeding at developing expert systems for production use. If we swing too far toward the production side, our systems will run aground from lack of technological breakthroughs and innovation. We will hit the limits of existing technology. If we swing too far toward the testbed side, our systems will fail from putting too many resources on experimentation and investment, and not enough on satisfying today's user needs and dependencies.

## HUMAN RESOURCE/ORGANIZATIONAL ISSUES

In an evolutionary environment, where managing change and managing learning are the name of the game (that is, where lack of norms is the norm. . . .), there are bound to be human resource and organizational challenges. The formula for success is to put energy into managing these challenges. For us, this has meant: be aware of the players and their roles and needs; identify the tasks, the processes, and the organizational structures needed to make the effort an ongoing success; and pay attention to the shifting sands—be sensitized to the impacts of the effort on *people;* notice when things are changing or should be changed.

### Key Roles

On the human resource side, clarity of roles is always an important factor. Based largely on the configuration systems experience, we have developed a model of the various key roles involved in an expert system development effort. This model reflects a broad perspective on involvement. It is a model of functions, not individuals; that is, one individual may play more than one role at any particular point in time, or one role may be played by more than one individual. The roles are as follows:

- The CHAMPION has strategic vision, a belief in what the technology can offer, political savvy, the ability to influence and/or provide a supportive, enabling environment, and influence over the sponsor.
- The SPONSOR has ownership of the business problem or vision, commitment to solve that problem or reach that vision, organizational stature and support, the appropriate resources (funding), and an understanding of managing change.
- The PROGRAM MANAGER is an integration role responsible for the overall goodness and deployment of the program, has more of a business than a technical focus, and manages the interfaces among the players.
- The TECHNICAL TEAM consists of two development roles:
  The KNOWLEDGE ENGINEER is the expert system technologist role which architects the AI portion of the system and performs the knowledge acquisition, knowledge representation, and knowledge base development and testing tasks; and does so using a rapid prototyping, iterative development process.
  The SOFTWARE SYSTEMS INTEGRATION ENGINEER is the more traditional software engineering role which owns the overall system architecture; designs and develops the traditional technology portions of the system (I/O-system and user and database interfaces, file handling, etc.); designs, develops, and manages the development environment (tools, hardware/software setup, etc.); performs release management tasks; and supports installed base system managers.
- The EXPERTS provide domain knowledge in terms of both the process of performing the task and the data content, as well as quality assurance, verification support.
- The USERS provide business knowledge in terms of the organization of the work being affected, how the system will fit into the current or future business process, and relevant job satisfaction issues.

It should be noted that in some cases the experts and the users may be the same people, but in other cases they may be different people, perhaps even in different parts of the company. For configuration systems, the primary experts are hardware design engineers and manufacturing engineers, whereas the primary users are salespersons, technical order validaters, and manufacturing build technicians.

We have found it important to look periodically at which roles are filled for the configuration systems effort and which are not. These things change over time, and some changes have caught us by surprise. The exercise includes assessing the impact of any gaps or holes which may be discovered, determining the exposure, and deciding what to do. At different points in the development cycle, we have found different roles may be more or less critical, but it has paid off for us to make those relative strength assessments consciously.

In expert systems development, it can be easy to get so focused on whether the technology can adequately address the problem and how to represent the knowledge effectively that the users' perspective gets inadequate attention. This happened in the early years of XCON and it took us several years to get back on track with the users in manufacturing. The expert system application exists to support a business need and be useable within the context of the appropriate business processes—the problem has not been solved until the users are using the system effectively. This is no different than in traditional software application development.

One way we have found to avoid this kind of imbalance is to set up clearly defined accountability relationships among the key roles. (Note that accountability does not necessarily imply a direct organizational reporting relationship.) There are many possible models of accountability and different ones will be more appropriate than others in different companies or on different projects. For us, the following relationships have been critical:

- The program manager must feel accountable to the sponsor and to the users.
- The technical team must feel responsible to the program manager.
- Users are probably ultimately accountable to the sponsor as part of the normal business structure.
- The champion may not have an accountability relationship with the other key roles.
- The same may be true with the experts—although, this can cause difficulties if a lot of their time is required working with knowledge engineers, especially in ongoing knowledge acquisition efforts.

**Key Role Evolution**

For us, the nature of these key roles has evolved over time, as the development effort has passed through various stages, when organizational growth has necessitated a re-evaluation of roles, and especially as each system went into production use. We have tried to understand and monitor this process as the development effort has proceeded. We have discovered that the incumbents may need help in understanding the change and feeling comfortable with it. In some cases, different people may be more suited to fill the roles. What we observed and learned from the configuration systems experience is generalized and summarized below:

The SPONSOR and CHAMPION roles do not evolve per se, but it is important to know what it takes to keep them supportive: maintain an understanding of their mission and the role expert systems can play, stay connected to their vision (it may change over time), keep them informed, and above all "deliver the goods" (this can include small successes along the way). Depending on the breadth of the expert system's applicability, there may eventually be more than one sponsor or champion. For the configuration systems, there are now several champions and a number of sponsors (representing the various constituencies and funding sources).

The PROGRAM MANAGER role evolution reflects the likelihood that a successful expert system will be visible, impact multiple functions and support a higher level of integration within the company. The emphasis may shift from a single project to a multi-project program, from setting schedules to setting expectations, from working tasks to working relationships, from providing individual contribution to motivating cooperation. A PROGRAM OFFICE may evolve to support the program manager, consisting of business analysts and implementation planning specialists. For the configuration systems, there are two program offices, one which supports the field users and one which supports the manufacturing users.

The TECHNICAL TEAM may grow to a size where a DEVELOPMENT or ENGINEERING MANAGER is needed.

The KNOWLEDGE ENGINEER may evolve from an individual contributor to a leader of multiple expert system technologists, may operate less in discovery mode and more in adaptive mode as the problem becomes better understood and the system design is established, and may become less of a novice and more of an expert in the subject domain. CSDG's most experienced knowledge engineers are recognized within the company as configuration experts.

The SOFTWARE SYSTEMS INTEGRATION ENGINEER role gets bigger and more complex as the system grows and broadens in scope, as the development environment must expand to support a larger technical team, as integration with traditional technology becomes more important, and as the system goes into production use. In the early years of the configuration systems effort, the importance of this role was inadequately understood and it was understaffed during some critical periods; it took us a long time to overcome the negative impacts on the operation.

The RESEARCHER/ADVANCED DEVELOPER is an optional role which evolves from a success base and deals with the initial application of new technology opportunities to the subject domain through major redesign of existing systems or major new system development. This role can consist of a team of knowledge engineers and software system integration engineers, as applicable. Within CSDG, both the RIME and XNET development efforts have been spearheaded by such teams.

The EXPERT role will always be to provide domain knowledge, but over time there will be additional emphasis on their influence on the system design and on the insight they gain from the technical team into the task being systematized. There will probably be an evolution from one or a few experts at early stages of development, to many experts once the system is in ongoing production use. For the configuration systems, there are literally hundreds of different experts in Manufacturing and Engineering which must be consulted for information during each quarterly release cycle. (A truly critical lesson we learned early on was that having only one expert initially can be potentially disastrous by falsely constraining the design and/or skewing the perspective which the system reflects.)

For USERS, the relative emphasis will shift from software functionality (can the expert system do the task?) to software quality (how accurate is the system?), and then from software quality to quality of delivery (how user-friendly is the system?). Overall, the main evolutionary issue for the users is how their business and their jobs change as a result of the use of the expert system.

As there are no norms, it took us a while to understand the skills and knowledge required in each role. We regularly assess the incumbents against these requirements to identify gaps and/or developmental needs.

**Development Tasks and Process**

As with the Key Roles Model, we have formulated a general model of expert systems development, based largely on the configuration systems experience. We believe there are four major expert systems development tasks. Within each major task, there are a few key sub-tasks we emphasize to insure continued success, as follows:

*Defining and redefining the system*
This includes determining how to exploit Expert Systems technology, determining where it is appropriate to use traditional software technology, and designing the system to satisfy a variety of requirements.

*Extending and refining the system*
This includes knowledge base management, ongoing knowledge acquisition, integration of multiple systems, and user and system interface management.

*Delivering the system*
This includes release management, release distribution, support of production installations, and support of users.

*Evaluating the system*
This includes looking at system accuracy, system performance, maintainability characteristics, and how well the system fits with the business need.

It has been our experience that these tasks, per se, are similar to those used in traditional software development. What is somewhat unique for expert systems is the process which must be set up to achieve these tasks. We have learned that the process of developing expert systems is likely to be even more iterative than traditional development for the following reasons:

- The technology is evolving,
- The problem is likely not well understood and of a knowledge-intensive nature,

**DEVELOPMENT GROUP STRUCTURE**

As the development process must reflect and facilitate achievement of the development tasks, the development group organizational structure must reflect and facilitate the processes used. We believe that there is no one organizational structure which will suffice for all time; CSDG has in fact changed its organizational structure a number of times over the years when the need has been apparent.

The CSDG currently has 59 members (excluding business management and administrative support) and is organized in the following functional subgroups:

KNOWLEDGE ENGINEERING—NEW SYSTEMS DEVELOPMENT designs and develops the AI aspects of new expert systems. This includes developing the overall design, acquiring knowledge from experts, producing user scripts to bound the system, iterative prototyping, implementation development (a transition phase) and releasing initial version into production use. There are six people in this group (10 percent).

KNOWLEDGE ENGINEERING—OPERATIONAL SYSTEMS DEVELOPMENT performs the knowledge engineering aspects of the extension and refinement of the systems in production use. This includes acquiring knowledge from experts, representing the knowledge, building the knowledge base, testing the systems, and providing regular releases. There are 27 people in this group (45 percent).

QUALITY ASSURANCE provides support for the production systems which includes processing and analyzing user problems, conducting production environment testing, developing and monitoring performance and success metrics, performing documentation administration, and updating and maintaining a project administration system. There are six people in this group (10 percent).

SOFTWARE SYSTEMS INTEGRATION ENGINEERING provides integration engineering and system deployment expertise. This includes monitoring the overall system architecture, developing and supporting all traditional software (for both new and production systems), developing interfaces to other software systems, extending, refining, and supporting the development environment, managing the release process, and supporting the system managers at production installation sites. There are 16 people in this group (28 percent).

ARCHITECTURES AND ADVANCED TECHNOLOGY insures appropriate use of state-of-the-art expert systems and traditional software engineering technology throughout CSDG. This includes definition of system architectures, involvement with various research efforts, awareness of other expert systems efforts inside and outside Digital, and architecture, design, and implementation consultation. There are four people in this group (7 percent).

- The match between technology and problem may be uncertain, and
- The business being affected will likely change significantly as a result of the use of the expert system.

The success of configuration systems at Digital would not have occurred had we not worked out a development process which allowed for iteration among all the tasks and which set expectations of all participants appropriately.

For the ongoing development of our production systems, we have used a process with basic ingredients: work planning and prioritization, software design/development/test, system quality review, and system release. We use a slightly different process for a new system's initial stages of development (pre-version 1). We have learned that the transition into production use is a real change, and our processes reflect that.

The development environment must support the overall development process and make the developers' lives as easy as possible. This is where the specialized expert systems languages and tools come into play. In CSDG, the following real-time, iterative daily knowledge engineer activities are supported: rule additions and modifications, database additions and modifications, rule and database compilations, testing, and selective saving of rules and data. In addition, there is a global nightly build which merges all validated rules and data, incorporates new database attributes, runs global tests, provides a "clean," stable version of the system to developers each morning, and generates run-time efficiency improvements.

## CONCLUSION

For Digital, the configuration systems experience has provided a model of both how much impact expert systems can have on a company, and how to successfully manage the ongoing development of expert systems in production use.

The value of the configuration systems to Digital can be stated as follows:

- Explicit focus on a task, and the related information, that had previously been distributed ineffectively among a variety of organizations.

  The configuration systems have provided a focus on system configuration across engineering groups, between manufacturing and engineering, between the field and manufacturing, and across geographies.
- Support for the corporation's *a la carte* marketing strategy.

  The configuration systems allow Digital to maintain its competitive edge during a time when our products and the solutions we sell are becoming increasingly complex.
- Process efficiencies, change enablement, and evolution to tomorrow's processes.

  The configuration systems are providing these kinds of benefits to the design and selection of systems to be ordered, the technical validation of system orders, and the fulfillment/build/installation processes for system orders.
- Testbed for application of expert systems technology and evolution of related software engineering languages, tools, and techniques.

  The configuration systems effort spans the full spectrum of software life cycles from research through production use. The configuration systems are a family of multiple cooperating expert systems with a common knowledge base. They utilize an architecture which integrates traditional and expert system technology. CSDG provides significant input to the development of the VAX OPS5 language and related tools. The configuration systems effort is a prime example of "programming in the large." CSDG is dealing with very high rates of change in the knowledge base/subject domain, the business environment, and the expert system technology used.

We have set up a highly successful enterprise providing reliable, regular releases of several extremely large expert systems which address a strategic business problem and are used every day in the corporation world-wide. The use of these systems, by a variety of user groups, is saving Digital tens of millions of dollars each year and helping us come up the learning curve in an exciting technology.

### THE ENGINEERING OF XCON

**Judith Bachant and Elliot Soloway**

As Barker and O'Connor point out, XCON provides critically important support for Digital's marketing strategy of selling *a la carte* systems; i.e., customers can put together a hardware/software system that is tailored to their specific needs. In effect, each system configuration is unique. Given that each such configuration may have hundreds of components, and that hundreds of systems are configured each day, this marketing philosophy would be difficult to manage without a high degree of automation.

In automating the configuration task, Digital needed to confront a number of serious issues: there are 30,000+ hardware and software parts that are drawn upon; there is a hefty body of knowledge about how to configure a system; and there is no way to identify beforehand what specific configurations might be produced—the combinatorics are substantial. A further complication involves coping with the following fact: the component database and the knowledge base must be continually updated to reflect new products, new marketing strategies, changing government regulations, new user requests, etc. These characteristics raise the question about the suitability of this task for automation. Prior to XCON, Digital attempted to tackle the configuration task using traditional procedural programming languages—without success. Rather, the breakthrough came when the configuration task was viewed from the perspective of production rule programming. In particular, OPS5, a production rule programming language, provided mechanisms for coping with a key aspect of automating the configuration task: the program deciding what to do and when to do it.

In general, customer orders are highly variable, and thus the determination of what actions need to be performed to configure an order must be made dynamically, at execution time, as the order is being processed. Deciding when an action can appropriately occur in relation to other actions is also sensitive to this variability in the customer order. While two system configurations may well need most of the same actions to occur, even ostensibly slight differences in the configurations may dictate variations in the sequence of activities due to complex interactions between components and constraints. Thus, procedural languages, with their commitment to pre-determined sequences of activities with relatively limited branching, do not provide the flexibility at run time that is needed to cope with the "what" and "when" characteristics of the configuration task confronting Digital.

In contrast, the production rule programming paradigm explicitly provides the dynamic, run-time decision-making that was essential. The foundation for processing in OPS5, a production rule language, is the recognize/act cycle. In the OPS5 language, the "working memory" holds global state information: inputs and results of rule actions. The conditional part of a production rule (the "if" part) specifies tests on that working memory; if all the conditions are satisfied by matches in the working memory, then the action part of the rule (the "then" part) is executed, which in turn changes working memory in some way. Changing working memory means updating or deleting existing elements that match conditions in the rule, or creating new elements. Furthermore, the method of selecting what to do next in OPS5 differs substantially from that in a procedural language. In the case of a procedural language, the amount of global state information needed for such a decision is, quite deliberately, severely limited: the program counter is incremented by one, or a small set of tests in a conditional statement is used to select what to do next.

In OPS5, the entire rule set is examined in light of the change to the working memory (global state), in order to select which rule to execute next. Each rule must carry its own complete triggering context in order to identify its scope of applicability. (This type of control will be referred to later as "situation recognition.") These properties of OPS5 provide the flexibility and variability needed for the task.

### COPING WITH COMPLEXITY AND CHANGE IN XCON

In Figure 1, we present a representative rule from pre-1988 XCON. (For ease of readability, the rules in all the figures are English renderings of actual OPS5 rules.) This rule deals with positioning a disk drive within an enclosure and connecting the disk to its controller. Notice first the number of test conditions in the conditional part of the rule; before this rule can activate, a great deal of information must exist in the global state. The situation described is complex and each condition is annotated to indicate why it is needed and what might happen if it were absent. Some of the conditions are needed in order to actually take the action specified. This may involve identifying what element in working memory needs to be updated. For example, the disk being configured needs to be identified (C4), since one action involves marking it as such and other actions use its identifiers in creating the connecting and containing relationships to other components. Other conditions, like C2, specify the general context of applicability for the entire rule. Still others look for cues signaling that related actions have occurred previously or have not yet occurred, in order to insure that this rule will activate at the appropriate time. Part of C4 specifies that a controller has already been assigned to the disk. This rule cannot activate until a controller has been assigned as a result of the activation of some other rule. C11 looks for specific unused spaces in a particular type of cabinet, since if there are such spaces, it is not yet time for this rule to execute. The OPS5 language effectively supports and efficiently processes this degree of conditional specification. XCON was successfully implemented in this manner.

As Barker and O'Connor point out, key to XCON's success has been its ability to grow and change in response to both Digital's product offerings and the ever expanding user base. Since XCON is continually evolving, the ability to modify, extend, and develop code efficiently is of paramount importance. Enhancing developer productivity became an increasingly important priority as the demands resulting from the success of the application mushroomed. Toward enhancing productivity, we needed to better manage the size and complexity of rules, and better manage the sheer

**FIGURE 1. Example of Pre-RIME XCON Rule (pp. 709–710)**

*Rule Name: R1a-unmounted-ubx-options*

| | IF | Comments |
|---|---|---|
| *C1* | The current step in the configuration process involves mounting options in containers; | *This condition is used to distinguish the group of rules that can potentially activate.* |
| *C2* | and the system being configured is not a vax11/780, vax11/782, vax11/785, vax8650, or vax8600; | *This rule is not applicable to those types of hardware systems.* |
| *C3* | and there is no unconfigured disk which sits on the idc bus; | *This condition insures that the rule will not activate before all disks on an idc bus have been configured ("Disk" actually means "disk drive".)* |
| *C4* | and there is an unconfigured r102-type disk which needs to mount inside a cabinet and whose pre-assigned controller sits on a unibus and it is the first disk assigned; | *This identifies the properties required of an appropriate disk to be configured by this rule.* |
| *C5* | and there is no unconfigured r102-type disk assigned to a controller that is placed closer to the cpu than the controller assigned to the aforementioned disk; | *Disks assigned to controllers that are closest to the cpu need to be placed first, in case there is insufficient capacity for all of them.* |
| *C6* | and there is a requirement to cable the disk to be configured to a controller; | *Part of the activity of this rule is to determine that cabling. There may be several possibilities.* |
| *C7* | and there has been no connection made between the disk to be configured and anything else; | *This indicates that some of the activities that this rule will perform have not yet occurred.* |
| *C8* | and there is a controller to which the disk to be configured has been pre-assigned and which sits on a unibus; | *This identifies the appropriate controller.* |
| *C9* | and there is a requirement to cable the controller to a disk whose type and quantity of cable match one of the possibilities specified for the disk; | *This identifies the type and quantity of cable needed for this particular disk/controller combination.* |
| *C10* | and there has been no connection created yet to this controller from any disk; | *Another indication that the activities to be performed by this rule have not occurred.* |
| *C11* | and there are no unused disk spaces in any unibus cabinet; | *This insures that any spaces appropriate for disks in this type of cabinet will be filled before the rule can activate.* |
| *C12* | and there is a description for the capacity of a disk cabinet, whose name is not "h9643"; | *This identifies a special type of cabinet that can only contain disks. An "h9643" is one variation of a cabinet to which the rule does not apply.* |
| *C13* | and there is an unconfigured disk cabinet; | *This identifies an appropriate cabinet in which the disk to be configured will be placed by the rule.* |
| *C14* | and the top space available for disk placement is unused; | *This identifies a location in the aforementioned cabinet where the disk to be configured can be placed. It needs to be on the top because of the removable medium.* |

**FIGURE 1. *continued***

| | THEN | *Comments* |
|---|---|---|
| *A1* | mark the disk configured; | |
| *A2* | and update the top space in the cabinet to be used; | *The location needs to be marked so that nothing else will be placed there.* |
| *A3* | and create a connection relationship between the disk and its controller, fully specifying the identifying information for the disk, controller, cabinet, and the type and quantity of the cable to be used for the connection; | *This establishes the connection between the disk and its controller. Other rules will determine the length and choose the exact cable(s).* |
| *A4* | and create a containing relationship between the disk and the cabinet, specifying the identifying information for the disk and cabinet as well as the location of the placement; | *This establishes the placement of the disk in the cabinet.* |
| *A5* | and create labels for the output diagram showing the disk within the cabinet for both the skyline view of the cabinet layout and the detailed view of the particular cabinet. | *This insures that the output diagram will display this information correctly.* |

quantity of rules. The RIME software engineering methodology [1, 12, 13] was developed to achieve these desired benefits. XCON was reimplemented utilizing this methodology and the new implementation has been in production use since January 1988. RIME was also used in the design and development of XNET (an expert system that configures computer networks—see Barker and O'Connor). We will now focus on two of RIME's major prescriptions: RIME's guidance in specifying control in a production rule context, and RIME's guidance in organizing a rule base.

## NEW CONTROL TECHNIQUES

### Problem-Solving Methods: Specifying Algorithmic Control

OPS5 supports "situation recognition" as its only form of control. Following the principles of *pure* production rule programming style, one should not force the firing of rules in a fixed sequence. However, the reality is that there are times when one wants to implement an algorithm, and thus execute a set of rules in some specific sequence. Rule developers did, in fact, use situation recognition to implement algorithm-like rule sequencing. What RIME has done is recognize that algorithms can and should be specifiable in a production rule context, and it provided explicit techniques for their definition. In RIME, pre-defined algorithms are referred to as problem-solving methods.

Problem-solving methods, then, are defined at development time—not at run time—and are composed of steps; each step of a method may contain one or more rules. Upon entry to a step, the rules fire (using "situation recognition") until all satisfied rules have been activated, and then processing proceeds to the next step. For example, in Figure 2 we present two rules from the "change-characteristic" problem-solving method used in XNET, an interactive system for specifying a computer network. This method allows a user to interact with XNET and change the characteristics of a part of the network (e.g., server, host, segment, etc.). The rule in Figure 2a is from the "ask-value" step of the method; in this step, the user is asked for a value of a network characteristic that the user wants to change. The rule in Figure 2b is from the "reset" step of this same method; as the last step it performs finalization activities, in this instance marking the characteristic as no longer identified as needing to be changed. There are also a number of other rules in each of these two steps.

Using this type of control reduces the amount of situation specification in the conditional part of the rule, since locating a rule within a pre-determined process eliminates the need for the individual rule to specify where it fits in that context. The individual rule's situation specification need not include reference to when it needs to activate in relation to rules in other steps of the process. In this case, without "algorithmic" control, one or more conditions would need to be added to the situation specification of the rule in Figure 2b to prevent it from activating before its time in the process (e.g., after the rule in Figure 2a fires).

### Deliberate Decision Making: Explicitly Choosing Among Alternatives

As the rule in Figure 1 illustrates, XCON rules tend to be complex. This rule actually makes a number of decisions implicitly in the course of recognizing its applicability (e.g., selecting an appropriate disk, selecting a cabinet in which to place it, selecting a particular place within the cabinet), all in order to configure a disk. In effect, each rule that dealt with configuring a component needed to make sure that a constellation of com-

**FIGURE 2a. Example of RIME XNET Rule**

*Rule Name: Change-characteristics:ask-value:300b:default-units*

| | IF | *Comments* |
|---|---|---|
| *C1* | The current step of the process of changing the characteristics involves asking for a value; | *The current activity of the system is to ask the user for a value of a characteristic.* |
| *C2* | and the characteristic to be changed involves length; | |
| *C3* | and a default has been specified; | |
| *C4* | and the default has not yet been expressed in terms of units; | |
| | **THEN** | |
| *A1* | change the default to be expressed in units. | *For example, if an appropriate cable has a length of 40 inches, the default to the user will read "3 feet, 4 inches".* |

**FIGURE 2b. Example of RIME XNET Rule**

*Rule Name: Change-characteristics:reset:100a:reset-characteristic*

| | IF | *Comments* |
|---|---|---|
| *C1* | The current step of the process of changing the characteristics involves resetting after a change was made; | *The current activity of the system is to reset after obtaining a new value.* |
| *C2* | and the characteristic to be changed is still marked as such; | |
| | **THEN** | |
| *A1* | reset the characteristic so that it is no longer identified for change. | *After this rule activates, the characteristic that was specified by the user will no longer be identified.* |

**FIGURE 3a. Example of RIME XCON Rule**

*Rule Name: Configure-device:propose:200a:select-device*

| | IF | *Comments* |
|---|---|---|
| *C1* | The current step of the process of configuring devices involves proposing alternatives; | *The current activity of the system is to propose tasks that will ultimately result in the configuration of a device.* |
| *C2* | and no device has yet been chosen; | |
| *C3* | and there is at least one unconfigured device; | *Not all of the devices on the customer order have been configured.* |
| *C4* | and the process of selecting a device has not yet been proposed; | |
| *C5* | and no problem has been identified concerning selecting a device; | *If there is already an identified problem with selecting a device, the task should not be proposed again until the problem has been resolved.* |
| | **THEN** | |
| *A1* | Propose to go through the process of selecting a device. | |

**FIGURE 3b. Example of RIME XCON Rule**

*Rule Name: Configure-device:propose:500b:select-container*

| | IF | *Comments* |
|---|---|---|
| *C1* | The current step of the process of configuring devices involves proposing alternatives; | *The current activity of the system is to propose tasks that will ultimately result in the configuration of a device.* |
| *C2* | and there is at least one unconfigured device that needs to be placed inside a container; | |
| *C3* | and no container has yet been chosen; | |
| *C4* | and no device in which other devices can be placed has been chosen as a container; | *There are some large tape drives that have a compartment in the bottom suitable for disk placement.* |
| *C5* | and the process of selecting a container has not yet been proposed; | |
| *C6* | and there has been no problem identified concerning selecting a container; | *If there is already an identified problem with selecting a container, the task should not be proposed again until the problem has been resolved.* |
| | **THEN** | |
| *A1* | Propose to go through the process of selecting a container. | |

ponents was available; such a need resulted in complex conditional parts of rules. Given the large number of rules that had such complex conditional parts, it became quite difficult to update the rules in light of new product announcements, etc.; it was hard to know if one had found all the rules that needed changing.

In contrast, RIME's philosophy is that complex rules need to be broken down; in particular, multiple tasks need to be factored out and each task needs to be made into an explicit, separate process. For example, in the new implementation of XCON, there is a set of rules that accomplishes the task of selecting a device (tape, disk, etc.), a set of rules that accomplishes the task of selecting a container for another component (cabinet, box, etc.), and another set of rules that accomplishes the task of selecting the particular location within the container to place the other component. Notice that all of these tasks are embedded in the conditional part of the rule in Figure 1.

The effect of accomplishing each of these tasks is to create intermediate results; components are selected, and made available to other tasks upon the completion of the task. In effect, these tasks work together to build up the set of components needed in order to perform the various activities involved in configuration. Thus, each rule can assume a certain amount of the specification as being accomplished; thus, rules, such as those in Figure 3, need only test those features of the state that are relevant to their specific task (e.g., selecting a particular disk).

Now that there are explicit tasks that need to be carried out, the question arises as to which tasks to execute and in what order. What RIME prescribes, in situations in which a choice must be made among competing alternatives, is that tasks to be accomplished are first proposed, and that there be an explicit arbitration process that examines the alternatives and selects one to carry out. We term this type of control technique "deliberate decision making" since we want to emphasize the need to have rules that deliberately examine the set of proposed tasks and decide, for specific, identifiable reasons why one task should be preferred over some others.

**Putting It All Together:**
**An Example Illustrating Three Types of Control**

The activity in the "propose-apply" problem-solving method provides examples of all three types of control techniques. Propose-apply was derived from the "universal weak method" developed by the researchers involved with the SOAR architecture [5]. The method is utilized fairly extensively in XCON because of the preponderance of complex decisions. The steps of the method include: proposing operators, eliminating the less desirable ones, selecting one, and performing the operation specified.

Figures 3, 4, and 5 present rules in three steps of the propose-apply method. The method, in this instance, is used for the task of configuring a device. The rules in Figures 3a and 3b are both from the propose step, and thus both put forth alternative suggestions. In this case, the alternatives are tasks themselves: 3a proposes to accomplish the task of selecting a device (tape, disk, etc.) to configure, while 3b proposes to accomplish the task of selecting a container (box, cabinet, etc.) in which to place a device. The rules in Figures 4a and 4b belong to a subsequent step (the eliminate step) in the method, and arbitrate between the two alternative tasks suggested in the previous step by the two rules in Figure 3. Deliberate decision making is this arbitration process: there are explicit rules that propose tasks, examine the proposed tasks, and choose which one to carry out.

Note in particular, that the rule in Figure 4a prefers one of the tasks proposed, while the rule in Figure 4b selects the other activity. The choice of whether 4a or 4b fires depends on the specific situation, (i.e., using situation recognition, these rules will fire depending on the details of the particular system configuration). Once the alternatives are narrowed to one, the apply step is entered. In this example, the rule in Figure 5 will activate since either alternative involves performing a new task. The new task will commence (either selecting a device or selecting a container) and when it is finished, control will return to the previous task, configuring a device.

After, for instance, the task of selecting a device completes and control returns to the task of configuring a device, other tasks may be proposed, and then eventually performed, until all of the required intermediate results are available. At this point, the task of actually performing the functionality of configuring a device will be proposed and selected. Once selected, the actions (corresponding to those performed by the "then" part of the rule in Figure 1) will be performed: actually marking the device configured, placing it in the cabinet, connecting it to its controller and specifying the appropriate cabling, etc. This method is used for the configuration of other types of components, and at its highest level for the process of configuring a system.

In summary, there are three forms of control that developers using RIME can employ. If the task they are implementing can be accomplished through a sequence of steps with little variation, using algorithmic control is encouraged. The developer makes decisions at development time about what should happen when

**FIGURE 4a. Example of RIME XCON Rule**

*Rule Name: Configure-device:eliminate:200g:prefer-select-device*

| | IF | *Comments* |
|---|---|---|
| *C1* | The current step of the process of configuring devices involves arbitrating between alternatives by pairwise elimination; | *The current activity of the system is to reduce the set of proposed alternatives by comparing two and preferring one over the other.* |
| *C2* | and the process of selecting a device has been proposed as an alternative; | |
| *C3* | and the process of selecting a container has been proposed as an alternative; | |
| *C4* | and the current goal of the process of configuring devices is to configure all of the rest of the devices that the customer ordered; | *This process of configuring devices iterates until the goal is achieved. In this case, the process will iterate until there are no more devices left to configure.* |
| | **THEN** | |
| *A1* | Eliminate selecting a container from consideration. | *This leaves selecting a device still a viable candidate.* |

**FIGURE 4b. Example of RIME XCON Rule**

*Rule Name: Configure-device:eliminate:200n:prefer-select-container*

| | IF | *Comments* |
|---|---|---|
| *C1* | The current step of the process of configuring devices involves arbitrating between alternatives by pairwise elimination; | *The current activity of the system is to reduce the set of proposed alternatives by comparing two and preferring one over the other.* |
| *C2* | and the process of selecting a container has been proposed as an alternative; | |
| *C3* | and the process of selecting a device has been proposed as an alternative; | |
| *C4* | and the current goal of the process of configuring devices is to fill a container with devices; | *This process of configuring devices iterates until the goal is achieved. In this case, the process will iterate until a container is filled with devices.* |
| | **THEN** | |
| *A1* | Eliminate selecting a device from consideration. | *This leaves selecting a container still a viable candidate.* |

during execution. Developers are encouraged to make these algorithms as general as possible to allow for their reuse in other instances. If there is significant variation in what activities need to occur when depending on different inputs, situation recognition or deliberate decision should be examined. Each of these provides a means for the program to participate in the decision process. Situation recognition should be used if the conditions and actions are straightforward and limited. Deliberate decision is most useful for managing complex situations with many variations and interactions. RIME has identified guidelines for aiding the developer in deciding between the last two forms of control.

**RIME's Guidelines for Organizing the Rule Base**

In addition to making explicit three types of control, RIME also prescribes explicit criteria for organizing the rule base. For many years, XCON developers have been in the habit of attempting to physically co-locate rules that had some commonality. However, as the complexity of the rules increased and the number of them grew, it became increasingly difficult to actually co-locate similar rules. It was hard to determine the most critical similarity since there were so many dimensions to choose from. There were no defined (and agreed upon) strategies for the organization so there was little consistency among different developers. Also, the reason for co-locating specific rules was not explicitly recorded. Another developer needed to infer the commonality from reading the rules. Since rules developed under RIME were less complex with the reduction in the number of conditions needing to be specified and with the limiting of functionality per rule, it was easier to see how they could be organized appropriately. The use of the control mechanisms already provided some organization based on that dimension. However, within a step in a method there may still be hundreds of rules for whom the sequence of their activation is irrelevant. The rules in the same step need to be grouped along some other dimension. Moreover, the dimensions may vary among the steps. RIME requires that the criteria for grouping be explicitly identified and recorded in "subgroup schemas." These schemas, much like database schemas, provide abstractions describing sets of rules that allow developers to efficiently index into the rule base. The schema in Figure 6 presents the organization for the "apply" rules for configuring a device. These rules actually perform the functionality of marking a device configured, connecting it to a controller, placing it in a container, etc. These actions are similar to the actions in the rule in Figure 1, but they are distributed among many rules. These rules are grouped according to their functionality. The action of a "200" rule would update the status of a component, a "320" rule would reduce the capacity available in the container in which the device was placed, etc. The dimensions for specifying organizing criteria may vary between steps. Since all of the "eliminate" rules (see Figures 4a and 4b) do exactly the

**FIGURE 5. Another Example of RIME XCON Rule**

*Rule Name: General:apply:100a:off-to-another-task*

| | **IF** | *Comments* |
|---|---|---|
| *C1* | The current step of any "propose-apply" process involves performing the task; | *This is a general rule in the system for any process that uses the propose-apply method. Examples of "performing the task" include marking an alternative chosen, doing the activities that realize the configuration, and transferring control to another process.* |
| *C2* | and the process chosen is different from the current one; | |
| | **THEN** | |
| *A1* | Transfer control to the new process as a subprocess. | *The new process will take over control and after it is finished, control will return to the current one.* |

**FIGURE 6. Partial Subgroup Schema Example**

*For the apply step of configuring a device*

| # | Level 1 | Level 2 | Level 3 |
|---|---|---|---|
| *100* | initialization | | |
| *200* | update-status | component | |
| *210* | | operator | |
| *220* | | restriction | |
| *230* | | template | |
| *300* | update-capacity | bus | |
| *310* | | power | |
| *320* | | space | drive |
| *321* | | | box |
| *330* | | load | ac |
| *331* | | | dc |
| *340* | | length | |
| *400* | update-containership | | |

same thing (actually removing from working memory the alternative matching C3) organizing by type of action would not be an effective strategy.

**THE BENEFITS OF RIME**

Recall that RIME was intended to provide guidance for the engineering of the evolving expert configuration systems at Digital. In particular, the objectives were to reduce the size and complexity of an average rule, and better manage the increasing number of rules. RIME's impact was felt dramatically in the reimplementation of XCON. For example, the appropriate use of the three available control techniques and the limiting of a rule's functionality led to smaller, more intelligible rules. Compare, for instance, the rule in Figure 1 with the RIME rules in subsequent figures. Both the use of the control techniques and the introduction of subgroup schemas aided in the management of large quantities of rules. While at first glance it may appear that the RIME methodology might require more rules and much more processing to perform the same task, that turned out not to be the case. The difference in quantity of rules was not significant: the smaller, more general rules can apply in a variety of situations. In fact, in adding new rules, one can now more easily take advantage of existing rules, and thus knowledge reuse results in a major productivity gain. The actual number of rule firings or activations did increase significantly. However, the actual processing time difference was negligible, since the OPS5 language can process the less complex rule network more efficiently. In fact, the time required per rule was an order of magnitude less, which compensated for the greater number of firings. When the newly reimplemented XCON was released, the users did not notice any change in performance either in accuracy or speed of execution. (The average cpu time to process a customer order, on a Vax 8800 with 128 MB of memory, is under a minute.) In contrast to the users, the developers definitely have noticed the difference in maintainability. The smaller rules are easier to understand, the differences between them are more pronounced, and they are much better organized.

**THE FUTURE:**
**VERY Large Configuration Expert Systems**

The RIME methodology continues to undergo change as we gain more experience with it in building industrial-strength, expert configuration systems. In addition, we are currently implementing a RIME Programming Environment that will help the developer better follow the RIME guidelines. In sum, our experiences with RIME support its utility in serving to increase both the productivity of our developers and the quality of the expert configuration systems. Inasmuch as we fully expect our configuration systems to have upwards of 20,000–30,000 rules in the near term, we believe that the RIME software development methodology can play a critical role in the engineering of this next generation of expert systems.

*Acknowledgments.* We are grateful to Bill Hanson, Digital's Vice President of Manufacturing, and Lou Gaviglia, Vice President of U.S. Manufacturing, for their commitment to and sponsorship of the configuration systems efforts over the years. This support has insured the positive environment which has enabled us to proceed, experiment, and make significant impacts. We would also like to thank John McDermott, Ken Gilbert, Bob Breau, and Anne Van Tine for their inputs on this article. And finally, it is important to acknowledge the ongoing dedication and hard work of all the members of the CSDG who have made this effort so successful and given us this story to tell.

## REFERENCES

1. Bachant, J. RIME: Preliminary work toward a knowledge-acquisition tool. In *Automating Knowledge Acquisition for Expert Systems,* S. Marcus, Ed. Kluwer Academic, 1988.
2. Bachant, J., and McDermott, J. R1 revisited: Four years in the trenches. *AI Mag. 5,* 3 (1984).
3. Feigenbaum, E., McCorduck, P., and Nii, H.P. *The Rise of the Expert Company.* Times Books, New York, 1988.
4. Kiskiel, M., Lynch, F., Marshall, C., and O'Connor, D. AI in manufacturing at Digital. *AI Mag. 7,* 5 (1986).
5. Laird, J., and Newell, A. A universal weak method. Tech. Rep. Carnegie-Mellon Univ., Dept. of Computer Science, 1983.
6. Leonard-Barton, D. Implementation as mutual adaptation of technology and organization. *Res. Policy 17,* 5 (Oct. 1988), 1–17.
7. Leonard-Barton, D. The case for integrative innovation: An expert system at Digital. *Sloan Manage. Rev. 29,* 1 (Fall 1987).
8. Leonard-Barton, D., and Sviokla, J.J. Putting expert systems to work. *Harvard Bus. Rev. 66,* 2 (Mar.–Apr. 1988).
9. McDermott, J. XSEL: A computer salesperson's assistant. In *Machine Intelligence,* J. Hayes and D. Michie, Eds. John Wiley and Sons, 1982.
10. McDermott, J. R1: The formative years. *AI Mag. 2,* 2 (1981).
11. McDermott, J. R1: A rule-based configurer of computer systems. *Artif. Intell. 19,* 1 (1982).
12. Soloway, E., Bachant, J., and Jensen, K. Assessing the maintainability of XCON-in-RIME: Coping with the problems of a very large rule-base. In *Proceedings of AAAI-87,* July, 1987.
13. van de Brug, A., Bachant, J., and McDermott, J. Taming of R1. *IEEE Expert* (Summer 1986).

# APPENDIX B

## ExperTAX$^{sm}$: An Expert System for Corporate Tax Planning

**Abstract:** *This paper describes the development of ExperTAX$^{sm}$, an expert system designed as a part of the service rendered by the audit and tax practices of the accounting firm of Coopers & Lybrand in the corporate tax accrual and planning function. The current operating environment is described and the expert system based solution is presented. The knowledge engineering process is described in detail and novel techniques for knowledge extraction are presented. The resulting system and its knowledge base is also presented together with a discussion on detailed knowledge acquisition and ongoing knowledge base maintenance facilities.*

### 1. Introduction

Recently, articles about the use of expert systems in accounting and auditing have begun to appear in the audit literature [2], and special audit research conferences focusing on the issue [3] have been scheduled. These trends are indicative of the growing degree of interest by researchers in the technology of these systems. An expert system is a system that handles real-world, complex problems requiring an expert's interpretation, and solves these problems using a computer model of expert human reasoning, reaching the same conclusions the expert would reach if faced with a comparable problem [4].

As additional artificial intelligence software tools for developing expert systems become available at reasonable cost, and the power, speed and portability of microcomputers increase, more and more audit and professional service tasks become likely candidates for assistance from

"ExperTAX$^{sm}$: An Expert System for Corporate Tax Planning" by D. Shpilberg, L. E. Graham, and H. Schatz, *Expert Systems,* July 1986, *3*(3), 136–151. 

expert systems. The potential gains in competitive advantage and productivity embodied in the use of this new technology, the ever-increasing complexity and volume of tax, regulatory, and professional accounting and auditing standards and the increasing sophistication of business environments combine to create a situation in which such systems will be most welcome. Various possible applications to the audit environment have been cited in the literature [5, 6]. Papers presented at the Symposium on Expert Systems and Audit Judgment (University of Southern California, February 1986) described some of the current expert systems work in public accounting [9, 10].

This paper presents a case study on the development of an expert system in an audit and tax environment. The study points out issues identified in the development process that are of interest to those researchers currently experimenting with expert systems. In addition, the case study may alert researchers to issues and areas of research related to expert systems where their efforts can lead to an advance in knowledge.

This paper describes the key issues surrounding the development of a knowledge-based expert system called ExperTAX$^{sm}$. It provides guidance and advice, through issue identification, to auditors and tax specialists in preparing the tax accrual for financial statement purposes. It also identifies relevant issues for tax planning, tax compliance and tax service purposes.

## 2. The problem

Tax accrual, the process of identifying tax-book differences and explaining differences between statutory and effective tax rates, is an audit task requiring specialized training and considerable time. In connection with tax services provided to most audit clients, the client's tax strategy, timely filing issues and planning opportunities are also identified during the course of the audit.

Many accounting firms have developed questionnaires, forms or checklists that facilitate the gathering of information necessary to conduct the tax accrual and tax planning functions. These questionnaires are usually completed by staff accountants in the field and may be brought back to the office or left in the field for analysis. At the client's location, an audit manager conducts the accrual analysis, and a tax manager, either in the office or at the client's location, reviews the analysis and identifies tax planning issues and opportunities. If these issues or opportunities are significant, the case is referred to more experienced personnel, such as the tax and audit partners, for further analysis and/or interaction with the client.

The problem is that practical realities limit the efficiency of the process. Tax accrual questionnaires are perceived by audit personnel to be long, complicated documents. On the other hand, tax professionals are concerned that such questionnaires attempt to simplify and standardize rather complex situations. Audit staff assigned to the task are concerned primarily with the tax accrual computation, and may not be aware of the detailed tax planning implications of some of the information collected. Other questions clearly address tax issues that are beyond their audit expertise and, while perhaps important to the tax function, may not be directly relevant to the task at hand.

After all the required information has been collected, its analysis by both the audit and tax managers on a timely basis is a complex task. While the tax accrual computation requires some time, identifying tax planning issues and opportunities is a much more demanding task. Reviewing the issues may necessitate several rounds of on-site information gathering to complete the questionnaires and answer follow-up questions. In the process of this review, the tax and audit reviewers must focus their expert attention on both simple and complex issues. The physical timing of this task creates considerable stress on tax planning efficiency, sometimes necessitating late hours and emergency meetings to meet critical deadlines.

## 3. The solution

Coopers & Lybrand has developed ExperTAX$^{sm}$, a knowledge-based expert system for supporting the corporate tax accrual and planning process. ExperTAX$^{sm}$ functions as an 'intelligent' questionnaire which guides the user through an information gathering process. It asks only those questions that are relevant to the client situation, is capable of sifting through issues that require clarification, and requests additional information when needed. It is also capable of explaining to the user why a question is being asked and why the response is relevant. In addition to its ability to gather information and identify tax accrual and planning issues, it keeps track of any relevant questions still unanswered and documents all the questions asked, answers given and user-generated 'marginal notes.'

ExperTAX$^{sm}$ enhances the current tax accrual and planning process by including the following two important features:

1) ExperTAX$^{sm}$ actively guides the staff accountant through the information gathering process, efficiently directing the individual to the relevant issues and pointing out the specific importance of the information requested. The accountant is motivated to obtain the data and become educated on the potential ramifications of the information requested. The system improves the staff accountant's productivity as well as the quality of the information gathered; it also accelerates the accountant's training process.
2) ExperTAX$^{sm}$ goes well beyond the efficient collection of information. It analyzes and synthesizes the information to identify relevant issues to be brought to the attention of audit and tax managers. It makes the process more efficient since ExperTAX$^{sm}$ routinely uncovers and describes most of the basic tax accrual and planning issues. The attention of the audit and tax managers is now directed at higher level issues, reviewing the conclusions rather than the raw data. This effectively eliminates the expert-resource-intensive task of routine information analysis, except for cases in which critical issues require the attention of highly specialized personnel.

ExperTAX$^{sm}$'s knowledge base consists of over 1000 frames, derived from knowledge engineering sessions conducted with over twenty senior tax and audit experts at Coopers & Lybrand. ExperTAX$^{sm}$ has been developed in common Lisp and runs on IBM-PC XT, AT or IBM-compatible personal computers. The following sections describe ExperTAX$^{sm}$ in greater detail.

## 4. Designing the product's environment

One of the first steps in knowledge engineering is designing the product's environment. This process includes:

- ○ Understanding the expert system's tasks
- ○ Exploring product delivery environments
- ○ Identifying the experts
- ○ Defining the structure of the knowledge base
- ○ Distilling technical requirements
- ○ Selecting software and hardware.

### *4.1 Understanding the expert system's tasks*

Prior to the introduction of ExperTAX$^{sm}$, the operating environment for the tax accrual process and related functions is summarized in Table 1. As can be seen from the Table, the process consisted of various phases and involved a number of professionals with an above average level of expertise. To aid in the conduct of the process, several supporting instruments were used and interim reports produced. All these factors and their interactions were considered in ExperTAX$^{sm}$'s development.

ExperTAX$^{sm}$ improves the tax accrual process by reducing the time devoted to specific tasks, reduces the time elapsed from start to finish, maintains the quality of the output and reduces the time demands and pressures on high-level expertise.

To improve data gathering, ExperTAX$^{sm}$ animates the questionnaire functions, asking only relevant questions and explaining the reasons for the required information in the context of the client's situation. The process allows more specialized questions to be asked, improves the average quality of the initial responses and tends to eliminate the need for additional data gathering sessions. ExperTAX$^{sm}$ allows the user to enter the required information in response to the multiple choice questions, supported by user-desired or required notes, explanations and schedules.

The most time-consuming tasks for managers are those associated with the analysis of the completed questionnaires. Over the course of the engagement, identifying and studying tax accrual and tax planning issues may take several days of expert time over several weeks of elapsed time. Since all the information used for these tasks is captured in the completed questionnaires, ExperTAX$^{sm}$ is able to conduct those tasks more efficiently, utilizing a knowledge base extracted from the experience and know-how of tax accrual and tax planning experts.

ExperTAX$^{sm}$ affects the process shown in Table 1. Step 3, Completing TAP Questionnaire, is directly replaced by ExperTAX$^{sm}$. The process

**Table 1.** *Manual Tax Accrual Process*

| | Task | Support Instruments | Output | Level of Expertise |
|---|---|---|---|---|
| Audit Strategy/Planning | | | | |
| 1. | Prepare Tax Strategy Summary | Prior-year info (summary, questionnaire, tax returns), preliminary financials, client discussion | Completed Tax Strategy Summary | Medium |
| 2. | Review Tax Strategy Summary and identify accrual issues and alternate tax strategies | Completed Tax Strategy Summary | Memoranda, possible client discussions | High |
| Preliminary Fieldwork | | | | |
| * 3. | Complete TAP questionnaire | Prior-year info, preliminary financials, client discussion | TAP questionnaire responses, notes, schedules | Medium |
| * 4. | Review data for tax accrual issues | Prior-year info, completed TAP | Memoranda | High |
| * 5. | Review data for tax planning/compliance issues and develop alternative tax strategies | Prior-year info, completed TAP | Memoranda, client discussions | High |
| Year-End Fieldwork | | | | |
| * 6. | Gather tax accrual data, compute accrual, and update questionnaire | Memoranda, financial statement data, updated TAP | Financial statement numbers, tax return schedules | Medium |
| * 7. | Perform a final review of tax accrual and TAP | Tax accrual workpapers, updated TAP | Memoranda | High |
| * 8. | Make a final identification of issues and alternative strategies | Updated TAP questionnaire | Reports to clients, memoranda | Very high |

* Steps affected by ExperTAX$^{sm}$

is greatly enhanced by the ExperTAX$^{sm}$'s 'smart' questionnaire and explanatory facilities.

Steps 4 and 5, the review for tax accrual, tax planning, and tax compliance issues, are redefined using ExperTAX$^{sm}$. Rather than reviewing raw input for issues, the issues uncovered by ExperTAX$^{sm}$ are presented to the audit manager for disposition. The audit manager reviews the issues to decide on implementation before year-end.

Step 6, the data gathering phase, also includes updating the questionnaire. ExperTAX$^{sm}$ facilitates changing answers to specific questions, and generates an updated list of issues based on the new information.

Steps 7 and 8, the final review of issues and strategies, is enhanced by ExperTAX$^{sm}$ providing to the audit and tax team a rich array of tax planning ideas and alternative tax strategies, matched to the client's particular situation.

### *4.2 Exploring product delivery environments*

By their nature, expert systems are serious consumers of computer power, and they function more efficiently using specialized hardware (e.g., Lisp machines) or fairly large dedicated general-purpose computers. Specialized hardware offers the added advantage of providing user-friendly software environments that are particularly productive in the context of quick prototyping of expert system functions. Several commercially available software environments (e.g., shells, artificial intelligence tools) contribute to making these programming environments even more productive.

When dealing with the issue of a delivery environment for ExperTAX$^{sm}$, however, one has to come to grips with the operational restrictions that the environment might impose. For the tax accrual function, the data gathering task takes place at the client's location and is generally carried out by a senior (in-charge) staff accountant. Only an expert system that can be resident in an easily obtained on-site computer will be feasible for this task. Hundreds of IBM-PC-compatible computers are currently utilized by staff at client sites. ExperTAX$^{sm}$ was designed to run on IBM-PC-compatible computers. See discussion below (Section 4.6) on selecting software and hardware.

### *4.3 Identifying the experts*

It is typical to find that very few experts are used while developing an expert system. This occurs for a number of reasons, usually due to the fact that experts are a scarce resource, and in many domains, one expert is all that's needed.

In the area of U.S. taxation, there are many areas of expertise, and this expertise is distributed throughout the Firm. ExperTAX$^{sm}$ used many experts during the construction of its knowledge base, and the knowledge base now represents their collected knowledge all in one place.

The task of identifying the professionals whose expertise should be tapped is significant. There are people who are 'experts' in the execution of the process; that is, they know what materials should be gathered, the order in which information should be collected and the most efficient order in which to answer the various questions. There are other 'experts' who know what questions to ask and why, and what follow-up questions may be required to identify a relevant issue. There is yet another group of 'experts' who are particularly good at summarizing the results and presenting the information for analysis. Finally, there are 'experts' who can construct viable alternative strategies, given the information presented to them.

All of those experts have a role in the tax accrual and planning process. Thus, for ExperTAX$^{sm}$ to satisfactorily perform its support tasks in the data gathering, analysis and planning modes, it incorporates expertise from several sources.

Although most tax managers could do a good job of performing the various tax accrual and planning tasks, they would probably not be as effective in each of the specific areas of the process as some specialized experts would be. Thus, it is conceivable that by bringing together the right experts for the right tasks, the resulting expert system could provide a consistent quality of response in a more efficient manner than would result from the experts acting alone. It is through the integration of the experts' collective specialized knowledge that ExperTAX$^{sm}$ comes alive.

### *4.4 Defining the structure of the knowledge base*

The most difficult task associated with the knowledge engineering function is to determine an adequate structure for the knowledge base. This task requires the most abstract level of knowledge acquisition, since neither the experts nor the knowledge engineer initially has a frame of reference on which to base their discussions.

In early exchanges with the experts, they described their tasks in holistic terms (i.e., 'focus on the main issues,' 'analyze all the relevant data,' 'base our analysis on experience,' 'react to the particular characteristcs of the client'). They described the process in terms that criticized the shortcomings of questionnaires and emphasized the value of unstructured, yet careful, analysis. However, the evidence clearly suggests that most analysis is based on the information gathered through the existing questionnaires and, on some occasions, through additional requests for specific data.

The structure of the expert system shell and knowledge base was designed with the help of an 'expert system simulation experiment'. This experiment is discussed in Section 6.

### *4.5 Distilling technical requirements*

The technical requirements for ExperTAX$^{sm}$ resulted from a careful analysis of the expert system simulation experiment. These technical requirements are summarized in Table 2.

**Table 2.** *ExperTAX$^{sm}$ Technical Requirements*

| *Requirement* | *Justification* |
|---|---|
| 'Smart' Questionnaire | Motivates user with relevant questions and explanations |
| Flexible user interface | System must perform maintained knowledge base |
| Frame-based organization | Provides easily maintained knowledge base |
| Large knowledge base | Initial estimate of 1,000 rules |
| Forward-chaining rules | Large number of conclusions from a large input data pool |

We decided the process should be driven by a 'smart' questionnaire. The ExperTAX$^{sm}$ has to continuously probe for information, deciding which questions to ask and in what order. In addition, it has to have the ability to explain 'why' a question is being asked and reveal some of the implications associated with the answers. This was found to be particularly important in motivating and guiding the user to gather the relevant data.

The user interface needs to be highly flexible. Staff auditors will spend considerable time interacting with the system and will be highly sensitive to the system's responses. The screen display should be simple and self-explanatory, yet allow the user to control the process at all times, permitting the insertion of free-flow text whenever the user considers it necessary to make a note. The 'why' explanations should be easily invoked but only at the user's request, since most auditors do not need to refer to this information for every question. The process sequence should be easily controllable by the user, allowing questions to be skipped for later completion.

We determined that a frame-based organization would be the best for ExperTAX$^{sm}$'s knowledge base. The frames were classified by the context of the knowledge (e.g., inventory, receivables) and the types of knowledge they represent (i.e., questions and issues). The slots in the frames were easy to define, and they represented items which our experts could understand. The knowledge base has to be easy to maintain, since the tax field is in constant flux and the audit and tax planning process was sure to be revised.

From our initial analysis, we estimated that the size of the knowledge base will be substantial, containing over 1000 frames. This size would impact the choice of expert system shells in which to implement the production version.

Figure 1 illustrates the aspects of ExperTAX$^{sm}$ which helped decide what type of control structure would best fit the shape of the knowledge base. ExperTAX$^{sm}$'s broad coverage of numerous subject areas, the fact it takes few questions to identify an issue, and the fact that ExperTAX$^{sm}$ would draw many conclusions from a large quantity of input data, made a forward chaining inference structure the best alternative.

The findings reported in this section were used to build the first ExperTAX$^{sm}$ prototype. It was used interactively during the knowledge acquisition sessions that followed. While the expert system continued to evolve throughout this process, it required only minor modifications to the user interface, inference engine and knowledge base structure.

### *4.6 Selecting software and hardware*

The analysis of the product delivery environment strongly suggested an IBM-compatible computer as the recommended hardware for the delivery of the ExperTAX$^{sm}$ system. Based on that requirement, commercially available expert system programming environments for the IBM-PC were carefully evaluated.

Several products such as ExpertEase, Exsys and M.1, ranging in price from \$150 to \$15,000 were identified and studied. First-cut prototypes

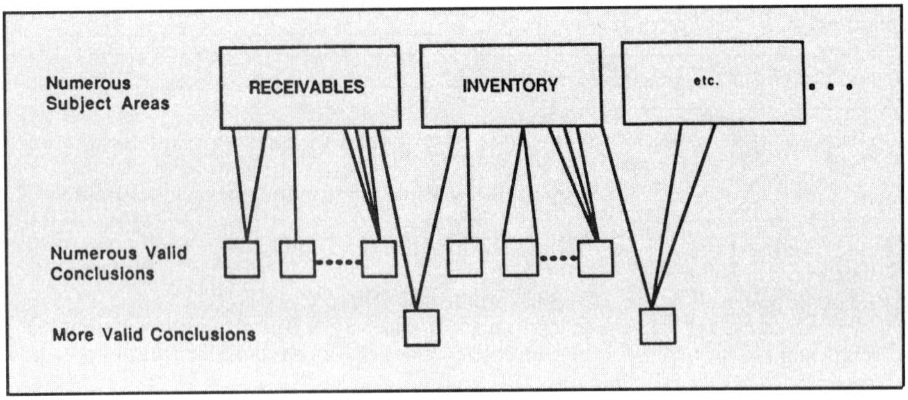


**Figure 1.** *ExperTAX$^{sm}$ Rationale for Forward Chaining Model*

were developed in those considered most promising. Several proved easy to use and versatile enough to accommodate some version of the desired prototype. However, they all failed to satisfy the technical specifications deemed essential for ExperTAX$^{sm}$. Screen design was not flexible enough to support the level of dialogue interaction required; response time was judged to be unbearably slow; the facility to explain the system's reasoning was rudimentary at best. In some, the size of the knowledge base was severely restricted, or the quality of displayed and printed output was unacceptable.

It was thus decided that the shell would have to be custom designed using a suitable programming language. Common Lisp was selected as the language to write ExperTAX$^{sm}$'s shell because it is relatively mature and versatile and is rapidly becoming the standard Lisp dialect for artificial intelligence work in the United States [7]. From among the Common Lisp implementation vehicles available for the IBM-PC, Gold Hill Computers' Golden Common Lisp [8] was selected for the project. It is a reasonable subset of Common Lisp and its code operates very efficiently in the IBM-PC environment.

IBM PC-AT's were used during the prototyping phase, but the product was designed to run on an IBM-PC-XT or compatible unit with 640 kilobytes of memory. The disk storage requirement for the knowledge base is under ten megabytes. To enhance the quality of the user interface, a high resolution color monitor is supported as optional equipment. A laser printer is the preferred output vehicle for printed reports.

## 5. ExperTAX$^{sm}$ components

ExperTAX$^{sm}$ consists of three main components, an expert system shell (called QShell), the knowledge base, and the knowledge base maintenance system. They are shown in Figure 2.

QShell is a rule-based expert system shell especially designed to accommodate the requirements of the tax accrual and planning process as conducted at Coopers & Lybrand. While it was specifically designed for ExperTAX$^{sm}$, QShell has been used as a flexible programming environment for other questionnaire-driven expert systems.

QShell is programmed in Gold Hill Common Lisp and runs on IBM-PC's, PC-XT's and IBM-

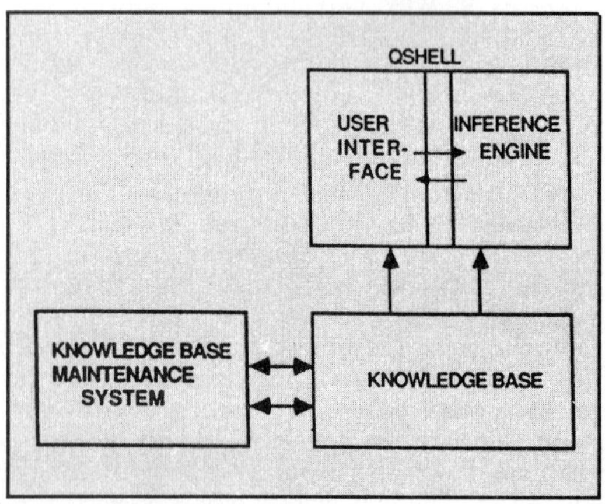


**Figure 2.** *ExperTAX$^{sm}$ Components*

compatible personal computers. It consists of two main components:

- The inference engine which controls the logic search through the knowledge base, firing the appropriate rules, tracking the inference process and communicating with the user through the user interface.
- The user interface which controls the screens and keyboard used by the system to communicate with the user, as well as the generation of all the printed reports. The information it displays comes directly from the knowledge base, and the information it takes in is used by the inference engine to direct its search processes and to enrich the output documentation.

The other two modules are separate from QShell:

- The knowledge base harbours all the frames, rules and facts that constitute the expertise of the system, and make them available upon request to the inference engine and the user interface.
- The knowledge base maintenance system supports the modification of frames, rules and facts in the knowledge base. It is independent from the other parts of the system and is designed to facilitate the maintenance of the knowledge base by the designated organizational group.

### *5.1 Inference engine*

QShell's inference engine is a forward-chaining, rule-based system. It incorporates a frame manager, a facts database and a rule interpreter.

Two types of frames are recognized by the frame manager, those associated with questions to be asked (question frames) and those associated with valid issues (issue frames). The frames can also be grouped in sections to be executed one at a time in any prescribed order. Within a section, the frame manager controls the execution of frames. The inferencing from question frames and issue frames takes place at different times.

The actual inferencing process is controlled by the rule interpreter, which uses the facts deposited in the facts database by the user interface. The rule interpreter focuses on the rules contained in the frames activated by the frame manager. It compares the left-hand side, or antecedent, of the rule (the 'IF' part of an 'IF; THEN' rule) with known facts in the database. When a match is found, the rule is executed. The execution of a rule, also known as rule firing, consists of implementing the instructions contained in the right-hand side of the rule (the THEN part or consequent). This can result in one of several actions: the set of known facts in the facts database may be modified, an information string may be sent to the user interface as output, the execution control may be transferred to the user interface, or a fact or documentation string may be requested from the user interface. The rule interpreter will continue to search the same section of frames in the knowledge base until it fires a rule that transfers control to the user interface.

The ExperTAX$^{sm}$ inference engine keeps track of the inference chain created by the successive firings of rules, allowing for the display of specific reasoning associated with conclusions. The inference engine permits interruption and resumption of the inference process at any stage and backtracking of the process for alternative fact evaluation.

### *5.2 User interface*

The user interface of ExperTAX$^{sm}$ controls the screen display used for communicating with the user and the printer commands necessary for formatting and issuing reports.

The screen layout consists of three active horizontal windows. The top window displays information identifying the section being analyzed. The middle window displays long and short forms of the questions being asked, the precondition that caused the current question rule and the valid answers. The lower window is used to present clarification messages (why messages), when requested, and to type in 'marginal note' information when requested by the system or the user. Figure 3 presents a sample screen display.

The user interface is operated through a system of nested menus that allows the user substantial control of the inference process. At virtually any point in the process, the user can return to a menu that allows for an orderly interruption of the process or for the resumption of the process at a different session or frame.

The printed reports generated by the user interface include lists of all issues identified by ExperTAX$^{sm}$, audit trails of all questions asked

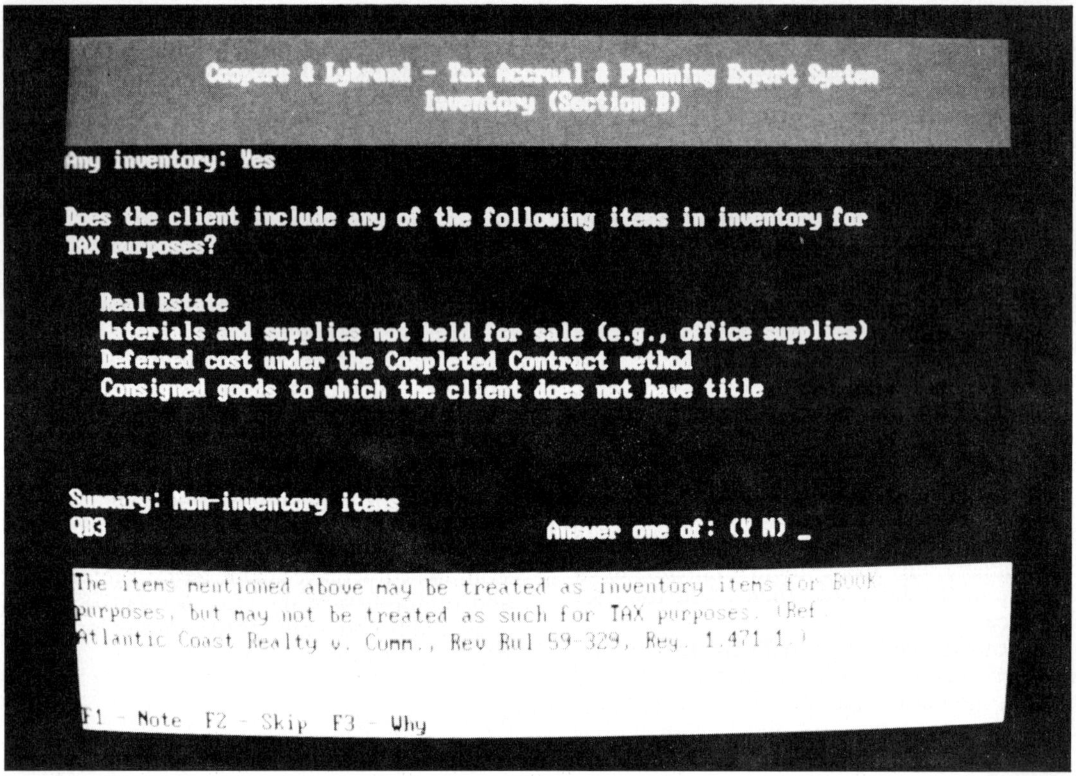


**Figure 3**

and answers received, notes taken during the sessions and specialized forms issued when additional documentation is required. An example appears in Section 7.

*5.3 Knowledge base*

The ExperTAX$^{\text{sm}}$ knowledge base stores information as 'frames.' There are several kinds of information attached to each frame. Some information relates to how and when to use the frame, some is used to determine what should happen next, some determines what to display or print. A frame can include several rules.

There are two types of frames in the ExperTAX$^{\text{sm}}$ knowledge base, question frames and issue frames. They differ in the number and type of attributes (also called slots), procedures and facts associated with them.

The question frames, an example of which is represented in Figure 4, include the following attributes:

- Questions
- A list of possible answers
- Pre-conditions, which appear as antecedents, and if true cause the question to be asked
- Rules which perform a variety of functions, including structure control, documentation control and others
- WHY messages

Figure 5 shows an example of an issue frame.

The issue frames are simpler than the question frames. They include only a Rule attribute and a Display attribute. The rule in the frame is tested, and if true, the display attribute appears on the screen or a printed report.

The frames are further classified by sections, which are groups of frames that share an execu-

Question:

What is client's bad-debt write-off method for TAX purposes?
S — Specific charge-off
R — Reserve Method

Possible Answers:

S — Specific charge-off
(Clarifying explanation required.)
R — Reserve Method
Followup Questions:
QA19 — Bad-debt reserve method
QA20 — Difference between BOOK and TAX reserve
QA21 — Bad-debt recoveries to reserve

WHY Message:

In a typical environment, the Reserve method over time will result in larger tax deductions than the Specific charge-off method.

**Figure 4.** *Sample Question Frame*

Rule:

(QB6 IS L) : Inventory valuing IS Lower of cost or market
AND
(QB14 IS L) : Method of accounting for inventory IS LIFO
OR
(QB14 IS B) : Method of accounting for inventory IS Both LIFO and FIFO

Display:

LIFO inventory may not be valued for tax purposes using the lower-of-cost-or-market method!! The IRS may terminate the taxpayer's LIFO election if LIFO inventory is valued at lower-of-cost-or-market. See Rev Proc 79-23. In limited situations, a taxpayer may be able to change to the Cost method and preclude the IRS from terminating its LIFO election. See Rev Proc 84-74. Market write-downs are required to be included in income under the provisions of Sec. 472(d) when LIFO is elected.

**Figure 5.** *Sample Issue Frame*

tion sequence. The number of frames in a section and number of sections in the knowledge base are restricted only by the storage limitation of the hardware and software environment.

### *5.4 Knowledge base maintenance system*

The ExperTAX$^{sm}$ knowledge base maintenance system is an independent software system designed to update, modify and expand the knowledge base. The system includes a frame editor, logic evaluator and rule interaction display.

The frame editor permits the user to state the different components of a frame in simple English. It edits the information entered for consistency and completeness and helps the user correct omissions or inconsistencies.

The logic evaluator checks for possible conflicts in logic between the rules in the frame being edited and the rules contained in currently valid frames. If an inconsistency is discovered, the evaluator suggests editorial actions that would resolve the situation.

For example, the system will diagnose the case where a question frame with a structure control rule would transfer to an undefined question, or cannot be asked due to an improper precondition. It will also diagnose the case where an issue frame contains a rule whose antecedent cannot be true (such as 'the answer to Q1 is a AND the answer to Q1 is B', and other more complex cases).

The rule interaction display allows the user to dynamically observe all the frames affected by changes in the frame being edited. This permits the user to better visualize the changes in operating procedure that could be implicit in modifications of a frame with several complex rules or follow-up routines.

## 6. Knowledge acquisition: building the knowledge base

During the knowledge acquisition phase of our project, the expert system was 'trained' until it was capable of delivering a level of performance we considered satisfactory for the task to be performed. In this phase of the project, detailed gathering of rules and facts took place. This process involved careful selection of experts, an expert system simulation experiment, exhaustive interactive sessions for knowledge capture, fine-tuning enhancements to QShell, and careful validation of the knowledge base logic, structure and information.

### *6.1 Selecting the experts*

A careful observation of the current tax accrual and planning process revealed several sources of expertise:

- The audit and tax specialists who design and maintain the support tools (e.g., questionnaires) used in the field.
- The engagement auditors who gather data for the process.
- The managers and partners who review the data and issue recommendations.
- The tax auditors and consultants who specialize in various complex areas of the tax planning process and are regularly used as expert resources by managers and partners on engagements.

As mentioned in Section 4.4, the initial attempt to infer a structure for the knowledge base utilized a simulation experiment. This experiment is described below.

The experts that participated in those sessions came from the four sources mentioned above. This allowed the knowledge engineering team to gain an understanding of the experts' likely role in the detailed knowledge acquisition process.

### *6.2 The expert system simulation experiment*

To bring structure to the process and to facilitate our understanding of the dynamics, a simulation experiment was conducted. An experienced auditor provided a real case for which the tax accrual process had recently been completed. He provided all the basic workpaper and tax return information that had been used to process the case. Two other experienced auditors, one in audit and one in tax, were asked to identify the specific information required to conduct a complete tax accrual process for the client in question.

A conference room with a long table in the middle was divided by a screen. All the case information was gathered and deposited on the left side of the table, including the forms and questionnaires deemed relevant. A staff accountant with no previous practice experience in the tax accrual process was selected at random and asked to sit at the left side of the table. Two experienced audit and tax people were given blank questionnaires and forms and were asked to sit at the right side of the table, separated by the screen from the staff accountant and the case data.

The staff accountant was informed that it was his responsibility to conduct a successful tax accrual process for the client. He was told that he currently had all the necessary information in front of him, and, most importantly, the resource of a panel of experts behind the screen. The experts were told that it was their responsibility to guide the staff accountant toward the successful completion of the tax accrual process. They were instructed to actively guide him with verbal advice and to answer questions when asked. They were unable to go to the other side of the screen to explain; only verbal communication was allowed.

The process was videotaped and observed by the knowledge engineering team. Several variations of the process were conducted for a total of twelve hours over three days. At the end of the experiment, the knowledge engineering team had a clear picture of the basic structure of the knowledge base and the minimum requirements for the user screen interface. A first prototype of the expert system could then be built.

From those sessions, it was concluded that the existing questionnaires constituted a good frame of reference for the tax accrual process. Thus, it was decided that the first source of expertise to be used for the ExperTAX$^{sm}$ knowledge base would be the existing tax accrual and planning support tools, such as the questionnaire (commonly referred to as the TAP, from which the name ExperTAX$^{sm}$ was derived) and the audit and tax specialists currently responsible for its maintenance and support.

The expert system simulation sessions also brought home the fact that the knowledge base had several clearly defined subsets or sections dealing with different areas of specialization (e.g., inventory, accounts receivable). Detailed problems related to these areas are routinely supported by different professionals acting as consultants on specific engagements.

To implement the process described above, the second source of expertise utilized was the one provided by the generalists. Audit and tax managers and partners who regularly conduct tax accrual and planning processes were consulted on the validity of the basic expertise structure of the questionnaire. These practitioners helped to validate the control process and use interaction features of the system and to identify some areas of cross-correlation between knowledge frames.

The largest pool of experts utilized were specialist tax consultants, who currently serve as expert resources supporting the practice managers and partners. These experts proved to be highly receptive to the structured question framework for knowledge acquisition, since it seems to resemble closely the process they often follow in acquiring information and giving advice over the telephone. By the end of the process, more than twenty experts had devoted over 1,000 hours to the project and had helped transform the prototype questionnaire-based knowledge base into an extensive pool of knowledge capable of efficiently supporting in-depth analysis in many areas of expertise.

The final group of experts asked to participate in the knowledge acquisition process were the staff auditors who currently gather data in the field. They, together with the tax and audit managers, participated in the field validation of successive versions of ExperTAX$^{sm}$, comparing and reporting on its performance *vis à vis* reports they had prepared for clients.

### *6.3 Interactive knowledge acquisition*

During interactive knowledge acquisition the expert system is 'trained' on site by the expert, with the help of the knowledge engineer, who acts as an information broker. The knowledge engineer ensures that the new knowledge is in phrases that are compatible with the structure of the expert system, elicits explanations and clarifications from the expert, questions the order of or need for the information supplied by the expert and runs the expert system continuously to let the expert observe the effects of the newly acquired knowledge.

All ExperTAX$^{sm}$ knowledge acquisition sessions (except for the simulation sessions described earlier) were conducted 'live' with the computer. The ideal knowledge acquisition session involved one knowledge engineer, a computer with the latest version of the expert system and one or two experts. The dynamics of these sessions were such that the experts often very quickly began to structure their responses to closely resemble the favored syntax and logic of the expert system structure. The experts became further motivated by observing their suggestions and comments being immediately introduced into the knowledge base. They saw how the expert system was 'learning' and how the system's advice began to closely resemble their own. They also observed when certain rules or facts put into the system affect the behavior of the system in undesirable ways (e.g., when such rules lead to 'blind alleys' or attempted to 'train' the system beyond the desired level of expertise). Thus, they could correct the mistake immediately, suggesting alternative approaches to address the point.

The net result is a highly efficient knowledge acquisition process in which the quality of the information exchange between the knowledge engineer and the experts is greatly enhanced by the instant feedback provided by the evolving expert system.

### *6.4 Enhancing the ExperTAX$^{sm}$ shell*

While the final version of ExperTAX$^{sm}$ closely resembled the original prototype, the programming environment provided by the ExperTAX$^{sm}$ shell in particular, and Lisp in general, made it feasible to expediently modify ExperTAX$^{sm}$ to accommodate new perceived user needs as the knowledge acquisiton process progressed.

When it became obvious that a new feature should be incorporated (e.g., the ability to go back to a previous question, add 'why' messages of extended length, or create special forms or schedules to be printed when required), it was added to the system by the knowledge engineering team immediately after the session. The additions were usually available for review at the next scheduled session.

The opportunity to observe emerging patterns of use by the experts testing the system permitted the search patterns and knowledge storage and retrieval rules to be designed to minimize system response times, without changing the hardware requirements.

This process of incremental software development yielded a final product closely tailored to the needs of the audit and tax professionals. Only the original prototype was based on a formal software system design. The final product was the result of incremental enhancements of the prototype, which were made possible by the interactive knowledge acquisitions sessions and the highly productive programming environment provided by the ExperTAX$^{sm}$ shell and Lisp.

### *6.5 Knowledge base validation*

The exhaustive validation of an expert system's knowledge base is a difficult task. Logic tests should be run to ensure the consistency of the knowledge base, and the system should be tested against the experts in an extensive array of situations.

One way, possibly the best way, to validate a pool of knowledge is for professionals that were not involved in the development process to conduct an independent validation of its performance. There are two potential problems with this approach. First, different professionals might have different approaches to arriving at a specific conclusion. Second, the sheer number of possible combinations of responses that the system is capable of producing makes it difficult to test the system exhaustively.

Our approach to the problem was to select a group of practice partners and managers in different offices and ask them to test the system for a representative set of their clients. A knowledge engineer supervised the process and ensured that all relevant comments made during the sessions were noted. The practice partners and managers familiarized themselves with ExperTAX$^{sm}$ by running random exercises and evaluating the system's responses. Once they were satisfied with the overall performance, they processed several client cases whose tax accrual and planning process had recently been completed and compared the system's responses with their personal evaluations of the cases. Some issues were raised as to the clarity of the wording of specific questions, explanations or recommendations. These issues were brought back to the experts who contributed those areas to the knowledge base and appropriate modifications of the knowledge base were made.

The results of the validation exercise indicated that ExperTAX$^{sm}$ and its knowledge base performed the task of collecting information better than the former paper method. The issues raised were reasonably comprehensive, and though they did not cover some of the finer points of tax law, at least issues were raised which pointed in their direction. These results were used in subsequent knowledge base maintenance passes, making the knowledge base an even stronger base of information.

## 7. ExperTAX$^{sm}$ at work: a sample session

ExperTAX$^{sm}$ starts with a choice between starting to work with a new client or continuing a job for a recurring client. To illustrate, assume we are starting with a new client, Artificial Company, a highly successful manufacturer of smart computers. ExperTAX$^{sm}$ would first ask some questions from the 'preliminary' section of its knowledge base. It would quickly find out that Artificial accounts for its transactions on an accrual basis, is a privately held company and is interested in tax minimization strategies. That general information helps ExperTAX$^{sm}$ structure its search procedures and access frame sections so as to minimize unnecessary paths and then loads into memory those subsets of the knowledge base that contain rules more likely to be fired.

Figure 6 joins an ExperTAX$^{sm}$ session where inventory questions related to the write-down of obsolete goods are being posed.

The user always has the option of answering the question, asking why the question is being asked, or skipping it altogether. He elects to answer C. ExperTAX$^{sm}$ changes its display to show Figure 7.

At this point, the user elects to press the 'Why' key. Why message appears as shown in Figure 8.

Having read the explanation, the user answers the question and continues in a similar manner until ExperTAX$^{sm}$ finishes with the section and returns to the selection menu.

Once the user has finished the inventory section, he might elect to continue with another section, to look at the issues raised so far, or to print those issues and the accompanying documentation. If he elects to look at the issues raised, they would appear in the middle window, one at a time, together with the specific answers that triggered them. Figure 9 shows a sample display.

Once the user has answered all relevant sections, a complete printed report can be generated. The report would list all issues raised, segmented by type (e.g., accrual, planning). It

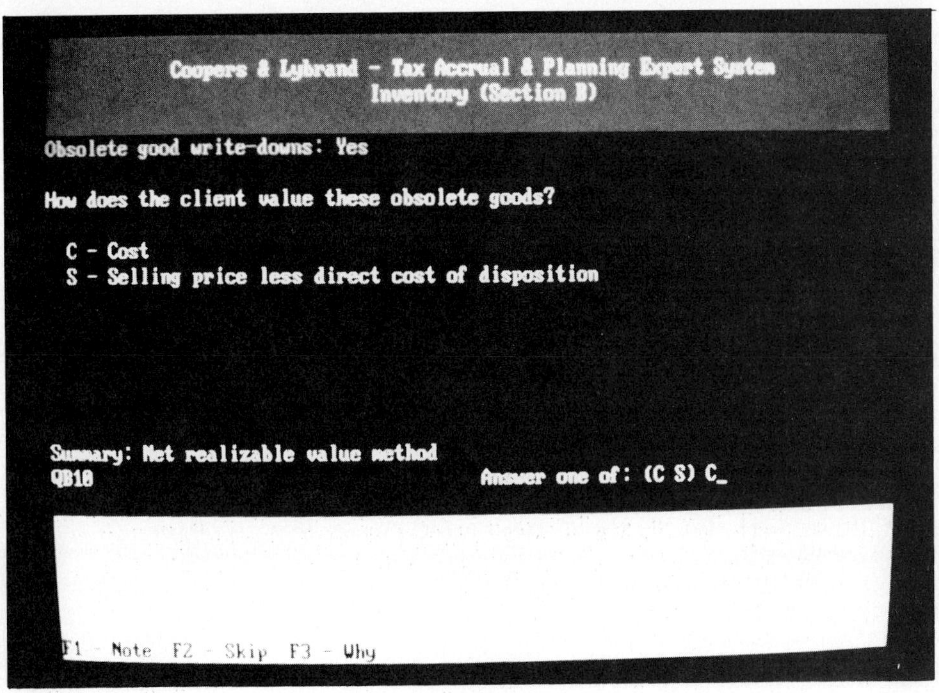


**Figure 6**

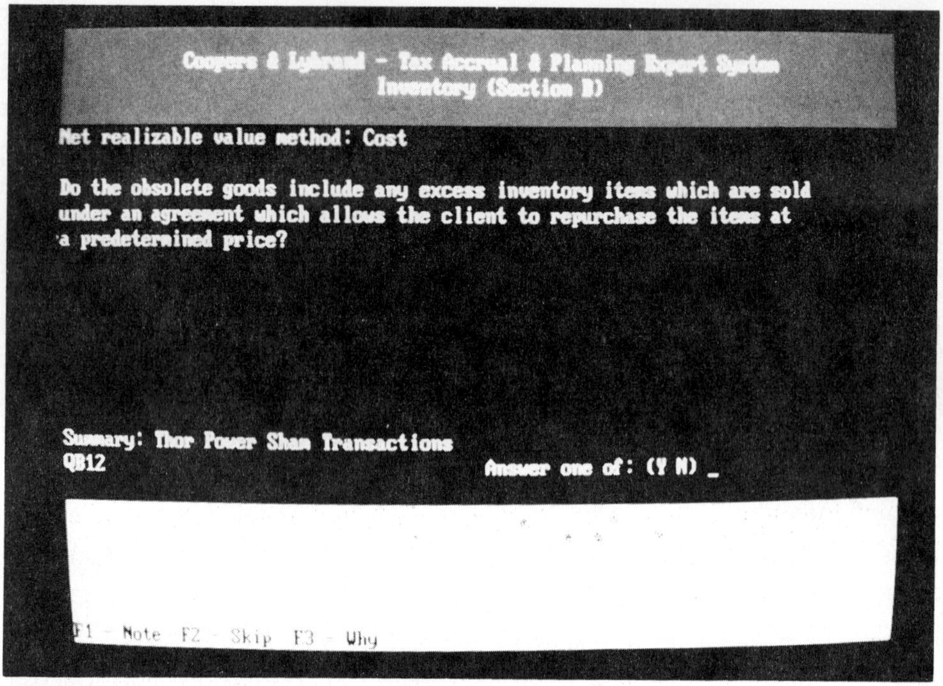


Figure 7

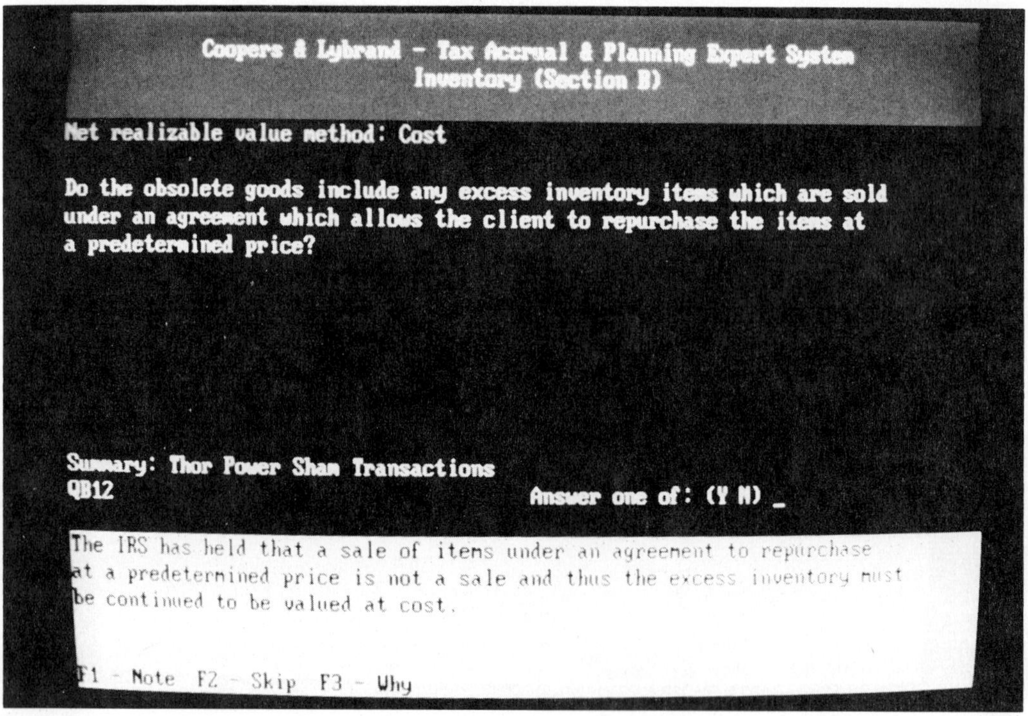


Figure 8

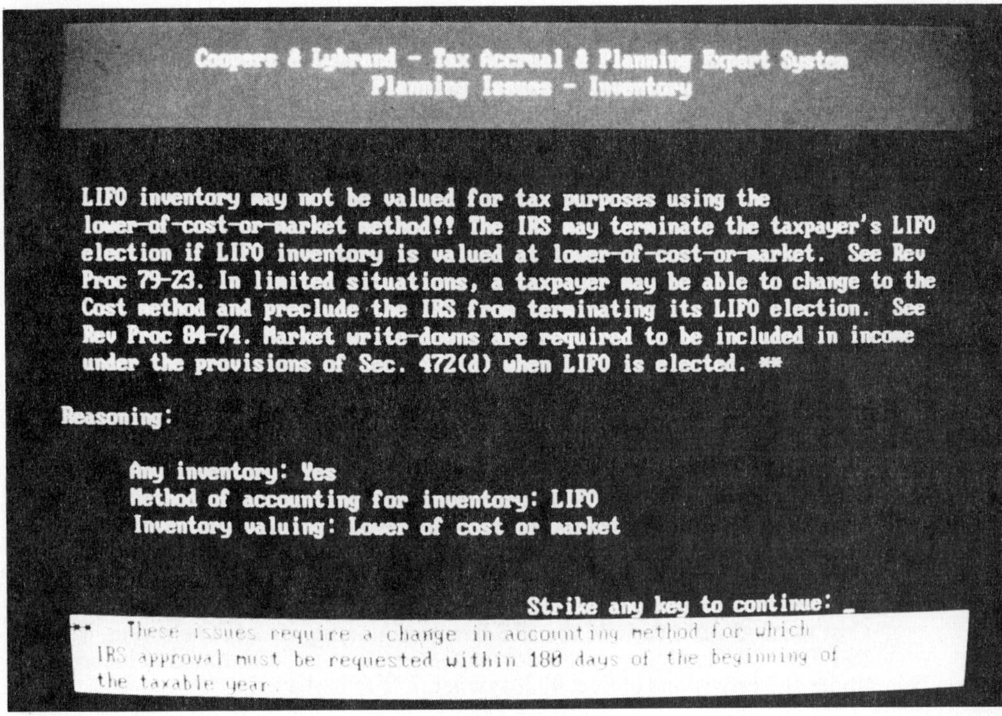


**Figure 9**

would also list all questions asked and responses received during the session and all notes taken by the user, whether voluntarily or because of prompts by the system to further explain an answer.

The ExperTAX$^{sm}$ report would then be used by the audit and tax managers or partners in charge of the engagement to prepare the final tax accrual and issue their tax planning recommendations to the client. Figure 10 shows part of the Planning Issues section of a typical ExperTAX$^{sm}$ report.

## 8. Issues and suggestions for further research

A number of observations came to mind during the development of ExperTAX$^{sm}$ that may be of interest to researchers in identifying areas for further scholarly research or to those interested in experimenting with the technology. Some of those issues are discussed further below.

### *8.1 Identifying the experts*

An important element in the development of an expert system is the identification of experts. It is illogical to attempt to develop an expert system if recognized expertise does not exist. The identification of experts in the accounting field is a complicated task, perhaps because often so many support mechanisms are used by practitioners for certain tasks (questionnaires, informal and formal consultations, texts, etc.). Together these support mechanisms contribute to the high quality of professional output. However, this may tend to make it difficult to identify a knowledge 'czar' whose estimates, processes or knowledge are clearly superior to what the system and mix of staff, support tools and consulting skills produce in the rendering of normal client service. Clearly, the delivery of consistent, high-

Coopers & Lybrand | ExperTAX Planning Issues and Ideas

April 8, 1986

The following planning ideas and issues should be reviewed to determine their applicability to the client.

Inventory

o Section 1.471-2(c) allows obsolete goods to be written down to bona fide selling price less direct cost of disposition. Such write-downs would reduce taxable income. However, excess inventory does not come under this provision. See Thor Power v. Comm. **

o LIFO inventory may not be valued for tax purposes using the lower-of-cost-or-market method!! The IRS may terminate the taxpayer's LIFO election if LIFO inventory is valued at lower-of-cost-or-market. See Rev proc 79-23. In limited situations, a taxpayer may be able to change to the Cost method and preclude the IRS from terminating its LIFO election. See Rev Proc 84-74. Market write-downs are required to be included in income under the provisions of Sec. 472(d) when LIFO is elected. **

** — These issues require a change in accounting method for which IRS approval must be requested within 180 days of the beginning of the taxable year.

**Figure 10.** *Sample 'Planning Issue' Report*

quality service is a primary objective for the practice of public accounting.

The more narrowly technical expertise is defined, the easier it may be to define an expert to begin the knowledge acquisition process. For example, a 'LIFO' expert may be easier to identify than an 'inventory' expert. But problems may arise if the LIFO expert is unfamiliar with the process being supported by the system. The expert may have little or no knowledge of the tax accrual or planning process and may be more attuned to the special project environment than the audit environment. Thus, identifying the right 'expert' may be a critical and difficult task in applying this technology to some types of problems.

### *8.2 Knowledge base management*

To justify the development of the initial system, knowledge base management and maintenance must be evaluated and considered feasible. From a distant vantage point, the development of an expert system may appear similar to the development process of any other software product. However, the parallels become blurred when one considers the specialized expertise necessary to evaluate or design system shells in a commercial environment, the interactive growth of the system (rather than the detailed design and programming stages), the more complicated issues of quality assurance and the technical expertise needed to supervise system growth and updating.

Groups such as the National organizations of the functional specializations (e.g., audit and tax), EDP development groups and Decision Support groups may all interact in the development process and are candidates for the continuing management and oversight of such systems. It remains an open but important question how the maintenance of such systems should be handled. The new technological environment provides an opportunity to reconsider the issue in light of organizational factors and efficiency.

*8.3 System distribution and security*

The existence of a competitive environment introduces significant issues into the expert system development process that are not encountered in more traditional software development environments. The handling of those issues may be influenced by whether the system will be sold commercially or will be resident only within the domain of the developer. One such issue that may be raised is whether the client will know (or care) that expert systems technology was applied during the engagement. This issue will affect the distribution process and publicity surrounding product releases.

Security is a heightened concern in expert systems. Such systems are no longer akin to computer software templates with only the capacity to manipulate numbers, but may also contain the accumulated knowledge of a firm. Communicating and distributing the product, protecting the software and at the same time providing an environment that does not constrain authorized users in its application is a practical problem. While the value of such a system may diminish over time if not continuously updated and maintained, the implications of the system's misappropriation or unauthorized use of transfer are more significant than with many other software products. Accordingly, organizational and hardware and/or software controls assume increased importance in the design and distribution of such systems.

*8.4 Issues for further research*

Some issues, such as the organization and mechanism by which projects are identified, assigned priority, managed and maintained, are very important to developers of support systems but may yield limited independent research opportunities. Other issues that may have research potential flow from some of the aforementioned topics — for example:

- The need to better understand what is meant by 'expertise.'
- More tools and techniques to evaluate and simulate real-world environments.
- Continued research into methods of extracting and capturing expertise.

The purpose of this paper has been to describe an application of AI technology (expert systems) to a real-world environment. It has attempted to go beyond a simple recitation of hardware and software options and capabilities, since that would hardly constitute a contribution to the research literature. However, the proprietary nature of ExperTAX$^{sm}$ precludes a higher level of detail than the one presented. We hope that the case presented will assist researchers in understanding more of the issues and areas that may be conducive to future research.

## 9. References

[1] Robert Longair, 'What 'Expert Systems' Will Mean for Auditors,' *Chartered Accountant in Australia*, November 1983.

[2] Greg Stoner, "Expert Systems': Jargon or Challenge?,' *Accountancy*, February 1985, pp. 142–145.

[3] *Symposium on Expert Systems and Audit Judgment*, University of Southern California, 1986; and *Symposium on Expert Systems and Audit Judgment Research*, University of Southern California, 1984.

[4] Shalom M. Weiss and Casimir A. Kulikowski, *A Practical Guide to Designing Expert Systems*, (Rowman and Allenhead 1984), p. 1.

[5] Robert K. Elliott and John A. Kielich, 'Expert Systems in Auditing, *Journal of Accountancy*, September 1985, pp. 130–131.

[6] Chris W.Dungan and John S. Chandler, 'Auditor: A Microcomputer Based Expert System to Support Auditors in the Field,' *Expert Systems*, 2, 4, October 1985, pp.210–221.

[7] Patrick H. Winston and Berthold K. Paul Horn, *LISP*, Second Edition (Addison-Wesley 1984).

[8] Gold Hill Computers, *Golden Common LISP* (Gold Hill Computers, Cambridge, Massachusetts 1985).

[9] Jesse F. Dillard and Jane F. Mutchler, 'Knowledge Based Expert Computer Systems for Audit Opinion Decision,' *Symposium on Expert Systems and Audit Judgment*, University of Southern California, February 1986.

[10] James V. Hansen, and William F. Messier Jr., 'A Preliminary Test of EDP-XPERT,' *Symposium on Expert Systems and Audit Judgment*, University of Southern California, February 1986.

# APPENDIX C

## The Ford Motor Company Direct Labor Management System

Ford Motor Co.'s Direct Labor Management System (DLMS) is one major subsystem of a multiphase manufacturing process planning system designed to assist production and planning personnel in all aspects of the manufacturing process. It will eventually support several thousand users. The ambitious system has profound implications for Ford; it aims to improve the assembly line and has targeted key areas in the planning process. Its five major objectives include:

- Standardizing process description and improving process sheets' clarity: The process sheet conveys assembly information from the initial process-planning stage to the plant's assembly lines. Process sheets and their derivatives should communicate information effectively at all the stages of construction.
- Creating work-allocation sheets: Detailed plant-floor instructions are automatically generated from the more abstract process sheet text.
- Estimating product and nonproduct labor times accurately: Product times represent effort directly associated with product assembly. Nonproduct times represent any indirect effort. Removing this essentially clerical task frees the industrial engineer to analyze assembly processes. Consistent process descriptions can help by highlighting inefficiencies.
- Processing generically: Process sheets are written at a fine level of granularity. The objective of generic processing is to provide higher-level process descriptions, standardizing assembly across vehicle types. Process sheets can now be written at any level of abstraction. Instructions can be written in

"The Ford Motor Company Direct Labor Management System" by W. P. Johnson, R. Woodhead, J. O'Brien, *AI Expert,* August 1989, pp. 42–52. 

terms of the assembly workers' micromotions (such as "grasp screw," "position screw," and so on), or as macrodescriptions applied to complete vehicle subsystems (such as "install brake system").

■ Translating: Automobile production is an international effort; translating process instructions into different languages involves considerable cost. The standard language is designed to simplify translation and the taxonomy is structured so it can serve as an interlingual form for all the target languages.

## SYSTEM ARCHITECTURE

An illustration of the system architecture is shown in Figure 1. The first steps in system development were to identify a grammar for describing assembly processes and a standard format for writing process descrip-

**FIGURE 1.**
DLMS software architecture.

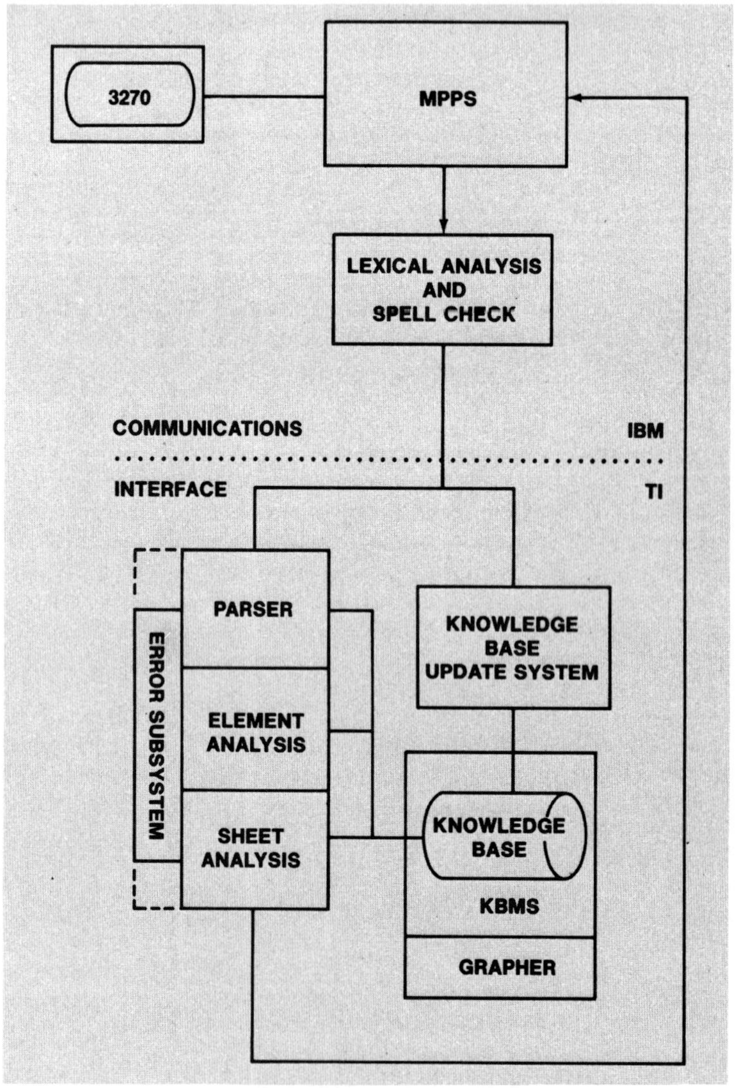

tions. These were originally written in free-form English and uninterpretable by computer. Process sheets in the reengineered system are described with a case grammar that meets automotive assembly requirements. English assembly instructions can be expressed at any level of detail. Potentially thousands of engineers with different educational levels will use this language; it needed to be clear but effective for all. Approximately 300 engineers have been trained to use the language without significant difficulties.

A typical process sheet is illustrated in Figure 2. Process data falls into two categories: process descriptions, specified in the body of the text and in "part" and "tools" areas of the sheet, and contextual data—for example, the sheet title and vehicle and plant information. Certain word categories

**FIGURE 2.** Typical process sheet.

**Sheet EJ540000000 Connect heater hoses to A/C evaporator assy.**

**10 Obtain lubricant from stored position**
**20 Spray lubricant onto A/C evaporator assembly nipples**
**30 Obtain 2 clamps from stock**
**40 Position 1 clamp onto outlet hose**
**60 Position existing clamp on hose between A/C evaporator assy. nipple and assy.**
**70 Secure outlet hose to heater nipple with 1 hose clamp**
**80 Position 1 clamp onto inlet hose**
**90 Seat hose to A/C evaporator assy.**
**100 Position existing clamp on inlet hose between A/C evaporator assy. nipple and assy.**
**110 Secure inlet hose to heater nipple with 1 hose clamp using a nutrunner**

**Tool (70 110) 1 P AAPTCA TSEQ rt angle nutrunner torque**
**shut off**
**Tool (70 110) 1 S 2H12E10H16B56 TSEQ 3/8 HEXSRT BDY 1/2**
**odlong lngth.**

**Process-prefix EJ**
**Repeat-opposite-side N**
**Plant AGO**
**Vehicle CQA**

in the language have very specific semantics defined by the engineers. Verbs are associated with specific assembly actions and modified by adverbs where appropriate. For instance, the fragments "inspect," "visually inspect," and "manually verify" have different interpretations. Important cases in the language are denoted by specific tokens. Sentence 110 from the example sheet is illustrated with its constituent cases in Figure 3. Other areas of the process sheet containing part, tool, vehicle, and other related information are parsed to provide extra detail and context for the sheet.

The DLMS system contains a large taxonomy of automotive assembly expertise, which maintains descriptions of concepts required to interpret the surface language and generate work instructions. Concepts in the taxonomy include parts, process equipment, standard operations, and geometric workstation models. A portion of the taxonomy is illustrated in Figure 4.

The DLMS knowledge-representation system is implemented on the NIKL[1,2] model. All concepts in the environment are described in terms of a Frame-based Description Language (FDL), a variation of the FL-language described by Brachman and Levesque.[3] It meets all the identified requirements for terminological reasoning and avoids the computational limitations implied by FL-.

Concepts in the taxonomy fall into two basic categories, primitive and nonprimitive. Primitive concepts have structures that contain necessary but not sufficient criteria for determining subsumption. This means the system will never automatically infer that a supplied concept is subsumed by a primitive concept, it must be specifically instructed to make the connection. The *operation* concept in Figure 4 is primitive.

Nonprimitive concepts are assumed to be fully defined by their descriptions, which contain necessary and sufficient criteria for determining subsumption. Nonprimitive concepts are defined by their roles, which describe properties of a concept by relating

**FIGURE 3.**
Example sentence and its constituent cases.

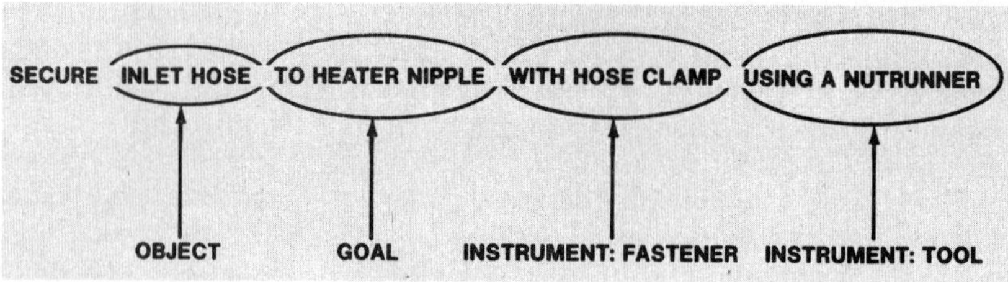


it to another concept. Roles correspond approximately to slots in a frame and form a subtaxonomy in their own right. A role is attached to a domain concept (the most general concept for which the role has meaning) and represents a set of fillers for each instance of that concept. Role restrictions constrain the set of values a filler can take. The *Secure threaded fastener using power tool* concept from Figure 4 is a nonprimitive concept. A partial description of the concept and some of its superconcepts are shown in Figure 5 (the notation follows Moser's example[1]).

Concepts can also be attributed with nondefinitional information; for example, a mini-process script can be associated with each standard operation. Because of the precisely specified semantics of the concept-description language, subsumption and an

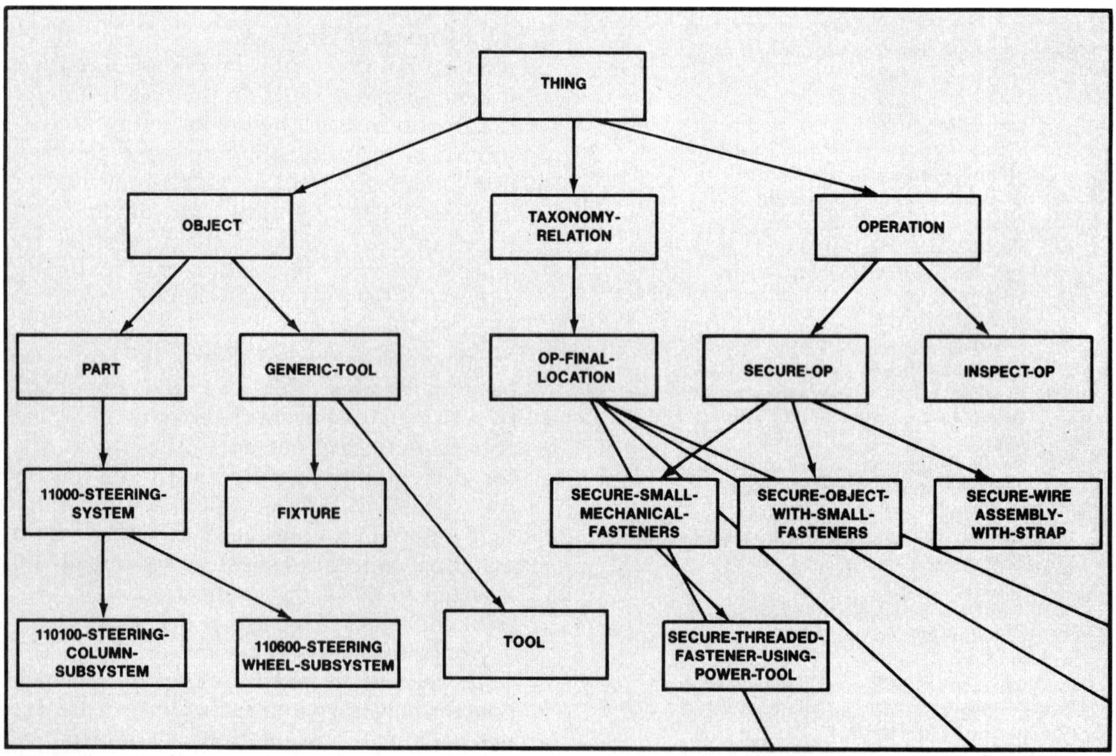


**FIGURE 4.**
Part of the DLMS taxonomy.

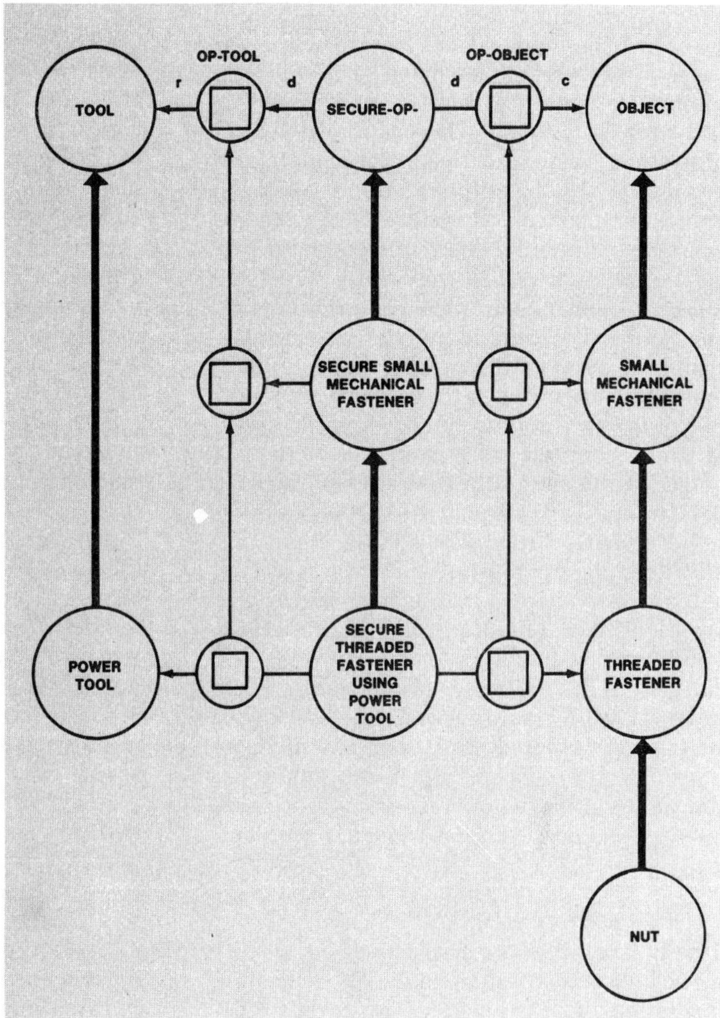


**FIGURE 5.** Taxonomy structure for secure operations.

associated classification procedure can be defined. Classification involves determining the most specific subsumers and most general subsumees of the current concept with the taxonomy.

Subsumption is intuitively clear:

```
Concept 1 subsumes Concept 2 <=> all objects that are
a Concept 2 are also a Concept 1
```

The test for subsumption used in this application is as follows:

```
Concept 1 subsumes Concept 2 if:
  All primitive concepts that subsume Concept 1 also
subsume Concept 2.
  For each roleset of Concept 1 and the correspond-
ing roleset of Concept 2, the value description of
Concept 1's roleset subsumes that of the value de-
scription of Concept 2's roleset.
```

The DLMS classifier is incremental. As concepts are added or modified, only inferences required to position the current concept and reclassify any related others are made. Two interfaces to the knowledge-based management system are provided. A procedural interface has been developed to support reasoning within the process sheet and user Knowledge Base Update (KBU) subsystems. An interactive graphic interface inspired by the ISI grapher[4] supports taxonomy maintenance for system development purposes. The number of concepts and the level of detail at which they must be represented is determined by the requirements of any standard operations and the need to discriminate between them. The set of defined operations determines the "granularity" of the resulting plan and hence the resolution of any associated time estimates. The required granularity or resolution can only be determined with respect to the processing requirements of any downstream client application. System resolution increases as significant derivatives of existing operations are identified. This leads to a definition of operational redundancy: a concept is redundant (for the purpose of creating work instructions) if no associated standard operation refers uniquely to it. For example, in Figure 5, the concept *nut* is redundant as the only significant operation refers to the concept *threaded fastener,* which subsumes *nut.*

## THE PARSING SUBSYSTEM

The parser produces a structure for grammatically correct sentences and provides information about the state of the parse to the error subsystem when parsing fails. It was designed primarily to process syntactically correct sentences efficiently and provide for flexible grammar extension. As the system is transaction-oriented and no direct user interaction is possible, any errors are processed as a group later in the analysis.

The parser is implemented as an Augmented Transition Network (ATN).[5,6] To improve the ATN's performance, the implementation includes a *cut* operator that eliminates backtracking in cases where traversing a specific arc clearly excludes all other alternatives. In addition, to eliminate the cost of undoing actions during backtracking, the parser defers most of its actions to a second phase, which it performs after a successful parse. This second phase generates a predicate-based representation of the parse tree used in the *element analysis* subsystem described later. The parser has an associated, rule-based, error-processing component tailored to match the standard grammar. It detects errors and suggests appropriate corrections to the user. No attempt was made to implement a general mechanism, for instance, like that proposed by Weischedel and Sonhdeimer.[7] Error-system requirements were derived by analyzing the types of errors made by process engineers during initial attempts to use the process-description language.

Data is passed to the error subsystem by the parser, which maintains a set of states representing the progress it has made in interpreting a given sentence. This set contains those partial parses with the greatest number of edges. If the parser is blocked, it reconstructs the partial parse tree for each of these states and applies rules to select one as the most likely intended interpretation. The error system proceeds by using information from the lexicon to identify case markers in the unparsed portion of the sentence. These case markers are then used to hypothesize any constituent phrases intended by the user from clues provided by the marker itself, the partial parse, and the phrase's position relative to other datum tokens (any verb or direct object, for instance). These hypotheses are tested using the appropriate transition subnetwork. When a complete hypothesis for the intended sentence structure has been determined and validated, it is translated into an error message and appropriate correction strategy for return to the user.

## ELEMENT ANALYSIS

Element analysis generates a set of atomic work elements representing the direct labor content implied by the process sheet. Direct labor encompasses all actions that contrib-

**FIGURE 6.**
Operation structure for sentence 110.

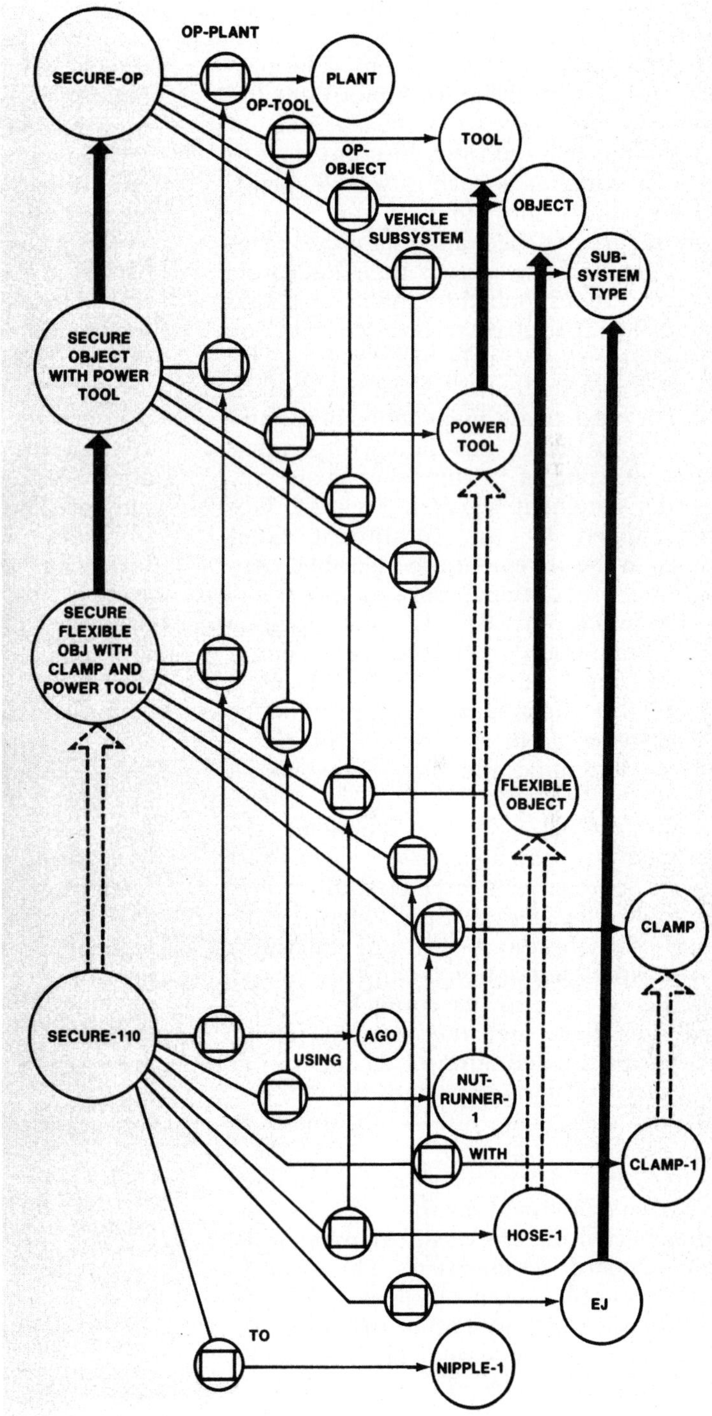

ute to automobile assembly. Indirect labor constitutes all the activities required to effect the associated direct actions. The process sheet shown in Figure 2 motivates the discussion.

A preliminary task identifies any significant contextual data (such as vehicle, plant, and functional subsystem of the vehicle) from the process sheet and establishes plausible defaults. The system then interprets the parse trees supplied by the parsing subsystem. The first phase resolves any weak or implied references in the sheet (ellipsis, intra- and intersentential anaphora, and so on). The next phase maps individual statements on the sheet into the corresponding operation concept within the taxonomy. Consider statement 110 from Figure 2. Objects implied by the constituent noun phrases in the statement are identified. Appropriate prepositional phrases are transformed into a normal noun-noun modifier form. Noun-noun modifiers are analyzed and individual concepts identified, using a precompiled dictionary structure. Finally, concept descriptions are created and classified to determine the closest taxonomic concept.

Significant cases in the statement are identified from the appropriate tokens and mapped onto their corresponding roles. Any tools associated with the statement are identified as necessary instrumental cases. An operation description is constructed and classified to identify its counterpart standard operation, and the assembly script stored with the definition of this operation is retrieved. The operation description created for statement 110 is illustrated in Figure 6.

After any necessary variable bindings have been established for the script, its constituent activities are classified to identify their standard counterparts. This process continues until a set of terminal scripts has been identified, representing the direct labor content of the statement. This set is then supplemented by adding any tool-handling information required to undertake the operation. The set of direct allocatable elements generated by statement 110 is shown in Figure 7. Redundant data is embedded in the output to maintain contextual information when the elements are split up into operator work allocations. The codes in parentheses represent the direct labor times associated with each element.

The assembly simulator elaborates the set of direct elements by generating any additional indirect work elements required to implement the current plan. The operator needs to make these motions to move around in the workstation. The first stage in this process is to identify the workstation configuration in which the assembly operation is assumed to take place from a taxonomy of standard configurations. Creating a workstation description from contextual information in the sheet and classifying it achieves this end. Each work element is then processed in sequence to identify any datum locations referred to in the text. The operator is assumed to relocate between datum locations in carrying out the assembly operation. The absence of a datum location for a given element is presumed to mean that the operator remains *in situ* for that element. Datum locations are once again identified by creating concept descriptions and classifying them, allowing a location to be associated with a concept at any level of detail. Figure 8 shows the complete set of elements for sentence 110 of Figure 2.

**FIGURE 7.** Direct elements for sentence 110.

**"Secure inlet hose to heater nipple with 1 hose clamp using a nutrunner"**

**Grasp power tool (rt angle nutrunner torque shut off) (01M4G1)**
**Position power tool (rt angle nutrunner torque shut off) to hose clamp**
**Secure inlet hose (01M4P2) to heater nipple using power tool (rt angle nutrunner torque shut off) with hose clamp (01M2P5M4P5M1P0)**
**Release power tool (rt angle nutrunner torque shut off) (01M4P0)**

**FIGURE 8.** Complete set of elements for sentence 110.

**Walk to power tool**
**Grasp power tool (rt angle nutrunner torque shut off)**
**(01M4G1)**
**Walk to heater**
**Position power tool (rt angle nutrunner torque shut off) to hose clamp**
**Secure inlet hose to heater nipple using power tool (rt angle nutrunner torque shut off) with hose clamp (01M2P5M4P5M1P0)**
**Release power tool (rt angle nutrunner torque shut off) (01M4P0)**

## UPDATING THE KNOWLEDGE BASE

The KBU is accessible to all process or industrial engineers who use the system. Users are allowed unrestricted access to maintain that part of the taxonomy directly related to their assembly expertise, necessitated because no single source of assembly expertise exists; in fact, several hundred assembly experts contribute. The KBU is divided into two basic areas of functionality. Process engineers maintain a common dictionary and describe parts, tools, and other assembly equipment. Industrial engineers maintain the part of the taxonomy containing standard operations. A query facility is universally available to facilitate knowledge-base interrogation.

The DLMS system is installed within the existing Ford systems network. An overview of the "back-end processor" architecture is shown in Figure 9.

The Texas Instruments Multi-Processor (MP) is the hardware platform. It uses a 16-slot Nubus architecture and allows four Explorer II processors to share a chassis and console. System software supports interprocessor communication and individual-processor rebooting; it also allows processors to share a common load band. Communication with the IBM host is effected via the TI SNA II processor, which acts as a 3274 terminal controller and terminal emulator. The rule-based system components were implemented from Inference Corp.'s ART. All other software was written in Common LISP.

## FUTURE DEVELOPMENT

DLMS was developed with continuous input from process and industrial engineers. Because the database required to describe all Ford vehicles is huge and its integrity of paramount importance, incremental deployment is critical. The system was introduced experimentally six months ago and is being used by a small subset of process and industrial engineers. Part of a major initiative at Ford, the system will continue to be enhanced for years to come.

*The authors thank Thomas S. Kaczmarek for his invaluable contribution to the initial specifi-*

**FIGURE 9.** DLMS deployment architecture.

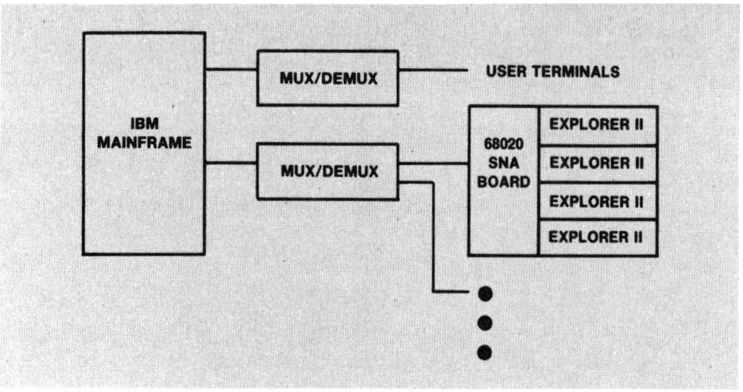

*cation and design of the DLMS system and Philip Klahr and Philip C. Jackson Jr., who were very helpful in criticizing early drafts of this paper.*

*This article is adapted from a paper presented at the Innovative Applications of AI conference held Mar. 28-30, 1989, at Stanford University, Palo Alto, Calif. © 1989 by AAAI, reprinted with permission.*

## REFERENCES

1. Moser, M.G. *An Overview of NIKL, the New Implementation of KL-ONE.* Cambridge, Mass.: Bolt Beranek and Newman Inc., 1983.

2. Kaczmarek, Thomas S., Raymond Bates, and Gabriel Robins. "Recent Developments in NIKL," in *AAAI-86 Proceedings,* Philadelphia, Pa.,1986.

3. Brachman, Ronald J., and Hector J. Levesque. "The Tractability of Subsumption in Frame-based Description Languages," in *AAAI-84 Proceedings,* Austin, Texas, 1984.

4. Robins, Gabriel. "The ISI Grapher and the ISI NIKL Browser," internal memo. Marina Del Rey, Calif.: USC/Information Sciences Institute, 1987.

5. Winograd, Terry. *Language as a Cognitive Process.* Reading, Mass.: Addison-Wesley, 1983.

6. Allen, James. *Natural Language Understanding.* New York, N.Y.: Benjamin Cummings, 1987.

7. Weischedel, Ralph M., and Norman K. Sondheimer. "Meta-rules as a Basis for Processing Ill-formed Input," *American Journal of Computational Linguistics 9,* (3-4): 161-177, 1983.

# APPENDIX D

## On-Line Expert Systems in Process Industries

The manufacturing sector of the economy can be divided broadly into two operation types: discrete parts (automobiles, airplanes, appliances, electronics, and computer hardware) and continuous or batch-process manufacturing (petroleum, chemicals, paper, pharmaceuticals, food, and utilities). These industries employ different manufacturing technologies and equipment that influence their application of automation technology, including AI and expert systems.

Within E.I. du Pont de Nemours & Co. Inc. (Du Pont) and the process industry in general, AI and expert systems are receiving much attention. Du Pont has an extensive program of expert-system applications, including advisory, scheduling, and process-control systems. Advisory systems encompass troubleshooting and product-selection applications that use off-line information from databases or data provided by question-and-answer keyboard input. Scheduling systems require information on the market forecast, customer orders, and plant equipment status. They establish practical constraints that narrow the search space and then search for an acceptable schedule. Scheduling systems run once a day to once every several days. Process-control systems include on-line expert systems that receive data primarily from sensor-based process monitoring and control systems and respond in real time to process problems.

This article focuses on applications of sensor-based, on-line, expert-system applications in the process-manufacturing environment. It describes various types of on-line

"On-Line Expert Systems in Process Industries" by D. A. Rowan, *AI Expert*, August 1989, pp. 30–38.

applications, examining the potential benefits, application experience, and tool requirements for implementing these applications. Du Pont views these expert-system applications as extensions to rather than replacements of process-control technology.

## MOTIVATION FOR APPLYING AI

The general demand for higher-quality domestic products is induced by worldwide competition. Improving quality requires us to have better data and analyze it to make appropriate decisions.

As discussed by Laffey *et al.*, real-time, on-line expert systems can benefit problem-solving situations in which humans suffer from cognitive overload, fail to monitor all available information or resolve conflicting constraints, are expensive or scarce, make high-cost mistakes, miss high-revenue opportunities, or cannot simultaneously manipulate all the relevant information to obtain optimal solutions or provide a solution quickly enough.[1] High-revenue opportunities certainly exist in the chemical and paper industries because many products are oversold; hence the economic incentive to improve plant utility. Automation in general and expert systems in particular do this by helping to prevent costly, unscheduled shutdowns due to equipment failure. Expert systems can also improve the percentage of time the process produces top-grade products by interpreting errant process behavior and advising corrective action. Companies understand that much of their competitive advantage results from knowledge about how to operate the process and process equipment most effectively. Because human expertise is perishable, interest in capturing this knowledge in expert systems is growing.

Much of the motivation for building on-line expert systems in the process industry is consistent with the published benefits for knowledge-based systems in general; that is, expertise is scarce, vague, and dispersed and should be preserved, made precise, focused, and applied continuously. Also, once captured, knowledge can be distributed among similar applications. Another motivating factor for applying on-line expert systems is reducing plant staffing. However, this is not a primary justification since operating labor typically represents a very small percentage of the total production cost. But reducing the routine technical assistance to manufacturing required of process engineers is of great interest. If expertise is leveraged in expert systems, engineers could move to more productive, creative, and valuable tasks. Domestic companies are also motivated by the fact that the Japanese are moving aggressively into the application of on-line expert systems.[2]

## PROCESS CONTROL

Improvements in process-control technology have been evolutionary. Before the 1940s, process parameters—flows, temperatures, and pressures—were controlled by human operators who adjusted valves manually while watching local instrument indicators, such as sight glasses and pressure gauges. In the 1940s and 1950s, pneumatic instrumentation was developed for sensing process parameters and providing feedback control. This gave operators hands-off control and allowed signal transmission to a remote control room, thus improving operator safety and comfort. With the advent of the transistor in the 1960s, analog electronic instrumentation became available on the market. Electronic instrumentation became more stable and precise than its pneumatic counterparts, and signals could be transmitted instantaneously over long distances. This allowed control areas to consolidate further, requiring less labor to operate the plant.

Beginning in the 1960s, digital computers were applied for process control. Computer inputs from process-measurement instrumentation and computer output signals to control valves were directly connected to the computer, providing direct digital control. Most process industries rejected this technique because having many control variables concentrated in a single computer was risky. This concern was alleviated in the 1970s when microprocessor technology allowed acceptable distribution of computing, control activity, and cost-effective redundancy, where required. Microprocessor-based, programmable logic controllers replaced discrete relays and other electronic logic systems for performing safety/process interlocks and sequencing operations for batch control. Distributed control systems consisting of CRT-based consoles and microprocessor-based controllers replaced panel boards of individual analog feedback controllers.

Today, digital-control systems dominate the industry. On larger processes, these systems typically feed data to a higher-level host computer for data archival, further data manipulation, and more sophisticated control manipulation. Sophisticated control strategies—linear and nonlinear optimizations, times-series analysis, control strategies based on process models, and statistical process-control techniques—reside at this level. These host computer systems are usually networked in a hierarchy of technical and business computing systems to make process information available to the appropriate technical and managerial personnel. Thus, many processes contain the necessary information networks to permit on-line, expert-system applications.

Even so, expert-system technology's entrance into process-control applications has been gradual and continues to evolve slowly. On the whole, this industry is rather conservative when it comes to using novel technology. Any misapplication can have severe consequences in terms of capital equipment and product loss, human safety, or possible environmental contamination. Despite this operating philosophy, the motivation for applying expert-systems technology is too compelling to disregard, and tools and techniques have evolved until beginning system implementation is cost-effective. Application areas that have benefitted include sensor validation, data reconciliation, on-line equipment diagnosis, and model-based knowledge systems. We routinely find applications with a 10:1 rate of return.

In the past, computer-based applications have approached what we call artificial intelligence today. In many cases, these systems were designed for one-of-a-kind applications related to a critical process problem. Generally, they take multiple-process sensor inputs, analyze the data, make nonroutine decisions about process operation conditions, and adjust process target values. In most cases, these applications have been written in procedural computer languages.

In one example, a water-cooled process reactor for an exothermic chemical reaction is operated at maximum cooling to gain the greatest product-to-ingredient yield. Increased cooling promotes a fouling problem that reduces heat transfer from the process fluid to the cooling water and eventually causes a severe loss of cooling and subsequent shutdown (with the potential for a runaway reaction). A supervisory computer monitors the differential temperatures of the process fluid and the cooling water to calculate a heat-transfer coefficient. When the supervisory computer determines that heat transfer is inadequate, it ramps the process temperature upward until the fouling clears and then gradually ramps the temperature back down to approach optimum yield once again. This system definitely embodies process expertise, though not designed as an expert system.

In the case of this computer program, the sensor data exists and changes fairly slowly with time; that is, the heat-transfer coefficient will change over tens of minutes. Such long time constants are typical for many petrochemical processes. However, much smaller time constants, on the order of tens of milliseconds, are involved in diagnosing electromechanical interlock systems. In one case, phantom shutdowns of a $3 million, 20,000 horse-power compressor result in down time costing $15,000 per hour. Capturing and quickly analyzing data for one of 40 possible interlock conditions capable of shutting down the compressor is absolutely necessary. A high-speed event recorder has been developed to log data such as vibration, stator temperature, over-voltage or over-current conditions, and high process temperature or pressure every millisecond.

This data collection rate is required to obtain sufficient resolution since the dropout time for the interlock relays is about 20 milliseconds. After an interlock event, experts determine the trip's cause. In this case, data analysis has not been reduced to an expert system, although such an operation is possible. The key to this application is having the available data with sufficient resolution to diagnose the problem. In this example, responding with any kind of corrective action during the tripping process is impossible; however, by aiding the postmortem analysis, the system reduces the mean time to repair, thereby increasing compressor availability.

In terms of process dynamics, we find some extremely long time constants in chemical processes with large residence times. These time constants can be several hours, meaning the process response to adjustments made by one operator may not be fully developed until hours later or perhaps until the next operating shift has taken over. (The new operator may not be aware of the previous action.) In these cases, great expertise and patience are required to control the process. The long time constants and large inertial loads of these processes make operating them much like navigating a supertanker: any need for corrective action must be anticipated and patience is required to allow process response to develop. Because these are not natural human tendencies, automatic process control and expert systems can benefit the operation of these processes.

These examples emphasize a point regarding real-time process-control systems, including expert systems: real time depends completely on the time constants of the process. A real-time system must collect and analyze data and issue a response within a time acceptable for resolving a problem.

## AI APPLICATIONS

Du Pont has explored many application areas: sensor validation, data reconciliation, process and equipment diagnosis, and model-based expert systems. Individual measurements generated by on-line process sensors are fundamental to on-line expert systems. These sensors range from basic physical measurement devices such as thermocouples to extremely complex devices such as on-stream process analyzers (complex chemical or electrical processes). The sensor's characteristic behavior reflects its design, specific installation, and process behavior. Many sensors are critical to process operation because they supply feedback and closed-loop control. In typical wet-chemical processes, about one-third of all process measurements serve as interlock sensors or are used in closed-loop control systems. These systems operate on the principle that the incoming measurement signal accurately reflects the process condition. Typically, these control systems only recognize a sensor fault for extreme conditions (open circuit, short circuit, and so on).

The objective of using expert systems for sensor validation is to improve the measurement system's overall reliability. This may simply mean recognizing that the sensor is suspect and an alternate measurement or control strategy should be instituted. A further objective is to improve the overall availability of the process measurement by providing troubleshooting assistance to the maintenance technician, thus reducing the mean time to repair. In general, systems that perform sensor validation can be used in multiple applications, generating more compelling economic incentives for their development.

Process engineers and plant operators develop experience in distinguishing normal from abnormal behavior of specific sensors. As an elementary example, consider the reactor temperature (Figure 1). Due to the large thermal inertia of the process, this signal is not expected to make an abrupt shift

**FIGURE 1.**
Reactor temperature trends.

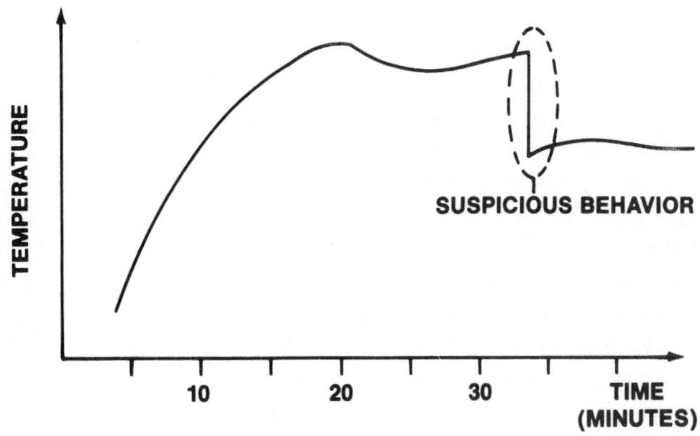


in value but will exhibit smooth, highly damped behavior. Therefore, any sudden shifts indicate a faulty signal (probably an electronic failure).

Other common physical-process measurements are pressure and flow detection. These signals exhibit a certain level of high frequency noise, as shown in Figure 2. A change in the noise band such as an increase or decrease in the noise level may indicate a faulty signal. A typical low noise level may indicate that the sensor has become detached from the process; for example, by a closed block valve. While the average pressure remains unchanged, the noise level will drop to zero. An increase in noise may indicate instability in the measurement. Engineers and operators recognize the typical signal patterns on strip-chart recorders or equivalent CRT displays. This process has been automated by developing algorithms to detect suspicious sensor behavior. With a short-term history of process data, these algorithms compute the rate of change, moving average and standard deviation, and other variables.

Du Pont also has an expert system that performs sensor validation on complex process analyzers. This system diagnoses mechanical and electronic failures in the analyzer, abnormal sample presentation to the analyzer, and adverse ambient conditions relative to the process or analyzer. The expert system is segmented into a monitoring

**FIGURE 2.**
Pressure and flow detection.

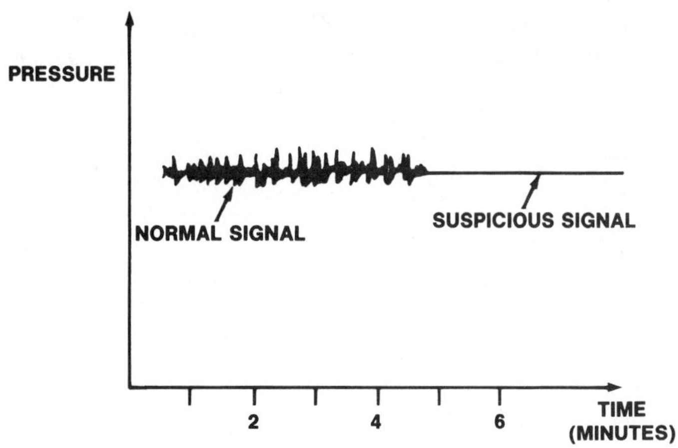

component that continuously scans and processes on-line data and a rule-base component that analyzes a snapshot of information and manually entered data. The expert system monitors on-line data for suspicious behavior, including the signal stability of the measurement and reference signal, and the characteristics of internal signals, such as the automatic gain control.

If the expert system determines that a fault has occurred, it alerts the operator. The maintenance technician can then activate the diagnostic expert system, which reads a snapshot of information from the on-line scanner, processes the data, and collects the additional information necessary to diagnose the problem from the technician. As in most other applications, human observation enhances on-line data. In most cases, a complete data set does not exist on line because some measurements or observations cannot be performed on line cost-effectively.

In a well-instrumented chemical process, redundant process data exists because of the process's inherent physical interaction. Consider the process by which inflow, outflow, and tank level are measured (Figure 3). These measurements are related by the mass-balance equation, which states that any difference between in-flow and out-flow results in a level change; the rate of level change is proportional to the difference in the two flows.

Any of the three measured variables could be calculated from the other two using the mass-balance equation; however, all three are usually measured. This creates redundant data, allowing cross-checks on all signals. Knowledge in the form of these governing equations is deep and provides additional information about the health of individual sensors and the process in general.

Drift in individual sensors may occur over a long period. Although it may not be detectable by sensor-validation techniques, it can often be detected by data-reconciliation techniques. Much work has been done in this area using both traditional data-reconciliation techniques[3] and expert-system methodology. In both approaches, noisy, imprecise measurements impede data reconciliation; however, sensor repeatability may be sufficient to allow data reconciliation even though sensor precision may be poor.[4] Relationships other than mass-balance relationships, such as energy-balance and reaction-rate equations, can reconcile process data. In addition, data-reconciliation techniques can be applied to process measurements and control-system outputs associated by feedback control. Since feedback-controller outputs often control variables such as pump speed or the automatic valve position, they provide a crude indication of process flow.

The reconciliation scheme can also include laboratory data. Since lab analysis is considered the ultimate proof that product properties meet specifications, lab data are of major importance. In addition, laboratory methods are sometimes required because

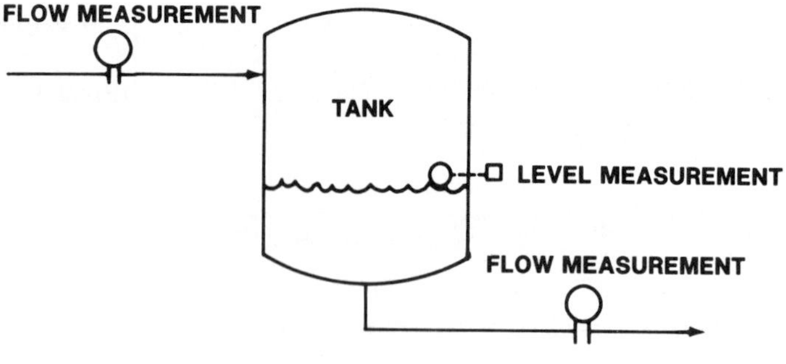


**FIGURE 3.** Tank-level measurement process.

techniques for on-line measurement of specific product composition may not be practical. In reconciling laboratory data with on-line process data, care must be taken that the data is adjusted in time. Because it may take several hours for the sample to be taken and processed in the lab and results returned, the lab data must be compared to the corresponding historical data taken on-line. Laboratory data can provide the final validation of on-line sensors and process operation.

Sensor validation and data-reconciliation techniques allow process measurements to be validated wherever measurement methods may fail or drift from the necessary accuracy. If measurement data are considered highly reliable, these steps may not be necessary. In any case, once process data have been judged reliable, individual data values may be combined into patterns, providing a higher information level. As a simple example, consider a liquid-flow process that normally operates under pressure. If the process flow increases and the pressure decreases rapidly, the process equipment or piping may have ruptured.

In another example, an exothermic batch reactor may be charged with ingredients and catalysts and then heated with steam to initiate the reaction. As the reaction begins, the process temperature increases rapidly. The expert system monitoring this process watches for the characteristic temperature profile when activation conditions have been met (the ingredients have been charged and the steam has been on long enough). Insufficient temperature rise indicates that not enough catalyst has been charged or that the catalyst's activity level is too low to initiate the reaction. These pattern-matching techniques are implemented in production-rule-based expert systems.

In addition to sensor data, these process-diagnostic applications often require observation by a human operator. This applies less to highly automated wet-chemical processes and more to sparsely instrumented mechanical operations, such as paper-manufacturing processes and film- or sheet-drying operations. In film- or sheet-processing applications, about 50% of the information required for a process diagnostic system must be entered manually. Expert systems for these applications must have a well-designed operator interface. Applications in the utility[5] and paper manufacturing industries[6] use manually entered data.

In addition to diagnosing process malfunctions that affect product quality, diagnosing supporting equipment, such as refrigeration machines, boilers, compressors, and instrumentation systems, is frequently desirable. The analyzer diagnostic system previously described is also an example of an equipment diagnostic application. Another example of this type of expert system is a diagnostic package for refrigeration equipment, which uses pressure and temperature data from both the process and refrigerant sides of the machine to detect degrading performance. Problems may occur in the compressor, condenser, evaporator, or purge unit and consist of abnormal conditions, such as compressor surging, loss of heat transfer, lubricating oil problems, and bearing failure. The system is being prototyped in an off-line mode but will be developed into an on-line system. Both of these examples represent systems that can be applied in many similar (though not all identical) applications because the supporting equipment is common to many processes and plants.

Model-based expert systems involve deep knowledge about the process. Models are derived from first-principle relationships of physics and chemical engineering and from empirical models based on statistical regression of process data. Incorporating this type of deep knowledge into an expert system allows for a very compact, precise system design. This has been proven true in diagnosing electronic circuits[7] and detecting chemical plant faults.[4] On-line models have been used for process-control strategies relying on the model to make process measurements unattainable on line with physical methods. Product properties or chemical compositions may be computed indirectly using available sensors to supply data for the model.

A simple example is using a model to calculate polymer viscosity from pressure, temperature, and flow measurements on a transfer pipeline. The biotechnology industry applies models to determine cell growth in bioreactors from the measurements of bulk properties, such as oxygen feed, ammonia evolution in the off-gas, and biomass temperature. Du Pont has developed expert systems that interact with process models and use the model-generated results as input information to the inference engine. On-line dynamic models can reason about the projection of process variables into the future. Modern AI tools allow model parameters to be included as object attributes (in an object-oriented tool). Combining the power of object-oriented modeling with an object-oriented expert system can be very powerful yet easy to understand and maintain.

## KNOWLEDGE-BASE DEVELOPMENT

Much has been written about knowledge extraction and knowledge-base development. Du Pont's experience has not been unique in these areas. We have found the accuracy and validity of the resulting expert systems to correlate directly with the quality of the domain expert's knowledge and ability to communicate this knowledge. Applying expert system technology demands the same understanding of the industrial process required when applying conventional control strategy and modeling techniques. In many cases, knowledge extraction has elucidated valuable information and produced new insights into the expert's reasoning. Therefore, performing initial problem analysis can be valuable even before the expert system is constructed. Du Pont has succeeded in staffing these projects by providing AI education to engineers experienced in process control. Using so-called knowledge engineers unfamiliar with this domain has proven impractical. In process-control AI application, domain experience outweighs AI experience. Other companies have come to similar conclusions.[8]

In many applications, existing domain expertise is adequate. It may exist in many forms: heuristics and empirical understanding from operating experience, fundamental understanding of first principles, existing models, and so forth. In our applications, most knowledge comes from engineers who have practical experience with the process or technical specialists who have studied it from a fundamental point of view. Senior operators' experience has also been included in some applications.

For applications in which cause-and-effect relationships are vague, we have run statistically designed experiments or less formal step tests to obtain better knowledge of these relationships and map cause and effect. Though these techniques are not novel AI technology, they clarify knowledge another way.

Du Pont has applied various tools and knowledge-representation techniques, including induction and rule-based, object-oriented, and frame-based systems. We have found that object-oriented knowledge powerfully represents the physical entities (such as sensors, pumps, valves, and pipes) and conceptual entities (such as mass and energy balances). The object structure affords much more efficient development of large applications. Logic has generally been represented in the form of production rules; however, we have seen the need for other pattern-matching techniques such as truth tables.

Du Pont has employed straightforward inferencing techniques for on-line expert systems. These systems are usually data-driven; they use forward chaining but employ some backward chaining for gathering data with respect to specific goals. Using tools that allow the knowledge base to be partitioned into compact modules that can be activated at the appropriate time has been very advantageous. Our expert systems run in several modes. Some systems run in a continuously scanning mode, monitoring for certain events to occur. Others are executed by periodic scanning when fresh data is available, usually once a minute (but perhaps more often). Some are activated by external events such as the input of lab data, while others are activated manually as needed. The inference engine must be able to continue processing real-time data while it seeks manually entered data; the system must not freeze under any conditions.

Several approaches to system validation have proven acceptable. For simple systems designed to detect process phenomena, some applications have been built simply and put on line. The performance of these systems is monitored as the particular process condition recurs. In most cases, however, capturing data related to process phenomena is desirable so the system can be tested off line. The sets provide case studies for alterations and refinements to the knowledge base. These data sets may be derived from archived plant data or captured during designed experiments. Validation of a system around very rare events, such as detection of catastrophic failure, requires process simulation as the only source of test data.

To validate the Falcon fault detection system, we used a benchmark data set of 11 sets of actual process data and 10 sets of simulated data.[4] Many interactions existed in this knowledge base and subtle changes were thoroughly tested using the benchmark data set. In general, we prefer testing the system in fast-forward mode (that is, faster than real time) to speed up the validation process.

## HUMAN-MACHINE INTERFACE

The ideal human-machine interface for plant operators would integrate directly with any existing control console. To date, this has not been achievable because control system vendors have not yet offered expert-system tools or capability. Many Du Pont process-control systems also include company-proprietary, host computer systems with additional consoles that display information generated by expert systems. Several plants use Digital Equipment Corp. (DEC) workstations (VAXstations) as expert-system operator interfaces.

Operators desire a very intuitive interface with basic functionality. Whereas system developers may function efficiently using a graphic interface with multiple overlaying windows, operators prefer an interface with hard boundaries and simple pushbuttons to call up other information on the screen. Display areas on the screen include scrollable, time-tagged, text-alarm messages; areas that will call up trend recordings, enter comments, and indicate the value of critical process variables; and facilities for activating these features. In addition, the engineers and production supervisors can call up an area of logged messages, including alarms and operator comments. In some instances, process graphics are also useful; however, these may appear on other control consoles and may not be duplicated in the expert system.

Since Du Pont regards the operator as the customer for these expert systems, we request assistance from operators when designing the human-machine interface for an application. Including operator suggestions in the design results in a more acceptable product and generates ownership by user contribution, which facilitates the technology transfer process.

The expert system explains its reasoning and conclusions. This explanation capability enhances the credibility of the expert system and is very valuable to operators. The value of explanation facilities has been recognized by the RESCU developers in the U.K.[9]

On-line, real-time system applications provide a genuine challenge for software designers building expert-system tools. Capabilities essential to these applications include data scanning over networks, temporal reasoning (collecting and analyzing time-varying data), calculation, logic solving in rule form, and other pattern-matching facilities. To handle time-varying data, the tool should have an internal historian for buffering data used to establish trends, rates of change, and other signal characteristics (like noise level). A library of common signal-processing functions is also useful. Highly desirable characteristics include an object-oriented structure allowing for multiple levels of classes, subclasses, and instances. Class (generic) rules are essential for efficiency when reasoning about common objects in the process; for example, a single rule should be able to check all temperature sensors against a high limit.

Though text editors may be a plausible development environment for small applications, graphic editors are decidedly more efficient and desirable. The editor should make as many syntactic and semantic checks as possible and provide on-line assistance for developing the proper rule grammar. Validation capability using canned data files and run-time debugging facilities such as break points, watch points, and single-step mode should be included. Facilities for constructing an operator interface as previously described are necessary; this interface should allow operator data entry.

Because these applications are critical, the on-line system and its tool must include facilities for error handling when communication errors occur, data supply systems go down, or bad data is returned from the process. Because these events are inevitable, the tool and application must be designed to cope with them, adding yet another level of complexity to the on-line application.

For more complex applications, Du Pont uses the commercial tool G2 from Gensym Corp. G2 offers most of the required functionality and runs on many platforms, including standard DEC VAX computer hardware platforms that prevail in our plants. Du Pont and Gensym have formed a working partnership to provide enhanced solutions to real-time AI applications. For smaller applications, we apply hybrid approaches by processing temporal data in an external program and calling an off-line tool such as Level5.

## VISION OF THE FUTURE

Du Pont applies a broad range of on-line expert systems. These initial successes create more interest and generate additional applications; therefore, we predict AI will become widespread in the company and the process industries in the future. Though we view AI and expert systems as extensions to conventional automation and process-control technology, new tools and improved application skills will allow further improvement in the rate of accomplishment.

*This article reflects the experience and efforts of J.T. Cardinal, R.K. Cox, K.A. Kosanovich, R.R. Lott, S.R. McBride, L.I. Morganstein, S. Padilla, P.D. Schnelle, R.J. Taylor, and B.D. Tyreus.*

## REFERENCES

1. Laffey, Thomas J., Preston A. Cox, James L. Schmidt, Simon M. Kao, and Jackson Y. Read. "Real-Time Knowledge-Based Systems," *AI Magazine*, Spring 1988, pp. 27-45.

2. Funakoshi, R. "Operation Instruction System: On-Line Process Monitoring and Fault Diagnosis," *Proceedings of AIChe Annual Meeting*, Paper 88G, Nov. 1987.

3. Tamhane, Ajit C., and Richard S. H. Mah. "Data Reconciliation and Gross Error Detection in Chemical Process Networks," *Technometrics*, 27(4): 409-422, Nov. 1985.

4. Rowan, Duncan A. "Applying On-Line Expert Systems: Technical Issues and Business Concerns," *Making Change Work* (Chemical Manufacturers Assoc. Sixth Process Control Users Forum), New Orleans, La., Apr. 1988.

5. Osborne, Robert L., Avelino J. Gonzalez, J.C. Bellows, and J.D. Chess. "On-Line Diagnosis of Instrumentation through Artificial Intelligence," *Proceedings of the ISA Meeting*, Paper #85-0985, 1985.

6. Myers, Douglas R., James F. Davis, and Charles E. Hurley. "Application of Artificial Intelligence to Malfunction Diagnosis of Sequential Operations which Involve Programmable Logic Controllers," *Extended Abstracts of AIChe Annual Meeting*, Abstract 37B, Apr. 1989.

7. Davis, Randall, Howard Shrobe, Walter Hamscher, Kären Wieckert, Mark Shirley, and Steve Polit. "Diagnosis Based on Description of Structure and Function," *Proceedings of the National Conference on AI*, pp. 137-142, 1982.

8. Ricketts, Grant V. "How to Do More in Less Time," *AI EXPERT*, Jan. 1988, pp. 46-52.

9. Shaw, Ray. "RESCU—On-Line Real-Time Artificial Intelligence," *Computer-Aided Engineering Journal*, 7(3): 29-30, 1987.

# APPENDIX E

## Rule-Based Structural Design in C

Computers are used extensively in the design process at Skidmore, Owings & Merrill, one of the largest architecture and engineering firms in the world. One application for which we write software is member design, basically the design of beams and columns. Over the years, we have had persistent maintenance and flexibility problems with these particular programs. Last year we decided to try something new: to write them as rule-based programs. Rather than use an off-the-shelf product, we wrote our own rule-based programming language in C. This language is not a toy or prototype; we use it to design office buildings with thousands of structural members. And now that this system has been in use for a few months, it has become clear that the new software has great advantages over our old FORTRAN and BASIC programs.

Most of the problems with our old member-design programs arose because they were written in FORTRAN. They were difficult to maintain—often a program could not be updated before another building-code revision was published. Another problem arose because users wanted to know in detail how a design program derived its results. We could not document the FORTRAN programs quickly enough, so the programmers spent a lot of time fielding questions about program internals. Finally, the programs were not extendible. A program cannot be modified when only the compiled form is available.

The root of our problem was that the data embodied in a FORTRAN program is inaccessible. A user who wanted to examine or change the way the program behaved could not be expected to search through thousands of lines of source code; anyone with a question about the behavior of such a program would have to go to the author, if the author were available.

Rule-based programming, in which design rules can be implemented as rules, looked like a possible solution. Representing our programs as rules has three crucial advantages:

- Users who want to know why the program comes up with a certain result can see, rule by rule, the reasoning that led to that result.
- Rule-based programs are easy to maintain because information about a particular design rule is localized in a few explicitly stated rules within the program.
- Users without much programming experience can read and even write the source code of a rule-based program—something only trained FORTRAN programmers could do before.

The value of a rule-based programming language is that it's halfway between a programming language and a user application. Like FORTRAN, programs can be written in the language, but like a spreadsheet, the language is accessible to nonprogrammers.

The core of our software is a 26,000-line C program called the Rule-Based Calculator (RBC). The RBC includes a programming language similar to OPS5 in its basic structure, an extensive trace facility, a way of displaying graphically what happens to variables at run time, and a structured query language (SQL) database interface. Intended from the start to be a general-purpose system, the RBC is currently used for five member-design applications and in a system for planning elevators. We are now considering it for stairwell design, toilet-room layout, and coordinated core design.

A rule-based programming language is based on two primary elements: the rule language and the inference strategy. A rule-based language becomes more powerful (and slower) as it supports more complex rules. The inference strategy used by a rule-based system does not directly affect its expressive power, but it does influence the problems for which it can be used. The following sections discuss the RBC along these two dimensions.

## RULE LANGUAGE

The simplest rule-based languages are similar in expressive power to propositional logic. In computer science terms, propositional-logic rules are rules that reason about the values of variables, for example:

```
IF   weather = cloudy
THEN prognosis = rain
```

Sometimes propositional-logic systems allow us to talk about variables being true with a certain degree of confidence, as in:

```
IF   weather = cloudy
THEN prognosis = rain, with confidence 0.7
```

but in their expressive power, these languages are still propositional-logic systems.

PROLOG and OPS5 offer a much richer form of logic called predicate logic, in which facts can be complex. Instead of just talking about the values of variables, relationships between them can be discussed. One test of whether or not a system supports predicate logic is to ask if it allows expression of the grandparent rule:

```
IF   x is the parent of y AND y is the parent of z
THEN x is the grandparent of z
```

This rule can be expressed in PROLOG and OPS5, but not in any propositional-logic system. However, predicate logic includes propositional logic, so a predicate-logic system can run any rule a propositional-logic system can.

Classical AI programs, meaning programs intended to exhibit some subset of intelligent behavior, had to represent facts in a notation at least as expressive as predicate logic. Without it, a program cannot discuss classes of objects or relationships between them. Unfortunately, pattern-matching is necessary to run predicate-logic rules. Looking at the grandparent rule, it should be clear that this rule demands more work of the computer than the rule about the weather. To run the weather rule, the system only has to check the value of the variable *weather.* To run the grandparent rule, it must check each pair of parent facts in the database.

Pattern-matching is not hard to implement, requiring less than 50 lines of LISP.[1] But pattern-matching is computationally expensive, so expensive that much of the research done on production systems is aimed at trying to make it faster. Charles Forgy, the author of OPS5, noted, "Some systems have been observed to spend more than nine-tenths of their total run-time performing...pattern-matching."[2]

If your domain can be represented in a restricted form of predicate logic, thereby avoiding pattern-matching, the resulting program will be faster. We did not need full predicate logic to represent our domain. We did need speed, however, because many of our applications use very large data sets.

One advantage of writing our own language was that we could tailor it to our specific projects. We decided to make the RBC support a subset of predicate logic, more expressive than propositional logic but sufficiently restricted that it requires no pattern-matching at run time.

The RBC's rule language is a compromise between speed and expressive power. It allows predicates of one argument. The consequences of this decision may not be obvious at first, but a few examples will make clear just what can be expressed in such a language.

First, the RBC allows simple propositional-logic rules:

```
RULE ''simplest''
IF   p
THEN q
```

Rules may also refer explicitly to the values of propositions, as in:

```
RULE ''employee status''
IF   age > 64
THEN retirement_age
```

So far we just have a regular propositional-logic system. The RBC allows us to go one step further and use some propositions as if they were vectors. The simplest case is the following:

```
RULE ''simple vector''
IF   p[2]
THEN q[4]
```

Like normal propositions, vector elements can have numeric values, so we can have rules like:

```
RULE ''check main tank''
IF   tank_contents[1] = 0
THEN main_tank_empty
```

The indices of vector variables can be variables in the sense of propositions, but not of pattern variables. The following example makes the distinction explicit:

```
RULE ''set biggest''
IF   true
THEN biggest_tank = 13

RULE ''test biggest''
IF   tank_contents[biggest_tank] = 0
THEN biggest_tank_empty
```

By assigning propositions integer values, the RBC can run more familiar examples:

```
RULE ''car starts implies battery working''
IF   status[starter] = working
THEN status[battery] = charged
```

Rules may not contain pattern variables like those found in OPS5, but they may contain wild cards, which is enough to make writing rules about object classes possible. Suppose we have a set of 20 pumps and we want to express the rule that if the flow in a pump falls below the pump's threshold, the pump is broken. In a purely propositional-logic system, we would have to use one rule per pump, yielding 20 nearly identical rules:

```
RULE ''check pump1''
IF   pump1_flow < pump1_threshold
THEN pump1_broken

RULE ''check pump2''
IF   pump2_flow < pump2_threshold
THEN pump2_broken
.
.
.
```

Using RBC vector variables, facts about the pumps can be expressed consistently. First, make a single vector of 20 elements called *pump_flow,* where the flow rate at pump *n* is stored in *pump_flow[n].* Then make similar vectors called *pump_threshold* and *pump_broken.* Using the RBC wild card *ANY,* the 20 propositional-logic rules can now be boiled down to one RBC rule that describes the whole class of pumps:

```
RULE ''pump example''
IF   pump_flow[ANY] < pump_threshold[ANY]
THEN pump_broken[ANY]
```

Paraphrased, this rule says that if the flow of any pump is less than the threshold for that pump, the pump is broken.

Suppose we want to add the further rule that any broken pump triggers an alert. In pure propositional logic, this rule would be unwieldy:

```
IF   pump1_broken
OR   pump2_broken
OR
.
.
.
OR   pump20_broken
THEN alert
```

Using the vector variables, the rule is reduced to two lines:

```
RULE ''alert example''
IF   pump_broken[ANY]
THEN alert
```

The case is similar when we want to test whether all the pumps are broken. The RBC approach is more concise and the rules need not be changed if the number of pumps changes. In fact, the number of pumps could be input by the user.

Finally, the RBC allows rules to refer to vector subranges. The following rule calculates the elevation of each floor in a building, from the height of each:

```
RULE ''height''
IF   true
THEN elev[1] = 0
AND  elev[2 TO floors] = elev[1 TO
     floors_less_one] + height[1 TO floors_less_one]
```

Vector variables also allow us to write rules that sum the values of elements, find the highest or lowest elements, and so on. Because these operations cannot be done with purely propositional logic, we thought we would require predicate logic with its attendant costs. Fortunately, this turned out not to be the case. The RBC works as fast as if it did only propositional logic. Its rule language represents an ideal compromise: the expressive power our applications demand and the speed of the simplest rule-based systems.

## INFERENCE STRATEGY

Roughly speaking, the inference strategy in a rule-based language determines the order in which conclusions are reached. The two most widely used inference strategies are backward chaining (used in PROLOG) and forward chaining (used in OPS5). Like its rule language, the RBC's inference strategy is a hybrid of existing approaches.

The rules used by backward- and forward-chaining systems look similar, but the ways they are used are quite different. Backward chaining is appropriate when the rules could create a larger (possibly infinite) number of conclusions than you need; forward chaining is well suited to problems that are like finding a needle in a haystack.

Forward chaining is used when a program should achieve its results by having side effects. Successive rule firings in a forward chainer eventually bring the desired conclusions. A backward chainer derives solutions, whereas a forward chainer assembles them. The distinction is not absolute—forward chaining can be simulated in PROLOG, as can backward chaining in OPS5—but the two strategies are rarely suited to the same problems. Backward chaining is useful when you know in advance what questions you want answered and you want to home in on them through a potentially large search space. We found that we wanted both properties so for the RBC, we designed an inference strategy that combines the best of both worlds.

The RBC uses both backward and forward chaining. Users give the RBC queries much as they would with a backward-chaining system. The RBC then tries to prove or disprove these queries by forward chaining. For example, suppose the RBC were given the following three rules about automobile insurance:

```
1. RULE ''determine if applicant is a high risk''
   IF    tickets > 2
   AND   accidents > 0
   THEN  risk = high
   AND    deductible = 500

2. RULE ''determine if record must be checked''
   IF    risk = high
   THEN  check driving record frequently

3. RULE ''set premium if high-risk applicant''
   IF    risk = high
   THEN premium = 2000
```

If we assert *tickets* = *4* and *accidents* = *1*, then ask the RBC to determine the premium, the sequence of events is as follows:

- The RBC knows that the third rule could assign a value to *premium* if *risk* were high.
- The RBC looks up how to establish *risk*. It sees that the first rule could do it if *tickets* > *2* and *accidents* > *0*.
- Finding it already established that *tickets* = *4* and *accidents* = *1* (and therefore *tickets* > *2* AND *accidents* > *0*), the RBC turns around and begins forward chaining through the path that it has followed thus far.
- The RBC fires the first rule, which asserts *risk* to be high and *deductible* to be $500.
- The RBC fires the third rule, which asserts *premium* to be 2,000.

The RBC forward chains like a production system, but it does so with the focus of a backward chainer. Its strategy could be called goal-directed forward chaining. The phrases "goal-directed" and "backward chaining" are often used as if they were synonomous, but the RBC's inference strategy shows that they are distinct concepts. A program is goal-directed if it knows where it is going, regardless of whether it gets there by query or by assertion. The RBC uses backward chaining to create the path through which it will forward chain. So when the RBC fires rules, it always does so with a particular goal in mind.

The usefulness of goal-directed forward chaining is not necessarily limited to our applications. Goal-directed forward chaining means that you no longer have to risk the assertion of lots of unneeded facts to enjoy the convenience and broader utility of forward chaining. Most production systems suffer to some degree from the proliferation of facts and, with many of them, the programmer does have some advance knowledge of what facts he or she eventually wants asserted. Wherever these two conditions hold, we can expect goal-directed forward chaining to cut down unnecessary assertions.

## SQL DATABASE INTERFACE

The last few years have seen an increasing emphasis on integrating rule-based programs with existing software. The RBC's structured query language interface is an example of this trend. SQL is a standard language for manipulating databases. The RBC allows SQL statements to be included directly in rules. The following SQL statement will yield a set of all item numbers from an inventory database with a retail cost of more than $2,000 and purchased before 1986:

```
SELECT item_no FROM inventory_db
WHERE retail_cost > 2000 AND yr_purchased < 1986
```

An SQL statement can be inserted wherever an assignment statement would normally be. As a simple example, this RBC rule will assign a value to the variable *item_no* an item number with a retail cost of more than $2,000 and in the inventory since before 1986:

```
IF    true
THEN  SQL ''SELECT item_no
FROM inventory_db
WHERE retail_cost > 2000
AND yr_purchased < 1986''
```

If *SELECT* yields more than one value, the variable *item_no* is set to the first one. If *SELECT* yields no values, the variable is set to *unknown.*

In addition to setting RBC variables, SQL statements can refer to the values of RBC variables using the key word *RBCVAL.* Suppose that *cost* is an RBC variable set to some number. The rule:

```
IF   true
THEN SQL ''SELECT item_no
FROM inventory_db
WHERE retail_cost > RBCVAL( cost )''
```

will set *item_no* to the item number of the first inventory item with retail cost greater than the value of *cost.* A fair amount of work may go on beneath the surface here. Because *cost* is an RBC variable, its value may depend on chains of other rules, which may in turn cause more rule firings and other SQL queries.

As well as querying databases, RBC rules can update, delete, and insert records within them. All these operations use standard SQL syntax.

Integrating a rule-based program with a database system offers many advantages. Often a rule-based program makes use of information most naturally represented in a table. Our member-design programs, for example, need to access tables of engineering data. By storing this information in an SQL database table, we can leave it in its most common form instead of coercing it into the RBC rule language. Putting these tables in the rules would also have the disadvantage of making the application larger and possibly slower.

Working with SQL databases is also advantageous because the RBC will be useful in a wider variety of applications. We can make an RBC program behave differently just by giving it different databases. It also means that in writing an RBC program, we need not always start from scratch. If our program can use information already stored in some database, that much of the work is already done.

## C IMPLEMENTATION

The RBC includes a rule compiler that reads ASCII files of rules and turns them into a compiled form, which the inference engine uses at run time. Compiled rules can be stored in a binary file and so do not require recompilation each time they are used. The RBC's two major data structures are the rule table and the datastore. The rule table contains an entry for each rule, and the datastore contains an entry for each variable used in the rules. The two data structures are outlined in Figure 1.

In addition to creating data structures the inference engine can operate on, the rule compiler figures out the data types of all variables and associates each rule and variable with information that makes chaining faster at run time.

**FIGURE 1.** The rule table and data store, the RBC's two major data structures.

**RULE TABLE ENTRY**

| LABEL | LHS | LHS VARIABLE DEPENDENCIES | RHS | RHS VARIABLE DEPENDENCIES | |
|---|---|---|---|---|---|

**DATASTORE ENTRY**

| LABEL | DATA TYPE | STATUS | VALUE | DEFINING RULES | |
|---|---|---|---|---|---|

The left-hand side (LHS) is the *if* part of a rule and the right-hand side (RHS) is the *then* part of a rule. The *LHS* and *RHS variable dependencies* fields of the rule structure each contain a list of the variables whose values must be known to evaluate the LHS of a rule and assert the RHS, respectively. When the inference engine runs a rule, it first tries to establish the value of each variable in the LHS. It loops through the list of LHS dependencies, checking the status of each variable. If the variable does not already have a value, the inference engine attempts to fire a rule that will define it. When the value of a variable depends on one rule, which in turn depends on the value of another variable, the result is backward chaining.

Assume the inference engine establishes the values of all the variables in the LHS. If the LHS is true, the RBC tries to establish the values of all the variables in the RHS. If it succeeds, the RBC fires the rule and begins to forward chain through the path it created by backward chaining.

The *defining rules* field of the variable structure is a list of all rules that, if fired, assign a value to that variable. This information is crucial to the speed of the inference engine; at run time, when the RBC needs to establish a variable, it already has a list of the rules that could affect its value.

## LESSONS

What's in store if you want to write a program like the RBC? This section tries to suggest an answer by presenting some of our experiences developing the RBC.

A program's specifications may change as it is written, often to a greater extent than its programmers remember afterward. The most important change in the specifications of the RBC was that we made the rule language more powerful. Early versions of the system supported only propositional-logic rules. When it became clear that propositional logic was not sufficient to describe our domain, we had to come up with a rule language that was slightly richer but would not require the program to be completely rewritten. The solution, using predicate logic for predicates of one integer argument, left the skeleton of the code untouched.

If you are planning to write a rule-based language like the RBC, it would be helpful to begin by writing some of the rules you expect to use. This will give you a clear idea of the features your language will need.

The implementation of the RBC also changed as the program matured. The most important change was the increasing emphasis on the rule compiler. To make applications as fast as possible at run time, the RBC compiles rules into a primitive procedural language, much like machine language, which is then interpreted at run time. This results in a trade-off between speed when rules are defined (if the rule compiler does not do much) and when they are run (if the compiler does a lot). Speed is important in our applications because they are computationally intensive and often deal with very large data sets. A typical request would be to design all beams and columns (approximately 2,000 ) in an 80-story building overnight. As time went on, the rule compiler grew more and more sophisticated, increasingly trading speed when rules were defined for speed when run.

Most rule-based applications will not require many new rules to be defined at run time. When this is the case (as with the RBC), it makes sense to do as much work ahead of time as possible. If you make a provision for storing the compiled forms of the rules in files and no new rules are defined, the hard work of compilation only has to be done once. The RBC compiles large (1,000-rule) rule bases in minutes, but it is able to load them in seconds.

One of the biggest surprises we encountered was the relative amounts of time spent writing the various parts of our program. At first we expected the writing of the RBC itself to take the longest. We predicted that the RBC would take 50% of the total hours, the five sets of member-design rules 15%, and the research for these rules 35%. In the end, the RBC took a much smaller proportion of the time than we had expected. The most time-consuming work was writing the rules. It turned out that each of the three tasks took roughly one-third of the time, meaning that writing the RBC required only half as many hours as writing the rules.

Another surprise was the effect of the rules on the program's performance. When we wanted to make our applications run faster, we assumed we had to make the RBC's inference engine faster. We continued to tune the RBC, squeezing out ever-smaller performance improvements until we discovered we could get greater speed increases by rewriting the rules. When we optimized one set of rules, it ran three times faster.

Anyone writing a program like the RBC should build in a trace facility from the beginning. Tracing rule firings helps programmers debug rules and helps users understand why the program gives the answers it does. But tracing is just as useful in debugging the inference engine itself, which is why it's worth including even before the system is finished. A basic trace facility is easy to write; we wrote our initial version, which printed out rule firings indented to show the depth of recursion, in one day. Time invested here will save time later in tracking down the most difficult bugs: those that might be in the inference engine or rules.

You should also think carefully about the data structures you use to represent rules and variables. Design them to make type checking as fast as possible, because this may take more time than you expect. And pay special attention to making the data structures small. When rules take up too much space, you may run into problems such as excessive paging or running out of memory, depending on your hardware configuration and operating system.

How much do you need to know about AI to write a program like the RBC? Frankly, not much. At one extreme, what people conventionally call "applied AI" is just very high-level programming. Most of the concepts in rule-based programming are familiar ones like abstraction, object-oriented programming, and data drivenness. To write a program like the RBC, you should understand at least the issues of rule language and inference strategies discussed here. In fact, you should understand these issues even if just trying to choose among existing languages. PROLOG and OPS5 are suited to different types of problems, and you want to decide which inference strategy works for you before choosing between them. It also helps to know AI history to get a feeling for the programming approach AI represents.

**REFERENCES**

1. Wilensky, R. *Common LISPcraft*, Norton, 1986.
2. Forgy, Charles L. "Rete: A Fast Algorithm for the Many Pattern/Many Object Pattern Match Problem," *Artificial Intelligence*, Vol. 19, 1982.

# APPENDIX F

## User-Developed Expert Systems

*Stripped of the magical aura that surrounds new technologies, expert systems turn out to be handy gadgets for a number of everyday tasks. Using a software tool that shifts the focus from programming to communicating information, a growing number of PC users are finding that they can build their own expert systems.*

*The results that come from user-built expert systems may not be as spectacular as those achieved by Schlumberger's oil well drilling advisor or American Express Corporation's credit authorizer's assistant, but development costs and associated risks are modest enough to be acceptable even to a small enterprise, and the payoffs can be just as great. Saving experts' energies for the hard problems, downloading routine tasks requiring judgment from human being to machine, and cutting training time where experienced personnel is scarce are among the benefits most often mentioned. This article will look at three such user-developed expert systems.*

### Troubleshooting PCs

In the St. Louis Public School System, three technicians and two PC experts were spread thin supporting some 2,000 PCs at 160 different locations. Now, thanks to Joseph Carr's Hardware Diagnosis System, technicians make thirty percent fewer service calls. The expert system shows PC users how to handle routine problems on their own. Reducing the number of trouble calls routed to the technicians was a priority for the school system's Information and Technology Development Department. Carr, networking specialist at the time and now an external consultant to the school board, spotted the opportunity to use an expert system.

Knowledge was abundantly available. The department maintained a service log for each call, listing symptoms, diagnosis, and cure. In addition, manuals were on file for every piece of computer equipment used in the school system. For the most difficult questions, the technicians were available to be interviewed.

Carr decided to learn as much as he could about troubleshooting PCs before he approached the experts. First he classified entries in the service log by symptom and cure. He estimated that between one-fourth and one-half of all calls received could have been handled by the users themselves, instead of dispatching trained technicians to the site.

Next, with advice from the technicians, Carr narrowed his list to include only PC problems that a well-instructed amateur could solve without any special equipment or software. The resulting list was the set of problems that the expert system was designed to handle.

Then Carr turned to the technical service manuals. He found it easy to translate the printed materials into problem/solution statements. However, because these materials assumed a certain level of knowledge on the part of the reader, they often lacked the detail that a novice PC user consulting an expert system would need. This detail had to be added to the expert system.

Getting information out of the technicians presented a different kind of problem. The technicians often recognized the significance of a set of symptoms without having to think about it, and it took some probing on Carr's part to get them to express in words knowledge that had become second nature to them.

Once he thought he had enough information to build the expert system, Carr grouped his problem/solution sets according to the related piece of equipment. Then he tried to solve problems listed in the log book, using only the information gleaned from manuals and technicians.

Where he found problems for which he had insufficient information, Carr did more interviews and text searches, until he could solve all the problems on his list.

Next, Carr built a diagram to show the logical steps the expert system would follow in seeking a solution. The diagram looks like a tree lying on its side (see figure 1). The trunk contains the name of the equipment, such as "keyboard." The first set of branches consists of symptoms; subsequent branches alternate between questions that the user can answer and suggested remedies or requests for additional diagnostic information.

A major failing of poorly-designed expert systems is their inability to recognize when they don't know enough to solve the problem at hand. Carr avoided this problem by making the instruction "Call Technology Development for service" one of the system's available choices.

Once the conceptual diagram was drawn, Carr was ready to select a software tool with

```
          |-...
          |                                   |-If yes, call for
          |                     |-            |  service
Keyboard-|                      |Is cable     |
          |  No keyboard -      |plugged in at -|
          |  operation.         |both ends?   |  If no, plug in cable
          |-                    |-            |-at both ends.
```

*Figure 1 (decision tree diagram)*

which to build the system. Because of the constraints of the job, the chosen system had to:

- Allow him to produce a prototype quickly
- Allow distribution on many machines at a modest cost
- Run on PCs equipped with only 256K bytes of RAM
- Provide a receptive user interface

He chose Paperback Software's VP-Expert.

Heeding the old programmer's dictum, "The sooner you start writing code, the longer the project will take," Carr spent about 40 hours designing the decision tree before he started coding the expert system. The rules he wrote came directly from the diagram (see figure 2).

Carr stresses the importance of providing for the possibility that the user may not know the answer to a particular question. "An expert system shell should allow you to use 'Unknown' as a value in your rule set," he says. "That way, the expert system can arrive at a conclusion even if the user doesn't have all the necessary information."

To keep the rule base manageable, Carr divided his diagnostic system into several sub-systems, each devoted to a single equipment or problem category. A consultation opens with a screen (see figure 3) that lists all the topics the expert system knows about and allows the user to select one or more problem areas to explore. The system routes the consultation to the first topic selected; once a conclusion is reached in that area, routing goes to the next topic, and so on.

Carr found that building an expert system involved several cycles of information collection, coding, and testing. "After I finished the different modules," he says, "I had to go back and conduct more interviews and do modifications again and again until I had a finished product." He spent about two weeks learning to use VP-Expert and exploit its features, and another two weeks extracting information from technical manuals and interviewing technicians. He spent 40 hours on conceptual design, creating diagrams to express the information that the expert system would contain. In all, Carr says, development took some 300 hours, counting his time and that of the technicians whose knowledge is built into the system. "Gathering the information tends to be the hardest part," Carr says. "Sometimes a person's opinion can vary from one day to another, or the technician may contradict what's in the manual. But that's why you have experts. There are things an expert

```
IF component = Keyboard and
   problem = No_operation and
   cable_plugged = yes then
   display "Call Technology Development for service";

IF component = Keyboard and
   problem = No_operation and
   cable_plugged = no then
   display "Make sure that the cable is plugged in at
    both ends.
    Try to type at the keyboard.
    If the keyboard does not work, call for service";
```

*Figure 2 (VP Expert rules corresponding to tree in figure 1)*

```
Starting Consultation - to end consultation press /Q

Select answers that come closest to your symptoms.

What area are you having a problem with?

No Power                PC not booting     Irregular beeping
POST Error Code         Software           Drive A or B
Hard disk               Printer            Display
Scanner                 Keyboard           Plotter
Communications port     Modem              Other

Exit diagnosis
```

*Figure 3 (Opening Screen)*

might know from experience that aren't in the manual."

The trick to knowledge acquisition, Carr adds, "is catering to the personality of the expert, to get him or her to open up and actually answer the questions. Primarily, it's a personal adjustment between you and the expert." Carr says the technicians were skeptical at first and reluctant to spend time downloading their knowledge. They doubted the system could answer questions faster than they could, and that an expert system could be built to contain all the information they brought to bear in solving a problem. "But of course," Carr remarks, "that depends on the quality of the knowledge gathering."

To gain their cooperation, Carr built a series of small prototypes based on problems in the service log. Then he showed the technicians how closely the expert system's analysis resembled their own solution. Once they had seen the prototypes, the technicians saw the value of taking part in the project.

Early response from the user community shows that people find the menu orientation of the expert system easy to use, and that they like the fact that the system will still try to find a solution even if the user can't answer all of its questions. Most have been pleased at the new-found competence the expert system imparts, but some still prefer human interaction. "We are still working on getting those users adjusted to the use of the PC for problem solving," Carr says.

Asked whether he would advise people to undertake a project such as his, Carr says, "I think expert systems are a great tool for saving time and money. But it's something that should be ventured into with a bit of hesitation, to prevent people from trying to create systems that are too large and broad. In other words, don't get too ambitious too fast."

### Repairing Winchester Drives

Not only can diagnostic systems economize on scarce human expertise, but they also make excellent teachers. Brian Gatza, president of TCE Company of Elgin, Illinois, is counting on an expert system to transfer senior technicians' expertise at repairing Winchester disk drives to unskilled novices.

"You can walk down the block in California and pass fifteen companies repairing disk drives, so skilled people are readily available there," Gatza says. "Not here. For all practical purposes, we're the only company in the Chicago area repairing Winchester drives. We had to do something about training in order to have the manpower necessary to grow at the rates we're projecting."

Gatza expects the system to cut by six months the time it takes to train novice service technicians to the point where they can work on their own. He notes that TCE's newest technician has a degree in electronics engineering, "and it's taken about nine months before we feel comfortable that he can operate completely independently."

Experienced technicians use the system, too. "Not on the day-to-day problems, because they are experts on those, but on the kind of problem that only shows up a half percent of the time." Human technicians can forget how they once solved a problem they rarely see, but an expert system, once told, will never forget. So while new employees use the expert disk diagnostics system as a trainer, experienced workers use the same system as a memory jogger.

When a disk drive comes in for repair, a TCE technician puts it through a set of 15 tests. Some combinations of test results can indicate several different problems; then the technician's expertise comes into play to decide which solution to try first. Picking the correct answer on the first try saves money both for the customer and for TCE.

For his software tool Gatza chose SuperExpert, an inductive tool that formulates IF/THEN rules from a table of example problems and their solutions. Gatza had looked at several tools before he met a representative of SoftSync, SuperExpert's vendor, at a Chicago computer show where he, too, was an exhibitor. "It was exactly what I was looking for," Gatza says. "It has flexibility; you can make it think your way, to come to the same logical conclusions."

The development team consisted of Gatza, TCE's service manager, and a technician. Their first step, Gatza says, was to list all the variables that tests evaluated, what values could be associated with each variable, and what conclusions a technician might reach. Matching a set of test values to a specific conclusion was the next step.

"That's the hard part," Gatza says. "After you do a thing for a long time, it becomes natural, instinctive, and you don't really think about it. Building an expert system forces you to define your decision process exactly. Once people get into the proper frame of mind it comes easily," he adds, "but it's tough at first."

Technicians sometimes disagree, Gatza acknowledged. Handling disagreements among experts is such a tricky task that knowledge engineers often shy away from working with more than one expert on a single system. Also, most inductive expert system tools stumble when a single set of parameters can lead to more than one conclusion.

The team at TCE met periodically to hammer out their disagreements. "Sometimes a test result could be caused by any of five different things," Gatza says. When two technicians disagreed on what cure to try first, both would be challenged to explain their reasoning. "We needed concrete reasons, not just feelings, about why each one thought his solution was the one to try first," he explains. "Eventually, in each case the team would agree to put one solution first and the other second."

Gatza guesses that the team has put in between 300 and 400 hours to build the system—95 percent of it in defining parameters and charting the flow of logic. He doubts the system will ever be finished. "We will always find another type of problem that occurs only once in six months, or a new type of disk drive that has its own little quirks, so there will always be something more to add to it. We're working with an electromechanical device," Gatza points out. "Who knows what's going to happen with those things?"

## Screening Graduate School Applicants

Fault diagnosis isn't the only kind of problem for user-built expert systems to tackle. Watching his wife screen graduate school admissions applications, Carl Disbrow sensed a problem crying out for an expert system solution. He manages the Center for Health Education, an organization engaged in planning and evaluating nutrition and public health services. The University of California at Berkeley's School of Public Health, where Doris Disbrow is on the faculty, is a major client of the Center.

As chair for the public health nutrition program's admissions committee, Doris Disbrow has a job involving reviewing application documents and writing a report of recommendations to accompany each application when the full committee came to consider it. That's not as simple as it sounds. A fair amount of discretion is involved. For example, grade point averages and prior schooling are important, but the admissions committee may choose to overlook marginal grades for a candidate with significant work experience in public health.

Doris Disbrow spent about a half hour on each application in a procedure that is boring and repetitive, but important, both to the applicant and to the school. The expert system can do the same job in a couple of minutes. "The computer doesn't make the decision," Carl Disbrow stresses. "It just pulls all the data together so that the faculty committee can see whether a student has the basic requirements or not."

To find a software tool that would help him, Disbrow went to a computer fair in San Francisco and visited every booth that seemed to have anything to do with AI. "Most of the people I talked to said you had to be able to program to do AI. My response was, 'Not me. I haven't gotten into programming and I don't intend to,'" Disbrow recalls. He adds, "The VP-Expert people had a booth there. They demonstrated that if/then/else logical programming was not a programming language as such, so I decided to try it."

Playing knowledge engineer to his wife's role as expert, Disbrow went through piles of applications, asking his wife about each piece of paper, "What do you do with this data? How significant is it? What is the minimum that you could accept in this area? What are the cutoff points?"

"I needed to know the cutoff points," Disbrow explains, "because the decisions being made were based primarily on whether the applicants had the basics. I had to have a very clear definition of what the basics were."

Disbrow says his first attempt "wasn't too satisfactory." He thought, incorrectly, that he had to use the conclusion to one rule as the premise of the next one. Also, instead of charting the logic that the system would follow, Disbrow tried to use VP-Expert's inductive system to create a matrix of examples and build the system's rules from them. "I had a table with about 30 lines and ten variables, and it just totally confused the program," he says. "It made the first 12 or 13 rules very nicely, and after that I just got garbage."

Disbrow talked with members of the local PC users group about his frustrations. One member offered to supply a rule set that worked. "When I looked at the first file, the light went on," Disbrow says. "It told me what I had to do. I did it and it worked the first time." (The first release of VP-Expert lacked good sample systems; that deficiency has since been corrected.)

Disbrow thinks that a sophisticated database would do the admissions screening job just as well as an expert system, except for one thing. An end user would have to know quite a bit about a database. With the expert system he built, anyone can run the application without knowing anything about the program. The user interface looks like a form to be completed. It asks for the prospective student's name, demographic data, and work experience, and for grades and credit hours earned in required courses. It calculates the applicant's grade point average and collects information on other credentials. Its output is a report setting out the applicant's strengths and deficiencies, much as Doris Disbrow would report them to the admissions committee.

Disbrow learned two things from his experience. First, he says, "I would definitely recommend that people make a logic chart before they start building the system. Moving from a logic chart to the rule base turned out to be a relatively simple matter." His second piece of advice is to seek good example rule sets from which to learn. Until he saw the rules furnished by the user group member, Disbrow thought that an expert system's usefulness would be severely limited. "That set of rules showed me that there's much more potential than was obvious at first," he says.

So, there you have it. Three different applications, three user-built expert systems. Expert system technology, not just for the computer expert, but for the "rest of us."

# Glossary

**Actions Block** A basic part of a VP-Expert knowledge base that sets the agenda for a consultation, such as displaying messages and instructing the program to find a goal.

**Algorithm** A set of rules, often mathematical, for solving a problem.

**Artificial intelligence** The capability of a device, such as a computer, to perform functions or tasks that would be regarded as intelligent, if they were observed in humans.

**Associative reasoning** The ability to identify a pattern in one area and apply that pattern to a new area.

**Attribute** The name of a data item and a specification of the type of data item in object-oriented systems; also called slots.

**Bias check** A review of a knowledge structure designed to eliminate any normal biases an expert may have in approaching a decision.

**Central processing unit (CPU)** The controller of the overall computer system, which performs the math and logic necessary to run a given application.

**Chaining** The linkage of two or more smaller, related knowledge bases to create an integrated system.

**Child class** The class being transferred to in an inheritance, in object-oriented systems.

**Class** In object-oriented systems, a template that gives an object its specific structure and behavior characteristics.

**Closed question** A question which sets limits on the type, level, and amount of information to be provided.

**Cognitive** Pertaining to the mental skills of perception, memory, judgment, and reasoning.

**Cognitive flexibility** The ability to use different problem-solving and modeling techniques based on the requirements of a situation.

**Cognitive map** Initial rough diagrams of an expert's ideas about primary relationships and concepts in a knowledge domain.

**Compatibility** The ability of one computer system component to integrate effectively with another.

**Compilation** The process by which the computer translates the programmer's instructions into machine language.

**Computer configuration** *See* Computer system.

**Computer system** The combination of selected computer components.

**Concept dictionary** A dictionary of concepts relevant to a knowledge domain under study, used as a reference tool in a KBS development project.

**Concept hierarchies** A "tree" of related concepts constructed by a knowledge engineer to help understand a domain expert's visualization of a domain's organization and subsystems.

**Conceptual framework** A specific structure for depicting categories of critical information to be analyzed to determine how an individual drew conclusions.

**Concurrent protocols** Verbal protocols obtained from an expert while he or she is solving a problem.

**Debugging** Correcting errors in a computer program, such as a KBS.

**Decision chart** A graphic representation of the knowledge segments and reasoning contained in the rule-set triangles of a dependency diagram.

**Decision situation diagram** The incrementally developed and refined diagram, or model, that represents the knowledge needed in a KBS development project.

**Declarative knowledge** Surface-level information that an expert can verbalize.

**Demon** Causes forward chaining in a knowledge base system; it executes whenever a monitored variable evaluates as true.

**Dependency diagrams** Indicates the relationship (or dependencies) among critical factors, all input questions, rules, values, and recommendations made by a KBS; it is a complete graphical "statement" of the KBS; it serves as the paper model for how to write or code the actual knowledge base.

**Domain expert** An individual who is widely recognized as having the knowledge and know-how necessary to solve a problem or make a decision in a specific knowledge domain.

**Dynamic memory** The most commonly used type of computer memory; also called random access memory (RAM).

**Encapsulation** The term used for the idea that an object should be a self-sufficient unit that contains both data and the methods to process that data.

**Encoding** Translating the rules developed for the knowledge base into a computer-readable format.

**Expert** In relation to KBS, a person who does his or her job very well or professionally, regardless of the nature of the particular job.

**Expert-driven** A KBS designed and developed by experts for their own use, without the assistance of specially trained outside personnel.

**Expert systems** A general term used to refer to knowledge-based systems, and to describe a wide range of advanced computer systems variously described as decision support systems, executive information systems, management information systems, and executive support systems.

**Feasibility study** A study undertaken to determine whether a planned KBS development project should proceed based on its chances of being successful.

**Fire** When a rule in a knowledge base evaluates as true, it is said to fire.

**Garbage collection** A facility which allows a computer system to reclaim for other use memory that is no longer needed by the application.

**Heuristics** Rules of thumb or other strategies used in problem solving and decision making.

**Hidden layer** The layer of a neural network where weighted inputs are evaluated and passed on to the output layer.

**Imbedded** Integration of a KBS into a larger conventional computer system.

**Incremental prototyping** The process of developing a KBS in stages, using small prototypes of the actual system, refining and extending the system over time.

**Indifference symbol** A mark, such as a hyphen, made on a decision table, which indicates that a condition has no bearing on an evaluation.

**Inference engine** A computer program that guides the manipulation of knowledge in a knowledge base.

**Inferential reasoning** The ability to draw inferences or implications from diverse areas perceived to be relevant to a decision area.

**Inheritance** The process by which one class transfers its structure and behavior characteristics to another class.

**Innovation assassin** An individual hostile to a newly introduced management system such as a KBS, who attempts to discourage others from making use of the system.

**In-program documentation** Typically any text in a KBS (preceded by an exclamation point in a VP-Expert KBS), used to document what is going on at that point in the program; also called remarks.

**Input layer** The "top" layer of a three-layer neural network, through which input values are weighted and passed on to the hidden layer.

**Instance** An object which contains specific values and inherits structure and behavior analogous to a database record with data in it.

**Integrated systems** KBS systems which are linked with other software or preexisting computer-based files and systems, such as spreadsheets or databases.

**Job analysis** Defining the skills required to perform a particular job.

**Knowledge base** A collection of expertise or expert knowledge.

**Knowledge-based system** A computer system that attempts to replicate specific human expert intelligent activities.

**Knowledge domain** A field of knowledge which can be defined by scope, range, depth, and/or breadth; also called problem space.

**Knowledge engineering** A term used to describe the KBS development jobs of situation analysis and representation, and computer system design and implementation.

**Knowledge intensive** A characteristic of a knowledge domain in which the reasoning processes tend to be heuristic and symbolic, rather than quantitative or process intensive.

**Machine language** The language actually understood by a computer.

**Message** A request from one method or object to another, or from a user, in an object-oriented system.

**Message passing** A technique for interconnecting methods that occur in different objects, or in the same object.

**Metaknowledge** Awareness of facts, heuristics, and/or rules, and the context within which they are used and manipulated.

**Method** A procedure associated with an attribute that can determine the attribute's value or execute a series of procedures when the attribute's value changes.

**Milestone chart** A screen displayed during neural network training that alerts the developer that training is progressing.

**Neural network** A trainable computer system that can be used to induce or extract a pattern of information from a structured set of data.

**Nodes** Points on the "internal map" of relationships between the input and output layers of a neural network, found by the hidden layer.

**Nonrecurring costs** One-time expenditures, such as site preparation, hardware and software acquisition, and training.

**Object** A data structure which represents anything tangible or abstract, encapsulating both data and procedures.

**OP** The operating system program that defines how the central processing unit (CPU) interacts with the other parts of the system.

**Open question** A question not seeking a specific answer, but encouraging a free-flowing response.

**Output layer** The layer of a neural network which produces the output results, such as predictions or classifications.

**Parent class** The class being transferred from in an inheritance.

**Peripheral equipment** The auxiliary devices connected to a computer system, such as printers or video displays.

**Permanent storage** Storage of computer programs or data on external media, such as magnetic disks or tape.

**Preliminary screening** An initial evaluation of feasibility, as part of a larger study; often suffices as the total feasibility study for smaller projects.

**Primary question** A question used to introduce, or move to another, general topic area.

**Problem space** *See* Knowledge domain.

**Procedural knowledge** Well-defined routine performance knowledge; often not easily verbalized by an expert because frequent performance tends to make the knowledge intuitive and reflexive.

**Process tracing** Any one of a set of techniques used in observing an expert to follow his or her train of thought or reasoning while a task is being performed.

**Project manager** In larger system development efforts, an individual other than the knowledge engineer who oversees and manages the multiple components of the project.

**Protocol analysis** The process of translating "thinking aloud" verbalizations into more accessible representations, such as decision scenarios.

**Prototype** A small KBS designed to replicate roughly a decision situation's broad outlines, or a small subsection of a decision situation, used to test the underlying structure and concept of a proposed system.

**Questions Block** The discrete section of a VP-Expert KBS program containing all the questions a user may be asked during a consultation.

**Random access memory (RAM)** The most commonly used type of memory; also called dynamic memory.

**Rapid prototyping** A knowledge acquisition strategy involving quickly creating computer prototypes or paper models of small segments or overall concepts of the proposed system.

**Rating matrices** Representations of an expert's view of a problem using a matrix or grid form.

**Reconceptualization phase** The phase of KBS development which involves transforming early rough situation models into computer-compatible situation diagrams; also called transformation phase.

**Recurring costs** Expenditures which are generated on a regular basis, such as wages and salaries, maintenance and repair, and most overhead costs.

**Remarks** *See* In-program documentation.

**Representation phase** *See* Situation reconceptualization.

**Retrospective protocols** Verbal protocols obtained by asking an expert to review records of previous verbalizations after a task is completed.

**Rules Block** The discrete section of a KBS program containing the encoded rules utilized by the inference engine.

**Sample cases** One of the components of the data set used for training a neural network.

**Scenario** The formal description of how a situation selected for KBS development operates.

**Secondary question** A probing question used to get more information in response to a primary or preceding secondary question.

**Semantic knowledge** Deep-level knowledge that involves structure, organization, and representation of cognitive or thinking processes.

**Situation analysis** The analysis of a business situation being replicated in a KBS; analogous to system analysis in conventional computer information systems development.

**Situation reconceptualization** The diagrams constructed during a KBS situation analysis and evaluation which help to give a more precise picture of how a decision is made or a task is performed.

**Slot** *See* Attribute.

**Static memory** The fastest type of computer memory available.

**Structured interview** An interview in which a knowledge engineer pursues specific goals and asks questions designed to elicit specific information.

**Syllogism** A form of symbolic reasoning in which two or more logically connected propositions are linked in a final proposition, or conclusion.

**Symbolic processor** A computer designed specifically for use in KBS development.

**Symbolic reasoning** The manipulation of symbols that represent concepts.

**Synaptic connection** The programmed interconnection between processing elements in a neural network; analogous to synapses in biological neurological systems.

**System analysis** The analysis of a situation being computerized.

**System design** The development of a computer system based on a system analysis.

**System proposal** The written statement detailing what is to be accomplished by a given KBS to be developed, and the resources which will be required for development.

**Task identification** The process of determining the nature of a task by breaking it down into its essential components.

**Task/time analysis** An evaluation of the effect of time on task completion.

**Taxonomies** Basic classification systems that are more detailed versions of conceptual frameworks.

**Training** The procedure whereby a neural network induces a working decision-making system.

**Transfer function** The rules that determine whether or not a given neural network processing element will fire.

**Transformation phase** *See* Reconceptualization phase.

**Unstructured interview** An interview in which spontaneous questions are asked in order to explore the knowledge involved in a situation in an open-ended way.

**User friendly** A computer system which attempts to facilitate use by nontechnical personnel through user interface improvements.

**User interface** All parts of a KBS a user will see on the screen and interact with during a consultation.

**Verbal protocols** Recorded verbalizations of an expert thinking aloud.

**Virtual memory** A technique or capability that allows the computer to use permanent memory as working memory.

**Working memory** Temporary storage of data within the computer's memory.

# Index

# About the Authors

**Dr. Robert J. Mockler** is a Professor at St. John's University Graduate School of Business and founder and director of the Strategic Management Research Institute's Center of Artificial Intelligence Systems for Business. He has written over twenty books and many articles in areas related to strategic corporate planning, management decision making, and computer systems' use for management decision making. His most recent publications concern knowledge-based systems developed for a variety of management decision-making areas. He has also worked extensively in his own businesses operating in highly competitive environments.

**Dr. Dorothy G. Dologite** is a Professor of Computer Information Systems at Baruch College, City University of New York. Her research efforts focus on human factors issues of user-developed knowledge-based systems. She has written nine books and many articles related to computer information systems as well as knowledge-based system development, training, and implementation. She has over 15 years of direct computer industry experience, including positions with computer hardware manufacturing and software development firms.

## GUIDE TO USING THE DISKS ACCOMPANYING THIS TEXT

The software accompanying this book may be installed on a hard drive or on diskettes. Hard drive installation requires 6 megabytes of available storage space. Diskette installation requires two high-density disk drives and three formatted high-density diskettes.

The two distribution diskettes contain so-called zipped or compressed files. These files must first be unzipped to be usable. This is accomplished by running the Install program. To run Install, place Disk #1 in the A: drive and, at the A:> prompt, type install <Enter>. Follow the instructions on the display.

The instructions for running the runtime and educational development versions of VP-Expert (Chapter 4), the special version of LEVEL5 OBJECT developed for this text (Chapter 21), the demonstration version of ObjectCraft (Chapter 21), and the runtime version of NeuroShell (Chapter 22) are found in their respective chapters. (NeuroShell can only be used with the example in Chapter 22 that uses VP-Expert software.) The instructions for running the educational development version of M.1 are as follows:

1. Load the M.1 expert system shell program and related M.1 data from the C:>, A:>, or other DOS prompt by typing "start" and pressing the Enter key. (Note: M.1 program and data files must be on the *same* disk drive.)

2. The M1> prompt appears on the screen. To load the desired system file, type

   M1> load file_name.extension
   Example:
   M1> load career.rev

   where file_name.extension represents the full DOS name of the M.1 file you wish to run (Note: lowercase letters must be used at all times while M.1 is running.) Press the Enter key. Loading the file can take from one to five minutes.

3. Once the file is finished loading, the M1> prompt reappears. Type "go" and press the Enter key.

4. Follow the instructions on the screen to run the knowledge-based system consultation. The prompt that appears on screen during the consultation is the >> prompt.

*Special functions available while running a consultation:*

- To go back to the M1> prompt while a consultation is in session, type "abort" at the >> prompt and press the Enter key.
- To exit M.1 and go back to DOS, type "exit" or "quit" at the M1> prompt or >> prompt and press the Enter key.
- To print out a consultation's reasoning steps, turn the printer on. Before typing "go", type "log printer" and press the Enter key. Then type "trace on" and press the Enter key. Typing "go" starts the consultation, which prints out as it appears on the screen. (To turn the trace function off, type "trace off" and press the Enter key.)

*Note:* If too many systems are loaded in a single session of M.1, the memory in your computer (RAM) may fill up, resulting in an error message ("Error 275"). In order to clear the memory, "quit" M.1 and begin again with Step 1.